HUMAN DEVELOPMENT
REPORT 2020

The next frontier

Human development and the Anthropocene

Team

Director and lead author
Pedro Conceição

Research and statistics
Jacob Assa, Cecilia Calderon, Fernanda Pavez Esbry, Ricardo Fuentes, Yu-Chieh Hsu, Milorad Kovacevic, Christina Lengfelder, Brian Lutz, Tasneem Mirza, Shivani Nayyar, Josefin Pasanen, Carolina Rivera Vázquez, Heriberto Tapia and Yanchun Zhang

Production, communications, operations
Rezarta Godo, Kristin Hagegård, Jon Hall, Seockhwan Bryce Hwang, Admir Jahic, Fe Juarez Shanahan, Sarantuya Mend, Anna Ortubia, Yumna Rathore, Dharshani Seneviratne and Marium Soomro

Foreword

Hidden in the long shadow of Covid-19, 2020 has been a dark year. Scientists have been forewarning a pandemic like this for years, pointing to the rise in zoonotic pathogens—those that jump from animals to humans—as a reflection of the pressures people put on planet Earth.

Those pressures have grown exponentially over the past 100 years. Humans have achieved incredible things, but we have taken the Earth to the brink. Climate change, rupturing inequalities, record numbers of people forced from their homes by conflict and crisis—these are the results of societies that value what they measure instead of measuring what they value.

In fact, the pressures we exert on the planet have become so great that scientists are considering whether the Earth has entered an entirely new geological epoch: the Anthropocene, or the age of humans. It means that we are the first people to live in an age defined by human choice, in which the dominant risk to our survival is ourselves.

Advancing human development while erasing such planetary pressures is the next frontier for human development, and its exploration lies at the heart of this 30th anniversary edition of UNDP's Human Development Report.

To survive and thrive in this new age, we must redesign a path to progress that respects the intertwined fate of people and planet and recognizes that the carbon and material footprint of the people who have more is choking the opportunities of the people who have less.

For example, the actions of an indigenous person in the Amazon, whose stewardship helps protect much of the world's tropical forest, offsets the equivalent of the carbon emissions of a person in the richest 1 percent of people in the world. Yet indigenous peoples continue to face hardship, persecution and discrimination.

Four thousand generations could live and die before the carbon dioxide released from the Industrial Revolution to today is scrubbed from our atmosphere, and yet decisionmakers continue to subsidize fossil fuels, prolonging our carbon habit like a drug running through the economy's veins.

And while the world's richest countries could experience up to 18 fewer days of extreme weather each year within our lifetime because of the climate crisis, the poorest countries face up to 100 extra days of extreme weather. That number could still be cut in half if the Paris Agreement is fully implemented.

It is time to make a change. Our future is not a question of choosing between people or trees; it is neither or both.

When the Human Development Report first challenged the primacy of growth as the measure of progress in 1990, the Cold War still shaped geopolitics, the World Wide Web had just been invented and very few people had heard of climate change. In that moment UNDP offered a forward-looking alternative to GDP, ranking all countries by whether people had the freedom and opportunity to live a life they valued. In so doing, we gave voice to a new conversation on the meaning of a good life and the ways we could achieve it.

Thirty years on, much has changed, but hope and possibility have not. If people have the power to create an entirely new geological epoch, then people also have the power to choose to change. We are not the last generation of the Anthropocene; we are the first to recognize it. We are the explorers, the innovators who get to decide what this—the first generation of the Anthropocene—will be remembered for.

Will we be remembered by the fossils we leave behind: swaths of species, long extinct, sunken and fossilized in the mud alongside plastic toothbrushes and bottle caps, a legacy of loss and waste? Or will we leave a much more valuable imprint: balance between people and planet, a future that is fair and just?

The Next Frontier: Human Development and the Anthropocene sets out this choice, offering a thought-provoking, necessary alternative to paralysis in the face of rising poverty and inequalities alongside alarming planetary change. With its new, experimental Planetary pressures–adjusted Human Development Index, we hope to open a new conversation on the path ahead for each country—a path yet unexplored. The way forward from Covid-19 will be the journey of a generation. We hope it is one that all people will choose to travel together.

Achim Steiner
Administrator
United Nations Development Programme

Acknowledgements

Every person, everywhere in the world, has been affected by the Covid-19 pandemic. Amidst untold suffering the process of producing a Human Development Report often appeared less urgent over the course of 2020. The Report team felt the need to document the unfolding and devastating impact of the pandemic on human development, supporting UNDP's response to the crisis. The well planned process of consultations and team meetings had to be scrapped or changed in unprecedented ways. This implied reinventing the Report's typical production process. At many points it seemed that the Report simply could not be finished on time. Doing so was possible only because of the conviction that the Report had something important to say that speaks to this year's crisis, the obligation to honour 30 years of Human Development Reports and the encouragement, generosity and contributions of so many, recognized only imperfectly and partially in these acknowledgments.

The members of our Advisory Board, led by Tharman Shanmugaratnam and A. Michael Spence as Co-Chairs, supported us in multiple and long virtual meetings, providing extensive advice on four versions of lengthy drafts. The other members of the Advisory Board were Olu Ajakaiye, Kaushik Basu, Haroon Bhorat, Gretchen C. Daily, Marc Fleurbaey, Xiheng Jiang, Ravi Kanbur, Jaya Krishnakumar, Melissa Leach, Laura Chinchilla Miranda, Thomas Piketty, Janez Potočnik, Frances Stewart, Pavan Sukhdev, Ilona Szabó de Carvalho, Krushil Watene and Helga Weisz.

Complementing the advice from our Advisory Board, the Report's Statistical Advisory Panel provided guidance on several methodological and data aspects of the Report, in particular related to the calculation of the Report's human development indices. We are grateful to all the panel members: Mario Biggeri, Camilo Ceita, Ludgarde Coppens, Koen Decancq, Marie Haldorson, Jason Hickel, Steve Macfeely, Mohd Uzir Mahidin, Silvia Montoya, Shantanu Mukherjee, Michaela Saisana, Hany Torky and Dany Wazen.

Many others without a formal advisory role offered advice, including Inês L. Azevedo, Anthony Cox, Andrew Crabtree, Erle C. Ellis, Eli Fenichel, Victor Galaz, Douglas Gollin, Judith Macgregor, Ligia Noronha, Belinda Reyers, Ingrid Robeyns, Paul Schreyer, Amartya Sen, Nicholas Stern, Joseph E. Stiglitz, Izabella Teixeira and Duncan Wingham.

We are thankful for especially close collaborations with our partners at the World Inequality Lab, including Lucas Chancel and Tancrède Voituriez, and with colleagues at the United Nations Environment Programme, including Inger Andersen, María José Baptista, Maxwell Gomera, Pushpam Kumar, Cornelia Pretorius, Steven Stone and Merlyn Van Voore, and at the International Science Council, including Eve El Chehaly, Mathieu Denis, Peter Gluckman, Heide Hackmann, Binyam Sisay Mendisu, Dirk Messner, Alison Meston, Elisa Reis, Asunción Lera St. Clair, Megha Sud and Zhenya Tsoy, with whom we partnered to initiate an ongoing conversation on rethinking human development. We are grateful for the opportunity to present to and receive feedback from the International Resource Panel and for the close collaboration with and support from the Stockholm Resilience Centre at Stockholm University.

Appreciation is also extended for all the data, written inputs and peer reviews of draft chapters to the Report, including those by Nuzhat Ahmad, Sabina Alkire, Simon Anholt, Edward Barbier, Scott Barrett, Kendon Bell, Joaquín Bernal, Christelle Cazabat, Manqi Chang, Ajay Chhibber, David Collste, Sarah Cornell, Bina Desai, Simon Dikau, Andrea S. Downing, Maria Teresa Miranda Espinosa, David Farrier, Katherine Farrow, John E. Fernández, Eduardo Flores Mendoza, Max Franks, William Gbohoui, Arunabha Ghosh, Oscar Gomez, Nandini Harihar, Dina Hestad, Solomon Hsiang, Inge Kaul, Axel Kleidon, Fanni Kosvedi, Jan. J. Kuiper, Timothy M. Lenton, Wolfgang Lutz, Khalid Malik, Wolf M. Mooij, Michael Muthukrishna, Karine Nyborg, Karen O'Brien, Carl Obst, José Antonio Ocampo, Toby Ord, Ian Parry, Catherine Pattillo, Jonathan Proctor, Francisco R. Rodríguez, Valentina Rotondi, Roman Seidl, Uno Svedin, Jeanette Tseng, Iñaki Permanyer Ugartemendia, David G. Victor, Gaia Vince and Dianneke van Wijk.

A number of virtual consultations with thematic and regional experts were held between February and September 2020, and physical consultations were held in New York; in the Republic of Korea, hosted by UNDP's Seoul Policy Centre; and in Zimbabwe, hosted by the United Nations Economic Commission for Africa. We are grateful for inputs during these consultations by Lilibeth Acosta-Michlik, Bina Agarwal, Sanghoon Ahn, Joseph Aldy, Alessandra Alfieri, Frans Berkhout, Steve Brumby, Anthony Cak, Hongmin Chun, Keeyong Chung, William Clark, Flavio Comin, Adriana Conconi, Fabio Corsi, Diane Coyle, Rosie Day, Fiona Dove, Paul Ekins, Marina Fischer-Kowalski, Enrico Giovannini, Pamela Green, Peter Haas, Raya Haffar El Hassan, Mark Halle, Stéphane

Hallegatte, Laurel Hanscom, Gordon Hanson, Ilpyo Hong, Samantha Hyde, Sandhya Seshadri Iyer, Nobuko Kajiura, Thomas Kalinowski, Simrit Kaur, Asim I. Khwaja, Yeonsoo Kim, Randall Krantz, Sarah Lattrell, Henry Lee, David Lin, Ben Metz, James Murombedzi, Connie Nshemereirwe, John Ouma-Mugabe, Jihyeon Irene Park, Richard Peiser, Richard Poulton, Isabel Guerrero Pulgar, Steven Ramage, Forest Reinhardt, Katherine Richardson, Jin Hong Rim, Giovanni Ruta, Sabyasachi Saha, Saurabh Sinha, Ingvild Solvang, Yo Whan Son, Tanja Srebotnjak, Jomo Kwame Sundaram, Philip Thigo, Charles Vörösmarty, Mathis Wackernagel, Robert Watson and Kayla Walsh.

Further support was also extended by others too numerous to mention here. Consultations are listed at http://hdr.undp.org/en/towards-hdr-2020, with more partners and participants mentioned at http://hdr.undp.org/en/acknowledgements-hdr-2020. Contributions, support and assistance from partnering institutions, including UNDP regional bureaus and country offices, are also acknowledged with much gratitude.

We are grateful for many colleagues in the UN family who supported the preparation of the Report by hosting consultations or providing comments and advice. They include Robert Hamwey, Maria Teresa Da Piedade Moreira, Henrique Pacini and Shamika Sirimanne at the United Nations Conference for Trade and Development; Astra Bonini, Sara Castro-Hallgren, Hoi Wai Jackie Cheng and Elliott Harris at the United Nations Department of Economic and Social Affairs; Manos Antoninis, Bilal Barakat, Nicole Bella, Anna Cristina D'Addio, Camila Lima De Moraes and Katharine Redman at the United Nations Educational, Scientific and Cultural Organization; Shams Banihani, Hany Besada, Jorge Chediek, Naveeda Nazir and Xiaojun Grace Wang at the United Nations Office for South-South Cooperation; Kunal Sen at the United Nations University–World Institute for Development Economics Research; and many colleagues from the United Nations Children's Fund and the United Nations Entity for Gender Equality and the Empowerment of Women.

Colleagues in UNDP provided advice and inputs. We are grateful to Babatunde Abidoye, Marcel Alers, Jesus Alvarado, Carlos Arboleda, Sade Bamimore, Betina Barbosa, Malika Bhandarkar, Bradley Busetto, Michele Candotti, Sarwat Chowdhury, Joseph D'Cruz, Abdoulaye Mar Dieye, Simon Dikau, Mirjana Spoljaric Egger, Jamison Ervin (who devoted much time to advise and contribute to the Report), Bakhodur Eshonov, Ahunna Eziakonwa, Almudena Fernández, Cassie Flynn, Bertrand Frot, Oscar A. Garcia, Raymond Gilpin, Balazs Horvath, Vito Intini, Artemy Izmestiev, Anne Juepner, Stephan Klingebiel, Raquel Lagunas, Luis Felipe López-Calva, Marion Marigo, George Gray Molina, Mansour Ndiaye, Sydney Neeley, Hye-Jin Park, Midori Paxton, Clea Paz, Isabel de Saint Malo de Alvarado, Tim Scott, Ben Slay, Anca Stoica, Bertrand Tessa, Anne Virnig, Mourad Wahba and Kanni Wignaraja.

We were fortunate to have the support of talented interns—Jadher Aguad, Cesar Castillo Garcia, Jungjin Koo and Ajita Singh—and fact checkers—Jeremy Marand, Tobias Schillings and Emilia Toczydlowska.

The Human Development Report Office also extends its sincere gratitude to the governments of Germany, the Republic of Korea, Portugal and Sweden for their financial contributions. Their ongoing support is much appreciated and remains essential.

We are grateful for the highly professional work of our editors and layout artists at Communications Development Incorporated—led by Bruce Ross-Larson with Joe Brinley, Joe Caponio, Meta de Coquereaumont, Mike Crumplar, Peter Redvers-Lee, Christopher Trott and Elaine Wilson. A special word of gratitude to Bruce, who edited the very first Report 30 years ago, and almost all the others since, bringing unparalleled scrutiny and wisdom—and, not infrequently, encouragement too.

To conclude, we are extremely grateful to UNDP Administrator Achim Steiner. His probing intellect and constant reminder that the Report needs to speak to people's concerns provided us the guideposts we needed to develop the arguments in a rigorous but practical way. He told us that this Report should matter in the context of the Covid-19 pandemic and beyond. That gave us the compass to navigate the production of the Report in a disorienting year—we hope to have been able to meet that aspiration, as we seek to contribute to advance the next frontier of human development in the Anthropocene.

Pedro Conceição
Director
Human Development Report Office

Contents

CONTENTS | ix

STATISTICAL ANNEX

Human development and Mahbub ul Haq

Amartya Sen, *Thomas W. Lamont University Professor, and Professor of Economics and Philosophy, at Harvard University*

That the Gross Domestic Product, or GDP, is a very crude indicator of the economic achievements of a nation is not a secret. Mahbub ul Haq knew all about it when he was an undergraduate, and as fellow students in Cambridge, we often talked about the misdirecting power of GDP as a popular measure. We also discussed how easily we could improve GDP as an indicator by replacing the values of commodities produced by aspects of the quality of life we had reason to value. We were ready from time to time to miss a class or two for the enjoyable exercise of proposing some simple improvements to GDP.

We ceased being undergraduates in 1955 and went in different directions, but remained close friends. I knew that Mahbub would get back to his favourite concern some day, and was not surprised when in the summer of 1989 Mahbub got in touch with me, with urgency in his voice, saying that I must drop everything and come and work with him immediately at the UNDP in a joint effort to clarify the understanding of indicators in general and to construct a good and useable index of the quality of life in particular. He had done considerable background work already (his knowledge of living conditions in different countries in the world was astounding), and he had also worked out how the analytical work I was then doing on welfare economics and social choice theory would relate closely to the task of constructing what we would later call a "human development index."

It was difficult for me to drop everything and join Mahbub in the UN, but eventually I managed to get together with him in regular intervals to try to help Mahbub in what he was hoping to construct. Combined with Chinese and South Asian meals (the restaurants were always chosen by Mahbub), I could enjoy the progress that we were making towards what Mahbub was trying to get, despite the evident scepticism of colleagues working with him in the UNDP. There were a number of other economists who joined us as consultants to the UNDP and who gave useful advice on what was emerging.

Mahbub and I agreed on most things, and where we disagreed, we did find ways of putting our respective inclinations together. One subject on which we did initially disagree was the usefulness of constructing an aggregate index as a comprehensive expression of "human development," in addition to all the disparate measurements to represent various aspects of it. Since human life has many different features, it seemed to me quite implausible to entertain the hope of getting one number which will reflect them all in some magically integrated way. A set of numbers and descriptions would do a better job, I argued, than one grand index in the form of one number. "Surely," I had to tell Mahbub, "you must see how vulgar this imagined single number must be in terms of trying to represent simultaneously so many distinct features of life!" To this Mahbub replied that it would indeed be vulgar, but we would never find an alternative to the GDP that would be widely used if it were not as simple—and as vulgar—as GDP itself. "People will pay tribute to the excellence of your multiple components, but when it comes to ready use," Mahbub insisted, "they will abandon your complicated world and choose the simple GDP number instead."

A better strategy, Mahbub argued, would be to compete with the GDP with another single number—that of human development—which would be no less vulgar than the GDP, but would contain more relevant information than the GDP managed to do. Once people get interested in the human development index, over-simple though it might be, they would have an interest, Mahbub argued, in the variety of tables with many different types of information that a Human Development Report would be presenting to the world. The Human Development Index must have some useful ingredients of social understanding and yet remain as easily useable as the GDP. "That is what," said Mahbub, "I am asking you to produce."

I was persuaded by Mahbub's reasoning, and though the follow up was complicated, my work was guided by my conversation with Mahbub. Even though I feel honoured by the fact that I sometimes get credit for the Human Development Index (HDI), I must emphasize that the HDI was driven entirely by Mahbub's vision, and (I must add here) also by his cunning about practical use. The simple HDI never tried to represent all that we wanted to capture in the indicator system, but it had much more to say about quality of life than GDP. It pointed to the possibility of thinking about more significant things regarding human life than just the market value of commodities bought and sold. The impacts of lower mortality, better health, more school education, and other elementary human concerns could be combined in some aggregate form, and the HDI did just that. Central to that aggregation was, of course, sensible choice of relative weights on different concerns (without overlooking the fact that different parts of our findings came expressed in very different units).

The UNDP's announcement in 1990 of the new Human Development Index, with concrete numbers for different countries' achievements, measured with transparency and relevance, was widely welcomed. There was clear vindication there of what Mahbub had hoped to get. He called me up in the morning to read to me from the front pages of several leading newspapers. What was particularly pleasing was the fact that all the newspaper reports supplemented the airing of HDI numbers—contrasted with GDP figures—by referring to some of the more detailed tables of particular aspects of human development (as Mahbub had predicted).

It was a great moment. Aside from celebrating what had just been achieved, I could not help recollecting, as Mahbub went on telling me about the news reports, the conversations we used to have as undergraduates 35 years earlier. There was, I thought, justification there for missing a class or two.

Human development and the Anthropocene

Human development and the Anthropocene

Structure of the 2020 Human Development Report

2020 HDR
Expanding human development, easing planetary pressures

Renewing human development for the Anthropocene

We are destabilizing the planetary systems we rely on for survival.

The strain on our planet mirrors that in societies.

These imbalances reinforce each other, amplifying the challenges.

Mechanisms of change to catalyse action

We need a just transformation in the way we live, work and cooperate.

New social norms, improved incentives and working with— not against—nature can take us there.

Exploring new metrics

A new era requires new measures of human development.

The Report proposes the Planetary pressures– adjusted Human Development Index and a new generation of dashboards.

We are at an unprecedented moment in the history of humankind and in the history of our planet. Warning lights—for our societies and the planet—are flashing red. They have been for some time, as we well know. The Covid-19 pandemic is the latest harrowing consequence of imbalances writ large. Scientists have long warned that unfamiliar pathogens will emerge more frequently from interactions among humans, livestock and wildlife,[1] interactions that have steadily increased in scale and intensity, ultimately squeezing local ecosystems so hard that deadly viruses spill out. The novel coronavirus may be the latest to do so, and unless we relax our grip on nature, it will not be the last.

New pathogens do not fall from the sky, nor do the epidemics they may cause. Covid-19 has spread quickly around an interconnected world, taking root wherever it has landed and thriving especially in the cracks in societies, exploiting and exacerbating myriad inequalities in human development. In too many cases those cracks have hamstrung efforts to control the virus (chapter 2).

While Covid-19 has absorbed the world's attention, pre-existing crises continue. Consider climate change. The 2020 Atlantic hurricane season either set new records or was on the verge of doing so, both in the number of storms and how many rapidly intensified.[2] Within the past 12 months extraordinary fires scorched enormous swaths of Australia, the Brazilian Pantanal, eastern Siberia in the Russian Federation and the West Coast of the United States.[3] The planet's biodiversity is plunging, with a quarter of species facing extinction, many within decades.[4] Numerous experts believe we are living through, or on the cusp of, a mass species extinction event, the sixth in the history of the planet and the first to be caused by a single organism—us.[5]

> " Warning lights—for our societies and the planet—are flashing red.

The strain on the planet mirrors the strain facing many of our societies. This is not mere coincidence. Indeed, planetary imbalances (the dangerous

Figure 1 Planetary and social imbalances reinforce each other

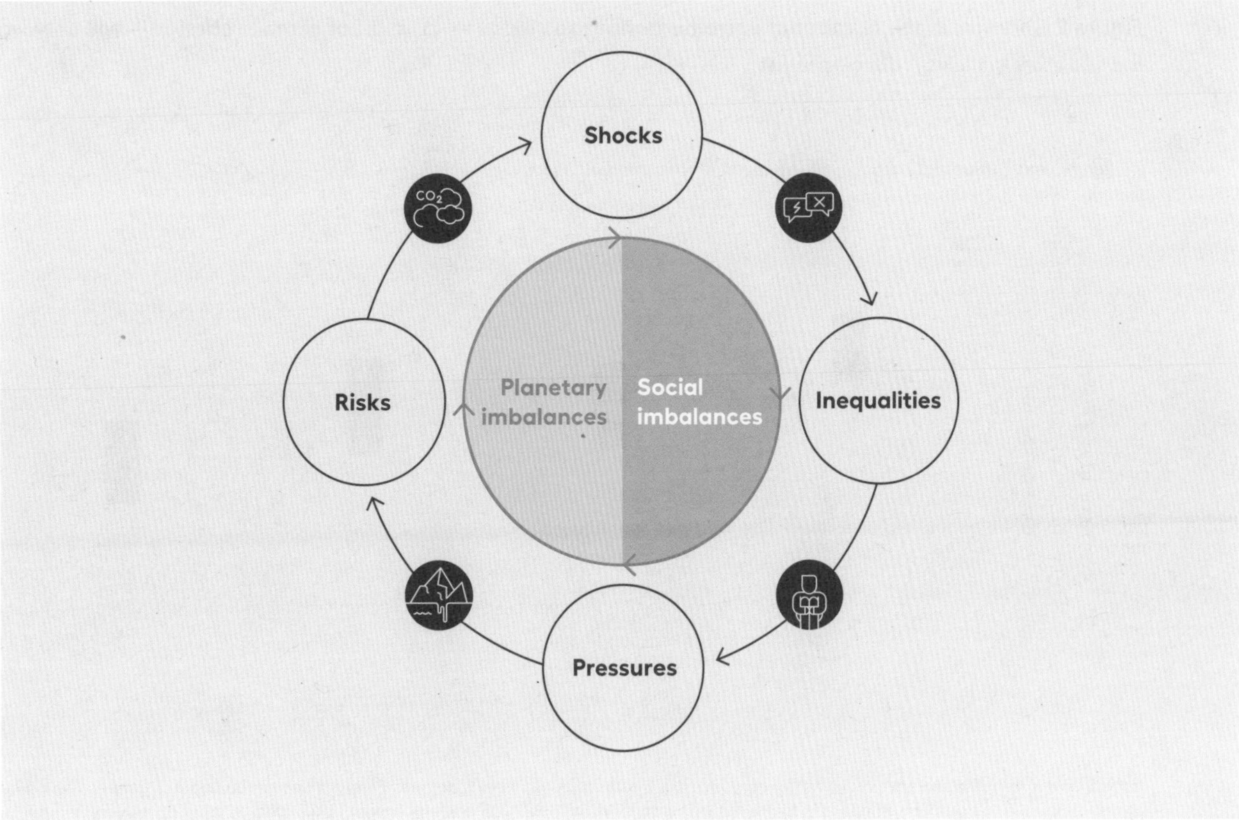

Source: Human Development Report Office.

planetary change for people and all forms of life) and social imbalances exacerbate one another (figure 1).[6] As the 2019 Human Development Report made plain, many inequalities in human development have been increasing and continue to do so.[7] Climate change, among other dangerous planetary changes, will only make them worse (figure 2).[8] Social mobility is down; social instability is up.[9] Ominous signs of democratic backsliding and rising authoritarianism are worrying.[10] Collective action on anything from the Covid-19 pandemic to climate change becomes more difficult against a backdrop of social fragmentation (chapter 1).[11]

> " A new normal is coming. Covid-19 is the tip of the spear.

There is talk of returning to "normal," as if some predetermined end date exists for the many crises gripping our societies and the planet, as if going back to normal is desirable or even possible. What or whose normal should that be? Lurching from crisis to crisis is one of the defining features of the present day, which has something to do with the "normalcy"

of the past, a return to which would seemingly consign the future to endless crisis management, not to human development.

Whether we wish it or not, a new normal is coming. Covid-19 is just the tip of the spear. Scientists generally believe that we are exiting the Holocene, which spanned some 12,000 years, during which human civilization as we know it came to be. They propose that we are now entering a new geologic epoch—the Anthropocene—in which humans are a dominant force shaping the future of the planet.[12] The question is: What do we do with this new age? Do we choose in the face of uncertain futures to embark on bold new paths that expand human freedoms while easing planetary pressures? Or do we choose to try—and ultimately fail—to go back to business as usual and be swept away, ill equipped and rudderless, into a dangerous unknown?

This Human Development Report is firmly behind the first choice, and its arguments go beyond summarizing well known lists of what can be done to realize it. We know that carbon pricing can be an effective and efficient policy measure for reducing carbon emissions. We know that fossil fuel subsidies

Figure 2 Changes in the number of extreme temperature days—a result of climate change—will only worsen inequalities in human development

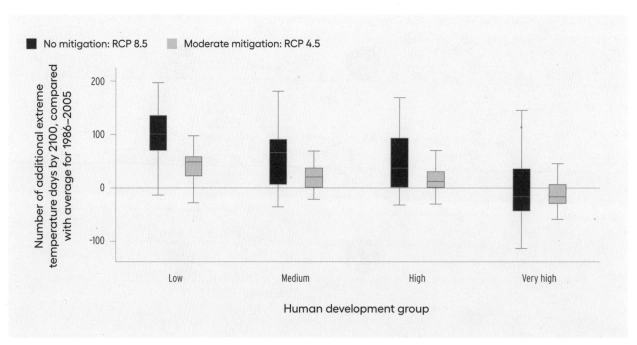

Note: Extreme temperature days are days during which the temperature is below 0 degrees Celsius or above 35 degrees Celsius. The figure shows the change between the actual number of extreme temperature days in 1986–2005 and the median projected number of extreme temperature days in 2080–2099.
Source: Human Development Report Office based on Carleton and others (2020).

encourage those very emissions and should be phased out (chapter 5). While the Report discusses various ways that societies can make different choices, its unique contribution is a human development lens, a lens that aims to unlock some of the deeper obstacles to advancing human flourishing while easing planetary pressures. It focuses on why much-discussed "solutions" are not being implemented fully—and in many cases not yet at the scale to make a difference.

The Report questions the very narrative around "solutions to a problem," which frames solutions to discrete problems as somehow external, somewhere "out there," disconnected from ourselves and from one another. Once solutions are discovered, the storyline goes, we need only implement them as panaceas everywhere. Technology and innovation matter—and matter a lot, as the Report argues—but the picture is much more complex, much more nonlinear, much more dynamic than simple plug-and-play metaphors. There can be dangerous unintended consequences from any single seemingly promising solution. We must reorient our approach from solving discrete siloed problems to navigating multidimensional, interconnected and increasingly universal predicaments.

In the face of complexity, progress must take on an adaptive learning-by-doing quality, fuelled by broad innovations, anchored in deliberative shared decisionmaking and buttressed by appropriate mixes of carrots and sticks. Getting there will not be easy. Fundamental differences loom large—in interests and around the responsiveness and accountability of current institutions. So do various forms of inequality, which restrict participation in decisionmaking, limit the potential for innovation and increase vulnerability to climate change and ecological threats (figure 3).[13] Development choices are often framed as if confined to a set of narrow, well trod but ultimately unsustainable paths. Deeper still are questions about what we value and by how much.[14]

" Human choices, shaped by values and institutions, have given rise to the interconnected planetary and social imbalances we face.

As Cassius famously remarks in Shakespeare's *Julius Caesar:* "The fault...is not in our stars/But in ourselves."[15] Consciously or not, human choices, shaped by values and institutions, have given rise to the interconnected planetary and social imbalances we face. Understanding and addressing them are impeded by

Figure 3 In countries with high ecological threats, there is also greater social vulnerability

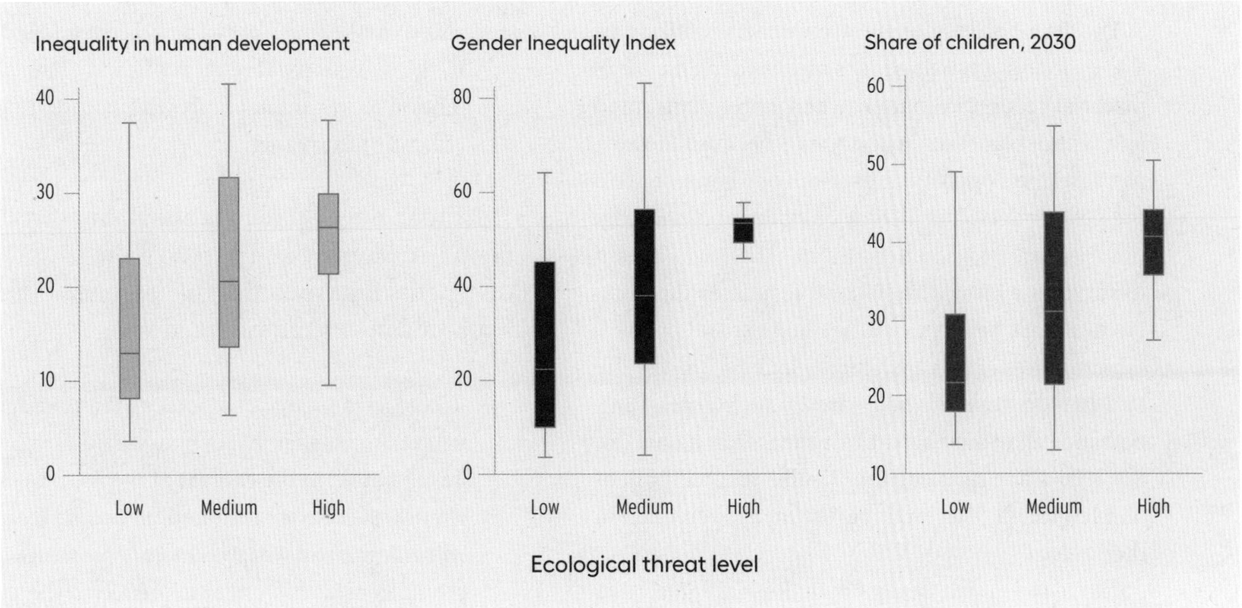

Note: Excludes outliers. Ecological threats include water stress, food insecurity, droughts, floods, cyclones, temperature rise, sea level rise and population growth. Levels are defined by number of threats faced by each country: low (zero to one threat), medium (two to three threats) and high (four or more threats). See IEP (2020).
Source: Human Development Report Office based on data from the United Nations Department of Economic and Social Affairs and IEP (2020).

rigidities in the very same values and institutions, rigidities that lend inertia to our past choices. We must critically examine the crucible of human values and institutions—specifically the way power is distributed and wielded—to accelerate implementation of the 2030 Agenda for Sustainable Development for people and planet.

The human development approach has much to contribute in addressing our collective paralysis in the face of alarming planetary change. Human development is about expanding human freedoms and opening more choices for people to chart their own development paths according to their diverse values rather than about prescribing one or more particular paths. Too often, development choices pit people against trees because the environment has been systematically undervalued while economic growth has had top billing. The human development concept emerged 30 years ago precisely as a counterpoint to myopic definitions of development. Economic growth is important, especially for developing countries; raising income levels is crucial for those living in poverty, in every country. But as the 2019 Human Development Report emphasized, the increasingly important questions for many countries are not about the overall size of the pie but the relative size of its slices.[16] In this year's Report, though not for the first time in its history, we also worry about the oven.

The human development approach reminds us that economic growth is more means than end. More material resources matter, when fairly distributed and within planetary boundaries,[17] because they expand people's opportunities, from one generation to the next. Indeed, the income component of the original Human Development Index (HDI) was meant to serve as a proxy for material resources that enable a suite of basic capabilities that expand people's opportunities. Two capabilities—living a healthy life and having an education—are of such critical importance that they have been measured as part of the HDI since its inception. Unlike income or economic growth, they are not just means but ends in themselves.

The 2019 Human Development Report argued that a new generation of enhanced capabilities is becoming more important for people to thrive in the digital age.[18] The central tenets of human development have not changed—its lodestar remains what people value. What has changed is the context. Consider that more than 1 billion people have been lifted out of extreme poverty within a generation,[19] unquestionably one of humanity's greatest accomplishments. But also consider that the Covid-19 pandemic may have pushed some 100 million people into extreme poverty, the worst setback in a generation.[20] Human development may have taken a big hit in 2020 (figure 4).[21] Eliminating poverty in all its forms—and keeping it eliminated in a dynamic world—remains central, but ambitions are continuously being raised, as they should be, alongside a firm commitment not to leave anyone behind in the process. Human development is an ongoing journey, not a destination. Its centre of gravity has always been about more than just meeting basic needs. It is about empowering people to identify and pursue their own paths for a meaningful life, one anchored in expanding freedoms. It challenges us to think of people as agents rather than as patients—a central theme of this year's Report.

The ground beneath us is shifting as we confront the unprecedented challenges of the apparent Anthropocene. This time, the way forward is not only about expanding people's capabilities to lead lives they value—that is, expanding choices available to people. We must also carefully consider two other critical dimensions of human development: agency (that is, the ability to participate in decisionmaking and to make one's desired choices) and values (that is, the choices that are most desired), with special attention to our interactions with nature, to our stewardship of the planet.

" Human development is about empowering people to identify and pursue their own paths for a meaningful life, one anchored in expanding freedoms.

Like a three-legged stool, capabilities, agency and values are inseparable in how we think about human development in the context of the Anthropocene. We cannot assume that expanding people's capabilities will automatically ease planetary pressures. The HDI provides clear historical evidence to the contrary—countries at the highest levels of the HDI have tended to exert more pressure over greater scales on the planet (figure 5).

Figure 4 The Covid-19 pandemic's unprecedented shock to human development

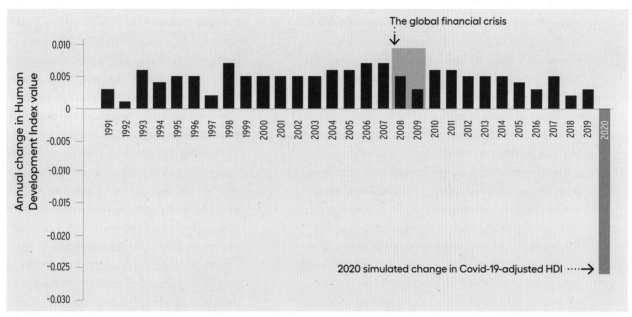

Figure 5 Countries with higher human development tend to exert more pressure over greater scales on the planet

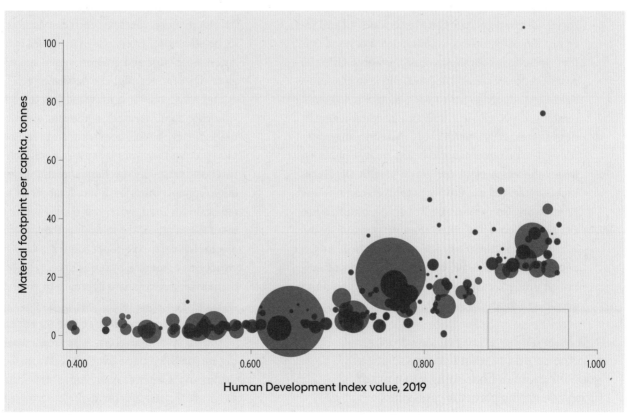

Note: Material footprint measures the amount of domestic and foreign extraction of materials (biomass, fossil fuels, metal ores and nonmetal ores) used to meet domestic final demand for goods and services within a country. Bubble size is proportional to country population. The green rectangle at the bottom right-hand corner represents the currently empty aspirational space for the human development journey in the Anthropocene (see box 1).

Nor can we simply assume that expanding agency on its own means that more empowered people will invariably choose, individually and collectively, to avoid dangerous planetary change. Values, especially how they stack up and interact, help provide the overall direction for the choices that empowered people make about their lives. Values are fundamental to our personal understanding of what it means to live a good life. But people cannot realize their values without having sufficient capabilities and agency.

The Report argues that to navigate the Anthropocene, humanity can develop the capabilities, agency and values to act by enhancing equity, fostering innovation and instilling a sense of stewardship of nature.[22] If these have greater weight within the ever widening choice sets that people create for themselves—if equity, innovation and stewardship become central to what it means to live a good life—then human flourishing can happen alongside easing planetary pressures.[23]

We have ample evidence that values can be changed purposefully and fairly quickly. Consider the sea change in many countries in tobacco-related social norms, regulations and behaviours.[24] Until recently, smoking tobacco commanded a coveted cultural position in countries around the world. Over the past decades, in varying degrees, smoking cigarettes has been reduced to junk status, though much work remains, especially in addressing residual inequalities in tobacco use, particularly in developing countries.[25] The first international health treaty negotiated under the auspices of the World Health Organization is dedicated exclusively to tobacco control—the Framework Convention on Tobacco Control. With 182 parties covering more than 90 percent of the world's people, the treaty is a testament to what science-based public health expertise, coupled with sustained and effective political leadership, can do to galvanize action on a globalized problem.[26]

" If equity, innovation and stewardship become central to what it means to live a good life, human flourishing can happen alongside easing planetary pressures.

Environmental values have witnessed similar upheavals. Take the publication of Rachel Carson's landmark *Silent Spring,* widely considered to have marked the advent of the modern environmental movement, whose roots are centuries older.[27] Distributional concerns soon came to the fore with the environmental justice movement. Each was in no small part a practical reaction to new realities, such as air and water pollution, happening in unprecedented ways and at unprecedented scales and often disproportionately impacting marginalized groups. Each broadened the idea of what constituted a good life by creating space for environmental stewardship, social justice and intergenerational responsibilities, laying the foundations for the sustainable development era. And each must continue to evolve in response to global planetary challenges that it, in its original incarnation, did not set out to address.

Now, in the context of the Anthropocene, it is essential to do away with stark distinctions between people and planet. Earth system approaches increasingly point to our interconnectedness as socioecological systems, a notion highly relevant to the Anthropocene.[28] Human development aligns well with such thinking. It has always been about breaking down silos and making connections. How could a development perspective centred on human possibility be otherwise? Every one of us moves in and out of social, economic and environmental spaces. On any given day a farmer might be navigating roles as mother and wife, collecting firewood and fetching water, worrying about weather and pests, negotiating the marketplace, buying medicine and textbooks. People, place and environment are not only connected in rural contexts. City dwellers, too, interact with their environment, often on a much larger or more varied scale for food, water, air quality, recreation and mental and physical health. It is the lens centred on any individual's experience, rather than institutional structures organized in terms of sectors, that allows the human development approach to break free from disciplinary and sectoral shackles. It aims to be development as seen through any of our own eyes.

And the system-level crises we are increasingly seeing are cause for alarm (chapter 2). We no longer have the luxury, if we ever really did, of solving problems as isolated, quasi-independent points in separate social and ecological spheres. Instead, they are nodes in an interdependent socioecological network that, as a whole, is flashing red.[29] The resilience of the system has been taken for granted, especially when only one part of it was under strain at a given time.[30] The homogenizing effect of our predominant models of production and consumption, which have been busy knitting the world together, have eroded the diversity —in all its forms, from biological to cultural—that is so vital to resilience.[31] Diversity increases redundancy, and while redundancy may not be good for business, it is good for system resilience in the face of shocks, which travel along the lines that connect people and nations.[32]

" In the Anthropocene, it is essential to do away with stark distinctions between people and planet.

Now, in little more than a decade, the global financial crisis, the climate crisis, the inequality crisis and the Covid-19 crisis have all shown that the resilience of the system itself is breaking down. Buffering systems are maxing out. Once-supple connections can become brittle, leaving them more inclined to break than to bend, further destabilizing the Earth system.[33] The result is that perturbations more easily become contagion—whether economic, environmental or viral—that slips indifferently through the porous borders of nation-states and scales illusory walls that divide people from planet.

Business as usual simply will not work. The same applies to the human development concept, which must be continually refreshed to respond to the challenges of our time. It is not about throwing out its central tenets, which remain vital to the many challenges of today, but rather drawing on them to help navigate a turbulent new geologic epoch. The goal of human development is as relevant as ever—for people to live lives they value. And within that goal lies the potential to navigate our predicament, if for no other reason than business as usual means that people, including future generations, will face ever narrowing instead of ever expanding sets of choices in their lives.

Easing planetary pressures implies understanding how all life on the planet—the biosphere—underpins so much of what we take for granted, like the air we breathe. This puts in sharp relief the importance of a biosphere that is regenerated, not depleted. It also implies understanding how societies use energy and materials. To what extent are sources of energy

renewable indefinitely—as from the sun—and to what extent are materials recycled rather than outcycled in waste and pollution? The accumulating carbon dioxide in the atmosphere and plastic in the oceans are just two of many examples that illustrate the risks of relying on fossil fuels and open material cycles. So is biodiversity loss, which often parallels loss of cultural and language diversity, impoverishing societies culturally.[34]

The Earth has gone through periods of instability before, evolving into new states. Planetary processes normally unfold over hundreds of thousands to millions of years, a timescale well beyond the reach of our species. For us, ancient is measured in thousands of years; our recorded history is a mere speck against the vastness of geologic time. Complicating matters is a backdrop of intrinsic climate instability. The Holocene, despite its apparent stability, is a warm blip within a changing climate regime, one in which oscillations between cooler glacial periods and warmer ones have become deeper and stronger. If the Earth's climate has already been characterized by abrupt change, then greenhouse gas emissions, along with other human-caused planetary disruptions to material cycles, add fuel to the fire, layering new instabilities on top of existing ones.

The Report calls for a just transformation that expands human freedoms while easing planetary pressures. It organizes its recommendations not around actors but around mechanisms for change—social norms and values, incentives and regulation, and nature-based human development. Each mechanism of change specifies multiple potential roles for each of us, for governments, for financial markets, for political and civil society leaders. It is not about pitting people against trees or about doing away with markets simply because they sometimes fail. Instead, it is about seeing how different approaches—using norms and values, using incentives and regulation, using nature itself—can be brought together in concert to expand human freedoms while mitigating planetary pressures.

Systems and complexity thinking applies equally to social norms, which are generated and reinforced across society, from what children learn in school, what people do online, what leaders say and enact by way of policy. Norms exhibit properties of stability and resilience, but they can be—and have been—nudged enough at critical points into new states, sometimes desirably, sometimes less so. Positive feedback loops can help accelerate change and stabilize new normative states, sometimes swiftly, as we have seen with tobacco norms. But, of course, reversion is possible. How do norms, as nebulous as they are powerful, change? What levers and mechanisms are available to policymakers and everyday citizens? This question animates chapter 4 of the Report. A first step is to expand choices available to people. Expanding choice—such as renewable energy sources and multimodal transportation networks—is in line with helping people realize their values. It is also in line with competitive well functioning markets.

" The Report calls for a just transformation that expands human freedoms while easing planetary pressures.

At the same time, moments of crisis can move systems closer to critical change thresholds. Consider many countries' experience in their progress towards universal health coverage, one of the Sustainable Development Goals. A recent analysis found that among 49 countries spanning different incomes, most moved towards universal health coverage as a result of disruption in the status quo, including when recovering from episodes of social instability.[35] Moreover, countries' transitions to universal health coverage have typically been easier when neighbours and peers have already achieved it—an example of both incentives and positive feedback effects. The overlapping crises we are facing now and facing most immediately in the Covid-19 pandemic give a chance for societies to re-evaluate norms and for policymakers to take spirited steps towards social and economic recoveries that invest in healthier, greener, more equitable futures—ones that expand human freedoms while easing planetary pressures.

Today almost 80 percent of the world's people believe that it is important to protect the planet. But only about half say they are likely to take concrete action to save it. There is a gap between people's values and their behaviour (see chapter 4). To help bridge the gap, to help empower people, the Report also looks at the ways incentives and regulation can prevent or promote people taking action based on their values (chapter 5). Incentives matter, even when

individuals do not change their minds or their values. Incentives—from fossil fuel subsidies to carbon prices, or a lack thereof—help explain current patterns of consumption, production and investment and other choices that lead to planetary and social imbalances. Take fossil fuel subsidies, which result in direct and indirect costs of over $5 trillion a year. Eliminating those subsidies in 2015 would have reduced global carbon emissions by 28 percent and fossil fuel air pollution deaths by 46 percent.[36]

The Report goes on to document how incentives and regulation could evolve in ways that would ease planetary pressures and move societies towards the transformative changes required to advance human development in the Anthropocene. It considers three domains shaped by incentives. The first is finance, which includes the incentives within financial firms as well as the regulatory authorities that oversee them. The second is prices, which rarely fully reflect social and environmental costs, thus distorting behaviour. The third is incentives for collective action, including at the international level.

Nature-based human development helps tackle three central challenges of the Anthropocene together —mitigating and adapting to climate change, protecting biodiversity and ensuring human wellbeing for all. Nature-based human development is about nesting human development—including social and economic systems—into ecosystems and the biosphere, building on a systemic approach to nature-based solutions that puts people's agency at the core. The potential is huge, with benefits ranging from climate change mitigation and disaster risk reduction to improving food security and increasing water availability and quality. A set of 20 cost-effective actions across global forests, wetlands, grasslands and agricultural lands could provide 37 percent of the mitigation needed through 2030 to keep global warming below 2 degrees Celsius above preindustrial levels and 20 percent of the mitigation needed through 2050 (figure 6).[37] About two-thirds of that mitigation potential (equivalent to one-fourth of total mitigation needs) is linked to forest pathways, mainly reforestation. The contribution per capita of indigenous peoples in the Amazon to climate change mitigation through their actions to preserve forests amounts to as much as the emissions per capita of the top 1 percent of the global income distribution (see chapter 6).

Figure 6 Twenty nature-based solutions could provide much of the mitigation needed to restrain global warming

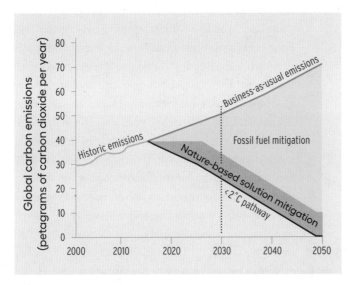

Source: Griscom and others 2017.

While the term "nature-based solutions" suffers from solutions-oriented language, it is not of that ilk. On the contrary, nature-based solutions, or approaches, are often rooted in socioecological system perspectives that recognize the many benefits and values of a healthy ecosystem for both people and planet. Yet it is the very complexity, and the multidimensionality of their benefits, that tend to make them the exception rather than the rule. It is admittedly difficult for their benefits to be properly aggregated and accounted for using traditional economic metrics and when benefits are dispersed across ministries of agriculture, environment, transport and infrastructure, development, tourism, health, finance—the list goes on. The problem, then, is not with nature-based solutions but with the inadequacy of our prevailing metrics and models of governance, and not recognizing people's agency in their implementation. Joined-up thinking and policymaking must become the norm for countries and people to succeed in the Anthropocene.

The Report focuses on mechanisms of action, rather than on specific actors, partly because human development in the Anthropocene will require whole-of-society responses. Even so, one set of actors plays a uniquely important leadership role: governments, especially national governments. Only governments have the formal authority and power to marshal collective action towards shared challenges, whether that is enacting and enforcing a carbon price, removing laws that marginalize and disenfranchise or setting up the policy and institutional frameworks, backed by public investment, to spur ongoing broadly shared innovation. Power goes hand-in-hand with responsibility and accountability.

But governments cannot go it alone. The challenges of the Anthropocene are too complex for white knights or for technological fixes only. Nor can we ignore the opportunity for and importance of social mobilization from the bottom up. Individuals, communities and social movements demand, pressure and support government action. But if government leadership and action are insufficient on their own, they are certainly necessary. Leadership by example matters. When governments subsidize fossil fuels, they send powerful signals beyond the obvious economic and environmental implications. They also send powerful messages about values. Several countries—including Chile, China, Japan and the Republic of Korea—have recently sent strong messages in the other direction by announcing bold new commitments to carbon neutrality.[38] The European Union has as well.[39] More government commitments—as well as commitments from the private sector that are picking up renewed interest in sustainable investment and in business practices that are mindful of environmental, social and governance impacts (chapter 5)—backed by action, can facilitate the normative changes needed to advance human development in the Anthropocene.

Development is dynamic; priorities and values shift. So should metrics. That is why the human development measurement toolkit has constantly evolved. The past decade has seen the launch of a suite of new dashboards and composite indices dedicated to measuring gender inequalities and women's empowerment. Since the 2010 Human Development Report, the Inequality-adjusted HDI has accounted for the distribution of human development within countries. A global Multidimensional Poverty Index was also introduced then to shift our attention from traditional income-based poverty measures towards a more holistic view of lived poverty.

The HDI remains useful for measuring a set of basic capabilities, but clearly we have moved beyond one indicator to rule them all. Indeed, the HDI never claimed to reflect the totality of human development. The challenges we face, and the possibilities before us, have always been more complex, much more multidimensional and interconnected than a single metric—or even a handful of metrics, no matter how good—could ever capture on its own. Complexity requires more lenses. New metrics help construct them.

" The Report presents an adjustment to the Human Development Index for planetary pressures, ushering it into a new geologic epoch.

What does the Report explore by way of new metrics? Among them is a new generation of dashboards, as well as metrics that adjust the income component of the HDI to account for the social costs of carbon or for natural wealth. Together they do not aim to make normative judgements about countries. Instead, as with all the other human development metrics, they help countries understand their own progress broadly over time, learn from other countries' experiences and raise their ambitions in advancing human development while accounting for people's interactions with the planet. They also help people and civil society organizations hold countries accountable for their commitments. While composite metrics, especially at the global level, are inherently unable to capture national and local complexities, such metrics nonetheless offer broad high-level and directional perspectives. At their best they can contribute to but do not substitute for the nitty-gritty of dialogue and policymaking, which must happen in every society.

Figure 7 The adjustment to standard Human Development Index values by the Planetary pressures–adjusted Human Development Index widens as human development levels increase

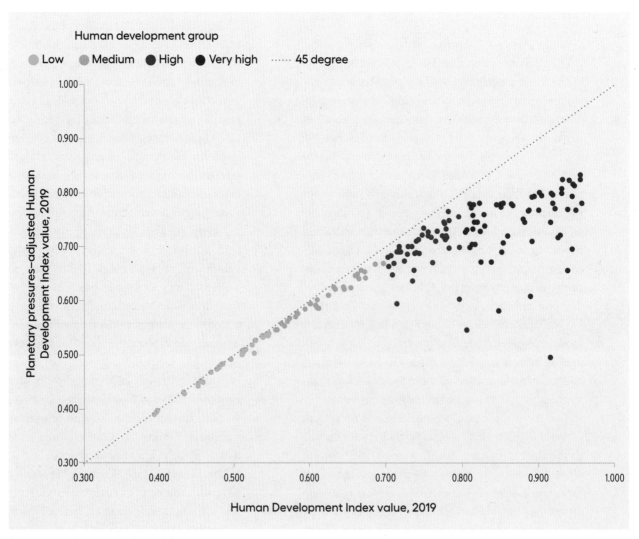

Source: Human Development Report Office.

Box 1 The Planetary pressures–adjusted Human Development Index: Signposts to navigate the Anthropocene

The Planetary pressures–adjusted Human Development Index (PHDI) provides a guiding metric towards advancing human development while easing planetary pressures—a combination that today corresponds to an "empty corner" when human development is contrasted with indicators of planetary pressure (the green rectangle in figure 5).[1] In the figure below the horizontal axis is HDI value, and the vertical axis is the index of pressures on the planet.[2] The contours of the shaded areas represent constant PHDI values that result from different combinations of HDI values and index of planetary pressures values. PHDI values increase as these lines move towards the bottom right corner, which corresponds to expanded capabilities and reduced planetary pressures. That corner, highlighted in green, is the aspirational destination of the human development journey in the Anthropocene. The curve corresponding to the average performance on the two indices for all countries moved towards that corner between 1990 and 2019.[3] But that movement was far too slow and modest. Further progress will require all countries to shift rapidly and substantially towards the bottom right corner. The PHDI and the HDI can help in assessing and, more importantly, in encouraging choices towards a human development journey in the Anthropocene that move us all in the direction of advancing human development while easing planetary pressures.

The world is moving far too slowly towards advancing human development while easing planetary pressures

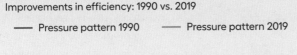

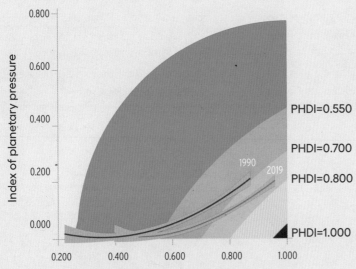

Human Development Index value, 2019

Note: Cross-sectional pressure patterns for 1990 and 2019 were calculated using polynomial regression models. Shaded areas are confidence intervals.
Source: Human Development Report Office.

Notes
1. See similar analysis in Lin and others (2018). As an image of aspirational space in development, it is also reminiscent of the idea of "casillero vacío" in Fajnzylber (1990). **2.** That is, one minus the adjustment factor for planetary pressures that is multiplied by the HDI to generate the PHDI. **3.** We thank Marina Fischer-Kowalski for insights on this pattern.

The Report presents an adjustment to the HDI for planetary pressures. The Planetary pressures-adjusted HDI (PHDI) retains the simplicity and clarity of the original HDI while accounting for some of the complex system-level dynamics discussed throughout the Report. By accounting for key planetary pressures, it ushers the HDI into a new geologic epoch.

" There are many opportunities for countries to expand capabilities-based human development while reducing planetary pressures. When agency and values are added to the mix, the opportunities become even greater.

The PHDI adjusts the standard HDI by a country's level of carbon dioxide emissions and material footprint, each on a per capita basis. For countries on the lower end of the human development spectrum, the impact of the adjustment is generally small. For high and very high human development countries the impact tends to become large, reflecting the various ways that their development paths impact the planet (figure 7 and box 1).

The good news is that there are many options and opportunities for countries to maintain and even expand traditional, capabilities-based notions of human development while reducing planetary pressures. When agency and values are added to the mix, as the Report demonstrates, the opportunities for expanding human freedoms while easing those pressures become even greater.

In his great postwar novel *The Plague,* Albert Camus wrote, "everyone has it inside himself, this plague, because no one in the world, no one, is immune."[40] If he were writing today, he could have easily been commenting on Covid-19 or climate change, though of course we understand that while everyone is affected, they are not affected equally. But while the stakes for humanity may unfortunately be much higher today than they were some 70 years ago, there is cause for hope—we need no longer be passive recipients of plagues or of development. Fate has been usurped by choice, which in turn is predicated on power. In this brave new geologic epoch of the Anthropocene—in this age of humans—inside our species, and our species uniquely, is the power to reimagine and rebuild our world, to choose justice and sustainability. This 2020 Human Development Report, coming at the close of a tumultuous year of layered global crises, helps signpost the way.

Renewing human development for the Anthropocene

Renewing human development for the Anthropocene

Part I has three chapters sequentially covering analytical, empirical and policy perspectives on how human development relates to the concept of and debates around the Anthropocene. Part II considers the implications for action, discussing three key mechanisms for change: social norms, incentives and nature-based human development. Part III explores implications for metrics of human development.

Chapter 1 argues that the human development journey (where we want to head) must now be considered in the context of an unprecedented moment in human history and in the planet's history—and that the human development approach opens fresh and empowering perspectives on how to get there. Complementing chapter 1's analysis, chapter 2 provides detailed evidence of unprecedented planetary and social imbalances and their interaction. It shows empirically that we are confronting something fundamentally new and that the natural world of the Anthropocene reflects imbalances in opportunities, wealth and power of the human world. Chapter 3 argues that working together in the pursuit of equity, innovation and planet stewardship can steer actions towards the transformational changes required to advance human development in the Anthropocene.

Charting human development in the Anthropocene

Charting human development in the Anthropocene

We are entering a new geologic age: the Anthropocene. The age of humans.

For the first time in our history the most serious and immediate risks are human made and unfold at planetary scales, from climate change to the Covid-19 pandemic to rising inequalities.

How can human development help us navigate the complexities of the Anthropocene?

This chapter argues that we must reimagine the human development journey and leverage the human development approach to support transformational change.

"The quandary of unsustainability may be our predicament, but the task of solving it is ours as well. The nature of the problem, its fuller appreciation and the ways and means of solving it all belong to us—humanity as a whole. If there is a subject on which collaboration and non-divisive commitments are needed, this surely is it. But in order to make this possible and effective, we need a vision of mankind not as patients whose interests have to be looked after, but as agents who can do effective things—both individually and jointly."[1]

Amartya Sen

"Most 'classic' writings on sustainability present people as the problem, not as a collective source of strength. [...They] frame the discourse in terms of the Earth's finite resources and rising population. [...] We have moved away from framing it exclusively around limits to growth and conserving natural resources. Instead, we emphasize the connections between communities, ecosystems and social justice."[2]

Harini Nagendra

The Covid-19 pandemic is a cautionary tale. For decades scientists have been predicting just such a pandemic, pointing to the rise of new diseases that jump from animals to humans[3]—and the virus that causes Covid-19 is likely one.[4] Indeed, the increasing transmission of disease from wildlife to humans reflects the pressures we are putting on the planet.[5]

It is a tale of the risks we confront as we go deeper into a new reality described as the Anthropocene, the age of humans, with the unprecedented planetary change in scope, scale and speed—as elaborated in chapter 2—driven by human activity posing risks to people and all forms of life.[6] But the risks do not affect everyone in the same way. Covid-19 was superimposed on a world with wide and growing inequalities in human development. And it is driving deeper wedges between those more able and those less able to cope. Meanwhile, the underlying drivers of shocks such as Covid-19 are rooted ultimately in unbalanced interactions between people and the planet. And these drivers feed off the imbalances in opportunities, wealth and power across people and countries.

Confronting this new reality of a self-reinforcing cycle of social imbalances and of planetary imbalances (the dangerous planetary change for people and all forms of life) calls for reimagining the human development journey (where do we want to go?).[7] It also calls for applying the human development approach to longstanding debates on sustainability (how do we want to get there?).

The human development journey—enlarging people's abilities and opportunities to be and do what they have reason to value—must be considered in the context of an unprecedented moment in human history and in the planet's history. This chapter asserts the importance of reconfiguring the material and energy flows now structurally linked to how we organize economies and societies. It details the transformational changes that need to be brought from the periphery to the centre of the human development journey. That journey cannot be separated from the web of life we are embedded in.

" The Anthropocene: the age of humans. For the first time in our history the most serious and immediate, even existential, risks are human made and unfolding at planetary scale.

The human development approach sets out an evaluative framework for development outcomes based on expanding capabilities, thus increasing wellbeing freedoms, the valuable opportunities to choose from. This takes us beyond notions of sustainability based on needs fulfilment and away from focusing on instrumental objectives such as economic growth. This chapter argues that a human development approach invites us to look beyond sustaining needs to expanding capabilities. To see people as agents—who act and bring about change. And to evaluate people's achievements in terms of their own values and goals. In that expansion and perspective lay both the goal of the human development journey and, instrumentally, the means to widen the scope of potential actions to change the drivers of pressures on the planet. In a broader set of motivations for human behaviour, market incentives as well as values, dignity and sense of worth are all important. Ultimately, people are agents of their individual and collective destiny, able to drive social change.

The Anthropocene: the age of humans. For the first time in our history the most serious and immediate, even existential, risks are human made and unfolding at planetary scale. The chapter argues that this new reality calls for reimagining the human development journey and leveraging the human development approach to support transformational social changes to ease pressures on the planet. The nature and process of change will be contested, resisted, promoted and driven by varied interests and values. This Report mobilizes human development analysis to marshal evidence and suggest options for individual and collective choices on how to redress both social and planetary imbalances. Thirty years ago the first Human Development Report placed people as the ultimate end of development. "People are the real wealth of nations," read the first line. It is time to draw on that real wealth of nations to transform our world, as called for in the 2030 Agenda for Sustainable Development.

Confronting a new reality: People versus trees?

"Unlike other concepts that have highlighted the impact of human pressures on the environment, the Anthropocene describes a state change in the Earth system, viewed as an interdependent, co-evolving social-ecological system, as well as a new way of thinking about our recent and current epoch. Anthropocene thinking takes us away from reductionist linear cause-effect analysis of equity and sustainability, to underline the fully intertwined character of human and ecological systems, and the co-evolving fates of sustainability and equity."[8]

Melissa Leach, Belinda Reyers and others

"It is people, not trees, whose future choices have to be protected" affirmed the first Human Development Report, published in 1990.[9] By setting human flourishing as the ultimate end of development, it asserted that development is not about the accumulation of material or natural resources. It is about enlarging people's ability to be and do what they have reason to value and expanding wellbeing freedoms. This fundamental premise of human development animates this Report. But the apposition of people and nature needs to be re-examined. Because leaving nature in the background—or, worse, presenting

choices as if they were between people and planet —will limit human flourishing for everyone. As the 1994 Human Development Report stated, "The strongest argument for protecting the environment is the ethical need to guarantee to future generations opportunities similar to the ones previous generation have enjoyed. This guarantee is the foundation of 'sustainable development.'"[10] But these impacts are no longer solely for future generations: Planetary imbalances are already hurting people today, driving some of the inequalities in human development analysed in the 2019 Human Development Report.[11] And those inequalities and social imbalances, in turn, are reflected in even sharper relief in planetary imbalances.

Over the years Human Development Reports have highlighted the interactions between environmental degradation and human development.[12] They have identified affluence in developed countries as a key environmental stressor. Two Reports have been devoted to water and climate change, and two have considered sustainability and resilience. The environment and the challenges of sustainability and climate have been forcefully advocated by social and political movements that have pushed these issues to the top of the development agenda. Natural hazards and environmental disasters have contributed to public awareness, and scientific evidence and understanding of key biophysical, economic and social impacts have accumulated (spotlight 1.1). The 2030 Agenda for Sustainable Development is a clear political statement of the universal consensus that has emerged as a result.

" This Report mobilizes human development analysis to marshal evidence and suggest options for individual and collective choices on how to redress both social and planetary imbalances.

Our dependence on nature is not in question. Amartya Sen put it bluntly: "It is not so much that humanity is trying to sustain the natural world, but rather that humanity is trying to sustain itself. It is us that will have to 'go' unless we can put the world around us in reasonable order. The precariousness of nature is *our* peril, *our* fragility."[13] But there are two new elements to consider.

First, the notion of the Anthropocene has forced a reframing of thinking—from standalone environmental and sustainability issues, such as climate change, to the recognition of a set of interdependent challenges resulting from underlying processes of planetary change driven by human pressures.[14] Indeed, the climate is changing in dangerous ways,[15] and urgent action is needed to curb the greenhouse gas emissions causing global warming.[16] Concentrations of carbon dioxide—a long-lived greenhouse gas—are high and increasing because the planetary processes that have maintained concentrations within a relatively narrow range (the carbon biogeochemical cycle) are being overwhelmed by rapid and large increases in anthropogenic emissions.[17] But other key biogeochemical cycles are being dramatically altered as well. Take nitrogen, essential for life and the most common yield-limiting nutrient in agriculture.[18] The use of synthetic fertilizers (which increased eightfold between 1960 and 2000) and the combustion of fossil fuels have produced the largest disturbance to the nitrogen biogeochemical cycle since it emerged 2.5 billion years ago.[19]

Most people now live longer and healthier lives than their predecessors, but the opposite is true for the vast majority of the rest of life on Earth.[20] Humans evolved over 300,000 years[21] amid a richness and diversity of life unprecedented in the planet's history, as measured by the absolute number of species.[22] That richness of life is now being destroyed at an alarming rate due to direct and indirect human action, with a quarter of species facing extinction, many within decades.[23] Biodiversity enhances nature's contributions to people.[24] In addition, language and culture have coevolved with biological diversity, so biological impoverishment parallels the loss of cultural and linguistic diversity.[25]

This Report's point of departure is that there is no clear pathway to avoid the dangerous planetary change of the Anthropocene. It is, as Julia Adeney Thomas argues, a predicament that needs to be navigated.[26] Or as Sharachchandra Lele put it, we need to move beyond a "narrowed framing of the problem: one value (sustaining future generations), one problem (climate change), one goal (reduce carbon emissions) and one solution (renewables)."[27] And that calls for a full understanding of the pressures we are putting on the planet and of our interdependence with nature.[28]

" As long as planetary imbalances persist, they engender risks that can materialize in shocks to human development, just as the Covid-19 pandemic has done. Superimposed on existing asymmetries of power and opportunity, they perpetuate and can even increase inequalities in human development.

Second, the notion of the Anthropocene emerges thanks to remarkable advances in Earth system and sustainability sciences.[29] In addition to documenting and explaining the impacts of human activities, these new fields are stimulating interdisciplinary work, encompassing natural and social sciences and the humanities, providing insights into how to mitigate those impacts while improving people's lives. The physical realities of the unprecedented pressure humans are putting on the planet have reawakened interest in understanding our dependence on nature now as well as in the past and what is likely to unfold in the future. Value systems go beyond conventionally looking at nature and the planet for only their instrumental value (service provision) or intrinsic value (inherent worth) to incorporate relational values ("associated with relationships, both interpersonal and as articulated by policies and social norms").[30] Bagele Chilisa has highlighted how knowledge systems rooted in African philosophies, worldviews and history have been marginalized in development discourse but hold the potential to enrich sustainability science.[31] And the interdependence of biological and cultural diversity has led to biocultural diversity (discussed later in the chapter) as a source of knowledge for scientists, local communities, civil society and policymakers interested in local and global sustainability.[32]

A key insight emerging from this vast and rapidly growing body of work is that social and natural systems are best seen not only as interacting and interdependent but also as embedded in each other. "Moving beyond the notion of sustainable development as separable human development targets constrained by environmental or natural resource limits, to an inseparable socio-ecological systems perspective on sustainable development, offers a fresh perspective on sustainable development. It further offers a novel and expanded opportunity space from which to address the challenges of the Anthropocene."[33]

An important implication is that as much as human activity is harming nature, it remains within our reach to be a positive regenerative force on the planet—looking at nature less as a constraint or something to be preserved in pristine form[34] and more as an asset with the potential to provide sources and resilience, and more choices, to navigate the Anthropocene.[35] More important, the emerging insights also point the way forward on what to do and how, in a way that avoids what Ruth DeFries and Harini Nagendra called the two traps of "falsely assuming a tame solution and inaction from overwhelming complexity."[36]

Considering the complex and interdependent relationship between people and planet, between socioeconomic and natural systems, points to the links between dangerous planetary and social imbalances, which interact and often reinforce each other. As long as planetary imbalances persist, they engender risks that can materialize in shocks to human development, just as the Covid-19 pandemic has done (figure 1.1). Superimposed on existing asymmetries of power and opportunity, they perpetuate and can even increase inequalities in human development. The pandemic is adjudged to have reversed development progress by decades. It has hit more harshly, more quickly and more deeply those already vulnerable, marginalized or with few resources and capabilities, increasing inequalities in human development.[37] That, in turn, has fed social imbalances.

Social dynamics result in actions that can either intensify or ease the pressures on the planet. Social imbalances feed inequalities in human development —which ultimately are gaps in empowerment—constraining the space for deliberative reasoning and collective action.[38] We all care about those close to us, but a key to solidarity and cooperation is how to extend pro-social behaviour beyond close-knit networks. That is determined in part by the position of those worse off and minorities in social structures and economic systems, along with the institutional arrangements that determine the extent of their political inclusion.[39] Instead, those who are more powerful (and for the most part benefit from the status quo) shape the framing of available information,

Figure 1.1 Planetary and social imbalances reinforce each other

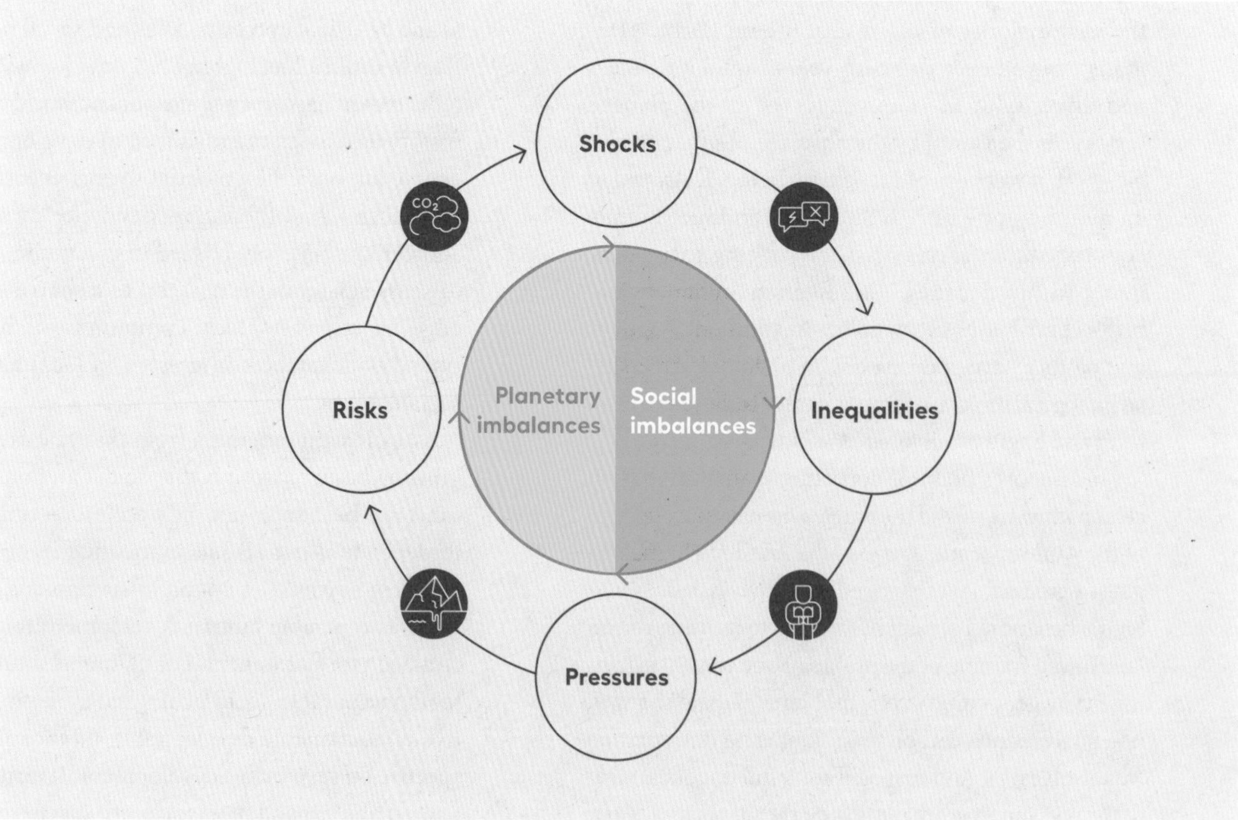

Source: Human Development Report Office.

including scientific evidence,[40] and leverage their resources and influence to preserve their power—often in ways that oppose transformation.[41] All of this perpetuates the pressures on the planet that further drive planetary imbalances. This, in turn, engenders risks, and the cycle starts afresh. Reframing the human development journey in the Anthropocene has the potential to break this cycle.

What does this mean for human development? First, it presents a challenge as to how to imagine and pursue human development. Addressing social imbalances, the hemisphere on the right in figure 1.1, has always been at the core of the human development journey. But until now the other hemisphere, planetary imbalances, has not been systematically brought into the human development journey. How to do it, and how that changes the journey, are addressed in the next section of this chapter.

Second, the human development approach has not yet been fully leveraged to inform how to address the challenges in the hemisphere on the left in figure 1.1. It can offer fresh perspectives on making expanded capabilities and human agency central to easing pressures on the planet, as addressed in the last section of this chapter.[42]

Human agency is thus at the core of the processes of change and transformation required to enhance equity in human development while easing pressures on the planet. This implies reassessing capabilities with a new sense of possibility and responsibility to respect the planet, to reach those who have the fewest opportunities and to eliminate the persistent patterns of inequality, discrimination and exclusion (including racism and patriarchy) that tear societies apart.[43]

Reimagining the human development journey: Bringing the planet back in

Decoupling economic growth from emissions and material use is key to easing pressures on the planet while improving living standards. The debate on the extent to which this is sufficient and feasible provides a natural starting point to explore whether decoupling helps rearticulate the human development journey in the Anthropocene.

The relative decoupling between GDP growth and both material use and carbon dioxide emissions is common (the economic growth rate is higher than the growth rate of material use or emissions). But absolute decoupling (economic growth alongside absolute reductions in material use or emissions) is partial, temporary and rare.[44] Interpretations of what the empirical findings imply vary. It is widely agreed that decoupling is vital and needs to be pursued.[45] Most agree also that future decoupling based on extrapolating current trends would be insufficient to meet goals such as those agreed to in the Paris Agreement[46] or the suite of international goals related to biodiversity loss.[47] But ultimately, it will be up to choices. A recent model suggested that a policy package on climate change mitigation would allow the world to reach net-zero emissions in 2050 at moderate transitional growth and employment costs, resulting in global net output gains of up to 13 percent of GDP by 2100 and with income transfers compensating the poor for the costs of the energy transition.[48]

Decoupling what?

The dominant view on decoupling is that green growth or green economy approaches hold promise by shifting towards more resource-efficient and less emission-intensive production and consumption, allowing for relative or absolute decoupling.[49]

A recent study identified 18 developed countries whose carbon dioxide emissions declined in absolute terms between 2005 and 2015, both for territorial emissions (those due to production within the country) and for consumption-based emissions (those that account for the effects of trade in shifting high-emission production activities to other countries and then importing goods produced elsewhere; figure 1.2).[50] Although slow growth contributed by reducing energy demand, absolute decoupling happened mainly as a result of targeted policies to promote renewable sources of energy and energy efficiency.[51] Another study looked at energy use and GDP in the aftermath of the 2008 global financial crisis, finding that although the countries worst affected economically had the largest reductions in energy use, those that rebounded more strongly had the highest energy efficiency gains.[52] Both studies cover a short period and limited set of countries, but they provide evidence for green growth patterns of development underpinned

Figure 1.2 Carbon dioxide emissions from fossil fuel combustion have fallen in several countries

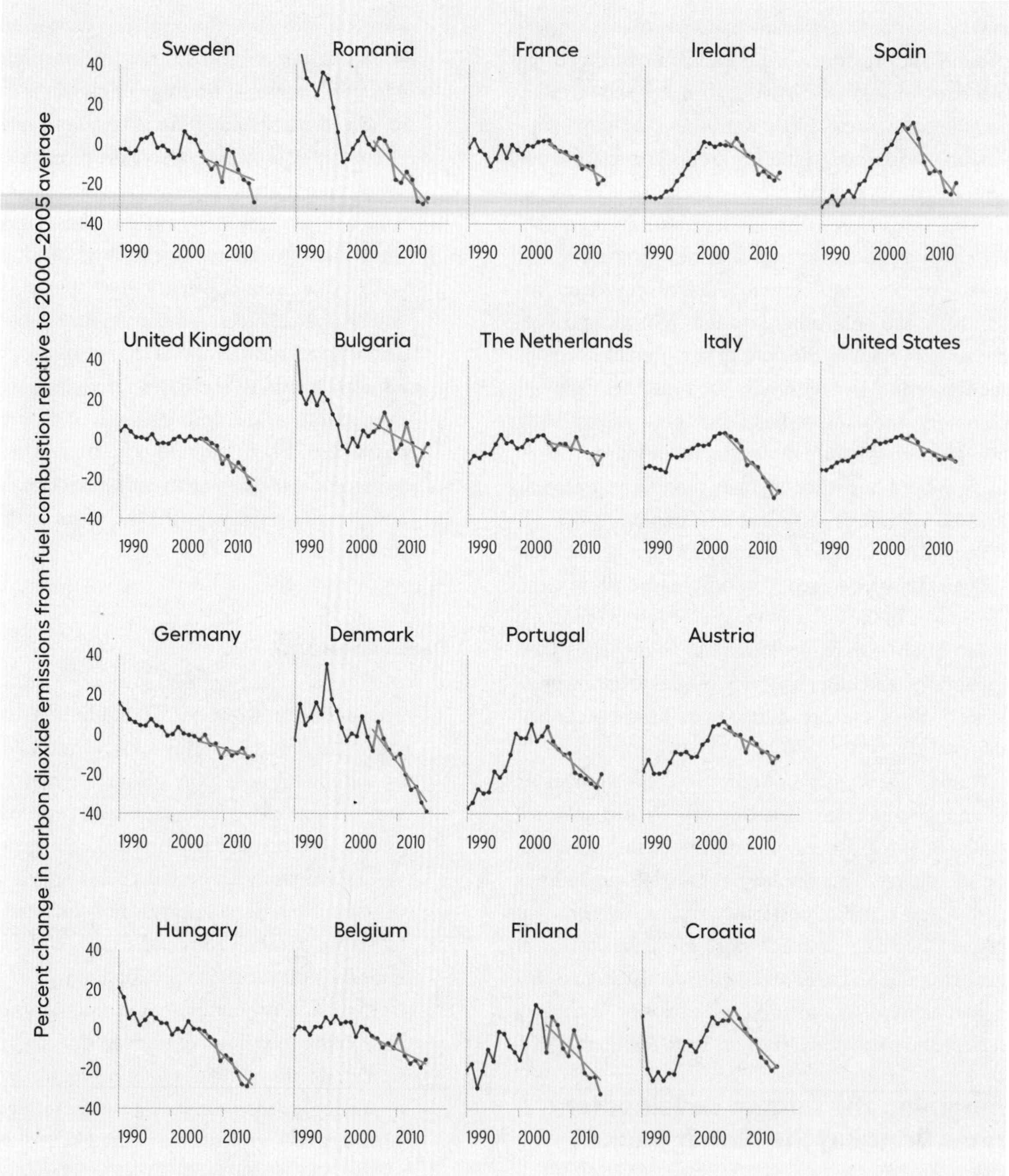

Source: Le Quéré and others 2019.

by more resource- and emission-efficient economies driven by policy interventions.[53]

It has been argued that efficiency gains based on known and safe technologies have proved insufficient (based on past trends and model-based projections) and that an overall downscaling in aggregate economic activity is also required.[54] This could be achieved through the degrowth of production and consumption in high-consuming countries and a shift away from growth-focused development in the Global South.[55] This conclusion is based primarily on scenarios of low energy demand[56] but is also informed by the broader research and advocacy on degrowth.[57]

The debate continues in part because economic models have limitations in incorporating key biophysical functions, and biophysical models remain limited in exploring the ranges of flexibility that can emerge as a result of changing economic and social behaviour, making clear that conclusions are difficult to reach.[58]

Can the decoupling framing help reimagine the human development journey? One way would be to replace economic growth with advances in human development. This shift has always been at the heart of the human development approach, and indeed the Human Development Index (HDI) can be, and has been, used instead of GDP.[59] Recent work that shifts the lens from decoupling growth and resource use to decoupling the determinants of wellbeing can illuminate pathways to improve people's lives in a less resource-intensive way.[60] Yet, these perspectives still underemphasize the role of human agency —the ability of individuals and communities to take the driver's seat in addressing challenges and seizing opportunities—that is central to the concept of human development.

Roughly speaking, human development comprises capabilities that relate to wellbeing and agency. Improvements in human development as measured by the HDI (which accounts only partially for agency) were fuelled by using resources that generated today's ecological crises (countries in rectangle B of figure 1.3). So a reimagined human development journey cannot occur along the same path for low human development countries (in rectangle A), and high human development countries cannot remain where they are. As elaborated later in chapter 2, inequalities in achievements in wellbeing mirror injustices in resource use. A reimagined human development journey thus calls on all countries to improve wellbeing equitably while easing pressures on the planet (moving to the empty rectangle C).

Taking that journey is a matter of choice. Simulations using shared socioeconomic pathways (SSP) scenarios to assess the impact of social and economic choices on greenhouse gas emissions and climate change illustrate the alternatives (figure 1.4).[61] SSP 5, the business-as-usual scenario, would move five world regions to high income status, but global warming would reach 3–5 degrees Celsius above preindustrial levels. SSP 1, the scenario in which social and

Figure 1.3 Where human development paths landed: High human development goes with high resource use

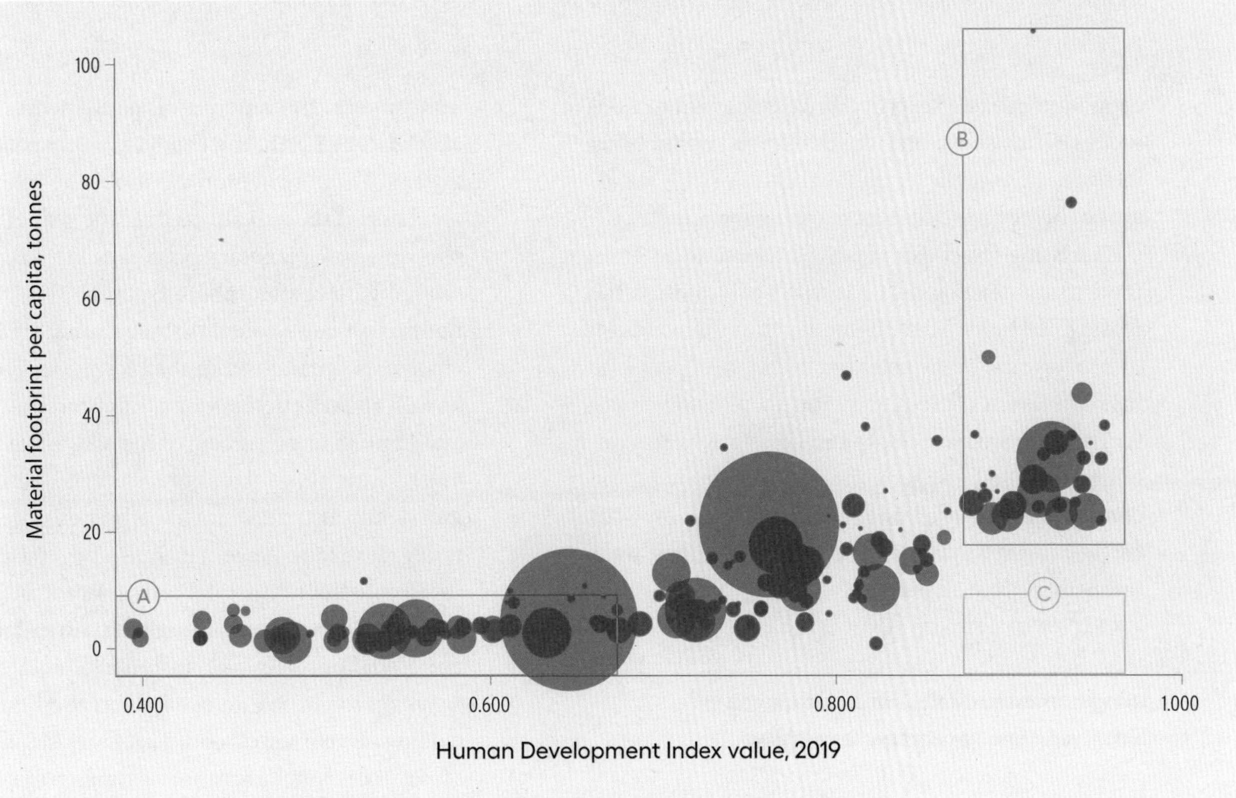

Note: Includes only countries with more than 1 million inhabitants. Bubble size is proportional to population.
Source: Human Development Report Office based on data from the United Nations Environment Programme.

Figure 1.4 Under the sustainability scenario, countries converge by 2100—with lower carbon dioxide emissions per capita and higher human development

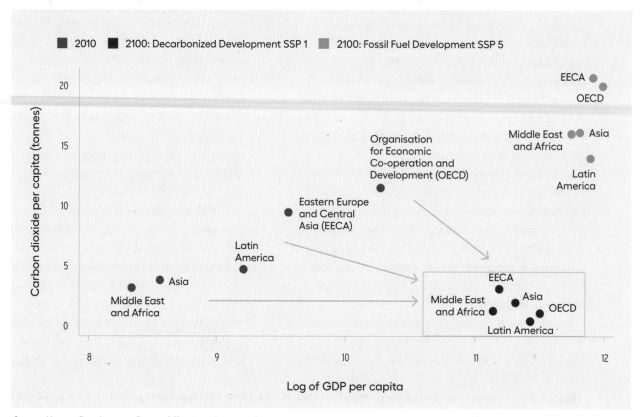

Source: Human Development Report Office based on data from the Shared Socioeconomic Pathways Database.

economic choices keep global warming within 2 degrees Celsius above preindustrial levels, would bring all five regions to the aspirational space of high standards of living and reduce pressures on the planet.

Exercising the choices that will take us away from the current development pathways and towards the reimagined human development journey depends on human agency, or the potential to empower people to make different choices, individually and collectively. To do so, we have to explore how societies, economies and the biosphere interact to understand the conditioning imposed by biophysical factors on what can be achieved in meeting people's aspirations: not a few people's, but all people's.

Mapping human societies' embeddedness in the biosphere: Energy and material flows

Life has created many of the features of the planet as we know them today: the gas composition of the atmosphere, the amount of sunlight reflected and absorbed by Earth, the chemical composition of the oceans. Timothy Lenton describes the role of life as a creator of these features over the planet's history, showing how planetary processes are deeply intertwined with the biosphere (spotlight 1.2). So it cannot be stressed enough that we cannot treat climate change as separate from the biosphere. The oceans absorb about 25 percent of annual carbon emissions and more than 90 percent of the additional heat generated from those emissions. Forests, wetlands and grasslands also draw down carbon dioxide, sequestering close to 30 percent of anthropogenic carbon dioxide emissions. The total carbon stored in terrestrial ecosystems in 2017 was almost 60 times larger than the global emissions of anthropogenic greenhouse gases (carbon dioxide equivalent). Soil carbon (including permafrost) is about 4.5 times larger than the atmospheric pool and about 5 times larger than the carbon in living plants and animals. The ocean holds a much larger carbon pool, about 38,000 gigatonnes.[62]

Human societies are embedded in the biosphere and depend on it. But by extracting from it for economic activities that shape consumption and production patterns, they have also been depleting it. Much of this happens in the background and seems invisible to social and individual choices, similar to forgetting our dependence on the air we breathe. To make the interactions between social and ecological systems more visible, it is useful to look at material and energy flows in our societies and their impact on planetary processes.

Every form of life takes up, transforms and expends energy and materials for its maintenance, growth and reproduction.[63] On land and in the seas, plants capture energy directly from sunlight, which combined with their use of materials[64] enable not only their growth and maintenance but also what is available to be consumed in succession by all other forms of life—generating waste products in the process. For the most part life consumes what is required for its biological existence, but human societies capture more energy and more material (figure 1.5) than they need to simply survive[65] on a scale that goes well beyond that of other species.[66]

For the planet the continuing flow of light from the sun ensures an essentially limitless flow of energy.[67] Looking at the evolution of the energy captured by the biosphere and by societies over major transitions, as well as the implications for material cycles, places the current moment in the context of both Earth history and human history (figure 1.6).[68] It highlights that the Anthropocene is unprecedented and shows how social dynamics drive planetary imbalances.[69] Major transitions correspond to increases in energy capture and changes in material cycles that surpassed the limiting conditions[70] prevailing before the transition. But these

Figure 1.5 Human societies are imbedded in the biosphere: Energy and biophysical resources are used to build stocks and provide benefits for humans while generating waste and emissions

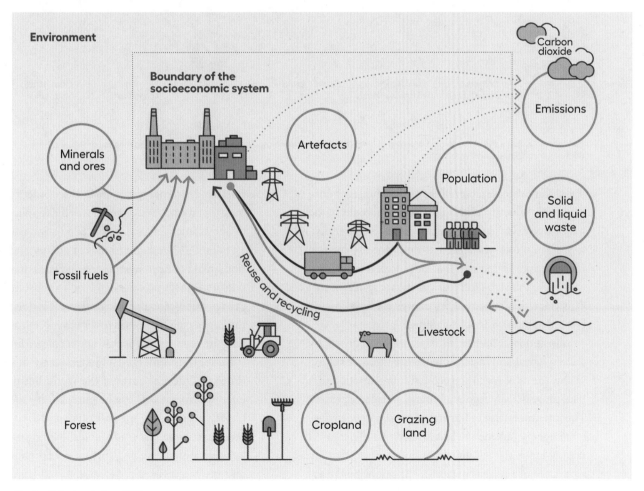

Source: Haberl and others 2019.

Figure 1.6 Energy captured in the biosphere and human society

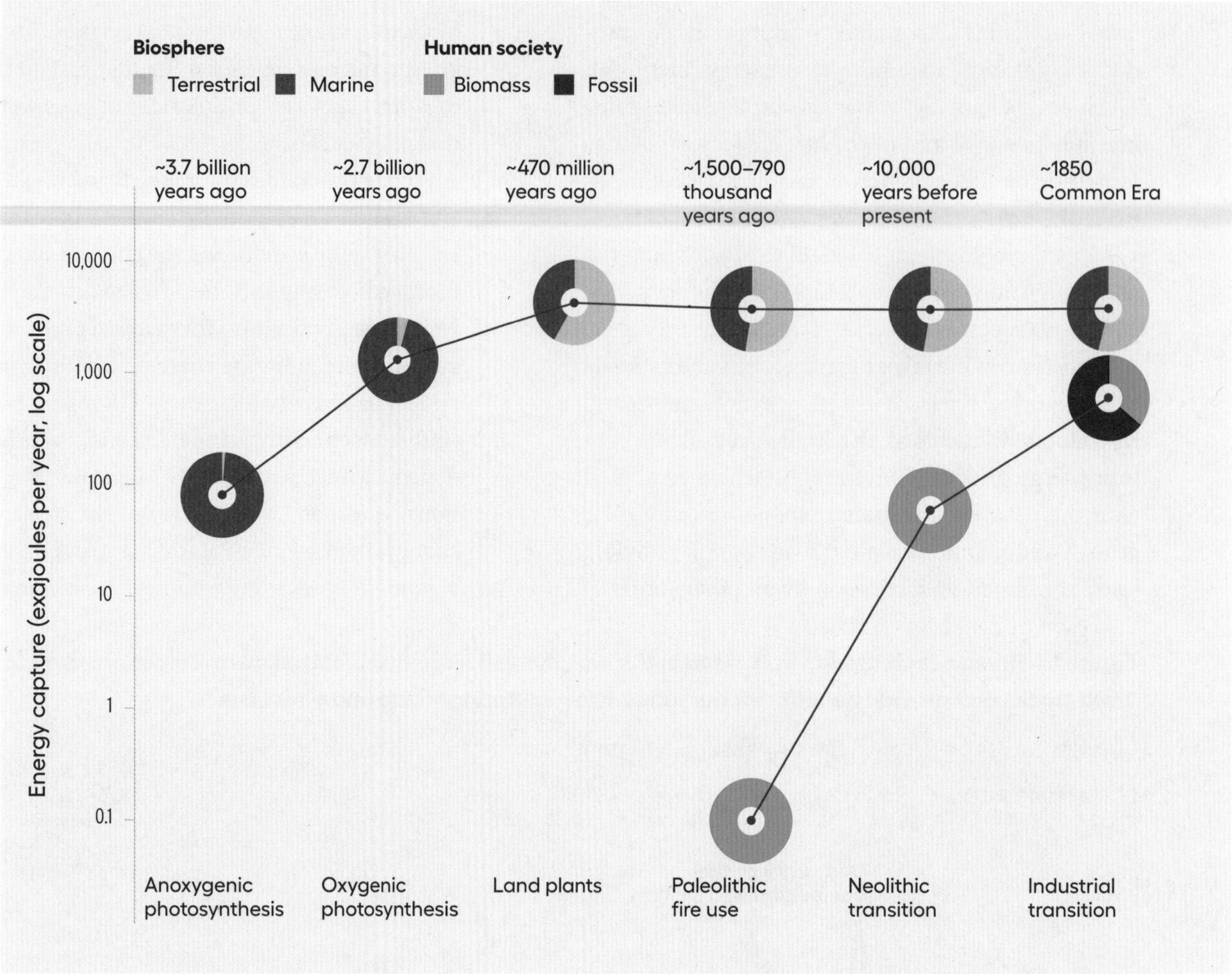

Note: Dates indicate the approximate beginning of each transition, with energy estimates for when energy regimes have matured.
Source: Lenton, Pichler and Weisz 2016.

transitions also destabilized the prevailing geochemical cycles. Timothy Lenton provides an account of the major transitions in Earth history, such as the transition from photosynthesis that does not use oxygen (anoxygenic) to the one that does (oxygenic, which took more than a billion years to evolve; spotlight 1.2). This transition increased the energy captured by the biosphere by an order of magnitude.[71]

Transitions in human history have been driven by technological and institutional innovations, resulting in new forms of social and economic organization that have progressively expanded energy and material use.[72] The intentional use of fire first allowed people to generate energy outside the human body[73] but increased energy input above human physiological needs only by a factor of 2–4 (see figure 1.6).[74] The transition to agriculture represented a fundamentally new stage that

raised human energy capture by three orders of magnitude (in around 1850, when it was the dominant mode of subsistence and the global population was around 1.3 billion).[75] The higher flows of energy and population linked to farming boosted societies' material inputs and waste products and led to substantial local (and possibly global) ecological impacts due in part to the large-scale changes in forest cover often associated with fire regimes that spread and managed fire.[76]

Agriculture emerged independently at different times in different parts of the world but generated energy surpluses. These heightened the social complexity in cities, the specialization and division of labour, exchange and trade, and the innovations such as writing that enabled further social stratification and provided for the expression and transmission of knowledge.[77] Still, the reliance on biomass from agriculture (requiring as much as 90 percent of the population to work in farming) linked the availability of energy surpluses to the land's productivity and expansion of its use, while transportation was limited by the need to balance the feed demands of animals with the distance they could travel.[78] These limiting conditions created quickly unfolding local negative feedbacks from resource use or destruction, holding down sustained material growth per person. Energy and material conditions imposed limiting constraints, but social change processes determined the actual production and demand for resources of different societies, which varied over time and across regions and were often shaped by inequalities in wealth distribution.[79]

As some societies increased economic demands and evolved social structures to sustain those demands, the limiting conditions could be overcome by using fossil fuels for energy and through industrialization. This decoupled energy use from land and human labour. As a result, global human energy capture rose 10-fold between 1850 and 2000, as the population grew by a factor of 4.6 and GDP per person by a factor of 8.3.[80] The total global energy flux through human societies is already one-third above the total that flows through all nonhuman and nonplant biomass. Along with energy, there have been unprecedented changes in global material cycles. Minerals have replaced biomass as the dominant material, and carbon dioxide emissions—which account for about 80 percent of the total annual flow of materials in industrial societies by weight—are the dominant waste product. Carbon dioxide emissions are overwhelming the carbon geochemical cycle and driving climate change, and the cycles for nitrogen and phosphorus have also been massively disrupted.

All this was underpinned by social and economic changes that drove, and were enabled by, technological and institutional innovations no less dramatic than those during the agricultural transition. But there is a key difference. The historical origins and initial diffusion of industrialization were concentrated geographically, leading to the Great Divergence between early industrializing countries and the rest of the world.[81] This divergence was exacerbated in some cases by colonialism and the intercontinental slave trade,[82] whose impacts persist to this day.[83] About two-thirds of the global population is undergoing the move from a predominantly agrarian society to an industrial one.[84]

But we are now confronting limiting conditions, determined by biophysical processes, to maintaining a resilient Earth system in a state conducive to human wellbeing. Overcoming those limiting conditions implies shifting away from fossil fuels[85] and closing material cycles.[86] Also essential is reducing pressure on the biosphere by protecting biodiversity and restoring landscapes and seascapes.[87]

Given the centrality of fossil fuels in industrial societies, it is crucial to keep policy and public attention on reducing carbon dioxide emissions. But this alone is insufficient to improve cycling for nitrogen, phosphorus and other materials, especially minerals. In fact, many energy-intensive processes—such as producing fertilizer, whose use contributes overwhelmingly to disruptions in the nitrogen and phosphorus cycles—could be made easier with greater availability of clean energy sources. Moreover, a transition to clean energy will likely boost demand for materials, especially minerals. Based on the International Energy Agency's scenarios through 2050 of shifts away from fossil fuels, targeting 15 electricity generation and 5 transport technologies would increase global total material requirements by up to 900 percent for electricity and 700 percent for transport, largely associated with greater use of copper, silver, nickel, lithium, cobalt and steel.[88] And the production processes could induce considerable greenhouse gas emissions.[89] Moreover, renewable energy technologies can come with other problems: They can be land use intensive[90] or require minerals from mines,[91] threatening biodiversity.[92]

That makes it essential to complement the focus on reducing carbon dioxide emissions with an explicit consideration of material flows. But there is a more fundamental point. Often the technological innovations that help address limiting constraints—overcoming the limitation of nitrogen in agriculture through fertilizers, the use of chlorofluorocarbons in refrigeration, fossil fuels to overcome the limiting energy constraints of agricultural societies—bring unintended consequences. As chapter 3 argues, this implies that in addition to expanding the use of known and proven technologies, it is crucial to continue to invest in science. The carbon stored in land, water and forests requires better management and stewardship by local communities and governments.

The demand of industrial societies for materials and fossil fuel energy is structurally determined, so focusing only on technological solutions can generate new problems.[93] Although end-of-pipe (meaning, at the end of production or consumption processes) approaches to treating waste and pollution (a focus of much environmental policy and advocacy) are important, they are not necessarily addressing the structurally determined uses of energy and demand for materials that generate planetary pressures.[94] Behavioural changes in production and consumption will also be crucial. But the structurally determined elements of industrial societies will not change unless the underlying mechanisms for capturing energy and using materials do—and this would likely imply another major transition.

A reimagined human development journey thus calls for a deeper connection between human development achievements and maintaining a resilient Earth system in a state conducive to human wellbeing. And the imperative of a major transition provides a sense of direction for the transformational change to ease planetary pressures.[95] One where the pursuit of improvements in wellbeing goes along with mobilizing human agency to implement that transition, where people are seen not only as users of resources, as rapacious of the environment, but also as able to reason individually and collectively to establish regenerative relationships with the biosphere. Human societies have had, and continue to have, visions of a good life, relational values with respect to nature (as discussed below), that go beyond seeing people as responding only to economic incentives or having a utilitarian perspective on the biosphere.

Learning from human and biological diversity

Biodiversity loss often parallels loss of cultural and language diversity, impoverishing societies culturally.[96] For instance, there is wide-ranging evidence that land-use intensification decouples productive landscapes from the natural processes in order to sustain production outcomes.[97] Gains in resource efficiency and production often affect the cultural diversity that underpins collective wellbeing (figure 1.7).[98] Biocultural approaches that emphasize the intertwining of human societies and ecological systems[99] and describe deeply interconnected ecological and social

dynamics where human livelihoods, landscapes and ecosystems have coevolved over long periods help explain this codependence. They move from a unidirectional utilitarian concept of nature towards acknowledging a plurality of worldviews and human-nature interactions.[100] Biocultural diversity is the "diversity of life in all its manifestations—biological, cultural, and linguistic—which are interrelated within a complex socio-ecological adaptive system."[101]

" The question is whether it is possible to marshal the social, political and economic changes towards a transition where societies can capture more energy from the sun, close material cycles and safeguard the biosphere. What would a human development journey look like as that transition unfolds? It requires a fundamental change in the role of humans on the planet.

These perspectives exemplify how the biosphere supports human development in nonmaterial ways—through learning and inspiration, physical and psychological experiences, and identities and sense of place.[102] People, through their experiences, derive meaning, a sense of belonging, identity and attachment to both place and the rhythms of nature.[103] Changes to the biosphere can affect a place's character and humans' relationship with it, since changes to the structure and function of an ecosystem can also affect the symbolic meaning and belonging created by the relationship with that place.[104] These kinds of change can lead to psychological and emotional distress,[105] including grief and anguish associated with loss of place, biodiversity and nature.[106] Sense of place connected to the biosphere affects how individuals and communities adapt to new conditions, determines whether relocation strategies are used or successful and influences shifts in livelihood strategies.[107] A strong attachment to particular meanings of a place and a feeling of belonging in nature inspire empathy[108] and motivate action and stewardship of ecosystems.[109]

Indigenous peoples' ways of knowing and being, and their governance systems, have supported biocultural diversity.[110] The decline in what the Intergovernmental Science-Policy Platform on Biodiversity and Ecosystem Services defines as nature has been lower in areas managed by indigenous peoples than in other lands, often as a result of practices that actively maintain or

Figure 1.7 Diversity in life, culture and language coevolve

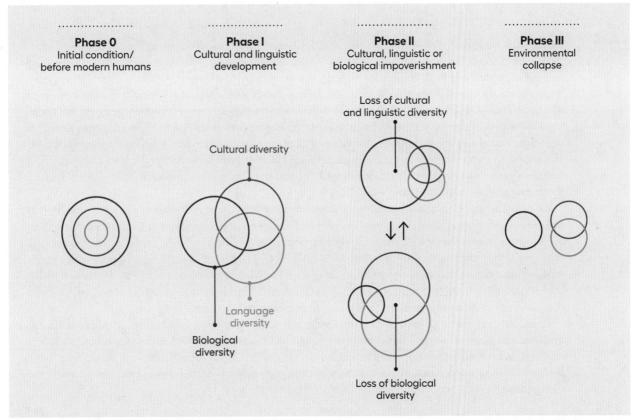

Note: The ancestral condition of humans is one in which culture and language reflect the local environment (phase 0). The evolution of culture and language partially detaches them from biological diversity, but it does not necessarily impoverish any of the three components (phase I). But losses in culture and language can occur when, for instance, more homogenous cultural populations overwhelm local diversity, from which loss in the diversity of life may follow (phase II). When the detachment becomes complete, all three dimensions lose in diversity (phase III).
Source: Frainer and others 2020.

enhance diversity.[111] Many of the world's healthiest ecosystems, especially those outside formally protected areas, involve lands of indigenous peoples and local communities.[112] And the customary lands of indigenous peoples and local communities encompass at least a quarter of the global land area, an important direct contribution to the global preservation of biocultural diversity,[113] even if indigenous peoples often resist nonindigenous peoples' unsustainable and unjust patterns of exploitation of the biosphere.[114] The cooperative management of centuries-old rice terraces in Bali extends beyond villages to entire watersheds. Decisions by local farmers evolved towards optimal harvests and preserved watersheds.[115]

Areas often perceived as wilderness or untouched are frequently the result of a long-term relationship between indigenous peoples and their territories.[116] But rather than extrapolating to a global scale what can be seen as isolated practices by indigenous peoples with little general relevance,[117] it is important to emphasize that indigenous peoples' knowledge systems reflect sophisticated governance practices that advance human wellbeing while maintaining biocultural diversity.[118] They open our eyes to the risks of reproducing the same socially, politically, culturally and economically engrained ways that have put pressures on the biosphere.[119] They give us an opportunity to better weave knowledge systems together (box 1.1)[120] and to broaden our understanding of the interdependence of the human development journey in the Anthropocene with the biosphere.

Envisioning the human development journey in the Anthropocene

The reality of the limiting constraints facing industrial societies is increasingly apparent, as chapter 2

Box 1.1 Indigenous and local knowledge systems and practices generate synergies between biodiversity and human wellbeing

Indigenous and local knowledge is a key link for building synergies between the wellbeing of local people and the conservation of ecosystems. To realize this potential for sustainable human development, indigenous and local knowledge needs to be embedded in and actively connected to ecosystem governance that recognizes their rights. The diverse social, cultural and environmental knowledge of indigenous peoples and local communities contributes to safeguarding ecosystem services and securing the multidimensional wellbeing of people across large parts of the globe.[1] The scope and content of indigenous and local knowledge bring insights of great relevance for ecosystem governance, as in controlling deforestation, reducing carbon dioxide emissions, understanding climate change and sustaining and restoring resilient landscapes.[2] For example, at least 36 percent of the world's intact forest landscapes are within indigenous peoples' lands.[3]

Despite the role of indigenous and local knowledge in conservation, indigenous and local governance systems are threatened and in decline—along with indigenous peoples' wellbeing.[4] Recognizing land tenure, access and resource rights; applying free, prior and informed consent; and improving collaboration and comanagement arrangements with indigenous peoples and local communities are critical. Indigenous peoples and local communities, and their knowledge systems and practices, have a major role in global biodiversity governance and conservation, from knowledge generation and assessment to policy formulation and decisionmaking and to implementation in practice.[5]

To realize this potential, new collaborative ways of mobilizing knowledge and learning across diverse systems can contribute innovations and new solutions to sustainable human development.[6] Involving multiple actors and knowledge can strengthen usefulness and legitimacy in decisionmaking and implementation.[7] Approaches and programmes that bridge diverse constituencies in resource governance along these lines are emerging in many parts of the world today.[8]

Notes
1. Díaz and others 2019b. **2.** Hill and others 2020. **3.** Fa and others 2020. **4.** Díaz and others 2019b. **5.** Hill and others 2020. **6.** Mistry and Berardi 2016; Sterling and others 2017; Tengö and others 2014. **7.** Danielsen and others 2005; Gavin and others 2018; Sterling and others 2017. **8.** Malmer and others 2020.
Source: Galaz, Collste and Moore 2020.

makes clear, and will condition the human development journey in the Anthropocene. The question is not whether that reality will continue to disrupt social and economic processes and drive further wedges in inequalities in human development. The question is whether it is possible to marshal the social, political and economic changes towards a transition where societies can capture more energy from the sun, close material cycles and safeguard the biosphere.

What would a human development journey look like as that transition unfolds? It requires a "fundamental change in the role of humans in the planet."[121] It takes us beyond ensuring the carrying capacity of an individual ecosystem or resource[122] to understanding the system dynamics for societies to expand human capabilities while supporting the planet's ability to provide for that expansion over time.[123]

The aspiration of a transition to a just and sustainable human environment has been discussed since at least the mid-1980s.[124] There has been much recent interest in the concept of just transitions (box 1.2). But we are now confronting a new reality. The Covid-19 pandemic seems to be one more example of the shocks we may be confronting, and there is a step-change in the nature of the risks we create because we are affecting the very planetary processes that enabled wellbeing to prosper in the first place. Global production systems, such as the food system, are growing increasingly homogeneous and concentrated, geared to yield high and predictable supplies of biomass in the short run, but are also entrenching long-term and pervasive risks.[125] For most of our existence the major risks were natural hazards—but they are now anthropocentric, and we are poorly prepared to cope (spotlight 1.3). The human development journey in the Anthropocene has to be fully aware of these risks and find ways to address them.

Box 1.2 A just transition

The idea of transforming our economies and societies must have equity or justice at its centre. The transition from the current unsustainable patterns of production and consumption to a more sustainable system is bound to have winners and losers. But what is just depends on one's perspective. Advocates of climate justice take a human rights approach to sharing the costs and benefits of adjusting to climate change. By contrast, energy justice usually focuses on access to energy as a human right. And environmental justice emphasizes the agency of people and seeks to involve them in environmental decisionmaking.[1]

All three approaches touch on the political economy of a transition to more sustainable economies and societies. Any just transition will be a delicate balancing act.[2] The concept of a just transition is not merely a technical process of moving from a fossil fuel–based to a low-carbon system—it is a political process. The status quo is not only disrupting planetary processes but also perpetuating inequalities.[3] With this in mind, green innovation alone would not suffice to make the transition happen in the first place or to ensure that it is just. A just transition would require creating political coalitions among social and environmental movements, minority groups, labour unions, people employed in the energy sectors and engaged local communities.[4]

In a way the idea of a just transition gets to the core of sustainability. Rather than a fixed state we are aiming to reach, sustainability can be seen as a process of debate and inclusive deliberation. This view of sustainability as a process of exploring social, technological and environmental pathways recognizes that different stakeholders view sustainability in different ways and have diverging narratives about what is or is not sustainable. This implies the need to identify, in each case, the actors, their framing of the situation and their emphasis. This socially complex view of sustainability also implies that governments are not the only policy agents and that there is an important role for citizen engagement and mobilization, protest and coalition building.[5]

Notes
1. Heffron and McCauley 2018. **2.** Consider phasing out fossil fuel use. On the one hand, attention must be paid to people living in energy poverty—those who presently do not have access to energy. On the other hand, many people's livelihoods currently depend on the fossil fuel economy, and they are thus vulnerable to any transition away from it. Furthermore, both current and future generations are at risk given the social and ecological instabilities of the Anthropocene (Newell and Mulvaney 2013). **3.** Healy and Barry 2017. **4.** Healy and Barry 2017. **5.** Leach, Sterling and Scoones 2010.

" The heightened risks combined with the narrow window of time to act instil a sense of urgency that is already well recognized for climate and biodiversity loss but is needed for a broader set of Anthropocene risks.

And we are unprepared for this. Take climate change. Both scientific and economic models, it is argued, have underestimated economic and social risks.[126] The call to shift the focus to lives and livelihoods and better incorporate risks[127] that we confront in the Anthropocene goes beyond climate change—and is consistent with how the interaction between social and planetary imbalances lies at the origin of these risks (see figure 1.1). Furthermore, not only are human-driven risks unprecedented and global in scale, but "social and technological trends and decisions occurring over the next decade or two could significantly influence the trajectory of the Earth system for tens to hundreds of thousands of years. And they could potentially lead to conditions that resemble planetary states that were last seen millions of years ago, conditions inhospitable to current human societies and to many other contemporary species."[128] The heightened risks combined with the narrow window of time to act instil a sense of urgency that is already well recognized for climate[129] and biodiversity loss[130] but is needed for a broader set of Anthropocene risks.[131]

Confronting these risks implies that enhancing resilience is central to the human development journey in the Anthropocene,[132] acknowledging that "[...] nonlinear, phased progress challenges the perception of linear incremental progressions from poverty to well-being, deforestation to reforestation, or fossil fuels to renewables. This insight highlights instead thresholds of change, where progress can involve the often invisible preparation for change, the navigation of change once past a threshold or tipping point, and finally a focus on building the resilience of the transformed system."[133]

The human development journey in the Anthropocene will benefit from the strong evidence of the transformational change at local scales that is being increasingly scaled up to national levels through policies and finance mechanisms.[134] This suggests that the process of change is adaptive, with social changes evolving through a combination of gradual changes and larger regime shifts, as many aspects of socioecological systems change together.[135] And this process is inherently political, with multiple interests pulling in different directions.[136]

Technological advances and renewable energy pricing now competitive with fossil fuels mean that the energy transformation is increasingly feasible, even if the effectiveness of some of the proposed technologies is contested (as chapter 3 discusses). A combination of renewable energy, greater efficiency and reduced energy demand would make such a transformation feasible[137]—even if it remains challenging to decarbonize some economic sectors,[138] including food systems.[139] In fact, a recent study suggested that even if fossil fuel emissions were immediately stopped, current emission trends in global food systems would likely preclude meeting the Paris Agreement goals.[140]

Closing material cycles—extracting less and recycling more—is less certain technically but is receiving increasing public and policy attention. The challenge stems in part from the fact that about half of materials extracted globally are used to build or renew in-use stocks (such as infrastructure), making them impossible to recycle in the short run. Material stocks increased 23-fold from 1900 to 2010 and would increase another 4-fold (to more than 150 times the 1900 stock) if there were global convergence to the level of stocks of developed countries.[141] And around 44 percent of processed materials (those not used to build stocks) are used to provide energy, making them unavailable for recycling as well.[142] Further, some materials remain essential for specific functions: No exemplary substitutes are available for all major uses of 62 metals.[143]

Despite being a major challenge,[144] closing material cycles shows the need for, and potential of, major product redesign. In fact, much evidence suggests that the opportunities are commensurate with the challenges, given that only 6 percent of globally extracted materials are recycled,[145] with clear opportunities for more efficient use and recycling in domains ranging from agriculture to green chemistry.[146] Analytical approaches such as the material stock-flow-service—focusing on the services that enhance wellbeing and then tracing back the flow of materials required and the minimum stocks needed—can also help identify opportunities to generate human benefits with less material use.[147]

Despite these challenges, the human development journey in the Anthropocene should be guided by exploration beyond the structural constraints of industrial societies—or it will be blind to what might be feasible. Living through the Industrial Revolution in England, Adam Smith, David Ricardo and others thought that diminishing marginal yields in agriculture would eventually bring industrialization to a halt.[148] They all saw the world through the lens of agricultural societies. Feasibility may be impossible to prove, but it is not disproved by using industrial societies as a frame of reference. It will be important to keep the future accessible and navigable[149] on the human development journey in the Anthropocene (box 1.3). And, as important, to recognize that new and unimagined institutions will support human aspirations for evolving conceptions of a good life.[150]

The human development journey in the Anthropocene will also hinge on broader social and economic transformations and their interactions with technologies, as during the agricultural and industrial transitions. Here, the insights from biocultural diversity approaches will be key to informing the transformations needed. Some elements of these changes may already be under way, such as the growing importance of intangible capital in many of today's economies[151] and the increasing economic value of digital goods and services (software, social networks, media, entertainment), even though it is unclear whether digitalization will substantially reduce demand for materials and energy.[152] Though the global population is growing, growth rates are falling (figure 1.8), with recent drops in fertility rates suggesting that the total population may even start falling in this century.[153] More and more people live in cities, so urban uses of energy and materials are particularly important,[154] as are the processes of economic and social change in cities.[155]

Box 1.3 Choosing inclusive futures for human development in the Anthropocene

By Andrea S. Downing, Stockholm Resilience Centre at Stockholm University and Global Economic Dynamics and the Biosphere programme at the Royal Swedish Academy of Sciences; Manqi Chang, Department of Aquatic Ecology at the Netherlands Institute of Ecology; David Collste, Stockholm Resilience Centre at Stockholm University; Sarah Cornell, Stockholm Resilience Centre at Stockholm University; Jan. J. Kuiper, Stockholm Resilience Centre at Stockholm University; Wolf M. Mooij, Department of Aquatic Ecology at the Netherlands Institute of Ecology and Department of Aquatic Ecology and Water Quality Management at Wageningen University; Uno Svedin, Stockholm Resilience Centre at Stockholm University; and Dianneke van Wijk, Department of Aquatic Ecology at the Netherlands Institute of Ecology

Presenting a choice between focusing on environmental conservation and focusing on poverty alleviation and human development is a false dichotomy. These two goals are indivisible: Either one chooses neither—for instance, by maintaining business-as-usual practices of consumption and production—or one chooses both.[1] This dependence is simple—long-term fair and just human development depends on relative stability in Earth system dynamics, which in turn can be ensured only through sustainable use of the environment—that is, maintaining rates of human resource extraction below rates of resource production, and rates of waste emissions below the environment's ability to absorb and transform the waste.[2] Overextraction and overemission compromise the biosphere's ability to produce the resources and sustain the services that societies need to thrive and survive.

Choices are nonetheless important, and the types of choices available differ according to scales and perspectives. At a generic, global level the Intergovernmental Panel on Climate Change community has been developing different representative concentration pathways and shared socioeconomic pathways that humanity might broadly take and have analysed the outcomes of those pathways in terms of climate change and biodiversity loss.[3] The pathways, ranging from no to high mitigation, are mutually exclusive and all lead to further deterioration of the natural world and frame sustainability as the outcome of policies that constrain present activities. The pathways—and their outcomes—are firmly anchored in the present and designed around alterations of current systems.

However, this is not only an exercise in fixing current unsustainable processes and controlling damage from the impacts of past overexploitations and injustices. It also requires active thought and planning of what sustainable futures can look like—irrespective of perceived constraints or norms that shape today's societies—and reflecting on how actions taken today build towards such futures or make them impossible. Clear goals of sustainable and just futures can help shape present action.[4] Furthermore, starting with a perspective on the desirable futures one aims for gears towards more transformative pathways of change,[5] acknowledging that gradual change is insufficient to ensure a safe and just world for all of humanity[6] or to achieve the Sustainable Development Goals.[7] Transformations would be the means to redesign systems to have justice and sustainability at their core rather than to gradually adjust systems to be less bad.

Though envisioning and choosing sustainable and just futures must be done across the world—indeed, all countries are developing countries in the context of the 2030 Agenda for Sustainable Development[8]—these are not global tasks. Indeed, the diversity of biogeophysical, socioeconomic and ethical contexts—and their possible combinations—clearly indicates that there is no silver bullet, no single realization of a sustainable future or transformation to guide all of humanity. Instead, each vision needs to suit the appropriate scales of biogeophysical dynamics, socioeconomic processes and ethical considerations.[9] This implies that a diversity of sustainable futures—and transformative pathways towards them—must coexist. From this perspective achieving the Sustainable Development Goals would be the outcome of realizing a diversity of desired sustainable development futures. Each pathway, transformation and realization of sustainable development must have at its core the inclusivity of other and different pathways and processes of sustainable human development.

Importantly, many of the processes and systems of today need to change: processes that overexploit and overemit, processes that benefit only the few, and the root causes and driving forces of these processes—such as consumerism, business models of unlimited economic growth and the displacement of impacts and dependencies across geographies and generations. Choosing away from an unsustainable present implies losses for those who disproportionately benefit or aim to benefit from business as usual. These can be seen as constraints—as in the framing of representative concentration pathways and shared socioeconomic pathways—but these unsustainable processes today all come at the cost of sustainable and just futures for all of humanity. Transformations are likely best navigated with an understanding of the unsustainable processes that must be lost and the sustainable and just processes that can be gained by using visions of inclusive, just and sustainable futures as compasses.

Notes

1. Downing and others 2020. **2.** Downing and others 2020; Rockström and others 2009a. **3.** Riahi and others 2017. **4.** Rodriguez-Gonzalez, Rico-Martinez and Rico-Ramirez 2020. **5.** Sharpe and others 2016. **6.** Holling, Clark and Munn 1986; Leach and others 2012. **7.** Hajer and others 2015; Randers and others 2019. **8.** United Nations 2015b. **9.** Häyhä and others 2016; Van Der Leeuw 2020.

Figure 1.8 Global population is growing, but growth rates are falling

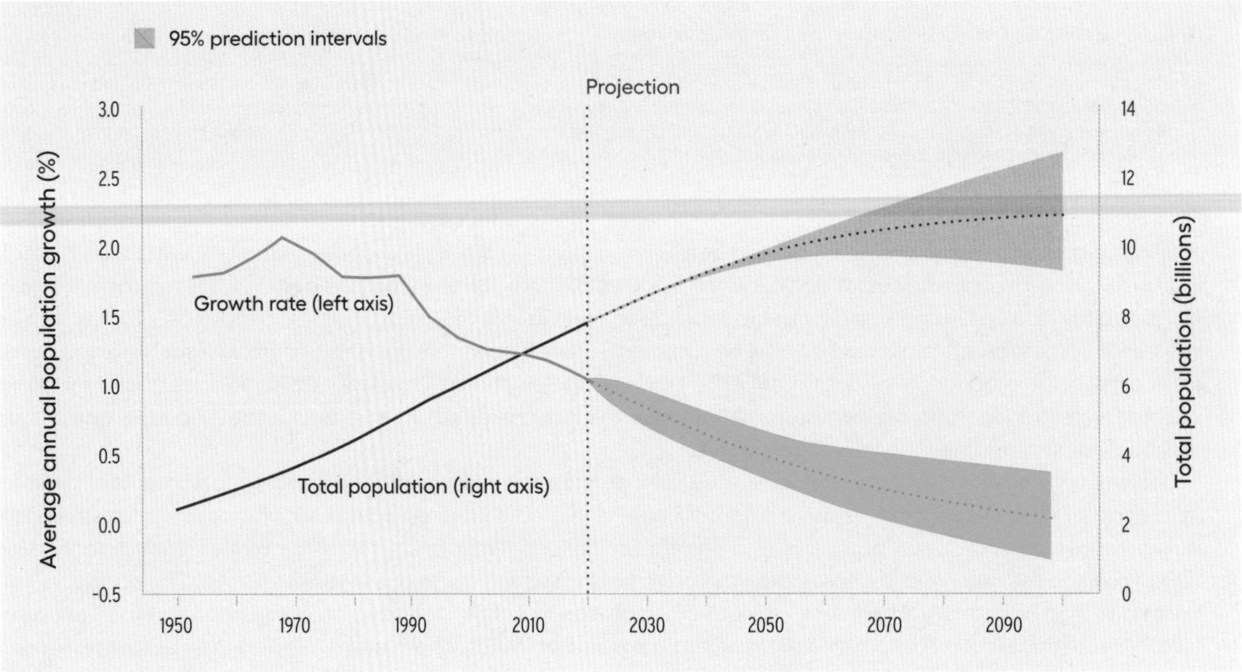

Source: UNDESA 2019b.

Studies suggest that cities do not necessarily "slow down" uniformly as the population grows, which is the typical pattern for colonies of hundreds of millions of organisms, such as termites, where the larger the colony, the slower the use of energy and materials relative to size.[156] Some aspects of city life do slow down as population grows, given that there are economies of scale (as with infrastructure networks), while increases in houses or jobs (associated with human needs) track population. But income, wages and rates of invention increase far faster than population.[157]

Urbanization's effects on pressures on the planet are currently mixed.[158] But as more people gather, particularly the more educated and interconnected they are, they generate a larger pool of potential ideas.[159] In fact, as cities grow, the complexity of social life increases, yielding even more innovations that can overcome constraints to further population growth in the same city.[160] This offers a glimpse of the opportunities that may emerge as more people become more educated and more connected, especially as digital technologies expand.[161] Seizing these opportunities calls for more than envisioning the human development journey in the Anthropocene. As argued next, it calls for leveraging the human development approach by seeing people as agents, not merely as patients.

Leveraging the human development approach for transformation: Beyond needs, beyond sustaining

The human development approach emphasizes expanding human freedoms and highlights inequalities in capabilities. Leveraging the human development approach takes us beyond notions of sustainability premised on meeting needs and striving for sufficiency and floors of subsistence alone—and towards empowering people to make choices that reduce planetary pressures and advance justice (addressing both planetary and social imbalances).

Meeting the needs of the present and the future: Is that all?

The Brundtland approach to defining sustainable development as "development that meets the needs of the present without compromising the ability of future generations to meet their own needs"[162] was a watershed moment.[163] It brought together the ethical imperative of fulfilling the basic subsistence requirements of people today—putting poverty eradication squarely at the centre of the concept—with an obligation to our descendants rooted in intergenerational justice. It put people at the core, instead of defining what needed to be sustained for consumption or production. And rather than asking for the preservation of a pristine state of nature, it emphasized the ability of each generation to use resources, allowing for some fungibility across resources.[164]

The two key ideas of the concept—sustain and needs—have been interpreted and reinterpreted in many ways. Sustain, when translated into notions that consumption is the thing to be made sustainable, puts the focus on disparities in consumption between developed and developing countries, informing approaches to deal with these asymmetries such as degrowth, discussed above. Robert Solow argued that a generalized capacity to produce wellbeing (or productive capacity) was the thing to be sustained into the indefinite future, allowing for the next generation to be left with what it takes to meet a standard of living at least as good as today's and to do so for the next generations similarly.[165]

There are also different interpretations of which needs should be sustained. Needs can be defined as encompassing not only the minimum required to survive but also a wider set of requirements.[166] However, moving the focus towards a wider conceptualization of needs—or completely away from needs to living standards or productive capacity—may diminish the ethical power of a formulation that emphasizes the minimum required to eliminate poverty in today's generation and every generation going forward.[167]

A focus on needs may lead to prioritizing social or economic floors, providing a minimum foundation to be shared by everyone, but it does not fully account for inequalities, and it downplays the potential of people as agents. For instance, the inspired and influential framework proposed by Kate Raworth sets a floor of essential human and social needs as a circle inside the planetary boundaries framework described in chapter 2.[168] The resulting "doughnut" defines an operating space that is not only safe, from the Earth system sciences perspective, but also socially just. People can strive in this safe and just operating space through a multitude of potential pathways.[169] But when interpreted as focused on enabling people to attain a minimum level of wellbeing, it puts less emphasis on inequalities.[170] Even when inequalities are considered in related frameworks, the emphasis is often on income inequality.[171]

But as the 2019 Human Development Report argued, it is important to go beyond inequalities in income and consider a broader set of inequalities in human development. The 2019 Report also argued that while setting a floor of minimum achievements is essential, it is not enough to address persistent, and in some cases increasing, inequalities.[172] As shown next, impressive achievements in reducing planetary pressures that are blind to distributional consequences are likely to leave existing inequalities in place, compounding the drivers of social imbalances.[173]

Reducing planetary pressures with persisting inequalities

As chapter 2 shows, environmental degradation and the negative effects of that degradation reflect, and often amplify, underlying inequalities that in turn are often underpinned by asymmetries in power. Asymmetries in power across economic sectors can also account for some of the heterogeneity in response to environmental challenges.

To take an example, racial and ethnic disparities in pollution exposure have long been documented in several countries. In the United States they were at the origin of the environmental justice movement and persist today. Non-Hispanic Whites experience about 17 percent less exposure to air pollution relative to their consumption, while Blacks and African Americans bear a pollution burden of 56 percent excess exposure relative to their consumption and Hispanics and Latinos, 63 percent.[174] The study also revealed the risks of looking at environmental action without considering equity implications. Although exposure to aggregate fine particulate matter (PM2.5) air pollution fell by 50 percent between 2002 and 2015, inequality in pollution exposure remained the same (figure 1.9).[175]

There are also large inequalities in the production side of the economy. Gross external damage[176] due to premature mortality caused by industrial emissions of pollutants, consistent with the reduction in pollution documented above, fell by about 20 percent between 2008 and 2014.[177] But the decline was driven by cleaning up electricity generation and utilities (figure 1.10), as a result of policy, economic and technological changes unique to the sector that may not be

Figure 1.9 Lower total pollution but persistent inequities in pollution exposure

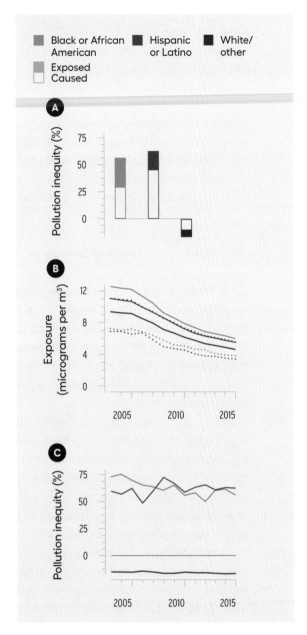

Note: (A) Contributions of differences in consumption (exposed and caused) to pollution inequity; (B) exposure of each racial/ethnic group to particle mass with aerodynamic diameter less than 2.5 microns (PM2.5) caused by the total combined personal consumption of all groups (solid lines) and total population exposure to PM2.5 caused by each group's population-adjusted consumption (dashed lines); (C) pollution inequity.
Source: Tessum and others 2019.

relevant to others.[178] By 2014, four sectors alone accounted for 75 percent of gross external damage but less than 20 percent of GDP; farms were the largest sector contributing to industrial pollution.[179]

In sum, aggregate reductions in pollution may leave existing inequalities in pollution exposure

Figure 1.10 Reduced economic damages from industrial pollution were driven by utilities without losing economic value added

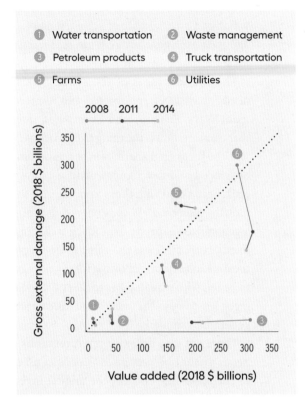

Source: Tschofen, Azevedo and Muller 2019.

intact. And there are asymmetries across sectors in how much they drive reductions in pollution (in the United States utilities reduced pollution sharply, while farms and oil did not). These inequalities and asymmetries result from the interplay of economic, technological and political factors. So considering inequalities in exposure and in actions to reduce environmental damages shows the importance of going beyond social floors for minimum needs—and how marginalization and exclusion that feed into the social imbalances are often a blind spot when meeting needs is what is intended to be sustained.

Expanding human freedoms to address social and planetary imbalances

Where to go beyond needs? What can we expand, beyond focusing on sustaining? How to account for persistent inequalities that feeds social imbalances? The human development approach offers a path to address these questions.

Human development takes us beyond notions of sustainability based on needs fulfilment and away from notions based on instrumental objectives such as consumption or economic activity (measured by growth in GDP, for instance).[180] By going beyond fulfilling basic needs, it also implies that the objective is to enable our children and their descendants to flourish, allowing for broader and evolving aspirations.

The approach is also fundamentally empowering in the realm of individual and social choice because it allows for the evolution of values (redefining parameters of worth and dignity) and of social norms that drive people's behaviour as much as, and sometimes more than, getting the prices right. People's commitments to certain values (honour, justice) can be absolute and inviolable.[181]

These values can encompass more than anthropocentric perspectives. Eileen Crist argued that a "human-centric worldview is blinding humanity to the consequences of our actions."[182] And Martha Nussbaum, an influential voice in the capabilities community, even argued for dropping "human" from the title of the *Journal of Human Development and Capabilities* to make it more inclusive of ethical views on the environment and the rights of nonhuman animals. This should be the case, she argued, even when they do not have a direct bearing on human capabilities because "the future of the planet and its sentient beings is one of the largest ethical issues facing humanity going forward."[183] These normative ethical concerns have acquired a heightened importance in the discussion surrounding the Anthropocene.[184]

Putting human freedoms at the core not only provides for a broader ethical and evaluative framing for sustainability but also, instrumentally, points the way towards changing the behaviours that are leading to unprecedented pressures on the planet. Surely the goal here is not to sustain these human freedoms, but rather to expand them as much as possible. For in that expansion lies the means to change both values and social norms, the possibility of widening the realm of action for change—whether through changes in individual behaviour or more consequentially through the expression of values and preferences in the political process or civil society advocacy and mobilization. Governments and policymakers are the central actors, but people's own will to shape their life can come together in organized ways through social movements. As Frances Stewart said, "Policy change is the outcome of a political struggle in which different groups (and individuals) provide support for particular changes. In this struggle, uncoordinated individuals are generally powerless. They are also powerless to improve the conditions they face in the market. Yet by getting together to support particular changes, individuals can acquire considerable power collectively."[185] It is in this sense that a human development approach not only allows but actually calls for going beyond sustaining towards "the goal of preparing a future that is not just as good as, but that is better than the present."[186]

> " Putting human freedoms at the core not only provides for a broader ethical and evaluative framing for sustainability but also, instrumentally, points the way towards changing the behaviours that are leading to unprecedented pressures on the planet.

Thus, it is important to develop a deeper awareness of our interdependence with the planet—one that is already held and sustained in part by values and social norms by communities around the world, as noted in the discussion on biocultural diversity, and it is also starting to percolate through the discourse on capabilities (box 1.4). These values and norms can find expression in individual and social choices—mediated through political and social processes that give further agency to people. Here, once again, redressing inequalities in human development is paramount, to avoid the capture of political processes by narrow interests that want to preserve the status quo—a process described in the 2019 Human Development Report.[187]

That change can happen does not mean that it will. It is conceivable, certainly based on past trends and current behaviour, that expanding human freedoms could result in a continuation of unsustainable patterns of consumption and production. But Amartya Sen has argued forcefully, using the decline in fertility rates, that empowering people and giving them enhanced agency not only avoid infringements of individual choice but can also effectively address the challenges of social choice.[188] Expanding human development—more education of women and girls, more economic empowerment of women, more

Box 1.4 Capabilities in a rapidly changing living planet

The task of identifying forward-looking capabilities is not trivial because there is a plurality of views.[1] A useful departure point is to draw on the differentiation among intrinsic, relational and instrumental values for nature,[2] which already reflect a plurality of voices.[3]

- **Intrinsic and relational.** Interaction with nature can be considered an essential capability based on normative principles. As argued above, nature and societies are interdependent, embedded in one another. Martha Nussbaum adopted the view of including nature as one of 10 central capabilities: "being able to live with concern for and in relation with animals, plants and the world of nature."[4]
- **Instrumental.** The interaction with the Earth system is a key factor defining other capabilities based on its instrumental role.[5] The erosion of biosphere integrity affects the ability to transform resources into functionings. For instance, more frequent and more intense extreme weather events as a result of climate change are likely to affect people's ability to inhabit certain places, cultivate certain products or sustain certain livelihoods. Air pollution affects health. When the instrumental role of a resource is omnipresent in the way of life, the resource may almost become a proxy of an essential capability. How we interact with nature conditions capabilities and functionings because its further erosion affects people's lives.
- **A new scientific consensus.** Scientists from a range of disciplines are showing with more precision the ways in which nature and people are interdependent, as discussed in chapter 2.[6] This emphasizes that humans and social actions are embedded in the biosphere[7] and that integration is key in dealing with complexity.
- **The political consensus.** Environmental sustainability appears at the same level of social and economic development objectives as part of an indivisible political global agenda. Since 2015 nature has been embedded in the Sustainable Development Goals.

Notes
1. Fukuda-Parr 2003. **2.** Following the typology in Brondizio and others (2019). **3.** This is consistent with the comparative analysis advocated by Amartya Sen (see Sen 2009). **4.** Nussbaum 2011, p. 33–34. **5.** Essential and instrumental roles can be intertwined in practice. This happens with the role of income in the human development approach. Though the capabilities approach makes an explicit effort to depart from considering commodities as a defining factor of development, income is acknowledged as a constitutive element of capabilities because of its importance in defining basic living standards. **6.** Díaz and others 2015. **7.** Dasgupta 2020.

---

bargaining power of young girls in households, reduced poverty[189]—contributed to lower fertility rates in India (especially in the state of Kerala) and Bangladesh. Crucially, social norms shifted in the context of public reasoning and deliberation.[190]

The evidence of the importance of social norms is particularly strong in Bangladesh, where community social interactions determined differences in fertility behaviour even within the same village. Each village was subject to the same interventions, access to information and services, including education. But social norms were largely associated with religious groups, and interactions rarely occurred across religious boundaries. This enabled a study to control for individual differences in education, age, wealth and other factors, resulting in the conclusion that a woman's behaviour was driven primarily by the predominant choice among other women in her religious group.[191]

This example is used not to suggest that it can simply be replicated as we confront the unprecedented challenges of the Anthropocene.[192] Rather, it shows that when people are the ultimate ends of development, progress in human development through expanded human freedoms also creates the means not only for people to become more productive economically and have higher standards of living but also to be more active participants in public reasoning and able to change social norms.[193] The quality of human agency is enhanced by better education, better health and higher standards of living,[194] dimensions that constitute the Human Development Index. Recall that longevity and education are capabilities that are valued in themselves—not just because they enable people to be more productive economically. As Sharachchandra Lele put it: "The purpose of education is not an instrumentalist 'skilling' to produce biddable masses for current economic and political systems to exploit. Its purpose is transformative: to imbue everyone with broad human values and critical thinking abilities. Only then can we overcome the confines of race, caste, gender and other prejudices, reconnect with our environment and become politically aware and active citizens."[195]

" The Anthropocene brings new evidence and concepts to inform public debate about the changes—normative, economic, technological, behavioural—needed to ease the unprecedented pressures we are putting on the planet. There can be no doubt that only people can effect these changes, but the Anthropocene and its planetary imbalances are superimposed on social imbalances and tensions.

The Anthropocene brings new evidence and concepts to inform public debate about the changes—normative, economic, technological, behavioural —needed to ease the unprecedented pressures we are putting on the planet. There can be no doubt that only people can effect these changes, but the Anthropocene and its planetary imbalances are superimposed on social imbalances and tensions. In some countries people are wealthier than ever, more educated than ever, healthier than ever—but not happier, and they are fearful about the future.[196]

There may not be a clear blueprint of what human development is and will be in the decades to come. Human development is permanently under construction, and the approach is open ended to new and emerging challenges and opportunities (spotlight 1.4). This chapter has attempted to sketch a vision of the human development journey in the Anthropocene in order to navigate towards a better planet for people and the rest of life. It has further argued that advancing human development is not only possible but also the way to address planetary and social imbalances. The vicious cycle in figure 1.1 can be broken.

Unprecedented—the scope, scale and speed of human pressures on the planet

Unprecedented—the scope, scale and speed of human pressures on the planet

The Anthropocene is ushering in new sets of complex, interconnected and universal predicaments. Social and ecological systems are ever more tightly coupled, within which inequalities form dangerous feedback loops. Systems thinking is in, siloed thinking out.

How does the Anthropocene impact human development, today and in the future?

This chapter shows that the Covid-19 pandemic has hit human development hard. Climate change is already dragging on economies, especially in developing countries. Hunger is rising, after decades of progress. Natural hazards are getting worse and threaten especially the more vulnerable, including women, ethnic groups and children.

Looking beneath the environment and sustainability: Human activity driving dangerous planetary change

The 21st century has seen a plethora of assessments and reports documenting multiple and worsening climate and ecological crises. Often seen as separate from one another, they mobilize public and policy attention to differing degrees. They are supported by distinct communities of advocates and civil society organizations. And they are sometimes presented as vindications of warnings made long ago about environmental degradation and climate change.

These challenges can be seen as manifestations of a more fundamental and integrated process of planetary change driven by human activity—leading to calls to designate our times as a new geological epoch: the Anthropocene. This chapter argues that we are confronting a fundamentally new set of challenges that cannot be seen simply as a continuation of past concerns about the environment and sustainability. This new reality compels reimagining the human development journey. And the case can be best made by laying out the evidence and describing the debates surrounding the Anthropocene concept.

The changes now unfolding reflect human pressures that are planetary (not just local) in scope, at a scale that is overwhelming the biosphere's regenerative ability and that has been unleashed with unprecedented speed.[1] The risk is that "[s]ociety may be lulled into a false sense of security by smooth projections of global change. Our synthesis of present knowledge suggests that a variety of tipping elements could reach their critical point within this century [...]."[2] The more that societies realize the implications of these changes, the more collectively self-aware they will be that we are shaping the future of the Earth system. This awareness corresponds to a completely new stage,[3] one in which the trajectory of the planet is clearly influenced by human agency and thus cannot be predicted using only biogeophysical processes.[4] Moreover, ecological challenges are often framed as a problem of the future, but the processes that need to be transformed are problems of today.[5] So the chapter marshals evidence to argue that the repercussions of the Anthropocene are already affecting human development prospects in the short run and in the long run —generating inequalities and social imbalances.

This evidence can feed into reasoned deliberations about both the challenges and the possibilities by reaching beyond researchers and policymakers dealing with the environment. As Amartya Sen notes, "There has been a serious failure in communicating the results of scientific analysis and in involving the general public in informed ethical reasoning."[6] Surely, the failure to act on this evidence has been aided by narrow interests that fear losing in this dialogue and public debate and that often mischaracterize the processes of scientific deliberation in ways that dilute the validity of results.[7] This impoverishes the debate on possible ways to confront the challenges of the Anthropocene.[8] And it can lead to a single-minded focus on a narrow set of high-profile issues that leaves the broader and far more consequential deep-seated determinants of those challenges in the background.[9]

> " Societies today have the ability to act on this evidence like never before—and to make choices that take us away from potentially catastrophic paths.

Societies today have the ability to act on this evidence like never before—and to make choices that take us away from potentially catastrophic paths. In doing so, it is important to go beyond panaceas, as Elinor Ostrom argues,[10] given that "configuring new spaces may require transformative changes in social norms, behaviours, governance and management."[11] And only by understanding the complexity of interactions between societies and ecosystems can we account for the unprecedented changes of the Anthropocene.

Enter the Anthropocene

"[T]he world is a complex, nonlinear system, in which the living and non-living components are tightly coupled [... with] important tipping points."[12]

Timothy M. Lenton

The story of the planet over time is told in the Geological Time Scale (figure 2.1). It records distinct periods in the Earth's history over timescales spanning thousands to millions of years, differentiated by characteristics ranging from climate to the emergence of life and stages in its evolution.[13] Earth system scientists

Figure 2.1 How the Anthropocene would fit in the Geological Time Scale corresponding to the Quaternary Period

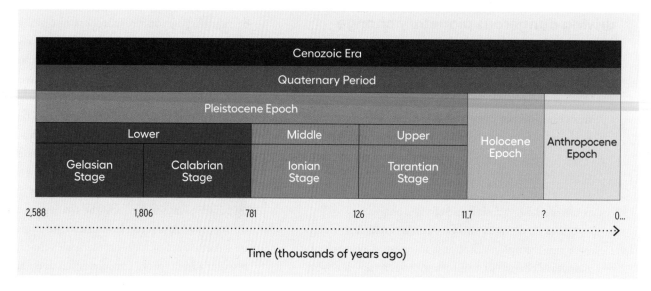

Source: Malhi 2017.

introduced the term Anthropocene at the turn of the 21st century (spotlight 2.1). They confronted a range of observations of recent changes to the planet that contrasted with the paleoenvironmental record of the Holocene (which is estimated to have started about 11,700 years ago) and indicated that the planet was operating in a no analogue state—that is, without precedent in the history of the planet.[14]

The Anthropocene is not yet formally established as a new geological epoch, but several geologists and Earth system scientists propose dating its beginning to the mid-20th century[15] with the growth in new anthropogenic materials as part of the evidence behind their proposal.[16] That would correspond to the Great Acceleration of human pressures on the planet that have the potential to leave a geological imprint (figure 2.2).

> " The Anthropocene is not yet formally established as a new geological epoch, but several geologists and Earth system scientists propose dating its beginning to the mid-20th century.

While the Anthropocene remains contested and subject to multiple interpretations, "the core concept that the term is trying to capture is that human activity is having a dominating presence on multiple aspects of the natural world and the functioning of the Earth system, and that this has consequences for how

we view and interact with the natural world—and perceive our place in it."[17] This reflects the use of the term in this Report.

Drawing on interdisciplinary evidence and analysis, Earth systems science, geology and ecology characterize the Anthropocene from distinct perspectives (table 2.1). Each brings something different, showing that considering diverse perspectives and approaches reveals the complexity and reach of the concept.[18]

Learning from Earth system science: Something new under the sun

Human societies have always been tightly linked to local environmental conditions, and many of the mechanisms at those scales are well understood.[19] These links have become less tight and more indirect as societies have modernized, urbanized and shifted their reliance from local ecosystems to more distant ones for food, water and energy (chapter 3).[20] But the notion that humans are now a dominant force in altering Earth system processes with likely detrimental impacts on human development is novel and brings whole new dimensions to the longstanding discussions of the interactions between people and nature. A key insight from Earth system science is that life and geophysical systems have interacted almost since life emerged on Earth[21]—and that these interactions

Figure 2.2 Dating the beginning of the Anthropocene to the mid-20th century would correspond to the Great Acceleration of human pressures on the planet that have the potential to leave a geological imprint

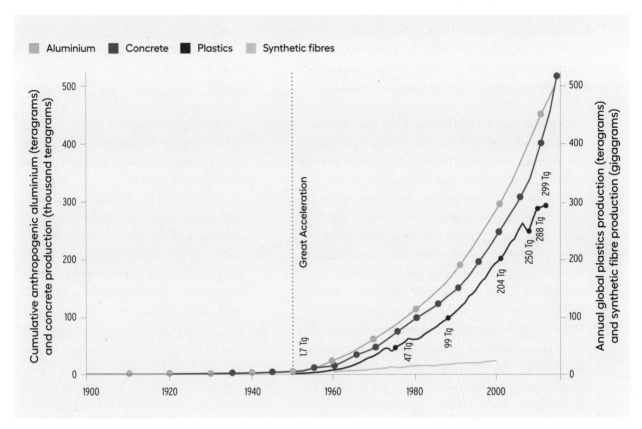

Source: Waters and others 2016.

Table 2.1 Perspectives from the natural sciences on the Anthropocene

Field	Focus	Evidence	Approaches and metrics
Earth system science	Planetary functions	Moving outside the range of variability of the Holocene → Climate change → Biogeochemical cycles disrupted (especially nitrogen and phosphorus) → Ocean acidification → Land use change → Biodiversity loss	→ Earth system tipping points and tipping elements → Planetary boundaries
Geology	Earth history	Identifying a contemporary change that is significant and detectable over Earth history timescales → Abundance of new materials of pure anthropogenic origin (aluminium, concrete, plastics) → Presence of radionuclides linked to atmospheric nuclear weapons testing	
Ecology	Biosphere	Altering the diversity, distribution, abundance and interactions of life on Earth → Conversion of ecosystems into agricultural or urban anthromes → Increasing species extinction rates → Habitat losses, overharvesting → Invasive species, global harmonization of flora and fauna	→ Biophysical reserve accounting (such as ecological footprint) → Human appropriation of net primary productivity → Rates of species extinction → Ecosystem services, nature's contributions to people

Source: Human Development Report Office based on Malhi (2017) and other sources in the text.

are now magnified by the dominant role of human activities.

> " An important characteristic of the climate system during the Holocene is the tight link between the whole web of life on the planet and in the atmosphere, regulating the carbon cycle.

Over the past 2.6 million years the planet's temperature has oscillated sharply, leading to alternating warmer and colder periods. But the Holocene has been both warmer and more stable in temperature. The climate system has also been more stable, despite massive hydrological variability that has had radical implications at the regional scale. For instance, the Sahara has not always been the dry desert we see today, and the Amazon had to confront severe droughts earlier in the Holocene.[22] In fact, an important characteristic of the climate system during the Holocene is the tight link between the whole web of life on the planet and in the atmosphere, regulating the carbon cycle. For instance, about a fifth of annual average precipitation falling on land is linked to plant-regulated water cycles, with many places now receiving half the precipitation from this type of cycle that they received before.[23]

A main focus of the Earth system community is to understand the parameters under which disruptions to planetary processes result in changes that could push some of these processes or the entire planet outside the range of variability that has characterized the Holocene. Evidence is drawn, for instance, from the analysis of climate change, alterations of biogeochemical cycles and ocean acidification. Analytical approaches emerging from the field include identifying tipping points, critical thresholds when small additional human-induced pressures can move a system to an entirely new state. A tipping point for the entire Earth system is difficult to establish—and may not even exist.[24] But several analyses of large-scale elements of the Earth system suggest tipping elements for parts of the Earth system—for example, the Greenland ice sheet and forest biomes such as the Amazon and boreal forests.[25] Something hopeful is emerging from the identification of tipping points. Though dangerous and harmful ones are to be avoided or reversed, the same dynamics can be harnessed to turn small

interventions into large impacts (such as a small conservation effort in the Apo Island in the Philippines, which resulted in a major restoration of marine life).[26]

A prominent framework to summarize how changes in the Earth system and the biosphere underpin human prosperity in fundamental ways is the planetary boundaries approach. In 2009 Johan Rockström and colleagues identified what they denoted a safe operating space for humanity.[27] This space is defined by several Earth system boundaries that, if transgressed, could undermine life-supporting conditions on our planet. This notion, refined over the years, remains one of the most influential framings for the challenges of the Anthropocene (box 2.1). Though the framework was designed explicitly for the global level only, there have been attempts to apply it at lower scales,[28] even though that is neither encouraged nor supported by the original proponents.[29] Still, the changes in the Earth system were not created by a homogeneous humanity, as can be clearly seen by the fact phosphorus and nitrogen (linked essentially to the use of fertilizers in agriculture) have breached the thresholds in several places around the world but remain far from levels of concern in many others.[30]

Understanding geological and ecological change

To specify the Anthropocene as a new geological epoch, geologists must identify a contemporary human-induced change that is significant and detectable over the timescales of Earth's history.[31] Mining, landfills, construction and urbanization have resulted in the greatest expansion of new minerals that do not exist in the natural world as rocks (in the geological sense of having the potential for long-term persistence).[32] Pure elemental aluminium is one of these materials, and as much as 98 percent of the aluminium on Earth has been produced since 1950. Another is plastics, whose current annual production equals the global human biomass.[33] The disruptions of the global biogeochemical cycles of carbon and nitrogen also leave detectable signals visible in ice cores, reflecting rapid increases in the concentrations of carbon dioxide and methane. A unique and globally dispersed geological signature corresponds to the

Box 2.1 The planetary boundaries framework

Earth system boundaries delineate a safe operating space for humanity (see figure). They quantify human-caused environmental changes that risk destabilizing the long-term dynamics of the Earth system. The framework proposes nine boundaries—limits to what the Earth system can support while maintaining the life-supporting functions of the Holocene—conducive for human development.

Climate change and biodiversity integrity loss are tightly coupled core boundaries, and human activities are currently pushing both of them into a high-risk zone. If humanity breaches planetary boundaries too far or for too long, it may disrupt planetary life support systems, with substantial risks for human life as we know it.

Nine planetary boundaries

■ Beyond zone of uncertainty (high risk) ■ Below boundary (safe)

■ In zone of uncertainty (increasing risk) ■ Boundary not yet quantified

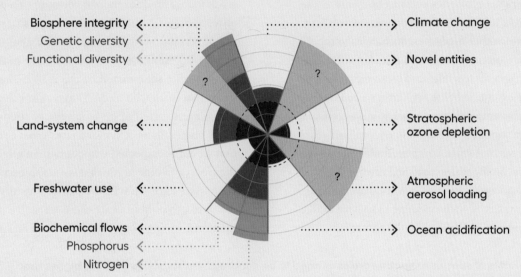

Note: The dotted area represents the safe operating space. The greater the human-caused perturbation, the greater the risk of large-scale abrupt and irreversible Earth system changes.
Source: Rockström and others 2009b; Steffen and others 2015.

The planetary boundaries framework has gained considerable attention and criticism since its inception in 2009. Some of the critiques parallel older debates about the limits to growth. But as Rockström and colleagues argue, limits to growth address neither the importance of ecosystems nor the possibility for abrupt nonlinear changes in the Earth system.[1] Other lines of criticism focus on the difficulties of defining global boundaries and the nonlinear dynamics for Earth system phenomena with such complex local and multiscale drivers, such as freshwater, biodiversity loss and land use change.[2]

The irreducible biophysical and social uncertainties associated with boundaries and global thresholds also spark debates about whether such framings can really motivate effective political action.[3] It has been argued that a focus on thresholds can lead to fatalism, unnecessary precaution and even perverse incentives that could contribute to their transgression. The international media and political debates about planetary boundaries in the runup to and during the United Nations Conference on Sustainable Development in June 2012 (Rio+20) vividly illustrate the interplay of scientific uncertainty about Earth system processes, differences in values and political conflict.[4]

Knowledge about various aspects of this safe operating space has increased rapidly over the past decade, including its applications for policymaking and business. Some of these scientific advances are related to single boundaries (including freshwater, biodiversity and nutrients) and to interactions between them.[5]

Notes
1. Rockström and others 2009b. **2.** Bass 2009; Blomqvist and others 2013; Molden 2009; Rockström and others 2018. **3.** Biermann 2012; Biermann and Kim 2020; Galaz 2014; Galaz and others 2012; Lewis 2012. **4.** Galaz 2014. **5.** Gerten and others 2013; Kahiluoto and others 2015; Lade and others 2020; Mace and others 2014; Nash and others 2017.
Source: Galaz, Collste and Moore 2020.

radioactive fallout from atmospheric nuclear weapons tested in the mid-20th century.

Geologists also consider changes in flora and fauna, both extinctions and the mixing of species across previously isolated continents and islands. Changes in periods in the geological timescale are often linked to sudden changes in the fossil record. While difficult to use as a marker for the Anthropocene with the precision of radionuclides, the magnitude and scale of the changes by humans to life on Earth may be the most enduring and obvious over the long term.

While Earth system science emphasizes the role of the biosphere on planetary functions and geologists look for markers, ecologists and sustainability scientists provide additional insights on human pressures by considering other fundamental changes to the diversity of life on the planet. The Anthropocene biosphere corresponds to a third and fundamentally new stage in the evolution of life on Earth.[34] The first was dominated by simple single-cell microbial organisms —from approximately 3.5 billion to 650 million years ago. In the second stage complex multicellular life emerged, becoming widespread and diverse after the Cambrian explosion 540 million years ago. Four characteristics make the Anthropocene biosphere unlike anything that has ever existed on the planet:

- Homogenization of flora and fauna through deliberate or accidental transfer of species across the globe.
- One species (humans) consuming 25–40 percent of land net primary productivity (that is, the biomass and energy made available by plants to all life on Earth).[35]
- Human-directed evolution of plants and animals, marginalizing natural biomes—something unprecedented in the last 2.4 billion years.[36]
- Increasing impact of new technologies as the biosphere interacts with the technosphere.[37]

In the Anthropocene biosphere, humans and livestock that is bred for human consumption outweigh all vertebrates combined (excluding fish), the mass of humans is an order of magnitude higher than that of all wild mammals and the biomass of domesticated poultry (dominated by chicken) is about three times that of all wild birds.[38] Rates of species extinction are estimated to be hundreds or thousands of times higher than background rates—that is, the rates that would be expected without human interference (figure 2.3).[39] Some argue that we are undergoing the sixth mass extinction in the planet's history.[40] Over the past 450 million years there were five mass extinctions, wiping out 70–95 percent of all species. It

Figure 2.3 Rates of species extinction are estimated to be hundreds or thousands of times higher than background rates

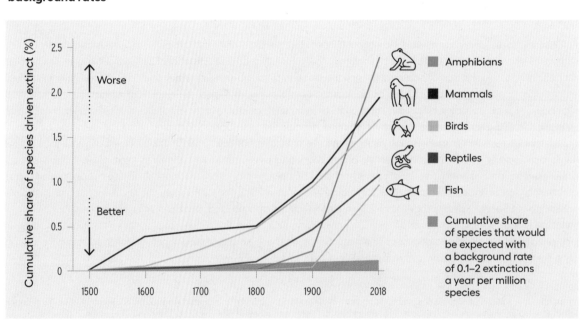

Note: Extinctions since 1500 for vertebrate groups. Rates for reptiles and fish have not been assessed for all species. See also Ceballos and others (2015).
Source: Díaz and others 2019b.

took millions of years for life to recover to the level of diversity before the extinction event. All five mass extinctions were due to natural causes, but the fact that humans may be driving a sixth raises profound ethical questions. And as a species disappears—a permanent loss—the ability of nature to provide some of its contributions on which we depend is also eroded.[41]

As much as three-quarters of the biosphere has been transformed into anthropogenic biomes—or anthromes.[42] Human societies have evolved to shape the ecology across that planet, with an impact that mirrors that of the climate, and are resetting evolutionary paths across the biosphere that will unfold, and have legacies, for hundreds of millions of years.[43]

Bringing the Anthro into the Anthropocene

But there is more to the Anthropocene than the accumulation of physical evidence of human activity's unprecedented impacts on the planet. That evidence is uncontested. And being aware of the scale and speed at which humans are changing the planet is crucial. The Anthropocene represents an unprecedented convergence of the timescales of human lives with those of historical, evolutionary and geological processes (spotlight 2.2).[44] The concept has also become a focal point of debate about how societies have evolved in their interaction with nature and how that evolution has shaped what we are today—and can inform what to envision going forward.[45]

Along with the physical evidence this added dimension of the Anthropocene is essential to framing a new human development narrative. It places people's interactions with nature in historical, social and economic contexts, informed by insights from the natural sciences.[46] This is reflected in new fields such as the climate-economy literature[47] and in the resurgence of interest in environmental history.[48]

Historical analysis places the current moment of the Anthropocene in perspective[49] but also shows how much of human history has been influenced by occurrences in the natural world. In the words of historian Kristina Sessa, "The idea that objects, animals, and other non-human entities (volcanoes, oak trees and solar radiation, for instance) shape the development of human affairs, that they possess historical agency in some form, has forced scholars to rethink some of their basic assumptions about government, power, and culture."[50]

" Human societies have evolved to shape the ecology across that planet, with an impact that mirrors that of the climate, and are resetting evolutionary paths across the biosphere that will unfold, and have legacies, for hundreds of millions of years.

But the interaction between people and nature has changed over time—and in dramatic ways during some major transitions (chapter 1). So the interaction runs in the other direction, too. The description of human activity's impact on the biosphere might suggest that the large-scale conversion of wildlands for human use is recent, but the Earth's latest transformation continues a process unfolding over time.[51] For instance, recent evidence suggests that rather than a geographic expansion of anthromes into uninhabited wildlands, the human impact on the biosphere can be described as an increasingly intensive use of land with already noticeable human impacts.[52] Even though some of this evidence remains contested,[53] it has led to the hypothesis that these early land use changes, starting at small scales thousands of years ago but unfolding over time to the global scale, drove substantial changes in greenhouse gas emissions and temperatures comparable to, and even higher, than in industrial times[54]—and that the Anthropocene should be used only as an informal term.

This historical perspective is also important to ensure that humans' impact on nature is not seen as a direct cause of modernity, industrialization or capitalism but as something more deeply embedded in our evolution and interaction with the natural world. Social, cultural and economic processes have enhanced environmental productivity by transforming ecosystems to meet human needs and wants.[55] While the scale of these transformations is unprecedented, having reached the entire planet, the underlying social and economic mechanisms remain relevant.[56]

For instance, the economic specialization and exchange that emerged deep in human history made it possible for most subsistence needs to be met with little direct interaction with ecosystems, in processes that eventually evolved to today's global supply chains. This has implications for both overexploitation of natural resources and violations of human rights (chapter 3), but the point to emphasize is the socioeconomic nature of the underlying processes. Looking at romantic notions of returning to some prior balance with nature or seeing the evolution of the human population as dependent on fixed environmental limits, as ecology does with other species, does not account for the fact that human pressures on the environment are defined by sociocultural processes.[57]

Thus, many argue that rather than looking at the Anthropocene as a precisely dated geological period, it would be better to consider it a process, or a continuous Holocene/Anthropocene, in order to understand the long (and ongoing) transition of the dialectical relationship between cultural, political and economic systems and the natural world.[58] Others reject the notion altogether, criticizing a narrative that lumps humanity together without attending to either existing inequalities or historical asymmetries in power and overexploitation of resources.[59] One common line of criticism is that the notion of the Anthropocene, especially the more science-based formulations such as planetary boundaries, do not strike at the heart of the problem, which is seen as capitalist modes of production as well as longstanding historical legacies of colonization.[60] Although Edward Barbier documents that the environmental record of centrally planned and collectivized economies has been no better than that of capitalist ones.[61]

Some of these differences in perspective reflect differences between the social sciences and the humanities, on the one hand, and the natural sciences, on the other.[62] The humanities see society and the economy as complex systems, with nature at best a contextual backdrop or something that can be analytically separated from societies, even if they are physically interdependent (box 2.2). The natural sciences

Box 2.2 Complexity in social and natural systems

The world has always been complex, but in recent decades our cumulative knowledge, tools and thinking about it have evolved to explicitly recognize that complexity. In the natural sciences—and more recently in the social sciences—people have realized that patterns that seem random on the surface may have a complex structure, resulting in surprising, abrupt shifts and cascades of change that are not easily recognizable or fully predictable, posing challenges for governance.[1]

One definition of complex (adaptive) systems is that they are "composed of multiple individual elements that interact with each other yet whose aggregate properties or behaviour is not predictable from the elements themselves."[2] The interactions of these elements (also known as agents)—be they people, animals, countries or molecules—often lead to results not directly predictable from the intentions or actions of any single agent. These results are known as emergent properties of the complex system.

The term emergence was coined in 1875 by G. H. Lewes, a British psychologist and philosopher, to describe phenomena that cannot be described or predicted by studying their underlying components. In other words the aggregate pattern is more than the sum of its parts.[3] In this view of the world, order and structured patterns can arise without any conscious design or any particular designer.[4]

The social sciences, especially economics, have not always looked at the world through the lens of complexity, often preferring top-down, equilibrium-based models rather than the bottom-up, agent-based models used in complexity research.[5] This analytical gap was pointed out in the aftermath of the global financial crisis, as economists and policymakers had been basing their models on past trends, assuming the economy evolves in a linear way.[6]

In reality, however, even Earth science models that include environmental dynamics in a complex way often represent the socioeconomic (human) world as a simple process of macroeconomic optimization.[7] As a result, many important features of complexity—such as interactions and feedback among human and ecological systems, economic and social networks, and even human agency—are left out.[8]

Part of the reason is that the dominant social narrative underlying such models is the same as in the standard economic models just described. But in reality human society is linked through many networks,

(continued)

Box 2.2 Complexity in social and natural systems *(continued)*

not just trade and information but also politics and infrastructure. Human behaviour—shaped by norms and values—causes changes in the functioning of the Earth system, which in turn has feedback effects on human norms, values and behaviours.

If we study the natural world and human world separately, ignoring the loops both within and between them—we risk missing emergent phenomena such as critical tipping points. One way to enrich our understanding of this human–nature interaction is to move beyond the assumption that human agency is concerned only with cost-optimization. Goals and desirable outcomes differ among people and groups, and those differences often result in conflict. Just having lots of money does not make you (or your neighbours) necessarily better off. A recent study found that neighbours of lottery winners were more likely to go bankrupt, mainly since the neighbours attempt to emulate the winner's lavish lifestyle and go too far.[9]

Such models are especially relevant for studying socioecological systems that link human behaviour and environmental dynamics. One study applied fuzzy cognitive mapping and agent-based modelling to simulate alternative policy options in a water-scarce farming community.[10] Another study looked at factors that affect the behaviour of people charging their electric vehicles. The agent-based model for the question analysed policy interventions, including smart automated charging, financial incentives and information campaigns. The model also included insight on psychological drivers of behaviour that is environmentally friendly.[11] Agent-based models are sometimes combined with social network analysis—as with, for example, a recent study on information sharing among conservation rangers patrolling hunting communities.[12]

The way forward involves a more socially differentiated representation of agency, going deeper into social and socioeconomic networks and accounting for the complexity of coevolutionary dynamics.[13] The models can include such phenomena as segregation, social learning, value changes and group dynamics.[14]

Notes

1. Galaz 2019. **2.** Wilensky and Rand 2015, p. 6. **3.** Wilensky and Rand 2015. **4.** Reynolds 1987; Stonedahl and Wilensky 2010. A classic example of complexity in the natural world is the flying pattern of some bird flocks. Thinking in a simple linear way would lead people who see geese flying in a V-formation to conclude that there is a leader bird (either the biggest one or the mother bird), and all other birds follow its direction. However, the reality is both simpler and more complex. Every bird in the flock just follows three basic directional rules (while maintaining the same speed). First, every bird aligns its flight direction to match that of nearby birds. Second, every bird separates when it is too close to other birds to avoid hitting them. And third, cohesion means birds move towards other birds nearby. If there is a conflict between the rules, separation overrides the other two, to avoid collisions. Another example involves the dynamic interactions of prey (sheep) and predator (wolves) populations (Dublin and Lotka 1925; Volterra 1926) with each other and with the environment (such as grass for the sheep to eat; Wilensky and Reisman 2006). A sustainable outcome depends not only on the sheep or the wolves but also on their interactions. If the wolves are too powerful and eat all the sheep, they will starve to death. Likewise, if the sheep multiply too fast, they will eat all the grass (before it has a chance to regenerate) and die. A similar pattern has been observed with lynx (predator) and snowshoe hare (prey) in Alaska (United States) and Canada, where the population of the lynx rises and falls with that of the hares (with a time lag of 1–2 years; US Department of the Interior 2017). **5.** Arthur 1999; Crépin and Folke 2015. **6.** Farmer and Foley 2009. **7.** Something that sustainability science seeks to consider more systematically (Clark and Harley 2020). **8.** Donges and others 2017b. **9.** Agarwal, Mikhed and Scholnick 2016. **10.** Mehryar and others 2020. **11.** Van Der Kam and others 2019. **12.** Dobson and others 2019. **13.** Donges and others 2017a; Nyborg and others 2016 ; Verburg and others 2016. **14.** Auer and others 2015; Schleussner and others 2016.

take the reverse perspective, with natural systems as interdependent and complex and human agency described in aggregate terms as causing generalized impacts or disturbances.[63] Others oppose conceptualizing the Anthropocene as a process because they view the concept's power as signifying a rupture with the past, thus indicating a contemporary state of the world that urgently needs fundamental changes at the risk of catastrophic consequences for nature.[64]

Where does this leave us? With the notion that the Anthropocene is something novel in two ways. First,

"the Anthropocene is an encapsulation of the concept that modern human activity is large relative to planetary processes, and therefore that human social, economic, and political decisions have become entangled in a web of planetary feedbacks. This global planetary entanglement is something new in human history and Earth history."[65] Second, the Anthropocene is a catalyst for systematic thinking about the interdependence of people and nature, including the Earth system. It is informed by a diversity of disciplines, going beyond linear and simplified narratives of progress, and invites framing the options that face us today as more than a choice between impending catastrophe or an easy decoupling of economic activity from planetary pressures.

" The Anthropocene is a catalyst for systematic thinking about the interdependence of people and nature, including the Earth system.

One implication of this understanding of the relationship between people and nature is the recent reframing of the conceptual approach of ecosystems as providers of services[66] to acknowledge nature's contributions to people.[67] This reframing also presents anthropogenic drivers of changes in nature as being embedded in institutions and governance systems. It recognizes the intrinsic value of preserving nature.

The remainder of this chapter brings the "Anthro into the Anthropocene" into even sharper relief, highlighting how dangerous planetary change already affects people's lived reality. It shows how different social groups and geographies are being affected and are likely to be affected in the future. Some of these differences are across countries, but most are across groups that are not separated by national borders. And most are expressed in an intersection of multiple characteristics that compound inequalities and differences in empowerment.

Anthropocene risks and human development

The Anthropocene implies enormous uncertainty for people and societies. Similarities to previous records provide some information on what is coming.[68] But unlike during other geological periods, the human factor—the one that took us to this point—will continue to be determinant.

Thus, the risks are not only greater; they are also different. The notion of risks faced by people is changing, as the risks reflect a new complex interrelation of planetary changes and social imbalances. Some scientists have proposed the notion of Anthropocene risk to reflect the new factors at play:[69] a new baseline of hazards (set of potential events), more complex exposure patterns resulting from the interconnection of the effects of social and planetary systems in different locations of Earth (telecoupling; see chapter 6) and

new ways to predict and perceive, with limited knowledge about the events and their probabilities.

Yet amid this uncertainty it is possible to discern some new trends. First, the Anthropocene is starting to have deep development impacts, disturbing societies at large and threatening development reversals. Second, these trends are expected to intensify over the rest of the century, even under moderate to high climate mitigation. Developing countries are expected to absorb the bulk of the human costs, exacerbating already destabilizing dynamics, as chapter 3 explains.

Unprecedented planetary change, unprecedented shocks on human development

Shocks emanating from disturbances in life systems and climate change are affecting people and changing societies. The Covid-19 pandemic has shown how the effects of large-scale shocks emerge out of ecological systems under pressure from social activities.[70] These shocks are affecting the main components of human development with unprecedented magnitude, synchronicity and global reach. Simulations of the pandemic's real-time impact suggest that during 2020, all the capabilities accounted for in the Human Development Index were severely affected (figure 2.4).[71]

However, even before the Covid-19 pandemic, systemic risk had been on the rise, often overshadowed by average progress in economic development and poverty reduction. There are indications on several fronts.[72]

Climate change is weakening economic progress and increasing inequality

There is evidence that economic development has already been systematically affected by climate change. In most countries GDP per capita is lower today than in the counterfactual without climate change —particularly in lower income countries, where it is estimated to be 17–31 percent lower. Overall, cross-country income inequality is estimated to be 25 percent higher because of climate change.[73]

Increasing hunger

After two decades of progress the number of people affected by hunger (undernourished people) has been

Figure 2.4 The Covid-19 pandemic's unprecedented shock to human development

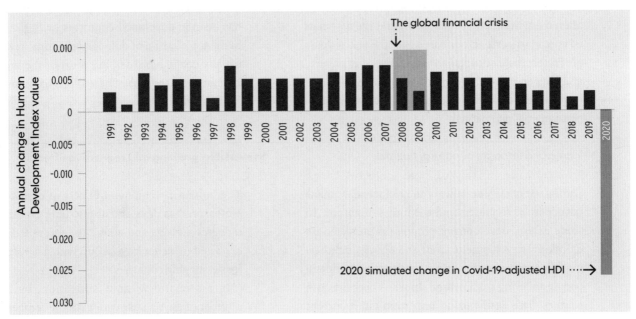

Source: Updated version of figure 3 in UNDP (2020b).

increasing since its low of 628 million in 2014. In 2019 the number was 688 million, up 60 million in only five years. Estimates for 2020 (including the effect of the Covid-19 pandemic) range from 780 million to 829 million (figure 2.5). By 2030, 900 million people could be undernourished. This trend is touching a large share of the global population: In 2019, 2 billion people were moderately or severely food insecure, 367 million more than in 2014.

The inflection point in the trajectory of progress in food security is due to multiple factors: stagnant or deteriorating economic conditions, weak positions in global value chains and large inequalities in the distribution of income, assets and resources. But

Figure 2.5 Hunger is on the rise

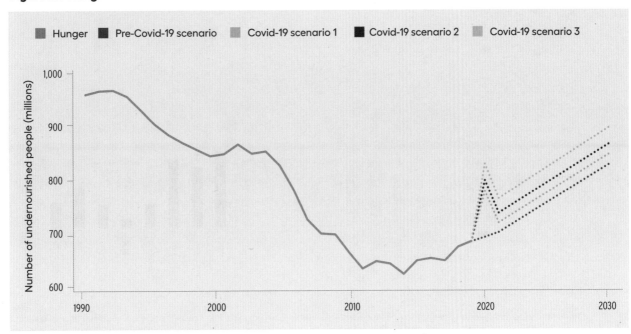

Source: Adapted from FAO and others (2020), using data for 1991–2001 from FAO (2020b) and UNDESA (2015).

anthropogenic shocks appear to be the newest driver: "increasing frequency of extreme weather events, altered environmental conditions, and the associated spread of pests and diseases over the last 15 years are factors that contribute to vicious cycles of poverty and hunger, particularly when exacerbated by fragile institutions, conflict, violence and widespread displacement of populations."[74]

Increasing impacts of natural hazards

During the relative stability of the Holocene, humans have learned to understand the forces of nature. To some extent, development progress is premised on delinking development from the shocks emanating from nature—which is reflected in the decline in people suffering from natural disasters over the 20th century. This resilience to uncertain but recurrent natural hazards has allowed for the reduction of inequalities in human development vulnerability.[75] But this is changing in the Anthropocene.

Recent scientific reports suggest that the effects of natural hazards have been increasing since the turn of the millennium.[76] Recorded damage and the number of affected people (including deaths,

injured and homeless) suggest an inflection point (figure 2.6). Most of the increased economic cost has been in developed countries (with the increase in the top quartile of damage reflecting new and unusually costly hazards), but most of the increase in human costs (people affected) has been in developing countries.

Irreversible, growing and regressive effects

The human development effects of climate change —measured as days of extreme temperatures below 0 degree Celsius and above 35 degrees Celsius—are expected to be heterogeneous, with a greater burden for developing countries.

In a scenario without mitigation, by 2100 the number of days a year with extreme temperatures is expected to increase by 100 in low human development countries, 66 in medium human development countries and 37 in high human development countries (median values). In very high human development countries the number is expected to fall by 16—driven by a reduction in extreme cold days greater than the increase in extreme hot days (figure 2.7).

Figure 2.6 The effects of natural hazards appear to be increasing

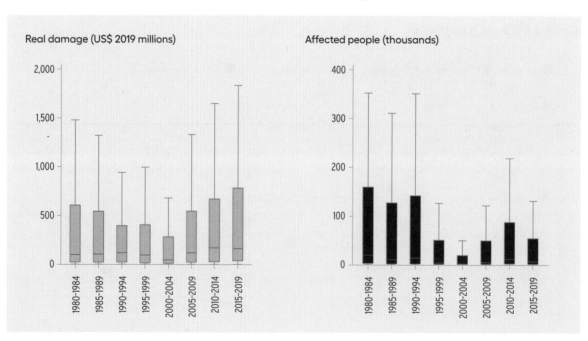

Note: Natural hazards excluding geophysical and extraterrestrial events. Each box plots the middle 50 percent of the distribution; the central line is the median. Outside the box, the extreme lines are the approximate minimum and maximum of the distribution. Outliers are not shown.
Source: Human Development Report Office based on data from the Centre for Research on the Epidemiology of Disasters's Emergency Events Database (http://www.emdat.be, accessed 11 October 2020).

Even under a scenario with mitigation that might be consistent with the Paris Agreement goals, the number of days with extreme temperatures in developing countries is expected to increase substantially by 2100: by 49 days in low human development countries and 21 days in medium human development countries.[77]

The effects on mortality are expected to be regressive, given the greater exposure and lower ability of poor countries to adapt. Indeed, in developed countries most of the health-related costs of climate change are expected to be economic—adaptation spending to cope with higher temperatures—with the number of deaths expected to decline by 2100. In low-income countries the economic burden of adaptation may be much lower, but the human cost in lives lost is likely to be extremely high, comparable to today's leading causes of death.[78]

Sea levels are expected to rise considerably in the coming decades. Climate change already caused a rise of 11–16 centimetres in the 20th century.[79] For the 21st century the estimated increase is much larger, in the range of 50–100 centimetres.[80] However, it could reach 2 metres in some (extreme) scenarios of no mitigation and early instability of the Antarctic ice sheet. More than a billion people live in low elevation coastal zones—contiguous areas along the coast that are less than 10 metres above sea level. More than three-quarters of them live in areas less than 5 metres above sea level,[81] vulnerable not only to average sea level rise but also to fluctuations caused by storms and high tides.

" Even under a scenario with mitigation that might be consistent with the Paris Agreement goals, the number of days with extreme temperatures in developing countries is expected to increase substantially by 2100.

The number of people vulnerable to permanent sea level rise is estimated to increase from 110 million today to more than 200 million by 2100.[82] These median values represent around a fifth of people in low elevation coastal zones in models with stable Antarctic conditions. In the case of Antarctic instability, between a quarter and a third of people in these zones become vulnerable. Even high mitigation scenarios project a large increase. Globally, the number of additional people on land at risk is expected to increase by 80 million in the high mitigation scenario (RCP 2.6),

Figure 2.7 By 2100 the number of days a year with extreme temperatures is expected to increase more in lower human development countries

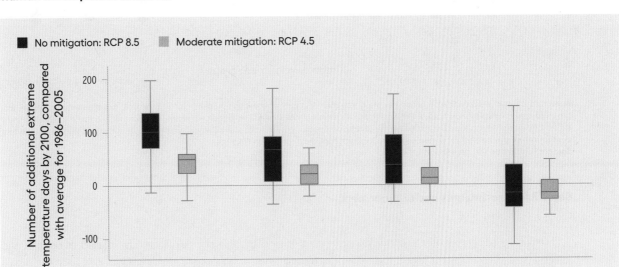

Note: Each box plots the middle 50 percent of the distribution; the central line is the median. Outside the box, the extreme lines are the approximate minimum and maximum of the distribution. Outliers are not shown. The figure compares the number of days of extreme temperature (below 0 degrees Celsius and above 35 degrees Celsius) between 1986 and 2005 (actual) and between 2080 and 2099 (median projected values).
Source: Human Development Report Office based on Carleton and others (2020).

by 90–140 million in the moderate mitigation scenario (RCP 4.5) and by 120–230 million people in the no mitigation scenario (RCP 8.5).[83]

The impacts are regressive (figure 2.8). Most of those vulnerable to the rise in sea level live in developing countries, particularly in Asia. Low human development countries are less exposed in absolute terms because they have much shorter coastlines than higher human development countries on average. But they face greater relative exposure per kilometre of coastline. People and societies adapt to changes. But adaptation can also be extremely costly in human development terms. Environmental shocks are already a leading source of forced displacement in the world (25 million people among only the internally displaced, in 2019; box 2.3). Some estimates indicate that 1 billion people worldwide could face forced displacement by 2050.[84]

The realities of the Anthropocene are overlaid on existing massive inequalities in human development. Nature's contributions to people are declining where people's needs for nature are now greatest, with up

Figure 2.8 Low human development countries have less exposure to sea level rise in absolute terms but greater relative exposure per kilometre of coastline

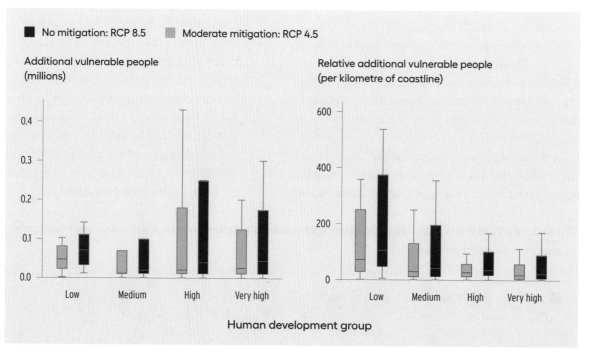

Note: Each box plots the middle 50 percent of the distribution; the central line is the median. Outside the box, the extreme lines are the approximate minimum and maximum of the distribution. Outliers are not shown. The panel on the right normalizes by coastline length to show that the vulnerability of people per kilometre of coastline is greater in lower human development countries. Estimates are based on the current population living in coastal zones and do not account for population growth or migration.
Source: Human Development Report Office based on Kulp and Strauss (2019).

Box 2.3 Natural hazards and displacement

Land degradation, water scarcity, natural hazards and biodiversity depletion are related to conflict, violence and migration.[1] Wetter coasts, higher temperatures, drier midcontinent areas and rising sea levels may cause the gravest effects of climate change by forcing sudden human displacement.[2] By 2070 extremely hot zones, similar to the Sahara, could cover nearly a fifth of the world's land, and a third of humanity could be living in unbearable conditions.[3] Shoreline erosion, river and coastal flooding, and severe drought have already displaced millions of people.[4] In 2019, 25 million people worldwide were internally displaced because of natural hazards.

(continued)

Box 2.3 Natural hazards and displacement *(continued)*

Disasters continued to trigger most new displacements in 2020. Cyclone Amphan hit Bangladesh and India, driving the largest single displacement event in the first half of the year, triggering 3.3 million pre-emptive evacuations. Several East African countries were hit by major floods and a locust infestation that aggravated food insecurity. And intense bushfires led to unprecedented displacement in Australia.[5] The expected annual number of people displaced after 2020 is about 13.7 million globally (see figure), most due to floods (72 percent).

Many people born in areas with low carbon footprints per capita are more likely to migrate to areas with higher carbon footprints. Migration is an adaptation strategy, but social patterns of discrimination and exclusion often persist even after people move.[6]

Africa is expected to experience a 10 percent decline in rainfall by 2050, potentially resulting in massive migration.[7] In Somalia drought episodes have forced entire communities to move to urban and periurban settlements.[8] New displacements in 2017 were 12 times larger than the previous year, reaching 899,000 people, and a million people were displaced in 2018 and in 2019. Informal urban settlements and displacement sites are creating new pressures on infrastructure and services, with evictions identified as a cause for secondary displacement.[9] Displaced people surveyed in Mogadishu experienced some improvements in access to education and health but faced reduced access to job opportunities and lower incomes.

Globally, about 13.7 million people a year are expected to be displaced after 2020, most due to floods

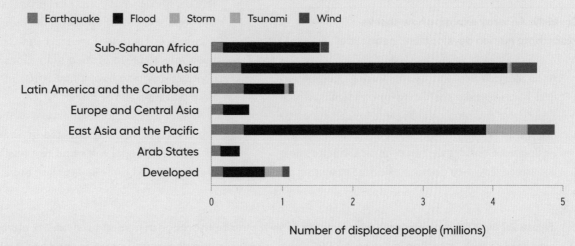

Source: IDMC 2020b.

Displacement can also differ by gender. Women's displacement can be linked to their role and status in society.[10] In 141 countries from 1981 to 2002, disasters killed more women than men on average.[11] Natural hazards with high female fatalities include the 1991 Cyclone Gorky in Bangladesh (91 percent women), the 2004 Indian Ocean Tsunami in Banda Aceh (75 percent) and the 2008 Cyclone Nargis in Myanmar (61 percent).[12] Women might be unwilling to evacuate for cultural reasons of not being able to swim or escape.[13]

But even when they survive, they are at greater risk of displacement. Women working in agriculture in Latin America, South Asia and Sub-Saharan Africa depend on forests, land, rivers and rainfall for their livelihoods.[14] Female migration intentions increase with the severity of food insecurity.[15] Changes in rainfall affect how women allocate time to paid work, unpaid care work and education, and girls can be forced to drop out of school to engage in household duties.[16]

Notes
1. Barbier and Homer-Dixon 1999; Barnett and Adger 2007; Gupta, Dellapenna and van den Heuvel 2016; Homer-Dixon 1991. **2.** IPCC 2014a. **3.** Xu and others 2020. **4.** IPCC 1995. **5.** IDMC 2020b. **6.** Singh and others 2012. **7.** Cechvala 2011. **8.** Hassan and Tularam 2017. **9.** Cortés Fernández 2020. **10.** Jungehülsing 2011. **11.** Neumayer and Plümper 2007. **12.** Oxfam 2005; Rex and Trohanis 2012. **13.** Alam and Rahman 2014; Chew and Ramdas 2005; Oxfam 2005. **14.** East Africa is defined in the cited article as generally including Burundi, Djibouti, Eritrea, Ethiopia, Kenya, Malawi, Rwanda, Somalia, South Sudan, Sudan, Tanzania, Uganda, Zambia and Zimbabwe (Abebe 2014). **15.** Smith and Floro 2020. **16.** Abebe 2014.
Source: Human Development Report Office.

to 5 billion people facing higher water pollution and insufficient pollination for nutrition under future scenarios of climate change and land use, particularly in Africa and South Asia.[85] Humans can survive within only a narrow temperature range,[86] and temperatures are projected to shift outside that range more over the next 50 years than in the past 6,000 years—negatively in developing countries, positively in developed countries (figure 2.9).

In summary, unprecedented global planetary change is posing existential risks to humans and all forms of life but also driving deeper wedges between those more and less prepared to cope with the change. The impacts are affecting not only the well-being of the most vulnerable people in the world; they are also disempowering them.

Covid-19: An x-ray exposing how shocks exacerbate human development inequalities

As an illustration of the disempowering effect of natural hazards, take the Covid-19 pandemic, which shows how environmental hazards exacerbate existing within-country inequalities, as the next section elaborates. Consider the two countries with the most confirmed Covid-19 deaths at the time of writing. In the United States Black and African American people and Hispanic and Latino people are nearly three times as likely as White people to test positive for Covid-19 and five times as likely to be hospitalized as White people.[87] In Brazil being of mixed ethnicity was the second most important risk factor (after age) for death among hospitalized Covid-19 patients.[88]

" When new shocks interact with intersecting horizontal inequalities, they reinforce patterns of disempowerment of specific groups—including ethnic minorities and indigenous populations, women, children and young people.

In Latin America the pandemic has spread across rural indigenous communities,[89] home to nearly 42 million people, 80 percent of them in Bolivia, Guatemala, Mexico and Peru.[90] In Peru 75–80 percent of the population in villages with the indigenous communities of Caimito, Pucacuro and Cantagallo has been infected.[91] In Mexico indigenous people who contract Covid-19 have a higher risk of pneumonia, hospitalization and death.[92]

As the next section elaborates, women and girls are disproportionately affected by shocks because of their traditional roles and responsibilities,[93] including around three-quarters of unpaid care work

Figure 2.9 By 2070 temperatures are projected to shift outside the range of human survivability more over the next 50 years than in the past 6,000 years—negatively in developing countries and positively in developed countries

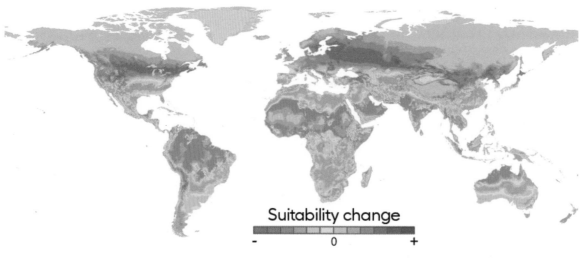

Suitability change

Source: Xu and others 2020.

Figure 2.10 The Covid-19 pandemic has erased decades of progress in the female labour force participation rate

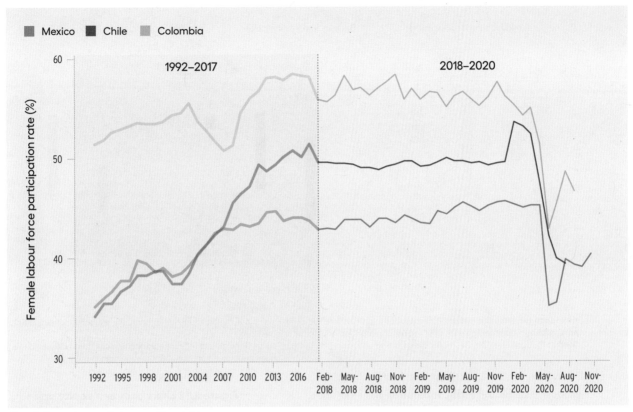

Note: Refers to the population ages 15 and older.
Source: Yearly data for 1992–2017 from the International Labour Organization's ILOSTAT database; monthly data for 2018–2020 from the National Institute of Statistics and Geography, the National Survey of Occupation and Employment and the Telephone Survey of Occupation and Employment for Mexico and from the ILOSTAT database for Colombia and Chile.

at home.[94] This burden, combined with the lockdowns, has reduced the female labour force participation rate in Mexico, Chile and Colombia by 10 percentage points, erasing decades of progress (figure 2.10).

School closures have affected approximately 90 percent of children worldwide. While some have had the opportunity to keep learning remotely, thanks to access to the internet, others have experienced an almost complete loss of formal learning through 2020. During the peak of the pandemic in countries with school closures, the estimated short-term out-of-school rate in primary education was 20 percent in high human development countries, compared with 86 percent in low human development countries.[95] Girls and young women are particularly vulnerable—to early pregnancy, child marriage and gender-based violence.[96] The education shock might result in a loss of key capabilities[97] and of effective empowerment for the first

generation embarking on the human development journey in the Anthropocene.

Planetary change is disempowering

The impacts of planetary change are diverse and context specific. For instance, countries with high ecological threats (defined by scenarios of resource scarcity and disasters linked to natural hazards) tend to be also countries with greater social vulnerability: where within-country inequalities in human development are larger, where women face larger empowerment gaps (proxied by the Gender Inequality Index) and where children—the new generation burdened by the responsibility to act—will represent a larger share of the population by 2030 (figure 2.11).

This poses a challenge in that it exacerbates inequalities in wellbeing. When new shocks interact with intersecting horizontal inequalities, they reinforce patterns of disempowerment of specific

Figure 2.11 Countries with higher ecological threats tend to have greater social vulnerability

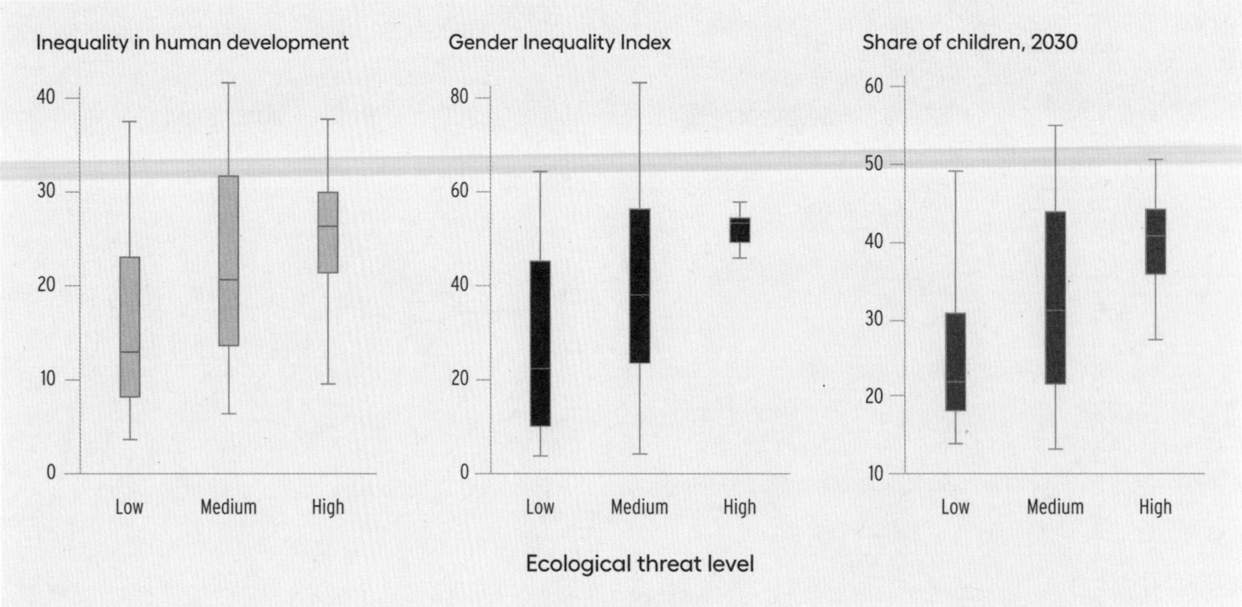

| Inequality in human development | Gender Inequality Index | Share of children, 2030 |

Ecological threat level

Note: Each box plots the middle 50 percent of the distribution; the central line is the median. Outside the box, the extreme lines are the approximate minimum and maximum of the distribution. Outliers are not shown.
Source: Human Development Report Office based data from the United Nations Department of Economic and Social Affairs and IEP (2020).

groups[98]—including ethnic minorities and indigenous populations, women, children and young people.[99] To see how, consider three forms of equity[100]— recognitional equity, distributional equity and procedural equity— each of which is directly linked to a key aspect of empowerment (figure 2.12).[101]

- Recognitional equity refers to recognition of interest holders and respect for their identity, values and associated rights. Empowerment is positively associated with the recognition of human rights and principles of nondiscrimination.[102]
- Distributional equity refers to the distribution of resources, costs and benefits among people and groups. Access to resources enhances an individual's ability to choose, so those resources are channels to exercise empowerment and agency.[103]
- Procedural equity relates to how decisions are being made in reference to institutions, governance and participation. Representation, power and voice are linked directly to empowerment—they shape communities' and individuals' ability to influence and participate in decisionmaking to achieve their desired outcomes and goals.[104]

As explored next, inequities in each of these three areas often reflect, and interact with, the asymmetric

Figure 2.12 Links between equity and empowerment

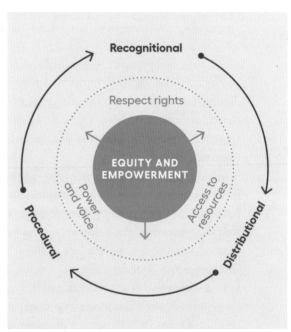

Source: Human Development Report Office based on Leach and others (2018).

impacts of planetary change, given the intertwined character of social and ecological systems.[105]

Recognitional equity and human rights

The lack of recognition of human rights amid dangerous planetary change perpetuates discrimination and injustice. Take the example of land. Though it is a source of livelihood and economic resilience linked to identities and tied to social and cultural rights, three-quarters of the world's people cannot prove that they own the land where they live or work.[106] And local efforts to manage common land, forests and fisheries have often been undermined by group-based inequities or class differences.[107] One of the biggest disadvantages faced by indigenous peoples is the lack of recognition and protection of their rights, including their right to land, which can disempower them and limit the opportunities to expand their capabilities.[108]

" The lack of recognition of human rights amid dangerous planetary change perpetuates discrimination and injustice.

This reflects longstanding patterns of discrimination, exclusion and nonrecognition of human rights linked to the fact that indigenous peoples have historically been denied the right to own land.[109] Only a few countries recognize indigenous peoples' land rights, but incomplete land demarcation and titling can mean that rights are not systematically protected and are vulnerable to changes in political leadership and policies. Even having legal title over land does not ensure indigenous peoples' security, as land can be leased by others without consulting them. Systemic discrimination permeates actions by governments and others, reflected, for instance, when indigenous peoples' ownership of land historically assumed to be worthless is disposed when that land is found to be rich in natural resources.

Ancestral relationships with the land have been a source of cultural and social identity for indigenous communities, as have their traditional knowledge systems. Even well intended policies have failed to acknowledge indigenous peoples' custodianship of ecosystems.[110] Conservation programmes can blunt indigenous peoples' rights, especially when excluding them in the design of conservation programmes or, worse, through forced evictions and other harms.[111] These challenges in recognitional equity extend beyond land. For example, indigenous peoples face lack of recognition of historical water uses and water rights, leading to conflicts over water in the Andes.[112]

Women in many countries also confront challenges in recognitional equity that are similar to those faced by indigenous peoples. In more than 90 countries female farmers lack equal rights to own land.[113] The asymmetries between women owning land and living off the land are striking. The lowest rates of land ownership occur in low and medium human development countries (16.4 percent and 14.4 percent) and the highest in very high human development countries (over 20 percent). But more than half of women live off the land in low human development countries compared with only 3.4 percent in very high human development countries (figure 2.13).[114] Statutory laws and restrictions on the ownership of land act as a mechanism for discrimination that exacerbates these inequalities. Even when laws are in place, enforcement can be lacking. Discriminatory social norms and practices are among the strongest barriers between women and their land rights.[115]

The implications of lack of recognitional equity disempower women in ways that have consequences beyond their wellbeing, because land use and management also determine agricultural productivity and the welfare of household members. Given that women are more likely to address their children's nutrition and education needs,[116] owning property gives them more bargaining power in their households to make decisions that benefit their families' long term capabilities.[117] Evidence from Colombia to India indicates that financial security and ownership of land improve women's security and reduce the risk of gender-based violence, clearly indicating that owning land can empower women.[118]

Distributional equity and access to resources

Inequalities in vulnerability to planetary change can be heightened by the uneven distribution of resources across groups (chapter 3).[119]

Consider indigenous peoples, who face a disproportionate burden of malnutrition.[120] Their food supply is diversified and linked to local ecosystems, which makes it highly vulnerable to environmental shocks.[121] Changes in rainfall, land degradation and

Figure 2.13 The asymmetries between women owning land and living off the land are striking

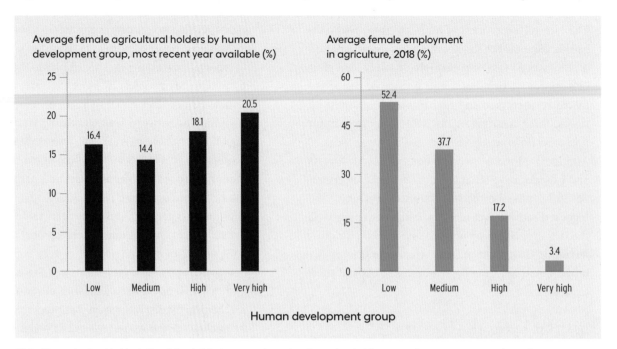

Note: The agricultural holder is the civil or juridical person who makes the major decisions regarding resource use and exercises management control over the agricultural holding.
Source: The Food and Agriculture Organization's Gender and Land Rights Database and the International Labour Organization's ILOSTAT database.

variations in ecosystem species and crops complicate indigenous peoples' access to their traditional food sources. In Australia indigenous mothers have a higher risk of giving birth to babies of low birthweight, and poor nutrition is higher among indigenous children.[122] The same happens in Asia, where indigenous children in Cambodia, India and Thailand show more malnutrition-related issues such as stunting and wasting.[123] These vulnerabilities extend to the lack of access to safe drinking water and wastewater treatment.[124] In Canada, a water-rich country, First Nations disproportionately risk exposure to contaminated and low-quality water. Water advisory alerts, informing communities when their water is unsafe to drink, were sent to 86 First Nation communities across the country in 2016.[125]

As with recognitional equity, women also confront systematic inequalities in access to resources and related vulnerabilities. Of the 2 billion food-insecure people worldwide in 2019, rural women were among the worst affected.[126] The prevalence of severe food insecurity in Africa, Asia and Latin America is slightly higher among women, with the largest differences in Latin America, where the gaps are rising.[127] Traditional gender roles can determine women's access to

food within the household—with consequences not just for their own food security and nutrition but also for their children's, as noted above. Women, along with their children, suffer the most from nutrient deficiencies, especially during reproductive years. While in some cases women must bargain for their fair share of food, they also are more likely to voluntarily relinquish food for their families.[128] In India different responses in parent behaviour as well as some disinvestment in girls' health and education have led to higher malnutrition among girls than among boys as a consequence of shocks likely linked to climate change.[129] In Rwanda girls born during crop failure showed more stunted growth than girls born when there was no crop failure.[130]

" Traditional gender roles can determine women's access to food within the household—with consequences not just for their own food security and nutrition but also for their children's.

The consequences of inequalities in access to resources are intensified when women are also producers of food. This often happens in countries with high shares of women employed in agriculture, typically with lower human development (see figure 2.13), mainly in South Asia and Sub-Saharan Africa, where rural women make up almost half of the agricultural labour force. Women farmers face challenges not only with the ownership of land, as discussed above, but also with accessing productive resources such as livestock, agricultural inputs, technology and finance.[131]

" When schools cannot reopen after a natural hazard, there is a long-term impact on students' learning. After 80 days of school closures, the children in areas affected by the 2005 earthquake in Pakistan were 1.5–2 years behind.

Unequal access to resources across groups also interacts with the costs and benefits linked to dangerous planetary change.[132] Consider the case of children, a vulnerable group, especially younger children who depend on adults for their survival and development.[133] Today, more than half a billion children live in extremely high flood occurrence zones, and nearly 160 million live in high or extremely high drought severity zones.[134] Changes in weather patterns, higher frequency of natural hazards and increased rainfall can interrupt children's education by displacing families (see box 2.3), destroying schools and pushing children into the labour force to help their families make ends meet.[135]

When schools cannot reopen after a natural hazard, there is a long-term impact on students' learning.[136] After 80 days of school closures, the children in areas affected by the 2005 earthquake in Pakistan were 1.5–2 years behind. Among children ages 3–5 whose mother had not completed at least primary education, those who lived close to the fault line scored significantly worse on academic tests than those who lived farther away; among children whose mother had completed at least primary education there was no gap in scores by distance. The gap is estimated to continue through adult life, leading to a 15 percent loss in lifetime earnings.[137] With the Covid-19 pandemic, school closures can create a multiplier effect on learning losses for millions of children.[138] Children may have to remain in unsafe conditions, and where there are no alternative childcare options, parents may be prevented

from returning to work, creating further economic stress and possibly forcing children to drop out of school—and in some cases be driven into the labour force.[139]

Procedural equity and representation, power and voice

Asymmetries in the distribution of power parallel inequities in the distribution of the impacts of a wide range of environmental hazards across population groups.[140] These, in turn, can exacerbate exclusion of and discrimination against ethnic minorities, those at the bottom of the income distribution and other groups that face horizontal inequalities.[141] These groups can be disproportionally affected through seemingly economic decisions, such as when chemical plants or waste deposits are built in low-income communities because it is cheaper, when in fact the choices are also due to differences in representation and voice. Polluting industries choose to locate in areas where they will face less resistance. Many vulnerable communities lack the financial resources and organizational clout to sustain a long-term fight when there is a threat to their wellbeing. And they have fewer advocates and lobbyists pushing for their interests at the national level.

Consider indigenous communities, which have been disproportionately subject to air, water and soil pollution and systematically excluded from healthy environments.[142] In Esmeraldas, Ecuador, home of the Afro Ecuadorian Wimbi community, a conflict started with a palm and wood company taking over territory. The company claimed ownership over the territory and replaced existing cacao plantations with others intended to extract palm oil.[143] The change in land use, which included deforestation, affected 57 percent of the territory of Esmeraldas, and the province has turned into a palm oil producer. Water sources around the area are highly polluted, which combined with the existing malfunctioning of safe water and sanitation systems puts the local population at high risk.[144] The Niger Delta, the largest wetland in Africa and home to the Ogoni communities, has suffered from oil spills, impairing water quality.[145] Several Ogoni communities have been drinking water with high hydrocarbon levels at 41 sites, and community members of Nisisioken Ogale have been drinking water with carcinogens.[146] The Peruvian Amazonia has also been affected by oil spills, which contaminated soil, water and the most important species for indigenous peoples' diets, with 50 percent of the general population and 64 percent of children in the area showing high levels of mercury.[147]

Women also face disproportionate burdens from planetary change due in part to the already prevailing uneven distribution of care work.[148] This includes caring for children, the elderly and the ill as well as household chores related to food production and fuel and water collection, activities that have become increasingly time consuming due to the impacts of climate change.[149] This not only reflects women's low bargaining power in household decisions but also further diminishes it. Women are left more vulnerable to external shocks and socially excluded because their higher household and care responsibilities affords them less time to participate in community decision-making or gain knowledge on adaptation strategies. They may also be excluded from the labour market, making them less independent.[150] Evidence bears out the relevance of these mechanisms. Ghanaian households headed by men were more resilient to climate shocks than those headed by women.[151] The differences were due to women's limited power in decisionmaking, coupled with low access to resources (illustrating how lack of distributional equity reinforces gaps in procedural equity).

Given that economic and political powerlessness can make poor and minority communities be seen as offering the path of least resistance for interests that pollute and degrade the environment,[152] the distribution of power is key.[153] Redressing these asymmetries in power has underpinned the environmental justice movement, which seeks to enhance the power of groups unseen, unheard and undervalued. Ethnicity can also reduce the options for minorities to "choose" a neighbourhood free of hazards.[154] Communities suffering environmental injustices do not lack agency; rather they are limited when they speak and act for justice by asymmetries in power that muffle their voices.[155]

This leaves some communities that have less power and voice disproportionally affected and exposed to toxic waste or excessive pollution,[156] as discussed in chapter 1. Racial disparities in environmental exposure have an impact on health: 5.6 percent of non-Hispanic Black and African American children have blood lead levels exceeding the US Centers for Disease Control and Prevention limit compared with 2.4 percent of non-Hispanic White children.[157] Possible reasons repeatedly documented for the disproportionate exposure of ethnic minorities to pollution are income inequality, discrimination, and costs of inputs, compliance and information. Disadvantaged populations can underestimate the effects that waste and pollution have on their households;[158] even when all households face the same lack of information, hidden pollution can lead to inequality.[159]

"Redressing asymmetries in power has underpinned the environmental justice movement, which seeks to enhance the power of groups unseen, unheard and undervalued.

In urban areas of Africa, Asia and Latin America, a high proportion of poor people face serious environmental hazards in their homes, surroundings and workplaces.[160] In some cases environmental inequities endure the passage of time and changes in values and political contexts. In 1980, under South Africa's apartheid regime, the Bisasar Road Landfill Site was created in the middle of a working-class Black African community to import waste from White communities. After the regime ended, and despite promises to the community to close the hazardous landfill, it has continued operations and developed further through the completion of an energy project to convert methane emissions into electricity on site. Exposure to the hazardous pollutants in the landfill has impaired the health of the surrounding community.[161]

This discussion has shown how gaps in procedural equity sustain control of voice and influence by those more powerful, leaving already disadvantaged populations further disenfranchised in the face of shocks linked to planetary change. In some cases those speaking and acting for these groups face threats to their physical integrity.[162] As discussed in chapter 3, supporting the agency and empowerment of disadvantaged populations—by respecting their human rights, increasing their access to resources and ensuring that they are represented and their voices are heard[163]—can break the vicious cycle of planetary and social imbalances identified in chapter 1.

Empowering people for equity, innovation and stewardship of nature

Empowering people for equity, innovation and stewardship of nature

This is the age of humans.

Human development puts people at the centre of development—people are agents of change.

But humans are pushing interdependent social and ecological systems into the danger zone.

How can we use our power to expand human freedoms while easing planetary pressures?

This chapter argues that we can do so by enhancing equity, fostering innovation and instilling a sense of stewardship of the planet.

Chapter 1 concluded that confronting the challenges of the Anthropocene by expanding human agency and freedoms widens the scope for action. The alternative of trying to "defend our way of life" would result instead in an exercise of facing constraints. This chapter argues that to steer actions towards transformational change, it is important to empower people in three ways: by enhancing equity, by pursuing innovation and by instilling a sense of stewardship of nature.

People can be agents of change if they have the power to act. But they are less likely or able to do so in ways that address the drivers of social and planetary imbalances if they are left out, if relevant technologies are not available or if they are alienated from nature. Conversely, equity, innovation and stewardship of nature each—and, more importantly, together—can break the vicious cycle of social and planetary imbalances (figure 3.1).

Equity is central in part because the inequalities documented in chapter 2 are reflected in asymmetries of power. The unequal distribution of nature's contributions to people and of environmental degradation's costs are often rooted in the power of a few to benefit without bearing the negative consequences—and in the disempowerment of the many that disproportionally bear the costs. The former group represents a minority of humans that biases collective decisions. Equity can rebalance these power asymmetries so that everyone can benefit from and contribute to easing planetary pressures. There is great potential to capture solar energy[1] and to expand forest areas to protect biodiversity and store carbon—if people are empowered to make those choices.[2]

" To steer actions towards transformational change, it is important to empower people in three ways: by enhancing equity, by pursuing innovation and by instilling a sense of stewardship of nature.

Innovation—which gave humans many of the tools to influence Earth systems—can be harnessed to ease planetary pressures. Beyond advances in science from multiple disciplines that can support capturing

Figure 3.1 Equity, innovation and stewardship of nature can break the vicious cycle of social and planetary imbalances

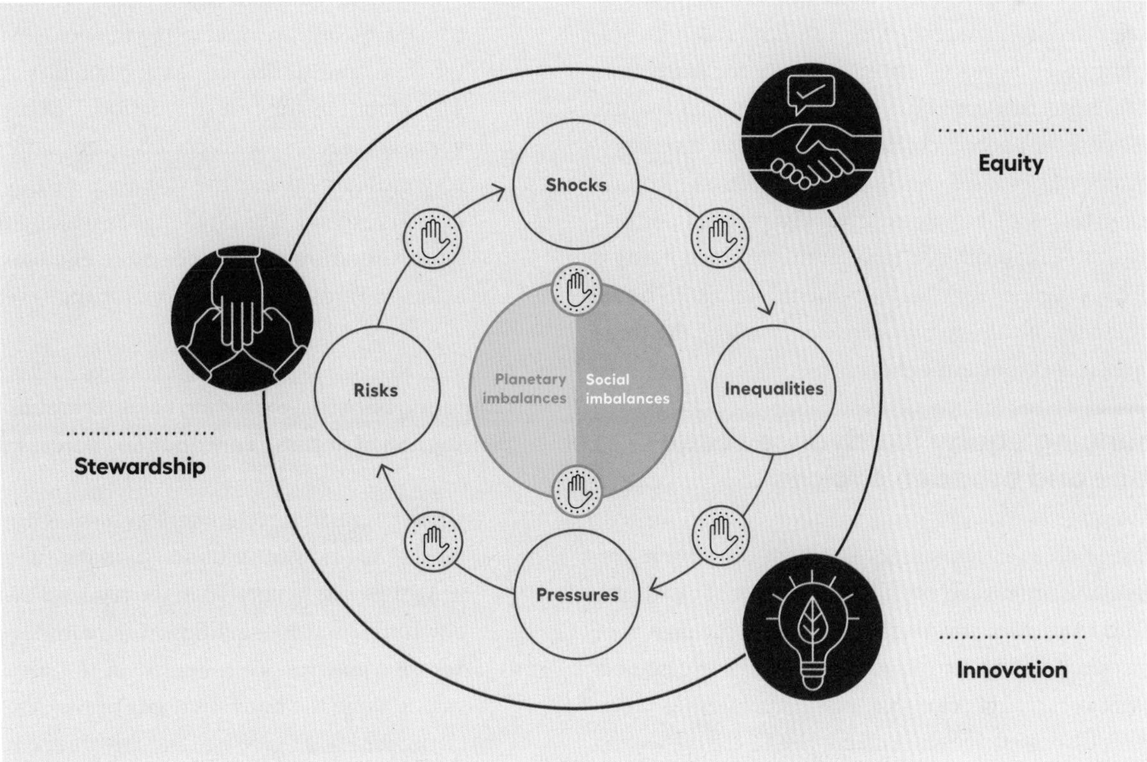

Source: Human Development Report Office.

energy from the sun and closing material cycles, innovation should be understood here also as a social process of change, resulting from advances in science and technology that are embedded in social and economic processes. Moreover, innovation is more than science and technology; it includes the institutional innovations that ultimately drive social and economic transformations.

Stewardship of nature echoes the often-unheard voices of indigenous peoples and the many communities and cultures over human history that see humans as part of a web of life on the planet. Evolution has encoded the lessons of billions of years in the biodiversity surrounding us (see spotlight 1.2). We depend on this biodiversity, even though we are accelerating its destruction. Instilling a sense of stewardship of nature can empower people to rethink values, reshape social norms and steer collective decisions in ways that ease planetary pressures.

Empowering people in these three ways is self-reinforcing. Inequalities bias investments in science and technology towards the powerful—and alienation from nature may shift priorities away from mobilizing human creativity to ease planetary pressures. Inequalities can facilitate elite capture, with powerful and privileged groups exercising undue influence over decisionmakers, which can limit market competition and create barriers to entry for innovators and firms that could drive transformational change. As chapter 1 noted, cultural and linguistic diversity—which has evolved jointly with biodiversity—implies that losses of biological diversity parallel cultural losses.[3] Empowering people in this way can harness human agency for transformational change.[4] The remainder of this chapter considers each of the three areas for empowerment in turn.

Enhancing equity to advance social justice and broaden choices

Inequalities in human development not only represent unfairness and social imbalances that can destabilize societies, affecting wellbeing and the dignity of people,[5] but they also play a role in how people interact with nature, impacting planetary pressures. As chapter 2 discussed, different inequalities (often reflecting relative disempowerment) determine the distribution of risks across the population in response to changes in the biosphere.[6] Disadvantaged groups tend to bear a larger burden. And as documented below, nature's degradation is often linked with power imbalances.

" An agenda centred on equity is important intrinsically, but it can also break socioenvironmental traps and ultimately ease planetary pressures.

The self-reinforcing cycle between social and planetary imbalances described in chapter 1 might also emerge as socioenvironmental traps at lower scales, making it difficult to escape from trajectories in which persistent inequalities compound behaviours that degrade nature and put pressure on the planet.[7]

In fact, Anthropocene risks and their consequences (see chapter 2) are intimately linked to how societies work. The asymmetries of power across groups can set the social conditions (the mix of incentives and narrow possibilities) that result in overexploitation of resources. For instance, people and communities experiencing deprivations or a lack of power may be drawn to use inefficient production practices or to generate dangerous pollutants because of the narrow set of choices they confront.[8]

So an agenda centred on equity is important intrinsically, but it can also break socioenvironmental traps and ultimately ease planetary pressures. The ambition for transformational change is universally relevant, with common but differentiated responsibility—due to the vast asymmetries in capacities to respond. The challenge is making the distribution of power and agency more equitable to steer action towards transformational change everywhere.

Capturing benefits, exporting costs: Unequal distribution of nature's contributions across countries

Higher human development countries concentrate most of nature's contributions without fully internalizing the costs generated in the process. Two tales of environmental inequalities in human development across countries are reflected in the dispersion of values along the horizontal axis of two environmental outcomes in figure 3.2. The Environmental Health Index measures the benefits of a sound relation with the planet in terms of clean air and water and

Figure 3.2 Two tales of environmental inequality

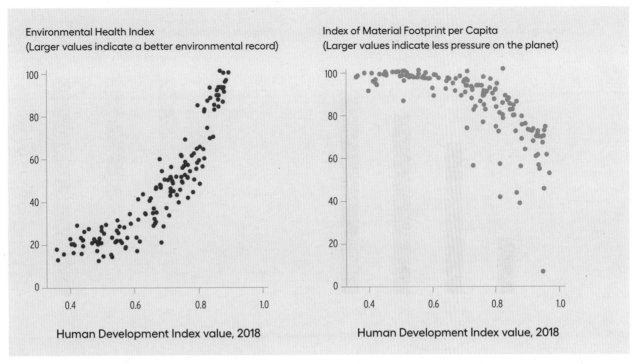

Environmental Health Index
(Larger values indicate a better environmental record)

Index of Material Footprint per Capita
(Larger values indicate less pressure on the planet)

Human Development Index value, 2018

Human Development Index value, 2018

Note: Includes countries with more than 1 million inhabitants.
Source: Human Development Report Office based on data from the Yale Center for Environmental Law and Policy and the United Nations Environment Programme.

effective management of waste and residuals. The Index of Material Footprint per Capita reflects use of materials for domestic consumption.[9]

Striking inequalities emerge across countries.[10] Low human development countries face substantial environmental challenges (they have low environmental health scores) and use much less material resources than countries at the other extreme. Higher human development countries have higher environmental health and material use scores.

> " The burden of planetary changes is not equally distributed across people. This is eminently destabilizing in that it rewards current production and consumption patterns.

And there is more: The burden of planetary changes is not equally distributed across people. Take climate change. On average, low human development countries are likely to have 50–100 additional days with extreme weather by century's end, while very high human development countries might see a decrease in the number of days with extreme weather (depending on the mitigation scenario).[11] The human

impact will be huge, even after adaptation efforts are taken into consideration: The number of excess deaths in poorer countries could be comparable to those from cancer today.[12]

This is eminently destabilizing in that it rewards current production and consumption patterns. And environmental inequalities are increasing across countries. For both the Environmental Health Index and the Index of Material Footprint per Capita, the gaps are widening (figure 3.3). This means that developed countries are improving their ability to benefit from nature (through cleaner water and air) faster than developing countries. At the same time, developed countries are increasing their already higher burden on the planet (in material footprint), despite some recent relative decoupling between greenhouse gas emissions and GDP growth in a few very high human development countries (chapter 1).[13]

These patterns are also present in integrated ecological footprint accounts,[14] which compare the demand for biocapacity (footprint) with its availability. The resulting biocapacity deficit (or reserve) can be decomposed into its noncarbon and carbon components: the noncarbon biocapacity deficit reflects

Figure 3.3 Growing environmental inequality

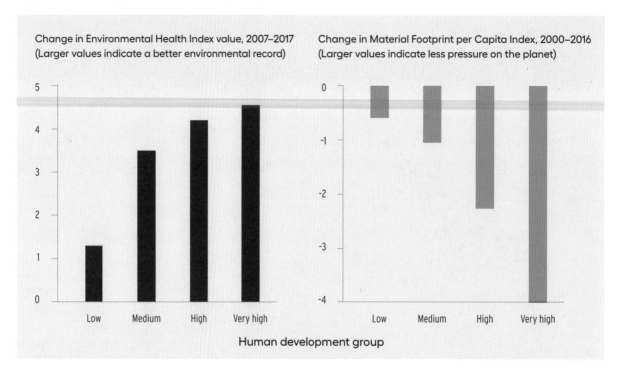

Change in Environmental Health Index value, 2007–2017
(Larger values indicate a better environmental record)

Change in Material Footprint per Capita Index, 2000–2016
(Larger values indicate less pressure on the planet)

Human development group

Note: Includes countries with more than 1 million inhabitants. Data are median values.
Source: Human Development Report Office based on data from the Yale Center for Environmental Law and Policy and the United Nations Environment Programme.

Figure 3.4 Unequal dynamics: Carbon footprint and biocapacity deficit

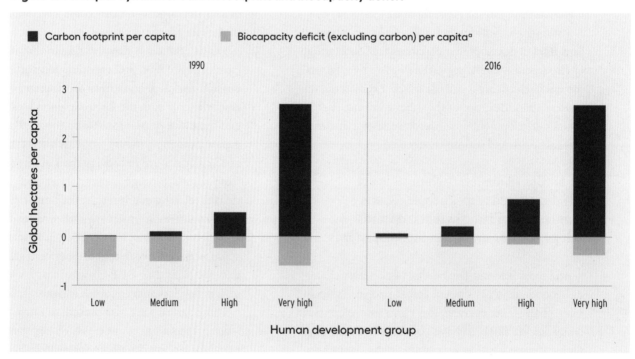

■ Carbon footprint per capita   ■ Biocapacity deficit (excluding carbon) per capita[a]

1990

2016

Global hectares per capita

Human development group

a. Equals domestic noncarbon footprint per capita minus domestic biocapacity per capita. Negative values indicate "reserve."
Note: Country-level data using the median to aggregate across human development groups. Balanced panel of 104 countries, based on production accounts.
Source: Human Development Report Office based on Global Footprint Network (2019).

predominantly domestic overuse when using production accounts, and the carbon component (carbon footprint) measures emissions, some of which can be absorbed domestically, but the rest becomes a planetary externality (figure 3.4).[15]

In 2016 very high human development countries had the largest noncarbon biocapacity reserves per capita and the largest carbon footprints per capita. Lower human development countries had smaller noncarbon biocapacity reserves and even smaller carbon footprints per capita.

From 1990 to 2016 global overshoot increased susbstantially, from 29 percent to 70 percent.[16] In per capita terms noncarbon biocapacity reserves decreased across all groups but decreased more in lower human development countries. In turn, carbon footprint per capita increased most in high human development countries.

Reducing horizontal inequalities to break socioenvironmental traps

Conceptualizing sustainable development as "development that meets the needs of the present without compromising the ability of future generations to meet their own needs"[17] acknowledges the interests of both present and future generations. But this conceptualization does not fully account for the complex relationship between intragenerational and intergenerational inequalities.[18] Neither the current generation nor future generations are homogeneous in their relationship with nature. The differentiated use of natural resources within societies and the resulting differences in environmental degradation are fundamental to understanding how inequalities can be passed from one generation to the next and the implications for the evolution of environmental pressures.

The process is complex. The nominal possession of natural resources is important, but it is far from sufficient for equitable wellbeing. There is some evidence of the so-called natural resource curse.[19] What matters in most cases is not the availability of natural resources as such but the distribution of costs and benefits associated with them. These are influenced heavily by the interests of different groups and the relative distribution of power among them, often manifest as horizontal (or intergroup) inequalities.

Some have deep historical roots, with origins in colonialism. The unequal distribution of power during colonial times was explicit, with colonies meant to provide natural resources for the colonial power.[20] Power imbalances meant that most benefits were concentrated in the colonial power. Colonies retained limited rents and had their natural capital progressively depleted. The differentiated dynamics in capital accumulation, in turn, affect people's wellbeing across generations (table 3.1).[21]

> " The differentiated use of natural resources within societies and the resulting differences in environmental degradation are fundamental to understanding how inequalities can be passed from one generation to the next and the implications for the evolution of environmental pressures.

Racism and classism reflect similar dynamics within countries—weakening long-term human development through exposure to environmental hazards, sometimes linked to extractive activities.[22] Some groups work in precarious conditions, degrading land and depleting natural resources as part of productive processes that yield rents for the elite or large companies.[23] In the process human rights violations intersect with unsustainable resource use. Exploitative labour practices, including slavery and human trafficking, have been documented, for instance, across seafood supply chains around the world.[24] Consumption often takes place in countries with strict sustainability requirements and a public sensitive to both resource overexploitation and poor working conditions, but

Table 3.1 Examples of horizontal inequalities and intergenerational inequalities connected to power imbalances

	Group concentrating and benefiting from power Colonial power Privileged groups Elites Large companies	Disadvantaged groups Colony Racial/ethnic minorities Low-earning workers Local communities
This generation	Extraction of benefits Often limited costs	Limited benefits External costs
Next generation Inherits:	High produced capital High human capital	Low produced capital Low human capital Depleted natural capital

Source: Human Development Report Office.

the complexity of supply chains weakens the price and information signals that link resource use and consumption. Worse, efforts to safeguard sustainability in a location can heighten resource overexploitation elsewhere. For instance, beginning in the late 1990s, concerns about cod stocks in the Baltic Sea led to a large reduction of local cod consumption in Sweden, after strong civil society mobilization. But overall cod consumption changed little, having been met through imports.[25] The complexity and opacity of seafood supply chains can increase even further with the growing commercial interest in marine resources.

And even with progress on the most egregious human rights violations, other more subtle violations can perpetuate discrimination or deny fair access to and sharing of marine benefits.[26]

Two long-term outcomes of these dynamics are inequality in human development and excessive resource use, potentially leading to biodiversity loss (box 3.1). Depletion of natural resources is likely to take place when the most powerful group has limited incentives to care about the consequences of overexploitation on others (including pollution, full depletion of reserves and other environmental damages).

Box 3.1 The Amazon's biodiversity loss and disempowerment

Critical ecosystems such as the Amazon face the risk of shifting from rainforest to savannah as forest loss increases, caused primarily by fires and changes in land use. Farmers and agricultural workers sometimes set fires to prepare land for replanting or to clear weeds. In 2018 and 2019 Bolivia and Brazil experienced high losses in primary forests—for Bolivia due to fires and large-scale agricultural activity and for Brazil mostly logging and clear-cut deforestation for new land use and agriculture (see map).[1]

Vanishing forests in the Amazon

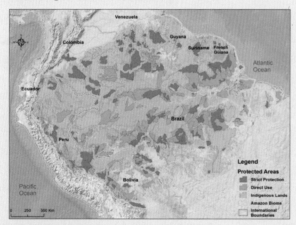

Source: World Wildlife Fund, based on WRI (2019).

Deforestation has led to biodiversity loss, habitat degradation, higher pollution, loss of water cycling and increased poverty.[2] A longitudinal study of Amazonian villages in Peru over 30 years finds strong evidence of path dependence in poverty traps.[3] Past household landholdings and assets can have a major impact on future land ownership and land use. Initially, land-poor households are typically limited to subsistence-oriented annual crops or cannot leave their land in fallow to restore soil nutrients. They can fall into land-use poverty traps. Poorer households' income relies more on fishing, day labour, small livestock and unsustainable harvesting of nontimber forest products.[4] These have direct effects on people's wellbeing as well as on the dynamics of tropical deforestation and secondary forest regrowth. One way poorer households have found to escape the trap is outmigration, which can also reduce pressures on the land.

Notes
1. Weisse and Dow Goldman 2020 ; WRI 2019. **2.** WWF 2020b. **3.** Coomes, Takasaki and Rhemtulla 2011. **4.** Barrett, Travis and Dasgupta 2011.

These outcomes have little to do with preferences about the wellbeing of future generations. The dominant groups can transmit their privileges to their descendants, and the disadvantaged groups face hugely restricted choices.

" Inequalities in empowerment today are at the root of environmental problems, many threatening the wellbeing of future generations. Important for a better tomorrow is to empower disadvantaged groups and actors today.

Case studies suggest that today's intragenerational inequalities are linked to intergenerational inequality and environmental degradation[27] through multiple channels, some of which are summarized in table 3.2. Generally, these are not about income inequality but about a variety of context-specific dynamics of inequality that produce a negative effect on nature, including the procedural and distributional inequalities analysed in chapter 2.[28] The local, national and global interactions underscore inequality's pervasive effects, including local environmental degradation, natural resource overexploitation and greenhouse gas emissions. In all the channels inequalities in empowerment today are at the root of environmental problems, many threatening the wellbeing of future generations. Therefore, an important part of the strategy for a better tomorrow is to empower disadvantaged groups and actors today.

These patterns can be exacerbated by climate change. As chapter 2 documented, disadvantaged groups face a disproportionate burden because of different forms of environmental imbalances, both across and within countries, which reinforce existing inequalities. One example is people living in less-favoured agricultural areas and rural low elevation coastal zones. These people are already suffering the effects of climate change, which exacerbate existing poverty-environment traps. One manifestation is that reduction of infant mortality is slower in these areas—precisely where the problem is more intense in the first place—widening gaps in human development (figure 3.5). The divergence in infant mortality contrasts sharply with the convergence observed on average across developing countries, with greater reductions in poorer countries[29]—underscoring how environmental factors affect social imbalances.

Table 3.2 Typologies of interaction dynamics between inequality and sustainability

How intragenerational inequality today affects sustainability		Response
Interaction dynamic	Sustainability consequences	Actors to be empowered
Resource distribution	Low environmental services	Disadvantaged groups
Ecological space	Greenhouse gases	Developing countries
Elite capture	Overexploitation, pollution	Majorities through social incentives
Marginalization	Low environmental services	Disadvantaged groups
Status and consumption	Overexploitation, greenhouse gases, pollution	Everyone through knowledge, change in norms and stewardship of nature
Environmental disconnection	Overexploitation, greenhouse gases, pollution	Everyone through knowledge, change in norms and stewardship of nature
Market imperfections	Overexploitation, greenhouse gases, pollution	Majorities through social incentives, local communities
Narrow environmental intervention	Low environmental services	Local communities
Collective action	Overexploitation, pollution	Disadvantaged groups, local communities
Morality–power–knowledge	Overexploitation, greenhouse gases, pollution	Indigenous peoples, local communities

Note: Resource distribution: inequality and unsustainability result from uneven distribution of resources, such as water and land, across groups. Ecological space: unequal distribution of "ecological space," such as greenhouse gas budget, reflects and reproduces economic, spatial and political inequalities. Elite capture: concentration of power and wealth in the hands of an elite facilitates pollution and environmental degradation with impunity. Marginalization: environmental shocks exacerbate existing inequalities, contributing to spirals of impoverishment and environmental degradation. Status and consumption: status hierarchies can drive unsustainable forms of material consumption. Environmental disconnection: urbanization can reduce people's direct reliance on nature, intensifying social inequities and reducing interest in sustainability. Market imperfections: deregulated markets can contribute to both economic inequality and environmental unsustainability. Narrow environmental intervention: interventions aimed only at environmental sustainability can lead to social exclusion. Collective action: inequalities can compromise sustainability by making cooperation more difficult. Morality–power–knowledge: potential disrespect for diverse moral options can contribute to political and knowledge inequalities and to unsustainability.

Source: Human Development Report Office based on Leach and others (2018).

Figure 3.5 In vulnerable areas in poorer countries, gaps in infant mortality are widening

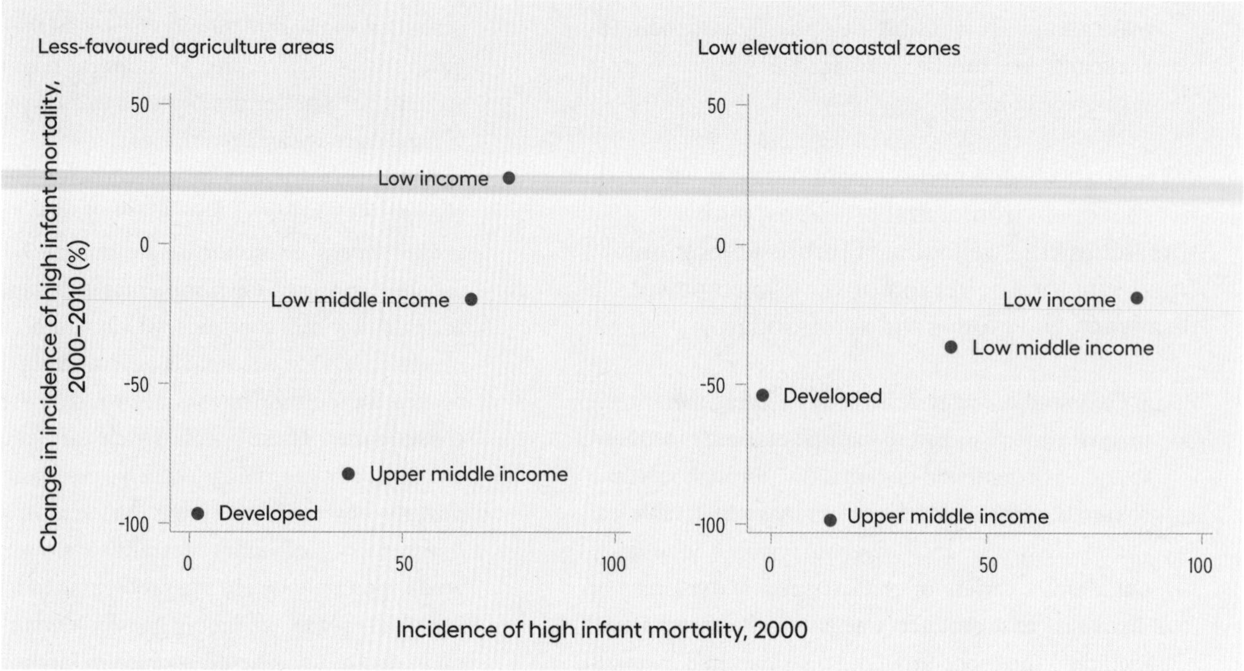

Note: High infant mortality refers to at least 32 deaths per 1,000 live births
Source: Human Development Report Office based on data from Barbier and Hochard (2018).

Thus, inequalities, particularly horizontal inequalities, can drive both environmental degradation and intergenerational inequality.[30] Enhancing equity can empower people to advance human development and ease planetary pressures. More cohesive societies have social mechanisms that can reduce gaps in empowerment encoded in legislation and policies, ranging from fiscal measures (both taxation and social protection) to regulation and competition policies (which preclude the excessive concentration of economic power in monopolies).[31] In less cohesive societies group-based inequalities, amplified by environmental factors, can generate social costs[32] that have inspired social mobilization, such as the environmental justice movement (box 3.2).

Redressing within country inequalities to ease pressures on the planet

But it is not only horizontal inequalities that matter. Addressing inequalities across people can also enable societies to advance human development while limiting planetary pressures. Consider the current frontiers of achievement in life expectancy at birth and mean years of schooling for different incomes (figure 3.6). For any income level there is wide variation in health and education outcomes, pointing to the potential for enhancing both without increasing income (and associated planetary pressures). In other words there is much potential at every income level for advancing human development by closing gaps in achievements in health and education, advancing equity in either dimension.

Progress in equity might also contribute to resetting priorities. Within-country inequality can be a factor behind the social need to increase material consumption[33] and the importance of economic growth in generating opportunities for those less well off.[34] With high inequality there are expenditure cascades[35] and moving targets: People make progress in material conditions, but it does not necessarily translate into greater capabilities[36] or sizeable increases in happiness.[37] In more unequal societies there is a greater search for status through consumption, sometimes leading people with low income to reduce caloric intake in favour of aspirational purchases.[38] Tragically, low-consuming and socially equitable communities, such as many indigenous peoples, have been increasingly marginalized.[39]

Box 3.2 The environmental justice movement

Environmental justice emerged in the last century as an international, intergenerational and multi-racial movement. It seeks to promote environmental, economic and social justice. It recognizes the links among environmental, economic and health issues and demands a safe, clean community and environment. Environmental justice evokes not just official regulations and policies but also social and cultural norms and values, behaviours and attitudes. From its early years environmental justice has been a hybrid, growing out of the civil rights movement in the United States into a social and political concept in the spheres of nongovernmental organizations and academia.[1]

The movement emerged in the 1960s when Black and African American communities in the United States were disproportionately affected by pollution from unwanted land use and waste facilities in their neighbourhoods. Blacks and African Americans mobilized against environmental injustice in Tennessee, where they advocated for better working conditions for garbage workers. Later in the 1980s a manufacturer of electrical transformers in North Carolina placed its toxic waste facility in a predominantly Black/African American town.[2] Around the same time Robert Bullard collected data for several civil rights lawsuits from 1930 to 1978 to show that 82 percent of the waste in Houston, Texas, was dumped in Black and African American neighbourhoods, a consistent pattern in the country's south.[3]

The movement expanded to the rest of the world around the 1990s, when it caught the attention of activists, researchers, academics and politicians. In 2002, 71 percent of Blacks and African Americans in the United States lived in counties that were in violation of federal air pollution standards.[4] These constitute examples of environmental injustice in which areas where vulnerable people live are chosen to place landfills or waste facilities that other areas would not allow. Now a field of study, environmental justice concerns itself with the "fair treatment and meaningful involvement of all people regardless of race, colour, national origin or income, with respect to the development, implementation and enforcement of environmental laws, regulations and policies."[5]

Notes
1. Rasmussen and Pinho 2016. **2.** Mayhew Bergman 2019. **3.** Bullard 1983. **4.** Southern Organizing Committee for Economic and Social Justice 2002. **5.** EPA 2020a.
Source: Human Development Report Office.

In sum, greater equity can be a powerful social stabilizing force and ease environmental pressures. It is not the only factor, and enhancing equity alone may not lead to these outcomes. That is why, along with equity, it is crucial to empower people through innovation and a sense of stewardship of nature. For instance, the equity lens is fundamental for transformations in the energy sector to achieve decarbonization. Indeed, some key instruments for decarbonization—such as carbon prices and reduced fossil fuel subsidies—have complex distributional impacts (chapter 5). This might feed a narrative of conflict between equity today and the wellbeing of future generations, complicating the political implementation of these measures. The tension can be relaxed if policymakers embed equity considerations in policy design.

Progressive taxation and transfers, for instance, will have key roles, something achievable with compensatory packages[40] and affordable alternatives to carbon-intensive goods and services.[41] Much of this can also be facilitated by innovation, be it renewable energy at competitive prices or innovations in allocating fiscal resources. Stewardship of nature should also have an equity component. As chapter 6 discusses, a new generation of bottom-up policies simultaneously targets the responsible use and protection of the environment and advancement of human development. In many cases, their success depends on empowering indigenous peoples and local communities.

Pursuing innovation to widen opportunities

The generation and diffusion of new ideas and technologies have improved people's wellbeing but have also given humanity the instruments to capture

Figure 3.6 Greater social efficiency of income (moving to the frontier) can enhance equity and ease planetary pressures

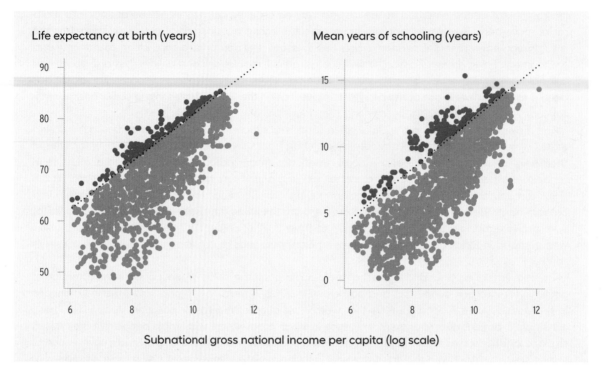

Note: The efficiency line approximates achievements in health and education at a given income, calculated using quantile regressions for the 90th percentile.
Source: Human Development Report Office based on calculations of subnational Human Development Index values by Smits and Permanyer (2019).

energy, use materials and put pressure on the biosphere that have resulted in today's unprecedented planetary imbalances.[42] Some were unintended consequences of technical change, as with synthetic fertilizers that vastly increased crop productivity but are now disrupting the nitrogen cycle. On a planet with bounded resources, ideas and the ability to use resources in ever more efficient ways have enabled human flourishing.[43] More important than any single idea or technology is the pursuit of innovation, broadly understood, in what Stiglitz and Greenwald call "learning societies."[44]

As chapter 1 discussed, shifting towards renewable energy and closing material cycles would be important manifestations of the transformational change to ease planetary pressures. For energy the goal should be decarbonization, ideally towards capturing energy directly from the sun, a limitless source of energy on human timescales. For materials the goal should be reducing waste and converging towards closed material cycles. These two goals require substantial technological innovation,[45] along with broader economic

and social innovations that ultimately determine the impact of new technologies on people and planet.

" Shifting towards renewable energy and closing material cycles would be important manifestations of the transformational change to ease planetary pressures. These two goals require substantial technological innovation, along with broader economic and social innovations.

The pace of technological change, for issues ranging from artificial intelligence to gene editing, is such that new institutions that cannot necessarily be predicted in advance may be required. This is in part because science has to confront normative and value-laden issues, and the challenges of the Anthropocene bring new dimensions.[46] The process of innovation, social and technological, is likely to continue to evolve and accelerate given that our "collective brain" expands and becomes more interconnected, facilitated by digital technologies.[47] For instance, a recently identified material exhibiting superconductivity at room temperature (but at high pressure) could dramatically reduce losses in energy transmission and the need for energy storage.[48]

In fact, digital technologies may directly ease planetary pressures and advance human development, even though there are also risks, as discussed below. From mobile payments to crowdfunding, digital technology is already a critical enabler in development.[49] During the Covid-19 pandemic digital technology has proved indispensable for work, education, health care and staying connected.[50] An expanded digital sphere has also eased planetary pressures, showing a way forward if temporary changes in behaviour can become more ingrained.[51] The UN Secretary-General's high-level Task Force on Digital Finance made several recommendations to leverage digital finance for attaining the Sustainable Development Goals.[52] It concluded that digitalization will give people greater control over how global finance—their own money—is used. The democratization of finance, enabled by digitalization, could empower people by ensuring that their values are translated into how global finance is channelled, as when taxpayers hold governments to account or investors hold financial institutions to account.

Shaping economies, societies and people's wellbeing

Modern communication technologies such as the internet have taken idea sharing and the democratization of production and access to knowledge to unprecedented heights.[53] The paths that modern societies follow going forward—and their pressures on the planet—rely on these knowledge networks. Digital technologies also have direct impacts on resource use. Innovation is constantly generating new applications that, if scaled, could lower the use of energy and other resources.[54] Remote meetings and telecommuting reduce air travel and commuting, cutting down energy use and carbon emissions.

Sharing resources, such as office space, with different sets of workers rotating through the same space, improves the efficiency of energy use and the use of space and other resources. In the aftermath of the Covid-19 pandemic, the trend for offices to have a smaller presence may continue. And shared vehicles, such as Didi Chuxing, Grab, LittleCab, Lyft,

Uber and Zipcar, can reduce car ownership, eventually leading to less resources needed to build cars and less fuel use.[55] Applications powered by artificial intelligence can improve energy and material efficiency. Smart appliances can considerably reduce energy use. Smart thermostats can detect when a building is occupied, learn occupants' preferences and encourage energy-efficient measures. In the United Kingdom smart heating controls in buildings could reduce carbon dioxide emissions by 1.2–2.3 percent.[56]

> " Technological breakthroughs without changes in regulations and behaviours are not enough to ease planetary pressures. Data and artificial intelligence applications also have a big impact from their own energy use.

The sharing economy has connected excess food that would likely go to waste with food-insecure households. In high-income countries most food waste is at the retail and consumer stages. OLIO, a popular food-sharing platform in the United Kingdom, has successfully distributed 60 percent of the 170,000 listings for food items on its website, diverting a substantial amount of food from waste.[57] Artificial intelligence–based technologies can also increase recycling rates.[58] Digital technologies can monitor resource use and illegal resource extraction.[59]

A note of caution. Technological breakthroughs without changes in regulations and behaviours are not enough to ease planetary pressures. Data and artificial intelligence applications also have a big impact from their own energy use. While there is no standard method for calculating internet-related energy consumption, estimates suggest that approximately 10 percent of global electricity in 2018 was consumed by information and communication technology.[60] The carbon footprint of training a single artificial intelligence system can be as much as 284 tonnes of carbon dioxide equivalent—five times the lifetime emissions of the average car.[61] Each year global online video streaming produces as much emissions as Spain.[62] And bitcoin energy use is alarming (figure 3.7). The digital economy also makes an impact through its material footprint—large and growing—including in the form of electronic waste (see box 3.3 later in this section).

Sometimes temporary incentives are enough to redirect technical choices towards clean technologies.

Figure 3.7 Bitcoin energy use is alarming

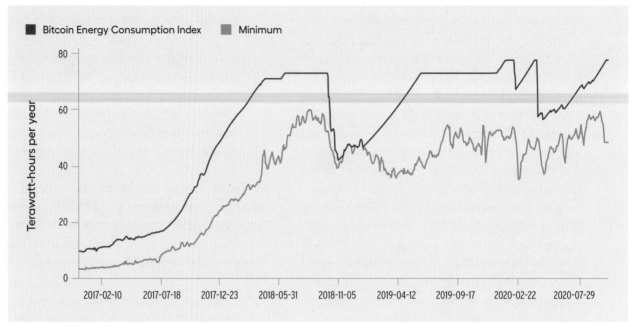

Note: The Index contains the aggregate of Bitcoin and Bitcoin Cash (other forks of the Bitcoin network are not included). The minimum is a lower bound calculated from the total network hashrate, assuming the only machine used in the network is Bitmain's Antminer S9 (drawing 1,500 watts each; Digiconomist 2020).
Source: Digiconomist 2020.

When two technologies, clean and dirty, are relatively substitutable, an unregulated economy would head towards environmental damage because the initial productivity advantage of dirty technologies would lead profit-maximizing firms to adopt them. However, with environmental regulation, taxes and subsidies, technical change can be redirected.[63] Once clean technologies are advanced enough, firms will adopt them and invest in research and development to cultivate them further.

Beyond innovation, diffusing new technology across an economy and across international borders is crucial. Many factors are at play.[64] One challenge is to make the economic, social and political systems that embed science and technological change cognizant of planetary pressures. The next two sections zoom in on technological innovations that can support the energy transition and the closing of material cycles.[65]

Advancing innovations for renewable energy

In 2018 the energy sector accounted for two-thirds of carbon dioxide emissions growth.[66] Switching from fossil fuel–based energy production to alternative sources requires new technologies and the diffusion and adaptation of existing technologies. Switching from mainstream established energy production can be challenging. Governments and investors with a long-term horizon can invest in new promising technologies, bringing them close to the point where they can compete in price with incumbent technologies. This is an example of a sensitive intervention point.[67]

Solar photovoltaics

Take investments in solar photovoltaics.[68] Deployment has clearly resulted in falling costs, and public policies could accelerate progress by neutralizing resistance to change based on economic costs.[69] The real cost of photovoltaic modules has dropped by more than a factor of 6,000 since 1956—and by 89 percent since 2010 (figure 3.8).[70] If their deployment continues to increase at the current rate, its price is likely to fall considerably.[71] In addition, the right sequence of policies can create political conditions for more ambitious climate policies in subsequent rounds of debate and policymaking,[72] as in California and the European Union, where policymakers first supported low-carbon technologies and

Figure 3.8 The real cost of photovoltaic modules has dropped 89 percent since 2010

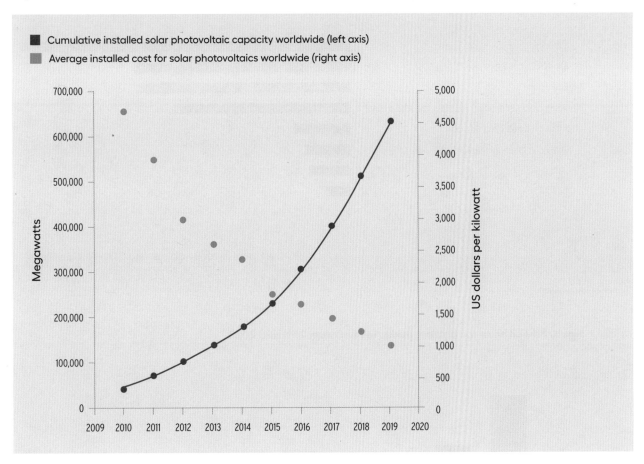

■ Cumulative installed solar photovoltaic capacity worldwide (left axis)
■ Average installed cost for solar photovoltaics worldwide (right axis)

Source: IRENA 2019b.

then carbon trading schemes.[73] And across the world, national policymaking has taken up the charge for promoting renewable energy (figure 3.9).

In 2008 India launched the National Action Plan on Climate Change, a sensitive intervention point because it was a formal recognition of the threat of climate change and the need to act at home, even as international negotiations were ongoing.[74] Under the Paris Agreement, India pledged to reduce the emission intensity of its GDP from the 2005 level by 33–35 percent by 2030 and to obtain 40 percent of electric power capacity from non-fossil fuel sources by 2030.[75] As part of the plan, the National Solar Mission aims to promote solar energy for power generation and other uses to make solar energy competitive with fossil fuel–based options.[76] Solar capacity in India increased from 2.6 gigawatts in March 2014 to 30 gigawatts in July 2019, achieving its target of 20 gigawatts four years ahead of schedule.[77] In 2019 India ranked fifth for installed solar capacity.[78]

Complementary storage and smart grids

With solar, wind and other intermittent sources of energy, complementary technologies such as storage systems (including lithium-ion batteries) are important—and here too prices are falling (figure 3.10). Integrating renewables in the mix of energy sources requires smart electric grid transmission systems that can integrate renewable and conventional sources of supply.[79] Smart grids are "electricity networks that can intelligently integrate behaviour and actions of all users connected to it—generators, consumers and those that do both—to efficiently deliver sustainable, economic and secure electricity supplies."[80] This involves a host of technologies, including smart meters, that measure output and consumption in real time, and algorithms to share and manage the data to unlock efficiency gains.[81]

Figure 3.9 Across the world, national policymaking has taken up the charge for promoting renewable energy

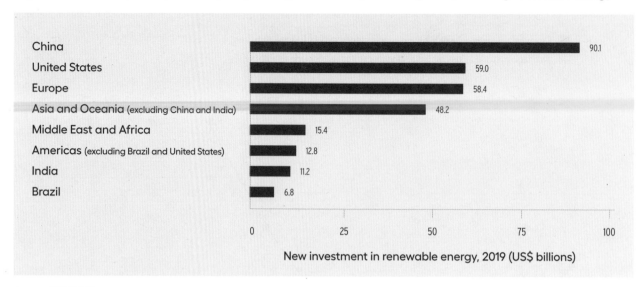

New investment in renewable energy, 2019 (US$ billions)

China — 90.1
United States — 59.0
Europe — 58.4
Asia and Oceania (excluding China and India) — 48.2
Middle East and Africa — 15.4
Americas (excluding Brazil and United States) — 12.8
India — 11.2
Brazil — 6.8

Source: REN21 2020.

Figure 3.10 Lithium-ion battery prices fell between 2011 and 2020

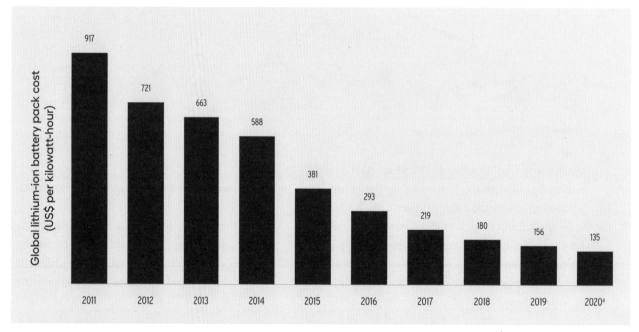

Global lithium-ion battery pack cost (US$ per kilowatt-hour)

2011 — 917
2012 — 721
2013 — 663
2014 — 588
2015 — 381
2016 — 293
2017 — 219
2018 — 180
2019 — 156
2020[a] — 135

a. Estimated.
Source: Statista 2020d.

Electricity markets may also need to be redesigned.[82] Nowadays, the price of electricity typically does not vary with supply and demand over short timeframes, but variable pricing (which adjusts frequently, even within the same day, in response to changes in demand and intermittent supply) may be more appropriate for systems that have a high share of energy from renewables.[83]

Despite these advances and future potential, challenges persist. The political economy of displacing established sources, such as coal-based power generation, is complex.[84] Economic growth will continue to put upward pressure on total energy demand and emissions. Energy efficiency is crucial in mitigating the rise of greenhouse gas emissions from the expanding pace of worldwide energy demand.[85]

But in 2018 primary energy intensity improved by just 1.2 percent, the slowest rate since 2010.[86] And as the technology frontier expands, access to the latest technologies by developing countries becomes ever more relevant. Developing countries face a dual challenge: Many of them are still working towards universal access to electric power while moving towards renewable energy. There are many impediments to accessing solar photovoltaics, batteries and smart grids. Financing (chapter 5) and intellectual property regimes[87] will be key to deploy these technologies at scale in developing countries.

" With solar, wind and other intermittent sources of energy, complementary technologies such as storage systems (including lithium-ion batteries) are important—and here too prices are falling.

Negative emissions technologies

Technological solutions have also been proposed for directly capturing carbon dioxide from the atmosphere—with negative emissions technologies, such as carbon capture and storage.[88] Some involve storing atmospheric carbon dioxide in geological formations.[89] Despite considerable research, carbon capture and storage have not been widely deployed due to a range of technical, economic and commercial challenges.[90] The UK Committee on Climate Change finds that the cost of meeting the United Kingdom's 2050 targets will be twice as high without carbon capture and storage as it would be with them.

Another negative emissions technology, bioenergy with carbon capture and storage, requires growing plant biomass to sequester carbon dioxide from the atmosphere, harvesting the biomass and burning it for energy, while capturing the carbon dioxide emissions from the power stations and storing the waste underground. The Intergovernmental Panel on Climate Change scenarios consistent with representative concentration pathway 2.6 (RCP 2.6), which offers the best chances of staying below the 2 degrees Celsius limit, rely on bioenergy with carbon capture and storage drawing excess carbon dioxide from the atmosphere in the second half of the century.[91]

Direct air capture requires stripping carbon dioxide out of the atmosphere with renewably powered open-air chemical engineering.[92] This idea is being implemented in experimental installations in Canada and Switzerland. One issue is that it requires a substantial amount of energy and water.[93]

As they currently stand, these technologies face scepticism and concerns that their claims on land use could compete with food production, drive biodiversity loss and deplete water.[94] Ultimately, the potential of negative emissions technologies will depend on adopting a portfolio of approaches (since relying on a single solution—such as bioenergy with carbon capture and storage—increases the risk of limited feasibility) and of further scientific and technical advances, which can be encouraged with structured incentives for innovation.[95]

Closing material cycles: The potential of circular economies

A circular economy can be key to decoupling production from planetary pressures.[96] Unlike the dominant linear extractive industrial approaches, circular principles require closing loops through reuse and recycling all along the supply chain to form circular supply chains (figure 3.11).[97] According to the European Commission, "the transition to a more circular economy, where the value of products, minerals and resources is maintained in the economy for as long as possible, and the generation of waste minimized, is an essential contribution to the EU's efforts to develop a sustainable, low carbon, resource efficient and competitive economy."[98] But strong incentives for a circular economy cannot simply displace linear economy activities to places lacking those incentives. For instance, firms headquartered in countries with strict environmental policies might perform their polluting activities abroad in countries with weaker policies, with evidence suggesting that when this happens, it is driven primarily by an incentive to avoid tight environmental policies in home countries rather than by purposefully pursuit of places with lenient environmental policies.[99]

" Strong incentives for a circular economy cannot simply displace linear economy activities to places lacking those incentives.

Figure 3.11 How the circular economy differs from the linear

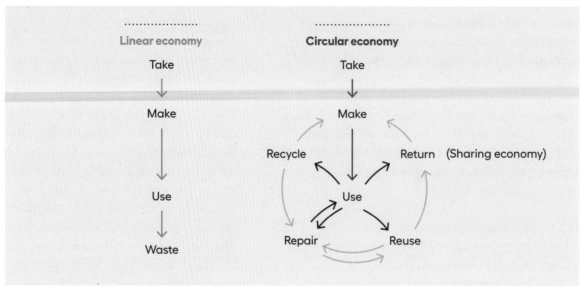

Source: Human Development Report Office.

Consider food systems. Nitrogen, phosphorus and potassium are essential for food production and life. About half the world's food production depends on mineral micronutrient fertilizers.[100] For the most part these fertilizers have been used with little consideration of their disruptive effects on biogeochemical cycles and even the local environment. Take nitrogen. The Earth's natural nitrogen cycle, with robust feedback and controls, is steered by a suite of microbial processes.[101] Providing the world's food supply disrupts that cycle, as noted in chapter 1. The use of nitrogen fertilizer increased by about 800 percent from 1960 to 2000, with its application to grow wheat, rice and maize accounting for half that.[102]

It was a technological breakthrough, the Haber-Bosch industrial process developed in the early 20th century, that enabled the production of ammonia, a chemically reactive, very usable form of nitrogen, to be synthesized using atmospheric nitrogen,[103] heralding the age of large-scale production and application of agricultural fertilizers.[104] Since the introduction of the process, reactive nitrogen in the Earth system has increased 120 percent over the Holocene baseline. As noted earlier in the Report, this influx has had the largest impact on the nitrogen cycle in 2.5 billion years.[105]

This reactive nitrogen largely ends up in nitrogen-limited ecosystems, leading to unintentional fertilization, loss of terrestrial biodiversity and lower quality surface and ground waters in coastal ecosystems.[106] Added to this are nitrogen oxides from fossil fuel combustion.[107] Globally, 4 million new paediatric asthma cases a year are attributable to nitrogen dioxide pollution, 64 percent of them in urban centres.[108]

❝ Opportunities for efficiency gains can be explored along the entire food chain —from more efficient use in cropping to reducing postharvest losses in storage.

But with much leakage and inefficiency at every stage, the potential for improvement is great.[109] In 2005 about 100 teragrams of nitrogen was applied in global agriculture, though humans consumed only 17 teragrams in crop, dairy and meat products.[110] The efficiency of nitrogen use for main crops is below 40 percent.[111] Most applied fertilizer is washed out or lost to the atmosphere. And a lot of agricultural output is simply wasted. Food waste accounts for 8 percent of global anthropogenic greenhouse gas emissions, 20 percent of freshwater consumption and 30 percent of global agricultural land use.[112] Opportunities for efficiency gains can be explored along the entire food chain—from more efficient use in cropping to reducing postharvest losses in storage. This extends to boosting the efficiency of food consumption patterns and improving the treatment of human and animal waste. Helpful approaches include some time-tested practices such as systematic crop rotation. For example, in maize production legume cropping supplies the nitrogen that would otherwise be provided by synthetic fertilizers.[113]

More generally, improving agricultural efficiency requires a broad range of innovations, encompassing also new food production processes (including precision agriculture).[114] Technologies could be harnessed to understand the current state of affairs (perhaps through satellite-based observation) and to advance efforts to reduce planetary pressures. Targeted breeding for old and new crops could provide reasonable avenues to meet human needs.[115] Dietary shifts could increase the efficiency of agricultural input use.[116]

This example shows the potential in food systems to move from a linear approach that begins with exploring and processing and ends with applying fertilizer towards a circular economy that could help close the cycle of resource use.[117] This potential is more broadly

Box 3.3 The potential in recycling electronic waste

Electrical and electronic equipment consumption is increasing by 2.5 million tonnes a year. After being used, it is disposed of as electronic waste (e-waste), a waste stream that contains hazardous as well as valuable materials. In 2019, 53.6 million tonnes of e-waste was generated globally, or 7.3 kilograms per capita. Fuelled by higher consumption, short lifecycles and few repair options, global e-waste has grown steadily, projected to double between 2014 and 2030.[1] Recycling is not keeping pace with the growth of e-waste (see figure). In 2019, 17.4 percent of e-waste was recycled globally, with variation across regions; the rest has adverse health and environmental impacts. In many countries e-waste is handled by informal sector workers, under inferior working conditions. There are also health impacts on children who live, work and play near e-waste.[2]

E-waste generation and recycling rates vary widely

Electronic waste generation per capita, 2019 (kilograms)

Electronic waste recycling rate, 2019[a] (%)

a. Estimates are based on limited cases.
Source: Human Development Report Office calculations based on United Nations Statistics Division (2020a).

In 2019 the value of raw materials in e-waste, including iron, copper and gold, was about $57 billion, roughly $10 billion of which was recovered through recycling.[3] Recovering some materials, such as germanium and indium, is challenging because of their dispersed use in products. Collecting and recycling e-waste can be economically viable for products with higher concentrations, but recycling rates are very low. For one, base metals such as gold, used in mobile phone and personal computers, have a relatively high concentration, about 280 grams per tonne of e-waste. But products are typically neither designed nor assembled with recycling in mind.

Notes
1. Forti and others 2020. **2.** Forti and others 2020. **3.** Forti and others 2020.

applicable to how societies extract and use resources (see box 3.3 for an example using e-waste). And as the German *Energiewende* (energy transition) illustrates, transitions of this nature call for government leadership and incentives.[118] Investing in new technologies and, through deployment, rendering them more competitive are essential parts of the process—in fact, sensitive intervention points[119]—but ones that need to be embedded in broader and more fundamental economic and social changes. That is why it is important to pursue innovation along with enhancing equity and stewardship of nature—to which we now turn.

Instilling a sense of stewardship of nature

Can you imagine a world where nature is understood as full of relatives not resources, where inalienable rights are balanced with inalienable responsibilities and where wealth itself is measured not by resources ownership and control, but by the number of good relationships we maintain in the complex and diverse life systems of this blue green planet? I can.

From the introduction to *Climate Change and Indigenous Peoples in the United States*[120]

The Human Development Report has a long tradition of thinking beyond the basic needs of people and how expanded freedoms, for everyone, align with stewardship of nature. The 2008 Human Development Report explored stewardship of the planet as a central pillar of a long-term inclusive solution for climate change.[121] We again take up empowering people through stewardship of nature—also referred to as environmental stewardship—as the responsible use and protection of the natural environment through conservation and sustainable practices to enhance ecosystem resilience and human wellbeing.[122] This stewardship is coupled with ambitions of social justice and expanded freedoms and control over people's own lives for current and future generations.

Stewardship can be supported by considering philosophical perspectives that value both thriving people and a thriving planet. This requires understanding how the relationship is and has been manifest in philosophical traditions, ancient knowledge (sometimes codified in religions and taboos) and social practices. Many religions around the world and over

time—including Buddhism, Christianity, Hinduism, Islam and Judaism—have developed complex views of intergenerational justice and shared responsibility for a shared environment. The Quaranic concept of "tawheed," or oneness, captures the idea of the unity of creation across generations. There is also an injunction that the Earth and its natural resources must be preserved for future generations, with human beings acting as custodians of the natural world.[123] The encyclical Laudato Si, issued in 2015, provides a Christian interpretation that speaks also to our embeddedness in nature and the notion of the planet as our common home, which we have a moral obligation to protect.[124]

Recognizing our humanity as part of a larger network of connections that include all living things is part of philosophical traditions worldwide.[125] These perspectives can help us rethink and reshape our places in this world. For many indigenous peoples, flourishing communities are grounded in equitable and sustainable relationships. Wellbeing and development begin where our lives with each other and with the natural environment meet. These intersections generate responsibilities for remembering and learning from the past and for creating equitable and sustainable conditions now and for the future. In Aotearoa, New Zealand, Māori philosophies ground the naming of Te Awa Tupua (the Whanganui River) and Te Urewera (previously a national park) as legal entities with rights.[126] At the root of rights of nature movements globally is the contention that navigating our complex responsibilities to people and other living things is fundamental to understanding ourselves and to leading lives we have reason to value.

" Recognizing our humanity as part of a larger network of connections that include all living things is part of philosophical traditions worldwide. These perspectives can help us rethink and reshape our places in this world.

Such understandings are not confined to indigenous communities. From global youth climate justice movements to local environmental protection and low-carbon initiatives—recognizing human–nature relationships can be found in communities and socioenvironmental movements worldwide. These renewed perspectives create space for us to reweave our intimate, caring connections with nonhuman-natures

Box 3.4 Human–nonhuman natures: Broadening perspectives

By Melissa Leach, Director, Institute of Development Studies, United Kingdom

A rethinking of our humanity can include its co-construction with nonhuman natures. This recognizes the intimate interconnectedness of human lives with all living things, their dynamism and agency, whether in our bodies, our homes or our communities; in landscapes and ecologies; and in biophysical processes extending up to the planetary, even cosmological scale. As recognized in growing bodies of work in multispecies ethnography[1] and "more than human" geography,[2] these interrelationships are often intimate, affective, emotional and embodied. They are important to our individual and collective senses of ourselves, wellbeing and identities as well as to the status and future of the plants, animals and other aspects of nonhuman nature with which they are inextricably entwined. Intersecting with advances in ecological and animal science that recognize modes of intelligence and communication among plants and animals, with each other and with humans, these perspectives in effect redefine humanity as part of nature, or at least as part of interconnected socionatural networks or assemblages[3] that question the boundaries between the human and the nonhuman.

It is important to avoid "othering" such perspectives into so-called indigenous societies and cultures. While understandings of human–nonhuman natures as deeply, intimately interconnected and their importance to human thriving and identity are sometimes most obviously found among such groups in the Amazon, Asia-Pacific region and beyond, they are by no means confined there. Among Māori people today, for instance, the dynamic agency that entwines human and nonhuman action extends to views of capabilities and rights, and court cases involving trees and rivers as claimants and right-sholders are commonplace. But there are plenty of similar cases in European history (the celebrated trial of a pig for murder in 15th century Britain is a well documented example[4]). And were we to think that these are outdated notions of the past, look at how people in so-called modern industrial societies relate to their pets,[5] accuse particular dogs of viciousness or attacks, engage with their garden plants and the animal life in cities and seek to protect particular, individual trees from road developments. In these examples[6] elements of nonhuman nature have personalities and communicative capacities, and people develop intimate connections with them that are important to their humanity.

One implication of these perspectives is the questioning of the widespread disconnection that results when "modern" Cartesian scientific and industrial cultures divide the human and the nonhuman. This disconnect underpins seeing nature as generalized "environment," "biodiversity" and "natural capital" —separate from humans and thus able to be commoditized, priced or exploited.[7] Instead, the new perspectives invite us to reweave our intimate, caring connections with nonhuman natures in all their characters and capabilities.

Notes
1. For example, Kirksey and Helmreich (2010), Lock (2018) and Locke and Muenster (2015). **2.** Dowling, Lloyds and Suchet-Pearson 2017. **3.** Haraway 2016. **4.** Cohen 1986; Sullivan 2013. **5.** Haraway 2003. **6.** Dowling, Lloyds and Suchet-Pearson 2017. **7.** More intertwined perspectives on human–nonhuman natures bring an important counter to views of nature as provider of discrete services as well as of current market logics in environmental governance for conservation and sustainability, which then disaggregate nonhuman natures into discrete units to which monetary value can be attached (Sullivan 2013).

in all their characters and capabilities (box 3.4). In doing so, they highlight the urgency and centrality of environmental concerns, the value of diverse knowledge and the need for local and global solutions. By transforming the way we think about our places in this world, these movements bring into focus how human flourishing concerns people, connected to each other, to nonhuman nature and ultimately to this planet. The magnitude and urgency of dangerous planetary change that we confront today require a broad response to reconnect with some of that knowledge.

Nurturing stewardship of nature

The vast literature on environmental stewardship provides frameworks and recommendations that are a helpful starting point.[127] Nathan J. Bennett and colleagues propose three fundamental elements— motivations, capacities and agents—that "are influenced by the socioecological context and that converge to produce both environmental and social outcomes" (figure 3.12).[128] These three elements can be explored through the lens of human development and agency.

For motivation there are two different but related ways to understand why we as humans should take care of the planet: intrinsic and extrinsic. Intrinsic motivations refer to the reasons associated with individual and collective wellbeing. They are closely related to belief systems and our fundamental values about what it means to live well. Extrinsic motivations are linked to external rewards or sanctions, be they social, legal or financial, as well as the evaluation of costs and benefits of stewarding the planet.

Intrinsic and extrinsic motivations are analytical categories because individuals, communities and societies have a mix of both. Separating them, though, allows identifying roadblocks and opportunities for strengthening the overall motivation in different contexts. Identifying the external and internal drivers and reasons to protect the environment also speaks to the concept of human development and agency, where a given development outcome, say education, is valued not only for its external rewards—employment and salaries—but also as something in itself, as a positive freedom.

There are several examples of both types of motivation to protect the planet. Illustrations of intrinsic motivation could refer to religious beliefs (briefly described above). Others to how indigenous peoples and other local communities have managed their relationship with natural entities. Indigenous socioenvironmental movements, grounded in indigenous philosophies, have become political signifiers able to express our shared humanity.[129] These philosophies are grounded in a profound respect for each other and the natural world. These movements place human-nature relationships at the centre. Such a relational approach draws out the interdependence of all things for wellbeing and the reciprocal relationships among people and between people and the planet.

In Aotearoa, New Zealand, the notion of "whakapapa" (to place in layers) sets out the connections among people, ecosystems and all flora and fauna.[130] The practices of "manaakitanga" (to care for) and "kaitiakitanga" (multispecies and intergenerational

Figure 3.12 A conceptual framework for local environmental stewardship

Socioecological context and change

Actors

LOCAL ENVIRONMENTAL STEWARDSHIP ACTIONS

Motivations

Capacity

Produces

ECOLOGICAL AND SOCIAL OUTCOMES OF STEWARDSHIP

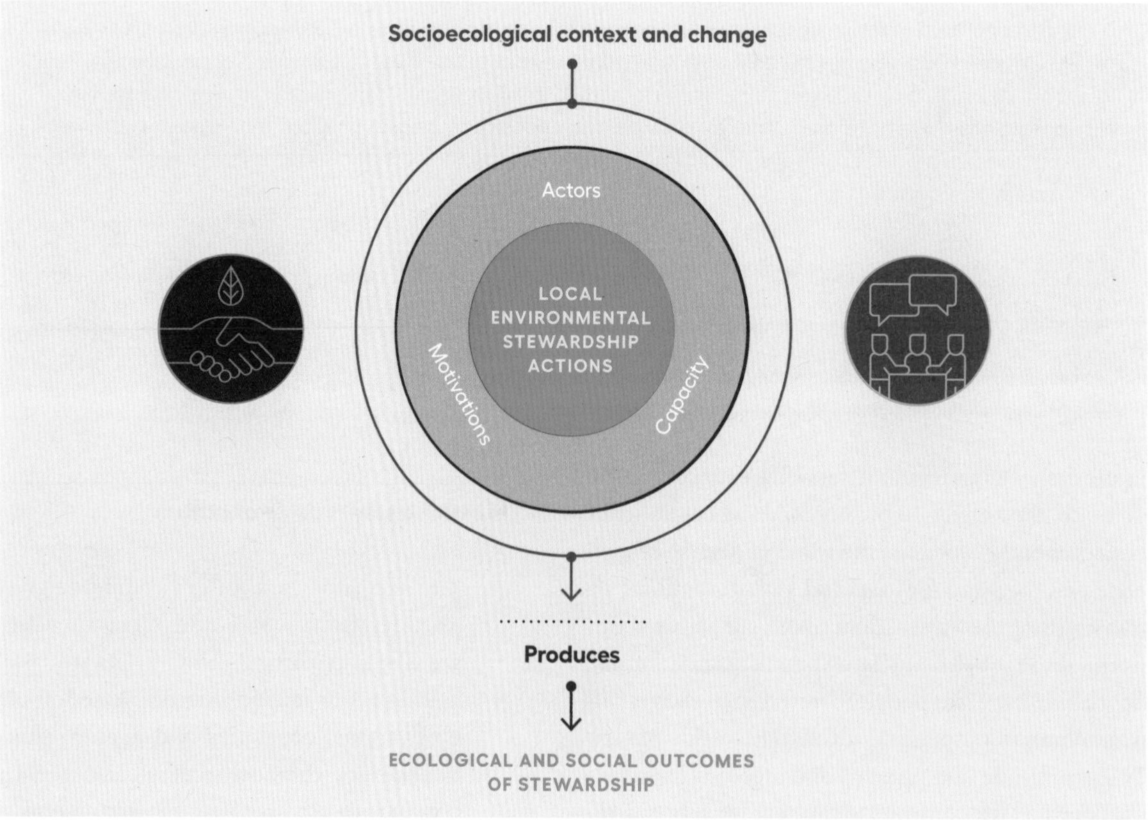

Source: Bennett and others 2018.

trusteeship) play key roles in articulating the responsibilities that fall out of these relationships.[131] These and other core concepts shape and centre collective responsibilities to protect and enhance socioenvironmental relationships.[132] Māori health models such as Te Whare Tapa Whā frame health and wellbeing around physical, spiritual, community and psychological dimensions.[133] Such multidimensional and community-engaged understandings of health continue to inform the delivery of health services and health policy in Aotearoa.[134] Other programmes of work build community and cultural capability to drive transitions to low-carbon futures.[135] A large part of their work is to detail the various ways in which local communities and relationships between people and the environment can be enhanced and protected through land and water development initiatives. The needs and aspirations of communities guided by intergenerational principles and practices seek to secure pathways towards sustainable and just futures.[136]

" In Aotearoa, New Zealand, the notion of 'whakapapa' (to place in layers) sets out the connections among people, ecosystems and all flora and fauna. Fundamental to the Quechua concept of 'Sumac Kawsay' (good living) is reciprocity, relationality and 'a profound respect of the differences (and an emphasis on the complementarities) among human beings and between human beings and the natural environment.'

Indigenous philosophies in Australia take as vital "collective responsibility and obligation to look after land, family, and community."[137] For the Yawuru community of Broome in Western Australia, wellbeing and development refer to the interconnectedness of "mabu buru" (strong country), "mabu ngarrungu" (strong community) and "mabu liyan" (strong spirit or good feeling).[138] Intergenerational transmission of knowledge and practice, as well as reciprocal sharing of gifts from lands and waters, exemplifies these connections. But these connections depend heavily on the freedom of the Yawuru to live in ways they value and to carry out these responsibilities.

The Anishinaabe concept of "Minobimaatisiiwin" (the good life) is similarly grounded in connections and the need for cooperation and justice among all beings.[139] The continuation of creation—and the relationships central to responsibilities to creation and re-creation—stem from the way all beings of Creation have duties and responsibilities to each other.[140] We see this philosophy in socioenvironmental movements and in governance and law.[141] According to Aimee Craft, Anishinaabe law and treatymaking are centrally about relationships and relationship-building, understood to include "relationships among and between ourselves, [as well as] relationships with other animal beings."[142]

Fundamental to the Quechua concept of "Sumac Kawsay" (good living) is reciprocity, relationality and "a profound respect of the differences (and an emphasis on the complementarities) among human beings and between human beings and the natural environment."[143] Similarly, "Ayni" (reciprocity) is "one of the most important tenets for the Andean people and is exemplified in the adage "what is received must be returned in equal measure."[144] According to Mariaelena Huambachano, these and other concepts enabled and ensured that Inca agricultural systems were grounded in sustainable production methods and food security.[145]

External incentives, where care of and respect for the Earth bring additional benefits, are also well documented. These include payments to enable certain management actions, payments for ecosystem services and market premiums for more environmentally sustainable products (chapter 5).

Beyond motivations, the environmental stewardship framework includes agents' capacity to actually undertake stewardship actions. This ability of people and communities to conduct specific activities in benefit of the planet will depend on the communal and individual assets—including infrastructure, technology, financing, income and wealth, rights, knowledge, skills, leadership and social relations—at their disposal as well as the decisionmaking structures within and across communities and groups.

Governance, understood as the process for state and nonstate actors to interact to reach and sustain agreements, is of particular importance.[146] These interactions shape and are being shaped by the distribution of power, as analysed earlier in this chapter and in chapter 2 (the agreements reached are typically called institutions). And wherever power imbalances are present, the poorer members of society end up losing more. The 2019 Human Development Report explored the elite capture of institutions, where the ability of government policy to address inequalities is constrained by powerful interest groups.[147] The policy outcomes then reflect the distribution of power in society. That is why enhancing equity, as underlined earlier in this chapter, is key.

" Reflecting the connectedness between nature and humanity, indigenous Hawaiians developed and applied a model for sustainable resource management, the ahupua'a system, designed more than 500 years ago to prevent overfishing and deforestation.

Again, there are lessons about governance from indigenous peoples. Making decisions in sync with the planet is part of indigenous cultures around the world —and it is the result not of chance but of finely tuned knowledge accumulated over long periods. Indigenous communities developed a deep understanding of their natural world to survive and ensure that it would provide resources in the future. This need to live sustainably is reflected in many practices and traditions that promote a general philosophy of subsistence not waste. In North America the Iroquois expected that a hunter who killed more deer than needed would be punished for it.[148] The Maasai pastoralist culture in East Africa has "always been one that has nurtured the land and used only the resources that were needed for the people. Abuse of the land or its animals and plants was frowned upon in the old days and still is by elders today."[149]

Reflecting the connectedness between nature and humanity, indigenous Hawaiians developed and applied a model for sustainable resource management, the ahupua'a system, designed more than 500 years ago to prevent overfishing and deforestation. Many other indigenous communities arrived at a similar concept of connectedness and used it to develop careful land and water use practices—and development approaches more generally.[150]

Other practices are more specific and demonstrate a profound knowledge of natural resources and sophisticated management practices, as with Amazonian communities that, to maintain healthy river ecosystems, "fish only for particular species in certain oxbow lakes at determined times of year. They also avoid certain parts of the rainforest altogether, ensuring that wildlife have a refuge where they can reproduce."[151] In Central Africa, when the Ba'aka dig up wild yams they return the stems to the ground so that the yams grow again. And they restrict "what you can hunt, when you can hunt it, who can hunt it ... a whole area of forest can be closed off from hunting or gathering activities in order to let it rest."[152]

These practices demonstrate a commitment to what Kyle Whyte refers to as "Collective Continuance" or "a community's capacity to be adaptive in ways sufficient for the livelihoods of its members to flourish into the future."[153] Not only does this require the capability to respond and adjust to changes as they arise, it also requires the ability to contest longstanding inequities (such as colonial hardships) and to build strong and cohesive relationships at all levels of engagement.

Promising initiatives link international law with indigenous communities through human rights. The International Labour Organization has led the global push for international law to recognize indigenous peoples' participation in decisions that affect them. Important advances have occurred in the context of Convention 169 on Indigenous and Tribal Peoples, adopted in 1989. Article 15 refers specifically to the participation rights of indigenous and tribal communities in managing and conserving the natural resources traditionally associated with them. The first element of the article reads, "The rights of the peoples concerned to the natural resources pertaining to their lands shall be specially safeguarded. These rights include the right of these peoples to participate in the use, management and conservation of these resources."[154]

Convention 169 demonstrates how different stakeholders' voices are given prominence through changes in decisionmaking processes—and is even more relevant since it refers to the rights of groups historically marginalized and discriminated against. And although much remains to be done to guarantee the rights of indigenous and tribal peoples—especially in societies with deep-seated inequalities—the convention has contributed. Under Convention 169, free, prior, informed consent responds to demands for self-determination, dignity and cultural integrity in international recognition of indigenous peoples' rights. It seeks to "regulate and operationalize the participation of indigenous peoples in environmental decisionmaking and political processes on questions where their interests are directly affected." While free, prior, informed consent is a welcome development in participatory processes, it still raises concerns and challenges. An adequate bottom-up approach would recognize indigenous peoples' right to self-determination while allowing the state to mediate and solve conflicts, strengthen local representative and democratic institutions, recognize existing national legislation and solve any contradiction emerging from the process. Moreover, free, prior, informed consent is not immune to elite capture, and with large power imbalances it can be detrimental.[155]

Knowledge is central to stewardship, and an opportunity exists for interchange between the types of knowledge just described and some of the tools of science. Recognizing both forms of knowledge can promote rich interactions and can give rise to relationships of trust able to navigate the shared opportunities and challenges that arise. This convergence of knowledge has been described variously, including as two-eyed seeing,[156] "He Awa Whiria"[157] and "Haudenosaunee Kaswentha."[158] As Priscilla Wehi notes, the convergence of multiple knowledges "can yield more comprehensive and detailed information" and "provides a strong ecological basis to quantify new hypotheses of ecological functioning, and add to the detailed information required in both conservation practice and restoration ecology."[159] We find such work undertaken by and with indigenous (and other local) communities all around the world.[160] This ongoing work remains critical since much of it must be undertaken on indigenous peoples' homelands.

Empowering agents as stewards

Stewardship of nature requires the commitment and will of billions of people around the world—from the communities and societies they construct, including leaders in every realm of society. It can unleash a new sense of agency and responsibility through a connection with nature, with the planet and with all living things. As Tim Lenton writes in spotlight 1.2, "To meet the challenge of expanding human freedoms in balance with the planet, there will surely need to be much learning-by-doing. Innovation usually happens from the 'bottom up,' driven by human

agency at small scales, and with the scope to spread if successful."

"Stewardship of nature requires the commitment and will of billions of people around the world—from the communities and societies they construct, including leaders in every realm of society.

Amartya Sen defines an agent as someone "who acts and brings about change, and whose achievements can be judged in terms of his or her own values and goals, whether or not we assess them in terms of some external criteria as well."[161] Sen has also argued that rethinking the relationship of people and the planet requires new ways of thinking, including recognizing agency as a central tenet. In his own words, "We must think not just about sustaining the fulfilment of our needs, but more largely about sustaining, and extending, our freedoms (including, of course, the freedom to meet our own needs, but going well beyond that). The sustaining of ecosystems and the preservation of species can be given new grounds by the recognition of human beings as reflective agents rather than as passive patients."[162] Sen's argument focuses on people's ability to act on their own volition and reasoning—and on what people have reason to value. It puts at the centre people, their freedoms and their capacity to be an agent of change.

Stewards could be individuals or a group organized at different scales. Their actions can occur at different levels (community, ecosystem, national or even global) and depend on capacities and institutional context. The examples described here suggest myriad possibilities for stewardship, reflecting the complex interaction between humans and the planet. Several levers could be harnessed to expand stewardship, including limiting the harvest of a species, establishing marine protected areas, managing comprehensive watersheds, and creating and maintaining urban green spaces and gardens (see chapter 6 on the potential of this type of interventions). Broader initiatives could span transboundary and regional scales. Successful stewardship requires not only motivated actors with the capacity to push the agenda but also a clear follow-up system in which metrics can evaluate social and environmental justice outcomes and provide the basis for learning and innovation.

Learning from sustainability science to guide sustainable human development

Andrea S. Downing, Stockholm Resilience Centre at Stockholm University and Global Economic Dynamics and the Biosphere programme at the Royal Swedish Academy of Sciences; **Manqi Chang,** Department of Aquatic Ecology at the Netherlands Institute of Ecology; **David Collste,** Stockholm Resilience Centre at Stockholm University; **Sarah Cornell,** Stockholm Resilience Centre at Stockholm University; **Jan. J. Kuiper,** Stockholm Resilience Centre at Stockholm University; **Wolf M. Mooij,** Department of Aquatic Ecology at the Netherlands Institute of Ecology and Department of Aquatic Ecology and Water Quality Management at Wageningen University; **Uno Svedin,** Stockholm Resilience Centre at Stockholm University; and **Dianneke van Wijk,** Department of Aquatic Ecology at the Netherlands Institute of Ecology

The 1960s mark a slow turning point for the "Western" world and international development in recognizing and understanding the interconnections among human wellbeing, the economy and the environment. In 1962 Rachel Carson linked industrial chemical pollution to biodiversity loss and human diseases in her highly influential book *Silent Spring*.[1] In 1968 the first Intergovernmental Conference for Rational Use and Conservation of the Biosphere took place, followed by the 1972 Stockholm Conference, where ecologically sustainable development was discussed in depth. International cooperation has evolved, coordinated and culminated in the United Nations 2030 Agenda for Sustainable Development[2] and the Paris Climate Agreement, which are soon to be complemented by the Post-2020 Global Biodiversity Framework of the Convention on Biological Diversity.

The timeline of scientific findings and international conferences is dotted and interwoven with human, economic and environmental catastrophes, including the 1973 Organization of the Petroleum Exporting Countries oil crisis; the 1984 drought in Ethiopia, which caused the loss of 1 million human lives; the fatal Bhopal toxic chemical leak that same year in India, which caused massive environmental damage; nuclear accidents; countless oil spills; epidemics; disproportionately extensive forest fires; and more.[3] At the time of writing, the Covid-19 pandemic is still spreading and has cost over 1.5 million lives, with an unprecedented economic downturn and social unrest in its wake.

Social movements calling for fair and sustainable development have grown and multiplied in parallel to these disasters: from Greenpeace's first civil protests (1971), the Chipko movement in India (1973), the greenbelt movement (1977), the Occupy Movement against inequality (2011), the climate march that preceded the UN Climate Change Conference in 2015 and many others (figure S1.1.1), culminating in today's global youth-led climate-related strikes and movements, which have engaged millions of people around the world, as well as worldwide protests against systemic racism and police brutality.

Over these decades scientific research has built an extensive body of knowledge on the connections between the biosphere—the thin layer of life that covers the earth—and human activities[4] and has taken multiple approaches to understanding the relations and dynamics between the two. Metabolic approaches describe a system's dynamics as generated from the flows of matter and energy between societies and their natural environments.[5] Human appropriation, metabolic approaches and planetary boundaries have common roots in the ecological and early Earth system sciences and in ecological economics (see figure S1.1.1). Planetary boundaries include resilience and complexity science. This implies analysing the dynamics that emerge from interactions and combinations of processes that constitute systems and how those dynamics in turn influence the processes and interactions that generated them. Complexity helps increase understanding of development in the face of both surprising and expected change and of the existence of alternative pathways.[6] Whatever the approach and regardless of whether it is used to eradicate poverty and hunger or for nature conservation, humanity and biosphere are indissociable. The

Figure S1.1.1 The knowledge, social will and political power needed to achieve sustainable development exists

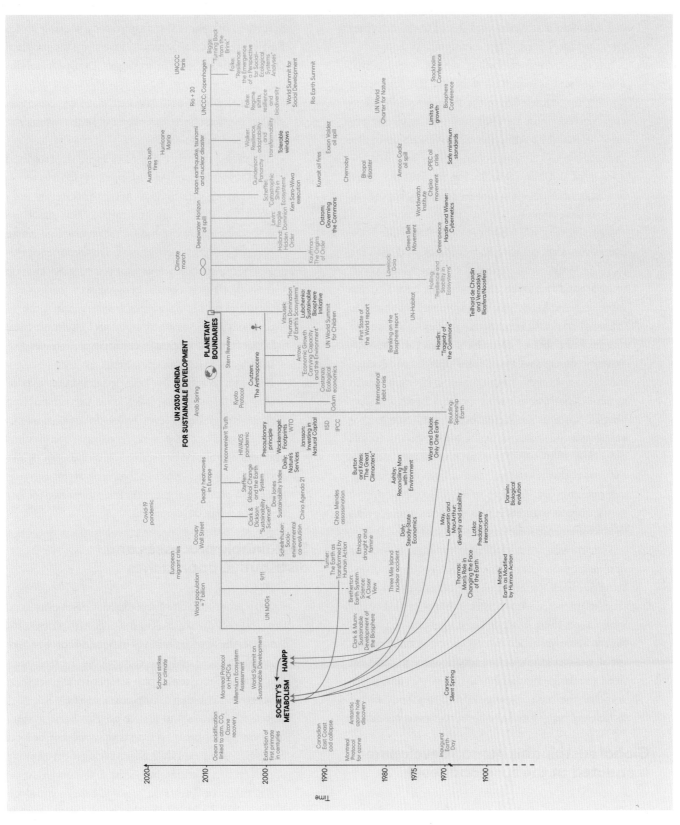

Note: Three interconnected branches of scientific inquiry—resilience (orange), human wellbeing through ecological economics (purple) and Earth system sciences (blue)—shape most of today's sustainability science and have common roots and shared knowledge (grey) dating back centuries. The mix of policy, social movements and disasters (red) speckle the timeline.

Source: Adapted from figure 1 in Downing and others (2020).

biosphere provides the energy and resources that constitute and support human life, and resource acquisition and matter disposal from human activities alter the biosphere and its functioning.

International cooperation, social movements, disasters and research all reinforce the consensus around and knowledge of the deep interdependencies between human wellbeing and environmental sustainability. Although we have known of the importance of the interdependencies between the biosphere and human wellbeing for over 60 years, unsustainable development has only increased, as human development has progressed at the cost of sustainability of the biosphere.[7] Climate-related disaster events are growing in frequency, and with the increased interconnectedness of socioecological systems around the globe, those systems have become more vulnerable to these environmental changes, to financial crises, to inequalities in society and to the unequal impacts of disturbances and disasters[8]— systemic shocks that are undoing decades of development. Unsustainable development is changing Earth system dynamics in such ways that Earth socioecological systems are increasingly unsuitable to provide equal and sufficient wellbeing for all.[9] All trends indicate that humanity is on an unsustainable development pathway that points away from human development goals. To meet sustainable development goals, transformations in how societies interact with the biosphere are necessary.

The problem is not a lack of knowledge, awareness or understanding of the threats that continued unsustainable development poses to societies worldwide (see figure S1.1.1). Across research, policy and social movements there has long been a general consensus that to achieve sustainable and just human development, the ways that socioeconomic systems function need to change fundamentally. Here we summarize some of the main messages from this body of research and bring forward where progress is needed.

Global sustainable human development is enacted at the subglobal level

The space view of planet Earth, which inspired Kenneth Boulding's "Spaceship Earth" in 1966[10] and many others, is a classic illustration of the global limits of resources and space. It continues to inspire the global footprint calculator[11] and the Earth Overshoot Day movement. That there is only one planet for humanity to live on and that humanity is using up 1.6 Earths are effective ways of illustrating the problem of unsustainability (for example, Earth Overshoot day[12]).

But at the subglobal level we have continuously shifted our baselines and overshot limits through at least three mechanisms:
- Adapting—changing our diets as we deplete food resources, for example (fishing down food webs).
- Relativizing situations to newer or different contexts. We shift or ignore limits to how much we can consume by expanding extraction and waste deposition across ecosystems. This is done regardless of the specific impacts of our consumption on individual resources and ecosystems.
- Pushing problems across borders and time[13]— displacing the socioeconomic and environmental impacts of production to countries with fewer regulations or to future generations.

It is time to act on the knowledge that unsustainability at the subglobal level leads to overshooting global limits. Process-level definitions of sustainability must hold across scales: ensuring the emissions and waste produced by human activities can be absorbed at balanced rates so that ecosystems can regulate and produce at rates that might suffice for fair and just human development.

Sustainable processes and distributive approaches

Research has a strong focus on identifying limits to unsustainability—such as limits to growth, emissions, land use, the appropriation of natural resources or energy, and more. This focus comes from the research's deep roots in environmental sciences and does little to bridge with human development needs.

Indeed, fairness and justice are not Earth system biogeophysical processes, and they are not default outcomes of sustainability, but taking a distributive approach to sustainability—and thus complementing a focus on limits to sustainability—could go hand-in-hand with addressing inequality.[14] Distributive approaches can measure the same variables as those that focus on limits but with attention to the process rates needed for individuals to thrive sustainably—that is, rates of (minimum) necessary resource extraction or of waste production that can be assimilated and processed—rather than identifying a total available amount of resources or total allowable depletion rate. Distributive approaches do not necessarily assume that all individuals require equal amounts of resources but account for context-specific differences in access to resources and in production of waste, information that may guide sustainable and equitable human development. Analysing how diverse needs and processes of sustainable consumption and production combine to shape global development can go beyond approaches that tend to maximize towards resource limits and from the deeply unequal and unequitable distribution of benefits and impacts that ensue.

Sustainable human development as forging new realities

Global perspectives on development are useful dashboards to indicate what is unsustainable—where limits are—and the risks posed by unsustainability, such as greater climate system variability and catastrophic shifts in the functioning of Earth system dynamics or social order.

Taking the next steps to identify what is sustainable and how to achieve it requires recognizing contexts, their differences and connections. Contexts are—especially in the Anthropocene—more than the "here and now" of specific situations: They include distal processes and historic legacies. Foreign and international policies, commodity prices abroad, conflicts or changes to land use and hydrology on a different continent, and much more influence national and local contexts. Past injustices, conflicts and ecosystem degradation can define what constitutes an acceptable or effective sustainable development option and for whom. A sustainable development process does not displace its social, economic, environmental or even discursive burdens across borders[15] or generations.[16] There is no panacea for achieving sustainable human development that fits the whole of humanity; instead, each approach must be fit to and evolve with the context in which it is set. Importantly, each approach must be inclusive of other approaches. Research on sustainable human development could then boost understanding of how different realizations of sustainable development combine to shape global development.

Using future goals to address present problems

An important objective of sustainability research is to clarify consequences of continued unsustainability, or projecting problems of unsustainability into the future, looking at what might happen when we cross limits of emissions or biodiversity loss, for example. Projecting problems rather than goals into the future is a critical issue in current sustainability and development discourses, as illustrated, for example, by the statement, "Two degrees warming will be a problem."

When the problem being addressed is seen as a present one, action can effectively be taken, such as the pesticide regulations that followed Rachel Carson's book or restrictions on chlorofluorocarbons triggered by the hole in the ozone layer.[17] More vividly, perhaps, the regulatory, governance, social, academic and financial responses to the Covid-19 pandemic have been unprecedented in speed and magnitude—though it is too early to assess their effectiveness. Just like the Covid-19 pandemic, unsustainable human development is a problem today that is affecting 7.8 billion people. It is not only a future risk or a problem elsewhere, as no country or region is developing sustainably. Understanding the problems as present and placing constructive goals in the future are framings that could trigger positive action towards solving today's unsustainability, poverty and injustice.

Understanding contexts as connected in time and space can inspire new thinking and designs of sustainable futures: What can sustainable and just futures look like in different contexts? What inequalities do different conceptions of futures bring to light? How, specifically, do these futures differ from present situations? Which processes need to be broken, and which need to be nurtured to achieve such futures?[18] Futures that are built on sustainable processes—that is, balanced rates of waste production and resource extraction—and that account for the distribution of access, impact, opportunities and responsibilities are engaging, constructive goals to work towards.

Transformative pathways for sustainable and just outcomes

Achieving sustainable development, and even meeting the Sustainable Development Goals, will require more than adaptations and gradual changes. It will require transformations that break current locked-in systems of unsustainability. Measures aimed solely at reducing carbon dioxide emissions and slowing biodiversity loss, for example, equate to "doing less bad" but do not represent "doing right." Compensation and offsetting mechanisms might have behavioural benefits—helping recognize the costs of specific unsustainable activities. But these mechanisms are neither sustainable nor transformative and cannot undo the unsustainability of the processes being offset or compensated for. We need to distinguish between end goals and outcomes. When reducing specific environmental and social impacts is a goal in itself, development still points in the wrong direction. Even optimistic scenarios of reduced consumption and material growth are likely to result in massive biodiversity loss[19]—and this may be an outcome of sustainability transformations, but it cannot be the goal. We need to aim for transformative changes in how societies relate to the biosphere, focus on distributive approaches and ensure extraction and emission rates align with the rates at which resources are produced and waste and emissions can be absorbed by the environment. Outcomes, such as biodiversity conservation and climate stabilization, can be measured as single variables, but the goals of sustainable human development must be rooted in integrated, transdisciplinary understandings of the connections of societies in the biosphere. Development pathways and goals will vary over time and space, as they are met or redefined. This requires adaptive management,[20] the ability to better understand, learn and act accordingly in an endless, iterative process.

All these findings apply to the 2030 Agenda: For the Sustainable Development Goals to be transformative, we must see them in their entirety as integral environmental, social and economic goals. They must be adapted to and consistent with the contexts in which they are being applied. Long-term sustainability is more than meeting quantitative targets; it requires reshaping the processes of development. Goals must be periodically re-evaluated in light of new knowledge and development to ensure that they represent just and sustainable futures for all.

Sustainable human development is not a checklist but a dynamic and continued process, and ample research, human will and political power—as well as urgency—exist to actively engage in that process.

NOTES

1 Carson 2002.

2 United Nations 2015b.

3 Creech 2012.

4 Downing and others 2020.

5 Fischer-Kowalski and Hüttler 1998.

6 Downing and others 2020; Holling 1973; Walker and others 2004.

7 Rockström and others 2009a.

8 Keys and others 2019.

9 Clark and Munn 1986; Rockström and others 2009a.

10 Boulding 1966.

11 http://www.footprintcalculator.org.

12 See https://www.overshootday.org.

13 Liu and others 2013; Pascual and others 2017.

14 Downing and others 2020.

15 Pascual and others 2017; Persson and Mertz 2019.

16 Brundtland Commission 1987.

17 Creech 2012; Downing and others 2020.

18 Sharpe and others 2016.

19 Powers and Jetz 2019.

20 Folke and others 2002.

Learning from Life—an Earth system perspective

Timothy M. Lenton, Director, Global Systems Institute, University of Exeter

Human development thus far has brought about the Anthropocene, a term that recognizes that humans are now a planetary force. It is highly unusual for one animal species to have global impacts, and we are certainly the first species to have a dawning collective awareness that it is changing the world. However, we are far from the first living things to change the planet. Rather, we exist—let alone develop—only because of the extraordinary consequences of 4 billion years of ongoing collective activity by other living things that have made the planet habitable for us. They range from the humblest bacteria to the mightiest trees—all unconsciously networked together. This totality of all living things is referred to here as "Life."

The idea that physics, chemistry, geology and climatology set a planetary stage on which Life has merely been an actor, adapting to what it is given, turns out to be an illusion. Instead, what we see as the nonliving physical world—the atmosphere, oceans, ice sheets, climate and even the continents—are (to varying degrees) created or affected by Life on Earth.[1] These factors in turn shape Life, closing myriad feedback loops (of varying strength). These closed loops of causality, in which the consequences of actions feedback to their originators or their descendants, can give rise to recognizable behaviour across a wide range of scales, right up to the planetary. Earth's history is characterized by long intervals of stable self-regulation interspersed with tipping points of abrupt change.

This new understanding has been unearthed over the last half century by the emerging field of Earth system science.[2] This perspective of Life in the Earth system offers some humbling yet empowering lessons on expanding human freedoms in balance with the planet.

How we got here

Humans owe our very existence to the activities of past and present life forms, which have created a world that we could inhabit.[3] This is true not just in the evolutionary sense that we are descended from earlier life forms but also in the Earth system sense that the atmosphere would be unbreathable and the climate intolerable were it not for the accumulated actions of other living things, past and present. Three pivotal revolutions stand out in Earth history, in which the Earth system was radically transformed. Each depended on the previous one, and without them we would not be here. They offer important lessons about the value of Life and about what supports its flourishing.

Life started on Earth remarkably soon after the planet formed 4.56 billion years ago and cooled enough to be inhabitable. The latest estimates put Life's origin at more than 4 billion years ago, and sedimentary rocks that could record the presence of Life, more than 3.7 billion years ago, suggest it was already there. Early Life was exclusively bacteria and archaea, the two kingdoms of prokaryotes (simple cells). All organisms need a supply of energy and materials to stay alive. The earliest cells probably got their energy in chemical form, from reacting compounds in their environment (just as humans burn fossil fuels with oxygen to power our societies today). However, a shortage of chemical energy at the time would have severely restricted the collective productivity of early Life.[4]

The first revolution started when some organisms evolved to harness the most abundant energy source on the planet—sunlight—and used it to fix carbon dioxide from the atmosphere in various forms of anoxygenic photosynthesis (which do not release oxygen).[5] At that point shortage of materials, rather than of energy, would have become limiting to global productivity. All forms of photosynthesis need a source of electrons (to reduce carbon), and the compounds used in the earliest forms of photosynthesis, such as hydrogen gas (H_2), were in short supply.[6] This illustrates a general problem for Life that is still with us today: The fluxes of materials coming to the surface of Earth from geologic (volcanic and metamorphic) processes are meagre, many orders of magnitude less than the needs of Life today—or indeed the needs of current human civilizations. There are two possible evolutionary answers to this problem: increase the inputs of materials needed or increase their recycling within the Earth system. Early Life's overwhelming answer was to evolve the means of recycling all the materials it needed to metabolize, using some of the energy captured in photosynthesis to power that recycling. This established what scientists call global biogeochemical cycles. A few scant clues suggest that global-scale recycling of hydrogen and carbon was in place by around 3.5 billion years ago. However, global productivity would still have been limited to less than 1 percent of today's.[7]

The second revolution started around 3 billion years ago with the evolution of oxygenic photosynthesis, which uses abundant water as a source of electrons.[8] This was a spectacularly difficult process to evolve[9] because splitting water requires more energy —that is, more high energy photons of sunlight—than any photosynthesis before. Around a billion years after the origin of Life, evolution chanced on a solution: wiring together two existing photosystems from completely different bacterial lineages in one cell and bolting on the front of them a remarkable piece of biochemical machinery that can rip apart water molecules.[10] The result was the first cyanobacterial cell: the ancestor of all organisms (cyanobacteria, algae and plants) performing oxygenic photosynthesis on the planet today. Life then became limited by the supply of different materials—the essential nutrients nitrogen and phosphorus—and new ways of recycling them evolved.

Production of the most abundant waste product of Life, oxygen, had begun. Yet oxygen did not rise in the atmosphere immediately or steadily. Instead, it remained a trace gas for hundreds of millions of years. Then in a spectacular transition around 2.4 billion years ago known as the Great Oxidation, oxygen rose abruptly and irreversibly to be the chemically dominant gas in the atmosphere.[11] This illustrates one of the key properties of the Earth system, which it shares with other complex systems: It possesses alternative stable states and occasionally passes tipping points when it goes abruptly from one (no

longer stable) state to another. At the Great Oxidation the Earth system tipped from a stable low oxygen state without an ozone layer to a stable high oxygen state with an ozone layer.[12] The tipping point was triggered when the balance of gaseous inputs to the atmosphere shifted from an excess of reductants (that is, electron-rich compounds) to an excess of oxygen. The transition was self-propelling thanks to self-amplifying (positive) feedback: Once enough oxygen built up for the ozone layer to start to form, this shielded the atmosphere below from ultraviolet light and slowed the chemical reactions that remove oxygen by reacting it with methane. More oxygen produced more ozone, letting through less ultraviolet light and further suppressing oxygen consumption in a runaway rise of oxygen. Among the consequences were severe ice ages, thanks to the removal of methane, a potent greenhouse gas.[13] A new stable state was established when a new sink (removal process) for oxygen kicked in: oxidation of sedimentary rocks and of the continents themselves. Oxygen may have overshot for hundreds of millions of years until a 1.5 billion year period of stability was established.[14]

The biosphere was supercharged by the Great Oxidation because respiration of organic matter with oxygen yields an order of magnitude more energy than breaking food down anaerobically. Key beneficiaries about 2 billion years ago were the first eukaryotes, complex cells. They evolved from a fusion of once free-living prokaryotes. Their energy factory (mitochondria) were once free-living aerobic bacteria, and the plastids where photosynthesis occurs in plant and algal cells were once free-living cyanobacteria. Using their larger energy supply, eukaryotes increased their genetic information storage and processing, copying many chromosomes in parallel (whereas prokaryotes copy their DNA in one long loop). This gave eukaryotes the capacity to create more complex, multicellular lifeforms. However, that capacity was suppressed under still low oxygen levels about 2 billion years ago to about 600 million years ago, while the deep ocean remained largely devoid of oxygen.[15]

The third revolution started around 700 million years ago in a period of extreme climate changes— "Snowball Earth" events during which the planet froze over completely—and a second rise in oxygen levels, when animals began to evolve.[16] The scientific details of what caused what in this revolution are still being untangled. Suffice to say there was (again) a link between environmental instability and the evolution of more complex life forms, which were themselves made up of pre-existing components (eukaryote cells). Furthermore, increased oxygen levels were a necessary condition for more complex forms of animal. The revolution did not finish until around 400 million years ago, when complex plants, in partnership with fungi, colonized the land and pushed oxygen up to modern levels, radically lowering carbon dioxide levels and cooling the climate. This land colonization hinged on evolving ways of extracting phosphorus from rocks and of efficiently recycling nutrients within terrestrial ecosystems. It doubled global productivity.[17] Through this success, plants created wildfire-supporting, carbon dioxide–limiting conditions, which entangled them in feedbacks that stabilize atmospheric oxygen, carbon dioxide and global temperature levels. The resulting stability and high oxygen levels were crucial for the further evolution of complex Life—including us.[18]

Why it is a bad time to perturb the planet

What can we draw out from this brief history of the Earth system? It was characterized by long intervals of stability and self-regulation, interspersed with tipping points of abrupt change. The most revolutionary changes were driven by Life, specifically new evolutionary innovations that increased energy and material consumption and generated new waste products (notably oxygen). Revolutions relied on some inherent instability in the Earth system to become planet changing. They sometimes took Life to the brink of total extinction in events such as "Snowball Earth." Stability was restored only when effective means of recycling materials were (re)established. Each revolution built on the previous one. Complex life forms are built from simpler ancestors. Greater biological complexity also relied on increased atmospheric oxygen and stronger environmental regulation (because complex life forms have narrower habitability requirements). Looking at the unfolding Anthropocene from this long-term vantage point raises the question: Could this be the start of another revolutionary change of the Earth system?

This is a bad time to be perturbing the Earth system because it is unusually unstable. Just as our hominin ancestors began to use stone tools around 2.6 million years ago, a roughly 40 million years cooling trend culminated in a series of Northern Hemisphere ice age cycles, initially every 40,000 years. Then as our ancestors were first taming fire, around a million years ago, these ice ages became more severe and less frequent, roughly every 100,000 years. This transition from a stable climate state to progressively deeper and stronger glacial-to-interglacial oscillations clearly indicates the Earth system's loss of stability.[19] These sawtooth oscillations—during which the climate cools progressively into an ice age then snaps rapidly out of it, only for the cycle to repeat soon after—are a classic example of a system that, despite being bounded by negative feedback, contains a strong amplifier (positive feedback), as should be familiar to students of electrical engineering. At the termination of an ice age, the Earth system goes into near runaway positive feedback, with carbon released from the deep ocean, amplifying global climate change. Looking at the last ice age, the sense of instability gets worse: It contained at least 20 abrupt climate change events[20] during which large areas of the Northern Hemisphere warmed markedly within a few years (followed later by abrupt cooling).[21]

Humans have unwittingly started the Anthropocene against this backdrop of long-term climate instability. Climate scientists often comfort themselves and their audience with the knowledge that the last 10,000 years of the Holocene interglacial period look climatically more stable[22] (until we started to mess it up). Indeed, a favoured origin story is that this stability provided an essential foundation for the multiple independent origins of agriculture and human civilizations. This Neolithic (agricultural) revolution controlled the means of (solar) energy input to societies and supported new levels of social organization (states). However, civilizations overwhelming arose in dry climates, often where the environment had been deteriorating. These novel complex social systems were then rather vulnerable to multiple internal and external factors, including abrupt regional climate changes. The path of human history too, it seems, is one of periods of stability interspersed with short intervals of abrupt, revolutionary change, with much trial and error.

A new, concentrated (but finite) source of energy —fossil fuels—propelled the industrial revolution, which continues to spread across the world today, increasing global energy and material consumption. Combusting fossil fuels breaks the natural (recycling) balance of the carbon cycle and generates our most abundant, invisible waste product: carbon dioxide. In industrial economies, about 80 percent of the total annual outflow of materials by weight is carbon dioxide[23] and global fossil fuel emissions account for around 35 billion tonnes of carbon dioxide a year, with another 5.5 billion from land use change.[24] The accumulation of this carbon dioxide and other anthropogenic greenhouse gases in the atmosphere and the resulting roughly 1 degree Celsius of global warming is already destabilizing the Earth system. Several tipping elements exist in the climate system that have alternative stable states and can pass tipping points between them.[25] Some involve abrupt shifts in modes of circulation of the ocean or atmosphere, some involve abrupt loss of parts of the cryosphere and some involve abrupt shifts in the biosphere. There is already evidence that parts of the West Antarctic and East Antarctic ice sheets may be in irreversible retreat, the Greenland ice sheet is shrinking at an accelerating rate, the overturning circulation of the Atlantic Ocean is weakening and the Amazon rainforest is burning.[26] In each case there is strong self-amplifying feedback within the system, which propels change.

For other crucial elemental cycles our collective activities exceed those of the rest of Life combined. We fix more reactive nitrogen from the atmosphere than the rest of the biosphere, and after it is added to our agricultural fields, most ends up elsewhere. Bacteria denitrify some of it back to atmospheric N_2 but also generate nitrous oxide, a potent, long-lived greenhouse gas. Other nitrogenous gases contribute to air pollution. Much reactive nitrogen leaks into fresh waters, estuaries and shelf seas, where it fuels productivity, often of cyanobacteria.[27] We also mine, refine and add to the Earth system about three times as much phosphorus as the natural processes of rock weathering. This also fuels productivity far beyond the fields where it is applied.[28] Together nitrogen and phosphorus loading contribute to eutrophication, deoxygenation of subsurface waters and toxic blooms. The deoxygenation of lakes and restricted shelf seas (such as the Baltic Sea) involves tipping point dynamics. As bottom waters deoxygenate, microbes in

sediments are triggered to recycle phosphorus back to the water column, adding to productivity and deoxygenation in a potent positive feedback cycle.[29]

Human activities have also made the Earth system —and our societies—less stable by forming more homogeneous and connected networks. All Life, including humanity, comprises interacting networks of actors. However, the stability of those networks depends crucially on the diversity (heterogeneity) or lack of it (homogeneity) within them and on how strongly connected they are. A more homogeneous and strongly connected network, though it may perform well at resisting small perturbations, is more prone to global collapse.[30] The Covid-19 pandemic has highlighted this for our interconnected, human societies. Today's dominant political economy has been busy homogenizing and interconnecting both the human world and the rest of the living world. About half the Earth's productive land surface is devoted to farming, dominated by a few staple crops and a handful of domesticated animal species. Those animals outweigh us, and we in turn outweigh all the remaining wild animal life. The resulting artificial ecosystems are vulnerable. Vast scientific efforts go into suppressing pathogens. Three-quarters of crops and 35 percent of crop production depend critically on natural pollinators,[31] which are often vulnerable to our pesticides.[32] The transfer of invasive species between continents is homogenizing Life. Our ongoing destruction of remaining natural habitats and our extraction and exchange of wild species as economic commodities (think the Wuhan wet market) are introducing new threats into the fragile networks we have created.

Given the Earth system's present underlying climate instability and our efforts to erode the stability of its networks, we need to confront the possibility that our actions could trigger a global tipping point. Already, the long lifetime of the carbon dioxide we have added to the atmosphere may have prevented the next ice age. If we burn all known fossil fuels, climate forcing from carbon dioxide could exceed anything the Earth has experienced in the last 400 million years.[33] Long before that happens, we risk tipping the Earth system into a hothouse state similar to those associated with past oceanic anoxic events and mass extinctions.[34] Our globalization and homogenization of the web of Life could also perhaps cause its networks to collapse in a mass extinction. We need to avoid such outcomes at all costs. Our very existence requires that Life survived such past scrapes with disaster,[35] but past survival provides no guarantee of future survival. After past close shaves, it typically took millions of years for the slow workings of evolution and Earth system dynamics to restore a well functioning, self-regulating biosphere. We do not have the luxury of waiting that long.

How we can save ourselves

This new knowledge emerging from Earth system science has important implications for how we can reduce the risks we pose to ourselves and other living beings. If we recognize the agency of humans, and all other Life, it can also show us a way forward to future flourishing.[36]

Energy and materials

If we continue to let our waste products accumulate, trouble will ensue—as it did during the revolutions that made the Earth. But what the biosphere illustrates is that solar energy and nearly closed material recycling are the basis of productivity and flourishing. Instead of just retreating to a world of lower energy and material consumption, we can open up a space for human flourishing—within planetary boundaries[37] —by changing our dominant source of energy and learning to recycle all the materials we need. The emphasis of industrial and agricultural activity needs to shift from increasing the inputs of carbon, nitrogen, phosphorus and other elements into the Earth system to increasing the recycling of these elements within the Earth system, powered by sustainable energy. Happily, the input of solar energy can far outstrip current fossil fuel energy consumption. Renewables are already cost-competitive with fossil fuel energy for electricity generation in much of the world—and will be much cheaper within a decade. There should thus be no long-term shortage of energy. Renewable energy is also more distributed than fossil fuels, offering the opportunity to (literally) put the power back with the people, democratizing energy supply. The challenge is to design and incentivize a transition to a circular economy. Waste products must become useful resources to make new products. Despite practical obstacles and thermodynamic constraints, there is huge potential to increase material recycling. Innovation and engineering need to shift attention to achieve nearly closed material cycling powered by sustainable energy.

Information and networks

The biosphere is built from adaptive networks of microbial actors that exchange materials, electrons and information—the latter through ubiquitous horizontal gene transfer. These microbial networks form the basis of the recycling loops that make up global biogeochemical cycles. Nowadays they are augmented by networks of macroscopic life, such as plants and mycorrhizal fungi. The topology of these networks and their feedback loops are persistent, even when the taxa performing particular functional roles within them change. Sufficient biodiversity to provide functional redundancy adds to network robustness. Self-regulation is a distributed property—that is, there is no centralized control—further adding to network robustness.[38] Humans have been busy creating more homogeneous, hierarchical—and therefore less stable—networks in the biosphere and their own realm. Shifting to more horizontal transfer of information, functional diversity with redundancy and distributed control will all likely be important to a successful circular economy. The challenge is to support diverse, autocatalytic networks of human agents that can propel transformations towards goals such as sustainable energy, fuelling the efficient cycling of resources. This is particularly challenging given the social and economic paradigm of short-term localized gain and weak global, unifying, long-term structures to counteract it.

Evolving solutions

All the living, networked actors in the Earth system continuously transform their stage in an interplay of action and reaction. Evolutionary experiments or innovations have consequences, and those consequences are filtered. Natural selection can help explain resource recycling and environmental regulation at small scales of space and time. But at larger space and time scales simpler dynamical mechanisms are at play: Systems that find self-stabilizing configurations tend to persist, and systems that persist have a greater likelihood of acquiring further persistence-enhancing properties.[39] Through these cruder filtering mechanisms, the Earth system appears to have acquired and accumulated stabilizing feedback mechanisms involving Life (including biogeochemical cycles). Major transitions in evolution[40] have created new levels of biological organization out of pre-existing components, including the eukaryote cell, multicellular complex life forms, social animal colonies, (human) states and who knows what next.

To meet the challenge of expanding human freedoms in balance with the planet, there will surely need to be much learning-by-doing. Innovation usually happens from the bottom up, driven by human agency at small scales and with the scope to spread if successful. These experiments will be subject to filtering, but we need to re-examine the values and priorities driving that filtering. If it is just the invisible hand of deregulated markets doing the filtering, based on short-term financial gains that concentrate power with the few, outcomes that promote sustainability, equity or collective flourishing are highly unlikely. After all, that filter got us into this mess in the first place. To change the filter will require conscious, collective leadership—and some things will need to be more tightly regulated than others.

Tipping positive change

While today's policymakers seem paralyzed by complexity, it should not be a barrier to action. The complex Earth system runs itself automatically.

Indigenous cultures worldwide have developed sophisticated ways of flourishing with the ecological complexity around them—for example, the Yap people of the Federated States of Micronesia have used adaptive management to sustain high population density in the face of scarce resources.[41] Contemporary science is developing a powerful toolkit to sense and understand complex systems and guide action. Frameworks such as adaptive management have been established. Perhaps a partial liberation for policymakers can come from realizing that action does not reside just with them; it continually comes—as it always has—from living free agents.

Improving our relationship with the rest of Life, as well as with each other, relies on having an advanced sensing capability. We need to be able to sense where things are going wrong—and where they are going right—to have any chance of correcting errors or charting a new course. More boldly, science has shown that tipping points in complex systems carry generic early warning signals.[42] Climate change and biosphere degradation have already advanced to the point where we are triggering damaging tipping points. Avoiding worse ones ahead will require finding and triggering positive tipping points towards sustainability in coupled social, technological and ecological systems.[43] The same methods that can provide early warning of damaging environmental tipping points could be used to detect when sociotechnical or socioecological systems are most sensitive to being deliberately tipped in a desirable direction. Participating in that deliberate tipping would expand human freedom. Policymakers have a special opportunity to provide a guiding framework, incentivizing some outcomes over others and thus playing a key part in tipping positive change.

NOTES

1	Lenton, Dutreuil and Latour 2020.	9	Allen and Martin 2007.
2	Lenton 2016.	10	Allen and Martin 2007; Lenton and Watson 2011.
3	Lenton and Watson 2011.	11	Goldblatt, Lenton and Watson 2006; Lenton and Watson 2011.
4	Lenton, Pichler and Weisz 2016.	12	Goldblatt, Lenton and Watson 2006.
5	Canfield, Rosing and Bjerrum 2006; Lenton and Watson 2011.	13	Lenton and Watson 2011.
6	Canfield, Rosing and Bjerrum 2006; Lenton and Watson 2011.	14	Lenton and Watson 2011.
7	Canfield, Rosing and Bjerrum 2006; Lenton, Pichler and Weisz 2016.	15	Lenton and Watson 2011.
8	Lenton and Watson 2011.	16	Lenton and Watson 2011.

17	Lenton, Pichler and Weisz 2016.
18	Lenton and Watson 2011.
19	Lenton and Watson 2011.
20	Dansgaard and others 1993.
21	Steffensen and others 2008.
22	Rockström and others 2009a.
23	Lenton, Pichler and Weisz 2016.
24	Friedlingstein and others 2019b.
25	Lenton and others 2008.
26	Lenton and others 2019.
27	Paerl and others 2011.
28	Paerl and others 2011.
29	Vahtera and others 2007.
30	Scheffer and others 2012.
31	Klein and others 2007.
32	Goulson and others 2015.
33	Foster, Royer and Lunt 2017.
34	Steffen and others 2018.
35	Lenton and Watson 2011.
36	Lenton and Latour 2018.
37	Rockström and others 2009a.
38	Barabás, Michalska-Smith and Allesina 2017.
39	Lenton and others 2018.
40	Maynard Smith and Szathmáry 1995.
41	Falanruw 1984.
42	Scheffer and others 2012.
43	Lenton 2020.

Existential risks to humanity

Toby Ord, Senior Research Fellow, The Future of Humanity Institute, University of Oxford

Humanity has a vast history, spanning hundreds of thousands of years. If all goes well, we can look forward to a future of equal or greater length. And just as our past saw profound expansions in our capabilities —through our lifespans, our education, our prosperity and our freedoms—so the future offers the possibility for this development to continue. We have the potential for every place on Earth to reach the highest standards seen today and to continue far beyond what has yet been achieved.

But this potential is at risk. Like every species, humanity has always been subject to the risk of extinction from natural catastrophes. And to this we have added risks of our own. Humanity's power over the world around us has increased tremendously over the past 200,000 years. In the 20th century, with the development of nuclear weapons, we became so powerful that we posed a threat to our own continued survival. This risk declined with the end of the Cold War but did not disappear. And it was joined by other risks that could threaten our continued existence, such as extreme climate change.

The 20th century thus ushered in a new period in which humanity has acquired the power to end its story without yet achieving the collective wisdom to ensure it does not. This period of heightened risk, known as the Precipice,[1] is closely related to the Anthropocene—indeed one suggested definition for the Anthropocene would have them begin at the same moment: 16 July 1945, when the first atomic bomb was detonated. Just as the Earth has entered a geological period in which humanity is the dominant force shaping the planet, so humanity has entered a historical period in which the dominant risks to its survival come from humanity itself. Both periods were triggered by our increasing power but may end at very different times: We could imagine a future in which humanity has found a path to safety, creating new institutions to govern global risks, such that while humanity continues to shape

the planet, it has ceased to pose a substantial risk to itself.

To understand humanity's predicament, it is helpful to define two terms:
- An existential catastrophe is the destruction of humanity's long-term potential.
- An existential risk is a risk that threatens the destruction of humanity's long-term potential.[2]

The most obvious form of existential catastrophe would be human extinction, for it is clear how that would permanently foreclose our potential (figure S1.3.1). But there could be other forms too. A global collapse of civilization would also count, if it were so deep and unrecoverable that it destroyed

Figure S1.3.1 Three types of existential catastrophe

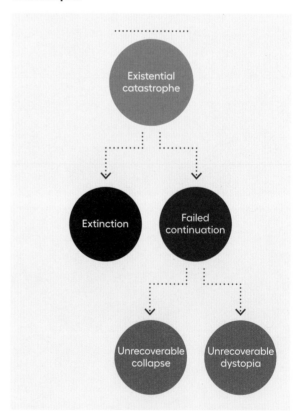

Source: Reproduced from Ord (2020).

(most of) humanity's potential. And it may also be possible for civilization to survive but be drawn into an unrecoverable dystopian future, with little value remaining.

What these outcomes have in common is that they would foreclose the possibility of human development. If such a catastrophe occurred even once, the great gains we have achieved would be permanently undone, and the possibility of reaching a more equal or more just world would be gone forever. Such risks thus threaten the most basic foundations on which almost all other value rests.

The risks

What risks could pose such a threat to our long-term potential? The most well understood are the natural risks. Take the possibility of a large asteroid impact. The mass extinction at the end of the Cretaceous 65 million years ago is widely agreed to have been caused by an asteroid, 10 kilometres in diameter, colliding with the Earth. The impact threw vast amounts of dust and ash into the stratosphere—so high that it could not be rained out. Atmospheric circulation spread this dark cloud around the planet and caused a massive global cooling, lasting years. The effects were so severe that all land-based vertebrates weighing more than 5 kilograms were killed.[3]

Scientists now have a good understanding of the chance that such an asteroid could hit us again. It is reassuringly low (table S1.3.1). In a typical century the chance of being struck by a 10 kilometre across asteroid would be just 1 in 1.5 million.[4] What about the next 100 years in particular? Scientists have modelled the orbits of all four known near-Earth asteroids of that size and confirmed that they will not hit the Earth in the next 100 years. So the remaining chance lies in the unlikely possibility that one remains undiscovered. The situation is somewhat less reassuring with asteroids between 1 and 10 kilometres across, for which detection and tracking are incomplete. Fortunately, they would also be less likely to cause a truly unrecoverable catastrophe.

Asteroids are the best-understood existential risk. They clearly pose a risk of human extinction (or unrecoverable collapse), but the risk is well understood and small. Moreover, they are the best managed existential risk: There is an effective international

Table S1.3.1 Progress in tracking large near-Earth asteroids

Asteroid diameter	Number	Percentage found	Chance of being struck in an average century	Change of being struck in next century
1–10 kilometres	~920	~95	1 in 6,000	1 in 120,000
10 or more kilometres	~4	> 99	1 in 1.5 million	< 1 in 150 million

Source: Adapted from Ord (2020).

research programme directly working on detecting and understanding these threats.

There are several other known natural existential risks, including comets and supervolcanic eruptions. These are less well understood than asteroids and may pose a greater risk. Because most of these risks were discovered only within the last century, there are presumably unknown natural risks too.

Fortunately, there is a way of using the fossil record to estimate an upper bound for the total extinction risk from all natural hazards—including those that have not yet been discovered. Since humanity has survived the entire array of natural risks for thousands of centuries, the chance of extinction per century must be correspondingly small. This produces a range of estimates depending on how broad we take "humanity" to be (table S1.3.2). We can also estimate this natural extinction risk via how long related species have survived, with a range of estimates depending on how closely related they are (table S1.3.3). Both techniques suggest that the total natural extinction risk is almost certainly below 1 in 300 per century and more likely to be 1 in 2,000 or lower.[5]

Unfortunately, there is no similar argument to help estimate the total anthropogenic risk because the track record is too short. Surviving 75 years since the invention of nuclear weapons does very little to

Table S1.3.2 Estimates and bounds of total natural extinction risk per century based on how long humanity has survived, using three conceptions of humanity

Conception of humanity	Years	Best guess of risk	99.9 percent confidence bound
Homo sapiens	200,000	< 1 in 2,000	< 1 in 300
Neanderthal split	500,000	< 1 in 5,000	< 1 in 700
Homo	2,000,000 – 3,000,000	< 1 in 20,000	< 1 in 4,000

Source: Adapted from Ord (2020).

Table S1.3.3 Estimates of total natural extinction risk per century based on the survival time of related species

Species	Years	Best guess of risk
Homo neanderthalensis	200,000	1 in 2,000
Homo heidelbergensis	400,000	1 in 4,000
Homo habilis	600,000	1 in 6,000
Homo erectus	1,700,000	1 in 17,000
Mammals	1,000,000	1 in 10,000
All species	1,000,000–10,000,000	1 in 100,000–1 in 10,000

Source: Adapted from Ord (2020).

constrain the amount of existential risk from nuclear weapons over a century. We therefore have to confront the possibility that this risk may be substantial.

In the early 1980s scientists discovered that nuclear war could create a global cooling effect similar to that of large asteroid impacts.[6] While initially controversial, subsequent research has mostly supported this "nuclear winter" effect in which ash from burning cities would rise into the stratosphere, causing severe cooling lasting for years.[7] This would cause massive crop failures and widespread starvation. Researchers studying nuclear winter now suggest that

a collapse of civilization might be possible, though it would be very difficult for nuclear winter to directly cause human extinction.[8]

Fortunately, the existential risk posed by nuclear war has been declining. Since the late 1980s the size of the nuclear arsenals has been substantially reduced, lowering the severity of an ensuing nuclear winter (figure S1.3.2). This appears to stem in part from concern about the existential risk the weapons posed, with both US President Ronald Reagan and USSR General Secretary Mikhail Gorbachev reporting that the possibility of nuclear winter weighed heavily on their minds.[9] Another major reduction in risk was the end of the Cold War, which has reduced the chance that the arsenals will be used at all. However, the chance has by no means been eliminated: Nuclear war could still begin through an accidental launch (and retaliation) or if tensions between great powers flare up once more.

Climate change may also pose an existential risk to humanity. Much of the scientific focus has been on the most likely scenarios. While these could be devastating by any normal measure, they would not be existential catastrophes. But some of the extreme possibilities may reach that threshold. For example,

Figure S1.3.2 While there have been substantial reductions in the number of active stockpiled nuclear warheads, the total number—especially in the Russian Federation and the United States—remains high

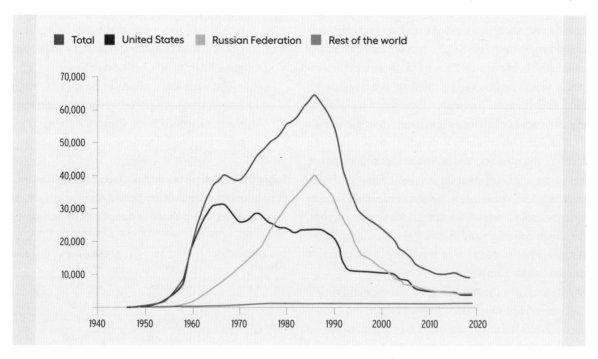

Source: Reproduced from Ord (2020) and adapted from Kristensen and Korda (2019).

we cannot yet rule out climate feedbacks taking us substantially beyond 6 degrees Celsius of warming —perhaps as far as 10 degrees Celsius or more.[10] It would be extremely valuable to have a better idea of the likelihood of such extreme scenarios and of whether civilization, or humanity itself, would survive them. But the lack of scientific research on them means existential risk from climate change remains poorly understood.

Several of the greatest catastrophes in human history have been caused by pandemics. The Black Death of 1347 killed 25–50 percent of people in Europe—about a tenth of the world's population.[11] The introduction of diseases from Europe (beginning in 1492) may have killed as much as 90 percent of the population in the Americas—again about a tenth of the world's population.[12] The 1918 flu killed roughly 3 percent of the world's population.[13]

So the current worldwide pandemic is not at all unprecedented. It is the worst pandemic in a century, but far from the worst in a millennium. Indeed, it is the idea that such catastrophes were left forever behind us that would have been unprecedented. Covid-19 shows us that this is false, that humanity is still vulnerable to global catastrophes. While we have made substantial improvements in medicine and public health (which have greatly reduced the burden of endemic disease), it is unclear whether we are any safer from pandemics. This is because there are also ways that human activity has made pandemics more dangerous, such as intensive farming, urbanization and rapid international travel. So even when pandemics are natural in origin, the argument for bounding natural extinction risk does not apply—that argument assumes the risk has been stable or declining over human history, which may not be true here. Though Covid-19 itself does not pose an existential risk to humanity, other pandemics might.[14]

And this situation looks considerably worse when we consider the possibility of engineered pandemics. Humanity has a long and dark history with using disease as a weapon, dating back at least 3,000 years.[15] Indeed, there are credible claims that the Black Death was introduced into Europe by catapulting plague-ridden bodies into the besieged city of Caffa on the Crimean Peninsula.[16] The 20th century saw many countries adopt major biological weapons programmes, and while these were officially outlawed by the Biological Weapons Convention of 1972, it would be a serious mistake to think that the convention has stopped all bioweapons programmes.[17] Though it is an important symbol and a useful forum, it is very under-resourced: with just four employees and a budget smaller than that of a typical McDonald's.

Biotechnology is advancing at an extremely rapid rate. And while these advances bear great promise for medical and industrial progress, they also aid progress in biological weaponry. This makes the weapons of a major state more powerful and opens up the possibility of extremely damaging weapons being deployed by small nations or subnational groups. If biotechnology continues to advance, this may create a very unstable strategic situation.

And there are other important technological risks on the horizon, such as those posed by advanced artificial intelligence and nanotechnology.[18] The sheer variety of these risks suggests that a piecemeal, siloed, approach—in which we hope that each risk will be dealt with separately by the relevant community —becomes increasingly hard, and a more unified approach is needed.

The anthropogenic risks are inherently more speculative than the natural risks, since it is impossible to acquire evidence of them having happened before. But this does not make them smaller. We saw that natural risk almost certainly totals less than 1 in 300 per century. How confident would we be that humanity could expect to survive 300 centuries like the 20th century? Or like the 21st? Using the fossil record, we can be more than 99.7 percent confident we will survive the natural risks of the next 100 years. How confident can we be that we survive the human-made risks? While we cannot be sure, reflections such as this make it seem likely that anthropogenic risks are now the greater threat to our future, posing an unsustainable level of risk (box S1.3.1).

Analysis

The world is only just beginning to understand the scale and severity of existential risk. The substantial work on the risks of nuclear war and climate change still pales in comparison with the importance of the topics. And little of this work has been directed to the parts of these problems most relevant to existential

Box S1.3.1 Existential risk as sustainability

Protecting humanity's long-term potential is a key form of sustainability. The current period of heightened anthropogenic risk is unsustainable—we can get lucky for a while, but eventually the odds are going to catch up with us. In many other cases people can do well by taking calculated risks, but here our entire bankroll is on the line, so if we eventually lose—even once—there is no coming back.

We could thus think of our accumulated existential risk over humanity's future as a kind of risk budget—a budget that has to last for our entire lifespan, the ultimate nonrenewable resource. Responsible stewardship of humanity's potential would involve lowering this risk as quickly as possible and setting in place the safeguards to keep it low in order to allow humanity to flourish for as long as possible.

risk (such as better understanding nuclear winter or extreme climate feedbacks).

It is helpful to look at why existential risk is so neglected.

First, protection from existential risk is an intergenerational global public good. Standard economic theory thus predicts a market failure in which individual nations cannot capture more than a small fraction of the benefits and are tempted to free-ride on each other, undersupplying this protection.

Second, many of the risks are inherently international—beyond any individual nation's ability to solve, were one even prepared to do so. International cooperation and coordination are thus required but move much slower than technology. If we remain in a paradigm in which a new agreement is required for each new risk and can be achieved only decades after the risk rises to prominence, we might forever be playing catchup.

Third, minimizing existential risk just feels like too big a task for most nations—something that is outside the scope of their usual responsibilities or "above the pay grade" of their leaders. Yet nations have not officially passed this responsibility up to the international level, entrusting an international institution with key tasks relating to monitoring, assessing or minimizing existential risks. Responsibility for protecting humanity's long-term potential thus falls through the cracks between the national and international spheres.

Fourth, the whole idea of existential risks to humanity is very recent. We have been exposed to anthropogenic existential risks for only 75 years, most of which was spent in the grip of a Cold War. Our ethics and our institutions have not had time to catch up.

As we begin to wake up to the present situation, we will face great challenges. But there will also be new opportunities. Responses that first seemed impossible may become possible—and in time even inevitable. As Ulrich Beck put it, "One can make two diametrically opposed kinds of assertion: global risks inspire paralysing terror, or: global risks create new room for action."[19]

We have seen that the rise in anthropogenic risk means that most of the existential risk we face likely arises from our own actions. While this is a disturbing trend, there is a flip side that should give us hope: Humanity's future is largely within humanity's control. If a 10 kilometre across asteroid were on a trajectory to hit the Earth in 10 years, there might truly be nothing we could do to stop it. But the risks from nuclear war, climate change and engineered pandemics arise from activities that humans perform—and thus that humans can stop.

There are serious challenges to doing so— challenges of international coordination, verification and policing—as well as the overarching challenge of creating the political will for action. But these are not insurmountable.[20] If we fail, it will not be because there was no way through but because we were distracted by other issues or were not willing to do the necessary work. If we set our minds to it, taking the risks with due seriousness and adopting the protection of humanity's long-term potential as one of the overarching missions of our time, then our generation could very well be the one that sets humanity on a path towards a long, secure future.

NOTES

1   Ord 2020.

2   The idea of existential risk was introduced by Bostrom (2002). Earlier work on the ethics of human extinction includes Leslie (1996), Parfit (1984), Sagan (1983) and Schell (1982).

3   Longrich, Scriberas and Wills 2016.

4   Stokes and others 2017.

5   See also Snyder-Beattie, Ord and Bonsall (2019).

6   Sagan 1983.

7   Robock, Oman and Stenchikov 2007.

8   For example, Richard Turco (Browne 1990): "My personal opinion is that the human race wouldn't become extinct, but civilization as we know it certainly would." And Alan Robock (Conn, Toon and Robock 2016): "Carl [Sagan] used to talk about extinction of the human species, but I think that was an exaggeration. ... But you wouldn't have any modern medicine. ... You wouldn't have any civilization."

9   Hertsgaard 2000; Reagan 1985.

10   See Ord 2020.

11   See Ord 2020.

12   See Ord 2020.

13   Taubenberger and Morens (2006) estimate 50 million deaths, which would be 2.8 percent of the 1918 world population of 1.8 billion.

14   Snyder-Beattie, Ord and Bonsall 2019.

15   Trevisanato 2007.

16   Kelly 2006.

17   Countries that are confirmed to have had bioweapons programmes include Canada (1940–1958), Egypt (1960s–?), France (1915–1966?), Germany (1915–1918), Iraq (1974–1991), Israel (1948–?), Italy (1934–1940), Japan (1934–1945), Poland (?), Rhodesia (1977), South Africa (1981–1993), Soviet Union (1928–1991), Syrian Arab Republic (1970s?–?), United Kingdom (1940–1957) and United States (1941–1971). See Carus (2017).

18   For more on existential risk from artificial intelligence, see Bostrom (2014) and Russell (2019). For existential risk from nanotechnology, see Drexler 2013.

19   Beck 2009, p. 57.

20   For a list of concrete policy and research proposals that would make a difference, see Ord (2020).

Conversations on rethinking human development: Ideas emerging from a global dialogue

The global dialogue was co-organized by the International Science Council and the United Nations Development Programme

In collaboration with the International Science Council, the United Nations Development Programme and the Human Development Report Office launched a platform to seek views, inputs and aspirations about what human development means today and how it can evolve in the future. Rethinking human development is not a one-off exercise. It is a continuing process requiring dialogue, a journey towards new understandings that hears a wide diversity of voices from the natural and social sciences, humanities, decisionmakers and wider public. This spotlight synthesizes inputs reflecting multiple perspectives on nine topics.

A fresh start for rethinking the meaning of development

Several contributions noted that the term "development" is loaded with history, values, politics and orthodoxies. The term has also become entrenched with ideas and ideologies that obscure important elements, such as the value of people's inner lives or the role of power relations in perpetuating poverty and vulnerability. Many argued for decolonizing development, which requires actively challenging these power relations, while recognizing development as positive change for everyone everywhere, nuanced by diverse societal priorities. Some further alternative meanings of the term emerging from evolutionary biology and social psychology were invoked. Others relate to its distinctive meaning in medicine and the human sciences, with passages from conception to birth to childhood to adulthood to old age and death. From the human sciences perspective the development and maintenance of good physical and psychological health are central. Indeed, concepts of personal, family and social wellbeing and happiness are closely linked to mental wellbeing, with the foundations created early in the life course.

Visionary rethinking of our humanity

As with the term "development," several contributions argued for the need to rethink "human," our humanity. Moving beyond the assumption that economic production is the primary driver of wellbeing to a deep dive into the conditions that make us humans living in diverse cultures who each need to be valued and that provided each of us with an identity that is key to our wellbeing. Rethinking our humanity includes recognizing the co-construction of human and nonhuman natures and the intimate connectedness, for our individual and collective wellbeing, with the natural environment, with all living things and their dynamism and agency, whether in our bodies, homes, communities, ecologies or planet. Connectedness to one another across societies in multicultural settings and the connectedness created by transnational webs leading to a global community of humans are fundamental elements of shaping human development in the 21st century.

Strengthening institutions and accountability

Moving to implementation, the contributions emphasized how institutions and accountability are central for operationalizing human development as freedom. Institutions work for humanity but also protect all the nonhuman elements that make humanity possible—functioning socioecological systems, including climate and biodiversity—and address the challenges of rapid technological change. Moreover, the measures to adapt to unavoidable climate change impacts and roll out the needed mitigation strategies to prevent catastrophic tipping points would be possible only with accountable institutions that create the needed incentives. These incentives require international, transnational and global institutions that take the world towards collective action, countering aggressive nationalism and revitalizing multilateralism, ensuring that global responsibilities are assumed in addressing global challenges.

Human development is possible only within planetary boundaries

The tendency to pit economic development against the environment has led the world towards a dead end. Several voices called to reinterweave them, just as humanity is interwoven with the health of nonhuman natures and ultimately the planet. The notion of responsible wellbeing was suggested as being cognizant of the implications of consumption and accountability and the ways to factor in the interests of future generations. Responsible wellbeing for people and planet is about internalizing environmental and social costs in the true value of goods and services, recognizing that the value extends well beyond the monetary. It is about conceptualizing the systems underpinning humanity as socioecological or socionatural systems—and development as positive change in those systems. If we wish to celebrate another 30 years of human development, attention must extend to all societies and to the behaviour of citizens who have already achieved high levels of human development on traditional measures.

Social cohesion and mitigating inequalities are enablers—not just prerequisites—for human development

It was frequently emphasized that a reconceptualization of human development that addresses cohesion across and within society—relations between countries or across generations and relations with nonhuman natures and ecologies—is threatened by a grossly unequal world and by the narratives, technologies and processes that perpetuate inequalities. Social cohesion requires vertical and horizontal trust within societies while respecting diversity of beliefs and worldviews. Enhancing social cohesion, mitigating inequalities and restoring the value of social and socionatural relations require the inclusion of multiple voices and perspectives. We have to seriously attend to the structural conditions and violence creating and perpetuating inequalities—and listen to and include the experiences and priorities of those most marginalized. Rethinking human development is an open journey for all, beyond governments and agencies, beyond experts and academics. It thus demands democratic deliberation.

Democratic deliberation is needed for resilient socioecological systems

Individual and community empowerment allowing for democratic deliberation—local, national and transnational—is a critical channel to get us there, many emphasized. This does not always or necessarily mean democracy, as defined by particular formal representative institutions and practices, or political and historical traditions, while recognizing that healthy institutions are necessary for us to live in large social and socioecological networks. Moreover, the broad rethinking of our humanity by and for all its members and recognizing our interconnectedness with nonhuman natures in legitimate democratic processes are key for generating the consensus and the institutions capable of doing the very difficult work of avoiding dangerous planetary change. The connectedness between people and planet and among societies—and the many other global interdependencies that have emerged in the past three decades—call for cultures of global cooperation and structures of global governance that enable transnational democratic deliberation.

Making the digital age work for human development

Big Data has become the new oil. As with fossil fuels, it has led to great advances and great harm, particularly threatening individual, social and institutional wellbeing. And as with fossil fuels, there is a need to address these matters in a way that transcends national boundaries. Yet just a few private companies dominate the digital sphere, driven by competitive short-term market gains, in a governance vacuum, without appropriate public and private regulation. Furthermore, human enhancement approaches, such as synthetic biology, genome research and digital technologies are coming together, which opens the possibility of transforming not just the planet but ourselves as humans, posing fundamental ethical and broader challenges. Hence the importance of moving towards fair and sustainable value chains for technology components, while redressing the huge technical and knowledge gaps. For many, even access to the internet is a challenge, and digital technologies and the capabilities to create, use and deploy them are still limited. But investments and innovation driven by a new conception of value can put technologies to work for human development.

Value—a new narrative

When GDP growth and macroeconomic stability are considered the key signposts of development, they are often presented as value-free concepts, desirable because of their efficiency in bringing about other positive outcomes. Yet GDP is used as a proxy for anything valuable while being presented as a measurement devoid of any normative context. This contradiction is a true sleight of hand. Our economies and public policy solutions are skewed against human development precisely because of the way we tend to understand "value," giving GDP growth a central role, discounting the future and any social and environmental harm. This misguided view of value, which considers activities harmful to people and to the environment as creating value, also fails to account for the true value of social services, social protection mechanisms or public goods.

The role of scientific knowledge

Science, in relation to human development, can be conceptualized broadly to include not just natural, health and technical sciences but also knowledge from the social sciences, arts and humanities. Several voices emphasized the need to learn to readjust and rebalance the interactions among the three major systems that shape our civilization: human systems, earth systems and technological and infrastructure systems. Science is not well prepared. There still is far too little cooperation between the natural and the social sciences and between the humanities and the medical sciences. Nor do all those sciences interact well with technology and engineering. Dominant scientific traditions must become more prepared to question their categories, languages and assumptions, including the relationship between human and nonhuman natures, and more open to dialogue with diverse scientific and other knowledge cultures. Transdisciplinary approaches must be promoted to break down the institutional barriers and reconcile the different logics of public and private research and innovation to progress in badly needed dialogue.

NOTE

For more information and a full account of the contributions, see https://stories.council.science/stories-human-development/. The global dialogue's steering group comprised Peter Gluckman, President-elect, International Science Council; Melissa Leach, Director, Institute of Development Studies; Dirk Messner, President, German Environmental Agency; Elisa Reis, Vice President, International Science Council; Binyam Sisay Mendisu, Program Officer, United Nations Educational, Scientific and Cultural Organization–International Institute for Capacity Building in Africa, Associate Professor of Linguistics, Addis Ababa University, Member of the Global Young Academy; Asunción Lera St. Clair, Program Director, Digital Assurance, DNV GL – Group Technology and Research; Heide Hackmann, Chief Executive Officer, International Science Council; Pedro Conceição, Director, Human Development Report Office, United Nations Development Programme.

A tale told to the future

David Farrier, author of *Footprints: In Search of Future Fossils,* Professor of Literature and the Environment at the University of Edinburgh

Imagine you could tell a story that would last for nearly 40,000 years.

The Gunditjmara people of southeastern Australia have a tale of four giants, creators of the early Earth, who arrived on land from the sea. Three strode off to other parts of the country, but one stayed behind. He lay down, and his body took the form of a volcano, called Tappoc in the Dhauwurd Wurrong language, while his head became another, called Budj Bim. When Budj Bim erupted, so the story goes, "the lava spat out as the head burst through the earth forming his teeth."[1]

The story occurs in the Dreaming, the mythic time in which the world was made, according to indigenous Australian cultures. But we can also place it in geological time. The discovery of a stone axe beneath tephra layers deposited when Budj Bim erupted around 37,000 years ago suggests that humans were living in the area and therefore could have witnessed the eruption. It would have been sudden; scientists think the volcano might have grown from ground level to tens of metres high in a matter of months or even just weeks.[2] Other Gunditjmara legends describe a time when the land shook and the trees danced. Budj Bim could be the oldest continually told story in the world.[3]

Many indigenous Australian peoples are thought to have lived on the same land for almost 50,000 years.[4] It is difficult to imagine that life in the developed world, governed by the propulsion of technological innovation and the spasms of election cycles, is as deeply embedded in time. Yet the cumulative effect of our occupation will be a legacy imprinted on the planet's geology, biodiversity and atmospheric and oceanic chemistry that will persist for hundreds of thousands of years—and in some cases even hundreds of millions.

Nearly 1,500 generations separate us from the people who first told the story of Budj Bim 37,000 years ago. In 100,000 years, or 4,000 generations from now, the Earth's atmosphere might still bear a trace of the carbon dioxide added to it since the Industrial Revolution.[5] The biologist Edward O. Wilson observed that it took tens of millions of years for biodiversity to recover following each of the last five major extinctions. Recovery from the most recent, the Cretaceous, which saw off the dinosaurs along with 75 percent of plant and animal species, took 20 million years.[6] If the current extinction crisis reaches the same pitch of ruin, 800,000 human generations would pass before our descendants live in a world as rich in life as the one we are destroying.

The ancient Gunditjmara story tells of the land remaking itself; ours will tell of the world remade by human action, a presence written so deeply in time that it will far outstrip the Gunditjmara's oldest tale.

The incredible extent of our reach through deep time is perhaps best illustrated by contemplating the fate of our cities. The world's megacities are dense concentrations of durable, artificial materials such as concrete, steel, plastic and glass. These are some of the largest cities that have ever existed, and they are threatened by seas that could rise by up to a metre by the end of the century and continue to rise for several centuries more. Shanghai, home to 26 million people, has sunk by more than 2.5 metres in the last 100 years, due to groundwater extraction and the weight of its immense skyscrapers, built on soft, boggy ground.[7]

Some megacities lie in regions being uplifted by geological processes. Over time they will be worn away just as hills and mountains are eroded. But others stand on ground that is sinking. If the waters rise to cover these cities, they will begin a long descent into the Earth, and a slow, patient process of fossilization. Thick mud will wash through the streets and the ground floors of buildings, coating them in preserving sediment. For thousands of years, abandoned towers will slowly crumble until there is nothing left above the surface. Anything beneath the ground, however, will submit to pressure and time, condensing over millions of years into what geologist Jan Zalasiewicz calls "the urban stratum," a layer of artificial materials in the geologic record.[8] In the foundations of tall buildings, concrete and brick will demineralize, glass will devitrify and iron reacting with sulphides will acquire the golden sheen of pyrite. The remains of subterranean shopping malls will be punctuated by the fossil outlines of countless everyday objects, from bottle caps to bicycle wheels; miles of subway tracks, perhaps even the twisted remains of a train carriage, will be preserved. Much will be lost, but even a fraction of this abundance will be enough to give the precise outlines of city life as it was once lived.

Life today will become the palaeontology of the future. One hundred million years from now, a city like Shanghai could be compressed into a metre-thick layer in the rock, hundreds of kilometres down.[9]

However, we do not need to peer this far ahead in order to glimpse the world to come. The future is hurtling towards us, and it looks to be a lot like the deep past. There is nothing that resembles the coming climate in all of human history; the nearest analogue would be the mid-Pliocene, 3 million years ago, when atmospheric carbon last exceeded 400 parts per million. The current emissions trajectory could render climates more like the Eocene by 2150, "effectively rewinding the climate clock by approximately 50 My [million years], reversing a multimillion year cooling trend in less than two centuries."[10]

Global warming is "scrambling our sense of time," writes David Wallace Wells.[11] It both accelerates and unwinds history, compressing millennia of change into decades and stretching time so that carbon burned to serve a moment of convenience will linger in the atmosphere and influence the climate for thousands of years.

Even as things accelerate, the present contains much more time than we tend to think. The situation calls us to cultivate a deep time perspective. We need long-term thinking in how we use resources, how we design our cities, how we trade and travel; intergenerational minds that accept the claim of the unborn on how we live now. To do this, we need to think about the stories we tell, and those we listen to. In fact, to really develop a frame of mind that spans generations, we need to change how we think about stories altogether.

In *Transcendence,* her account of the evolution of human culture, Gaia Vince writes that the first stories were exercises in time travel, as the very first storytellers found it was to their advantage to direct the attention of the group to a threat or an opportunity that lay beyond the here and now.[12] Stories gave us time, shaping our capacity for narrative, which in turn shaped how we came to perceive the world, providing our ancestors with both a cultural memory bank and a predictive tool.

Stories provide both an inheritance and a window onto possible futures. What if we were to think of our material traces—our plastic waste or carbon emissions—not as the byproducts of a developed way of life, or even as the pollution that future generations will be forced to contend with, but as stories, as tales told to the future? Embracing this way of thinking would mean we were better placed to choose the kind of world we will pass on.

For too long we have listened to a single story, one in which land is only ever tap or sink and growth overthrows balance. It is essentially the story of a minority who, in pursuit of a particular way of life, put all life on the planet at risk. In *Braiding Sweetgrass,* botanist and member of the Citizen Potawatomi Nation Robin Wall Kimmerer recounts the Anishinaabe legend of the Windigo, who was transformed from a man into a creature of pure appetite. Ten feet tall, with lips chewed ragged and bloody by his insatiable hunger, the Windigo stalks people through "the hungry time" of winter. The more he eats, the greater his hunger becomes, Kimmerer says, so that the Windigo represents a kind of positive feedback. Today he walks wherever we find feedback loops, from melting permafrost accelerating warming by releasing methane, to melting ice darkening the poles and absorbing more heat. But perhaps the greater feedback loop is in the developed world's growth-driven economic model. "Windigo," Kimmerer writes, "is the name for that within us which cares more for its own survival than for anything else."[13]

Climate change confronts us with a fundamental truth: that our individual stories are braided with the stories of every living thing on the planet and of countless lives yet to be born. Decisions taken in the next decades will shape the story of life on Earth for generations to come. Like the graphs that plot different warming trajectories, 1.5, 2, 3 degrees Celsius or more, the threads of many different future Earths spool out from this moment. The thread we follow will connect us to people living decades, generations, even millennia in the future. It will determine whether our descendants will be riding in a tourist boat through the drowned streets of an abandoned Venice, fighting in water wars caused by the loss of Himalayan glaciers or fleeing with millions of others from storm, drought and flood or whether they will live in cities designed to be sustainable, in a world that is damaged but moving closer each day towards balance, in which fossil fuels, rather than megafauna, are a distant memory.

Climate change is also a matter of temporal equality. The human climate niche—the narrow climate window that permitted human societies to develop and flourish since the end of the last ice age—is closing, but not for all; or at least, not at the same time. Without action to arrest emissions, over the course of the next 50 years 1–3 billion people (overwhelmingly in the Global South) could be "left outside the climate conditions that have served humanity well over the past 6,000 years,"[14] as large parts of the planet would become uninhabitable. Already, the very worst effects of global warming are focused on some of the poorest nations.[15] By 2070 we could see a situation of global temporal apartheid, as the Global North continues (although probably only temporarily) to enjoy something like the world as human societies have always known it, while the Global South is exiled to a version of the planet unlike anything that humans have ever experienced before.[16]

Unheeding consumption cannot be the only story. Kimmerer also recounts the Mayan creation myth: When the gods set out to populate the Earth, they made a people of mud, who melted in the rain. Next the gods made a people of wood and reed, whose cleverness filled the world with made things but who lacked compassion in their hearts. So the gods made a people of light, who were so beautiful, and proud of their beauty, that they thought they could do without the gods altogether. Finally, the gods made a people from corn. These people could sing praise and offer gratitude to the world that sustained them; "and so," Kimmerer says, "they were the people who were sustained upon the earth."[17]

Indigenous peoples' creation stories, Kimmerer writes, imagine time as a lake rather than a river—a pooling of past, present and future. The story of the people of corn is both history and prophecy: which people are we, the people of wood or the people of corn, and which could we become?[18] It invites us to contemplate a different relationship to time; to realize that moment by moment the present in which we live is accompanied by the deep past and the distant future. Facing this reality is the first step to deciding which story we want to tell.

We enter this crucial period with life reconfigured by the Covid-19 pandemic. The human cost has been intolerable, and much of the world has yet to truly reckon with the challenge of living in the long term with the virus. But the disruption of the pandemic has also emphasized the scale of the environmental challenge. Despite the massive drop in heavy industry, air traffic and consumption, global greenhouse gas emissions will have declined by only 8 percent by the end of 2020,[19] roughly equivalent to the annual reduction we need to achieve between now and 2050 if we are to limit global mean temperature rise to 1.5 degrees Celsius.[20]

Still, the window has been opened, just a crack, on a world driven by care for the most vulnerable rather than by the illusion of infinite growth. "If a New World were discovered now, would we be able to *see it?*" Italo Calvino once asked.[21] We cannot help but acknowledge the new world before us. We are stewards of a story we did not begin, and we have no choice but to carry it forward. Yet we can also have a say in how the story goes.

Walter Benjamin writes of an Egyptian king, Psammenitus, who, according to Herodotus, was defeated by the Persians and made to watch as his people were led into slavery. He remained impassive even while first his daughter, then his son were led past. Only when he saw an old man, a former servant, stumble along at the procession's tale, did king's grief break over him. Successive generations have wondered why Psammenitus wept at the suffering of the old man and not at those closest to him, Benjamin recounts.[22] Future generations might also wonder how we could be unmoved by the procession of disaster, as the waves engulf low-lying nations, crops fail and whole regions become uninhabitable. Or might they tell the story of how, finally, we were shaken from our inertia by those at the tail end of the procession of development but at the frontline of climate change?

The world is a gift that we can only pass on. Every material and chemical trace, each remade landscape and coastline, is a tale told to the future, so long lasting it will resemble a kind of continuous occupation like that of the Gunditjmara. But the world does not stand still. Stories can be changed in the telling.

NOTES

1   Gunditjmara People and Wettenhall (2010), quoted in Matchan and others (2020, p. 390).

2   Gunditjmara People and Wettenhall (2010), quoted in Matchan and others (2020).

3   Gunditjmara People and Wettenhall (2010), quoted in Matchan and others (2020).

4   Tobler and others 2017.

5   Archer 2005.

6   Wilson 1999.

7   Farrier 2020.

8   Zalasiewicz and Freedman 2009.

9   Zalasiewicz and Freedman 2009.

10   Burke and others 2018, p. 13288.

11   Wallace-Wells 2020.

12   Vince 2020.

13   Kimmerer 2013, p. 304.

14   Xu and others 2020, p. 11350.

15   UNFCCC 2018.

16   Xu and others 2020.

17   Kimmerer 2013, p. 343.

18   Kimmerer 2013.

19   IEA 2020c.

20   UNFCCC 2019.

21   Calvino 2013, p. 10.

22   Benjamin 1973.

Developing humanity for a changed planet

Gaia Vince, science writer and author of *Transcendence: How Humans Evolved through Fire, Language, Beauty and Time* and *Adventures in the Anthropocene: A Journey to the Heart of the Planet We Made*

For the endangered olive ridley sea turtle, life is a challenge faced alone. From the moment a clutch of eggs is deposited in a sandy beach pit, each embryo faces its own private battle for survival. The odds are stacked against it even surviving long enough to be born. During the turtle's 50-day gestation, the eggs are frequently damaged or dug up by dogs and birds or harvested by people for their value as a delicacy. Any hatchling that emerges undisturbed must then unbury itself and cross the open beach to reach the ocean—all without being eaten. Only a tiny percentage of turtle eggs will go on to become adults that live as long as 50 years.

What counts as a good life for the solitary olive ridley turtle? Perhaps, living long enough to successfully mate with one of the vanishingly few others of its type and producing living descendants. Perhaps it is to be pain-free; to escape boat damage, plastic pollution and fishing net entanglement; to be able to satisfy its hunger in overfished and depleted seas. Its existence is driven entirely by its biology and environment, a lifestyle of swimming, feeding and occasionally mating, that remains almost unchanged since the species evolved more than 30 million years ago.

Humans, though, are different. We, who wonder about the life lived by a turtle, want more for our own lives. We have become exceptionally good at survival, but this is not enough—it has never been enough for our species. Humans have needs and desires that go far beyond receiving an adequate number of calories. We want these needs to be met for ourselves and our families, but we also want this for strangers in distant lands whom we will never meet.

The needs, rights and desires of humans have changed and evolved over time, unlike those of the olive ridley turtle. But for both species, at its most fundamental, a good life rests on having a safe environment in which to thrive. For humans this includes not just the physical environment but also the social environment. We want people to be able to live a good life with their basic needs met, such as clean water and sanitation, and their human rights respected, such as access to education. We hope to achieve this and more for every human on Earth through "development."

What does human development mean? What does it mean to develop as a person? These are two different but entwined questions, and they go to the heart of what it means to be a human rather than, say, a turtle, on this rapidly transforming planet.

All life evolves as biology adapts to environmental pressures. This is how the turtle got its hard shell and we got our sweating skin. Over billions of years, a great diversity of life forms has evolved, each adapted for its niche within complex ecosystems in the grander biosphere. Deep in our ancestry, hominins diverged from the evolutionary path taken by all other creatures and pioneered a new type of development driven by cumulative culture. Just as genetic information is passed down through generations of families, humans also pass a whole suite of cultural information through societies and down the generations, including knowledge, behaviours, tools, languages and values. By learning from each other, teaching each other and relying on each other for resources, human culture ratchets up in complexity and diversity over generations to produce increasingly more efficient solutions to life's challenges.

In this way human cultural evolution allows us to solve many of the same adaptive problems as genetic evolution, only faster and without speciation. Our societies of cooperating, interconnected individuals work collectively, enjoying great efficiencies in the way they harvest energy and resources. It is our collective culture, even more than our individual intelligence, that makes us smarter than the other animals, and it is this that creates the extraordinary nature of us: a species with the ability to be not simply the objects of a transformative cosmos, but agents of our own transformation.

Our cumulative culture relies on an exceptional degree of cooperation and our ability to communicate and learn from each other. We are not just stronger together; we are utterly dependent on each other from birth. Human development took an evolutionary path that prioritized cooperation and group reliance instead of individual strength, as a way of getting the most energy and resources from our environment for the least individual effort.

Humans do not operate within their ecosystems in the same way as other species, even other top-level predators. We do not have an ecological niche; rather, we dominate and alter the local—and now, global—ecosystem cumulatively to suit our lifestyles and make it safer, including though habitat loss, introduction of invasive species, climate change, industrial-scale hunting, burning, planting, infrastructure replacement and countless other modifications. It means that while other species do not naturally cause extinctions, humans currently threaten 1 million of the world's 8 million species.[1]

Over tens of thousands of years, this has helped make us the most successful big species. Humans now operate as a globalized network of nearly 8 billion hyperconnected individuals. We have effectively become a superorganism in our interactions with the natural world. We now dominate the planet and have pushed it into the Anthropocene, the Age of Humans. No part of Earth is untouched by human activity. About four-tenths of the planet's land surface is used to grow our food.[2] We have interfered with most of the world's major river systems.[3] We have harnessed more than a quarter of the entire biological productivity of the planet's land.[4] Our material changes alone—including roads, buildings and croplands—weigh an estimated 30 trillion tonnes[5] and allow us to live in an ultraconnected global population that is heading for 9 billion.

In changing the Earth we have been able to live longer and healthier than ever before. Through human development, a 72-year-old Japanese man today has the same chances of dying as a 30-year-old caveman.[6] The chance of a child dying before age 5 has declined five-fold since 1950, and the number of women dying in childbirth has been almost halved globally since 1990.[7] In many ways the world is becoming safer for a human to live and grow up in, due largely to harnessing energy, modern medicine and affordable, plentiful food.

We have made the planet safer for humans in a number of ways, but we have also made it worse: depleting its resources, killing its biodiversity, polluting it with waste and straining its capacity to support us. We have added hundreds of billions of tonnes of carbon dioxide to the atmosphere since industrialization—we currently add at least 36 billion tonnes a year[8]—progressively heating the planet, producing stronger storms, with extreme and erratic weather (including droughts and floods), sea level rise, melting ice caps, heatwaves and wildfires, all of which directly threaten the safety of humans or the ecosystems we rely on.

In 2019 nation-sized wildfires blazed across the northern hemisphere and Australia. Summer heatwaves produced temperatures above 45 degrees Celsius in Europe[9]—and above 50 degrees Celsius in Australia,[10] India and Pakistan[11]—breaking temperature records and killing hundreds of people. Heatwaves and intense rains boosted giant swarms of locusts, the size of New York City, which have since devastated crops from Kenya to Iran. Meanwhile, Arctic sea ice has melted to its second lowest extent in the 40-year satellite record,[12] alongside alarming melting of Greenland's ice sheet. A crippling drought coupled with poor infrastructure in Chennai, India—home to 10 million people—caused water shortages so severe that there were street clashes.[13] Meanwhile, the heaviest monsoon in 25 years produced catastrophic floods and the loss of at least 1,600 lives across 13 Indian states; in Kerala more than 100,000 people had to be evacuated. In September Hurricane Lorenzo became the largest and most powerful hurricane to make it so far east in the Atlantic that it reached Ireland and the United Kingdom,[14] just weeks after Hurricane Dorian devastated the Bahamas. This is the best scenario we can hope for if we reduce our carbon emissions to net-zero; if they continue to climb, it will only get worse.

No one decided to heat the planet and degrade our natural environment; it emerged from our collective cultural evolution. Human development has made us healthier and wealthier but also ushered in a global social system that constrains us. The environmental problems we face are systemic: a mixture of physical, chemical, biological and social changes that all interact and feed back on each other. Trying to understand how our impacts in one area, such as river extraction, affect another, such as food provision, is a complex task. But while our problematic practices in one area can impact many other areas, the good news is that so can our restorative ones: improving biodiversity in a wetland ecosystem can also reduce water pollution and soil erosion and protect crops against storm damage, for instance.

Earth's biosphere operates systemically, but so does human culture. Our numbers, how we are networked and our position in this network of humanity as individuals and societies, all produce their own effects. This is important because human interactions with their ecosystems are culturally driven. We attach subjective values to things of no or little survival value, such as gold, mahogany and turtle eggs. And we spread these invented values through our networks, just as we spread our resources, genes and germs. We are each individuals with our own motivations and desires, and yet much of our autonomy is an illusion. We are formed in our society's cultural "developing bath," which we will ourselves then help fashion and maintain—a grand social project without direction or goal that has nevertheless produced the most successful species on Earth.

In some societies humans are understood as part of the ecosystem they inhabit, an integral player like the fish or turtle. In others humans are part of an economic and social system that is seen as separate and external to nature. Many economic and development models, including the Human Development Index, do not factor in the environment or nature at all. Meanwhile, many societies measure progress or development with the gross domestic product metric, which does not value the biodiversity of the river or the cleanliness of the beach, only the price the fish or eggs obtain in a formal market. In reality the human economy is a wholly owned subsidiary of the environment, not the reverse.

Human development is ongoing, of course. It is possible for people in prosperous countries to order food from an app in air-conditioned comfort only because their recent ancestors developed by exploiting the natural wealth of other places and people. Rich nations continue to import resources from poorer nations, offloading the environmental damage of global consumption onto the people with the least power. As each generation of nation develops, this pattern has been followed, with richer Asian countries importing materials at the environmental expense of poorer Asian and African nations. But the poorest nations will have nowhere else to exploit. Earth, we are realizing, is finite.

Thus far, a key feature of human development has been inequality. By contrast, for most of our ancestry, the evidence suggests we lived as equals—today's hunter-gatherer communities are notable for their lack of social or gender-based hierarchies. However, as people began settling, and it became possible to own and store more resources, and the land itself, hierarchies developed, and people became valued according to the amount of stuff they possessed. Although the numbers living in extreme poverty have fallen, today's global inequality is at record levels, with 40 percent of total wealth in the hands of billionaires and nearly half of humanity living on less than $5.50 a day.[15]

This matters because the richest people in the world are doing the most to damage the environment that we all rely on for clean air, water, food and other resources. Yet they experience few consequences and the least danger from this environmental damage. The richest 10 percent of the world's population are responsible for half of carbon emissions, while the poorest 50 percent are responsible for just 10 percent.[16] At the same time the wealthiest people contribute less socially, paying in the least to the collective pot. In relatively equal Scandinavia the richest 0.01 percent illegally evade 25 percent of the taxes they owe, far higher than the average evasion rate of 2.8 percent.[17] In the United States the richest 400 families pay a lower effective tax rate than any other income group.[18] An estimated $9–$36 trillion is stored in tax havens around the world.[19] Delivering social justice and protecting the environment are closely linked: How poor people get rich will strongly shape the Anthropocene.

A useful thought experiment is to imagine you are in an antechamber waiting to be born, but first you must create the global society in which you will live. You do not know who you will be born as (what sex, skin colour, wealth, or nationality you will be or what skills or intelligence you will possess) or where you will be born (with rich soils and clean rivers or with toxic ponds and filthy air). Would you design today's world with its palaces and slums, knowing you are far more likely to end up in a slum with no sanitation than with a gold-plated toilet bowl?[20]

In 2015 UN Member States agreed to 17 Sustainable Development Goals (SDGs) for 2030 in a plan to achieve a better future for all, recognizing that all our needs are intertwined with each other's and with our environment. The SDGs seek to address the global challenges we face, including those related to poverty, inequality, climate, environmental degradation, prosperity, and peace and justice. We are a third of the way to 2030, and despite progress in some areas, progress in others has been too slow or has even been reversed. For instance, even though extreme poverty has reached its lowest point since monitoring began, we are still not on track to end it by 2030; meanwhile, malnutrition rates are creeping upwards again for the first time in years, even as the amount of food produced per capita increases. The unequal impacts of the Covid-19 pandemic may push a further 100 million people into extreme poverty, effectively wiping out progress made since 2017 and exacerbating child hunger.[21]

So perhaps we should now ask what does it mean to develop as a person? Every human life begins small, vulnerable and dependent on others, as we slowly mature physically, cognitively and socially throughout our lives. For a human to thrive, she needs a safe physical environment that does not risk her health and a safe social environment that does not constrain her potential. The two are linked: Life-path studies suggest that socioeconomic circumstances are embedded in our biology—disadvantage does not just make life worse; it makes it shorter. Humans are now the main driver of planetary change, and human systems must be targeted to do something about it. That means addressing societal systems, including populism, finance and information transmission, alongside the practices and technologies that emit polluting gases, from fossil fuel burning to food production.

As individuals there is little we can do about glaring inequalities of opportunity, climate change and environmental degradation—these are systemic issues that will be solved only through large-scale structural change. But even such major reformations of how society functions start with the individual agency of voters, consumers, gardeners, parents and witnesses. We are a vast global population facing unprecedented environmental challenges, yet we still have the time and capability to prevent extreme outcomes, such as runaway climate change and wildlife extinctions. Even if some environmental changes feel too locked in or overwhelming to reverse, we have the power to change the social justice systems that underlie and manage their impacts on us.

We cannot protect our environment unless we also protect the needs of the humans that rely on it. Take the illegal trade in wildlife, which is worth an estimated $19 billion a year[22] and threatens the stability of governments as well as human health—some 75 percent of infectious diseases have zoonotic origins,[23] including Covid-19.[24] This trade is often conducted by well organized criminal networks that undermine government efforts to halt other illegal trades, such as arms and drug trafficking, and help finance regional conflicts.

In the past 20 years the population of olive ridley turtles has fallen by a third. Around the world females are slaughtered on the beach for their meat, skins and shells, and their eggs are traded as a valuable delicacy. One of the species' few remaining nesting sites is Ostional beach in Costa Rica, home to a poor village wedged on the coast between mountains and rivers and entirely cut off during seasonal floods. The villagers once subsisted on fishing and turtle eggs but stopped after egg-harvesting was prohibited by international conservation laws. Many villagers deserted Ostional to find work in the cities; those who remained lived in fear as it became besieged by poachers and violent criminal gangs.

In desperation, women from the village banded together to form the Ostional Development Association and approached biologists studying the turtles to see whether there was a way to legalize egg collecting within sustainable parameters. A plan was drawn up with the government to allow families to harvest a limited number of eggs, and as part of the agreement, the community cleans the beach, protects the turtles and their eggs from poachers and manages the many tourists that now descend on Ostional during monthly egg-layings. The eggs harvested are licensed for sale at the same price as chicken eggs to deter the black market, and the proceeds are used for community development projects. Egg licencing has given people a living wage and paid for training, maternity cover and pensions. Residents have a vested interest in protecting eggs and turtles,[25] and the population of baby turtles has risen, while other wildlife has returned.[26] People, too, are returning to the village and making new lives for themselves.

As we negotiate a path between the needs of the human and natural worlds, Ostional shows us that resilience relies on recognizing the interdependence of the two. To protect wildlife, you must also protect human life. Our environmental crisis is a test of our uniquely human development, of our ability to come together, cooperate and adapt to a different way of sharing this one planetary home. We live in our own small local environments that we can ourselves defile, restore or enhance. Each is a part of the bigger whole, just as we are part of a bigger humanity.

NOTES

1   United Nations 2019c.

2   Ramankutty and others 2008; World Bank 2016a.

3   Millennium Ecosystem Assessment 2003.

4   Krausmann and others 2013.

5   Zalasiewicz and others 2017.

6   Burger, Baudisch and Vaupel 2012.

7   Roser, Ritchie and Dadonaite 2013.

8   Friedlingstein and others 2019b; Ritchie and Roser 2020.

9   Pacorel 2019.

10   Government of Australia 2019.

11   NASA Earth Observatory 2019.

12   Witze 2020b.

13   Yeung and Gupta 2019.

14   Fortin 2019.

15   Oxfam 2020.

16   See spotlight 7.2. See also Chakravarty and others (2009), Kartha and others (2020) and SEI (2020).

17   Alstadsæter, Johannesen and Zucman 2019.

18   Saez and Zucman 2019.

19   Shaxson 2019.

20   Rawls 1971.

21   On poverty, see World Bank (2020c); on child hunger, see Fore and others (2020).

22   Dalberg 2012.

23   Taylor, Latham and Woolhouse 2001.

24   Burki 2020.

25   Sardeshpande and MacMillan 2019.

26   Bézy, Valverde and Plante 2015.

The future we want—the United Nations we need

Perspectives from commemorations of the 75th anniversary of the United Nations

Across this anniversary year, we have engaged in a global conversation. And the results are striking. People are thinking big—they are also expressing an intense yearning for international cooperation and global solidarity. Now is the time to respond to these aspirations and realize these aims. In this 75th anniversary year, we face our own 1945 moment. We must meet that moment. We must show unity like never before to overcome today's emergency, get the world moving and working and prospering again, and uphold the vision of the Charter.

UN Secretary-General António Guterres

In January 2020 UN Secretary-General António Guterres launched the UN75 initiative, not as a celebration but as the world's largest conversation about current global challenges—and the gap between the future we want and where we are headed if current trends continue.

Through formal and informal surveys and dialogues held around the world, the exercise took stock of global concerns and gained views on what sort of global cooperation is required. It was also intended to reimagine the UN role in addressing global challenges.

To date, more than 1 million people in all UN Member and Observer States have taken the one-minute survey, and more than 1,000 dialogues have been held in 82 countries. In addition, 50,000 people in 50 countries took part in independent polling by Edelman and the Pew Research Center, and artificial intelligence analysis of social and traditional media was conducted in 70 countries, along with academic and policy research mappings in all regions.

Together, they represent the most ambitious attempt by the United Nations to undertake a global reality check and hear from "we the peoples" on their priorities and suggested solutions to global challenges, providing unique insights into the future we want and the United Nations we need.

The key findings align with the main topics of the 2020 Human Development Report, including people's concern for both climate and social issues such as poverty and inequality as well as the importance of multilateralism and global cooperation. The findings identify some optimism for the future and belief that we can improve current social and planetary trajectories though stronger global leadership, innovation and inclusiveness in the multilateral arena.

Ten key findings

1. Amid the Covid-19 pandemic the immediate priority of most respondents everywhere is improved access to basic services: health care, safe water and sanitation, and education.

2. The next main priority is greater international solidarity and increased support to the places hardest hit by the pandemic. This includes tackling poverty, reducing inequalities and boosting employment.

3. Respondents were hopeful about progress in access to public health services. They also believe access to education and women's rights will improve.

4. Respondents' priorities for the future corresponded to the areas they believe will worsen. Most participants across all regions are worried about the future impact of climate change. The most overwhelming medium- and long-term concern is our inability to stem the climate crisis and the destruction of the natural environment.

5. Other major priorities for the future include ensuring greater respect for human rights, settling conflicts, tackling poverty and reducing corruption.

6. Younger participants and participants in developing countries tended to be more optimistic about the future than older participants and participants in developed countries.

7. Some 87 percent of respondents believe international cooperation is vital to deal with today's challenges. And the majority of respondents believe the Covid-19 pandemic has made international cooperation even more urgent.

8. About 60 percent of respondents believe the United Nations has made the world a better place, and 74 percent see the United Nations as essential in tackling global challenges. At the same time over half see the United Nations as remote from their lives and say they do not know much about it. Moreover, while just under half currently see the United Nations as contributing somewhat to advancing key global challenges, only about a third see it as contributing a lot in this regard. The United Nations is perceived to be contributing most to upholding human rights and promoting peace.

9. Dialogue participants overwhelmingly called for the United Nations to be more inclusive of the diversity of actors in the 21st century. They identified in particular the need for greater inclusion of civil society, women, young people, vulnerable groups, cities and local authorities, businesses, regional organizations and other international organizations.

10. Dialogue participants also called for the United Nations to innovate in other ways, with stronger leadership and more consistency in exercising its moral authority to uphold the UN Charter. There were calls for increased accountability, transparency and impartiality, including through better engagement and communication with communities, as well as strengthening implementation of programmes and operations.

NOTE

The UN75 initiative gathered the data synthesized here through five channels between January and August 2020. This spotlight reflects the analysis of more than 800,000 survey responses collected between 2 January and 1 September 2020. It also analyses more than 1,000 dialogues in 82 countries with groups representing street children, indigenous peoples, grassroots activists, youth networks, nongovernmental organizations, schools and universities, cities and local authorities, and businesses. It also includes an analysis of a survey by Edelman, a global communications firm, of 35,777 people in 36 countries as well as a Pew survey of 14,276 adults ages 18 and older.

Acting for change

Acting for change

Part I of the Report showed how the human development journey in the Anthropocene involves transformational changes and argued that people can generate change by acting through social, economic and political processes—a notion at the core of the human development approach. Therefore, expanding human agency and freedoms—with a compass for enhancing equity, innovation and stewardship of the planet—is central to enabling that transformation.

Part II of the Report explores mechanisms of change[1] that can mobilize action by individuals, communities, governments, civil society and businesses. In emphasizing mechanisms, the aim is to provide a broader template of choices, for multiple actors, that is consistent with the perspective of this Report: that the Anthropocene is a predicament to be navigated, not a policy problem to be solved. In doing so, the chapters draw from, but attempt to go beyond, long-standing discussions on the environment and sustainability. Three specific mechanisms of change are considered.

First, social norms, which frame socially permissible—or forbidden—behaviours. Sometimes understood as informal institutions, they have been less explored as a mechanism for change than formal institutions based on authority (exercised as government regulation, for instance) or prices (providing consumption and production incentives). Chapter 4 reports recent findings that social norms are powerful determinants of people's choices and can change faster than commonly assumed. And new forms of information sharing can support social processes of ethical reasoning (while also presenting risks).

Second, incentives for change. Incentives determine in part what consumers choose to buy, what firms produce and trade, where investors put their money and how governments cooperate. Incentives and social norms interact with one another, but incentives are also crucial in their own right: Even if people do not change their minds, they may still respond to incentives based on what they can afford

and where they see opportunities to meet their aspirations. Chapter 5 considers how existing incentives help explain current patterns of consumption, production, investment and other choices that lead to the planetary pressures documented in part I. It also explores how these incentives could evolve in ways that would ease planetary pressures and move societies towards the transformative changes required for human development in the Anthropocene. It considers three domains shaped by considerations related to incentives: finance, prices and international collective action.

Third, just as social norms and incentives can be harnessed for transformational change, so can a new generation of nature-based solutions. They can protect, sustainably manage and restore ecosystems, simultaneously promoting wellbeing and mitigating biosphere integrity loss. They embrace equity, innovation and stewardship of nature, the three elements of the compass for empowerment outlined in chapter 3. They boost the regeneration of nature by protecting and responsibly using resources. And they rely on the participation and initiative of indigenous peoples and local communities. Chapter 6 illustrates a range of experiences with nature-based solutions and argues that even though they are bottom-up and context-specific, they can contribute to transformational scale at higher levels for two reasons. First, many local and community decisions add up to substantial global impact. Second, planetary and social and economic systems are interconnected, and local decisions can have impacts elsewhere and at multiple scales. But to realize their potential as mechanisms for large-scale transformative change, there has to be a systematic approach to their contribution, what we call nature-based human development. It is premised on acknowledging the systemic role of indigenous peoples and local communities and narrower gaps in empowerment between those fighting against, and those working towards, preserving biosphere integrity while advancing human development.

Empowering people, unleashing transformation

CHAPTER 4

Empowering people, unleashing transformation

Social norms are powerful. They can also be harmful —to the planet and to people, especially to those with less power.

Imagine if such norms were changed. Imagine the possibilities for unleashing society-wide transformations geared towards equity, innovation and stewardship of the planet.

How can this be done?

This chapter emphasizes the importance of education and identifies ways in which catalytic action can ripple across society, helping to shift norms and empower people to act on their values.

People care about the environment. Media attention and the spread of information about the consequences of human pressures on the planet have increased awareness of planetary imbalances, contributing to values that generally favour easing planetary pressures. The Fridays for Future movement and organizations such as Extinction Rebellion have mobilized millions of people around the globe as an expression of this awareness and how much it matters to so many people.[1] Yet, these values are rarely reflected in people's behaviour, both individually and collectively. Is it because they do not care enough? Because they do not have options to change their behaviour? Because they see their actions as inconsequential unless others act, too?

This chapter explores how social norms that inform choices on transportation, production and consumption can evolve towards norms that reduce planetary imbalances. It does so by addressing three questions: How willing are people to assume responsible stewardship of the planet? What has led them to this attitude? And how can even more change be unleashed that ultimately contributes to transformation? Examining the role of social norms does not imply that they alone will suffice. Or that no other elements are needed for change. For example, social norms may not change the behaviour of someone who really cares about the planet and wants to comply with a new social standard if she has no option to take public transportation or to use something other than kerosene at home. Changing social norms should be seen as one potentially powerful mechanism to address planetary imbalances, but one that interacts with—and in some ways may depend on—others, several of which are considered in the other two chapters of part II.

Understanding the dynamics of collective behaviour change[2] is key to appreciating the potential of social norms. In principle, if a certain action is adopted by enough individuals, it can lead to behavioural tipping and turn into a social norm, generating positive feedback loops that reinforce the same behaviour in societies.[3] In reality, however, this process is accompanied by power struggles within and between governments and among civil society organizations, consumers and businesses, reflecting different material interests, emotional attachments and moral values.[4] This chapter thus highlights the potential of social norms for transformation and identifies ways to seize that potential, but it does not claim that these changes will inevitably happen. An appreciation of the underlying processes that lead to the evolution of social norms and how they shape people's choices will prove useful when drawing on them as a mechanism for change, driving at equity, innovation and stewardship, as discussed in chapter 3.

" Most people align their behaviour with that of their peers, leading to fairly persistent social norms—"things that are fit and proper to be done" in society.

This chapter first covers different concepts of social norms. It then argues that education and lifelong learning have contributed to the formation of values that support the idea of stewardship of the planet. Following the capabilities approach, a crucial link to operationalize these values and turn them into self-reinforcing social norms is agency—people's actions that lead to change.[5] Theories of collective action and the experience of the Covid-19 pandemic may help explain why this has not yet happened at the societal level. And social psychology and economics literature as well as voices from civil society provide insights on what can be done to empower people to act on their values.

From theory to change

Social psychology finds that most people align their behaviour with that of their peers, leading to fairly persistent social norms. Those norms are what people believe to be "normal" (descriptive norms), either because of their own perception or because they received the information that it is commonly approved behaviour (injunctive norms).[6] In other words, social norms are "things that are fit and proper to be done" in a given society.[7] Game theorists explain the persistence of social norms as a behavioural equilibrium: "Everyone wants to play their part given the expectation that everyone else will continue to play theirs. It is, in short, an equilibrium of a game."[8]

But how do social norms emerge? And how can they be changed? Recently, holistic multidisciplinary approaches have blurred the traditional divide between *homo sociologicus*—a person who is pushed by social forces and sticks to prescribed behaviour—and *homo economicus*—a rational actor who acts to maximize his or her own interests and benefits.[9] Amartya Sen adds that some behaviour is based on other people's goals or common goals, through "a matter of social living, social intercourse, of social cooperation [...]."[10] "[...] what we value can extend far beyond our own interests and needs."[11] Both self-interest and common goals, among many other factors, contribute to the formation of values, which in turn shape behaviours.[12]

Another variable that contributes to the formation of values is education.[13] But this does not refer only to the formal education system; education at home and continued learning in adulthood are also included. For simplicity, we call all of this learning. The resulting values should, in the best case, lead to agency, since values "serve as standards or criteria to guide not only action but also judgment, choice, attitude, evaluation, argument, exhortation, rationalization, and, one might add, attribution of causality."[14] However, this does not always happen because, among other reasons, businesses, governments and civil society organizations push for their interests in ways that may make agency difficult or impossible.[15] Collective action problems pose an additional challenge at the societal level (chapter 5), and at the individual level there are psychological obstacles such as the persistence of old behavioural patterns or habits and the perception that only a powerful external entity can bring about change, which pro-environmental behavioural researchers refer to as external locus of control.[16]

Social norms are known to be persistent and hard to change, surviving through economic development and political regimes.[17] But when they change, it can happen quickly, usually when new public information becomes available, as during the Covid-19 pandemic. Behavioural tipping points—that is, when enough people have strong enough attitudes against an existing social norm (or towards a new one)—are decisive for norm change.[18] They may be followed by a norm cascade, where more and more people adopt the new norm, leading to self-reinforcement.[19] Through self-reinforcement, positive feedback loops, and trial and error, one or several equilibria of behaviour can be reached without external intervention.[20] By adopting new behavioural patterns, one or more individuals can shape population-level dynamics, leading to

transformational change in behaviour at the societal level.[21] In some cases not enough people adopt desired behaviour, so those who initially changed their behaviour revert to old habits, or status quo behaviour, because that is what seems socially acceptable. Overcoming such a status quo–conserving effect is crucial to incentivizing transformation.[22] All of this happens in a context of external situational factors and facilitating conditions that may consist of policies that incentivize certain behaviour.[23] Examples include provision of recycling facilities, access to energy-efficient lights and appliances, and availability of public transport services.

> " Education has more than an instrumental role—its purpose is transformative through exposure to broad human values and the promotion of critical thinking, to make for politically aware and active people.

To sum up, self-interest, goals of others and common goals, and learning lead to value formation (figure 4.1). Learning can also shape common goals and even self-interest when informing about rights. Different actors feed their interests into the potential transformation of values to agency and thus social norms. Persistent habits and an external locus of control as well as collective action problems constitute an additional challenge for transformation. When enough people act on their values and express agency, a tipping point is reached, leading to self-reinforcing social norms that trigger actions from even more people. Equal access to facilitating conditions is key to generating change with equity throughout society.

But what if the status quo, the prevailing set of social norms, is detrimental to the planet? How do social norms change when the equilibrium is self-reinforcing? To address these questions, we take several steps back to observe how and if pro-planet values have been formed and whether they have challenged and changed existing social norms throughout society and, if not, how this can be accomplished.

From learning to value formation

In the capabilities approach, education for sustainable development is defined as "educational practice that results in the enhancement of human well-being,

Figure 4.1 From learning to self-reinforcing social norms

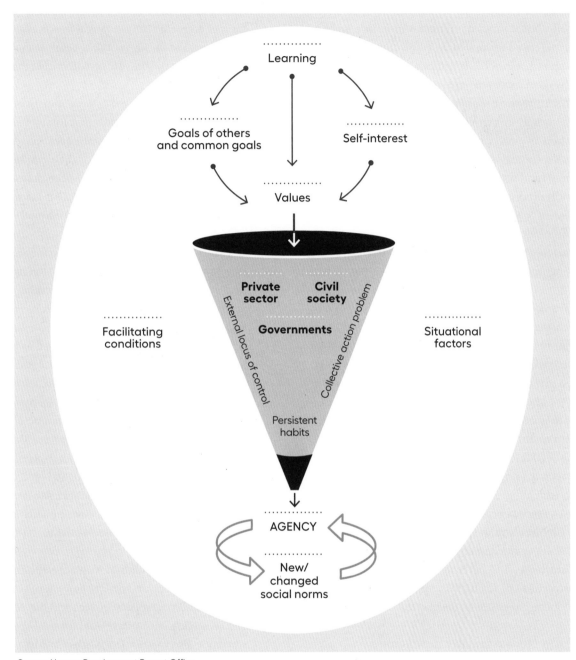

Source: Human Development Report Office.

conceived in terms of the expansion of individuals' agency, capabilities and participation in democratic dialogue, both for now and for future generations."[24] Other literature, focusing more on education in the formal education system, uses narrower concepts and definitions, such as climate change education or environmental education.[25] We use the broader definition from the capabilities approach, and we assess knowledge acquisition that occurs outside the formal education system. As chapter 1 emphasized,

education has more than an instrumental role—its purpose is transformative through exposure to broad human values and the promotion of critical thinking, to make for politically aware and active people.

Where do children learn?

The home is where developmental foundations originate and interests, sensitivities and values towards the environment may emerge if parents and caregivers teach and foster them.[26] This can happen intentionally, but at times it is inherent in culture and has been practised for millennia at the community level (chapters 1, 3 and 6). Intentional practices have recently been shown to have significant effects on children's attitudes towards environmental protection. They usually comprise three components: training children on environmental ethics, mitigation and adaptation strategies; modelling pro-environmental behaviour; and seeking and buying of environmentally friendly products and food for children.[27]

The effects of these practices start very early in children's lives and are carried through to adulthood. Children whose parents expose them to wild nature (hiking or camping) or domesticated nature (planting flowers) during early childhood develop greater awareness of nature and the need to preserve it, which they sustain throughout the course of life.[28] Children also form pro-environmental values when talking about environmental protection at home and when given access to relevant books and other media.[29] Although they may not have reached voting age, they are more likely to politically support pro-environmentalist views when their parents do the same.[30] Older children and teenagers who feel more connected to nature behave in a more sustainable way, which appears to have positive psychological consequences because they also report being happier.[31] Children's values then contribute to worldviews that shape understanding and assumptions about the world that lead to perceptions, interpretations and constructions of reality that can be more supportive of reducing pressures on the planet.[32]

" Education for sustainable development helps develop the right knowledge, skills and technical solutions. But equal access to quality education remains a challenge.

Education for sustainable development in schools is at least as important as learning at home. "It helps develop the right knowledge, skills and technical solutions [...], [...] is clearly shown to be the best tool for climate change awareness, and [...] improves disaster preparedness and reduces vulnerability to climate-related disasters. [Moreover], green schools, well-designed curricular and hands-on learning

outside of school can strengthen people's connection with nature."[33] It does not necessarily have to take the form of a specific subject taught in school but can be mainstreamed throughout the overall school curricula, focusing on the breadth of skills rather than specific knowledge.[34]

Education for sustainable development is not new. As early as 1977 the world's first Intergovernmental Conference on Environmental Education, organized by the United Nations Educational, Scientific and Cultural Organization (UNESCO) and the United Nations Environment Programme, took place in Georgia, but it was not until later that many school curricula included aspects of environmental sustainability.[35] During the United Nations Decade of Education for Sustainable Development (2005–2014), additional funding for initiatives on education for sustainable development was mobilized, and initiatives were further strengthened and scaled up by the Global Action Programme on Education for Sustainable Development led by UNESCO (2015–2019).[36] The Sustainable Development Goals endorse education for sustainable development in target 4.7, which aims to ensure that all learners acquire the knowledge and skills needed to promote sustainable development by 2030.[37]

Children from backgrounds with weaker interests in or knowledge about environmental protection can benefit from including sustainable development in school curricula, which can have equalizing effects. As in many other areas, schools can thus flatten gradients in knowledge on the planet. However, this benefit applies only to children with access to the formal education system. In 2018, 17 percent of the world's children and young people were still out of primary and secondary education.[38] And the quality of formal education also varies.[39] During the Covid-19 pandemic in 2020, 91 percent of children worldwide were affected by temporary school closures.[40] Equal access to quality education remains paramount. Education is important not only for environmental protection and climate change mitigation but also for climate change adaptation; it can even reduce the number of fatalities due to natural disasters (box 4.1). It is thus a critical aspect of equity.

Educational interventions that seek to increase awareness and knowledge about the planet are most successful when based on tangible, personally relevant and meaningful information that fits the local

Box 4.1 How education can save lives

Education is essential not only for environmental protection and climate change mitigation but also for climate change adaptation. It may be even more important than income and wealth for reducing vulnerability to natural hazards.[1] The higher the average level of education in a country, the fewer deaths due to disasters, even after income, life expectancy at birth, exposure to climate related risks, population density, the political system, the region and whether a country is landlocked are taken into account.

The importance of education for disaster resilience is valid for both slow and rapid onset cases.[2] There are several potential causal mechanisms behind this. Learning basic reading, writing and abstraction skills raises the efficiency of cognitive processes and logical reasoning, thus enhancing cognitive capacity.[3] Probably as a result, more educated people usually have better personal planning skills and are willing to change potentially risky behaviour.[4] They are also more prepared for hazards because they tend to establish, for example, a family evacuation plan or stockpile emergency supplies.[5] And they can access early warning systems and seasonal predictions more easily, which directly helps prevent fatalities.

Female education at a certain age, typically the childrearing years, is especially important in preventing disaster-related deaths (see figure) as well as in building long-term resilience because of women's active role in improving the overall "[...] quality of institutions and social networks for mutual assistance [...]."[6] In this sense there is a spillover effect that works through social interaction when members of a community benefit from their peers' higher education levels, which can facilitate access to information and knowledge as well as to institutions that help reduce disaster risk.[7] This is important because diverse forms of knowledge obtained from, for instance, social networks and boundary organizations can greatly reduce vulnerability through two-way communication, improving mitigation as well as adaptation.[8]

Female education can save lives

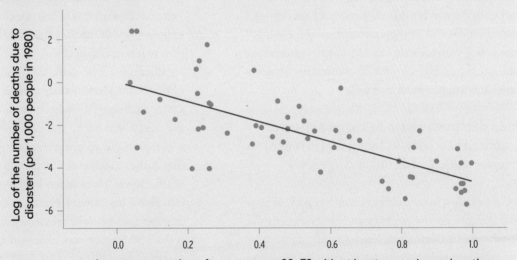

Note: Includes 63 countries with one or more disasters on average per year for 1980–2010.
Source: Striessnig, Lutz and Patt 2013.

Education also increases sociopsychological resilience. Better educated individuals affected by the 2004 Indian Ocean tsunami were more able to cope with psychological stress in the long term. Though education was not related to whether people developed posttraumatic stress symptoms immediately after the disaster, it was decisive for how they dealt with the trauma during the following years (a fact that cannot be attributed to better access to mental health services, since counselling was hardly available).

(continued)

Box 4.1 How education can save lives *(continued)*

Better educated individuals were also less likely to live in camps or other temporary housing a few years after the tsunami, and they were economically more resilient (their household consumption did not decrease as much as that of less educated individuals).[9] Other aspects of education that contribute to economic resilience include a wider set of skills among better educated individuals, which allows them to take up jobs in sectors other than agriculture,[10] as well as easier access to certain resources due to social networks, including government financial assistance or informal loans from social networks.[11]

Notes
1. Striessnig, Lutz and Patt 2013. This empirical study showed that the education component of the Human Development Index (HDI) explains most of the variance in deaths due to natural disasters, even after several other variables are controlled for, including the other components of the HDI (life expectancy at birth and income), exposure to climate-related risks, whether a country is landlocked, population density, the political system and the region. For forward-looking projects using different population scenarios, see Lutz, Muttarak and Striessnig (2014). A review of 11 studies on the same subject confirms the importance of education for adaptation to climate change (Muttarak and Lutz 2014). For a study comparing the effects of education and wealth on disaster resilience in Nepalese communities, see KC (2013). **2.** Muttarak and Lutz 2014. **3.** Baker, Salinas and Eslinger 2012. **4.** Striessnig, Lutz and Patt 2013. **5.** Muttarak and Pothisiri 2013. **6.** Pichler and Striessnig 2013, p. 31. The study of three Caribbean island states—Cuba, the Dominican Republic and Haiti—confirmed the results about the effects of female education on climate risk vulnerability and revealed that women's education also contributes to long-term resilience. See also Striessnig, Lutz and Patt (2013). **7.** Lutz, Muttarak and Striessnig 2014. **8.** Thomas and others 2018. **9.** Frankenberg and others 2013. **10.** Van der Land and Hummel 2013. **11.** Garbero and Muttarak 2013.

context and that children can put in practice in their daily life.[41] Active and engaging teaching methods such as open discussions are important because students feel that they can participate in decision-making, which empowers them to assume a sense of stewardship of the planet.[42] By contrast, a lack of participation can impede ownership of success and eventually lead to a programme's loss of meaning.[43] Interacting with scientists to address misconceptions and implementing school and community projects have shown to be effective as well.[44]

> " Action solutions need to be suggested, tried and practised in schools as living labs in order to empower students and unleash agency.

Case studies from different countries provide specific insights on the benefits and challenges in the classroom. In Germany a learning module on biodiversity strengthened students' knowledge on the subject. It also enhanced students' values on appreciation and preservation of nature and diminished attitudes and values that would support its exploitation.[45] A study from Singapore shows that knowledge, attitudes, skills and competencies are transmitted and should lead, in the best case, to pro-environmental action.[46] This is not always the case, however. Empirical research from China shows that with increasing age, knowledge about the environment grows, but positive experiences in nature

and thus concerns about its protection decrease.[47] And a Programme for International Student Assessment study shows that students who perform better in environmental science tend to be less optimistic about the possibility of easing planetary pressures in the coming decades. A potential explanation is that better understanding of the issues may lead to greater awareness of the complexity of the challenge and thus to less optimism.[48]

Education for sustainable development has been criticized for a lack of evaluation of its effectiveness.[49] Other challenges include students and teachers feeling overwhelmed by the concept of sustainability—comparing it to a never ending staircase, which diminishes motivation for action due to the sense that little can be changed by one person[50]—and the perceived disconnect between environmental education and personal responsibility.[51] Teaching in India and Mexico was observed to often be rather disciplinary and textbook based, which has led to a neglect of a more systemic approach to study causes and solutions.[52] In Austria and Germany students have shown a lack of knowledge about the links between consumption and production networks, which has impeded change in consumption and production patterns, despite precise knowledge of sustainability and the importance of sustainable behaviour.[53] Other challenges especially relevant for low and medium human development countries include a lack of time, money, teacher training and government support.[54]

Apart from additional funding, there is a need for substantial transformation of how education leaders and participants look at systems and processes of planetary change. Such transformation requires releasing existing assumptions and beliefs through experiential processes, allowing for the evolution of education processes rather than the creation of new ones.[55] Many school curricula focus on knowledge transmission, not action competence, which is insufficient to change behaviour. Action solutions need to be suggested, tried and practised in schools as living labs in order to empower students and unleash agency.[56] Reforms could be implemented using such a strategy to strengthen the link between academic content and personal responsibility in order to respect and protect the planet on the one hand and create awareness of one's own power of action on the other.

One approach is to use the Sustainable Development Goals as the destination and develop a strategy that takes several steps back. The first step could be agreeing on a common vision of sustainability by all parties involved, followed by identifying required competences and developing appropriate learning strategies to integrate in the curricula. Monitoring and evaluation are vital to any such strategy and should track the effectiveness of specific initiatives, allowing for adjustment and improvement.[57]

Where do adults learn?

Apart from continued learning in the formal education system, youth and adult learning about planetary pressures can happen through multiple other channels, including the workplace (trainings, seminars), social interaction (including social media), or public policies and government communication (such as governmental awareness campaigns or political discourse). Firms can also contribute to adult learning on sustainability. When a company tries to improve its environmental record, information and awareness influence employees' attitudes and behaviour, not only at the workplace but also in their daily lives. One explanation for this is the leadership role that employers assume for their employees.[58]

Social media have become an important channel of social interaction and thus offer opportunities for learning on topics around sustainability.[59] But they can also contribute to user polarization, which can diminish the learning effect. A large study on Twitter users showed that mostly people with strong opinions on climate change (either climate change mitigation activists or climate change deniers) and global warming engage in conversations on these topics and that they self-segregate into groups of like-minded users in an echo chamber (figure 4.2).[60] User polarization and echo chamber building has also been observed on other social media platforms such as Facebook and YouTube, where users cluster around content that is shared, liked and commented on by like-minded users. Algorithms for content promotion are partly responsible for this, but more and more insights on cognitive factors such as confirmation bias also explain echo chamber building.[61] Instead of contributing to learning, social media can thus also increase polarization among societies when users are exposed to only certain content.

" The Fridays for Future movement has not only influenced many adults' attitudes and public opinion on climate change around the globe but also contributed substantially to changing the spirit of large international forums.

Another important channel of adult learning is intergenerational interaction. When children and young people enjoy education for sustainable development at school, parents are indirectly exposed to information, learn from their children's newly acquired skills and witness potential change in behaviour. This way, the effect of education can spread throughout communities.[62] Though this reversed way of learning may seem counterintuitive, the evidence that children and young people can influence their parents' awareness and behaviour around sustainability issues has been well established for decades.[63]

Sometimes, young people influence awareness and behaviour on a large scale by integrating activism into existing systems and power structures (dutiful dissent), by contesting prevailing social norms to change policies and outcomes (disruptive dissent) or by creating new and alternative systems that challenge or even undermine existing power structures, mobilizing citizens to create and follow new norms and values (dangerous dissent).[64] A compelling case is that of young activist Greta Thunberg. Under her

Figure 4.2 Social media platforms can contribute to polarization

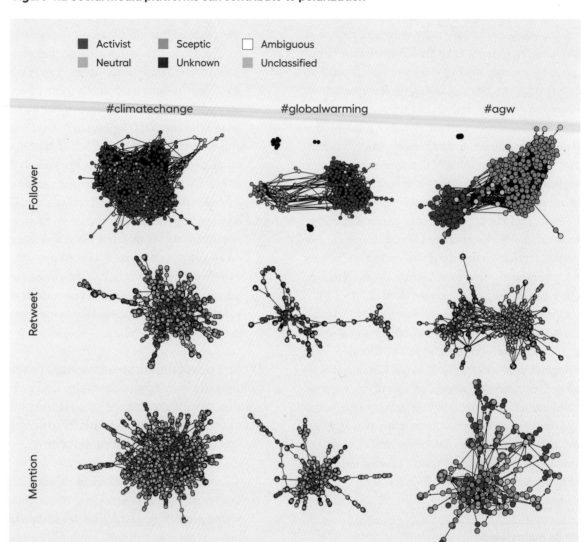

Note: Distribution of attitudes across interaction networks of Twitter users communicating about climate change. Rows show follower, retweet and mention networks, and columns show networks for #climatechange, #globalwarming and #agw (anthropogenic global warming). Each node represents a user, and each edge indicates an interaction between a pair of users. Nodes are coloured by user attitude classification. Network layouts are based solely on network topology and are independent of user attitudes. Networks are filtered for visualization: follower networks show only users with more than [35, 12, 4] tweets, and retweet and mention networks show only edges with weights greater than [2, 1, 0] retweets and [1, 0, 0] mentions for [#climatechange, #globalwarming, #agw], respectively.
Source: Williams and others 2015.

leadership the Fridays for Future movement has not only influenced many adults' attitudes and public opinion on climate change around the globe but also contributed substantially to changing the spirit of large international forums such as the 2019 United Nations Climate Change Conference COP25, the 2019 UN Climate Action Summit and the 2019 and 2020 World Economic Forums.[65] While the impact of Thunberg's seemingly simple school strike is impressive, it probably was also just the right moment for such a phenomenon—the world was ready for it.

There is also a learning effect from public policies and government communication. Making widely accepted scientific information available to the public is critical to gaining support for certain policies.[66] Narratives can be a powerful instrument to mobilize and empower people.[67] But they are not enough to empower people and unleash change.[68] And political discourse can pull in the other direction when leaders question scientific evidence and provide "alternative facts," especially in the context of post-truth politics.[69] Together with the suggested polarizing effect of social media, this risks producing a distorted picture of what people value.

" Social media can be a learning tool for young people and adults, but it can also contribute to polarization among societies.

In fact, scientific evidence is processed at many levels of society and policymaking. As Helga Weisz put it: "The climate does not speak to us. Society would not know about climate change had not certain climate phenomena resonated in parts of society and had not these parts of society started communicating about it. The first resonance of a possible induced climate change occurred in parts of the science system, more precisely in atmospheric chemistry. [...] Once the topic of climate change turned into a political issue, it was picked up—as a topic—by other reference systems, the policy and economic systems."[70] Communicating and engaging with scientific evidence are essential parts of societal learning about planetary change. But at the same time it is crucial to understand that the values some people hold may be inconsistent with the implications of scientific evidence (for instance, someone with the view that governments should not meddle in markets who therefore opposes climate regulation) without that signifying that they reject the scientific consensus (denying that climate change is anthropogenic).[71]

These dynamics can then associate positions on reducing planetary pressures with partisanship identity, which appears to shape opinions about the dangers and importance of climate change, regardless of scientific evidence,[72] leading to the bundling of opposition to market regulation and views that are more sceptical of climate change.[73] But even here, interestingly enough, education moderates this association.[74]

If leaders, national or local, are on board with stewardship for the planet, awareness campaigns can help, say, with litter reduction[75] or water conservation[76]—especially campaigns that use participatory approaches such as events, competitions and exhibitions.[77] Activities around the international Earth Day, for instance, have been shown to affect people's attitudes towards protecting the planet in as early as 1970.[78] Likewise, art projects have enhanced critical thinking and increased awareness of people's own actions that affect the planet.[79] Communicating these types of participatory projects and sharing the outcomes—in exhibitions, for example—can expand the positive effects to the community. They can even be emulated in events and competitions in senior communities.[80]

Where do we stand with our values?

Where do societies stand, after all, on values and attitudes towards reducing planetary imbalances? Evidence of support for protecting the environment is impressive. Data from a global survey show that the vast majority—on average about 78 percent of the total respondents from 59 low, medium, high and very high human development countries—agree that it is important to look after the environment (figure 4.3). There was no significant difference in support across countries or human development groups or between men and women.[81]

Apart from the high overall support for protecting the planet, what is striking is that this support is not new. By the early 1990s on average about 77 percent of people in an admittedly much smaller sample of selected countries said that they would give part of their income to protect the planet, independent of levels of human development.[82] Whereas the question from the more recent global survey asked only whether people agree with the importance of looking after the environment, the question from the 1990s asked whether people were willing to give part of their income for this cause, a much more serious commitment (figure 4.4).

These surveys reflect values. When it comes to concrete action, the picture looks different. In 2020 single-use plastic bags, containers, cups, cutlery and other items; idling cars; and wasteful consumption patterns still form part of many societies' social norms, especially in higher human development countries. Global production of plastic (an extremely lightweight material) was 359 million tonnes in 2018, up from 1.5 million tonnes in 1950,[83] even though it is widely known that plastic seriously harms ecosystems, especially oceans, marine life and even drinking water. More than 8 million tonnes of plastic leak into the ocean each year[84]—equal to dumping a garbage truck of plastic every minute[85]—and recent estimates show that 14 million tonnes of microplastic already reside on the ocean floor.[86] Fish and other species ingest and get entangled in plastic, and the

Figure 4.3 Most people agree that it is important to protect the planet, regardless of their country's level of human development

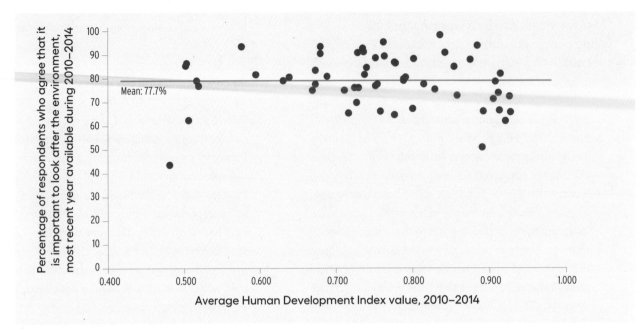

Note: The survey question reads: "It is important to this person looking after the environment." "Would you please indicate [...] whether that person is very much like you, like you, somewhat like you, not like you, or not at all like you?" The figure includes people in the first three categories (very much like you, like you and somewhat like you). The average breakdown of responses across the sample of 59 countries was 24.7 percent for very much like me, 29.8 percent for like me, 23.2 percent for somewhat like me, 13.6 percent for a little like me, 5.9 percent for not like me and 2.8 percent for not at all like me (see annex figure A4.1 at the end of the chapter).
Source: Human Development Report Office calculations based on data from the World Value Survey Wave 6 (Inglehart 2014b).

Figure 4.4 Lost opportunity: People would have given part of their income to protect the planet in the 1990s, regardless of levels of human development

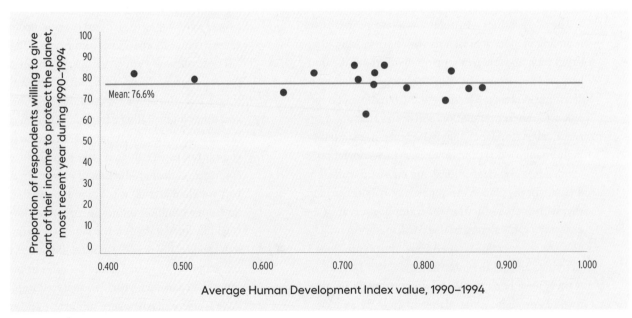

Note: Covers 16 low, medium, high and very high human development countries.
Source: Human Development Report Office with data from the World Value Survey Wave 2 (Inglehart 2014a).

micro particles can be ingested by humans who consume fish or seafood.[87] Plastic particles also reach tap water in many areas—more than 80 percent of samples from five continents are contaminated.[88] Ingesting plastic particles can have direct consequences on human health, as it may cause cancer, reproductive problems, asthma, obesity and other health issues.[89] And although a few countries have already witnessed a change in some social norms (plastic bags are seen as offensive, are charged for or are prohibited altogether; neighbours may tell you not to idle your car in the morning; and the like), we are still far from the systemic transformation needed.

In fact, the proportion of people who are likely to take concrete action is much smaller than the proportion who express values for the environment (figure 4.5). Across all the suggested areas that could reduce planetary pressures, the average percentage of people who are likely to take action is only about 47 percent.[90] And the likelihood of taking action rarely even reflects the actual action people engage in. A potential explanation for both discrepancies is that people are less likely to act on their values when action implies personal sacrifice, financial cost, increased effort or inconvenience.[91] Many people hesitate to take on such a burden for long-term collective benefits, especially without knowing what others will do—that is, before social norms are established and made explicit.[92] This is often called a social dilemma.[93]

"Worldwide about 78 percent of people agree that it is important to look after the environment.

Insights from social neuroscience provide additional evidence and explanation for the discrepancy between self-reported values and behaviour at the societal level. Consumers who self-reportedly prefer eco-friendly products were exposed in an experiment to advertisements of green and conventional products.[94] Although they reported liking the green products better, magnetic resonance imaging showed that only the conventional products

Figure 4.5 Fewer people are likely to take concrete actions that reduce planetary pressures

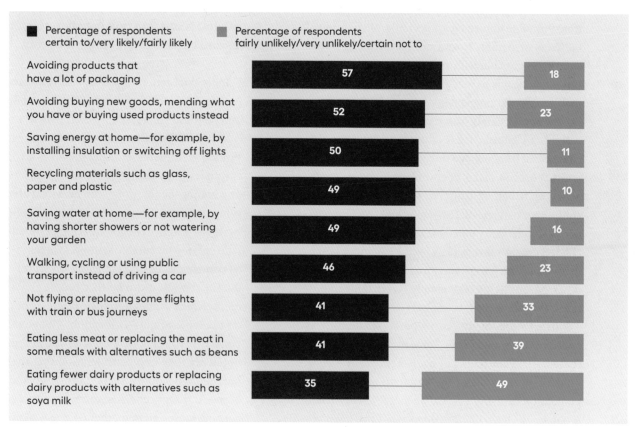

Note: Reflects online responses by 20,590 adults ages 16–74 to the question "Thinking about things you might do in order to limit your own contribution to climate change, how likely or unlikely would you be to make the following changes within the next year?"
Source: IPSOS Global Advisor 2020.

activated the parts of the brain responsible for value and reward, most likely leading to a purchase. Similar inconsistencies between values and purchase behaviour have been widely documented for quite some time.[95] One possible explanation is the association between green products and higher prices. But two other factors may be at play. One is social bias, the fact that self-reporting may be biased by perceptions of social desirability, with people assuming that preferring green products is more socially accepted. The other is the perception that one person's purchase of a green product will make little difference for the planet.[96] The next section assesses this last argument in the context of agency from a capabilities perspective. Agency may just be a missing link between supportive values and behavioural change that, once activated in enough people, can lead to behavioural tipping, changing social norms for some time to come.

From values to self-reinforcing social norms

"Social arrangements inherited from the past are transformable human creations rather than immutable facts of nature,"[97] so a change in social norms should be possible with supportive values in place. But many people expect governments to take action first, as with the implementation of the Sustainable Development Goals (see figure 4.6). Psychologists call this an external locus of control—the sense that change can be generated only by a powerful external entity.[98] But the quality of governance—important for action on behalf of nature, as shown by biodiversity conservation—varies across countries.[99] And on some occasions planetary imbalances may not be a national government's first priority because of more immediate issues such as poverty and hunger,[100] whereas other governments may simply reject their importance altogether.

Furthermore, many people perceive themselves and their communities as "too small to make a difference."[101] They feel "[...] overwhelmed by a combination of the scale of the problems and a limited perception of their personal agency."[102] This vision problem has been identified as one of the main obstacles to pro-environmental behaviour for decades.[103] It undermines people's agency because they rely on an overarching entity to take action. But the vision is not necessarily true. Individual action can indeed drive change towards transformation, but only if emulated and, of course, only if directed towards protecting the planet. The planet is affected by the accumulation of myriad acts of individual consumption.[104] For example, changes in western diets that are based heavily on animal products and processed foods could reduce greenhouse gas emissions by at least 40 percent.[105] About 70 percent of Unilever's greenhouse gas footprint depends on consumer choices—on which product consumers purchase, how they use it and how they dispose of it.[106] The private sector thus also constitutes a channel through which behaviour and social norms can change. And people indeed see other entities, apart from governments, as agents of change, indicating potential for partnerships (figure 4.6; see also box 4.2 later in the chapter).[107] There have been successful cases, such as the global science–business initiative for ocean stewardship.[108]

" The percentage of people who are likely to take concrete actions is much smaller—only about 47 percent. A missing link between supportive values and behavioural change is agency.

Individual action can be especially impactful when people drive change in organizations, communities and politics.[109] Embracing disagreement among pluralistic constituencies with different interests such as firms, governments and civil society is an opportunity rather than a challenge in this regard. One person, or a homogeneous group, can be wrong about something, whereas truly pluralistic constituencies that form coalitions to negotiate, cooperate and coordinate provide favourable settings to tackle a challenge as complex as easing planetary pressures.[110] A conducive condition can be that people's moral judgement, which shapes decisionmaking, is based partly on the logic of universalization: "What would happen if everybody acted that way?" So at times people implicitly take into consideration that their behaviour could become a social norm.[111] As the realities of the Anthropocene, and the risks that it generates, become more apparent, there is a real chance for cooperation to move the needle towards reducing planetary pressures.

Figure 4.6 People expect governments to take action, but there is room for partnerships

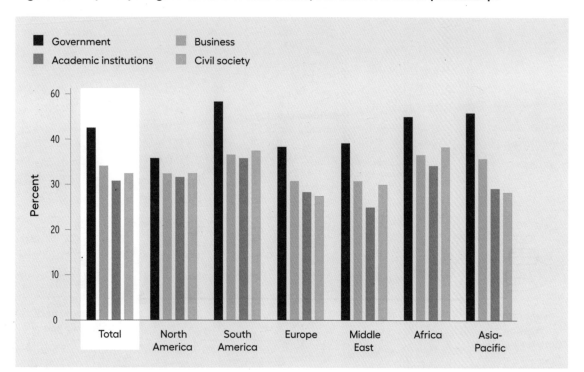

Note: Reflects responses by 26,374 individuals worldwide to the survey question "Who do you expect to push forward the implementation of the SDGs in your country?"
Source: Frank and Cort 2020.

Harnessing agency

When people have agency, they support policies that are aligned with their values and act on them.[112] "Activating conscious human agency that is critically reflective of individual and shared assumptions, beliefs and paradigms is a powerful way to shift norms [...]."[113]

" In some countries the combined annual marketing expenditure of only two large companies is more than the annual government budget for environmental protection.

But individuals do not act in a vacuum. Behaviours are shaped by social, economic, technological and institutional factors. People are deeply embedded in social and economic structures that can either constrain or foster their actions, either restrict them or empower them to act as agents of change. The social structures have three interconnected layers: institutional (rules, norms, traditions, customs), organizational (governance structures, networks) and technosphere (technology and infrastructure). Some changes are fairly easy, while others can be more difficult. The former can accelerate the latter, but the latter can also slow down the former.[114]

Within this structure, agency can play out in two dimensions, each with two extremes: One is everyday agency (daily decisionmaking) as opposed to strategic and political agency (long-term planning), and the other is personal agency (individual choices) as opposed to collective agency (people's capacity to trigger sweeping change; figure 4.7).[115] Collective agency has the greatest potential to change social norms. But the collective is also the strongest force to defend conserving the status quo. Individual choices are not independent of collective ones because they are made within a sociocultural context that shapes behaviour through such mechanisms as peer effects, lifestyles and social norms[116] that emerge within and are reinforced by people's communities, neighbourhoods, information groups and networks of friends and professionals.[117] In times of increased political polarization in many countries,[118] which is often reflected in environmental issues,[119] power struggles can emerge between polarized groups, one defending the status quo and practicing

Figure 4.7 Agency plays out in a social structure and can take two dimensions

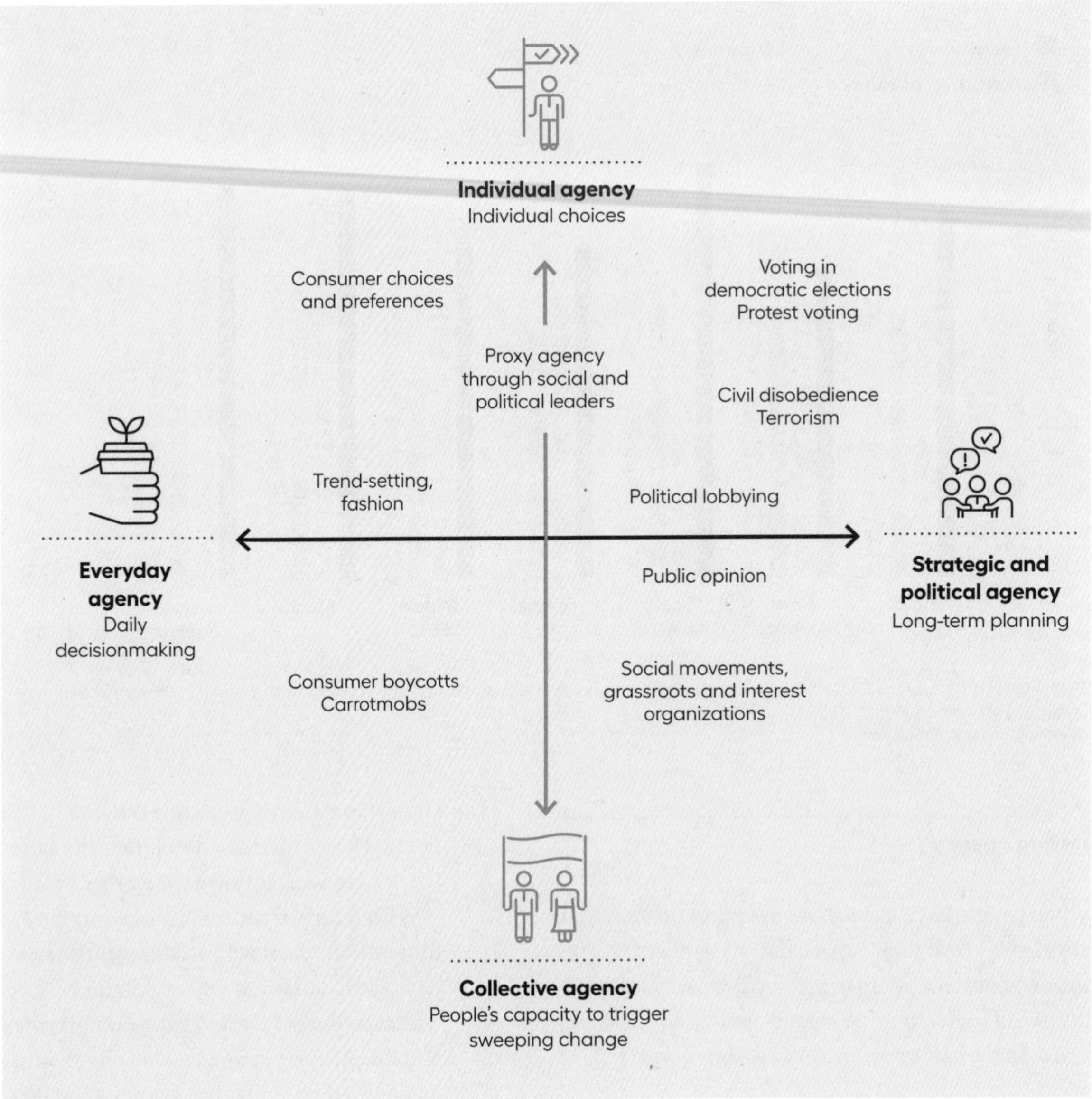

Individual agency
Individual choices

Consumer choices and preferences

Voting in democratic elections
Protest voting

Proxy agency through social and political leaders

Civil disobedience
Terrorism

Trend-setting, fashion

Political lobbying

Everyday agency
Daily decisionmaking

Public opinion

Strategic and political agency
Long-term planning

Consumer boycotts
Carrotmobs

Social movements, grassroots and interest organizations

Collective agency
People's capacity to trigger sweeping change

Source: Otto and others 2020c.

existing norms, and the other seeking change and trying to model behaviour in the hope that others follow.

There are also incentives that work subconsciously against some people's values. In this sense not all agency eases planetary pressures, especially when firms and consumers face economic incentives, such as subsidized fossil fuels, that rationally lead to overuse (see chapter 5). But more is at work than confronting the wrong prices. Firms themselves may drive perceptions of what constitutes social needs. Consider the marketing efforts of large companies for allegedly necessary products or convenient services. The combined annual marketing spending of two large global companies in the United States ($11.16 billion) is more than the annual budget of the country's Environmental Protection Agency ($8.84 billion).[120] In Brazil the combined marketing expenditure of only two companies ($1.48 billion) is almost eight times the budget of the Ministry for the Environment ($0.19 billion).[121] This marketing spending, designed to increase consumption, has to be seen against the level of resources available to public authorities whose duty is to safeguard the environment. Another example is the struggle over leaded gasoline, which was found to cause substantial damage to the planet as early as the 1960s. It took several decades until it was phased out in most countries, in large part because of considerable resistance and attacks by powerful companies defending their interests in maintaining the status quo.[122] A similar case is the ongoing struggle between activists and lobbying companies over the use of some pesticides.[123]

Unleashing change through policies

So how can policies help people act on their values despite these obstacles and counterincentives? Among the conventional solutions to overcoming social dilemmas are legal reforms that restrict or regulate certain behaviour. One recent success story is plastic bag bans, for which government enforcement was key. Another is carbon taxes in European countries. Thirty years later, there has been no negative effect on GDP or employment growth, and the $40 tax per tonne of carbon dioxide covering 30 percent of emissions has reduced cumulative emissions by 4–6 percent.[124] This type of tax constitutes an incentive intended to direct economic activity towards sustainable production patterns (see chapter 5). It can also lead to a change in consumer behaviour when customers respond to green advertisements from competing companies.

But other regulations may create public resistance.[125] That is why regulations are often adopted only if supported by a large enough segment of the population —so the political system itself is also responsive to values and social norms. Support for policies usually varies depending on the restrictiveness of the legislation and the personal sacrifice that compliance requires. At the same time information asymmetries create a wedge between what is in the public interest and individual choice, and governments have a responsibility to safeguard the public interest. This is the driving motivation for restrictions on tobacco use indoors, where initial resistance was overwhelmed by a new social norm.

> " Expanding choices can empower people to act on their values.

The discussion is less about whether legal restrictions should be implemented and more about how and when. When support in society is already broad, this will be much easier and likely more effective. Clear and transparent communication can leverage support for certain policies, based on individual or social rationality, as long as people perceive the policy as appropriate to tackle the problem.[126] Support can also be generated through culture, defined as "socially transmitted information, which can include beliefs, values, behaviours, and knowledge and—more specific to sustainability science—the technologies, lifestyles, consumption patterns, norms, institutions, and worldviews that ultimately shape human impacts on the environment."[127] And support can be guided when individuals or groups deliberately create new practices by researching or learning (as with eco-parenting).[128] On some occasions behaviour even changes before regulations are implemented, such as during the Covid-19 pandemic in many places of the world (see below).

Expanding choices

Expanding choices can empower people to act on their values. When people do not have enough options, their agency is externally limited by a lack of choice. For example, in some places the only option for takeout food is a plastic container because bringing your own container is prohibited due to hygienic precautions. Innovation is critical here. If the private sector develops biodegradable food trays or finds other solutions, that would be at least a second-best option for consumers. And if those options were communicated in an attractive way and adopted by community leaders and role models, more people might choose to follow until a tipping point is reached, leading to a positive feedback loop.

Likewise, if carbon, hydro and wind power are the only ways power is produced in a given country, consumers and the private sector do not have the option to use more sustainable energy sources, though they may know that the available ones may harm ecosystems, either directly through adverse effects or through externalities.[129] Here, incentives for innovation such as seed money are needed, together with subsidies that lower the cost of the resulting innovative sources of energy.[130] While technological innovations can be a double-edged sword—not least because they have contributed to the enormous pressures that humans have been putting on the planet—they are also an opportunity on the way towards transformation (chapter 3).[131]

> " Empowered people can unleash real world transformation by changing social norms.

Governments can also directly contribute to increasing people's choices—for instance, through investment in certain infrastructure.[132] When more bike lanes are constructed, people can try biking and learn about its benefits, which may lead to more demand for bicycle lanes and yet more investment in their construction. Policies thus can offer reasons for people to change their behaviour, which can trigger large-scale behavioural tipping without major coercion or enforcement efforts.[133] Amsterdam has arrived at an equilibrium of very high bike use (box 4.2). Apart from the necessary infrastructure, one reason is that moral motivation can be socially learned. Interviews with representatives from neighbourhood recycling programmes in Norway show how participation was reinforced through social interaction. Even though responsibility for recycling was assumed only reluctantly (duty orientation was identified as the most important motive for recycling), once adopted by a few, others followed, especially when there was certainty about other group members' compliance.[134]

But sometimes the social structures can counter the desired norm change—for example, with good quality and accessible public transport systems. If fewer people drive to work or school, this leads to less congestion, which can incentivize those who shifted to public transport to avoid traffic to go back to using their cars. So complementary regulations such as toll roads, road pricing, ecotaxes and subsidies for public transportation may be necessary in some cases to reinforce existing values and provide incentives for the majority of the population to act on them. There is no silver bullet that works for all situations in all societies.

Framing choices

Change through policy is not only about more choices —it is also about how those choices are framed. Examples include nudging and boosting. Nudges are "interventions designed to steer people in a particular direction while preserving their freedom of choice."[135] Boosting aims "to foster people's competence to make their own choices—that is, to exercise their own agency."[136] Certain default options can change habits through cues by changing the choice architecture.[137] In Germany 94 percent of 150,000 private and business customers stuck to the default option of green energy supply, even though a slightly cheaper option was available.[138] Likewise, restaurants can offer paper straws (or none at all) and provide plastic ones only on request, and companies can make paperless billing the default.[139] These default options could be legally required by supportive governments. The key is to make sustainable options easier for consumers, just like placing more recycle bins than trash cans on the street. Some legislation can also shape decisions in nonregulated areas, thus serving as a learning tool. After laws restricted smoking in certain areas, smokers were generally more considerate with their smoking behaviour, even in nonrestricted areas. The new restriction triggered an initial change in attitudes and behaviour that was large enough to cause tipping and cascading.[140] This way, regulations can signal what is considered socially acceptable behaviour.[141]

In both cases, when expanding and framing choices, it is key to focus on high-impact behaviour—such as changes in lifestyle—and behaviours that have high impact when they are aggregated over time.[142] For example, changes in ways of transportation, such as replacing short flights with low-carbon alternatives, walking or cycling instead of driving short distances and reducing speed when driving could make a considerable difference in achieving net zero emissions by 2050.[143] But policies need to incentivize enough people to join until societywide behavioural tipping sets in and positive feedback loops are triggered. Otherwise the few that adopt the new behaviour tend to feel inappropriate and can fall back into previous behavioural patterns (conserving the status quo).[144]

The focus on empowering people may seem at odds with the emphasis on policies steered mostly by governments. Since the context for change consists of the complex and interactive construct of human society with varying levels of governmental support, both approaches will likely be needed.[145] Still, much can be learned from the local level (box 4.3).

Crises as drivers for transformation

The Covid-19 pandemic is an extreme example of the conditions under which society can support drastic

Box 4.2 Real world transformation, unleashed by empowered people

Many people have heard of Amsterdam as Europe's bicycle capital. Perhaps fewer people know that Portland, Oregon, in the United States is a similar case. The story of how both cities became paradises for bikers is similar, only that Amsterdam did so 30 years earlier. In both cases activists played a crucial role in initiating bottom-up change. In both cases newly established social norms ensured that more and more people, including newcomers, reinforced the equilibrium.

When the Dutch economy boomed in the postwar era, cars flooded Dutch cities, but casualties due to traffic accidents also increased considerably. In 1971 more than 400 children were killed in traffic accidents, triggering the movement Stop de Kindermoord (stop child murder), which eventually led to the formation of the country's first cyclists' union.[1] In Portland, activist groups such as Active Right of Way, Friends of Barbur, Swift Planning Group and the bike festival PedalPalooza, which started in 2002, were important in expanding the habit of biking throughout society.[2] But as in Amsterdam, support from local governments was also key, not least for infrastructure and traffic laws. Social scientists speak here of sensitive intervention points, when a small kick can generate great and long-lasting impact throughout society.[3] One of the challenges is finding the circumstances for social movements to change legislation or social norms, even without support from governments.[4]

In Portland and Amsterdam riding a bike has become a social norm, something that is socially expected, "hip," and part of people's identity.[5] About 6.3 percent of commuters use bikes in Portland compared with 0.5 percent nationally in the United States.[6] And 38 percent of all trips are by bike in Amsterdam compared with 2 percent in the United Kingdom.[7] The norm is reinforcing as it attracts more bike-loving people, while newcomers adopt the same behaviour in order to fit in to their new environment.[8] Another mechanism of reinforcement is the early exposure of children to biking, which is a strong predictor of bicycle use in adulthood.[9] Through children the social norm of biking is perpetuated in societies.

There are also examples from developing countries in which civil society, governments and the private sector worked together, generating a change in social norms. Many countries from the global South, such as Bhutan (1999), Bangladesh and India (2002), Rwanda (2004) and Eritrea (2003) implemented plastic bag bans long before higher human development countries, such as China (2008) and Australia (2009, in the state of South Australia), followed by Italy (2013) and France (2016), did.[10] In most cases this has not been a top-down decision by governments but a result of national public pressures. Since most of these countries lack adequate infrastructure for waste collection and recycling, plastic contamination was much more visible and affected the population directly. Sewers clogged by plastic waste were breeding points for mosquitos, increasing the risk of malaria, and cattle and sheep were dying from eating plastic, leading to substantial economic losses for farmers.[11] African countries in particular do not have a strong plastic lobby, so the status quo–conserving effect was weak. Yet, the bans have not come without challenges. Viable alternatives to plastic bags are still scarce, which leads to suboptimal replacements such as bags made of other synthetic fibres, resistance from some businesses and at times even smuggling of plastic.[12] Partnerships can play an important role, as in Kenya where the United Nations Environment Programme, Safaricom and the National Environment Management Agency are working together towards a comprehensive solution for hard plastic waste.[13]

Notes
1. Van der Zee 2015. **2.** Andersen 2013. **3.** Farmer and others 2019. Elsewhere, similar mechanisms have been called social tipping interventions (Otto and others 2020a). **4.** Otto and others 2020b. **5.** Pelzer 2010. **6.** Portland Bureau of Transportation 2019. **7.** Van der Zee 2015. **8.** Nello-Deakin and Nikolaeva 2020. **9.** Pelzer 2010. **10.** Knoblauch, Mederake and Stein 2018. **11.** Knoblauch, Mederake and Stein 2018. **12.** de Freytas-Tamura 2017; Watts 2018. **13.** UNEP 2018a.

restrictions, leading to changes in social norms within a very short timeframe.[146] During several lockdowns air travel was restricted in the majority of countries, consumption of material goods and services dramatically declined and life was temporarily reduced to meeting only essential needs such as food and shelter. For indispensable services, such as doctor appointments and education, alternative solutions, such as teleconferences, have been found, albeit only for those with access to the necessary

Box 4.3 What we need to do—learning from locals

Many approaches to reducing planetary imbalances take countries as a whole and focus on the nations that pollute most.[1] Poverty, environmental justice and governance are often missing in these approaches, while conversations about increasing consumption by some and deprivation of others are frequently avoided. But many local initiatives, several led by women, have been successful—for example, an Indian project led by Kudumbashree, which empowers women farmers, fishers and grazers to assume leadership in public decisionmaking.[2] Other initiatives move from the local through the national to the regional level.

In March 2018 the first environmental treaty for Latin America and the Caribbean, the Regional Agreement on Access to Information, Public Participation and Access to Justice in Environmental Matters, known as the Escazú Agreement, was approved.[3] United Nations Secretary-General António Guterres called this agreement "a valuable tool to seek people-centred solutions grounded in nature."[4] To make participation possible, the Economic Commission for Latin America and the Caribbean established and coordinated the Regional Public Mechanism, which let civil society representatives participate in the meetings alongside country delegates, but without being able to vote in the decisionmaking. Still, more than 30 civil society organizations, known as the LACP10 network, had a substantial impact on the agreement. They brought proposals to the table, some picked up directly, others shaping the positions of government delegates.[5]

Locally informed perspectives also suggest strategic approaches to tackling planetary imbalances.[6] First is the need to shift our way of thinking—away from the belief that self-interest eventually leads in all cases to the common good, away from the perception that higher consumption leads to greater overall wellbeing and towards an integrated approach of development that takes into account not only economics but all social sciences, including the humanities. Second, structural change in the ownership of productive assets can be supportive of easing planetary pressures. Cases in India and Nepal show that environmental decisionmaking can be democratized when control over the means of production is transferred to local communities, which can lead to more sustainable outcomes. Participation is key for strengthening transparency and accountability—among politicians but also among scientists and engineers, who need to consider socioenvironmental challenges in their work. Third, education is paramount.[7] It is not so much a matter of teaching certain skills, reducing resource consumption being an important one. Rather, its purpose is transformative: It is about dismantling unsustainable perspectives of growth and development and constructing new worldviews that ease planetary pressures while advancing human development.

Notes
1. UNDP 2019c. **2.** Nagendra 2018. **3.** CIVICUS 2020. The agreement follows Principle 10 of the 1992 Rio Declaration on Environment and Development, which seeks to ensure access to information, citizen participation and access to justice in environmental matters (ECLAC 2020). **4.** United Nations 2020c, p. 19. **5.** CIVICUS 2020. **6.** Lele 2020. **7.** Lele 2020; Nagendra 2018.

---

technology, which is doomed to increase inequalities in outcomes. Within a few weeks the pandemic also led to an unprecedented change in socially acceptable behaviour and social norms—as with the change of common salutations such as handshakes and hugs and kisses and the use of face masks in public—based on information and recommendations from experts and governments. Some variations in compliance can be observed across countries depending on culture and the form of government. Still, in an impressively short timeframe the vast majority of people adopted new social norms that came with substantial personal sacrifice in order to slow the spread of the virus.[147]

Why are responses to the Covid-19 pandemic so much more pervasive than responses to the pressures that humans put on the planet? Both, controlling a communicable disease and climate stability, are global public goods,[148] so their provision comes with similar challenges of collective action, such as free riding.[149] Yet, there is a decisive difference between the two: the immediate nature of the threat that Covid-19 poses to each individual. People have been dying by the minute, and many more people have gotten infected every second.[150] The spread is overwhelming and carries the virus right to everyone's front door. The threat from climate change, and the pressure humans put on the planet more broadly, is much more gradual and abstract—though this is changing. The pandemic itself may reflect the risks associated with planetary pressures. Some communities have already experienced the consequences in the form of adverse health effects from air pollution or extreme weather events such as hurricanes, floods and droughts. But, tragically, those are precisely the groups that typically have less voice and less power in society, impeding more substantial calls for action (box 4.4).[151] Inequalities shape who has agency and who lacks it and vice versa.[152] These are the social imbalances highlighted in chapters 1 and 2 that shape action (or a lack thereof) in addressing planetary pressures.

History has shown that risks, including perceived risks, "serve as a pivot to reorient social actors and how they interact with one another and the natural environment."[153] Indeed, perceived risks from climate change are statistically associated with higher support for mitigation policies and improved pro-environmental behaviour.[154] The perception of risk depends on the social context in which individuals and communities are embedded.[155] Greta Thunberg's wakeup calls, which painted a horrific picture of climate change's threat, might have had an impact on the thinking and behaviour of many, as shown by the notable participation in Fridays for Future demonstrations around the world. Yet, there is no comparison to the dramatic change in social norms observed during the Covid-19 pandemic. But since more and more studies, and thus also the media, relate the pandemic to the pressures that we put on our planet, particularly to the loss in biodiversity,[156] values can turn increasingly into action and consequently into social norms—because of the connection between the two crises (chapter 1).

" Inequalities shape who has agency and who lacks it. Still, crises can be opportunities for transformation.

The Covid-19 pandemic can thus drive people to revise their relationship with the planet. For policymakers this is a good time to create facilitating conditions for change. "The capacity to undergo a radical restructuring [...] is a unique feature distinguishing social systems from organic or mechanical ones. Restructuring the social structure is a product of human agency and is grounded in the interaction between structures and human actions that produces change in a system's given form, structure or state. [...] the transition of institutions is frequently driven by crises."[157] The next section takes up the example of the Covid-19 pandemic, looking at how, when and by whom social norms changed during the crisis.

From existential risks to transformation

So how can we encourage change in social norms in a context of strong values, weak agency and easy free riding? And who is best equipped to do so? One perspective on collective action is that an external entity needs to take this role, enforcing rule compliance. But alternative approaches show that self-organization can also be effective.[158] Specifically, the organization in polycentric systems of governance—"several centers of decision-making which are formally independent of each other"—can mitigate collective action problems that many large administrations face.[159] Each unit, such as a family, a company or a local government, establishes norms and rules with considerable independence. Chapters 1, 3 and 6 documented the numerous communities around the world, particularly indigenous peoples, that have preserved both cultural and biological diversity. Part of the explanation for their effectiveness is that they integrate local knowledge, peer learning and trial-and-error learning.[160] Since they act at the local level, they also benefit from some social success factors because in smaller entities it is possible to establish trust and reciprocity, which foster agency and collective action, often without needing external enforcement and sanctions (box 4.5).

People's attachment to their place of living implies an awareness of the value of territory, local identity and a sense of community, fostering stewardship for the planet. This combined with a participatory approach to decisionmaking as well as institutional respect for people and organized groups, for their identity and for their local culture constitutes a favourable setting for collective action at the local level.[161] Such an approach is also well equipped to foster the complex and intertwined relationship between equity and sustainability in a way that unleashes positive synergies between the two.[162] It is thus a promising way to foster agency among those who are

Box 4.4 Less voice, less power, more suffering

As chapter 2 noted, some groups suffer disproportionally from the continued pressures humans put on the planet, which exacerbates group-based inequalities, also known as horizontal inequalities.[1] This happens through three main channels: disadvantaged groups' increased exposure to climate change, their higher susceptibility to potential damages caused by the pressure humans put on the planet and their lower ability to cope and recover from adverse climate events.[2]

Most affected are populations that depend on natural resources, such as coastal agricultural, pastoral and forest communities, because of adverse effects on food, water and infrastructure.[3] Many times, these populations are already disadvantaged—as with some indigenous peoples—when it comes to culturally adequate education, health services or infrastructure. This increases multidimensional horizontal inequalities. For example, in rural communities of Burkina Faso and in mountainous areas of Nepal, livelihood options are limited, and many people rely on weather-dependent agriculture for their own food safety and to generate resources to cover other living expenses. Adaptive capacity is typically low in these communities due to low levels of education and information.[4] Rural populations are also more vulnerable to the climate's adverse effects on health, as seen in the Hindu Kush–Himalayas area.[5]

But natural resource–dependent communities are not the only ones that suffer disproportionally. The consequences of human pressures on the planet affect some social groups more than others in resources and livelihoods. These differences emerge from social hierarchies based on race, caste and gender discrimination as well as poverty and power differentials.[6] For instance, in some communities women may be unable to escape from floods or other disasters due to restrictions of movement without a male chaperone, or they may not be allowed to seek shelter where they would have to cohabit with unknown men.[7] As chapter 1 noted, in the United States air pollution harms disproportionally more Black and African American people and Hispanic and Latino people than non-Hispanic White people, relative to each group's consumption, due mainly to geographic location.[8]

Agency of minority groups is often demotivated due to the biased public perception that environmentalist civil society organizations consist mostly of affluent Whites. This undermines their concern for these issues, and it marginalizes them from civic participation.[9]

Inequities can be reinforcing because personal experience shapes behaviour. For example, a person who has already experienced the consequences of climate change, say during a flood, is more likely to believe scientific research on it and adopt pro-environmental behaviour. Therefore, those who bear the biggest burden of degradation are likely to pollute less.[10] Power differentials increase existing inequalities and inequities, as protection measures may target certain communities. More influential communities tend to be better able to gather resources for sea walls, dikes or flood channels to protect their livelihood, deflecting the risk to communities that are already more vulnerable.[11]

In addition to distributional equity, recognitional and procedural fairness are important in challenging power relations that persistently shape the rules of the game in favour of elite groups (see chapter 2).[12] When people from all affected groups actively engage in decisionmaking processes, the resulting policies will likely be better accepted, supported and complied with throughout society[13] because support for policies depends heavily on distributional, recognitional and procedural justice.[14]

Preferences to reduce environmental inequality are stronger when framed in terms of benefits than harms.[15] That is, most people have a weaker preference for initiatives that direct inevitable harm towards communities that so far have been less affected than for measures that alleviate environmental harm for adversely affected communities.[16]

Notes
1. Stewart 2016. Horizontal inequalities were initially defined as inequalities between ethnic groups (Stewart 2005). This definition has been amplified throughout the years and is currently used for inequalities between groups distinguished by their history, religion, language, race, region and the like (Stewart 2016). 2. Islam and Winkel 2017. 3. UNEP 2019c. 4. Gentle and Maraseni 2012; Tankari 2018. 5. Ebi and others 2007. 6. Thomas and others 2018. 7. Sultana 2014. 8. Tessuma and others 2019. 9. A study on public perception in the United States shows that people widely underestimate the environmental concerns of Blacks and African Americans, Hispanics and Latinos, and other minority groups. This can have implications for civic engagement of minorities, who may feel excluded by images of White affluent American environmentalists (Pearson and others 2018). 10. Hamilton-Webb and others 2017; Spence and others 2011. 11. Atteridge and Remling (2018), cited in Thomas and others (2018). See also Leach and others (2018). 12. Leach and others 2018. 13. Steg 2016. 14. For a detailed explanation of each sphere of justice within the capabilities approach, see Walker and Day (2012). 15. Steg 2016. 16. Makov, Newman and Zauberman 2020. In that study participants were told that having a water treatment plant in the community increased water quality in the community by one unit-change. There were two scenarios with a tight budget: In one scenario, one treatment plant had to close; in the other there was only enough funding to open one additional plant. People had a general preference for equal outcomes. But their preference for opening a treatment plant in a community with lower water quality was much higher than their preference for closing down a plant in a community that enjoyed good water quality, both with the end of enhancing equality.

Box 4.5 Why polycentric systems work: Insights from social psychology

Social psychology provides detailed insights on how the mechanisms behind polycentric systems work at the individual level. Free riding is less common among small groups because it violates absolute and inviolable values, risks negative sanctions from others and counters the desire to receive the respect of other group members, among other reasons.[1] Communication within the group about intentions, sentiments, action and outlook is key.[2] In this regard, different forms of trust are important. Social trust—trust in neighbours and strangers—as well as trust in institutions are associated with stronger support for some sustainability policies and can be built through fair processes and clear communication based on scientific assessments.[3]

Moreover, behavioural rules need to be salient in order to be followed.[4] In other words, norms must be explicit—for instance, when an entity, small as it might be, informs people of other people's desirable or commonly approved behaviour (injunctive norm), this shapes the perception of the appropriate thing to do.[5] This sort of communication can also help correct misperceptions about what others do and approve of, leading to a change in normative beliefs.[6] Reciprocity and maintaining one's reputation can be important motives to limit free riding if one's behaviour is observable by others.[7] When individuals receive the information that more and more people are doing something that is desirable,[8] in the best case, this will lead to emerging dynamic norms that trigger certain behaviour leading to behavioural tipping and norms cascades. Injunctive norms can prevent boomerang effects—people who initially performed better than others do not reverse their behaviour when they realize that they are contributing more to a public good than others.[9] When community leaders or other role models take the lead, participation may increase, and behavioural tipping may become more likely given their influential position within the community.[10]

Notes
1. Stroebe and Frey 1982. **2.** Wang and others 2020. **3.** Dietz, Shwom and Whitley 2020; Firestone and others 2020. Smith and Mayer (2018) found that social trust is an even stronger predictor of support for climate change mitigation policies than institutional trust is. Social trust is also a strong predictor of pro-environmental behaviour. **4.** Cialdini and Goldstein 2004, p. 597. **5.** Aasen and Vatn 2018; Chabay and others 2019. **6.** Lapinski and Rimal 2005; Legros and Cislaghi 2020. **7.** Yoeli and others 2013. **8.** One study observed that the use of reusable coffee mugs increased by 17.3 percent after a dynamic norms intervention (Loschelder and others 2019). **9.** Reno, Cialdini and Kallgren 1993; Schultz and others 2007. **10.** Legros and Cislaghi (2020) highlight the importance of role models for changing social norms in all stages of their lifecycle.

typically disadvantaged in society, with the possibility of reducing group-based inequalities and easing planetary pressures.

Most of us have probably observed some of the mechanisms described in box 4.3 during the Covid-19 pandemic in our immediate circles of contact, such as the workplace, school, friends and family. Many social norms that emerged during this time were already being practised before being made explicit by governments (such as social distancing, avoiding handshakes, using hand sanitizer), and they were also practised by many people in countries in which governments were hesitant to implement stronger restriction. This happened mostly through exchange of information and opinions, as well as conversations and discussions, which is what the capabilities approach suggests for the transition to sustainability: "The role of public discussion and participation [...] can be crucial in behavioural change and in the use of responsible agency. [...] The medieval distinction between seeing human beings as 'agents' and as 'patients' has not lost its relevance in the contemporary world. The reach of reason and interactive agency can indeed be remarkably extensive, and it can be particularly crucial for our transition to sustainability."[163]

This does not mean, however, that governments and other community leaders are condemned to lean back and wait for slow progress. The Covid-19 pandemic differs from the situation regarding the planet because of its strong individual incentives to take action. In the absence of these, and in view of strong counterincentives, responsible stewardship of the planet needs to be nurtured[164] by making certain behaviour "[...] more feasible, more attractive, and more profitable for individuals and groups."[165] Governments can choose to create the conditions that allow people to expand their capabilities with equity while assuming caring stewardship of the planet.

" Instead of seeing people as patients that need to be treated or objects that need to be changed, they need to be empowered to act as agents of change who trigger real systemic transformation.

Instead of seeing people as patients that need to be treated or objects that need to be changed, they need to be empowered to act as agents of change who trigger real systemic transformation.[166] This is particularly important because framings that suggest inexorable collapse are disempowering and not borne out by evidence of past environmental crises.[167] In fact, recent evidence suggests that historical societal collapses—to the extent the term collapse even has meaning—are seldom the direct consequence of ecological stress.[168] Societies that have confronted dramatic environmental challenges "improve[d] societal resilience, increasing opportunities for learning and innovation, to broaden the repertoire of adaptive responses. Collapse is not an inevitable result of transformations."[169] "Societies have avoided collapse by revitalizing a common will to overcome adversity, drawing from both old experience and new information to revise or develop collective strategies for survival. [...] Solutions ultimately are cognitive and collaborative. However, solutions to acute crises of sustainability cannot be devised or implemented if remedial response is modelled with stereotypic assumptions about human behaviour."[170]

In some cases severe power differentials need to be overcome in order to establish equity (that is what makes equity one of the key dimensions of empowerment identified in chapter 3). History shows that societies can be resilient, but some groups that have been notoriously deprived of power—such as indigenous peoples—are among those with the knowledge required to build that resilience. As argued in chapter 6, they will need a booster of empowerment that puts decisionmaking in their hands in order to fulfil principles of distributional, recognitional and procedural justice.[171]

To sum up, learning, self-interest and common goals or goals of others shape values. When it comes to easing planetary pressures, there seems to be a gap between people's values and their agency. Values are most likely to result in action for change and eventually in widespread behaviour and social norm change when:

- There is public discussion of challenges and their potential solutions that includes all groups of society with equity.
- Governments create facilitating conditions by making behavioural change feasible, attractive and profitable for the majority of people.
- Agency is enabled by participatory approaches in small entities and groups.
- Desirable behaviour and innovations are fostered by incentives.
- Behaviour is reinforced after tipping points through:
  ○ The observable behaviour of others.
  ○ The risk of negative sanctions from others.
  ○ A guilty conscience.
  ○ A desire to receive the respect of other group members.
- New or changed norms are salient, injunctive and dynamic.

Systemic transformation that aims to ease planetary pressures while equitably advancing human development can happen within the complex and interdependent structure of today's societies in which multiple actors push for their interests. First, self-interest and common interests nurtured through information and knowledge, among others, shape people's values. Policies, consisting of incentives for certain behaviour and for innovations, as well as transparent communication about scientific evidence, can empower people to act on their values by creating facilitating conditions for doing so. If enough people change their behaviour, positive feedback loops set

" The voices, empowerment and agency of typically disadvantaged groups are crucial on the way towards transformation with equity because these are the people who suffer most from the pressure humans are putting on the planet.

in, behaviour is reinforced and social norms start to change. At that point, they are weighed against pressures to maintain the status quo, which is decisive for whether the system tips over and transformation takes place (figure 4.8). The voices, empowerment and agency of typically disadvantaged groups are crucial on the way towards transformation with equity because these are the people who suffer most from the pressure humans are putting on the planet.

Figure 4.8 Tipping the balance towards transformation

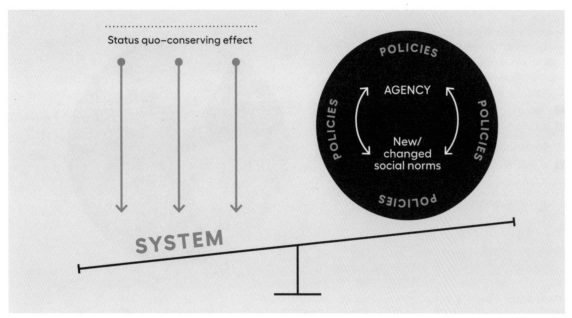

Source: Human Development Report Office.

Seeing the pressures that humans put on the planet as a global phenomenon, we have to ask, however, to what extent can the insights about participatory education, polycentric systems and public discussion travel to the global level? Are they applicable to an environment in which states are expected to cooperate and nurture social norms beyond borders?

What can be done when some states are not willing to cooperate due to different worldviews or other public policy priorities? Could civil society and nongovernmental organizations partly substitute for state actors? What in the end is the role of incentives? These and other questions are addressed in chapter 5.

Annex figure A4.1 Disaggregated data for survey question in figure 4.3

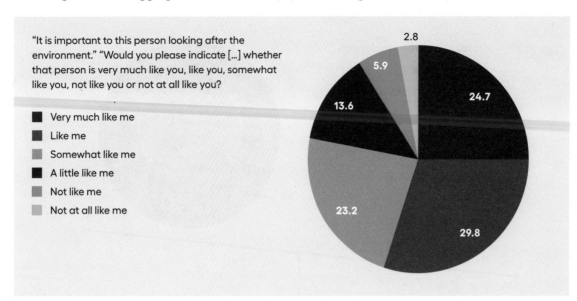

"It is important to this person looking after the environment." "Would you please indicate [...] whether that person is very much like you, like you, somewhat like you, not like you or not at all like you?

- Very much like me
- Like me
- Somewhat like me
- A little like me
- Not like me
- Not at all like me

2.8
5.9
13.6
24.7
23.2
29.8

Note: Data are percentages for the most recent year available during 2010–2014.
Source: Human Development Report Office calculations based on data from the World Value Survey Wave 6 (Inglehart 2014b).

Shaping incentives to navigate the future

CHAPTER 5

Shaping incentives to navigate the future

Like norms, incentives and regulation are powerful. By preventing or promoting specific actions, they influence behavior directly. They also operate indirectly by reinforcing norms or signaling their change.

How can incentives and regulation advance human development in the Anthropocene?

This chapter explores three areas of opportunity: in finance, so that resources are directed toward investments that reduce planetary pressures; in prices, so that they better capture social and environmental costs; and in collective action, especially at the international level.

What consumers choose to buy, what firms produce and trade, where investors put their money and how governments cooperate are all shaped by incentives. They are not the only drivers of behaviour—social norms matter a great deal (chapter 4)—but even if people do not change their minds, they may still respond to incentives that can either increase or ease planetary pressures. This chapter focuses on how incentives help explain current patterns of consumption, production and investment and other choices that lead to the planetary and social imbalances documented in part I. It explores how these patterns could evolve in ways that would ease planetary pressures and advance human development in the Anthropocene. It does this by considering three domains: finance, prices and international collective action.

" This chapter focuses on how incentives help explain current patterns of consumption, production and investment and other choices that lead to the planetary and social imbalances documented in part I. It explores how these patterns could evolve in ways that would ease planetary pressures and advance human development in the Anthropocene. It does this by considering three domains: finance, prices and international collective action.

First, finance, which encompasses mobilizing resources from firms and savings from people to reward investments that reduce planetary pressures and to penalize or restrict investments that increase those pressures. What is the role of public entities that oversee financial markets and of monetary authorities? And what developments in financial markets indicate the direction of change that may already be occurring? For instance, highly carbon intensive firms listed on European stock exchanges (such as oil extraction, air transport and petroleum refining firms) suffered larger than average declines in stock value after the outbreak of Covid-19, possibly signalling that financial markets see carbon-intense industries as not having as bright a future as others.[1] And with the Covid-19 pandemic there has been a sharp slowdown in economic activity, especially in transport and mobility, so sharp that seismic monitors have picked it up.[2] That raises the potential for locking in some of the behavioural changes

that have eased pressure on the planet during the pandemic.

Second, current market prices do not reflect the social costs of planetary pressures, distorting economic decisions and leading to overuse of resources and excessive environmental degradation relative to what would occur if prices reflected those costs. Even worse, government subsidies compound the distortions. For example, subsidies for fossil fuels are not only a large fiscal burden—at over $317 billion in 2019[3]—but they also encourage behaviour that impedes the transition to renewable energy sources, with direct and indirect costs to people amounting to $4.7 trillion globally in 2015 (6.3 percent of global GDP) and $5.2 trillion in 2017 (6.5 percent).[4] Eliminating subsidies would have reduced global carbon emissions by 28 percent and deaths due to fossil fuel air pollution by 46 percent in 2015.[5] Further, since a very large share of the benefits in developing countries accrues to higher income households, subsidies exacerbate inequalities.[6]

So the chapter discusses the potential for reflecting in market prices the social costs of greenhouse gas emissions and incorporating in economic decisions the value of biodiversity. A key obstacle to removing fossil fuel subsidies is the political economy of addressing the short-term and immediate financial implications for those who benefit from the subsidies, which are easier to navigate in a context of historically low oil prices during the Covid-19 pandemic.[7]

Third, international collective action, addressing the structure of incentives that countries face when they make decisions with implications beyond their borders. This challenge has been studied extensively in the context of providing global public goods.[8] Examples of achievements through international collective action include eradicating smallpox in 1980[9] and adopting the Montreal Protocol to address depletion of the ozone layer. International cooperation is needed because a single country removing all fossil fuel subsidies and putting in place measures that account for the social cost of carbon would not be enough—and in most cases would do very little—to ease planetary pressures.[10] So countries have to come together in some way. The landmark Paris Agreement on climate change[11] has offered a beacon of hope,[12] bringing an unprecedented number of countries on board but only after long negotiations.[13] Even then, the pledges—the nationally determined contributions—under the agreement do not guarantee that its goals will be reached, though they represent the single largest ever commitment to mitigation.[14] Recent studies warn that even if global emissions are reduced enough to keep global temperature rise below the agreement's 2 degrees Celsius goal, dangerous scenarios are probably avoidable only by getting greenhouse gas emissions to net zero by 2050.[15] Thus, it is important to understand how incentives can support international collective action.

Harnessing finance to incentivize transformation

Mobilizing financial resources is essential for the investment in people, infrastructure, technology and broader social change required to transform our world, as called for by the 2030 Agenda for Sustainable Development.[16] So is ensuring that those resources are channelled in ways to advance that transformation. For example, cumulative global investment in low-carbon power between 2020 and 2040, based on stated energy policies, is about $16 trillion (figure 5.1). But to reach net-zero emissions by 2050, that would have to increase to more than $27 trillion, with other shifts in energy efficiency and grid networks as well as lower investment in

fossil fuel power and oil transport and refining. Such shifts call for a wide range of changes in incentives, with governments playing a key role, but they can also emerge as a result of pressure from the investors who entrust their savings to financial firms.[17]

" Mobilizing financial resources is essential for the investment in people, infrastructure, technology and broader social change required to transform our world, as called for by the 2030 Agenda for Sustainable Development. So is ensuring that those resources are channelled in ways to advance that transformation.

Drawing on financial markets

That investment in renewable energy sources remains below future needs, especially in developing countries, opens up opportunities.[18] In 2018 lower-middle-income and low-income countries, with well over 40 percent of the world's people, accounted for less than 15 percent of renewable energy investment, while high-income countries, with just over 15 percent of the world's people, accounted for more than 40 percent.[19] The difference comes largely from a lack of access to funding in

Figure 5.1 Incentives are required to shift finance towards low-carbon energy

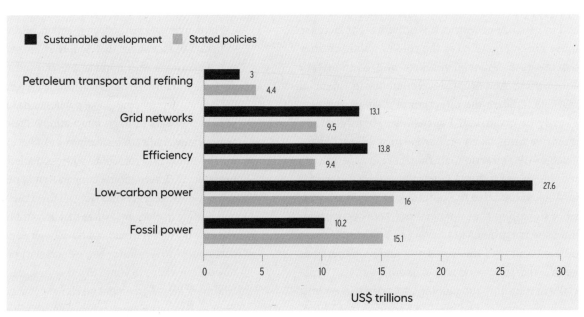

Source: Fickling 2020.

developing countries, which in turn has major impacts on the price and competitiveness of green energy.

Take India, where financing costs account for 50–65 percent of renewable energy tariffs (figure 5.2).[20] Solar tariffs have consistently fallen in India since 2010.[21] But since a high share of the tariff is the cost of capital, even big declines in equipment costs could lower tariffs only so much. The cost of capital is high, even with a maturing market, partly because of the perceived risks in renewable energy investments. So policy had to reduce risk perceptions and improve the bankability of renewable energy projects. Large solar parks were attractive to international investors, and when the bids were backed by central and state government guarantees or credible offtakers (such as the Delhi Metro Rail Corporation), tariffs fell sharply.[22] The government aimed to improve the availability and pricing of project debt finance over time, facilitating lower cost investment.[23]

Incentives can thus lower the cost of finance and improve access to domestic and foreign institutional capital. Options include pooled de-risking of projects across different geographies; solar parks that allow developers to adopt a plug-and-play model and shorten construction timelines; and greater transparency about policies, deployment and project performance to reduce perceived risk.[24]

Opposition is growing to allocating savings to investments linked to fossil fuels or activities that threaten sustainability. Younger people, such as those born in the 1980s and 1990s, are more than twice as likely as those in other generations to invest in companies or funds that target social or environmental outcomes— and they will inherit as much as $24 trillion in wealth over the next decade and a half or so.[25] Some of this wealth is now channelled through financial intermediaries (such as pension funds and asset managers holding mutual funds) that manage savings on behalf of households, especially in the United States (figure 5.3). Partly because of investor pressure, large pension funds, both public and private, have divested some or all of their fossil fuel–related investments. For example, the National Employment Savings Trust—the United Kingdom's largest pension fund— recently decided to ban investments in any company participating in arctic drilling, tar sand extraction or coal mining. With 9 million members, the trust will shift £5.5 billion towards more climate-friendly

Figure 5.2 The cost of finance accounts for the largest share of historically low solar tariffs in India

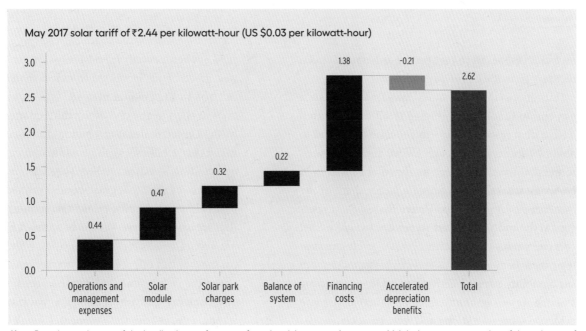

May 2017 solar tariff of ₹2.44 per kilowatt-hour (US $0.03 per kilowatt-hour)

Note: Based on estimates of the levelized cost of energy of an electricity generation asset, which is the net present value of the unit cost of electricity over the lifetime of an asset. Several factors determine the levelized cost of energy or tariff of grid-connected solar power plants. This figure is the component-wise breakdown of the solar tariff in India in 2017. It includes operations and management, solar module, solar park charges, balance of system (costs related to civil works, mounting structures and other preoperative expenses), and financing costs and accelerated depreciation benefit (government incentives that lower the tax burden in the early years of a project).
Source: CEEW 2020.

Figure 5.3 Financial intermediaries hold an increasing share of savings on behalf of households in the United States

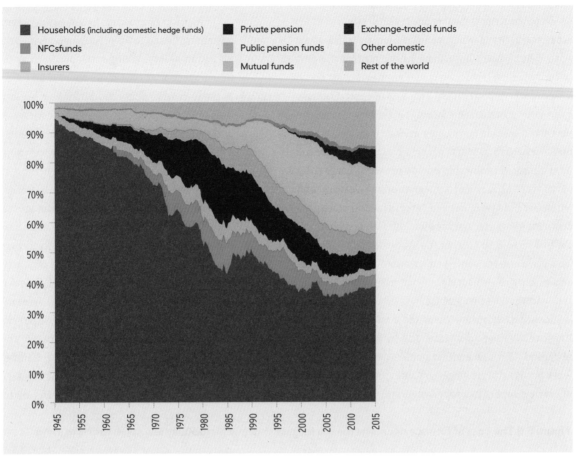

Source: Braun 2020.

investments, based in part on the anticipated green recovery from the Covid-19 pandemic.[26]

Institutional investors under public mandates, such as pension funds and sovereign wealth funds, often have a dual responsibility—to generate profit and to abide by international agreements, including environmental treaties.[27] Large intermediaries that hold company stocks have acquired a larger share of the ownership of firms—in the United States, from 1 percent in the 1990s to almost 10 percent today for S&P 500 companies.[28] They have a greater say in the strategic management of firms and can pressure for more sustainability-focused activity. In addition to strong statements of commitment to sustainability, some evidence suggests a strong and robust association between firm ownership by the three largest asset managers and subsequent reductions in carbon emissions.[29]

Green bonds—first issued in 2007 by the European Investment Bank—are debt securities designed to

fund environmentally friendly investments. Issues of new green bonds increased from less than $1 billion in 2008 to $143 billion in 2018.[30] Green bond issuance in 2020 by the end of the third quarter was led by the United States ($32.3 billion) followed by Germany ($21.4 billion), with an estimated cumulative outstanding issuance totaling $948 billion.[31] Recent evidence suggests that green bonds certified by third parties improve the environmental footprints of firms (but are issued at a premium over ordinary bonds and are held more closely).[32] Certification is thus a critical mechanism of green bond market governance.[33] Given the lack of standardization in the field, some governments and international organizations are stepping up, as with the European Union's consultation on the establishment of a Green Bond Standard.[34]

Additional efforts are under way to scientifically assess the impact of green bonds and other sustainable investments, given the phenomenon of greenwashing—unverifiable assertions by some firms about the sustainability of their investments. Specifically, the environmental performance of green bonds can be more accurately assessed by metrics on their outputs, outcomes and impacts. For wastewater treatment these criteria would cover the volume of wastewater treated (in cubic metres per day), reductions in pollutant concentration in affected water (milligrams per litre), the size of downstream beneficiary populations (in thousands) and the length of improved fish habitat stream (kilometres).[35]

One reason that incentives are changing in financial markets is the growing realization that financial assets are themselves vulnerable to the risks of climate change. A 2015 study projects that climate change will pose a risk of cumulative losses until 2100 that could range from $4.2 trillion to $43 trillion.[36] A more recent report estimates that more than half the world's GDP—around $44 trillion—is either moderately or highly dependent on nature and ecoservices.[37] Climate risks are now being incorporated even in mutual funds that aggregate government debt, with one firm recently launching an exchange-traded fund focused on sovereign bonds, which weights countries based on their climate change risk. Two sovereign bond indices, one weighted by climate risk and the other unweighted, show significant differences in the weights of different countries, based on the assumption that climate change can substantially affect governments' finances and therefore their creditworthiness.[38]

Engaging financial and monetary authorities

Financial and monetary policy to manage climate risks—and to shape incentives for financial players and investment more broadly—has been increasing (spotlight 5.1). Central banks can reduce both financial and climate risks, since many of them are hybrid institutions, combining public and private elements. The Network for Greening the Financial Sector, launched in 2017, comprises central banks and supervisors working together to help countries cope with the economic and financial impacts of climate change. A recent network report analysing the risks in mitigating climate change found that costs can be lowered if the transition starts early and is orderly.[39]

Central banks can deploy several tools to cope with such risks, including adjusting interest rates or expanding balance sheets by purchasing bonds. Unfortunately, only a few central banks (12 percent of 135 surveyed) have taken the financial risks associated with climate change into account and introduced mandates explicitly addressing sustainability.[40] Nearly half the central banks have no explicit or implicit objectives related to sustainability. But many have recently started to integrate environmental risks into their core policy frameworks.[41]

> " Central banks can reduce both financial and climate risks, since many of them are hybrid institutions, combining public and private elements.

Central banks can also coordinate with governments, academia, private firms and civil society so that monetary policy works with fiscal, prudential and carbon policies to support an energy transition.[42] And as financial regulators, central banks can monitor market conditions (the liquidity and premiums of green bonds), catalyse a stable scaleup of green financing and identify obstacles to the emergence of green markets.[43]

The Finance Initiative of the United Nations Environment Programme is another relevant example.[44] This partnership with 300 global financial actors—including banks, investors and insurance companies—mobilizes private finance for sustainable development. Its goal is to make the global financial sector fit-for-purpose in serving both people and the planet. The partnership supports several principles for the global financial sector, including:

- Principles for responsible banking, covering a third of all global banking.
- Principles for sustainable insurance, covering 25 percent of the world's insurance firms.
- Principles for responsible investment, covering 50 percent of the world's institutional investors.

The Financial Stability Board, an international body that advises key institutions of the global financial system, created the Task Force on Climate-Related Financial Disclosures to help companies voluntarily disclose climate-related financial risks to their lenders, investors and insurers (box 5.1).

The Group of Thirty recently published a report on mainstreaming the transition to a net-zero economy,

Box 5.1 The Task Force on Climate-Related Financial Disclosure

The Task Force on Climate-Related Financial Disclosure is a voluntary market-led initiative for firms to disclose pertinent and prospective information on potential financial impacts of climate change.[1] It comprises commercial companies from various sectors, financial entities and investment fund managers. They bring to the present the issues arising from future climate change (through the analysis of various possible scenarios) and emphasize risks and opportunities related to the transition to a lower carbon economy.

The task force's motivation is to give investors and external stakeholders a basis for properly valuating assets and investment projects. That would better guide the market in mobilizing financial resources to facilitate the transition to more sustainable and resilient activities.

The task force invites companies to disclose estimates of three impacts of their production processes: direct emissions generated by the companies (scope 1), indirect emissions (scope 2) and emissions generated throughout the entire value chain, backwards through suppliers and outsourced processes and forward to the companies' consumers and distribution logistics (scope 3).

The task force's 2019 progress report recognizes the difficulty of revealing information on environmental sustainability and identifying valid scenarios to carry out its analysis and make forecasts. It also recognizes that the first steps in this direction are only just being taken, that the methodologies for evaluating the financial risk spreads between green and brown assets are incipient, that the data are limited and that there are no common standards.

However, surveys by the task force indicate that the number of companies implementing its recommendations is increasing and that the main motivations are the reputational benefit and the pressure from investors to provide information on climate-related risks and to recognize how important they are or will be. Financial regulators and supervisors are expected to require that the recommended disclosures be formally incorporated in company reports. Risk-rating firms may also soon begin to incorporate the disclosures in their evaluations. The (UK) HM Treasury (along with the Bank of England and other regulators) issued a roadmap towards mandatory climate-related disclosures in line with the task force recommendations for all major UK companies and financial institutions by 2025.[2]

Notes
1. Bernal-Ramirez and Ocampo 2020; TCFD 2019. **2.** United Kingdom HM Treasury 2020.

---

exploring how the decisions of investors, financial institutions, regulators and governments will affect sustainability in the short and medium terms. Those decisions are important not only for the planet but also for the sustainability of economies. The report's recommendations can accelerate countries' transitions to net-zero emissions and improve their long-term economic and financial prospects.[45]

The International Monetary Fund's Global Financial Stability Report went even further, suggesting that companies be mandated to disclose their climate risk exposure because voluntary efforts were not enough.[46] That view is based on the major financial market failure of inadequate representation of climate risks in asset prices and financial balance sheets. This lack of transparency implies that investments affected by climate risk are de facto subsidized.

The European Central Bank president recently questioned the principle of market neutrality—where central banks purchase assets that mirror the composition of the bond market on the grounds that trusting markets that do not price in climate change and its effects is increasingly risky.[47] And the US Federal Reserve Board issued a report concluding that climate change increases the likelihood of dislocations and disruptions in the economy, which in turn are likely to increase financial shocks and financial system vulnerabilities.[48]

The Bank for International Settlements—an international organization coordinating financial and monetary cooperation among central banks—points out that integrating the analysis of risks related to climate change into existing monitoring of financial stability is particularly hard. Climate change has physical, social and economic dimensions characterized by radical uncertainty and involves complex dynamics.[49]

Traditional backward-looking risk assessments are thus insufficient for predicting how climate risks will evolve. "Green swan" risks are climate-related events that could create extreme financial disruptions and cause future global financial crises.[50] Central banks can help both by developing forward-looking risk assessment tools and by coordinating systemwide policies to mitigate climate change. Examples include developing new international financial mechanisms, integrating sustainability into accounting and financial practices and pricing carbon.

The Sustainability Accounting Standards Board, an independent body, ratifies accounting standards to better reflect the impact of various economic processes on sustainability. A current project involves assessing the interest of investors in incorporating risks and opportunities related to the use of plastic in standards for the paper and chemicals industries. As regulations and consumer preferences for packaging shift away from plastic, this line of research can help investors more accurately assess the risks and opportunities of investing in these industries.[51]

The SDG Impact Standards for private equity, debt and venture capital funds can help their managers consider the positive or negative effects of investment practices on people and the planet. The four standards focus on strategy and purpose, operations and management, transparency and performance reporting, and governance practices.[52]

Impact investing is another recent innovation in investments related to social or environmental aims. For example, social impact bonds pay returns to investors depending on prespecified social or environmental objectives. More than 80 such bonds have a total investment value of $375 million.[53] Especially when the costs of a project cannot be covered with private benefits—the bonds allow governments or other entities interested in social benefits to support a positive net present value for investors, which traditional debt financing cannot.

Multilateral development banks are also very important in the ecosystem of climate finance. In 2019 they accounted for $61.6 billion in climate financing, 67 percent of which was invested in low- and middle-income countries. More than three-quarters of the total financing was directed at mitigating climate change. The remaining quarter went to climate change adaptation.[54]

Finally, a recent trend in investment and credit analysis involves taking into account environmental, social and governance criteria in assessing risk, returns and impact. Environmental, social and governance analysis allows the identification of emerging risks to credit quality as well as the preparedness of firms to cope with such risks. This can reduce portfolio risk as issues in these areas can often cause sudden changes in regulation and consumer tastes, so incorporating them into investment strategies reduces exposure to such risks—which may be rare but could be very large.[55]

In contrast to the specialized sphere of green bonds, environmental, social and governance investing is becoming part of mainstream processes, especially for investors in fixed-income products.[56]

Making choices during the response to and recovery from the Covid-19 pandemic

Financial and monetary authorities are playing a central role during the Covid-19 pandemic. Their choices shape incentives that can encourage a transitioning to a net-zero emissions economic system and reducing socioeconomic inequalities (box 5.2; see also spotlight 5.2).[57]

" Financial and monetary authorities are playing a central role during the Covid-19 pandemic. Their choices shape incentives that can encourage a transitioning to a net-zero emissions economic system and reducing socioeconomic inequalities.

It has been argued that, in addition to aligning banking business models with a green and inclusive recovery, financial institutions can support this process in four ways. First, they can rebuild public trust by supporting households and firms through the difficult process of recovery. Second, they can more closely align shareholder engagements with the broader interests of all stakeholders, such as customers and staff. Third, the banking sector can focus on helping small businesses, workers and communities. Fourth, banks can offer new products and services so

Box 5.2 The Covid-19 pandemic and a green recovery

By José Antonio Ocampo and Joaquín Bernal

The Covid-19 pandemic has provided vivid evidence of the fragility of global systems and raised awareness of the possible shocks for the global economy in reaching tipping points if nothing is done to reduce greenhouse gas emissions. The pandemic and climate change both affect human lives and economic wellbeing, and both have a substantial negative distributional impact. They have both also made evident the need for policymakers to cooperate on building more holistic approaches to identify and manage global risks that have been neither fully considered nor priced in a framework of multilateral cooperation.[1]

The time is now for national and international authorities to take climate change into account in engineering a green recovery to the pandemic. Their coordination is needed, alongside business and civil society, to align their response measures with the Paris Agreement and the Sustainable Development Goals.

A wide variety of policy actions can be taken in this direction. Reducing the carbon footprint by promoting sustainable investments, with a longer term view of returns on investment projects that includes putting a floor on the carbon price (or reducing emission ceilings), phasing out subsidies to carbon-intensive sectors and conditioning support for businesses to survive the current crisis on their moving towards a more sustainable future. And for financial and monetary policy, authorities could advance climate-related prudential regulation and supervision to minimize financial institutions' climate-related risks. They could also adopt ecological accounting frameworks, with the possible obligation of all agents to disclose their exposure to brown activities. And they could have central banks more accurately reflect climate risks in their balance sheets and operations.

Note
1. Pereira Da Silva 2020.

---

that households and firms can save and invest in ways that support that transition.[58]

More broadly, the response need not stop at supply-side solutions for shifting economies and technologies; it can also pursue demand-side transformations in societies and human behaviours. The starting point could be human aspirations—individual or communal—that by interacting with economic and energy processes aggregate into changes at scale. This broadened approach also calls for knowledge to be codeveloped with people from marginalized communities.[59]

A review of 130 studies relating to green and inclusive recoveries highlighted several options that would encourage structural reforms supportive of this transition:[60]

- Increasing the price of carbon dioxide and reducing carbon subsidies that harm the environment.
- Removing regulatory obstacles to green investments and introducing such regulatory requirements as a minimum quota for electric cars.

- Offering training and continuing education programmes for people who lost or will lose their jobs.
- Making the financial system sustainable by pricing environmental risks into investment and lending decisions.
- Increasing corporate transparency in reporting on social and environmental aspects of their operations.

Otherwise, fiscal measures of countries recovering from the Covid-19 pandemic could entrench the fossil fuel–intensive economic system. A recent survey of 25 major fiscal recovery packages assessed their implementation speed, economic impact, potential for climate impact and overall desirability. Several policies had a high potential for both economic and climate impact: investing in education, training and natural capital; green physical infrastructure; green research and development; and energy efficiency retrofits for residential and commercial purposes. But in low- and middle-income countries investing in rural support was seen as more important than clean research and development.[61]

For the Group of 20 countries the recovery from the Great Recession offers useful lessons, pointing to the need for much more than short-term fiscal stimuli. A green and inclusive transition would require long-term commitments (5–10 years) for reforming pricing and public spending. Correctly pricing pollution and carbon emissions and removing subsidies for fossil fuels can accelerate the transition process, lower its cost and yield resources for public investment. Public spending could prioritize developing smart grids and transport systems, supporting private sector efforts in innovating and green infrastructure, and investing in sustainable cities and networks of charging stations.[62]

Indeed, some policies can help countries face both the Covid-19 pandemic and climate change. Labour-intensive green infrastructure projects, planting trees, lowering labour taxes and pricing carbon emissions can boost economic recovery from the pandemic. Helping some low-emission yet labour-intensive service sectors such as restaurants, culture, education and health care can help fight climate change.[63] Some proactive measures are being taken, such as the European Union's €750 billion recovery package, which includes support for wind energy.[64]

Shifting prices, changing minds

Greenhouse gas emissions continue to rise, with no sign of peaking.[65] The overall emissions gap is wide—in 2030 annual emissions need to be 15 gigatonnes of carbon dioxide equivalent lower than what countries have collectively committed to in order to meet the 2 degrees Celsius goal and 32 gigatonnes of carbon dioxide equivalent lower for the 1.5 degrees Celsius goal.[66]

Regulations and pricing are both essential and can be self-reinforcing in reducing emissions. In fact, the majority of environmental policies around the world take the form of regulation.[67] Designing effective regulations on, for example, air quality, land use or deforestation and setting emissions standards can play a broader role in bringing about technical advances to deal with carbon emissions. What began as efforts in California to address smog eventually turned into a national-scale regulatory effort in the United States, with the creation of the US Environmental Protection Agency (1970), the Clean Air Act (1970) and its eventual amendments. Despite initial resistance from

automobile companies and complaints that technology to meet the demanding regulations on automobile emissions did not exist, these regulatory actions eventually spurred technological innovation to meet the regulatory standards.[68] This shows that regulation can not only lead directly to reductions in emissions but also drive technological change.[69]

" The overall emissions gap is wide—in 2030 annual emissions need to be 15 gigatonnes of carbon dioxide equivalent lower than what countries have collectively committed to in order to meet the 2 degrees Celsius goal and 32 gigatonnes of carbon dioxide equivalent lower for the 1.5 degrees Celsius goal.

Reflecting the social costs of emissions in carbon prices could dramatically shift incentives for what is consumed, produced and invested in—helping correct what Nicholas Stern has called the greatest market failure in history.[70] Such a change would shift incentives in a decentralized way, giving societies and economies new parameters for determining how to steer creativity and innovation and which firms and economic activities are viable and potentially changing behaviours ranging from how people move around to what they eat.

Pricing carbon: Potential and reality

Advancing carbon pricing—having market prices for carbon that more closely reflect the social costs of emissions—can be achieved in various ways, including cap and trade programmes or carbon taxes. A cap and trade programme sets the maximum allowable emissions and lets emissions permits be traded. Companies receive a certain amount of permits—low emitters sell their permits to high emitters at a price that emerges from the exchanges. The market mechanism sets the price. For carbon taxes governments set a tax on emissions, making their price more closely reflect social costs to discourage reliance on fossil fuels. The world now has 61 carbon pricing programmes, 48 of them national,[71] covering 20 percent of global greenhouse gas emissions. But less than 5 percent of them are priced at levels consistent with reaching the Paris Agreement goals.

Setting a carbon price is highly contentious. Theoretically the price of carbon should be equal to the social cost of carbon, in order to limit emissions to the desired level and increase the relative price of high-emissions products. In 2016 the Interagency Working Group on the Social Cost of Carbon—a partnership of US government agencies—estimated the social cost of carbon at $51 per tonne. That year, at the recommendation of the 22nd session of the Conference of the Parties, a high-level commission on carbon prices was established to guide countries in developing carbon pricing instruments.[72] The commission—through consultation with experts in the field—concluded that the price should be at least $40–$80 per tonne of carbon dioxide by 2020 (and $50–$100 by 2030), accompanied by a supportive policy environment to be effective.[73] Yet in 2020 only four countries had a price above $40 (table 5.1). (See also chapter 7 for more on estimates of the social cost of carbon.)

Only a few countries report substantially lower emissions after introducing carbon prices, likely because the prices are too low. Part of the reason is that it is politically difficult to raise prices to levels that could make deep decarbonization possible.[74] But carbon pricing alone may not work, or have political support, if people lack alternatives and are simply asked to bear a higher burden. So carbon pricing would be best implemented as part of a broader set of policies and programmes that can elicit wider public support and greater behaviour changes (box 5.3).

Sweden has the highest price, $138 a tonne. Carbon prices were set in 1991 with tax rates increasing over time, which disincentivized high emissions in homes and industries.[75] The government of Sweden also reduced taxes in other sectors, such as labour taxes, to balance the rising costs due to higher energy taxes. By 2017 emissions were 26 percent lower than in 1991, while the economy was 75 percent larger.[76] Fossil fuels for heating have been slowly phased out, down 85 percent since 1990 and now only 2 percent of total emissions. In 2013 the United Kingdom introduced carbon taxes on electricity produced from coal. The tax rate was increased to $18 per tonne of carbon by 2015 and led to the gradual reduction of coal-fuelled electricity from 40 percent to 3 percent by 2019.[77]

Public acceptability of carbon prices is key.[78] Well designed carbon pricing programmes can help counter adverse distributional effects through redistributive efforts (transfers or public services, including public transport) or pay for equivalent tax cuts in other areas to compensate for higher energy prices, which can boost public support.[79] These programmes could include cash transfers, labour tax cuts, carbon dividends or installation of clean energy equipment such as rooftop solar, solar heating or biogas or distribution of energy-efficient stoves.[80] When carbon taxes are part of more comprehensive policies to curb emissions, they become more widely supported. Transparency and clear communications on how these revenues are used also boosts acceptability among the public. Tax progressivity may also matter at the international level. The world's 10 largest emitters account for 45 percent of total emissions while the bottom 50 percent account for only 13 percent.[81] This highlights the dual challenge of curbing emissions and addressing environmental inequality. However, the distributional impact of carbon pricing across countries is not determined by emissions level or income alone, with great heterogeneity across countries, even in the same income group, depending on the structure of their economies and trade patterns.[82]

> " Public acceptability of carbon prices is key. Well designed carbon pricing programmes can help counter adverse distributional effects through redistributive efforts (transfers or public services, including public transport) or pay for equivalent tax cuts in other areas to compensate for higher energy prices, which can boost public support.

There is also concern that carbon pricing will affect the competitiveness of the private sector. But the impact on the economy is expected to be positive, as highlighted in spotlight 5.3. Economists suggest that carbon taxes will in fact spur technological innovation and advance large-scale infrastructure development.[83] In British Columbia, Canada, the loss of industrial competitiveness hurt only a few companies. The region is now home to a thriving community of 200 clean energy producers generating more than $1.7 billion in total revenue.[84] Carbon pricing creates long-term competitiveness by lowering costs, increasing efficiency and enhancing product quality.[85] And as it pushes markets towards newer forms of technology, it also incentivizes

Table 5.1 Carbon prices vary and are much lower than estimated social costs of emissions

Country or subregion	2020 price ($ per tonne of carbon dioxide)	Year of implementation	Greenhouse gas emissions covered in the jurisdiction	
			Million tonnes of carbon dioxide	Percent
Carbon taxes				
British Columbia (Canada)	30	2008	42	70
Chile	5	2017	58	39
Denmark	28	1992	25	40
Finland	73	1990	40	36
France	53	2014	171	35
Iceland	31	2010	1	29
Ireland	31	2010	32	49
Latvia	11	2004	3	15
Mexico	3	2014	378	46
Norway	60	1991	47	62
Poland	0	1990	17	4
Portugal	28	2015	23	29
South Africa	7	2019	512	80
Sweden	138	1991	44	40
Emissions trading systems				
Alberta (Canada)	22	2007	132	48
Australia	11	2016	344	50
Beijing (China)	13	2013	85	45
California (United States)	17	2012	375	85
Chongqing (China)	2	2014	122	50
European Union, Iceland, Liechtenstein and Norway	31	2005	2,255	45
Fujian (China)	4	2016	200	60
Guangdong, except Shenzhen (China)	4	2013	367	60
Hubei (China)	4	2014	208	45
Kazakhstan	1	2013	182	50
Korea, Republic of	18	2015	489	70
Massachusetts (United States)	8	2018	15	20
New Zealand	23	2008	45	51
Quebec (Canada)	17	2013	66	85
Regional Greenhouse Gas Initiative[a]	6	2009	108	18
Saitama (Japan)	6	2011	7	18
Shanghai (China)	6	2013	170	57
Shenzhen (China)	5	2013	61	40
Switzerland	20	2008	6	11
Tianjin (China)	4	2013	118	55
Tokyo (Japan)	6	2010	13	20

a. A cooperative effort among the US states of Connecticut, Delaware, Maine, Maryland, Massachusetts, New Hampshire, New Jersey, New York, Rhode Island, Vermont and Virginia.
Note: The sources of carbon emissions covered vary largely across countries. When implementing carbon prices, policymakers often start with the power sector and large industrial firms but exclude other emissions sources such as energy-intensive manufacturing.
Source: Human Development Report Office based on data from the World Bank Carbon Pricing Dashboard.

Box 5.3 Impediments to effective carbon pricing mechanisms

By William Gbohoui and Catherine Pattillo, Fiscal Affairs Department, International Monetary Fund

While carbon pricing is the most well known climate change mitigation tool, it is not generating investment at the pace and scale needed for transition to a cleaner energy system.

To maximize the efficiency of carbon pricing, several market impediments and government failures need to be addressed:

- **Knowledge spillovers.** Knowledge and research and development in renewable investment cannot be left only to the private sector, as they are public goods to some extent. Spillovers from research and development and technology diffusion could prevent companies from capturing the entire return of their investment, leading to suboptimal investment in the absence of public support. While these spillovers are common to emerging technologies—and may be addressed to some extent by intellectual property protection and other regulations—public research and development support and targeted fiscal incentives (such as capital grants, tax credits and feed-in tariffs) are warranted to stimulate private investment in long-lived, low-carbon technologies whose future returns are uncertain because of changing mitigation policies. For example, setting carbon prices while providing public research and development spending in renewable technologies has proven successful in mobilizing investment in emerging markets.[1]

- **Entry barriers.** Economies of scale and sunk costs favour established traditional technologies because energy-efficient power generation and renewable energy often involve higher upfront costs (such as the fixed costs of setting up factories, assembly lines and supply chains for parts of electric vehicles) and larger uncertainties, deterring firms from investing until they are confident of the market size of clean technologies. Thus, public support and regulations (for example on renewable generation shares) that provide more certainty on demand for clean technologies are critical. For example, banning incandescent lights bulbs could ensure that the demand for efficient LED light bulbs is sustainable and promote the development of affordable and highly efficient LEDs.

- **Network externalities.** Coordination failures could prevent market forces alone from deploying interlocked network technologies in which additional infrastructure needed for one investor can benefit other firms, as with electric vehicles and charging infrastructure. Public investment in such infrastructure as robust power grids and charging stations for electric vehicles, as well as international coordination, would be essential.

- **Market distortions and government failures.** Lack of information; misalignment across policies, regulations and markets; and unsuitable investment conditions hamper investment in renewables. Regulations that improve information disclosure about product energy efficiency or carbon content could allow agents to make informed choices and boost adoption of low-carbon technologies. Regulations that impose disproportionately higher costs on new entrants—such as the 2015 rule in Canada that requires investment in carbon capture and storage in new coal plants while allowing long adjustment periods for existing firms—are a deterrent.[2] Removing inconsistent policy incentives, such as simultaneously subsidizing renewables and fossil fuels, will be crucial for public credibility and support for the transition to low-carbon energy.

- **Financial market imperfections.** Incomplete and imperfect capital markets, long-run uncertainties, political risks and insufficient knowledge to assess low-carbon projects hamper their financing. Crucial to addressing financial sector short-termism and mobilizing private financing are financial instruments (prototype green bond contracts and benchmark indices of environmentally friendly securities) that reduce the risk-weighted capital costs of low-carbon investments and rebalance risk perceptions between low-carbon and brown projects, along with regulations to encourage disclosure of stranded asset risks in fossil fuels.[3] Also needed are shifts in the portfolio choices of central banks and institutional investors and further participation of multilateral or national development banks to act as trusted conveners to bring in other financing institutions.

(continued)

Box 5.3 Impediments to effective carbon pricing mechanisms *(continued)*

- **Distributional effects.** Carbon pricing will inevitably increase energy prices, at least in the short term, and could affect consumer purchasing power. Complementary policies are needed to protect the most vulnerable (households, regions and businesses), to ease their transition and to overcome resistance and opposition (from specific groups, such as owners and employees in the coal industry and fishers and farmers who depend on diesel).[4]

Policies to overcome the bottlenecks should be appropriately designed, scaled and targeted but should remain flexible. Governments should avoid policies that lock in particular technologies, fuel choices and technology-specific targets.[5] In this respect, fixed subsidies per kilowatt-hour of renewable energy are more flexible than investment-based incentives, regulations that force the adoption of new technologies regardless of their future costs and feed-in tariffs that guarantee minimum prices per kilowatt-hour but do not permit supply responses to changing market conditions.[6]

Governments should increase research and development support initially and then gradually reduce support once technologies are widely deployed and used by firms and households.[7] As renewable-based electricity approaches cost parity with fossil fuel–generated power, subsidies could be shifted from research and development to deployment and then progressively phased out. Supporting upstream development and manufacturing of clean technologies tends to be more cost effective than supporting downstream consumption because upstream providers face less competition.[8] While conditioning agricultural subsidies on adopting environmentally friendly practices can help reduce negative environmental impacts, removing environmentally harmful subsidies could prove more effective.

Today's historically low interest rates combined with the need to kickstart the global economy offer a unique opportunity for governments to transition to low-carbon pathways. Governments could attach green strings to fiscal supports—bailouts, grants, loans, tax breaks or equity purchases—to push industry towards a viable low-carbon future. To further incentivize companies to adopt cleaner technologies, stimulus packages could consider provisions to convert the type of aid provided—loans can be converted to equity, and grants to loans—if climate change–related conditions are not met.

Notes

1. Ang, Röttgers and Burli 2017. **2.** OECD 2017. **3.** Bhattacharya and others 2016; Stiglitz and others 2017. **4.** See, for example, IMF (2019b) and OECD (2017) for simulation outcomes. **5.** Pomázi 2009. **6.** IMF 2019b. **7.** Acemoglu and others 2012; Acemoglu and others 2016. **8.** Fischer 2016; Requate 2005.

---

education gains and skill-based development, which advances development.[86]

Despite the implementation challenges, the evolution towards carbon pricing continues around the world. Building on its regional experience, China launched its first National Energy Trading System in 2017.[87] The programme, linked to the country's nationally determined contributions under the Paris Agreement, covers 3 billion tonnes of carbon dioxide from the energy sector, making it the world's largest, nearly twice the size of the next largest (the EU Emissions Trading System).[88] China's programme is expected to affect 30 percent of national emissions.[89]

Canada's new Pan-Canadian Framework on Clean Growth and Climate Change enacted a nationwide tax on oil, coal and gas, starting at $15 per tonne of carbon dioxide in 2019 and rising to $38 by 2022.[90] The initiative aims to be revenue neutral by returning all the proceeds to households and businesses as rebates, thereby strengthening public acceptability and minimizing regressive impacts of the tax.

Interest in and momentum for market mechanisms to manage carbon are increasing across Africa. More than 34 countries have indicated an interest in market mechanisms for their nationally determined contributions.[91] Many international entities are providing knowledge and capacity-building support to develop the enabling conditions for these tools. South Africa is the only country in the region with a carbon pricing programme. Since less than half of Africa is electrified, the technology and resources used to expand electricity will have a huge bearing on future emissions.[92]

As noted earlier, an important step towards shifting incentives in addition to carbon pricing is removing fossil fuel subsidies. But the sharp decline in fossil fuel consumption during the Covid-19 pandemic in 2020 will lead to an estimated $180 billion decline in fossil fuel subsidies, a drop of 43 percent, compared with 27 percent in 2019.[93] As noted above, this period of low fuel and energy consumption provides for a favourable context to make a decisive move towards phasing out fossil fuel subsidies.[94]

Making biodiversity economically visible

As chapter 2 noted, biodiversity is being lost at an alarming rate.[95] The latest Intergovernmental Science-Policy Platform on Biodiversity and Ecosystem Services report found that 1 million species are threatened with extinction, many within a few decades.[96] Stocktaking of progress by the Global Biodiversity Outlook suggests that the world has not achieved a single one of the Aichi Biodiversity Targets.[97]

Changing incentives to preserve biodiversity is difficult given the complexity of the fabric of life. A key challenge is that biodiversity remains undervalued in current markets, despite the increasing appreciation of its contributions to people—thanks to such initiatives as The Economics of Ecosystems and Biodiversity,[98] the European Union's Mapping and Assessment of Ecosystems and Their Services[99] and the comprehensive mapping of nature's contributions to people.[100] In turn, better measurement of policy interventions is crucial (spotlight 5.4).

" Changing incentives to preserve biodiversity is difficult given the complexity of the fabric of life. A key challenge is that biodiversity remains undervalued in current markets, despite the increasing appreciation of its contributions to people.

Incentives to preserve biodiversity can assume different forms—and need not be shaped only through the recognition of the benefits that the biosphere and its diverse ecosystems bring to humans. As the pathbreaking Economics of Ecosystems and Biodiversity initiative argued, where there is strong recognition of the fundamental dependence of people on the diversity of life, through cultural or spiritual values, there is no need to invoke benefits.[101] For instance, the preservation of natural parks that host wildlife has benefitted from the shared value that society puts on them, without any incentive linked to prices. But appreciating the benefits and vast economic values that ecosystems provide can help change incentives.

Consider how our understanding and valuing of wetlands has changed over time. Wetlands were historically considered places that bred diseases (such as malaria and yellow fever) and were to be avoided. Now science has established that wetlands are rich ecosystems that serve as habitats for diverse species and provide a variety of services such as wastewater treatment, flood protection and removal of excess nitrogen and phosphorous from water. And they are a rich food source for a variety of animals, birds and plants as well as a shelter for migratory animals.[102] Pantanal, the largest wetland in the world, is a rich ecosystem that spans Bolivia, Brazil and Paraguay and is home to 4,700 species. Attracting many tourists and contributing to soybean production and cattle farming, the economic activities in this wetland generated $70 billion in 2015.[103]

Valuing biodiversity has also taken on much political importance in several countries. In 2020 the United Kingdom's Chancellor of the Exchequer commissioned an independent global review of the economics of biodiversity. It analysed the sustainability of the services we receive from nature and what needs to be done to safeguards the world's natural wealth. An important reminder of the report is that human actions are derived from human knowledge and understanding of our nature.[104] Echoing the discussion in chapter 4, part of the problem in undervaluing nature results from our perceptions, shaped in part by what we are taught as children. The report suggests starting with reforms in the education system that deepen the appreciation and understanding of nature from a young age. Growing urbanization has detached us and our children from nature, and major changes in behaviour and social norms would come from bringing this understanding into our nurturing and education systems.

Historically, governments have regulated biodiversity conservation by protecting key habitats. About 15 percent of the earth's terrestrial and inland water and 4 percent of the world's oceans are protected.[105] But incentives can also be harnessed to protect biodiversity through a range of market mechanisms. Regulatory frameworks that set a cap on the impact on species or habitat create incentives in which owners of land or habitats can exchange offsetting credits with those who need to mitigate their impacts. Still, these mechanisms may be seen to violate ethical stances that value nature's intrinsic and relational values (chapters 1 and 3).[106] The design and implementation of the programmes are critical to avoid adverse selection and moral hazard.

" For climate change and biodiversity loss, individual actions and even national actions will not do enough to ease planetary pressures.

Payments for ecosystem services provide incentives for biodiversity preservation. The beneficiaries of the ecosystem services pay those who facilitate their provision (box 5.4). For example, farmers upstream are paid to reduce the amount of fertilizer they use and thus help maintain the water quality downstream. Beneficiaries are those farther downstream, such as fishers, water plants or communities, who make the payments. While some basic forms of payments for ecosystem services existed earlier, they came into the mainstream in the mid-1990s. Since then, payments for ecosystem services programmes have grown considerably, with as many as 550 around the world making payments of more than $36 billion.[107]

Enhancing international and multiactor collective action

For climate change and biodiversity loss, individual actions and even national actions will not do enough to ease planetary pressures. This section explores the challenges in activating collective action that transcends borders and the possible incentives to mitigate those challenges.[108]

Chapter 4 described how learning translates to values that may turn into stable social norms. It is important to recognize the link between those norms and international collective action. The norms are not restricted to one country. Particularly in the information age, where ideas zip across borders, the formation of norms can transcend national borders.

Powerful norms—whether on conserving energy, using electric vehicles or reducing meat consumption—can then galvanize global public policy. It can be argued that recent international agreements such as the Paris Agreement on climate change are responses to heightened concerns about climate change.

That the vast majority of countries have signed international environmental agreements to ease planetary pressures suggests that we are not confronting a challenge at all (figure 5.4). Clearly, what is needed is not an examination of the act of signing but an understanding of differences in effectiveness across agreements—why some seem to provide stronger incentives than others. The Convention on Biological Diversity was signed at the 1992 Rio Earth Summit.[109] As we approach the end of the United Nations Decade on Biodiversity 2011–2020, progress towards global biodiversity targets, including those under the Sustainable Development Goals, has been lacking, as noted above.

Also important to consider: the evolution of agreements and how they may embed opportunities to respond to challenges, such as the flexibility that the Paris Agreement affords countries in approaching climate change.[110] It is setting in motion a catalytic process in which past action creates fertile ground for future action, leading to virtuous cycles of ambition and national climate commitments and action.[111]

Despite its flexibility, the Paris Agreement is based on voluntary compliance and lacks an enforcement structure or even Kyoto Protocol–like targets for individual countries.[112] This may result in freeriding, or some parties making little or no effort to address the challenges. Trade restrictions, such as those included in the Montreal Protocol, are a possible enforcement mechanism to prevent freeriding.[113] They were also discussed for the Kyoto Protocol.[114] Such restrictions would involve generalized tariffs imposed on countries that do not participate. This approach could give incentives for all countries to engage in an international agreement to cut emissions.[115]

Yet such a broad-based tariff restriction may also face challenges (box 5.5). In 2015 the Kigali Amendment to the Montreal Protocol was negotiated to phase out hydrofluorocarbons—a potent greenhouse gas—that the Kyoto Protocol did not include. With the trade restrictions in place, the protocol includes strong incentives for compliance.[116] This chapter

Box 5.4 Payments for ecosystem services in New York and Tanzania

Land management in the Catskills for clean water supply

A programme of land management in the Catskills region of New York state is an early example of payments for ecosystem services. New York City's water is regarded among the cleanest in the world, comparable to bottled mineral water. About 90 percent of the city's water comes from the Catskills–Delaware Watershed: 1.1 billion gallons are delivered every day to 9 million New York City residents.[1] The purity and cleanliness of this water are of great significance for the healthy lives of city residents.

The search for a clean sustained source of water for the city started in the 1830s, when it was decided to find water farther north rather than using unreliable local sources that would have met only short-term needs. In the 1980s the city began to worry about the quality of various water sources, including the Croton River and the Catskills–Delaware Watershed. A big challenge with the Catskills area was that only 30 percent of the land was owned by the public; the rest was used for private farming, woodlot forestry and tourism. Facing growing competition, Catskills farmers were using intensive agricultural practices and concentrated livestock management that increased pollutant runoff into soil, streams and lakes. Unsustainable land management and forestry, with the added pressure of a growing tourism industry and road construction, continued to degrade the environment, thus increasing nonpoint pollution.[2] Because of concerns about the safety of this water, consensus began to emerge that the water needed to be filtered.

But the cost of a filtration facility was very high, estimated at $5 billion, plus annual operating costs of $250 million. The water authority wondered whether it might be more efficient to manage the pollution sources rather than allow the water to be polluted and then spend resources to clean it up. Many water regulators thought it would be too difficult to track and manage the various sources of pollution. Even so, the commissioner of the New York City Department of Environment Protection conducted a series of education sessions with local farmers and businesses during which the department expressed concerns and options and the farmers shared their side of the story about competition and costs.

The open consultation expanded both parties' knowledge and understanding and allowed both to think collectively about solutions. A better environment with sustained local business opportunities was of interest for all. Eventually, the Whole Farm Program was established in the early 1990s, a proposal by local farmers to tackle pollution while helping local businesses thrive. Each farmer received a technical team to provide guidance on pollution control and advice on integrated business management. This enabled farmers to lower pollution without any additional costs. The city paid for the staff costs and capital costs for the pollution control, and farmers joined the programme on a voluntary basis, with the condition that at least 85 percent join within five years to ensure a critical mass for success.[3]

The ingenuity of this payments for ecosystem services programme enabled the city to maintain the high quality of its water and the region to enjoy a better quality environment. Filtration was no longer an issue. The model gained global recognition. Delegations from around the world, including Chile, Colombia, India, Ireland, France, the Republic of Korea, Singapore and Uzbekistan, have visited the region to learn about its innovative practices.[4]

Ecotourism in Tanzania

The United Republic of Tanzania is among the most biodiverse countries on the planet, and about 38 percent of the country's land area is protected for conservation.[5] But as in many countries, concerns have been raised that the protected areas may not be fully respected when there are no local incentives for conservation.

The Simanjiro Plains border a protected national park and are home to important wet season grazing areas for wildebeest and zebra. The plains are managed mainly by the Maasai, whose traditional livestock practices include seasonal grazing that protects the area. But the land has come under growing pressure from smallholder farming conversion. And the plains are an attractive tourist spot with operators running wildlife tours. Increased smallholder farming threatens the ecosystem, resulting in less grazing areas for wildlife, less area for the Maasai's traditional livestock practices and fewer opportunities for wildlife tourism.

(continued)

Box 5.4 Payments for ecosystem services in New York and Tanzania *(continued)*

A project in which tour operators pay local villages a fee for preventing agricultural production and illegal hunting on the plains was tested in the area of Terrat. The details of the agreement, including the fee level, number of instalments and who should manage the funds, were decided collectively by local tour operators, local villages and civil society organizations working in the area. Involving the local community was crucial for building support and ensuring compliance. Including tour operators and civil society organizations already known in the area created trust among the stakeholders. The fee was set low enough that operators could contribute but high enough to create a discretionary income stream for the local village. This built further support for the project, as the village could decide collectively on where to allocate the funds.[6]

The payments for ecosystem services scheme has since been expanded to other villages in the area and remains a model for similar projects to preserve biodiversity while supporting local economic development and poverty reduction.

Notes
1. Watershed Agricultural Council 2019. **2.** Appleton 2002. **3.** See also Chichilnisky and Heal (1998). **4.** Dunne 2017. **5.** FAO 2016. **6.** Ingram and others 2014.

Figure 5.4 Most countries have ratified international environmental treaties

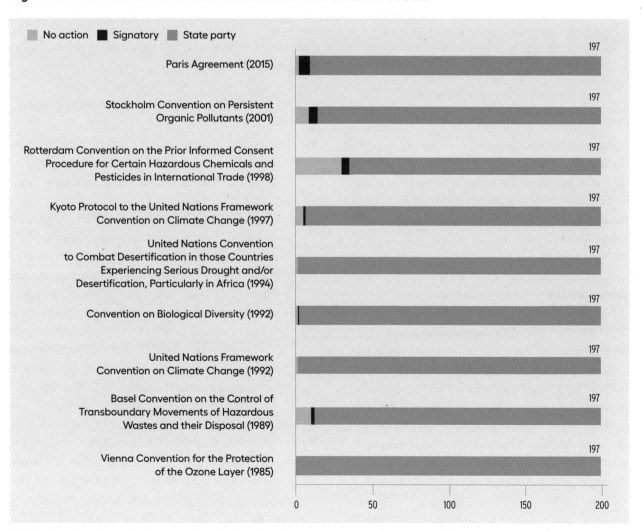

Note: Includes the 197 countries that are parties to the United Nations Framework Convention on Climate Change.
Source: Human Development Report Office based on United Nations (n.d.).

Box 5.5 Trade-related incentives in international treaties—credible and effective?

Leakage is one issue that international agreements confront. Suppose there is an international treaty in which parties agree to reduce their carbon emissions by putting in place appropriate domestic policies. A country that is not a party to the treaty will not adjust domestically with a carbon tax or a permits system, and goods imported from that country would have an unfair advantage over goods produced by countries that are parties to the agreement. A country that is a party might impose carbon tariffs on imported goods or adjust border taxes applied to imports from countries that are not parties to the treaty.

Border tax adjustments would neutralize the leakage. But they have to be comprehensive and based on emissions embedded in the production of a whole range of imported goods. They are hard to estimate.

Trade restrictions can also be designed to deter nonparticipation directly. This would involve broad restrictions, such as no trading privileges for a country that does not participate or a country that has joined but then is found to be in noncompliance. The problem is that this may fail to be a credible threat. Broadly, countries also harm themselves when they suspend the trading privileges of a country not joining.

If economically powerful countries do not participate in treaties or are not in compliance, these threats are not credible. Ending trade relations with an important trading partner is likely to be costly. These incentives also apply in the case of groups addressing a collective action problem in general.

Moreover, adding strong enforcement and penalties can have other consequences. Parties may want to water down the agreement during the negotiation in order to ensure the punishments are not imposed. The trade-related provisions in the Montreal Protocol were effective, turning the phasing out of chlorofluorocarbons into a coordination game characterized by tipping points. The effectiveness of across-the-board climate-related trade restrictions remains to be tested.

Source: Barrett 2008; Kotchen and Segerson 2020.

explores different dimensions of what may stand in the way of countries coming together. It illustrates the broader challenges in achieving international collective action to ease planetary pressures and points to possible ways of changing incentives to encourage shared action.

Reducing uncertainty, targeting groups

One challenge related to climate change—but relevant more broadly—involves uncertainties in the underlying planetary processes and their implications. In the case of the climate system, there is uncertainty about how much temperatures will increase with growing atmospheric concentrations of greenhouse gases (called climate sensitivity)[117] and about possible thresholds after which the consequences of those increases in temperature would be catastrophic (see chapter 2 for more on tipping points in the Earth system).[118] Collective action is harder when uncertainty about this type of threshold is large, so reducing this

uncertainty can enhance incentives to bring about behavioural changes to address climate change.[119]

When uncertainty about the threshold is large, abatement is a prisoner's dilemma. Even if every country plays its part in reducing the risk of crossing a threshold, each country has an incentive to scale back on its abatement. By doing so, a country reduces its abatement costs considerably but increases the chance of catastrophe only slightly. When every country faces these incentives, the most likely outcome is low overall abatement effort.[120] But when the threshold is less uncertain, incentives change: It turns from a prisoner's dilemma into a challenge of coordination, which might be easier to achieve than cooperation.

Given the key role of the level of uncertainty, early warning signals can be pivotal in reducing uncertainty. A Climate Risk Atlas for Developing Countries has been proposed to measure vulnerability to climate shocks.[121] This international exercise could feed into national and regional processes to develop climate risk indices.[122] These would then be linked to disaster risk reduction plans. For developing countries this would fill a critical gap in measuring vulnerability to climate change and could also act as an early warning system for climate shocks.

" But many examples of cooperation in managing natural shared resources have been documented, by self-organized mechanisms of incentives to oversee common resources at small and medium scales. One reason is that behaviour is driven not only by self-interest but also by how others behave, taking us back to social norms.

Group-level policies, based on group performance rather than individual practices, could enhance incentives for collective action.[123] In these instances rewards or penalties are based on rights allocated to a group. This can be done when group outcomes are more easily monitored than actions of individuals or countries within the group or when transaction costs are lower in dealing with the group. For example, monitoring individual farms to determine the contribution to a water pollution problem (nonpoint pollution) may not be feasible. But the quality of the affected water body is easily monitored.

An example of group-level arrangements is collective payments for ecosystem services programmes, discussed above. In a study of the impact of payments for biodiversity conservation in Chiapas, Mexico, communities that participated in a payments for ecosystem services programme had lower deforestation rates than nonparticipating communities.[124] And Ecuadorian farmer communities that participated in a collective payments programme strengthened their grazing restrictions.[125]

Learning from the local level

The examples also show that a variety of mechanisms can provide incentives for cooperation. The challenge of cooperation is often framed as a tragedy of the commons: Actions by individuals result in socially suboptimal outcomes. There is at least one outcome that yields higher returns for all involved, but individual choices do not produce that outcome. This has been used extensively for the study of climate change and the governance of natural resources.[126]

But many examples of cooperation in managing natural shared resources have been documented, by self-organized mechanisms of incentives to oversee common resources at small and medium scales.[127] One reason is that behaviour is driven not only by self-interest but also by how others behave, taking us back to social norms.[128] This also means that the mechanisms are very context specific, and since they often are based on incentives requiring trust and reciprocity, they may work only at smaller scales.[129]

But even for challenges at the global scale, such as climate change and biodiversity loss, much can be done even when global cooperation is difficult. As Elinor Ostrom puts it, "Rather than only a global effort, it would be better to self-consciously adopt a polycentric approach to the problem of climate change in order to gain the benefits to multiple scales as well as to encourage experimentation and learning from diverse policies adopted at multiple scales."[130]

There are also benefits to addressing global challenges at the local level.[131] For example, efforts to reduce greenhouse gas emissions also reduce particulate matter pollution in a city or region, providing local cobenefits.[132] A review of 239 peer-reviewed studies found that the cobenefits of climate mitigation policies alone—reduced air pollution, enhanced biodiversity, increased energy security and improved water quality—often outweigh the mitigation costs.[133] In the United States, among all the major Clean Air Act rules issued by the Environment Protection Agency over 1997–2019, cobenefits make up a sizeable share of the monetized benefits in the cost-benefit analysis.[134] These are examples of the provision of joint goods—actors' contributions provide both a public good and a private benefit to the contributor.[135] Many mitigation actions entail cobenefits, which provide incentives for communities to come together to invest in, say, renewable sources of power for household energy use. Power that is not needed is contributed to the network, potentially reducing costs for everyone. These actions also reduce greenhouse gas emissions. Similarly, investment in better waste disposal facilities generates local benefits and helps reduce global emissions.[136] Discussions and initiatives at the community level matter.[137]

It is also important to recognize the asymmetries in preferences, benefits and costs across actors.[138] For example, Costa Rica has already harnessed hydropower and largely decarbonized electricity production.[139] There are also differences between nation-states and other kinds of actors such as multinational corporations and civil society organizations. National governments may be susceptible to political capture by narrow interests, with fossil fuel interests opposing climate action.[140] Given that fossil fuel industries are geographically concentrated, the opposition to cooperative action may also be concentrated. Where those interests are not present or do influence power, collective action may emerge more easily.

Leveraging increasing returns: The more the merrier

Many collective action problems exhibit increasing returns, meaning that benefits for any actor grow as the number of actors that contribute expands.[141] This changes the incentives for cooperation from where individual benefits are independent of the number of contributors (figure 5.5).

Increasing returns to actions can emerge from feedback loops. These can include incremental decline in costs following deployment of new technologies, such as green energy or new agricultural processes (chapter 3). In the international arena, learning effects can be a powerful channel of increasing returns. Denmark, for example, passed on to China's electric grid operators what it had learned about operating a grid with variable wind power.[142] In developing its national emissions trading system, China has drawn on a great deal of international expertise.[143]

Increasing returns can also accrue through network effects. Catalytic converters introduced in the 1970s dramatically reduced harmful automobile emissions.[144] Catalytic converters and unleaded fuel are complementary technologies. After the technology was introduced in Germany, gas stations in Italy, responding to tourism business from Germany, started providing unleaded fuel, making the eventual adoption of unleaded fuel in Italy far easier, due to the network effects.[145] For electric cars, once a critical

Figure 5.5 Catalytic cooperation with increasing returns

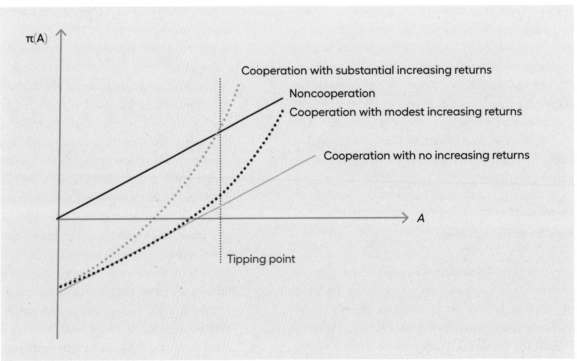

Note: The vertical axis represents the payoff to actor *i* from collective action as a function of *A* (how much others are contributing—the horizontal axis). Without increasing returns the individual payoff to actor *i* from not cooperating is always higher than that from cooperating. But increasing returns imply that the payoffs to individual *i*'s actions depend on *A*—that is, how much has been contributed already. If increasing returns are strong enough, the cooperation curve intersects the noncooperation curve at a certain level of *A*, a tipping point occurs for cooperation to become strictly preferable.
Source: Hale 2020.

threshold is reached for charging stations, network benefits can help lock in the new technology. Through the choice of technical equipment, some international agreements—such as the International Convention for the Prevention of Pollution from Ships —have leveraged network externalities to achieve international cooperation.[146] Prior action can also change norms and political processes, pointing to another route to increasing returns.[147]

" Many collective action problems exhibit increasing returns, meaning that benefits for any actor grow as the number of actors that contribute expands. This changes the incentives for cooperation from where individual benefits are independent of the number of contributors.

Recognizing and leveraging increasing returns can help shape more effective incentives to mobilize international cooperation—with substantial gains attained incrementally and dynamically.[148] For some actors—state or nonstate—private benefits may be high enough for them to act as first movers. On climate, based on recent efforts, the European Union can be seen as a first mover with enough scale to trigger increasing returns.[149] And the actions of the first movers can change the parameters enough for other actors, both governments and firms, to also contribute to collective action.[150]

In this sense the Paris Agreement can be seen as catalytic, a pivot providing opportunities for increasing returns to take hold, especially as awareness of the cobenefits of climate action increases. In allowing for voluntary, flexible national commitments while also bringing into the fold nonstate and subnational actors such as cities, regions and activist groups, it broadens the range of actors engaged.[151] Reflecting the dynamic and changing nature of preferences, the agreement allows actors to update their pledges. It is thus a pledge, review and ratchet mechanism. It can lead to a virtuous, upward spiral of ambition.[152]

The risk: Increasing returns do not take hold, and there is a race to the bottom instead.[153] But recognizing the potential for increasing returns opens the possibility for new mechanisms to provide incentives for international collective action and for seeing existing agreements, such as the Paris Agreement, in a new light. Using the logic of increasing returns, catalytic

incentives to encourage unilateral, early mover actions and then enhance the diffusion of increasing returns from the actions of early movers to more recalcitrant actors could help reach a tipping point of comprehensive or near-comprehensive action. Flexible, nonpunitive international agreements provide space for actors for whom individual benefits may exceed the costs of action. Allowing nonstate and subnational actors—including civil society organizations, multinational corporations and cities—to demonstrate policy actions increases the likelihood of prodding first-mover champions, who can change the incentives for other to join in once increasing returns take hold.

Recognizing differentiated responsibilities and abilities

Climate change is a challenge shared by everyone, but countries have recognized that there are differentiated responsibilities. Group of 20 members account for 78 percent of global emissions.[154] Most of the carbon dioxide emissions in the atmosphere today are a result of historical emissions from developed countries.[155] And developing countries are at the receiving end of the impacts of climate change, as the 2019 Human Development Report documented and this Report highlights.[156] So the climate change challenge is fundamentally one of climate justice.[157]

To address these differences, the Montreal Protocol incorporated the principle of common but differentiated responsibilities and respective capabilities, which recognized the unequal distribution of responsibility between industrialized and developing countries.[158] Developing countries were given easier initial limits and expected to eventually get to the same final endpoints as rich countries. The Kyoto Protocol took this a step further, with no limits on emissions from developing countries.[159] But this may have diminished developed countries' commitment to its success.[160]

The balancing act between designing equitable and efficient governance systems and the realities of international negotiations has played out in the discussions on climate change. As countries negotiated the post–Kyoto Protocol regime at the 15th session of the Conference of the Parties in Copenhagen in 2009, disagreements on key issues and deep mistrust led to a flawed and weak deal. The following years, negotiators fought their way back from the brink with the Cancun Agreements then the Durban Platform, which laid the foundation for the Paris Agreement in 2015. Among the key issues at stake was differentiation, or the various levels of commitments by richer and poorer countries. This was delicately addressed in the Paris Agreement negotiations and paved the way for it to become the first universal deal and to launch an entirely new era of climate action.[161]

Innovating to enhance collective action

As noted, local leaders and stakeholders are often able to self-organize to manage a common resource through effective rules. Looking at the factors that make these arrangements possible may suggest innovations to bring about collective action at other scales. For instance, the sustainability of the systems devised depends on the quality of monitoring and enforcement. It also depends on actors' willingness and ability to monitor one another.[162]

Monitoring and enforcement are also crucial for the success of global agreements. Many of the mechanisms in the Paris Agreement—including the monitoring and review mechanisms—have not been fully defined, which may hamper its effectiveness. As noted, the agreement is built on a pledge, review and ratchet structure. Parties are expected to adhere to their nationally determined contributions, publish biennial reports tracking emissions and progress towards implementation and update their nationally determined contributions in a five-year cycle. The biennial reports are subject to technical review and feedback. This review process is expected to feed into a five-year global stocktaking. But many of the details still need to be filled in. The evolution of the transparency and accountability mechanisms and the global stocktaking could make the agreement more effective.[163] The pledge and review process on the global stage would add peer pressure and help raise ambitions but could also empower domestic constituencies by providing a hook to hold policymakers to account.[164]

In the first opportunity for countries to upgrade their nationally determined contributions in 2020, some countries have announced increased ambitions. China announced that it will peak its emissions before 2030 and achieve carbon neutrality by 2060.[165] Saudi Arabia is setting up its first utility-scale wind power farm, which will be the largest in the Middle East.[166] Japan, the world's third largest economy, announced its commitment to net-zero emissions by 2050.[167] The Republic of Korea, the world's 11th largest economy, also committed to net-zero emissions by 2050.[168] Their revised nationally determined contributions, to be submitted by the 26th session of the Conference of the Parties in 2021, are expected be consistent with these aims. As noted above, action by some countries can create favourable conditions for others to act.

" Monitoring and enforcement are also crucial for the success of global agreements. Many of the mechanisms in the Paris Agreement —including the monitoring and review mechanisms—have not been fully defined, which may hamper its effectiveness.

A hallmark of the Paris Agreement is that it diversifies climate leadership and includes nonstate and subnational actors, including civil society, the private sector and city governments.[169] All will have to step up their ambition and action. The United Nations Framework Convention on Climate Change process continues to engage with nonstate stakeholders and leverages their participation, while civil society organizations and others can tailor their advocacy towards the model of national pledges, implementation and review. Many stakeholders are stepping up. During Climate Week 2020 some of the world's biggest companies—including AT&T, Morgan Stanley and Walmart—adopted aggressive timetables for reducing emissions. General Electric announced that it will no longer build new coal-fired power plants.[170] Building on the potential for multiactor engagement can strengthen incentives for cooperation, especially given the ease of global communication across people and civil society and the economic interconnections associated with global value chains—though incentives to cooperate are also shaped by broader geopolitical developments and the connection of international commitments to interests of national constituencies.[171]

Addressing inequalities can also play an instrumental role in enhancing incentives for cooperation.

Inequality reduces the space for deliberative thinking and collective action (chapter 1). As the 2019 Human Development Report noted, higher inequality is associated with less communication and information sharing among different interest groups.[172] This results in less willingness to contribute to public goods.[173] Chapter 3 shows how inequalities parallel losses in biosphere integrity.[174]

Inequality also shapes perceptions of unfairness across countries. Differentiated responsibility and climate as justice will continue to shape the international dialogue. Under the Paris Agreement, countries make voluntary commitments while being mindful of their national capacities.[175] Differences across countries can be narrowed also with better access to technology and innovations that enable decarbonizing pathways (chapter 3). There is great potential for increasing developing countries' access to technology, credit and finance to close these gaps, which could also enhance incentives for cooperation.[176]

Trust and reciprocity are central to collective action.[177] Norms of trust and reciprocity, how they come about, what policies help promote them and how they can be sustained are important elements in the success or failure of collective action. They have direct implications for incentives for international cooperation. The stronger the reciprocal preferences of governments, the more effective systems of pledging, reporting, reviewing and stocktaking will be. Addressing climate change as a challenge of justice and reducing inequalities within and across countries may enhance actors' willingness to reduce emissions in a way that increases others' willingness to do the same.[178] This would be a more general template in which to frame incentives in order to enhance international collective action to ease planetary pressures.

Building nature-based human development

Building nature-based human development

So far, the focus has been on norms, incentives and regulation.

But what can the flourishing of nature itself contribute to advancing human development in the Anthropocene?

As this chapter argues: a lot. It makes the case for nature-based human development and for the cumulative impacts that local initiatives can have at global levels. It highlights the contributions indigenous communities around the world are making every day to protect the planet.

Social norms and incentives can be harnessed for transformational change, and so can a new generation of nature-based solutions—actions to protect, sustainably manage and restore ecosystems while simultaneously promoting wellbeing.[1] These are a manifestation of people empowered in ways that enhance equity, foster innovation and are rooted in a sense of stewardship of nature (figure 6.1).

Nature-based solutions are typically bottom-up, with a proliferation of new initiatives in different contexts. They often rely on the participation and initiative of indigenous peoples and local communities. They are implemented across countries at all levels of human development and are nested in social and economic systems, complementing human-made engineered solutions.

When local becomes global

Local nature-based solutions have the potential to contribute to transformational change, even at the global level—for two reasons. First, many local and community decisions can add up to substantial global impact. Second, planetary and socioeconomic systems are interconnected, and local decisions can have impacts elsewhere and at multiple scales.

As an illustration of the first effect, consider how a set of 20 cost-effective actions across global forests, wetlands, grasslands and agricultural lands can provide 37 percent of the mitigation needed through 2030 to keep global warming below 2 degrees Celsius above preindustrial levels and 20 percent of the mitigation needed through 2050 (figure 6.2).[2] About two-thirds of that mitigation potential is linked to forest pathways.[3]

And for the second effect, consider the decisions in small-scale, coastal aquaculture—perhaps the world's most vibrant food sector today, especially in Southeast Asia (figure 6.3).[4] Coastal aquaculture puts stress on land (due to the need for terrestrial crops for feed) and on the local environment (destroying coastal vegetation—mangroves, in particular) in ways that scale up to the national or even global level (by incubating diseases that may spread to other species

Figure 6.1 Nature-based solutions and the potential for a virtuous cycle between people and planet

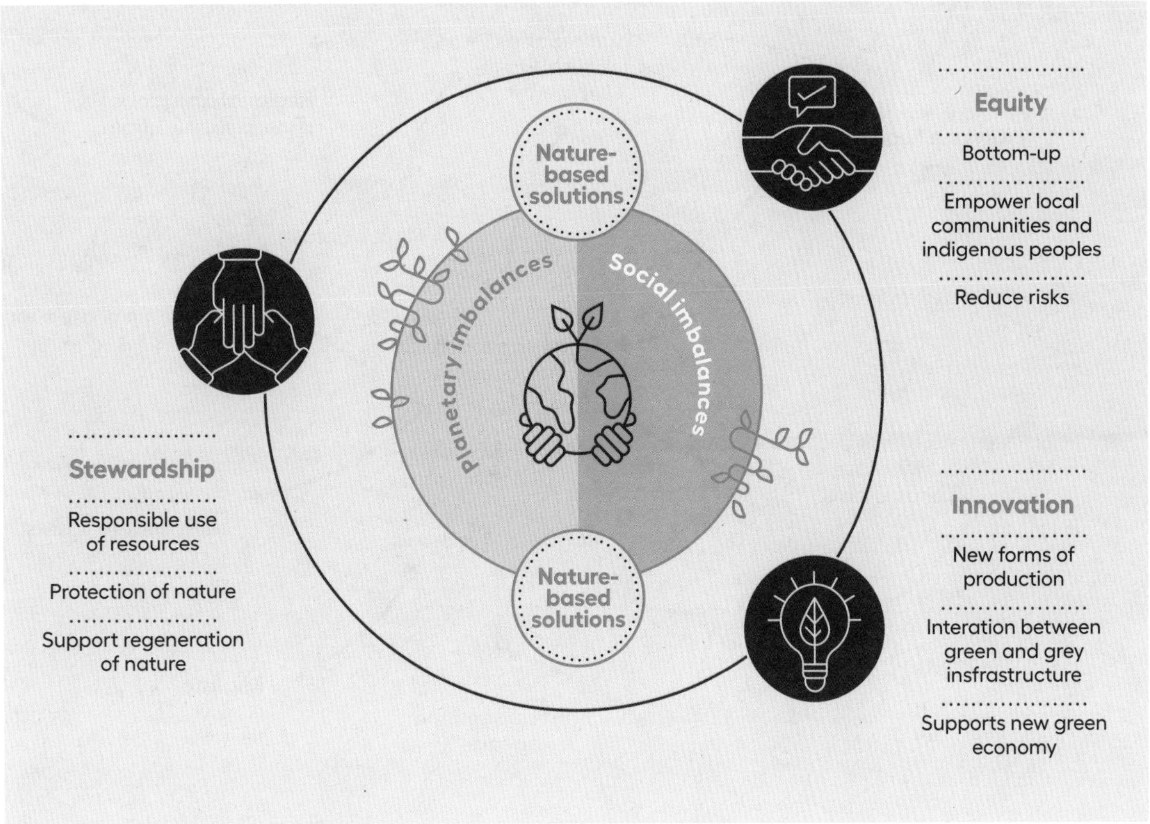

Source: Human Development Report Office.

Figure 6.2 Twenty nature-based solutions can provide some of the mitigation needed to restrain global warming

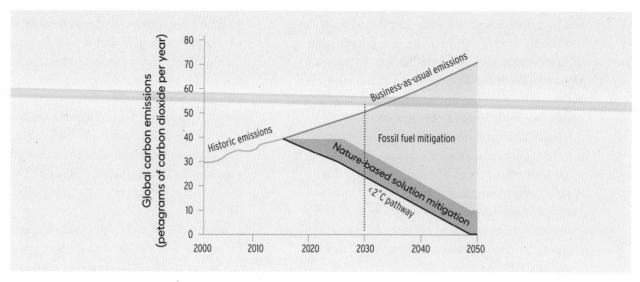

Source: Griscom and others 2017, figure 2.

Figure 6.3 The local and the global are deeply interconnected

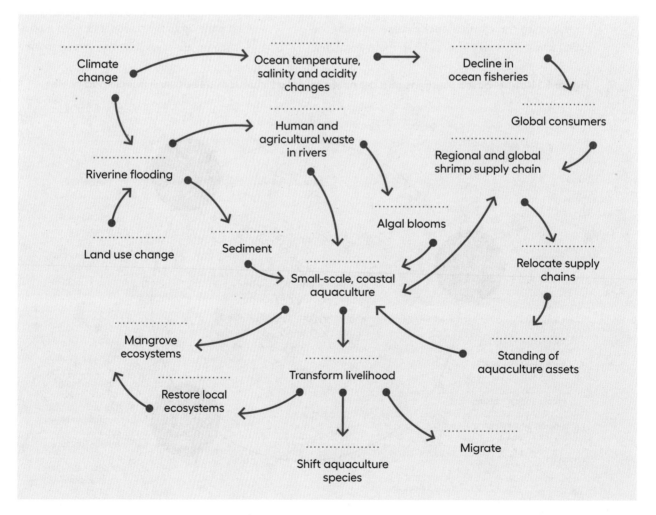

Source: Keys and others 2019, figure 3b.

and by using antimicrobials in ways that cause resistance). But aquaculture practices that provide livelihoods and better address these risks can have regional and global benefits. This is part of the more general pattern of telecoupling: the global interconnection of ecological and social systems (box 6.1).

A systematic approach to nature-based solutions can leverage their potential for large-scale transformative change—what this chapter calls "nature-based human development."

" A systematic approach to nature-based solutions can leverage their potential for large-scale transformative change—what this chapter calls "nature-based human development."

The next section provides evidence on how nature-based solutions are being implemented and the ways they advance human development while protecting ecosystem integrity. The final section addresses the potential to turn a cloud of fragmented solutions into an integrated system of nature-based human development, underscoring the role of indigenous peoples and local communities. This systemic integration requires structural support, involving the coordination and contributions of various actors and institutions so that nature-based solutions not only provide multiple benefits to multiple stakeholders but are also harnessed for transformative change at the global scale.

Avoiding biosphere integrity loss, empowering people

Nature-based solutions show that human development can be advanced while safeguarding the integrity of ecosystems. This section describes how nature-based solutions are helping manage risks from natural hazards, improve water availability and quality and enhance food security.

Managing risks from natural hazards

Natural hazards such as heat waves, severe flooding, storms, landslides and droughts drive risks that affect migration, urbanization, inequality and the degradation of ecosystems, including soil erosion.[5] A

Box 6.1. Telecoupling between Indian farmers and rainfall in East Africa

How do the agricultural practices of farmers in India affect rainfall in East Africa? The link is atmospheric moisture recycling, the process of evaporation in which water enters the atmosphere, travels along prevailing winds and falls as rain elsewhere. Farmers in India rely on groundwater for irrigation. This water then evaporates into the atmosphere, where it is carried to East Africa to fall again as rain. This process could be interrupted if groundwater were unexpectedly and rapidly drained. In other words, Indian farmers might unexpectedly discover that their groundwater pumps cannot reach the water table any longer, leaving them unable to irrigate their fields. This could eliminate the supply of evaporated water and lead to a substantial decline in rainfall in East Africa, with corresponding consequences for the productivity of local ecosystem services—for example, water for animals, agriculture and trees. Such an interruption in rainfall could also have regional impacts: It might trigger migration and conflict over resources. An unexpected outcome could be the loss of livestock in Somaliland.

Source: Galaz, Collste and Moore 2020.

hazard combined with exposure and vulnerability becomes a risk that can cause loss, damage and death.[6] Worldwide the number of disasters linked to natural hazards has increased by 75 percent over the past 20 years.[7] In the past two decades these disasters have affected more than 4 billion people, claiming 1.23 million lives and causing close to $3 trillion in economic losses.[8] Disasters are one of the main triggers of displacement, with almost 23 million people displaced on average every year as a result of natural hazards in 2009–2019.[9] Actions for national and local disaster risk reduction strategies are thus crucial, as called for by the Sendai Framework (box 6.2).

The role of ecosystems in reducing risks from disasters has been widely recognized in recent years as climate change has increased the frequency, intensity and magnitude of natural hazards.[10] In this context, maintaining ecosystem integrity can provide cost-effective measures that, if complemented by other policies, can enhance community preparedness and resilience.[11] It is an investment: In the United States every $1 spent on preparedness saves $4 in natural

Box 6.2 The Sendai Framework

Disaster risk reduction has been as a global policy priority since the late 1980s. In March 2015 in Sendai, Japan, UN member states adopted the Framework for Disaster Risk Reduction, laying out a voluntary pathway for reducing risks from natural hazards during the following 15 years. The framework, following the Hyogo Framework for Action 2005–2015, was signed in the same year as the Sustainable Development Goals. Although the Hyogo Framework led to more proactive and coordinated international efforts to reduce disaster risk, the achievements were uneven across countries. The Sendai Framework renewed the sense of urgency with seven targets: reduce global disaster mortality, reduce the number of affected people globally, reduce direct disaster economic loss as a share of global GDP, reduce disaster damage to critical infrastructure and disruption of basic services, increase the number of countries with national and local disaster risk reduction strategies, enhance international cooperation to developing countries and increase the availability of and access to early warning systems and disaster risk information.[1]

In the first five years of the agreement, countries were to shape national and local strategies to implement in the next 10 years. This year, 2020, is the deadline, requiring immediate and focused action to reduce natural disaster risk. The main challenge for the next 10 years revolves around international coordination, since the framework's targets are collective.

The Covid-19 pandemic adds another layer to the challenges but can also be used as an example of country capacities in risk management. The Sendai Framework mechanisms and strategies for disaster resilience can complement and enhance current responses to the Covid-19 pandemic.[2] The Sendai Framework treats epidemics and pandemics explicitly as biological hazards that can lead to disaster. Several aspects of the framework can be used in responding to biological hazards, such as risk assessment (to have stronger knowledge of the crisis), multistakeholder and regional coordination mechanisms, the resilience of critical infrastructure and the preparation of inclusive recovery plans. Finally, social systems and links shape community perceptions of risk,[3] so community-based models for disaster risk reduction can be applied for Covid-19 assessment, preparedness and management, important in reducing deaths and losses from natural hazards.

Notes
1. Mysiak and others 2016. **2.** Djalante, Shaw and DeWit 2020. **3.** Scherer and Cho 2003.

---

disaster costs,[12] and the ratio is higher for flooding and hurricane-related disasters.

Green areas to manage extreme temperatures risk

Heat waves, a dangerous natural hazard, killed more than 166,000 people between 1998 and 2017. About 125 million more people faced exposure to heat waves in 2016 than in 2000.[13] Besides being lethal, heat waves can cause fatigue, nausea, dehydration and heat stroke and aggravate chronic respiratory diseases. Patients with mental health issues could be at higher risk of heat-related morbidities and undesirable effects of psychiatric medications.[14] Risks are also expected from vectorborne and waterborne diseases and through malnutrition, given the expected impacts on food security.[15]

> " Nature-based solutions can mitigate the health impacts of extreme weather.

Extreme heat events are particularly severe in cities because they become urban heat islands. Buildings, roads and other structures absorb and re-emit the sun's heat typically more than natural landscapes do. Areas with a higher concentration of these structures and limited greenery become islands of greater heat than other areas.[16] Due to urban heat islands, urban populations, particularly more vulnerable social groups, face greater health risks from heat exposure than rural populations do.[17] Nature-based solutions can mitigate the health impacts of extreme weather.

Cooling systems, such as air conditioning, are often used to cope with extreme temperatures, especially during heat waves. Since parts of the population cannot access or afford air conditioning systems (which can triple annual energy costs for heating and cooling), this solution can exacerbate inequalities in exposure to heat waves. And air conditioning aggravates the underlying cause of extreme temperatures by releasing heat energy into the outdoor environment of the city and hindering the natural cooling that happens after sunset. It creates a vicious cycle in which the mechanism to cope with heat waves contributes to extreme temperatures.[18]

A viable and effective nature-based solution to mitigate the effects of urban heat islands is to create, restore and protect vegetation within cities. Evapotranspiration draws heat from the air, naturally decreasing the temperature of surrounding areas. Plants and trees absorb solar radiation and shade the ground beneath, and trees affect wind and can reduce heating energy in winter by shading wind. Vegetation also assimilates carbon dioxide and produces oxygen, lowering greenhouse gas concentration in the atmosphere.[19] Thus, green spaces such as urban parks and forests are an effective way to both cope with the effects of urban heat islands and mitigate anthropogenic planetary pressures.

" Conserving forests and other vegetation can help with both rapid- and slow-onset disasters, since vegetation reduces the risk of landslides after earthquakes and during droughts.

Multiple studies have documented the effects of urban green areas on cooling cities. In Nagoya, in central Japan, temperatures were up to 1.9 degrees Celsius higher in urban areas than in green areas. Differences were larger during the day than at night, and greater during the summer. In the winter temperature differences fell due to the loss of tree foliage, which reduces shading and evapotranspiration, causing a relative increase in green space air temperature and a decrease in differences with urban area temperatures. The cooling effect of green areas appeared to extend 200–300 metres from the green area into urban areas at night and 300–500 metres during the day.[20] A study in London assessing the cooling effects of a large urban green space found that the mean temperature difference between urban and green spaces was about 1.1 degrees Celsius in the summer—and as much as 4 degrees on some nights—with the estimated cooling reaching 20–440 metres into the urban

area.[21] Studies of the physiological equivalent temperature, which describes human thermal perceptions and is used as an indicator of human comfort under temperature variation,[22] showed considerable impacts of urban green spaces. In the Yunan Dynasty City Walls Relics Park in Shanghai, China, the physiological equivalent temperature fell by 2 degrees Celsius on average and by up to 15.6 degrees at 14:00 on a hot summer day in August. The biggest factor reducing the physiological equivalent temperature was the presence of high trees.[23]

Ecosystems for disaster risk reduction

Ecosystem-based disaster risk reduction is the sustainable management, conservation and restoration of ecosystems to reduce disaster risk.[24] Conserving forests and other vegetation can help with both rapid- and slow-onset disasters, since vegetation reduces the risk of landslides after earthquakes and during droughts.[25] Wetlands are critical to regulating and controlling floods and drought.[26] Coastal vegetation such as sand dunes and mangrove forests can prevent damage to crops by coastal storms.[27]

Sustainably managing ecosystems in seas, wetlands and rivers can boost fish stocks, support livelihoods dependent on fisheries, reduce the risks of flooding and benefit tourism and the economy. Oyster and coral reefs, salt marshes, dunes, barrier islands, floodplains, wetlands, forests and mangroves are natural defenders and can reduce the risk of a hazard turning into a disaster by protecting the shoreline against storms, winds and erosion; bolstering food security; and providing a high level of carbon storage.[28] For example, in the Gulf of Nicoya in Costa Rica, where 34 percent of the mangrove forests are threatened by agricultural expansion,[29] Conservation International started a mangrove restoration project, building capacity and creating an education programme so local stakeholders could replant mangroves.[30] Other countries have recently implemented innovative approaches to manage risks, expanding the use of insurance mechanisms (box 6.3).

Ecosystem-based disaster risk reduction can be leveraged by empowering women, drawing on their risk awareness, social networking practices, extensive knowledge of their communities and tasks related to managing natural environmental resources and

Box 6.3 The first reef insurance policy to protect coastal communities in Mexico

Hurricanes Emily, Stan and Wilma hit the Caribbean coast of Mexico in 2005, causing about $8 billion in damage, closing restaurants and hotels in an area whose income depends mostly on tourism.[1]

But one of the ports, Puerto Morelos, protected by its coral reef, suffered less damage. A healthy coral reef can reduce the energy of a wave by 97 percent (the reef crest alone reduces it by 86 percent),[2] so waves are much less destructive when they reach the shoreline. Coral reefs can provide similar or better wave attenuation than artificial defences such as breakwaters.

But coral reefs can also be damaged or destroyed by natural hazards such as storms and by pollution, overfishing and bleaching—as of 2018, 50 percent of Mexico's reefs were in poor or critical condition.[3] Since this destruction compromises the safety of coastal communities and their livelihoods, in 2018 the Nature Conservancy, the insurance company Swiss Re and Mexico's state governments partnered to protect the coral reefs in the Yucatan Peninsula.[4] Several reefs were at risk of dying because of pollution and storm damage.

The partnership offers an insurance solution. The state of Quintana Roo established the Coastal Zone Management Trust in 2018 to manage funds collected for coral reef maintenance and reconstruction. In 2019 the trust purchased the first coral reef insurance policy in the world.[5] The policy will ensure the repair of coral reefs after severe storms, providing the community the financial resources to manage the reefs and prevent erosion to coastlines. The policy covers six municipalities and 160 kilometres of coastline, including the city of Cancún and the municipality of Puerto Morelos.

Key lessons of this experience are the opportunity to use financial mechanisms to protect nature and the importance of different stakeholders collaborating. Such initiatives have important implications for the 840 million people around the world who live with the risk of coastal flooding and for economies that rely on tourism (coral reef tourism generates $36 billion a year).[6] Similar partnerships are being considered in Asia, Australia, the Caribbean and the United States.

On Mexico's Caribbean coast, volunteer squads of divers are learning to repair the coral reefs that shield the shore. The Nature Conservancy gathered fishers, researchers, hotel owners, tour operators, local government representatives and coral specialists and designed a training course for volunteers to repair reefs and the surrounding infrastructure. The divers learned skills such as using pneumatic drills underwater and inserting metal rods to keep larger pieces of reattached coral in place, setting them like broken bones. They practised with cement and marine epoxy on pieces of dead coral and learned to inflate nylon lift bags to move large pieces of coral and storm debris.[7]

Notes
1. Healthy Reefs 2020. 2. Ferrario and others 2014. 3. Healthy Reefs 2020. 4. Swiss Re Group 2019. 5. The Nature Conservancy 2019b.
6. The Nature Conservancy 2019b. 7. Smith 2018.

caring for the community. In Nepal climate change is associated with rainfall variability that has increased the risk of floods, affecting water and food scarcity. The US Agency for International Development, in partnership with the World Wildlife Fund and CARE International, started the Hariyo Ban Program in 2011 to help the government work with civil society to use existing ecosystems to build resilience to floods and landslides through natural resource management groups.[31] More than 12,000 women were supported and empowered to ensure their meaningful representation in decisionmaking, and the groups' internal governance was led mostly by women (70 percent).[32]

Biodiversity contributes to resilience

Biodiversity has a role in reducing disaster risk, fostering ecological resilience and enhancing ecosystem protective functions and community resilience. For instance, seagrass ensures the generation of oxygen, affects fisheries' efficiency and captures sand, dirt and silt particles, thus improving water quality. Its roots trap and stabilize sediment, reducing erosion and buffering the coastline against storms. Indonesia is home to the world's largest concentration of seagrass—more than 30,000 square kilometres, 10 percent of the world's seagrass.[33] But only 40 percent of Indonesian seagrass is healthy.[34] In

2013 researchers from the University of California, Davis, and Hasanuddin University started a pilot programme for restoring seagrass in Sulawesi, Indonesia, by transplanting different combinations of seagrass species to determine which performed best.[35] The survival and coverage of seagrass increased with the number of species transplanted, signalling that species richness can be important for restoration.[36]

Africa is home to crop diversity that reduces the potential impact of climate stressors and is adaptive,[37] as different genotypes create more resistance to changing conditions.[38] But diversity losses have been reported in crop varieties, mainly because of improved varieties displacing local ones. In Burkina Faso and Mali sorghum and millet face genetic erosion given high rainfall variability, among other factors.[39] Bioversity International partnered with local governments and universities in Burkina Faso, Mali and Niger in a project to encourage farmers to experiment with and evaluate diverse crop varieties. The project trained farmers in producing quality seed to adapt to local conditions.[40] Several farmers have formed their own seed production groups and set up community seedbanks.[41] In Mali the project continued without external financial support, and local community leaders have integrated the approach into development plans.[42]

Improving water availability and quality

While water covers 70 percent of the Earth's surface, less than 1 percent is available as freshwater.[43] This vital resource is under increasing pressure from households and productive activities.[44] Global water use has risen sixfold over the past 100 years,[45] and 80 percent of wastewater is released back into the environment without treatment,[46] while about half of accessible freshwater is appropriated for human use each year.[47] Water pollution in rivers rose more than 50 percent between 1990 and 2010 in Africa, Asia and Latin America, driven by agriculture, economic activity, population growth and an increase in untreated sewage discharge.[48] Since 1900, 64–71 percent of natural wetland area worldwide has been lost due to human activity.[49] As a result, about 4 billion people—60 percent of the world's population—live in regions with nearly permanent water stress,[50] and 3 billion people lack basic handwashing facilities at

home.[51] By 2030 global demand for water is expected to exceed supply by 40 percent,[52] and about 6 billion people might face clean water scarcity by 2050.[53] Enhancing water's availability and quality is thus a major challenge.

" The integrated management of hydric resources can often offer multiple benefits to different communities. Bearing this in mind is important to shape innovative collective financing mechanisms being used to scale up nature-based solutions.

Neither nature nor human-built infrastructure alone will address this challenge.[54] Nature-based solutions for water security benefit from ecosystem processes and functions for providing and managing water. In some cases, rather than building infrastructure to manage water, relying on such ecosystems as grasslands, mountains and rivers would be better for water management.[55] Some nature-based approaches provide the main or only viable solution, such as landscape restoration to combat land degradation and desertification. Still, infrastructure will always be required for some purposes, such as supplying water for households through pipes and taps.

Green infrastructure watershed banks or a global water ecosystem services observatory could support the adoption of more efficient and sustainable water futures.[56] A global assessment that mapped the water catchments and watersheds supplying water for more than 1.7 billion people across 4,000 of the world's largest cities estimated that source water conservation and restoration could reduce sediment pollution in at least 70 percent of watershed areas in Africa, Asia, Europe and Latin America.[57] That could benefit 780 million people who live in urban watersheds in countries in the bottom decile of the Human Development Index (as of 2014). The integrated management of hydric resources can often offer multiple benefits to different communities. Bearing this in mind is important to shape innovative collective financing mechanisms being used to scale up nature-based solutions (box 6.4).

Managing water availability

Nature-based solutions focused on water availability address water supply by managing water

Box 6.4. Using collective financing mechanisms to scale up nature-based water management

In Ecuador the Fund for the Protection of Water was created in 2000 to preserve the watershed that provides water for the Metropolitan District of Quito, where almost 15 percent of the country's population resides. The fund, a collective financing mechanism, gathers public and private resources and prioritizes investment in green infrastructure as the core of water management. It has recovered and restored more than 15,000 hectares through diverse projects in water management, sustainable hydric conservation, green cover restoration and environmental education.[1] One of the first funds created for sustainable management of watersheds, the fund today operates with an annual budget of $2 million.[2] The strategy has been replicated throughout Ecuador, and in 2015 a fund was set up for the conservation of the Daule River, which feeds the city of Guayaquil. The fund also works as a participatory multisector financial tool dedicated to conserving hydric resources and the watershed that supplies the population.[3]

A regional alliance for water funds was set up to scale up this initiative. The Alianza Latinoamericana de Fondos de Agua provides seed capital and technical assistance for the creation of water funds, mostly in Latin America and the Caribbean. At least 25 funds exist throughout the region in Argentina, Brazil, Chile, Colombia, Costa Rica, the Dominican Republic, Ecuador and Guatemala.[4] Water funds build evidence on water security, help develop a shared and actionable vision for water security, gather diverse stakeholders and encourage political will for positive change. They influence water governance, promote green infrastructure projects and offer an attractive and cost-efficient investment opportunity.[5]

Another organization, Rare, uses blended finance and reciprocity arrangements as innovative ways to promote conservancy. For example, in the Cauca Valley in Colombia, a programme was set up for downstream users to fund incentives for upstream farmers to set aside some of their land for conservation. This helps farmers transition to more sustainable practices and protects the quality of the water that reaches downstream users.[6]

Notes
1. FONAG n.d. 2. The Nature Conservancy 2019a. 3. Alianza Latinoamericana de Fondos de Agua 2020a. 4. Alianza Latinoamericana de Fondos de Agua 2020b. 5. Alianza Latinoamericana de Fondos de Agua 2018. 6. National Geographic 2014.

storage, infiltration and transmission to improve the location, timing and quantity of water for human needs. For instance, natural wetlands, improvements in soil moisture and groundwater recharge are ecosystem-friendly methods of storing water that are cheaper and more sustainable than building and maintaining dams.[58]

In China the per capita availability of water resources is just a fourth the world average.[59] Nationally, 83 percent of surface water and 28 percent of ground water do not meet standards for safe water.[60] A partnership between Chinese government institutions and the International Union for Conservation of Nature developed a project to use natural infrastructure to secure long-term supplies of drinking water. By rehabilitating and protecting the Miyun and Jiaquan Watersheds, the project aimed to ensure sustainable water supplies in 30–50 Chinese megacities. It created long-term management and financing mechanisms to protect drinking water sources and

enhanced local capacities by teaching 500 farmers safe pesticide and fertilizer use and water source protection to prevent pollution.[61]

Urban settlements are another area for water management. Although cities account for only 2 percent of global land,[62] they will absorb most of the population growth in the coming years, and their water demand will also grow, putting pressure on supplies.[63] Nature-based solutions for cities include catchment management, water recycling and green infrastructure. Catchment measures are traditionally used to improve water supply, but they can also store water and control regular water flows to a city. Urban green infrastructure is incorporated in infiltration, bioretention, permeable pavements, designing new areas, constructing wetlands and connecting rivers and floodplains.

Revitalizing and restoring riverbanks can provide water for cities and urban areas. Revitalizing the Ślepiotka River valley in Katowice, Poland, reestablished natural habitats on the riverbanks and in the river basin. By bringing together multiple actors, including individuals, engineers and planners, the project was planned to store water and mitigate flood risks. Previously abandoned spaces along the riverbanks were regenerated with citizens' help.[64] In the Netherlands the sealed surfaces of urban riverbanks of Boompjes Promenade were restored to a green riverfront area. The promenade was part of the country's "Give space back to the river" programme and its implementation in Rotterdam. As in Poland, the riverbank was used for water retention as well as for green urban recreation space.[65]

Ensuring water quality

While water availability considers the quantity of demand and supply, water quality relates to pollution and health. Protecting water sources through nature-based solutions can improve water quality. The process can reduce water treatment costs for urban suppliers and improve access to safe drinking water, mainly for rural communities.

Agricultural pesticides and wastewater from food processing and livestock add considerably to water pollution. Wetlands and grasslands can be managed to enable soils and crops to reduce sediment loading, capture and retain pollutants, and recycle nutrients that improve water quality and reduce demand for fertilizers.

Of Peru's 32 million people, 2.5 million lack access to safe water, and 5 million lack access to improved sanitation facilities.[66] In 2015 the water utility serving Lima approved Latin America's largest investment in natural infrastructure, funded by monthly tariffs.[67] The project is restoring wetlands and grasslands and rehabilitating and replicating infiltration channels in the Chillon, Rimac and Alto Mantaro Rivers, which provide water to Lima. It has also developed a tool, Cuantificación de Beneficios Hidrológicos de Intervenciones en Cuencas (Quantification of Hydrological Benefits of Interventions in Watersheds), to estimate the impacts of the most common nature-based solutions, such as grassland, forest or wetland conservation and restoration, infiltration trenches, riparian buffers and permeable reservoirs. The tool allows practitioners and decisionmakers to know what they are getting for their investments in nature and to compare it with alternatives.

As with water availability, green infrastructure in new spaces in cities can reduce urban pollution. For instance, through green walls, roof gardens, vegetated infiltration and drainage basins, nature-based solutions support the treatment and recycling of wastewater. Urban water pollution control is mostly an "end of pipe" solution with intensive wastewater treatment, but nature-based solutions offer alternatives. Constructed wetlands are among the solutions that can be incorporated into urban design to manage polluted water from rainfall, by biodegrading or filtering pollutants.[68]

" Protecting water sources through nature-based solutions can improve water quality. The process can reduce water treatment costs for urban suppliers and improve access to safe drinking water, mainly for rural communities.

Constructed wetlands are engineered systems built to use natural processes mimicking natural wetland systems that filter runoff before it reaches open water. Used for rainwater treatment, they combine sewer overflow treatment, cleaning outflows from water treatment plants and greywater treatment.[69] They typically can remove up to 88 percent of suspended solids, 92 percent of organic matter, 46–90 percent of phosphorus and 16–84 percent of nitrogen,[70] and they can remove pathogens.[71] Constructed wetlands have become a common nature-based alternative to help obtain clean and reusable water, safeguarding human health and preserving hydric resources.

Studies in water-stressed areas in the Arab States region have shown the potential for constructed wetlands to treat wastewater and polluted water and to preserve freshwater by producing reusable effluents for irrigation. In Oman constructed wetlands treat the wastewater from workers' camps at oil production facilities. In the United Arab Emirates a constructed wetland serves a residential area of 100 villas, producing effluent water reused to irrigate green areas.[72] The solutions are used across the region for wastewater from sludge, residential areas, and oil and gas activities, which are among the largest industrial sources of wastewater worldwide. Implementing such solutions in water-stressed environments has additional challenges, including increased evapotranspiration due to high temperatures and higher plant biomass production.[73] But the benefits come in areas where water scarcity and quality are obstacles to human development.

Enhancing food security

Biological diversity—including soil microbial diversity; genetic seed diversity; pollinator diversity; crop, livestock and fish diversity; and more—underpins food security at all levels. Although humans have evolved to eat more than 7,000 species, just three—wheat, rice and maize—now provide more than half our calories,[74] and just 12 plant crops and 5 animal species account for 75 percent of our entire planetary food system.[75] We are losing genetic diversity within species. For example, seed growers in 1900 offered 3,879 varieties of 10 common vegetables in the United States, but in 1983 that number was reduced more than tenfold to 310.[76] We are losing the populations of wild crop and livestock relatives, plants and animals.[77]

The sharp decline of pollinators due to pesticides and habitat loss threatens food security and nutrition around the world.[78] Of the leading global food crops consumed directly by humans and traded on the global market, 85 percent rely on animal pollination. Without pollinators, production would fall by more than 90 percent for 12 percent of leading global crops.[79] The decline of pollinators affects both production and nutrition. Pollinated crops account for 35 percent of global food production, more than 90 percent of available vitamin C and more than 70 percent of available vitamin A.[80]

"We are losing genetic diversity within species. For example, seed growers in 1900 offered 3,879 varieties of 10 common vegetables in the United States, but in 1983 that number was reduced more than tenfold to 310.

Forests are essential to global food security. More than 1.25 billion people depend directly on forests for shelter, livelihoods, water, fuel and food security.[81] Wild foods harvested from forests provide a wide range of nutrients and micronutrients,[82] especially important to the more than 2 billion people who experience micronutrient malnutrition.[83] Wild animals, or bush meat, provide more than 6 million tonnes of food a year to communities in the Congo and Amazon Basins alone.[84] Yet tropical forest loss has been accelerating, taking more than 60 million hectares since 2002.[85]

Pastoralist activities are carried out by more than 200 million people worldwide and are essential to food security, especially in dryland areas such as the Horn of Africa. But they are also some of the most vulnerable to climate change.[86] As the demand for animal products keeps increasing,[87] climate-related phenomena such as droughts and climate variability put pressure on pastoralist systems, causing losses of livestock and poor reproductive performance, partially hindering their adaptive capacity.[88]

Farming is the occupation that engages the most people on the planet.[89] But rural farmers disproportionately face the brunt of agrobiodiversity loss, especially soil microbial diversity loss. More than 1.3 billion people live on degraded agricultural land with limited fertility,[90] and more than half of agricultural land worldwide is moderately or severely affected by land degradation and desertification.[91] Poor farmers, when trapped in a vicious cycle, are forced to use ever-increasing inputs of chemical pesticides and fertilizers, further degrading microbial diversity and in turn undermining long-term crop productivity and requiring even more inputs, causing more degradation.[92] The next section reviews options to improve agricultural practices on and off the farm and provides examples related to fisheries. Both farming and fishing are key to enhancing food security.

Improving agricultural practices

Nature-based solutions to improve agricultural practices while enhancing food security include regenerative agriculture, agroforestry, silvopasture, habitat protection for pollinators, protection of crop wild relatives and promotion of agrobiodiversity.

Regenerative agriculture—farming that increases soil fertility and productive capacity over time—provides substantial long-term gains for farmers by releasing them from the land degradation trap. Farmers save money by spending less on chemical inputs and see increased crop productivity.[93]

Agroforestry—growing crops on land interspersed with trees—provides many benefits for food and reduces inequality. Agroforestry improves crop yields by increasing soil fertility and providing pollinator habitat. It strengthens farmers' economic resilience by diversifying the type and timing of their crops and reducing the risk of crop failures, and it improves farmer nutrition by offering a wider range of foods, especially protein from nut trees. Forest and grassland protection provides a range of benefits. Many pollinators depend on forest habitat, while strips of forest, as well as large forest blocks, have multiple benefits for many crops, such as coffee.[94]

" Regenerative agriculture, agroforestry and silvopasture—yield many of the same benefits, including increased diversity of farmer income, improved nutrition, enhanced resilience to climate change, more carbon sequestration and greater biodiversity.

Silvopasture integrates trees, forests, forage and grazing livestock in mutually beneficial ways. It yields multiple benefits, including more efficient use of mixed woodlands, greater wildlife abundance and diversity, increased carbon sequestration, improved animal health and nutrition, better weed and vegetation control and reduced labour inputs. Farm productivity can be enhanced by planting fruit and nut trees on pasture lands.[95]

All three approaches—regenerative agriculture, agroforestry and silvopasture—yield many of the same benefits, including increased diversity of farmer income, improved nutrition, enhanced resilience to climate change, more carbon sequestration and greater biodiversity.[96] They provide an alternative approach to today's most common agricultural practices, which favour high-chemical fertilizers and pesticides, crop monocultures, simplified seed genetic diversity, mechanized equipment that prevents trees growth, and high tillage and other practices that reduce soil microbial health and fertility. A broad array of tax incentives, market and pricing structures, land use policies and perverse agricultural subsidies inhibit agricultural nature-based solutions around the world and can keep farmers trapped on degraded lands.[97]

Preserving fisheries

More than 90 percent of the world's fisheries have been fully exploited, have been overexploited or have collapsed altogether.[98] Overfishing has profound impacts on the world's food systems. About 3.1 billion people rely on fish for 20 percent of their daily protein intake.[99] Globally, consumption of seafood per capita is over 15 times higher in indigenous coastal communities than in nonindigenous communities.[100]

Sustainable fisheries and protected marine areas ensure that fish populations can regenerate and provide sustainable yields. Protecting coastal and marine areas such as mangroves, coral reefs, seagrass beds and seamounts—particularly the sites of fish spawning, nursery and aggregation—is crucial to various parts of fish lifecycles. Fish biomass can be as much as 670 percent higher in effectively managed marine protected areas than in unprotected areas, providing a source population for local fisheries.[101] Expanding marine protected areas by 5 percent could yield at least a 20 percent increase in future catch.[102]

Towards nature-based human development

Nature-based solutions can add up to a substantial impact. For instance, reforestation and land neutrality can curb climate risks, with several mitigation actions potentially adding up to a considerable reduction in net greenhouse gas emissions. Those mitigation actions are heterogenous across regions and levels of development, depending largely on geographic characteristics (figure 6.4), with several of the globally relevant ecosystems transcending national borders.[103]

Even though mitigation actions are cost-effective, implementing them is challenging because they contribute to global benefits (climate change mitigation) but have local costs. And with ecosystems shared across countries, action by one country alone does not ensure ecosystem integrity. Moreover, multiple interests are at play. Large differences in wealth and power have been operating for centuries, distorting incentives and often biasing decisions towards overexploiting forest resources. With the individuals interested in protecting the forest, such as indigenous peoples and local communities, historically disempowered, large business interests typically enjoy more power.

Forest area has been decreasing over the past few decades in developing countries, reflecting national or local development priorities. This underlying

Figure 6.4 The mitigation potential of eight climate change interventions is widely distributed across countries in different regions and at different levels of development

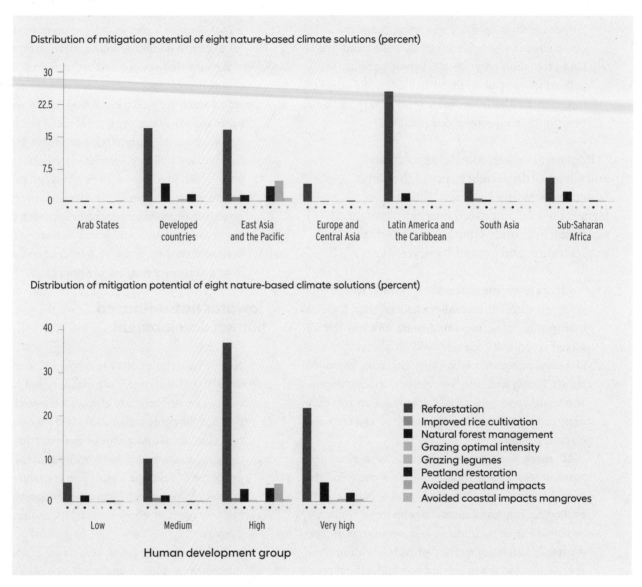

Note: This is a subset of the 20 cost-effective solutions that are geolocalized.
Source: Human Development Report Office based on Griscom and others (2017).

reality presents a challenge for the mitigation potential offered by nature-based solutions (figure 6.5). To enhance human development, reforestation or large-scale afforestation cannot be dissociated from socioeconomic development of forest- and grassland-dependent communities.[104] Instead, reforestation must be part of a broader social and economic development effort, supporting local communities and supported by them, with socioeconomic empowerment and the protection of nature coming together. There is great potential for this, as close to 295 million people live on tropical forest restoration opportunity land in the Global South.[105] But global incentives also matter. If reforestation is pursued only locally, carbon leakage is a risk: Market interests might simply finance deforestation in a different location. Aligning incentives would be easier with actions towards reducing the need for pasture, which in turn depend on systemic support for improving beef production efficiency or changing dietary preferences to reduce beef consumption.[106] In fact, achieving land degradation neutrality goes beyond reforestation; it also depends on combatting desertification and restoring degraded land and soil.[107]

Figure 6.5 The decrease in forest area in developing countries presents a challenge for the mitigation potential offered by nature-based solutions

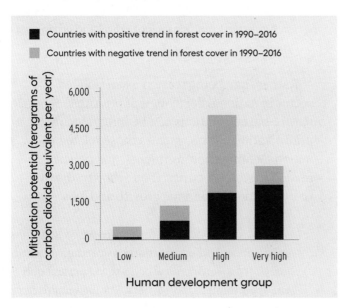

Source: Human Development Report Office based on FAO (2020b) and Griscom and others (2017).

This discussion of the potential and challenges of land use illustrates a broader point: how a systemic approach that considers asymmetries of power and incentive structures at multiple scales is crucial to unleash the potential of nature-based solutions for transformational change. The rest of this chapter explores how to do so through nature-based human development, which shifts the focus from specific solutions towards human agency and to the broader determinants of local empowerment to advance human development and preserve the integrity of the biosphere.

Leveraging interventions for transformational change

The value of nature-based solutions goes beyond their contributions to local communities. If their effects are scaled up, they can contribute to transformational change. Promoting innovative ideas and diffusing knowledge of existing nature-based solutions are first steps. But only a systemic approach will enable nature-based solutions to have impacts at larger scales. Creating systemic conditions that provide the socioeconomic support for this to happen is referred to here as nature-based human development.

Having plausible and cost-effective nature-based solutions is not enough to ensure their implementation. Despite the overwhelmingly compelling social, economic and ecological case for these solutions, only about $120–$150 billion a year is spent globally on biodiversity conservation. There is an estimated gap of about $600–$820 billion a year to increase protected areas,[108] improve the productive management of landscapes and seascapes and protect biodiversity in areas of high human impact.[109] The benefits of this investment might outweigh the costs by a factor of five,[110] with many of the benefits accruing to those who need it most—often poor rural communities that depend directly on nature for their livelihoods. Yet nature-based solutions have been largely ignored by governments, firms and investors alike. This is not new, as countries' natural resource endowments have often been associated with a "curse" obstructing human progress.[111]

A systemic approach would ease constraints that limit the adoption of nature-based solutions, including the fact that the social value (typically widely shared across communities) is larger than the private value that accrues to direct beneficiaries, leading to underinvestment. Moreover, extant interests in managing natural resources are encoded in regulations, subsidies and taxes that reflect current distributions in wealth and power, with a bias to preserving the status quo of resource over-exploitation for larger private gains. The political economy challenge is compounded because developing countries and poor communities lack resources—the origin of environmental poverty traps[112]—and because the compounding negative impacts of human pressures on the planet further erode their agency.[113]

Nature-based human development complements the mechanisms of change discussed in chapters 4 and 5 by highlighting the importance of placing the preservation of ecosystem integrity at the core of multiple economic and social processes.

Leveraging business and finance

This means using regulations and incentive mechanisms to hold financial institutions accountable for their impacts on nature. A key step to increase transparency and accountability is a new task force—the Informal Working Group for the Taskforce on Nature-related Financial Disclosure[114]—that will be launched in 2021 to steer finance towards nature-positive outcomes. It also means reducing business-related risks from nature losses. As noted in chapter 5, nearly half of global GDP might already be at risk as a result of degrading nature.[115] But by prioritizing nature, businesses could unlock $10 trillion in financial opportunities and create 395 million jobs by 2030.[116] Placing nature at the heart implies phasing out governments' nature-harmful incentives, which present an enormous barrier to transformative change, such as the fossil fuel subsidies discussed in chapter 5 as well as many agricultural subsidies.

Embedding ecosystem integrity into
sustainable development policymaking

Rather than being treated as an isolated sector in national development priorities, nature-based solutions can be integrated into prioritization efforts, such as those related to national climate commitments, and policies related to water security, food security, disaster risk reduction, economic growth and jobs. Investing in nature- and climate-aligned Covid-19 stimulus packages can yield returns of $2–$10 per $1 invested.[117] To achieve this, multiple government sectors can align their policies and priorities around a coherent framework, as Costa Rica

and Uganda have done.[118] For instance, Costa Rica recently undertook an extensive mapping of essential life support areas, identifying opportunities for protecting, restoring and managing nature through nature-based solutions in both rural and urban areas (figure 6.6).

" Rather than being treated as an isolated sector in national development priorities, nature-based solutions can be integrated into prioritization efforts, such as those related to national climate commitments, and policies related to water security, food security, disaster risk reduction, economic growth and jobs.

There is no blueprint for nature-based solutions governance, and each country's economic, institutional, social and political context will present different opportunities and barriers. But high multisector participation and incentives for nature-based solutions implementation at scale are important everywhere.[119] The International Institute for Applied Systems Analysis has identified three governance enablers for implementing nature-based solutions: polycentric governance (echoing the discussion in chapter 4), participatory codesign (for example, at the municipal level in Costa Rica, constant stakeholder involvement and technical knowledge transfer have been vital)[120] and financial incentives (as noted above).[121]

Figure 6.6 Costa Rica's high-resolution mapping of national nature-based solutions priorities

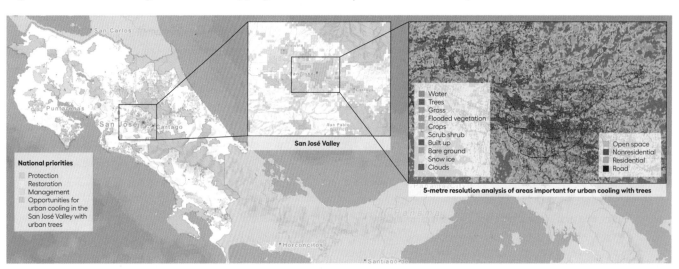

Source: Maps provided by the United Nations Biodiversity Lab.

People's values in relation to nature can shape the attitudes of stakeholders towards nature-based solutions. There is evidence that people who value stewardship or the conservation of nature have a higher preference for nature-based solutions than for conventional approaches.[122] Education also seems to have a positive association with perceptions of nature-based solutions[123]—stressing the importance of knowledge in the Anthropocene.[124] The mechanisms for changing social norms described in chapter 4 can be harnessed by increasing awareness and education of nature-based solutions to catalyse transformational change.

Elevating efforts to the regional and global levels

Internationally, actors ranging from UN agencies to multilateral development banks have developed collaboration tools and made financial resources available for interested countries. The International Union for Conservation of Nature has launched the first-ever global standard for nature-based solutions and has facilitated communication between governments and civil society organizations, providing key knowledge, research and tools, in addition to carrying out its own projects in more than 160 countries. The Intergovernmental Science-Policy Platform on Biodiversity and Ecosystem Services, established in 2012, works on assessments and identifies policy-relevant tools to build capacity and knowledge for its 94 member states.[125] Several UN agencies work on nature-based solutions. The United Nations Environment Programme works to implement nature-based solutions and coleads the United Nations Decade on Ecosystem Restoration 2021–2030, together with the Food and Agriculture Organization (which has produced substantive work on nature-based solutions focused on agricultural practices, water and food). The United Nations Development Programme's Equator Initiative highlights nature-based solutions among indigenous peoples and local communities and has produced toolkits and research to support the implementation of nature-based solutions.

International efforts have also aimed to protect agents of change that have been historically disempowered, specifically through international agreements to protect indigenous peoples. The Indigenous

" The Indigenous and Tribal Peoples Convention, adopted in 1989 by the International Labour Organization and ratified by most of Latin America and a few other countries worldwide, is an important international law on indigenous peoples' rights.

and Tribal Peoples Convention, adopted in 1989 by the International Labour Organization and ratified by most of Latin America and a few other countries worldwide, is an important international law on indigenous peoples' rights (chapter 3). Among multilateral development banks, the World Bank has had a nature-based solutions programme since 2017 to inform its operations, advice and investments.[126] Regional development banks have also become active promoters. In 2018 the Inter-American Development Bank launched the Natural Capital Lab, a platform to bring government and businesses together to create high-risk, high-reward approaches for preserving natural capital.[127] The African Development Bank has funded several initiatives prioritizing the restoration of damaged ecosystems, the conservation of biodiversity and integrated natural resources management.[128] The Asian Development Bank has partnered with the International Centre for Environmental Management and the Nordic Development Fund to build capacity for green infrastructure across Asian cities and to share knowledge for implementation from international good practices.

Closing gaps in empowerment: Indigenous peoples as shapers and defenders of nature

As part I of this Report argues, the Anthropocene compels a reimaging of the human development journey in which our embeddedness in nature is brought to the fore. Doing so by expanding human agency implies empowering people by enhancing equity, fostering innovation and instilling a sense of stewardship for nature. Complementing social norms and incentives, this chapter argues for a systemic approach to nurture and expand nature-based solutions to deliver transformational change. Over human history and in many places around the world today, those systemic approaches have emerged, providing social benefits while preserving ecosystems. One example is the contribution of many indigenous peoples and local communities to preserving nature

For example, biodiversity richness has a higher estimated value in indigenous lands than in protected areas, despite differences across indigenous peoples' contribution in the same country (figure 6.7).[129] This is the result of interactions between people and nature that have evolved over millennia and are tied to biocultural diversity (chapter 1).[130] Thus, supporting the practices of indigenous peoples that sustain biodiversity is key, especially since lands managed by indigenous peoples—around 25 percent of global land area—host an estimated 80 percent of global biodiversity.[131]

Consider Colombia, one of the world's most biodiverse countries. It is home to more than 50 million ethnically and linguistically diverse people, and it has a leading regional and global role in environmental stewardship and climate change leadership. Deforestation continues to be the largest source of greenhouse gas emissions in Colombia, accounting for 27 percent of annual emissions, equivalent to 69 megatonnes of carbon dioxide. Despite sustained efforts to set aside large portions of the country's lands for environmental protection, key carbon sinks are under severe stress. Colombia has drafted detailed plans to reduce carbon emissions 20 percent by 2030, primarily through reduced deforestation, which also protects biodiversity and natural watersheds and secures a future for communities that depend directly on the forest. Success will require the participation of a multitude of indigenous peoples across the country.[132]

" Supporting the practices of indigenous peoples that sustain biodiversity is key, especially since lands managed by indigenous peoples— around 25 percent of global land area—host an estimated 80 percent of global biodiversity.

Over the past few decades indigenous peoples have been on the front line of defending the Amazon rainforest. Territories across nine countries sharing the Amazon Basin and managed by indigenous peoples barely lost stored carbon between 2003 and 2016 (a fall of 0.1 percent), reflecting minor forest loss. Protected areas not managed by indigenous peoples experienced a loss of 0.6 percent.[133] The rest of the Amazon experienced a loss of 3.6 percent.[134] Translating indigenous peoples' contribution to forest preservation in terms of its impact on climate change mitigation—a rather narrow and limited

Figure 6.7 Biodiversity richness is greatest under indigenous peoples' management regimes

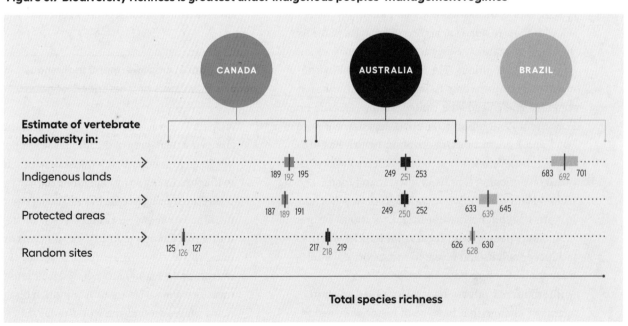

Note: Regression-based estimates. Boxes represent 95 percent confidence intervals.
Source: Schuster and others 2019.

exercise, in that it does not account for many other contributions, including avoiding biocultural diversity loss—suggests that indigenous peoples' per capita contribution as a carbon sink through forest preservation in the Amazon is roughly equal to the average per capita emissions by the top 1 percent of the income distribution (figure 6.8).

The large-scale indigenous peoples' contribution to carbon storage is an example of how local decisions and nature-based solutions can add up to substantial easing of planetary pressures. Where the role of indigenous peoples supports ecosystem preservation, it provides a useful template for how to think about systemic approaches for nature-based human development. In those instances, every single leverage point recently identified by the Intergovernmental Science-Policy Platform on Biodiversity and Ecosystem Services seems to be at play (figure 6.9).

The behaviour of indigenous peoples and local communities is not only about a single solution but also about wellbeing while preserving ecosystem integrity in coupled social and ecological systems. Understanding the drivers of behaviour—which work outside formal market-mediated incentives—has the potential to inform the system approach to nature-based solutions that can unleash transformational change (table 6.1 and box 6.5).

Despite numerous well documented instances of the multiple benefits of indigenous peoples' actions, their perseverance and contributions are hugely undervalued by most societies. As the United Nations Declaration on the Rights of Indigenous Peoples sets out, self-determination lies at the heart of

Figure 6.8 The per capita contribution by indigenous peoples preserving forest storage capacity in the Amazon is roughly equal to per capita greenhouse gas emissions by the top 1 percent of the income distribution

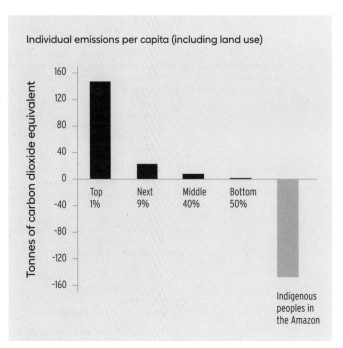

Individual emissions per capita (including land use)

Source: Human Development Report Office based on data in spotlight 7.2 with estimates for 2020 of individual distribution of carbon dioxide emissions. Estimates of contributions of indigenous peoples are based on data for 2003–2016 from Walker and others (2020).

Figure 6.9 Indigenous peoples and local communities move the leverage points to build global sustainability

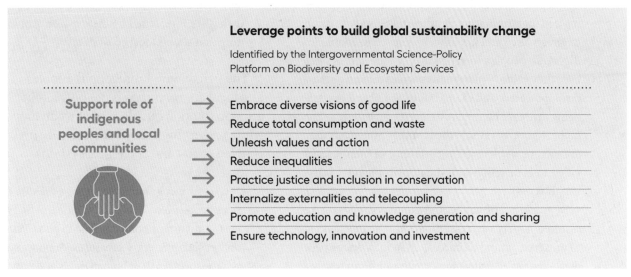

Source: Human Development Report Office based on Brondizio and others (2019).

Table 6.1 Examples of nature-based solutions by indigenous peoples and local communities

Solution	Contributions to human development	Preservation of ecosystem integrity	Examples in indigenous and local communities
Agroforestry	→ Food security → Sustainable livelihoods for small-scale farmers → Higher productivity of trees, crops and livestock → Greater product diversity for farmers	→ Preserving biodiversity and increasing diversity → Reducing soil erosion → Reducing loss of water, soil material, organic matter and nutrients → Reducing insect pests → Maintaining soil fertility → Increasing carbon sequestration	→ Bolivia, Consejo Indigena del Pueblo Tacana[a] → Cameroon, Riba[b] → Cameroon, Gender and Environment Watch[c] → Jamaica, Jeffrey Town Farmers Association[d] → Mexico, Koolel-Kab/Muuchkambal[e] → Nigeria, Environmental Management and Development Trust[f] → Phillipines, Camalandaan Agroforestry Farmers' Association[g]
Protection of coastal ecosystems for disaster risk reduction	→ Safeguarding lives, homes and livelihoods by mitigating the impacts of tsunamis, typhoons and other hydrometeorological disasters on human settlements → Supporting livelihoods through timber and nontimber product availability	→ Protecting and stabilizing coastal zones → Supporting unique and rich ecosystems and biodiversity → Storing carbon	→ Federated States of Micronesia, Tamil Resources Conservation Trust[h] → Indonesia, West Kalimantan[i] → Thailand, Community Mangrove Forest Conservation of Baan Bang La[j]
Sustainable land management	→ Optimizing social and economic benefits from nature's ecosystem services → Increasing community resilience and ensuring the continued availability of food, water and other natural products → Establishing practices and knowledge that can be replicated and inherited through changes in administration and across generations → Participatory management of natural assets	→ Protecting and conserving ecosystems → Safeguarding nature's ecosystem services and species' ability to regenerate	→ Bolivia, La Paz[k] → Ghana, Greater Accra Region[l] → Northwestern Nicaragua[m]

Notes
a. See UNDP (2015a). **b.** See UNDP (2010a). **c.** See UNDP (2019a). **d.** See UNDP (2014c). **e.** See UNDP (2014d). **f.** See UNDP (2019b). **g.** See UNDP (2008). **h.** See UNDP (2019d). **i.** See UNDP (2017b). **j.** See UNDP (2017a). **k.** See UNDP (2010b). **l.** See UNDP (2014b). **m.** See UNDP (2012).
Source: Human Development Report Office literature review.

development for and by indigenous peoples. Achieving self-determination requires the transformation of governance and law as well as space to enable indigenous peoples to articulate, pursue and realize lives they value.[135] Indigenous peoples remain notably disempowered, and the 1.3 billion indigenous people living in areas endowed with forests have some of the highest poverty rates in the world.[136] Moreover, they are victims of violence, with several of their leaders killed in connection with their environmental activism (box 6.6).

Degradation of nature and biodiversity loss have resulted largely from disempowering many seeking to preserve natural resources, often indigenous peoples (chapter 2). Indigenous communities managing their territories typically have limited power to face extractive industries, and their livelihoods and wellbeing are threatened by the expansion of infrastructure that strains local ecosystems.[137]

" The behaviour of indigenous peoples and local communities is not only about a single solution but also about wellbeing while preserving ecosystem integrity in coupled social and ecological systems.

Greater recognition and support are due to indigenous peoples and local communities, in line with their past and current contributions to conserving nature and easing planetary pressures. Support starts with basic respect for their human rights and ensuring their freedom from violence. Yet the opposite has been the

Box 6.5 Holistic approaches to nature can deliver multiple impacts

The Lashihai Watershed, in the southwestern province of Yunnan, China, is home to about 10,000 indigenous people, mostly Naxi and the Yi peoples. Lashihai Lake, also part of the watershed, plays a vital role in sustaining biodiversity in the area because it has the greatest bird diversity in the country and is an important migration passage, breeding ground and wintering habitat for many goose and duck species.

In 1998 a dam was built in the area, flooding farmland and displacing communities, who moved to hillsides to farm and began to overfish the lake using illegal nets. This, in turn, led to mudslides, soil erosion and the depletion of fish populations, increasing poverty and tensions between the communities and local governments.

In 2000 the Green Watershed organization began working with the local governments and established an indigenous peoples' watershed management model to include local indigenous communities in the management of resources while also considering economic development objectives. The initiative founded indigenous peoples' autonomous organizations, included participatory methods to promote self-management of resources and generated positive results.

Water security. The initiative ensured the irrigation of surrounding farmland during five consecutive years of drought. Agroforestry and ecological cultivation were promoted, curbing soil erosion and reducing wetland sediment deposition. The Fishermen's Association restored the ecological balance of the wetlands, which guaranteed food for 100,000 wintering birds of more than 76 species.

Food security. The Yi people could ensure only about four months of food into the future. High-quality potato seeds were introduced to Yi households, and production increased fivefold in the span of a year. Moreover, a ban on the use of illegal nets by the Fishermen's Association protected fish populations, resources and related livelihoods, restoring fish to numbers last seen 20 years before.

Sustainable livelihoods. The Naxi community built slit dams to control soil erosion, planted forests, implemented household methane biodigesters and developed agroforestry. The Yi villages developed animal husbandry, cultivated Chinese herbal medicines and opened an ecotourism enterprise to diversify their livelihoods in the face of natural and market risks. The average income per capita of both groups increased tenfold.

Disaster risk reduction. Water storage ponds mitigated the effects of droughts. Fortified houses were built to withstand earthquakes. Afforestation was encouraged to mitigate flooding and mudslide risks. And livelihood diversification was encouraged to help the communities face the potential losses of livelihood due to disaster.

Source: Human Development Report Office based on UNDP (2015c).

norm. Between 2002 and 2017, 1,558 people across 50 countries were killed for defending their environment and lands.[138] The loss is tragic for the community but no less so for all of us and our descendants. We miss taking full advantage of learning from their knowledge and principles, precisely when a sense of stewardship for nature is becoming paramount to ease planetary pressures. A greater space for indigenous peoples and local communities adds voices that have often been silenced or unheard in public deliberation and that tend to be marginalized by other ways of knowing based on technologies and the advancement of science.[139]

Recognizing and supporting the direct contributions of indigenous peoples and local communities in the preservation of biosphere integrity are key to easing planetary pressures.[140] Just as important is recognizing the ongoing injustices suffered by these communities and the ways these injustices shape their agency and ability to thrive in ways valuable to them.[141] Only then might we begin to learn with humility from what they and many others over our 300,000 year history have done. That is the aspiration—and promise—of nature-based human development.

Box 6.6 Environmental activists are being killed

In 2019 a record 212 people—more than four a week—were killed defending their land and environment.[1] Violence against environmental activists has increased, with the annual death toll more than tripling since the early 2000s (see figure).

Indigenous peoples have an important presence in environmental activism, and they are disproportionately at risk of violence, attacks and killings for their activism. In 2019, 40 percent of murdered defenders belonged to indigenous communities, and more than a third of fatal attacks between 2015 and 2019 targeted indigenous peoples.[2] In 2018 the United Nations Special Rapporteur on the rights of indigenous peoples expressed grave concern at the targeting of indigenous peoples through attacks and violence in the context of large-scale projects of extractive industries and mounting competition to exploit natural resources.[3]

The number of killings of environmental activists has more than tripled since the early 2000s

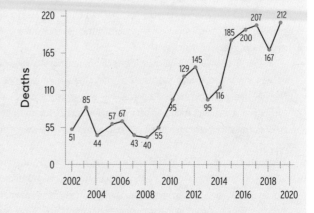

Source: Human Development Report Office based on data from Global Witness's annual land and environmental defenders reports 2002–2019, accessed on 23 November 2020.

Notes
1. Global Witness 2020. **2.** Global Witness 2019. **3.** UN Human Rights Council 2018.
Source: Human Development Report Office based on data from Global Witness. Data from Global Witness on environmental defenders' killing has been cited in studies by Butt and others (2019), Scheidel and others (2020) and the UN Special Rapporteur on the situation of human rights defenders (Forst and Tognoni 2016) and in media such as CNN (Guy 2020b), *The Guardian* (Watts 2019) and *Time* magazine (Godin 2020).

Implications of climate change for financial and monetary policy

Joaquín Bernal, Advisor to the Governor of Banco de la República (Central Bank of Colombia), and **José Antonio Ocampo,** Professor at the School of International and Public Affairs, Columbia University, and Chair of the United Nations Committee for Development Policy

Climate change generates widely known physical risks, particularly disasters associated with hydro-meteorological events such as hurricanes, tornadoes, cyclones, monsoons, floods and avalanches—and, conversely, desertification and increasing aridity. These impacts are wide ranging and affect all agents and sectors of the economies in all geographies of the planet—though in an uneven way. These major events, as well as more gradual but persistent changes in temperatures, have structural impacts on economic activity, labour productivity and people's wellbeing. In addition, the process of adjustment towards a lower carbon economy—prompted by climate-related policies, technological disruptions and shifts in consumer preferences—generates what in the literature are called transition risks.[1]

These risks have major macroeconomic and financial implications that have been recognized in the Paris Agreement (article 2, c), which states that, in order to strengthen the global response to the threat of climate change, it is essential to make "finance flows consistent with a pathway towards low greenhouse gas emissions and climate resilient development." Financial policies play a key role in mobilizing mainstream finance to move towards the needed large-scale transformation in the productive structure of the economy. It is also key to generate a concomitant change in the underlying financial asset structure by leveraging market mechanisms to increase efficiency in allocating resources for and costs of mitigating climate change.[2]

Financial policies encompass macroprudential, financial regulation and supervision, governance and financial market development policies. They include policies aimed at redressing possible underpricing and the lack of transparency of climate risks in financial markets and regulatory prudential frameworks. They are also intended to develop a taxonomy of economic activities to advance markets for green financial instruments. And they help reduce the short-term

bias and improve the governance frameworks of financial institutions. Monetary policy can also contribute to these goals. It may include instruments related to the central bank balance sheet—such as collateral policy, asset purchases and commercial bank access to the central bank balance sheet—and in some countries credit allocation.[3] These financial and monetary policies to promote green investments should complement—but not substitute for—tax and fiscal policies and government investment responsibilities.

Financial policies

A first group of financial policies standardizes climate-related risks disclosures and makes them mandatory. These policies can support and improve the pricing and transparency of these risks.[4] Gathering and disseminating relevant climate-related financial data could also enhance risk assessment in financial regulation and stress tests. In addition, laying solid foundations is instrumental in defining an adequate taxonomy of "green" and sustainable assets in relation to climate and other environmental considerations and for the development of green bonds and markets, as well as carbon pricing.

In this regard, the efforts of the Task Force on Climate-related Financial Disclosure should be particularly highlighted. Its recommendations, developed by the market for the market, aim to ensure that climate-related risks are understood and discussed at a broad level, considered in risk management and investment decisions and embedded into firms' strategies. The recommendations may allow investors and external stakeholders to better value assets and investment projects and to mobilize financial resources to facilitate the transition to more sustainable and resilient activities.

Supervisors should verify that individual institutions under their purview identify exposures to climate-related risks, assess the potential losses should those risks materialize, ensure adequate management of the risks and take mitigating action where appropriate. Authorities should set supervisory expectations based on a prudent approach to climate-related and environmental risks.[5]

In addition, central banks and supervisors should gradually develop tools to map the transmission channels of physical and transition risks within the financial system and conduct quantitative climate-related risk analysis to size the risks across the financial system and how the impact of climate change can be included in macroeconomic modelling, forecasting and financial stability monitoring.[6] Some leading central banks—those in Brazil, the United Kingdom (Bank of England), France and the Netherlands—are also preparing to apply these tools on stress test scenarios for the financial firms they supervise.

A second group of policies support the development of a taxonomy of economic activities and the advancement of markets for green financial instruments. Financial regulators and supervisors can take a leading role in bringing together relevant stakeholders and experts to develop a taxonomy that enhances the transparency around which economic activities contribute to the transition to a "green" (low-carbon and environmentally sustainable) economy and in which others are more exposed to climate-related risks ("brown"). Such a taxonomy[7] would facilitate financial institutions' identification, assessment and management of climate and environment-related risks and mobilize capital for green and low-carbon investments.[8]

For prudential regulation some analysts have proposed adapting micro- and macro-prudential policies to explicitly consider climate-related risks and internalize systemic climate risk. "Tools could include reserve, liquidity and capital adequacy requirements, loan-to-value ratios, and caps on credit growth, as well as sectoral capital buffers targeting credit to particularly climate-exposed sectors."[9] Similarly, green supporting and brown penalizing factors could be included in capital requirements, and regulation could determine that minimum amounts of green assets should be held on financial institutions' balance sheets.[10]

There is controversy, however, over the effectiveness of these climate-related prudential regulations, as they "may only very partially contribute to hedging financial institutions from 'green swan' events."[11]

Other analysts consider that "lowering capital requirements on bank loans to green sectors could undermine macroprudential policy goals and financial risk mitigation. The Basel Committee has consistently adopted an approach in which prudential rules are based only on risk considerations, to shield them from influences like industrial policy goals or political interference in banks' lending practices."[12]

In this respect, a recent survey by the Basel Committee on Banking Supervision found that "The majority of authorities considered it appropriate to address climate-related financial risks within their existing regulatory and supervisory framework.[...] However, it is important to note that the majority of members have not factored, or have not yet considered factoring, the mitigation of such risks into the prudential capital framework."[13]

The third group of financial policies can reduce financial institutions' short-term bias and improve their governance. This can be done through prudential and corporate governance reforms and by adopting environmental, social and governance standards in the financial sector, especially among pension funds and other asset managers. Depending on a country's institutional framework, some central banks and regulators can also be catalysts for sound scaling up of green finance.[14]

Private sector moves towards long termism and supporting the values of sustainable finance are also under way. Some of the largest wealth managers have publicly announced a series of initiatives to place sustainability at the centre of their investment approach, liquidate investments that present a high risk to sustainability and commit to disclosure guidelines in accordance with the Task Force on Climate-related Financial Disclosure, among others.[15]

According to the Institute of International Finance, "with the Covid-19 pandemic serving as a real-life "stress test" for ESG [environmental, social and governance] investing strategies, the relative performance of sustainable assets has been remarkable" during the atypical first half of 2020."[16]

Monetary policy

Climate-related physical and transition risks will most likely progressively have an impact on prices, actual and potential economic growth, and financial stability, all of which are core objectives of most central banks. Increasingly, therefore, central banks have to analyse and discuss whether and what they can and should do to confront climate change in order to efficiently and successfully safeguard price and financial stability.[17]

As mentioned above, central banks can use the valuable arsenal of policy tools at their disposal to respond to the challenges arising from climate-related shocks, even within a restricted interpretation of their mandates. These tools include adjusting interest rates, expanding balance sheets through bond purchases and extending loans to companies via banks. They also include providing funding schemes for banks that invest in low-carbon projects and even allowing credit allocation policies to favour low-carbon investments (either directly or indirectly through guarantees).

Other more specific aspects of the discussion on ways central banks could proactively support the transition to a low-carbon economy relate to how they can reflect climate risks in monetary policy frameworks. They can integrate climate risk analytics into collateral frameworks—for instance, by adjusting haircuts and valuations on brown assets and even excluding them from the pool of eligible collateral. They can use sustainability criteria in their large-scale asset purchases and refinancing operations to exclude carbon-intensive assets and favour green assets (also referred to as green quantitative easing).

And they can implement parallel asset purchase programmes focused on low-carbon assets.[18]

However, the mainstream literature does not consider monetary policy best suited for long-term climate change mitigation efforts and believes it should remain focused on short-term stabilization. And the use of central bank balance sheets to tackle "green swan" events or to further green investments and markets is highly controversial. It may imply stretching central banks' mandates, raising questions of governance, and may risk distorting markets.[19]

Other actions that central banks can consider are coordinating macroeconomic policies and prudential regulations to support an environmental transition.[20] To do so, central banks need to coordinate their own actions with a broad set of fiscal, prudential and carbon regulations to be implemented by other players (governments, private sector, academia, civil society and the international community), keeping in mind that this is a collective action problem.

Finally, central banks and supervisors have a role in leading by example by incorporating sustainability and environmental, social and governance criteria into their own investment portfolios and operational activities. Examples are managing corporate portfolios and pension funds, integrating green requirements into their management framework, targeting green financing, reducing their carbon footprint as companies and publicly disclosing their engagement regarding the previous items.[21]

NOTES

1 Batten and others 2016; NGFS 2019a, 2019b.

2 Krogstrup and Oman 2019.

3 Krogstrup and Oman 2019.

4 Krogstrup and Oman 2019.

5 NGFS 2020a.

6 NGFS 2019a, 2020a.

7 China and the European Union have outlined green taxonomies. There are also some market-driven taxonomies, such as the Climate Bonds Standards (released by the Climate Bonds Initiative) and the International Capital Market Association's Green Bond Principles.

8 NGFS 2019a.

9 Krogstrup and Oman 2019, p. 26.

10 Dikau and Volz 2019.

11 Bolton and others 2020, p. 53.

12 Krogstrup and Oman 2019, p. 29.

13 BCBS 2020, p. 1.

14 Krogstrup and Oman 2019.

15 Fink 2020; *The Economist* 2020a.

16 IIF 2020, p. 1.

17 Bolton and others 2020; Dikau, Robins and Volz 2020; Dikau and Volz 2019; NGFS 2019b, 2020b.

18 Dikau, Robins and Volz 2020; Krogstrup and Oman 2019.

19 Bolton and others 2020; Krogstrup and Oman 2019; Pereira da Silva 2020.

20 Bolton and others 2020.

21 These are considered under workstream 3 (mainstreaming green finance) of the Network for Greening the Financial System (NGFS 2019c).

The role of carbon pricing in climate change mitigation

Ian Parry, Fiscal Affairs Department, International Monetary Fund

The public health and economic crisis precipitated by the Covid-19 pandemic has not altered the basic need for transitioning to clean energy systems by mid-century to contain the risk of dangerous and irreversible instability in the global climate system. Indeed, with governments likely to bring forward investment plans to help boost their economies, the pandemic has added to the urgency of ensuring that this new investment is appropriately allocated to low-carbon technologies rather than locking in emissions-intensive capital. Carbon pricing provides a critical incentive in this regard, and the revenue it yields can also help meet fiscal needs—needs that are especially pressing because of the crisis and in the wider context of meeting the Sustainable Development Goals. But to maximize effectiveness, pricing needs to be part of a comprehensive policy package and coordinated across large emitters.

Emissions trends and the Paris Agreement

An emissions pathway consistent with limiting future global warming to 1.5–2 degrees Celsius would require cutting fossil fuel–based carbon dioxide and other greenhouse gas emissions to 25–50 percent of their 2018 levels by 2030,[1] with continued rapid reductions thereafter. Emissions are projected to be about 8 percent lower in 2020 than in 2019,[2] due to both lower GDP and structural shifts in the economy, such as increased remote working. However, this dent in the flow hardly affects the stock of carbon dioxide in the atmosphere, which continues to rise precipitously. And emissions are likely to start rising again in 2021 as economies recover and some of the structural shifts are partially reversed (figure S5.2.1).

Figure S5.2.1 Emissions are likely to start rising again in 2021 as economies recover and some structural shifts are partially reversed

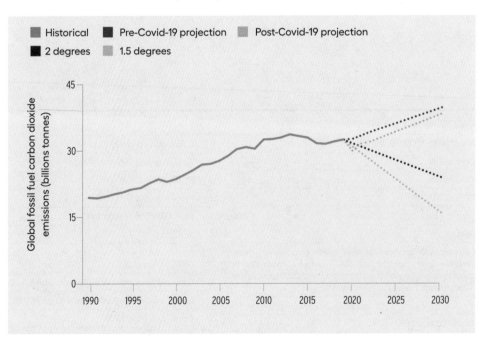

Source: International Monetary Fund staff calculations and IEA (2020b) and IPCC (2018).

The 2015 Paris Agreement provides the international framework for meaningful action on climate mitigation. The heart of the agreement is commitments by 188 parties to reduce their emissions. These pledges are due to be revised ahead of the 26th UN Climate Change Conference of the Parties (COP26), in November 2021. Although the immediate challenge is for countries to implement current pledges, ambition at the global level needs to be scaled up considerably. Even if current pledges are fully achieved, the emissions gap in 2030 to the 2 degrees Celsius target would be cut by only a third.[3]

The case for carbon pricing

As argued in the chapter, carbon pricing can play a pivotal role in mitigation strategies by providing a critical price signal for redirecting investment and consumption towards low-carbon technologies. A carbon price of, say, $50 per tonne of carbon dioxide emissions in 2030 could increase projected prices in Group of 20 (G20) countries by about 140 percent for coal, 45 percent for natural gas, 30 percent for electricity and 10 percent for gasoline.[4]

The carbon prices consistent with countries' mitigation pledges vary widely due to both differences in the stringency of commitments and the responsiveness of emissions to pricing (for example, emissions are more price responsive in countries using a lot of coal, such as China, India and South Africa). For example, a $25 carbon price would exceed the level needed to meet mitigation commitments in China, India, South Africa and the United States, but $75 per tonne would fall short of what is needed in Canada, France, Italy and the Republic of Korea (figure S5.2.2).

Carbon pricing could also raise significant revenue, typically 0.5–2 percent of GDP in G20 countries for a $50 tax in 2030. That revenue can be used productively to offset the harmful macroeconomic effects of higher energy prices—for example, by funding general or green public investments or lowering taxes on work effort and investment.

Many studies suggest that carbon pricing has a small overall impact, or perhaps even a positive impact, on GDP.[5] The economic efficiency costs of carbon pricing—the value of foregone benefits to fuel users minus savings in supply costs—are also not that large, typically around 0.5 percent of GDP or less for

a $50 carbon price in 2030 (figure S5.2.3). Moreover, for many countries these efficiency costs are more than offset by the domestic environmental benefits, such as reduced mortality due to local air pollution. In short, many countries can move ahead unilaterally with some level of carbon pricing that makes them better off, before even counting the global warming benefits.

Although more than 60 carbon tax and trading systems are in operation at the national, subnational and regional levels in various countries, the average price on emissions worldwide is only $2 per tonne.[6] The International Monetary Fund has called for measures equivalent to a global carbon price of at least $75 per tonne by 2030 to keep global warming below 2 degrees Celsius.[7] The difference between current and needed prices underscores the political difficulty of ambitious pricing, as elaborated in the chapter. Where carbon pricing is politically constrained, policymakers could reinforce it with other approaches that do not impose a new tax burden on energy and therefore avoid large increases in energy prices.

One flexible and cost-effective approach of this kind is (revenue-neutral) "feebates," which provide a sliding scale of fees on products or activities with above-average emissions intensity and a sliding scale of rebates for products or activities with below-average emissions intensity. Feebates are especially valuable for sectors that are difficult to decarbonize through carbon pricing alone, such as the transport sector. By altering the relative price of vehicles with high- and low-emissions rates, feebates could provide powerful incentives for consumers to buy electric or other zero-emissions vehicles without a new tax burden on the average motorist or the fiscal costs associated with tax rebate or subsidy programmes for zero- or low-emissions vehicles. Several countries, including France, the Netherlands and Norway, have introduced elements of feebates for the vehicle sector.

Broader components of green recovery programmes

In addition to carbon pricing and reinforcing mitigation instruments, as well as developing a new and ambitious climate plan for COP26, there are several other potential ingredients to a green recovery programme.

Figure S5.2.2 The carbon prices consistent with countries' mitigation pledges vary widely

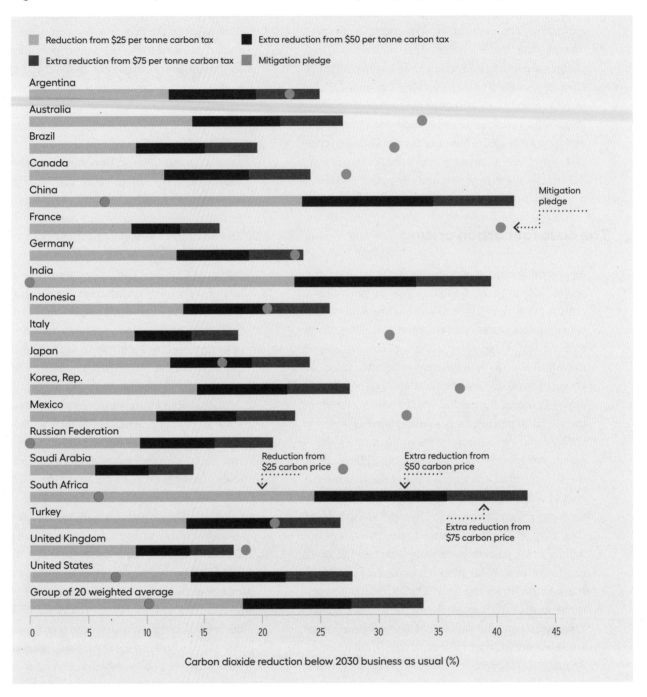

Note: Mitigation pledges are from the Paris Agreement or subsequent national pledges.
Source: Updated from IMF (2019b).

One is measures to enhance the effectiveness and credibility of carbon pricing. These include public investment in clean energy infrastructure (grid extensions to link renewable generation sites, pipelines for carbon capture and storage, charging stations for electric vehicles), instruments to promote the development and deployment of clean energy technologies (prizes for energy storage technologies, fiscal incentives to encourage deployment of immature technologies) and instruments to lubricate climate finance from financial markets (carbon disclosures, futures markets for carbon pricing, loans for residential retrofitting). Carbon pricing or feebates can also be extended to other emissions sources as monitoring

Figure S5.2.3 The economic efficiency costs of carbon pricing are more than offset by domestic environmental benefits

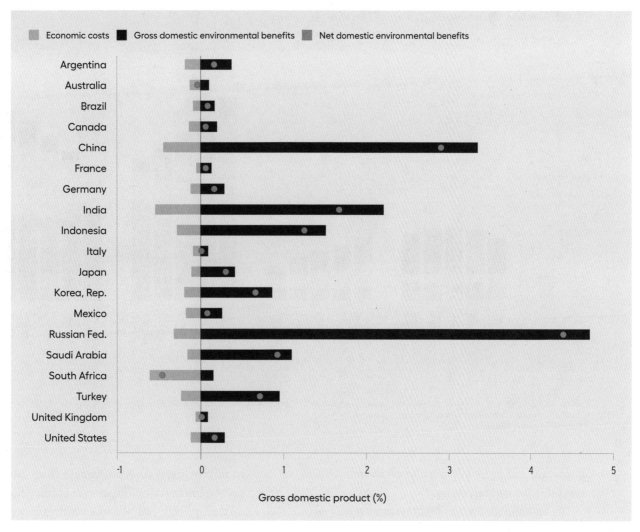

Source: Updated from IMF (2019b).

capacity is developed (for forestry, industrial process emissions, fugitive emissions from extractive industries). Where monitoring is inherently difficult, as in agriculture, proxy emissions fees or feebates might be based on farm-level inputs to promote less emissions-intensive methods (poultry or crop farming instead of cattle and pig farming) and "sin taxes" at the consumer level might discourage meat consumption.

Besides prioritizing climate investments in national budgeting procedures, government support might also be greened, where appropriate, by making business loans conditional on environmental improvement (for example, emissions reductions for airline companies).

The overall carbon mitigation package needs to be equitable within countries—both for its own sake

and to enhance the acceptability of reform. Incidence analyses suggest that carbon pricing can be anything from moderately regressive (China, the United States), to distribution-neutral (Canada) to moderately progressive (India, where wealthier households have greater access to electricity; figure S5.2.4). The recycling of carbon pricing revenues should be tilted towards lower income households in the former cases to keep the overall policy reform fair from a distributional perspective. Adverse impacts on displaced workers (from coal mining) and regions (rural areas lacking access to public transport) are also a major concern. An upfront package of targeted assistance measures (stronger social safety nets, worker retraining programmes, tax relief for commuters) is

Figure S5.2.4 Carbon pricing can be moderately regressive, distribution-neutral or moderately progressive

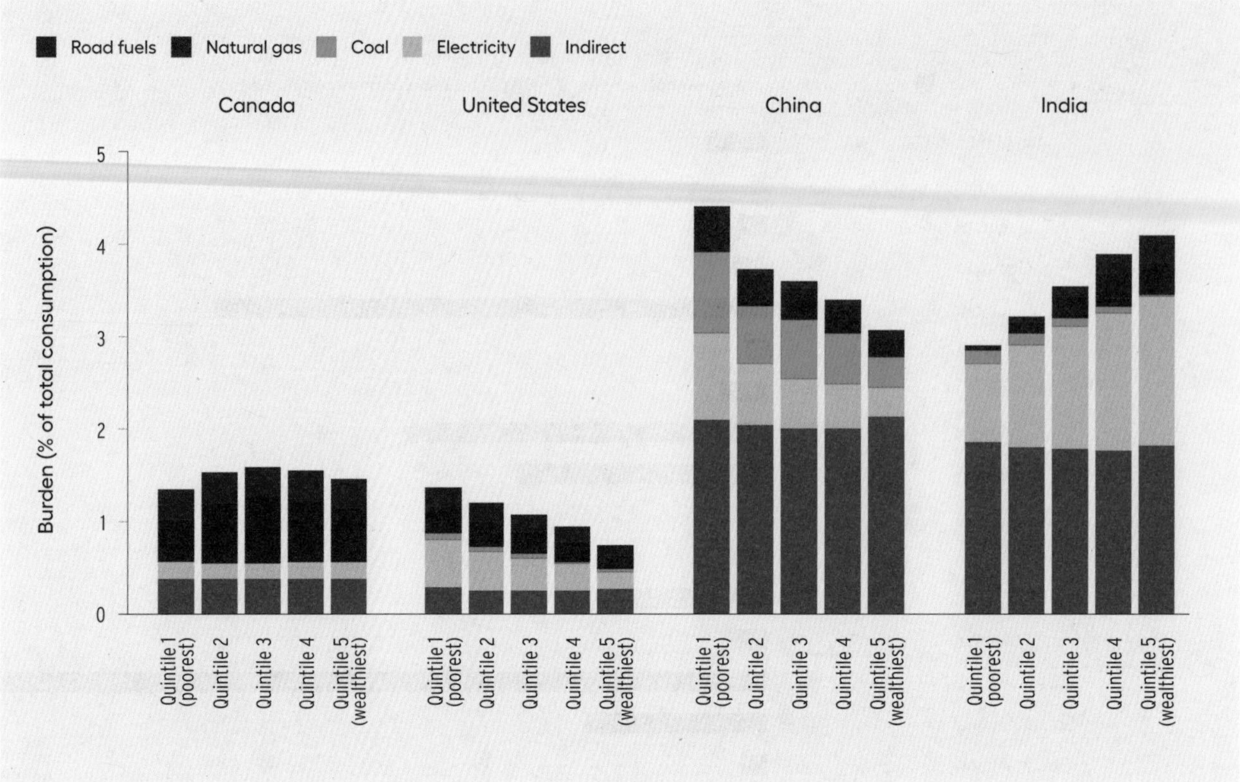

Note: "Indirect" refers to the increased price of consumer goods from higher energy costs. Burdens are estimated prior to the use of carbon tax revenue; a full passthrough of taxes to consumer prices is assumed.
Source: Updated from IMF (2019b).

important and need only use a small fraction of the revenue from carbon pricing.

The appropriate timing of carbon pricing will vary with international conditions (reform may be easier when oil prices are low) and national circumstances (reform may be delayed until recovery is well under way for countries able to finance stimulus packages through debt). And consultations with business interests and labour organizations, as well as an extensive public communications programme, may help to overcome opposition to the reform.

Advancing policy internationally —a carbon price floor

At the international level the Paris Agreement mitigation process could be strengthened and reinforced with a carbon price floor arrangement among large-emitting countries. This arrangement would guarantee a minimum level of effort among participants and provide some reassurance against losses

in international competitiveness from introducing carbon pricing. Coordination over price floors rather than price levels allows countries to exceed the floor if this is needed to meet their Paris Agreement mitigation pledges. And the floor could be designed equitably, with stricter requirements for advanced countries, and flexibly, to accommodate different approaches at the national level if they achieve the same emissions outcome as would have occurred under the floor price. There are some monitoring challenges—for example, countries would need to agree on procedures to account for possible exemptions in carbon pricing schemes and changes in pre-existing energy taxes that might offset, or enhance, the effectiveness of carbon pricing. But these analytical challenges should be manageable.

The price floor could be strikingly effective. For example, if advanced and developing G20 countries were subject to (relatively modest) carbon floor prices of $50 and $25 per tonne of carbon dioxide respectively, mitigation effort by 2030 would still be twice as much as reductions implied by meeting current mitigation pledges.[8] The prospective border carbon adjustment in the European Union could be a potential mechanism for promoting participation in such an arrangement, through exemptions for those with adequate carbon pricing.

NOTES

1	IPCC 2018.		5	For example, Metcalf and Stock (2020).
2	IEA 2020b.		6	World Bank 2020d.
3	UNEP 2019a.		7	Georgieva 2020.
4	IMF 2019b.		8	IMF 2019b.

How do governments' responses to the Covid-19 pandemic address inequality and the environment?

Tancrède Voituriez, International Research Center for Agriculture and Development, Institute for Sustainable Development and International Relations, World Inequality Lab, Paris School of Economics, and **Lucas Chancel,** World Inequality Lab, Paris School of Economics

Around the globe the Covid-19 pandemic has exacerbated several forms of health, social, gender and racial inequality. The worse-off, with less access to health care, have been hit particularly hard.[1] The consequences of the pandemic for the environment are more ambiguous. The Great Lockdown led to a temporary drop in global greenhouse gas emissions, but it is still unclear whether environmental protection will increase thanks to the pandemic. So to what extent do Covid-19 economic policy responses integrate inequality reduction and environmental protection, two central dimensions of the Sustainable Development Goals?

Colourless stimulus packages hide polarized endeavours for green transition

The global Covid-19 pandemic has imposed unprecedented constraints on social and economic activity—particularly mobility—with severe impacts on energy use. Global energy demand is expected to contract by 6 percent in 2020, the largest drop in more than 70 years. The decline in greenhouse gas emissions in the short term is a mechanical scale effect of the economic contraction and physical lockdown—particularly limited surface transport. Globally, greenhouse gas emissions are expected to fall by 8 percent in 2020,[2] roughly the cut needed every year from 2020 to 2030 to be on track for the Paris Agreement on climate change objective to keep global warming below 1.5 degree Celsius.[3]

This expected reduction in greenhouse gas emissions is the highest relative to major historical wars and epidemics.[4] Annual carbon dioxide emissions dropped by 3 percent during World War II (1939–1945) and by 4 percent during the 1980–1982 recession.[5] They fell by only 1 percent during the 1991–1992

recession and the 2009 global financial crisis. Despite the dip in emissions seen in 2020, the sector with the highest emissions—electricity—had one of the smallest changes in activity,[6] making decarbonizing the power sector a burning emergency. In addition, there was a postlockdown rebound in countries such as China, where fossil and cement emissions were higher in May 2020 than a year before.[7]

In one study of more than 300 policies in Group of 20 countries, only 8 percent were deemed green or brown (4 percent green and 4 percent brown), while 92 percent were deemed colourless.[8] Although lockdown measures and particularly restrictions on mobility have reduced greenhouse gas emissions in 2020, the overall climate impact will be driven by investment choices and the greenness of recovery packages, when existing. Climate experts warn that pollution and emissions could bounce back after the Covid-19 pandemic due to a carbon-driven recovery[9] and the relaxation of environmental regulation.[10]

A limited number of policy responses targeted the environment. Take Kenya, where $8 million was spent to enhance the provision of water facilities, $9 million for flood control measures and $5 million for a Greening Kenya Campaign.[11] Barbados announced a massive environmental cleanup program.[12] Some measures actually harmed the environment in the short term. In Viet Nam a deduction of 30 percent of the current environmental protection tax was allowed for jet fuel between August and December 2020.[13] In Fiji the government cut the environmental tax but at the same time eased credit for renewable energy businesses.[14]

The greenness of emergency rescue packages should be much higher than the documented 4 percent share. Clean physical renovations and retrofits, education and training, natural capital and ecosystem resilience, and clean research and development are pinpointed as key investment priorities.[15]

Screening the policy responses collated by the International Monetary Fund Policy Tracker,[16] a few of these normative policy types turn up in actual recovery packages. Limited in number, the green recovery packages and financial measures encompass investment in green infrastructure, incentives for consumer purchases, support to green jobs and credit facilities for green sectors or activities, including research and development. Strikingly, they are found almost exclusively in a few high-income countries; Fiji, Kenya and Uganda are exceptions (table S5.3.1).

There is a marked difference between the haves and the have nots—governments having the financial and institutional capacity to plan and green their long-term economic pathway in the follow-up to the Covid-19 pandemic, and the others.

How social can green recovery policies be?

It is unclear whether green policies will affect socioeconomic inequalities—and in which direction.

Infrastructure investment can turn out to be pro-poor environmental policies. In Sweden investments in urban renewable heating networks in the 1970s and 1980s made it possible for households to reduce their energy bill and shift to low-carbon energy technologies.[17] A carbon tax in the 1990s with support schemes for households (followed by a tax reduction for low-income households in 2004) made Sweden one of the rare industrialized countries to have reduced its carbon dioxide emissions between 1990 and the early 2010s, while sustaining growth and keeping inequalities under control. However, other forms of low-carbon investments may favour the better-off: high-speed trains connecting large urban centres may benefit urban elites more than rural communities. On a similar reasoning, credit facilities for green sectors or research and development subsidies can be critical to develop green innovation and jobs. And yet, in dual economies with formal and informal sectors, such policies may deepen the gap.

The economic transformation sparked by the Covid-19 pandemic and its diverse responses will

Table S5.3.1 A breakdown of green recovery measures

Country or economy	Investment in green infrastructure	Incentives for consumer purchases	Support to green jobs	Credit facilities for green sectors or activities, including research and development
Australia	✔			
Barbados	✔			
Canada (British Columbia)				✔
France	✔	✔		
Germany	✔	✔		
Kuwait				✔
Ireland				✔
Italy				✔
Korea, Rep.	✔			
Luxemburg	✔	✔		
Norway	✔	✔		
Spain				✔
Sweden			✔	
United Kingdom	✔		✔	
Euro Area	✔	✔		
Fiji				✔
Kenya				✔
Uganda				✔

Source: Authors' creation based on the International Monetary Fund Policy Tracker.

move some countries closer to the Sustainable Development Goals pathway, while pushing others farther away from it. As in any crisis, the drivers of positive societal change are playing out. The expansion of social registers is part of it, as in Angola and Nigeria, and the same holds for higher public health spending, including capital spending, partly because of long-lasting scrutiny of Covid-19's resurgence, as in Senegal and Tunisia. A structural transformation is under way in Uganda, where the government provided additional funding to the Uganda Development Bank, recapitalized the Uganda Development Cooperation and accelerated the development of industrial parks while boosting funding for agriculture.[18] Fiji raised its Import Substitution and Export Finance Facility by FJ$100 million to provide credit to exporters, large-scale commercial agricultural farmers, public transportation and renewable energy businesses at concessional rates.[19]

Making the Covid-19 recovery an opportunity for countries to harness the transformation called for by the 2030 Agenda for Sustainable Development and the Sustainable Development Goals is a crying emergency. Lack of financial resources, policy coordination and knowledge put the fragile momentum for building back better at risk. In order to maximize policies' effectiveness at reaching interdependent sustainable development goals, we must increase understanding of how social and environmental impacts of stimulus and recovery packages are playing out and could be magnified.

To this aim, we propose a socioenvironmental policy assessment matrix, narrowing environmental policy to sustainable energy for all, and identify from the deep decarbonization literature three broad pathways to achieving sustainable energy for all: increasing energy access and efficiency, decarbonizing existing energy carriers and switching to low-carbon energy carriers (table S5.3.2).[20] To design the matrix, each pathway considers whether specific environmental policies might affect inequality by looking at the incidence of impacts at the bottom, middle and top of the income distribution, following the economic inequality literature.[21]

The matrix enables mapping of what transformative decarbonization measures were taken or planned in Covid-19 responses, what kind of inequality is affected and, as important, what complementary measures could be envisaged to ensure that the recovery phase genuinely supports the Sustainable Development Goals. Our takeaway from the Covid-19 response trackers is that, the Euro Area/European Union aside, most green measures fall in the energy access and efficiency pathway (in bold). Progressive funding measures are still not considered at this stage. This leaves ample room to innovate and experiment with recovery packages in meeting the sustainable development challenges of our times.

Table S5.3.2 A matrix of environmental and inequality reduction policies, with a focus on energy transition in developing countries

		Pathway to low-carbon and inclusive energy systems		
		Increase energy efficiency and access	Decarbonize energy supply	Large-scale switch in end uses (building, transport, industry)
What kind of inequality is impacted?	Bottom	→ **Cash transfers** → Clean cooking solutions → Rural electrification (solar)	→ Decentralized off-grid/mini-grid	→ Green bus rapid transit
	Middle	→ Overhaul of power distribution → Energy-efficient buildings → **Electricity bill relief**	→ On-grid renewable energy deployment	→ Railway development → Circular economy
	Top	→ Wealth taxes (to finance the above) → **Removal of fossil fuel subsidies**	→ Carbon-based corporate taxes → Wealth taxes (to finance the above)	→ Energy-positive buildings → Electric vehicles subsidies → Carbon-based flight (business) ticket taxes → Wealth taxes (to finance the above)

Source: Authors' creation.

NOTES

1. See, for instance, evidence from Opportunity Insights data (at https://tracker.opportunityinsights.org). In the United States low-wage employment (below $27,000 a year) dropped by 35 percent in April, while high-wage employment (above $60,000 a year) fell by close to 13 percent in the same month. Employment rebounded by the end of August to pre-Covid levels for high-wage earners, while they remained significantly lower for low-wage earners.

2. IEA 2020b.

3. UNEP 2019a.

4. Boden and other 2017; Liu and others 2020; Pongratz and others 2011.

5. Boden and others 2017.

6. Le Quéré and others 2020.

7. Myllyvirta 2020.

8. Hepburn and others 2020.

9. Liu and others 2020.

10. Le Quéré and others 2020.

11. SET 2020

12. KPMG 2020.

13. IMF 2020b.

14. IMF 2020b.

15. Hepburn and others 2020.

16. IMF 2020b.

17. Chancel 2020.

18. Cases of Angola, Nigeria, Senegal, Tunisia and Uganda are based on SET (2020).

19. IMF 2020b.

20. Energy Transitions Commission 2018; Waisman and others 2019.

21. Particularly Blanchard and Rodrik (forthcoming) and World Inequality Lab and World Inequality Database (2018).

Policymaking for sustainable development 2.0

Kendon Bell, Global Policy Laboratory, Goldman School of Public Policy, University of California, Berkeley; Manaaki Whenua, Landcare Research; **Jeanette Tseng,** Global Policy Laboratory, Goldman School of Public Policy, University of California, Berkeley; and **Solomon Hsiang,** Global Policy Laboratory, Goldman School of Public Policy, University of California, Berkeley, and National Bureau of Economic Research

As policymakers around the world strive for global sustainability, research in support of this goal is racing ahead, driven by new and exciting innovations. Advances in data collection and computing capabilities and the integration of science with economics are transforming how we think about managing the planet.

A key step is to focus our attention on critical sustainability issues rather than trying to answer interesting but impractical questions. A large body of research has focused on pricing the total annual value produced by the world's natural systems—for example, how much the world values the totality of global rainforests or all biodiversity on the planet (see also chapter 7 and spotlight 7.3).[1] These tasks are both ambitious and inspiring, but they are almost impossible, from both a practical and a theoretical standpoint— and more important, they are unnecessary for guiding the world towards achieving sustainability.

What is essential for achieving sustainability is properly valuing natural resource assets that might be affected by decisions today. In the language of economics, we need to think about planetary resource management "on the margin." If a resource might be used or polluted by humans, we need to ask whether the benefits of that decision outweigh the costs, both direct and indirect. If we can ensure that we satisfy this sustainability criterion at every decision point, we are guaranteed to achieve long-term sustainability as a global society.[2] In this way achieving sustainability is like following a compass on a journey: Each time you choose a path, if you check that you are traveling north, you are guaranteed to keep moving northward. Similarly, if we ensure that each economic project is increasing the wellbeing of future generations, we will achieve sustainability.

New empirical research is illuminating how environmental conditions affect economic outcomes. If human activities alter the environment, the environment may in turn alter the economy. For example, recent findings illustrate how industrial pollution lowers the productivity of workers,[3] how changes in sunlight—either by pollution or intentional geoengineering—affect crop yields,[4] how living forests increase the value of real estate,[5] how fisheries provide labour opportunities for would-be pirates,[6] how groundwater depletion drives poverty,[7] how windblown dust increases child mortality,[8] how El Niño droughts increase the risk of civil conflict,[9] how rainfall during early life improves women's long-term health outcomes[10] and how hurricanes slow GDP growth.[11] All these data-driven insights result from innovations in how environmental science is integrated with more traditional economic analyses.

Among these findings the role of temperature has stood out as a major environmental factor influencing human development around the world.[12] High temperatures have been found to cause crop failures;[13] increase violence,[14] suicide,[15] all-cause mortality[16] and asylum applications;[17] reduce cognitive performance,[18] learning,[19] industrial productivity[20] and economic growth;[21] and strain the basic functioning of governance systems[22] and infrastructure.[23] Taken together, this collection of findings suggests that climate change, through its direct effect on increasing temperature alone, may be a major obstacle to future development. For context, in a high greenhouse gas emissions scenario, temperatures are projected to climb to unprecedented levels throughout the developing world by the end of the century, with future Mexico hotter than historical Iraq and future Bangladesh hotter than historical Mali (figure S5.4.1). Future Sudan will be so hot that there is no historical country it can be compared to. Figure S5.4.2 depicts the projected global mortality consequences of this warming.

The explosion of empirical findings have raced ahead of our theoretical understanding of how

Figure S5.4.1 In a high greenhouse gas emissions scenario, temperatures are projected to climb to unprecedented levels throughout the developing world by the end of the century

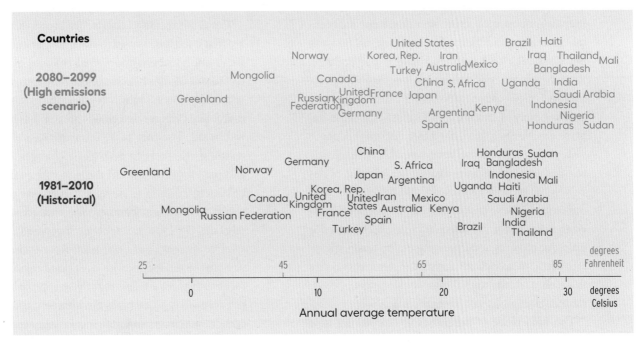

Source: Reproduced from Hsiang and Kopp (2018).

Figure S5.4.2 Average mortality risk due to climate change in 2100, accounting for both the costs and the benefits of adaptation

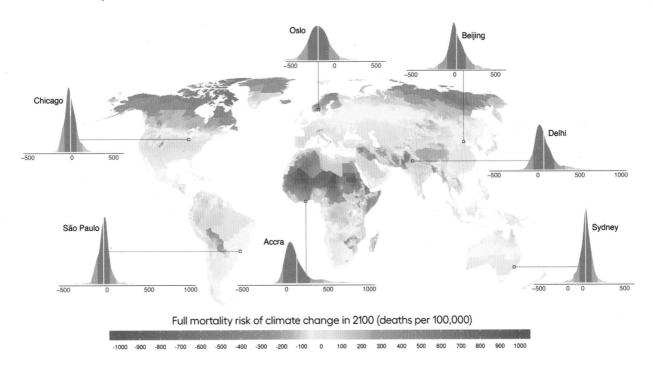

Full mortality risk of climate change in 2100 (deaths per 100,000)

Note: Density plots for select regions indicate the full probabilistic distribution of estimated impacts across simulations.
Source: Reproduced from Carleton and others (2020).

environmental changes should be integrated into development planning and economic decisionmaking. Achieving the sustainability criterion means that the human influence on these numerous environmental conditions, and their subsequent impact on wellbeing, should be accounted for in major projects. Researchers are now developing the methods necessary to "price" these externalities using the rapidly growing body of empirical findings, so that these impacts can be easily integrated into decisionmaking.[24] This pricing effort allows decisionmakers to explicitly weigh these externalities against the benefits of development projects, provided those benefits are also monetized. These approaches can be further adjusted to account for the unequal costs and benefits of different projects, incorporating equity and justice.[25] Furthermore, as new links are uncovered, our ability to account for the multidimensional impact of environmental changes will strengthen.

The final piece of the puzzle is monitoring how human actions are altering the environment around the world in real time, so that the impacts can be fully accounted for. At present the global community has no system for measuring the comprehensive wealth of countries—that is, tracking changes to environmental assets alongside humanmade assets—so even if we were achieving the sustainability criterion, we would not know. Developing such a system is a major challenge, but it is an essential step towards building global institutions that can account for global environmental changes while balancing the economic interests of current and future generations.

The dual obstacles to assembling such a system are that it must be sensitive and granular enough that small and local environmental changes can be detected but comprehensive enough in both scale and scope that it meaningfully captures the extent of environmental changes that could threaten future human wellbeing. For this task, innovations in machine learning are likely to be a game changer, enabling automated systems to sift through vast quantities of unstructured data to develop structured measurements that are environmentally and economically relevant. For example, applying machine learning to satellite imagery has been fruitful for gathering development-related metrics over large regions,[26] and recent advances suggest that these approaches could be extended to study many environmental and development outcomes simultaneously using current satellite systems.[27]

Just as integrating environmental science with economics revolutionized our understanding of environmental impacts, integrating machine learning will likely revolutionize real-time monitoring of global environmental systems. Together, these elements will empower decisionmakers to integrate the sustainability criterion into their everyday decisionmaking, guiding us towards true sustainable development.

NOTES

1 For example, Costanza and others (1997).

2 Dasgupta 2009; Hartwick 1977; Solow 1986.

3 Graff Zivin and Neidell 2012.

4 Burney and Ramanathan, 2014; Proctor and others 2018.

5 Druckenmiller 2020.

6 Axbard 2016.

7 Blakeslee and others 2020.

8 Heft-Neal and others 2020.

9 Hsiang and others 2011.

10 Maccini and Yang 2009.

11 Hsiang and Jina 2014.

12 Carleton and Hsiang 2016.

13 Schlenker and Lobell 2010.

14 Hsiang and others 2013.

15 Burke and others 2018; Carleton 2017.

16 Carleton and others 2020.,

17 Missirian and Schlenker 2017.

18 Graff Zivin and others 2018.

19 Fishman and others 2019; Park and others 2020.

20 Zhang and others 2018.

21 Burke and others 2015; Hsiang 2010.

22 See Obradovich and others (2018) for an analysis of both extremely hot and cold temperatures

23 See Aufhammer and others (2017) for the case of electricity infrastructure.

24 Bell and others 2020; Carleton and others 2020; Deryugina and Hsiang 2017; Fenichel and Abbott 2014; Hsiang and others 2017; Muller and others 2011.

25 For example, Anthoff and others (2009), Hsiang and others (2017) and Hsiang and others (2019).

26 Blumenstock 2018; Burke and others 2020.

27 Rolf and others 2020.

Measuring human development and the Anthropocene

Measuring human development and the Anthropocene

The first Human Development Report, published 30 years ago, presented the concept and measurement of human development. Since then, the connection between the two has evolved, and proposals have been made to adjust or change human development metrics, including to account for sustainability.

This Report began by looking at the new reality underpinning proposals for the Anthropocene and what that means for human development. It argued for reimagining the human development journey as one in which people are embedded in the biosphere. And it made the case that expanding human freedoms is central to confronting the unprecedented challenges we now face.

This concluding part of the Report explores implications for measuring human development. Chapter 7 sets out a framework for advancing the agenda of human development metrics in the Anthropocene. It starts by reaffirming the continuing relevance of the Human Development Index (HDI), as long as it is interpreted to measure what it was meant to—a partial set of key capabilities—and not as encompassing the totality of the human development concept. The chapter then explores metrics of human development that are informed by the analysis in this Report. It concludes with a proposal for a new experimental index that accounts for both human development achievements and planetary pressures.

Augmenting the chapter are five spotlights on some of its key concepts. The first looks at the HDI as it turns 30, arguing that it has aged well and remains relevant. The second explores inequalities in greenhouse gas emissions across people, highlighting the need to look beyond country aggregate emissions. The third considers developments in the conceptualization and measurement of comprehensive wealth, including natural capital. The fourth reviews some of the metrics introduced to account for the environment and sustainability, and the fifth reviews proposals to incorporate these dimensions in the HDI.

Towards a new generation of human development metrics for the Anthropocene

Towards a new generation of human development metrics for the Anthropocene

Human development is dynamic. So the way we measure it must be, too. Over the years, new dashboards and indices have been introduced.

How do we measure human development in the Anthropocene?

In line with a central theme of the report, there is no one-size-fits-all tool or metric. Instead, this chapter introduces and explores a suite of possibilities, including an experimental Planetary pressures-adjusted Human Development Index.

One index to rule them all?

Confronting the Anthropocene calls for a new generation of human development metrics. The Human Development Index (HDI) introduced in 1990 was intended to be a general index for global assessment and critique based on a minimal listing of capabilities focused on enjoying a basic quality of life.[1] Clear and simple, and focused on income, education and health, it shaped public and political debate and reoriented objectives and actions. It has since been augmented by the Inequality-adjusted HDI, the Gender Development Index, the Gender Inequality Index and the Multidimensional Poverty Index (spotlight 7.1).

The inclusion of income in the HDI was intended only as a proxy for capabilities other than education and health, as something instrumentally important for achievements in those other capabilities. But gross national income (GNI) does not account for planetary pressures. So this chapter considers possible adjustments to the HDI's income component, subtracting the social costs of carbon from GNI and discussing options to account for changes in total wealth that include natural capital.

The chapter also presents an adjustment to the HDI that uses indicators of greenhouse gas emissions and material footprint. The adjustment is made by multiplying the HDI by an adjustment factor that accounts for planetary pressures. This adjustment factor is calculated as the arithmetic mean of indices measuring carbon dioxide emissions per capita—which speaks to the challenge of shifting away from fossil fuels for energy—and the material footprint per capita—which relates to the challenge of closing material cycles. This Planetary pressures–adjusted HDI provides a sense of the possibilities for achieving high HDI values with lower emissions and resource use.

The HDI was not meant to encompass the totality of the human development approach since no single measure can do that.[2] But it has served as a powerful device to shape public and political debate, encouraging a reorienting of objectives and action. Because supporting that reorientation remains vital, it is important to reaffirm the original intent of the HDI (spotlight 7.1). But as we confront the Anthropocene, the original reorientation is no longer enough. The transformational changes required to ease planetary pressures and redress social imbalances call for another reorientation of goals and choices like the one that the HDI encouraged 30 years ago.

> " The transformational changes required to ease planetary pressures and redress social imbalances call for another reorientation of goals and choices like the one that the HDI encouraged 30 years ago.

Confronting the Anthropocene calls for a new generation of human development metrics, guided by three considerations. First, as the 2019 Human Development Report argued, we need a revolution in metrics, going beyond averages to inequalities both across and within countries (part I).[3] The inequalities reflect the unequal consequences of dangerous planetary change and the differences in power that frame choices driving planetary pressures. And they are manifest not only in inequalities in income and wealth but also in enhanced capabilities—today's new necessities in a rapidly changing and increasingly digital world. Particularly important is to emphasize horizontal (intergroup) inequalities, since they often reflect longstanding patterns of exclusion and discrimination. And it is important to go beyond national averages more than ever—for even countries contributing little to total greenhouse gas emissions may have large individual emitters (spotlight 7.2).

Second, while longstanding debates on sustainability are crucial, we need to go beyond sustaining —meaning, aspiring for a better future for our descendants, not merely avoiding a decline as the objective—and beyond needs (chapter 1). Sustainability cannot be assessed without defining what is to be sustained. Different approaches suggest different indicators: No unique measure is applicable to all definitions of sustainability.[4] Nor can sustainability be assessed without forecasting the future, for what will matter then is not necessarily what matters for us today, but what will matter for future generations.[5] These are not mere technical challenges. If the metrics are to influence those making choices in the real world, these challenges are consequential and cannot be brushed aside.[6] And there simply is no way of assessing any notion of sustainability based on past or current indicators without making assumptions about the future.[7] Going beyond "sustaining," and consistent with the findings of this Report, measuring human development in the Anthropocene should be guided towards measures of planetary pressures and those that incorporate human agency.[8]

Third, although composite indices are powerful political signalling devices, relying on them exclusively can be misleading. The shortcomings of relying only on GDP were emphasized by Joseph Stiglitz, Amartya Sen and Jean Paul Fitoussi's *Report of the Commission on the Measurement of Economic Performance and Social Progress*[9] and further strengthened in more recent work by Stiglitz, Fitoussi and Martine Durand.[10] Dashboards can complement single indicators, including composite indices,[11] particularly when thinking about measures of current and future wellbeing (with the latter meant in some sense to reflect sustainability). Sen, Fitoussi and Stiglitz used the analogy of a driver relying on a car's dashboard for information on speed and on how much fuel is in the tank.[12] Both pieces of information are valuable separately, but it is difficult to see how they could be combined in a way that warns the driver of both whether he or she is speeding or running out of fuel.

These considerations define a broad framework for the evolution of metrics of human development in the Anthropocene, and this chapter makes an initial and partial contribution. To take the third consideration first, a new dashboard of indicators can be organized according to the findings of this Report.[13] Composite indices impose normative assumptions for the choice and aggregation of the indicators, including the weights for different components. They are rarely transparent or even explicit.[14] Dashboards, by contrast, make it possible to inspect different dimensions simultaneously, recognizing that different people can give different weights to each dimension depending on context and aspiration.[15]

This chapter suggests a new dashboard on human development and the Anthropocene, with indicators aimed at capturing the complex interactions between people and ecosystems and at monitoring individual country progress towards easing planetary pressures and social imbalances. The information is organized in four dimensions: status of human development, energy systems, material cycles and transforming our future (figure 7.1). An initial implementation of this dashboard is available online, with the choice of indicators guided in part by data availability.[16]

Figure 7.1 New dashboard on human development and the Anthropocene

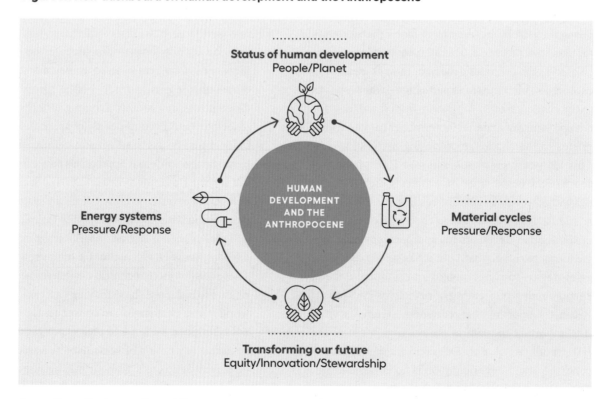

Source: Human Development Report Office.

Also important is presenting the information in a way that helps decisionmakers and the public, and harnessing the power of digital data platforms provides an opportunity to innovate. The Covid-19 Dashboard of the Center for Systems Science and Engineering at Johns Hopkins University presents data from multiple sources and combines spatial data visualizations and data modelling.[17] With a real-time tracking map of Covid-19 cases and deaths, it uses open data principles, offering data downloads with transparent explanations of its sources and documentation. Our World in Data, a University of Oxford initiative, combines data and research to inform global audiences and inspire change. It presents in a transparent and engaging way data and knowledge that would be otherwise hidden in databases and scientific papers.[18]

" The chapter concludes by proposing a new index to adjust the HDI for planetary pressures. It is a crude but simple way of bringing together a central theme of this Report—reimagining the human development journey as one in which the expanding human freedoms also eases planetary pressures.

The chapter next explores how the analysis of human development in the Anthropocene in parts I and II can inform adjustments to the income component of the HDI. These adjustments are informed by recent developments in comprehensive wealth accounting (which includes natural capital, reviewed in more detail in spotlight 7.3) and by advances in the measurement of sustainability and environmental degradation (spotlight 7.4). Both open a new perspective for metrics of human development in the Anthropocene. The chapter concludes by proposing a new index to adjust the HDI for planetary pressures. It is a crude but simple way of bringing together a central theme of this Report—reimagining the human development journey as one in which the expanding human freedoms also eases planetary pressures.

Broadening the vista on the Human Development Index: The income component and planetary pressures

This section builds on proposals to add environmental and sustainability dimensions to the HDI (spotlight 7.4) but explores metrics guided by the importance of going beyond sustaining.[19] It focuses on the implications of accounting for planetary pressures[20] by adjusting the income component of the HDI (box 7.1 shows and discusses an adjustment to the HDI through the health component that could be linked to the drivers and impact of planetary pressures).[21]

Since the HDI presents an alternative to GDP, its income component has been a source of controversy.[22] Including income in the HDI has been criticized as encouraging unaimed opulence—that is, "attempting to maximize economic growth without paying any direct attention to the transformation of greater opulence into better living conditions. Unaimed opulence generally is a roundabout, undependable and wasteful way of improving the living standards of the poor."[23] But including income in the HDI was intended as a proxy for capabilities other than health and education (spotlight 7.1). It does not represent human thriving directly but something instrumentally important to enable achievements in other capabilities. And it is included in the HDI in a way that recognizes that such instrumentality declines as income rises.[24]

Thus, this apparent difficulty would be resolved if the original intent of including income as an index of nonhealth and noneducation capabilities were retained. A more fundamental issue is that GNI does not account for planetary pressures. So this section considers possible adjustments to the income component of the HDI. First, by subtracting from GNI the social costs of carbon. Second, by discussing recent developments in wealth accounting that open the possibility of replacing GNI with measures that account for changes in total wealth, inclusive of natural capital, representing net changes in a more comprehensive measure of capital than the gross investment in physical capital that goes into GNI.

Accounting for the social cost of carbon

The HDI's indicator for the income dimension is GNI. "Gross" is the rogue word in this concept because it fails to account for the depreciation of capital assets[25] and ignores natural capital (spotlight 7.2) and the social costs (borne by everyone) of environmental damage.[26] Other income-based indicators take a

Box 7.1 Would health-adjusted longevity better reflect the impact of planetary pressures?

The Human Development Index (HDI) includes a measure of length of life—life expectancy at birth—but not how healthy people are when they are alive. Environmental pressures are important determinants of health inequalities, and the very consumption patterns that are ecologically damaging (such as meat consumption, discussed in the 2019 Human Development Report[1]) may also relate to deteriorating health in noncommunicable diseases.[2]

The determinants of morbidity are complex and multifaceted, but if the focus is on the capability to live a long and healthy life, this capability might be better captured by healthy life expectancy, an indicator that looks at both the length of life and the quality of health during life. It adjusts life expectancy to account for illness or disability. Using healthy life expectancy instead of life expectancy at birth lowers HDI values for all countries.[3] But the HDI and the healthy life expectancy–adjusted HDI are highly correlated, suggesting only very small changes in rank (see figure).

Healthy life expectancy broadly preserves the ranking of countries by Human Development Index value

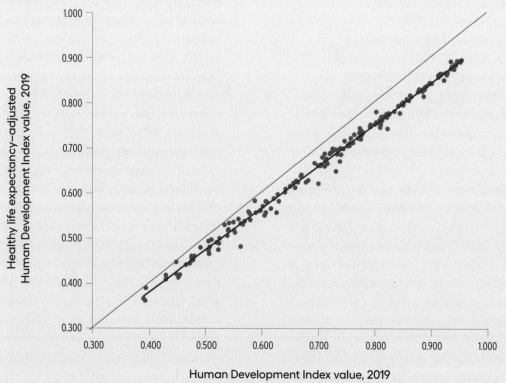

Correlation coefficient = 0.997

Note: Covers 186 countries with Human Development Index (HDI) values. Healthy life expectancy is not available for Liechtenstein and Hong Kong Special Administrative Region, China; Nigeria is excluded because the value for healthy life expectancy (produced by the Institute for Health Metrics and Evaluation) is higher than the value for life expectancy (produced by the United Nations Department of Economic and Social Affairs and included in the HDI).
Source: Human Development Report Office calculations based on HDI values from table 1 in the statistical annex and healthy life expectancy data from IHME (2020).

Notes
1. UNDP 2019c. **2.** Springmann and others 2016. We are grateful to Marc Fleurbaey for this suggestion. The education component could also be adjusted to reflect more directly not only learning but also innovation. And the income component could be adjusted by deducting the social cost of greenhouse gas emissions—something explored later in this chapter. **3.** Given that healthy life expectancy is lower than life expectancy. The slope of the green line depends on the choice for the maximum goalpost in the health dimension—these results assume the same maximum goalpost as the one used for life expectancy in the HDI.

broader view of net flows from capital and adjust for natural resource depletion and damage from emissions and pollution.[27] Here we explore a simpler and more direct adjustment to GNI by subtracting the social costs of carbon dioxide emissions.[28] Again, this is driven by the importance of encouraging a transformation in energy use to lower greenhouse gas emissions. This is not meant to accurately capture the full social costs of environmental damage or the overuse of resources not in GNI. For simplicity the adjustment considers emissions from each country, not the actual damages to each country caused by global aggregate emissions.[29]

The social cost of carbon is the economic cost attributable to an additional tonne of carbon dioxide emissions or its equivalent. Estimates of this cost depend on several assumptions and parameter choices and span a wide range.[30] Here we consider two estimates.[31] One proposed by the International Monetary Fund sets the cost of carbon in 2030 at $75 per tonne of carbon dioxide—in 2017 US dollars and covering all fossil fuels (spotlight 5.1). It is based on a model showing that the impact of a global carbon tax at this level would be consistent with countries meeting their Paris Agreement pledges. The other estimate is from a recent application of the Dynamic Integrated Climate-Economy integrated assessment model.[32] It includes the latest climate science and reflects a broad range of expert recommendations on social discount rates—a key parameter in the model that weighs the value today of future benefits and costs.[33] The median expert view on discount rates gives a carbon social cost of around $200 per tonne of carbon dioxide in 2020 (in 2010 international dollars).[34]

The adjustment to the income component of the HDI subtracts the social cost of carbon dioxide emissions (measured as the product of the country's carbon dioxide emissions per capita and the social cost of carbon) from GNI per capita (and so does not account for the costs of other greenhouse gases). With the social cost set at $75 per tonne of carbon dioxide,[35] the adjustment to the income component would not change a country's HDI value substantially. The changes are generally small, even with the higher social price of carbon of $200 per tonne (figure 7.2). The small changes also suggest that an HDI adjusted only for the social costs of carbon in these price ranges

would not send strong enough signals to encourage behaviour change. Something more comprehensive may be required. The next section explores changes in comprehensive wealth that involve natural capital, which more inclusively accounts for the social costs of the depletion of natural capital than carbon dioxide emissions alone does.

Accounting for changes in comprehensive— and natural—wealth

Recent analytical and empirical advances in wealth accounting offer exciting new avenues to explore human development metrics. Measures of economic activity and social welfare are becoming available that include contributions from nature, the costs of extraction from it and how pollution depreciates capital.[36] They relate to the measurement of comprehensive wealth (sometimes called inclusive or total wealth), which includes natural capital[37] along with produced and human capital.[38] Natural capital comprises nature's assets.[39] These approaches have a long tradition in economics.[40] Irving Fisher started his 1906 book on the nature of capital and income by using fisheries in the Newfoundland Banks as an example of a stock.[41] But the pace picked up from the late 1960s, fuelled in part by debates on how to link social welfare to measures of economic activity and consumption[42] as well as by growing awareness and concerns over ecological degradation.[43]

" Recent analytical and empirical advances in wealth accounting offer exciting new avenues to explore human development metrics.

Partha Dasgupta and Karl-Göran Mäler have built on this tradition, proposing a model in which changes in comprehensive wealth are equivalent to changes in social welfare (meaning that the changes encompass the social welfare of the current generation and all future ones).[44] This is the foundation for much conceptual and empirical work. On the conceptual front, Dasgupta extends the model to include both the values and ethics of population levels and growth and empirical estimates of the planet's human carrying capacity under different normative and parametric assumptions.[45] Empirical estimates of comprehensive

Figure 7.2 The changes to Human Development Index values after subtracting the social costs of carbon at $200 per tonne of carbon dioxide emissions are generally small

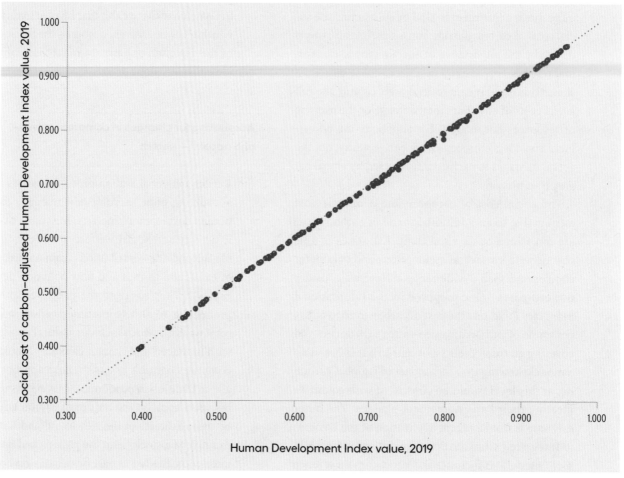

Source: Human Development Report Office calculations based on Human Development Index values from table 1 in the statistical annex and data on production-based carbon dioxide emissions from GCP (2020).

wealth were informed by pioneering work on genuine savings[46] and have evolved to encompass not only cases for some countries[47] but also estimates for several countries. The United Nations Environment Programme (UNEP) and the World Bank now issue country-level estimates.[48] Table 7.1 describes the measures of inclusive wealth released by the UNEP and the measures of total wealth estimated by the World Bank. Both organizations emphasize that their approaches likely greatly underestimate natural capital. A separate but related development is the growing interest in directly measuring wellbeing (box 7.2).

The various components that make up inclusive wealth show different trends (figure 7.3). For most countries and for the world at large, inclusive wealth grows more slowly than GDP. Although the increase in physical capital is on par with GDP, the growth of

human capital is slower. More troubling, these estimates suggest that natural capital has been steadily declining over time (spotlight 7.3).

Changes in inclusive wealth offer a more comprehensive approach than simply subtracting the social costs of carbon dioxide emissions discussed above. Explorations could include adjusting the income component of the HDI by replacing GNI with measures that account for changes in comprehensive wealth. But given that changes in comprehensive wealth reflect broader implications for human wellbeing than just the effect of planetary pressures, how to introduce this broader concept in an index of capabilities like the HDI requires further analysis. These explorations remain under study also because of empirical challenges. To begin with, estimates of inclusive wealth are likely lower bounds, as noted

Table 7.1 Estimates of comprehensive wealth

Measure	Institution	Data	Description
Inclusive wealth	United Nations Environment Programme	140 countries 1990–2014	Inclusive wealth aims to measure wellbeing by monitoring the productive base for future generations. A country's inclusive wealth is the social value of all its capital assets (valued through shadow prices[a]). These include natural capital (fossil fuels, minerals, forests, agricultural land, fisheries), human capital (health, education) and produced capital (equipment, machineries, roads). Of importance for analysis is the change in wealth.
			In 2014 about 20 percent of global inclusive wealth was accounted for by produced capital, 60 percent by human capital and 20 percent by natural capital. Even though 135 of 140 countries showed growth in inclusive wealth in 2014, natural capital declined in 127 of the 140 countries.
Total wealth	World Bank	141 countries 1995–2014	World Bank wealth accounts include the following asset categories: produced capital and urban land (machinery, buildings, equipment, residential and nonresidential urban land—measured at market prices), natural capital (energy and minerals, agricultural land, forests, terrestrial protected areas—measured as the discounted sum of the value of the rents generated over the lifetime of the asset), human capital (disaggregated by gender and employment status—measured as the discounted value of earnings over a person's lifetime) and net foreign assets (for example, foreign direct investment, reserve assets).
			In 2014 about 27 percent of total wealth was produced capital, 64 percent was human capital and 9 percent was natural capital, with natural capital accounting for 47 percent of the wealth in low-income countries and 27 percent in lower-middle-income countries.

a. The shadow price or value of a capital asset is the monetary measure of the contribution a marginal unit of that asset is forecast to make to human wellbeing (UNEP 2018b).
Source: UNEP 2018b; World Bank 2018.

above. For instance, the social cost of carbon used to estimate the damages from carbon emissions in inclusive wealth is $50—using the $200 value as above would multiply the change in inclusive wealth due to this factor by four. And the information on changes in comprehensive wealth from the UNEP and World Bank estimates often vary greatly for some countries, not only in magnitude but also on whether there was a decrease or increase over some time periods. Still the ongoing advances in wealth accounting hold great potential to explore new avenues to incorporate into human development metrics the challenges that we confront in the Anthropocene.

Adjusting the Human Development Index as a whole

The HDI is an example of what James Foster has called "intentional measurement."[49] Its construction was driven by its intended purpose and desired characteristics. The purpose was to shift objectives and action towards a view of development that put people at the centre. Two of its main desired characteristics were clarity and simplicity. A criterion for the validity of such indices is whether they are actually used and adopted over time. And by that standard—despite the modifications made over the years—the HDI has stood the test of time (spotlight 7.1).

So now is the chance to step back and reflect on the intent of adjusting the HDI. Put simply the intent is to have a measure that accounts for how people are doing and for the unprecedented pressures people are imposing on the planet. To account for capabilities, the HDI is the obvious choice. And for the other component, the biophysical and socioeconomic processes that produce planetary pressures should inform the choice. We consider two summary measures: carbon dioxide emissions and material footprint, both on a per capita basis, informed by the discussion in chapter 1. It is crucial to keep in mind the clarity of message and simplicity of understanding.

The adjustment to the HDI is a signalling device for positive change, encouraging the expansion of capabilities while reducing planetary pressures.[50] The focus on greenhouse gases and material flows does not imply that all other environmental concerns are less important or urgent—as is the case for losses in biosphere integrity and several other urgent concerns, as reflected in the Sustainable Development Goals. But reductions in the flows of greenhouse gases and more efficient material use would eventually reflect the outcomes of the broader economic and societal transformation to ease planetary pressures.[51]

The Planetary pressures–adjusted Human Development Index

The adjustment corresponds to multiplying the HDI by an adjustment factor, creating the Planetary

Box 7.2 Measuring wellbeing

Efforts to measure societies' wellbeing have involved government, civil society, academia and international organizations, often working in collaboration. Though some initiatives have sought to measure wellbeing, others have assessed related concepts, including progress, quality of life or sustainable development. For the purposes here, there is little to choose among the measures used for these themes —each initiative has sought to provide an index, or set of indicators, that paints a broader picture of national wellbeing than GDP provides.

Official statistical offices have often been at the forefront of this work, keen to see a richer, fact-based debate about key aspects of life. An early effort came from the United Kingdom, which produced Quality of Life Accounts in 1999.[1] In 2002 the Australian Bureau of Statistics produced "Measuring Australia's Progress."[2] Ireland's Central Statistics Office followed a year later with "Measuring Ireland's Progress."[3]

In 2005 the Organisation for Economic Co-operation and Development (OECD) began its Global Project on Measuring the Progress of Society[4] to catalyse growing interest in going beyond GDP. In 2007 the OECD, along with the European Commission, the United Nations, the United Nations Development Programme (UNDP), the World Bank and others, cosigned a declaration on the importance of measuring the progress of societies.[5] Later that year the European Union held a conference—Beyond GDP—on developing indicators that are as clear and appealing as GDP but more inclusive of environmental and social aspects of progress.[6]

There has been much work since then. Some, such as the 2009 Commission on the Measurement of Economic Performance and Social Progress,[7] has been driven by political leaders. Others, such as the Canadian Wellbeing Index, have been driven by civil society and academia.[8]

International organizations have also been active. UNDP aside—many would argue that the Human Development Index is a measure of wellbeing—the OECD began compiling its Better Life Index in 2011 to bring together internationally comparable measures of wellbeing.[9]

Bhutan's Gross National Happiness work is a well known project from the Global South. What began as a remark by Bhutan's King—"Gross national happiness is more important than GNP"—gained traction as a policy goal, and the Centre for Bhutan Studies developed a survey to measure the population's overall wellbeing that covers four pillars: promotion of sustainable development, preservation and promotion of cultural values, conservation of the natural environment and establishment of good governance. These four pillars consist of nine general contributors to happiness, including psychological wellbeing, health, education, cultural diversity and resilience, time use, community vitality, living standard, and ecological diversity and resilience. And these ideas are embedded into national policy.[10]

Central government agencies are also becoming interested in wellbeing. For example, the government of New Zealand recently made a strong political commitment to go beyond GDP, with its Treasury using the OECD's Living Standard Framework, which measures wellbeing, capital stocks, and risk and resilience to inform budget decisions.[11] Its commitment to engaging with diverse communities within Aotearoa, New Zealand, will help transformation towards an even richer conceptualization and measure of wellbeing.

Around the world the development of wellbeing indicators for children,[12] older people,[13] people with disabilities[14] and indigenous communities[15] is ongoing, sometimes building on a long tradition of work. So too are wellbeing initiatives undertaken by local communities, such as indigenous communities, that are also undertaking socioenvironmental wellbeing surveys.[16] These and other communities are developing wellbeing indicators to understand the needs and aspirations of their communities in the widest sense.[17]

Notes

1. UK Department of the Environment, Transport and the Regions 1999. **2.** Trewin 2002. **3.** Ireland Central Statistics Office 2004. **4.** OECD 2020a. **5.** OECD 2007. **6.** European Commission 2009. **7.** Stiglitz, Sen and Fitoussi 2009. **8.** CIW 2020. **9.** OECD 2020b. **10.** Centre for Bhutan Studies and GNH Research 2016. **11.** New Zealand Treasury 2020. **12.** Biggeri, Ballet and Comim 2011. **13.** ICECAP-O 2020. **14.** Trani and others 2011. **15.** Breslow and others 2016; Durie 1995; Yap and Yu 2016a. **16.** Durie 1995; Yap and Yu 2016a. **17.** Kukutai and Taylor 2016.

Figure 7.3 The steady decline in natural capital

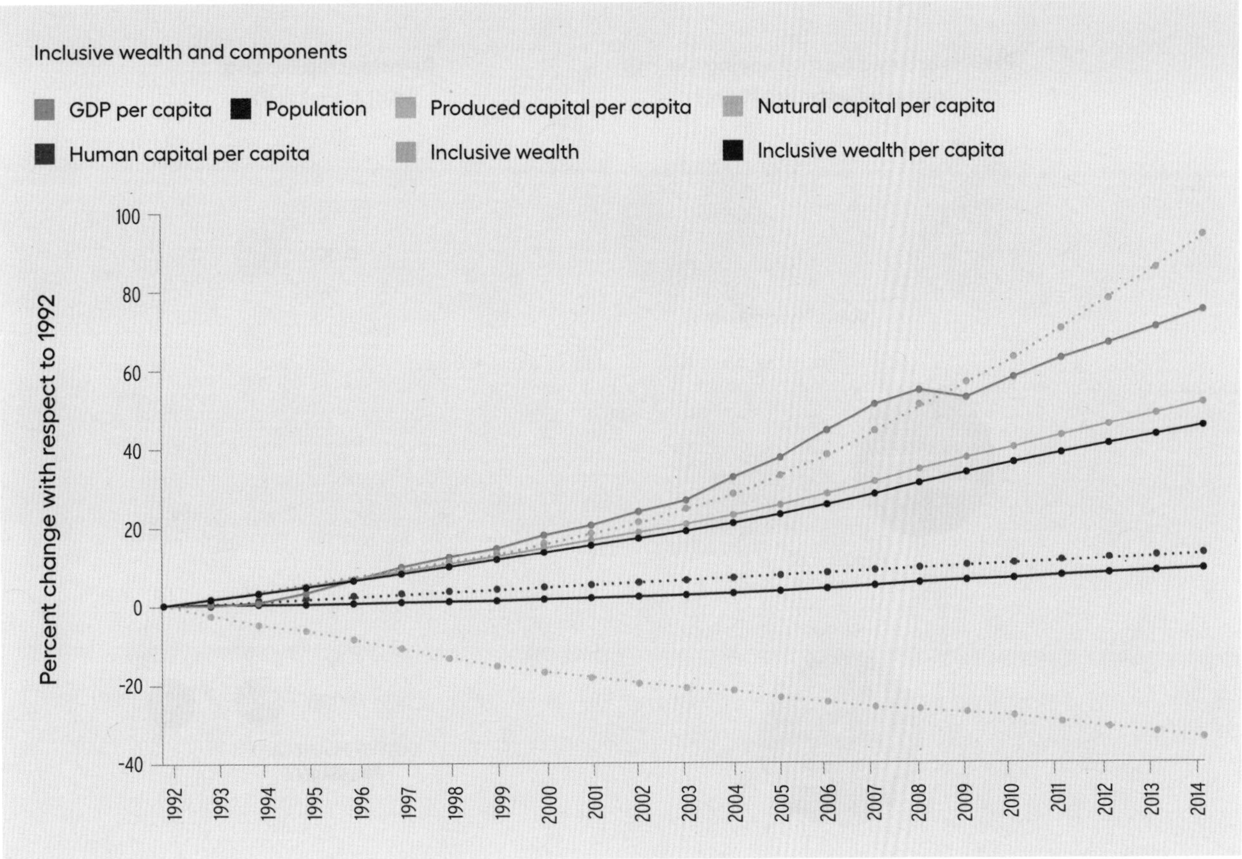

Inclusive wealth and components

- GDP per capita
- Population
- Produced capital per capita
- Natural capital per capita
- Human capital per capita
- Inclusive wealth
- Inclusive wealth per capita

Source: UNEP 2018b.

pressures-adjusted HDI (PHDI; figure 7.4).[52] If a country puts no pressure on the planet, its PHDI and HDI would be equal, but the PHDI falls below the HDI as pressure rises. The adjustment factor is calculated as the arithmetic mean of indices measuring carbon dioxide emissions per capita, which speaks to the energy transition away from fossil fuels, and material footprint per capita, which relates to closing material cycles.[53] A country's material footprint measures the amount of material extracted (biomass, fossil fuels, metal ores and nonmetal ores) to meet domestic final demand for goods and services, regardless of where extraction occurs. It is a consumption-based measure that accounts for international trade. It also indicates pressures on the biosphere exerted by socioeconomic activities, since it includes the use of biomass—thus indirectly reflecting impacts of actions such as land use change on the loss of biosphere integrity.[54]

The literature has often justified adjustments to the HDI of this type as a penalty for pollution,[55] as in

proposals to multiply the HDI by a loss function associated with carbon dioxide emissions above a country's "fair share."[56] Discounting the HDI could be interpreted as similar to the adjustments in the Inequality-adjusted HDI (IHDI).[57] The IHDI adjustment is motivated by intragenerational inequality, lowering each component of the HDI by the inequality in that component. By analogy, discounting the HDI for planetary pressures could be interpreted as reflecting a concern for intergenerational inequality.

> " If a country puts no pressure on the planet, its PHDI and HDI would be equal, but the PHDI falls below the HDI as pressure rises.

But "one should be careful not to interpret [this type of adjustment] in terms of moral appraisal of countries, because some may have little choice but to deplete their capital."[58] The interpretation proposed here for the adjustment for planetary pressures is

Figure 7.4 Visual representation of the Planetary pressures–adjusted Human Development Index

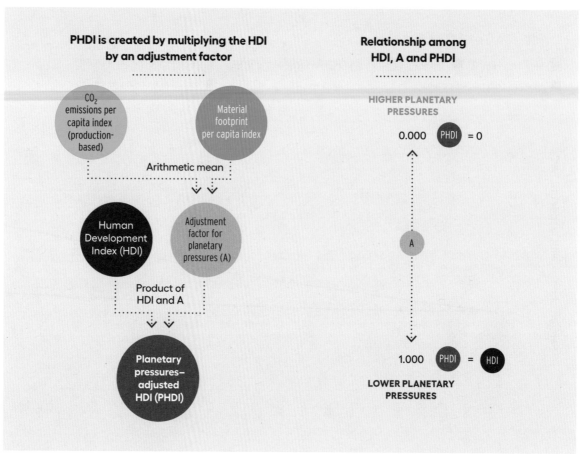

Source: Human Development Report Office.

intended to incentivize change by providing a metric for countries to assess their own progress over time and highlighting countries that are moving in the right direction so that others can learn from them.[59] It provides a sense of possibility for how to achieve high HDI values with lower emissions and resource use. This approach also avoids imposing what will always be ultimately arbitrary constraints on each country, blind to their historic responsibilities, within-country inequalities—which often reflect longstanding patterns of racial, gender and other types of discrimination—and resource and economic circumstances.[60]

PHDI values are very close to HDI values for countries with an HDI value of 0.7 or lower (figure 7.5). Differences start to open up at higher HDI values, with wider divergence at very high HDI values. But caution must be used in interpreting these numbers because the adjustment does not account for individual country responsibilities—current or historical.[61]

Annex table A7.1 at the end of the chapter presents the values and ranks of countries on the PHDI. Costa Rica has a very large increase in rank from the HDI to the PHDI, while the opposite is true for countries that depend heavily on hydrocarbons. Luxembourg and Singapore demonstrate this more sharply, in large part reflecting their exceptional circumstances, given that both are small, highly open economies with high income per capita and a structural dependence on hydrocarbons for energy.[62]

Human development progress based on the Planetary pressures–adjusted Human Development Index: A new lens

The global PHDI offers a summary view of the evolution in human development and the associated planetary pressures—the world has consistently increased planetary pressures per capita over the

Figure 7.5 Planetary pressures–adjusted Human Development Index values are very close to Human Development Index values for countries with a Human Development Index value of 0.7 or lower

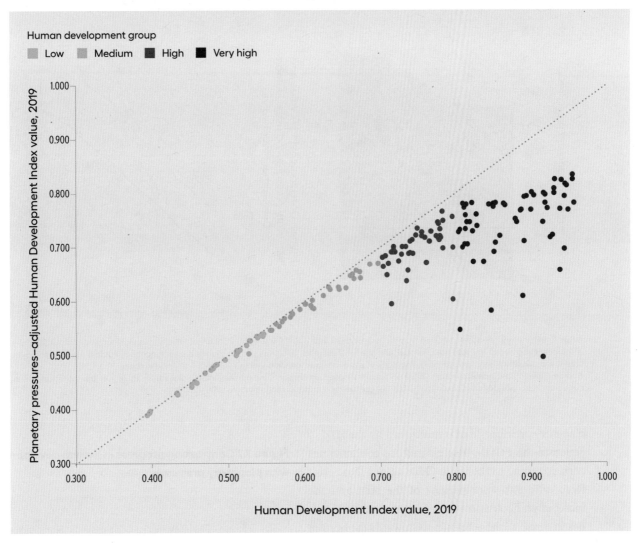

Note: The Planetary pressures–adjusted Human Development Index covers 169 countries with Human Development Index (HDI) values. Data on material footprint are not available for 19 countries with HDI values, and Guyana is excluded from the analysis due to unrealistically high values for material footprint.
Source: Human Development Report Office calculations based on HDI values from table 1 in the statistical annex, data on carbon dioxide emissions from GCP (2020) and data on material footprint from UNEP (2020d).

past three decades (figure 7.6, left panel).[63] The PHDI is not only lower than the HDI; it is also growing more slowly (figure 7.6, right panel). The gap between the conventional assessment of development (the HDI) and the new perspective to navigate the Anthropocene (the experimental PHDI) has been widening.

From an evaluative perspective these trends reflect both gains in the space of basic capabilities and general material conditions and the increasing anthropogenic planetary pressures. As discussed in chapter 2, the negative effects of climate change and losses in

biosphere integrity are starting to emerge in different aspects of human development not captured in the HDI.

From a policy perspective the PHDI provides a guiding metric towards advancing human development while easing planetary pressures—a combination that today corresponds to an "empty corner" when human development is contrasted with indicators of planetary pressures, as chapter 1 highlighted.[64] In figure 7.7 the horizontal axis shows the HDI, and the vertical axis shows the index of planetary pressures (which is one minus the adjustment factor for

Figure 7.6 Planetary pressures have increased with gains on the Human Development Index

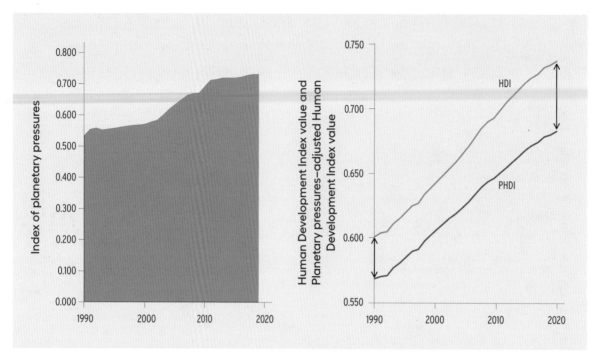

Note: The Planetary pressures–adjusted Human Development Index (PHDI) values for 2018 and 2019 use material footprint data for 2017, the most recent year for which data are available, and the PHDI value for 2019 uses carbon dioxide emissions per capita data for 2018, the most recent year for which data are available. The index of planetary pressures is equal to 1 – A, with A defined in figure 7.4
Source: Human Development Report Office calculations based on Human Development Index values from table 2 of the statistical annex, data on carbon dioxide emissions from GCP (2020) and data on material footprint from UNEP (2020d).

planetary pressures that is multiplied by the HDI to generate the PHDI). Also plotted are contour lines corresponding to the same PHDI values that result from different combinations of the HDI and the index of planetary pressures (isoquants). PHDI values increase as these lines move towards the bottom right corner. This corner (highlighted in green in the figure) is the "empty space" identified in chapter 1 as the aspirational destination of the human development journey in the Anthropocene. For instance, countries in positions A and B have very different HDI values (0.55 and 0.85) but the same PHDI value (0.55) because the greater progress in HDI in country B has been coupled with much greater planetary pressures. This simple example shows the importance of a joint assessment of socioeconomic and planetary pressure indicators as part of a single framework.

Figure 7.8 shows how human development (in its traditional interpretation, characterized by the HDI) is intimately connected with planetary pressures. Of the more than 60 very high human development countries, only 10 are still classified as very high

Figure 7.7 Contrasting progress in human development with planetary pressures

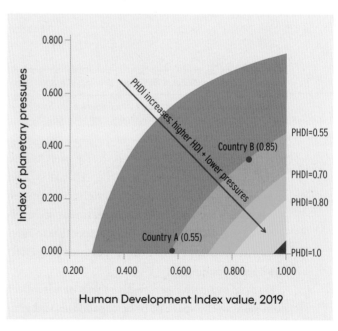

Human Development Index value, 2019

Note: The index of planetary pressures is equal to 1 – A, with A defined in figure 7.4
Source: Human Development Report Office.

human development on the PHDI. And even in those 10 countries the PHDI is still far from the aspirational bottom-right corner.

Looking at the trajectory of countries over the past three decades shows different paths across human development groups. Low and medium human development countries have been able to improve social and economic conditions substantially without a high burden on planetary pressures. But in high and very high human development countries, improvements on the HDI have been coupled with rising planetary pressures (figure 7.9, left panel).

Although absolute planetary pressures have been growing, two aspects reflect some progress. First, after the 2008 global financial crisis a few developed countries have shown some decoupling of human development gains from planetary pressures.[65] For instance, on average, the top 10 countries on the PHDI have increased their HDI value and reduced their planetary pressures over the last decade (figure 7.9, right panel).[66] Second, there is some evidence more broadly of relative decoupling.[67] The curve corresponding to the average performance on the HDI and planetary pressures for all countries moved slightly

Figure 7.8 Of the more than 60 very high human development countries in 2019, only 10 are still classified as very high human development on the Planetary pressures–adjusted Human Development Index

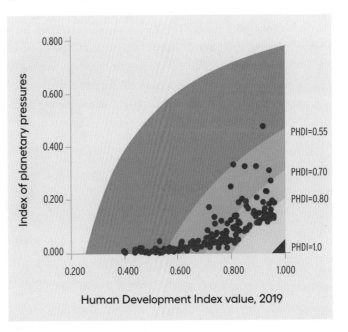

Note: The index of planetary pressures is equal to 1 – A, with A defined in figure 7.4
Source: Human Development Report Office calculations based on Human Development Index values from table 1 of the statistical annex, data on carbon dioxide emissions from GCP (2020) and data on material footprint from UNEP (2020d).

Figure 7.9 Human Development Index and Planetary pressures–adjusted Human Development Index trajectories are coupled in very high human development countries

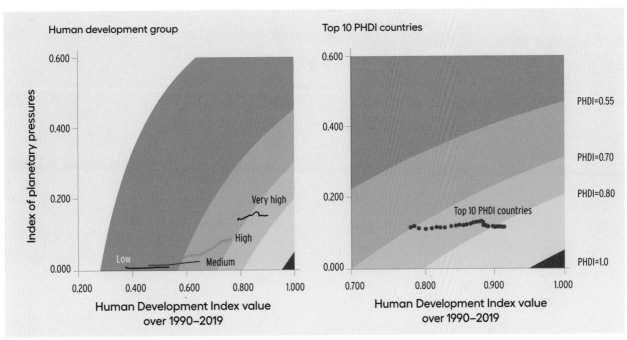

Note: The index of planetary pressures is equal to 1 – A, with A defined in figure 7.4. The lines on the left panel and the dots on the right panel represent the evolution of the two indices over 1990–2019.
Source: Human Development Report Office calculations based on Human Development Index values from table 2 of the statistical annex, data on carbon dioxide emissions from GCP (2020) and data on material footprint from UNEP (2020d).

towards the bottom right-hand corner between 1990 and 2019 (figure 7.10).

But the movement has been far too slow and modest. Further progress will require all countries to rapidly shift substantially towards the bottom-right corner. The PHDI and the HDI can help assess and, more important, encourage choices towards a human development journey in the Anthropocene that move us all in the direction of advancing human development while easing planetary pressures.

Figure 7.10 The world is moving far too slowly towards advancing human development while easing planetary pressures

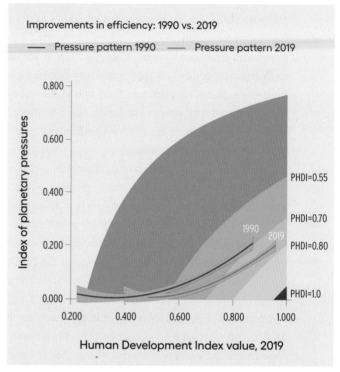

Improvements in efficiency: 1990 vs. 2019

— Pressure pattern 1990   — Pressure pattern 2019

Note: Cross-sectional pressure patterns for 1990 and 2019 were calculated using a polynomial regression model. Shaded areas are confidence intervals. The index of planetary pressures is equal to 1 – A, with A defined in figure 7.4
Source: Human Development Report Office calculations based on Human Development Index values from table 2 of the statistical annex, data on carbon dioxide emissions from GCP (2020) and data on material footprint from UNEP (2020d).

Planetary pressures-adjusted Human Development Index

		Human Development Index (HDI)	Planetary pressures-adjusted HDI (PHDI)			Adjustment factor for planetary pressures	SDG 9.4 Carbon dioxide emissions per capita (production)	Carbon dioxide emissions (production) index	SDG 8.4, 12.2 Material footprint per capita	Material footprint index
		Value	Value	Difference from HDI value (%)	Difference from HDI rank	Value	(tonnes)	Value	(tonnes)	Value
HDI RANK		2019	2019	2019	2019ª	2019	2018	2018	2017	2017
Very high human development										
1	Norway	0.957	0.781	18.4	−15	0.816	8.3	0.881	37.9	0.752
2	Ireland	0.955	0.833	12.8	1	0.872	8.1	0.884	21.5	0.859
2	Switzerland	0.955	0.825	13.6	0	0.864	4.3	0.938	32.1	0.790
4	Hong Kong, China (SAR)	0.949	..	..	..	..	5.9	0.916	..	
4	Iceland	0.949	0.768	19.1	−26	0.809	10.8	0.846	34.8	0.772
6	Germany	0.947	0.814	14.0	−1	0.859	9.1	0.869	23.0	0.849
7	Sweden	0.945	0.817	13.5	1	0.865	4.1	0.941	32.2	0.789
8	Australia	0.944	0.696	26.3	−72	0.737	16.9	0.758	43.4	0.716
8	Netherlands	0.944	0.794	15.9	−6	0.842	9.5	0.864	27.7	0.819
10	Denmark	0.940	0.824	12.3	5	0.876	6.1	0.913	24.6	0.839
11	Finland	0.938	0.770	17.9	−19	0.821	8.5	0.878	36.1	0.763
11	Singapore	0.938	0.656	30.1	−92	0.700	7.1	0.898	76.1	0.501
13	United Kingdom	0.932	0.825	11.5	10	0.885	5.6	0.919	22.7	0.851
14	Belgium	0.931	0.800	14.1	4	0.859	8.7	0.876	24.1	0.842
14	New Zealand	0.931	0.808	13.2	6	0.867	7.3	0.895	24.5	0.840
16	Canada	0.929	0.721	22.4	−40	0.776	15.3	0.781	34.9	0.771
17	United States	0.926	0.718	22.5	−45	0.775	16.6	0.763	32.5	0.787
18	Austria	0.922	0.771	16.4	−11	0.837	7.7	0.889	32.9	0.784
19	Israel	0.919	0.797	13.3	7	0.867	7.7	0.890	23.9	0.843
19	Japan	0.919	0.781	15.0	2	0.850	9.1	0.869	25.9	0.830
19	Liechtenstein	0.919	..	..	..	..	4.0	0.942	..	..
22	Slovenia	0.917	0.800	12.8	11	0.873	6.9	0.901	23.7	0.845
23	Korea (Republic of)	0.916	0.746	18.6	−19	0.814	12.9	0.816	28.6	0.813
23	Luxembourg	0.916	0.495	46.0	−131	0.541	15.9	0.773	105.6	0.308
25	Spain	0.904	0.795	12.1	11	0.880	5.7	0.918	24.1	0.842
26	France	0.901	0.801	11.1	16	0.889	5.2	0.926	22.5	0.853
27	Czechia	0.900	0.768	14.7	−5	0.853	9.9	0.858	23.0	0.849
28	Malta	0.895	0.794	11.3	13	0.887	3.6	0.948	26.5	0.826
29	Estonia	0.892	0.711	20.3	−40	0.797	14.8	0.788	29.6	0.806
29	Italy	0.892	0.792	11.2	12	0.888	5.6	0.920	21.9	0.857
31	United Arab Emirates	0.890	0.609	31.6	−87	0.685	21.3	0.694	49.6	0.675
32	Greece	0.888	0.768	13.5	0	0.865	7.0	0.899	25.8	0.831
33	Cyprus	0.887	0.767	13.5	−2	0.865	6.3	0.910	27.5	0.820
34	Lithuania	0.882	0.746	15.4	−8	0.846	4.8	0.931	36.3	0.762
35	Poland	0.880	0.752	14.5	−5	0.855	9.1	0.870	24.5	0.839
36	Andorra	0.868	..	..	..	..	6.1	0.912	..	..
37	Latvia	0.866	0.777	10.3	9	0.897	3.7	0.947	23.2	0.848
38	Portugal	0.864	0.780	9.7	15	0.903	5.0	0.929	18.7	0.878
39	Slovakia	0.860	0.720	16.3	−21	0.837	6.6	0.905	35.3	0.769
40	Hungary	0.854	0.781	8.5	21	0.915	5.1	0.926	14.9	0.903
40	Saudi Arabia	0.854	0.707	17.2	−33	0.827	18.4	0.736	12.4	0.919
42	Bahrain	0.852	0.691	18.9	−42	0.811	19.8	0.717	14.4	0.906
43	Chile	0.851	0.774	9.0	14	0.910	4.6	0.934	17.5	0.885
43	Croatia	0.851	0.779	8.5	19	0.916	4.5	0.936	16.0	0.895
45	Qatar	0.848	0.581	31.5	−84	0.685	38.0	0.456	13.2	0.913
46	Argentina	0.845	0.778	7.9	20	0.920	4.4	0.937	14.7	0.904
47	Brunei Darussalam	0.838	0.672	19.8	−49	0.802	18.5	0.735	20.0	0.869
48	Montenegro	0.829	0.738	11.0	−1	0.890	3.2	0.954	26.7	0.825
49	Romania	0.828	0.760	8.2	11	0.917	3.8	0.946	16.9	0.889
50	Palau	0.826	..	..	..	..	13.2	0.811	..	..
51	Kazakhstan	0.825	0.672	18.5	−46	0.815	17.6	0.749	18.1	0.881
52	Russian Federation	0.824	0.728	11.7	−4	0.883	11.7	0.832	9.9	0.935
53	Belarus	0.823	0.781	5.1	33	0.949	6.9	0.901	0.4	0.997
54	Turkey	0.820	0.746	9.0	10	0.910	5.2	0.926	16.2	0.894
55	Uruguay	0.817	0.704	13.8	−20	0.862	2.0	0.971	37.7	0.753
56	Bulgaria	0.816	0.745	8.7	9	0.913	6.3	0.910	12.8	0.916
57	Panama	0.815	0.778	4.5	30	0.955	2.6	0.963	8.0	0.947
58	Bahamas	0.814	0.733	10.0	6	0.900	4.7	0.933	20.2	0.868
58	Barbados	0.814	0.758	6.9	18	0.932	4.5	0.936	11.1	0.927

Continued →

HDI RANK	Human Development Index (HDI)	Planetary pressures–adjusted HDI (PHDI)			Adjustment factor for planetary pressures	Carbon dioxide emissions per capita (production)	Carbon dioxide emissions (production) index	Material footprint per capita	Material footprint index
	Value	Value	Difference from HDI value (%)	Difference from HDI rank	Value	(tonnes)	Value	(tonnes)	Value
	2019	2019	2019	2019[a]	2019	2018	2018	2017	2017
60 Oman	0.813	0.704	13.4	–15	0.866	13.9	0.801	10.4	0.932
61 Georgia	0.812	0.772	4.9	30	0.951	2.6	0.962	9.1	0.940
62 Costa Rica	0.810	0.779	3.8	37	0.961	1.6	0.977	8.3	0.946
62 Malaysia	0.810	0.699	13.7	–18	0.863	8.1	0.884	24.2	0.842
64 Kuwait	0.806	0.547	32.1	–74	0.678	23.7	0.661	46.5	0.696
64 Serbia	0.806	0.732	9.2	10	0.908	5.2	0.926	16.7	0.891
66 Mauritius	0.804	0.727	9.6	9	0.904	3.8	0.945	20.8	0.864
High human development									
67 Seychelles	0.796	0.699	12.2	–13	0.879	6.7	0.903	22.3	0.854
67 Trinidad and Tobago	0.796	0.603	24.2	–54	0.758	31.3	0.552	5.6	0.963
69 Albania	0.795	0.756	4.9	28	0.951	1.6	0.977	11.4	0.925
70 Cuba	0.783	0.749	4.3	27	0.957	2.5	0.964	7.8	0.949
70 Iran (Islamic Republic of)	0.783	0.698	10.9	–12	0.891	8.8	0.874	14.1	0.908
72 Sri Lanka	0.782	0.765	2.2	34	0.979	1.1	0.984	4.1	0.973
73 Bosnia and Herzegovina	0.780	0.718	7.9	8	0.920	6.5	0.907	10.2	0.933
74 Grenada	0.779	..	..	..	..	2.4	0.965	..	..
74 Mexico	0.779	0.733	5.9	22	0.941	3.8	0.946	9.8	0.936
74 Saint Kitts and Nevis	0.779	..	..	..	..	4.6	0.934	..	..
74 Ukraine	0.779	0.720	7.6	13	0.924	5.1	0.927	12.1	0.920
78 Antigua and Barbuda	0.778	0.713	8.4	7	0.917	5.9	0.916	12.5	0.918
79 Peru	0.777	0.743	4.4	28	0.956	1.7	0.975	9.6	0.937
79 Thailand	0.777	0.716	7.9	9	0.921	4.2	0.941	15.0	0.902
81 Armenia	0.776	0.745	4.0	32	0.960	1.9	0.973	8.2	0.947
82 North Macedonia	0.774	0.720	7.0	19	0.930	3.5	0.950	13.8	0.910
83 Colombia	0.767	0.729	5.0	26	0.951	2.0	0.972	10.7	0.930
84 Brazil	0.765	0.710	7.2	10	0.927	2.2	0.969	17.4	0.886
85 China	0.761	0.671	11.8	–16	0.881	7.0	0.899	20.9	0.863
86 Ecuador	0.759	0.718	5.4	19	0.947	2.5	0.965	11.0	0.928
86 Saint Lucia	0.759	..	..	..	..	2.3	0.967	..	..
88 Azerbaijan	0.756	0.720	4.8	24	0.953	3.7	0.947	6.3	0.959
88 Dominican Republic	0.756	0.727	3.8	28	0.962	2.3	0.967	6.6	0.957
90 Moldova (Republic of)	0.750	0.734	2.1	36	0.979	1.3	0.982	3.8	0.975
91 Algeria	0.748	0.721	3.6	29	0.963	3.7	0.947	3.1	0.980
92 Lebanon	0.744	0.688	7.5	–2	0.924	3.5	0.949	15.4	0.899
93 Fiji	0.743	0.713	4.0	21	0.959	2.4	0.966	7.2	0.953
94 Dominica	0.742	..	..	..	..	2.5	0.964	..	..
95 Maldives	0.740	0.689	6.9	1	0.931	3.0	0.958	14.5	0.905
95 Tunisia	0.740	0.710	4.1	19	0.960	2.7	0.961	6.3	0.959
97 Saint Vincent and the Grenadines	0.738	..	..	..	..	2.0	0.971	..	..
97 Suriname	0.738	0.687	6.9	1	0.931	3.1	0.956	14.2	0.907
99 Mongolia	0.737	0.657	10.9	–10	0.891	8.9	0.873	13.9	0.909
100 Botswana	0.735	0.637	13.3	–18	0.867	3.0	0.958	34.1	0.776
101 Jamaica	0.734	0.700	4.6	18	0.954	2.8	0.960	7.9	0.948
102 Jordan	0.729	0.700	4.0	19	0.961	2.4	0.965	6.7	0.956
103 Paraguay	0.728	0.686	5.8	5	0.943	1.1	0.985	15.1	0.901
104 Tonga	0.725	..	..	..	..	1.3	0.981	..	..
105 Libya	0.724	0.673	7.0	3	0.929	8.1	0.884	3.9	0.974
106 Uzbekistan	0.720	0.691	4.0	15	0.960	2.8	0.960	6.0	0.960
107 Bolivia (Plurinational State of)	0.718	0.695	3.2	17	0.968	2.0	0.972	5.5	0.964
107 Indonesia	0.718	0.691	3.8	16	0.963	2.3	0.967	6.3	0.959
107 Philippines	0.718	0.701	2.4	24	0.977	1.3	0.982	4.4	0.971
110 Belize	0.716	0.690	3.6	16	0.964	1.5	0.979	7.8	0.949
111 Samoa	0.715	0.690	3.5	17	0.965	1.3	0.981	7.9	0.948
111 Turkmenistan	0.715	0.595	16.8	–18	0.832	13.7	0.805	21.5	0.859
113 Venezuela (Bolivarian Republic of)	0.711	0.670	5.8	7	0.942	4.8	0.931	7.3	0.952
114 South Africa	0.709	0.648	8.6	–1	0.914	8.1	0.884	8.5	0.945
115 Palestine, State of	0.708	..	..	..	..	0.7	0.991	..	..
116 Egypt	0.707	0.684	3.3	15	0.967	2.4	0.965	4.8	0.968
117 Marshall Islands	0.704	..	..	..	..	2.6	0.963	..	..
117 Viet Nam	0.704	0.664	5.7	7	0.943	2.2	0.969	12.7	0.917
119 Gabon	0.703	0.680	3.3	16	0.967	2.5	0.964	4.5	0.971
Medium human development									
120 Kyrgyzstan	0.697	0.669	4.0	11	0.960	1.6	0.977	8.7	0.943
121 Morocco	0.686	0.668	2.6	11	0.974	1.8	0.974	3.9	0.975
122 Guyana	0.682	..	..	..	..	3.1	0.955	..[b]	..
123 Iraq	0.674	0.642	4.7	3	0.953	5.3	0.924	2.8	0.982
124 El Salvador	0.673	0.654	2.8	8	0.972	1.1	0.984	6.3	0.959
125 Tajikistan	0.668	0.657	1.6	12	0.984	0.6	0.991	3.7	0.976

Continued →

HDI RANK	Human Development Index (HDI) Value 2019	Planetary pressures–adjusted HDI (PHDI) Value 2019	Difference from HDI value (%) 2019	Difference from HDI rank 2019[a]	Adjustment factor for planetary pressures Value 2019	SDG 9.4 Carbon dioxide emissions per capita (production) (tonnes) 2018	Carbon dioxide emissions (production) index Value 2018	SDG 8.4, 12.2 Material footprint per capita (tonnes) 2017	Material footprint index Value 2017
126 Cabo Verde	0.665	0.641	3.6	5	0.964	1.2	0.983	8.6	0.944
127 Guatemala	0.663	0.650	2.0	10	0.980	1.1	0.985	3.9	0.975
128 Nicaragua	0.660	0.647	2.0	9	0.980	0.9	0.988	4.3	0.972
129 Bhutan	0.654	0.624	4.6	4	0.954	1.6	0.977	10.4	0.932
130 Namibia	0.646	0.621	3.9	4	0.961	1.7	0.975	8.2	0.946
131 India	0.645	0.626	2.9	8	0.971	2.0	0.972	4.6	0.970
132 Honduras	0.634	0.621	2.1	6	0.980	1.0	0.985	4.0	0.974
133 Bangladesh	0.632	0.625	1.1	9	0.988	0.5	0.992	2.4	0.985
134 Kiribati	0.630	..	..	..	..	0.6	0.991	..	..
135 Sao Tome and Principe	0.625	0.610	2.4	6	0.976	0.6	0.992	5.9	0.961
136 Micronesia (Federated States of)	0.620	..	..	..	..	1.3	0.981	..	..
137 Lao People's Democratic Republic	0.613	0.586	4.4	-2	0.956	2.7	0.961	7.5	0.951
138 Eswatini (Kingdom of)	0.611	0.587	3.9	0	0.961	1.1	0.985	9.6	0.937
138 Ghana	0.611	0.601	1.6	5	0.984	0.6	0.991	3.6	0.977
140 Vanuatu	0.609	0.592	2.8	3	0.971	0.5	0.992	7.6	0.950
141 Timor-Leste	0.606	..	..	..	..	0.4	0.994	..	..
142 Nepal	0.602	0.595	1.2	7	0.988	0.3	0.995	2.8	0.982
143 Kenya	0.601	0.594	1.2	6	0.988	0.4	0.995	3.0	0.980
144 Cambodia	0.594	0.584	1.7	3	0.984	0.6	0.991	3.6	0.976
145 Equatorial Guinea	0.592	..	..	..	..	4.3	0.938	..	..
146 Zambia	0.584	0.576	1.4	1	0.986	0.3	0.996	3.5	0.977
147 Myanmar	0.583	0.578	0.9	3	0.992	0.5	0.993	1.4	0.991
148 Angola	0.581	0.570	1.9	2	0.981	1.1	0.984	3.4	0.978
149 Congo	0.574	0.567	1.2	2	0.988	0.6	0.991	2.2	0.986
150 Zimbabwe	0.571	0.562	1.6	2	0.983	0.8	0.988	3.2	0.979
151 Solomon Islands	0.567	..	..	..	..	0.3	0.996	..	..
151 Syrian Arab Republic	0.567	0.554	2.3	1	0.977	1.7	0.976	3.4	0.978
153 Cameroon	0.563	0.558	0.9	3	0.991	0.3	0.995	1.9	0.987
154 Pakistan	0.557	0.547	1.8	2	0.982	1.1	0.985	3.2	0.979
155 Papua New Guinea	0.555	0.547	1.4	3	0.985	0.9	0.987	2.6	0.983
156 Comoros	0.554	..	..	..	..	0.3	0.996	..	..
Low human development									
157 Mauritania	0.546	0.539	1.3	1	0.987	0.6	0.991	2.5	0.984
158 Benin	0.545	0.535	1.8	-1	0.981	0.6	0.991	4.4	0.971
159 Uganda	0.544	0.539	0.9	3	0.991	0.1	0.998	2.5	0.983
160 Rwanda	0.543	0.537	1.1	2	0.989	0.1	0.999	3.1	0.980
161 Nigeria	0.539	0.532	1.3	0	0.987	0.6	0.991	2.7	0.982
162 Côte d'Ivoire	0.538	0.535	0.6	3	0.995	0.3	0.995	0.9	0.994
163 Tanzania (United Republic of)	0.529	0.526	0.6	1	0.994	0.2	0.997	1.4	0.991
164 Madagascar	0.528	0.526	0.4	2	0.996	0.2	0.998	0.8	0.994
165 Lesotho	0.527	0.503	4.6	-4	0.954	1.3	0.982	11.4	0.925
166 Djibouti	0.524	0.518	1.1	2	0.988	0.7	0.990	2.3	0.985
167 Togo	0.515	0.509	1.2	2	0.989	0.4	0.994	2.5	0.984
168 Senegal	0.512	0.505	1.4	0	0.987	0.7	0.989	2.4	0.984
169 Afghanistan	0.511	0.508	0.6	3	0.994	0.3	0.996	1.2	0.992
170 Haiti	0.510	0.507	0.6	3	0.994	0.3	0.996	1.4	0.991
170 Sudan	0.510	0.500	2.0	0	0.980	0.5	0.993	5.0	0.967
172 Gambia	0.496	0.491	1.0	0	0.990	0.3	0.996	2.3	0.985
173 Ethiopia	0.485	0.483	0.4	0	0.997	0.1	0.998	0.8	0.995
174 Malawi	0.483	0.481	0.4	0	0.996	0.1	0.999	1.2	0.992
175 Congo (Democratic Republic of the)	0.480	0.477	0.6	0	0.993	0.0	1.000	2.0	0.987
175 Guinea-Bissau	0.480	..	..	..	..	0.2	0.997	..	..
175 Liberia	0.480	0.476	0.8	-1	0.993	0.3	0.995	1.6	0.990
178 Guinea	0.477	0.473	0.8	0	0.991	0.3	0.996	2.3	0.985
179 Yemen	0.470	0.467	0.6	0	0.994	0.4	0.995	1.1	0.993
180 Eritrea	0.459	0.449	2.2	-1	0.978	0.2	0.997	6.2	0.959
181 Mozambique	0.456	0.452	0.9	1	0.992	0.3	0.996	2.0	0.987
182 Burkina Faso	0.452	0.446	1.3	0	0.986	0.2	0.997	4.0	0.974
182 Sierra Leone	0.452	0.442	2.2	-1	0.978	0.1	0.998	6.4	0.958
184 Mali	0.434	0.427	1.6	-2	0.984	0.2	0.997	4.6	0.970
185 Burundi	0.433	0.431	0.5	1	0.994	0.0	0.999	1.6	0.990
185 South Sudan	0.433	0.430	0.7	0	0.993	0.2	0.998	1.6	0.989
187 Chad	0.398	0.396	0.5	0	0.994	0.1	0.999	1.5	0.990
188 Central African Republic	0.397	0.393	1.0	0	0.991	0.1	0.999	2.6	0.983
189 Niger	0.394	0.390	1.0	0	0.989	0.1	0.999	3.2	0.979
Other countries or territories									
Korea (Democratic People's Rep. of)	..	..	..	..	0.988	1.2	0.983	1.0	0.993
Monaco	..	..	..	..	..	..	..	..	..

Continued →

HDI RANK	Human Development Index (HDI) Value 2019	Planetary pressures–adjusted HDI (PHDI) Value 2019	Difference from HDI value (%) 2019	Difference from HDI rank 2019[a]	Adjustment factor for planetary pressures Value 2019	SDG 9.4 Carbon dioxide emissions per capita (production) (tonnes) 2018	Carbon dioxide emissions (production) index Value 2018	SDG 8.4, 12.2 Material footprint per capita (tonnes) 2017	Material footprint index Value 2017
Nauru	..	..	..	..	..	4.7	0.933	..	..
San Marino	..	..	..	..	..	..	..	..	..
Somalia	..	..	..	..	0.992	0.0	0.999	2.3	0.985
Tuvalu	..	..	..	..	..	1.0	0.986	..	..
Human development groups									
Very high human development	0.898	0.760	15.4	–	0.846	10.4	0.851	24.2	0.841
High human development	0.753	0.688	8.6	–	0.914	5.1	0.927	15.2	0.900
Medium human development	0.631	0.615	2.5	–	0.975	1.6	0.977	4.0	0.974
Low human development	0.513	0.508	1.0	–	0.990	0.3	0.996	2.2	0.985
Developing countries	0.689	0.651	5.5	–	0.944	3.4	0.952	9.6	0.937
Regions									
Arab States	0.705	0.666	5.5	–	0.944	4.8	0.931	6.5	0.958
East Asia and the Pacific	0.747	0.676	9.5	–	0.905	5.5	0.921	16.9	0.890
Europe and Central Asia	0.791	0.728	8.0	–	0.920	5.5	0.921	12.2	0.920
Latin America and the Caribbean	0.766	0.720	6.0	–	0.940	2.8	0.960	12.4	0.919
South Asia	0.641	0.622	3.0	–	0.971	2.0	0.972	4.6	0.970
Sub-Saharan Africa	0.547	0.539	1.5	–	0.985	0.8	0.988	2.8	0.982
Least developed countries	0.538	0.533	0.9	–	0.990	0.3	0.995	2.3	0.985
Small island developing states	0.728	0.680	6.6	–	0.935	3.2	0.954	12.9	0.915
Organisation for Economic Co-operation and Development	0.900	0.766	14.9	–	0.851	9.5	0.864	24.8	0.838
World	**0.737**	**0.683**	**7.3**	**–**	**0.927**	**4.6**	**0.934**	**12.3**	**0.919**

Notes

a   Based on countries for which a Planetary pressures–adjusted Human Development Index value is calculated.

b   Not reported.

Definitions

Human Development Index (HDI): A composite index measuring average achievement in three basic dimensions of human development—a long and healthy life, knowledge and a decent standard of living. See *Technical note 1* at http://hdr.undp.org/sites/default/files/hdr2020_technical_notes.pdf for details on how the HDI is calculated.

Planetary pressures–adjusted HDI (PHDI): HDI value adjusted by the level of carbon dioxide emissions and material footprint per capita to account for excessive human pressures on the planet. It should be seen as an incentive for transformation. See *Technical note* at http://hdr.undp.org/sites/default/files/phdi_tn.pdf for details on how the PHDI is calculated

Difference from HDI value: Percentage difference between the PHDI value and the HDI value.

Difference from HDI rank: Difference in ranks on the PHDI and the HDI, calculated only for countries for which a PHDI value is calculated.

Adjustment factor for planetary pressures: Arithmetic average of the carbon dioxide emissions index and the material footprint index, both defined below. A high value implies less pressure on the planet.

Carbon dioxide emissions per capita (production): Carbon dioxide emissions produced as a consequence of human activities (use of coal, oil and gas for combustion and industrial processes, gas flaring and cement manufacture) divided by midyear population. Values are territorial emissions, meaning that emissions are attributed to the country in which they physically occur.

Carbon dioxide emissions (production) index: Carbon dioxide emissions per capita (production-based) expressed as an index using a minimum value of 0 and a maximum value of 69.85 tonnes per person. A high value implies less pressure on the planet.

Material footprint per capita: Material footprint is the attribution of global material extraction to domestic final demand of a country. The total material footprint is the sum of the material footprint for biomass, fossil fuels, metal ores and nonmetal ores. Material footprint is calculated as raw material equivalent of imports plus domestic extraction minus raw material equivalents of exports. Material footprint per capita describes the average material use for final demand.

Material footprint index: Material footprint per capita expressed as an index using a minimum value of 0 and a maximum value of 152.58 tonnes per person. A high value implies less pressure on the planet.

Sources

Column 1: Human Development Report Office calculations based on data from UNDESA (2019b), UNESCO Institute for Statistics (2020), United Nations Statistics Division (2020b), World Bank (2020g), Barro and Lee (2018) and IMF (2020d).

Column 2: Calculated as the product of the HDI and the adjustment factor presented in column 5.

Column 3: Calculated based on data in columns 1 and 2.

Column 4: Calculated based on PHDI values and recalculated HDI ranks for countries for which a PHDI value is calculated.

Column 5: Calculated based on data in columns 7 and 9.

Column 6: GCP 2020.

Column 7: Calculated based on data in column 6.

Column 8: UNEP 2020d.

Column 9: Calculated based on data in column 8.

The Human Development Index at 30: Ageing well?

Amartya Sen argued that presenting an alternative to the exclusive concentration on utility (and its "younger brother," real income) in the evaluation of wellbeing and development was key for the success of the first 10 years of the Human Development Report. The genius of Mahbub Ul Haq, Sen argued, was to confederate "large armies of discontent" with the single-minded focus on income and to put forward a "broad and permissive framework for social evaluation" open to multiple concerns—a framework that makes it possible "to have many different things as being simultaneously valuable."[1] The approach came with proposals on accounting for differences and progress in human development that reflected this spirit and were informed by the capability approach.

The Human Development Index (HDI) was introduced to account for a basic set of capabilities—longevity, education and "command over resources to enjoy a decent standard of living."[2] Proxied by income per capita, this third component of the HDI was to be interpreted "strictly as a residual catch-all, to reflect something of other basic capabilities not already incorporated in the measures of longevity and education."[3] Thus, while the indicators for health and education directly reflect capabilities, income is included as something with instrumental value, as a "causal antecedent for basic human capabilities" to account for other "basic concerns that have to be captured in an accounting of elementary capabilities."[4] Those concerns could include freedom from hunger, having shelter, mobility or Adam Smith's notion that "the clothing and other resources one needs 'to appear in public without shame' depends on what other people standardly wear, which in turn could be more expensive in rich societies than in poor ones."[5]

Before starting the Human Development Report, Haq was an influential voice in framing the sustainability debate in terms that reflected the perspective of developing countries.[6] This evolved towards the more recent formulations that tie environmental sustainability with social and economic sustainability, culminating in the 2030 Agenda for Sustainable Development. But as chapter 1 argued, the Report has integrated concerns with environmental degradation and sustainability from the very beginning. Over the years the Report has followed a dual approach in implementing Haq's vision of enhancing human lives through more freedom and opportunity—presenting alternative human development metrics and applying the human development approach to a development theme.[7]

With its visibility and relevance, the HDI has been subjected to its own dose of critical scrutiny. A perennial observation is that the HDI does not include important dimensions of development. The list is long but includes poverty, human rights, happiness, governance, security, environment, wellbeing and social cohesion, among many others.[8] Motivated in part by these "missing" dimensions and in part by the proven success of composite indices and country rankings, the HDI is now released among a plethora of other measures that purport to serve as alternative focal points of measurement either for development or for some particular dimension.

Adding something would inevitably dilute the significance of the constitutive dimensions of human development of the HDI. Additions would thus also diminish its distinctiveness in the now fairly well populated ecosystem of composite indices.[9] It is unclear which missing dimensions could be characterized as a capability.[10] Many, if not most, have been addressed in the narrative parts of Human Development Reports.[11] Thus the HDI has been retained over the years as it was initially intended—an index of basic capabilities, with health and education at their core and income used instrumentally as a residual that accounts for other elemental capabilities.

While the three dimensions have been retained, several modifications have been made. Some were simple changes to the indicators, aimed at better reflecting achievements in the capabilities accounted for in the index. For instance, the literacy rate was dropped as an indicator of education, replaced by a combination of mean years of schooling and expected years of schooling.[12] The Sustainable Development Goals have further shifted education aims away from enrolment rates towards targets related to learning. While that is also the relevant capability that years of schooling meant to capture, more direct measures of learning achievements would take us closer. But data availability remains a challenge.[13] This example is not meant to be settled here but to illustrate the dynamic and iterative process involved in the choice of indicators included in the HDI. This process reflects advances in measurement that better capture capabilities, improvements in our empirical understanding of the real achievement (and shortfalls) that are relevant and the data availability that allows for reasonably comprehensive coverage of countries over time.[14]

In debates over sustainability and environmental pressure, including income in the HDI is seen by some as particularly problematic.[15] But as noted, income should be understood as an index of other basic capabilities beyond health and education. It is crucial to reiterate that the production and command over commodities are seen as instrumental—one of the contributions of the Human Development Report has been to document the very different ways societies make use of their ability to produce commodities to yield very different achievements in capabilities. Furthermore, conversion rate of income into basic capabilities decreases as income rises—which is one reason why income per capita enters into the HDI in logarithmic form.[16] Conversely, additional income is likely to make a big difference in enabling capabilities at low incomes. In fact, the first version of the HDI gave zero weight to income per capita above a certain threshold—defined for the 1990 Report as the mean of the poverty lines in a few high-income countries.[17]

This first version of the HDI could also be interpreted as an expression of the ethical concern for those who have the least, which permeates not only the human development approach but also has broad ethical appeal. It is reflected in the aspiration to "leave no one behind and reach the furthest behind first" of the 2030 Agenda for Sustainable Development, and in Sustainable Development Goal 10, for which one target is having the bottom 40 percent of the population increase its income at a rate greater than the average. But by the second Human Development Report, the constraint of giving zero weight to incomes above the poverty line of rich countries was relaxed because it implied that human development gains above that poverty line were essentially worthless, which was inconsistent with the broader framing of striving for longer and better lives for everyone.[18] There are thus good reasons to include income with logarithmic transformation in the HDI.

The HDI has been complemented over the years with other indices, statistical tables and statistical dashboards to provide a more comprehensive perspective of the relevant data to assess countries on human development. To shine a spotlight on poverty, the Human Development Report introduced in 2010 the Multidimensional Poverty Index, which measures deprivations without including income. In the same year it introduced the Inequality-adjusted HDI, which addresses another criticism of the HDI—it is based on average achievements and does not consider disparities across the population. The Inequality-adjusted HDI discounts the average achievement in each dimension by the level of inequality in that dimension. Building on the pioneering 1995 Human Development Report on gender, which also proposed indices to measure gender inequalities in both wellbeing and agency, the Report now includes two indices on gender, one accounting for differences between men and women on the HDI dimensions, the other a composite of inequalities in empowerment and wellbeing.

In practical terms the Human Development Report has always considered the single index versus dashboards a false dichotomy. Since the beginning, the Report has presented both composite indices (often several) and dashboards (initially in the form of statistical tables aggregated by topics relevant for human development, now complemented by full-fledged dashboards).[19] Improving the metrics of human development implies continuing work on both fronts.

Thus the HDI at 30 years is ageing well. It remains effective as a partial index of basic capabilities essential for wellbeing to be complemented by a broader set of indices and statistics that give a fuller account of the state and prospects of human development.

NOTES

1. This paragraph is based on Sen (2000), with direct quotations from this work. See also Stewart, Ranis and Samman (2018).

2. UNDP 1990, p. 1.

3. Anand and Sen 2000b, p. 86.

4. Anand and Sen 2000b, p. 86.

5. Sen 2005, p. 154. Of course, clothing is used as an example of a broader point: The experience of not living in poverty includes a dimension of social inclusion, of dignity, for which the level of command over commodities is higher in countries with higher income. People may have reasons to value higher incomes far beyond what is required to meet basic subsistence needs.

6. Fukuda-Parr and Muchhala 2020.

7. Haq 1995. Ironically, the success of the HDI may have generated its very own dominance, of the sort that Mahbub Ul Haq rebelled against in the form of income, often overshadowing the narrative component of many Human Development Reports and in the process partially obscuring the critical scrutiny of the human development approach to a wide range of policies, practices and features in areas ranging from the international financial and economic system to intellectual property rights that stand in the way of enhancing human lives and freedoms.

8. See, for instance, Ranis, Stewart and Samman (2006).

9. Kanbur 2020.

10. For a discussion in the context of sustainability, see Malik (2020).

11. Sometimes accompanied by introducing innovative measures of human development related to them.

12. Differences across countries in literacy rates had shrunk considerably by the time this change was implemented in 2010, which partially motivated the drop of literacy, but even a change as simple as this inevitably implies that something is lost. In this case there is no information on learning achievements—for which literacy, however imperfectly, provided some. Recent evidence suggests that as many as 53 percent of 10-year-olds in low- and middle-income countries—and as many as 80 percent in some of the lowest income countries—cannot read and understand a simple written paragraph (World Bank 2019a).

13. Even if there have been some recent advances in the direct measurement of literacy and numeracy, such as those used in the measure of quality of education in producing the World Bank's Human Capital Index (World Bank 2020a). But data are available only for recent years and for a limited number of countries, and the measures used contested.

14. The modification of the way the three components are combined into a single index was more substantial. One strand of critical scrutiny targets the assumption of equal weights across the three dimensions of the HDI. Another persistent line of argument was that the assumption of perfect substitutability, as reflected in the use of the arithmetic mean to aggregate the HDI in the 1990–2010 Human Development Reports allowed for perfect substitutability across the three dimensions. The shift from an arithmetic mean to a geometric one to aggregate the three components of the index was meant, in part, to address this line of concern (Klugman, Rodríguez and Choi 2011; UNDP 2010c). But it generated its own rebuttals, with a debate that continues today (Ravallion 2012). For a recent perspective on the debate, see Rodriguez (2020). Anand (2018) provides a forceful argument for the advantages of the arithmetic mean, showing that using the geometric mean suggests that improvements in life expectancy in lower income countries are "worth" less—when evaluated in terms of income, as implied by the geometric mean aggregation—than in richer countries. This goes against the fundamental human development principle of equality of life claims. Fleurbaey (2019) counters that it is possible to look at this result with a different ethical lens, suggesting that the lower value of life expectancy in a poorer country simply reflects that an impartial observer would rather live a year more of life in a rich country than in a poorer country. As a matter of empirical fact, however, differences in rankings of countries obtained with either method—or with some of the other alternatives proposed—are not very significant (Klasen 2018). But the objections to the geometric mean deserve careful consideration as we think about the future of the HDI, bearing in mind the original objective to have a measure that was simple to communicate and understand by the public, a rough and ready indicator, which the use of the geometric mean does not help with. And worrying too much about substitutability goes against the idea of having many different things as being simultaneously valuable. As Basu and Lòpez-Calva (2011) argue, the capabilities approach compels us to think about sets and to move away from framing welfare evaluation as the maximization of a single variable that is a function of factors that are subject to tradeoffs and marginal rates of substitution.

15. Chhibber 2020.

16. One consequence of this—more than the use of the geometric mean to aggregate the different components of the HDI—is the very low implicit valuation of life expectancy at low income levels (and very high implicit valuation at high income levels). Thus, proposals have been made to use a different transformation of income, such as x to the power of a, where $0 < a < 1$ (see Rodriguez 2020), but those transformations would imply a constant marginal rate of contribution of income to the HDI.

17. Anand and Sen 2000a.

18. The income component has been treated in different ways over the years, with a transition phase in which different weights were used at different levels of income (Anand and Sen 2000a), but the logarithmic transformation now in use represents a balance between a plausible index for basic capabilities beyond health and education (which includes income-relative notions of social standing and dignity), while incorporating the idea that the rate at which incomes can reasonably be seen as indexing those capabilities decreases as incomes go up.

19. The Human Development Report now publish several dashboards, including a dashboard on environmental sustainability and a dashboard on socioeconomic sustainability. The main distinction of these dashboards is the partial ordering and the colour-coding of tercile groups in each indicator for easy visualization and comparison of the country's achievements. The Report's dashboards allow partial grouping of countries by indicator—rather than complete ranking by a composite measure, such as the HDI—that combines multiple indicators after making them commensurable. A complete ranking depends on how component indicators are combined; in contrast, a partial grouping does not require assumptions about normalization, weighting or the functional form of the composite index. Generally, a partial grouping may depend on the predefined values used as thresholds for grouping, expressing what is considered good performance or a target to be achieved. The dashboards divide countries into three groups of approximately equal size (terciles) for each indicator in the dashboard: the top third, the middle third and the bottom third. The intention is not to suggest thresholds or target values for the indicators but to allow a crude assessment of a country's performance relative to others. Three-colour coding is used to visualize the partial grouping of countries by indicator—a simple tool to help users immediately discern a country's performance.

Global inequality in carbon emissions: Shifting from territorial to net emissions by individuals

Lucas Chancel, World Inequality Lab, Paris School of Economics

From territorial emissions to net national emissions

Global carbon emissions from human activities —energy, transport, agriculture, industry, waste, deforestation—today amount to about 56 gigatonnes of carbon dioxide equivalent, or about 7 tonnes per capita a year.[1] Where do these emissions come from? Emissions can be seen in terms of territorial emissions, which include all emissions happening within national boundaries, and net emissions (or carbon footprint), which include emissions produced abroad and incorporated in the goods and services consumed at home.[2] Net emissions provide a more reliable picture of each country's responsibilities for carbon dioxide emissions.[3]

At the global level territorial emissions must by definition equal net emissions, since the world does not trade with another planet. But gaps between territorial and net emissions at the regional and national levels are meaningful, and shifting from one representation to the other might reveal significantly different trends depending on a region's integration into global value chains and economic development.

To what extent does moving from territorial emissions to net emissions reveal different regional trends in greenhouse gas emissions? Today, total territorial emissions are 7.2 gigatonnes of carbon dioxide equivalent for North America, about 15 percent of the world total,[4] and 4.8 gigatonnes of carbon dioxide equivalent for Europe, 10 percent of the world total (figure S7.2.1). Taking into account imported emissions, net emissions are 8 percent above territorial emissions in North America and 27 percent above territorial emissions in Europe.

While territorial emissions show a relatively clear downward trend in Europe since 1990, net emissions associated with Europeans' lifestyles have actually been stable over the past 30 years. In the United States the apparent stability of territorial emissions also masks important variations and a slight increase

overall in net emissions over the past 30 years. This focus on net emissions therefore invites us to reconsider regions' effectiveness at curbing emissions.

Unlike rich countries, which import more carbon than they export, large emerging countries are net exporters (figure S7.2.2). China's net emissions (8 gigatonnes) are 34 percent below its territorial emissions (12.5 gigatonnes) compared with 19 percent in India and 15 percent in Sub-Saharan Africa. Although in China and India net emissions are lower than territorial emissions, the two measures have followed a similar trend over the past three decades—a sharp increase in the 1990s and 2000s followed by relative stability.

Factoring in international trade has implications for global climate policy discussions, as it might change representations of countries' responsibilities in the face of climate change. A better understanding of imported emissions can also be key for domestic policy: In July 2020 EU countries agreed to a carbon tax on emissions imported from abroad (also known as "carbon border adjustment") to finance the Covid-19 recovery package.[5]

While extremely useful, aggregate net emissions figures remain incomplete measures of carbon emissions, just as GDP is insufficient as an indicator of a country's income and wealth dynamics. Ultimately, all carbon flows serve an economic function, which in turn serves individuals when they consume goods and services—whether privately or collectively—or when they invest in the economy. In designing global or national climate mitigation policies, it is thus necessary to go beyond national or regional totals and averages[6] to focus on individuals' emissions and the inequality of those emissions.

Attributing net carbon emissions to individuals

Researchers and statistical offices have combined total net emissions figures such as those presented

Figure S7.2.1 Greenhouse gas emissions and international trade: Europe, North America, Central Asia and other rich countries, 1990–2019

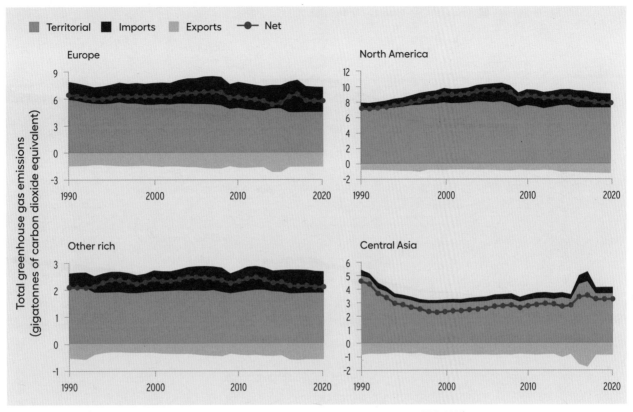

Note: Emissions exclude land use change (about 6 gigatonnes of carbon dioxide equivalent a year in 2015–2020).
Source: World Inequality Lab and Human Development Report Office using the Eora Global Supply Chain Database.

above with inequality statistics to determine emissions levels associated with individuals' consumption.[7] Recent research has found, for instance, that the richest 1 percent of EU households have an annual carbon footprint of 55 tonnes of carbon dioxide equivalent per capita, and only 5 percent of EU households live within sustainable climate targets, estimated at 2.5 tonnes of carbon dioxide equivalent per capita a year. But this analysis focuses on a subset of net emissions because it excludes government and investment-related emissions, which ultimately accrue to individuals. Government and investment-related emissions (called "institutional sectors" in the language of national accounting) account for 35–45 percent of emissions throughout the world. Investment-related emissions have surged over the past two decades in China while remaining broadly stable in Europe and the United States.

To assess individuals' responsibilities associated with climate change, and to design fair and politically sustainable climate mitigation policies, it also seems

critical to factor in investment-related emissions, as much as government expenditure emissions. The emissions associated with investments in machines, buildings and factories, for instance, are the result of decisions by individuals (or groups of individuals) who have power over how capital is invested. So, it seems only logical to attribute the resulting emissions to the individuals who make those decisions rather than to consumers.

If a government or an institution wanted to determine individuals' emissions based on what they consume and how they invest in stocks, for example, they would first need information on those individuals' asset ownership. In a handful of countries such information on the ultimate beneficiaries of asset ownership is available (Norway), while in most it remains extremely opaque after decades of financial deregulation and disinterest in financial transparency matters. This highlights the importance of data transparency in the fight against both tax evasion and extreme inequality on the one hand and climate change on the other.

Figure S7.2.2 Large emerging countries are net exporters of carbon

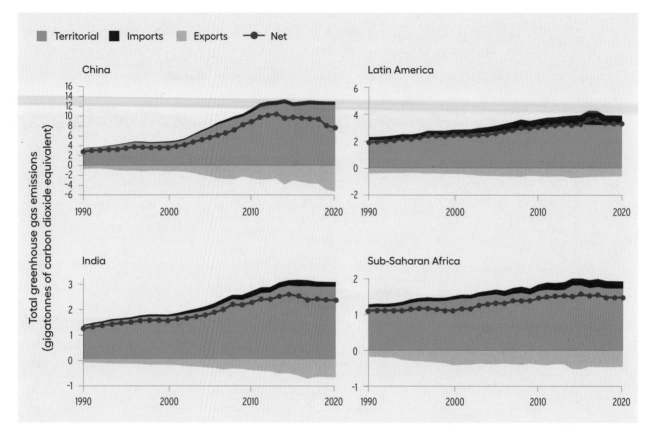

Note: Emissions exclude land use change (about 6 gigatonnes of carbon dioxide equivalent a year in 2015–2020).
Source: World Inequality Lab and Human Development Report Office using the Eora Global Supply Chain Database.

While governments need to move towards more transparency, it is already possible to develop methods to approximate how different income or wealth groups emit carbon dioxide, taking into account consumption, government spending and investment.[8]

Global inequality in individual net carbon emissions

Using net emissions data and the World Inequality Database on global income and wealth inequality, we obtain net emission totals, related both to investment and to private and public consumption for different income groups across countries and world regions. Such numbers should indeed be read with care given the various underlying scenarios.[9]

Emissions at the top of the income distribution may be quite substantial once emissions associated with wealth ownership and investment are factored in. In the benchmark scenario the annual emissions of the wealthiest 1 percent of individuals in 2019

averaged 146 tonnes of carbon dioxide equivalent per capita, up from 110 in 1980 (figure S7.2.3). This group is responsible for more than 20 percent of global emissions.

At the other end of the income distribution, the global poorest 50 percent emits on average 1.4 tonnes of carbon dioxide equivalent per capita a year, a hundredth of what the wealthiest 1 percent emit and just 9 percent of global emissions. Over the past 50 years this group's emissions have remained stable. The world's poorest individuals emit about as much today as they did in 1980, whereas the annual emissions of the richest 1 percent of individuals has increased by 35 tonnes per capita on average.

In 2020 individuals in the middle 40 percent of the income distribution emitted 7 tonnes of carbon dioxide equivalent per capita on average, or about 41 percent of global emissions. The top wealthiest 10 percent emitted 37 tonnes per capita, or 51 percent of global emissions. The top 0.1 percent emits

Figure S7.2.3 The wealthiest 1 percent of individuals worldwide emit 100 times as much carbon dioxide each year as the bottom 50 percent

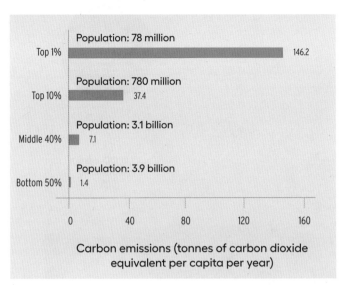

Carbon emissions (tonnes of carbon dioxide equivalent per capita per year)

Source: World Inequality Lab and Human Development Report Office based on the World Inequality Database and the Eora Global Supply Chain Database.

an average of 687 tonnes a year, or 9 percent of global emissions.

While the emissions of the bottom 50 percent can essentially be traced to fossil fuels for heating, cooking, transportation and the consumption of goods, this is not the case higher on the income distribution. The richer individuals are, the more their emissions are embedded in the assets they own and the investments they make. Investment-related emissions totalled 73 tonnes of carbon dioxide equivalent per capita among the wealthiest 1 percent of individuals, or about half of their total emissions. This share has been rising over the past four decades; hence the focus on emissions from investments and not only from consumption (figures S7.2.4 and S7.2.5).

The rise of the middle class in emerging countries has increased that group's emissions. At the same time greater energy efficiency and sluggish income growth among the working and middle classes in rich

Figure S7.2.4 Emissions from the bottom 50 percent over 1975–2020: Small and linked predominantly to consumption

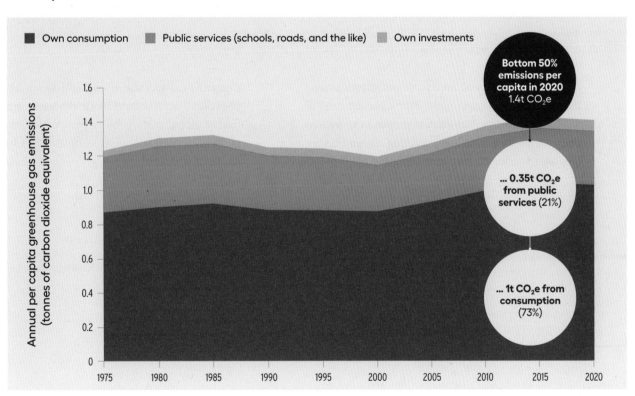

Source: World Inequality Lab and Human Development Report Office based on the World Inequality Database and the Eora Global Supply Chain Database.

Figure S7.2.5 For the wealthiest 1 percent of individuals, the share of investment-related emissions in total emissions has been rising over the past four decades

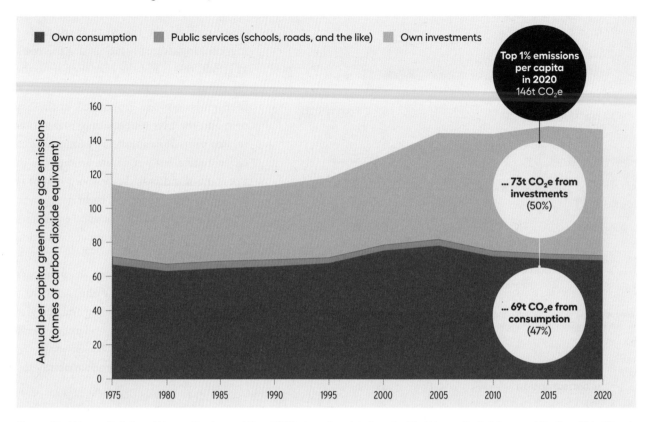

Source: World Inequality Lab and Human Development Report Office based on data from the World Inequality Database and the Eora Global Supply Chain Database.

countries has reduced emissions per capita among these groups. The top 1 percent of earners worldwide have recorded substantial growth in emissions because of increased consumption as well as increased emissions from their wealth and investments (figure S7.2.6). While rising emissions among the poorest 50 percent worldwide represent a challenge from a global sustainability perspective, the importance of emissions among wealthiest 1 percent should not be downplayed.

Figure S7.2.6 The highest income earners worldwide have recorded substantial growth in emissions because of increased consumption as well as increased emissions from their wealth and investments

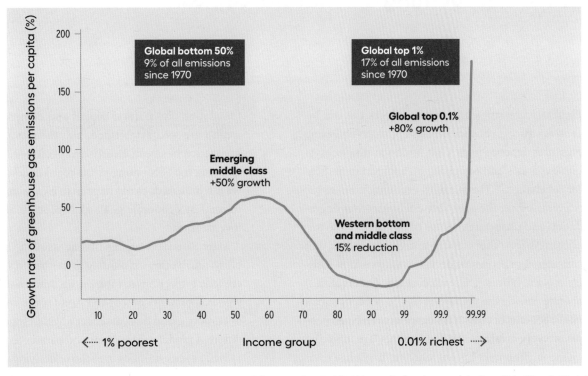

Source: World Inequality and Human Development Report Office based on the World Inequality Database and the Eora Global Supply Chain Database.

NOTES

1   Including land use change, (such as deforestation), the global total is close to 56 gigatonnes of carbon dioxide equivalent today—that is, an extra tonne per capita per year.

2   The underlying method, based on the pioneering work of Nobel Prize–winning economist Wassily Leontief (1936). Leontief (1970) starts from territorial emissions and subtracts all the carbon exported and adds the carbon imported from abroad, by each sector of the economy, to obtain net national emissions, also known as national carbon footprint or consumption-based emissions. See also Bullard and Herendeen (1975) and Krey and others (2014).

3   There is no single standard source of net national emissions, but there exist a few providers of multiregion input output tables, which provide results with similar trends and order of magnitudes but which can differ slightly among each other, because of different methodological choices, imputation methods or raw data. Such providers include the Global Trade Analysis Project, the Eora Global Value Chain Database, the World Input-Output Database, the Organisation for Economic Co-operation and Development Inter-Country Input-Output database and the EXIOBASE database (Lenzen and others 2013). Below, international trade and emissions data are mobilized from the Eora Global Value Chain Database (the only database providing global coverage of all countries between 1990 and today) and from the World Inequality Database.

4   These values do not include emissions associated with deforestation and land use change.

5   European Council 2020.

6   UNDP 2019c.

7   Ivanova and Wood 2020; Wiedenhofer and others 2017.

8   Net emissions related to investments in a country can be attributed in proportions to individuals' share of wealth in the country, for instance. Put simply, if person A owns 1 percent of the wealth in her country, she will be attributed 1 percent of all private investment–related emissions. This is imperfect, but when focusing on anonymized groups of individuals (top 0.1 percent, middle 40 percent and the like), it can provide valuable insights into who is actually responsible for emissions. The allocation of government related emissions also poses several questions. Certain forms of government interventions can be individualized, but others cannot. In which case, who benefits from government emissions associated with defence or justice? As a first approximation, one can assume that these emissions are shared equally across the population.

9   See Chancel (2020) for details on the methodology.

Wealth accounting and natural capital

Planetary pressures are weakly reflected in the incentive structure of societies, and progress on easing pressures depends in part "on understanding ecosystem dynamics and on relying on appropriate indicators of change."[1] The standard economic framework is premised on the idea that environmental degradation and unsustainable use of resources have implications for others, today and in the future, not considered in economic decisions with current institutions and norms. These implications (externalities) operate outside the market—prices do not fully signal either benefits or costs. This happens even when people are very aware of the damage they are inflicting on the environment but are reluctant to change their behaviour for fear others will not do so (a collective action problem).

Viewed from the perspective in which individuals pursue their self-interest and behave rationally, the social costs of degrading nature (essentially those shared by everyone) are not borne by the individuals deriving personal benefits from its use, leading to the tragedy of the commons.[2] This is the foundation for a vast literature on environmental and resource economics that considers how to structure economic incentives to avoid or mitigate the tragedy of the commons (through prices, regulation and assigning property rights to common resources). But market prices cannot fully account for many decisions that put pressure on the environment.[3] So, in the spirit of Elinor Ostrom[4] and as argued in parts I and II of the Report, different institutions and norms as well as assumptions on what drives human behaviour can lead to the identification of mechanisms other than markets to encourage individual consumers and producers to consider, and incorporate in their decision-making, the damage they do to nature and the full benefits they derive from it.

Advances in wealth accounting and measurement of natural capital can shift incentives and open new perspectives for human development metrics.[5] The foundations for natural capital and comprehensive wealth are well established, and their applicability in practice has been clearly demonstrated.[6] But uncovering the accounting prices required to construct wealth indices does not happen in a vacuum. It is informed by economic goals and resource allocation mechanisms.[7]

Marc Fleurbaey argues that in assessing sustainability, uncovering accounting prices has to somehow embody projections of future paths and how they vary with components of wealth.[8] And for the social cost of carbon, estimates can cover a wide range, due to different model assumptions and parameter choices, as well as uncertainties over the underlying geophysical processes modelled.[9] The role of economic inequalities (typically ignored) in estimating the social cost of carbon can have implications as great as those that relate to differences around the discount rate.[10] Ethical stances on future population growth can also have implications of the same order of magnitude,[11] showing the relevance of ethical discussions beyond those related to discount rates.[12] And even migration policy can influence the exposure and vulnerability to climate change that are used to inform climate damages in integrated assessment models.[13]

Part of the limitation in uncovering prices is the representation of the complexity of natural systems, given that the loss or even substantial reduction in the stocks of a species can have dramatic implications for overall ecosystem functioning. Natural systems are rife with bifurcations when critical thresholds or tipping points are reached.[14] Still, these challenges are less important when pricing natural capital to consider changes in value at the margin.[15] Recent climate models have incorporated nonlinear tipping points, such as the melting of the Greenland ice sheet.[16]

Sudhir Anand and Amartya Sen have argued that nondeclining wealth—and understanding sustainability as preserving the opportunity for a certain standard of living—may be relevant from a human development perspective. They do not reject or exclude the concepts but find them lacking for two reasons: "(i) in terms of the limitation of the means-ends relations, and (ii) in terms of the inadequacy of the notion of overall living standards as the thing to be sustained."[17] The limitation of the means-ends relations is due to the nonuniqueness of wealth as a means to the end of human development (even if it can have an important instrumental role) and the contingent nature of its effectiveness as a means (which depends on distribution and the uses to which wealth is put).

While some of the work on natural capital and comprehensive wealth is a collaboration between economists and ecologists, there are critical views, even from within these disciplines. A central objection is that even when the concept of natural capital is accepted, the substitutability of different forms of capital implicit in the notion of preserving comprehensive wealth as the criterion for sustainability settles for a notion of "weak sustainability." That is, it is acceptable to draw down nature's assets as long as the buildup of other forms of capital compensates for those losses.[18]

But the prices considered in building a comprehensive wealth index are not market prices; rather, they reflect the social value of the asset given its current stock level.[19] So prices would increase as stocks decline, admitting different degrees of substitutability

and even complementarity—an extreme form of nonsubstitutability—across different assets (it is even possible to use the framework to incorporate into an asset's price how its stock depends on the interactions across stocks). As an illustration, Seong Do Yun and others calculated the wealth stored in Baltic Sea fisheries, incorporating into the prices of three species of fish the way they interact in the ecosystem.[20] While the two prey species (sprat and herring) were substitutes, they were each complements with cod, the predator species (figure S7.3.1). Moreover, the shadow prices of sprat and herring adjusted when the stock of one species went down, so that the decline in one could compensate for the other, but not at a fixed ratio.[21]

One possible approach to strong versus weak sustainability is to consider the issue an empirical matter and try to determine the degree of substitutability empirically. Francois Cohen, Cameron J. Hepburn and Alexander Teytelboym report a bias in the economic literature towards considering that substitutability is high, but that is based on strong assumptions (perhaps reflecting initial priors on the potential for substitutability) that are subject to challenge or methodological approaches that are far from robust.[22] But the disagreements appear to run deeper.

Consider an exchange reflecting different views on the evolution of modern agriculture. Kenneth Arrow and others cite modern agriculture as an example of

Figure S7.3.1 Contours of shadow prices for different species of fish in the Baltic Sea

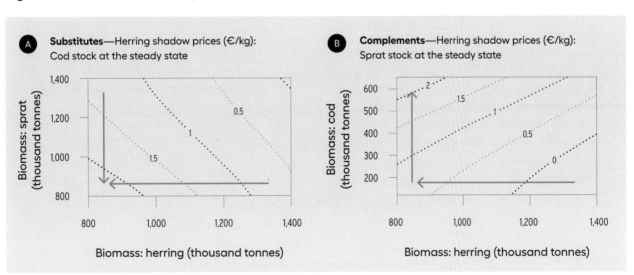

Note: Contours of shadow prices calculated by fixing the cod stock in A and the sprat stock in B. Red arrows are the increasing direction of shadow prices. Downward sloping curves show substitute relationships, and upward sloping curves show complementary relationships.
Source: Yun and others 2017.

how deploying knowledge and capital has enabled agricultural productivity to more than keep up with population growth since the middle of the 20th century.[23] As a result the Malthusian concern (that population growth would run ahead of agricultural production) that re-emerged in more comprehensive formulations in the limits to growth[24] and "population explosion"[25] warnings did not come to pass. But Herman E. Daly and others write: "We, on the contrary, consider modern agriculture a case of substituting one resource base (nonrenewable fossil fuels and fertilizers) for another (renewable sunlight and soil)—not a case of substituting capital funds for resource flows."[26]

The reality for many is that it is simply not possible in the limit to substitute the services provided by ecosystems. The difference between ecological and economic perspectives may be due to ecologists focusing on limit behaviour and economists emphasizing a marginal concept.[27] And if one conceives of strong sustainability as "insisting on preserving every detailed component of natural capital, this would make sustainability totally impossible, in an uninteresting way."[28] In the end, both notions might be relevant, depending on how close one is from critical thresholds or tipping points in natural systems, if we know how close we are.[29]

NOTES

1   Arrow and others 1995, p. 521.

2   A term coined by Hardin (1968), but the idea really harks back to Gordon (1954). We are grateful to Eli Fenichel for this reference.

3   Dietz, Shwom and Whitley 2020; Dietz and Whitley 2018; Nielsen and others 2020; Stern 1986; Stern and others 2016.

4   Ostrom 1990.

5   They are underpinned by clear analytical frameworks and theory—which is not the case for some estimates, such as those presented in Costanza and others 1997 (in fact, Toman 1998 quipped that those estimates seriously underestimate infinity).

6   Fenichel and Abbott 2014; Fenichel, Abbott and Yun 2018.

7   Arrow, Dasgupta and Mäler 2003; Fenichel and Hashida 2019.

8   Fleurbaey 2020; Scovronick and others 2019.

9   Palmer and Stevens 2019.

10   Dennig and others 2015.

11   Scovronick and others 2017.

12   Fleurbaey and others 2019.

13   Benveniste, Oppenheimer and Fleurbaey 2020.

14   A much studied example is the collapse in the population of cod in the Baltic Sea, attributed to passing a threshold linked to the equilibrium between predator (cod) and prey (sprat; Lade and others 2015). Reusch and others (2018) suggest that this could be a model to understand marine systems more broadly. For a conceptual visualization, see Millennium Ecosystem Assessment (2003).

15   As shown in Fenichel and Abbott (2014).

16   Nordhaus 2019.

17   Anand and Sen 2000a, p. 2037.

18   See, for instance, Daly and others (2007), who also pose the question more generally, if neoclassical economics is able to account for physical limits of the scale of production imposed by the natural world. These questions are at the heart of ecological economics, with Daly (1992), arguing that scale should be a key objective of economic analysis and policy, along with efficient allocation and equitable distribution.

19   Fenichel and Abbott 2014; Fenichel, Abbott and Yun 2018.

20   Yun and others 2017.

21   Maher and others (2020) extend this type of analysis to a system with caribou, wolves, deer and oil production.

22   Cohen, Hepburn and Teytelboym 2019.

23   Arrow and others 2007.

24   Such as those presented in Meadows and others (1972).

25   Ehrlich 1968.

26   Daly and others 2007, p. 1362.

27   As argued in Fenichel and Zhao (2015).

28   Fleurbaey 2020, p. 16.

29   Barbier and Hochard 2019.

Evolving metrics to account for environmental degradation and sustainability

How best to reflect concerns with environmental degradation and sustainability in indicators of development? The wealth accounting and natural capital measurement reviewed in chapter 7 and spotlight 7.3 provide an answer, but several other approaches have been considered: dashboards, composite indices, indices that adjust GDP or other existing metrics and indices that focus on measuring how much we overconsume our resources.[1]

An obvious argument for a dashboard approach is to recognize that no single indicator or index can provide a good and comprehensive enough measure. The Sustainable Development Goals implicitly reflect this assumption, proposing 169 targets and more than 230 indicators. Still, having many indicators in a dashboard is always a challenge because it makes interpretation and policy use difficult and because

of the high risk of missing values for many countries. For example, of the 93 Sustainable Development Goal indicators related to the environment, 30 percent lack an agreed methodology, and most that have one lack sufficient data to assess progress.[2]

So interest in composite indices seeks to complement dashboards by providing comprehensible summary indicators that combine relevant information. Some composite indices combine economic, social and environmental dimensions. Much innovation is being applied subnationally, with estimates of a gross ecosystem product, which summarizes the value of the contributions of nature to economic activity, already informing investments in conservation and restoration across China, but it is designed to be applied at the national level and thus could have global applicability.[3] Table S7.4.1 presents an illustrative set of

Table S7.4.1 Composite indices that combine economic, social and environment dimensions

Index	Institution	Data coverage	Description and comments
Green Economy Progress Index[a]	United Nations Environment Programme and Partnership for Action on the Green Economy	105 countries	The Green Economy Progress Index measures progress in improving the wellbeing of current generations relative to economic opportunities, social inclusiveness and environmental protection. It comprises 13 indicators that capture critical issues faced in achieving an inclusive green economy transition (material footprint, energy use, air pollution, protected areas, gender inequality, green trade, renewable energy, Palma ratio, environmental patents, life expectancy, mean years of schooling, pension coverage and access to basic services). It focuses on country progress towards a target set for each individual indicator. A companion dashboard of sustainability includes six indicators (inclusive wealth index, freshwater withdrawals, greenhouse gas emissions, nitrogen emissions, land use, ecological footprint) that track the sustainability of any progress achieved by the index.
Sustainable Society Index[b]	Sustainable Society Foundation	154 countries	The Sustainable Society Index depicts countries' current level of sustainability. It is built up by 21 indicators clustered in seven categories (basic needs, health, personal and social development, natural resources, climate and energy, transition, economy) and finally in three dimensions (human, environmental and economic wellbeing).
Environmental Performance Index[c]	Yale and Columbia Universities	180 countries	The 2020 edition of the Environmental Performance Index ranks 180 countries and is based on 32 indicators—7 cover environmental health and 25 cover ecosystem vitality. The indicators establish how close countries are to established environmental policy goals.
Red List Index	International Union for Conservation of Nature	195 countries	The Red List Index, based on the International Union for Conservation of Nature's Red List of Threatened Species, measures the changing state of global biodiversity. It defines the conservation status of major species groups and measures trends in extinction risk, reporting under Sustainable Development Goal indicator 15.5.1.

a. PAGE 2017.
b. World Bank 2020f.
c. https://epi.yale.edu.
Source: Human Development Report Office.

composite indices at the national level for more than 100 countries.

The HDI is positively associated with some of these indices (figure S7.4.1), perhaps reflecting that higher human development enhances the ability to invest in both people and ecosystems. But for the most part these indices inform about a mix of current environmental quality or pressure on resources but do not indicate whether a country is actually on a sustainable path.

A related approach is adjusting GDP (or GNI) to account for environmental degradation and natural resource depletion.[4] The System of Economic and Environmental Accounts proposes doing so as an extension of the concept of net domestic product. Just as GDP (gross) is turned into net domestic product by accounting for the consumption of fixed capital (depreciation of produced capital), an environmentally adjusted GDP considers the flow of damages to the environment. Adjusted net savings, also known as genuine savings or genuine investment, builds on these concepts but reformulates them as stocks of wealth rather than flows of income or consumption. It is computed as net national savings plus education expenditure and minus energy depletion, mineral depletion, net forest depletion and carbon dioxide and particulate emissions damage (table S7.4.2).

An accounting shortcoming of adjusted net savings is that the adjustment for environmental degradation is limited to a restricted set of pollutants. The calculations do not include other important sources of environmental degradation, such as underground water depletion, unsustainable fisheries, soil degradation or biodiversity loss. And the World Bank adds current education spending to indicate investment in human capital but not health expenditures.[5] If the logic is that education spending improves education, then if human capital is depreciating through morbidity and mortality, health spending that potentially increases life expectancy could also be seen as increasing human capital.[6] Similarly, as discussed in spotlight 7.3, pricing environmental degradation is tricky because the relevant prices are not necessarily those provided by current market valuations, which undervalue nature and are myopic relative to the future. Shadow prices that fully account for the social value of capital could be used, and these can adjust unboundedly when some stock approaches a critical value.

Figure S7.4.1 The Human Development Index is positively associated with the Environmental Performance Index

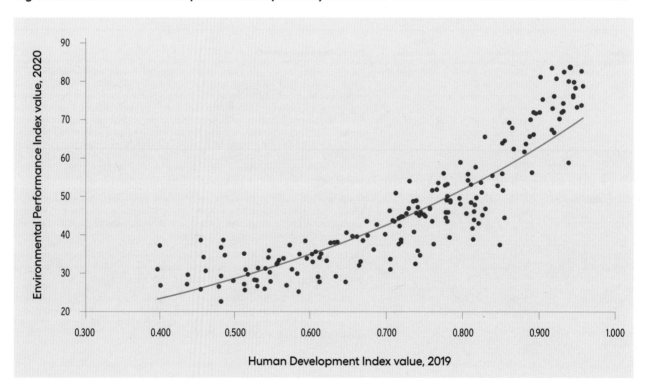

Source: Human Development Report Office calculations based on Human Development Index values from table 1 in the statistical annex and Environmental Performance Index data from Wendling and others (2020).

Table S7.4.2 Indicators of national savings

Index	Institution	Data coverage	Description and comments
Adjusted net savings (current $, percent of GNI)	World Bank, Organisation for Economic Co-operation and Development	More than 150 countries	Adjusted net savings equals net national savings plus education expenditure and minus energy depletion, mineral depletion, net forest depletion, and carbon dioxide and particulate emissions damage.
Net national savings (current $, current local currency unit, percent of GDP)	World Bank, Organisation for Economic Co-operation and Development	Up to 194 countries	Net national savings equals gross national savings minus consumption of fixed capital.
Gross savings (current $, current local currency unit, percent of GDP)	World Bank, Organisation for Economic Co-operation and Development	Up to 194 countries	Gross national savings equals GNI minus final consumption expenditure (former total consumption) plus net transfers.
Gross domestic savings (current $, current local currency unit, percent of GDP)	World Bank, Organisation for Economic Co-operation and Development	Up to 194 countries	Gross domestic savings equals GDP minus final consumption expenditure.
Adjusted net national income (current $, current local currency unit)	World Bank	Up to 194 countries	Adjusted net national income equals GNI minus consumption of fixed capital and natural resources depletion.

Source: Compiled by the Human Development Report Office based on metadata available at World Bank (2020f).

Indices that measure how much we are overconsuming our resources include estimates of footprints as indicators of the pressure of human activities on the environment. The ecological footprint tracks demand for biocapacity compared with availability of biocapacity.[7] It measures how much "area" of biologically productive land and water that human activities require in order to produce all the resources consumed and to absorb the waste generated.[8] Put another way, the ecological footprint measures human appropriation and the biosphere's supply of ecosystem products and services as the bioproductive land and sea area needed to supply these products and services.[9] Biocapacity is a measure of the amount of biologically productive land and sea area available to provide ecosystem services.

Global demand for biocapacity, as measured by the ecological footprint, is largely explained by carbon dioxide emissions, expressed in hectares of forest needed for carbon sequestration (figure S7.4.2).[10] These are conservative accounts: biocapacity is overestimated because it does not consider land degradation and long-term sustainability of resource extraction. In turn, the ecological footprint might be underestimated because it does not measure human demand of freshwater consumption, soil erosion or emissions of greenhouse gases other than carbon

dioxide.[11] However, the aggregate magnitude of ecological footprint is sensitive to the methodology used to estimate the effect of carbon emissions.[12]

Measures of carbon footprint are designed to account for greenhouse gas emissions that are caused directly and indirectly by an activity or accumulated over the lifecycle of a product.[13] It has become a widely referenced environmental protection indicator, benefiting mostly from the work of the Intergovernmental Panel on Climate Change and the climate change community. The carbon footprint considers emissions of the seven greenhouse gases framed by the Kyoto Protocol (carbon dioxide, methane, nitrous oxide, perfluorocarbons, hydrofluorocarbons, sulphur hexafluoride and nitrogen trifluoride).[14] Emissions are typically accounted for through a lifecycle perspective, including all stages—from raw material extraction to the end of production. The carbon footprint is quantified using global warming potential,[15] which represents the quantities of greenhouse gas emissions that contribute to climate change. A specific time horizon is usually considered, such as 100 years.[16] The carbon footprint also has an interesting feature of being computable at any level of disaggregation. This makes it a powerful instrument for monitoring the behaviour of individual actors.

Figure S7.4.2 Global demand for biocapacity as measured by the ecological footprint is largely explained by carbon dioxide emissions

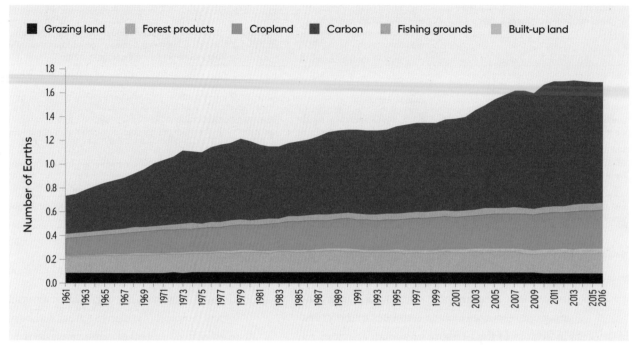

■ Grazing land   ■ Forest products   ■ Cropland   ■ Carbon   ■ Fishing grounds   ■ Built-up land

Source: Global Footprint Network 2019.

NOTES

1   For a recent review, see Dizdaroglu (2017).

2   UNEP 2019d.

3   Ouyang and others 2020. This is part of the broader efforts to draw on the value of natural capital to inform sustainable development in China (Guerry and others 2015; Ouyang and others 2016; Zheng and others 2019). See also D'Odorico and others (2020) for estimates of the value of water. See Mohan and others (2020) for an alternative approach.

4   See, for instance, Muller, Mendelsohn, and Nordhaus (2011).

5   Kraay 2018.

6   Although this is challenging to do, as illustrated also in Jones (2016).

7   Wackernagel and Rees 1996; Wackernagel and others 2019.

8   Lin and others 2018; Wackernagel and Rees 1996.

9   Borucke and others 2013.

10   Extracted from Global Footprint Network 2019.

11   Borucke and others 2013.

12   Blomqvist and others 2013.

13   Fang, Heijungs and De Snoo 2015. One example is the carbon footprint computed by the Global Footprint Network as an input for the ecological footprint (https://www.footprintnetwork.org/our-work/climate-change/).

14   WRI 2013.

15   Høgevold 2003.

16   These greenhouse gases, weighted by their global warming potential value, are expressed in carbon dioxide equivalents. See explanations in Our World in Data (2020a, b). "The GWP [global warming potential] measures the relative warming impact of one molecule or unit mass of a greenhouse gas relative to carbon dioxide over a given timescale—usually over 100 years. For example, one tonne of methane would have 34 times the warming impact of a tonne of carbon dioxide over a 100-year period. GWP100 values are used to combine greenhouse gases into a single metric of emissions called carbon dioxide equivalents (CO2-eq). CO2-eq is then derived by multiplying the mass of emissions of a specific greenhouse gas by its equivalent GWP100 factor. The sum of all gases in their CO2-eq form provides a measure of total greenhouse gas emissions."

Adding environmental and sustainability dimensions to the Human Development Index

Proposals to adjust the Human Development Index (HDI) by adding environmental dimensions include the variant proposed by Casilda Lasso De La Vega and Ana Marta Urrutia, who replaced the standard of living term with a harmonic mean of income and an environmental behaviour indicator, defined as 1 minus a normalized measure of carbon dioxide emissions per capita.[1] The harmonic mean is a special case of the constant elasticity of substitution function, which introduces imperfect substitutability but no complementarity between income and the environment indicator. This adjustment penalizes uneven patterns of economic development (those where progress in environmental behaviour far outstrips progress in economic growth).

An alternative approach added a fourth component to the index to account for air pollution, water pollution, soil pollution from agriculture and energy consumption.[2] The authors also suggested modifying the health index by adding a measure of employment, which they argue allows the health component to work as a proxy for social stability. Similarly, Ajay Chhibber and Rachid Laajaj's Global Development Index included a fourth dimension, environment, with four indicators in the HDI.[3] They distinguished two aspects of environmental costs—those related to damages that the country inflicted on its own nature and people through unsustainable development, such as air pollution, soil erosion or poor water quality, and those related damages to other countries through carbon dioxide emissions, ocean acidification or biodiversity loss. Two indicators in the first environmental subdimension related to local impact are sulphur dioxide emissions and water scarcity (measured by water withdrawal as a share of renewable water resources), and two indicators in the global impact subdimension are carbon dioxide emissions per capita and share of renewable energy in total energy consumption. A simple average with equal weights allowed perfect substitutability between

four dimensions. Chhibber and Laajaj also suggested replacing life expectancy with health-adjusted life expectancy.

Another proposal involved simply adding carbon dioxide emissions per capita to the HDI using the territorial allocation of the production-based carbon emissions as a summary measure of all other degradation of environment, including loss of biodiversity and pollution.[4] The justification for this simplicity parallels one usually given for using life expectancy as a representative of healthy longevity in the HDI. The authors interpreted the addition of carbon emissions as accounting for the cost of one country's quality of life to another's, because the high quality of life enjoyed in a country with high carbon emissions comes at a price for the quality of life in other countries, particularly developing countries, and for future generations.

Giangiacomo Bravo's critical review of this index found a very high correlation with the HDI (.98)[5] and its components but a low correlation with environmental indices and indicators. Bravo concluded that "a little is better than nothing" but that it is adding little to distinguish between ecosystem destruction and welfare.

More recent research has further explored adding an environmental dimension—carbon dioxide emissions per capita—and the freedom dimension based on human and political rights.[6] For an environmentally-centred sustainable HDI the authors suggested a novel method of aggregation implying that the degree of substitutability is linked directly to a country's general level of wellbeing. This form penalizes heterogeneity, so the environmentally-centred sustainable HDI heavily penalized countries with high carbon dioxide emissions. It was calculated using data for 2013 and resulted in substantial changes in country ranks compared with the HDI.

Eric Neumayer suggested leaving the HDI as it is and adding sustainability concerns as an external qualification to the achieved level of human development.[7] His proposal is to complement the HDI with one or preferably two pieces of additional information on sustainability—one that he considered to reflect weak sustainability, the other strong sustainability.

As a weak measure of sustainability, Neumayer suggested genuine savings (adjusted net savings) because it is available for a large sample of countries over a long period.[8] Some of its notable weaknesses were mentioned in spotlight 7.4: The coverage of both nonrenewable and renewable resources is limited.[9] High and very high human development countries typically have high net saving rates (figure S7.5.1), but if more pollutants were taken into account, the picture would likely change. And adjusted net savings is based on a social cost of carbon of $30 per tonne, far below other estimates, as discussed in chapter 7.

As a measure for what he considered strong sustainability, Neumayer suggested the ecological footprint. Although the ecological footprint uses land area instead of money as a yardstick, there is possible substitutability within the considered natural capital, which may be problematic in the strong sustainability

sense.[10] The focus of the ecological footprint is consumption, so the consumer rather than the producer is "billed" for the impact on nature.[11] Neumayer suggested constructing a table with values of the HDI, ecological footprint and adjusted net savings. He then suggested that the sustainability measures to partially rank countries in two groups—sustainable and unsustainable. This proposal can be further developed by considering the individual gaps of countries from the available biocapacity or from a 0 value of the adjusted net savings. Countries could also be partially ranked by each sustainability measure (table S7.5.1).

Planetary boundaries

This spotlight concludes with an exploration built on the planetary boundary framework described in chapter 2. An index of planetary pressure is proposed here that can be compared with the HDI in the same way that Neumayer proposed.[12] Planetary boundaries are interdependent, but two of them, climate change and biodiversity, are considered core boundaries in part because action aimed at addressing

Figure S7.5.1 High human development index values go along with positive adjusted net savings

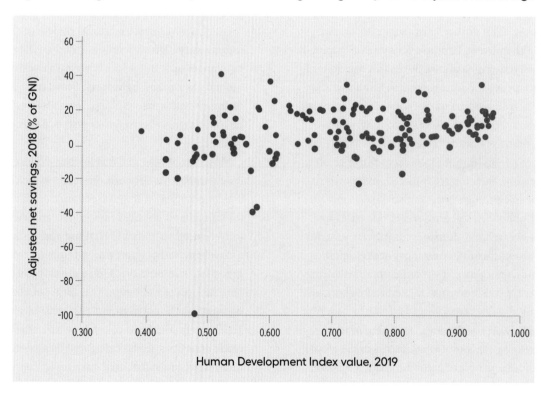

Note: Data for adjusted net savings refer to 2018 or the most recent year available.
Source: Human Development Report Office calculations based on Human Development Index values from table 1 in the statistical annex and adjusted net savings data from World Bank (2020e).

Table S7.5.1 Gaps from sustainable values of the ecological footprint and adjusted net savings

HDI rank, 2019	Country	Adjusted net savings		Ecological footprint		
		Value	Rank[a]	Global hectares per person	Rank[a]	Ecological reserve[b]
1	Norway	18.2	31	5.5	152	-3.9
2	Ireland	16.1	41	5.1	147	-3.5
2	Switzerland	16.9	36	4.6	142	-3.0
6	Germany	14.4	52	4.8	145	-3.2
7	Sweden	17.8	32	6.5	164	-4.9
8	Australia	4.4	98	6.6	165	-5.0
8	Netherlands	19.2	28	4.8	144	-3.2
10	Denmark	19.4	25	6.8	167	-5.2
11	Finland	10.8	64	6.3	162	-4.7
11	Singapore	34.7	4	5.9	157	-4.3
13	United Kingdom	3.0	109	4.4	136	-2.8
14	Belgium	11.1	62	6.3	161	-4.7
14	New Zealand	10.1	69	4.7	143	-3.1
16	Canada	6.0	86	7.7	170	-6.1
17	United States	5.6	87	8.1	171	-6.5
175	Congo (Democratic Republic of the)	-7.9	141	0.7	6	0.9
175	Guinea-Bissau	-2.2	128	1.5	46	0.1
175	Liberia	-99.4	154	1.1	28	0.5
178	Guinea	-10.2	145	1.6	50	0.0
181	Mozambique	5.1	91	0.8	10	0.8
182	Burkina Faso	0.6	116	1.2	33	0.4
182	Sierra Leone	-20.3	150	1.2	32	0.4
184	Mali	2.5	112	1.6	51	0.0
185	Burundi	-16.9	148	0.7	3	0.9
185	South Sudan	-9.2	144	1.5	45	0.1
189	Niger	7.2	78	1.7	55	-0.1

a. Calculated by the Human Development Report Office.
b. Biocapacity minus ecological footprint. Measured in global hectares per person.
Note: Among the top and bottom countries by Human Development Index (HDI) rank, the most unsustainable countries according to each measure are in red. Data for adjusted net savings refer to 2018 or the most recent year available since 2008. Data for ecological footprint accounts refer to 2016.
Source: Human Development Report Office based on HDI values from table 1 of the statistical annex, adjusted net savings data from World Bank (2020e) and ecological footprint data (consumption-based) from Global Footprint Network (2019).

them would also alleviate pressure on others—as reducing carbon dioxide emissions would reduce the risk of ocean acidification.[13] One challenge with the planetary boundary approach is its validity at scales other than global, as is the case for nitrogen and phosphorus cycles (chapter 2). Thus proposals to bring the boundaries from the global to the national level have limitations and must be interpreted with some caution. Still, assessing the extent to which planetary boundaries are being transgressed when global boundaries are brought to the national level provides useful information on countries' contribution to planetary pressures: avoiding the transgression of regional and national boundaries "would thus contribute to an aggregate outcome within a planetary-level safe operating space."[14] The definition of national boundaries follows proposals in the literature,[15] and excessive pressure is measured by the extent to which the values of component indicators exceed each planetary boundary.[16] The index of excessive pressure on the planet proposed here combines indicators of carbon dioxide emissions,

nitrogen use, land use, freshwater withdrawals and material footprint—the last of which is not part of the planetary boundaries framework. Table S7.5.2 summarizes planetary boundaries and their expressions per capita or per area unit.[17] It also shows the number of countries within boundaries for these indicators. Only four countries are within boundaries for all five indicators—Gambia, Ghana, Republic of Moldova and Rwanda.

The indicator values are standardized by the corresponding boundary expressed per capita or per area unit. The standardized value represents the order of transgression by which the country's emissions, environmental degradation or overconsumption exceed the boundaries.[18] Among the 142 countries with information on all five index of excessive pressure on the planet indicators, the index equals the quadratic mean order of overshooting across all considered indicators (table S7.5.3).

When ranked by index of excessive pressure on the planet value (the quadratic mean order of transgressions), 6 of the 10 countries in the table would be

Table S7.5.2 Planetary boundaries per capita or per area unit

Biophysical indicator	Planetary boundary	Per capita or per area unit boundary	Countries with data	Countries within boundaries[a]
Carbon dioxide emissions (production)	2 degrees Celsius warming	1.61 tonnes per year	193	74
Nitrogen as fertilizer nutrient	62 teragrams per year	39.4 tonnes per 1,000 hectares of cropland per year	152	71
Freshwater withdrawals	4,000 cubic kilometres per year	565 cubic metres	179	122
Change in forest area	47.9 million square kilometres by 2050	Annual average growth of forest area by 0.25 percent since 1990	187	53
Material footprint[b]	50 gigatonnes per year	7.2 tonnes per year	172	72

a. Data refer to 2018 or the most recent year available.
b. Material footprint is not part of the planetary boundaries framework, so this is a maximum sustainable value.
Source: Human Development Report Office calculations based on Human Development Index values from table 1 in the statistical annex, carbon dioxide emissions data from GCP (2020), nitrogen and freshwater withdrawals data from FAO (2020a), forest area data from World Bank (2020e) and material footprint data from UNEP (2020d).

Table S7.5.3 Balance sheet of transgressions of the top 10 Human Development Index–ranked countries with information on all five index of excessive pressure on the planet indicators

Country	Human Development Index, 2019		Order of transgression					Index of excessive pressure on the planet		Number of transgressed boundaries
	Value	Rank	Carbon dioxide emissions (production)	Nitrogen as fertilizer nutrient	Freshwater withdrawals	Change in forest area	Material footprint	Value	Rank	
Norway	0.957	1	5.2	3.2	1.1	2.0	5.3	3.7	121	5
Switzerland	0.955	2	2.7	2.7	0.0	0.0	4.5	2.6	84	3
Iceland	0.949	4	6.7	2.5	1.4	0.0	4.8	3.9	122	4
Germany	0.947	6	5.7	2.9	0.0	1.8	3.2	3.3	109	4
Sweden	0.945	7	2.6	1.8	0.0	2.0	4.5	2.6	83	4
Australia	0.944	8	10.5	1.1	1.2	2.4	6.0	5.6	135	5
Denmark	0.940	10	3.8	2.0	0.0	0.0	3.4	2.4	73	3
Finland	0.938	11	5.3	1.6	2.2	1.8	5.0	3.6	118	5
United Kingdom	0.932	13	3.5	4.3	0.0	0.0	3.2	2.9	95	3
Belgium	0.931	14	5.4	4.9	0.0	1.6	3.3	3.7	120	4

Note: Covers 142 countries with data for all five indicators. A value of 0 indicates no transgression.
Source: Human Development Report Office calculations based on Human Development Index values from table 1 in the statistical annex, carbon dioxide emissions data from GCP (2020), nitrogen and freshwater withdrawals data from FAO (2020a), forest area data from World Bank (2020e) and material footprint data from UNEP (2020d).

ranked below 100, and all of them would be ranked below 70. Other important information provided by the index is the number of boundaries that each country transgressed. Six of the 10 countries in the table have their largest transgression in carbon dioxide emissions, three have their largest transgression in material footprint and one (United Kingdom) has their largest in nitrogen.

NOTES

1. de La Vega and Urrutia 2001.

2. Costantini and Monni 2005.

3. Chhibber and Laajaj 2008.

4. Bravo 2014; Togtokh 2011; Togtokh and Gaffney 2010.

5. Bravo 2014.

6. Biggeri and Mauro 2018.

7. Neumayer 2013.

8. Neumayer 2013.

9. For example, forests are an important renewable resource that are included in adjusted net savings, but water, soil and biodiversity are also important renewables and should be included into the calculation. Similarly, loss of natural capital due to environmental pollution is underestimated, since only two pollutants are included. Ideally, damage from emissions of, for example, sulphur oxides, nitrogen oxides, faecal coliforms and particulate matter should also be included.

10. Neumayer 2013.

11. This is quite different from adjusted net savings, which attributes natural capital depreciation from resource extraction to the extracting, not the consuming country, according to the capital maintenance principle. Recently, the economic footprint has been produced, accounting for the impact of production as well. But perhaps, more importantly, the economic footprint measures a country's contribution to global strong unsustainability rather than how a country is affected by strong unsustainability of others. A good example is the Maldives, a country that is likely to become a victim of the strong unsustainability of others in the future, although it does not have an unsustainably high ecological footprint. What matters to countries like the Maldives is whether globally there is strong unsustainability in the form of, for example, unsustainably high greenhouse gas emissions, not so much their own contribution to it. So the reasoning is that by identifying contributors to the global unsustainability, the progress towards strong sustainability can be made globally if the high contributors reduce their own contributions.

12. The framework identifies nine critical boundaries related to essential planetary processes at the global scale. Only seven boundaries are currently measured: climate change (carbon dioxide concentration in the atmosphere less than 350 parts per million), ocean acidification (mean surface seawater saturation state with respect to aragonite at least 80 percent of preindustrial levels), stratospheric ozone (less than 5 percent reduction in ozone concentration from preindustrial level of 290 Dobson units), biogeochemical nitrogen cycle (limit industrial and agricultural fixation of N_2 to 35 teragrams per year) and phosphorus cycle (annual phosphorus inflow to oceans not to exceed 10 times the natural background weathering of phosphorus), global freshwater use (less than 4,000 cubic kilometres per year of consumptive use of runoff resources), land system change (less than 15 percent of the ice-free land surface under cropland) and the rate at which biological diversity is lost (less than 10 extinctions per million species per year). The two additional planetary boundaries for which scientists have not yet been able to determine a boundary level are chemical pollution and atmospheric aerosol loading.

13. Steffen and others 2015.

14. Steffen and others 2015, p. 2.

15. O'Neill and others 2018; Steffen and others 2015.

16. This work is inspired and based on works of Hickel (2019a, 2020b) and O'Neill and others (2018).

17. For carbon dioxide emissions we adopt the approach by O'Neill and others (2018) and consider the planetary boundary derived from the target of limiting global warming to 2 degrees Celsius, as emphasized in the Paris Agreement. This target roughly translates to emissions per capita of 1.61 tonnes of carbon dioxide per year. In Steffen and others (2015) the planetary boundary for nitrogen is set at 62 teragrams per year. O'Neill and others (2018) expressed this quantity as 8.9 kilograms per capita per year. Because nitrogen is an active compound in the fertilizers used in agriculture, it seems that it would be better to express it per area unit of agricultural land than per capita. However, not all types of agricultural land require fertilizers, so we opted to look at the planetary boundary expressed in tonnes per 1,000 hectares of cropland—that is, arable land plus permanent cropland. In 2016 the size of cropland at the global level was 1,575,238,243 hectares, so the planetary boundary for the nitrogen can be expressed as 39.4 tonnes per 1,000 hectares of arable land.

Rockström and others (2009a) specified the planetary boundary for freshwater use as a maximum global withdrawal of 4,000 cubic kilometres per year of blue water, which is water from rivers, lakes, reservoirs and renewable groundwater stores. Despite thorough debates, research findings and proposed revisions in the literature, the practical implications on assessment of the planetary boundaries were, overall, minor (O'Neill and others 2018). Although we recognized that the research is still in progress, we decided to follow the originally established global boundary of 4,000 cubic kilometres per year. Data on annual freshwater withdrawal available from the Food and Agriculture Organization of the United Nations AQUASTAT database cover many countries, but the most recent available year of data is scattered in a large time interval, from 1990 to 2017. Using the global population of 2012 (median year of the latest data on withdrawal available) of 7.086 billion, we arrived at a per capita boundary of 565 cubic metres per year. This is slightly lower than the 574 cubic metres used by O'Neill and others (2018).

The area of forested land that is maintained on the ice-free land surface is expressed as a percentage of the potential area of forested land in the Holocene. Based on previous research, the planetary boundary was set at 75 percent of potential forest cover, meaning that approximately 47.9 million square kilometres of the ice-free land surface of Earth should be maintained as forest. This boundary has been constructed as a weighted aggregate of three individual biome boundaries. For tropical and boreal forests the boundary was set at 85 percent of potential forest cover, while for temperate forests the boundary was proposed as 50 percent of the potential forest cover. A challenging issue is how to determine the national share of the planetary boundary so that it is possible to identify countries that are transgressing. With the idea to increase the global forest to the extent of 47.9 million square kilometres by 2050, it means that the average annual growth rate of area under forest should be about 0.25 percent since 1990.

Material footprint is an indicator of strong sustainability that does not link directly to a planetary boundary. However, we include it in the index of excessive pressure on the planet analysis because material use is an important indicator of the environmental pressure exerted by socioeconomic activities.

Following O'Neill and others (2018), we adopt a global target of 50 gigatonnes per year, although we caution that the literature is not very mature in this area. This value leads to a per capita target of 7.2 tonnes per year, assuming a world population of 7 billion people.

18. For each indicator, except for change in forest area, the standardized value equals the observed value divided by the boundary. For change in forest area, the standardized value equals 2 minus the ratio between the observed value and the boundary.

Notes
and
references

Notes

OVERVIEW

1   Berger 2020; Carroll and others 2018; Cheng and others 2007; Johnson and others 2020; Morse and others 2012.

2   Dolce 2020; Guzman 2020; Lam 2020; Norman 2020.

3   Bloch 2020; Guy 2020a; Mega 2020; Witze 2020a.

4   Díaz and others 2019a. See also Díaz and others 2019b.

5   As argued in Kolbert (2014). See also Ceballos, Ehrlich and Raven (2020) and Torres-Romero and others (2020) .

6   Social imbalances refer to asymmetries in opportunities, wealth and power across groups of people. The term "balance" is used recognizing that the Earth system has displayed many different states over time and that the planet and its subsystems (including the biosphere, which comprises all life on Earth) are dynamic and constantly evolving. So it should not be seen as aiming to capture a "balance of nature" concept or a return to some prior state of a more desirable equilibrium. It is meant simply as shorthand for dangerous planetary change for life on Earth, including for people. We are grateful to Victor Galaz of the Stockholm Resilience Centre and Erle C. Ellis of the University of Maryland for help clarifying this concept and terminology.

7   UNDP 2019c.

8   Carleton and others 2020.

9   For the interaction between equity and sustainability, see Leach and others (2018).

10 Hyde 2020.

11 See also the discussion in the 2019 Human Development Report (UNDP 2019c) on how inequalities make acting on climate change more difficult.

12 As a compelling symbolic characterization of the Anthropocene, by the end of 2020 the mass material output of human activities (which has doubled every 20 years in the recent past) will for the first time ever overtake natural biomass (Elhacham and others 2020). See the discussion in chapter 2 of the Report. For an early framing of the concept of the Anthropocene, see (Steffen, Crutzen and McNeill 2007). The original proposal was made by Crutzen (2002) and Crutzen and Stoermer (2000). See also Steffen and others (2016). Zalasiewicz and others (2008) raised the possibility of formalizing a new geological epoch, and Zalasiewicz came to lead the Working Group on the Anthropocene that formally provisionally recommended in August 2016 to the International Union of Geological Sciences the designation of the Anthropocene as the new geological epoch, with a start date in the mid-20th century. This was followed by a binding vote of the working group affirming these recommendations in May 2019 (http://quaternary.stratigraphy.org/working-groups/anthropocene/). For a recent review, see Ellis (2018a).

13 IEP 2020.

14 And how to work together towards a better future when our values and perspectives differ. See Ellis (2018b, 2019a).

15 This observation is also relevant in the context of narratives of societal collapse, as discussed in chapter 4 of the Report. See Butzer and Endfield (2012).

16 UNDP 2019c.

17 Steffen and others 2015.

18 UNDP 2019c.

19 United Nations 2020i.

20 World Bank 2020b. In addition, countries might experience a setback equivalent to 9 years of progress on the Multidimensional Poverty Index (UNDP and OPHI 2020).

21 UNDP 2020b.

22 Amartya Sen (Sen 2013., p. 7) emphasized the importance of this shift in seeing people as agents, rather than patients, as we confront the challenges of the Anthropocene: "The quandary of unsustainability may be our predicament, but the task of solving it is ours as well. The nature of the problem, its fuller appreciation and the ways and means of solving it all belong to us—humanity as a whole. If there is a subject on which collaboration and non-divisive commitments are needed, this surely is it. But in order to make this possible and effective, we need a vision of mankind not as patients whose interests have to be looked after, but as agents who can do effective things—both individually and jointly."

23 See also Ellis (2019b).

24 As discussed in WHO (2019b) and Wipfli and Samet (2016).

25 Bilano and others 2015.

26 World Health Organization 2018, 2020.

27 See Carson (1962), Turner and Isenberg (2020) and Wills (2020).

28 Fischer-Kowalski and Weisz 1999; Leach and others 2018; Weisz and Clark 2011.

29 Downing and others 2020; Lele 2020; Steffen and others 2018.

30 Cai, Lenton and Lontzek 2016; Lenton 2013.

31 Nyström and others 2019.

32 On the importance of biocultural diversity, see Merçon and others (2019) and (Maffi 2005). On broader perspectives on resilience, see Folke (2016), Lenton (2020) and Reyers and others (2018).

33 Lenton and others 2008; Steffen and others 2018.

34 Galaz, Collste and Moore 2020. See also Maffi (2005).

35 McDonnell 2019.

36 Coady and others 2019. Jewell and others (2018) found a smaller impact on emissions than that reported by Coady and others (2017), but Parry (2018) explains the discrepancy in terms of the scope of the consideration of the impact of subsidies in the two studies, with Coady and others (2019) having a broader perspective, and reiterates the large impact of subsidies on emissions .

37 Griscom and others 2017.

38 Climate Action Tracker 2020, McCurry 2020a, b; Sengupta 2020.

39 European Commission 2019 .

40 de Botton 2020.

CHAPTER 1

1   Sen 2013, p. 7.

2   Nagendra 2018, p. 486.

3   Carroll and others 2018; Morse and others 2012.

4   Berger 2020; Cheng and others 2007.

5   In part as a result of new areas being opened up to people to exploit wildlife: "Exploitation of wildlife through hunting and trade facilitates close contact between wildlife and humans, and our findings provide further evidence that exploitation, as well as anthropogenic activities that have caused losses in wildlife habitat quality, have increased opportunities for animal–human interactions and facilitated zoonotic disease transmission" (Johnson and others 2020, p. 1924).

6   For an early framing of the concept of the Anthropocene, see Steffen, Crutzen and McNeill (2007). Chapter 2 presents the evidence and discusses different perspectives—from Earth systems science, from ecology and geology and from the social sciences and humanities—around the concept.

7   The term "balance" is used recognizing that the Earth system has displayed many different

states over time and that the planet and its subsystems (including the biosphere, which comprises all life on Earth) are dynamic and constantly evolving. So it should not be seen as aiming to capture a "balance of nature" concept or a return to some prior state of a more desirable equilibrium. It is meant simply as shorthand for dangerous planetary change for life on Earth, including for people. We are grateful to Victor Galaz of the Stockholm Resilience Centre and Erle C. Ellis of the University of Maryland for help clarifying this concept and terminology.

8   Leach and others 2018, p. 2.

9   UNDP 1990, p. 7.

10 UNDP 1994, p. 13.

11 UNDP 2019c.

12 Based on the review in Galaz, Collste and Moore (2020).

13 Sen 2013, p. 6.

14 Amply documented, including in Díaz and others (2019b), IPCC (2014a), Oberle and others (2019) and UNEP (2019b, 2020a), on which this Report draws extensively.

15 The five climate change assessments completed by the Intergovernmental Panel on Climate Change (IPCC) show the quickly increasing impacts and risks of climate change, from more frequent and intense extreme weather events to collapsing of ecosystems (IPCC 1990, 1995, 2001, 2007, 2014a). (The sixth assessment is currently under way.) Drawing on this evidence, the 2015 Paris Agreement aimed at holding global average temperature increases "well below 2 °C above pre-industrial levels and pursuing efforts to limit the temperature increases to 1.5 °C above pre-industrial levels, recognizing that this would significantly reduce the risks and impacts of climate change." In late 2018 the IPCC prepared a special report on the impacts of global warming of 1.5 degrees Celsius above preindustrial levels and related global greenhouse gas emission pathways in the context of strengthening the global response to the threat of climate change, sustainable development and efforts to eradicate poverty. It confirmed that the risks and impacts would increase substantially more if the 1.5 degrees Celsius ceiling were breached, and it reached the preliminary conclusion that restraining global average temperature increase to below that threshold would be much less costly than the damages due to inaction (Hoegh-Guldberg and others 2019).

16 Carbon dioxide emissions have been increasing, threatening the Paris Agreement targets (Friedlingstein and others 2019a; Jackson and others 2019). Le Quéré and others (2020) document a sharp decrease in emissions (by about 17 percent) during the first half of 2020 due to the decline in economic activity as a result of the Covid-19 pandemic. But this would still correspond to the level of emissions in 2006. They argue that this drop is likely to be temporary, because the underlying energy and economic structures remained largely in place, and that the rebound in economic activity will result in emissions picking back up. Still, the decline shows the potential for social changes to affect emissions, even though they are insufficient without more structural changes in economic and energy systems, which still rely on burning fossil fuels, the main source of carbon dioxide emissions.

17 Atmospheric concentration of carbon dioxide is now above 400 parts per million (Marangoni and others 2017), and carbon dioxide is being emitted at the highest rate in the last 65 million years. Concentrations remained stable until 1850, having increased slowly from 260 parts per million about 9,000 years ago to 285 parts per million (Waters and others 2016).

18 Smil 2002.

19 Canfield, Glazer and Falkowski 2010. Waters and others (2016) show that in addition to carbon and nitrogen, anthropogenic perturbations extend to a broad set of key biogeochemical cycles—the biological and geological processes that regulate the flows of chemicals on the planet. Human-induced changes are imperceptible until approximately 250 years ago, coinciding with the Industrial Revolution, when a slow increase emerged, followed by a sharp acceleration of anthropogenic disturbance by the middle of the 20th century (see chapter 2).

20 Ellis 2019.

21 Based on recent estimates suggesting that humans emerged much earlier than previously thought (Brooks and others 2018; Deino and others 2018; Potts and others 2018). See also Potts and others (2020).

22 Ceballos, Ehrlich and Raven 2020.

23 Díaz and others 2019a. See also Brondizio and others (2019).

24 Cardinale and others 2012; Díaz and others 2015.

25 Frainer and others 2020.

26 Thomas 2019.

27 Lele 2020, p. 61.

28 Thomas (2019) also suggested that this navigation required scientists, policymakers, humanists and community leaders to collaborate.

29 Bettencourt and Kaur (2011, p. 19541) argue that sustainability emerged as a unified field in 2000, with the number of publications growing exponentially ever since and roughly doubling in just over eight years. The related field of sustainability economics, which emerged in the early 1970s, has also shown a regular increase in publications that has accelerated since 2005 or so (Drupp and others 2020). Other branches include Earth system science (Schellnhuber 1999; Steffen and others 2020), discussed in more detail in chapter 2. See also spotlight 1.2.

30 Chan and others 2016, p. 1462. A good illustration of this evolution is the change from the framing of ecosystem services of the Millennium Ecosystem Assessment (2005) to the 2015 Intergovernmental Science-Policy Platform on Biodiversity and Ecosystem Services analytical framework (Díaz and others 2015) of nature's contributions to people, culminating in Brondizio and others (2019).

31 Chilisa 2017.

32 Merçon and others 2019.

33 Reyers and others 2018, p. 272.

34 The planet, including the biosphere, has changed and continues to change in ways that are independent of humans. In fact, for many years human activity had less impact on the planet than, say, elephant or mammoth activity did (Malhi 2014). And given that humans have been transforming the environment since emerging as a species, and even before then by other ancestors of the *homo* genus, this implies that "few, if any, regions be characterized as pristine" (Boivin and others 2016, p. 6389).

35 For example, if major pressures—including climate change—are mitigated, recovery rates of marine ecosystems after conservation interventions suggest that substantial recovery of the abundance, structure and function of marine life could be achieved by 2050 (Duarte and others 2020).

36 From DeFries and Nagendra (2017, p. 265), who used the notion of the two traps in the management of ecosystems as a wicked problem, which applies with even more force to navigating the Anthropocene. See also DeFries (2014).

37 See, for instance, UNDP (2020c).

38 The 2019 Human Development Report (UNDP 2019c) reviews the evidence, but for a recent analysis of this interplay in urban settings, see Schell and others (2020).

39 Baldassarri 2020; Baldassarri and Abascal 2020. Andy Stirling (2019) emphasizes access by the least powerful to the capacities to challenge power as a key determinant of the ability to transform incumbency.

40 See the discussion in chapter 4 on the distortion of scientific processes and findings to serve particular interests, including action against climate change. The availability of information and the framing are crucial because there is ambiguous evidence on whether experiencing temperature changes is enough to change people's minds on the reality of climate change (Howe and others 2019). Some recent evidence suggests that as temperature increases, people adapt their expectations of what is normal and perceive the dramatic changes that are taking place as unremarkable (Kaufmann and others 2017; Moore and others 2019). This has been referred to as the "boiling frog effect, with respect to the human experience of climate change [...] whereby the negative effects of a gradually changing environment become normalized so that corrective measures are never adopted, even when those affected would have chosen to avoid these impacts ex-ante" (Moore and others 2019, p. 4909). A similar shifting baseline of normalization of environmental damages has been documented for biodiversity loss (Papworth and others 2009) and for ecosystems such as fisheries (Pauly 1995).

41 Resistance to action on climate is aided by framings that portray it as a threat to "our way of life," but it would be equally possible to reframe action as patriotic and welfare enhancing (Feygina, Jost and Goldsmith 2010).

Support for environmental action in some countries emerged initially with support from more politically conservative stances (Turner 2018). So it is less the inherent implications of action and more the framing that drives public perceptions for or against action, and the messenger increasingly determines the public perceptions more than the message does (Swire-Thompson and others 2020).

42 The human development journey and approach are, of course, not only interrelated but also inseparable. Taken together, they move us beyond framings focused on current versus future generations, placing inequalities in human development and power asymmetries in each generation at the centre, given their fundamental role in framing choices and defining opportunities (Leach and others 2018).

43 As forcefully argued in Guterres (2020).

44 Haberl and others 2020.

45 Jackson and Victor 2019.

46 Haberl and others 2020. One objection to the idea of extrapolation is based on evidence of a saturation point (meaning that resource stock and flows per person move towards a peak, stabilize and then decline as the economy continues to expand) in the use of some resources. For instance, Bleischwitz and others (2018) found that saturation starts at $12,000 per capita for cement and steel and at $20,000 per capita for copper, based on evidence from Germany, Japan, the United Kingdom and the United States. Evidence also suggests that saturation for steel and copper is emerging in China. Gleick (2018) showed that in the United States, annual water withdrawals increased with GDP from 1900 but peaked in 1980 and have declined by 25 percent since then and that water use per capita for all purposes dropped from its peak in 1975 by almost half. Still, this evidence is limited to specific resources and countries. Moreover, there is also evidence of a rebound effect—for instance, in energy use—in which efficiency gains lead to income and substitution effects that increase overall energy consumption (Brockway and others 2017; Chitnis, Fouquet and Sorrell 2020; Sorrell, Gatersleben and Druckman 2020).

47 Chan and others 2020.

48 IMF 2020c.

49 Dominant because, according to Haberl and others (2020), it is included in about two-thirds of the literature on decoupling.

50 Le Quéré and others 2019. The difference between the two can be considerable, with estimates suggesting that over 20 percent of global carbon dioxide emissions result from production that is consumed elsewhere (Davis and Caldeira 2010; Davis, Peters and Caldeira 2011; Peters, Davis and Andrew 2012). In developed countries territorial emissions tend to be lower than consumption-based emissions, whereas the reverse happens in developing countries (Davis and Caldeira 2010), although the rise of South–South trade is making this dichotomy less stark (Meng and others 2018). While this has been important historically (for instance, average elasticities of GDP for greenhouse gas emissions are negative in high-income countries, suggesting absolute decoupling, when territory-based emissions are used but not when consumption-based emissions are used (Haberl and others 2020), the transfer of emissions through trade from developed to developing countries has stabilized since 2005 (Friedlingstein and others 2019b; Le Quéré and others 2018)—the elasticities of GDP in high-income countries are actually lower for consumption-based carbon dioxide emissions than for production-based emissions (Haberl and others 2020). Still, beyond carbon dioxide and greenhouse gas emissions, the shift of resource-intensive production from developed to developing countries persists (Dorninger and others 2021; Schandl and others 2018).

51 About half of the reduction in emissions was driven by the decline in the share of fossil fuels in final energy use, while decreased energy use (combining gains in efficiency with reductions in demand, due in part to the low growth associated with the 2008 global financial crisis) accounted for a little over a third. The drivers of absolute decoupling represent a structural change from historical trends since 1960 in that they are characterized by a sustained and large decrease in the fossil fuel share. Furthermore, the study analysed energy use and emissions for two groups of developing countries, low growth and high growth. Higher energy use accounted for 75 percent of the increase in carbon dioxide emissions in low-growth countries, compared with 79 percent in high-growth countries. So the GDP growth rate was not a determining factor in carbon dioxide emissions, but higher energy use was. This points to the potential for gains in efficiency and meeting energy demand through non–fossil fuel sources.

52 Andreoni, Nikiforakis and Siegenthaler 2020.

53 Cohen and others 2018. Krausmann and others (2017a) also found that scenario analysis suggests that a well designed mix of policies, including pricing, investments and incentives in resource efficiency, as well as demand shifts, could enable economic growth while slowing the increase in global material use.

54 Hickel and Kallis 2020.

55 Steinberger and others (2013) make a similar argument but to achieve dematerialization—that is, decoupling economic growth and the use of materials.

56 Grubler and others 2018.

57 The degrowth research agenda and movement, which seeks a "radical political and economic reorganization leading to reduced resource and energy use" (Kallis and others 2018, p. 291), dates back to the writings of Serge Latouche in the 1990s (Latouche 2009). Degrowth is sometimes presented as a utopian (Mair, Druckman and Jackson 2020) imaginary of hope (Kallis and March 2015). Evidence suggests that the concept is capturing the imagination, and speaking to the anxieties, of many, especially the more affluent in developed countries (Cassidy 2020; Correia 2012). But given the urgency of the challenges, some have questioned whether there is enough time before those imaginaries are realized

(Schwartzman 2012, 2014). D'Alessandro and others (2020) contrast models of degrowth, green growth and strong policies for social equity. While the degrowth model achieves the largest reductions in greenhouse gas emissions, the models with strong policies for social equity and green growth are not far behind, and the model with strong policies has the same growth rate as the green growth model (about 1 percent a year) but achieves a lower unemployment rate than even the degrowth model (in which GDP growth is negative at some point). A recent comprehensive review suggests that degrowth perspectives account for less than 3 percent of the literature on decoupling (Haberl and others 2020) but is shared by a wider community of scholars (Ehrlich and Ehrlich 2016).

58 Wiedenhofer and Fischer-Kowalski 2015.

59 Bergh and Botzen 2018; Costa, Rybski and Kropp 2011. However, a mechanistic replacement of one indicator by another is not fully informative as to what needs to be added. Moreover, the HDI is a proxy for a set of limited capabilities that does not speak to the entirety of the human development concept (as elaborated in chapter 7).

60 Brand-Correa and Steinberger 2017; Lamb and Steinberger 2017; O'Neill and others 2018; Steinberger, Lamb and Sakai 2020; Steinberger and Roberts 2010; Vita and others 2019.

61 For details, see Riahi and others (2017).

62 Folke and others 2020.

63 This is biological metabolism. Metabolic analysis provides a basis for using fundamental principles of physics, chemistry and biology to connect the biology of individual mechanisms to the ecology of populations, communities and ecosystems (Brown and others 2004).

64 Nutrients, including carbon, nitrogen and phosphorus. In addition to plants, other forms of life—for example, some bacteria—have the same ability as plants. A few forms of life capture thermal energy directly from the planet.

65 This can be analysed using a socioeconomic metabolic approach, which considers the exchanges of energy and materials between socioeconomic systems and ecological systems: how energy and materials are used and transformed within society, generating waste products in the process (Fischer-Kowalski and Hüttler 1998; Fischer-Kowalski and Weisz 1999; Haberl and others 2016). This is a systemic approach that provides a biophysical basis for analysing both socioeconomic and ecological processes, which can ensure that the challenges of reducing and changing the use of the Earth's resources while fulfilling human aspirations are not addressed separately—or at the expense of each other—but are understood in their mutual interdependencies. By integrating knowledge across disciplines from the natural and social sciences and humanities, socioeconomic metabolic research is applicable at different scales (from global to urban, from economic sectors to the supply chains of specific materials) and has guided the development of models, indicators and databases (Haberl and others 2019).

66   This does not mean that this is the only way in which humans are distinct or that biology cannot account at least in part for traits seen as exclusively attributable to human cognition. For instance, Waal (2009) argues that ethical behaviour and human morality evolved out of mammalian societies. But our ability to learn from each other—through cultural adaptation and very large-scale cooperation—is what makes human societies unique (Boyd 2019; Vince 2020). That is why a socioeconomic metabolic approach and conceptual framework, more than a theory that encompasses or aims to explain everything, provides insights for interpreting human development in the context of the Anthropocene (Fischer-Kowalski, Krausmann and Pallua 2014).

67   This means that the Earth system is a thermodynamically closed, but not isolated, system, which implies that there are not necessarily the theoretical thermodynamic limits to economic and social activity (Kåberger and Månsson 2001; Schwartzman 2008) that some have invoked.

68   The discussion in this paragraph follows Lenton, Pichler and Weisz (2016).

69   Fischer-Kowalski, Krausmann and Pallua 2014.

70   For either biological or cultural/social evolution.

71   It changed the chemical composition of the atmosphere in part because oxygenic photosynthesis led to the production of oxygen as a waste product—resulting in an increase in the oxygen level by over three orders of magnitude. After land plants evolved, another major transition increased the energy captured now in both the marine and terrestrial biospheres and further raised oxygen levels to atmospheric concentrations above 15 percent—enabling, along with the increase of food supply of land plants, animal complexity to evolve from aerobic pathways (Lenton, Pichler and Weisz 2016).

72   This paragraph is based on Fischer-Kowalski, Krausmann and Pallua (2014) and Lenton, Pichler and Weisz (2016).

73   Biggs and others 2016. It played a key role in human evolution, enabling cooking, contributing to brain development and furthering social interactions (Wrangham 2009).

74   And although it transformed land substantially, it had a small impact on global human energy capture, in part because population numbers were also small.

75   Lenton, Pichler and Weisz 2016.

76   We are grateful to Erle C. Ellis for this observation. See Ellis, Beusen and Goldewijk (2020), Ellis and others (2010) and Ruddiman and others (2016), which is contested, as reviewed in Lenton (2016).

77   Why societies moved from hunter-gathering to agriculture remains an unresolved question, especially given that early agriculturalists had worse health and nutrition and likely participated in more arduous labour than hunter-gatherers (Larsen 1995; Mummert and others 2011). Explanations range from climatic changes (as argued by Scott 2017, but see Lilley 2017) for what Scott (2017) described as Boserup (1965)'s "back against the wall" hypothesis (forced by economic incentives to shift to agriculture) to explanations based on locally contingent complex adaptive systems (Ullah, Kuijt and Freeman 2015). Regardless of the initial trigger, life in the early cities was difficult for the majority of the population, with high mortality rates due to disease, lack of sanitation, poor nutrition and the long work hours required to keep the fragile farms and livestock (Algaze 2018). Scott (2017) argued that city walls may have been constructed to keep people inside cities as much as or more than to protect them. Early cities were fragile, with epidemics and local ecological stresses (erosion as result of depletion of forests upstream from rivers and salination as a result of irrigation, which might have explained the transition from wheat to the more salt-tolerant barley in early Mesopotamia) dispersing the population of several of these cities and even of entire civilizations (often characterized as collapse, though this is at odds with the duration and complexity of these processes; Butzer 2012a, b; Butzer and Endfield 2012), and the negative connotation of the term betrays the assumption that people were better off in cities prior to dispersal—Diamond (1987) went as far as suggesting that the transition to agriculture was the worst mistake in human history. Thus, for millennia the transition to agriculture looked far from certain. While mortality rates were very high in early cities, birth rates were just enough higher (in part because there was no need to limit the number of children, as hunter-gatherers did due to the need to move young children) to enable a demographic transition that over time led to sustained increases in sedentary population, ultimately locking in the processes of city and state growth (Bocquet-Appel 2011).

78   The transition to agriculture as the main means of subsistence for a large segment of the population did not happen until 1500 CE (Lenton, Pichler and Weisz 2016), and many population groups remained nomadic until much later. These groups were often designated then as "barbarians," reflecting a bias of the historical record, as told by those "civilized" living in cities (see Beckwith 2009 for an account of this dynamic in Eurasia).

79   For instance, Goldstone (2002) described periods and places, such as the Roman Empire and the Dutch Golden Age, of what he called "efflorescence"—where sophisticated specialization and efficient exchange increased income per capita above historical standards for agricultural societies—but they all came to confront the limits of the socioeconomic metabolic regime based on agriculture.

80   Based on the estimates in Lenton, Pichler and Weisz 2016. In 1850 the population was 1.3 billion, and GDP per capita was $800 in international dollars; in 2000 the population was 6 billion, and GDP per capita was $6,600 in international dollars.

81   As discussed in the 2019 Human Development Report (UNDP 2019c).

82   Nunn 2020a, b.

83   Butt and others 2019.

84   Haberl and others 2011.

85   Over the very long run that probably implies harnessing energy directly from the sun (including what solar radiation does to atmospheric circulation, including wind and precipitation). Nuclear fission is limited by the amount of fissionable material and the challenging of cycling that material (how to handle nuclear waste). Nuclear fusion presents fewer challenges because hydrogen is abundant and the waste product, helium, is an inert gas, but the scientific and technological challenges at scale remain.

86   As Kleidon (2010, p. 1303) put it: "Matter mixes, water flows downhill and wood burns into ashes. If nothing else were to take place, sooner or later all matter would end up in a uniform mix of everything, water would collect in the world's oceans and all biomass would be burnt to ashes. All processes would lead to a 'dead' Earth state with no gradients present to drive fluxes and no free energy available to run life. That the Earth system is not in a 'dead' state [...] some processes need to take place that create gradients and sources of free energy [...]. These processes need to perform physical and chemical work in order to separate matter, to move water up the hill, or to produce wood out of ashes or, in general terms, create gradients to keep global cycling of matter going. In such a 'living' state of the Earth system [...,]" we owe to the radiative forcing of the sun a constant flow of free energy that makes these processes possible. Earth's thermal energy can also be harnessed. But, ultimately, the only free energy at scale entering the Earth system comes from the sun. See also Kleidon (2012).

87   See, for instance, UNEP (2020c). On forests, see Kemppinen and others (2020) and Cook-Patton and others (2020). On oceans, see Österblom, Wabnitz and Tladi (2020).

88   Watari and others 2019.

89   Beylot and others 2019.

90   Rehbein and others 2020.

91   Sonter and others 2020.

92   Sovacool and others 2020.

93   Krausmann and Fischer-Kowalski 2013.

94   Weisz, Suh and Graedel 2015.

95   "Transformation" or "transformational change" can be defined by contrasting it with adaptation. Adaptation is about adjusting responses to changing external drivers and internal processes (of, for example, a business, community, city or economy) in order to remain on the current development path. An example of this is when farmers switch to more drought-tolerant crops or when insurance companies raise their premiums to adapt to climate change. Transformation, on the other hand, involves creating a fundamentally new system when ecological, economic or social conditions make continuing the existing system untenable. This could challenge the behaviours, business models and mindsets that generated dangerous planetary change in the first place. As such, transformations are characterized by radical changes in everything

from power and resource flows to roles and routines. Shifts must take place at different levels of society, from practices and behaviours to rules and regulations to values and worldviews. Research also emphasizes that to succeed, transformations need to change the relationships both among humans and between humans and nature (Folke and others 2010; Olsson and others 2017). We are grateful to Victor Galaz for this formulation of the term "transformation." The term "transformation" has its critics, who claim that it is being used and abused in development discourse (Blythe and others 2018).

96 This section and box 1.1 are adapted from Galaz, Collste and Moore (2020). See also Maffi (2005).

97 Nyström and others 2019.

98 For more on the link between biocultural approaches and wellbeing, see Sterling and others (2017).

99 Merçon and others 2019.

100 Maffi and Woodley 2012; Merçon and others 2019; Pungetti 2013.

101 Maffi 2005, p. 602.

102 Cunsolo Willox and others 2012; Speldewinde and others 2009.

103 Masterson and others 2017; Njwambe, Cocks and Vetter 2019; Stedman 2003.

104 Stedman 2016.

105 Albrecht and others 2007; Jacquet and Stedman 2014; Marshall and others 2019.

106 Albrecht and others 2007.

107 Adger and others 2013; Adger and others 2009; Clayton and others 2015.

108 Brown and others 2019.

109 Enqvist and Ziervogel 2019. Some evidence suggests that changes in sense of place, belonging and identity are unequally borne out and more directly affect economically and socially vulnerable people (Njwambe, Cocks and Vetter 2019). The sense of attachment can also create a strong affinity for the status quo and reveal cultural social and psychological limits to adaptation to biosphere change (Adger and others 2013), which can thus pose a barrier to transformation (Turner and others 2016).

110 Brondizio and Tourneau 2016.

111 Garnett and others 2018.

112 Fa and others 2020. See also Garnett and others (2018) and Brondizio and others (2019).

113 Díaz and others 2019b, p. 14. Without adequate alternatives for improving wellbeing and with social and economic pressures to survive or "develop," some indigenous peoples and local communities may convert (or be unable to resist the conversion of) biodiverse-rich lands to landscapes for resource-intensive activities, including agriculture, mining and more (Brondizio and others 2019; Heinimann and others 2017).

114 Bargh 2007; Simpson 2017.

115 Lansing and others 2017.

116 Borrows and Rotman 1997; Brondizio and others 2019; Thornton and Deur 2015; Toniello and others 2019.

117 Indeed, approximately 72 percent of the selected indicators that the Intergovernmental Science-Policy Platform on Biodiversity and Ecosystem Services uses to monitor biodiversity loss still showed a decline in areas occupied by indigenous peoples, indicating that global drivers of change can ultimately override local management efforts by indigenous peoples and local communities (Brondizio and others 2019).

118 Brondizio and others 2016; Brondizio and Tourneau 2016; Mistry and Berardi 2016.

119 Latulippe and Klenk 2020.

120 Tengö and others 2014.

121 Steffen and others 2018, p. 8254. As Downing and others (2020) argued, it is more than just returning to Holocene-like dynamics by establishing Holocene-like conditions with transformed socioecological system interactions and processes.

122 All ecosystems, and the biosphere as a whole, regenerate. In an early formulation of the concept of sustainable development, the 1980 World Conservation Strategy, the framing was that nature should be used (not left untouched) but allowed to be renewed indefinitely (IUCN and others 1980). Borrowing a concept from ecology—that of carrying capacity of an ecosystem, defined roughly as the maximum population level that an ecological system can sustain—there have been attempts to estimate the human carrying capacity of the planet, which would provide a benchmark against which to assess current pressures. However, estimating that carrying capacity is not straightforward, precisely because of the complexity of social processes and their interaction with ecological systems. The relevant concept here may be, as Daily and Ehrlich (1996) put it, social carrying capacity. Cohen (1995, p. 343) elaborates further: "Human carrying capacity depends both on natural constraints, which are not fully understood, and on individual and collective choices concerning the average level and distribution of material well being, technology, political institutions, economic arrangements, family structure, migration and other demographic arrangements, physical, chemical, and biological environments, variability and risk, the time horizon, and values, tastes, and fashions. How many people Earth can support depends in part on how many will wear cotton and how many polyester; on how many will eat meat and how many bean sprouts; on how many will want parks and how many will want parking lots. These choices will change in time and so will the number of people Earth can support. [...] Human carrying capacity cannot be defined for a nation independently of other regions if that nation trades with others and shares the global resources of the atmosphere, ocean, climate, and biodiversity."

123 Downing and others 2020.

124 Robert Kates was writing about this in the mid-1980s (Burton and Kates 1986). By 2012 he was already arguing that transformational change

was needed in light of the insufficiency of incremental steps—in the context of adaptation to climate change (Kates, Travis and Wilbanks 2012).

125 Nyström and others 2019.

126 Battiston and others 2017; Monasterolo 2020; Stern 2013; WEF 2020d.

127 Stern 2013.

128 Steffen and others 2018, p. 8253.

129 Lenton and others 2019.

130 Brondizio and others 2019.

131 Keys and others 2019.

132 In the form articulated by Holling (1973), staying within a magnitude of disturbances before a coupled economic and social system shifts from a stable state to another equilibrium. Articulated more fully in Folke (2016), Arrow and others (1995) argued that a coupled economic and ecosystem can be considered sustainable if it is resilient in this sense. Because some variance and change are essential for diversity and innovation to occur over the long run, stability should not be misunderstood to imply stagnation or regression (Anderies 2015). Carpenter and others (2015) argue for the importance of allowing for some variance for evolution and innovations to take place. From history, fundamental restructurings of the way in which humans interact with ecosystems (Biggs and others 2016) would require fundamental and large-scale reconfiguration of human–nature interactions (Westley and others 2011). Still, some ecologists object to this definition of resilience due to its multidimensionality combining persistence, resistance and local stability across multiple equilibria (Donohue and others 2016).

133 Reyers and others 2018, p. 276 . See also Lenton (2020).

134 Mandle and others 2019.

135 We are grateful to Erle C. Ellis for this formulation.

136 As shown in Scoones (2016) and Scoones and others (2020). See also Ellis, Pascual and Mertz (2019) in the context of land's and nature's contributions to people.

137 Lenton, Pichler and Weisz 2016.

138 Davis and others 2018.

139 Poore and Nemecek 2018.

140 Clark and others 2020. See also Theurl and others (2020) for more on the potential of changing in diets to reduce emissions from food systems.

141 Krausmann and others 2017b. Zalasiewicz and others (2017) suggest that the physical weight of the technosphere—everything physically built by humans on the planet—is five orders of magnitude larger than the human biomass.

142 Haas and others 2015.

143 Graedel and others 2015.

144 Because there are no substitutes, all of them are perfect complements to the intended uses, so price increases in the face of growing scarcity, for instance, will not be effective in shifting to other metals.

145 Haas and others 2015.

146 Lenton, Pichler and Weisz 2016; Weisz, Suh and Graedel 2015.

147 Krausmann, Wiedenhofer and Haberl 2020.

148 Lenton, Pichler and Weisz 2016. And in the case of Thomas Malthus, probably also due to little recognition of the role of human agency.

149 Weisz and Clark 2011.

150 We are grateful to Ligia Noronha of the United Nations Environment Programme for this formulation. This statement also echoes Ellis and others (2018).

151 Haskel and Westlake 2018.

152 Court and Sorrell 2020.

153 Vollset and others 2020.

154 Haberl and others 2019. Ecological concerns have often been associated with population, even if what matters most is the way in which population interacts with other factors (Bongaarts and O'Neill 2018). Sometimes this is expressed through the IPAT equation, which suggests that ecological human impact (I) equals the product of population (P), affluence (A) and technology (T). Emanating from the ecological and environmental sciences, the IPAT equation was meant to formalize the compounding effects of the three elements, making clear that what ultimately matters at any point in time are the levels in each dimension. Early formulations of the IPAT equation emerged from the debates between Commoner (1971) and Ehrlich and Holdren (1971), who highlighted the role of population and consumption. For the potential and limitations of the approach, see, for instance, Fischer-Kowalski and Amann (2001) and Fischer-Kowalski, Krausmann and Pallua (2014). Dietz (2017) provides an account of further evolutions of the IPAT equation to consider stochastic dynamics and as well as several applications and frameworks derived from it. Stubblefield (2018) criticizes the approach because there is no assessment of history, culture or social and economic relations needed to understand how, why and to what extent humans impact nature.

155 Elmqvist and others 2019.

156 Malhi 2014. For the argument that our societies are, indeed, slowing down, see Dorling (2020).

157 Bettencourt 2013; Bettencourt and others 2007. For an integrated perspective of emergent statistics in cities, see Bettencourt (2020).

158 Seto and others 2017.

159 Ord 2014. This is also the logic behind several endogenous growth models (Jones and Romer 2010; Kremer 1993). And, conversely, declining population could spell the end of economic growth, as argued by Jones (2020).

160 Bettencourt 2013; Bettencourt and others 2007.

161 Malhi 2014. As Kenneth Arrow wrote to Partha Dasgupta, every person born in this world comes with one mouth—but also two arms and one brain (Dasgupta 2019).

162 WCED 1987, p. 1.

163 Malik 2020.

164 This paragraph and much of this subsection follow the arguments of Sen (2013, 2014).

165 Solow 1993, p. 168. Sustainability thus implies a criterion different from that of maximizing welfare, resulting in different development pathways than those implied by a welfare maximization objective.

166 Gough 2015, 2017, 2019.

167 Anand and Sen (2000) showed that setting a minimum standard of living as a criterion may violate sustainability. This is shown in the context of models of intertemporal allocation of resources. They compare three criteria: minimum standard of living, sustainability and optimality. They find that none can be derived from the others and that they are logically independent. And it is possible to generate paths of very low, or even zero, consumption, if consumption paths imply putting people's lives at risk, as in Jones (2016), where even though the model is related to the development of life-threatening technologies, the results can still be interpreted in the broader context of sustainability.

168 Raworth 2017.

169 Leach, Raworth and Rockström 2013.

170 Pasgaard and Dawson 2019. This point is also made in a different way in Leach and others (2018), who note that equity is missing from the approach.

171 As in Coote (2015).

172 UNDP 2019c.

173 Important contributions have been made using a capability approach (in the sense described by Robeyns 2016, 2017) to establish links with sustainability. See, for instance, Crabtree (2012, 2013, 2020), Lessmann and Rauschmayer (2013) and Rauschmayer and Lessmann (2013).

174 Tessum and others 2019.

175 For more examples, see Anderson and others (2020) and Schell and others (2020).

176 Gross external damage is based on the environmental accounting literature and is calculated as the sum of the products of marginal damages and emissions by pollutant and source location. Marginal damages for each pollutant are calculated using integrated assessment models that specify the full economic damages of each source.

177 Moreno-Cruz 2019; Tschofen, Azevedo and Muller 2019.

178 Holland and others 2020.

179 Tschofen, Azevedo and Muller 2019. Two caveats. First, it is difficult to fully attribute the contributions to a single sector, given that production networks link industries through supply chains (Baqaee and Farhi 2019). Thus, a sector such as agriculture, with a ratio of gross external damage to value added higher than 1 (meaning that the economic damages it causes are greater than the value it creates) may be due in part to the fact that the value of agriculture generated outside the sector (in enabling services, for example) may not

be fully accounted for. Second, local pollution may be affected by atmospheric transport of pollution from distant sources, with international trade further complicating attribution. Global estimates of premature deaths related to PM2.5 pollution found that 12 percent were related to air pollutants emitted in a region other than where the deaths occurred and 22 percent were related to goods and services produced in one region and meant to be consumed in another (Zhang and others 2017).

180 Rather than needs, as Sen (2013, p. 9–10) put it, human development emphasizes "the freedom of future generations to live the way they like and to what they have reason to value (no matter whether this corresponds to their own conception of their 'needs', not to mention our conception of their 'needs')."

181 Tetlock 2003.

182 Crist 2018, p. 1242. See also Crist (2007) and Crist, Mora and Engelman (2017).

183 Nussbaum 2019, p. 125.

184 Babcock (2020), for instance, calls for a new ontology for the Anthropocene that uncovers the anthropogenic biases of the Enlightenment (advanced by Kant, Hume and Descartes), with formulations of reality, causality and the human mind that separated humans from the natural world. The new ontology, he argues, should be based on nonanthropocentric conceptualizations of the same constructs, highlighting the dialectical relationship between humans and the natural world.

185 Stewart 2013, p. 7.

186 Fleurbaey 2020, p. 3.

187 UNDP 2019c.

188 Sen 2013.

189 Lutz 2017; Lutz, Muttarak and Striessnig 2014.

190 Barrett and others 2020b. Sen (2013, p. 17) argued that "effectiveness of reasoning cannot be dissociated from the freedom and power to participate in the decision-making." Daw and others (2015, p. 6953) also noted that "value pluralism and deliberative environmental governance […] has a greater chance of achieving socially equitable and sustainable decision making."

191 This is based on Barrett and others (2020a) and Munshi and Myaux (2006).

192 Within the variety of cultures and values across countries and people, the fact that inequalities persist in contributions to planetary pressures and vulnerability to their effects is not a reason to circumscribe the realm of public reasoning to within country borders or to use countries as the unit of analysis. Sen (2005) exposed the dangers of building uncrossable barriers between the values or moral claims of different cultures—also because that obliterates the differences within countries: Even within the same country deep racial and other horizontal inequalities persist. And thus they are not manifested only in differences across countries in patterns of industrialization and colonization. The Anthropocene, as a universally shared challenge, is also fundamentally an invitation to universal

processes of scrutiny and public reasoning within and across borders.

193 "The significance of human development as an end should not, however, be construed as a denial of the importance of human development as a means" (Anand and Sen 2000a, p. 2039).

194 Anand and Sen 2000a.

195 Lele 2020, p. 63.

196 In the United States 44 percent of the population expect standards of living to get worse over the next 30 years, 35 percent expect conditions to stay about the same and only 20 percent expect an improvement (Parker, Morin and Horowitz 2019).

CHAPTER 2

1 The chapter presents more evidence on all three accounts, but briefly. On moving from localized to global impact, neobiota expansion is now global (Williams and others 2015). On the scale of impact, the industrial transition represents for the Earth system a transition in the nature of life on Earth comparable to the colonization of land by plants (Malhi 2017). The amount of reactive nitrogen has introduced the greatest perturbation of the nitrogen cycle since the major pathways of the modern nitrogen cycle emerged about 2.7 billion years ago (Canfield, Glazer and Falkowski 2010), and transfer of phosphates from rock strata to surface soil is unprecedented (Steffen and others 2015). The present anthropogenic release rate of carbon is unprecedented in the last 66 million years and puts the climate system in a no analogue state (Steffen and others 2016). Humans and our domesticated animals have about 30 times the living mass of all existing wild mammals, which need resources and space that is increasingly being take up by us (Bar-On, Phillips and Milo 2018; Ceballos, Ehrlich and Raven 2020). On speed, the expansion of neobiota is nearly synchronous on a geological timescale (Williams and others 2015). Some recent research suggests that the magnitude of the disruption to the Earth's carbon cycle is not proportional to the external forcing or external perturbation but rather to the intrinsic dynamics of the cycle (in particular, once the addition of carbon dioxide to the oceans passes a threshold, the rate of amplification and the severity of the change are independent of the detailed history of the perturbation). "The consequences of the ongoing fast forcing at human timescales may be similar to the outcome of slow forcing at geological timescales" (Rothman 2019, p. 14813).

2 Lenton and others 2008, p. 1792.

3 Lenton and Latour 2018.

4 Steffen and others 2016.

5 Downing and others 2020.

6 Sen 2014.

7 Mildenberger 2020; Oreskes and Conway 2011.

8 Oreskes 2019.

9 Sen 2014. This reflects an awakening that is also going on in the biodiversity/conservation community about how they have built their own narratives and evidence and not empowered the knowledge and action needed. See https://luchoffmanninstitute.org/biodiversity -revisited/. We are grateful to Belinda Reyers for this observation.

10 Ostrom 2007.

11 Dearing 2018, p. 62.

12 Lenton 2019, p. 62.

13 This is typically done by geologists studying ancient rocks and fossil records, looking at glacier ice cores and geological strata, layers of rock or soil that have distinctive characteristics (including fossil records). They are used to identify stratigraphic signatures that enable geologists to characterize distinct stages in the evolution of the planet. The emergence of Earth system science (Schellnhuber 1999) brings together many scientific disciplines to describe and understand the evolution of Earth as a complex system, driven by interactions among energy, matter and life (Steffen and others 2020).

14 Crutzen 2002; Crutzen and Stoermer 2000.

15 Steffen and others 2016. Zalasiewicz and others (2008) raised the possibility of formalizing a new geological epoch, and Zalasiewicz came to lead the Working Group on the Anthropocene that formally provisionally recommended in August 2016 to the International Union of Geological Sciences the designation of the Anthropocene as the new geological epoch, with a start date in the mid-20th century. This was followed by a binding vote of the working group affirming these recommendations in May 2019 (http://quaternary.stratigraphy.org/ working-groups/anthropocene/).

16 Farrier (2020) provides a narrative account of the evidence. See also Biello (2016) and Ripple and others (2017).

17 Malhi 2017, p. 78.

18 The review follows the discussion in Malhi (2017).

19 The title of this section is taken from McNeill (2000).

20 Radkau (2008) describes how humans have been interacting with the environment since the Paleolithic and how that interaction is fundamental to understanding human history. Barbier (2011) describes economic development as a process of exploiting natural resources and confronting scarcities by expanding into new frontiers, both horizontally (claiming more of the biosphere for human activities) and vertically (mining and exploitation of fossil fuels). Scott (2017) documents how throughout much of the Neolithic transition, over thousands of years, urban agglomerations had to confront both disease and ecological constraints (irrigation led to salination of fertile land and tree cutting to erosion and protection from floods), leading to the dissipation of multiple urban agglomerations.

21 Lenton 2019.

22 On environmental changes in Africa over the Holocene, see Hoag and Svenning (2017). On the Amazon, see Bush (2019).

23 Keys, Wang-Erlandsson and Gordon 2016. Williams and Burke (2019, p. 136) argue that rather than a more stable climate, "the Pleistocene-Holocene transition should be viewed [...] as a fundamental shift in the type and drivers of climate variability, from a cold glacial world characterized by large temperature swings and positive feedbacks strongly governed by ice sheet dynamics and cryosphere-ocean-atmosphere feedbacks to a warm interglacial world characterized by a wetter and more energetic atmosphere and governed by vegetation-atmosphere and ocean-atmosphere feedbacks."

24 Williams and Lenton 2010. But see also Steffen and others (2018) for just such a possibility.

25 Lenton and others 2008. See also Biggs, Peterson and Rocha (2018), Cai, Lenton and Lontzek (2016), Rocha, Peterson and Biggs (2015) and Rocha and others (2018).

26 Lenton 2013; Wintle and others 2019.

27 Rockström and others 2009b; Steffen and others 2015.

28 See, for instance, Cooper and Dearing (2019), Dearing (2018), Dearing and others (2014) and Hossain and others (2017).

29 Rockström and others 2018.

30 Steffen and others 2015.

31 Boundaries in the Geological Time Scale are preferably indicated by Global Stratigraphic Section and Points (also informally called "golden spikes") that correspond to well preserved and distinct geological sections. When these cannot be defined, a Global Standard Stratigraphic Age is designated (these have been used to designate boundaries for very ancient periods in the Earth's history, when it is difficult to find well preserved sections; Malhi 2017).

32 Waters and others 2016.

33 Data in this paragraph are from Malhi (2017).

34 Williams and others 2015.

35 These estimates are uncertain and disputed (Smil 2011, 2013).

36 See Bull and Maron (2016). A precedent is found going back to the Great Oxygenation Event, when life evolved towards photosynthesis that uses carbon dioxide as an input and oxygen as an output, changing the chemical composition of the atmosphere and the oceans to the make it oxygen rich. During this event anaerobic microbes (previously dominant) were pushed to where oxygen was low, while aerobic organisms became dominant (see spotlight 1.2).

37 Haff 2014. For Haff the technosphere is equivalent to other components of the Earth system, such as the atmosphere, and it "includes all large-scale interconnected technological systems such as those involved in energy, transportation and agriculture, the devices, human beings and institutions directly and indirectly involved in their operation, and the anthropogenically altered environment that sustains and supports all of these" (Szerszynski 2016, p. 92).

38 Bar-On, Phillips and Milo 2018.

39 A model of extinctions over the past 126,000 years shows that human population size predicts past extinctions with 96 percent accuracy, suggesting a near-term escalation in extinctions of unprecedented magnitude (Andermann and others 2020).

40 Ceballos, Ehrlich and Raven 2020; Torres-Romero and others 2020. See also Barnosky and others (2011), Ceballos and others (2015), Ceballos, Ehrlich and Dirzo (2017), Dirzo and others (2014), Kolbert (2014), Pimm and others (2014) and Young and others 2016. However, the recent Intergovernmental Science-Policy Platform on Biodiversity and Ecosystem Services global assessment showed that this may not actually be the case (Díaz and others 2019b).

41 Cardinale and others 2012.

42 Ellis 2019; Ellis and Ramankutty 2008.

43 Malhi 2017.

44 For instance, in the next 200 years carbon dioxide concentrations could approach or even exceed those during the Eocene (49–53 million years ago) or even mid-Cretaceous (90 million years ago) under the fossil fuel–intensive SSP 5/RCP 8.5 scenario, when global mean surface temperature was close to, or above, twice today's value (Duffy and others 2019; Tierney and others 2020a; Tierney and others 2020b).

45 Ellis and others 2016.

46 Haldon and others 2018. An example is the account of key events in the evolution of the Roman Empire and their relationship with changes in climate and disease (Harper 2017). While the devastating impact of the first global pandemic, which became known as the Justinian Plague because it reached the Roman Empire in the early 540s (and recurred occasionally over the next two centuries), is well documented in the historical record, only recent work by paleogeneticists has been able to unambiguously identify in skeletal remains from the sixth century the DNA of the bubonic plague and use phylogenetic profiling to trace the origin of the disease to Asia (Feldman and others 2016; Keller and others 2019). The same tools being used to understand Covid-19 are helping illuminate our past. Another example corresponds to work dating the emergence of measles in humans to as far back as the 6th century BCE, when the historical record of the disease does not date back any earlier that the late 9th century CE. This is important because it establishes a link with early domestication of animals and possibly coincides with the rise of large cities (Düx and others 2020).

47 Dell, Jones and Olken 2014.

48 For accounts of the evolution of environmental history prior to this resurgence, see, for instance, Crosby (1995). For a more recent account of the field, including a suggestion that it may have gone overboard in the direction of environmental determinism, see Sessa (2019).

49 Davis 2019; Rick and Sandweiss 2020; Turvey and Saupe 2019.

50 Sessa 2019, pp. 217–218.

51 Including the impact on biological extinction (Turvey and Crees 2019).

52 Ellis, Beusen and Goldewijk 2020; Ellis and others 2010; Stephens and others 2019. One way of interpreting this evidence is to see the long-term trend of increasing population and land intensification as a succession of regimes—characterized by institutions, technology and natural resource use—and within each regime is a three-phase evolution of land productivity and population. The first stage corresponds to intensification, with the adoption of more productive technologies that make land yields increase faster than population—as inspired by Boserup (1965). She proposed that agriculturalists sought increases in productivity only when "their backs were against the wall," saving on the use of labour and technology (even if it was available) until population growth demanded it. It was, therefore, an alternative to the Malthusian formulation that considers agricultural productivity the limiting factor of population growth. While rarely applied today in its original formulation, Boserup's hypothesis inspired intensification theories across many disciplines (Turner and Fischer-Kowalski 2010). This stage would be followed by a period of involution, when technology-driven productivity increases are exhausted (Geertz 1963), culminating in the third stage, with a Malthusian process once productivity gains cannot keep up with population growth. The shift to a new regime makes it possible to move from the Malthusian trap, where the cycle repeats. Thus, this interpretation portrays the interaction between people and nature as more complex and dynamic than one that must follow ineluctably a Malthusian process spelling doom or collapse. Moreno-Cruz and Taylor (2020) provide evidence that Malthusian dynamics accounted for the levels of population and settlement patterns in Medieval England, as an example of what happens towards the end of the Malthusian cycle. Ellis and others (2013) argue that the theory is applicable over the long run to account for the evolution of land intensification.

53 Roberts 2019.

54 Ruddiman 2013; Ruddiman and others 2016.

55 This process has been described as sociocultural niche construction. Most species engage in some form of niche construction, the alteration of ecological patterns or processes seeking evolutionary advantages (nests built by termites and dams by beavers are examples). Humans are unique in that this process is not primarily biological, chemical or physical but rather social and cultural (Ellis 2015).

56 Ellis and others 2018.

57 Ellis and others 2016.

58 Braje 2015, 2016, 2018. In a direct response to Braje (2016). Zalasiewicz and Waters (2016) counter that drawing on evidence and data that suggest a new and distinct geological record implies the need to use a different name—and that doing so does not deny the importance of the historical and natural processes that have accumulated over time.

59 Malm and Hornborg 2014. Lorimer (2017) provides a comprehensive review of the debate in the humanities.

60 Stubblefield 2018.

61 Barbier 2011.

62 Fischer-Kowalski and Weisz 1999. Although one characteristic of the Anthropocene debate is that it is leading to calls for much stronger engagement and collaboration across these boundaries (Brondizio and others 2016; Görg and others 2020; Palsson and others 2013).

63 Moreover, there are increasing interactions with social sciences and the humanities, and even the arts, even if not yet fully accomplished (Castree and others 2014). This is helping clarify the role of humans as they interact with nature (Leach, Sterling and Scoones 2010).

64 Hamilton 2016; Hamilton, Gemenne and Bonneuil 2015. Dalby (2016) discusses the implications of these pessimistic framings as well as optimistic ones, subscribed to by ecomodernists, who argue that technologies can be deployed to decouple economic activity from pressures on the environment (Asafu-Adjaye and others 2015) and that both represent extremes that are unlikely to characterize how the Anthropocene plays out (Bennett and others 2016; Pereira and others 2019; Raudsepp-Hearne and others 2020) discuss a middle ground of how to envision seeds of a good Anthropocene.

65 Malhi 2017, p. 97.

66 On nature's contributions to people's wellbeing, the Millennium Ecosystem Assessment (2005) classified services provided by ecosystems to human wellbeing, defined as benefits to humans that are derived from ecological processes (Daily 1997) into four categories: provisioning, regulating, cultural and supporting (see also Millennium Ecosystem Assessment 2003). This has remained an influential characterization, in part because it highlights the variety of benefits we derive from nature (even if, in this case, it is circumscribed to ecosystems). Carpenter and others (2009) propose expanding and reconceptualizing this approach in terms of nature's contributions to people, adding the intrinsic value of nature and proposing an even more tightly coupled relationship between people and nature. This is the foundation for the conceptual approach of the more recent global assessment of biodiversity and ecosystem services by the Intergovernmental Science-Policy Platform on Biodiversity and Ecosystem Services (Brondizio and others 2019).

67 Díaz and others 2015.

68 In the context of climate change, see Tierney and others (2020a).

69 Keys and others 2019.

70 As discussed, in chapter 1, even though the specific Anthropogenic origin of the SARS-CoV-2 virus is under study, it represents a manifestation of a risk scientist have been warning of for years, a result of human pressure on the planet. Zoonotic diseases are substantial threats to human health, with vector-borne diseases accounting for approximately 17 percent of all infectious diseases and causing an estimated 700,000 deaths a year globally. See Brondizio and others (2019).

71 UNDP 2020b.

72   Amid the greater uncertainty linked to the Anthropocene, we present some estimates based on simulation scenarios that measure possible change over the 21st century. Like all projection exercises, they rely on a set of assumptions that include mitigation scenarios and adaptation conditions. They are not official and are subject to debate among scientists. Despite the space for error, they are useful for indicating potential effects of ongoing changes, with emphasis on their distribution, and give an idea of the space for public policies going forward.

73   Diffenbaugh and Burke 2019.

74   FAO and others 2020, p. 7.

75   Human Development Report 2019 discusses this improvement as a case of convergence in basic capabilities (UNDP 2019c).

76   See a study on economic effects in Coronese and others (2019), which presented a graphical analysis of the data, taken as a model here. See also IPCC (2014a).

77   Currently, very high human development countries have more days with extremely low temperatures (69 days on average) than low human development countries (5 days on average). On the other hand, low human development countries have more days with very hot temperatures (76 days on average) than very high human development countries (16 days on average). Based on information from Carleton and others (2020).

78   The adaptation scenarios assume that socioeconomic conditions evolve according to SSP 3/RCP 4.5 and SSP 3/RCP 8.5. See Carleton and others (2020).

79   Kulp and Strauss 2019.

80   Scenarios of medium or no mitigation (RCP 4.5 and RCP 8.5).

81   See Kulp and Strauss (2019). Previous estimates of people in low elevation coastal zones were on the order of 600 million.

82   Other estimates focus on the number of people vulnerable to episodic coastal flooding caused by storms—for instance, Kirezci and others (2020) estimate the number of people exposed to episodic coastal flooding by 2100: 202 million in the RCP 4.5 scenario and 225 million in the RCP 8.5 scenario. Again, the conclusion is a large impact on people even with substantial mitigation.

83   Variations within each mitigation scenario are given by the degree of Antarctic stability. See Kulp and Strauss (2019).

84   An estimated 1.2 billion people are at risk of displacement by 2050 (IEP 2020).

85   Chaplin-Kramer and others 2019.

86   Sherwood and Huber 2010.

87   CDC 2020. See also Artiga, Corallo and Pham (2020) and Rubian-Miller and others (2020).

88   Baqui and others 2020.

89   Most of the countries in the region do not have official disaggregated data by ethnicity, but some rough estimates are presented according to regions, states or municipalities that have higher representation of indigenous peoples (OHCHR and RISIU 2020).

90   Iglesias-Osores and Saavedra-Camacho 2020; Meneses-Navarro and others 2020.

91   Cherofsky 2020; Galdos and Somra 2020; Mucushua and Huerta 2020.

92   Ortiz-Hernández and Pérez-Sastré 2020.

93   IIED 2017.

94   See chapter 4 of UNDP (2015b).

95   UNDP 2020b.

96   United Nations 2020a.

97   World Bank 2020a.

98   Ballet, Dubois and Mahieu 2011.

99   The analysis of the implications of global change on development also requires recognizing that the unequal accumulation of benefits and consequences affects different groupings and that inequality emerges from the intersection of various social groupings, including but not limited to age, ethnicity, religion, seniority, marital status and livelihood. See Galaz, Collste and Moore (2020).

100   Leach and others 2018; McDermott, Mahanty and Schreckenberg 2013.

101   Empowerment is used as an inclusive concept that, from a capabilities approach perspective, groups agency and means. Some empowerment discourses can be reminiscent of a colonizer narrative that assumes a dominant in the position to give and bestow the power to those whom it has subjugated in the first place (Kayumova, McGuire and Cardello 2019).

102   Alsop, Bertelsen and Holland 2005; Dery and others 2020; Desai 2010.

103   Dery and others 2020; Kabeer 2005.

104   Alsop, Bertelsen and Holland 2005; Kabeer 2005.

105   Dery and others 2020; Williams 2018.

106   Villa 2017.

107   Ostrom 1990.

108   ILO 2017. The 370 million indigenous people—roughly 5 percent of the world's population—occupy more than a quarter of the world's land surface and account for more than 15 percent of the world's extreme poor. They contribute little to greenhouse gas emissions but are among the first to experience the direct impacts of climate change (FAO and others 2019; UNPFII 2016b). See also the discussion in Whyte (2017b).

109   Vermeylen 2019.

110   McLean 2012.

111   In Brazil social movements have pushed for land rights as well as access to and control over natural resources since 1970, but indigenous peoples still inhabit common land exploited by powerful economic groups for agribusiness, mining and hydropower, threatening their subsistence (Rasmussen and Pinho 2016).

112   Jiménez, Cortobius and Kjellén 2014.

113   Villa 2017.

114   Estimates of land ownership are from the Food and Agriculture Organization and based on Living Standards Measurement Studies Integrated Surveys on Agriculture, but availability is limited. A farmholder is the person who makes most of the decisions about farm operations.

115   FAO 2002; World Bank 2019c.

116   Komatsu, Malapit and Theis 2018; Malapit and Quisumbing 2015.

117   Allendorf 2007; Deere and Twyman 2012; Doss, Summerfield and Tsikata 2014; Doss and others 2015.

118   Habitat for Humanity 2016.

119   Leach and others 2018.

120   Anderson and others 2016.

121   FAO and others 2019.

122   Wise 2013.

123   Pasricha and Biggs 2010.

124   Jiménez, Cortobius and Kjellén 2014.

125   Klasing 2016.

126   FAO and others 2020.

127   See FAO and others (2020).

128   UN Women 2019.

129   Datar and others 2013.

130   Girls born during crop failure had 0.86 standard deviation lower height-for-age z-scores, with no adverse impacts noted among boys (Akresh, Verwimp and Bundervoet 2011).

131   OHCHR and UN Women 2020.

132   Benefits from local ecosystems, responses, adaptation, resilience to change and vulnerability to environmental degradation often differ across groups. Resilience and preparedness are key when environmental shocks, such as natural hazards happen. Overlapping identities interact to amplify risks. Poor households (associated with higher risks for flood and drought), which have the fewest resources to be resilient and cope with climate change, face higher exposure to the consequences over human development. See Galaz, Collste and Moore (2020).

133   Some of the life-threatening dangers they face are related to natural hazards, food insecurity, malnutrition, air pollution, disrupted access to safe water and higher risk of vector-borne diseases.

134   Rees and Anthony 2015.

135   Kousky 2016.

136   Onigbinde 2018.

137   Andrabi, Daniels and Das 2020.

138   So it is key for schools to recognize the knowledge level of returning students, so that learning can restart at that point and not where the curriculum expected them to be when the crisis started (Pritchett 2020).

139   Kousky 2016.

140   Bullard 2008; Chakraborty and others 2014; Grineski 2007; Houston and others 2016; ISSC, IDS and UNESCO 2016; Leach and others 2018;

United Church of Christ Commission for Racial Justice 1987; US General Accounting Office 1983.

141 Hajat, Hsia and O'Neill 2015; Mohai and Saha 2015.

142 Research from 367 case studies across 141 indigenous communities provides a recent and comprehensive review. Most cases of environmental injustice and pollution were reported in North America, South America and Africa. Across these cases pollutants ranged from heavy metals to organic matter. Most of the health impacts came from consumption of polluted food and water, and exposure to other pollutants elevated the risks for immune system diseases, cancer, endocrine disruptions and generally higher mortality (see Fernández-Llamazares and others 2020).

143 Brown 2018.

144 Moreno Parra 2019.

145 Osuagwu and Olaifa 2018.

146 UNEP 2011.

147 O'Callaghan-Gordo and others 2018; Orta-Martínez and others 2018.

148 As with other household decisions, environmentally relevant decisions and behaviours are negotiated unequally between women and men, filtered through gender norms and roles. The decisions include water management and use, division of labour, energy source choices and financial allocations for agricultural adaptation. Intrahousehold dynamics are important for resources and their use, conservation, consumption and the ways women and men might act as agents of change (Seager and others 2016; UN Women 2015, 2019).

149 Resulting in increased time poverty for women, depriving women of time needed to invest in new resilient livelihoods (UNDP 2018, 2020a).

150 UNEP and others 2020. See also Paavola (2008).

151 Tambo 2016; FAO and others 2018.

152 Roberts 1998.

153 Empowerment is used as an inclusive concept that, from a capabilities approach perspective, groups agency and means. Some empowerment discourses can be reminiscent of a colonizer narrative that assumes a dominant in a position to give and bestow the power to those whom it has subjugated in the first place (Kayumova, McGuire and Cardello 2019).

154 There are systemic forces at play. For instance, Crowder and Downey (2010) find that in the United States minorities tend to move into neighbourhoods with significantly higher hazard levels. Hamilton (1995) finds that polluting firms tend to move to areas with larger minorities. There is no clear evidence of minorities' different propensity to move away from environmental hazards (see Hunter and others 2003).

155 Kayumova, McGuire and Cardello 2019; Kayumova and others 2015.

156 Mitchell 2011; Ramirez-Andreotta 2019.

157 Nigra 2020.

158 A cross-sectional study that analysed inequities in the exposure of same-sex partner households to hazardous air pollutants in the United States found cancer and respiratory risks from those pollutants for same-sex partners are 12.3 percent and 23.8 percent greater, respectively, than for heterosexual partners. See Collins, Grineski and Morales (2017).

159 Hausman and Stolper 2020.

160 Satterthwaite 2003.

161 Bond and Sharife 2012.

162 See discussion in chapter 6 and in Butt and others (2019).

163 To achieve this, a real compromise for institutional transformation is necessary to translate minority concerns into public policies, going beyond participatory mechanisms for specific projects that alone will be unable to provide more power of decision. See Merino (2018).

CHAPTER 3

1 Sen 2014.

2 See discussion in chapter 6. See also Griscom and others (2017).

3 Frainer and others 2020.

4 Moving us away from the dichotomies between green growth and degrowth considered in chapter 1, which tend to be associated with varying values and cosmogonies of the relationship between humans and nature, Mann (2018) suggests an interesting contrast: ideas for "green growth" (by the so-called Wizards) are based on faith in innovation and human ingenuity as a way to tackle development challenges; ideas for "degrowth" (by the so-called Prophets) are based on the emphasis on preserving ecological balances as a necessary condition for subsistence.

5 UNDP 2019c.

6 See also the survey in Hamann and others (2018).

7 Socioenvironmental traps nest a wide set of cases, including poverty–environment traps (see Barbier 2010; Barbier and Hochard 2019), but they also include a wider set of cases in which the core element is inequality in empowerment: More resources will not suffice to restore imbalances (see Chancel 2020; Duraiappah 1998; Leach and others 2018).

8 See Duraiappah 1998.

9 To provide an idea of relative performance, the Index of Material Footprint per Capita is a min-max transformation of material footprint per capita, calculated as (maximum – observed value) / (maximum – minimum), using sample minimum and maximum over 2000–2016. It goes from 0 to 100. The larger the index, the lower the pressure on the planet's resources.

10 Smith and Ezzati (2005) explore these relationships in the context of health. They find a negative correlation between development and environmental risks for household issues, such as sanitation: greater income, lower risks. For community issues, such as pollution, they report an inverted-U relationship (with some exceptions). In the case of global environmental issues, such as greenhouse gases emissions, they report a negative relationship.

11 See analysis in chapter 2, based on Carleton and others (2020).

12 See discussion in chapter 2, based on data from Carleton and others (2020).

13 Harberl and others 2020; Wiedenhofer and others 2020.

14 Ecological footprint accounts—which measure biocapacity and ecological footprint in a common unit (global hectares)—allow biocapacity deficit to be calculated for each country (footprint minus biocapacity). See Lin and others (2018).

15 The aggregation across large country groups using the median is intended to capture the situation of countries at different levels of development, beyond specific country endowments.

16 See Lin and others (2018) and updated data from https://data.footprintnetwork.org (accessed 28 December 2020). The total global biocapacity deficit is the product of net per capita demand and the number of people, which also increased over the period.

17 Brundtland 1987, p. 54.

18 In 1991 Robert Solow warned about how difficult it is in practice to face the tension between intra- and inter- generational inequalities (Solow 1991). Three decades later, progress has been limited. As pointed out by Leach and others (2018, p. 1), "There is remarkably little work on the interlinkages between sustainability and equity." The 2011 Human Development Report is an exception (UNDP 2011).

19 See discussion and evidence in Frankel (2011) and Venables (2016).

20 Trade is typically controlled by the "metropolis" and the resulting asymmetry the "goal" of colonialism. For an assessment of this hypothesis in the 20th century, see Kleiman (1976).

21 There is path dependence in development linked to inequalities. See, for instance, Acemoglu and others (2001) and Engerman and Sokoloff (2005).

22 Cole and Foster 2001; Newell 2005.

23 Murphy 2009. For an empirical analysis across occupations, see Stanbury and Rosenman (2014).

24 Marschke and Vandergeest 2016; Sutton and Siciliano 2016. This would not have constituted a surprise to Oreskes (2019, p. 158), who wrote, "The Old Testament—the foundation of the world's three great monotheistic religions—begins with Creation and so do the organizing myths and stories of most human societies. Whether we call it biodiversity or Creation or the Dreamtime or Mother Earth, climate change threatens it. Everything we know—from science, from history, from literature, from ethics—tells us that caring for our fellow citizen and caring for the environment are the same thing. The dichotomy of man versus environment, or jobs versus environment, or prosperity versus environment is a dangerous fiction constructed to justify greed. It cynically warrants destruction in the name of the false prophet of progress."

25 Crona and others 2016.

26 Teh and others 2019. Businesses, therefore, will have an important role to play in ocean stewardship, including in dialogue with scientists (Österblom and others 2017).

27 Leach and others 2018.

28 Leach and others 2018.

29 See UNDP (2019c).

30 Horizontal inequalities are used here in a specific sense, linked to empowerment or agency to allocate natural capital and distribute its costs and benefits. In some of the foregoing examples, these group-based inequalities coincide with social horizontal inequalities related to the distribution of other outcomes (income, education, health and the like). This is common but not always the case. Even with relative equality in outcomes or relative affluence, some groups might be disempowered in their ability to influence the way their environment is affected, taking the burden of decisions by others. This could be further aggravated by global production structures and phenomena such as telecoupling, where a change in productive dynamics of one industry can such produce environmental impacts on the other side of the world where resources for that industry are being extracted.

31 See discussion about the mechanisms to achieve societies with lower inequality in human development in UNDP (2019c).

32 See, for instance, Sen (2007, 2008).

33 Leach and others 2018.

34 See Stewart (2014).

35 Levine, Frank and Dijk 2010.

36 UNDP 2019c.

37 Income growth has been shown to have a positive but very small impact on happiness in the long run (Beja 2014).

38 See Bellet and Colson-Sihra (2018) and Levine, Frank and Dijk (2010).

39 Leach and others 2018.

40 See discussion in chapter 5 and spotlight 7.2 in UNDP (2019c).

41 See Chancel (2020).

42 When accounting for the drivers of economic growth, Solow (1957) and Kuznets (1971) estimated that the residual accounted for as much as 80 percent of US growth. Interpreting the residual as technological change paints a very optimistic picture of the potential for future growth, as long as technological change continues. However, many attributed the very high residual to imperfect measurement of capital (for example, Dasgupta and Mäler 2000). More recent estimates that included the adoption of capital services as a capital input turn the contribution of multifactor productivity to 20 percent, reversing the earlier estimates (Jorgenson 2018).

43 Romer 1990. For a model in which the social or reciprocal character of intellectual activity drives economic growth, see Lucas (2009). For other models in which the diffusion of ideas across individuals fuels growth, see Caicedo, Lucas and Rossi-Hansberg (2019) and Garicano and Rossi-Hansberg (2006).

44 Stiglitz and Greenwald 2014.

45 Innovation takes place in a complex system. While centred on firms, the national innovation system encompasses research and education systems, government, financial and regulatory bodies, civil society and consumers. The effectiveness of the national innovation system in learning, adopting and disseminating knowledge and technologies rests very much on the capabilities of these actors, the connections among them and the enabling environment for innovation that they create. See UNCTAD (2018) and UNDP (2019c).

46 J. Renn 2020; O. Renn and others 2020; Seidl and others 2013.

47 Muthukrishna and Henrich 2016.

48 Snider and others 2020.

49 Rotondi and others (2020) show that access to mobile phones is associated with advances in empowerment-related Sustainable Development Goals. On the potential of information and communication technology for sustainable development, see Fernández-Portillo and others (2019).

50 On India's efforts in inclusive digital health care, see Agrawal (2020).

51 Due to the contraction in economic activity and transport, greenhouse gas emissions are expected to fall by 8 percent in 2020. This would be six times larger than the previous record reduction, in 2009, due to the financial crisis (IEA 2020b). More generally, studies have urged caution in equating digital with less energy consumption. See Court and Sorrell (2020).

52 United Nations Sustainable Development Group 2020.

53 Studies have tried to quantify the benefits of digital technology for sustainable economic growth (see Fernández-Portillo and others 2019). Rotondi and others (2020) found that improved mobile phone access and coverage can be powerful tools for empowerment and development, particularly for women.

54 Although expanding this sector can itself drive the demand for energy, as highlighted in the example of bitcoin detailed below.

55 The final effect of these new tools will depend on context and how they are implemented. Evidence about the effects of these platforms on car sales is mixed (see Guo, Xin and Li 2019). Also, there are social effects linked to these platforms. See UNDP (2015b, 2019c).

56 United Nations 2020d.

57 Makov and others 2020.

58 WEF 2019.

59 United Nations 2020b.

60 Andrae 2019.

61 Strubell, Ganesh and McCallum 2019.

62 Efoui-Hess 2019.

63 Acemoglu and others 2012.

64 Sometimes, early adopters play a key role, and as use increases, quality improves and the cost of adoption falls. Some technologies complement a trained labour force and are adopted more easily in regions or countries with a more educated workforce (Stokey 2020).

65 The Rio+20 Declaration, The Future We Want, stresses the need to ensure food, water and energy security while limiting the adverse impacts on nature, including biodiversity and the climate. These objectives are among the 169 targets of the 17 Sustainable Development Goals. For example, to fulfil Goal 13, if the global economy grows by 3 percent a year, as per Goal 8, achieving sufficient emission reduction requires decoupling (or decarbonization) of 7.29 percent per year, about six times faster than historical rates. Sustainable Development Goals 8 and 9 require growth and more industrialization; Sustainable Development Goals 6, 12, 13,14 and 15 address sustainability (Hickel 2019b).

66 IEA 2019c.

67 Farmer and others 2019; van Ginkel and others 2020.

68 In addition to solar energy, there are other emerging renewable energy technologies that could support the energy transition. They include new wind power technologies (such as floating offshore turbines), third generation biofuels, low-impact hydropower dams, marine energy, microbial fuel cells, hydrogen (for heat and transport applications), artificial photosynthesis and cellulosic ethanol energy extraction. See, for instance, UNCTAD (2019).

69 Another example of a sensitive intervention point is government incentives to develop phosphorus recycling technologies, which have recently entered a stage of recycling that is viable (Kabbe, Kraus and Remy 2017). Over the next 12–15 years the learning curve is likely to accelerate, and the technology to improve substantially (Scholz and Wellmer 2019; see the next subsection). There is also the related concept of sustainability transition policy, which recognizes that a low-carbon transition must involve multiple and coevolving social and technological change, including on the one hand, support for emerging innovations and their deployment, and on the other hand, decommissioning existing technologies and infrastructure (Rosenbloom and others 2020).

70 Bloomberg 2019; Lafond and others 2018.

71 Lafond and others 2018.

72 Meckling, Sterner and Wagner 2017.

73 This sequence can be driven by two factors. First, government support for low-carbon technologies fosters interest groups or constituencies that support the expansion of low-carbon policy, which extends to carbon prices. Second, policy helps drive down costs through economies of scale and learning by doing (Meckling, Sterner and Wagner 2017).

74 CEEW 2020.

75 Government of India 2015. The Paris Agreement commits the world to keeping global warming to no more than 2 degrees Celsius

above preindustrial levels. It went into force in 2016 (see chapter 5).

76 Also, within the National Action Plan for Climate Change, the National Mission for Enhanced Energy Efficiency regulates large energy-consuming industries, with an arrangement for companies to trade energy-saving certificates (CEEW 2020).

77 Government of India 2020.

78 IRENA 2019a.

79 Barbier 2020.

80 Jenkins, Long and Wu 2015, p. 414.

81 Clastres 2011.

82 Cramton 2017.

83 Fripp and Roberts 2018.

84 For instance, in India coal is the largest source in both power generation and industry, accounting for 70 percent of energy-related carbon dioxide emissions in 2017 (IEA 2020d). Since 2017 government support for fossil fuels has increased by 65 percent while support for renewables has declined by 35 percent (Vibhuti Garg 2020). Coal subsidies have remained stable since 2014, declining only marginally from INR 15,660 crore to INR 15,456 crore in 2019. The public company Coal India Ltd. employs 300,000 people and enjoys political support (CEEW 2020).

85 For instance, there is a large space of action in the definition of more efficient relative prices, as discussed in chapter 5 and IMF (2019b). Also, there are approaches that combine different dimensions of public action, such as personal carbon trading (Parag and Fawcett 2014).

86 Compare with the 2.5 percent improvement in 2016 and the 1.7 percent improvement in 2017 (IEA 2019b).

87 See the discussion on intellectual property rights in UNDP (2019c).

88 For discussions on negative emissions technologies, see Carton and others (2020, Field and others (2020), Fuss and others (2018) and Minx and others (2018).

89 Rogelj and others 2018.

90 Bui and others 2018.

91 IPCC 2014b.

92 *The Economist* 2020b.

93 Fuhrman and others 2020.

94 European Commission 2018; Hickel 2019b; Van Vuuren and others 2018.

95 Hänsel and others 2020.

96 See United Nations (2020d).

97 De Angelis 2018.

98 European Commission 2018, p. 9. Similar approaches can also be found in developing countries. See, for instance, an analysis of circular economy strategy for Lao PDR in UNDP and Lao PDR Ministry of Energy and Mines (2017).

99 Ben-David, Kleimeier and Viehs 2018.

100 Erisman and others 2008; Scholz and Wellmer 2019. Smil (2002) estimated that the Haber-Bosch synthesis of ammonia supports about 40 percent of humanity. It is also pointed out that these are global average estimates, hiding many differences. Affluent countries consume about 35 percent of all nitrogen fertilizers, which supports unnecessarily protein-rich diets. In contrast, in low-income countries the supply of dietary protein remains inadequate. In large food-producing countries equitable access to nutritious food would go a long way in addressing these nutritional deficiencies.

101 Canfield, Glazer and Falkowski 2010.

102 Canfield, Glazer and Falkowski 2010. Fertilizer use is only expected to grow. The Food and Agriculture Organization (FAO 2017b) estimated that demand for nitrogen would grow by 1.5 percent a year on average from 2015 to 2020, phosphorus by 2.2 percent and potassium by 2.4 percent.

103 Erisman and others 2008.

104 About 80 percent of the total nitrogen manufactured by the Haber-Bosch process is used in the production of agricultural fertilizers (Erisman and others 2008).

105 Waters and others 2016.

106 Erisman and others 2008.

107 Waters and others 2016.

108 Achakulwisut and others 2019. This accounts for 13 percent of global incidence. The greatest burdens were estimated in Lima, Peru, Shanghai, China, and Bogota, Colombia. Covid-19 lockdowns have been found to lower nitrogen dioxide level (Venter and others 2020).

109 Similar arguments can be made with respect to phosphorus. The resource efficiency of phosphorus is very low in food production. The total nutrient use efficiency of phosphorus —the ratio of the amount of phosphorus in digested human food to the amount in phosphate rock mined for human fertilizer and feed additives—is 5–10 percent. There are losses all along the supply chain, including the mines. For several importing countries recycling offers a diversified source of supply. And large consumer countries have higher potential for recycling (Scholz and Wellmer 2019).

110 Erisman and others 2008.

111 Canfield, Glazer and Falkowski 2010.

112 FAO 2013, 2018.

113 Smil 2002.

114 See UNCTAD (2017).

115 Eshed and Lippman 2019.

116 Berners-Lee and others 2018; Shepon and others 2018.

117 Geissler and others 2018.

118 Farmer and others 2019.

119 Acting on this principle, the German government has adopted a law that makes Germany the first EU country to make phosphorus recovery compulsory under the law. After a transition phase of 12–15 years, 50 percent of the phosphate in sewage water must recovered for any larger German sewage treatment plant (500 of 9,300 existing plants treating two-thirds of Germany's sewage), if phosphorus concentrations in sewage sludge are 20 milligrams of phosphorus per kilogram of dry matter or higher. Such incentives are needed to develop phosphorus recycling technologies and to promote industries to recycle beyond the present economic optimum (Scholz and Wellmer 2019).

120 Maldonado, Colombi and Pandya 2014.

121 UNDP 2007.

122 Chapin and others 2010.

123 UNDP 2007.

124 Pope Francis 2016, p. 266.

125 Huambachano 2015; Kawharu 2000; McGregor 2009.

126 Ruru 2014.

127 Bennett and others 2018. Although the authors refer to local environmental stewardship, the framework is also useful for thinking about stewardship, agency and human development at a broader scale.

128 Bennett and others 2018, p. 599.

129 Watene and Merino 2019.

130 Wehi and others 2020.

131 Watene 2016; Watene and Yap 2015.

132 Kawharu 2002; Waitangi Tribunal 2011.

133 Durie 1998.

134 Watene, Rochford and Tamariki 2017.

135 Hall 2019; Kawharu 2019. See also National Science Challenges 2020.

136 Hall 2018.

137 Graham 2013, p. 4.

138 Yap and Yu 2016b; Yawuru RNTBC 2011.

139 Watene and Merino 2019.

140 McGregor 2009.

141 Craft 2019.

142 Craft 2013, p. 16.

143 Watene and Merino 2019, p. 139.

144 Huambachano 2015, p. 106.

145 Huambachano 2015.

146 Following the definition of governance in World Development Report 2017 (World Bank 2017b). See also McGregor (2009).

147 UNDP 2019c.

148 Lee 1994.

149 Lesisa, Kairung, and Cowell, 2016.

150 Dussault 2017.

151 Dussault 2017.

152 Taylor 2011.

153 Whyte 2013, p. 10. See also Whyte (2017a).

154 ILO 1989.

155 Fontana and Grugel 2016.

156 Bartlett, Marshall and Marshall 2012.

157 Macfarlane, Macfarlane and Gillon 2015.

158 Ransom and Ettenger 2001.

159 Wehi and others 2020, p. 2.

160 Breslow and others 2016; Frank 2005; Gratani and others 2014; Hikuroa and Slade 2010; Kawagley, Norris-Tull and Norris-Tull 1998; Ngāi Tahu 2001; Ngāti Whātua Ōrākei 2019; Ransom and Ettenger 2001; Rayne and others 2020; Tuhoe 2014; Waikato-Tainui 2013; Whyte and others 2017.

161 Sen 2001, p.19

162 Sen 2014.

PART II

1 The concept of "mechanism" is inspired by the contrast between a catalogue of political regimes and a catalogue of mechanisms, which Elster (1993) claimed to be a sounder and more helpful tool to understand and guide action. The three mechanisms of change discussed align with the concepts proposed as levers of change towards more effective governance in World Bank (2017b): incentives, norms (preferences and beliefs) and contestability in the policy arena (bringing interested actors to the table). The discussion about effective governance (institutions that coordinate expectations, induce voluntary compliance [cooperation] and are capable of sustaining agreements over time [commitment]) are extremely relevant for the analysis in this part of the Report.

CHAPTER 4

1 Extinction Rebellion 2020; Thunberg 2020.

2 Chabay and others 2019, p. 2.

3 Farrow, Grolleau and Ibanez 2017. Social norms are considered institutions in the social science literature. For an analysis of this perspective, see Vatn (2009).

4 Based on the five categories of human–nature connections in Ives and others (2018)—material, experiential, cognitive, emotional and philosophical—interpreted here more broadly for social norms in general.

5 Sen 2013.

6 See Cialdini and Goldstein (2004). The literature also distinguishes between social norms as an individual construct and social norms as a collective construct. The former is often used in psychological research, given that it focuses on the underlying mechanisms that lead to normative behaviour in the individual; the latter is used to study how norms evolve over time at the population level. For studies on international development such as the Human Development Report, it is useful to combine both approaches, as the main purpose is to study how people's beliefs are influenced by institutions and vice versa, thus shaping people's behaviour at both the individual and collective levels (Legros and Cislaghi 2020).

7 Klamer 1989, p. 144.

8 Young 1998, p. 821.

9 Elster 1989, p. 102. See also Basu (2018).

10 Klamer 1989, p. 144.

11 Sen 2010, p. 8.

12 The underlying factors that contribute to sustainable behaviour and lifestyles have been studied for several decades (Hedlund-de Witt 2012). The concept of values (that is, important life goals or standards; Rokeach 1973) is used here rather than worldviews, environmental attitudes, beliefs and others because values are more concrete than worldviews ("sets of beliefs and assumptions that describe reality"; Koltko-Rivera 2004, p. 3). Values are actually part of worldviews and are thus better quantifiable (as with, for example, the World Value Survey). But values are less specific than environmental attitudes ("the collection of beliefs, affect, and behavioural intentions a person holds regarding environmentally related activities or issues"; Schultz and others 2004, p. 32), which also form part of worldviews and are thus more compatible with the Report's broader framework, which goes beyond environmental protection.

13 UNESCO 2016.

14 Rokeach 2008, p. 2.

15 Otto and others 2020b.

16 Kollmuss and Agyeman 2002. Human behaviour is so multifaceted that numerous other factors play a role in determining behaviour (see figure 7 in the cited article). They cannot all be included in the model of social norms change. The purpose of the model is to come to a broad understanding of how social norms emerge, persist and potentially change, based on a wide variety of perspectives from the social sciences. For details on habits, see Jackson (2005).

17 Aggregators of public opinion (such as the outcome of elections) can lead to a rapid change in otherwise sticky social norms when what appears to be publicly acceptable behaviour or expression of opinion changes (Bursztyn, Egorov and Fiorin 2017). See also Denton and others (2020).

18 Behavioural tipping occurs for several reasons. New behaviours may be associated with success (payoff-based transmission), they may be what is now most common throughout the population or they may be modelled by prestigious individuals (even though an individual's prestige may be unrelated to the behaviour; Legros and Cislaghi 2020).

19 See, for example, Legros and Cislaghi (2020), Nyborg and others (2016) and Young (2015). Tipping refers to the point at which a crucial threshold is reached and enough people adopt a certain behaviour that is then reinforced by positive feedback loops. This logic was first introduced in Schelling (1978, 1980), though in a slightly different context.

20 Young 2015.

21 Brooks and others 2018.

22 Nyborg 2020. Status quo–conserving effect is equivalent to the vicious cycle described in the article.

23 Jackson 2005.

24 Landorf, Doscher and Rocco 2008, p. 232.

25 See, for example, Eppinga, de Scisciolo and Mijts (2019), Lundholm (2019), Mochizuki and Bryan (2015), Monroe and others (2019) and Vaughter (2016).

26 Güven and Yılmaz 2017; Kola-Olusanya 2005.

27 These practices have been referred to as eco-parenting (Nche, Achunike and Okoli 2019). For more empirical evidence, see Matthies, Selge and Klöckner (2012).

28 Wells and Lekies 2006.

29 Eagles and Demare 1999.

30 Pettifor 2012. The study refers to parents that are partisans to the Green Party in England, Scotland and Wales. No causal relationship has been established. For more evidence on parents' intergenerational transmission of values, attitudes and behaviours, see Grønhøj and Thøgersen (2009).

31 Barrera-Hernández and others 2020. The study analysed 296 Mexican children ages 9–12. Connectedness to nature was measured by a scale consisting of 16 items that included, for instance, the pleasure of seeing wildflowers and wild animals, hearing sounds of nature, touching animals and plants and considering that human beings are part of the natural world. The measure of sustainable behaviour consisted of four components: altruism, equity, frugality and pro-ecological behaviour. Happiness was measured by three items of the Subjective Happiness Scale.

32 O'Brien (2018) describes this as one of three spheres of transformation. She highlights that these do not have to be fixed and unchangeable but are transformable.

33 UNESCO 2016, p. 18.

34 Email conversation with the United Nations Educational Scientific and Cultural Organization's Global Education Monitoring Report team in September 2020.

35 Kioupi and Voulvoulis 2019; Lundholm 2019.

36 The United Nations Decade of Education for Sustainable Development (2005–2014) sought to mobilize additional education resources to enhance sustainable development (UNESCO 2014). The Global Action Programme on Education for Sustainable Development (2015–2019) aimed to generate and scale up initiatives to accelerate progress towards sustainable development. It was based on five priority action areas: advancing policy, transforming learning and training environments, building capacities of educators and trainers, empowering and mobilizing youth, and accelerating sustainable solutions at the local level (UNESCO 2020a).

37 United Nations 2015a.

38 United Nations 2020h.

39 For data on quality of education see dashboard 1 in the statistical annex of UNDP (2019c).

40 United Nations 2020h.

41 Keller and others 2019; Monroe and others 2019.

42   Cincera and Krajhanzl 2013. See also Monroe and others (2019).

43   Cincera and others 2019.

44   Monroe and others 2019. These findings are based on observations from the EcoSchool programme, one of the biggest programmes on environmental education worldwide, in Czechia. Launched in 1994, the programme has spread to 64 countries, with 49,000 schools participating and approximately 16 million students involved.

45   The study used a small and homogenous sample of 276 grade 10 students in schools that prepare students for university ("gymnasiums") in rural areas and small towns in northern Bavaria (Schneiderhan-Opel and Bogner 2020). See also Dasgupta (2020), who argues that a deeper understanding and appreciation of nature is necessary to protect biodiversity, which can be partly achieved by transformative education.

46   Nguyen 2019; Wi and Chang 2019.

47   Clayton and others 2019. Bratman and others (2019) show how exposure to nature has positive effects on mental health in children and adults. It also mentions that the possibilities of experiencing nature have decreased in frequency and intensity (due to rapid urbanization, among other reasons) and that creating opportunities for these experiences and prioritizing projects with strongest positive impact on mental health should form part of urban and city planning.

48   OECD 2012.

49   Kioupi and Voulvoulis 2019.

50   Seatter and Ceulemans 2017.

51   Blumstein and Saylan 2007.

52   Benavides Lahnstein 2018; Haydock and Srivastava 2019.

53   Kowasch and Lippe 2019.

54   Anderson and Jacobson 2018.

55   O'Brien and others 2013. A more ambitious suggestion is to change the base of education. Following this approach, research in the natural sciences should integrate the humanities in an interdisciplinary approach, including the human dimension, to ensure that human behaviour, habits and emotions are considered in earth science studies to pave the path towards sustainability (Castree and others 2014).

56   Vaughter 2016. It has even been suggested that the reformed education processes include an inner dimension consisting of mindfulness and contemplation exercises such as body scan, breathing, gratitude, deep listening and compassion meditation, which have been shown to be critical for sustainability education and were well received by students in a small teaching experiment (Wamsler 2020).

57   Kioupi and Voulvoulis 2019.

58   Robertson and Barling 2013.

59   Anderson 2017.

60   Williams and others 2015.

61   Bessi and others 2016. Anderson 2017.

62   Ballantyne, Connell and Fien 1998. See also Gentry and Benenson (1993).

63   Ballantyne, Connell and Fien 1998; Damerell, Howe and Milner-Gulland 2013; Uzzell 1994.

64   O'Brien, Selboe and Hayward 2018.

65   Han and Ahn 2020; Trihartono, Viartasiwi and Nisya 2020; WEF 2020c. Thunberg's engagement did not, however, translate into successful negotiations at the country level at COP25, which testifies to the difficulty of securing international cooperation to address climate change (United Nations 2019b).

66   Druckman, Bayes and Bolsen 2019. There is the risk that large information campaigns backfire with those who already have an opinion or prefer believing their like-minded network (Druckman, Bayes and Bolsen 2019).

67   Chabay and others 2019.

68   The information deficit model, which assumes that the public needs more and higher quality information in order to overcome scepticism on (new) scientific topics, has received substantial critique during the past two decades. With regards to climate change, it has been concluded that providing information and knowledge is necessary but not sufficient to foster active behavioural engagement (Moser and Dilling 2011).

69   Lockie 2017; Prasad 2019.

70   Weisz 2011, p. 331.

71   Oreskes 2019.

72   Bolsen and Druckman 2018; Guber 2017.

73   Lockwood 2018; Milfont, Davies and Wilson 2019; Smith and Mayer 2019.

74   Smith and Mayer 2019.

75   Willis and others 2018.

76   Katz and others 2016. This study found that water conservation campaigns are as effective as price increases but usually last longer due to education effects. People have also been found to be more cooperative after the campaign than after the price increase.

77   Veiga and others 2016. This was a Europewide project, involving 15 countries with the aim of raising awareness and co-responsibility about marine litter through a variety of participatory activities.

78   Hungerman and Moorthy 2020. Good weather on the inaugural Earth Day is said to have led to less opposition to government spending as well as to higher donations to protect the planet with a long-lasting effect. Other studies find mixed results of initiatives on this day (Tortell 2020).

79   Bentz and O'Brien 2019.

80   Vaughter 2016.

81   Data from World Value Survey Wave 6 (Inglehart 2014b). For a review of other measures of environmental values, including the widely used New Environmental Paradigm Scale, see Bernstein (2020).

82   Data from World Value Survey Wave 2 (Inglehart 2014a).

83   Statista 2020b.

84   UNEP 2017.

85   United Nations 2017.

86   Barrett and others 2020a.

87   UNEP 2017.

88   Tyree and Morrison 2020.

89   European Commission 2011.

90   IPSOS Global Advisor 2020.

91   Steg 2016.

92   Lundholm 2019. For a theoretical framework for these claims, see discussions on the social dilemma from psychology and sociology literature—for example, Dawes (1980) and Kollock (1998). See also Huckelba and Van Lange (2020).

93   Dawes 1980; Kollock 1998.

94   Vezich, Gunter and Lieberman 2017.

95   See, for example, European Commission (2008), Derksen and Gartrell (1993), Rex and Baumann (2007) and and Schlegelmilch, Bohlen and Diamantopoulos (1996).

96   Vezich, Gunter and Lieberman 2017.

97   Wright (2010), cited in O'Brien (2018), p. 154; O'Brien, Selboe and Hayward (2018).

98   Kollmuss and Agyeman 2002.

99   While the quality of national governance is hard to measure, with different metrics heavily debated and contested, using the World Bank's Worldwide Governance Indicators shows that the quality of governance using this measure is positively associated with public and private investment in biodiversity conservation after several other socioeconomic variables are controlled for. While this relation is significant, the governance indicators are even more significant in combination with GDP per capita and a measure of globalization (Baynham-Herd and others 2018).

100   About 1.3 billion people across 107 developing countries—22 percent of their population—lived in multidimensional poverty in 2018 (UNDP and OPHI 2020). According to current estimates, about 690 million people—approximately 8.9 percent of the world's population—suffer from hunger (United Nations 2020g).

101   Remark by Greta Thunberg cited in Hungerman and Moorthy (2020, p. 1).

102   O'Brien 2020, p. 81.

103   Schwab, Dustin and Bricker 2017.

104   World Bank 2010. See also Jackson (2005).

105   The study refers to changes in diets of adults from the United Kingdom and that country's greenhouse gas emissions (Green and others 2015). For a study on the contribution of food to annual greenhouse gas emissions, see IPCC (2018) and Poore and Nemecek (2018). Another study provides evidence that what is often considered an excuse for inaction is actually true to some extent: Environmental self-identity is a strong indicator of environmental

behaviour; however, that behaviour seems to have low impact on the environment, as environmental self-identity does not predict overall energy use or the size of one's carbon footprint. The authors come to the conclusion that policies should focus on incentivizing high-impact behaviour as well as behaviour patterns and lifestyles (Moser and Kleinhückelkotten 2018).

106 White 2019.

107 Frank and Cort 2020.

108 Österblom and others 2017. See also Folke and others (2019).

109 This is directly related to the 2019 Human Development Report's topic of inequality, including inequality in political power and elite capture of institutions (UNDP 2019c). There is a vast difference between powerful and resource-rich people and the ordinary individual in leveraging resources and action for encouraging behavioural change (Nielsen and others 2020; Otto and others 2020c).

110 Brush 2020; Proctor 2020.

111 Levine and others 2020.

112 Hicks and others 2016.

113 O'Brien 2018, p. 158.

114 Otto and others 2020c.

115 Otto and others (2020c), based on Lister and Campling (2017) and Coulthard (2012).

116 Jorgenson and others 2018.

117 Huckelba and Van Lange 2020.

118 Böttcher and others 2020; McCoy, Rahman and Somer 2018.

119 Cook and Lewandowsky 2016; Dunlap, McCright and Yarosh 2016.

120 Data are for 2019. The companies are Amazon and Procter & Gamble (a consumer goods corporation specializing in personal care and hygiene products; Ad Age Datacenter 2020 and Statista 2020a, d). Budget data can be found at EPA (2020b).

121 Data for advertisement spending are for 2018. The companies are Genomma and Hypera Pharma (both pharmaceutical and personal care products; Kantar IBOPE Media 2019 and Statista 2020c). Budget data are for 2017 (Brazil MMA 2020).

122 Tortell 2020.

123 Tortell 2020.

124 Metcalf and Stock 2020.

125 Evidence is mixed on the effectiveness of legal restrictions on changing social norms. They might, for example, cause those who believe in the existing (damaging) norms to follow them secretly, making undesirable behaviour more difficult to reveal. This can hinder rather than help a change in these norms, because revelation would have led to disapproval by wider society, which would have ultimately been more effective in discouraging them (Legros and Cislaghi 2020).

126 Aasen and Vatn 2018. There is also evidence from two examples (the German transition to renewable energies and Cape Town's response to water scarcity) that positively framed communication strategies are more effective than collapse scenarios, since the latter lead to apathy and inaction (Strunz, Marselle and Schröter 2019).

127 Brooks and others 2018, p. 3.

128 Brooks and others 2018.

129 For critical reviews of these energy sources, see Botelho and others (2017), Goodale and Milman (2016), Jumani and others (2017), Kaldellis and others (2016), Rudberg and others (2014) and Sharma and Thakur (2017).

130 This is another example of a sensitive intervention point (Farmer and others 2019).

131 Westley and others 2011.

132 Steg 2016.

133 Nyborg and others 2016.

134 Brekke, Kipperberg and Nyborg 2010.

135 Hertwig and Grüne-Yanoff 2017, p. 973. Some authors have criticized nudging as being manipulative, curtailing people's choices (see, for example, Wilkinson 2013). Others have found that nudging can be justified to protect people's health or to preserve their autonomy (Nys and Engelen 2017).

136 Hertwig and Grüne-Yanoff 2017, p. 973. Boosting may be more respectful of people's autonomy than nudging because boosting emphasizes agency.

137 White and others 2019.

138 Pichert and Katsikopoulos 2008.

139 Regarding paperless billing, making opting out of paperless billing the default option has been shown to be effective in getting consumers to go paperless (Theotokis and Manganari 2015).

140 Nyborg and Rege 2003.

141 Funk 2007.

142 Moser and Kleinhückelkotten 2018. Dietz, Shwom and Whitley (2020) make a similar recommendation for the chain of production, consumption and waste disposal, as do Nielsen and others (2020), who point at social learning effects that set in when lifestyles change (for example, diet or transportation). These authors identify different timeframes for assessing individuals' impact, as some behaviour effects become significant only after accumulating over time.

143 IEA 2020e.

144 Nyborg 2020.

145 Patterson and others 2017.

146 Pew Research Center 2020.

147 UNDP 2020b.

148 Chen, Evans and Cash 1999; Galea 2016; Zacher 1999. Public health does not refer to individual health services, which are indeed not always a public good. Rather, it refers to the state of health in society—for example, the absence of communicable diseases.

149 Free riding is "the temptation to share in the consumption of the public good without contributing to its provision" (Stroebe and Frey 1982, p. 121). See chapter 5.

150 Reuters 2020.

151 Stewart 2016.

152 Piketty 2014.

153 Fisher and Jorgenson 2019, p. 350. The authors call this the anthro-shift. They point out that these shifts are multidirectional and can be reversed easily by other or new social events.

154 Lubell and others 2006; O'Connor, Bord and Fisher 1999; Smith and Mayer 2018.

155 Wright and Boudet 2012.

156 Grandcolas and Justine 2020; Vidal 2020; Perrings, Levin and Daszak 2018; Zhou and others 2020.

157 Otto and others 2020c, p. 4. Based on Archer and Archer (1996) and Beddoe and others (2009).

158 Ostrom (2009a), who shows this by means of numerous examples on sustainable management of natural resources.

159 Ostrom, Tiebout and Warren 1961, pp. 831–832.

160 Ostrom 2010.

161 Tiberio and others 2020.

162 Leach and others 2018.

163 Sen 2013, p. 18.

164 Basu 2020.

165 Huckelba and Van Lange, p. 18.

166 O'Brien 2018; Sen 2013.

167 Diamond 2011. For other past examples of societal declines, collapses, migrations and resettlements linked to severe regional environmental stresses, see Latorre, Wilmshurst and von Gunten (2016). For an example from the Arabian Peninsula, see Petraglia and others (2020). On how climate fluctuations (primarily cooling) between 1500 and 1800 can be linked to a series of human crises in Europe, see Parker (2013) and Zhang and others (2011). See also the review of this work by Pomeranz (2013).

168 The paradigmatic illustration used by Diamond (2011) included the collapse of Easter Island. The argument was that overuse of natural resources (in particular deforestation in part to build and move the well known monumental statues) generated ecological crises that ultimately led to the collapse of the human population. But more recent evidence suggests, instead, that the history of Easter Island was one of remarkable environmental resilience among indigenous peoples before slave hunters raided the island and introduced disease that destroyed that society (DiNapoli and others 2020; Garlinghouse 2020; Hunt 2007). More recent models attempt to incorporate the effect of inequalities with environmental stress, allowing for a more nuanced treatment of the dynamics of collapse Motesharrei, Rivas and Kalnay (2014).

169 Butzer 2012a; Butzer and Endfield 2012, p. 3630.

170 Butzer and Endfield 2012, p. 3631. As Haldon and others (2018, p. 7) argue, "[s]ocietal decline

or collapse is never monocausal and never predetermined. Rather, the environment is a continuous factor with which human societies interact. While it can adversely affect those societies, the causal relationship between them is complex, malleable, and has a different impact within a given society. [... Interpreting] causal relationships underlying how past societies mitigated their challenges, contemporary policymakers can develop more resilient and robust strategies to tackle the challenges of our own changing environment."

171 For a detailed explanation on the principles of distributional, recognitional and procedural justice, see Day, Walker and Simcock (2016).

CHAPTER 5

1 Mukanjari and Sterner 2020. Although the underperformance of oil companies may also be related to the oil price decline at the beginning of 2020.

2 See Denolle and Nissen-Meyer (2020) and Lecocq and others (2020).

3 https://www.iea.org/topics/energy-subsidies.

4 Coady and others 2019.

5 Coady and others 2019. Jewell and others (2018) found a smaller impact on emissions than those reported by Coady and others (2017), but Parry (2018) explains the discrepancy in terms of the scope of the impact of subsidies.

6 Coady, Flamini and Sears 2015.

7 Mintz-Woo and others 2000. See also Abdallah, Coady and Le (2020) and Derviş and Strauss (2020).

8 See, for example, Kaul and others (2003).

9 Fenner and others 1988. The international collaboration to eradicate smallpox was an impressive feat and "arguably the single most successful instance of superpower collaboration in Cold War history" (Manela 2010, p. 301). The two superpowers at the time facilitated mass production of vaccines as well as a programme to vaccinate people throughout the world (Manela 2010).

10 There is evidence that carbon dioxide emissions have been declining in the United States and some European countries (Le Quéré and others 2019), but those countries are unable to offset the growth in emissions in other countries. Global greenhouse gas emissions have grown every year since 2009. They are dominated by fossil fuel carbon dioxide emissions from both energy use and industry, which after growing 1.5 percent a year for a decade and 2 percent in 2018, are at a record 37.5 gigatonnes (UNEP 2019a). With the world on lockdown for many weeks due to the Covid-19 pandemic, global carbon dioxide emissions are on track to fall this year—but by only 5.5 percent (see Evans 2020). The fact is that utilities are still running, and electricity and heat are still being provided to homes.

11 The Paris Agreement aims at "holding the increase in the global average temperature to well below 2°C" and "to pursue efforts to limit the temperature increase to 1.5°C" (UNFCCC Secretariat 2015). The overarching temperature goal was a big accomplishment of the Paris Agreement in 2015, under the umbrella of the United Nations Framework Convention on Climate Change in 1992. The 2 degrees Celsius target had also been set in the Copenhagen Accord of 2009 (Gao, Gao and Zhang 2017). But the Paris Agreement went further, adding that states will attempt to hold temperature increases "well below" 2 degrees Celsius and including an aspirational target of limiting global warming to 1.5 degrees Celsius above preindustrial levels.

12 Slaughter 2015.

13 Hale, Held and Young 2013; Held and Roger 2013; Kotchen and Segerson 2019.

14 Höhne and others 2018; Rogelj and others 2016. The Paris Agreement, which came into effect on 4 November 2016, laid a high-potential framework for action on climate change (Held and Roger 2018).

15 Masson-Delmotte and others 2018; McKibben 2020; Schröder and Storm 2020; Steffen and others 2018.

16 United Nations 2015b.

17 Much financial activity and credit are short-term investing in financial assets, stock buybacks or real estate purchases—meant merely to capitalize on equity gains (Bezemer 2014). The challenge is to regulate finance and provide incentive through which financial market activities translate into higher and more sustainable investments to ease planetary pressures and advance human development (Jerneck 2017).

18 IRENA 2020.

19 Chawla and Ghosh 2019.

20 Chawla and Ghosh 2019.

21 Chawla and Ghosh 2017. India announced in 2019 that it would aim for renewable energy capacity of 450 gigawatts, more than double the original goal of 175 GW by 2022 (CEEW 2020).

22 CEEW 2020.

23 Dutt, Lucila and Barath 2019. Between 2014 and 2018 interest rate spreads over bank benchmark lending rates also fell by 75–125 basis points for both wind and solar photovoltaic, and loan tenures increased as lenders became more comfortable extending longer term loans.

24 Chawla and Ghosh 2019.

25 Lagarde 2019.

26 Collinson and Ambrose 2020.

27 Galaz and others 2015.

28 Braun 2020.

29 Azar and others 2020. The three largest asset managers are BlackRock, Vanguard and State Street.

30 Flammer 2020.

31 Climate Bonds Initiative 2020. Ehlers, Mojon and Packer (2020) find that current labels for green bonds do not necessarily signal a lower or decreasing carbon intensity, measured as emissions relative to revenue, and suggest that rating firms, rather than bonds, on their carbon emissions could provide a useful signal to investors and encourage companies to increase their carbon efficiency.

32 Baker and others 2018.

33 Flammer 2020.

34 European Commission 2019; European Union 2020.

35 Vörösmarty and others 2018.

36 This corresponds to the net present value of losses accruing up to 2100. The lower value results from applying a higher discount rate, typically used by private investors, while the higher value uses a lower discount rate, in the range used by government authorities (EIU 2015).

37 WEF 2020a, b.

38 Johnson 2020. The two funds, issued by Black-Rock, are the Eurozone Government Bond Index (which does not account for climate risk) and the Advanced Climate Eurozone Government Bond Index, which reweights the contributions to the fund by climate risk.

39 NGFS 2019b.

40 Dikau and Volz 2019; IMF 2019a.

41 Dikau and Volz 2019.

42 Bernal-Ramirez and Ocampo 2020 (see spotlight 5.1).

43 Krogstrup and Oman 2019.

44 UNEP 2020b.

45 G30 2020.

46 IMF 2020a.

47 Look 2020.

48 US Federal Reserve Board 2020.

49 Bolton and others 2020.

50 Bolton and others 2020.

51 Sustainability Accounting Standards Board 2020.

52 SDG Impact Standards 2020.

53 Tortorice and others 2020.

54 EBRD 2020.

55 Jagannathan, Ravikumar and Sammon 2017.

56 Inderst and Stewart 2018.

57 One encouraging development has been how the European Union has come together to ease fiscal pressures (Wallace and Minczeski 2020).

58 Robins and others 2020.

59 Nikas and others 2020.

60 Burger, Kristof and Matthey 2020.

61 Hepburn and others 2020.

62 Barbier 2020.

63 Engström and others 2020.

64 WEF 2020a.

65 UNEP 2019a.

66 UNEP 2019a.

67 Fullerton and Muehlegger 2019.

68 Johnson 2016.

69   See Mazzucato (2011).

70   Stern and others 2006.

71   World Bank 2020d.

72   Conference of the Parties refers to the 197 countries that have signed on to the 1992 United Nations Framework Convention on Climate Change (UNFCCC 2020).

73   Stiglitz and others 2017.

74   Carbon pricing initiatives are often met with backlash from the public. In France, for example, increases in carbon taxes led to what became the Gilet Jaunes movement. Carbon taxes were introduced in 2014 at $8 per tonne of carbon dioxide and increased to $50 by 2018. The public claimed that a large portion of the cost burden was falling on the middle class, given that the reform was introduced simultaneously with broader tax cuts that benefitted the wealthy. The government's plans to increase these prices up to $97 per tonne of carbon dioxide by 2022 have now been halted. In 2015, 92 percent of Swiss voters rejected a tax on nonrenewable energy. In Washington state a carbon tax has been opposed twice—in 2016 and 2018. While polls suggest stronger support for protecting the environment, when it comes to actual voting, people tend to oppose taxes (Anderson, Marinescu and Shor 2019).

75   IMF 2019b; World Bank 2019b.

76   Government of Sweden 2020.

77   Gissey and others 2019.

78   Carattini, Kallbekken and Orlov 2019.

79   Klenert and others 2018.

80   Boyce 2019.

81   Chancel and Piketty 2015.

82   Fullerton and Muehlegger 2019.

83   Climate Leadership Council 2019.

84   Carbon Pricing Leadership Coalition 2016.

85   Carbon Pricing Leadership Coalition 2016.

86   Borissov, Brausmann and Bretschger 2019.

87   IEA 2020a.

88   Timperley 2018.

89   International Carbon Action Partnership 2020.

90   Plumer and Popovich 2019.

91   Carbon Pricing Leadership Coalition 2019.

92   ACRP 2020.

93   IEA 2020b.

94   IEA 2020b.

95   The Living Planet Report found that the population size of nonhuman species has dropped by 68 percent since 1970 to 2016. These data are constructed from the monitored populations of birds, mammals, amphibians, reptiles and fish (WWF 2020d). However, recent analysis suggests that this may be an overestimation, given that it is based on the construction of a mean global index that hides variation across different species. Leung and others (2020) find that the estimate is driven by less than 3 percent of vertebrate populations, and if these are excluded, the global mean trend

turns to an increase. For more comprehensive assessments of biodiversity loss, see the discussion in chapter 2.

96   IPBES 2020b.

97   Hirsch, Mooney and Cooper 2020.

98   De Groot and others 2010.

99   Maes and others 2016.

100   Díaz and others 2018.

101   De Groot and others 2010.

102   Cherry 2011; EPA 2020d.

103   WWF 2020c.

104   Dasgupta 2020.

105   UNEP-WCMC 2016.

106   Karlsson and Edvardsson Björnberg 2020.

107   Salzman and others 2018.

108   The case of climate change illustrates the nature of the challenge. If and once catastrophic climate change is averted, all countries will benefit. This complicates incentives. It is tempting to free ride. Each country is tempted to not bear the costs (reducing emissions, changing technologies, imposing carbon taxes), hoping it can enjoy the benefits when climate change is averted. Also, each country knows that others are tempted to take advantage in the same way. With each country reasoning in this manner, the result is that no one has the incentive to bear the costs. Several strategies have been explored, both theoretical and practical, to change these underlying incentives in a way that advances the provision of global public goods such as climate stability (Kaul and others 2003). There are numerous instances of successful collective action. Many are at the regional, national and community levels, such as successful shepherding of common resources (forests, fisheries, pastures; Ostrom 2009a). Anholdt (2020) has argued that leaders of countries have a dual mandate whereby they are accountable not just to their own citizens but also responsible for working towards solutions to global challenges.

109   Convention on Biological Diversity 2020.

110   Victor and others 2017.

111   Hale 2020; Held and Roger 2018.

112   The Kyoto Protocol required reduced emissions in industrialized countries (called Annex I countries) over 2008–2012. It was hoped that even non–Annex I countries would eventually agree to limit their emissions. The protocol's targets for reducing emissions (about 5 percent a year) were limited, and the idea was to successively build on them (Barrett 2008). But the treaty lacked enforcement mechanisms, and the problems of nonparticipation and noncompliance were never resolved. The Kyoto Protocol implemented a strict interpretation of the principle of common but differentiated responsibilities and respective capabilities (see subsection below). Developing countries were exempt from obligations, even voluntary ones. This was against a backdrop in which many of them were emerging as large greenhouse gas emitters. The fact that large emerging economies were not part of the agreement

contributed to undermining of the agreement and lack of legitimacy (Held and Roger 2018; Rajamani 2012a).

113   It has been argued that the initial conditions, in the case of Montreal Protocol, were very favourable to international cooperation. For example, damages from ozone depletion such as skin cancer were felt by all countries, including influential developed countries. The costs of substituting ozone-depleting chemicals were modest. The companies manufacturing ozone-depleting chemicals also happened to be best placed to develop and make their replacements, and viable technologies to do so were within reach (Barrett 2007, 2008). The trade restrictions integrated into the agreement—banning trade in ozone-depleting substances between parties and nonparties—also acted as a credible threat (Benedick 1998; Werksman 1992). The threat to impose the trade restrictions were credible due to the issue of leakage (see box 5.2) (Barrett 2008).

114   Barrett 2008. The Kyoto Protocol expired in 2012. Its implementation phase was 2008–2012. Under the Doha Amendment to the Kyoto Protocol, a second commitment period, 2013–2020 was agreed on. During that period countries were to commit to reducing greenhouse gas emissions by 18 percent compared to 1990 levels. However, to come into force, the Doha Amendment required ratification by 144 countries, a threshold that was not reached until October 2020, when it was ratified by Jamaica and Nigeria (UNFCCC 2020).

115   Barrett 2016; Nordhaus 2015.

116   Barrett 2016.

117   For recent estimates of climate sensitivity that narrow the range of uncertainty of earlier estimates, see Sherwood and others (2020).

118   Barrett 2008.

119   Barrett and Dannenberg 2014.

120   Barrett 2016.

121   Ghosh 2020b. The inputs to design such an atlas would come from the United Nations Framework Convention on Climate Change as well as from the United Nations Convention on Biological Diversity, the United Nations Convention to Combat Desertification, the United Nations Development Programme and the United Nations Environment Programme, among others, in order to ensure institutional coordination.

122   Germanwatch, a think tank, produces the Climate Risk Index (Eckstein and others 2019). However, more work is needed to improve coverage for developing countries.

123   Kotchen and Segerson 2019.

124   Costedoat and others 2015.

125   Hayes, Murtinho and Wolff 2015.

126   Schelling 2006.

127   Ostrom 2009a.

128   Ostrom 2009b.

129   Behavioural and experimental studies have documented that reciprocal preferences—the desire to repay kind intentions by kind actions

and mean intentions by mean actions—are prevalent among individuals. See Falk, Fehr and Fischbacher (2003, 2008), Fehr and Gächter (2000) and Sobel (2005). Widespread reciprocity may also affect international negotiations and the prospects for collective action (Nyborg 2018).

130 Ostrom 2009b, p. 32.

131 Ostrom 2009b.

132 Green 2015.

133 Karlsson, Alfredsson and Westling 2020.

134 Aldy and others 2020. Among these cobenefits, those associated with reductions in adverse health effects due to fine particulate matter are the most important.

135 Hale 2020.

136 Ostrom 2009b.

137 Households may decide to invest in energy-saving appliances and better insulation. Neighbouring groups may decide to carpool to some destinations, instead of taking one car per person.

138 Hale 2020. Consider small island nations, coastal regions and arid regions, which already bear the brunt of climate change. They are likely to view the cost-benefit estimation of climate action quite differently from how inland regions do. There can also be differences in the private benefits, as described before.

139 CEPAL 2019.

140 Hale 2020.

141 Bernstein and Hoffmann 2018; Hale and Urpelainen 2015.

142 Victor 2019.

143 Biedenkopf and others 2017.

144 For an account of how technologies such as the catalytic converter developed in response to automobile emissions regulation in the 1970s, see Johnson (2016).

145 Heal 1999.

146 See Barrett (2003) and Mitchell (1992).

147 That preferences are unchanging over time is often a standard assumption. However, here past actions by others can change preferences for some actors, and institutions can facilitate this (see chapter 4).

148 Hale 2020.

149 In December 2019, just before Covid-19 reached Europe, the European Commission announced the Green Deal, committing to decarbonization and emissions neutrality by 2050 (European Commission 2019). In July 2020 the European Union unveiled its Covid-19 recovery plan and pledged that 30 percent of the package would go towards climate policies (European Commission 2020). The EU package has been criticized by some as lacking in detailed follow-up actions (Taylor 2020). In fact, many of the details have been left to national policymaking (Treyer 2020). The interaction between the Green Deal and the Covid-19 recovery package, and the net effects, will depend on the details of national policies (Kluth 2020).

150 Soon after the Montreal Protocol was signed, US company DuPont announced that that it would stop making chlorofluorocarbons. DuPont was the world's largest producer of chlorofluorocarbons, and this action had considerable knock-on effects. Later that year, a coalition of US producer and user companies announced support for a phaseout. European companies later followed (Barrett 2003).

151 Hale 2016.

152 Held and Roger 2018.

153 A dynamic, agent-based model of the Paris Agreement finds that the process delivers sufficient ambition and ratchet-up to achieve the 2 degrees Celsius goal only under a very restricted set of conditions. A key result is that if ambition is not increased from the start of implementation, the model does not produce any scenario that achieves the goal (Scælen 2020).

154 UNEP 2019a.

155 According to one study of historical emissions (from 1850), the United States is responsible for 40 percent of the overshoot in emissions over the planetary boundary (350 parts per million). By this approach, a majority of the world's countries have a climate credit. India is in credit of 90 billion tonnes of carbon dioxide (34 percent of total credit; Hickel 2020a).

156 UNDP 2019c. There is a high prevalence of recent catastrophic events such as floods, cyclones and locust attacks in India and Pakistan. In 2018 India was the fifth most affected by extreme weather, with 2,100 deaths and $38 billion in losses in purchasing power terms (Ghosh 2020a). The likelihood of catastrophic events is shaped by multiple stressors—which include climate change as well as local environmental factors. In India the state of Uttarakhand, for example, has become more vulnerable to flash floods due to land use changes such as deforestation and urbanization patterns, and the flash floods are likely more intense due to climate change (Dubash 2019; Najib 2019).

157 CEEW 2020.

158 Tortell 2020.

159 Barrett 2008.

160 Harrison 2010; Parks and Roberts 2008.

161 Dubash 2009; Held and Roger 2018; Rajamani 2012b, 2016. The Kigali Amendment to the Montreal Protocol is an example of the compromises that can be struck. India took a stand deciding to be part of a multilateral solution without compromising on differentiation. Even if unabated, India's hydrofluorocarbon emissions would be 7 percent of the world's total, and China's would be 31 percent. So in the final deal India agreed to freeze its hydrofluorocarbon emissions by 2030 (Chaturvedi and Sharma 2015).

162 Ostrom 2009a.

163 Much seems to hinge on how the review processes will work. Barrett and Dannenberg (2016) examine in the laboratory how well a pledge-and-review process similar to the Paris Agreement's works. They find that although the review process may increase the collective target chosen and the ambition of players' pledges, in the end it has only a small impact on contributions. Many other factors can determine the success or failure of these mechanisms (Hale 2017).

164 Dai 2010; Falkner 2016; Keohane and Oppenheimer 2016.

165 Sengupta 2020.

166 Malek 2020.

167 McCurry 2020a.

168 McCurry 2020b.

169 Held and Roger 2018.

170 Morgan Stanley declared that the emissions of clients and projects it finances would equal net-zero by 2050 (Mufson and Dennis 2020).

171 As mentioned in the 2014 Human Development Report, "the national orientation of public policymaking is increasingly at odds with the global nature of policy challenges" (UNDP 2014a, p. 114).

172 UNDP 2019c.

173 For experimental evidence, see Anderson, Mellor and Milyo (2008) and Tavoni and others (2011). For how these mechanisms operate in an urban setting, see Schell and others (2020).

174 See also Ostrom (2009a) on how divisions make collective action problems harder.

175 Held and Roger 2018; Rajamani 2016.

176 Under the United Nations Framework Convention for Climate Change, the Green Climate Fund is one mechanism to assist developing countries in mitigation and adaptation. Only $10.4 billion for mitigation and $4.4 billion for adaptation funding out of the $100 billion in climate financing promised under the fund has been raised over 2013–2018 (CEEW 2020).

177 Rabin 1993. showed that with strong enough reciprocal preferences, the standard prisoner's dilemma (two player) turns into a coordination game, with the real possibility of cooperation.

178 Nyborg 2018.

CHAPTER 6

1 Nature-based solutions boost the regeneration of nature through protection and responsible use of resources. They can help with mitigation of and adaption to climate change and with protection of biodiversity, while contributing to human wellbeing (Seddon and others 2020).

2 Griscom and others 2017.

3 Earth's oceans and lands are substantial global carbon sinks. Without their combined role the rate of increase of atmospheric carbon dioxide would double, and the current concentration would be 500 parts per million compared with 411 today. Anthropogenic use of land is also a substantial source of greenhouse gas emissions. Agriculture, forestry and other land use account for about 13 percent of global anthropogenic carbon dioxide emissions, 44 percent of global anthropogenic methane emissions and 81 percent of global anthropogenic nitrous oxide emissions (Shukla and others 2019).

4   This example is based on Keys and others (2019).

5   Ras 2017; UNCCD 2017.

6   McGlade and others 2019.

7   The most common in very high human development countries are storms, floods, wildfires and extreme temperatures. In low human development countries floods and epidemics are more common. Hazard events have taken a high toll on human lives. Some 1.94 million lives were lost between 1970 and 2012 because of climate, weather and water-based hazards (Whitmee and others 2015; WMO and UCL 2014), and 1.35 million were lost between 1994 and 2013 (CRED 2020).

8   UNDRR 2020. Some 92 percent of the mortality attributed to internationally reported disasters associated with natural hazards occurred in low- and middle-income countries, mainly in Africa and the Asia-Pacific region (McGlade and others 2019). Most deaths in very high human development countries are from extreme temperatures (67 percent) and earthquakes (22 percent), and most deaths in high human development countries are from earthquakes (69 percent) and flooding (15 percent). In contrast, most deaths in medium human development countries are due to storms (55 percent) and earthquakes (22 percent), and most deaths in low human development countries are from earthquakes (58 percent) and epidemics (33 percent).

9   IDMC 2020a.

10 UNDRR 2020.

11 Adger, Arnell and Tompkins 2005; US Department of Homeland Security 2016.

12 Multihazard Mitigation Council 2017.

13 WHO 2020a.

14 Petkova, Morita and Kinney 2014.

15 UNESCO 2020b.

16 EPA 2020c.

17 Heaviside, Macintyre and Vardoulakis 2017.

18 Szkordilisz 2014.

19 Szkordilisz 2014.

20 The measurements refer to the shortest distance between the edge of the green area and each measurement point used by the authors in the urban area around the green space studied (Hamada and Ohta 2010).

21 Doick, Peace and Hutchings 2014.

22 Aram and others 2019.

23 Chen and others 2015; Mahmoud 2011; Sun and others 2017.

24 Monty and others 2017.

25 Rapid-onset disasters refer to disasters due to natural hazards such as earthquakes, cyclones, floods, landslides, avalanches, volcanic eruptions and certain types of disease epidemics. They occur suddenly, often with very little warning. While slow-onset disasters refer mostly to food shortage or famine triggered by drought or pest attacks on crops, where the crisis builds up over several weeks

or months, they can also cover disasters caused by environmental degradation or pollution (Twigg 2004).

26 Murti and Buyck 2014.

27 Duncan, Dash and Tompkins 2014.

28 Das and Crépin 2013.

29 Venegas-Li, Morales-Barquero and Martínez-Fernández 2013.

30 Conservation International 2020.

31 CARE Interational 2016; WWF 2017.

32 Six women's learning centres were established for them to engage as community catalysts to change the perception of conservation and motivate community members to get involved in forest management. The programme helped women build their capacity for recovery, encouraging them to participate in decisionmaking, engage in advocacy on local issues and contribute to recovery in their community. Recognizing that promoting gender equality depends also on engaging men and decisionmakers as champions for the cause, the programme launched a pilot framework for men and decisionmaker engagement to support the leadership of women and marginalized groups as well as initiatives against gender-based violence (WWF 2017).

33 Alongi and others 2016.

34 Mowbray 2017.

35 Williams 2013.

36 Williams and others 2017.

37 Commission on Genetic Resources for Food and Agriculture 2015.

38 When different species in an ecosystem perform similar functions, the resistance of the ecosystem will be higher. This is known as the insurance effect (Oliver and others 2015). Genetic diversity has the same insurance effect, since an ecosystem with different genotypes resists changes easily (Hoffmann and Sgro 2011). Therefore, when developing risk reduction strategies, countries can take advantage of species diversity, since it ensures variation of traits within ecosystems. For instance, roots differing in thickness, orientation and depth are important for soil bioengineering since they can be used to make slopes more stable or as watersheds (Ghestem and others 2014; Stokes and others 2009).

39 Sultan and others 2013.

40 Bioversity International 2008.

41 In the community seedbanks female farmers have specialized in the domestication of wild species. Women have the knowledge of the best time to plant certain species, how densely to plant them and how to select good quality seeds for future use. Thanks to the programme they have become seed producers and vendors in the area, and several of them ended up selling vegetables in local and regional markets (Bioversity International 2014).

42 Commission on Genetic Resources for Food and Agriculture 2015.

43 UNEP 2016a.

44 Economic activities such as agriculture and energy production are water intensive. About 70 percent of global water withdrawals are used for agricultural irrigation (FAO 2017a; World Bank 2017a).

45 UN-Water 2018; Wada and others 2016.

46 Díaz and others 2019b.

47 Whitmee and others 2015.

48 UNEP 2016c.

49 UN-Water 2018.

50 Regions are classified as under water stress when net withdrawals of surface and groundwater meet or exceed the available supply, which implies no additional water available for ecosystem use or to meet future demand (World Bank 2016b).

51 WHO and UNICEF 2019. Contaminated drinking water causes an estimated 485,000 diarrhoeal deaths a year, a number that grows to 829,000 when diarrhoeal deaths caused by poor sanitation and hand hygiene are included. In 2017 more than 220 million people required treatment for schistosomiasis, an acute and chronic disease caused by parasitic worms acquired through exposure to infested water (WHO 2019a).

52 UNEP 2016a,b.

53 Throughout the early-mid 2010s, about 1.9 billion people (27 percent of the global population) lived in potential severely water-scarce areas, and in 2050 this could increase to some 2.7–3.2 billion. However, if monthly variability is taken into account, 3.6 billion people worldwide (nearly half the global population) are already living in potential water-scarce areas at least one month per year, and this could increase to some 4.8–5.7 billion in 2050 (UN-Water 2018).

54 Coates and Smith 2012.

55 UN-Water 2018.

56 Vörösmarty and others 2018.

57 Abell and others 2017; Abell and others 2019.

58 IUCN 2016. In addition to increasing supply to meet demand, it is important to improve efficiency, especially in activities intensive in water use, such as agriculture. So nature-based solutions have focused on water management for irrigation, which requires large withdrawals of water. Rainfed systems serving small farms and households also present opportunities for improving the efficiency of water use in agriculture.

59 Sun, Fang and Lv 2017.

60 IUCN 2016.

61 China Ministry of Environmental Protection and Stockholm International Water Institute 2017.

62 UN-Habitat 2011.

63 McDonald and others 2014.

64 Frantzeskaki 2019.

65 Frantzeskaki 2019.

66 Water.org 2020.

67 Moss 2020.

68 Oral and others 2020.

69 Masi, Rizzo and Regelsberger 2018.

70 Oral and others 2020.

71 Maiga, Sperling and Mihelcic 2017.

72 Stefanakis 2020.

73 Stefanakis 2020.

74 Sunderland 2011; Sunderland and others 2013a; Vira and others 2015.

75 Bioversity International 2017.

76 Sharp 2011.

77 More than 70 percent of the wild relative species of essential crops urgently need protection and risk extinction (Castañeda-Álvarez and others 2016).

78 Potts and others 2016b; Soroye, Newbold and Kerr 2020.

79 Potts and others 2016a.

80 FAO 2019.

81 WWF 2020a.

82 Sunderland and others 2013b.

83 Von Grebmer and others 2014.

84 Nasi, Taber and Van Vliet 2011.

85 Butler (2020) and Weisse and Dow Goldman (2020) using data from the World Resources Institute.

86 FAO 2019.

87 FAO 2020c.

88 Nassef, Anderson and Hesse 2009.

89 There are roughly 2.5 billion farmers (IFAD and UNEP 2013). Of the approximately 570 million farms, 84 percent are smaller than 2 hectares. Three-quarters of the world's agricultural land is home to family farms (Lowder, Skoet and Raney 2016).

90 UNCCD 2017.

91 TEEB for Agriculture & Food 2018.

92 Radosavljevic and others 2020.

93 Keesstra and others 2018.

94 Ricketts and others 2004.

95 Cheng and others 2017; Jose and Dollinger 2019.

96 Cheng and others 2017; Elevitch, Mazaroli and Ragone 2018; Losada 2019; Mosquera-Losada and others 2018.

97 See, for instance, Gupta (2019) and Ricker-Gilbert (2020).

98 Kituyi and Thomson 2018.

99 Sustainable Fisheries. n.d.

100 Cisneros-Montemayor and others 2016.

101 Sala and Giakoumi 2018.

102 Cabral and others 2020.

103 The mitigation measures considered in figure 6.4 include only cost-effective actions with abatement cost below $100 per megagram of carbon dioxide as of 2030.

104 Lele 2020. Investments in community-based forest management arrangements in Nepal have contributed to positive outcomes for both the reduction of poverty and deforestation (Oldekop and others 2019). Benefits also seem to be produced in the other direction as improving rural health care was shown to reduce illegal logging and conserve carbon in the tropical forest in Borneo (Jones and others 2020).

105 Erbaugh and others 2020.

106 Griscom and others 2017.

107 The United Nations Convention to Combat Desertification is leading the international community in this regard; so far 124 countries have set targets for land degradation neutrality (UNCCD 2020).

108 See Deutz and others (2020).

109 See Deutz and others (2020).

110 See Waldron and others (2020). The cost range: "the investment needed to implement the 30% target through protected areas ranges from $103 billion per year to $178 billion," and the benefit range: "projected 2050 revenues from all four sectors combined were between $64 billion and $454 billion higher than under the no-PA-expansion alternative (depending on scenario)." These numbers are obtained from a very specific type of project: "expansion of conservation areas to 30% of the earth's surface by 2030 (hereafter the "30% target"), using protected areas (PAs) and other effective area-based conservation measures (OECMs)."

111 Venables 2016.

112 Wamsler and others 2017.

113 Barbier 2010; Barbier and Hochard 2019.

114 See https://tnfd.info/.

115 WEF 2020d.

116 WEF 2020d.

117 Levy, Brandon and Studart 2020.

118 See Ogwal, Okurut and Rodriguez (2020).

119 See, for instance, Lambin, Leape and Lee (2019).

120 Neumann and Hack 2020.

121 IIASA 2019.

122 De Groot 2012.

123 Duan and others 2018.

124 Han and Kuhlicke 2019.

125 IPBES 2020a.

126 Jongman, Ellison and Ozment 2019.

127 IADB 2019, 2020.

128 AfDB 2019.

129 Schuster and others 2019.

130 Brondizio and others 2019.

131 UNDESA 2019a.

132 IDEAM and others 2017.

133 See Maxwell and others (2020) for a discussion on the limits of protected areas.

134 Walker and others 2020.

135 Anaya 2004; Merino 2015; Watene and Merino 2019.

136 Chao 2012.

137 The consequences of this dynamic are reflected in the negative trends in 72 percent of indicators developed by indigenous peoples and local communities to track the role of nature. See Brondizio and others (2019).

138 See also Butt and others (2019).

139 There is also an opportunity to introduce important and powerful technologies in partnership with indigenous peoples. Novel inventions and innovations are needed in the development of devices for real-time data acquisition and processing to assist in effective interdiction of illegal forest-clearing activities. An example includes the use of geographic information system mapping and three-dimensional visualizations in public consultations with indigenous communities in British Columbia, Canada, to enhance communication on and understanding of possible future landscapes scenarios (Lewis and Sheppard 2006).

140 Nobre and others 2016.

141 Anaya 2004.

CHAPTER 7

1 It is worthwhile hearing from Amartya Sen about the original motivation and intent: "[…] when my friend Mahbub ul Haq asked me, in 1989, to work with him on indicators of human development, and in particular to help develop and general index for global assessment and critique, it was clear to me that we were involved in a particular exercise of specific relevance. So the 'Human Development Index' was based on a very minimal listing of capabilities, with a particular focus on getting at a minimally basic quality of life, calculable from available statistics, in a way that the Gross National Product of Gross Domestic Product failed to capture" (Sen 2005, p. 159).

2 And the "success" of the HDI may have led to an identification of human development with wellbeing only—and even more narrowly with the dimensions included in the HDI—which was used by many to argue for increases in public spending on health and education and provide for basic needs, to the point that human development in the minds of many may have been equated simply with social sectors.

3 UNDP 2019c.

4 Anand and Sen 2000a; Fleurbaey 2015, 2020.

5 Fleurbaey 2020; Irwin, Gopalakrishnan and Randall 2016.

6 Fenichel and Horan 2016.

7 This being the case, Fleurbaey (2020) advocates for constructing and contrasting scenarios of possible future pathways for human development over several decades as the means to contextualize choices today. The process of "discovery" that is required is universally shared, and merely considering past pathways of countries that today have

high human development is not appropriate to inform future paths.

8   Mahbub ul Haq in the context of early Human Development Reports explored the design of a separate index that would speak more to agency. See the discussion in Sen (2000) of Haq's initiative to propose an index of political freedom. Despite the persistent reiteration that both the agency and wellbeing aspects of human development matter—and that in fact some of the more powerful critical analyses emanating from the approach are provided through the agency angle—that part of his project remains unfulfilled.

9   Stiglitz, Sen and Fitoussi 2009.

10 Durand, Fitoussi and Stiglitz 2018; Stiglitz, Fitoussi and Durand 2018.

11 As an illustration of the risks of relying on a single measure, consider the evolution of median earnings in a country, which is a reliable indicator of the income of a typical family and is distribution sensitive (by using the median and not the mean). It is well documented that this indicator has stagnated in many developed countries. But in the initial months of 2020, there was a sharp rise in median earnings in some countries, even as job losses accumulated. The reason for the increase was job losses concentrated in occupations with low earnings—thus pushing the median up (Crust, Daly and Hobijn 2020). That one should look at both price and quantity changes to assess an aggregate indicator may seem obvious, but once one specific metric becomes entrenched in public perceptions and discourses on wellbeing, that makes it ever more important to rely on dashboards of indicators.

12 Also used by Heal (2011). Or in flying a plane, as in Matson, Clark and Andersson (2016).

13 For instance, Fenichel and others (2020) argue for a dashboard approach to provide economic information on the ocean economy, including wealth but not collapsing all relevant information into a single metric to assess system provision and sustainability. A prototype is available at https://environment.yale.edu/data-science/norwegian-ocean-economy-dashboard/.

14 And even more rarely are they based on axiomatic foundations.

15 Since 2016 the Human Development Report has presented a new generation of five full-fledged human development dashboards in the statistical annex. They provide a more comprehensive perspective of the relevant data to assess countries on human development. The Human Development Report Office recently introduced two sets of new dashboards to capture the impacts of the Covid-19 pandemic on human development, one on countries' preparedness to respond to Covid-19 and their vulnerability to pandemics (http://hdr.undp.org/en/content/covid-19-human-development-exploring-preparedness-vulnerability) and one on the Covid-19 crisis and women's capabilities at risk and measures of safe space, balanced care work and the agency of women and girls (http://hdr.undp.org/en/content/gender-inequality-and-covid-19-crisis-human-development-perspective).

16 Available at http://hdr.undp.org.

17 https://coronavirus.jhu.edu/map.html.

18 https://ourworldindata.org/about. For another important dashboard, see http://www.oecdbetterlifeindex.org/#/01111111111.

19 The title of this section, "Broadening the vista," is borrowed from Chhibber (2020).

20 Thus leaving for future analysis the development of indices related to nonhuman life or the integrity of the biosphere as well as the incorporation of human agency into human development metrics.

21 It can be argued that this might help capture a wider range of impacts on people from the challenges of the Anthropocene than relying on longevity alone.

22 Ravallion 2010; Stiglitz, Sen and Fitoussi 2010.

23 Drèze and Sen 1990, p. 269.

24 Due to the logarithmic transformation of income when it enters the index. This also captures the idea that income works less well as a proxy for basic capabilities as income rises.

25 It is gross investment that is accounted for in GNI.

26 Borrowing from Dasgupta (2019).

27 One example is adjusted net savings, which "are derived from standard national accounting measures of gross savings by making four adjustments. First, estimates of fixed capital consumption of produced assets are deducted to obtain net savings. Second, current public expenditures on education are added to net savings (in standard national accounting these expenditures are treated as consumption). Third, estimates of the depletion of a variety of natural resources are deducted to reflect the decline in asset values associated with their extraction and harvest. And fourth, deductions are made for damages from carbon dioxide emissions and local pollution" (https://data.worldbank.org/indicator/NY.ADJ.SVNG.GN.ZS).

28 Following a suggestion by Fleurbaey (2020). We are grateful for the suggestion by Eli Fenichel of Yale University that this would map closely to the concept of income by Hicks (1939). See also Heal (1998).

29 In other words a country can emit very little and still suffer substantially from climate change due to emissions from others because carbon dioxide mixes in the atmosphere without respecting national borders. An example of estimates of the distributions of damages from climate change is Nordhaus and Boyer (2000). Moreover, most of the social cost of carbon comes from harms in the future. Deducting the social cost of carbon from current GNI is capturing the wellbeing of the current generation not only net of the cost of emissions on itself but also net of the cost of pollution to its descendants.

30 Nordhaus (2017) suggests a social cost of carbon of $31 per tonne in 2015 (in 2010 prices), increasing at 3 percent a year to 2050 (using a 2.5 percent discount rate and an integrated assessment model approach). Pindyck (2019) prefers the modelling approach, a method

based on a survey of experts, finding values as high as $200 per tonne of carbon dioxide. Hsiang and Kopp (2018) describe the key characteristics of the physical climate processes relevant for economic analysis, and Pindyck (2020) highlights some of the remaining uncertainties that are relevant for economic analysis of climate—in particular, climate sensitivity, how much temperature is likely to increase with a doubling of carbon dioxide concentrations. Jaakkola and Millner (2020) propose a method to incorporate new information over time to narrow the range of estimates of the social cost of carbon. World Bank (2020e) assumes the cost of damage due to carbon dioxide emissions from fossil fuel use and the manufacture of cement to be $30 per tonne of carbon dioxide (the unit damage in 2014 US dollars for carbon dioxide emitted in 2015). The Stiglitz–Stern Commission proposed carbon prices of $40–$80 for 2016 and 2020 (Stiglitz and others 2017).

31 Both for a global cost of carbon, even though the heterogeneous geography of climate change and of contributions to emissions would suggest the importance of considering country-specific prices (Ricke and others 2018).

32 Refers to the update to Nordhaus (2017) by Hänsel and others (2020).

33 Hänsel and others 2020.

34 As noted, this value is also within the range of those obtained by Pindyck (2019).

35 For Iceland, for instance, this would reduce the contribution of GNI to the HDI from $54,682 to $53,872, given its emissions of 10.8 tonnes of carbon dioxide per capita ($54,682 – [10.8*$75]).

36 For an early account of these efforts, see Daily (1997) and Daily and others (2000); for a recent review, see Barbier (2016) and Irwin, Gopalakrishnan and Randall (2016). See also Costanza and others (2014), Daly (1977), Daly, Cobb and Cobb (1994), Dasgupta (2014) and Stiglitz, Sen and Fitoussi (2010).

37 The Natural Capital Coalition defines it as "the stock of renewable and non-renewable resources that combine to yield a flow of benefits to people" (NCC 2020). See also Barbier (2019).

38 Fenichel, Abbott and Yun 2018. Because "inclusive" is often associated with more broadly shared outcomes (as in inclusive growth) and "total" could imply that there are no disputes on considering parts of nature as capital, we use "comprehensive wealth."

39 The System of Environment Economic Accounting is a "satellite" of the System of National Accounts (Turchin and others 2018), the international standard of economic accounts for measures such as GDP coordinated by the United Nations (for a comprehensive account of the key institutions and architecture, see Jorgenson 2018). There is very active and fast-paced ongoing work under the System of Environment Economic Accounting, including on experimental ecosystem accounting (see https://seea.un.org). Under this system a difference is established between natural resources or assets (say, oil deposits or the stock of a particular species of fish) and ecosystem

assets (the Baltic Sea ecosystem, for instance, comprising several species of animals, plants and abiotic, meaning nonliving, elements). This is an important distinction because the economic valuation of ecosystems is vastly more complex, depending on not only the number or species but also their interactions with one another. Here we use "nature's assets" as a broad category to include both as well as others that might be considered in the future (United Nations 2018, 2019a, 2020f).

40 Daly (2020) "defends" the notion of natural capital against those that object to it for perceiving the notion as one that "commoditizes" nature. Guerry and others (2015) illustrate the policy relevance of the concept.

41 To quote: "Wealth, then, includes all those parts of the material universe which have been appropriated to the uses of [humankind] It does not include the sun, the moon, or stars because [nobody] owns them. It is confined [...] to the appropriated portions of the earth's surface and the appropriated objects upon it. The appropriation need not be complete; it is often only partial and for a particular purpose, as in the case of the Newfoundland Banks, which are appropriated only in the sense that the fishermen of certain nations have the right to take fish in their vicinity" (Fisher 1906, p. 4).

42 As noted, economists have grappled with these issues going back at least to Irving Fisher at the beginning of the 20th century. The modern debate was reinvigorated when, along with economic theory, national accounting, formalized in the 1950s, made measures such as gross national product or GDP, meant to measure economic activity, widely available. GDP growth has often been equated with economic performance by policymakers and the public, who use GDP to assess differences in development across countries. GDP growth assumed heightened significance because it is key to understand the business cycle, the management of which became a primary focus of economic policy. People can also relate more directly to periods of GDP expansion as being associated with lower unemployment and higher earnings and periods of contraction with increased unemployment and economic difficulties. GDP growth may have been somehow more directly linked to improvements in welfare in the post–World War II recovery period (Coyle 2015), which may have entrenched it as a marker of development, or convergence (Spence 2011) for developing countries, many of which were newly independent after World War II, making GDP growth a universal aspiration. Economic theory, though, was always more careful and nuanced. In the early 1960s Samuelson (1961) was making the point that net national product, rather than GDP, could be used to assess social welfare, because GDP measures production while net national product accounts for consumption, which is what matters for welfare. Sen (1976) emphasized the importance of inequality and considered the distribution of real income, and Weitzman (1976) formalized the notion of equivalence between net national product and welfare. Weitzman (1998) argued that the equivalence between net national product and welfare would hold even under uncertainty and with a "comprehensive" net national product that accounted for the depletion of environmental assets.

43 Nordhaus and Tobin (1973) already asked in the early 1970s whether growth was obsolete and laid out proposals for measuring social welfare that drew in part from subcomponents of the System of National Accounts but that also estimated the value of leisure and some nonmarket activities. They also considered how to incorporate environmental damages and natural resource use. Anticipating much of the debate that unfolded over the ensuing decades and that persists today (for a good summary, see Jorgenson and others 2018), they raised questions such as the extent to which natural capital and other forms of capital can be substitutes for one another and the role of prices and technology in providing incentives for less environmental damaging modes of consumption and production.

44 Dasgupta and Mäler 2000. Crucially, these results extend to nonoptimal paths. They are based, as those in Arrow and others (2004), on an approach in which sustainability means that intertemporal social welfare (defined as the discounted utilitarian sum of utilities) is currently nondecreasing. In contrast, Pezzey (1997, 2004) relied on the Bruntlandt-like approach discussed in chapter 1, defining sustainability as the possibility for future generations to sustain at least the welfare of the current generation. Fleurbaey (2015) discusses the differences and the link between these two approaches to sustainability. We are grateful to Marc Fleurbaey for discussions on this topic. Genuine savings can serve as a sustainability criterion for both approaches (but with specific accounting prices for capital in each approach).

45 Dasgupta (2019), building on, among others, on Dasgupta (2001, 2014), with Barrett and others (2020a) presenting a synthesis and elaboration of the main results.

46 Hamilton and Clemens 1999.

47 Arrow and others (2012) analyse the wealth of nations by looking into the growth of different forms of capital: not only reproducible and physical capital but also natural capital, health improvements and technological change. By analysing data for five countries (Brazil, China, India, the United States and Venezuela), the authors demonstrate that looking into these additional forms of capital offers different conclusions on whether these nations are "getting richer" from what would be drawn by relying on changes in GDP only. See also Arrow and others (2004) and Dasgupta (2001).

48 Lange, Wodon and Carey 2018; Managi and Kumar 2018. These institutional efforts are complemented by very active ongoing research on global environmental accounting, such as Mohan and others (2020) and Ouyang and others (2020).

49 We are grateful to Luis Felipe Lopes-Calva for this insight. James Foster used this expression during the 2019 Human Development and Capability Association Conference.

50 Recent research shows that high HDI values can be achieved with moderate energy use and carbon emissions. Decoupling the HDI from per capita energy and carbon use has been documented from 1975 to 2005, and the carbon and energy needed to enhance human development are projected to decrease by 2030 (Steinberger and Roberts 2010). Therefore, a strong correlation between human development and emissions at one point in time does not imply the same relationship over the long run. For example, only a quarter of the increase in life expectancy between 1971 and 2014 can be attributed to higher energy use and related carbon emissions, though energy use and income growth are strongly correlated (Lamb and Steinberger 2017; O'Neill and others 2018; Steinberger, Lamb and Sakai 2020).

51 This is one of the contributions of the socioeconomic metabolic approach, discussed in chapter 1, which suggests what indicators could be used. See also Pauliuk and Hertwich (2015).

52 An alternative is to take the HDI as a whole and compare it with indicators of planetary pressures. An experimental approach to do this is included in spotlight 7.5.

53 For carbon dioxide emissions per capita the values are normalized in the same way as the components of the HDI, through a min-max transformation, leading to an index calculated as (maximum value – observed value) / (maximum value – minimum value). As a minimum, zero was set. The maximum corresponds to the maximum value observed historically for all countries since 1990, in line with the similar approaches in the literature, as in Biggeri and Mauro (2018). The same procedure is applied to material footprint per capita. The ranking of countries is sensitive to the selection of the minimum and the maximum; in the case of the maximum, it enters both the numerator and the denominator of the min-max transformation. Other aggregation approaches such as the geometric mean (which produces results nearly identical to those of the arithmetic mean), the minimum and the product (which produces an even larger adjustment) of the two indices were considered. A similar pattern of changes in the rankings was observed through these different aggregation approaches. Using carbon footprint instead of carbon emissions produces similar results (since the correlation with production-based carbon footprint is .99 and with consumption-based footprint is .95, both statistically significant at 1 percent), but coverage drops to 153 countries. Also, the latest year with available data for carbon footprint is 2016.

54 United Nations 2020e. For the conceptual foundation of the metric, grounded on sociometabolic analysis, see Haberl and others (2019). O'Neill and others (2018) provide a discussion of material use in the context of the planetary boundaries framework.

55 An alternative would be to add a dimension to the three components of the HDI that is aggregated with the other three dimensions in the same way. For instance, Biggeri and Mauro (2018) propose adding carbon dioxide emissions. But that would mix pollution with capabilities, creating conceptual difficulties (Malik 2020).

56 Pineda 2012. Hickel (2019a, 2020b) adds material consumption to carbon dioxide emissions, as here, and justifies the adjustment in a similar way as Pineda (2012).

57 Rodriguez 2020.

58 Fleurbaey 2020, p. 18. The quote refers to the context of assessing each country's contribution to preserving the natural capital of the whole planet.

59 This interpretation is also consistent with the open-endedness of the human development journey in the Anthropocene, in which the outcomes of the transformations that are needed can be understood, but a prescriptive indication as to how they should be implemented cannot.

60 And it is flexible, allowing countries to explore their own paths, as opposed to prescribing one particular option. For instance, changing the composition of economic growth by promoting clearly unbounded, and not very resource intensive, activities in art, culture and science, can advance human flourishing while easing planetary pressures.

61 For instance, the size of a nation's population is not included here. And the larger the population the greater the environmental impact, all else being equal. If population were included, it would tend to dominate the "loss function" (Pineda 2012).

62 In Luxembourg's case a high number of cross-border workers and a lower fuel tax also help explain its high emissions per capita. Singapore has virtually no natural resources, is a net importer of most goods and raw materials and has a large volume of visitors. Singapore also imports and refines crude oil as feedstock for its large petrochemical export industry, which contributes to the country's high emissions per capita.

63 Total pressure (not displayed), which is a product of pressure per capita and population, has grown even more as global population has increased substantially in the past 30 years.

64 See similar analysis in Lin and others (2018). As an image of aspirational space in development, it is also reminiscent of the idea of "casillero vacío" in Fajnzylber (1990). The aspiration corner should be understood in a stylized and illustrative sense, not literally, since all countries will have some level of emissions (what matters is net emissions) and need to use materials. Further refinements to the adjustment may take this into account.

65 See the discussion in chapter 1 and Andreoni (2020).

66 See chapter 1 for a discussion about relative and absolute decoupling in comparison to GDP. Overall, absolute decoupling appears to be partial, temporary and rare.

67 We thank Marina Fischer-Kowalski for insights on this pattern.

References

Aasen, M., and Vatn, A. 2018. "Public Attitudes toward Climate Policies: The Effect of Institutional Contexts and Political Values." *Ecological Economics* 146: 106–114.

Abdallah, C., Coady, D., and Le, N.-P. 2020. "The Time Is Right! Reforming Fuel Product Pricing under Low Oil Prices." Special Series on COVID-19, International Monetary Fund, Washington, DC. https://www.imf.org/~/media/Files/Publications/covid19-special-notes/enspecial-series-on-covid19the-time-is-right-reforming-fuel-product-pricing-under-low-oil-prices.ashx. Accessed 23 November 2020.

Abebe, M. A. 2014. "Climate Change, Gender Inequality and Migration in East Africa." *Washington Journal of Environmental Law and Policy* 4(1): 104.

Abell, R., Asquith, N., Boccaletti, G., Bremer, L., Chapin, E., Erickson-Quiroz, A., Higgins, J., and others. 2017. *Beyond the Source: The Environmental, Economic and Community Benefits of Source Water Protection*. Arlington, VA: The Nature Conservancy.

Abell, R., Vigerstol, K., Higgins, J., Kang, S., Karres, N., Lehner, B., Sridhar, A., and Chapin, E. 2019. "Freshwater Biodiversity Conservation through Source Water Protection: Quantifying the Potential and Addressing the Challenges." *Aquatic Conservation: Marine and Freshwater Ecosystems* 29(7): 1022–1038.

Acemoglu, D., Aghion, P., Bursztyn, L., and Hemous, D. 2012. "The Environment and Directed Technical Change." *American Economic Review* 102(1): 131–66.

Acemoglu, D., Akcigit, U., Hanley, D., and Kerr, W. 2016. "Transition to Clean Technology." *Journal of Political Economy* 124(1): 52–104.

Acemoglu, D., Johnson, S., and Robinson, J. A., 2001. "The Colonial Origins of Comparative Development: An Empirical Investigation." *American Economic Review* 91(5): 1369–1401.

Achakulwisut, P., Brauer, M., Hystad, P., and Anenberg, S. C. 2019. "Global, National, and Urban Burdens of Paediatric Asthma Incidence Attributable to Ambient NO2 Pollution: Estimates from Global Datasets." *The Lancet Planetary Health* 3(4): e166–e178.

ACRP (African Climate Reality Project). 2020. "Market Incentives to Decarbonize African Economies." Johannesburg. https://climatereality.co.za/carbon-pricing/. Accessed 23 November 2020.

Ad Age Datacenter. 2020. "Leading National Advertisers 2020 Fact Pack." https://s3-prod.adage.com/s3fs-public/2020-07/lnafp_aa_20200713_locked.pdf. Accessed 11 November 2020.

Adger, W. N., Arnell, N. W., and Tompkins, E. L. 2005. "Successful Adaptation to Climate Change across Scales." *Global Environmental Change* 15(2): 77–86.

Adger, W. N., Barnett, J., Brown, K., Marshall, N., and O'Brien, K. 2013. "Cultural Dimensions of Climate Change Impacts and Adaptation." *Nature Climate Change* 3(2): 112–117.

Adger, W. N., Dessai, S., Goulden, M., Hulme, M., Lorenzoni, I., Nelson, D. R., Naess, L. O., and others. 2009. "Are There Social Limits to Adaptation to Climate Change?" *Climatic Change* 93(3–4): 335–354.

AfDB (African Development Bank). 2019. "Are Nature Based Solutions the Key to Africa's Climate Response?" https://www.afdb.org/en/news-and-events/are-nature-based-solutions-key-africas-climate-response-33090. Accessed 25 November 2020.

Agarwal, S., Mikhed, V., and Scholnick, B. 2016. "Does Inequality Cause Financial Distress? Evidence from Lottery Winners and Neighboring Bankruptcies." Working Paper 16-4, Federal Reserve Bank of Philadelphia, Philadelphia, PA.

Agrawal, A. 2020. "Bridging Digital Health Divides." *Science* 369(6507): 1050–1052.

Akresh, R., Verwimp, P., and Bundervoet, T. 2011. "Civil War, Crop Failure, and Child Stunting in Rwanda." *Economic Development and Cultural Change* 59(4): 777–810.

Alam, K., and Rahman, M. H. 2014. "Women in Natural Disasters: A Case Study from Southern Coastal Region of Bangladesh." *International Journal of Disaster Risk Reduction* 8: 68–82.

Albrecht, G., Sartore, G.-M., Connor, L., Higginbotham, N., Freeman, S., Kelly, B., Stain, H., and others. 2007. "Solastalgia: The Distress Caused by Environmental Change." *Australasian Psychiatry* 15(sup1): S95–S98.

Aldy, J. E., Kotchen, M., Evans, M. F., Fowlie, M., Levinson, A., and Palmer, K. 2020. "Co-Benefits and Regulatory Impact Analysis: Theory and Evidence from Federal Air Quality Regulations." Working Paper 27603, National Bureau of Economic Research, Cambridge, MA.

Algaze, G. 2018. "Entropic Cities: The Paradox of Urbanism in Ancient Mesopotamia." *Current Anthropology* 59(1): 23–54.

Alianza Latinoamericana de Fondos de Agua. 2018. "Amèrica Latina: Fondos de Agua." https://ipmcses.fiu.edu/conferencia-alcaldes/anteriores/presentaciones-2018/nature-conservancy.pdf. Accessed 25 November 2020.

Alianza Latinoamericana de Fondos de Agua. 2020a. "Fondo para la Conservación del Agua de Guayaquil." https://www.fondosdeagua.org/es/los-fondos-de-agua/mapa-de-los-fondos-de-agua/fondo-para-la-conservacion-del-agua-de-guayaquil/. Accessed 25 November 2020.

Alianza Latinoamericana de Fondos de Agua. 2020b. "Nuestros Fondos." https://www.fondosdeagua.org/es/los-fondos-de-agua/mapa-de-los-fondos-de-agua/. Accessed 25 November 2020.

Allen, J. F., and Martin, W. 2007. "Evolutionary Biology: Out of Thin Air." *Nature* 445(7128): 610–612.

Allendorf, K. 2007. "Do Women's Land Rights Promote Empowerment and Child Health in Nepal?" *World Development* 35(11): 1975–1988.

Alongi, D., Murdiyarso, D., Fourqurean, J., Kauffman, J., Hutahaean, A., Crooks, S., Lovelock, C., and others. 2016. "Indonesia's Blue Carbon: A Globally Significant and Vulnerable Sink for Seagrass and Mangrove Carbon." *Wetlands Ecology and Management* 24(1): 3–13.

Alsop, R., Bertelsen, M., and Holland, J. 2005. *Empowerment in Practice: From Analysis to Implementation*. Washington, DC: World Bank.

Alstadsæter, A., Johannesen, N., and Zucman, G. 2019. "Tax Evasion and Inequality." *American Economic Review* 109(6): 2073–2103.

Anand, S. 2018. "Recasting Human Development Measures." Discussion Paper. United Nations Development Programme, Human Development Report Office, New York. http://hdr.undp.org/sites/default/files/anand_recasting_human_development_measures.pdf. Accessed 30 November 2020.

Anand, S., and Sen, A. 2000a. "Human Development and Economic Sustainability." *World Development* 28(12): 2029–2049.

Anand, S., and Sen, A. 2000b. "The Income Component of the Human Development Index." *Journal of Human Development* 1(1): 83–106.

Anaya, S. J. 2004. *Indigenous Peoples in International Law*. New York: Oxford University Press.

Anderies, J. M. 2015. "Managing Variance: Key Policy Challenges for the Anthropocene." *Proceedings of the National Academy of Sciences* 112(47): 14402–14403.

Andermann, T., Faurby, S., Turvey, S. T., Antonelli, A., and Silvestro, D. 2020. "The Past and Future Human Impact on Mammalian Diversity." *Science Advances* 6(36): eabb2313.

Andersen, M. 2013. "What Caused Portland's Biking Boom?" https://bikeportland.org/2013/07/02/what-caused-portlands-biking-boom-89491. Accessed 14 October 2020.

Anderson, A. A. 2017. "Effects of Social Media Use on Climate Change Opinion, Knowledge, and Behavior." In *Oxford Research Encyclopedia of Climate Science*. Oxford, UK: Oxford University Press.

Anderson, C., and Jacobson, S. 2018. "Barriers to Environmental Education: How Do Teachers' Perceptions in Rural Ecuador Fit into a Global Analysis?" *Environmental Education Research* 24(12): 1684–1696.

Anderson, I., Robson, B., Connolly, M., Al-Yaman, F., Bjertness, E., King, A., Tynan, M., and others. 2016. "Indigenous and Tribal Peoples' Health (The Lancet–Lowitja Institute Global Collaboration): A Population Study." *The Lancet* 388(10040): 131–157.

Anderson, L. R., Mellor, J. M., and Milyo, J. 2008. "Inequality and Public Good Provision: An Experimental Analysis." *The Journal of Socio-Economics* 37(3): 1010–1028.

Anderson, P., Charles-Dominique, T., Ernstson, H., Andersson, E., Goodness, J., and Elmqvist, T. 2020. "Post-Apartheid Ecologies in the City of Cape Town: An Examination of Plant Functional Traits in Relation to Urban Gradients." *Landscape and Urban Planning* 193: 103662.

Anderson, S. T., Marinescu, I., and Shor, B. 2019. "Can Pigou at the Polls Stop Us Melting the Poles?" Working Paper 26146, National Bureau of Economic Research, Cambridge, MA.

Andrabi, T., Daniels, B., and Das, J. 2020. "Human Capital Accumulation and Disasters: Evidence from the Pakistan Earthquake of 2005." Working Paper Series 20/039, Research on Improving Systems of Education, London.

Andrae, A. S. 2019. "Predictions on the Way to 2030 of Internet's Electricity Use." https://www.researchgate.net/publication/331564853_Predictions_on_the_way_to_2030_of_internet's_electricity_use. Accessed 4 December 2020.

Andreoni, J., Nikiforakis, N., and Siegenthaler, S. 2020. "Predicting Social Tipping and Norm Change in Controlled Experiments." Working Paper 27310, National Bureau of Economic Research, Cambridge, MA.

Andreoni, V. 2020. "The Energy Metabolism of Countries: Energy Efficiency and Use in the Period That Followed the Global Financial Crisis." *Energy Policy* 139: 111304.

Ang, G., Röttgers, D., and Burli, P. 2017. "The Empirics of Enabling Investment and Innovation in Renewable Energy." OECD Environment Working Paper 123, OECD Publishing, Paris.

Anholdt, S. 2020. "Measuring Countries' Contribution to Addressing Common Global Challenges." Background paper for Human Development Report 2018, United Nations Development Programme, Human Development Report Office, New York.

Anthoff, D., Hepburn, C., and Tol, R. S. J. 2009. "Equity Weighting and the Marginal Damage Costs of Climate Change." *Ecological Economics* 68(3): 836–849.

https://doi.org/10.1016/j.ecolecon.2008.06.017. Accessed 1 December 2020.

Appleton, A. F. 2002. "How New York City Used an Ecosystem Services Strategy Carried out through an Urban-Rural Partnership to Preserve the Pristine Quality of Its Drinking Water and Save Billions of Dollars and What Lessons It Teaches About Using Ecosystem Services." Presented at the Katoomba Conference, Tokyo, November 2002. https://vtechworks.lib.vt.edu/bitstream/handle/10919/66907/2413_pes_in_newyork.pdf. Accessed 1 December 2020.

Aram, F., García, E. H., Solgi, E., and Mansournia, S. 2019. "Urban Green Space Cooling Effect in Cities." *Heliyon* 5(4): e01339.

Archer, D. 2005. "Fate of Fossil Fuel CO_2 in Geologic Time." *Journal of Geophysical Research: Oceans* 110(C9).

Archer, M. S., and Archer, M. S. 1996. *Culture and Agency: The Place of Culture in Social Theory*. Cambridge, UK: Cambridge University Press.

Arrow, K. J., Bolin, B., Costanza, R., Dasgupta, P., Folke, C., Holling, C. S., Jansson, B.-O., and others. 1995. "Economic Growth, Carrying Capacity, and the Environment." *Ecological Economics* 15(2): 91–95.

Arrow, K. J., Daily, G., Dasgupta, P., Ehrlich, P., Goulder, L., Heal, G., Levin, S., and others. 2007. "Consumption, Investment, and Future Well-Being: Reply to Daly Et Al." *Conservation Biology* 21(5): 1363–1365.

Arrow, K. J., Dasgupta, P., Goulder, L., Daily, G., Ehrlich, P., Heal, G., Levin, S., and others. 2004. "Are We Consuming Too Much?" *Journal of Economic Perspectives* 18(3): 147–172.

Arrow, K. J., Dasgupta, P., Goulder, L. H., Mumford, K. J., and Oleson, K. 2012. "Sustainability and the Measurement of Wealth." *Environment and Development Economics* 17(3): 317–353.

Arrow, K. J., Dasgupta, P., and Mäler, K.-G. 2003. "Evaluating Projects and Assessing Sustainable Development in Imperfect Economies." *Environmental and Resource Economics* 26(4): 647–685.

Arthur, W. B. 1999. "Complexity and the Economy." *Science* 284(5411): 107–109.

Artiga, S., Corallo, B., and Pham, O. 2020. "Racial Disparities in Covid-19: Key Findings from Available Data and Analysis." Kaiser Family Foundation, 17 August. https://www.kff.org/report-section/racial-disparities-in-covid-19-key-findings-from-available-data-and-analysis-issue-brief/. Accessed 19 November 2020.

Asafu-Adjaye, J., Blomquist, L., Brand, S., Brook, B. W., Defries, R., Ellis, E., Foreman, C., and others. 2015. "An Ecomodernist Manifesto." https://www.ecomodernism.org. Accessed 19 November 2020.

Atteridge, A., and Remling, E. 2018. "Is Adaptation Reducing Vulnerability or Redistributing It?" *Wiley Interdisciplinary Reviews: Climate Change* 9(1): 500–20.

Auer, S., Heitzig, J., Kornek, U., Schöll, E., and Kurths, J. 2015. "The Dynamics of Coalition Formation on Complex Networks." *Scientific Reports* 5: 13386.

Auffhammer, M., Baylis, P., and Hausman, C. H. 2017. "Climate Change Is Projected to Have Severe Impacts on the Frequency and Intensity of Peak Electricity Demand across the United States." *Proceedings of the National Academy of Sciences* 114(8): 1886–1891. https://doi.org/10.1073/pnas.1613193114. Accessed 1 December 2020.

Australians Together. 2020. "The Importance of Land." https://australianstogether.org.au/discover/indigenous-culture/the-importance-of-land/. Accessed 16 November 2020.

Axbard, S. 2016. "Income Opportunities and Sea Piracy in Indonesia: Evidence from Satellite Data." *American Economic Journal: Applied Economics* 8(2): 154–194. https://doi.org/10.1257/app.20140404. Accessed 1 December 2020.

Azar, J., Duro, M., Kadach, I., and Ormazabal, G. 2020. "The Big Three and Corporate Carbon Emissions around the World." *Journal of Financial Economics*. https://papers.ssrn.com/sol3/papers.cfm?abstract_id=3553258. Accessed 1 December 2020.

Babcock, M. 2020. "A New Ontology for the Anthropocene: Seeing Beyond the Enlightment's Anthropocentrism to Reconceptualize Reality, Causality and the Human Mind." *St Antony's International Review* 15(2): 12–41.

Baker, D. P., Salinas, D., and Eslinger, P. J. 2012. "An Envisioned Bridge: Schooling as a Neurocognitive Developmental Institution." *Developmental Cognitive Neuroscience* 2: S6–S17.

Baker, M., Bergstresser, D., Serafeim, G., and Wurgler, J. 2018. "Financing the Response to Climate Change: The Pricing and Ownership of US Green Bonds." Working Paper 25194, National Bureau of Economic Research, Cambridge, MA.

Baldassarri, D. 2020. "Market Integration Accounts for Local Variation in Generalized Altruism in a Nationwide Lost-Letter Experiment." *Proceedings of the National Academy of Sciences* 117(6): 2858–2863.

Baldassarri, D., and Abascal, M. 2020. "Diversity and Prosocial Behavior." *Science* 369(6508): 1183–1187.

Ballantyne, R., Connell, S., and Fien, J. 1998. "Students as Catalysts of Environmental Change: A Framework for Researching Intergenerational Influence through Environmental Education." *Environmental Education Research* 4(3): 285–298.

Ballet, J., Dubois, J.-L., and Mahieu, F.-R. 2011. "Socially Sustainable Development: From Omission to Emergence." *Mondes en developpement* (4): 89–110.

Baqaee, D. R., and Farhi, E. 2019. "The Macroeconomic Impact of Microeconomic Shocks: Beyond Hulten's Theorem." *Econometrica* 87(4): 1155–1203.

Baqui, P., Bica, I., Marra, V., Ercole, A., and van Der Schaar, M. 2020. "Ethnic and Regional Variations in Hospital Mortality from Covid-19 in Brazil: A Cross-Sectional Observational Study." *The Lancet Global Health* 8(8): e1018–e1026.

Barabás, G., Michalska-Smith, M. J., and Allesina, S. 2017. "Self-Regulation and the Stability of Large Ecological Networks." *Nature Ecology & Evolution* 1(12): 1870–1875.

Barbier, E. B. 2010. "Poverty, Development, and Environment." *Environment and Development Economics* 15(6): 635–660.

Barbier, E. B. 2011. *Scarcity and Frontiers: How Economies Have Developed through Natural Resource Exploitation.* New York: Cambridge University Press.

Barbier, E. B. 2016. "Sustainability and Development." *Annual Review of Resource Economics* 8(1): 261–280.

Barbier, E. B. 2019. "The Concept of Natural Capital." *Oxford Review of Economic Policy* 35(1): 14–36.

Barbier, E. B. 2020. "Greening the Post-Pandemic Recovery in the G20." *Environmental and Resource Economics* 76(4): 685–703.

Barbier, E. B., and Hochard, J. P. 2018. "The Impacts of Climate Change on the Poor in Disadvantaged Regions." *Review of Environmental Economics and Policy* 12(1): 26–47.

Barbier, E. B., and Hochard, J. P. 2019. "Poverty-Environment Traps." *Environmental and Resource Economics* 74(3): 1239–1271.

Barbier, E. B., and Homer-Dixon, T. F. 1999. "Resource Scarcity and Innovation: Can Poor Countries Attain Endogenous Growth?" *Ambio* 28(2): 144–147.

Bargh, M. 2007. *Resistance: An Indigenous Response to Neoliberalism.* Wellington: Huia Publishers.

Barnett, J., and Adger, W. N. 2007. "Climate Change, Human Security and Violent Conflict." *Political Geography* 26(6): 639–655.

Barnosky, A. D., Matzke, N., Tomiya, S., Wogan, G. O. U., Swartz, B., Quental, T. B., Marshall, C., and others. 2011. "Has the Earth's Sixth Mass Extinction Already Arrived?" *Nature* 471(7336): 51–57.

Bar-On, Y. M., Phillips, R., and Milo, R. 2018. "The Biomass Distribution on Earth." *Proceedings of the National Academy of Sciences* 115(25): 6506–6511.

Barrera-Hernández, L. F., Sotelo-Castillo, M. A., Echeverría-Castro, S. B., and Tapia-Fonllem, C. O. 2020. "Connectedness to Nature: Its Impact on Sustainable Behaviors and Happiness in Children." *Frontiers in Psychology* 11: 276.

Barrett, C. B., Travis, A. J., and Dasgupta, P. 2011. "On Biodiversity Conservation and Poverty Traps." *Proceedings of the National Academy of Sciences* 108(34): 13907–13912.

Barrett, J., Chase, Z., Zhang, J., Banaszakholl, M. M., Willis, K. A., Williams, A., Hardesty, B. D., and Wilcox, C. 2020a. "Microplastic Pollution in Deep-Sea Sediments from the Great Australian Bight." *Frontiers in Marine Science* 7: 808.

Barrett, S. 2003. *Environment and Statecraft: The Strategy of Environmental Treaty-Making: The Strategy of Environmental Treaty-Making.* Oxford, UK: Oxford University Press.

Barrett, S. 2007. *Why Cooperate? The Incentive to Supply Global Public Goods.* Oxford, UK: Oxford University Press.

Barrett, S. 2008. "Climate Treaties and the Imperative of Enforcement." *Oxford Review of Economic Policy* 24(2): 239–258.

Barrett, S. 2016. "Collective Action to Avoid Catastrophe: When Countries Succeed, When They Fail, and Why." *Global Policy* 7: 45–55.

Barrett, S., and Dannenberg, A. 2014. "Sensitivity of Collective Action to Uncertainty About Climate Tipping Points." *Nature Climate Change* 4(1): 36–39.

Barrett, S., and Dannenberg, A. 2016. "An Experimental Investigation into 'Pledge and Review'in Climate Negotiations." *Climatic Change* 138(1-2): 339–351.

Barrett, S., Dasgupta, A., Dasgupta, P., Adger, W. N., Anderies, J., Bergh, J. v. d., Bledsoe, C., and others. 2020b. "Social Dimensions of Fertility Behavior and Consumption Patterns in the Anthropocene." *Proceedings of the National Academy of Sciences* 117(12): 6300–6307.

Barro, R. J., and J.-W. Lee. 2018. Dataset of Educational Attainment, June 2018 Revision. www.barrolee.com. Accessed 20 July 2020.

Bartlett, C., Marshall, M., and Marshall, A. 2012. "Two-Eyed Seeing and Other Lessons Learned within a Co-Learning Journey of Bringing Together Indigenous and Mainstream Knowledges and Ways of Knowing." *Journal of Environmental Studies Science* 2(2012): 331–340.

Bass, S. 2009. "Planetary Boundaries: Keep Off the Grass." *Nature Climate Change* 1(910): 113–114.

Basu, K. 2018. *The Republic of Beliefs: A New Approach to Law and Economics.* Princeton, NJ: Princeton University Press.

Basu, K. 2020. "How the Pandemic Should Shake up Economics." https://www.project-syndicate.org/commentary/covid19-pandemic-shows-markets-depend-on-tacit-social-norms-by-kaushik-basu-2020-06. Accessed 23 June 2020.

Basu, K., and Lòpez-Calva, L. F. 2011. "Functionings and Capabilities." In Arrow, K. J., Sen, A., and Suzumura, K., (eds.), *Handbook of Social Choice and Welfare, Vol. 2.* New York: Elsevier.

Batten, S., R. Sowerbutts, R., and M. Tanaka. 2016. "Let's Talk about the Weather: The Impact of Climate Change on Central Banks." Staff Working Paper 603, Bank of England, London. https://www.bankofengland.co.uk/working-paper/2016/lets-talk-about-the-weather-the-impact-of-climate-change-on-central-banks. Accessed 1 December 2020.

Battiston, S., Mandel, A., Monasterolo, I., Schütze, F., and Visentin, G. 2017. "A Climate Stress-Test of the Financial System." *Nature Climate Change* 7(4): 283–288.

Baynham-Herd, Z., Amano, T., Sutherland, W., and Donald, P. 2018. "Governance Explains Variation in National Responses to the Biodiversity Crisis." *Environmental Conservation* 45(4): 407–418.

BCBS (Basel Committee on Banking Supervision). 2020. "Climate-Related Financial Risks: A Survey on Current Initiatives." Bank for International Settlements, Basel, Switzerland. https://www.bis.org/bcbs/publ/d502.pdf. Accessed 1 December 2020.

Beck, U. 2009. *World at Risk.* Cambridge, UK: Polity.

Beckwith, C. I. 2009. *Empires of the Silk Road: A History of Central Eurasia from the Bronze Age to the Present.* Princeton, NJ: Princeton University Press.

Beddoe, R., Costanza, R., Farley, J., Garza, E., Kent, J., Kubiszewski, I., Martinez, L., and others. 2009. "Overcoming Systemic Roadblocks to Sustainability: The Evolutionary Redesign of Worldviews, Institutions, and Technologies." *Proceedings of the National Academy of Sciences* 106(8): 2483–2489.

Beja, E. L. 2014. "Income Growth and Happiness: Reassessment of the Easterlin Paradox." *International Review of Economics* 61(4): 329–346.

Bell, K., Sum, S., Tseng, J., and Hsiang, S. 2020. "Empirically Valuing the Contribution of Natural Capital to Firm Production." Unpublished manuscript, Global Policy Laboratory, University of California–Berkeley.

Bellet, C., and Colson-Sihra, E. 2018. "The Conspicuous Consumption of the Poor: Forgoing Calories for Aspirational Goods." Working Paper. https://www.idc.ac.il/he/schools/economics/research/documents/eve_colson_shira.pdf. Accessed 16 November 2020.

Benavides Lahnstein, A. I. 2018. "Conceptions of Environmental Education in Mexican Primary Education: Teachers' Views and Curriculum Aims." *Environmental Education Research* 24(12): 1697–1698.

Ben-David, I., Kleimeier, S., and Viehs, M. 2018. "Exporting Pollution: Where Do Multinational Firms Emit CO_2?" Working Paper 25063. National Bureau of Economic Research, Cambridge, MA.

Benedick, R. E. 1998. *Ozone Diplomacy.* Cambridge, MA: Harvard University Press.

Benjamin, W. 1973. *Illuminations.* London: Fontana.

Bennett, E. M., Solan, M., Biggs, R., McPhearson, T., Norström, A. V., Olsson, P., Pereira, L., and others. 2016. "Bright Spots: Seeds of a Good Anthropocene." *Frontiers in Ecology and the Environment* 14(8): 441–448.

Bennett, N. J., Whitty, T. S., Finkbeiner, E., Pittman, J., Bassett, H., Gelcich, S., and Allison, E. H. 2018. "Environmental Stewardship: A Conceptual Review and Analytical Framework." *Environmental Management* 61(4): 597–614.

Bentz, J., and O'Brien, K. 2019. "Art for Change: Transformative Learning and Youth Empowerment in a Changing Climate." *Elementa: Science of the Anthropocene* 7(1).

Benveniste, H., Oppenheimer, M., and Fleurbaey, M. 2020. "Effect of Border Policy on Exposure and Vulnerability to Climate Change." *Proceedings of the National Academy of Sciences* 117(43): 26692–26702.

Berger, K. 2020. "The Man Who Saw the Pandemic Coming." *Nautilus*, 12 March. http://nautil.us/issue/83/intelligence/the-man-who-saw-the-pandemic-coming. Accessed 23 November 2020.

Bergh, J. C. J. M. v. d., and Botzen, W. J. W. 2018. "Global Impact of a Climate Treaty If the Human Development Index Replaces GDP as a Welfare Proxy." *Climate Policy* 18(1): 76–85.

Bernal-Ramirez, J., and Ocampo, J. A. 2020. "Climate Change: Policies to Manage Its Macroeconomic and Financial Effects." Background paper for Human Development Report 2020, United Nations Development Program, Human Development Report Office, New York.

Berners-Lee, M., Kennelly, C., Watson, R., and Hewitt, C. 2018. "Current Global Food Production Is Sufficient to Meet Human Nutritional Needs in 2050 Provided There Is Radical Societal Adaptation." *Elementa: Science of the Anthropocene* 6(1).

Bernstein, J. 2020. "(Dis) Agreement over What? The Challenge of Quantifying Environmental Worldviews." *Journal of Environmental Studies and Sciences* 10: 169–177.

Bernstein, S., and Hoffmann, M. 2018. "The Politics of Decarbonization and the Catalytic Impact of Subnational Climate Experiments." *Policy Sciences* 51(2): 189–211.

Bessi, A., Zollo, F., Del Vicario, M., Puliga, M., Scala, A., Caldarelli, G., Uzzi, B., and Quattrociocchi, W. 2016. "Users Polarization on Facebook and Youtube." *PLOS ONE* 11(8).

Bettencourt, L. M. A. 2013. "The Origins of Scaling in Cities." *Science* 340(6139): 1438–1441.

Bettencourt, L. M. A. 2020. "Urban Growth and the Emergent Statistics of Cities." *Science Advances* 6(34): eaat8812.

Bettencourt, L. M. A., and Kaur, J. 2011. "Evolution and Structure of Sustainability Science." *Proceedings of the National Academy of Sciences* 108(49): 19540–19545.

Bettencourt, L. M. A., Lobo, J., Helbing, D., Kühnert, C., and West, G. B. 2007. "Growth, Innovation, Scaling, and the Pace of Life in Cities." *Proceedings of the National Academy of Sciences* 104(17): 7301–7306.

Beylot, A., Guyonnet, D., Muller, S., Vaxelaire, S., and Villeneuve, J. 2019. "Mineral Raw Material Requirements and Associated Climate-Change Impacts of the French Energy Transition by 2050." *Journal of Cleaner Production* 208: 1198–1205.

Bezemer, D. J. 2014. "Schumpeter Might Be Right Again: The Functional Differentiation of Credit." *Journal of Evolutionary Economics* 24(5): 935–950.

Bézy, V. S., Valverde, R. A., and Plante, C. J. 2015. "Olive Ridley Sea Turtle Hatching Success as a Function of the Microbial Abundance in Nest Sand at Ostional, Costa Rica." *PLOS ONE* 10(2): e0118579.

Bhattacharya, A., Meltzer, J. P., Oppenheim, J., Qureshi, Z., and Stern, N. 2016. *Delivering on Sustainable Infrastructure for Better Development and Better Climate.* Washington, DC: Brookings Institution.

Biedenkopf, K., Müller, P., Slominski, P., and Wettestad, J. 2017. "A Global Turn to Greenhouse Gas Emissions Trading? Experiments, Actors, and Diffusion." *Global Environmental Politics* 17(3): 1–11.

Biello, D. 2016. *The Unnatural World: The Race to Remake Civilization in Earth's Newest Age.* New York: Simon and Schuster.

Biermann, F. 2012. "Planetary Boundaries and Earth System Governance: Exploring the Links." *Ecological Economics* 81: 4–9.

Biermann, F., and Kim, R. E. 2020. "The Boundaries of the Planetary Boundary Framework: A Critical Appraisal of Approaches to Define a "Safe Operating Space" for Humanity." *Annual Review of Environment and Resources* 45(1).

Biggeri, M., Ballet, J., and Comim, F. 2011. *Children and the Capability Approach.* New York: Springer.

Biggeri, M., and Mauro, V. 2018. "Towards a More 'Sustainable' Human Development Index: Integrating the Environment and Freedom." *Ecological Indicators* 91: 220–231.

Biggs, R., Boonstra, W., Peterson, G., and Schlüter, M. 2016. "The Domestication of Fire as a Social-Ecological Regime Shift." *Past Global Change Magazine* 24(1): 22–23.

Biggs, R., Peterson, G. D., and Rocha, J. C. 2018. "The Regime Shifts Database: A Framework for Analyzing Regime Shifts in Social-Ecological Systems." *Ecology and Society* 23(3): 9.

Bilano, V., Gilmour, S., Moffiet, T., d'Espaignet, E. T., Stevens, G. A., Commar, A., Tuyl, F., and others. 2015. "Global Trends and Projections for Tobacco Use, 1990–2025: An Analysis of Smoking Indicators from the WHO Comprehensive Information Systems for Tobacco Control." *The Lancet* 385(9972): 966–976.

Bioversity International. 2008. *Implementing the Agricultural Biodiversity Programme of Work: The Contribution of Bioversity International and its Partners.* Rome.

Bioversity International. 2014. "Women Farming Wild Species in West Africa." Press Release, 21 June. https://www.bioversityinternational.org/news/detail/women-farming-wild-species-in-west-africa/. Accessed 25 November 2020.

Bioversity International. 2017. *Mainstreaming Agrobiodiversity in Sustainable Food Systems: Scientific Foundations for an Agrobiodiversity Index.* Rome.

Blakeslee, D., Fishman, R., and Srinivasan, V. 2020. "Way Down in the Hole: Adaptation to Long-Term Water Loss in Rural India." *American Economic Review* 110(1): 200–224. https://doi.org/10.1257/aer.20180976. Accessed 1 December 2020.

Blanchard, O., and Rodrik, D., (eds.). Forthcoming. Combating Inequalities. Cambridge, MA: MIT Press.

Bleischwitz, R., Nechifor, V., Winning, M., Huang, B., and Geng, Y. 2018. "Extrapolation or Saturation: Revisiting Growth Patterns, Development Stages and Decoupling." *Global Environmental Change* 48: 86–96.

Bloch, M., Reinhard, S., Tompkins, L., Pietsch, B., and McDonnell Nieto del Rio, G. 2020. "Fire Map: California, Oregon and Washington." *New York Times.* https://www.nytimes.com/interactive/2020/us/fires-map-tracker.html. Accessed 18 November 2020.

Blomfield, M. 2019. *Global Justice, Natural Resources, and Climate Change.* New York: Oxford University Press.

Blomqvist, L., Brook, B. W., Ellis, E. C., Kareiva, P. M., Nordhaus, T., and Shellenberger, M. 2013. "Does the Shoe Fit? Real Versus Imagined Ecological Footprints." *PLOS Biology* 11(11): e1001700.

Bloomberg. 2019. *New Energy Outlook 2019.* New York.

Blumenstock, J. 2018. "Don't Forget People in the Use of Big Data for Development." *Nature* 561: 170–172.

Blumstein, D. T., and Saylan, C. 2007. "The Failure of Environmental Education (and How We Can Fix It)." *PLOS Biology* 5(5).

Blythe, J., Silver, J., Evans, L., Armitage, D., Bennett, N. J., Moore, M.-L., Morrison, T. H., and Brown, K. 2018. "The Dark Side of Transformation: Latent Risks in Contemporary Sustainability Discourse." *Antipode* 50(5): 1206–1223.

Bocquet-Appel, J.-P. 2011. "When the World's Population Took Off: The Springboard of the Neolithic Demographic Transition." *Science* 333(6042): 560–561.

Boden, T. A., G. Marland, and R. J. Andres. 2017. "Global, Regional, and National Fossil-Fuel CO2 Emissions." US Department of Energy, Oak Ridge National Laboratory, Oak Ridge, TN.

Boivin, N. L., Zeder, M. A., Fuller, D. Q., Crowther, A., Larson, G., Erlandson, J. M., Denham, T., and Petraglia, M. D. 2016. "Ecological Consequences of Human Niche Construction: Examining Long-Term Anthropogenic Shaping of Global Species Distributions." *Proceedings of the National Academy of Sciences* 113(23): 6388–6396.

Bolsen, T., and Druckman, J. N. 2018. "Do Partisanship and Politicization Undermine the Impact of a Scientific Consensus Message about Climate Change?" *Group Processes & Intergroup Relations* 21(3): 389–402.

Bolton, P., Despres, M., da Silva, L. A. P., Svartzman, R., and Samama, F. 2020. *The Green Swan: Central Banking and Financial Stability in the Age of Climate Change.* Bank for International Settlements. https://www.bis.org/publ/othp31.pdf. Accessed 1 December 2020.

Bond, P., and Sharife, K. 2012. "Africa's Biggest Landfill Site: The Case of Bisasar Road." *Le Monde diplomatique,* 27 April. https://mondediplo.com/outsidein/africa-s-biggest-landfill-site-the-case-of. Accessed 19 November 2020.

Bongaarts, J., and O'Neill, B. C. 2018. "Global Warming Policy: Is Population Left out in the Cold?" *Science* 361(6403): 650–652.

Borissov, K., Brausmann, A., and Bretschger, L. 2019. "Carbon Pricing, Technology Transition, and Skill-Based Development." *European Economic Review* 118: 252–269.

Borrows, J., and Rotman, L. I. 1997. "The Sui Generis Nature of Aboriginal Rights: Does It Make a Difference." *Alberta Law Review* 36(1): 9–45.

Borucke, M., Moore, D., Cranston, G., Gracey, K., Iha, K., Larson, J., Lazarus, E., and others. 2013. "Accounting for Demand and Supply of the Biosphere's Regenerative Capacity: The National Footprint Accounts' Underlying Methodology and Framework." *Ecological Indicators* 24: 518–533.

Boserup, E. 1965. *The Conditions of Agricultural Growth: The Economics of Agrarian Change under Population Pressure.* London: George All & Unwin, Ltd.

Bostrom, N. S. 2002. "Existential Risks: Analyzing Human Extinction Scenarios and Related Hazards." *Journal of Evolution and Technology* 9(1).

Bostrom, N. S. 2014. *Paths, Dangers, Strategies.* Oxford, UK: Oxford University Press.

Botelho, A., Ferreira, P., Lima, F., Pinto, L. M. C., and Sousa, S. 2017. "Assessment of the Environmental Impacts Associated with Hydropower." *Renewable and Sustainable Energy Reviews* 70: 896–904.

Böttcher, L., Montealegre, P., Goles, E., and Gersbach, H. 2020. "Competing Activists—Political Polarization." *Physica A: Statistical Mechanics and its Applications* 545: 123713.

Boulding, K. E. 1966. "The Economics of the Coming Spaceship Earth." In Jarrett, H., (ed.), *Environmental Quality in a Growing Economy.* Baltimore, MD: Resources for the Future/Johns Hopkins University Press.

Boyce, J. K. 2019. *The Case for Carbon Dividends.* Medford, MA: Polity Press.

Boyd, R. 2019. *A Different Kind of Animal: How Culture Transformed Our Species.* Princeton, NJ: Princeton University Press.

Braje, T. J. 2015. "Earth Systems, Human Agency, and the Anthropocene: Planet Earth in the Human Age." *Journal of Archaeological Research* 23(4): 369–396.

Braje, T. J. 2016. "Evaluating the Anthropocene: Is There Something Useful About a Geological Epoch of Humans?" *Antiquity* 90(350): 504–512.

Braje, T. J. 2018. "The Anthropocene as Process: Why We Should View the State of the World through a Deep Historical Lens." *Revista de Estudos e Pesquisas Avançadas do Terceiro Setor* 1(1): 4–20.

Brand-Correa, L. I., and Steinberger, J. K. 2017. "A Framework for Decoupling Human Need Satisfaction from Energy Use." *Ecological Economics* 141: 43–52.

Bratman, G. N., Anderson, C. B., Berman, M. G., Cochran, B., De Vries, S., Flanders, J., Folke, C., and others. 2019. "Nature and Mental Health: An Ecosystem Service Perspective." *Science Advances* 5(7): 1–14.

Braun, B. 2020. "American Asset Manager Capitalism." *SocArXiv,* 18 June. https://osf.io/preprints/socarxiv/v6gue. Accessed 1 December 2020.

Bravo, G. 2014. "The Human Sustainable Development Index: New Calculations and a First Critical Analysis." *Ecological Indicators* 37: 145–150.

Brazil MMA (Ministério do Meio Ambiente). 2020. "Orçamento." https://www.mma.gov.br/mma-em-numeros/or%C3%A7amento. Accessed 12 August 2020.

Brekke, K. A., Kipperberg, G., and Nyborg, K. 2010. "Social Interaction in Responsibility Ascription: The Case of Household Recycling." *Land Economics* 86(4): 766–784.

Breslow, S. J., Sojka, B., Barnea, R., Basurto, X., Carothers, C., Charnley, S., Coulthard, S., and others. 2016. "Conceptualizing and Operationalizing Human Wellbeing for Ecosystem Assessment and Management." *Environmental Science & Policy* 66: 250–259.

Brockway, P. E., Saunders, H., Heun, M. K., Foxon, T. J., Steinberger, J. K., Barrett, J. R., and Sorrell, S. 2017. "Energy Rebound as a Potential Threat to a Low-Carbon Future: Findings from a New Exergy-Based National-Level Rebound Approach." *Energies* 10(1): 51.

Brondizio, E. S., O'Brien, K., Bai, X., Biermann, F., Steffen, W., Berkhout, F., Cudennec, C., and others. 2016. "Re-Conceptualizing the Anthropocene: A Call for Collaboration." *Global Environmental Change* 39: 318–327.

Brondizio, E. S., Settele, J., Díaz, S., and H. T. Ngo. 2019. *Global Assessment Report on Biodiversity and Ecosystem Services.* Bonn, Germany: Intergovernmental Science-Policy Platform on Biodiversity and Ecosystem Services Secretariat.

Brondizio, E. S., and Tourneau, F.-M. L. 2016. "Environmental Governance for All." *Science* 352(6291): 1272–1273.

Brooks, A. S., Yellen, J. E., Potts, R., Behrensmeyer, A. K., Deino, A. L., Leslie, D. E., Ambrose, S. H., and others. 2018. "Long-Distance Stone Transport and Pigment Use in the Earliest Middle Stone Age." *Science* 360(6384): 90–94.

Brooks, J. S., Waring, T. M., Mulder, M. B., and Richerson, P. J. 2018. "Applying Cultural Evolution to Sustainability Challenges: An Introduction to the Special Issue." *Sustainability Science* 13(1): 1–8.

Brown, J. H., Gillooly, J. F., Allen, A. P., Savage, V. M., and West, G. B. 2004. "Toward a Metabolic Theory of Ecology." *Ecology* 85(7): 1771–1789.

Brown, K. 2018. "El Pequeño Pueblo Que Lucha Contra Un Gigante Del Aceite De Palma En Ecuador." Mongabay Latam Periodismo Ambiental Independiente.

Brown, K., Adger, W. N., Devine-Wright, P., Anderies, J. M., Barr, S., Bousquet, F., Butler, C., and others. 2019. "Empathy, Place and Identity Interactions for Sustainability." *Global Environmental Change* 56: 11–17.

Browne, M. W. 1990. "Nuclear Winter Theorists Pull Back." *New York Times,* 23 January.

Brundtland Commission. 1987. "Report of the World Commission on Environment and Development: Our Common Future." New York: United Nations.

Brundtland, G. 1987. *Our Common Future: Report of the World Commission on Environment and Development.* New York: United Nations. https://sustainabledevelopment.un.org/content/documents/5987our-common-future.pdf. Accessed 16 November 2020.

Brush, E. 2020. "Inconvenient Truths: Pluralism, Pragmatism, and the Need for Civil Disagreement." *Journal of Environmental Studies and Sciences* 10: 160–168.

Bui, M., Adjiman, C. S., Bardow, A., Anthony, E. J., Boston, A., Brown, S., Fennell, P. S., and others. 2018. "Carbon Capture and Storage (CCS): The Way Forward." *Energy & Environmental Science* 11(5): 1062–1176.

Bull, J. W., and Maron, M. 2016. "How Humans Drive Speciation as Well as Extinction." *Proceedings of the Royal Society B: Biological Sciences* 283: 1–10.

Bullard III, C. W., and Herendeen, R. A. 1975. "The Energy Cost of Goods and Services." *Energy Policy* 3(4): 268–278.

Bullard, R. D. 1983. "Solid Waste Sites and the Black Houston Community." *Sociological Inquiry* 53(2–3): 273–288.

Bullard, R. D. 2008. *Dumping in Dixie: Race, Class, and Environmental Quality.* Boulder, CO: Westview Press.

Burger, A., Kristof, K., and Matthey, A. 2020. *The Green New Consensus: Study Shows Broad Consensus on Green Recovery Programmes and Structural Reforms.* Berlin: German Federal Environment Agency. https://www.conpolicy.de/en/news-detail/the-green-new-consensus-study-shows-broad-consensus-on-green-recovery-programmes-and-structural-ref/. Accessed 23 November 2020.

Burger, O., Baudisch, A., and Vaupel, J. W. 2012. "Human Mortality Improvement in Evolutionary Context." *Proceedings of the National Academy of Sciences* 109(44): 18210–18214.

Burke, K., Williams, J., Chandler, M., Haywood, A., Lunt, D., and Otto-Bliesner, B. 2018. "Pliocene and Eocene Provide Best Analogs for near-Future Climates." *Proceedings of the National Academy of Sciences* 115(52): 13288–13293.

Burke, M., Driscoll, A., Lobell, D., and Ermon, S. 2020. "Using Satellite Imagery to Understand and Promote Sustainable Development." Working Paper w27879, National Bureau of Economic Research, Cambridge, MA.

Burke, M., González, F., Baylis, P., Heft-Neal, S., Baysan, C., Basu, S., and Hsiang, S. 2018. "Higher Temperatures Increase Suicide Rates in the United States and Mexico." *Nature Climate Change* 8(8): 723–729. https://doi.org/10.1038/s41558-018-0222-x. Accessed 1 December 2020.

Burke, M., Hsiang, S. M., and Miguel, E. 2015. "Global Non-Linear Effect of Temperature on Economic Production." *Nature* 527(7577): 235–239. https://doi.org/10.1038/nature15725. Accessed 1 December 2020.

Burki, T. 2020. "The Origin of SARS-CoV-2." *The Lancet Infectious Diseases* 20(9): 1018–1019.

Burney, J., and V. Ramanathan. 2014. "Recent Climate and Air Pollution Impacts on Indian Agriculture." *Proceedings of the National Academy of*

Sciences 111(46): 16319–16324. https://doi.org/10.1073/pnas.1317275111. Accessed 1 December 2020.

Bursztyn, L., Egorov, G., and Fiorin, S. 2017. "From Extreme to Mainstream: How Social Norms Unravel." Working Paper 23415, National Bureau of Economic Research, Cambridge, MA. https://www.nber.org/system/files/working_papers/w23415/w23415.pdf. Accessed 11 November 2020.

Burton, I., and Kates, R. W. 1986. "The Great Climacteric, 1798–2048: The Transition to a Just and Sustainable Human Environment." Geography, Resources, and Environment. Chicago, IL: University of Chicago Press.

Bush, M. B. 2019. "A Neotropical Perspective on Past Human-Climate Interactions and Biodiversity." In Lovejoy, T. E., and Hannah, L., (eds.), Biodiversity and Climate Change: Transforming the Biosphere. New Haven, CT: Yale University Press.

Butler, R. 2020. "How Much Rainforest Is Being Destroyed?" Mongabay News, 10 June. https://news.mongabay.com/2020/06/how-much-rainforest-is-being-destroyed/. Accessed 25 November 2020.

Butt, N., Lambrick, F., Menton, M., and Renwick, A. 2019. "The Supply Chain of Violence." Nature Sustainability 2(8): 742–747.

Butzer, K. W. 2012a. "Collapse, Environment, and Society." Proceedings of the National Academy of Sciences 109(10): 3632–3639.

Butzer, K. W. 2012b. "Reply to Pearson and Pearson: Reflections on Historical vs. Contemporary Information." Proceedings of the National Academy of Sciences 109(30): E2032–E2032.

Butzer, K. W., and Endfield, G. H. 2012. "Critical Perspectives on Historical Collapse." Proceedings of the National Academy of Sciences 109(10): 3628–3631.

Cabral, R. B., Bradley, D., Mayorga, J., Goodell, W., Friedlander, A. M., Sala, E., Costello, C., and Gaines, S. D. 2020. "A Global Network of Marine Protected Areas for Food." Proceedings of the National Academy of Sciences 117(45): 28134–28139.

Cai, Y., Lenton, T. M., and Lontzek, T. S. 2016. "Risk of Multiple Interacting Tipping Points Should Encourage Rapid CO_2 Emission Reduction." Nature Climate Change 6(5): 520–525.

Caicedo, S., Lucas Jr, R. E., and Rossi-Hansberg, E. 2019. "Learning, Career Paths, and the Distribution of Wages." American Economic Journal: Macroeconomics 11(1): 49–88.

Calvino, I. 2013. Collection of Sand: Essays. New York: Houghton Mifflin Harcourt.

Canfield, D. E., Glazer, A. N., and Falkowski, P. G. 2010. "The Evolution and Future of Earth's Nitrogen Cycle." Science 330(6001): 192–196.

Canfield, D. E., Rosing, M. T., and Bjerrum, C. 2006. "Early Anaerobic Metabolisms." Philosophical Transactions of the Royal Society B: Biological Sciences 361(1474): 1819–1836.

Carattini, S., Kallbekken, S., and Orlov, A. 2019. "How to Win Public Support for a Global Carbon Tax." Nature, 16 January. https://www.nature.com/articles/d41586-019-00124-x?sf206102567=1. Accessed 1 December 2020.

Carbon Pricing Leadership Coalition. 2016. "What Is the Impact of Carbon Pricing on Competitiveness?" Executive Briefing. http://pubdocs.worldbank.org/en/759561467228928508/CPLC-Competitiveness-print2.pdf. Accessed 23 November 2020.

Carbon Pricing Leadership Coalition. 2019. "Carbon Pricing in Africa Webinar Series." https://www.carbonpricingleadership.org/calendar/2019/10/3/carbon-pricing-in-africa-webinar-series-carbon-pricing-101. Accessed 23 November 2020.

Cardinale, B. J., Duffy, J. E., Gonzalez, A., Hooper, D. U., Perrings, C., Venail, P., Narwani, A., and others. 2012. "Biodiversity Loss and Its Impact on Humanity." Nature 486(7401): 59–67.

CARE International 2016. The Benefits and Challenges of Integrating an Ecosystem Approach in Community Climate Adaptation in Two Landscapes in Nepal. Kathmandu: CARE International, United States Agency for International Development and World Wildlife Fund.

Carleton, T. A. 2017. "Crop-Damaging Temperatures Increase Suicide Rates in India." Proceedings of the National Academy of Sciences 114(33): 8746–8751. https://doi.org/10.1073/pnas.1701354114. Accessed 1 December 2020.

Carleton, T. A., and S. M. Hsiang. "Social and Economic Impacts of Climate." Science 353(6304): aad9837–aad9837. https://doi.org/10.1126/science.aad9837. Accessed 1 December 2020.

Carleton, T. A., Jina, A., Delgado, M. T., Greenstone, M., Houser, T., Hsiang, S. M., Hultgren, A., and others. 2020. "Valuing the Global Mortality Consequences of Climate Change Accounting for Adaptation Costs and Benefits." Working Paper 27599, National Bureau of Economic Research, Cambridge, MA. https://doi.org/10.3386/w27599. Accessed 1 December 2020.

Carpenter, S. R., Brock, W. A., Folke, C., van Nes, E. H., and Scheffer, M. 2015. "Allowing Variance May Enlarge the Safe Operating Space for Exploited Ecosystems." Proceedings of the National Academy of Sciences 112(46): 14384–14389.

Carpenter, S. R., Mooney, H. A., Agard, J., Capistrano, D., DeFries, R. S., Diaz, S., Dietz, T., and others. 2009. "Science for Managing Ecosystem Services: Beyond the Millennium Ecosystem Assessment." Proceedings of the National Academy of Sciences 106(5): 1305–1312.

Carroll, D., Daszak, P., Wolfe, N. D., Gao, G. F., Morel, C. M., Morzaria, S., Pablos-Méndez, A., and others. 2018. "The Global Virome Project." Science 359(6378): 872–874.

Carson, R. 2002. Silent Spring. New York: Houghton Mifflin Harcourt.

Carter, L. 2019. "He korowai o Matainaka/The Cloak of Matainaka." New Zealand Journal of Ecology 43(3): 1–8.

Carton, W., Asiyanbi, A., Beck, S., Buck, H. J., and Lund, J. F. 2020. "Negative Emissions and the Long History of Carbon Removal." Wiley Interdisciplinary Reviews: Climate Change 11(6): e671.

Carus, W. S. 2017. "A Century of Biological-Weapons Programs (1915–2015): Reviewing the Evidence." The Nonproliferation Review 24(1–2): 129–153.

Cassidy, J. 2020. "Can We Have Prosperity without Growth?" The New Yorker, 3 February. https://www.newyorker.com/magazine/2020/02/10/can-we-have-prosperity-without-growth. Accessed 18 November 2020.

Castañeda-Álvarez, N. P., Khoury, C. K., Achicanoy, H. A., Bernau, V., Dempewolf, H., Eastwood, R. J., Guarino, L., and others. 2016. "Global Conservation Priorities for Crop Wild Relatives." Nature Plants 2(4): 1–6.

Castree, N., Adams, W. M., Barry, J., Brockington, D., Büscher, B., Corbera, E., Demeritt, D., and others. 2014. "Changing the Intellectual Climate." Nature Climate Change 4(9): 763–768.

CDC (United States Centers for Disease Control and Prevention). 2020. "Covid-19 Cases, Hospitalization, and Death by Race/Ethnicity, Updated 6 August 2020." https://www.cdc.gov/coronavirus/2019-ncov/covid-data/investigations-discovery/hospitalization-death-by-race-ethnicity.html. Accessed 28 November 2020.

Ceballos, G., Ehrlich, P. R., Barnosky, A. D., García, A., Pringle, R. M., and Palmer, T. M. 2015. "Accelerated Modern Human–Induced Species Losses: Entering the Sixth Mass Extinction." Science Advances 1(5): e1400253.

Ceballos, G., Ehrlich, P. R., and Dirzo, R. 2017. "Biological Annihilation via the Ongoing Sixth Mass Extinction Signaled by Vertebrate Population Losses and Declines." Proceedings of the National Academy of Sciences 114(30): E6089–E6096.

Ceballos, G., Ehrlich, P. R., and Raven, P. H. 2020. "Vertebrates on the Brink as Indicators of Biological Annihilation and the Sixth Mass Extinction." Proceedings of the National Academy of Sciences 117(24): 13596–13602.

Cechvala, S. 2011. "Rainfall & Migration: The Somali-Kenyan Conflict." ICE Case Number 256, Mandala Project.

CEEW (Council on Energy Environment and Water). 2020. "The Road to Net Zero Emissions? View from India." Background paper for Human Development Report 2020. United Nations Development Programme, Human Development Report Office, New York.

Centre for Bhutan Studies and GNH Research. 2016. A Compass Towards a Just and Harmonious Society: 2015 GNH Survey Report. Thimphu: Centre for Bhutan Studies & GNH Research.

CEPAL (Comisión Económica para América Latina y el Caribe). 2019. Estadísticas de producción de electricidad de los países del Sistema de la Integración Centroamericana (SICA): datos preliminares a 2019. Mexico City.

Chabay, I., Koch, L., Martinez, G., and Scholz, G. 2019. "Influence of Narratives of Vision and

Identity on Collective Behavior Change." *Sustainability* 11(20): 5680.

Chakraborty, J., Collins, T. W., Grineski, S. E., Montgomery, M. C., and Hernandez, M. 2014. "Comparing Disproportionate Exposure to Acute and Chronic Pollution Risks: A Case Study in Houston, Texas." *Risk Analysis* 34(11): 2005–2020.

Chakravarty, S., Chikkatur, A., De Coninck, H., Pacala, S., Socolow, R., and Tavoni, M. 2009. "Sharing Global CO_2 Emission Reductions among One Billion High Emitters." *Proceedings of the National Academy of Sciences* 106(29): 11884–11888.

Chan, K. M. A., Balvanera, P., Benessaiah, K., Chapman, M., Díaz, S., Gómez-Baggethun, E., Gould, R., and others. 2016. "Opinion: Why Protect Nature? Rethinking Values and the Environment." *Proceedings of the National Academy of Sciences* 113(6): 1462–1465.

Chan, K. M. A., Boyd, D. R., Gould, R. K., Jetzkowitz, J., Liu, J., Muraca, B., Naidoo, R., and others. 2020. "Levers and Leverage Points for Pathways to Sustainability." *People and Nature* 2(3): 693–717.

Chancel, L. 2020. *Unsustainable Inequalities: Social Justice and the Environment.* Cambridge, MA: Belknap Press and Harvard University Press.

Chancel, L., and Piketty, T. 2015. "Carbon and Inequality: From Kyoto to Paris. Trends in the Global Inequality of Carbon Emissions (1998–2013) and Prospects for an Equitable Adaptation Fund." World Inequality Lab, Paris. http://piketty.pse.ens.fr/files/ChancelPiketty2015.pdf. Accessed 23 November 2020.

Chao, S. 2012. *Forest Peoples: Numbers across the World.* Moreton-in-Marsh, UK: Forest Peoples Programme.

Chapin III, F. S., Carpenter, S. R., Kofinas, G. P., Folke, C., Abel, N., Clark, W. C., Olsson, P., and others. 2010. "Ecosystem Stewardship: Sustainability Strategies for a Rapidly Changing Planet." *Trends in Ecology & Evolution* 25(4): 241–249.

Chaplin-Kramer, R., Sharp, R. P., Weil, C., Bennett, E. M., Pascual, U., Arkema, K. K., Brauman, K. A., and others. 2019. "Global Modeling of Nature's Contributions to People." *Science* 366(6462): 255–258.

Chaturvedi, V., and Sharma, M. 2015. "China's Role in Global HFC Emissions Matters for Phase-Down Proposals." Policy Brief, Council on Energy, Environment and Water, New Delhi.

Chawla, K., and Ghosh, A. 2017. "Celebrate Progress... With Caution." *Business Standard*, 20 February. https://www.business-standard.com/article/opinion/arunabha-ghosh-kanika-chawla-celebrate-progress-with-caution-117022001223_1.html. Accessed 1 December 2020.

Chawla, K., and Ghosh, A. 2019. "Greening New Pastures for Green Investments." Issue Brief, Council on Energy, Environment and Water, New Delhi.

Chemhuru, M., and Masaka, D. 2010. "Taboos as Sources of Shona People's Environmental Ethics." *Journal of Sustainable Development in Africa* 12(7): 121–133.

Chen, L., Evans, T., and Cash, R. 1999. "Health as a Global Public Good." In Kaul, I., Grunberg, I., and Stern, M., (eds.), *Global Public Goods. International Cooperation in the 21st Century.* Oxford, UK: Oxford University Press.

Chen, L., Wen, Y., Zhang, L., and Xiang, W.-N. 2015. "Studies of Thermal Comfort and Space Use in an Urban Park Square in Cool and Cold Seasons in Shanghai." *Building and Environment* 94: 644–653.

Cheng, S. H., Ahlroth, S., Onder, S., Shyamsundar, P., Garside, R., Kristjanson, P., McKinnon, M. C., and Miller, D. C. 2017. "What Is the Evidence for the Contribution of Forests to Poverty Alleviation? A Systematic Map Protocol." *Environmental Evidence* 6(1): 10.

Cheng, V. C. C., Lau, S. K. P., Woo, P. C. Y., and Yuen, K. Y. 2007. "Severe Acute Respiratory Syndrome Coronavirus as an Agent of Emerging and Reemerging Infection." *Clinical Microbiology Reviews* 20(4): 660–694.

Cherofsky, J. 2020. "Abandoned by Government, Peru's Indigenous Peoples Lead Powerful Covid-19 Response." *Cultural Survival*, 3 September. https://www.culturalsurvival.org/news/abandoned-government-perus-indigenous-peoples-lead-powerful-covid-19-response. Accessed 19 November 2020.

Cherry, J. A. 2011. "Ecology of Wetland Ecosystems: Water, Substrate, and Life." *Nature Education Knowledge* 3(1): 6. https://www.nature.com/scitable/knowledge/library/ecology-of-wetland-ecosystems-water-substrate-and-17059765/. Accessed 18 November 2020.

Chew, L., and Ramdas, K. N. 2005. *Caught in the Storm: The Impact of Natural Disaster on Women.* San Francisco, CA: Global Fund for Women.

Chhibber, A. 2020a. "Development Indicators: Broadening the Vista." Background paper for Human Development Report 2020, United Nations Development Programme, Human Development Report Office, New York.

Chhibber, A. 2020b. "Variations on the HDI for the Anthropocene: Broadening the Vista." Background paper for Human Development Report 2020, United Nations Development Programme, Human Development Report Office, New York.

Chhibber, A., and Laajaj, R. 2008. "A Global Development Index: Extending the Human Development Index with Environment and Social Structures." https://www.researchgate.net/publication/237710031_A_Global_Development_Index_Extending_the_Human_Development_Index_with_Environment_and_Social_Structures. Accessed 8 December 2020.

Chichilnisky, G., and Heal, G. 1998. "Economic Returns from the Biosphere." *Nature* 391(6668): 629–630.

Chilisa, B. 2017. "Decolonising Transdisciplinary Research Approaches: An African Perspective for Enhancing Knowledge Integration in Sustainability Science." *Sustainability Science* 12(5): 813–827.

China Ministry of Environmental Protection and Stockholm International Water Institute. 2017. *EU–China Environmental Sustainability Program Flagship Policy Report: Lot 1 Water Quality Management.* https://www.siwi.org/wp-content/uploads/2017/05/EU-China-ESP-Flagship-Policy-Report.pdf. Accessed 25 November 2020.

Chitnis, M., Fouquet, R., and Sorrell, S. 2020. "Rebound Effects for Household Energy Services in the UK." *The Energy Journal* 41(4).

Cialdini, R. B., and Goldstein, N. J. 2004. "Social Influence: Compliance and Conformity." *Annual Review of Psychology* 55: 591–621.

Cincera, J., Boeve-de Pauw, J., Goldman, D., and Simonova, P. 2019. "Emancipatory or Instrumental? Students' and Teachers' Perceptions of the Implementation of the Ecoschool Program." *Environmental Education Research* 25(7): 1083–1104.

Cincera, J., and Krajhanzl, J. 2013. "Eco-Schools: What Factors Influence Pupils' Action Competence for Pro-Environmental Behaviour?" *Journal of Cleaner Production* 61: 117–121.

Cisneros-Montemayor, A. M., Pauly, D., Weatherdon, L. V., and Ota, Y. 2016. "A Global Estimate of Seafood Consumption by Coastal Indigenous Peoples." *PLOS ONE* 11(12): e0166681.

CIVICUS. 2020. "Escazú Agreement." https://www.civicus.org/index.php/es/component/tags/tag/escazu-agreement. Accessed 13 October 2020.

CIW (Canadian Index of Wellbeing). 2020. "Canadian Index of Wellbeing." https://uwaterloo.ca/canadian-index-wellbeing/. Accessed 2 December 2020.

Clapcott, J., Ataria, J., Hepburn, C., Hikuroa, D., Jackson, A.-M., Kirikiri, R., and Williams, E. 2018. "Mātauranga Māori: Shaping Marine and Freshwater Futures." *Journal New Zealand Journal of Marine and Freshwater Research* 52(4): 457–466.

Clark, M. A., Domingo, N. G. G., Colgan, K., Thakrar, S. K., Tilman, D., Lynch, J., Azevedo, I. L., and Hill, J. D. 2020. "Global Food System Emissions Could Preclude Achieving the 1.5° and 2°C Climate Change Targets." *Science* 370(6517): 705–708.

Clark, W. C., and Harley, A. G. 2020. "Sustainability Science: Toward a Synthesis." *Annual Review of Environment and Resources* 45: 331–386.

Clark, W. C., and Munn, R. E. 1986. *Sustainable Development of the Biosphere.* Cambridge, UK: Cambridge University Press.

Clastres, C. 2011. "Smart Grids: Another Step towards Competition, Energy Security and Climate Change Objectives." *Energy Policy* 39(9): 5399–5408.

Clayton, S., Bexell, S. M., Xu, P., Tang, Y. F., Li, W. J., and Chen, L. 2019. "Environmental Literacy and Nature Experience in Chengdu, China." *Environmental Education Research* 25(7): 1105–1118.

Clayton, S., Devine-Wright, P., Stern, P. C., Whitmarsh, L., Carrico, A., Steg, L., Swim, J., and Bonnes, M. 2015. "Psychological Research and Global Climate Change." *Nature Climate Change* 5(7): 640–646.

Climate Action Tracker. 2020. "Climate Action Tracker: Chile." https://climateactiontracker.org/countries/chile/pledges-and-targets/. Accessed 23 November 2020.

Climate Bonds Initiative. 2020. "Green Bonds Market Summary - Q3 2020." https://www.climatebonds.net/resources/reports/green-bonds-market-summary-q3-2020. Accessed 1 December 2020.

Climate Leadership Council. 2019. "Economists Statement on Carbon Dividends." https://www.econstatement.org. Accessed 23 November 2020.

Coady, D., Flamini, V., and Sears, L. 2015. "The Unequal Benefits of Fuel Subsidies Revisited: Evidence for Developing Countries." Working Paper WP/15/250, International Monetary Fund, Washington, DC.

Coady, D., Parry, I., Le, N.-P., and Shang, B. 2019. "Global Fossil Fuel Subsidies Remain Large: An Update Based on Country-Level Estimates." Working Paper WP/19/89, International Monetary Fund, Washington, DC. https://www.imf.org/en/Publications/WP/Issues/2019/05/02/Global-Fossil-Fuel-Subsidies-Remain-Large-An-Update-Based-on-Country-Level-Estimates-46509. Accessed 23 November 2020.

Coady, D., Parry, I., Sears, L., and Shang, B. 2017. "How Large Are Global Fossil Fuel Subsidies?" World Development 91: 11–27. https://doi.org/10.1016/j.worlddev.2016.10.004. Accessed 1 December 2020.

Coates, D., and Smith, M. 2012. "Natural Infrastructure Solutions for Water Security." In Ardakanian, R., and Jaeger, D., (eds.), Water and the Green Economy: Capacity Development Aspects. Bonn, Germany: UN-Water Decade Programme on Capacity Development).

Cohen, E. 1986. "Law, Folklore and Animal Lore." Past and Present 110: 6–37.

Cohen, F., Hepburn, C. J., and Teytelboym, A. 2019. "Is Natural Capital Really Substitutable?" Annual Review of Environment and Resources 44(1): 425–448.

Cohen, G., Jalles, J. T., Loungani, P., and Marto, R. 2018. "The Long-Run Decoupling of Emissions and Output: Evidence from the Largest Emitters." Energy Policy 118: 58–68.

Cohen, J. E. 1995. "Population Growth and Earth's Human Carrying Capacity." Science 269(5222): 341–346.

Cole, L. W., and Foster, S. R. 2001. From the Ground Up: Environmental Racism and the Rise of the Environmental Justice Movement. New York: NYU Press.

Collins, T. W., Grineski, S. E., and Morales, D. X. 2017. "Environmental Injustice and Sexual Minority Health Disparities: A National Study of Inequitable Health Risks from Air Pollution among Same-Sex Partners." Social Science & Medicine 191: 38–47.

Collinson, P., and Ambrose, J. 2020. "UK's Biggest Pension Fund Begins Fossil Fuels Divestment." The Guardian, 29 July. https://www.theguardian.com/environment/2020/jul/29/national-employment-savings-trust-uks-biggest-pension-fund-divests-from-fossil-fuels. Accessed 1 December 2020.

Commission on Genetic Resources for Food and Agriculture 2015. Coping with Climate Change: The Roles of Genetic Resources for Food and Agriculture. Rome: Food and Agriculture Organization of the United Nations.

Commoner, B. 1971. "Economic Growth and Ecology—a Biologist's View." Monthly Labor Review 94(11): 3–13.

Conn, A., Toon, B., and Robock, A. 2016. "Transcript: Nuclear Winter Podcast with Alan Robock and Brian Toon." 31 October. Future of Life Institute. https://futureoflife.org/2016/10/31/transcript-nuclear-winter-podcast-alan-robock-brian-toon/. Accessed 30 November 2020.

Conservation International. 2020. "Blue Carbon: Mitigating Climate Change along Our Coasts." Arlington, VA: Conservation International. https://www.conservation.org/projects/blue-carbon#:~:text=Blue%20Carbon%20in%20the%20Gulf,that%20country's%20most%20productive%20estuary.&text=Conservation%20efforts%20are%20currently%20focused,through%20mangrove%20restoration%20and%20conservation. Accessed 25 November 2020.

Convention on Biological Diversity. 2020. "The Convention on Biological Diversity." https://www.cbd.int/convention/. Accessed 2 December 2020.

Cook, J., and Lewandowsky, S. 2016. "Rational Irrationality: Modeling Climate Change Belief Polarization Using Bayesian Networks." Topics in Cognitive Science 8(1): 160–179.

Cook-Patton, S. C., Leavitt, S. M., Gibbs, D., Harris, N. L., Lister, K., Anderson-Teixeira, K. J., Briggs, R. D., and others. 2020. "Mapping Carbon Accumulation Potential from Global Natural Forest Regrowth." Nature 585(7826): 545–550.

Coomes, O. T., Takasaki, Y., and Rhemtulla, J. M. 2011. "Land-Use Poverty Traps Identified in Shifting Cultivation Systems Shape Long-Term Tropical Forest Cover." Proceedings of the National Academy of Sciences 108(34): 13925–13930.

Cooper, G. S., and Dearing, J. A. 2019. "Modelling Future Safe and Just Operating Spaces in Regional Social-Ecological Systems." Science of the Total Environment 651: 2105–2117.

Coote, A. 2015. "People, Planet, Power: Toward a New Social Settlement." The International Journal of Social Quality 5(1): 8–34.

Coronese, M., Lamperti, F., Keller, K., Chiaromonte, F., and Roventini, A. 2019. "Evidence for Sharp Increase in the Economic Damages of Extreme Natural Disasters." Proceedings of the National Academy of Sciences 116(43): 21450–21455.

Correia, D. 2012. "Degrowth, American Style: No Impact Man and Bourgeois Primitivism." Capitalism Nature Socialism 23(1): 105–118.

Cortés Fernández, P. 2020. No Land, No Water, No Pasture, the Urbanisation of Drought Displacement in Somalia. Geneva: Internal Displacement Monitoring Centre.

Costa, L., Rybski, D., and Kropp, J. P. 2011. "A Human Development Framework for CO_2 Reductions." PLOS ONE 6(12): e29262.

Costantini, V., and Monni, S. 2005. "Sustainable Human Development for European Countries." Journal of Human Development 6(3): 329–351.

Costanza, R., d'Arge, R., De Groot, R., Farber, S., Grasso, M., Hannon, B., Limburg, K., and others. 1997. "The Value of the World's Ecosystem Services and Natural Capital." Nature 387(6630): 253–260.

Costanza, R., De Groot, R., Sutton, P., Van der Ploeg, S., Anderson, S. J., Kubiszewski, I., Farber, S., and Turner, R. K. 2014. "Changes in the Global Value of Ecosystem Services." Global Environmental Change 26: 152–158.

Costedoat, S., Corbera, E., Ezzine-de-Blas, D., Honey-Rosés, J., Baylis, K., and Castillo-Santiago, M. A. 2015. "How Effective Are Biodiversity Conservation Payments in Mexico?" PLOS ONE 10(3): e0119881.

Coulthard, S. 2012. "Can We Be Both Resilient and Well, and What Choices Do People Have? Incorporating Agency into the Resilience Debate from a Fisheries Perspective." Ecology and Society 17(1).

Court, V., and Sorrell, S. 2020. "Digitalisation of Goods: A Systematic Review of the Determinants and Magnitude of the Impacts on Energy Consumption." Environmental Research Letters 15(4): 043001.

Coyle, D. 2015. GDP: A Brief but Affectionate History— Revised and Expanded Edition. Princeton, NJ: Princeton University Press.

Crabtree, A. 2012. "A Legitimate Freedom Approach to Sustainability: Sen, Scanlon and the Inadequacy of the Human Development Index." The International Journal of Social Quality 2(1): 24–40.

Crabtree, A. 2013. "Sustainable Development: Does the Capability Approach Have Anything to Offer? Outlining a Legitimate Freedom Approach." Journal of Human Development and Capabilities 14(1): 40–57.

Crabtree, A. 2020. "Sustainability Indicators, Ethics and Legitimate Freedoms." In Crabtree, A., (ed.) Sustainability, Capabilities and Human Security. Cham, Switzerland: Springer International Publishing.

Craft, A. 2013. Breathing Life into the Stone Fort Treaty: An Anishnabe Understanding of Treaty One. Saskatoon, SK: Purich Publishing.

Craft, A. 2019. "Navigating Our Ongoing Sacred Legal Relationship with Nibi (Water)." In Borrows, J., Chartrand, L., Fitgerald, O., and Schwarts, R., (eds.), Braiding Legal Orders: Implementing the United Nations Declaration on the Rights of Indigenous Peoples. Waterloo, ON: Centre for International Governance Innovation.

Cramton, P. 2017. "Electricity Market Design." Oxford Review of Economic Policy 33(4): 589–612.

CRED (Center for Research on the Epidemiology of Disasters). 2020. "EM-DAT: The International Disaster database." https://www.emdat.be/. Accessed September 10 2020.

Creech, H. 2012. "Sustainable Development Timeline." International Institute of Sustainable Development, Winnipeg, MB.

Crépin, A.-S., and Folke, C. 2015. "The Economy, the Biosphere and Planetary Boundaries: Towards Biosphere Economics." International Review of Environmental and Resource Economics 8(1): 57–100.

Crist, E. 2007. "Beyond the Climate Crisis: A Critique of Climate Change Discourse." *Telos* 2007(141): 29–55.

Crist, E. 2018. "Reimagining the Human." *Science* 362(6420): 1242–1244.

Crist, E., Mora, C., and Engelman, R. 2017. "The Interaction of Human Population, Food Production, and Biodiversity Protection." *Science* 356(6335): 260–264.

Crona, B. I., Daw, T. M., Swartz, W., Norström, A. V., Nyström, M., Thyresson, M., Folke, C., and others. 2016. "Masked, Diluted and Drowned out: How Global Seafood Trade Weakens Signals from Marine Ecosystems." *Fish and Fisheries* 17(4): 1175–1182.

Crosby, A. W. 1995. "The Past and Present of Environmental History." *The American Historical Review* 100(4): 1177–1189.

Crowder, K., and Downey, L. 2010. "Interneighborhood Migration, Race, and Environmental Hazards: Modeling Microlevel Processes of Environmental Inequality." *American Journal of Sociology* 115(4): 1110–1149.

Crust, E. E., Daly, M. C., and Hobijn, B. 2020. "The Illusion of Wage Growth." FRBSF Economic Letter 2020-26, Federal Reserve Bank of San Francisco.

Crutzen, P. 2002. "Geology of Mankind." *Nature* 415(6867): 23–23.

Crutzen, P., and Stoermer, E. 2000. "The 'Anthropocene.'" *Global Change Newsletter* 41: 17–18.

Cunsolo Willox, A., Harper, S. L., Ford, J. D., Landman, K., Houle, K., and Edge, V. L. 2012. "'From This Place and of This Place': Climate Change, Sense of Place, and Health in Nunatsiavut, Canada." *Social Science & Medicine* 75(3): 538–547.

D'Alessandro, S., Cieplinski, A., Distefano, T., and Dittmer, K. 2020. "Feasible Alternatives to Green Growth." *Nature Sustainability* 3(4): 329–335.

D'Odorico, P., Chiarelli, D. D., Rosa, L., Bini, A., Zilberman, D., and Rulli, M. C. 2020. "The Global Value of Water in Agriculture." *Proceedings of the National Academy of Sciences* 117(36): 21985–21993.

Dai, X. 2010. "Global Regime and National Change." *Climate Policy* 10(6): 622–637.

Daily, G. C. (Ed.). 1997. *Nature's Services*. Washington, DC: Island Press.

Daily, G. C., and Ehrlich, P. R. 1996. "Socioeconomic Equity, Sustainability, and Earth's Carrying Capacity." *Ecological Applications* 6(4): 991–1001.

Daily, G. C., Söderqvist, T., Aniyar, S., Arrow, K., Dasgupta, P., Ehrlich, P. R., Folke, C., and others. 2000. "The Value of Nature and the Nature of Value." *Science* 289(5478): 395–396.

Dalberg, W. 2012. "Fighting Illicit Wildlife Trafficking: A Consultation with Governments." WWF International, Gland, Switzerland.

Dalby, S. 2016. "Framing the Anthropocene: The Good, the Bad and the Ugly." *The Anthropocene Review* 3(1): 33–51.

Daly, H. E. 1977. "Steady State Economy." San Francisco, CA.

Daly, H. E. 1992. "Allocation, Distribution, and Scale: Towards an Economics That Is Efficient, Just, and Sustainable." *Ecological Economics* 6(3): 185–193.

Daly, H. E. 2020. "A Note in Defense of the Concept of Natural Capital." *Ecosystem Services* 41: 101051.

Daly, H. E., Cobb Jr, J. B., and Cobb, J. B. 1994. *For the Common Good: Redirecting the Economy toward Community, the Environment, and a Sustainable Future*. Boston, MA: Beacon Press.

Daly, H. E., Czech, B., Trauger, D. L., Rees, W. E., Grover, M., Dobson, T., and Trombulak, S. C. 2007. "Are We Consuming Too Much: For What?" *Conservation Biology* 21(5): 1359–1362.

Damerell, P., Howe, C., and Milner-Gulland, E. J. 2013. "Child-Orientated Environmental Education Influences Adult Knowledge and Household Behaviour." *Environmental Research Letters* 8(1): 015016.

Danielsen, F., Jensen, A. E., Alviola, P. A., Balete, D. S., Mendoza, M., Tagtag, A., Custodio, C., and Enghoff, M. 2005. "Does Monitoring Matter? A Quantitative Assessment of Management Decisions from Locally-Based Monitoring of Protected Areas." *Biodiversity & Conservation* 14(11): 2633–2652.

Dansgaard, W., Johnsen, S. J., Clausen, H. B., Dahl-Jensen, D., Gundestrup, N. S., Hammer, C. U., Hvidberg, C. S., and others. 1993. "Evidence for General Instability of Past Climate from a 250-Kyr Ice-Core Record." *Nature* 364(6434): 218–220.

Das, S., and Crépin, A.-S. 2013. "Mangroves Can Provide Protection against Wind Damage during Storms." *Estuarine, Coastal and Shelf Science* 134: 98–107.

Dasgupta, P. 2001. *Human Well-Being and the Natural Environment*. Oxford, UK: Oxford University Press.

Dasgupta, P. 2009. "The Welfare Economic Theory of Green National Accounts." *Environmental and Resource Economics* 42(1): 3–38. https://doi.org/10.1007/s10640-008-9223-y. Accessed 1 December 2020.

Dasgupta, P. 2014. "Measuring the Wealth of Nations." *Annual Review of Resource Economics* 6(1): 17–31.

Dasgupta, P. 2019. *Time and the Generations: Population Ethics for a Diminishing Planet*. New York: Columbia University Press.

Dasgupta, P. 2020. "The Dasgupta Review–Independent Review on the Economics of Biodiversity Interim Report." https://www.gov.uk/government/publications/interim-report-the-dasgupta-review-independent-review-on-the-economics-of-biodiversity. Accessed 15 October 2020.

Dasgupta, P., and Mäler, K.-G. 2000. "Net National Product, Wealth, and Social Well-Being." *Environment and Development Economics* 5(1): 69–93.

Datar, A., Liu, J., Linnemayr, S., and Stecher, C. 2013. "The Impact of Natural Disasters on Child Health and Investments in Rural India." *Social Science & Medicine* 76: 83–91.

Davis, D. S. 2019. "Studying Human Responses to Environmental Change: Trends and Trajectories of Archaeological Research." *Environmental Archaeology* 25: 367–380.

Davis, S. J., and Caldeira, K. 2010. "Consumption-Based Accounting of CO_2 Emissions." *Proceedings of the National Academy of Sciences* 107(12): 5687–5692.

Davis, S. J., Lewis, N. S., Shaner, M., Aggarwal, S., Arent, D., Azevedo, I. L., Benson, S. M., and others. 2018. "Net-Zero Emissions Energy Systems." *Science* 360(6396).

Davis, S. J., Peters, G. P., and Caldeira, K. 2011. "The Supply Chain of CO_2 Emissions." *Proceedings of the National Academy of Sciences* 108(45): 18554–18559.

Daw, T. M., Coulthard, S., Cheung, W. W. L., Brown, K., Abunge, C., Galafassi, D., Peterson, G. D., and others. 2015. "Evaluating Taboo Trade-Offs in Ecosystems Services and Human Well-Being." *Proceedings of the National Academy of Sciences* 112(22): 6949–6954.

Dawes, R. M. 1980. "Social Dilemmas." *Annual Review of Psychology* 31(1): 169–193.

Day, R., Walker, G., and Simcock, N. 2016. "Conceptualising Energy Use and Energy Poverty Using a Capabilities Framework." *Energy Policy* 93: 255–264.

De Angelis, R. 2018. *Business Models in the Circular Economy: Concepts, Examples and Theory*. Cham: Switzerland: Springer.

de Botton, A. 2020. "Camus on the Coronavirus." *New York Times*, 19 March. https://www.nytimes.com/2020/03/19/opinion/sunday/coronavirus-camus-plague.html. Accessed 8 December 2020.

de Freytas-Tamura, K. 2017. "Public Shaming and Even Prison for Plastic Bag Use in Rwanda." *New York Times*, 28 October. https://www.nytimes.com/2017/10/28/world/africa/rwanda-plastic-bags-banned.html. Accessed 15 October 2020.

De Groot, M. 2012. "Exploring the Relationship between Public Environmental Ethics and River Flood Policies in Western Europe." *Journal of Environmental Management* 93(1): 1–9.

De Groot, R. S., Fisher, B., Christie, M., Aronson, J., Braat, L., Haines-Young, R., Gowdy, J., and others. 2010. "Integrating the Ecological and Economic Dimensions in Biodiversity and Ecosystem Service Valuation." *The Economics of Ecosystems and Biodiversity (TEEB): Ecological and Economic Foundations*. New York: Routledge.

de La Vega, M. L., and Urrutia, A. M. 2001. "HDPI: A Framework for Pollution-Sensitive Human Development Indicators." *Environment, Development and Sustainability* 3(3): 199–215.

Dearing, J. A. 2018. "Limits and Thresholds: Setting Global, Local and Regional Safe Operating Spaces." In Schreckenberg, K., Mace, G., and Poudyal, M., (eds.), *Ecosystem Services and Poverty Alleviation: Trade-Offs and Governance*. London: Routledge.

Dearing, J. A., Wang, R., Zhang, K., Dyke, J. G., Haberl, H., Hossain, M. S., Langdon, P. G., and others. 2014. "Safe and Just Operating Spaces for

Regional Social-Ecological Systems." *Global Environmental Change* 28: 227–238.

Deere, C. D., and Twyman, J. 2012. "Asset Ownership and Egalitarian Decision Making in Dual-Headed Households in Ecuador." *Review of Radical Political Economics* 44(3): 313–320.

DeFries, R. 2014. *The Big Ratchet: How Humanity Thrives in the Face of Natural Crisis.* New York: Basic Books.

DeFries, R., and Nagendra, H. 2017. "Ecosystem Management as a Wicked Problem." *Science* 356(6335): 265–270.

Deino, A. L., Behrensmeyer, A. K., Brooks, A. S., Yellen, J. E., Sharp, W. D., and Potts, R. 2018. "Chronology of the Acheulean to Middle Stone Age Transition in Eastern Africa." *Science* 360(6384): 95–98.

Dell, M., Jones, B. F., and Olken, B. A. 2014. "What Do We Learn from the Weather? The New Climate-Economy Literature." *Journal of Economic Literature* 52(3): 740–798.

Dennig, F., Budolfson, M. B., Fleurbaey, M., Siebert, A., and Socolow, R. H. 2015. "Inequality, Climate Impacts on the Future Poor, and Carbon Prices." *Proceedings of the National Academy of Sciences* 112(52): 15827–15832.

Denolle, M. A., and Nissen-Meyer, T. 2020. "Quiet Anthropocene, Quiet Earth." *Science* 369(6509): 1299–1300.

Denton, K. K., Ram, Y., Liberman, U., and Feldman, M. W. 2020. "Cultural Evolution of Conformity and Anticonformity." *Proceedings of the National Academy of Sciences* 117(24): 13603–13614.

Derksen, L., and Gartrell, J. 1993. "The Social Context of Recycling." *American Sociological Review* 58(3): 434–442.

Derviş, K., and Strauss, S. 2020. "The Carbon-Tax Opportunity." *Project Syndicate*, 6 May. https://www.project-syndicate.org/commentary/low-oil-prices-opportunity-for-carbon-tax-by-kemal-dervis-and-sebastian-strauss-2020-05. Accessed 23 November 2020.

Dery, F., Bisung, E., Dickin, S., and Dyer, M. 2020. "Understanding Empowerment in Water, Sanitation, and Hygiene (WASH): A Scoping Review." *Journal of Water, Sanitation and Hygiene for Development* 10(1): 5–15.

Deryugina, T., and Hsiang, S. 2017. "The Marginal Product of Climate." Working Paper 24072, National Bureau of Economic Research, Cambridge, MA. https://doi.org/10.3386/w24072. Accessed 1 December 2020.

Desai, M. A. 2010. "Hope in Hard Times: Women's Empowerment and Human Development." Human Development Research Paper 2010/14, United Nations Development Programme, New York.

Deutz, A., Heal, G., Niu, R., Swanson, E., Townshend, T., Li, Z., Delmar, A., and others. 2020. *Financing Nature: Closing the Global Biodiversity Financing Gap.* The Paulson Institute, The Nature Conservancy, and the Cornell Atkinson Center for Sustainability. https://www.paulsoninstitute.org/key-initiatives/financing-nature-report/. Accessed 25 November 2020.

Diamond, J. 1987. "The Worst Mistake in the History of the Human Race." *Discover Magazine* May: 64–66.

Diamond, J. 2011. *Collapse: How Societies Choose to Fail or Succeed.* New York: Penguin Books.

Díaz, S., Demissew, S., Carabias, J., Joly, C., Lonsdale, M., Ash, N., Larigauderie, A., and others. 2015. "The IPBES Conceptual Framework—Connecting Nature and People." *Current Opinion in Environmental Sustainability* 14: 1–16.

Díaz, S., Pascual, U., Stenseke, M., Martín-López, B., Watson, R. T., Molnár, Z., Hill, R., and others. 2018. "Assessing Nature's Contributions to People." *Science* 359(6373): 270–272.

Díaz, S., Settele, J., Brondízio, E. S., Ngo, H. T., Agard, J., Arneth, A., Balvanera, P., and others. 2019a. "Pervasive Human-Driven Decline of Life on Earth Points to the Need for Transformative Change." *Science* 366(6471).

Díaz, S., Settele, J., Brondízio, E. S., Ngo, H. T., Guèze, M., Agard, J., Arneth, A., and others, (eds.). 2019b. "Summary for Policymakers of the Global Assessment Report on Biodiversity and Ecosystem Services of the Intergovernmental Science-Policy Platform on Biodiversity and Ecosystem Services." Bonn, Germany: Intergovernmental Science-Policy Platform on Biodiversity and Ecosystem Services Secretariat. https://uwe-repository.worktribe.com/output/1493508/summary-for-policymakers-of-the-global-assessment-report-on-biodiversity-and-ecosystem-services-of-the-intergovernmental-science-policy-platform-on-biodiversity-and-ecosystem-services. Accessed 9 December 2020.

Dietz, T. 2017. "Drivers of Human Stress on the Environment in the Twenty-First Century." *Annual Review of Environment and Resources* 42(1): 189–213.

Dietz, T., Shwom, R. L., and Whitley, C. T. 2020. "Climate Change and Society." *Annual Review of Sociology* 46: 135–158.

Dietz, T., and Whitley, C. T. 2018. "Environmentalism, Norms, and Identity." *Proceedings of the National Academy of Sciences* 115(49): 12334–12336.

Diffenbaugh, N. S., and Burke, M. 2019. "Global Warming Has Increased Global Economic Inequality." *Proceedings of the National Academy of Sciences* 116(20): 9808–9813.

Digiconomist. 2020. "Bitcoin Energy Consumption Index." https://digiconomist.net/bitcoin-energy-consumption/. Accessed 11 November 2020.

Dikau, S., Robins, N., and Volz, U. 2020. "A Toolbox for Sustainable Crisis Response Measures for Central Banks and Supervisors, Second Edition: Lessons from Practice." Inspire Briefing Paper, Grantham Research Institute on Climate Change and the Environment, London School of Economics and Political Science and SOAS Centre for Sustainable Finance, London. https://www.climateworks.org/wp-content/uploads/2020/11/INSPIRE-toolbox_-2nd-Edition-2.pdf. Accessed 1 December 2020.

Dikau, S., and Volz, U. 2020. "Central Bank Mandates, Sustainability Objectives and the Promotion of Green Finance." Working Paper 232, SOAS Department of Economics, London. https://www.soas.ac.uk/economics/research/workingpapers/file145514.pdf. Accessed 1 December 2020.

DiNapoli, R. J., Rieth, T. M., Lipo, C. P., and Hunt, T. L. 2020. "A Model-Based Approach to the Tempo of 'Collapse': The Case of Rapa Nui (Easter Island)." *Journal of Archaeological Science* 116: 105094.

Dirzo, R., Young, H. S., Galetti, M., Ceballos, G., Isaac, N. J. B., and Collen, B. 2014. "Defaunation in the Anthropocene." *Science* 345(6195): 401–406.

Djalante, R., Shaw, R., and DeWit, A. 2020. "Building Resilience against Biological Hazards and Pandemics: COVID-19 and Its Implications for the Sendai Framework." *Progress in Disaster Science* 6: 100080.

Dobson, A. D., de Lange, E., Keane, A., Ibbett, H., and Milner-Gulland, E. 2019. "Integrating Models of Human Behaviour between the Individual and Population Levels to Inform Conservation Interventions." *Philosophical Transactions of the Royal Society B* 374(1781): 20180053.

Doick, K. J., Peace, A., and Hutchings, T. R. 2014. "The Role of One Large Greenspace in Mitigating London's Nocturnal Urban Heat Island." *Science of the Total Environment* 493: 662–671.

Dolce, C. 2020. "All the Records the 2020 Hurricane Season Has Broken So Far." *The Weather Channel*, 6 October. https://weather.com/storms/hurricane/news/2020-09-21-atlantic-hurricane-season-2020-records. Accessed 18 November 2020.

Donges, J. F., Lucht, W., Müller-Hansen, F., and Steffen, W. 2017a. "The Technosphere in Earth System Analysis: A Coevolutionary Perspective." *The Anthropocene Review* 4(1): 23–33.

Donges, J. F., Winkelmann, R., Lucht, W., Cornell, S. E., Dyke, J. G., Rockström, J., Heitzig, J., and Schellnhuber, H. J. 2017b. "Closing the Loop: Reconnecting Human Dynamics to Earth System Science." *The Anthropocene Review* 4(2): 151–157.

Donohue, I., Hillebrand, H., Montoya, J. M., Petchey, O. L., Pimm, S. L., Fowler, M. S., Healy, K., and others. 2016. "Navigating the Complexity of Ecological Stability." *Ecology Letters* 19(9): 1172–1185.

Dorling, D. 2020. *Slowdown: The End of the Great Acceleration—and Why It's Good for the Planet, the Economy, and Our Lives.* New Haven, CT: Yale University Press.

Dorninger, C., Hornborg, A., Abson, D. J., von Wehrden, H., Schaffartzik, A., Giljum, S., Engler, J.-O., and others. 2021. "Global Patterns of Ecologically Unequal Exchange: Implications for Sustainability in the 21st Century." *Ecological Economics* 179: 106824.

Doss, C., Kovarik, C., Peterman, A., Quisumbing, A., and Van Den Bold, M. 2015. "Gender Inequalities in Ownership and Control of Land in Africa: Myth and Reality." *Agricultural Economics* 46(3): 403–434.

Doss, C., Summerfield, G., and Tsikata, D. 2014. "Land, Gender, and Food Security." *Feminist Economics* 20(1): 1–23.

Dowling, R., Lloyd, K., and S. Suchet-Pearson. 2017. "Qualitative Methods II: 'More-than-Human'

Methodologies and/in Praxis." *Progress in Human Geography* 41(6): 823–831.

Downing, A. S., Chang, M., Kuiper, J. J., Campenni, M., Häyhä, T., Cornell, S., Svedin, U., and Mooij, W. 2020. "Learning from Generations of Sustainability Concepts." *Environmental Research Letters* 15(8).

Drexler, K. E. 2013. *Radical Abundance: How a Revolution in Nanotechnology Will Change Civilization.* New York: Public Affairs.

Drèze, J., and Sen, A. 1990. *Hunger and Public Action.* Oxford, UK: Clarendon Press.

Druckenmiller, H. 2020. "Estimating an Economic and Social Value of Forests: Evidence from Tree Mortality in the American West." Unpublished manuscript, University of California–Berkeley.

Druckman, J., Bayes, R., and Bolsen, T. 2019. "A Research Agenda for Climate Change Communication and Public Opinion: The Role of Consensus Messaging and Beyond." Working Paper 19-28, Northwestern University Institute for Policy Research, Evanston, IL. https://www.ipr.northwestern.edu/documents/working-papers/2019/wp-19-28.pdf. Accessed 2 May 2020.

Drupp, M. A., Baumgärtner, S., Meyer, M., Quaas, M. F., and von Wehrden, H. 2020. "Between Ostrom and Nordhaus: The Research Landscape of Sustainability Economics." *Ecological Economics* 172: 106620.

Duan, J., Wang, Y., Fan, C., Xia, B., and de Groot, R. 2018. "Perception of Urban Environmental Risks and the Effects of Urban Green Infrastructures (UGIs) on Human Well-being in Four Public Green Spaces of Guangzhou, China." *Environmental Management* 62(3): 500–517.

Duarte, C. M., Agusti, S., Barbier, E., Britten, G. L., Castilla, J. C., Gattuso, J.-P., Fulweiler, R. W., and others. 2020. "Rebuilding Marine Life." *Nature* 580(7801): 39–51.

Dubash, N. K. 2009. "Copenhagen: Climate of Mistrust." *Economic and Political Weekly* 44(52): 8–11.

Dubash, N. K. 2019. *India in a Warming World: Integrating Climate Change and Development.* Oxford, UK: Oxford University Press.

Dublin, L. I., and Lotka, A. J. 1925. "On the True Rate of Natural Increase: As Exemplified by the Population of the United States, 1920." *Journal of the American Statistical Association* 20(151): 305–339.

Duffy, P. B., Field, C. B., Diffenbaugh, N. S., Doney, S. C., Dutton, Z., Goodman, S., Heinzerling, L., and others. 2019. "Strengthened Scientific Support for the Endangerment Finding for Atmospheric Greenhouse Gases." *Science* 363(6427).

Duncan, J., Dash, J., and Tompkins, E. L. 2014. "Mangrove Forests Enhance Rice Cropland Resilience to Tropical Cyclones: Evidence from the Bhitarkanika Conservation Area." In Murti, R. and Buyck, C., (eds.), *Safe Havens: Protected Areas for Disaster Risk Reduction and Climate Change Adaptation.* Gland, Switzerland: International Union for Conservation of Nature.

Dunlap, R. E., McCright, A. M., and Yarosh, J. H. 2016. "The Political Divide on Climate Change: Partisan Polarization Widens in the Us." *Environment: Science and Policy for Sustainable Development* 58(5): 4–23.

Dunne, A. 2017. "Delegation from India Wants to Learn About Catskills Watershed." *WAMC Northeast Public Radio,* 26 April. https://www.wamc.org/post/delegation-india-wants-learn-about-catskills-watershed. Accessed 1 December 2020.

Duraiappah, A. K. 1998. "Poverty and Environmental Degradation: A Review and Analysis of the Nexus." *World Development* 26(12): 2169–2179.

Durand, M., Fitoussi, J.-P., and Stiglitz, J. E. 2018. *For Good Measure: Advancing Research on Well-Being Metrics Beyond GDP.* Paris: Organisation for Economic Co-operation and Development.

Durie, M. H. 1995. "Te Hoe Nuku Roa Framework a Maori Identity Measure." *The Journal of the Polynesian Society* 104(4): 461–470.

Durie, M. H. 1998. *Whaiora: Māori Health Development.* Auckland, New Zealand: Oxford University Press.

Dussault, J. 2017. "Is Culture Missing from Conservation? Scientists Take Cues from Indigenous Peoples." *Christian Science Monitor,* 24 November. https://www.csmonitor.com/Environment/2017/1124/Is-culture-missing-from-conservation-Scientists-take-cues-from-indigenous-peoples. Accessed 16 November 2020.

Dutt, A., Lucila, A., and Barath, M. 2019. *Clean Energy Investment Trends: Evolving Risk Perceptions for India's Grid-Connected Renewable Energy Projects.* New Delhi: Council on Energy, Environment and Water; Paris: International Energy Agency. https://www.ceew.in/sites/default/files/CEEW-Clean-Energy-Investment-Trends-2019.pdf. Accessed 1 December 2020.

Düx, A., Lequime, S., Patrono, L. V., Vrancken, B., Boral, S., Gogarten, J. F., Hilbig, A., and others. 2020. "Measles Virus and Rinderpest Virus Divergence Dated to the Sixth Century BCE." *Science* 368(6497): 1367–1370.

Eagles, P. F., and Demare, R. 1999. "Factors Influencing Children's Environmental Attitudes." *The Journal of Environmental Education* 30(4): 33–37.

Earth Overshoot Day. n.d. "I Join the #Movethedate Movement." https://www.overshootday.org/portfolio/i-join-the-solutions-to-movethedate-movement. Accessed 30 November 2020.

Ebi, K. L., Woodruff, R., von Hildebrand, A., and Corvalan, C. 2007. "Climate Change-Related Health Impacts in the Hindu Kush–Himalayas." *EcoHealth* 4(3): 264–270.

EBRD (European Bank for Reconstruction and Development). 2020. "MDBs' Climate Finance in Low- and Middle-Income Countries in 2019 Reaches US$ 41.5 Billion." Press Release, 6 August. https://www.ebrd.com/news/2020/mdbs-climate-finance-in-low-and-middleincome-countries-in-2019-reaches-us-415-billion.html. Accessed 23 November 2020.

Eckstein, D., Künzel, V., Schäfer, L., and Winges, M. 2019. "Global Climate Risk Index 2020." Bonn, Germany: Germanwatch. https://www.germanwatch.org/en/17307. Accessed 1 December 2020.

ECLAC (Economic Commission for Latin America and the Caribbean). 2020. "Principle 10 of the Rio Declaration on Environment and Development." https://www.cepal.org/en/infografias/principio-10-la-declaracion-rio-medio-ambiente-desarrollo. Accessed 13 October 2020.

The Economist. 2020a. "Grantham on Divesting from Big Oil: A Contrarian Investor on the Hazards of Owning Fossil-Fuel Stocks." 9 January. https://www.economist.com/finance-and-economics/2020/01/09/jeremy-grantham-on-divesting-from-big-oil. Accessed 1 December 2020.

The Economist. 2020b. "Humanity's Immense Impact on Earth's Climate and Carbon Cycle." 9 May. https://www.economist.com/schools-brief/2020/05/09/humanitys-immense-impact-on-earths-climate-and-carbon-cycle. Accessed 17 November 2020.

Efoui-Hess, M. 2019. *Climate Crisis: The Unsustainable Use of Online Video: The Practical Case for Digital Sobriety.* Paris: The Shift Project. https://theshiftproject.org/wp-content/uploads/2019/07/2019-02.pdf. Accessed 16 November 2020.

Ehlers, T., Mojon, B., and Packer, F. 2020. "Green Bonds and Carbon Emissions: Exploring the Case for a Rating System at the Firm Level." *BIS Quarterly Review,* September 2020.

Ehrlich, P. R. 1968. *The Population Bomb Keeps Ticking.* New York: Ballantine Books.

Ehrlich, P. R., and Ehrlich, A. H. 2016. "Population, Resources, and the Faith-Based Economy: The Situation in 2016." *BioPhysical Economics and Resource Quality* 1(1): 3.

Ehrlich, P. R., and Holdren, J. P. 1971. "Impact of Population Growth." *Science* 171(3977): 1212–1217.

EIU (Economist Intelligence Unit). 2015. "The Cost of Inaction: Recognizing the Value at Risk from Climate Change." London.

Elevitch, C. R., Mazaroli, D. N., and Ragone, D. 2018. "Agroforestry Standards for Regenerative Agriculture." *Sustainability* 10(9): 3337.

Elhacham, E., Ben-Uri, L., Grozovski, J., Bar-On, Y. M., and Milo, R. 2020. "Global Human-Made Mass Exceeds All Living Biomass." *Nature.* https://doi.org/10.1038/s41586-020-3010-5. Accessed 10 December 2020.

Ellis, E. C. 2015. "Ecology in an Anthropogenic Biosphere." *Ecological Monographs* 85(3): 287–331.

Ellis, E. C. 2018a. *Anthropocene: A Very Short Introduction.* New York: Oxford University Press.

Ellis, E. C. 2018b. "Science Alone Won't Save the Earth. People Have to Do That." *New York Times,* 11 August. https://www.nytimes.com/2018/08/11/opinion/sunday/science-people-environment-earth.html. Accessed 23 November 2020.

Ellis, E. C. 2019. "To Conserve Nature in the Anthropocene, Half Earth Is Not Nearly Enough." *One Earth* 1(2): 163–167.

Ellis, E. C. 2019a. "Sharing the Land between Nature and People." *Science* 364(6447): 1226–1228.

Ellis, E. C. 2019b. "To Conserve Nature in the Anthropocene, Half Earth Is Not Nearly Enough." *One Earth* 1(2): 163–167.

Ellis, E. C., Beusen, A. H. W., and Goldewijk, K. K. 2020. "Anthropogenic Biomes: 10,000 BCE to 2015 CE." *Land* 9(5): 129.

Ellis, E. C., Fuller, D. Q., Kaplan, J. O., and Lutters, W. G. 2013. "Dating the Anthropocene: Towards an Empirical Global History of Human Transformation of the Terrestrial Biosphere." *Elementa: Science of the Anthropocene* 1(0): 000018.

Ellis, E. C., Goldewijk, K. K., Siebert, S., Lightman, D., and Ramankutty, N. 2010. "Anthropogenic Transformation of the Biomes, 1700 to 2000." *Global Ecology and Biogeography* 19(5): 589–606.

Ellis, E. C., Magliocca, N. R., Stevens, C. J., and Fuller, D. Q. 2018. "Evolving the Anthropocene: Linking Multi-Level Selection with Long-Term Social–Ecological Change." *Sustainability Science* 13(1): 119–128.

Ellis, E. C., Maslin, M., Boivin, N., and Bauer, A. 2016. "Involve Social Scientists in Defining the Anthropocene." *Nature* 540(7632): 192–193.

Ellis, E. C., Pascual, U., and Mertz, O. 2019. "Ecosystem Services and Nature's Contribution to People: Negotiating Diverse Values and Trade-Offs in Land Systems." *Current Opinion in Environmental Sustainability* 38: 86–94.

Ellis, E. C., and Ramankutty, N. 2008. "Putting People in the Map: Anthropogenic Biomes of the World." *Frontiers in Ecology and the Environment* 6(8): 439–447.

Elmqvist, T., Andersson, E., Frantzeskaki, N., McPhearson, T., Olsson, P., Gaffney, O., Takeuchi, K., and Folke, C. 2019. "Sustainability and Resilience for Transformation in the Urban Century." *Nature Sustainability* 2(4): 267–273.

Elster, J. 1989. "Social Norms and Economic Theory." *Journal of Economic Perspectives* 3(4): 99–117.

Elster, J. 1993. *Political Psychology*. Cambridge, UK: Cambridge University Press.

Energy Transitions Commission. 2018. *Mission Possible: Reaching Net-Zero Carbon Emissions from Harder-to-Abate Sectors by Mid-Century*. Energy Transitions Commission. http://www.energy-transitions.org/mission-possible. Accessed 1 December 2020.

Engerman, S. L., and Sokoloff, K. L. 2005. "Colonialism, Inequality, and Long-Run Paths of Development." Working Paper 11057, National Bureau of Economic Research, Cambridge, MA.

Engström, G., Gars, J., Jaakkola, N., Lindahl, T., Spiro, D., and van Benthem, A. A. 2020. "What Policies Address Both the Coronavirus Crisis and the Climate Crisis?" *Environmental and Resource Economics* 76(4): 789–810.

Enqvist, J. P., and Ziervogel, G. 2019. "Water Governance and Justice in Cape Town: An Overview." *Wiley Interdisciplinary Reviews: Water* 6(4): e1354.

EPA (United States Environmental Protection Agency). 2020a. "Environmental Justice." https://www.epa.gov/environmentaljustice. Accessed 30 November 2020.

EPA (United States Environmental Protection Agency). 2020b. "EPA's Budget and Spending." https://www.epa.gov/planandbudget/budget. Accessed 6 August 2020.

EPA (United States Environmental Protection Agency). 2020c. "Heat Islands." https://www.epa.gov/heatislands/learn-about-heat-islands. Accessed 25 November 2020.

EPA (United States Environmental Protection Agency). 2020d. https://www.epa.gov. Accessed 18 November 2020.

Eppinga, M. B., de Scisciolo, T., and Mijts, E. N. 2019. "Environmental Science Education in a Small Island State: Integrating Theory and Local Experience." *Environmental Education Research* 25(7): 1004–1018.

Erbaugh, J., Pradhan, N., Adams, J., Oldekop, J., Agrawal, A., Brockington, D., Pritchard, R., and Chhatre, A. 2020. "Global Forest Restoration and the Importance of Prioritizing Local Communities." *Nature Ecology & Evolution* 4(11): 1472–1476.

Erisman, J. W., Sutton, M. A., Galloway, J., Klimont, Z., and Winiwarter, W. 2008. "How a Century of Ammonia Synthesis Changed the World." *Nature Geoscience* 1(10): 636–639.

Eshed, Y., and Lippman, Z. B. 2019. "Revolutions in Agriculture Chart a Course for Targeted Breeding of Old and New Crops." *Science* 366(6466).

European Commission. 2008. "Special Eurobarometer 295. Attitudes of European Citizens Towards the Environment." https://ec.europa.eu/commfrontoffice/publicopinion/archives/ebs/ebs_295_en.pdf. Accessed 11 November 2020.

European Commission. 2009. "Conference Proceedings: Beyond GDP Measuring Progress, True Wealth, and the Wellbeing of Nations. 19-20 November, 2007." https://ec.europa.eu/environment/beyond_gdp/proceedings/bgdp_proceedings_full.pdf. Accessed 2 December 2020.

European Commission. 2011. "Plastic Waste: Ecological and Human Health Impacts." https://ec.europa.eu/environment/integration/research/newsalert/pdf/IR1_en.pdf. Accessed 11 November 2020.

European Commission. 2018. "Report on Critical Raw Materials and the Circular Economy." Commission Staff Working Document. https://ec.europa.eu/commission/publications/report-critical-raw-materials-and-circular-economy_en. Accessed 17 November 2020.

European Commission. 2019. "Communication from the Commission to the European Parliament, the European Council, the Council, the European Economic and Social Committee and the Committee of the Regions. The European Green Deal. Com/2019/640 Final." Brussels: European Commission. https://eur-lex.europa.eu/legal-content/EN/TXT/?uri=COM%3A2019%3A640%3AFIN. Accessed 23 November 2020.

European Commission. 2020. "Recovery Plan for Europe." https://ec.europa.eu/info/strategy/recovery-plan-europe_en. Accessed 2 December 2020.

European Council. 2020. "Conclusions. Special Meeting of the European Council: July 17-21 2020." https://www.consilium.europa.eu/media/45109/210720-euco-final-conclusions-en.pdf. Accessed 30 November 2020.

European Union. 2020. "Targeted Consultation on the Establishment of an EU Green Bond Standard." Brussels: European Union. https://ec.europa.eu/info/consultations/finance-2020-eu-green-bond-standard_en. Accessed 23 November 2020.

Evans, S. 2020. "Analysis: Coronavirus Set to Cause Largest Ever Annual Fall in CO2 Emissions." Carbon Brief 9. https://www.carbonbrief.org/analysis-coronavirus-set-to-cause-largest-ever-annual-fall-in-co2-emissions. Accessed 23 November 2020.

Extinction Rebellion. 2020. "Rebellion Global." https://rebellion.global. Accessed 5 August 2020.

Fa, J. E., Watson, J. E., Leiper, I., Potapov, P., Evans, T. D., Burgess, N. D., Molnár, Z., and others. 2020. "Importance of Indigenous Peoples' Lands for the Conservation of Intact Forest Landscapes." *Frontiers in Ecology and the Environment* 18(3): 135–140.

Fajnzylber, F. 1990. "Industrialización en América Latina: de la 'caja negra' al 'casillero vacío': comparación de patrones contemporáneos de industrialización." United Nations Economic Commission for Latin America and the Caribbean, Santiago.

Falanruw, M. V. C. 1984. "People Pressure and Management of Limited Resources on Yap." In McNeely, J. A. and Miller, K. R., (eds.), *National Parks, Conservation, and Development: The Role of Protected Areas in Sustaining Society*. Washington, DC: The Smithsonian Institution Press.

Falk, A., Fehr, E., and Fischbacher, U. 2003. "On the Nature of Fair Behavior." *Economic Inquiry* 41(1): 20–26.

Falk, A., Fehr, E., and Fischbacher, U. 2008. "Testing Theories of Fairness—Intentions Matter." *Games and Economic Behavior* 62(1): 287–303.

Falkner, R. 2016. "The Paris Agreement and the New Logic of International Climate Politics." *International Affairs* 92(5): 1107–1125.

Fang, K., Heijungs, R., and De Snoo, G. R. 2015. "Understanding the Complementary Linkages between Environmental Footprints and Planetary Boundaries in a Footprint–Boundary Environmental Sustainability Assessment Framework." *Ecological Economics* 114: 218–226.

FAO (Food and Agriculture Organization of the United Nations). 2002. "Gender and Access to Land." FAO Land Tenure Studies. Rome.

FAO (Food and Agriculture Organization of the United Nations). 2013. *Food Wastage Footprint: Impacts on Natural Resources*. Rome.

FAO (Food and Agriculture Organization of the United Nations). 2016. "Tanzania Biodiversity Information Management Tool (BIMT): Access Data Delineating Areas of High Biodiversity Conservation Priority in Tanzania." Rome. http://aims.fao.org/activity/blog/tanzania-biodiversity-information-management-tool-bimt-access-data-delineating-areas. Accessed 18 November 2020.

FAO (Food and Agriculture Organization of the United Nations). 2017a. Water for Sustainable Food and Agriculture. Rome.

FAO (Food and Agriculture Organization of the United Nations). 2017b. World Fertilizer Trends and Outlook to 2020: Summary Report. Rome.

FAO (Food and Agriculture Organization of the United Nations). 2018. Food Loss and Waste and the Right to Adequate Food: Making the Connection. Rome.

FAO (Food and Agriculture Organization of the United Nations). 2019. The State of the World's Biodiversity for Food and Agriculture. Rome.

FAO (Food and Agriculture Organization of the United Nations). 2020a. "AQUASTAT Database." http://www.fao.org/nr/water/aquastat/data/query/index.html?lang=en. Accessed 7 December 2020.

FAO (Food and Agriculture Organization of the United Nations). 2020b. "FAOSTAT Statistical Database." http://www.fao.org/faostat/en/. Accessed 25 November 2020.

FAO (Food and Agriculture Organization of the United Nations). 2020c. Innovative Pastoralism: Achieving Productivity and Sustainability for Food Security. Rome.

FAO (Food and Agriculture Organization of the United Nations), IFAD (International Fund for Agricultural Development), UNICEF (United Nations Children's Fund), WFP (World Food Programme) and WHO (World Health Organization). 2018. The State of Food Security and Nutrition in the World 2018: Building Climate Resilience for Food Security and Nutrition. Rome: FAO.

FAO (Food and Agriculture Organization of the United Nations), IFAD (International Fund for Agricultural Development), UNICEF (United Nations Children's Fund), WFP (World Food Programme) and WHO (World Health Organization). 2019. The State of Food Security and Nutrition in the World 2019: Safeguarding against Economic Slowdowns and Downturns. Rome: FAO.

FAO (Food and Agriculture Organization of the United Nations), IFAD (International Fund for Agricultural Development), UNICEF (United Nations Children's Fund), WFP (World Food Programme) and WHO (World Health Organization). 2020. The State of Food Security and Nutrition in the World 2020: Transforming Food Systems for Affordable Healthy Diets. Rome: FAO.

Farmer, J. D., and Foley, D. 2009. "The Economy Needs Agent-Based Modelling." Nature 460(7256): 685–686.

Farmer, J., Hepburn, C., Ives, M., Hale, T., Wetzer, T., Mealy, P., Rafaty, R., and others. 2019. "Sensitive Intervention Points in the Post-Carbon Transition." Science 364(6436): 132–134.

Farrier, D. 2020. Footprints: In Search of Future Fossils. New York: Farrar, Straus and Giroux.

Farrow, K., Grolleau, G., and Ibanez, L. 2017. "Social Norms and Pro-Environmental Behavior: A Review of the Evidence." Ecological Economics 140: 1–13.

Fehr, E., and Gächter, S. 2000. "Fairness and Retaliation: The Economics of Reciprocity." Journal of Economic Perspectives 14(3): 159–181.

Feldman, M., Harbeck, M., Keller, M., Spyrou, M. A., Rott, A., Trautmann, B., Scholz, H. C., and others. 2016. "A High-Coverage Yersinia Pestis Genome from a Sixth-Century Justinianic Plague Victim." Molecular Biology and Evolution 33(11): 2911–2923.

Fenichel, E. P., and Abbott, J. K. 2014. "Natural Capital: From Metaphor to Measurement." Journal of the Association of Environmental and Resource Economists 1(1/2): 1–27. https://doi.org/10.1086/676034. Accessed 1 December 2020.

Fenichel, E. P., Abbott, J. K., and Yun, S. D. 2018. "The Nature of Natural Capital and Ecosystem Income." In Dasgupta, P., Pattanayak, S. K., and Smith, V. K., (eds.), Handbook of Environmental Economics. New York: Elsevier.

Fenichel, E. P., Addicott, E. T., Grimsrud, K. M., Lange, G.-M., Porras, I., and Milligan, B. 2020. "Modifying National Accounts for Sustainable Ocean Development." Nature Sustainability 3: 889–895.

Fenichel, E. P., and Hashida, Y. 2019. "Choices and the Value of Natural Capital." Oxford Review of Economic Policy 35(1): 120–137.

Fenichel, E. P., and Horan, R. D. 2016. "Tinbergen and Tipping Points: Could Some Thresholds Be Policy-Induced?" Journal of Economic Behavior & Organization 132: 137–152.

Fenichel, E. P., and Zhao, J. 2015. "Sustainability and Substitutability." Bulletin of Mathematical Biology 77(2): 348–367.

Fenner, F., Henderson, D. A., Arita, I., Jezek, Z., and Ladnyi, I. D. 1988. Smallpox and Its Eradication. Geneva: World Health Organization.

Fernández-Llamazares, Á., Garteizgogeascoa, M., Basu, N., Brondizio, E. S., Cabeza, M., Martínez-Alier, J., McElwee, P., and Reyes-García, V. 2020. "A State-of-the-Art Review of Indigenous Peoples and Environmental Pollution." Integrated Environmental Assessment and Management 16(3): 324–341.

Fernández-Portillo, A., Almodóvar-González, M., Coca-Pérez, J. L., and Jiménez-Naranjo, H. V. 2019. "Is Sustainable Economic Development Possible Thanks to the Deployment of ICT?" Sustainability 11(22): 6307.

Ferrario, F., Beck, M. W., Storlazzi, C. D., Micheli, F., Shepard, C. C., and Airoldi, L. 2014. "The Effectiveness of Coral Reefs for Coastal Hazard Risk Reduction and Adaptation." Nature Communications 5(1): 1–9.

Feygina, I., Jost, J. T., and Goldsmith, R. E. 2010. "System Justification, the Denial of Global Warming, and the Possibility of 'System-Sanctioned Change.'" Personality and Social Psychology Bulletin 36(3): 326–338.

Fickling, D. 2020. "Capitalism Caused Climate Change; It Must Also Be the Solution." Bloomberg, 14 October. https://www.bloomberg.com/opinion/articles/2020-10-14/capitalism-caused-climate-change-it-must-also-be-the-solution. Accessed 1 December 2020.

Field, J. L., Richard, T. L., Smithwick, E. A. H., Cai, H., Laser, M. S., LeBauer, D. S., Long, S. P., and others. 2020. "Robust Paths to Net Greenhouse Gas Mitigation and Negative Emissions via Advanced Biofuels." Proceedings of the National Academy of Sciences 117(36): 21968–21977.

Fink, L. 2020. "Sustainability as Blackrock's New Standard for Investing, 2020 Letter to CEOs." https://www.blackrock.com/corporate/investor-relations/blackrock-client-letter. Accessed 1 December 2020.

Firestone, J., Hirt, C., Bidwell, D., Gardner, M., and Dwyer, J. 2020. "Faring Well in Offshore Wind Power Siting? Trust, Engagement and Process Fairness in the United States." Energy Research & Social Science 62: 101393.

Fischer, C. 2016. "Strategic Subsidies for Green Goods." Discussion Paper 16-12, Resources for the Future, Washington, DC. https://www.rff.org/publications/working-papers/strategic-subsidies-for-green-goods/. Accessed 1 December 2020.

Fischer-Kowalski, M., and Amann, C. 2001. "Beyond IPAT and Kuznets Curves: Globalization as a Vital Factor in Analysing the Environmental Impact of Socio-Economic Metabolism." Population and Environment 23(1): 7–47.

Fischer-Kowalski, M., and Hüttler, W. 1998. "Society's Metabolism: The Intellectual History of Materials Flow Analysis, Part II, 1970–1998." Journal of Industrial Ecology 2(4): 107–136.

Fischer-Kowalski, M., Krausmann, F., and Pallua, I. 2014. "A Sociometabolic Reading of the Anthropocene: Modes of Subsistence, Population Size and Human Impact on Earth." The Anthropocene Review 1(1): 8–33.

Fischer-Kowalski, M., and Weisz, H. 1999. "Society as Hybrid between Material and Symbolic Realms: Toward a Theoretical Framework of Society-Nature Interrelation." Advances in Human Ecology 8: 215–251.

Fisher, D. R., and Jorgenson, A. K. 2019. "Ending the Stalemate: Toward a Theory of Anthro-Shift." Sociological Theory 37(4): 342–362.

Fisher, I. 1906. The Nature of Capital and Income. Norwood, MA: Norwood Press.

Fishman, R., Carrillo, P., and Russ, J. 2019. "Long-Term Impacts of Exposure to High Temperatures on Human Capital and Economic Productivity." Journal of Environmental Economics and Management 93: 221–238. https://doi.org/10.1016/j.jeem.2018.10.001. Accessed 1 December 2020.

Flammer, C. 2020. "Green Bonds: Effectiveness and Implications for Public Policy." Environmental and Energy Policy and the Economy 1(1): 95–128.

Fleurbaey, M. 2015. "On Sustainability and Social Welfare." *Journal of Environmental Economics and Management* 71: 34–53.

Fleurbaey, M. 2019. "On Human Development Indicators." United Nations Development Programme, Human Development Report Office, New York. http://hdr.undp.org/sites/default/files/on_human_development_indicators_m_fleurbaey.pdf. Accessed 30 November 2020.

Fleurbaey, M. 2020. "Sustainabililty and Human Development." Background paper for Human Development Report 2020, United Nations Development Programme, Human Development Report Office, New York.

Fleurbaey, M., Ferranna, M., Budolfson, M., Dennig, F., Mintz-Woo, K., Socolow, R., Spears, D., and Zuber, S. 2019. "The Social Cost of Carbon: Valuing Inequality, Risk, and Population for Climate Policy." *The Monist* 102(1): 84–109.

Flinders University. 2019. "What We Can Learn from Indigenous Land Management: Lessons from First Nations Governance in Environmental Management." https://www.sciencedaily.com/releases/2019/11/191105075838.htm. Accessed 17 November 2020.

Folke, C. 2016. "Resilience (Republished)." *Ecology and Society* 21(4).

Folke, C., Carpenter, S. R., Chapin, F., Gaffney, O., Galaz, V., Hoffmann, H., Lamont, M., and others. 2020. "Our Future in the Anthropocene Biosphere: Global Sustainability and Resilient Societies." Discussion Paper 272, Beijer Institute of Ecological Economics, Stockholm. https://scholar.harvard.edu/files/lamont/files/folke_et_al_2020_beijer_disc_paper.pdf. Accessed 9 December 2020.

Folke, C., Carpenter, S., Elmqvist, T., Gunderson, L., Holling, C. S., and Walker, B. 2002. "Resilience and Sustainable Development: Building Adaptive Capacity in a World of Transformations." *Ambio* 31(5): 437–440.

Folke, C., Carpenter, S., Walker, B., Scheffer, M., Chapin, T., and Rockström, J. 2010. "Resilience Thinking: Integrating Resilience, Adaptability and Transformability." *Ecology and Society* 15(4).

Folke, C., Österblom, H., Jouffray, J.-B., Lambin, E. F., Adger, W. N., Scheffer, M., Crona, B. I., and others. 2019. "Transnational Corporations and the Challenge of Biosphere Stewardship." *Nature Ecology & Evolution* 3(10): 1396–1403.

FONAG (Fondo Para la Protección del Agua). n.d. "FONAG en cifras." http://www.fonag.org.ec/web/conocenos-2/fonag-en-cifras/. Accessed 25 November 2020.

Fontana, L. B., and Grugel, J. 2016. "The Politics of Indigenous Participation through 'Free Prior Informed Consent': Reflections from the Bolivian Case." *World Development* 77: 249–261.

Fore, H. H., Dongyu, Q., Beasley, D. M., and Ghebreyesus, T. A. 2020. "Child Malnutrition and Covid-19: The Time to Act Is Now." *The Lancet* 396(10250): 517–518.

Forst, M., and Tognoni, G. 2016. "They Spoke Truth to Power and Were Murdered in Cold Blood." *Assistenza Infermieristica e Ricerca: AIR* 35(4): 209–213.

Forti, V., Balde, C. P., Kuehr, R., and Bel, G. 2020. "The Global E-waste Monitor 2020: Quantities, Flows and the Circular Economy Potential." http://ewastemonitor.info/wp-content/uploads/2020/07/GEM_2020_def_july1_low.pdf. Accessed 17 November 2020.

Fortin, J. 2019. "Hurricane Lorenzo Has Broken Records in the Atlantic." *New York Times*, 30 September. https://www.nytimes.com/2019/09/30/world/europe/hurricane-lorenzo-path.html. Accessed 10 December 2020.

Foster, G. L., Royer, D. L., and Lunt, D. J. 2017. "Future Climate Forcing Potentially without Precedent in the Last 420 Million Years." *Nature Communications* 8: 14845.

Frainer, A., Mustonen, T., Hugu, S., Andreeva, T., Arttijeff, E.-M., Arttijeff, I.-S., Brizoela, F., and others. 2020. "Opinion: Cultural and Linguistic Diversities Are Underappreciated Pillars of Biodiversity." *Proceedings of the National Academy of Sciences* 117(43): 26539–26543.

Frank, K. 2005. "The Effect of Residential and Agricultural Runoff on the Microbiology of a Hawaiian Ahupua'a." *Water Environment Research* 77(7): 2988–2995.

Frank, T., and Cort, T. 2020. *Report of Results Global Survey on Sustainability and the SDGs.* Hamburg, Germany: Schlange & Co. GmbH.

Frankel, J. 2011. "Natural Resource Curse: A Survey of the Literature." In Arezki, R., Pattillo, C. A., and Quintyn, M. G., (eds.), *Commodity Prices and Inclusive Growth in Low-Income Countries.* Washington, DC: International Monetary Fund.

Frankenberg, E., Sikoki, B., Sumantri, C., Suriastini, W., and Thomas, D. 2013. "Education, Vulnerability, and Resilience after a Natural Disaster." *Ecology and Society: A Journal of Integrative Science for Resilience and Sustainability* 18(2): 16.

Frantzeskaki, N. 2019. "Seven Lessons for Planning Nature-Based Solutions in Cities." *Environmental Science & Policy* 93: 101–111.

Friedlingstein, P., Allen, M., Canadell, J. G., Peters, G. P., and Seneviratne, S. I. 2019a. "Comment on 'The Global Tree Restoration Potential.'" *Science* 366(6463).

Friedlingstein, P., Jones, M. W., O'Sullivan, M., Andrew, R. M., Hauck, J., Peters, G. P., Peters, W., and others. 2019b. "Global Carbon Budget 2019." *Earth System Science Data* 11(4): 1783–1838.

Fripp, M., and Roberts, M. J. 2018. "Variable Pricing and the Cost of Renewable Energy." Working Paper 24712, National Bureau of Economic Research, Cambridge, MA.

Fuhrman, J., McJeon, H., Patel, P., Doney, S. C., Shobe, W. M., and Clarens, A. F. 2020. "Food–Energy–Water Implications of Negative Emissions Technologies in a +1.5°C Future." *Nature Climate Change* 10: 1–8.

Fukuda-Parr, S. 2003. "The Human Development Paradigm: Operationalizing Sen's Ideas on Capabilities." *Feminist Economics* 9(2–3): 301–317.

Fukuda-Parr, S., and Muchhala, B. 2020. "The Southern Origins of Sustainable Development Goals: Ideas, Actors, Aspirations." *World Development* 126: 104706.

Fullerton, D., and Muehlegger, E. 2019. "Who Bears the Economic Burdens of Environmental Regulations?" *Review of Environmental Economics and Policy* 13(1): 62–82.

Funk, P. 2007. "Is There an Expressive Function of Law? An Empirical Analysis of Voting Laws with Symbolic Fines." *American Law and Economics Review* 9(1): 135–159.

Fuss, S., Lamb, W. F., Callaghan, M. W., Hilaire, J., Creutzig, F., Amann, T., Beringer, T., and others. 2018. "Negative Emissions—Part 2: Costs, Potentials and Side Effects." *Environmental Research Letters* 13(6): 063002.

G30 (Group of Thirty). 2020. *Mainstreaming the Transition to a Net-Zero Economy.* Washington, DC. https://group30.org/images/uploads/publications/G30_Mainstreaming_the_Transition_to_a_Net-Zero_Economy.pdf. Accessed 23 November 2020.

Galaz, V. 2014. *Global Environmental Governance, Technology and Politics: The Anthropocene Gap.* Cheltenham, UK: Edward Elgar Publishing.

Galaz, V. 2019. *Global Challenges, Governance, and Complexity: Applications and Frontiers.* Cheltenham, UK: Edward Elgar Publishing.

Galaz, V., Biermann, F., Crona, B., Loorbach, D., Folke, C., Olsson, P., Nilsson, M., and others. 2012. "'Planetary Boundaries'—Exploring the Challenges for Global Environmental Governance." *Current Opinion in Environmental Sustainability* 4(1): 80–87.

Galaz, V., Collste, D., and Moore, M.-L. 2020. "Planetary Change and Human Development." Unpublished manuscript, Stockholm University, Stockholm Resilience Centre.

Galaz, V., Gars, J., Moberg, F., Nykvist, B., and Repinski, C. 2015. "Why Ecologists Should Care About Financial Markets." *Trends in Ecology & Evolution* 30(10): 571–580.

Galdos, G., and Somra, G. 2020. "In This Indigenous Village, Two Nurses Care for Hundreds of Covid-19 Patients." *CNN*, 23 June. https://www.cnn.com/2020/06/23/americas/peru-coronavirus-caimito-nurse-intl/index.html. Accessed 19 November 2020.

Galea, S. 2016. "Public Health as a Public Good." https://www.bu.edu/sph/2016/01/10/public-health-as-a-public-good/#:~:text=It%20is%20then%20incumbent%20upon,the%20production%20and%20consumption%20of. Accessed 25 May 2020.

Gao, Y., Gao, X., and Zhang, X. 2017. "The 2 C Global Temperature Target and the Evolution of the Long-Term Goal of Addressing Climate Change—From the United Nations Framework Convention on Climate Change to the Paris Agreement." *Engineering* 3(2): 272–278.

Garbero, A., and Muttarak, R. 2013. "Impacts of the 2010 Droughts and Floods on Community Welfare in Rural Thailand: Differential Effects of Village Educational Attainment." *Ecology and Society* 18(4).

Garg, V., Beaton, C., Sharma, S., Bridle, R., Viswanathan, B., Narayanaswamy, D., and Ganesan, K. 2020. *Mapping India's Energy Subsidies 2020: Fossil Fuels, Renewables and Electric Vehicles.* Winnipeg, MB: International Institute for Sustainable Development).

Garicano, L., and Rossi-Hansberg, E. 2006. "Organization and Inequality in a Knowledge Economy." *The Quarterly Journal of Economics* 121(4): 1383–1435.

Garlinghouse, T. 2020. "Rethinking Easter Island's Historic 'Collapse.'" https://www.scientificamerican.com/article/rethinking-easter-islands-historic-collapse/. Accessed 21 October 2020.

Garnett, S. T., Burgess, N. D., Fa, J. E., Fernández-Llamazares, Á., Molnár, Z., Robinson, C. J., Watson, J. E., and others. 2018. "A Spatial Overview of the Global Importance of Indigenous Lands for Conservation." *Nature Sustainability* 1(7): 369.

Gavin, M. C., McCarter, J., Berkes, F., Mead, A. T. P., Sterling, E. J., Tang, R., and Turner, N. J. 2018. "Effective Biodiversity Conservation Requires Dynamic, Pluralistic, Partnership-Based Approaches." *Sustainability* 10(6): 1846.

GCP (Global Carbon Project). 2020. "Global Carbon Project." https://www.globalcarbonproject.org. Accessed 30 November 2020.

Geissler, B., Hermann, L., Mew, M. C., and Steiner, G. 2018. "Striving toward a Circular Economy for Phosphorus: The Role of Phosphate Rock Mining." *Minerals* 8(9): 395.

Gentle, P., and Maraseni, T. N. 2012. "Climate Change, Poverty and Livelihoods: Adaptation Practices by Rural Mountain Communities in Nepal." *Environmental Science & Policy* 21: 24–34.

Gentry, D. B., and Benenson, W. A. 1993. "School-to-Home Transfer of Conflict Management Skills among School-Age Children." *Families in Society* 74(2): 67–73.

Georgieva, K. 2020. "New Priorities for the Global Economy." Speech at the Workshop on New Forms of Solidarity, Vatican City, 5 February. http://www.imf.org/en/News/Articles/2020/02/05/sp-200205-kristalina-georgieva-new-priorities-for-the-global-economy. Accessed 1 December 2020.

Gerten, D., Hoff, H., Rockström, J., Jägermeyr, J., Kummu, M., and Pastor, A. V. 2013. "Towards a Revised Planetary Boundary for Consumptive Freshwater Use: Role of Environmental Flow Requirements." *Current Opinion in Environmental Sustainability* 5(6): 551–558.

Ghestem, M., Veylon, G., Bernard, A., Vanel, Q., and Stokes, A. 2014. "Influence of Plant Root System Morphology and Architectural Traits on Soil Shear Resistance." *Plant and Soil* 377(1-2): 43–61.

Ghosh, A. 2020a. "India Needs a Plan for Extreme Weather Caused by Climate Change." *Nikkei Asian Review*, 27 June. https://asia.nikkei.com/Opinion/India-needs-a-plan-for-extreme-weather-caused-by-climate-change. Accessed 1 December 2020.

Ghosh, A. 2020b. "Multilateralism for Chronic Risks." UN75 Global Governance Innovation Perspectives, International Order and Conflict Issue Brief, Stimson Center. https://www.stimson.org/wp-content/uploads/2020/06/GloCo-Issue-Brief-June-2020-Multilateralism-R4-WEB.pdf. Accessed 1 December 2020.

Gissey, G. C., Guo, B., Newbery, D., Lipman, G., Montoya, L., Dodds, P., Grubb, M., and Ekins, P. 2019. "The Value of International Electricity Trading." Office of Gas and Electricity Markets, University College London and University of Cambridge. https://www.ofgem.gov.uk/system/files/docs/2019/10/value_of_international_electricity_trading.pdf. Accessed 1 December 2020.

Gleick, P. H. 2018. "Transitions to Freshwater Sustainability." *Proceedings of the National Academy of Sciences* 115(36): 8863–8871.

Global Footprint Network. 2019. "National Footprint and Biocapacity Accounts." https://data.footprintnetwork.org. Accessed 10 October 2020.

Global Witness. 2019. "Defending Tomorrow." https://www.globalwitness.org/en/campaigns/environmental-activists/defending-tomorrow/. Accessed 25 November 2020.

Global Witness. 2020. "Global Witness Records the Highest Number of Land and Environmental Activists Murdered in One Year—with the Link to Accelerating Climate Change of Increasing Concern." Press Release, 29 July. https://www.globalwitness.org/en/press-releases/global-witness-records-the-highest-number-of-land-and-environmental-activists-murdered-in-one-year-with-the-link-to-accelerating-climate-change-of-increasing-concern/. Accessed 25 November 2020.

Godin, M. 2020. "Record Number of Environmental Activists Killed in 2019." *Time*, 29 July. https://time.com/5873137/record-number-killing-environmental-activists-2019/. Accessed 25 November 2020.

Goldblatt, C., Lenton, T. M., and Watson, A. J. 2006. "Bistability of Atmospheric Oxygen and the Great Oxidation." *Nature* 443: 683–686.

Goldstone, J. A. 2002. "Efflorescences and Economic Growth in World History: Rethinking the 'Rise of the West' and the Industrial Revolution." *Journal of World History* 13(2): 323–389.

Goodale, M. W., and Milman, A. 2016. "Cumulative Adverse Effects of Offshore Wind Energy Development on Wildlife." *Journal of Environmental Planning and Management* 59(1): 1–21.

Gordon, H. S. 1954. "The Economic Theory of a Common-Property Resource: The Fishery." *Journal of Political Economy* 62(2): 124–142.

Görg, C., Plank, C., Wiedenhofer, D., Mayer, A., Pichler, M., Schaffartzik, A., and Krausmann, F. 2020. "Scrutinizing the Great Acceleration: The Anthropocene and Its Analytic Challenges for Social-Ecological Transformations." *The Anthropocene Review* 7(1): 42–61.

Gough, I. 2015. "Climate Change and Sustainable Welfare: The Centrality of Human Needs." *Cambridge Journal of Economics* 39(5): 1191–1214.

Gough, I. 2017. "Recomposing Consumption: Defining Necessities for Sustainable and Equitable Well-Being." *Philosophical Transactions of the Royal Society A: Mathematical, Physical and Engineering Sciences* 375(2095): 20160379.

Gough, I. 2019. "Universal Basic Services: A Theoretical and Moral Framework." *The Political Quarterly* 90(3): 534–542.

Goulson, D., Nicholls, E., Botías, C., and Rotheray, E. L. 2015. "Bee Declines Driven by Combined Stress from Parasites, Pesticides, and Lack of Flowers." *Science* 347(6229): 1255957.

Government of Australia. 2019. "Daily Extremes." http://www.bom.gov.au/cgi-bin/climate/extremes/monthly_extremes.cgi?climtab=tmax_high&area=aus&year=2019&mon=12. Accessed 10 December 2020.

Government of India. 2015. "India's Intended Nationally Determined Contribution: Working towards Climate Justice." *Vikaspedia*. https://vikaspedia.in/energy/environment/climate-change/india2019s-intended-nationally-determined-contribution. Accessed 17 November 2020.

Government of India. 2020. "Solar Energy Current Status." Delhi. https://mnre.gov.in/solar/current-status/. Accessed 10 November 2020.

Government of Sweden. 2020. "Carbon Taxation in Sweden." March 2020. Stockholm: Government Offices of Sweden. https://www.government.se/492a01/contentassets/419eb2cafa93423c891c09cb9914801b/200224-carbon-tax-sweden---general-info.pdf. Accessed November 18 2020.

Graedel, T. E., Harper, E. M., Nassar, N. T., and Reck, B. K. 2015. "On the Materials Basis of Modern Society." *Proceedings of the National Academy of Sciences* 112(20): 6295–6300.

Graff Zivin, J., and Neidell, M. 2012. "The Impact of Pollution on Worker Productivity." *American Economic Review* 102(7): 3652–3673. https://doi.org/10.1257/aer.102.7.3652. Accessed 1 December 2020.

Graff Zivin, J., Hsiang, S. M., and Neidell, M. 2018. "Temperature and Human Capital in the Short and Long Run." *Journal of the Association of Environmental and Resource Economists* 5(1): 77–105. https://doi.org/10.1086/694177. Accessed 1 December 2020.

Graham, M. 2013. "Australian Aboriginal Concept of Ethics." http://colourise.com.au/landed/wp-content/uploads/2013/06/CustodialNavigator.pdf. Accessed 17 November 2020.

Grandcolas, P., and Justine, J.-L. 2020. "Covid-19 or the Pandemic of Mistreated Biodiversity." *The Conversation*, 29 April. https://theconversation.com/covid-19-or-the-pandemic-of-mistreated-biodiversity-136447. Accessed 12 November 2020.

Gratani, M., Bohensky, E. L., Butler, J. R. A., Sutton, S. G., and Foale, S. 2014. "Experts' Perspectives on the Integration of Indigenous Knowledge and Science in Wet Tropics Natural Resource Management." *Australian Geographer* 45(2): 167–184.

Green, F. 2015. "Nationally Self-Interested Climate Change Mitigation: A Unified Conceptual Framework." Grantham Research Institute on Climate Change and the Environment, Leeds, UK.

Green, R., Milner, J., Dangour, A. D., Haines, A., Chalabi, Z., Markandya, A., Spadaro, J., and Wilkinson, P. 2015. "The Potential to Reduce Greenhouse Gas Emissions in the UK through Healthy and Realistic Dietary Change." *Climatic Change* 129(1–2): 253–265.

Grineski, S. E. 2007. "Incorporating Health Outcomes into Environmental Justice Research: The Case of Children's Asthma and Air Pollution in Phoenix, Arizona." *Environmental Hazards* 7(4): 360–371.

Griscom, B. W., Adams, J., Ellis, P. W., Houghton, R. A., Lomax, G., Miteva, D. A., Schlesinger, W. H., and others. 2017. "Natural Climate Solutions." *Proceedings of the National Academy of Sciences* 114(44): 11645–11650.

Grønhøj, A., and Thøgersen, J. 2009. "Like Father, Like Son? Intergenerational Transmission of Values, Attitudes, and Behaviours in the Environmental Domain." *Journal of Environmental Psychology* 29(4): 414–421.

Grubler, A., Wilson, C., Bento, N., Boza-Kiss, B., Krey, V., McCollum, D. L., Rao, N. D., and others. 2018. "A Low Energy Demand Scenario for Meeting the 1.5 °C Target and Sustainable Development Goals without Negative Emission Technologies." *Nature Energy* 3(6): 515–527.

Guber, D. L. 2017. "Partisan Cueing and Polarization in Public Opinion About Climate Change." *Oxford Research Encyclopedia of Climate Science*. Oxford, UK: Oxford University Press.

Guerry, A. D., Polasky, S., Lubchenco, J., Chaplin-Kramer, R., Daily, G. C., Griffin, R., Ruckelshaus, M., and others. 2015. "Natural Capital and Ecosystem Services Informing Decisions: From Promise to Practice." *Proceedings of the National Academy of Sciences* 112(24): 7348–7355.

Gunditjmara People, and Wettenhall, G. 2010. *The People of Budj Bim: Engineers of Aquaculture, Builders of Stone House Settlements and Warriors Defending Country*. Ballarat, Australia: em PRESS Publishing.

Guo, Y., Xin, F., and Li, X. 2019. "The Market Impacts of Sharing Economy Entrants: Evidence from USA and China." *Electronic Commerce Research* 20: 1–21.

Gupta, G. S. 2019. "Land Degradation and Challenges of Food Security." *Review of European Studies* 11(1): 63.

Gupta, J., Dellapenna, J. W., and van den Heuvel, M. 2016. "Water Sovereignty and Security, High Politics and Hard Power: The Dangers of Borrowing Discourses!" *Handbook on Water Security*. Cheltenham, UK: Edward Elgar Publishing.

Guterres, A. 2020. "Secretary-General's Nelson Mandela Lecture: 'Tackling the Inequality Pandemic: A New Social Contract for a New Era.'" 18 July. https://www.un.org/sg/en/content/sg/statement/2020-07-18/secretary-generals-nelson-mandela-lecture-%E2%80%9Ctackling-the-inequality-pandemic-new-social-contract-for-new-era%E2%80%9D-delivered. Accessed 18 November 2020.

Güven, S., and Yılmaz, N. 2017. "Role and Importance of Family at Preschool Children Environmental Education." *European Journal of Sustainable Development* 6(4): 105–105.

Guy, J. 2020a. "Nearly Three Billion Animals Killed or Displaced by Australia's Fires." *CNN*, 28 July. https://www.cnn.com/2020/07/28/asia/australia-fires-wildlife-report-scli-intl-scn/index.html. Accessed 18 November 2020.

Guy, J. 2020b. "Record Number of Environmental Activists Killed in 2019." *CNN*, 29 July. https://www.cnn.com/2020/07/29/world/global-witness-2019-defenders-report-scli-intl/index.html. Accessed 25 November 2020.

Guzman, J. 2020. "Zeta Becomes 27th Storm This Year. The Atlantic Hasn't Experienced This Many Storms for Nearly Two Decades." *The Hill*, 26 October. https://thehill.com/changing-america/sustainability/environment/522795-zeta-becomes-27th-storm-this-year-the-atlantic. Accessed 18 November 2020.

Haas, W., Krausmann, F., Wiedenhofer, D., and Heinz, M. 2015. "How Circular Is the Global Economy? An Assessment of Material Flows, Waste Production, and Recycling in the European Union and the World in 2005." *Journal of Industrial Ecology* 19(5): 765–777.

Haberl, H., Fischer-Kowalski, M., Krausmann, F., Martinez-Alier, J., and Winiwarter, V. 2011. "A Socio-Metabolic Transition Towards Sustainability? Challenges for Another Great Transformation." *Sustainable Development* 19(1): 1–14.

Haberl, H., Fischer-Kowalski, M., Krausmann, F., and Winiwarter, V. 2016. *Social Ecology: Society–Nature Relations across Time and Space*. New York: Springer.

Haberl, H., Wiedenhofer, D., Pauliuk, S., Krausmann, F., Müller, D. B., and Fischer-Kowalski, M. 2019. "Contributions of Sociometabolic Research to Sustainability Science." *Nature Sustainability* 2(3): 173–184.

Haberl, H., Wiedenhofer, D., Virág, D., Kalt, G., Plank, B., Brockway, P., Fishman, T., and others. 2020. "A Systematic Review of the Evidence on Decoupling of GDP, Resource Use and GHG Emissions, Part II: Synthesizing the Insights." *Environmental Research Letters* 15(6): 065003.

Habitat for Humanity. 2016. *Shelter Report 2016: Level the Field: Ending Gender Inequality in Land Rights*. Atlanta, GA: Habitat for Humanity.

Haff, P. K. 2014. "Technology as a Geological Phenomenon: Implications for Human Well-Being." *Geological Society, London, Special Publications* 395(1): 301–309.

Hajat, A., Hsia, C., and O'Neill, M. S. 2015. "Socioeconomic Disparities and Air Pollution Exposure: A Global Review." *Current Environmental Health Reports* 2(4): 440–450.

Hajer, M., Nilsson, M., Raworth, K., Bakker, P., Berkhout, F., De Boer, Y., Rockström, J., and others. 2015. "Beyond Cockpit-Ism: Four Insights to Enhance the Transformative Potential of the Sustainable Development Goals." *Sustainability* 7(2): 1651–1660.

Haldon, J., Mordechai, L., Newfield, T. P., Chase, A. F., Izdebski, A., Guzowski, P., Labuhn, I., and Roberts, N. 2018. "History Meets Palaeoscience: Consilience and Collaboration in Studying Past Societal Responses to Environmental Change." *Proceedings of the National Academy of Sciences* 115(13): 3210–3218.

Hale, T. 2016. "All Hands on Deck: The Paris Agreement and Nonstate Climate Action." *Global Environmental Politics* 16(3): 12–22.

Hale, T. 2017. "Under What Conditions Does International Review Alter National Policy? Refining Concepts and Building Theory." Presented at the 10th Annual Conference on the Political Economy of International Organizations, Bern, Switzerland.

Hale, T. 2020. "Catalytic Cooperation." *Global Environmental Politics* 20(4): 73–98.

Hale, T., and Urpelainen, J. 2015. "When and How Can Unilateral Policies Promote the International Diffusion of Environmental Policies and Clean Technology?" *Journal of Theoretical Politics* 27(2): 177–205.

Hale, T., Held, D., and Young, K. 2013. *Gridlock: Why Global Cooperation Is Failing When We Need It Most*. Oxford, UK: Polity Press.

Hall, D. 2018. "The Interwoven World | Te Ao I Whiria: Towards an Integrated Landscape Approach in Aotearoa New Zealand." Auckland, New Zealand.

Hall, D. 2019. "A Careful Revolution: Towards a Low-emissions Future." Wellington.

Hamada, S., and Ohta, T. 2010. "Seasonal Variations in the Cooling Effect of Urban Green Areas on Surrounding Urban Areas." *Urban Forestry & Urban Greening* 9(1): 15–24.

Hamann, M., Berry, K., Chaigneau, T., Curry, T., Heilmayr, R., Henriksson, P. J. G., Hentati-Sundberg, J., and others. 2018. "Inequality and the Biosphere." *Annual Review of Environment and Resources* 43(1): 61–83.

Hamilton, C. 2016. "The Anthropocene as Rupture." *The Anthropocene Review* 2(1): 59–72.

Hamilton, C., Gemenne, F., and Bonneuil, C. 2015. *The Anthropocene and the Global Environmental Crisis: Rethinking Modernity in a New Epoch*. London: Routledge.

Hamilton, J. T. 1995. "Testing for Environmental Racism: Prejudice, Profits, Political Power?" *Journal of Policy Analysis and Management* 14(1): 107–132.

Hamilton, K., and Clemens, M. 1999. "Genuine Savings Rates in Developing Countries." *World Bank Economic Review* 13(2): 333–356.

Hamilton-Webb, A., Manning, L., Naylor, R., and Conway, J. 2017. "The Relationship between Risk Experience and Risk Response: A Study of Farmers and Climate Change." *Journal of Risk Research* 20(11): 1379–1393.

Han, H., and Ahn, S. W. 2020. "Youth Mobilization to Stop Global Climate Change: Narratives and Impact." *Sustainability* 12(10): 4127.

Han, S., and Kuhlicke, C. 2019. "Reducing Hydro-Meteorological Risk by Nature-Based Solutions: What Do We Know about People's Perceptions?" *Water* 11(12): 2599.

Hänsel, M. C., Drupp, M. A., Johansson, D. J. A., Nesje, F., Azar, C., Freeman, M. C., Groom, B., and Sterner, T. 2020. "Climate Economics Support for the UN Climate Targets." *Nature Climate Change* 10(8): 781–789.

Haq, M. u. 1995. *Reflections on Human Development*. Oxford, UK: Oxford University Press.

Haraway, D. 2003. *The Companion Species Manifesto: Dogs, People, and Significant Otherness*. Chicago, IL: Prickly Paradigm Press.

Haraway, D. 2016. *Staying with the Trouble: Making Kin in the Chthulucene*. Durham, NC: Duke University Press.

Hardin, G. 1968. "The Tragedy of the Commons." *Science* 162(3859): 1243–1248.

Harper, K. 2017. *The Fate of Rome: Climate, Disease & the End of an Empire*. Princeton, NJ: Princeton University Press.

Harrison, K. 2010. "The United States as Outlier: Economic and Institutional Challenges to US Climate Policy." In *Global Commons, Domestic Decisions: The Comparative Politics of Climate Change*, 67–103. Cambridge, MA: MIT Press.

Hartwick, J. M. 1977. "Intergenerational Equity and the Investing of Rents from Exhaustible Resources." *The American Economic Review* 67(5): 972–974.

Haskel, J., and Westlake, S. 2018. *Capitalism without Capital*. Princeton, NJ: Princeton University Press.

Hassan, O. M., and Tularam, G. A. 2017. "Impact of Rainfall Fluctuations and Temperature Variations on People Movement in Sub-Saharan Africa: A Time Series Analysis of Data from Somalia and Ethiopia." 22nd International Congress on Modelling and Simulation, Hobart, Tasmania, Australia, 3–8 December 2017. https://mssanz.org.au/modsim2017/A5/hassan.pdf. Accessed 20 November 2020.

Hausman, C., and Stolper, S. 2020. "Inequality, Information Failures, and Air Pollution." Working Paper 26682, National Bureau of Economic Research, Cambridge, MA.

Haydock, K., and Srivastava, H. 2019. "Environmental Philosophies Underlying the Teaching of Environmental Education: A Case Study in India." *Environmental Education Research* 25(7): 1038–1065.

Hayes, T., Murtinho, F., and Wolff, H. 2015. "An Institutional Analysis of Payment for Environmental Services on Collectively Managed Lands in Ecuador." *Ecological Economics* 118: 81–89.

Häyhä, T., Lucas, P. L., van Vuuren, D. P., Cornell, S. E., and Hoff, H. 2016. "From Planetary Boundaries to National Fair Shares of the Global Safe Operating Space: How Can the Scales Be Bridged?" *Global Environmental Change* 40: 60–72.

Heal, G. M. 1998. *Valuing the Future: Economic Theory and Sustainability*. New York: Columbia University Press.

Heal, G. M. 1999. "New Strategies for the Provision of Public Goods." In *Global Public Goods: International Cooperation in the 21st Century*. New York: Oxford University Press.

Heal, G. M. 2011. Sustainability and Its Measurement. Cambridge, MA: National Bureau of Economic Research.

Healthy Reefs. 2020. *Mesoamerican Reef Report Card Evaluation of Ecosystem Health*. https://www.healthyreefs.org/cms/wp-content/uploads/2020/02/2020_Report_Card_MAR.pdf. Accessed 25 November 2020.

Healy, N., and Barry, J. 2017. "Politicizing Energy Justice and Energy System Transitions: Fossil Fuel Divestment and a 'Just Transition.'" *Energy Policy* 108: 451–459.

Heaviside, C., Macintyre, H., and Vardoulakis, S. 2017. "The Urban Heat Island: Implications for Health in a Changing Environment." *Current Environmental Health Reports* 4(3): 296–305.

Hedlund-de Witt, A. 2012. "Exploring Worldviews and Their Relationships to Sustainable Lifestyles: Towards a New Conceptual and Methodological Approach." *Ecological Economics* 84: 74–83.

Heffron, R. J., and McCauley, D. 2018. "What Is the 'Just Transition'?" *Geoforum* 88: 74–77.

Heft-Neal, S., Burney, J., Bendavid, E., Voss, K. K., and Burke, M. 2020. "Dust Pollution from the Sahara and African Infant Mortality." *Nature Sustainability* 3(10): 863–871. https://doi.org/10.1038/s41893-020-0562-1. Accessed 1 December 2020.

Heinimann, A., Mertz, O., Frolking, S., Egelund Christensen, A., Hurni, K., Sedano, F., Parsons Chini, L., and others. 2017. "A Global View of Shifting Cultivation: Recent, Current, and Future Extent." *PLOS ONE* 12(9): e0184479.

Held, D., and Roger, C. 2013. *Global Governance at Risk*. Oxford, UK: Polity Press.

Held, D., and Roger, C. 2018. "Three Models of Global Climate Governance: From Kyoto to Paris and Beyond." *Global Policy* 9(4): 527–537.

Hepburn, C., O'Callaghan, B., Stern, N., Stiglitz, J., and D. Zenghelis. 2020. "Will Covid-19 Fiscal Recovery Packages Accelerate or Retard Progress on Climate Change?" *Oxford Review of Economic Policy* 16(S1): S359–S381.

Hertsgaard, M. 2000. "Mikhail Gorbachev Explains What's Rotten in Russia." Salon.com, 7 September.

Hertwig, R., and Grüne-Yanoff, T. 2017. "Nudging and Boosting: Steering or Empowering Good Decisions." *Perspectives on Psychological Science* 12(6): 973–986.

Hickel, J. 2019a. "Is It Possible to Achieve a Good Life for All within Planetary Boundaries?" *Third World Quarterly* 40(1): 18–35.

Hickel, J. 2019b. "The Contradiction of the Sustainable Development Goals: Growth versus Ecology on a Finite Planet." *Sustainable Development* 27(5): 873–884.

Hickel, J. 2020a. "Quantifying National Responsibility for Climate Breakdown: An Equality-Based Attribution Approach for Carbon Dioxide Emissions in Excess of the Planetary Boundary." *The Lancet Planetary Health* 4(9): e399–e404.

Hickel, J. 2020b. "The Sustainable Development Index: Measuring the Ecological Efficiency of Human Development in the Anthropocene." *Ecological Economics* 167: 106331.

Hickel, J., and Kallis, G. 2020. "Is Green Growth Possible?" *New Political Economy* 25(4): 469–486.

Hicks, C. C., Levine, A., Agrawal, A., Basurto, X., Breslow, S. J., Carothers, C., Charnley, S., and others. 2016. "Engage Key Social Concepts for Sustainability." *Science* 352(6281): 38–40.

Hicks, J. R. 1939. "Value and Capital: An Inquiry into Some Fundamental Principles of Economic Theory." Oxford, UK: Clarendon Press.

Hikuroa, D., and Slade, A. 2010. "Restoring the Mauri to Rotoitipaku (Industrial Waste Site): Implementing Matauranga in a Scientific Paradigm." http://www.maramatanga.ac.nz/project/restoring-mauri-rotoitipaku-industrial-waste-site. Accessed 17 November 2020.

Huambachano, M. 2015. "Food Security and Indigenous Knowledge: El Buen Vivir-Sumaq Kawsay in Peru and Tē Atānoho New Zealand, Māori-New Zealand." *The International Journal of Food Studies: An Interdisciplinary Journal* 5(3): 33–47.

Hill, R., Adem, Ç., Alangui, W. V., Molnár, Z., Aumeeruddy-Thomas, Y., Bridgewater, P., Tengö, M., and others. 2020. "Working with Indigenous, Local and Scientific Knowledge in Assessments of Nature and Nature's Linkages with People." *Current Opinion in Environmental Sustainability* 43: 8–20.

Hirsch, T., Mooney, K., and Cooper, D. 2020. *Global Biodiversity Outlook 5*. Montreal, QC: Secretariat of the Convention on Biological Diversity.

Hoag, C., and Svenning, J.-C. 2017. "African Environmental Change from the Pleistocene to the Anthropocene." *Annual Review of Environment and Resources* 42(1): 27–54.

Hoegh-Guldberg, O., Jacob, D., Taylor, M., Bolaños, T. G., Bindi, M., Brown, S., Camilloni, I. A., and others. 2019. "The Human Imperative of Stabilizing Global Climate Change at 1.5°C." *Science* 365(6459).

Hoffmann, A. A., and Sgro, C. M. 2011. "Climate Change and Evolutionary Adaptation." *Nature* 470(7335): 479–485.

Høgevold, N. M., 2003. "A Corporate Effort towards a Sustainable Business Model: A Case Study from the Norwegian Furniture Industry." *International Journal of Operations and Production Management* 23(4): 392–400.

Höhne, N., Fekete, H., den Elzen, M. G., Hof, A. F., and Kuramochi, T. 2018. "Assessing the Ambition of Post-2020 Climate Targets: A Comprehensive Framework." *Climate Policy* 18(4): 425–441.

Holland, S. P., Mansur, E. T., Muller, N. Z., and Yates, A. J. 2020. "Decompositions and Policy Consequences of an Extraordinary Decline in Air Pollution from Electricity Generation." *American Economic Journal: Economic Policy* 12(4): 244–274.

Holling, C. S. 1973. "Resilience and Stability of Ecological Systems." *Annual Review of Ecology and Systematics* 4(1): 1–23.

Holling, C. S., Clark, W., and Munn, R. 1986. *Sustainable Development of the Biosphere.* Cambridge, UK: Cambridge University Press.

Homer-Dixon, T. F. 1991. "On the Threshold: Environmental Changes as Causes of Acute Conflict." *International Security* 16(2): 76–116.

Horan, R. D., Fenichel, E. P., Drury, K. L. S., and Lodge, D. M. 2011. "Managing Ecological Thresholds in Coupled Environmental-Human Systems." *Proceedings of the National Academy of Sciences* 108(18): 7333–7338. https://doi.org/10.1073/pnas.1005431108. Accessed 1 December 2020.

Hossain, M. S., Dearing, J. A., Eigenbrod, F., and Johnson, F. A. 2017. "Operationalizing Safe Operating Space for Regional Social-Ecological Systems." *Science of the Total Environment* 584–585: 673–682.

Houston, D., Wu, J., Ong, P., and Winer, A. 2016. "Structural Disparities of Urban Traffic in Southern California: Implications for Vehicle-Related Air Pollution Exposure in Minority and High-Poverty Neighborhoods." *Journal of Urban Affairs* 26(5): 565–592.

Howe, P. D., Marlon, J. R., Mildenberger, M., and Shield, B. S. 2019. "How Will Climate Change Shape Climate Opinion?" *Environmental Research Letters* 14(11): 113001.

Hsiang, S. M. 2010. "Temperatures and Cyclones Strongly Associated with Economic Production in the Caribbean and Central America." *Proceedings of the National Academy of Sciences* 107(35): 15367–15372. https://doi.org/10.1073/pnas.1009510107. Accessed 1 December 2020.

Hsiang, S. M., Burke, M., and Miguel, E. 2013. "Quantifying the Influence of Climate on Human Conflict." *Science* 341(6151): 1235367. https://doi.org/10.1126/science.1235367. Accessed 1 December 2020.

Hsiang, S. M., and Jina, A. 2014. "The Causal Effect of Environmental Catastrophe on Long-Run Economic Growth: Evidence From 6,700 Cyclones." Working Paper 20352, National Bureau of Economic Research, Cambridge, MA. https://doi.org/10.3386/w20352. Accessed 1 December 2020.

Hsiang, S. M., and Kopp, R. E. 2018. "An Economist's Guide to Climate Change Science." *Journal of Economic Perspectives* 32(4): 3–32. https://doi.org/10.1257/jep.32.4.3. Accessed 1 December 2020.

Hsiang, S. M., Kopp, R., Jina, A., Rising, J., Delgado, M., Mohan, S., Rasmussen, D. J., and others. 2017. "Estimating Economic Damage from Climate Change in the United States." *Science* 356(6345): 1362–1369.

Hsiang, S. M., Meng, K. C., and Cane, M. A. 2011. "Civil Conflicts Are Associated with the Global Climate." *Nature* 476(7361): 438–441. https://doi.org/10.1038/nature10311. Accessed 1 December 2020.

Hsiang, S. M., Oliva, P., and R. Walker. 2019. "The Distribution of Environmental Damages." *Review of Environmental Economics and Policy* 13(1): 83–103.

Huckelba, A. L., and Van Lange, P. A. 2020. "The Silent Killer: Consequences of Climate Change and How to Survive Past the Year 2050." *Sustainability* 12(9): 3757–3778.

Hungerman, D. M., and Moorthy, V. S. 2020. "Every Day Is Earth Day: Evidence on the Long-Term Impact of Environmental Voluntarism." Working Paper 26979, National Bureau of Economic Research, Cambridge, MA.

Hunt, T. L. 2007. "Rethinking Easter Island's Ecological Catastrophe." *Journal of Archaeological Science* 34(3): 485–502.

Hunter, L. M., White, M. J., Little, J. S., and Sutton, J. 2003. "Environmental Hazards, Migration, and Race." *Population and Environment* 25(1): 23–39.

Hyde, S. D. 2020. "Democracy's Backsliding in the International Environment." *Science* 369(6508): 1192–1196.

IADB (Inter-American Development Bank). 2019. "The Government of France Becomes Founding Donor of the IDB's Natural Capital Lab." Press Release, 2 December. https://www.iadb.org/en/news/government-france-becomes-founding-donor-idbs-natural-capital-lab. Accessed 25 November 2020.

IADB (Inter-American Development Bank). 2020. *A 12-Step Technical Guidance Document for Project Developers: Increasing Infrastructure Resilience with Nature-Based Solutions (NbS).* Washington, DC.

ICECAP-O (Icepop Capability Measure for Older People). 2020. "Icepop Capability Measure for Older People." https://www.birmingham.ac.uk/research/activity/mds/projects/HaPS/HE/ICECAP/ICECAP-O/index.aspx#:~:text=The%20ICECAP%2DO%20(ICEpop%20CAPability,broader%20sense%2C%20rather%20than%20health. Accessed 2 December 2020.

IDEAM (Instituto de Hidrología, Meteorología y Estudios Ambientales), PNUD (Programa de las Naciones Unidas para el Desarrollo), MADS (Colombia Ministerio de Ambiente y Desarrollo Sostenible), DNP (Colombia Departamento Nacional de Planeación) and Cancillería. 2017. "Resumen ejecutivo Tercera Comunicación Nacional de Colombia a la Convención Marco de las Naciones Unidas sobre Cambio Climático (CMNUCC)." Tercera Comunicación Nacional de Cambio Climático. Bogotá.

IDMC (Internal Displacement Monitoring Centre). 2020a. "Global Internal Displacement Database." Geneva. https://www.internal-displacement.org/database. Accessed 25 November 2020.

IDMC (Internal Displacement Monitoring Centre). 2020b. *Internal Displacement 2020: Mid-Year Update.* Geneva.

IEA (International Energy Agency). 2019a. *Bitcoin Energy Use: Mined the Gap.* Paris.

IEA (International Energy Agency). 2019b. *Energy Efficiency 2019.* Paris.

IEA (International Energy Agency). 2019c. *Global Energy and CO$_2$ Status Report 2019.* Paris.

IEA (International Energy Agency). 2020a. "China's Emissions Trading Scheme." https://www.iea.org/reports/chinas-emissions-trading-scheme. Accessed 23 November 2020.

IEA (International Energy Agency). 2020b. *Global Energy Review 2020: The Impacts of the Covid-19 Crisis on Global Energy Demand and CO$_2$ Emissions.* Paris. https://www.iea.org/reports/global-energy-review-2020 Accessed 30 November 2020.

IEA (International Energy Agency). 2020c. "The Impact of the Covid-19 Crisis on Clean Energy Progress." https://www.iea.org/articles/the-impact-of-the-covid-19-crisis-on-clean-energy-progress. Accessed 1 December 2020.

IEA (International Energy Agency). 2020d. *India 2020: Energy Policy Review.* Paris.

IEA (International Energy Agency). 2020e. *World Energy Outlook 2020.* Paris. https://www.iea.org/reports/world-energy-outlook-2020/achieving-net-zero-emissions-by-2050#abstract. Accessed 22 October 2020.

IEP (Institute for Economics & Peace). 2020. *Ecological Threat Register 2020: Understanding Ecological Threats, Resilience and Peace.* Sydney, Australia.

IFAD (International Fund for Agricultural Development) and UNEP (United Nations Environment Programme). 2013. *Smallholders, Food Security and the Environment.* Rome.

Iglesias-Osores, S., and Saavedra-Camacho, J. L. 2020. "Covid-19 en Comunidades Indígenas del Perú: Casos y Accesibilidad a Servicios de Salud." *Anales de la Facultad de Medicina* 81(2): 181–183.

IHME (Institute for Health Metrics and Evaluation). 2020. "Global Burden of Disease Collaborative Network. Global Burden of Disease Study 2019 (GBD 2019) Disability-Adjusted Life Years and Healthy Life Expectancy 1990-2019." Seattle, WA.

IIASA (International Institute for Applied Systems Analysis) 2019. "Governance Innovation through Nature-Based Solutions." Policy Brief 25, Laxenburg, Austria. https://phusicos.eu/wp-content/uploads/2019/12/PB_25_Governance-innovation-through-nature-based-solutions_web.pdf. Accessed 25 November 2020.

IIED (International Institute for Environment and Development). 2017. *Development and Climate Days: Global Ambition. Local Action. Climate Resilience for All.* Bonn, Germany.

IIF (Institute of International Finance). 2020. "ESG Funds Deliver!" IIF Green Weekly Insight, 18 June. https://www.iif.com/Portals/0/Files/content/200618WeeklyInsight_vf.pdf. Accessed 1 December 2020.

ILO (International Labour Organization). 1989. *Convention Concerning Indigenous and Tribal Peoples in Independent Countries.* Convention 169. Geneva.

ILO (International Labor Organization). 2017. *Indigenous Peoples and Climate Change: From Victims to Change Agents through Decent Work*. Geneva.

ILO (International Labour Organization). 2020. ILOSTAT database. https://ilostat.ilo.org/data/. Accessed 21 July 2020.

IMF (International Monetary Fund). 2019a. Central Bank Legislation Database. https://extauth.imf.org/extranetlogin/LoginForm.aspx?TYPE=33554433&REALMOID=06-78cf8e6b-d5a7-4e1c-9842-d5b0f4eedc96&GUID=&SMAUTHREASON=0&METHOD=GET&SMAGENTNAME=SMz8McW5UizZfWw9PNNAkv11JVcxioFxgDQ3saO6fHoZpeeZA4NaBTGbVlbf/OhtIF&Redirect=SMhttps://www-extranet.imf.org/default.aspx&TARGET2=SMhttps://www-extranet.imf.org/&TARGET=SMhttps://www-extranet.imf.org/. Accessed 15 October 2020.

IMF (International Monetary Fund). 2019b. *Fiscal Monitor, October 2019: How to Mitigate Climate Change*. Washington, DC.

IMF (International Monetary Fund). 2020a. *Global Financial Stability Report*. Washington, DC.

IMF (International Monetary Fund). 2020b. "Policy Responses to Covid-19." https://www.imf.org/en/Topics/imf-and-covid19/Policy-Responses-to-COVID-19. Accessed 18 November 2020.

IMF (International Monetary Fund). 2020c. *World Economic Outlook, October 2020: A Long and Difficult Ascent*. Washington, DC.

IMF (International Monetary Fund). 2020d. World Economic Outlook database. Washington, DC. www.imf.org/external/pubs/ft/weo/2020/01/weodata/index.aspx. Accessed 15 July 2020.

Inderst, G., and Stewart, F. 2018. "Incorporating Environmental, Social and Governance Factors into Fixed Income Investment." Press Release, 19 April. https://www.worldbank.org/en/news/feature/2018/04/19/incorporating-environment-social-and-governance-esg-factors-into-fixed-income-investment. Accessed 23 November 2020.

Indigenous Corporate Training. 2015. "First Nation Relationship to the Land." https://www.ictinc.ca/blog/first-nation-relationship-to-the-land. Accessed 17 November 2020.

Inglehart, R., Haerpfer, C., Moreno, A., Welzel, C., Kizilova, K., Diez-Medrano, J., Lagos, M., and others (eds.). 2014a. *World Values Survey: Round Two—Country-Pooled Datafile 1990–1994*. Madrid: JD Systems Institute. http://www.worldvaluessurvey.org/WVSOnline.jsp. Accessed 15 May 2020.

Inglehart, R., Haerpfer, C., Moreno, A., Welzel, C., Kizilova, K., Diez-Medrano, J., Lagos, M., and others. 2014b. *World Values Survey: Round Six—Country-Pooled Datafile 2010–2014*. Madrid: JD Systems Institute. http://www.worldvaluessurvey.org/WVSOnline.jsp. Accessed 15 May 2020.

Ingram, J. C., Wilkie, D., Clements, T., McNab, R. B., Nelson, F., Baur, E. H., Sachedina, H. T., Peterson, D. D., and Foley, C. A. H. 2014. "Evidence of Payments for Ecosystem Services as a Mechanism for Supporting Biodiversity Conservation and Rural Livelihoods." *Ecosystem Services* 7: 10–21.

International Carbon Action Partnership. 2020. "China's National ETS." https://icapcarbonaction.com/en/?option=com_etsmap&task=export&format=pdf&layout=list&systems%5B%5D=55. Accessed 18 November 2020.

IPBES (Intergovernmental Science-Policy Platform on Biodiversity and Ecosystem Services). 2019a. *Global Assessment Report on Biodiversity and Ecosystem Services*. Bonn, Germany: IPBES Secretariat.

IPBES (Intergovernmental Science-Policy Platform on Biodiversity and Ecosystem Services). 2019b. "Summary for Policymakers of the Global Assessment Report on Biodiversity and Ecosystem Services." Bonn, Germany: IPBES Secretariat.

IPBES (Intergovernmental Science-Policy Platform on Biodiversity and Ecosystem Services). 2020a. "About the Intergovernmental Science-Policy Platform on Biodiversity and Ecosystem Services." https://ipbes.net/about. Accessed 25 November 2020.

IPBES (Intergovernmental Science-Policy Platform on Biodiversity and Ecosystem Services). 2020b. "Media Release: Nature's Dangerous Decline 'Unprecedented.'" https://ipbes.net/news/Media-Release-Global-Assessment. Accessed November 18 2020.

IPCC (Intergovernmental Panel on Climate Change). 1990. *FAR Climate Change: The IPCC Scientific Assessment*. New York: Cambridge University Press.

IPCC (Intergovernmental Panel on Climate Change). 1995. *SAR Climate Change 1995: Economic and Social Dimensions of Climate Change*. New York: Cambridge University Press.

IPCC (Intergovernmental Panel on Climate Change). 2001. *TAR Climate Change 2001: The Scientific Basis*. New York: Cambridge University Press.

IPCC (Intergovernmental Panel on Climate Change). 2007. *AR4 Climate Change 2007: Mitigation of Climate Change*. New York: Cambridge University Press.

IPCC (Intergovernmental Panel on Climate Change). 2014a. *AR5 Climate Change 2014: Impacts, Adaptation and Vulnerability*. Contribution of Working Group II to the Third Assessment Report of the Intergovernmental Panel on Climate Change. New York: Cambridge University Press.

IPCC (Intergovernmental Panel on Climate Change). 2014b. "Mitigation of Climate Change." Contribution of Working Group III to the Fifth Assessment Report of the Intergovernmental Panel on Climate Change, 1454.

IPCC (Intergovernmental Panel on Climate Change). 2018. *Global Warming of 1.5 °C*. Special Report. Geneva. https://www.ipcc.ch/sr15/. Accessed 11 November 2020.

IPSOS Global Advisor. 2020. "Earth Day 2020: How Does the World View Climate Change and Covid-19?" https://www.ipsos.com/sites/default/files/ct/news/documents/2020-04/earth-day-2020-ipsos.pdf. Accessed 10 November 2020.

Ireland Central Statistics Office. 2004. "Measuring Ireland's Progress." Dublin.

IRENA (International Renewable Energy Agency). 2019a. *2019 Country Rankings*. Abu Dhabi.

IRENA (International Renewable Energy Agency). 2019b. *Renewable Power Generation Costs in 2018*. Abu Dhabi.

IRENA (International Renewable Energy Agency). 2020. "Renewable Energy Finance." Renewable Energy Finance Brief 2, International Renewable Energy Agency, Abu Dhabi.

Irwin, E. G., Gopalakrishnan, S., and Randall, A. 2016. "Welfare, Wealth, and Sustainability." *Annual Review of Resource Economics* 8(1): 77–98.

Islam, N., and Winkel, J. 2017. "Climate Change and Social Inequality." Working Paper 152, United Nations Department of Economic and Social Affairs, New York. https://www.un.org/esa/desa/papers/2017/wp152_2017.pdf. Accessed 11 November 2020.

ISSC (International Social Science Council), IDS (Institute of Development Studies) and UNESCO (United Nations Educational, Scientific and Cultural Organization). 2016. *World Social Science Report 2016: Challenging Inequalities: Pathways to a Just World*. Paris: UNESCO Publishing.

IUCN (International Union for Conservation of Nature). 2016. "Nature-Based Solutions for Sustainable Drinking Water." https://www.iucn.org/asia/countries/china/nature-based-solutions-sustainable-drinking-water. Accessed 25 November 2020.

IUCN (International Union for the Conservation of Nature and Natural Resources), UNEP (United Nations Environment Programme), WWF (World Wildlife Fund), FAO (Food and Agriculture Organization of the United Nations) and UNESCO (United Nations Educational, Scientific and Cultural Organization). 1980. *World Conservation Strategy: Living Resource Conservation for Sustainable Development*. Gland, Switzerland: IUCN.

Ivanova, D., and Wood, R. 2020. "The Unequal Distribution of Household Carbon Footprints in Europe and Its Link to Sustainability." *Global Sustainability* 3.

Ives, C. D., Abson, D. J., von Wehrden, H., Dorninger, C., Klaniecki, K., and Fischer, J. 2018. "Reconnecting with Nature for Sustainability." *Sustainability Science* 13(5): 1389–1397.

Jaakkola, N., and Millner, A. 2020. "Nondogmatic Climate Policy." Cambridge, MA: National Bureau of Economic Research.

Jackson, A.-M., Stewart, G. T., Hakopa, H., Phillips, C., Parr-Brownlie, L. C., Russell, P., Hulbe, C., and others. 2019. "Towards Building an Indigenous Science Tertiary Curriculum." *New Zealand Science Review* 75(4).

Jackson, R. B., Friedlingstein, P., Andrew, R. M., Canadell, J. G., Quéré, C. L., and Peters, G. P. 2019. "Persistent Fossil Fuel Growth Threatens the Paris Agreement and Planetary Health." *Environmental Research Letters* 14(12): 121001.

Jackson, T. 2005. "Motivating Sustainable Consumption: A Review of Evidence on Consumer Behaviour and Behavioural Change." *Sustainable Development Research Network* 29: 30.

Jackson, T., and Victor, P. A. 2019. "Unraveling the Claims for (and against) Green Growth." *Science* 366(6468): 950–951.

Jacquet, J. B., and Stedman, R. C. 2014. "The Risk of Social-Psychological Disruption as an Impact of Energy Development and Environmental Change." *Journal of Environmental Planning and Management* 57(9): 1285–1304.

Jagannathan, R., Ravikumar, A., and Sammon, M. 2017. "Environmental, Social, and Governance Criteria: Why Investors Are Paying Attention." Working Paper 24063, National Bureau of Economic Research, Cambridge, MA.

Jenkins, N., Long, C., and Wu, J. 2015. "An Overview of the Smart Grid in Great Britain." *Engineering* 1(4): 413–421.

Jerneck, M. 2017. "Financialization Impedes Climate Change Mitigation: Evidence from the Early American Solar Industry." *Science Advances* 3(3): e1601861.

Jewell, J., McCollum, D., Emmerling, J., Bertram, C., Gernaat, D. E. H. J., Krey, V., Paroussos, L., and others. 2018. "Limited Emission Reductions from Fuel Subsidy Removal except in Energy-Exporting Regions." *Nature* 554(7691): 229–233.

Jiménez, A., Cortobius, M., and Kjellén, M. 2014. "Water, Sanitation and Hygiene and Indigenous Peoples: A Review of the Literature." *Water International* 39(3): 277–293.

Johnson, A. 2016. "Environmental Regulation and Technological Development in the U.S. Auto Industry." In *The Causes and Consequences for Sustained Economic Development*. Washington, DC: Washington Center for Equitable Growth.

Johnson, C. K., Hitchens, P. L., Pandit, P. S., Rushmore, J., Evans, T. S., Young, C. C. W., and Doyle, M. M. 2020. "Global Shifts in Mammalian Population Trends Reveal Key Predictors of Virus Spillover Risk." *Proceedings of the Royal Society B: Biological Sciences* 287(1924): 20192736.

Johnson, S. 2020. "Blackrock ETF Thrusts Climate Change into Political Sphere." *Financial Times*, 6 October. https://www.ft.com/content/112e536a-91db-426a-aef6-3106f0717972. Accessed 1 December 2020.

Jones, C. I. 2016. "Life and Growth." *Journal of Political Economy* 124(2): 539–578.

Jones, C. I. 2020. "The End of Economic Growth? Unintended Consequences of a Declining Population." Working Paper 26651, National Bureau of Economic Research, Cambridge, MA.

Jones, C. I., and Romer, P. M. 2010. "The New Kaldor Facts: Ideas, Institutions, Population, and Human Capital." *American Economic Journal: Macroeconomics* 2(1): 224–245.

Jones, I. J., MacDonald, A. J., Hopkins, S. R., Lund, A. J., Liu, Z. Y.-C., Fawzi, N. I., Purba, M. P., and others. 2020. "Improving Rural Health Care Reduces Illegal Logging and Conserves Carbon in a Tropical Forest." *Proceedings of the National Academy of Sciences* 117(45): 28515–28524.

Jongman, B., Ellison, G., and Ozment, S. 2019. "Nature-Based Solutions for Disaster Risk Management: Booklet." Washington, DC: World Bank. http://documents1.worldbank.org/curated/en/253401551126252092/pdf/134847-NBS-for-DRM-booklet.pdf. Accessed 25 November 2020.

Jorgenson, A. K., Fiske, S., Hubacek, K., Li, J., McGovern, T., Rick, T., Schor, J. B., and others. 2018. "Social Science Perspectives on Drivers of and Responses to Global Climate Change." *Wiley Interdisciplinary Reviews: Climate Change* 10(1): e554.

Jorgenson, D. W. 2018. "Production and Welfare: Progress in Economic Measurement." *Journal of Economic Literature* 56(3): 867–919.

Jose, S., and Dollinger, J. 2019. "Silvopasture: A Sustainable Livestock Production System." *Agroforestry Systems* 93(1): 1–9.

Jumani, S., Rao, S., Machado, S., and Prakash, A. 2017. "Big Concerns with Small Projects: Evaluating the Socio-Ecological Impacts of Small Hydropower Projects in India." *Ambio* 46(4): 500–511.

Jungehülsing, J. 2011. *Women Who Go, Women Who Stay: Reactions to Climate Change*. Berlin: Heinrich Böll Foundation.

Kabbe, C., Kraus, F., and Remy, C. 2017. "Circular Economy: Challenges and Opportunities for Phosphorus Recovery & Recycling from Wastes in Europe." International Phosphorus Workshop, 2017.

Kabeer, N. 2005. "Gender Equality and Women's Empowerment: A Critical Analysis of the Third Millennium Development Goal 1." *Gender & Development* 13(1): 13–24.

Kåberger, T., and Månsson, B. 2001. "Entropy and Economic Processes: Physics Perspectives." *Ecological Economics* 36(1): 165–179.

Kahiluoto, H., Kuisma, M., Kuokkanen, A., Mikkilä, M., and Linnanen, L. 2015. "Local and Social Facets of Planetary Boundaries: Right to Nutrients." *Environmental Research Letters* 10(10): 104013.

Kaldellis, J., Apostolou, D., Kapsali, M., and Kondili, E. 2016. "Environmental and Social Footprint of Offshore Wind Energy: Comparison with Onshore Counterpart." *Renewable Energy* 92: 543–556.

Kallis, G., Kostakis, V., Lange, S., Muraca, B., Paulson, S., and Schmelzer, M. 2018. "Research on Degrowth." *Annual Review of Environment and Resources* 43(1): 291–316.

Kallis, G., and March, H. 2015. "Imaginaries of Hope: The Utopianism of Degrowth." *Annals of the Association of American Geographers* 105(2): 360–368.

Kanbur. 2020. "The Index Ecosystem and the Commitment to Development Index." Policy Papers, Center for Global Development, Washington, DC. https://www.cgdev.org/publication/index-ecosystem-and-commitment-development-index. Accessed 30 November 2020.

Kantar IBOPE Media. 2019. "Retrospectiva & Perspectiva 2018." https://www.kantaribopemedia.com/wp-content/uploads/2019/05/retrospectiva_2018_FINAL.pdf. Accessed 11 November 2020.

Karlsson, M., Alfredsson, E., and Westling, N. 2020. "Climate Policy Co-Benefits: A Review." *Climate Policy* 20(3): 292–316.

Karlsson, M., and Edvardsson Björnberg, K. 2020. "Ethics and Biodiversity Offsetting." *Conservation Biology*. https://conbio.onlinelibrary.wiley.com/doi/full/10.1111/cobi.13603?af=R. Accessed 1 December 2020.

Kartha, S., Kemp-Benedict, E., Ghosh, E., Nazareth, A., and Gore, T. 2020. "The Carbon Inequality Era." https://www.sei.org/publications/the-carbon-inequality-era/. Accessed 10 December 2020.

Kates, R. W., Travis, W. R., and Wilbanks, T. J. 2012. "Transformational Adaptation When Incremental Adaptations to Climate Change Are Insufficient." *Proceedings of the National Academy of Sciences* 109(19): 7156–7161.

Katz, D., Grinstein, A., Kronrod, A., and Nisan, U. 2016. "Evaluating the Effectiveness of a Water Conservation Campaign: Combining Experimental and Field Methods." *Journal of Environmental Management* 180: 335–343.

Kaufmann, R. K., Mann, M. L., Gopal, S., Liederman, J. A., Howe, P. D., Pretis, F., Tang, X., and Gilmore, M. 2017. "Spatial Heterogeneity of Climate Change as an Experiential Basis for Skepticism." *Proceedings of the National Academy of Sciences* 114(1): 67–71.

Kaul, I., Conceicao, P., Le Goulven, K., and Mendoza, R. U. 2003. *Providing Global Public Goods: Managing Globalization*. Oxford, UK: Oxford University Press.

Kawagley, A., Norris-Tull, D., and Norris-Tull, R. 1998. "The Indigenous Worldview of Yupiaq Culture: Its Scientific Nature and Relevance to the Practice and Teaching of Science." *Journal of Research Science* 35(2): 133–144.

Kawharu, M. 2000. "Kaitiakitanga: A Maori Anthropological Perspective of the Maori Socioenvironmental Ethic of Resource Management." *Journal of the Polynesian Society* 110(4): 349–370.

Kawharu, M. 2019. "Reinterpreting the Value Chain in an Indigenous Community Enterprise Context." *Journal of Enterprising Communities* 13(3): 242–262. http://doi.org/10.1108/jec-11-2018-0079. Accessed 17 November 2020.

Kayumova, S., Karsli, E., Allexsaht-Snider, M., and Buxton, C. 2015. "Latina Mothers and Daughters: Ways of Knowing, Being, and Becoming in the Context of Bilingual Family Science Workshops." *Anthropology & Education Quarterly* 46(3): 260–276.

Kayumova, S., McGuire, C. J., and Cardello, S. 2019. "From Empowerment to Response-Ability: Rethinking Socio-Spatial, Environmental Justice, and Nature-Culture Binaries in the Context of STEM Education." *Cultural Studies of Science Education* 14(1): 205–229.

KC, S. 2013. "Community Vulnerability to Floods and Landslides in Nepal." *Ecology and Society* 18(1).

Keesstra, S., Nunes, J., Novara, A., Finger, D., Avelar, D., Kalantari, Z., and Cerdà, A. 2018. "The Superior Effect of Nature Based Solutions in Land Management for Enhancing Ecosystem Services." *Science of the Total Environment* 610: 997–1009.

Keller, L., Stötter, J., Oberrauch, A., Kuthe, A., Körfgen, A., and Hüfner, K. 2019. "Changing Climate Change Education: Exploring Moderate Constructivist and Transdisciplinary Approaches through the Research-Education Co-Operation Kidz 21." *GAIA – Ecological Perspectives for Science and Society* 28(1): 35–43.

Keller, M., Spyrou, M. A., Scheib, C. L., Neumann, G. U., Kröpelin, A., Haas-Gebhard, B., Päffgen, B., and others. 2019. "Ancient Yersinia Pestis Genomes from across Western Europe Reveal Early Diversification during the First Pandemic (541–750)." *Proceedings of the National Academy of Sciences* 116(25): 12363–12372.

Kelly, J. 2006. *The Great Mortality: An Intimate History of the Black Death.* New York: HarperCollins.

Kemppinen, K. M. S., Collins, P. M., Hole, D. G., Wolf, C., Ripple, W. J., and Gerber, L. R. 2020. "Global Reforestation and Biodiversity Conservation." *Conservation Biology* 34(5): 1221–1228.

Keohane, R. O., and Oppenheimer, M. 2016. "Paris: Beyond the Climate Dead End through Pledge and Review?" *Politics and Governance* 4(3): 142–151.

Keys, P. W., Galaz, V., Dyer, M., Matthews, N., Folke, C., Nyström, M., and Cornell, S. E. 2019. "Anthropocene Risk." *Nature Sustainability* 2(8): 667–673.

Keys, P. W., Wang-Erlandsson, L., and Gordon, L. J. 2016. "Revealing Invisible Water: Moisture Recycling as an Ecosystem Service." *PLOS ONE* 11(3): e0151993.

Kimmerer, R. W. 2013. *Braiding Sweetgrass: Indigenous Wisdom, Scientific Knowledge and the Teachings of Plants.* Minneapolis, MN: Milkweed Editions.

Kioupi, V., and Voulvoulis, N. 2019. "Education for Sustainable Development: A Systemic Framework for Connecting the SDGs to Educational Outcomes." *Sustainability* 11(21): 6104.

Kirezci, E., Young, I. R., Ranasinghe, R., Muis, S., Nicholls, R. J., Lincke, D., and Hinkel, J. 2020. "Projections of Global-Scale Extreme Sea Levels and Resulting Episodic Coastal Flooding over the 21st Century." *Scientific Reports* 10(1): 1–12.

Kirksey, S. E., and Helmreich, S. 2010. "The Emergence of Multispecies Ethnography." *Cultural Anthropology* 25: 545–76.

Kituyi, M., and Thomson, P. 2018. "90% of Fish Stocks Are Used Up—Fisheries Subsidies Must Stop Emptying the Ocean." World Economic Forum Global Agenda, 13 July. https://www.weforum.org/agenda/2018/07/fish-stocks-are-used-up-fisheries-subsidies-must-stop/. Accessed 25 November 2020.

Klamer, A. 1989. "A Conversation with Amartya Sen." *Journal of Economic Perspectives* 3(1): 135–150.

Klasen, S. 2018. "Human Development Indices and Indicators: A Critical Evaluation." United Nations Development Programme, Human Development Report Office, New York. http://hdr.undp.org/sites/default/files/klasen_final.pdf. Accessed 30 November 2020.

Klasing, A. M. 2016. *Make It Safe: Canada's Obligation to End the First Nations Water Crisis.* Human Rights Watch. https://www.hrw. org/report/2016/06/07/make-it-safe/canadas-obligation-end-first-nations-water-crisis. Accessed 20 November 2020.

Kleidon, A. 2010. "A Basic Introduction to the Thermodynamics of the Earth System Far from Equilibrium and Maximum Entropy Production." *Philosophical Transactions of the Royal Society B: Biological Sciences* 365(1545): 1303–1315.

Kleidon, A. 2012. "How Does the Earth System Generate and Maintain Thermodynamic Disequilibrium and What Does It Imply for the Future of the Planet?" *Philosophical Transactions of the Royal Society A: Mathematical, Physical and Engineering Sciences* 370(1962): 1012–1040.

Kleiman, E. 1976. "Trade and the Decline of Colonialism." *The Economic Journal,* 86(343): 459–480.

Klein, A.-M., Vaissière, B. E., Cane, J. H., Steffan-Dewenter, I., Cunningham, S. A., Kremen, C., and Tscharntke, T. 2007. "Importance of Pollinators in Changing Landscapes for World Crops." *Proceedings of the Royal Society B: Biological Sciences* 274(1608): 303–313.

Klenert, D., Mattauch, L., Combet, E., Edenhofer, O., Hepburn, C., Rafaty, R., and Stern, N. 2018. "Making Carbon Pricing Work for Citizens." *Nature Climate Change* 8(8): 669–677.

Klugman, J., Rodríguez, F., and Choi, H.-J. 2011. "The HDI 2010: New Controversies, Old Critiques." *The Journal of Economic Inequality* 9(2): 249–288.

Kluth, A. 2020. "Will the Coronavirus Turn out Green or Brown?" *Bloomberg,* 16 September. https://www.bloomberg.com/opinion/articles/2020-09-16/eu-could-turn-coronavirus-recovery-green-if-it-chooses. Accessed 1 December 2020.

Knoblauch, D., Mederake, L., and Stein, U. 2018. "Developing Countries in the Lead—What Drives the Diffusion of Plastic Bag Policies?" *Sustainability* 10(6): 1994.

Kola-Olusanya, A. 2005. "Free-Choice Environmental Education: Understanding Where Children Learn Outside of School." *Environmental Education Research* 11(3): 297–307.

Kolbert, E. 2014. *The Sixth Extinction: An Unnatural History.* New York: Henry Holt and Company.

Kollmuss, A., and Agyeman, J. 2002. "Mind the Gap: Why Do People Act Environmentally and What Are the Barriers to Pro-Environmental Behavior?" *Environmental Education Research* 8(3): 239–260.

Kollock, P. 1998. "Social Dilemmas: The Anatomy of Cooperation." *Annual Review of Sociology* 24(1): 183–214.

Koltko-Rivera, M. E. 2004. "The Psychology of Worldviews." *Review of General Psychology* 8(1): 3–58.

Komatsu, H., Malapit, H. J. L., and Theis, S. 2018. "Does Women's Time in Domestic Work and Agriculture Affect Women's and Children's Dietary Diversity? Evidence from Bangladesh, Nepal, Cambodia, Ghana, and Mozambique." *Food Policy* 79: 256–270.

Kotchen, M. J., and Segerson, K. 2019. "On the Use of Group Performance and Rights for Environmental Protection and Resource Management." *Proceedings of the National Academy of Sciences* 116(12): 5285–5292.

Kotchen, M. J., and Segerson, K. 2020. "The Use of Group-Level Approaches to Environmental and Natural Resource Policy." Working Paper 27142, National Bureau of Economic Research, Cambridge, MA.

Kousky, C. 2016. "Impacts of Natural Disasters on Children." *The Future of Children* 26(1): 73–92.

Kowasch, M., and Lippe, D. F. 2019. "Moral Impasses in Sustainability Education? Empirical Results from School Geography in Austria and Germany." *Environmental Education Research* 25(7): 1066–1082.

KPMG. 2020. "Barbados: Government and Institution Measures in Response to COVID-19." https://home.kpmg/xx/en/home/insights/2020/04/barbados-government-and-institution-measures-in-response-to-covid.html. Accessed 30 November 2020.

Kraay, A. 2018. *Methodology for a World Bank Human Capital Index.* Washington, DC: World Bank.

Krausmann, F., Erb, K.-H., Gingrich, S., Haberl, H., Bondeau, A., Gaube, V., Lauk, C., Plutzar, C., and Searchinger, T. D. 2013. "Global Human Appropriation of Net Primary Production Doubled in the 20th Century." *Proceedings of the National Academy of Sciences* 110(25): 10324–10329.

Krausmann, F., and Fischer-Kowalski, M. 2013. "Global Socio-Metabolic Transitions." In Singh, S. J., Haberl, H., Chertow, M., Mirtl, M., and Schmid, M., (eds.), *Long Term Socio-Ecological Research.* Dordrecht: Springer Netherlands.

Krausmann, F., Schandl, H., Eisenmenger, N., Giljum, S., and Jackson, T. 2017a. "Material Flow Accounting: Measuring Global Material Use for Sustainable Development." *Annual Review of Environment and Resources* 42(1): 647–675.

Krausmann, F., Wiedenhofer, D., Lauk, C., Haas, W., Tanikawa, H., Fishman, T., Miatto, A., and others. 2017b. "Global Socioeconomic Material Stocks Rise 23-Fold over the 20th Century and Require Half of Annual Resource Use." *Proceedings of the National Academy of Sciences* 114(8): 1880–1885.

Kremer, M. 1993. "Population Growth and Technological Change: One Million B.C. To 1990." *The Quarterly Journal of Economics* 108(3): 681–716.

Krey, V., Masera, O., Blanford, G., Bruckner, T., Cooke, R., Fisher-Vanden, K., Haberl, H., and others. 2014. "Annex 2-Metrics and Methodology." In *Climate Change 2014: Mitigation of Climate Change.* IPCC Working Group III Contribution to AR5. Cambridge, UK: Cambridge University Press.

Krogstrup, S., and Oman, W. 2019. "Macroeconomic and Financial Policies for Climate Change Mitigation: A Review of the Literature." Working Paper No. 19/185, International Monetary Fund, Washington, DC. https://www.imf.org/en/Publications/WP/Issues/2019/09/04/Macroeconomic-and-Financial-Policies-for-Climate-Change-Mitigation-A-Review-of-the-Literature-48612. Accessed 1 December 2020.

Kukutai, T., and Taylor, J. 2016. "Data Sovereignty for Indigenous Peoples: Current Practice and Future

Needs." In Kukutai, T., and Taylor, J., (eds.), *Indigenous Data Sovereignty*. Acton, Australia: ANU Press.

Kulp, S. A., and Strauss, B. H. 2019. "New Elevation Data Triple Estimates of Global Vulnerability to Sea-Level Rise and Coastal Flooding." *Nature Communications* 10(1): 4844.

Kuznets, S. 1971. *Economic Growth of Nations: Total Output and Production Structure*. Cambridge, MA: Belknap Press of Harvard University Press.

Lade, S. J., Niiranen, S., Hentati-Sundberg, J., Blenckner, T., Boonstra, W. J., Orach, K., Quaas, M. F., and others. 2015. "An Empirical Model of the Baltic Sea Reveals the Importance of Social Dynamics for Ecological Regime Shifts." *Proceedings of the National Academy of Sciences* 112(35): 11120–11125.

Lade, S. J., Steffen, W., de Vries, W., Carpenter, S. R., Donges, J. F., Gerten, D., Hoff, H., and others. 2020. "Human Impacts on Planetary Boundaries Amplified by Earth System Interactions." *Nature Sustainability* 3(2): 119–128.

Lafond, F., Bailey, A. G., Bakker, J. D., Rebois, D., Zadourian, R., McSharry, P., and Farmer, J. D. 2018. "How Well Do Experience Curves Predict Technological Progress? A Method for Making Distributional Forecasts." *Technological Forecasting and Social Change* 128: 104–117.

Lagarde, C. 2019. "The Financial Sector: Redefining a Broader Sense of Purpose." Speech at the 32nd World Traders' Tacitus Lecture, London, 28 February. https://www.imf.org/en/News/Articles/2019/02/21/sp022819-md-the-financial-sector-redefining-a-broader-sense-of-purpose. Accessed 18 November 2020.

Lam, L. 2020. "Hurricane Epsilon Is the Seventh Atlantic Storm to Rapidly Intensify in 2020." *The Weather Channel*, 21 October. https://weather.com/storms/hurricane/news/2020-10-21-rapid-intensification-atlantic-2020. Accessed 18 November 2020.

Lamb, W. F., and Steinberger, J. K. 2017. "Human Well-Being and Climate Change Mitigation." *Wiley Interdisciplinary Reviews: Climate Change* 8(6): e485.

Lambin, E. F., Leape, J., and Lee, K. 2019. "Amplifying Small Solutions for Systemwide Change." In Mandle, L. A., Ouyang, Z., Salzman, J. E., and Daily, G. C., (eds.), *Green Growth That Works*. Washington, DC: Island Press.

Landorf, H., Doscher, S., and Rocco, T. 2008. "Education for Sustainable Human Development: Towards a Definition." *Theory and Research in Education* 6(2): 221–236.

Lange, G.-M., Wodon, Q., and Carey, K., (eds.). 2018. *The Changing Wealth of Nations 2018: Building a Sustainable Future*. Washington, DC: World Bank.

Lansing, J. S., Thurner, S., Chung, N. N., Coudurier-Curveur, A., Karakaş, Ç., Fesenmyer, K. A., and Chew, L. Y. 2017. "Adaptive Self-Organization of Bali's Ancient Rice Terraces." *Proceedings of the National Academy of Sciences* 114(25): 6504–6509.

Lapinski, M. K., and Rimal, R. N. 2005. "An Explication of Social Norms." *Communication Theory* 15(2): 127–147.

Larsen, C. S. 1995. "Biological Changes in Human Populations with Agriculture." *Annual Review of Anthropology* 24(1): 185–213.

Latorre, C., Wilmshurst, J., and von Gunten, L. 2016. "Climate Change and Cultural Evolution." *PAGES (Past Global Changes) Magazine* 24: 1–32.

Latouche, S. 2009. *Farewell to Growth*. Cambridge, UK: Polity.

Latulippe, N., and Klenk, N. 2020. "Making Room and Moving Over: Knowledge Co-Production, Indigenous Knowledge Sovereignty and the Politics of Global Environmental Change Decision-Making." *Current Opinion in Environmental Sustainability* 42: 7–14.

Le Quéré, C., Andrew, R. M., Friedlingstein, P., Sitch, S., Pongratz, J., Manning, A. C., Korsbakken, J. I., and others. 2018. "Global Carbon Budget 2017." *Earth System Science Data* 10(1): 405–448.

Le Quéré, C., Jackson, R. B., Jones, M. W., Smith, A. J. P. Abernethy, S., Andrew, R. M., De-Gol, A. J., and others. 2020. "Temporary Reduction in Daily Global CO_2 Emissions during the Covid-19 Forced Confinement." *Nature Climate Change* 10: 647–653.

Le Quéré, C., Korsbakken, J. I., Wilson, C., Tosun, J., Andrew, R., Andres, R. J., Canadell, J. G., and others. 2019. "Drivers of Declining CO_2 Emissions in 18 Developed Economies." *Nature Climate Change* 9(3): 213–217.

Leach, M., Raworth, K., and Rockström, J. 2013. "Between Social and Planetary Boundaries: Navigating Pathways in the Safe and Just Space for Humanity." In *World Social Science Report 2013: Changing Global Environments*. Paris: OECD Publishing.

Leach, M., Reyers, B., Bai, X., Brondizio, E. S., Cook, C., Díaz, S., Espindola, G., and others. 2018. "Equity and Sustainability in the Anthropocene: A Social–Ecological Systems Perspective on Their Intertwined Futures." *Global Sustainability* 1.

Leach, M., Rockström, J., Raskin, P., Scoones, I., Stirling, A. C., Smith, A., Thompson, J., and others. 2012. "Transforming Innovation for Sustainability." *Ecology and Society* 17(2).

Leach, M., Sterling, A., and Scoones, I. 2010. *Dynamic Sustainabilities: Technology, Environment, Social Justice*. London: Earthscan.

Lecocq, T., Hicks, S. P., Noten, K. V., Wijk, K. V., Koelemeijer, P., Plaen, R. S. D., Massin, F., and others. 2020. "Global Quieting of High-Frequency Seismic Noise due to COVID-19 Pandemic Lockdown Measures." *Science* 369 (6509): 1338–1343.

Lee, G. 1994. "Did Early Native Americans Live in Harmony with Nature?" *Washington Post*, 5 December. https://www.washingtonpost.com/archive/politics/1994/12/05/did-early-native-americans-live-in-harmony-with-nature/2981bdb7-3466-42a7-9e16-30cc75c06761/. Accessed 17 November 2020.

Legros, S., and Cislaghi, B. 2020. "Mapping the Social-Norms Literature: An Overview of Reviews." *Perspectives on Psychological Science* 15(1): 62–80.

Lele, S. 2020. "Environment and Well-Being: A Perspective from the Global South." *New Left Review* 123(May–June): 41–63.

Lenton, T. M. 2013. "Environmental Tipping Points." *Annual Review of Environment and Resources* 38(1): 1–29.

Lenton, T. M. 2013. "Environmental Tipping Points." *Annual Review of Environment and Resources* 38(1): 1–29.

Lenton, T. M. 2016. *Earth System Science: A Very Short Introduction*. Oxford, UK: Oxford University Press.

Lenton, T. M. 2019. "Biodiversity and Global Change: From Creator to Victim." In Dasgupta, P., Raven, P. H., and Mcivor, A. L., (eds.), *Biological Extinction: New Perspectives*. Cambridge, UK: Cambridge University Press.

Lenton, T. M. 2020. "Tipping Positive Change." *Philosophical Transactions of the Royal Society B: Biological Sciences* 375(1794): 20190123.

Lenton, T. M., Daines, S. J., Dyke, J. G., Nicholson, A. E., Wilkinson, D. M., and Williams, H. T. P. 2018. "Selection for Gaia across Multiple Scales." *Trends in Ecology & Evolution* 33(8): 633–645.

Lenton, T. M., Dutreuil, S., and Latour, B. 2020. "Life on Earth Is Hard to Spot." *The Anthropocene Review* 7(3): 248–272.

Lenton, T. M., Held, H., Kriegler, E., Hall, J., Lucht, W., Rahmstorf, S., and Schellnhuber, H. J. 2008. "Tipping Elements in the Earth's Climate System." *Proceedings of the National Academy of Sciences* 105(6): 1786–1793.

Lenton, T. M., and Latour, B. 2018. "Gaia 2.0." *Science* 361(6407): 1066–1068.

Lenton, T. M., Pichler, P. P., and Weisz, H. 2016. "Revolutions in Energy Input and Material Cycling in Earth History and Human History." *Earth System Dynamics* 7(2): 353–370.

Lenton, T. M., Rockstrom, J., Gaffney, O., Rahmstorf, S., Richardson, K., Steffen, W., and Schellnhuber, H. J. 2019. "Climate Tipping Points—Too Risky to Bet Against." *Nature* 575(7784): 592–595.

Lenton, T. M., and Watson, A. J. 2011. *Revolutions That Made the Earth*. Oxford, UK: Oxford University Press.

Lenzen, M., Moran, D., Kanemoto, K., and Geschke, A. 2013. "Building Eora: A Global Multi-Region Input–Output Database at High Country and Sector Resolution." *Economic Systems Research* 25(1): 20–49.

Leontief, W. W. 1936. "Quantitative Input and Output Relations in the Economic Systems of the United States." *The Review of Economic Statistics* 18(3): 105–125.

Leontief, W. W. 1970. "Environmental Repercussions and the Economic Structure: An Input-Output Approach." *The Review of Economics and Statistics* 52(3): 262–271.

Lesisa, S., Kairung, K., and Cowell, G. 2016. "Elephants and the Maasai Culture: Today's Problems,

Tomorrow's Solutions." *National Geographic*, 6 June. https://blog.nationalgeographic.org/2016/06/06/elephants-and-the-maasai-culture-todays-problems-tomorrows-solutions/. Accessed 17 November 2020.

Leslie, J. 1996. *The End of the World: The Science and Ethics of Human Extinction*. New York: Routledge.

Lessmann, O., and Rauschmayer, F. 2013. "Re-Conceptualizing Sustainable Development on the Basis of the Capability Approach: A Model and Its Difficulties." *Journal of Human Development and Capabilities* 14(1): 95–114.

Leung, B., Hargreaves, A. L., Greenberg, D. A., McGill, B., Dornelas, M., and Freeman, R. 2020. "Clustered Versus Catastrophic Global Vertebrate Declines." *Nature*: 1–5.

Levine, A. S., Frank, R. H., and Dijk, O. 2010. "Expenditure Cascades." https://papers.ssrn.com/sol3/papers.cfm?abstract_id=1690612. Accessed 17 November 2020.

Levine, S., Kleiman-Weiner, M., Schulz, L., Tenenbaum, J., and Cushman, F. 2020. "The Logic of Universalization Guides Moral Judgment." *Proceedings of the National Academy of Sciences* 117(42): 26158–26169.

Levy, J., Brandon, C., and Studart, R. 2020. "Designing the COVID-19 Recovery for a Safer and More Resilient World." https://www.wri.org/news/designing-covid-19-recovery-safer-and-more-resilient-world. Accessed 25 November 2020.

Lewis, J. L., and Sheppard, S. R. 2006. "Culture and Communication: Can Landscape Visualization Improve Forest Management Consultation with Indigenous Communities?" *Landscape and Urban Planning* 77(3): 291–313.

Lewis, S. L. 2012. "We Must Set Planetary Boundaries Wisely." *Nature* 485(7399): 417–417.

Lilley, I. 2017. "Palaeoecology: Agriculture Emerges from the Calm." *Nature Ecology & Evolution* 1(3): 1–2.

Lin, D., Hanscom, L., Murthy, A., Galli, A., Evans, M., Neill, E., Mancini, M. S., and others. 2018. "Ecological Footprint Accounting for Countries: Updates and Results of the National Footprint Accounts, 2012–2018." *Resources* 7(3): 58.

Lister, R., and Campling, J. 2017. *Citizenship: Feminist Perspectives*. London: Macmillan International Higher Education.

Liu, J., Hull, V., Batistella, M., DeFries, R., Dietz, T., Fu, F., Hertel, T. W., and others. 2013. "Framing Sustainability in a Telecoupled World." *Ecology and Society* 18(2): 26.

Liu, Z., Ciais, P., Deng, Z., Lei, R., Davis, S.J., Feng, S., Zheng, B., and others. 2020. "Near-Real-Time Monitoring of Global CO_2 Emissions Reveals the Effects of the COVID-19 Pandemic." *Nature Communications* 11(1): 1–12.

Lock, M. 2018. "Mutable Environments and Permeable Human Bodies." *Journal of the Royal Anthropological Institute* 24(3): 449–474.

Locke, P., and Muenster, U. 2015. "Multispecies Ethnography." Oxford Bibliographies. https://www.oxfordbibliographies.com/view/document/obo-9780199766567/obo-9780199766567-0130.xml. Accessed 17 November 2020.

Lockie, S. 2017. "Post-Truth Politics and the Social Sciences." *Environmental Sociology* 3(1): 1–5.

Lockwood, M. 2018. "Right-Wing Populism and the Climate Change Agenda: Exploring the Linkages." *Environmental Politics* 27(4): 712–732.

Longrich, N., Scriberas, J., and Wills, M. 2016. "Severe Extinction and Rapid Recovery of Mammals across the Cretaceous–Palaeogene Boundary, and the Effects of Rarity on Patterns of Extinction and Recovery." *Journal of Evolutionary Biology* 29(8): 1495–1512.

Look, C. 2020. "Lagarde Says ECB Needs to Question Market Neutrality on Climate." *Bloomberg Economics*, 14 October. https://www.bloomberg.com/news/articles/2020-10-14/lagarde-says-ecb-needs-to-question-market-neutrality-on-climate. Accessed 1 December 2020.

Lorimer, J. 2017. "The Anthropo-Scene: A Guide for the Perplexed." *Social Studies of Science* 47(1): 117–142.

Losada, M. R. M. 2019. "Agroforestry: A Nature Based Solution for Sustainability." UN Secretary-General Climate Action Summit. https://wedocs.unep.org/handle/20.500.11822/28868?show=full. Accessed 28 Nov 2020.

Loschelder, D. D., Siepelmeyer, H., Fischer, D., and Rubel, J. A. 2019. "Dynamic Norms Drive Sustainable Consumption: Norm-Based Nudging Helps Café Customers to Avoid Disposable to-Go-Cups." *Journal of Economic Psychology* 75: 102146.

Lowder, S. K., Skoet, J., and Raney, T. 2016. "The Number, Size, and Distribution of Farms, Smallholder Farms, and Family Farms Worldwide." *World Development* 87: 16–29.

Lubell, M., Vedlitz, A., Zahran, S., and Alston, L. T. 2006. "Collective Action, Environmental Activism, and Air Quality Policy." *Political Research Quarterly* 59(1): 149–160.

Lucas Jr., R. E. 2009. "Ideas and Growth." *Economica* 76(301): 1–19.

Lundholm, C. 2019. "Where to Look and What to Do? Blank and Bright Spots in Research on Environmental and Climate Change Education." *Environmental Education Research* 25(10): 1427–1437.

Lutz, W. 2017. "Global Sustainable Development Priorities 500 Y after Luther: Sola Schola Et Sanitate." *Proceedings of the National Academy of Sciences* 114(27): 6904–6913.

Lutz, W., Muttarak, R., and Striessnig, E. 2014. "Universal Education Is Key to Enhanced Climate Adaptation." *Science* 346(6213): 1061–1062.

Maccini, S., and Yang, D. 2009. "Under the Weather: Health, Schooling, and Economic Consequences of Early-Life Rainfall." *American Economic Review* 99(3): 1006–1026. https://doi.org/10.1257/aer.99.3.1006. Accessed 1 December 2020.

Mace, G. M., Reyers, B., Alkemade, R., Biggs, R., Chapin III, F. S., Cornell, S. E., Díaz, S., and others. 2014. "Approaches to Defining a Planetary Boundary for Biodiversity." *Global Environmental Change* 28: 289–297.

Macfarlane, S., Macfarlane, A., and Gillon, G. 2015. "Sharing the Food Baskets of Knowledge: Creating Space for a Blending of Streams." In Macfarlane, A., Macfarlane, S., and Webber, M., (eds.), *Sociocultural Realities: Exploring New Horizons*. Christchurch, New Zealand: Canterbury University Press.

Maes, J., Liquete, C., Teller, A., Erhard, M., Paracchini, M. L., Barredo, J. I., Grizzetti, B., and others. 2016. "An Indicator Framework for Assessing Ecosystem Services in Support of the EU Biodiversity Strategy to 2020." *Ecosystem Services* 17: 14–23.

Maffi, L. 2005. "Linguistic, Cultural, and Biological Diversity." *Annual Review of Anthropology* 34(1): 599–617.

Maffi, L., and Woodley, E. 2012. *Biocultural Diversity Conservation: A Global Sourcebook*. New York: Routledge.

Maher, S. M., Fenichel, E. P., Schmitz, O. J., and Adamowicz, W. L. 2020. "The Economics of Conservation Debt: A Natural Capital Approach to Revealed Valuation of Ecological Dynamics." *Ecological Applications* 30(6): e02132.

Mahmoud, A. H. A. 2011. "Analysis of the Microclimatic and Human Comfort Conditions in an Urban Park in Hot and Arid Regions." *Building and Environment* 46(12): 2641–2656.

Maiga, Y., Sperling, M. v., and Mihelcic, J. 2017. "Constructed Wetlands." In Haas, C., Mihelcic, J., and Verbyla, M., (eds.), *Global Water Pathogen Project*. East Lansing, MI: Michigan State University.

Mair, S., Druckman, A., and Jackson, T. 2020. "A Tale of Two Utopias: Work in a Post-Growth World." *Ecological Economics* 173: 106653.

Makov, T., Newman, G. E., and Zauberman, G. 2020. "Inconsistent Allocations of Harms Versus Benefits May Exacerbate Environmental Inequality." *Proceedings of the National Academy of Sciences* 117(16): 201911116.

Makov, T., Shepon, A., Krones, J., Gupta, C., and Chertow, M. 2020. "Social and Environmental Analysis of Food Waste Abatement via the Peer-to-peer Sharing Economy." *Nature Communications* 11(1): 1–8.

Malapit, H. J. L., and Quisumbing, A. R. 2015. "What Dimensions of Women's Empowerment in Agriculture Matter for Nutrition in Ghana?" *Food Policy* 52: 54–63.

Maldonado, J., Colombi, B., and Pandya, R. 2014. *Climate Change and Indigenous Peoples in the United States: Impacts, Experiences, and Actions*. Heidelberg, Germany: Springer.

Malek, C. 2020. "Saudi Wind Farm's Progress Heralds a New Era in Clean Energy." *Arab News*, 5 October. https://www.arabnews.com/node/1744636/saudi-arabia. Accessed 1 December 2020.

Malhi, Y. 2014. "The Metabolism of a Human-Dominated Planet." In Goldin, I., (ed.) *Is the Planet Full?* Oxford, UK: Oxford University Press.

Malhi, Y. 2017. "The Concept of the Anthropocene." *Annual Review of Environment and Resources* 42(1): 77–104.

Malik, K. 2020. "Sustainability and Human Development." Background paper for Human Development Report 2020, United Nations Development Programme, Human Development Report Office, New York.

Malm, A., and Hornborg, A. 2014. "The Geology of Mankind? A Critique of the Anthropocene Narrative." *The Anthropocene Review* 1(1): 62–69.

Malmer, P., Masterson, V., Austin, B., and Tengo, M. 2020. "Mobilisation of Indigenous and Local Knowledge as a Source of Useable Evidence for Conservation Partnerships." *Conservation Research, Policy and Practice*: 82.

Managi, S., and Kumar, P., (eds.). 2018. *Inclusive Wealth Report 2018: Measuring Progress toward Sustainability.* New York: Routledge.

Mandle, L., Ouyang, Z., Daily, G. C., and Salzman, J. E. 2019. *Green Growth That Works: Natural Capital Policy and Finance Mechanisms around the World.* Washington, DC: Island Press.

Manela, E. 2010. "A Pox on Your Narrative: Writing Disease Control into Cold War History." *Diplomatic History* 34(2): 299–323.

Mann, C. C. 2018. *The Wizard and the Prophet: Two Remarkable Scientists and their Dueling Visions to Shape Tomorrow's World.* New York: Knopf.

Manuelli, R. E., and Seshadri, A. 2014. "Frictionless Technology Diffusion: The Case of Tractors." *American Economic Review* 104(4): 1368–91.

Marangoni, G., Tavoni, M., Bosetti, V., Borgonovo, E., Capros, P., Fricko, O., Gernaat, D. E. H. J., and others. 2017. "Sensitivity of Projected Long-Term CO_2 Emissions across the Shared Socioeconomic Pathways." *Nature Climate Change* 7(2).

Marschke, M., and Vandergeest, P. 2016. "Slavery Scandals: Unpacking Labour Challenges and Policy Responses within the Off-Shore Fisheries Sector." *Marine Policy* 68: 39–46.

Marshall, N., Adger, W. N., Benham, C., Brown, K., Curnock, M. I., Gurney, G. G., Marshall, P., and others. 2019. "Reef Grief: Investigating the Relationship between Place Meanings and Place Change on the Great Barrier Reef, Australia." *Sustainability Science* 14(3): 579–587.

Masi, F., Rizzo, A., and Regelsberger, M. 2018. "The Role of Constructed Wetlands in a New Circular Economy, Resource Oriented, and Ecosystem Services Paradigm." *Journal of Environmental Management* 216: 275–284.

Masson-Delmotte, T., Zhai, P., Pörtner, H., Roberts, D., Skea, J., Shukla, P., Pirani, A., and others. 2018. "IPCC, 2018: Summary for Policymakers." In *Global Warming of 1.5°C: An IPCC Special Report on the Impacts of Global Warming of 1.5°C above Pre-Industrial Levels and Related Global Greenhouse Gas Emission Pathways, in the Context of Strengthening the Global Response to the Threat of Climate Change, Sustainable Development, and Efforts to Eradicate Poverty.* Geneva: Intergovernmental Panel on Climate Change.

Masterson, V. A., Stedman, R. C., Enqvist, J., Tengö, M., Giusti, M., Wahl, D., and Svedin, U. 2017. "The Contribution of Sense of Place to Social-Ecological Systems Research: A Review and Research Agenda." *Ecology and Society* 22(1).

Matchan, E. L., Phillips, D., Jourdan, F., and Oostingh, K. 2020. "Early Human Occupation of Southeastern Australia: New Insights from 40ar/39ar Dating of Young Volcanoes." *Geology* 48(4): 390–394.

Matson, P., Clark, W. C., and Andersson, K. 2016. *Pursuing Sustainability: A Guide to the Science and Practice.* Princeton, NJ: Princeton University Press.

Matthies, E., Selge, S., and Klöckner, C. A. 2012. "The Role of Parental Behaviour for the Development of Behaviour Specific Environmental Norms–the Example of Recycling and Re-Use Behaviour." *Journal of Environmental Psychology* 32(3): 277–284.

Maxwell, S. L., Cazalis, V., Dudley, N., Hoffmann, M., Rodrigues, A. S. L., Stolton, S., Visconti, P., and others. 2020. "Area-Based Conservation in the Twenty-First Century." *Nature* 586(7828): 217–227.

Mayhew Bergman, M. 2019. "They Chose Us Because We Were Rural and Poor: When Environmental Racism and Climate Change Collide." *The Guardian*, 8 March. https://www.theguardian.com/environment/2019/mar/08/climate-changed-racism-environment-south. Accessed 17 November 2020.

Maynard Smith, J., and Szathmáry, E. 1995. *The Major Transitions in Evolution.* Oxford, UK: Freeman.

Mazzucato, M. 2011. "The Entrepreneurial State." *Soundings* 49(49): 131–142.

McCoy, J., Rahman, T., and Somer, M. 2018. "Polarization and the Global Crisis of Democracy: Common Patterns, Dynamics, and Pernicious Consequences for Democratic Polities." *American Behavioral Scientist* 62(1): 16–42.

McCurry, J. 2020a. "Japan Will Become Carbon Neutral by 2050, PM Pledges." *The Guardian*, 26 October. https://www.theguardian.com/world/2020/oct/26/japan-will-become-carbon-neutral-by-2050-pm-pledges. Accessed 18 November 2020.

McCurry, J. 2020b. "South Korea Vows to Go Carbon Neutral by 2050 to Fight Climate Emergency." *The Guardian*, 28 October. https://www.theguardian.com/world/2020/oct/28/south-korea-vows-to-go-carbon-neutral-by-2050-to-fight-climate-emergency. Accessed 18 November 2020.

McDermott, M., Mahanty, S., and Schreckenberg, K. 2013. "Examining Equity: A Multidimensional Framework for Assessing Equity in Payments for Ecosystem Services." *Environmental Science & Policy* 33: 416–427.

McDonald, R. I., Weber, K., Padowski, J., Flörke, M., Schneider, C., Green, P. A., Gleeson, T., and others. 2014. "Water on an Urban Planet: Urbanization and the Reach of Urban Water Infrastructure." *Global Environmental Change* 27: 96–105.

McDonnell, A. U., Ana F., and Samman, E. 2019. "Reaching Universal Health Coverage: A Political Economy Review of Trends across 49 Countries." Working Paper 570, Overseas Development Institute, London.

McGlade, J., Bankoff, G., Abrahams, J., Cooper-Knock, S., Cotecchia, F., Desanker, P., Erian, W., and others. 2019. *Global Assessment Report on Disaster Risk Reduction 2019.* Geneva: United Nations Office for Disaster Risk Reduction.

McGregor, D. 2009. "Honouring Our Relations: An Anishnaabe Perspective on Environmental Justice." In Agyeman, J., Cole, P., and Haluza-Delay, R., (eds.), *Speaking for Ourselves: Environmental Justice in Canada.* Vancouver, BC: University of British Columbia Press.

McKibben, B. 2020. "How Fast Is the Climate Changing? It's a New World, Each and Every Day." *The New Yorker.* 3 September. https://www.newyorker.com/news/annals-of-a-warming-planet/how-fast-is-the-climate-changing-its-a-new-world-each-and-every-day. Accessed 1 December 2020.

McLean, K. G. 2012. "Land Use, Climate Change Adaptation and Indigenous Peoples." United Nations University, 30 October. https://unu.edu/publications/articles/land-use-climate-change-adaptation-and-indigenous-peoples.html. Accessed 20 November 2020.

McNeill, J. R. 2000. *Something New Under the Sun: An Environmental History of the Twentieth-Century World.* New York: W. W. Norton & Company.

Meadows, D. H., Meadows, D. L., Randers, J., and Behrens, W. W. 1972. *The Limits to Growth: A Report for the Club of Rome's Project on the Predicament of Mankind.* New York: Universe Books.

Meckling, J., Sterner, T., and Wagner, G. 2017. "Policy Sequencing toward Decarbonization." *Nature Energy* 2(12): 918–922.

Mega, E. R. 2020. "'Apocalyptic' Fires Are Ravaging the World's Largest Tropical Wetland." *Nature*, 25 September. https://www.nature.com/articles/d41586-020-02716-4. Accessed 18 November 2020.

Mehryar, S., Schwarz, N., Sliuzas, R., and van Maarseveen, M. 2020. "Making Use of Fuzzy Cognitive Maps in Agent-Based Modeling." In Verhagen, H., Borit, M., Bravo, G., and Wijermans, N., (eds.), *Advances in Social Simulation.* New York: Springer.

Meneses-Navarro, S., Freyermuth-Enciso, M. G., Pelcastre-Villafuerte, B. E., Campos-Navarro, R., Meléndez-Navarro, D. M., and Gómez-Flores-Ramos, L. 2020. "The Challenges Facing Indigenous Communities in Latin America as They Confront the Covid-19 Pandemic." *International Journal for Equity in Health* 19: 1–3.

Meng, J., Mi, Z., Guan, D., Li, J., Tao, S., Li, Y., Feng, K., and others. 2018. "The Rise of South–South Trade and Its Effect on Global CO_2 Emissions." *Nature Communications* 9(1): 1871.

Merçon, J., Vetter, S., Tengö, M., Cocks, M., Balvanera, P., Rosell, J., and Ayala-Orozco, B. 2019. "From Local Landscapes to International Policy: Contributions of the Biocultural Paradigm to Global Sustainability." *Global Sustainability* 2(e7): 1–11.

Merino, R. 2015. "The Politics of Extractive Governance: Indigenous Peoples and Socio-Environmental Conflicts." *The Extractive Industries and Society* 2(1): 85–92.

Merino, R. 2018. "Re-Politicizing Participation or Reframing Environmental Governance? Beyond Indigenous' Prior Consultation and Citizen Participation." *World Development* 111: 75–83.

Metcalf, G. E., and Stock, J. H. 2020. "The Macroeconomic Impact of Europe's Carbon Taxes." Working Paper 27488, National Bureau of Economic Research, Cambridge, MA.

Mildenberger, M. 2020. *Carbon Captured: How Business and Labor Control Climate Politics.* Cambridge, MA: MIT Press.

Milfont, T. L., Davies, C. L., and Wilson, M. S. 2019. "The Moral Foundations of Environmentalism." *Social Psychological Bulletin* 14(2): 1–25.

Millennium Ecosystem Assessment. 2003. *Ecosystems and Human Well-Being: A Framework for Assessment.* Report of the Conceptual Framework Working Group of the Millennium Ecosystem Assessment. Washington, DC: Island Press.

Millennium Ecosystem Assessment. 2005. *Our Human Planet.* Summary for Decision Makers of the Millennium Ecosystem Assessment. Washington, DC: Island Press.

Mintz-Woo, K., Dennig, F., Liu, H., and Schinko, T. 2020. "Carbon Pricing and Covid-19." *Climate Policy.*

Minx, J. C., Lamb, W. F., Callaghan, M. W., Fuss, S., Hilaire, J., Creutzig, F., Amann, T., and others. 2018. "Negative Emissions—Part 1: Research Landscape and Synthesis." *Environmental Research Letters* 13(6): 063001.

Missirian, A., and Schlenker, W. 2017. "Asylum Applications Respond to Temperature Fluctuations." *Science* 358(6370): 1610–1614. https://doi.org/10.1126/science.aao0432. Accessed 1 December 2020.

Mistry, J., and Berardi, A. 2016. "Bridging Indigenous and Scientific Knowledge." *Science* 352(6291): 1274–1275.

Mitchell, G. 2011. "Environmental Justice: An Overview." *Encyclopedia of Environmental Health—Reference Module in Earth Systems and Environmental Sciences* 2011: 449–458.

Mitchell, R. B. 1992. "Intentional Oil Pollution of the Oceans." *Environment: Science and Policy for Sustainable Development* 34(4): 29–29.

Mochizuki, Y., and Bryan, A. 2015. "Climate Change Education in the Context of Education for Sustainable Development: Rationale and Principles." *Journal of Education for Sustainable Development* 9(1): 4–26.

Mohai, P., and Saha, R. 2015. "Which Came First, People or Pollution? A Review of Theory and Evidence from Longitudinal Environmental Justice Studies." *Environmental Research Letters* 10(12): 125011.

Mohan, A., Muller, N. Z., Thyagarajan, A., Martin, R. V., Hammer, M. S., and van Donkelaar, A. 2020. "The Growth of Nations Revisited: Global Environmental Accounting from 1998 to 2018." Cambridge, MA: National Bureau of Economic Research.

Molden, D. 2009. "Planetary Boundaries: The Devil Is in the Detail." *Nature Climate Change* 1(910): 116–117.

Monasterolo, I. 2020. "Climate Change and the Financial System." *Annual Review of Resource Economics* 12(1): 299–320.

Monroe, M. C., Plate, R. R., Oxarart, A., Bowers, A., and Chaves, W. A. 2019. "Identifying Effective Climate Change Education Strategies: A Systematic Review of the Research." *Environmental Education Research* 25(6): 791–812.

Monty, F., Murti, R., Miththapala, S., and Buyck, C. 2017. "Ecosystems Protecting Infrastructure and Communities: Lessons Learned and Guidelines for Implementation." Gland, Switzerland: International Union for Conservation of Nature.

Moore, F. C., Obradovich, N., Lehner, F., and Baylis, P. 2019. "Rapidly Declining Remarkability of Temperature Anomalies May Obscure Public Perception of Climate Change." *Proceedings of the National Academy of Sciences* 116(11): 4905–4910.

Moreno Parra, M. 2019. "Racismo Ambiental: Muerte Lenta y Despojo de Territorio Ancestral Afroecuatoriano en Esmeraldas." *Íconos. Revista de Ciencias Sociales* (64): 89–109.

Moreno-Cruz, J. 2019. "Understanding the Industrial Contribution to Pollution Offers Opportunities to Further Improve Air Quality in the United States." *Proceedings of the National Academy of Sciences* 116(40): 19768–19770.

Moreno-Cruz, J., and Taylor, M. S. 2020. "Food, Fuel and the Domesday Economy." Working Paper 27414, National Bureau of Economic Research, Cambridge, MA.

Morse, S. S., Mazet, J. A., Woolhouse, M., Parrish, C. R., Carroll, D., Karesh, W. B., Zambrana-Torrelio, C., and others. 2012. "Prediction and Prevention of the Next Pandemic Zoonosis." *The Lancet* 380(9857): 1956–1965.

Moser, S., and Dilling, L. 2011. "Communicating Climate Change: Closing the Science-Action Gap." *The Oxford Handbook of Climate Change and Society.* Oxford, UK: Oxford University Press.

Moser, S., and Kleinhückelkotten, S. 2018. "Good Intents, but Low Impacts: Diverging Importance of Motivational and Socioeconomic Determinants Explaining Pro-Environmental Behavior, Energy Use, and Carbon Footprint." *Environment and Behavior* 50(6): 626–656.

Mosquera-Losada, M., Santiago-Freijanes, J., Rois-Díaz, M., Moreno, G., den Herder, M., Aldrey-Vázquez, J., Ferreiro-Domínguez, N., and others. 2018. "Agroforestry in Europe: A Land Management Policy Tool to Combat Climate Change." *Land Use Policy* 78: 603–613.

Moss, S. 2020. "Launch: CUBHIC Tools Support Rapid Assessment of Water Quantity and Quality Benefits of Nature-Based Solutions." *Forest Trends Blog,* 13 February. https://www.forest-trends.org/blog/launch-cubhic-tools-support-rapid-assessment-of-water-quantity-and-quality-benefits-of-nature-based-solutions/. Accessed 25 November 2020.

Motesharrei, S., Rivas, J., and Kalnay, E. 2014. "Human and Nature Dynamics (Handy): Modeling Inequality and Use of Resources in the Collapse or Sustainability of Societies." *Ecological Economics* 101: 90–102.

Mowbray, S. 2017. "Indonesians Plant Trees to Nurse Seagrass Back to Health in Wakatobi." *Mongabay News,* 31 October. https://news.mongabay.com/2017/10/indonesians-plant-trees-to-nurse-seagrass-back-to-health-in-wakatobi/. Accessed 25 November 2020.

Mucushua, E., and Huerta, E. 2020. "Coronavirus: Unos 600 Habitantes De Pucacuro En Loreto Tienen Síntomas De Covid-19, Informó El Apu De La Comunidad." https://rpp.pe/peru/actualidad/coronavirus-unos-600-habitantes-de-pacacuro-en-loreto-tienen-sintomas-de-covid-19-informo-apu-de-la-comunidad-noticia-1268259. Accessed 20 November 2020.

Mufson, S., and Dennis, B. 2020. "U.S. Companies Make New Vows to Tackle Carbon Emissions Even as Global Action Falls Short." *The Washington Post,* 22 September. https://www.washingtonpost.com/climate-environment/2020/09/22/climate-clock-week/. Accessed 1 December 2020.

Mukanjari, S., and Sterner, T. 2020. "Charting a 'Green Path' for Recovery from Covid-19." *Environmental and Resource Economics* 76(4): 825–853.

Muller, N. Z., Mendelsohn, R., and Nordhaus, W. 2011. "Environmental Accounting for Pollution in the United States Economy." *American Economic Review* 101(5): 1649–1675.

Multihazard Mitigation Council. 2017. *Natural Hazard Mitigation Saves: 2017 Interim Report.* Washington, DC: National Institute of Building Sciences.

Mummert, A., Esche, E., Robinson, J., and Armelagos, G. J. 2011. "Stature and Robusticity During the Agricultural Transition: Evidence from the Bioarchaeological Record." *Economics & Human Biology* 9(3): 284–301.

Munshi, K., and Myaux, J. 2006. "Social Norms and the Fertility Transition." *Journal of Development Economics* 80(1): 1–38.

Murphy, J. 2009. "Environment and Imperialism: Why Colonialism Still Matters." *Sustainability Research Institute* 20: 1–27.

Murti, R., and Buyck, C. 2014. *Safe Havens: Protected Areas for Disaster Risk Reduction and Climate Change Adaption.* Gland, Switzerland: International Union for Conservation of Nature.

Muthukrishna, M., and Henrich, J. 2016. "Innovation in the Collective Brain." *Philosophical Transactions of the Royal Society B: Biological Sciences* 371(1690): 20150192.

Muttarak, R., and Lutz, W. 2014. "Is Education a Key to Reducing Vulnerability to Natural Disasters and Hence Unavoidable Climate Change?" *Ecology and Society* 19(1): 42.

Muttarak, R., and Pothisiri, W. 2013. "The Role of Education on Disaster Preparedness: Case Study of 2012 Indian Ocean Earthquakes on Thailand's Andaman Coast." *Ecology and Society* 18(4).

Myllyvirta, L. 2020. "Analysis: China's CO_2 Emissions Surged past Pre-Coronavirus Levels in May." Carbon-Brief Post, 29 June 2020. https://www.carbonbrief.org/analysis-chinas-co2-emissions-surged-past-pre-coronavirus-levels-in-may#:~:text=China's%20CO2%20emissions%20have%20surged,and%20power%20plants%20reduced%20output. Accessed 1 December 2020.

Mysiak, J., Surminski, S., Thieken, A., Mechler, R., and Aerts, J. C. 2016. "Brief Communication: Sendai Framework for Disaster Risk Reduction–Success or Warning Sign for Paris?" *Natural Hazards and Earth System Sciences* 16(10): 2189–2193.

Nagendra, H. 2018. "The Global South Is Rich in Sustainability Lessons That Students Deserve to Hear." *Nature* 557(7706): 485–488.

Najib, R. 2019. "Navroz Dubash: Climate Change Is Really a Here and Now Problem." *The Hindu Business Line*, 6 December. https://www.thehindubusinessline.com/blink/know/navroz-dubash-climate-change-is-really-a-here-and-now-problem/article30212160.ece. Accessed 1 December 2020

NASA (US National Aeronautics and Space Administration) Earth Observatory. 2019. "Heatwave in India." https://earthobservatory.nasa.gov/images/145167/heatwave-in-india)%E2%80%94breaking. Accessed 10 December 2020.

Nash, K. L., Cvitanovic, C., Fulton, E. A., Halpern, B. S., Milner-Gulland, E., Watson, R. A., and Blanchard, J. L. 2017. "Planetary Boundaries for a Blue Planet." *Nature Ecology & Evolution* 1(11): 1625–1634.

Nasi, R., Taber, A., and Van Vliet, N. 2011. "Empty Forests, Empty Stomachs? Bushmeat and Livelihoods in the Congo and Amazon Basins." *International Forestry Review* 13(3): 355–368.

Nassef, M., Anderson, S., and Hesse, C. 2009. *Pastoralism and Climate Change: Enabling Adaptive Capacity.* London: Overseas Development Institute.

National Geographic. 2014. "Reciprocal Water Agreements for Watershed Protection." *National Geographic Blog*, 17 June. https://blog.nationalgeographic.org/2014/06/17/reciprocal-water-agreements-for-watershed-protection/. Accessed 25 November 2020.

National Science Challenges. 2020. "Our Land and Water." https://www.mbie.govt.nz/science-and-technology/science-and-innovation/funding-information-and-opportunities/investment-funds/national-science-challenges/the-11-challenges/our-land-and-water/. Accessed 3 December 2020.

The Nature Conservancy. 2019a. "Estrategia Hídrica en Ecuador." Press Release, 2 May. https://www.nature.org/es-us/sobre-tnc/donde-trabajamos/tnc-en-latinoamerica/ecuador/estrategia-hidrica/. Accessed 25 November 2020.

The Nature Conservancy. 2019b. "Insuring Nature to Ensure a Resilient Future: The World's First Insurance Policy on a Coral Reef Is Now in Place in Mexico." *Perspectives* [blog], 3 September. https://www.nature.org/en-us/what-we-do/our-insights/perspectives/insuring-nature-to-ensure-a-resilient-future/. Accessed 25 November 2020.

NCC (Natural Capital Coalition). 2020. "What Is Natural Capital?" https://naturalcapitalcoalition.org/natural-capital-2/. Accessed 2 December 2020.

Nche, G. C., Achunike, H. C., and Okoli, A. B. 2019. "From Climate Change Victims to Climate Change Actors: The Role of Eco-Parenting in Building Mitigation and Adaptation Capacities in Children." *The Journal of Environmental Education* 50(2): 131–144.

Nello-Deakin, S., and Nikolaeva, A. 2020. "The Human Infrastructure of a Cycling City: Amsterdam through the Eyes of International Newcomers." *Urban Geography*: 1–23. https://doi.org/10.1080/02723638.2019.1709757. Accessed 12 November 2020.

Neumann, V. A., and Hack, J. 2020. "A Methodology of Policy Assessment at the Municipal Level: Costa Rica's Readiness for the Implementation of Nature-Based-Solutions for Urban Stormwater Management." *Sustainability* 12(1): 230.

Neumayer, E. 2013. *Weak and Strong Sustainability. Exploring the Limits of Two Opposing Paradigms.* Northampton, MA: Edward Elgar.

Neumayer, E., and Plümper, T. 2007. "The Gendered Nature of Natural Disasters: The Impact of Catastrophic Events on the Gender Gap in Life Expectancy, 1981–2002." *Annals of the Association of American Geographers* 97(3): 551–566.

New Zealand Treasury. 2020. "Wellbeing Budget 2020: Rebuilding Together." https://www.treasury.govt.nz/publications/wellbeing-budget/wellbeing-budget-2020. Accessed 2 December 2020.

Newell, P. 2005. "Race, Class and the Global Politics of Environmental Inequality." *Global Environmental Politics* 5(3): 70–94.

Newell, P., and Mulvaney, D. 2013. "The Political Economy of the 'Just Transition.'" *The Geographical Journal* 179(2): 132–140.

Ngāi Tahu. 2001. "Tino Rangatiratanga—'Mō tātou, ā, mō kā uri ā muri ake nei' (Tino Rangatiratanga—'For Us and Our Children after Us')." https://ngaitahu.iwi.nz/wp-content/uploads/2013/06/NgaiTahu_20251.pdf. Accessed 30 November 2020.

Ngāti Whātua Ōrākei. 2019. "Ngāti Whātua Ōrākei ki Tua 5 Year Plan 2019–2024." http://ngatiwhatuaorakei.com/wp-content/uploads/2020/02/Ng%C4%81ti-Wh%C4%81tua-%C5%8Cr%C4%81kei-5-Year-Plan.pdf. Accessed 30 November 2020.

NGFS (Network for Greening the Financial System). 2019a. "A Call for Action: Climate Change as a Source of Financial Risk." London. https://www.ngfs.net/en/first-comprehensive-report-call-action. Accessed 1 December 2020.

NGFS (Network for Greening the Financial System). 2019b. "Macroeconomics and Financial Stability Implications of Climate Change." Technical Supplement to the First Comprehensive Report, London. https://www.ngfs.net/en/technical-supplement-first-ngfs-comprehensive-report. Accessed 1 December 2020.

NGFS (Network for Greening the Financial System). 2019c. "A Sustainable and Responsible Investment Guide for Central Banks' Portfolio Management." Technical Document, London. https://www.ngfs.net/sites/default/files/medias/documents/ngfs-a-sustainable-and-responsible-investment-guide.pdf. Accessed 1 December 2020.

NGFS (Network for Greening the Financial System). 2020a. "Guide for Supervisors: Integrating Climate-Related and Environmental Risks into Prudential Supervision." London. https://www.ngfs.net/en/guide-supervisors-integrating-climate-related-and-environmental-risks-prudential-supervision. Accessed 1 December 2020.

NGFS (Network for Greening the Financial System). 2020b. "NGFS Climate Scenarios for Central Banks and Supervisors." London. https://www.ngfs.net/en/ngfs-climate-scenarios-central-banks-and-supervisors. Accessed 1 December 2020.

Nguyen, T. P. 2019. "Searching for Education for Sustainable Development in Vietnam." *Environmental Education Research* 25(7): 991–1003.

Nielsen, K. S., Clayton, S., Stern, P. C., Dietz, T., Capstick, S., and Whitmarsh, L. 2020. "How Psychology Can Help Limit Climate Change." *American Psychologist.* https://doi.org/10.1037/amp0000624. Accessed 12 November 2020.

Nigra, A. E. 2020. "Environmental Racism and the Need for Private Well Protections." *Proceedings of the National Academy of Sciences* 117(30): 17476–17478.

Nikas, A., Lieu, J., Sorman, A., Gambhir, A., Turhan, E., Baptista, B. V., and Doukas, H. 2020. "The Desirability of Transitions in Demand: Incorporating Behavioural and Societal Transformations into Energy Modelling." *Energy Research & Social Science* 70: 101780.

Njwambe, A., Cocks, M., and Vetter, S. 2019. "Ekhayeni: Rural–Urban Migration, Belonging and Landscapes of Home in South Africa." *Journal of Southern African Studies* 45(2): 413–431.

Nobre, C. A., Sampaio, G., Borma, L. S., Castilla-Rubio, J. C., Silva, J. S., and Cardoso, M. 2016. "Land-use and Climate Change Risks in the Amazon and the Need of a Novel Sustainable Development Paradigm." *Proceedings of the National Academy of Sciences* 113(39): 10759–10768.

Nordhaus, W. D. 2015. "Climate Clubs: Overcoming Free-Riding in International Climate Policy." *American Economic Review* 105(4): 1339–70.

Nordhaus, W. D. 2017. "Revisiting the Social Cost of Carbon." *Proceedings of the National Academy of Sciences* 114(7): 1518–1523.

Nordhaus, W. D. 2019. "Economics of the Disintegration of the Greenland Ice Sheet." *Proceedings of the National Academy of Sciences* 116(25): 12261–12269.

Nordhaus, W. D., and Boyer, J. 2000. *Warming the World: Economic Models of Global Warming.* Cambridge, MA: MIT Press.

Nordhaus, W. D., and Tobin, J. 1973. "Is Growth Obsolete?" In Moss, M., (ed.), *The Measurement of*

Economic and Social Performance. Cambridge, MA: MIT Press.

Norman, G., and Chinchar, A. 2020. "With Two Months Left, the 2020 Hurricane Season Has a Chance to Set the Record for Most Named Storms." *CNN*, 3 October. https://www.cnn.com/2020/10/03/weather/gamma-rapid-intensification-on-record-season/index.html. Accessed 18 November 2020.

Nunn, N. 2020a. "The Historical Roots of Economic Development." *Science* 367(6485).

Nunn, N. 2020b. "History as Evolution." Working Paper 27706, National Bureau of Economic Research, Cambridge, MA.

Nussbaum, M. C. 2011. *Creating Capabilities.* Cambridge, MA: Harvard University Press.

Nussbaum, M. C. 2019. "Preface: Amartya Sen and the HDCA." *Journal of Human Development and Capabilities* 20(2): 124–126.

Nyborg, K. 2018. "Reciprocal Climate Negotiators." *Journal of Environmental Economics and Management* 92: 707–725.

Nyborg, K. 2020. "No Man Is an Island: Social Coordination and the Environment." *Environmental and Resource Economics* 76(1): 177–193.

Nyborg, K., Anderies, J. M., Dannenberg, A., Lindahl, T., Schill, C., Schlüter, M., Adger, W. N., and others. 2016. "Social Norms as Solutions." *Science* 354(6308): 42–43.

Nyborg, K., and Rege, M. 2003. "On Social Norms: The Evolution of Considerate Smoking Behavior." *Journal of Economic Behavior & Organization* 52(3): 323–340.

Nys, T. R., and Engelen, B. 2017. "Judging Nudging: Answering the Manipulation Objection." *Political Studies* 65(1): 199–214.

Nyström, M., Jouffray, J.-B., Norström, A. V., Crona, B., Søgaard Jørgensen, P., Carpenter, S. R., Bodin, Ö., and others. 2019. "Anatomy and Resilience of the Global Production Ecosystem." *Nature* 575(7781): 98–108.

O'Brien, K. 2018. "Is the 1.5 C Target Possible? Exploring the Three Spheres of Transformation." *Current Opinion in Environmental Sustainability* 31: 153–160.

O'Brien, K. 2020. "You Matter More Than You Think: Quantum Social Science in Response to a World Crisis." Forthcoming manuscript. https://www.youmattermorethanyouthink.com/. Accessed 11 November 2020.

O'Brien, K., Reams, J., Caspari, A., Dugmore, A., Faghihimani, M., Fazey, I., Hackmann, H., and others. 2013. "You Say You Want a Revolution? Transforming Education and Capacity Building in Response to Global Change." *Environmental Science & Policy* 28: 48–59.

O'Brien, K., Selboe, E., and Hayward, B. M. 2018. "Exploring Youth Activism on Climate Change." *Ecology and Society* 23(3).

O'Callaghan-Gordo, C., Flores, J. A., Lizárraga, P., Okamoto, T., Papoulias, D. M., Barclay, F.,

Orta-Martínez, M., and others. 2018. "Oil Extraction in the Amazon Basin and Exposure to Metals in Indigenous Populations." *Environmental Research* 162: 226–230.

O'Connor, R. E., Bord, R. J., and Fisher, A. 1999. "Risk Perceptions, General Environmental Beliefs, and Willingness to Address Climate Change." *Risk Analysis* 19(3).

O'Neill, D. W., Fanning, A. L., Lamb, W. F., and Steinberger, J. K. 2018. "A Good Life for All within Planetary Boundaries." *Nature Sustainability* 1(2): 88–95.

Oberle, B., Bringezu, S., Hatfield-Dodds, S., Hellweg, S., Schandl, H., Clement, J., Cabernard, L., and others. 2019. *Global Resources Outlook 2019: Natural Resources for the Future We Want.* Nairobi: United Nations Environment Programme.

Obradovich, N., Tingley, D., and Rahwan, I. 2018. "Effects of Environmental Stressors on Daily Governance." *Proceedings of the National Academy of Sciences* 115(35): 8710–8715. https://doi.org/10.1073/pnas.1803765115. Accessed 1 December 2020.

OECD (Organisation for Economic Co-operation and Development). 2012. "Do Today's 15-Year-Olds Feel Environmentally Responsible?" https://www.oecd-ilibrary.org/docserver/5k918xhzk88t-en.pdf?expires=1599669863&id=id&accname=guest&checksum=14F98BEA0F9301B3EEC0DF619F650026. Accessed 9 September 2020.

OECD (Organisation for Economic Co-operation and Development). 2007. "The Istanbul Declaration." https://www.oecd.org/newsroom/38883774.pdf. Accessed 2 December 2020.

OECD (Organisation for Economic Co-operation and Development). 2017. "Policies for Scaling up Low-Emission and Resilient Investment." In *Investing in Climate, Investing in Growth.* Paris: OECD Publishing.

OECD (Organisation for Economic Co-operation and Development). 2020a. "A Global Project on 'Measuring the Progress of Societies: The OECD World Forum on Statistics, Knowledge, and Policy.'" Paris.

OECD (Organisation for Economic Co-operation and Development). 2020b. "OECD Better Life Index." http://www.oecdbetterlifeindex.org. Accessed 2 December 2020.

Ogwal, F., Okurut, T., and Rodriguez, C. M. 2020. "Mapping Nature to Create a Global Biodiversity Framework." United Nations Development Programme blog, 28 August. https://www.undp.org/content/undp/en/home/blog/2020/mapping-nature-to-create-a-global-biodiversity-framework.html. Accessed 25 November 2020.

OHCHR (Office of the United Nations High Commisioner for Human Rights) and RISIU (Red de Investigaciones sobre Indígenas Urbanos) 2020. "Contribución Continental al Informe del Relator Especial sobre los Derechos de los Pueblos Indígenas sobre el Impacto de Covid-19 en los Pueblos Indígenas." https://www.clacso.org/contribucion-continental-al-informe-del-relator-especial-sobre-los-derechos-de-los-pueblos-indigenas/. Accessed 20 November 2020.

OHCHR (Office of the United Nations High Commisioner for Human Rights) and UN Women (United Nations Entity for Gender Equality and the Empowerment of Women) 2020. *Realizing Women's Rights to Land and Other Productive Resources.* Second Edition. New York and Geneva.

Oldekop, J. A., Sims, K. R., Karna, B. K., Whittingham, M. J., and Agrawal, A. 2019. "Reductions in Deforestation and Poverty from Decentralized Forest Management in Nepal." *Nature Sustainability* 2(5): 421–428.

Oliver, T. H., Heard, M. S., Isaac, N. J., Roy, D. B., Procter, D., Eigenbrod, F., Freckleton, R., and others. 2015. "Biodiversity and Resilience of Ecosystem Functions." *Trends in Ecology & Evolution* 30(11): 673–684.

Olsson, P., Moore, M.-L., Westley, F. R., and McCarthy, D. D. P. 2017. "The Concept of the Anthropocene as a Game-Changer: A New Context for Social Innovation and Transformations to Sustainability." *Ecology and Society* 22(2).

Onigbinde, L. 2018. "The Impacts of Natural Disasters on Educational Attainment: Cross-Country Evidence from Macro Data." Master's Thesis 1078. University of San Francisco, CA. https://repository.usfca.edu/thes/1078. Accessed 1 December 2020.

Oral, H. V., Carvalho, P., Gajewska, M., Ursino, N., Masi, F., Hullebusch, E. D. v., Kazak, J. K., and others. 2020. "A Review of Nature-Based Solutions for Urban Water Management in European Circular Cities: A Critical Assessment Based on Case Studies and Literature." *Blue-Green Systems* 2(1): 112–136.

Ord, T. 2014. "Overpopulation or Underpopulation." *Is the Planet Full*: 46–60.

Ord, T. 2020. *The Precipice: Existential Risk and the Future of Humanity.* New York: Hachette Books.

Oreskes, N. 2019. *Why Trust Science.* Princeton, NJ: Princeton University Press.

Oreskes, N., and Conway, E. M. 2011. *Merchants of Doubt: How a Handful of Scientists Obscured the Truth on Issues from Tobacco Smoke to Global Warming.* New York: Bloomsbury Press.

Orta-Martínez, M., Rosell-Melé, A., Cartró-Sabaté, M., O'Callaghan-Gordo, C., Moraleda-Cibrián, N., and Mayor, P. 2018. "First Evidences of Amazonian Wildlife Feeding on Petroleum-Contaminated Soils: A New Exposure Route to Petrogenic Compounds?" *Environmental Research* 160: 514–517.

Ortiz-Hernández, L., and Pérez-Sastré, M. A. 2020. "Inequidades Sociales en la Progresión de la Covid-19 en Población Mexicana." *Revista Panamericana de Salud Pública* 44.

Österblom, H., Jouffray, J.-B., Folke, C., and Rockström, J. 2017. "Emergence of a Global Science–Business Initiative for Ocean Stewardship." *Proceedings of the National Academy of Sciences* 114(34): 9038–9043.

Österblom, H., Wabnitz, C., and Tladi, D. 2020. "Towards Ocean Equity." Washington, DC: World Resources Institute. https://www.oceanpanel.org/sites/default/files/2020-04/towards-ocean-equity.pdf. Accessed 9 December 2020.

Ostrom, E. 1990. *Governing the Commons: The Evolution of Institutions for Collective Action*. Cambridge, UK: Cambridge University Press.

Ostrom, E. 2007. "A Diagnostic Approach for Going Beyond Panaceas." *Proceedings of the National Academy of Sciences* 104(39): 15181–15187.

Ostrom, E. 2009. "A General Framework for Analyzing Sustainability of Social-Ecological Systems." *Science* 325(5939): 419–422.

Ostrom, E. 2009b. "A Polycentric Approach for Coping with Climate Change." Policy Research Working Paper 5095, World Bank, Washington, DC.

Ostrom, E. 2010. "Polycentric Systems for Coping with Collective Action and Global Environmental Change." *Global Environmental Change* 20(4): 550–557.

Ostrom, V., Tiebout, C. M., and Warren, R. 1961. "The Organization of Government in Metropolitan Areas: A Theoretical Inquiry." *American Political Science Review* 55(4): 831–842.

Osuagwu, E. S., and Olaifa, E. 2018. "Effects of Oil Spills on Fish Production in the Niger Delta." *PLOS ONE* 13(10): e0205114.

Otto, I. M., Donges, J. F., Cremades, R., Bhowmik, A., Hewitt, R. J., Lucht, W., Rockström, J., and others. 2020a. "Social Tipping Dynamics for Stabilizing Earth's Climate by 2050." *Proceedings of the National Academy of Sciences* 117(5): 2354–2365.

Otto, I. M., Donges, J. F., Lucht, W., and Schellnhuber, H. J. 2020b. "Reply to Smith et al.: Social Tipping Dynamics in a World Constrained by Conflicting Interests." *Proceedings of the National Academy of Sciences* 117(20): 10631–10632.

Otto, I. M., Wiedermann, M., Cremades, R., Donges, J. F., Auer, C., and Lucht, W. 2020c. "Human Agency in the Anthropocene." *Ecological Economics* 167: 106463.

Our World in Data. 2020a. "CO_2 and Other Greenhouse Gas Emissions." https://ourworldindata.org/co2-and-other-greenhouse-gas-emissions. Accessed 7 December 2020.

Our World in Data. 2020b. "You Want to Reduce the Carbon Footprint of Your Food? Focus on What You Eat, Not Whether Your Food Is Local." https://ourworldindata.org/food-choice-vs-eating-local. Accessed 7 December 2020.

Ouyang, Z., Song, C., Zheng, H., Polasky, S., Xiao, Y., Bateman, I. J., Liu, J., and others. 2020. "Using Gross Ecosystem Product (GEP) to Value Nature in Decision Making." *Proceedings of the National Academy of Sciences* 117(25): 14593–14601.

Oxfam. 2005. "The Tsunami's Impact on Women." Oxfam Briefing Note 14. https://policy-practice.oxfam.org.uk/publications/the-tsunamis-impact-on-women-115038. Accessed 20 November 2020.

Oxfam. 2020. "5 Shocking Facts About Extreme Global Inequality and How to Even It Up." https://www.oxfam.org/en/5-shocking-facts-about-extreme-global-inequality-and-how-even-it. Accessed 30 November 2020.

Paavola, J. 2008. "Livelihoods, Vulnerability and Adaptation to Climate Change in Morogoro, Tanzania." *Environmental Science & Policy* 11(7): 642–654.

Pacorel, J. 2019. "Mercury Tops 45c in France as Deadly Heatwave Roasts Europe." https://phys.org/news/2019-06-all-time-hottest-temperature-france-443c.html. Accessed 10 December 2020.

Paerl, H. W., Xu, H., McCarthy, M. J., Zhu, G., Qin, B., Li, Y., and Gardner, W. S. 2011. "Controlling Harmful Cyanobacterial Blooms in a Hyper-Eutrophic Lake (Lake Taihu, China): The Need for a Dual Nutrient (N & P) Management Strategy." *Water Research* 45(5): 1973–1983.

PAGE (Partnership for Action on Green Economy). 2017. *The Green Economy Progress Measurement Framework Methodology*. Nairobi: United Nations Environment Programme.

Palmer, T., and Stevens, B. 2019. "The Scientific Challenge of Understanding and Estimating Climate Change." *Proceedings of the National Academy of Sciences* 116(49): 24390–24395.

Palsson, G., Szerszynski, B., Sörlin, S., Marks, J., Avril, B., Crumley, C., Hackmann, H., and others. 2013. "Reconceptualizing the 'Anthropos' in the Anthropocene: Integrating the Social Sciences and Humanities in Global Environmental Change Research." *Environmental Science & Policy* 28: 3–13.

Papworth, S. K., Rist, J., Coad, L., and Milner-Gulland, E. J. 2009. "Evidence for Shifting Baseline Syndrome in Conservation." *Conservation Letters* 2(2): 93–100.

Parag, Y., and Fawcett, T. 2014. "Personal Carbon Trading: A Review of Research Evidence and Real-World Experience of a Radical Idea." *Energy and Emission Control Technologies* 2: 23–32.

Parfit, D. 1984. *Reasons and Persons*. Oxford, UK: Oxford University Press.

Park, R. J., Goodman, J., and Behrer, A. P. 2020. "Learning Is Inhibited by Heat Exposure, Both Internationally and within the United States." *Nature Human Behaviour*, 5 October. https://doi.org/10.1038/s41562-020-00959-9. Accessed 1 December 2020.

Park, R. J., Goodman, J., Hurwitz, M., and Smith, J. 2020. "Heat and Learning." *American Economic Journal: Economic Policy* 12(2): 306–339. https://doi.org/10.1257/pol.20180612. Accessed 1 December 2020.

Parker, G. 2013. *Global Crisis: War, Climate Change, & Catastrophe in the Seventeenth Century*. New Haven, CT: Yale University Press.

Parker, K., Morin, R., and Horowitz, J. M. 2019. "Looking to the Future, Public Sees an America in Decline on Many Fronts." *Pew Research Center,* 21 March. https://www.pewsocialtrends.org/2019/03/21/public-sees-an-america-in-decline-on-many-fronts/. Accessed 18 November 2020.

Parks, B. C., and Roberts, J. T. 2008. "Inequality and the Global Climate Regime: Breaking the North–South Impasse." *Cambridge Review of International Affairs* 21(4): 621–648.

Parry, I. 2018. "Fossil-Fuel Subsidies Assessed." *Nature* 554(7691): 175–176. https://doi.org/10.1038/d41586-018-01495-3. Accessed 1 December 2020.

Pascual, U., Palomo, I., Adams, W. M., Chan, K. M., Daw, T. M., Garmendia, E., Gómez-Baggethun, E., and others. 2017. "Off-Stage Ecosystem Service Burdens: A Blind Spot for Global Sustainability." *Environmental Research Letters* 12(7): 075001.

Pasgaard, M., and Dawson, N. 2019. "Looking Beyond Justice as Universal Basic Needs Is Essential to Progress towards 'Safe and Just Operating Spaces.'" *Earth System Governance* 2: 100030.

Pasricha, S. R., and Biggs, B. A. 2010. "Undernutrition among Children in South and South-East Asia." *Journal of Paediatrics and Child Health* 46(9): 497–503.

Patterson, J., Schulz, K., Vervoort, J., Van Der Hel, S., Widerberg, O., Adler, C., Hurlbert, M., and others. 2017. "Exploring the Governance and Politics of Transformations Towards Sustainability." *Environmental Innovation and Societal Transitions* 24: 1–16.

Pauliuk, S., and Hertwich, E. G. 2015. "Socioeconomic Metabolism as Paradigm for Studying the Biophysical Basis of Human Societies." *Ecological Economics* 119: 83–93.

Pauly, D. 1995. "Anecdotes and the Shifting Baseline Syndrome of Fisheries." *Trends in Ecology & Evolution* 10(10): 430.

Pearson, A. R., Schuldt, J. P., Romero-Canyas, R., Ballew, M. T., and Larson-Konar, D. 2018. "Diverse Segments of the US Public Underestimate the Environmental Concerns of Minority and Low-Income Americans." *Proceedings of the National Academy of Sciences* 115(49): 12429–12434.

Pelzer, P. 2010. "Bicycling as a Way of Life: A Comparative Case Study of Bicycle Culture in Portland, OR and Amsterdam." Paper Presented at the 7th Cycling and Society Symposium, Oxford, UK. https://www.ris.uu.nl/ws/files/31021264/Bicycling_as_a_way_of_life.pdf. Accessed 11 November 2020.

Pereira Da Silva, L. 2020. "Green Swan 2: Climate Change and Covid-19: Reflections on Efficiency Versus Resilience." Speech based on remarks at the OECD Chief Economists Talk Series, Paris, 23 April, and a Research Webinar at the Bank for International Settlements, 13 May. https://www.bis.org/speeches/sp200514.htm. Accessed 1 December 2020.

Pereira, L., Bennett, E., Biggs, R., Mangnus, A., Norstrom, A. V., Peterson, G., Raudsepp-Hearne, C., and others. 2019. "Seeding Change by Visioning Good Anthropocenes." *Solutions Journal* 10(3).

Perrings, C., Levin, S., and Daszak, P. 2018. "The Economics of Infectious Disease, Trade and Pandemic Risk." *Ecohealth* 15(2): 241–243.

Persson, J., and Mertz, O. 2019. "Discursive Telecouplings." In Friis, C., and Nielsen, Jonas Ø., (eds.), *Telecoupling*. Cham, Switzerland: Springer.

Peters, G. P., Davis, S. J., and Andrew, R. 2012. "A Synthesis of Carbon in International Trade." *Biogeosciences* 9(8): 3247–3276.

Petkova, E. P., Morita, H., and Kinney, P. L. 2014. "Health Impacts of Heat in a Changing Climate:

How Can Emerging Science Inform Urban Adaptation Planning?" *Current Epidemiology Reports* 1(2): 67–74.

Petraglia, M. D., Groucutt, H. S., Guagnin, M., Breeze, P. S., and Boivin, N. 2020. "Human Responses to Climate and Ecosystem Change in Ancient Arabia." *Proceedings of the National Academy of Sciences* 117(15): 8263–8270.

Pettifor, H. 2012. "Do Parents Affect the Early Political Prioritisation of Nature in Their Children?" ISER Working Paper Series, University of Essex, Colchester, UK. https://www.iser.essex.ac.uk/research/publications/working-papers/iser/2012-11.pdf. Accessed 11 November 2020.

Pew Research Center. 2020. "Most Approve of National Response to Covid-19 in 14 Advanced Economies." https://www.pewresearch.org/global/2020/08/27/most-approve-of-national-response-to-covid-19-in-14-advanced-economies/. Accessed 9 October 2020.

Pezzey, J. C. V. 1997. "Sustainability Constraints Versus "Optimality" Versus Intertemporal Concern, and Axioms Versus Data." *Land Economics* 73(4): 448–466.

Pezzey, J. C. V. 2004. "One-Sided Sustainability Tests with Amenities, and Changes in Technology, Trade and Population." *Journal of Environmental Economics and Management* 48(1): 613–631.

Pichert, D., and Katsikopoulos, K. V. 2008. "Green Defaults: Information Presentation and Pro-Environmental Behaviour." *Journal of Environmental Psychology* 28(1): 63–73.

Pichler, A., and Striessnig, E. 2013. "Differential Vulnerability to Hurricanes in Cuba, Haiti, and the Dominican Republic: The Contribution of Education." *Ecology and Society* 18(3).

Piketty, T. 2014. *Capital in the 21st Century*. Translated by Arthur Goldhammer. New York: Belknap Press.

Pimm, S. L., Jenkins, C. N., Abell, R., Brooks, T. M., Gittleman, J. L., Joppa, L. N., Raven, P. H., and others. 2014. "The Biodiversity of Species and Their Rates of Extinction, Distribution, and Protection." *Science* 344(6187).

Pindyck, R. S. 2019. "The Social Cost of Carbon Revisited." *Journal of Environmental Economics and Management* 94: 140–160.

Pindyck, R. S. 2020. "What We Know and Don't Know About Climate Change, and Implications for Policy." Cambridge, MA: National Bureau of Economic Research.

Pineda, J. 2012. "Sustainability and Human Development: A Proposal for a Sustainability Adjusted Human Development Index." *Theoretical and Practical Research in Economic Fields* 3(06): 71–98.

Plumer, B., and Popovich, N. 2019. "These Countries Have Prices on Carbon: Are They Working?" *New York Times*, 2 April. https://www.nytimes.com/interactive/2019/04/02/climate/pricing-carbon-emissions.html. Accessed 1 December 2020.

Pomázi, I. 2009. "OECD Environmental Outlook to 2030." *Hungarian Geographical Bulletin* 58(2): 139–140.

Pomeranz, K. 2013. "Weather, War, and Welfare: Persistence and Change in Geoffrey Parker's Global Crisis." *Historically Speaking* 14(5): 30–33.

Pongratz, J., Caldeira, K., Reick, C., and Claussen, M. 2011. "Coupled Climate–Carbon Simulations Indicate Minor Global Effects of Wars and Epidemics on Atmospheric CO_2 between AD 800 and 1850." *The Holocene* 21(5): 843–851.

Poore, J., and Nemecek, T. 2018. "Reducing Food's Environmental Impacts through Producers and Consumers." *Science* 360(6392): 987–992.

Pope Francis. 2016. "Laudato Si': On Care For Our Common Home." *Perspectives on Science and Christian Faith* 68(4).

Portland Bureau of Transportation. 2019. "Bicycles in Portland Fact Sheet." https://www.portlandoregon.gov/transportation/article/407660. Accessed 11 November 2020.

Potts, R., Behrensmeyer, A. K., Faith, J. T., Tryon, C. A., Brooks, A. S., Yellen, J. E., Deino, A. L., and others. 2018. "Environmental Dynamics During the Onset of the Middle Stone Age in Eastern Africa." *Science* 360(6384): 86–90.

Potts, R., Dommain, R., Moerman, J. W., Behrensmeyer, A. K., Deino, A. L., Riedl, S., Beverly, E. J., and others. 2020. "Increased Ecological Resource Variability During a Critical Transition in Hominin Evolution." *Science Advances* 6(43).

Potts, S. G., Imperatriz-Fonseca, V., Ngo, H., Biesmeijer, J. C., Breeze, T., Dicks, L., Garibaldi, L., and others. 2016a. *The Assessment Report of the Intergovernmental Science-Policy Platform on Biodiversity and Ecosystem Services (IPBES) on Pollinators, Pollination and Food Production: Summary for Policymakers*. Bonn, Germany: Intergovernmental Science-Policy Platform on Biodiversity and Ecosystem Services Secretariat.

Potts, S. G., Ngo, H. T., Biesmeijer, J. C., Breeze, T. D., Dicks, L. V., Garibaldi, L. A., Hill, R., Settele, J., and Vanbergen, A. 2016b. *The Assessment Report of the Intergovernmental Science-Policy Platform on Biodiversity and Ecosystem Services on Pollinators, Pollination and Food Production*. Bonn, Germany: Intergovernmental Science-Policy Platform on Biodiversity and Ecosystem Services Secretariat.

Powers, R. P., and Jetz, W. 2019. "Global Habitat Loss and Extinction Risk of Terrestrial Vertebrates under Future Land-Use-Change Scenarios." *Nature Climate Change* 9(4): 323–329.

Prasad, A. 2019. "Denying Anthropogenic Climate Change: Or, How Our Rejection of Objective Reality Gave Intellectual Legitimacy to Fake News." *Sociological Forum* 34(S1): 1217–1234.

Pritchett, L. 2020. "Developing Country Schools Need to Reopen with Different Teaching." Research on Improving Systems of Education Programme, 12 June. https://riseprogramme.org/blog/developing-country-schools-reopen. Accessed 20 November 2020.

Proctor, J. D. 2020. "Introduction: The Value of Environmental Disagreement." *Journal of Environmental Studies and Sciences* 10: 156–159.

Proctor, J. D., Hsiang, S., Burney, J., Burke, M., and Schlenker, W. 2018. "Estimating Global Agricultural Effects of Geoengineering Using Volcanic Eruptions." *Nature* 560(7719): 480–483. https://doi.org/10.1038/s41586-018-0417-3. Accessed 1 December 2020.

Pungetti, G. 2013. "Biocultural Diversity for Sustainable Ecological, Cultural and Sacred Landscapes: The Biocultural Landscape Approach." In Fu, B., and Jones, B. K., (eds.), *Landscape Ecology for Sustainable Environment and Culture*. New York: Springer.

Rabin, M. 1993. "Incorporating Fairness into Game Theory and Economics." *The American Economic Review* 83(5): 1281–1302.

Radkau, J. 2008. *Nature and Power: A Global History of the Environment*. New York: Cambridge University Press.

Radosavljevic, S., Haider, L. J., Lade, S. J., and Schlüter, M. 2020. "Effective Alleviation of Rural Poverty Depends on the Interplay between Productivity, Nutrients, Water and Soil Quality." *Ecological Economics* 169: 106494.

Rajamani, L. 2012a. "The Changing Fortunes of Differential Treatment in the Evolution of International Environmental Law." *International Affairs* 88(3): 605–623.

Rajamani, L. 2012b. "The Durban Platform for Enhanced Action and the Future of the Climate Regime." *International & Comparative Law Quarterly* 61(2): 501–518.

Rajamani, L. 2016. "Ambition and Differentiation in the 2015 Paris Agreement: Interpretative Possibilities and Underlying Politics." *International & Comparative Law Quarterly* 65(2): 493–514.

Ramankutty, N., Evan, A. T., Monfreda, C., and Foley, J. A. 2008. "Farming the Planet: 1. Geographic Distribution of Global Agricultural Lands in the Year 2000." *Global Biogeochemical Cycles* 22(1).

Ramirez-Andreotta, M. 2019. "Environmental Justice." In Brusseau, M. L., Pepper, I. L., and Gerba, C. P., (eds.), *Environmental and Pollution Science*. Cambridge, MA: Elsevier.

Randers, J., Rockström, J., Stoknes, P.-E., Goluke, U., Collste, D., Cornell, S. E., and Donges, J. 2019. "Achieving the 17 Sustainable Development Goals within 9 Planetary Boundaries." *Global Sustainability* 2.

Ranis, G., Stewart, F., and Samman, E. 2006. "Human Development: Beyond the Human Development Index." *Journal of Human Development* 7(3): 323–358.

Ransom, J., and Ettenger, K. 2001. "'Polishing the Kaswentha': A Haudenosaunee View of Environmental Cooperation." *Environmental Science & Policy* 4(4-5): 219–228.

Ras, M. 2017. "Natural Disasters Don't Exist but Natural Hazards Do." *Our Perspectives* [blog], 18 May. https://www.undp.org/content/undp/en/home/blog/2017/5/18/

Natural-disasters-don-t-exist-but-natural-hazards-do.html#:~:text=Because%20the%20fact%20is%20that,due%20to%20risk%2Dblind%20development. Accessed 9 September 2020.

Rasmussen, M. B., and Pinho, P. F. 2016. "Introduction: Environmental Justice and Climate Change in Latin America." *LASA Forum* 47(4): 8–11.

Raudsepp-Hearne, C., Peterson, G. D., Bennett, E. M., Biggs, R., Norström, A. V., Pereira, L., Vervoort, J., and others. 2020. "Seeds of Good Anthropocenes: Developing Sustainability Scenarios for Northern Europe." *Sustainability Science* 15(2): 605–617.

Rauschmayer, F., and Lessmann, O. 2013. "The Capability Approach and Sustainability." *Journal of Human Development and Capabilities* 14(1): 1–5.

Ravallion, M. 2010. *Troubling Tradeoffs in the Human Development Index*. Washington, DC: World Bank.

Ravallion, M. 2012. "Troubling Tradeoffs in the Human Development Index." *Journal of Development Economics* 99(2): 201–209.

Rawls, J. 1971. *A Theory of Justice*. Cambridge, MA: Harvard University Press.

Raworth, K. 2017. *Doughnut Economics: Seven Ways to Think Like a 21st-Century Economist*. White River Junction, VT: Chelsea Green Publishing.

Rayne, A., Byrnes, G., Collier-Robinson, L., Hollows, J., McIntosh, A., Ramsden, M., Rupene, M., and others. 2020. "Centring Indigenous Knowledge Systems to Re-imagine Conservation Translocations." *People and Nature* 2(3).

Reagan, R. 1985. "Transcript of Interview with President Reagan on a Range of Issues." Interview with Weinraub, B., *New York Times*, 12 February.

Rees, N., and Anthony, D. 2015. *Unless We Act Now: The Impact of Climate Change on Children*. New York: United Nations Children's Fund.

Rehbein, J. A., Watson, J. E. M., Lane, J. L., Sonter, L. J., Venter, O., Atkinson, S. C., and Allan, J. R. 2020. "Renewable Energy Development Threatens Many Globally Important Biodiversity Areas." *Global Change Biology* 26(5): 3040–3051.

REN21. "Key Findings of the Renewables 2020 Global Status Report." Paris.

Renn, J. 2020. *The Evolution of Knowledge: Rethinking Science for the Anthropocene*. Princeton, NJ: Princeton University Press.

Renn, O., Chabay, I., van der Leeuw, S., and Droy, S. 2020. "Beyond the Indicators: Improving Science, Scholarship, Policy and Practice to Meet the Complex Challenges of Sustainability." *Sustainability* 12(2): 578.

Reno, R. R., Cialdini, R. B., and Kallgren, C. A. 1993. "The Transsituational Influence of Social Norms." *Journal of Personality and Social Psychology* 64(1): 104.

Requate, T. 2005. "Timing and Commitment of Environmental Policy, Adoption of New Technology, and Repercussions on R&D." *Environmental and Resource Economics* 31(2): 175–199.

Reusch, T. B. H., Dierking, J., Andersson, H. C., Bonsdorff, E., Carstensen, J., Casini, M., Czajkowski, M., and others. 2018. "The Baltic Sea as a Time Machine for the Future Coastal Ocean." *Science Advances* 4(5): eaar8195.

Reuters. 2020. "The Pace of Death." https://graphics.reuters.com/HEALTH-CORONAVIRUS/DEATHS/xlbpgobgapq/. Accessed 3 November 2020.

Rex, E., and Baumann, H. 2007. "Beyond Ecolabels: What Green Marketing Can Learn from Conventional Marketing." *Journal of Cleaner Production* 15(6): 567–576.

Rex, H. C., and Trohanis, Z. 2012. *Making Women's Voices Count: Integrating Gender Issues in Disaster Risk Management: Overview and Resources for Guidance Notes*. Washington, DC: World Bank.

Reyers, B., Folke, C., Moore, M.-L., Biggs, R., and Galaz, V. 2018. "Social-Ecological Systems Insights for Navigating the Dynamics of the Anthropocene." *Annual Review of Environment and Resources* 43(1): 267–289.

Reynolds, C. W. 1987. "Flocks, Herds and Schools: A Distributed Behavioral Model." *Proceedings of the 14th Annual Conference on Computer Graphics and Interactive Techniques*, 25–34. https://dl.acm.org/doi/10.1145/37401.37406. Accessed 20 November 2020.

Riahi, K., Van Vuuren, D. P., Kriegler, E., Edmonds, J., O'Neill, B. C., Fujimori, S., Bauer, N., and others. 2017. "The Shared Socioeconomic Pathways and Their Energy, Land Use, and Greenhouse Gas Emissions Implications: An Overview." *Global Environmental Change* 42: 153–168.

Rick, T. C., and Sandweiss, D. H. 2020. "Archaeology, Climate, and Global Change in the Age of Humans." *Proceedings of the National Academy of Sciences* 117(15): 8250–8253.

Ricke, K., Drouet, L., Caldeira, K., and Tavoni, M. 2018. "Country-Level Social Cost of Carbon." *Nature Climate Change* 8(10): 895–900.

Ricker-Gilbert, J. 2020. "Inorganic Fertiliser Use Among Smallholder Farmers in Sub-Saharan Africa: Implications for Input Subsidy Policies." In Gomez y Paloma, S., Riesgo, L., and Louhichi, K., (eds.), *The Role of Smallholder Farms in Food and Nutrition Security*. Cham, Switzerland: Springer.

Ricketts, T. H., Daily, G. C., Ehrlich, P. R., and Michener, C. D. 2004. "Economic Value of Tropical Forest to Coffee Production." *Proceedings of the National Academy of Sciences* 101(34): 12579–12582.

Ripple, W. J., Wolf, C., Newsome, T. M., Galetti, M., Alamgir, M., Crist, E., Mahmoud, M. I., and Laurance, W. F. 2017. "World Scientists' Warning to Humanity: A Second Notice." *BioScience* 67(12): 1026–1028.

Ritchie, H., and Roser, M. 2020. "Co2 Emissions." https://ourworldindata.org/co2-emissions. Accessed 10 December 2020.

Roberts, N. 2019. "How Humans Changed the Face of Earth." *Science* 365(6456): 865–866.

Roberts, R. G. 1998. "Environmental Justice and Community Empowerment: Learning from the Civil Rights Movement." *American University Law Review* 48 (1): 229–267.

Robertson, J. L., and Barling, J. 2013. "Greening Organizations through Leaders' Influence on Employees' Pro-Environmental Behaviors." *Journal of Organizational Behavior* 34(2): 176–194.

Robeyns, I. 2016. "Capabilitarianism." *Journal of Human Development and Capabilities* 17(3): 397–414.

Robeyns, I. 2017. *Wellbeing, Freedom and Social Justice: The Capability Approach Re-Examined*. Cambridge, UK: Open Book Publishers.

Robins, N., Tickell, S., Irwin, W., and Sudmant, A. 2020. *Financing Climate Action with Positive Social Impact: How Banking Can Support a Just Transition in the UK*. London: Grantham Research Institute on Climate Change and the Environment. https://www.lse.ac.uk/granthaminstitute/wp-content/uploads/2020/07/Financing-climate-action-with-positive-social-impact_How-banking-can-support-a-just-transition-in-the-UK-1.pdf. Accessed 1 December 2020.

Robock, A., Oman, L., and Stenchikov, G. L. 2007. "Nuclear Winter Revisited with a Modern Climate Model and Current Nuclear Arsenals: Still Catastrophic Consequences." *Journal of Geophysical Research: Atmospheres* 112(D13).

Rocha, J. C., Peterson, G. D., and Biggs, R. 2015. "Regime Shifts in the Anthropocene: Drivers, Risks, and Resilience." *PLOS ONE* 10(8): e0134639.

Rocha, J. C., Peterson, G. D., Bodin, Ö., and Levin, S. 2018. "Cascading Regime Shifts within and across Scales." *Science* 362(6421): 1379–1383.

Rockström, J., Richardson, K., Steffen, W., and Mace, G. 2018. "Planetary Boundaries: Separating Fact from Fiction. A Response to Montoya et al." *Trends in Ecology & Evolution* 33(4): 233–234.

Rockström, J., Steffen, W., Noone, K., Persson, Å., Chapin III, F. S., Lambin, E., Lenton, T. M., and others. 2009a. "A Safe Operating Space for Humanity." *Nature* 461(7263): 472–475.

Rockström, J., Steffen, W., Noone, K., Persson, Å., Chapin III, F. S., Lambin, E., Lenton, T. M., and others. 2009b. "Planetary Boundaries: Exploring the Safe Operating Space for Humanity." *Ecology and Society* 14(2).

Rodriguez-Gonzalez, P. T., Rico-Martinez, R., and Rico-Ramirez, V. 2020. "Effect of Feedback Loops on the Sustainability and Resilience of Human-Ecosystems." *Ecological Modelling* 426: 109018.

Rodriguez, F. 2020. "Human Development and Capabilities: Conceptual and Measurement Advances." Background paper for Human Development Report 2020, United Nations Development Programme, Human Development Report Office, New York.

Rogelj, J., Den Elzen, M., Höhne, N., Fransen, T., Fekete, H., Winkler, H., Schaeffer, R., and others. 2016. "Paris Agreement Climate Proposals Need a Boost to Keep Warming Well Below 2°C." *Nature* 534(7609): 631–639.

Rogelj, J., Shindell, D., Jiang, K., Fifita, S., Forster, P., Ginzburg, V., Handa, C., and others. 2018. "Mitigation Pathways Compatible with 1.5°C in the Context of Sustainable Development." In *Global Warming of 1.5°C: An IPCC Special Report on the Impacts of Global Warming of 1.5°C above Pre-industrial Levels and Related Global Greenhouse Gas Emission Pathways, in the Context of Strengthening the Global Response to the Threat of Climate Change, Sustainable Development, and Efforts to Eradicate Poverty*. Geneva: Intergovernmental Panel on Climate Change.

Rokeach, M. 1973. *The Nature of Human Values*. New York: Free Press.

Rokeach, M. 2008. *Understanding Human Values*. New York: Simon and Schuster.

Rolf, E., Proctor, J., Bolliger, I., Shankhar, V., Ishihara, M., Recht, B., and Hsiang, S. 2020. "A Generalizable and Accessible Approach to Machine Learning with Global Satellite Imagery." https://www.researchgate.net/profile/Ian_Bolliger/publication/344734239_A_Generalizable_and_Accessible_Approach_to_Machine_Learning_with_Global_Satellite_Imagery/links/5f9746e7299bf1b53e49771e/A-Generalizable-and-Accessible-Approach-to-Machine-Learning-with-Global-Satellite-Imagery.pdf. Accessed 7 December 2020.

Romer, P. M. 1990. "Endogenous Technological Change." *Journal of Political Economy* 98(5, Part 2): S71–S102.

Rosenbloom, D., Markard, J., Geels, F. W., and Fuenfschilling, L. 2020. "Opinion: Why Carbon Pricing Is Not Sufficient to Mitigate Climate Change—and How 'Sustainability Transition Policy' Can Help." *Proceedings of the National Academy of Sciences* 117(16): 8664–8668.

Roser, M., Ritchie, H., and Dadonaite, B. 2013. "Child and Infant Mortality." Our World in Data. https://ourworldindata.org/child-mortality#child-mortality-around-the-world-since-1800. Accessed 10 December 2020.

Rothman, D. H. 2019. "Characteristic Disruptions of an Excitable Carbon Cycle." *Proceedings of the National Academy of Sciences* 116(30): 14813–14822.

Rotondi, V., Kashyap, R., Pesando, L. M., Spinelli, S., and Billari, F. C. 2020. "Leveraging Mobile Phones to Attain Sustainable Development." *Proceedings of the National Academy of Sciences* 117(24): 13413–13420.

Rubian-Miller, L., Alban, C., Artiga, S., and Sullivan, S. 2020. "Covid-19 Racial Disparities in Testing, Infection, Hospitalization, and Death: Analysis of Epic Patient Data." https://www.kff.org/report-section/covid-19-racial-disparities-in-testing-infection-hospitalization-and-death-analysis-of-epic-patient-data-issue-brief/. Accessed 20 November 2020.

Rudberg, P. M., Escobar, M., Gantenbein, J., and Ni-iro, N. 2014. "Mitigating the Adverse Effects of Hydropower Projects: A Comparative Review of River Restoration and Hydropower Regulation in Sweden and the United States." *Georgetown International Environmental Law Review* 27: 251.

Ruddiman, W. F. 2013. "The Anthropocene." *Annual Review of Earth and Planetary Sciences* 41(1): 45–68.

Ruddiman, W. F., Fuller, D. Q., Kutzbach, J. E., Tzedakis, P. C., Kaplan, J. O., Ellis, E. C., Vavrus, S. J., and others. 2016. "Late Holocene Climate: Natural or Anthropogenic?" *Reviews of Geophysics* 54(1): 93–118.

Ruru, J. 2014. "Tūhoe-Crown Settlement – Te Urewera Act 2014." *Māori Law Review*, October 2014. http://maorilawreview.co.nz/2014/10/tuhoe-crown-settlement-te-ureweraact-2014/. Accessed 17 November 2020.

Russell, S. 2019. *Human Compatible: Artificial Intelligence and the Problem of Control*. New York: Penguin.

Sælen, H. 2020. "Under What Conditions Will the Paris Process Produce a Cycle of Increasing Ambition Sufficient to Reach the 2°C Goal?" *Global Environmental Politics* 20(2): 83–104.

Saez, E., and Zucman, G. 2019. *The Triumph of Injustice: How the Rich Dodge Taxes and How to Make Them Pay*. New York: WW Norton & Company.

Sagan, C. 1983. "Nuclear War and Climatic Catastrophe: Some Policy Implications." *Foreign Affairs* 62(2): 257–292.

Sala, E., and Giakoumi, S. 2018. "No-Take Marine Reserves Are the Most Effective Protected Areas in the Ocean." *ICES Journal of Marine Science* 75(3): 1166–1168.

Salzman, J., Bennett, G., Carroll, N., Goldstein, A., and Jenkins, M. 2018. "The Global Status and Trends of Payments for Ecosystem Services." *Nature Sustainability* 1(3): 136–144.

Samuelson, P. A. 1961. "The Evaluation of 'Social Income': Capital Formation and Wealth." In Lutz, F. A., and Hague, D. C., (eds.), *The Theory of Capital: Proceedings of a Conference Held by the International Economic Association*. London: Palgrave Macmillan UK.

Sardeshpande, M., and MacMillan, D. 2019. "Sea Turtles Support Sustainable Livelihoods at Ostional, Costa Rica." *Oryx* 53(1): 81–91.

Satterthwaite, D. 2003. "The Links between Poverty and the Environment in Urban Areas of Africa, Asia, and Latin America." *The Annals of the American Academy of Political and Social Science* 590(1): 73–92.

Schandl, H., Fischer-Kowalski, M., West, J., Giljum, S., Dittrich, M., Eisenmenger, N., Geschke, A., and others. 2018. "Global Material Flows and Resource Productivity: Forty Years of Evidence." *Journal of Industrial Ecology* 22(4): 827–838.

Scheffer, M., Carpenter, S. R., Lenton, T. M., Bascompte, J., Brock, W., Dakos, V., van de Koppel, J., and others. 2012. "Anticipating Critical Transitions." *Science* 338(6105): 344–348.

Scheidel, A., Del Bene, D., Liu, J., Navas, G., Mingorría, S., Demaria, F., Avila, S., and others. 2020. "Environmental Conflicts and Defenders: A Global Overview." *Global Environmental Change* 63: 102–104.

Schell, C. J., Dyson, K., Fuentes, T. L., Des Roches, S., Harris, N. C., Miller, D. S., Woelfle-Erskine, C. A., and Lambert, M. R. 2020. "The Ecological and Evolutionary Consequences of Systemic Racism in Urban Environments." *Science* 369(6510).

Schell, J. 1982. "The Fate of the Earth; II—The Second Death." *The New Yorker*, 8 February.

Schelling, T. C. 1978. "Micromotives and Macrobehavior." New York: W.W. Norton & Company.

Schelling, T. C. 1980. *The Strategy of Conflict*. Cambridge, MA: Harvard University Press.

Schelling, T. C. 2006. *Micromotives and Macrobehavior*. New York: W.W. Norton & Company.

Schellnhuber, H. J. 1999. "'Earth System' Analysis and the Second Copernican Revolution." *Nature* 402(6761): C19–C23.

Scherer, C. W., and Cho, H. 2003. "A Social Network Contagion Theory of Risk Perception." *Risk Analysis: An International Journal* 23(2): 261–267.

Schlegelmilch, B. B., Bohlen, G. M., and Diamantopoulos, A. 1996. "The Link between Green Purchasing Decisions and Measures of Environmental Consciousness." *European Journal of Marketing* 30(5): 35–55.

Schlenker, W., and Lobell, D. B. 2010. "Robust Negative Impacts of Climate Change on African Agriculture." *Environmental Research Letters* 5(1): 014010. https://doi.org/10.1088/1748-9326/5/1/014010. Accessed 1 December 2020.

Schleussner, C.-F., Lissner, T. K., Fischer, E. M., Wohland, J., Perrette, M., Golly, A., Rogelj, J., and others. 2016. "Differential Climate Impacts for Policy-Relevant Limits to Global Warming: The Case of 1.5°C and 2°C." *Earth System Dynamics* 7: 327–351.

Schneiderhan-Opel, J., and Bogner, F. X. 2020. "The Relation between Knowledge Acquisition and Environmental Values within the Scope of a Biodiversity Learning Module." *Sustainability* 12(5): 2036.

Scholz, R. W., and Wellmer, F. W. 2019. "Although There Is No Physical Short-Term Scarcity of Phosphorus, Its Resource Efficiency Should Be Improved." *Journal of Industrial Ecology* 23(2): 313–318.

Schröder, E., and Storm, S. 2020. "Economic Growth and Carbon Emissions: The Road to "Hothouse Earth" Is Paved with Good Intentions." *International Journal of Political Economy* 49(2): 153–173.

Schultz, P. W., Nolan, J. M., Cialdini, R. B., Goldstein, N. J., and Griskevicius, V. 2007. "The Constructive, Destructive, and Reconstructive Power of Social Norms." *Psychological Science* 18(5): 429–434.

Schultz, P. W., Shriver, C., Tabanico, J. J., and Khazian, A. M. 2004. "Implicit Connections with Nature." *Journal of Environmental Psychology* 24(1): 31–42.

Schuster, R., Germain, R. R., Bennett, J. R., Reo, N. J., and Arcese, P. 2019. "Vertebrate Biodiversity on Indigenous-Managed Lands in Australia, Brazil, and Canada Equals That in Protected Areas." *Environmental Science & Policy* 101: 1–6.

Schwab, K., Dustin, D., and Bricker, K. 2017. "Reframing Humankind's Relationship with Nature: Contributions from Social Exchange Theory." *Journal of Sustainability Education* 12.

Schwartzman, D. 2008. "The Limits to Entropy: Continuing Misuse of Thermodynamics in Environmental and Marxist Theory." *Science & Society* 72(1): 43–62.

Schwartzman, D. 2012. "A Critique of Degrowth and Its Politics." *Capitalism Nature Socialism* 23(1): 119–125.

Schwartzman, D. 2014. "Is Zero Economic Growth Necessary to Prevent Climate Catastrophe?" *Science & Society* 78(2): 235–240.

Scoones, I. 2016. "The Politics of Sustainability and Development." *Annual Review of Environment and Resources* 41(1): 293–319.

Scoones, I., Stirling, A., Abrol, D., Atela, J., Charli-Joseph, L., Eakin, H., Ely, A., and others. 2020. "Transformations to Sustainability: Combining Structural, Systemic and Enabling Approaches." *Current Opinion in Environmental Sustainability* 42: 65–75.

Scott, J. C. 2017. *Against the Grain: A Deep History of the Earliest States*. New Haven, CT: Yale University Press.

Scovronick, N., Budolfson, M. B., Dennig, F., Fleurbaey, M., Siebert, A., Socolow, R. H., Spears, D., and Wagner, F. 2017. "Impact of Population Growth and Population Ethics on Climate Change Mitigation Policy." *Proceedings of the National Academy of Sciences* 114(46): 12338–12343.

Scovronick, N., Vasquez, V. N., Errickson, F., Dennig, F., Gasparrini, A., Hajat, S., Spears, D., and Budolfson, M. B. 2019. "Human Health and the Social Cost of Carbon: A Primer and Call to Action." *Epidemiology* 30(5): 642–647.

SDG Impact. 2020. "SDG Impact Standards for Privte Equity Funds." https://sdgimpact.undp.org/private-equity.html. Accessed 1 December 2020.

Seager, J., Bechtel, J., Bock, S., and Dankelman, I. 2016. *Global Gender and Environment Outlook*. Nairobi: United Nations Environment Programme.

Seatter, C. S., and Ceulemans, K. 2017. "Teaching Sustainability in Higher Education: Pedagogical Styles That Make a Difference." *Canadian Journal of Higher Education* 47(2): 47–70.

Seddon, N., Chausson, A., Berry, P., Girardin, C. A., Smith, A., and Turner, B. 2020. "Understanding the Value and Limits of Nature-Based Solutions to Climate Change and Other Global Challenges." *Philosophical Transactions of the Royal Society B* 375(1794): 20190120.

SEI (Stockholm Environment Institute). 2020. "Carbon Emissions of Richest One Percent More Than Double the Emissions of the Poorest Half of Humanity." Press release, 21 September. https://www.sei.org/about-sei/press-room/carbon-emissions-of-richest-1-percent-more-than-double-the-emissions-of-the-poorest-half-of-humanity/. Accessed 20 December 2020.

Seidl, R., Brand, F. S., Stauffacher, M., Krütli, P., Le, Q. B., Spörri, A., Meylan, G., and others. 2013. "Science with Society in the Anthropocene." *Ambio* 42(1): 5–12.

Sen, A. 1976. "Real National Income." *The Review of Economic Studies* 43(1): 19–39.

Sen, A. 2000. "A Decade of Human Development." *Journal of Human Development* 1(1): 17–23.

Sen, A. 2001. *Development as Freedom*. New York: Oxford Paperbacks.

Sen, A. 2005. "Human Rights and Capabilities." *Journal of Human Development* 6(2): 151–166.

Sen, A. 2007. *Identity and Violence: The Illusion of Destiny*. Delhi: Penguin Books India.

Sen, A., 2008. "Violence, Identity and Poverty." *Journal of Peace Research* 45(1): 5–15.

Sen, A. 2009. *The Idea of Justice*. Cambridge, MA: Harvard University Press.

Sen, A. 2010. "Sustainable Development and Our Responsibilities." *Notizie di Politeia* 26(98): 129–137.

Sen, A. 2013. "The Ends and Means of Sustainability." *Journal of Human Development and Capabilities* 14(1): 6–20.

Sen, A. 2014. "Global Warming Is Just One of Many Environmental Threats That Demand Our Attention." *The New Republic,* 22 August. https://newrepublic.com/article/118969/environmentalists-obsess-about-global-warming-ignore-poor-countries. Accessed 18 November 2020.

Sengupta, S. 2020. "China, in Pointed Message to U.S., Tightens Its Climate Targets." *New York Times*, 22 September. https://www.nytimes.com/2020/09/22/climate/china-emissions.html . Accessed 1 December 2020.

Sessa, K. 2019. "The New Environmental Fall of Rome: A Methodological Consideration." *Journal of Late Antiquity* 12(1): 211–255.

SET (Supporting Economic Transformation). 2020. "Country Policy Responses to Covid-19." https://set.odi.org/wp-content/uploads/2020/09/Country-fiscal-and-monetary-policy-responses-to-coronavirus_12-Aug-2020-.pdf. Accessed 30 November 2020.

Seto, K. C., Golden, J. S., Alberti, M., and Turner, B. L. 2017. "Sustainability in an Urbanizing Planet." *Proceedings of the National Academy of Sciences* 114(34): 8935–8938.

Sharma, A. K., and Thakur, N. 2017. "Assessing the Impact of Small Hydropower Projects in Jammu and Kashmir: A Study from North-Western Himalayan Region of India." *Renewable and Sustainable Energy Reviews* 80: 679–693.

Sharp, G. 2011. "Loss of Genetic Diversity in U.S. Food Crops." *Sociological Images* [blog], 19 July. https://thesocietypages.org/socimages/2011/07/19/loss-of-genetic-diversity-in-u-s-food-crops/. Accessed 25 November 2020.

Sharpe, B., Hodgson, A., Leicester, G., Lyon, A., and Fazey, I. 2016. "Three Horizons: A Pathways Practice for Transformation." *Ecology and society* 21(2): 32.

Shaxson, N. 2019. "Tackling Tax Havens." *Finance & Development* 56(3): 6–10.

Shepon, A., Eshel, G., Noor, E., and Milo, R. 2018. "The Opportunity Cost of Animal Based Diets Exceeds All Food Losses." *Proceedings of the National Academy of Sciences* 115(15): 3804–3809.

Sherwood, S. C., and Huber, M. 2010. "An Adaptability Limit to Climate Change Due to Heat Stress." *Proceedings of the National Academy of Sciences* 107(21): 9552–9555.

Sherwood, S. C., Webb, M. J., Annan, J. D., Armour, K., Forster, P. M., Hargreaves, J. C., Hegerl, G., and others. 2020. "An Assessment of Earth's Climate Sensitivity Using Multiple Lines of Evidence." *Reviews of Geophysics* 58(4): e2019RG000678.

Shukla, P., Skea, J., Calvo Buendia, E., Masson-Delmotte, V., Pörtner, H., Roberts, D., Zhai, P., and others. 2019. *Climate Change and Land: An IPCC Special Report on Climate Change, Desertification, Land Degradation, Sustainable Land Management, Food Security, and Greenhouse Gas Fluxes in Terrestrial Ecosystems*. Geneva: Intergovernmental Panel on Climate Change.

Simpson, L. B. 2017. *As We Have Always Done: Indigenous Freedom through Radical Resistance*. Saint Paul, MN: University of Minnesota Press.

Singh, N. J., Börger, L., Dettki, H., Bunnefeld, N., and Ericsson, G. 2012. "From Migration to Nomadism: Movement Variability in a Northern Ungulate across Its Latitudinal Range." *Ecological Applications* 22(7): 2007–2020.

Slaughter, A.-M. 2015. "The Paris Approach to Global Governance." *Project Syndicate* 28: 15–12.

Smil, V. 2002. "Nitrogen and Food Production: Proteins for Human Diets." *Ambio* 31(2): 126–131.

Smil, V. 2011. "Harvesting the Biosphere: The Human Impact." *Population and Development Review* 37(4): 613–636.

Smil, V. 2013. *Harvesting the Biosphere: What We Have Taken from Nature*. Cambridge, MA: MIT Press.

Smith, E. K., and Mayer, A. 2018. "A Social Trap for the Climate? Collective Action, Trust and Climate Change Risk Perception in 35 Countries." *Global Environmental Change* 49: 140–153.

Smith, E. K., and Mayer, A. 2019. "Anomalous Anglophones? Contours of Free Market Ideology, Political Polarization, and Climate Change Attitudes in English-Speaking Countries, Western European and Post-Communist States." *Climatic Change* 152(1): 17–34.

Smith, J. 2018. "Bracing for Impact on Mexico's Caribbean Coast, Volunteer Squads of Divers Are Learning to Repair the Coral Reefs that Shield the Shore." The Nature Conservancy, 15 November. https://www.nature.org/en-us/magazine/magazine-articles/bracing-for-impact/. Accessed 25 November 2020.

Smith, K. R., and Ezzati, M. 2005. "How Environmental Health Risks Change with Development: The Epidemiologic and Environmental Risk Transitions Revisited." *Annual Review of Environment and Resources* 30: 291–333.

Smith, M. D., and Floro, M. S. 2020. "Food Insecurity, Gender, and International Migration in Low-and Middle-Income Countries." *Food Policy* 91: 101837.

Smits, J., and Permanyer, I. 2019. "The Subnational Human Development Database." *Scientific Data* 6: 190038.

Snider, E., Dasenbrock-Gammon, N., McBride, R., Debessai, M., Vindana, H., Vencatasamy, K., Lawler, K. V., and others. 2020. "Room-Temperature Superconductivity in a Carbonaceous Sulfur Hydride." *Nature* 586(7829): 373–377.

Snyder-Beattie, A. E., Ord, T., and Bonsall, M. B. 2019. "An Upper Bound for the Background Rate of Human Extinction." *Scientific Reports* 9(1): 1–9.

Sobel, J. 2005. "Interdependent Preferences and Reciprocity." *Journal of Economic Literature* 43(2): 392–436.

Solow, R. M. 1957. "Technical Change and the Aggregate Production Function." *The Review of Economics and Statistics* 39(3): 312–320.

Solow, R. M. 1986. "On the Intergenerational Allocation of Natural Resources." *The Scandinavian Journal of Economics* 88(1): 141. https://doi.org/10.2307/3440280. Accessed 1 December 2020.

Solow, R. M. 1991. *Sustainability: An Economist's Perspective.* Woods Hole, MA: Marine Policy Center.

Solow, R. M. 1993. "An Almost Practical Step toward Sustainability." *Resources Policy* 19(3): 162–172.

Sonter, L. J., Dade, M. C., Watson, J. E. M., and Valenta, R. K. 2020. "Renewable Energy Production Will Exacerbate Mining Threats to Biodiversity." *Nature Communications* 11(1): 4174.

Soroye, P., Newbold, T., and Kerr, J. 2020. "Climate Change Contributes to Widespread Declines among Bumble Bees across Continents." *Science* 367(6478): 685–688.

Sorrell, S., Gatersleben, B., and Druckman, A. 2020. "The Limits of Energy Sufficiency: A Review of the Evidence for Rebound Effects and Negative Spillovers from Behavioural Change." *Energy Research & Social Science* 64: 101439.

Southern Organizing Committee for Economic and Social Justice. 2002. "Air of Injustice." http://www.energyjustice.net/files/coal/Air_of_Injustice.pdf. Accessed 17 November 2020.

Sovacool, B. K., Ali, S. H., Bazilian, M., Radley, B., Nemery, B., Okatz, J., and Mulvaney, D. 2020. "Sustainable Minerals and Metals for a Low-Carbon Future." *Science* 367(6473): 30–33.

Speldewinde, P. C., Cook, A., Davies, P., and Weinstein, P. 2009. "A Relationship between Environmental Degradation and Mental Health in Rural Western Australia." *Health & Place* 15(3): 880–887.

Spence, A., Poortinga, W., Butler, C., and Pidgeon, N. F. 2011. Perceptions of Climate Change and Willingness to Save Energy Related to Flood Experience. *Nature Climate* 1(1): 46–49.

Spence, M. 2011. *The Next Convergence: The Future of Economic Growth in a Multispeed World.* New York: Farrar, Straus and Giroux.

Springmann, M., Godfray, H. C. J., Rayner, M., and Scarborough, P. 2016. "Analysis and Valuation of the Health and Climate Change Cobenefits of Dietary Change." *Proceedings of the National Academy of Sciences* 113(15): 4146–4151.

Stanbury, M., and Rosenman, K. D. 2014. "Occupational Health Disparities: A State Public Health-based Approach." *American Journal of Industrial Medicine,* 57(5): 596–604.

Statista. 2020a. "Amazon's Advertising Spending in the United States from 2012 to 2019." https://www.statista.com/statistics/192254/us-ad-spending-of-amazon/. Accessed 6 August 2020.

Statista. 2020b. "Global Plastic Production from 1950 to 2018." https://www.statista.com/statistics/282732/global-production-of-plastics-since-1950/#statisticContainer. Accessed 11 November 2020.

Statista. 2020c. "Leading Advertisers in Brazil in 2018, Based on Advertising Spending." https://www.statista.com/statistics/257475/leading-advertisers-in-brazil/. Accessed 12 August 2020.

Statista. 2020d. "Lithium-Ion Battery Pack Costs Worldwide between 2011 and 2020." https://www.statista.com/statistics/883118/global-lithium-ion-battery-pack-costs/. Accessed 16 October 2020.

Statista. 2020d. "Procter & Gamble's Advertising Spending in the United States from 2009 to 2019." https://www.statista.com/statistics/191998/ad-spending-of-procter-and-gamble-in-the-us/. Accessed 6 August 2020.

Stedman, R. C. 2003. "Sense of Place and Forest Science: Toward a Program of Quantitative Research." *Forest Science* 49(6): 822–829.

Stedman, R. C. 2016. "Subjectivity and Social-Ecological Systems: A Rigidity Trap (and Sense of Place as a Way Out)." *Sustainability Science* 11(6): 891–901.

Stefanakis, A. I. 2020. "Constructed Wetlands for Sustainable Wastewater Treatment in Hot and Arid Climates: Opportunities, Challenges and Case Studies in the Middle East." *Water* 12(6): 1665.

Steffen, W., Crutzen, P. J., and McNeill, J. R. 2007. "The Anthropocene: Are Humans Now Overwhelming the Great Forces of Nature." *Ambio* 36(8): 614–621.

Steffen, W., Leinfelder, R., Zalasiewicz, J., Waters, C. N., Williams, M., Summerhayes, C., Barnosky, A. D., and others. 2016. "Stratigraphic and Earth System Approaches to Defining the Anthropocene." *Earth's Future* 4(8): 324–345.

Steffen, W., Richardson, K., Rockström, J., Cornell, S. E., Fetzer, I., Bennett, E. M., Biggs, R., and others. 2015. "Planetary Boundaries: Guiding Human Development on a Changing Planet." *Science* 347(6223): 1259855.

Steffen, W., Richardson, K., Rockström, J., Schellnhuber, H. J., Dube, O. P., Dutreuil, S., Lenton, T. M., and Lubchenco, J. 2020. "The Emergence and Evolution of Earth System Science." *Nature Reviews Earth & Environment* 1(1): 54–63.

Steffen, W., Rockström, J., and Costanza, R. 2011. "How Defining Planetary Boundaries Can Transform Our Approach to Growth." *The Solutions Journal* 2(3): 59–65.

Steffen, W., Rockström, J., Richardson, K., Lenton, T. M., Folke, C., Liverman, D., Summerhayes, C. P., and others. 2018. "Trajectories of the Earth System in the Anthropocene." *Proceedings of the National Academy of Sciences* 115(33): 8252–8259.

Steffensen, J. P., Andersen, K. K., Bigler, M., Clausen, H. B., Dahl-Jensen, D., Fischer, H., Goto-Azuma, K., and others. 2008. "High-Resolution Greenland Ice Core Data Show Abrupt Climate Change Happens in Few Years." *Science* 321: 680–684.

Steg, L. 2016. "Values, Norms, and Intrinsic Motivation to Act Proenvironmentally." *Annual Review of Environment and Resources* 41: 277–292.

Steinberger, J. K., and Roberts, J. T. 2010. "From Constraint to Sufficiency: The Decoupling of Energy and Carbon from Human Needs, 1975–2005." *Ecological Economics* 70(2): 425–433.

Steinberger, J. K., Krausmann, F., Getzner, M., Schandl, H., and West, J. 2013. "Development and Dematerialization: An International Study." *PLOS ONE* 8(10): e70385.

Steinberger, J. K., Lamb, W. F., and Sakai, M. 2020. "Your Money or Your Life? The Carbon-Development Paradox." *Environmental Research Letters* 15(4): 044016.

Stephens, L., Fuller, D., Boivin, N., Rick, T., Gauthier, N., Kay, A., Marwick, B., and others. 2019. "Archaeological Assessment Reveals Earth's Early Transformation through Land Use." *Science* 365(6456): 897–902.

Sterling, E. J., Filardi, C., Toomey, A., Sigouin, A., Betley, E., Gazit, N., Newell, J., and others. 2017. "Biocultural Approaches to Well-Being and Sustainability Indicators across Scales." *Nature Ecology & Evolution* 1(12): 1798–1806.

Stern, N. 2013. "The Structure of Economic Modeling of the Potential Impacts of Climate Change: Grafting Gross Underestimation of Risk onto Already Narrow Science Models." *Journal of Economic Literature* 51(3): 838–859.

Stern, N. H., Peters, S., Bakhshi, V., Bowen, A., Cameron, C., Catovsky, S., Crane, D., and others. 2006. *Stern Review: The Economics of Climate Change.* Cambridge, MA: Cambridge University Press.

Stern, P. C. 1986. "Blind Spots in Policy Analysis: What Economics Doesn't Say About Energy Use." *Journal of Policy Analysis and Management* 5(2): 200–227.

Stern, P. C., Janda, K. B., Brown, M. A., Steg, L., Vine, E. L., and Lutzenhiser, L. 2016. "Opportunities and Insights for Reducing Fossil Fuel Consumption by Households and Organizations." *Nature Energy* 1(5): 1–6.

Stewart, F. 2005. "Horizontal Inequalities: A Neglected Dimension of Development." *Wider Perspectives on Global Development.* Springer.

Stewart, F. 2013. "Capabilities and Human Development: Beyond the Individual-the Critical Role of Social Institutions and Social Competencies." UNDP–HDRO Occasional Papers 2013/03. United Nations Development Programme–Human Development

Report Office, New York. http://hdr.undp.org/sites/default/files/hdro_1303_stewart.pdf. Accessed 9 December 2020.

Stewart, F. 2014. "Sustainability and Inequality." *Development* 57(3-4): 344–361.

Stewart, F. 2016. "The Dynamics of Horizontal Inequalities." http://hdr.undp.org/en/content/dynamics-horizontal-inequalities. Accessed 11 November 2020.

Stewart, F., Ranis, G., and Samman, E. 2018. *Advancing Human Development: Theory and Practice.* Oxford, UK: Oxford University Press.

Stiglitz, J. E., Fitoussi, J.-P., and Durand, M. 2018. *Beyond GDP: Measuring What Counts for Economic and Social Performance.* Paris: OECD Publishing.

Stiglitz, J. E., and Greenwald, B. C. 2014. *Creating a Learning Society: A New Approach to Growth, Development, and Social Progress.* New York: Columbia University Press.

Stiglitz, J. E., Sen, A., and Fitoussi, J.-P. 2009. *Report by the Commission on the Measurement of Economic Performance and Social Progress.* https://www.economie.gouv.fr/files/finances/presse/dossiers_de_presse/090914mesure_perf_eco_progres_social/synthese_ang.pdf. Accessed 2 December 2020.

Stiglitz, J. E., Sen, A., and Fitoussi, J.-P. 2010. *Mismeasuring Our Lives: Why GDP Doesn't Add Up.* New York: The New Press.

Stiglitz, J. E., Stern, N., Duan, M., Edenhofer, O., Giraud, G., Heal, G. M., la Rovere, E. L., and others. 2017. *Report of the High-Level Commission on Carbon Prices.* Carbon Pricing Leadership Coalition. Washington, DC: World Bank.

Stirling, A. 2019. "How Deep Is Incumbency? A 'Configuring Fields' Approach to Redistributing and Reorienting Power in Socio-Material Change." *Energy Research & Social Science* 58: 101239.

Stokes, A., Atger, C., Bengough, A. G., Fourcaud, T., and Sidle, R. C. 2009. "Desirable Plant Root Traits for Protecting Natural and Engineered Slopes against Landslides." *Plant and Soil* 324(1–2): 1–30.

Stokes, G., Barbee, B., Bottke Jr, W., Buie, M., Chesley, S., and Chodas, P. 2017. "Update to Determine the Feasibility of Enhancing the Search and Characterization of NEOs." Report of the Near-Earth Object Science Definition Team, US National Aeronautics and Space Administration, Washington, DC.

Stokey, N. 2020. "Technology Diffusion." Working Paper 27466, National Bureau of Economic Research, Cambridge, MA.

Stonedahl, F., and Wilensky, U. 2010. "Finding Forms of Flocking: Evolutionary Search in ABM Parameter-Spaces." In Bosse, T., Geller, A., and Jonker, C. M., (eds.), *Multi-Agent-Based Simulation XI: MABS 2010.* Lecture Notes in Computer Science, Volume 6532. Berlin: Springer. https://doi.org/10.1007/978-3-642-18345-4_5.

Striessnig, E., Lutz, W., and Patt, A. G. 2013. "Effects of Educational Attainment on Climate Risk Vulnerability." *Ecology and Society* 18(1).

Stroebe, W., and Frey, B. S. 1982. "Self-Interest and Collective Action: The Economics and Psychology of Public Goods." *British Journal of Social Psychology* 21(2): 121–137.

Strubell, E., Ganesh, A., and McCallum, A. 2019. "Energy and Policy Considerations for Deep Learning in NLP." https://arxiv.org/abs/1906.02243. Accessed 17 November 2020.

Strunz, S., Marselle, M., and Schröter, M. 2019. "Leaving the 'Sustainability or Collapse' Narrative Behind." *Sustainability Science* 14(3): 1–12.

Stubblefield, C. 2018. "Managing the Planet: The Anthropocene, Good Stewardship, and the Empty Promise of a Solution to Ecological Crisis." *Societies* 8(2): 38.

Sullivan, M. J. P., Lewis, S. L., Affum-Baffoe, K., Castilho, C., Costa, F., Sanchez, A. C., Ewango, C. E. N., and others. 2020. "Long-Term Thermal Sensitivity of Earth's Tropical Forests." *Science* 368(6493): 869–874.

Sullivan, S. 2013. "Nature on the Move III: (Re)countenancing an Animate Nature." *New Proposals: Journal of Marxism and Interdisciplinary Inquiry* 6 (1-2): 50–71.

Sultan, B., Roudier, P., Quirion, P., Alhassane, A., Muller, B., Dingkuhn, M., Ciais, P., and others. 2013. "Assessing Climate Change Impacts on Sorghum and Millet Yields in the Sudanian and Sahelian Savannas of West Africa." *Environmental Research Letters* 8(1): 014040.

Sultana, F. 2014. "Gendering Climate Change: Geographical Insights." *The Professional Geographer* 66(3): 372–381.

Sun, S., Fang, C., and Lv, J. 2017. "Spatial Inequality of Water Footprint in China: A Detailed Decomposition of Inequality from Water Use Types and Drivers." *Journal of Hydrology* 553: 398–407.

Sun, S., Xu, X., Lao, Z., Liu, W., Li, Z., García, E. H., He, L., and Zhu, J. 2017. "Evaluating the Impact of Urban Green Space and Landscape Design Parameters on Thermal Comfort in Hot Summer by Numerical Simulation." *Building and Environment* 123: 277–288.

Sunderland, T. C. 2011. "Food Security: Why Is Biodiversity Important?" *International Forestry Review* 13(3): 265–274.

Sunderland, T. C., Abanda, F., de Camino, R., Matakala, F., and May, P. 2013a. "Sustainable Forestry and Food Security and Nutrition." Technical Report 11, Committee on World Food Security, High Level Panel of Experts on Food Security and Nutrition, Food and Agriculture Organization of the United Nations, Rome.

Sunderland, T. C., Powell, B., Ickowitz, A., Foli, S., Pinedo-Vasquez, M., Nasi, R., and Padoch, C. 2013b. *Food Security and Nutrition.* Bogor, Indonesia: Center for International Forestry Research.

Sustainability Accounting Standards Board. 2020. "Active Projects." https://www.sasb.org/standard-setting-process/current-projects/?utm_medium=email&_hsmi=90943966&_hsenc=p2ANqtz-8Zs7ZvZ_mV-fvIaq4CWN-JhSlB9gjQSmWy-kmhendrHs6Jv3YmSBmnLsbVu3TkQd8d6OObNltnMxUJu5FBEvn0BH3mfQ&utm_content=90943560&utm_source=hs_email. Accessed November 18 2020.

Sustainable Fisheries. n.d. "What Does the World Eat?" https://sustainablefisheries-uw.org/seafood-101/what-does-the-world-eat/. Accessed 25 November 2020.

Sutton, T., and Siciliano, A. 2016. "Seafood Slavery: Human trafficking in the International Fishing Industry." Center for American Progress. https://www.americanprogress.org/issues/green/reports/2016/12/15/295088/seafood-slavery/. Accessed 17 November 2020.

Swire-Thompson, B., Ecker, U. K. H., Lewandowsky, S., and Berinsky, A. J. 2020. "They Might Be a Liar but They're My Liar: Source Evaluation and the Prevalence of Misinformation." *Political Psychology* 41(1): 21–34.

Swiss Re Group. 2019. "Designing a New Type of Insurance to Protect the Coral Reefs, Economies and the Planet." Press Release, 10 December. https://www.swissre.com/our-business/public-sector-solutions/thought-leadership/new-type-of-insurance-to-protect-coral-reefs-economies.html. Accessed 25 November 2020.

Szerszynski, B. 2016. "Viewing the Technosphere in an Interplanetary Light." *The Anthropocene Review* 4(2): 92–102

Szkordilisz, F. 2014. "Mitigation of Urban Heat Island by Green Spaces." *Pollack Periodica* 9(1): 91–100.

Tambo, J. A. 2016. "Adaptation and Resilience to Climate Change and Variability in North-East Ghana." *International Journal of Disaster Risk Reduction* 17: 85–94.

Tankari, M. 2018. "Rainfall Variability and Farm Households Food Insecurity in Burkina Faso: The Nonfarm Enterprises as Coping Strategy." *Food Security* 12: 567–578.

Taubenberger, J. K., and Morens, D. M. 2006. "1918 Influenza: The Mother of All Pandemics." *Revista Biomedica* 17(1): 69–79.

Tavoni, A., Dannenberg, A., Kallis, G., and Löschel, A. 2011. "Inequality, Communication, and the Avoidance of Disastrous Climate Change in a Public Goods Game." *Proceedings of the National Academy of Sciences* 108(29): 11825–11829.

Taylor, D. 2011. "Pygmies of Central Africa Driven from Ancestral Jungles." *Voice of America*, 11 April. https://www.voanews.com/africa/pygmies-central-africa-driven-ancestral-jungles. Accessed 17 November 2020.

Taylor, L. H., Latham, S. M., and Woolhouse, M. E. 2001. "Risk Factors for Human Disease Emergence." *Philosophical Transactions of the Royal Society of London. Series B: Biological Sciences* 356(1411): 983–989.

Taylor, M. 2020. "Greta Thunberg Says EU Recovery Plan Fails to Tackle Climate Crisis." *The Guardian*, 21 July. https://www.theguardian.com/environment/2020/jul/21/greta-thunberg-says-eu-recovery-plans-climate-provisions-inadequate. Accessed 1 December 2020.

TCFD (Task Force on Climate-Related Financial Disclosures). 2019. *Task Force on Climate-Related Financial Disclosures: Status Report.* Basel, Switzerland: Bank for International Settlements.

TEEB for Agriculture & Food. 2018. "An Initiative of 'The Economics of Ecosystems and Biodiversity (TEEB).'" http://teebweb.org/agrifood/. Accessed 25 November 2020.

Teh, L. C. L., Caddell, R., Allison, E. H., Finkbeiner, E. M., Kittinger, J. N., Nakamura, K., and Ota, Y. 2019. "The Role of Human Rights in Implementing Socially Responsible Seafood." *PLOS ONE* 14(1): e0210241.

Tengö, M., Brondizio, E. S., Elmqvist, T., Malmer, P., and Spierenburg, M. 2014. "Connecting Diverse Knowledge Systems for Enhanced Ecosystem Governance: The Multiple Evidence Base Approach." *Ambio* 43(5): 579–591.

Tessum, C. W., Apte, J. S., Goodkind, A. L., Muller, N. Z., Mullins, K. A., Paolella, D. A., Polasky, S., and others. 2019. "Inequity in Consumption of Goods and Services Adds to Racial–Ethnic Disparities in Air Pollution Exposure." *Proceedings of the National Academy of Sciences* 116(13): 6001–6006.

Tetlock, P. E. 2003. "Thinking the Unthinkable: Sacred Values and Taboo Cognitions." *Trends in Cognitive Sciences* 7(7): 320–324.

Theotokis, A., and Manganari, E. 2015. "The Impact of Choice Architecture on Sustainable Consumer Behavior: The Role of Guilt." *Journal of Business Ethics* 131(2): 423–437.

Theurl, M. C., Lauk, C., Kalt, G., Mayer, A., Kaltenegger, K., Morais, T. G., Teixeira, R. F. M., and others. 2020. "Food Systems in a Zero-Deforestation World: Dietary Change Is More Important Than Intensification for Climate Targets in 2050." *Science of the Total Environment* 735: 139353.

Thomas, J. A. 2019. "Why the "Anthropocene" Is Not "Climate Change" and Why It Matters." *AsiaGlobal Online*, 10 January. https://www.asiaglobalonline.hku.hk/anthropocene-climate-change/. Accessed 18 November 2020.

Thomas, K., Hardy, R. D., Lazrus, H., Mendez, M., Orlove, B., Rivera-Collazo, I., Roberts, J. T., and others. 2018. "Explaining Differential Vulnerability to Climate Change: A Social Science Review." *Wiley Interdisciplinary Reviews: Climate Change* 10(2): 565–583.

Thornton, T., and Deur, D. 2015. "Introduction to the Special Section on Marine Cultivation among Indigenous Peoples of the Northwest Coast." *Human Ecology* 43(2).

Thunberg, G. 2020. "Fridays for Future." https://fridaysforfuture.org. Accessed 5 August 2020.

Tiberio, L., De Gregorio, E., Biresselioglu, M. E., Demir, M. H., Panno, A., and Carrus, G. 2020. "Psychological Processes and Institutional Actors in the Sustainable Energy Transition: A Case-Study Analysis of a Local Community in Italy." *Frontiers in Psychology* 11: 980.

Tierney, J. E., Poulsen, C. J., Montañez, I. P., Bhattacharya, T., Feng, R., Ford, H. L., Hönisch, B., and others. 2020a. "Past Climates Inform Our Future." *Science* 370(6517).

Tierney, J. E., Zhu, J., King, J., Malevich, S. B., Hakim, G. J., and Poulsen, C. J. 2020b. "Glacial Cooling and Climate Sensitivity Revisited." *Nature* 584(7822): 569–573.

Timperley, J. 2018. "Q&A: How Will China's New Carbon Trading Scheme Work?" *Carbon Brief*, 29 January. https://www.carbonbrief.org/qa-how-will-chinas-new-carbon-trading-scheme-work. Accessed 1 December 2020.

Tobler, R., Rohrlach, A., Soubrier, J., Bover, P., Llamas, B., Tuke, J., Bean, N., and others. 2017. "Aboriginal Mitogenomes Reveal 50,000 Years of Regionalism in Australia." *Nature* 544(7649): 180–184.

Togtokh, C. 2011. "Time to Stop Celebrating the Polluters." *Nature* 479(7373): 269.

Togtokh, C., and Gaffney, O. 2010. "2010 Human Sustainable Development Index." United Nations University. https://ourworld.unu.edu/en/the-2010-human-sustainable-development-index. Accessed 7 December 2020.

Toman, M. 1998. "Why Not to Calculate the Value of the World's Ecosystem Services and Natural Capital." *Ecological Economics* 1(25): 57–60.

Toniello, G., Lepofsky, D., Lertzman-Lepofsky, G., Salomon, A. K., and Rowell, K. 2019. "11,500 Y of Human–Clam Relationships Provide Long-Term Context for Intertidal Management in the Salish Sea, British Columbia." *Proceedings of the National Academy of Sciences* 116(44): 22106–22114.

Torres-Romero, E. J., Giordano, A. J., Ceballos, G., and López-Bao, J. V. 2020. "Reducing the Sixth Mass Extinction: Understanding the Value of Human-Altered Landscapes to the Conservation of the World's Largest Terrestrial Mammals." *Biological Conservation* 249: 108706.

Tortell, P. D. 2020. "Earth 2020: Science, Society, and Sustainability in the Anthropocene." *Proceedings of the National Academy of Sciences* 117(16): 8683–8691.

Tortorice, D. L., Bloom, D. E., Kirby, P., and Regan, J. 2020. "A Theory of Social Impact Bonds." Working Paper 27527, National Bureau of Economic Research, Cambridge, MA.

Trani, J.-F., Bakhshi, P., Bellanca, N., Biggeri, M., and Marchetta, F. 2011. "Disabilities through the Capability Approach Lens: Implications for Public Policies." *Alter* 5(3): 143–157.

Trevisanato, S. I. 2007. "The 'Hittite Plague', an Epidemic of Tularemia and the First Record of Biological Warfare." *Medical Hypotheses* 69(6): 1371–1374.

Trewin, D. 2002. "Measuring Australia's Progress." Australian Bureau of Statistics. https://www.abs.gov.au/ausstats/abs@.nsf/94713dd445ff1425ca2568200192af2/61bc26e9785accc5ca256bdc001223ed!OpenDocument. Accessed 2 December 2020.

Treyer, S. 2020. "Green and Social Recovery: The European Union and Its Member States at the Forefront." IDDRI blog, 1 September. https://www.iddri.org/en/publications-and-events/blog-post/green-and-social-recovery-european-union-and-its-member-states. Accessed 23 November 2020.

Trihartono, A., Viartasiwi, N., and Nisya, C. 2020. "The Giant Step of Tiny Toes: Youth Impact on the Securitization of Climate Change." *IOP Conference Series: Earth and Environmental Science* 485(1): 012007.

Tschofen, P., Azevedo, I. L., and Muller, N. Z. 2019. "Fine Particulate Matter Damages and Value Added in the US Economy." *Proceedings of the National Academy of Sciences* 116(40): 19857–19862.

Tuhoe. 2014. "Te Kawa o Te Urewera." https://www.ngaituhoe.iwi.nz/te-kawa-o-te-urewera. Accessed 17 November 2020.

Turchin, P., Currie, T. E., Whitehouse, H., François, P., Feeney, K., Mullins, D., Hoyer, D., and others. 2018. "Quantitative Historical Analysis Uncovers a Single Dimension of Complexity That Structures Global Variation in Human Social Organization." *Proceedings of the National Academy of Sciences* 115(2): E144–E151.

Turner, B. L., and Fischer-Kowalski, M. 2010. "Ester Boserup: An Interdisciplinary Visionary Relevant for Sustainability." *Proceedings of the National Academy of Sciences* 107(51): 21963–21965.

Turner, J. M. 2018. *The Republican Reversal: Conservatives and the Environment from Nixon to Trump.* Cambridge, MA: Harvard University Press.

Turner, J. M., and Isenberg, A. C. 2020. "Earth Day at 50." *Science* 368(6488): 215.

Turner, R. A., Addison, J., Arias, A., Bergseth, B. J., Marshall, N. A., Morrison, T. H., and Tobin, R. C. 2016. "Trust, Confidence, and Equity Affect the Legitimacy of Natural Resource Governance." *Ecology and Society* 21(3).

Turvey, S. T., and Crees, J. J. 2019. "Extinction in the Anthropocene." *Current Biology* 29(19): R982–R986.

Turvey, S. T., and Saupe, E. E. 2019. "Insights from the Past: Unique Opportunity or Foreign Country?" *Philosophical Transactions of the Royal Society B: Biological Sciences* 374(1788): 20190208.

Twigg, J. 2004. *Disaster Risk Reduction: Mitigation and Preparedness in Development and Emergency Programming.* London: Overseas Development Institute.

Tyree, C., and Morrison, D. 2020. "Plastic Invasion." https://orbmedia.org/stories/Invisibles_plastics/. Accessed 11 November 2020.

UK Department of the Environment, Transport and the Regions. 1999. "Quality of Life Counts: Indicators for a Strategy for Sustainable Development for the United Kingdom: A Baseline Assessment." London.

Ullah, I. I. T., Kuijt, I., and Freeman, J. 2015. "Toward a Theory of Punctuated Subsistence Change." *Proceedings of the National Academy of Sciences* 112(31): 9579–9584.

UN Women (United Nations Entity for Gender Equality and the Empowerment of Women). 2015. *Progress of the World's Women 2015–2016: Transforming Economies, Realizing Rights.* New York.

UN Women (United Nations Entity for Gender Equality and the Empowerment of Women). 2019. *Progress* of the World's Women 2019–2020: Families in a Changing World. New York.

UN-Habitat (United Nations Human Settlement Program). 2011. Hot Cities: Battle-Ground for Climate Change. Nairobi.

UN-Water. 2018. 2018 UN World Water Development Report: Nature-Based Solutions for Water. Geneva.

UNCCD (United Nations Convention to Combat Desertification). 2017. Global Land Outlook. Bonn, Germany.

UNCCD (United Nations Convention to Combat Desertification). 2020. "The Land Degradation Neutrality (LDN) Target Setting Programme." https://www.unccd.int/actions/ldn-target-setting-programme. Accessed 25 November 2020.

UNCTAD (United Nations Conference on Trade and Development). 2017. The Role of Science, Technology and Innovation in Ensuring Food Security by 2030. Geneva.

UNCTAD (United Nations Conference on Trade and Development). 2018. Technology and Innovation Report 2018: Harnessing Frontier Technologies for Sustainable Development. Geneva.

UNCTAD (United Nations Conference on Trade and Development). 2019. The Role of Science, Technology and Innovation in Promoting Renewable Energy by 2030. Geneva.

UNDESA (United Nations Department of Economic and Social Affairs). 2015. "Millennium Development Goals Indicators Website." https://unstats.un.org/unsd/mdg/default.aspx. Accessed 20 October 2020.

UNDESA (United Nations Department of Economic and Social Affairs). 2019a. "EGM: Conservation and the Rights of Indigenous Peoples 23–25 January 2019 Nairobi, Kenya." https://www.un.org/development/desa/indigenouspeoples/news/2018/12/egm-conservation-and-the-rights-of-indigenous-peoples-23-25-january-2019-nairobi-kenya/. Accessed 25 November 2020.

UNDESA (United Nations Department of Economic and Social Affairs). 2019b. World Population Prospects: The 2019 Revision. Rev 1. New York. https://population.un.org/wpp/Publications/Files/WPP2019_Highlights.pdf. Accessed 9 December 2020.

UNDESA (United Nations Department of Economic and Social Affairs). 2020. "SDG Indicators Global Database." https://unstats.un.org/sdgs/indicators/database/. Accessed 20 October 2020.

UNDP (United Nations Development Programme). 1990. Human Development Report 1990: Concept and Measurement of Human Development. New York: Oxford University Press.

UNDP (United Nations Development Programme). 1994. Human Development Report 1994: New Dimensions of Human Security. New York: Oxford University Press.

UNDP (United Nations Development Programme). 2007. Human Development Report 2007/2008: Fighting Climate Change: Human Solidarity in a Divided World. New York.

UNDP (United Nations Development Programme). 2008. "Camalandaan Agroforestry Farmers' Association (CAFA)." Equator Initiative Case Studies, New York. https://www.equatorinitiative.org/2017/05/27/camalandaan-agroforestry-farmers-association-cafa/. Accessed 25 November 2020.

UNDP (United Nations Development Programme). 2010a. "Centre de Ressources en Agroforesterie de Riba (Riba Agroforestry Resource Centre)." Equator Initiative Case Studies, New York. https://www.equatorinitiative.org/2017/05/27/centre-de-ressources-en-agroforesterie-de-riba-riba-agroforestry-resource-centre/. Accessed 25 November 2020.

UNDP (United Nations Development Programme). 2010b. "Consejo Regional Tsimané Mosetene (CRTM, Tsimané Mosetene Regional Council of Pilón Lajas)." Equator Initiative Case Studies, New York. https://www.equatorinitiative.org/2017/05/28/consejo-regional-tsimane-mosetene-crtm-tsimane-mosetene-regional-council-of-pilon-lajas/. Accessed 25 November 2020.

UNDP (United Nations Development Programme). 2010c. Human Development Report 2010. The Real Wealth of Nations: Pathways to Human Development. New York.

UNDP (United Nations Development Programme). 2011. Human Development Report 2011: Sustainability and Equity, A Better Future for All. New York.

UNDP (United Nations Development Programme). 2012. "Alexander Von Humboldt Center." Equator Initiative Case Studies, New York. https://www.equatorinitiative.org/wp-content/uploads/2017/05/case_1370356204-1.pdf. Accessed 25 November 2020.

UNDP (United Nations Development Programme). 2014a. Human Development Report 2014: Sustaining Human Progress: Reducing Vulnerabilities and Building Resilience. New York. http://hdr.undp.org/sites/default/files/hdr14-report-en-1.pdf. Accessed 4 December 2020.

UNDP (United Nations Development Programme). 2014b. "Integrated Development in Focus." Equator Initiative Case Studies, New York. https://www.equatorinitiative.org/wp-content/uploads/2017/05/case_1459268655.pdf. Accessed 25 November 2020.

UNDP (United Nations Development Programme). 2014c. "Jeffrey Town Farmers Association." Equator Initiative Case Studies, New York. https://www.equatorinitiative.org/2017/05/30/jeffrey-town-farmers-association/. Accessed 25 November 2020.

UNDP (United Nations Development Programme). 2014d. "Koolel-Kab/Muuchkambal." Equator Initiative Case Studies, New York. https://www.equatorinitiative.org/2017/05/30/koolel-kabmuuchkambal/. Accessed 25 November 2020.

UNDP (United Nations Development Programme). 2015a. "Consejo Indígena del Pueblo Tacana (CIPTA)." Equator Initiative Case Studies, New York. https://www.equatorinitiative.org/wp-content/uploads/2017/05/CIPTA-Bolivia.pdf. Accessed 25 November 2020.

UNDP (United Nations Development Programme). 2015b. Human Development Report 2015: Work for Human Development. New York.

UNDP (United Nations Development Programme). 2015b. Human Development Report 2015: Work for Human Development. New York.

UNDP (United Nations Development Programme). 2015c. "Yunnan Green Watershed Management Research and Promotion Centrer (Green Watershed)." Equator Initiative Case Studies, New York. https://www.equatorinitiative.org/wp-content/uploads/2017/05/Green-Watershed-China.pdf. Accessed 25 November 2020.

UNDP (United Nations Development Programme). 2017a. "Community Mangrove Forest Conservation of Baan Bang La." Equator Initiative Case Studies, New York. https://www.equatorinitiative.org/2017/06/28/community-mangrove-forest-conservation-of-baan-bang-la/. Accessed 25 November 2020.

UNDP (United Nations Development Programme). 2017b. "Yayasan Planet Indonesia." Equator Initiative Case Studies, New York. https://www.equatorinitiative.org/wp-content/uploads/2019/02/Yayasan-Planet-Indonesia-Case-Study-English-r3.pdf. Accessed 25 November 2020.

UNDP (United Nations Development Programme). 2018. "Turning Unpaid Domestic and Care Work into Development Dividends." New York. https://www.undp.org/content/dam/rbap/docs/gender/RBAP-Gender-2018-Unpaid-Domestic-and-Care-Work-Brochure.pdf. Accessed 20 November 2020.

UNDP (United Nations Development Programme). 2019a. "Cameroon Gender and Environment Watch." Equator Initiative Case Studies, New York. https://www.equatorinitiative.org/2019/07/30/cameroon-gender-and-environment-watch/. Accessed 25 November 2020.

UNDP (United Nations Development Programme). 2019b. "Environmental Management and Development Trust." Equator Initiative Case Studies, New York. https://www.equatorinitiative.org/2019/07/29/environmental-management-and-development-trust/. Accessed 25 November 2020.

UNDP (United Nations Development Programme). 2019c. Human Development Report 2019: Beyond Income, Beyond Averages, Beyond Today: Inequalities in Human Development in the 21st Century. New York.

UNDP (United Nations Development Programme). 2019d. "Tamil Resources Conservation Trust." Equator Initiative Case Studies, New York. https://www.equatorinitiative.org/2019/07/30/tamil-resources-conservation-trust/. Accessed 25 November 2020.

UNDP (United Nations Development Programme). 2020a. "Climate Change Adaptation Impact Gender: Time Poverty." https://www.adaptation-undp.org/Impact2/topics/time.html. Accessed 20 November 2020.

UNDP (United Nations Development Programme). 2020b. Covid-19 and Human Development: Assessing the Crisis, Envisioning the Recovery. 2020 Human Development Perspectives. New York. http://hdr.undp.org/en/hdp-covid. Accessed 9 December 2020.

UNDP (United Nations Development Programme) and Lao PDR Ministry of Energy and Mines 2017.

Circular Economy Strategies for Lao PDR: A Metabolic Approach to Redefine Resource Efficient and Low-Carbon Development. https://www.undp.org/content/undp/en/home/librarypage/climate-and-disaster-resilience-/circular-economy-strategies-for-lao-pdr.html. Accessed 17 November 2020.

UNDP (United Nations Development Programme) and OPHI (Oxford Poverty and Human Development Initiative). 2020. Global Multidimensional Poverty Index 2020: Charting Pathways out of Multidimensional Poverty: Achieving the SDGs. New York. http://hdr.undp.org/sites/default/files/2020_mpi_report_en.pdf. Accessed 9 September 2020.

UNDRR (United Nations Office for Disaster Risk Reduction). 2020. Human Cost of Disasters: An Overview of the Last 20 Years, 2000–2019. Geneva.

UNEP (United Nations Environment Programme). 2011. Environmental Assessment of Ogoniland. Nairobi.

UNEP (United Nations Environment Programme). 2016a. "Half the World to Face Severe Water Stress by 2030 Unless Water Use Is "Decoupled" from Economic Growth, Says International Resource Panel." Press Release, 21 March. https://www.unenvironment.org/news-and-stories/press-release/half-world-face-severe-water-stress-2030-unless-water-use-decoupled. Accessed 25 November 2020.

UNEP (United Nations Environment Programme). 2016b. Options for Decoupling Economic Growth from Water Use and Water Pollution. Nairobi.

UNEP (United Nations Environment Programme). 2016c. Snapshot of the World's Water Quality: Towards a Global Assessment. Nairobi.

UNEP (United Nations Environment Programme). 2017. "UN Declares War on Ocean Plastic." https://www.unenvironment.org/news-and-stories/press-release/un-declares-war-ocean-plastic-0#:~:text=23%20February%202017%20E2%80%93%20UN%20Environment,plastic%20by%20the%20year%202022. Accessed 3 November 2020.

UNEP (United Nations Environment Programme). 2018a. "Africa Is on the Right Path to Eradicate Plastics." https://www.unenvironment.org/news-and-stories/story/africa-right-path-eradicate-plastics. Accessed 10 October 2020.

UNEP (United Nations Environment Programme). 2018b. Inclusive Wealth Report 2018. Nairobi.

UNEP (United Nations Environment Programme). 2019a. Emissions Gap Report 2019. Nairobi. https://www.unenvironment.org/resources/emissions-gap-report-2019. Accessed 4 December 2020.

UNEP (United Nations Environment Programme). 2019b. Global Chemicals Outlook II: From Legacies to Innovative Solutions. Nairobi. https://www.unenvironment.org/resources/report/global-chemicals-outlook-ii-legacies-innovative-solutions. Accessed 9 December 2020.

UNEP (United Nations Environment Programme). 2019c. "Global Environment Outlook—Geo-6: Healthy Planet, Healthy People." https://www.unenvironment.org/global-environment-outlook. Accessed 11 November 2020.

UNEP (United Nations Environment Programme). 2019d. Measuring Progress: Towards Achieving the Environmental Dimension of the SDGs. Nairobi.

UNEP (United Nations Environment Programme). 2020a. The Global Biodiversity Outlook 5. Montreal, QC: Secretariat of the Convention on Biological Diversity. https://www.cbd.int/gbo5. Accessed 9 December 2020.

UNEP (United Nations Environment Programme). 2020b. "UNEP Finance Initiative." Nairobi. https://www.unepfi.org/. Accessed 4 December 2020.

UNEP (United Nations Environment Programme). 2020c. "United Nations Ramps up Drive to Restore the Natural World." https://www.unenvironment.org/news-and-stories/story/united-nations-ramps-drive-restore-natural-world. Accessed 18 November 2020.

UNEP (United Nations Environment Programme). 2020d. "World Environment Situation Room, Data Downloader." https://environmentlive.unep.org/downloader. Accessed 7 December 2020.

UNEP (United Nations Environment Programme), UN Women (United Nations Entity for Gender Equality and the Empowerment of Women), DPPA (United Nations Department of Political and Peacebuilding Affairs) and UNDP (United Nations Development Programme). 2020. Gender, Climate & Security: Sustaining Inclusive Peace on the Frontlines of Climate Change. New York. https://www.unwomen.org/-/media/headquarters/attachments/sections/library/publications/2020/gender-climate-and-security-en.pdf?la=en&vs=215. Accessed 28 November 2020.

UNEP-WCMC (United Nations Environment Programme World Conservation Monitoring Centre) and IUCN (International Union for the Conservation of Nature). 2016. Protected Planet Report 2016: How Protected Areas Contribute to Achieving Global Targets for Biodiversity. Cambridge, UK and Gland, Switzerland: UNEP-WCMC and IUCN.

UNESCO (United Nations Educational, Scientific and Cultural Organization). 2014. "UN Decade of Education for Sustainable Development." https://en.unesco.org/themes/education-sustainable-development/what-is-esd/un-decade-of-esd. Accessed 4 May 2020.

UNESCO (United Nations Educational, Scientific and Cultural Organization). 2016. Education for People and Planet: Creating Sustainable Futures for All. Paris. https://unesdoc.unesco.org/ark:/48223/pf0000245752. Accessed 11 September 2020.

UNESCO (United Nations Educational, Scientific and Cultural Organization). 2020a. "Global Action Programme on Education for Sustainable Development (2015–2019)." https://en.unesco.org/globalactionprogrammeoneducation. Accessed 3 May 2020.

UNESCO (United Nations Educational, Scientific and Cultural Organization). 2020b. United Nations World Water Development Report 2020: Water and Climate Change. Paris.

UNESCO (United Nations Educational, Scientific and Cultural Organization) Institute for Statistics. 2020. Data Centre. http://data.uis.unesco.org. Accessed 21 July 2020.

UNFCCC (United Nations Framework Convention on Climate Change). 2015. Synthesis Report on the Aggregate Effect of the Intended Nationally Determined Contributions. Bonn, Germany: United Nations Framework Convention on Climate Change. https://unfccc.int/resource/docs/2016/cop22/eng/02.pdf. Accessed 1 December 2020.

UNFCCC (United Nations Framework Convention on Climate Change). 2018. "Low-Income Countries Hit Hardest by Soaring Costs of Climate-Related Disasters." https://unfccc.int/news/low-income-countries-hit-hardest-by-soaring-costs-of-climate-related-disasters. Accessed 1 December 2020.

UNFCCC (United Nations Framework Convention on Climate Change). 2019. "Cut Global Emissions by 7.6 Percent Every Year for Next Decade to Meet 1.5°C Paris Target - UN Report." https://unfccc.int/news/cut-global-emissions-by-76-percent-every-year-for-next-decade-to-meet-15degc-paris-target-un-report. Accessed 1 December 2020

UNFCCC (United Nations Framework Convention on Climate Change). 2020. "Ratification of Multilateral Climate Agreement Gives Boost to Delivering Agreed Climate Pledges and to Tackling Climate Change." UN Climate Press Release, 2 October. https://unfccc.int/news/ratification-of-multilateral-climate-agreement-gives-boost-to-delivering-agreed-climate-pledges-and. Accessed 1 December 2020.

UNHRC (United Nations Human Rights Council). 2018. "Report of the Special Rapporteur on the Rights of Indigenous Peoples." New York. https://undocs.org/A/HRC/39/17. Accessed 25 November 2020.

United Church of Christ Commission for Racial Justice 1987. Toxic Wastes and Race in the United States: A National Report on the Racial and Socio-Economic Characteristics of Communities with Hazardous Waste Sites. Public Data Access. https://www.nrc.gov/docs/ML1310/ML13109A339.pdf. Accessed 20 November 2020.

United Kingdom HM Treasury. 2020. A Roadmap Towards Mandatory Climate-Related Disclosures. https://assets.publishing.service.gov.uk/government/uploads/system/uploads/attachment_data/file/933783/FINAL_TCFD_ROADMAP.pdf. Accessed 23 November 2020.

United Nations Statistics Division. 2020a. Global SDG Indicators Database. https://unstats.un.org/sdgs/indicators/database/. Accessed 28 September 2020.

United Nations Statistics Division. 2020b. National Accounts Main Aggregates Database. http://unstats.un.org/unsd/snaama. Accessed 15 July 2020.

United Nations Sustainable Development Group. 2020. People's Money: Harnessing Digitalization to Finance a Sustainable Future. https://unsdg.un.org/resources/peoples-money-harnessing-digitalization-finance-sustainable-future. Accessed 17 November 2020.

United Nations. 2015a. "Sustainable Development Goals." https://sustainabledevelopment.un.org/sdgs. Accessed 5 May 2020.

United Nations. 2015b. Transforming Our World: The 2030 Agenda for Sustainable Development. New York. https://sustainabledevelopment.un.org/

post2015/transformingourworld/publication. Accessed 9 December 2020.

United Nations. 2017. "Factsheet: Marine Pollution." https://sustainabledevelopment.un.org/content/documents/Ocean_Factsheet_Pollution.pdf. Accessed 11 November 2020.

United Nations. 2018. "The Valuation of Ecosystem Services and Assets for SEEA Ecosystem Accounting." New York.

United Nations. 2019a. "Natural Capital and Ecosystem Services FAQ." https://seea.un.org/content/natural-capital-and-ecosystem-services-faq. Accessed 2 December 2020.

United Nations. 2019b. "Statement by the UN Secretary-General António Guterres on the Outcome of COP25." https://unfccc.int/news/statement-by-the-un-secretary-general-antonio-guterres-on-the-outcome-of-cop25. Accessed 23 September 2020.

United Nations. 2019c. "UN Report: Nature's Dangerous Decline 'Unprecedented'; Species Extinction Rates 'Accelerating'." https://www.un.org/sustainabledevelopment/blog/2019/05/nature-decline-unprecedented-report/. Accessed 30 November 2020.

United Nations. 2020a. "Education During Covid-19 and Beyond." Policy Brief, New York.

United Nations. 2020b. "Exploring Space Technologies for Sustainable Development and the Benefits of International Research Collaboration in This Context." New York.

United Nations. 2020c. "Policy Brief: The Impact of Covid-19 on Latin America and the Caribbean." https://www.un.org/sites/un2.un.org/files/sg_policy_brief_covid_lac.pdf. Accessed 13 October 2020.

United Nations. 2020d. Report of the UN Economist Network for the UN 75th Anniversary: Shaping the Trends of Our Time. New York.

United Nations. 2020e. "SDG Indicators Metadata Repository." https://unstats.un.org/sdgs/metadata/. Accessed 2 December 2020.

United Nations. 2020f. "SEEA Experimental Ecosystem Accounting Revision 2020: Revision Issues Note-Final." New York.

United Nations. 2020g. "Sustainable Development Goals, Goal 2: Zero Hunger." https://www.un.org/sustainabledevelopment/hunger/. Accessed 11 September 2020.

United Nations. 2020h. "Sustainable Development Goals, Goal 4: Quality Education." https://www.un.org/sustainabledevelopment/education/. Accessed 11 September 2020.

United Nations. 2020i. "We Can End Poverty: Millennium Development Goals and Beyond 2015." https://www.un.org/millenniumgoals/poverty.shtml. Accessed 18 November 2020.

United Nations. n.d. "United Nations Treaty Collection." https://treaties.un.org/. Accessed 17 November 2020.

UNPFII (United Nations Permanent Forum on Indigenous Issues). 2016a. Backgrounder: Climate Change and Indigenous Peoples. New York.

UNPFII (United Nations Permanent Forum on Indigenous Issues). 2016b. State of the World's Indigenous Peoples: Indigenous People's Access to Health Services. New York.

US Department of Homeland Security. 2016. "Draft Interagency Concept for Community Resilience Indicators and National-Level Measures." Washington, DC.

US Department of the Interior. 2017. "Dynamics of Lynx Populations in Relation to Snowshoe Hare Abundance in the Boreal Forest." https://eros.usgs.gov/doi-remote-sensing-activities/2017/fws/dynamics-lynx-populations-relation-snowshoe-hare-abundance-boreal-forest.

US Federal Reserve Board. 2020. "Financial Stability Report – November." https://www.federalreserve.gov/publications/2020-november-financial-stability-report-near-term-risks.htm. Accessed 2 December 2020.

US General Accounting Office. 1983. "Siting of Hazardous Waste Landfills and Their Correlation with Racial and Economic Status of Surrounding Communities." RCED-83-168, Gaithersburg, MD.

Uzzell, D. 1994. "Children as Catalysts of Environmental Change: Final Report." https://cordis.europa.eu/docs/projects/files/EV5V/EV5V0157/34266871-6_en.pdf . Accessed 25 November 2020.

Vahtera, E., Conley, D. J., Gustafsson, B. G., Kuosa, H., Pitkänen, H., Savchuk, O. P., Tamminen, T., and others. 2007. "Internal Ecosystem Feedbacks Enhance Nitrogen-Fixing Cyanobacteria Blooms and Complicate Management in the Baltic Sea." Ambio 36(2): 186–194.

Van Der Kam, M., Peters, A., Van Sark, W., and Alkemade, F. 2019. "Agent-Based Modelling of Charging Behaviour of Electric Vehicle Drivers." Journal of Artificial Societies and Social Simulation 22(4).

Van der Land, V., and Hummel, D. 2013. "Vulnerability and the Role of Education in Environmentally Induced Migration in Mali and Senegal." Ecology and Society 18(4).

Van Der Leeuw, S. 2020. Social Sustainability, Past and Future: Undoing Unintended Consequences for the Earth's Survival. Cambridge, UK: Cambridge University Press.

Van der Zee, R. 2015. "How Amsterdam Became the Bicycle Capital of the World." The Guardian, 5 May. https://www.theguardian.com/cities/2015/may/05/amsterdam-bicycle-capital-world-transport-cycling-kindermoord. Accessed 11 November 2020.

van Ginkel, K. C., Botzen, W. W., Haasnoot, M., Bachner, G., Steininger, K. W., Hinkel, J., Watkiss, P., and others. 2020. "Climate Change Induced Socio-Economic Tipping Points: Review and Stakeholder Consultation for Policy Relevant Research." Environmental Research Letters 15(2): 023001.

Van Vuuren, D. P., Stehfest, E., Gernaat, D. E., Van Den Berg, M., Bijl, D. L., De Boer, H. S., Daioglou, V., and others. 2018. "Alternative Pathways to the 1.5

°C Target Reduce the Need for Negative Emission Technologies." Nature Climate Change 8(5): 391–397.

Vatn, A. 2009. "Cooperative Behavior and Institutions." The Journal of Socio-Economics 38(1): 188–196.

Vaughter, P. 2016. "Climate Change Education: From Critical Thinking to Critical Action." Policy Brief 4, United Nations University, Institute for the Advanced Study of Sustainability, Tokyo. https://www.uncclearn.org/wp-content/uploads/library/unuias_pb_4.pdf. Accessed 11 November 2020.

Veiga, J. M., Vlachogianni, T., Pahl, S., Thompson, R. C., Kopke, K., Doyle, T. K., Hartley, B. L., and others. 2016. "Enhancing Public Awareness and Promoting Co-Responsibility for Marine Litter in Europe: The Challenge of Marlisco." Marine Pollution Bulletin 102(2): 309–315.

Venables, A. J. 2016. "Using Natural Resources for Development: Why Has It Proven So Difficult?" Journal of Economic Perspectives 30(1): 161–84.

Venegas-Li, R., Morales-Barquero, L., and Martínez-Fernández, D. 2013. "Mapping Mangrove Species Composition with Rapideye Satellite Images in the Nicoya Gulf, Costa Rica: How Far Can We Go?" Association for Tropical Biology and Conservation. https://www.researchgate.net/publication/257128663_Mapping_Mangrove_Species_Composition_with_Rapideye_Satellite_Images_in_the_Nicoya_Gulf_Costa_Rica_How_far_can_we_go. Accessed 25 November 2020.

Venter, Z. S., Aunan, K., Chowdhury, S., and Lelieveld, J. 2020. "COVID-19 Lockdowns Cause Global Air Pollution Declines with Implications for Public Health Risk." medRxiv. https://www.medrxiv.org/content/10.1101/2020.04.10.20060673v1.full.pdf. Accessed 17 November 2020.

Verburg, P. H., Dearing, J. A., Dyke, J. G., Van Der Leeuw, S., Seitzinger, S., Steffen, W., and Syvitski, J. 2016. "Methods and Approaches to Modelling the Anthropocene." Global Environmental Change 39: 328–340.

Vermeylen, S. 2019. "Special Issue: Epistemic Violence and Environmental Justice." Local Environment: The International Journal of Justice and Sustainability 24(2): 89–93.

Vezich, I. S., Gunter, B. C., and Lieberman, M. D. 2017. "The Mere Green Effect: An Fmri Study of Pro-Environmental Advertisements." Social Neuroscience 12(4): 400–408.

Victor, D. G. 2019. "We Have Climate Leaders. Now We Need Followers." New York Times, 13 December. https://www.nytimes.com/2019/12/13/opinion/climate-change-madrid.html. Accessed 1 December 2020.

Victor, D. G., Akimoto, K., Kaya, Y., Yamaguchi, M., Cullenward, D., and Hepburn, C. 2017. "Prove Paris Was More Than Paper Promises." Nature News 548(7665): 25.

Vidal, J. 2020. "'Tip of the Iceberg': Is Our Destruction of Nature Responsible for Covid-19?" The Guardian, 18 March. https://www.theguardian.com/environment/2020/mar/18/tip-of-the-iceberg-is-our-destruction-of-nature-responsible-for-covid-19-aoe. Accessed 11 November 2020.

Villa, M. 2017. "Women Own Less Than 20% of the World's Land: It's Time to Give Them Equal Property Rights." Davos, Switzerland: World Economic Forum.

Vince, G. 2020. *Transcendence: How Humans Evolved through Fire, Language, Beauty, and Time.* New York: Basic Books.

Vira, B., Agarwal, B., Jamnadas, R., Kleinschmit, D., McMullin, S., Mansourian, S., Neufeldt, H., and others. 2015. "Introduction." In Vira, B., Wildburger, C., and Mansourian, S., (eds.), *Forests, Trees and Landscapes for Food Security and Nutrition,* IUFRO World Series Vol. 33: 14–23. Vienna: International Union of Forest Research Organizations.

Vita, G., Hertwich, E. G., Stadler, K., and Wood, R. 2019. "Connecting Global Emissions to Fundamental Human Needs and Their Satisfaction." *Environmental Research Letters* 14(1): 014002.

Vollset, S. E., Goren, E., Yuan, C.-W., Cao, J., Smith, A. E., Hsiao, T., Bisignano, C., and others. 2020. "Fertility, Mortality, Migration, and Population Scenarios for 195 Countries and Territories from 2017 to 2100: A Forecasting Analysis for the Global Burden of Disease Study." *The Lancet* 396(10258): 1295–1306.

Volterra, V. 1926. "Fluctuations in the Abundance of a Species Considered Mathematically." *Nature* 119(12–13).

Von Grebmer, K., Saltzman, A., Birol, E., Wiesman, D., Prasai, N., Yin, S., Yohannes, Y., and others. 2014. *2014 Global Hunger Index: The Challenge of Hidden Hunger.* Washington, DC: International Food Policy Research Institute.

Voosen, P. 2020. "No Asteroids Needed: Ancient Mass Extinction Tied to Ozone Loss, Warming Climate." *Science,* 27 May. https://www.sciencemag.org/news/2020/05/no-asteroids-or-volcanoes-needed-ancient-mass-extinction-tied-ozone-loss-warming. Accessed 20 November 2020.

Vörösmarty, C. J., Osuna, V. R., Cak, A. D., Bhaduri, A., Bunn, S. E., Corsi, F., Gastelumendi, J., and others. 2018. "Ecosystem-Based Water Security and the Sustainable Development Goals (SDGs)." *Ecohydrology & Hydrobiology* 18(4): 317–333.

Vörösmarty, C. J., Osuna, V. R., Koehler, D., Klop, P., Spengler, J., Buonocore, J., Cak, A., and others. 2018. "Scientifically Assess Impacts of Sustainable Investments." *Science* 359(6375): 523–525.

Waal, F. d. 2009. *Primates and Philosophers: How Morality Evolved.* Princeton, NJ: Princeton University Press.

Wackernagel, M., Lin, D., Evans, M., Hanscom, L., and Raven, P. 2019. "Defying the Footprint Oracle: Implications of Country Resource Trends." *Sustainability* 11(7): 2164.

Wackernagel, M., and Rees, W. 1996. *Our Ecological Footprint: Reducing Human Impact on the Earth.* New Society Publishers.

Wada, Y., Flörke, M., Hanasaki, N., Eisner, S., Fischer, G., Tramberend, S., Satoh, Y., and others. 2016. "Modeling Global Water Use for the 21st Century: The Water Futures and Solutions (WFaS) Initiative and Its Approaches." *Geoscientific Model Development* 9(1): 175–222.

Waikato-Tainui. 2013. "Tai Timu, Tai Pari, Tai Ao: Waikato-Tainui Environmental Plan." https://waikatotainui.com/wp-content/uploads/2020/11/Tai-Tumu-Tai-Pari-Tai-Ao-PLAN-ENGLISH.pdf. Accessed 30 November 2020.

Waisman, H., Bataille, C., Winkler, H., Jotzo, F., Shukla, P., Colombier, M., Buira, D. and others. 2019. "A Pathway Design Framework for National Low Greenhouse Gas Emission Development Strategies." *Nature Climate Change* 9: 261–268.

Waitangi Tribunal. 2011. "Ko Aotearoa tēnei: A Report into Claims Concerning New Zealand Law and Policy Affecting Māori Culture and Identity." https://forms.justice.govt.nz/search/Documents/WT/wt_DOC_68356416/KoAotearoaTeneiTT2Vol1W.pdf. Accessed 17 November 2020.

Waldron, A., Adams, V., Allan, J., Arnell, A., Asner, G., Atkinson, S., Baccini, A., and others. 2020. "Protecting 30% of the Planet for Nature: Costs, Benefits and Economic Implications." http://pure.iiasa.ac.at/id/eprint/16560/1/Waldron_Report_FINAL_sml.pdf. Accessed 25 November 2020.

Walker, B., Holling, C. S., Carpenter, S. R., and Kinzig, A. 2004. "Resilience, Adaptability and Transformability in Social–Ecological Systems." *Ecology and Society* 9(2): 5.

Walker, G., and Day, R. 2012. "Fuel Poverty as Injustice: Integrating Distribution, Recognition and Procedure in the Struggle for Affordable Warmth." *Energy Policy* 49: 69–75.

Walker, W. S., Gorelik, S. R., Baccini, A., Aragon-Osejo, J. L., Josse, C., Meyer, C., Macedo, M. N., and others. 2020. "The Role of Forest Conversion, Degradation, and Disturbance in the Carbon Dynamics of Amazon Indigenous Territories and Protected Areas." *Proceedings of the National Academy of Sciences* 117(6): 3015–3025.

Wallace, J., and Minczeski, P. 2020. "Why Common Bonds Signal a New Era for Europe." *The Wall Street Journal,* 22 July. https://www.wsj.com/articles/why-common-bonds-signal-a-new-era-for-europe-11595410330. Accessed 1 December 2020.

Wallace-Wells, D. 2020. "Global Warming Is Melting Our Sense of Time." *New York,* 27 June. https://nymag.com/intelligencer/2020/06/global-warming-is-melting-our-sense-of-time.html. Accessed 1 December 2020.

Wamsler, C. 2020. "Education for Sustainability: Fostering a More Conscious Society and Transformation Towards Sustainability." *International Journal of Sustainability in Higher Education* 21(1): 112–130.

Wamsler, C., Pauleit, S., Zölch, T., Schetke, S., and Mascarenhas, A. 2017. "Mainstreaming Nature-Based Solutions for Climate Change Adaptation in Urban Governance and Planning." *Nature-Based Solutions to Climate Change Adaptation in Urban Areas.* Cham, Switzerland: Springer.

Wang, Z., Jusup, M., Guo, H., Shi, L., Geček, S., Anand, M., Perc, M., and others. 2020. "Communicating Sentiment and Outlook Reverses Inaction against Collective Risks." *Proceedings of the National Academy of Sciences* 117(30): 17650–17655.

Watari, T., McLellan, B. C., Giurco, D., Dominish, E., Yamasue, E., and Nansai, K. 2019. "Total Material Requirement for the Global Energy Transition to 2050: A Focus on Transport and Electricity." *Resources, Conservation and Recycling* 148: 91–103.

Watene, K. 2016. "Valuing Nature: Māori Philosophy and the Capability Approach." *Oxford Development Studies* 44(3): 287–296.

Watene, K., and Merino, R. 2019. "Indigenous People: Self-determination, Decolonization, and Indigenous Philosophies." In Drydyk, J., and Keleher, L., (eds.), *Routledge Handbook of Development Ethics.* Boca Raton, FL: Routledge.

Watene, K., Rochford, T., and Tamariki, N. 2017. *Whānau Ora: Transforming Health and Well-Being, in Stephen Chadwick, How Should We Live? Ethical Issues in Aotearoa New Zealand.* Auckland, New Zealand: Massey University Press.

Watene, K., and Yap, M. 2015. "Culture and Sustainable Development: Indigenous Contributions." *Journal of Global Ethics* 11(1): 51–55.

Water.org. 2020. "Peru's Water and Sanitation Crisis." https://water.org/our-impact/where-we-work/peru/#:~:text=With%20a%20total%20population%20of,access%20to%20safe%20piped%20water. Accessed 27 August 2020.

Waters, C. N., Zalasiewicz, J., Summerhayes, C., Barnosky, A. D., Poirier, C., Gałuszka, A., Cearreta, A., and others. 2016. "The Anthropocene Is Functionally and Stratigraphically Distinct from the Holocene." *Science* 351(6269).

Watershed Agricultural Council. 2019. "Overview." https://www.nycwatershed.org/about-us/overview/. Accessed 18 November 2020.

Watts, J. 2018. "Eight Months on, Is the World's Most Drastic Plastic Bag Ban Working?" *The Guardian,* 25 April. https://www.theguardian.com/world/2018/apr/25/nairobi-clean-up-highs-lows-kenyas-plastic-bag-ban. Accessed 15 October 2020.

Watts, J. 2019. "Environmental Activist Murders Double in 15 Years." *The Guardian,* 5 August. https://www.theguardian.com/environment/2019/aug/05/environmental-activist-murders-double. Accessed 25 November 2020.

WCED (World Commission on Environment and Development). 1987. *Our Common Future.* Oxford, UK: Oxford University Press.

WEF (World Economic Forum). 2019. "Here's How Digitilization Can Boost Recycling Rates." https://www.weforum.org/agenda/2019/01/here-s-how-digitization-can-boost-recycling-rates/. Accessed 17 November 2020.

WEF (World Economic Forum). 2020a. "Global Leaders Must Act Fast to Ensure a Green Recovery." Press Release, 13 July. https://www.weforum.org/agenda/2020/07/global-leaders-act-fast-green-recovery/. Accessed 23 November 2020.

WEF (World Economic Forum). 2020b. *The Global Risks Report 2020.* Geneva. https://www.weforum.org/reports/the-global-risks-report-2020. Accessed 4 December 2020.

WEF (World Economic Forum). 2020c. "The Greta Effect? Why Businesses Are More Committed to Climate Action in 2020." https://www.weforum.org/agenda/2020/02/greta-effect-business-climate-action/. Accessed 11 September 2020.

WEF (World Economic Forum). 2020d. *New Nature Economy Report II: The Future of Nature and Business.* Geneva.

Wehi, P., Whaanga, H., Watene, K., and Steeves, T. 2020. "Mātauranga as Knowledge, Process and Practice in Aotearoa New Zealand." In Thornton, T., and Bhagwat, S., (eds.), *Handbook of Indigenous Environmental Knowledge: Global Themes and Practice.* London: Routledge.

Weisse, M., and Dow Goldman, E. 2020. "We Lost a Football Pitch of Primary Rainforest Every 6 Seconds in 2019." World Resources Institute blog, 2 June. https://www.wri.org/blog/2020/06/global-tree-cover-loss-data-2019. Accessed 17 November 2020.

Weisz, H. 2011. "The Probability of the Improbable: Society-Nature Coevolution." *Geografiska Annaler: Series B, Human Geography* 93(4): 325–336.

Weisz, H., and Clark, E. 2011. "Society–Nature Co-evolution: Interdisciplinary Concept for Sustainability." *Geografiska Annaler: Series B, Human Geography* 93(4): 281–287.

Weisz, H., Suh, S., and Graedel, T. E. 2015. "Industrial Ecology: The Role of Manufactured Capital in Sustainability." *Proceedings of the National Academy of Sciences* 112(20): 6260–6264.

Weitzman, M. L. 1976. "On the Welfare Significance of National Product in a Dynamic Economy." *The Quarterly Journal of Economics* 90(1): 156–162.

Weitzman, M. L. 1998. "On the Welfare Significance of National Product under Interest-Rate Uncertainty." *European Economic Review* 42(8): 1581–1594.

Wells, N. M., and Lekies, K. S. 2006. "Nature and the Life Course: Pathways from Childhood Nature Experiences to Adult Environmentalism." *Children Youth and Environments* 16(1): 1–24.

Wendling, Z. A., Emerson, J. W., de Sherbinin, A., Esty, D. C., and others. 2020. "2020 Environmental Performance Index." Yale Center for Environmental Law & Policy, New Haven, CT. https://epi.yale.edu. Accessed 10 December 2020.

Werksman, J. D. 1992. "Trade Sanctions under the Montreal Protocol." *Review of European Community & International Environmental Law* 1(1): 69–72.

Westley, F., Olsson, P., Folke, C., Homer-Dixon, T., Vredenburg, H., Loorbach, D., Thompson, J., and others. 2011. "Tipping toward Sustainability: Emerging Pathways of Transformation." *Ambio* 40(7): 762.

White, K., Hardisty, D., and Habib, R. 2019. "The Elusive Green Consumer." *Harvard Business Review* 2019(July–August): 124–133.

Whitmee, S., Haines, A., Beyrer, C., Boltz, F., Capon, A. G., de Souza Dias, B. F., Ezeh, A., and others. 2015. "Safeguarding Human Health in the Anthropocene Epoch: Report of The Rockefeller Foundation–Lancet Commission on Planetary Health." *The Lancet* 386(10007): 1973–2028.

WHO (World Health Organization). 2018. *2018 Global Progress Report on Implementation of the WHO Framework Convention on Tobacco Control.* Geneva.

WHO (World Health Organization). 2019a. "Drinking-Water." https://www.who.int/news-room/fact-sheets/detail/drinking-water. Accessed 25 November 2020.

WHO (World Health Organization). 2019b. *WHO Report on the Global Tobacco Epidemic, 2019.* Geneva.

WHO (World Health Organization). 2020a. "Heatwaves." https://www.who.int/health-topics/heatwaves#tab=tab_1. Accessed 25 November 2020.

WHO (World Health Organization). 2020b. *WHO Framework Convention on Tobacco Control.* Geneva. https://www.who.int/fctc/text_download/en/. Accessed 18 November 2020.

WHO (World Health Organization) and UNICEF (United Nations Children's Fund). 2019. *Progress on Household Drinking Water, Sanitation and Hygiene 2000–2017: Special Focus on Inequalities.* Geneva.

Whyte, K. P. 2013. "Justice Forward: Tribes, Climate Adaptation and Responsibility." *Climatic Change* 120: 517–530.

Whyte, K. P. 2017. "Food Sovereignty, Justice and Indigenous Peoples: An Essay on Settler Colonialism and Collective Continuance." In Barnhill, A., Doggett, T., and Egan, A., (eds.), *Oxford Handbook on Food Ethics.* Oxford, UK: Oxford University Press.

Whyte, K. P. 2017b. "Indigenous Climate Change Studies: Indigenizing Futures, Decolonizing the Anthropocene." *English Language Notes* 55(1): 153–162.

Whyte, K. P., Reo, N., McGregor, D., Smith, M., and Jenkins, J. 2017. "Seven Indigenous Principles for Successful Cooperation in Great Lakes Conservation Initiatives." In Freedman, E., and Neuzil, M., (eds.), *Biodiversity, Conservation and Environmental Management in the Great Lakes Basin.* London: Routledge.

Wi, A., and Chang, C.-H. 2019. "Promoting Pro-Environmental Behaviour in a Community in Singapore: From Raising Awareness to Behavioural Change." *Environmental Education Research* 25(7): 1019–1037.

Wiedenhofer, D., and Fischer-Kowalski, M. 2015. "Achieving Absolute Decoupling? Comparing Biophysical Scenarios and Macro-Economic Modelling Results." Working Paper 86, WWWforEurope, Vienna. https://www.wifo.ac.at/bibliothek/archiv/36247/WWWforEurope_WP_086.pdf. Accessed 9 December 2020.

Wiedenhofer, D., Guan, D., Liu, Z., Meng, J., Zhang, N., and Wei, Y.-M. 2017. "Unequal Household Carbon Footprints in China." *Nature Climate Change* 7(1): 75–80.

Wiedenhofer, D., Virág, D., Kalt, G., Plank, B., Streeck, J., Pichler, M., Mayer, A., and others. 2020. "A Systematic Review of the Evidence on Decoupling of GDP, Resource Use and GHG Emissions, Part I: Bibliometric and Conceptual Mapping." *Environmental Research Letters* 15(6): 063002.

Wilensky, U., and Rand, W. 2015. *An Introduction to Agent-Based Modeling: Modeling Natural, Social, and Engineered Complex Systems with Netlogo.* Cambridge, MA: MIT Press.

Wilensky, U., and Reisman, K. 2006. "Thinking Like a Wolf, a Sheep, or a Firefly: Learning Biology through Constructing and Testing Computational Theories—an Embodied Modeling Approach." *Cognition and Instruction* 24(2): 171–209.

Wilkinson, T. M. 2013. "Nudging and Manipulation." *Political Studies* 61(2): 341–355.

Williams, H. T., and Lenton, T. M. 2010. "Evolutionary Regime Shifts in Simulated Ecosystems." *Oikos* 119(12): 1887–1899.

Williams, H. T., McMurray, J. R., Kurz, T., and Lambert, F. H. 2015. "Network Analysis Reveals Open Forums and Echo Chambers in Social Media Discussions of Climate Change." *Global Environmental Change* 32: 126–138.

Williams, J. W., and Burke, K. D. 2019. "Past Abrupt Changes in Climate and Terrestrial Ecosystems." In Lovejoy, T. E., and Hannah, L., (eds.), *Biodiversity and Climate Change: Transforming the Biosphere.* New Haven, CT: Yale University Press.

Williams, L. 2018. "Empowerment and Social-Ecological Resilience in the Anthropocene." *Resilient Systems, Resilient Communities* 134.

Williams, M., Zalasiewicz, J., Haff, P., Schwägerl, C., Barnosky, A. D., and Ellis, E. C. 2015. "The Anthropocene Biosphere." *The Anthropocene Review* 2(3): 196–219.

Williams, S. L. 2013. "A New Collaboration for Indonesia's Small Islands." *Frontiers in Ecology and the Environment* 11(5): 274–275.

Williams, S. L., Ambo-Rappe, R., Sur, C., Abbott, J. M., and Limbong, S. R. 2017. "Species Richness Accelerates Marine Ecosystem Restoration in the Coral Triangle." *Proceedings of the National Academy of Sciences* 114(45): 11986–11991.

Willis, K., Maureaud, C., Wilcox, C., and Hardesty, B. D. 2018. "How Successful Are Waste Abatement Campaigns and Government Policies at Reducing Plastic Waste into the Marine Environment?" *Marine Policy* 96: 243–249.

Wills, M. 2020. "The First Earth Day, and the First Green Generation." *JSTOR Daily*, 15 April. https://daily.jstor.org/the-first-earth-day-and-the-first-green-generation/. Accessed 23 November 2020.

Wilson, E. O. 1999. *The Diversity of Life.* New York: W.W. Norton & Company.

Wintle, B. A., Kujala, H., Whitehead, A., Cameron, A., Veloz, S., Kukkala, A., Moilanen, A., and others. 2019. "Global Synthesis of Conservation Studies Reveals the Importance of Small Habitat Patches for Biodiversity." *Proceedings of the National Academy of Sciences* 116(3): 909–914.

Wipfli, H., and Samet, J. M. 2016. "One Hundred Years in the Making: The Global Tobacco Epidemic." *Annual Review of Public Health* 37: 149–166.

Wise, S. 2013. "Improving the Early Life Outcomes of Indigenous Children: Implementing Early Childhood Development at the Local Level." Australian Institute of Health and Welfare. https://www.aihw.gov.au/reports/indigenous-australians/improving-early-life-outcomes-indigenous-australia/contents/table-of-contents. Accessed 20 November 2020.

Witze, A. 2020a. "The Arctic Is Burning Like Never Before—and That's Bad News for Climate Change." Nature, 10 September. https://www.nature.com/articles/d41586-020-02568-y. Accessed 18 November 2020.

Witze, A. 2020b. "Arctic Sea Ice Hits Second-Lowest Level on Record." Nature, 22 September. https://www.nature.com/articles/d41586-020-02705-7. Accessed 10 December 2020.

WMO (World Meteorological Organization) and UCL (Université catholique de Louvain). 2014. Atlas of Mortality and Economic Losses from Weather, Climate and Water Extremes, 1970–2012. Geneva.

World Bank. 2010. World Development Report 2010: Development and Climate Change. Washington, DC. https://openknowledge.worldbank.org/handle/10986/4387. Accessed 21 November 2020.

World Bank. 2016a. "Agricultural Land (% of Land Area)." https://data.worldbank.org/indicator/AG.LND.AGRI.ZS. Accessed 30 November 2020.

World Bank. 2016b. High and Dry: Climate Change, Water, and the Economy. Washington, DC.

World Bank. 2017a. "Chart: Globally, 70% of Freshwater is Used for Agriculture." https://blogs.worldbank.org/opendata/chart-globally-70-freshwater-used-agriculture. Accessed 25 November 2020.

World Bank. 2017b. World Development Report 2017: Governance and the Law. Washington, DC. https://www.worldbank.org/en/publication/wdr2017. Accessed 21 November 2020.

World Bank. 2018. The Changing Wealth of Nations: Building a Sustainable Future. Washington, DC.

World Bank. 2019a. "Brief on Learning Poverty." https://www.worldbank.org/en/topic/education/brief/learning-poverty. Accessed 30 November 2020.

World Bank. 2019b. State and Trends of Carbon Pricing 2019. Washington, DC. https://openknowledge.worldbank.org/handle/10986/31755. Accessed 4 December 2020.

World Bank. 2019c. "Women in Half the World Still Denied Land, Property Rights Despite Laws." Washington, DC. https://www.worldbank.org/en/news/press-release/2019/03/25/women-in-half-the-world-still-denied-land-property-rights-despite-laws. Accessed 20 November 2020.

World Bank. 2020a. The Human Capital Index 2020 Update: Human Capital in the Time of Covid-19. Washington, DC.

World Bank. 2020b. Poverty and Shared Prosperity 2020: Reversals of Fortune. Washington, DC.

World Bank. 2020c. "Projected Poverty Impacts of Covid-19 (Coronavirus)." https://www.worldbank.org/en/topic/poverty/brief/projected-poverty-impacts-of-COVID-19#:~:text=Estimates%20based%20on%20growth%20projections,million%20under%20the%20downside%20scenario. Accessed 30 November 2020.

World Bank. 2020d. State and Trends of Carbon Pricing 2020. Washington, DC. https://openknowledge.worldbank.org/handle/10986/33809. Accessed 4 December 2020.

World Bank. 2020e. "Wealth Accounting and Valuation of Ecosystems (WAVES)." https://www.wavespartnership.org. Accessed 2 December 2020.

World Bank. 2020f. "World Bank Open Data." https://data.worldbank.org. Accessed 20 November 2020.

World Bank. 2020g. World Development Indicators database. Washington, DC. http://data.worldbank.org. Accessed 22 July 2020.

World Inequality Lab and World Inequality Database. 2018. World Inequality Report 2018. https://wir2018.wid.world. Accessed 1 December 2020.

Wrangham, R. 2009. Catching Fire: How Cooking Made Us Human. New York: Basic Books.

WRI (World Resources Institute). 2013. "Required Greenhouse Gases in Inventories: Accounting and Reporting Standard Amendment." London.

WRI (World Resources Institute). 2019. Global Forest Watch: 2019 Treecover Loss Data. Washington, DC.

Wright, E. O. 2010. Envisioning Real Utopias. London: Verso.

Wright, R. A., and Boudet, H. S. 2012. "To Act or Not to Act: Context, Capability, and Community Response to Environmental Risk." American Journal of Sociology 118(3): 728–777.

WWF (World Wildlife Fund for Nature). 2017. Biodiversity, People and Climate Change: Final Technical Report of the Hariyo Ban Program, First Phase. Kathmandu.

WWF (World Wildlife Fund for Nature). 2020a. "Deforestation and Forest Degradation." https://www.worldwildlife.org/threats/deforestation-and-forest-degradation. Accessed 25 November 2020.

WWF (World Wildlife Fund for Nature). 2020b. "Forests Burn, Soils Dwindle and People Suffer." https://wwf.panda.org/knowledge_hub/where_we_work/amazon/amazon_threats/#:~:text=Among%20the%20threats%20behind%20environmental,and%20enforce%20legislation%20for%20nature. Accessed 17 November 2020.

WWF (World Wildlife Fund for Nature). 2020c. Living Planet Report 2020: Bending the Curve of Biodiversity Loss. Gland, Switzerland.

WWF (World Wildlife Fund for Nature). 2020d. "The Pantanal: Saving the World's Largest Tropical Wetland." https://www.worldwildlife.org/projects/the-pantanal-saving-the-world-s-largest-tropical-wetland. Accessed 23 November 2020.

Xu, C., Kohler, T. A., Lenton, T. M., Svenning, J.-C., and Scheffer, M. 2020. "Future of the Human Climate Niche." Proceedings of the National Academy of Sciences 117(21): 11350–11355.

Yap, M., and Yu, E. 2016a. "Community Wellbeing from the Ground Up: A Yawuru Example." Bentley, Australia: Bankwest Curtin Economics Centre.

Yap, M., and Yu, E. 2016b. "Data Sovereignty for the Yawuru in Western Australia." In Kukutai, T., and Taylor, J., (eds.), Indigenous Data Sovereignty: Towards an Agenda. Canberra: ANU Press.

Yawuru RNTBC (Yawuru Native Title Holders Aboriginal Corporation Native Title Prescribed Body Corporation). 2011. "Walyjala-jala buru jayida jarringgun Nyamba Yawuru ngan-ga mirlimirli: Planning for the Future—Yawuru Cultural Management Plan." Broome, Australia: Pindan Printing.

Yeung, J., and Gupta, S. 2019. "More Than 500 Arrested after Protests and Clashes as India Water Crisis Worsens." https://edition.cnn.com/2019/06/20/india/chennai-water-crisis-intl-hnk/index.html. Accessed 10 December 2020.

Yoeli, E., Hoffman, M., Rand, D. G., and Nowak, M. A. 2013. "Powering up with Indirect Reciprocity in a Large-Scale Field Experiment." Proceedings of the National Academy of Sciences 110(Supplement 2): 10424–10429.

Young, H. P. 1998. "Social Norms and Economic Welfare." European Economic Review 42(3–5): 821–830.

Young, H. P. 2015. "The Evolution of Social Norms." Economics 7(1): 359–387.

Young, H. S., McCauley, D. J., Galetti, M., and Dirzo, R. 2016. "Patterns, Causes, and Consequences of Anthropocene Defaunation." Annual Review of Ecology, Evolution, and Systematics 47(1): 333–358.

Yun, S. D., Hutniczak, B., Abbott, J. K., and Fenichel, E. P. 2017. "Ecosystem-Based Management and the Wealth of Ecosystems." Proceedings of the National Academy of Sciences 114(25): 6539–6544.

Zacher, M. 1999. "Global Epidemiological Surveillance." In Kaul, I., Grunberg, I., and Stern, M., (eds.), Global Public Goods: International Cooperation in the 21st Century. Oxford, UK: Oxford University Press.

Zalasiewicz, J., and Freedman, K. 2009. The Earth after Us: What Legacy Will Humans Leave in the Rocks? Oxford, UK: Oxford University Press.

Zalasiewicz, J., and Waters, C. N. 2016. "Geology and the Anthropocene." Antiquity 90(350): 512–514.

Zalasiewicz, J., Williams, M., Smith, A., Barry, T. L., Coe, A. L., Bown, P. R., Brenchley, P., and others. 2008. "Are We Now Living in the Anthropocene." GSA Today 18(2): 4.

Zalasiewicz, J., Williams, M., Waters, C. N., Barnosky, A. D., Palmesino, J., Rönnskog, A.-S., Edgeworth, M., and others. 2017. "Scale and Diversity of the Physical Technosphere: A Geological Perspective." The Anthropocene Review 4(1): 9–22.

Zhang, D. D., Lee, H. F., Wang, C., Li, B., Pei, Q., Zhang, J., and An, Y. 2011. "The Causality Analysis of Climate Change and Large-Scale Human Crisis." Proceedings of the National Academy of Sciences 108(42): 17296–17301.

Zhang, P., Deschenes, O., Meng, K., and Zhang, J. 2018. "Temperature Effects on Productivity and Factor Reallocation: Evidence from a Half Million Chinese Manufacturing Plants." *Journal of Environmental Economics and Management* 88: 1–17. https://doi.org/10.1016/j.jeem.2017.11.001. Accessed 1 December 2020.

Zhang, Q., Jiang, X., Tong, D., Davis, S. J., Zhao, H., Geng, G., Feng, T., and others. 2017. "Transboundary Health Impacts of Transported Global Air Pollution and International Trade." *Nature* 543(7647): 705–709.

Zhou, P., Yang, X.-L., Wang, X.-G., Hu, B., Zhang, L., Zhang, W., Si, H.-R., and others. 2020. "A Pneumonia Outbreak Associated with a New Coronavirus of Probable Bat Origin." *Nature* 579(7798): 270–273.

Statistical annex

Statistical annex

Readers guide

The statistical tables in this annex depict the state of human development before the Covid-19 pandemic based on available data for 2019 and earlier years. Data reflecting changes caused by the pandemic and its socioeconomic fallout in 2020 will be available in 2021 and will be presented in tables and related analyses of the 2021 Human Development Report.

The tables provide an overview of key aspects of human development. The first six tables contain the family of composite human development indices and their components estimated by the Human Development Report Office (HDRO). The sixth table is produced in partnership with the Oxford Poverty and Human Development Initiative (OPHI). The remaining tables present a broader set of indicators related to human development. The five dashboards use colour coding to visualize partial groupings of countries according to performance on each indicator.

Tables 1–6 and dashboards 1–5 are part of the 2020 Human Development Report. The full set of 20 statistical tables is available for download at http://hdr.undp.org/en/2020-report. Unless otherwise noted, tables use data available to the HDRO as of 15 July 2020. All indices and indicators, along with technical notes on the calculation of composite indices and additional source information, are available at http://hdr.undp.org/en/data.

Countries and territories are ranked by 2019 Human Development Index (HDI) value. Robustness and reliability analysis has shown that for most countries differences in HDI are not statistically significant at the fourth decimal place. For this reason countries with the same HDI value at three decimal places are listed with tied ranks.

Sources and definitions

Unless otherwise noted, the HDRO uses data from international data agencies with the mandate, resources and expertise to collect national data on specific indicators.

Definitions of indicators and sources for original data components are given at the end of each table, with full source details in *Statistical references*.

Gross national income per capita in purchasing power parity terms

In comparing standard of living across countries, the income component of the HDI uses gross national income (GNI) per capita converted into purchasing power parity (PPP) terms to eliminate differences in national price levels.

The International Comparison Programme (ICP) survey, the world's largest statistical initiative under the coordination by the World Bank, in the 2017 cycle has produced internationally comparable price level indices and estimates of PPP-based GDP and its major expenditure components in aggregate and per capita terms for 176 participating economies. The 2020 Human Development Report uses GNI per capita in constant 2017 PPP terms.

Methodology updates

The 2020 Report retains all the composite indices from the family of human development indices—the HDI, the Inequality-adjusted Human Development Index (IHDI), the Gender Development Index (GDI), the Gender Inequality Index (GII) and the Multidimensional Poverty Index (MPI). The methodology used to compute the indices is the same as the one used in the 2019 Human Development Report. For details, see *Technical notes 1–5* at http://hdr.undp.org/sites/default/files/hdr2020_technical_notes.pdf.

The 2020 Report has five colour-coded dashboards (quality of human development, life-course gender gap, women's empowerment, environmental sustainability and socioeconomic sustainability). For details on the methodology used to create them, see

Technical note 6 at http://hdr.undp.org/sites/default/files/hdr2020_technical_notes.pdf.

Comparisons over time and across editions

Because national and international agencies continually improve their data series, the data—including the HDI values and ranks—presented in this report are not comparable to those published in earlier editions. For HDI comparability across years and countries, see table 2, which presents trends using consistent data, or http://hdr.undp.org/en/data, which presents interpolated consistent data.

Discrepancies between national and international estimates

National and international data can differ because international agencies harmonize national data using a consistent methodology and occasionally produce estimates of missing data to allow comparability across countries. In other cases international agencies might not have access to the most recent national data. When HDRO becomes aware of discrepancies, it brings them to the attention of national and international data authorities.

Country groupings and aggregates

The tables present weighted aggregates for several country groupings. In general, an aggregate is shown only when data are available for at least half the countries and represent at least two-thirds of the population in that grouping. Aggregates for each grouping cover only the countries for which data are available.

Human development classification

HDI classifications are based on HDI fixed cutoff points, which are derived from the quartiles of distributions of the component indicators. The cutoff points are HDI of less than 0.550 for low human development, 0.550–0.699 for medium human development, 0.700–0.799 for high human development and 0.800 or greater for very high human development.

Regional groupings

Regional groupings are based on United Nations Development Programme regional classifications. Least Developed Countries and Small Island Developing States are defined according to UN classifications (see www.unohrlls.org).

Developing countries

The aggregates for developing countries are based on information from all developing countries that are included in a regional grouping.

Organisation for Economic Co-operation and Development

Of the 37 Organisation for Economic Co-operation and Development members, 33 are considered developed countries and 4 (Chile, Colombia, Mexico and Turkey) are considered developing countries. Aggregates refer to all countries from the group for which data are available.

Country notes

Data for China do not include Hong Kong Special Administrative Region of China, Macao Special Administrative Region of China or Taiwan Province of China.

As of 2 May 2016, Czechia is the short name to be used for the Czech Republic.

As of 1 June 2018, the Kingdom of Eswatini is the name of the country formerly known as Swaziland.

As of 14 February 2019, the Republic of North Macedonia (short form: North Macedonia) is the name of the country formerly known as the former Yugoslav Republic of Macedonia.

Symbols

A dash between two years, as in 2010–2019, indicates that the data are from the most recent year available during the period specified. A slash between years, as in 2015/2020, indicates that the data are the average for the years shown. Growth rates are usually average annual rates of growth between the first and last years of the period shown.

The following symbols are used in the tables:

..	Not available
0 or 0.0	Nil or negligible
—	Not applicable

Statistical acknowledgements

The Report's composite indices and other statistical resources draw on a wide variety of the most respected international data providers in their specialized fields. HDRO is particularly grateful to the Centre for Research on the Epidemiology of Disasters; Economic Commission for Latin America and the Caribbean; Eurostat; Food and Agriculture Organization; Gallup; ICF Macro; Institute for Criminal Policy Research; Institute for Health Metrics and Evaluation; Internal Displacement Monitoring Centre; International Labour Organization; International Monetary Fund; International Telecommunication Union; Inter-Parliamentary Union; Luxembourg Income Study; Office of the United Nations High Commissioner for Human Rights; Office of the United Nations High Commissioner for Refugees; Organisation for Economic Co-operation and Development; Socio-Economic Database for Latin America and the Caribbean; Syrian Center for Policy Research; United Nations Children's Fund; United Nations Conference on Trade and Development; United Nations Department of Economic and Social Affairs; United Nations Economic and Social Commission for West Asia; United Nations Educational, Scientific and Cultural Organization Institute for Statistics; United Nations Entity for Gender Equality and the Empowerment of Women; United Nations Office on Drugs and Crime; United Nations World Tourism Organization; World Bank; and World Health Organization. The international education database maintained by Robert Barro (Harvard University) and Jong-Wha Lee (Korea University) was another invaluable source for the calculation of the Report's indices.

Statistical tables

The first six tables relate to the five composite human development indices and their components. Since the 2010 Human Development Report, four composite human development indices—the HDI, the IHDI, the GII and the MPI for developing countries—have been calculated. The 2014 Report introduced the GDI, which compares the HDI calculated separately for women and men.

The remaining tables present a broader set of human development indicators and provide a more comprehensive picture of a country's human development.

For indicators that are global Sustainable Development Goals indicators or can be used in monitoring progress towards specific goals, the table headers include the relevant goals and targets.

Table 1, Human Development Index and its components, ranks countries by 2019 HDI value and details the values of the three HDI components: longevity, education (with two indicators) and income per capita. The table also presents the difference in rankings by HDI value and gross national income per capita, as well as the rank on the 2018 HDI, calculated using the most recently revised historical data available in 2020.

Table 2, Human Development Index trends, 1990–2019, provides a time series of HDI values allowing 2019 HDI values to be compared with those for previous years. The table uses the most recently revised historical data available in 2020 and the same methodology applied to compute 2019 HDI values. The table also includes the change in HDI rank over the last five years and the average annual HDI growth rate across four time intervals: 1990–2000, 2000–2010, 2010–2019 and 1990–2019.

Table 3, Inequality-adjusted Human Development Index, contains two related measures of inequality—the IHDI and the overall loss in HDI due to inequality. The IHDI looks beyond the average achievements of a country in longevity, education and income to show how these achievements are distributed among its residents. The IHDI value can be interpreted as the level of human development when inequality is accounted for. The relative difference between IHDI and HDI values is the loss due to inequality in distribution of the HDI within the country. The table presents the coefficient of human inequality, which is the unweighted average of inequalities in the three dimensions. In addition, the table shows each country's difference in rank on the HDI and the IHDI. A negative value means that taking inequality into account lowers a country's rank on the HDI. The

table also presents the income shares of the poorest 40 percent, the richest 10 percent and the richest 1 percent of the population, as well as the Gini coefficient.

Table 4, Gender Development Index, measures disparities on the HDI by gender. The table contains HDI values estimated separately for women and men, the ratio of which is the GDI value. The closer the ratio is to 1, the smaller the gap between women and men. Values for the three HDI components—longevity, education (with two indicators) and income per capita—are also presented by gender. The table includes five country groupings by absolute deviation from gender parity in HDI values.

Table 5, Gender Inequality Index, presents a composite measure of gender inequality using three dimensions: reproductive health, empowerment and the labour market. The reproductive health indicators are maternal mortality ratio and adolescent birth rate. The empowerment indicators are the percentage of parliamentary seats held by women and the percentage of population with at least some secondary education by gender. The labour market indicator is participation in the labour force by gender. A low GII value indicates low inequality between women and men, and vice-versa.

Table 6, Multidimensional Poverty Index, captures the multiple deprivations that people in developing countries face in their health, education and standard of living. The MPI shows both the incidence of nonincome multidimensional poverty (a headcount of those in multidimensional poverty) and its intensity (the average deprivation score experienced by poor people). Based on deprivation score thresholds, people are classified as multidimensionally poor, in severe multidimensional poverty or vulnerable to multidimensional poverty. The table includes the contribution of deprivation in each dimension to overall multidimensional poverty. It also presents measures of income poverty—population living below the national poverty line and population living on less than $1.90 in purchasing power parity terms per day. MPI values are based on a revised methodology developed in partnership with OPHI. For details, see *Technical note 5* at http://hdr.undp.org/sites/default/files/mpi2020_technical_notes.pdf.

Table 7, Population trends, contains major population indicators including total population, median age, dependency ratios and total fertility rates, which can help assess the burden of support that falls on the labour force in a country.

Table 8, Health outcomes, presents indicators of infant health (percentage of infants who are exclusively breastfed in the 24 hours prior to the survey, percentage of infants who lack immunization for DTP and measles, and infant mortality rate) and of child health (percentage of children under age 5 who are stunted and under-five mortality rates). The table also contains indicators of adult health (adult mortality rates by gender, mortality rates attributable to noncommunicable diseases by gender, incidence of malaria and tuberculosis, and HIV prevalence rates). Finally, it includes healthy life expectancy at birth and current health expenditure as a percentage of GDP.

Table 9, Education achievements, presents standard education indicators. The table provides indicators of educational attainment—adult and youth literacy rates and the percentage of the adult population with at least some secondary education. Gross enrolment ratios at each level of education are complemented by primary school dropout rate and survival rate to the last grade of lower secondary general education. The table also presents government expenditure on education as a percentage of GDP.

Table 10, National income and composition of resources, covers several macroeconomic indicators such as gross domestic product (GDP), labour share of GDP (which includes wages and social protection transfers), gross fixed capital formation, and taxes on income, profit and capital gains as a percentage

of total tax revenue. Gross fixed capital formation is a rough indicator of national income that is invested rather than consumed. In times of economic uncertainty or recession, gross fixed capital formation typically declines. General government final consumption expenditure (presented as a percentage of GDP and as average annual growth) is an indicator of public spending. In addition, the table presents two indicators of debt—external debt stock and total debt service, both measured as a percentage of GNI. The consumer price index, a measure of inflation, is also presented.

Table 11, Work and employment contains indicators on five topics: employment, unemployment, work that is a risk to human development, skill-level employment and employment-related social security. The employment indicators are employment to population ratio, labour force participation rate, employment in agriculture and employment in services. The unemployment indicators are total unemployment, youth unemployment and youth not in school or employment. The indicators on work that is a risk to human development are child labour, the working poor and proportion of informal employment in nonagricultural employment. The indicator on skill-level employment is high-skill to low-skill employment ratio. The indicator on employment-related social security is the percentage of the eligible population that receives an old-age pension.

Table 12, Human security, reflects the extent to which the population is secure. The table begins with the percentage of births that are registered, followed by the number of refugees by country of origin and the number of internally displaced people. It then shows the size of the homeless population due to natural disasters, the population of orphaned children and the prison population. It also provides homicide and suicide rates (by gender), an indicator on justification of wife beating and an indicator on the depth of food deficit (average dietary energy supply adequacy).

Table 13, Human and capital mobility, provides indicators of several aspects of globalization. International trade is captured by measuring exports and imports as a percentage of GDP. Financial flows are represented by net inflows of foreign direct investment and flows of private capital, net official development assistance and inflows of remittances. Human mobility is captured by the net migration rate, the stock of immigrants, the net number of tertiary students from abroad (expressed as a percentage of total tertiary enrolment in the country) and the number of international inbound tourists. International communication is represented by the percentages of the total and female populations that use the Internet, the number of mobile phone subscriptions per 100 people and the percentage change in mobile phone subscriptions between 2010 and 2018.

Table 14, Supplementary indicators: perceptions of wellbeing, includes indicators that reflect individuals' perceptions of relevant dimensions of human development—education quality, health care quality, standard of living, personal safety, freedom of choice and overall life satisfaction. The table also presents indicators reflecting perceptions about community and government.

Table 15, Status of fundamental human rights treaties, shows when countries ratified key human rights conventions. The 11 selected conventions cover basic human rights and freedoms related to elimination of all forms of racial and gender discrimination and violence and protection of the rights of children, migrant workers and persons with disabilities. They also cover torture and other cruel, inhuman and degrading treatment as well as protection from enforced disappearance.

Dashboard 1, Quality of human development, contains a selection of indicators associated with the quality of health, education and standard of living. The indicators on quality of health are lost health expectancy, number of physicians and number of hospital beds. The indicators on quality of education are pupil–teacher ratio in primary schools; primary school teachers trained to teach; the percentages of primary schools and of secondary schools with access to the Internet; and Programme for International Student Assessment (PISA) scores in reading, mathematics and science. The indicators on quality of standard of living are the percentage of employment that is in vulnerable employment, the percentage of rural population with access to electricity, the percentage of population using safely managed drinking-water services and the percentage of population using safely managed sanitation facilities. A country in the top third of an indicator distribution has performed better than at least two-thirds of countries globally. A country that is in the top third group on all indicators can be considered a country with the highest quality of human development. The dashboard shows that not all countries in the very high human development group have the highest quality of human development across all quality indicators and that many countries in the low human development group are in the bottom third of all quality indicators in the table.

Dashboard 2, Life-course gender gap, contains a selection of indicators that indicate gender gaps in choices and opportunities over the life course—childhood and youth, adulthood and older age. The indicators refer to health, education, labour market and work, political decisionmaking, time use and social protection. Most indicators are presented as a ratio of female to male values. Sex ratio at birth is an exception to grouping by tercile—countries are divided into two groups: the natural group (countries with a value of 1.04–1.07, inclusive) and the gender-biased group (all other countries). Deviations from the natural sex ratio at birth have implications for population replacement levels; they can suggest possible future social and economic problems and may indicate gender bias. Countries with values of a parity index concentrated around 1 form the group with the best achievements in that indicator. Deviations from parity are treated equally regardless of which gender is overachieving.

Dashboard 3, Women's empowerment, contains a selection of woman-specific empowerment indicators that allows empowerment to be compared across three dimensions: reproductive health and family planning, violence against girls and women and socioeconomic empowerment. Most countries have at least one indicator in each tercile, which implies that women's empowerment is unequal across indicators and countries.

Dashboard 4, Environmental sustainability, contains a selection of indicators that cover environmental sustainability and environmental threats. The environmental sustainability indicators present fossil fuel energy consumption, carbon dioxide emissions, forest area, fresh water withdrawals, use of fertilizer nutrient and domestic material consumption. The

environmental threats indicators are mortality rates attributed to household and ambient air pollution and to unsafe water, sanitation and hygiene services, the number of deaths and missing persons attributed to disasters, the percentage of land that is degraded mostly by human activities and practices, and the International Union for Conservation of Nature Red List Index value, which measures aggregate extinction risk across groups of species.

Dashboard 5, Socioeconomic sustainability, contains a selection of indicators that cover economic and social sustainability. The economic sustainability indicators are adjusted net savings, total debt service, gross capital formation, skilled labour force, diversity of exports and expenditure on research and development. The social sustainability indicators are old age dependency ratio projected to 2030, ratio of education and health expenditure to military expenditure, change in overall loss in HDI value due to inequality and changes in gender and income inequality.

Human development composite indices

TABLE 1

Human Development Index and its components

	Human Development Index (HDI)	SDG 3 Life expectancy at birth	SDG 4.3 Expected years of schooling	SDG 4.4 Mean years of schooling	SDG 8.5 Gross national income (GNI) per capita	GNI per capita rank minus HDI rank	HDI rank
	Value	(years)	(years)	(years)	(2017 PPP $)		
HDI RANK	2019	2019	2019[a]	2019[a]	2019	2019	2018
Very high human development							
1 Norway	0.957	82.4	18.1[b]	12.9	66,494	7	1
2 Ireland	0.955	82.3	18.7[b]	12.7	68,371	4	3
2 Switzerland	0.955	83.8	16.3	13.4	69,394	3	2
4 Hong Kong, China (SAR)	0.949	84.9	16.9	12.3	62,985	7	4
4 Iceland	0.949	83.0	19.1[b]	12.8[c]	54,682	14	4
6 Germany	0.947	81.3	17.0	14.2	55,314	11	4
7 Sweden	0.945	82.8	19.5[b]	12.5	54,508	12	7
8 Australia	0.944	83.4	22.0[b]	12.7[c]	48,085	15	7
8 Netherlands	0.944	82.3	18.5[b]	12.4	57,707	6	9
10 Denmark	0.940	80.9	18.9[b]	12.6[c]	58,662	2	10
11 Finland	0.938	81.9	19.4[b]	12.8	48,511	11	11
11 Singapore	0.938	83.6	16.4	11.6	88,155[d]	-8	12
13 United Kingdom	0.932	81.3	17.5	13.2	46,071	13	14
14 Belgium	0.931	81.6	19.8[b]	12.1[e]	52,085	6	13
14 New Zealand	0.931	82.3	18.8[b]	12.8[c]	40,799	18	14
16 Canada	0.929	82.4	16.2	13.4[c]	48,527	5	14
17 United States	0.926	78.9	16.3	13.4	63,826	-7	17
18 Austria	0.922	81.5	16.1	12.5[c]	56,197	-3	18
19 Israel	0.919	83.0	16.2	13.0	40,187	14	21
19 Japan	0.919	84.6	15.2	12.9[f]	42,932	9	20
19 Liechtenstein	0.919	80.7[g]	14.9	12.5[h]	131,032[d,i]	-18	19
22 Slovenia	0.917	81.3	17.6	12.7	38,080	15	24
23 Korea (Republic of)	0.916	83.0	16.5	12.2	43,044	4	22
23 Luxembourg	0.916	82.3	14.3	12.3[e]	72,712	-19	23
25 Spain	0.904	83.6	17.6	10.3	40,975	6	25
26 France	0.901	82.7	15.6	11.5	47,173	-1	26
27 Czechia	0.900	79.4	16.8	12.7[c]	38,109	9	26
28 Malta	0.895	82.5	16.1	11.3	39,555	6	28
29 Estonia	0.892	78.8	16.0	13.1[c]	36,019	9	30
29 Italy	0.892	83.5	16.1	10.4[j]	42,776	0	29
31 United Arab Emirates	0.890	78.0	14.3	12.1	67,462	-24	30
32 Greece	0.888	82.2	17.9	10.6	30,155	14	33
33 Cyprus	0.887	81.0	15.2	12.2	38,207	2	32
34 Lithuania	0.882	75.9	16.6	13.1	35,799	5	35
35 Poland	0.880	78.7	16.3	12.5[e]	31,623	8	34
36 Andorra	0.868	81.9[g]	13.3[k]	10.5	56,000[l]	-20	36
37 Latvia	0.866	75.3	16.2	13.0[c]	30,282	8	37
38 Portugal	0.864	82.1	16.5	9.3	33,967	2	38
39 Slovakia	0.860	77.5	14.5	12.7[c]	32,113	3	39
40 Hungary	0.854	76.9	15.2	12.0	31,329	4	42
40 Saudi Arabia	0.854	75.1	16.1	10.2	47,495	-16	40
42 Bahrain	0.852	77.3	16.3	9.5	42,522	-12	41
43 Chile	0.851	80.2	16.4	10.6	23,261	16	43
43 Croatia	0.851	78.5	15.2	11.4[e]	28,070	6	44
45 Qatar	0.848	80.2	12.0	9.7	92,418[d]	-43	45
46 Argentina	0.845	76.7	17.7	10.9[c]	21,190	16	46
47 Brunei Darussalam	0.838	75.9	14.3	9.1[f]	63,965	-38	47
48 Montenegro	0.829	76.9	15.0	11.6[m]	21,399	13	48
49 Romania	0.828	76.1	14.3	11.1	29,497	-1	49
50 Palau	0.826	73.9[g]	15.8[j]	12.5[j]	19,317	15	52
51 Kazakhstan	0.825	73.6	15.6	11.9[j]	22,857	9	53
52 Russian Federation	0.824	72.6	15.0	12.2[j]	26,157	2	49
53 Belarus	0.823	74.8	15.4	12.3[m]	18,546	14	49
54 Turkey	0.820	77.7	16.6[c]	8.1	27,701	-4	54
55 Uruguay	0.817	77.9	16.8	8.9	20,064	9	56
56 Bulgaria	0.816	75.1	14.4	11.4	23,325	2	55
57 Panama	0.815	78.5	12.9	10.2[f]	29,558	-10	58
58 Bahamas	0.814	73.9	12.9[n]	11.4[j]	33,747	-17	58
58 Barbados	0.814	79.2	15.4	10.6[o]	14,936	20	60
60 Oman	0.813	77.9	14.2	9.7[f]	25,944	-5	56
61 Georgia	0.812	73.8	15.3	13.1	14,429	22	63
62 Costa Rica	0.810	80.3	15.7	8.7	18,486	6	61

Continued →

TABLE 1 / HUMAN DEVELOPMENT INDEX AND ITS COMPONENTS   343

TABLE 1

HDI RANK		Human Development Index (HDI)	SDG 3 Life expectancy at birth	SDG 4.3 Expected years of schooling	SDG 4.4 Mean years of schooling	SDG 8.5 Gross national income (GNI) per capita	GNI per capita rank minus HDI rank	HDI rank
		Value	(years)	(years)	(years)	(2017 PPP $)		
		2019	2019	2019[a]	2019[a]	2019	2019	2018
62	Malaysia	0.810	76.2	13.7	10.4	27,534	-11	63
64	Kuwait	0.806	75.5	14.2	7.3	58,590	-51	62
64	Serbia	0.806	76.0	14.7	11.2	17,192	8	65
66	Mauritius	0.804	75.0	15.1	9.5[f]	25,266	-10	66
High human development								
67	Seychelles	0.796	73.4	14.1	10.0[k]	26,903	-15	69
67	Trinidad and Tobago	0.796	73.5	13.0[j]	11.0[f]	26,231	-14	67
69	Albania	0.795	78.6	14.7	10.1[p]	13,998	18	68
70	Cuba	0.783	78.8	14.3	11.8[j]	8,621[q]	45	71
70	Iran (Islamic Republic of)	0.783	76.7	14.8	10.3	12,447	26	70
72	Sri Lanka	0.782	77.0	14.1	10.6	12,707	23	73
73	Bosnia and Herzegovina	0.780	77.4	13.8[k]	9.8	14,872	7	76
74	Grenada	0.779	72.4	16.9	9.0[n]	15,641	3	74
74	Mexico	0.779	75.1	14.8	8.8	19,160	-8	76
74	Saint Kitts and Nevis	0.779	74.8[q]	13.8[j]	8.7[n]	25,038	-17	75
74	Ukraine	0.779	72.1	15.1[j]	11.4[o]	13,216	19	78
78	Antigua and Barbuda	0.778	77.0	12.8[j]	9.3[k]	20,895	-15	80
79	Peru	0.777	76.7	15.0	9.7	12,252	19	78
79	Thailand	0.777	77.2	15.0[j]	7.9	17,781	-10	80
81	Armenia	0.776	75.1	13.1	11.3	13,894	9	72
82	North Macedonia	0.774	75.8	13.6	9.8[m]	15,865	-7	82
83	Colombia	0.767	77.3	14.4	8.5	14,257	3	83
84	Brazil	0.765	75.9	15.4	8.0	14,263	1	84
85	China	0.761	76.9	14.0[j]	8.1[f]	16,057	-11	87
86	Ecuador	0.759	77.0	14.6[o]	8.9	11,044	19	84
86	Saint Lucia	0.759	76.2	14.0[j]	8.5[j]	14,616	-4	86
88	Azerbaijan	0.756	73.0	12.9[j]	10.6	13,784	3	88
88	Dominican Republic	0.756	74.1	14.2	8.1[j]	17,591	-18	89
90	Moldova (Republic of)	0.750	71.9	11.5	11.7	13,664	2	91
91	Algeria	0.748	76.9	14.6	8.0[m]	11,174	13	91
92	Lebanon	0.744	78.9	11.3	8.7[n]	14,655	-11	90
93	Fiji	0.743	67.4	14.4[n]	10.9	13,009	1	93
94	Dominica	0.742	78.2[q]	13.0[p]	8.1[k]	11,884	7	94
95	Maldives	0.740	78.9	12.2[p]	7.0[p]	17,417	-24	98
95	Tunisia	0.740	76.7	15.1	7.2	10,414	14	94
97	Saint Vincent and the Grenadines	0.738	72.5	14.1[j]	8.8[j]	12,378	0	96
97	Suriname	0.738	71.7	13.2	9.3[m]	14,324	-13	98
99	Mongolia	0.737	69.9	14.2[j]	10.3[m]	10,839	7	97
100	Botswana	0.735	69.6	12.8[j]	9.6[o]	16,437	-27	102
101	Jamaica	0.734	74.5	13.1[j]	9.7[j]	9,319	13	98
102	Jordan	0.729	74.5	11.4[p]	10.5[f]	9,858	8	103
103	Paraguay	0.728	74.3	12.7[m]	8.5	12,224	-4	104
104	Tonga	0.725	70.9	14.4[j]	11.2[f]	6,365	25	105
105	Libya	0.724	72.9	12.9[n]	7.6[o]	15,688	-29	106
106	Uzbekistan	0.720	71.7	12.1	11.8	7,142	17	107
107	Bolivia (Plurinational State of)	0.718	71.5	14.2[r]	9.0	8,554	9	108
107	Indonesia	0.718	71.7	13.6	8.2	11,459	-4	110
107	Philippines	0.718	71.2	13.1	9.4	9,778	4	111
110	Belize	0.716	74.6	13.1	9.9[m]	6,382	18	108
111	Samoa	0.715	73.3	12.7[j]	10.8	6,309	19	113
111	Turkmenistan	0.715	68.2	11.2[j]	10.3[m]	14,909	-32	112
113	Venezuela (Bolivarian Republic of)	0.711	72.1	12.8[n]	10.3	7,045[s]	11	101
114	South Africa	0.709	64.1	13.8	10.2	12,129	-14	115
115	Palestine, State of	0.708	74.1	13.4	9.2	6,417	12	114
116	Egypt	0.707	72.0	13.3	7.4[f]	11,466	-14	117
117	Marshall Islands	0.704	74.1[q]	12.4[n]	10.9[j]	5,039	21	116
117	Viet Nam	0.704	75.4	12.7[j]	8.3[f]	7,433	3	118
119	Gabon	0.703	66.5	13.0[n]	8.7[f]	13,930	-30	119
Medium human development								
120	Kyrgyzstan	0.697	71.5	13.0	11.1[m]	4,864	23	120
121	Morocco	0.686	76.7	13.7	5.6[f]	7,368	1	121
122	Guyana	0.682	69.9	11.4[j]	8.5[m]	9,455	-10	121
123	Iraq	0.674	70.6	11.3[m]	7.3[j]	10,801	-16	123

Continued →

TABLE 1

HDI RANK	Human Development Index (HDI) Value 2019	SDG 3 Life expectancy at birth (years) 2019	SDG 4.3 Expected years of schooling (years) 2019a	SDG 4.4 Mean years of schooling (years) 2019a	SDG 8.5 Gross national income (GNI) per capita (2017 PPP $) 2019	GNI per capita rank minus HDI rank 2019	HDI rank 2018
124 El Salvador	0.673	73.3	11.7	6.9	8,359	-6	124
125 Tajikistan	0.668	71.1	11.7 j	10.7 p	3,954	25	126
126 Cabo Verde	0.665	73.0	12.7	6.3 j	7,019	-1	125
127 Guatemala	0.663	74.3	10.8	6.6	8,494	-10	128
128 Nicaragua	0.660	74.5	12.3 f	6.9 f	5,284	6	127
129 Bhutan	0.654	71.8	13.0	4.1	10,746	-21	131
130 Namibia	0.646	63.7	12.6 j	7.0 f	9,357	-17	129
131 India	0.645	69.7	12.2	6.5 j	6,681	-5	130
132 Honduras	0.634	75.3	10.1	6.6	5,308	1	132
133 Bangladesh	0.632	72.6	11.6	6.2	4,976	7	134
134 Kiribati	0.630	68.4	11.8 m	8.0 m	4,260	12	133
135 Sao Tome and Principe	0.625	70.4	12.7 j	6.4 j	3,952	16	135
136 Micronesia (Federated States of)	0.620	67.9	11.5 k	7.8 n	3,983	13	136
137 Lao People's Democratic Republic	0.613	67.9	11.0	5.3 f	7,413	-16	137
138 Eswatini (Kingdom of)	0.611	60.2	11.8 j	6.9 m	7,919	-19	139
138 Ghana	0.611	64.1	11.5	7.3 f	5,269	-3	138
140 Vanuatu	0.609	70.5	11.7 n	7.1	3,105	20	140
141 Timor-Leste	0.606	69.5	12.6 j	4.8 p	4,440	3	141
142 Nepal	0.602	70.8	12.8	5.0 j	3,457	13	143
143 Kenya	0.601	66.7	11.3 p	6.6 f	4,244	5	141
144 Cambodia	0.594	69.8	11.5 p	5.0 f	4,246	3	144
145 Equatorial Guinea	0.592	58.7	9.7 n	5.9 k	13,944	-57	145
146 Zambia	0.584	63.9	11.5 p	7.2 p	3,326	10	145
147 Myanmar	0.583	67.1	10.7	5.0 p	4,961	-6	148
148 Angola	0.581	61.2	11.8 p	5.2 p	6,104	-17	145
149 Congo	0.574	64.6	11.7 n	6.5 o	2,879	13	149
150 Zimbabwe	0.571	61.5	11.0 m	8.5	2,666	14	150
151 Solomon Islands	0.567	73.0	10.2 j	5.7 m	2,253	17	151
151 Syrian Arab Republic	0.567	72.7	8.9 j	5.1 m	3,613 t	2	152
153 Cameroon	0.563	59.3	12.1	6.3 m	3,581	1	153
154 Pakistan	0.557	67.3	8.3	5.2	5,005	-15	154
155 Papua New Guinea	0.555	64.5	10.2 p	4.7 f	4,301	-10	156
156 Comoros	0.554	64.3	11.2	5.1 n	3,099	5	154
Low human development							
157 Mauritania	0.546	64.9	8.6	4.7 f	5,135	-21	157
158 Benin	0.545	61.8	12.6	3.8 p	3,254	0	158
159 Uganda	0.544	63.4	11.4 p	6.2 p	2,123	15	160
160 Rwanda	0.543	69.0	11.2	4.4 j	2,155	12	159
161 Nigeria	0.539	54.7	10.0 p	6.7 p	4,910	-19	161
162 Côte d'Ivoire	0.538	57.8	10.0	5.3 f	5,069	-25	161
163 Tanzania (United Republic of)	0.529	65.5	8.1	6.1 f	2,600	2	164
164 Madagascar	0.528	67.0	10.2	6.1 n	1,596	16	163
165 Lesotho	0.527	54.3	11.3 j	6.5 m	3,151	-6	165
166 Djibouti	0.524	67.1	6.8 j	4.1 n	5,689	-34	166
167 Togo	0.515	61.0	12.7	4.9 m	1,602	12	168
168 Senegal	0.512	67.9	8.6	3.2 j	3,309	-11	167
169 Afghanistan	0.511	64.8	10.2	3.9 f	2,229	0	169
170 Haiti	0.510	64.0	9.7 j	5.6 p	1,709	7	170
170 Sudan	0.510	65.3	7.9 j	3.8 f	3,829	-18	171
172 Gambia	0.496	62.1	9.9 p	3.9 m	2,168	-1	172
173 Ethiopia	0.485	66.6	8.8 j	2.9 m	2,207	-3	174
174 Malawi	0.483	64.3	11.2 j	4.7 f	1,035	13	174
175 Congo (Democratic Republic of the)	0.480	60.7	9.7 j	6.8	1,063	11	174
175 Guinea-Bissau	0.480	58.3	10.6 m	3.6 m	1,996	1	178
175 Liberia	0.480	64.1	9.6 n	4.8 f	1,258	8	173
178 Guinea	0.477	61.6	9.4 m,p	2.8 p	2,405	-12	177
179 Yemen	0.470	66.1	8.8 j	3.2 f	1,594 t	2	179
180 Eritrea	0.459	66.3	5.0 j	3.9 n	2,793 u	-17	180
181 Mozambique	0.456	60.9	10.0	3.5 j	1,250	3	181
182 Burkina Faso	0.452	61.6	9.3	1.6 p	2,133	-9	183
182 Sierra Leone	0.452	54.7	10.2 f	3.7 f	1,668	-4	182
184 Mali	0.434	59.3	7.5	2.4 m	2,269	-17	184
185 Burundi	0.433	61.6	11.1	3.3 p	754	4	184

Continued →

TABLE 1 / HUMAN DEVELOPMENT INDEX AND ITS COMPONENTS

TABLE 1

	Human Development Index (HDI)	SDG 3 Life expectancy at birth	SDG 4.3 Expected years of schooling	SDG 4.4 Mean years of schooling	SDG 8.5 Gross national income (GNI) per capita	GNI per capita rank minus HDI rank	HDI rank
	Value	(years)	(years)	(years)	(2017 PPP $)		
HDI RANK	2019	2019	2019[a]	2019[a]	2019	2019	2018
185 South Sudan	0.433	57.9	5.3[n]	4.8[n]	2,003[u]	-10	186
187 Chad	0.398	54.2	7.3	2.5[p]	1,555	-5	187
188 Central African Republic	0.397	53.3	7.6[j]	4.3[f]	993	0	188
189 Niger	0.394	62.4	6.5	2.1[j]	1,201	-4	189
Other countries or territories							
Korea (Democratic People's Rep. of)	..	72.3	10.8[j]	..	..	..	..
Monaco	..	..	..	..	..	..	..
Nauru	..	..	11.2[j]	..	16,237	..	..
San Marino	..	..	13.0	..	..	..	..
Somalia	..	57.4	..	..	..	..	..
Tuvalu	..	..	12.3[j]	..	6,132	..	..
Human development groups							
Very high human development	0.898	79.6	16.3	12.2	44,566	–	–
High human development	0.753	75.3	14.0	8.4	14,255	–	–
Medium human development	0.631	69.3	11.5	6.3	6,153	–	–
Low human development	0.513	61.4	9.4	4.9	2,745	–	–
Developing countries	0.689	71.3	12.2	7.5	10,583	–	–
Regions							
Arab States	0.705	72.1	12.1	7.3	14,869	–	–
East Asia and the Pacific	0.747	75.4	13.6	8.1	14,710	–	–
Europe and Central Asia	0.791	74.4	14.7	10.4	17,939	–	–
Latin America and the Caribbean	0.766	75.6	14.6	8.7	14,812	–	–
South Asia	0.641	69.9	11.7	6.5	6,532	–	–
Sub-Saharan Africa	0.547	61.5	10.1	5.8	3,686	–	–
Least developed countries	0.538	65.3	9.9	4.9	2,935	–	–
Small island developing states	0.728	72.0	12.3	8.7	16,825	–	–
Organisation for Economic Co-operation and Development	0.900	80.4	16.3	12.0	44,967	–	–
World	**0.737**	**72.8**	**12.7**	**8.5**	**16,734**	**–**	**–**

Notes

a   Data refer to 2019 or the most recent year available.

b   In calculating the HDI value, expected years of schooling is capped at 18 years.

c   Based on data from OECD (2019b).

d   In calculating the HDI value, GNI per capita is capped at $75,000.

e   Updated by HDRO based on data from Eurostat (2019).

f   Based on projections from Barro and Lee (2018).

g   Value from UNDESA (2011).

h   Imputed mean years of schooling for Austria.

i   Estimated using the purchasing power parity (PPP) rate and projected growth rate of Switzerland.

j   Updated by HDRO based on data from UNESCO Institute for Statistics (2020).

k   Based on data from the national statistical office.

l   Estimated using the PPP rate and projected growth rate of Spain.

m   Updated by HDRO based on data from United Nations Children's Fund (UNICEF) Multiple Indicator Cluster Surveys for 2006–2019.

n   Based on cross-country regression.

o   Updated by HDRO using projections from Barro and Lee (2018).

p   Updated by HDRO based on data from ICF Macro Demographic and Health Surveys for 2006–2019.

q   Based on cross-country regression and the projected growth rate from UNECLAC (2020).

r   Updated by HDRO based on data from CEDLAS and World Bank (2020).

s   HDRO estimate based on data from World Bank (2020a) and United Nations Statistics Division (2020b) and UNECLAC (2020).

t   HDRO estimate based on data from World Bank (2020a) and United Nations Statistics Division (2020b) and the projected growth rate from UNESCWA (2020).

u   HDRO estimate based on data from World Bank (2020a), United Nations Statistics Division (2020b) and IMF (2020).

Definitions

Human Development Index (HDI): A composite index measuring average achievement in three basic dimensions of human development—a long and healthy life, knowledge and a decent standard of living. See *Technical note 1* at http://hdr.undp.org/sites/default/files/hdr2020_technical_notes.pdf for details on how the HDI is calculated.

Life expectancy at birth: Number of years a newborn infant could expect to live if prevailing patterns of age-specific mortality rates at the time of birth stay the same throughout the infant's life.

Expected years of schooling: Number of years of schooling that a child of school entrance age can expect to receive if prevailing patterns of age-specific enrolment rates persist throughout the child's life.

Mean years of schooling: Average number of years of education received by people ages 25 and older, converted from education attainment levels using official durations of each level.

Gross national income (GNI) per capita: Aggregate income of an economy generated by its production and its ownership of factors of production, less the incomes paid for the use of factors of production owned by the rest of the world, converted to international dollars using PPP rates, divided by midyear population.

GNI per capita rank minus HDI rank: Difference in ranking by GNI per capita and by HDI value. A negative value means that the country is better ranked by GNI than by HDI value.

HDI rank for 2018: Ranking by HDI value for 2018, calculated using the same most recently revised data available in 2020 that were used to calculate HDI values for 2019.

Main data sources

Columns 1 and 7: HDRO calculations based on data from UNDESA (2019a), UNESCO Institute for Statistics (2020), United Nations Statistics Division (2020b), World Bank (2020a), Barro and Lee (2018) and IMF (2020).

Column 2: UNDESA (2019a).

Column 3: UNESCO Institute for Statistics (2020), ICF Macro Demographic and Health Surveys, UNICEF Multiple Indicator Cluster Surveys and OECD (2019b).

Column 4: UNESCO Institute for Statistics (2020), Barro and Lee (2018), ICF Macro Demographic and Health Surveys, UNICEF Multiple Indicator Cluster Surveys and OECD (2019b).

Column 5: World Bank (2020a), IMF (2020) and United Nations Statistics Division (2020b).

Column 6: Calculated based on data in columns 1 and 5.

TABLE 2

Human Development Index trends, 1990–2019

		Human Development Index (HDI)								Change in HDI rank	Average annual HDI growth (%)			
				Value										
HDI RANK		1990	2000	2010	2014	2015	2017	2018	2019	2014-2019ᵃ	1990-2000	2000-2010	2010-2019	1990-2019
Very high human development														
1	Norway	0.849	0.915	0.940	0.944	0.947	0.954	0.956	0.957	0	0.75	0.27	0.20	0.41
2	Ireland	0.773	0.867	0.901	0.928	0.935	0.947	0.951	0.955	7	1.15	0.39	0.65	0.73
2	Switzerland	0.840	0.898	0.941	0.942	0.947	0.949	0.955	0.955	0	0.67	0.47	0.16	0.44
4	Hong Kong, China (SAR)	0.784	0.830	0.904	0.926	0.930	0.941	0.946	0.949	7	0.57	0.86	0.54	0.66
4	Iceland	0.807	0.867	0.898	0.931	0.934	0.943	0.946	0.949	4	0.72	0.35	0.62	0.56
6	Germany	0.808	0.876	0.927	0.937	0.938	0.943	0.946	0.947	-3	0.81	0.57	0.24	0.55
7	Sweden	0.821	0.903	0.911	0.935	0.938	0.942	0.943	0.945	-3	0.96	0.09	0.41	0.49
8	Australia	0.871	0.903	0.930	0.933	0.938	0.941	0.943	0.944	-2	0.36	0.30	0.17	0.28
8	Netherlands	0.836	0.882	0.917	0.932	0.934	0.939	0.942	0.944	-1	0.54	0.39	0.32	0.42
10	Denmark	0.806	0.870	0.917	0.935	0.933	0.936	0.939	0.940	-6	0.77	0.53	0.28	0.53
11	Finland	0.790	0.864	0.916	0.928	0.930	0.935	0.937	0.938	-2	0.90	0.59	0.26	0.59
11	Singapore	0.721	0.821	0.909	0.926	0.931	0.933	0.936	0.938	0	1.31	1.02	0.35	0.91
13	United Kingdom	0.781	0.874	0.912	0.925	0.923	0.926	0.928	0.932	0	1.13	0.43	0.24	0.61
14	Belgium	0.813	0.880	0.910	0.918	0.922	0.929	0.930	0.931	1	0.80	0.34	0.25	0.47
14	New Zealand	0.826	0.876	0.906	0.916	0.921	0.926	0.928	0.931	3	0.59	0.34	0.30	0.41
16	Canada	0.850	0.867	0.901	0.918	0.921	0.926	0.928	0.929	-1	0.20	0.39	0.34	0.31
17	United States	0.865	0.886	0.916	0.920	0.921	0.924	0.925	0.926	-3	0.24	0.33	0.12	0.24
18	Austria	0.803	0.847	0.904	0.913	0.915	0.919	0.921	0.922	0	0.53	0.65	0.22	0.48
19	Israel	0.801	0.861	0.895	0.909	0.910	0.913	0.916	0.919	1	0.72	0.39	0.29	0.48
19	Japan	0.818	0.858	0.887	0.906	0.908	0.915	0.917	0.919	2	0.48	0.33	0.39	0.40
19	Liechtenstein	..	0.862	0.904	0.911	0.911	0.916	0.919	0.919	0	..	0.48	0.18	..
22	Slovenia	0.774	0.832	0.889	0.894	0.894	0.907	0.912	0.917	2	0.73	0.66	0.35	0.59
23	Korea (Republic of)	0.732	0.823	0.889	0.904	0.907	0.912	0.914	0.916	-1	1.18	0.77	0.33	0.78
23	Luxembourg	0.797	0.860	0.898	0.903	0.906	0.913	0.913	0.916	0	0.76	0.43	0.22	0.48
25	Spain	0.761	0.832	0.872	0.888	0.895	0.903	0.905	0.904	1	0.90	0.47	0.40	0.60
26	France	0.786	0.849	0.879	0.893	0.895	0.897	0.898	0.901	-1	0.77	0.35	0.28	0.47
27	Czechia	0.738	0.804	0.870	0.888	0.891	0.896	0.898	0.900	-1	0.86	0.79	0.38	0.69
28	Malta	0.752	0.795	0.853	0.874	0.880	0.888	0.894	0.895	2	0.56	0.71	0.54	0.60
29	Estonia	0.735	0.787	0.852	0.871	0.877	0.885	0.889	0.892	2	0.69	0.80	0.51	0.67
29	Italy	0.776	0.838	0.879	0.882	0.882	0.886	0.890	0.892	-1	0.77	0.48	0.16	0.48
31	United Arab Emirates	0.723	0.782	0.820	0.847	0.859	0.881	0.889	0.890	6	0.79	0.48	0.91	0.72
32	Greece	0.761	0.804	0.865	0.875	0.877	0.879	0.881	0.888	-3	0.55	0.73	0.29	0.53
33	Cyprus	0.735	0.804	0.856	0.862	0.865	0.878	0.885	0.887	0	0.90	0.63	0.40	0.65
34	Lithuania	0.738	0.762	0.831	0.859	0.862	0.873	0.876	0.882	0	0.32	0.87	0.66	0.62
35	Poland	0.718	0.790	0.840	0.858	0.863	0.873	0.877	0.880	0	0.96	0.62	0.52	0.70
36	Andorra	..	0.813	0.837	0.863	0.862	0.863	0.867	0.868	-4	..	0.29	0.40	..
37	Latvia	0.711	0.735	0.824	0.845	0.849	0.859	0.863	0.866	3	0.33	1.15	0.55	0.68
38	Portugal	0.718	0.792	0.829	0.847	0.854	0.858	0.860	0.864	-1	0.99	0.46	0.46	0.64
39	Slovakia	0.741	0.765	0.831	0.847	0.850	0.855	0.858	0.860	-2	0.32	0.83	0.38	0.51
40	Hungary	0.708	0.772	0.831	0.838	0.842	0.846	0.850	0.854	1	0.87	0.74	0.30	0.65
40	Saudi Arabia	0.697	0.743	0.809	0.852	0.859	0.852	0.854	0.854	-4	0.64	0.85	0.60	0.70
42	Bahrain	0.749	0.795	0.800	0.820	0.848	0.854	0.852	0.852	6	0.60	0.06	0.70	0.45
43	Chile	0.706	0.756	0.803	0.837	0.842	0.847	0.849	0.851	0	0.69	0.60	0.65	0.65
43	Croatia	0.677	0.757	0.815	0.835	0.840	0.845	0.848	0.851	2	1.12	0.74	0.48	0.79
45	Qatar	0.750	0.816	0.834	0.835	0.839	0.848	0.845	0.848	0	0.85	0.22	0.19	0.42
46	Argentina	0.718	0.781	0.829	0.836	0.840	0.843	0.842	0.845	-2	0.84	0.60	0.21	0.56
47	Brunei Darussalam	0.767	0.802	0.827	0.838	0.838	0.838	0.836	0.838	-6	0.45	0.31	0.15	0.31
48	Montenegro	..	..	0.802	0.813	0.816	0.822	0.826	0.829	2	..	..	0.37	..
49	Romania	0.708	0.716	0.805	0.811	0.815	0.821	0.823	0.828	2	0.11	1.18	0.31	0.54
50	Palau	..	0.744	0.786	0.825	0.820	0.822	0.822	0.826	-3	..	0.55	0.55	..
51	Kazakhstan	0.690	0.685	0.764	0.798	0.806	0.815	0.819	0.825	7	-0.07	1.10	0.86	0.62
52	Russian Federation	0.735	0.722	0.781	0.807	0.809	0.820	0.823	0.824	1	-0.18	0.79	0.60	0.39
53	Belarus	..	0.686	0.795	0.814	0.814	0.819	0.823	0.823	-4	..	1.49	0.39	..
54	Turkey	0.583	0.660	0.739	0.796	0.801	0.814	0.817	0.820	5	1.25	1.14	1.16	1.18
55	Uruguay	0.694	0.743	0.782	0.803	0.806	0.814	0.816	0.817	1	0.68	0.51	0.49	0.56
56	Bulgaria	0.708	0.720	0.788	0.806	0.809	0.811	0.813	0.816	-2	0.17	0.91	0.39	0.49
57	Panama	0.675	0.735	0.774	0.795	0.799	0.811	0.812	0.815	5	0.86	0.52	0.58	0.65
58	Bahamas	..	0.797	0.805	0.805	0.808	0.812	0.812	0.814	-3	..	0.10	0.12	..
58	Barbados	0.732	0.771	0.797	0.808	0.809	0.810	0.810	0.814	-6	0.52	0.33	0.23	0.37
60	Oman	..	0.693	0.782	0.802	0.814	0.819	0.813	0.813	-3	..	1.22	0.43	..
61	Georgia	..	0.690	0.751	0.783	0.790	0.799	0.805	0.812	7	..	0.85	0.87	..
62	Costa Rica	0.665	0.721	0.765	0.796	0.797	0.804	0.808	0.810	-3	0.81	0.59	0.64	0.68

Continued →

TABLE 1 / HUMAN DEVELOPMENT INDEX AND ITS COMPONENTS

TABLE 2

HDI RANK		Human Development Index (HDI) Value								Change in HDI rank	Average annual HDI growth (%)			
		1990	2000	2010	2014	2015	2017	2018	2019	2014-2019[a]	1990-2000	2000-2010	2010-2019	1990-2019
62	Malaysia	0.643	0.723	0.772	0.791	0.796	0.805	0.805	0.810	1	1.18	0.66	0.54	0.80
64	Kuwait	0.705	0.781	0.788	0.796	0.801	0.805	0.807	0.806	-5	1.03	0.09	0.25	0.46
64	Serbia	0.722	0.716	0.766	0.784	0.789	0.798	0.803	0.806	3	-0.08	0.68	0.57	0.38
66	Mauritius	0.624	0.678	0.751	0.789	0.789	0.797	0.801	0.804	-2	0.83	1.03	0.76	0.88
High human development														
67	Seychelles	..	0.714	0.764	0.775	0.786	0.789	0.790	0.796	2	..	0.68	0.46	..
67	Trinidad and Tobago	0.668	0.717	0.784	0.785	0.792	0.795	0.795	0.796	-1	0.71	0.90	0.17	0.61
69	Albania	0.650	0.671	0.745	0.787	0.788	0.790	0.792	0.795	-4	0.32	1.05	0.72	0.70
70	Cuba	0.680	0.691	0.781	0.767	0.772	0.777	0.781	0.783	5	0.16	1.23	0.03	0.49
70	Iran (Islamic Republic of)	0.565	0.658	0.742	0.774	0.774	0.787	0.785	0.783	1	1.54	1.21	0.60	1.13
72	Sri Lanka	0.629	0.691	0.754	0.773	0.776	0.775	0.779	0.782	0	0.94	0.88	0.41	0.75
73	Bosnia and Herzegovina	..	0.679	0.721	0.758	0.761	0.774	0.777	0.780	8	..	0.60	0.88	..
74	Grenada	..	..	0.754	0.766	0.770	0.770	0.773	0.779	2	..	..	0.36	..
74	Mexico	0.656	0.708	0.748	0.761	0.766	0.771	0.776	0.779	4	0.77	0.55	0.45	0.59
74	Saint Kitts and Nevis	..	..	0.746	0.768	0.768	0.770	0.773	0.779	0	..	..	0.48	..
74	Ukraine	0.725	0.694	0.755	0.771	0.765	0.771	0.774	0.779	-1	-0.44	0.85	0.35	0.25
78	Antigua and Barbuda	..	..	0.763	0.760	0.762	0.768	0.772	0.778	1	..	..	0.22	..
79	Peru	0.613	0.679	0.721	0.760	0.759	0.767	0.771	0.777	0	1.03	0.60	0.83	0.82
79	Thailand	0.577	0.652	0.724	0.742	0.749	0.765	0.772	0.777	8	1.23	1.05	0.79	1.03
81	Armenia	0.654	0.669	0.747	0.764	0.768	0.769	0.771	0.776	-4	0.23	1.11	0.42	0.59
82	North Macedonia	..	0.677	0.743	0.755	0.761	0.767	0.770	0.774	2	..	0.93	0.46	..
83	Colombia	0.603	0.666	0.729	0.753	0.756	0.763	0.764	0.767	2	1.00	0.91	0.57	0.83
84	Brazil	0.613	0.685	0.727	0.756	0.756	0.761	0.762	0.765	-2	1.12	0.60	0.57	0.77
85	China	0.499	0.588	0.699	0.731	0.739	0.750	0.755	0.761	12	1.65	1.74	0.95	1.47
86	Ecuador	0.648	0.675	0.726	0.756	0.764	0.760	0.762	0.759	-4	0.41	0.73	0.50	0.55
86	Saint Lucia	..	0.695	0.730	0.735	0.747	0.759	0.758	0.759	6	..	0.49	0.43	..
88	Azerbaijan	..	0.635	0.726	0.740	0.744	0.754	0.754	0.756	1	..	1.35	0.45	..
88	Dominican Republic	0.599	0.659	0.706	0.730	0.738	0.746	0.751	0.756	10	0.96	0.69	0.76	0.81
90	Moldova (Republic of)	0.690	0.643	0.713	0.737	0.736	0.743	0.746	0.750	0	-0.70	1.04	0.56	0.29
91	Algeria	0.572	0.637	0.721	0.736	0.740	0.745	0.746	0.748	0	1.08	1.25	0.41	0.93
92	Lebanon	..	..	0.766	0.748	0.744	0.748	0.747	0.744	-6	..	..	-0.32	..
93	Fiji	0.662	0.695	0.715	0.733	0.737	0.740	0.742	0.743	1	0.49	0.28	0.43	0.40
94	Dominica	..	0.703	0.740	0.741	0.739	0.736	0.738	0.742	-6	..	0.51	0.03	..
95	Maldives	..	0.622	0.685	0.718	0.724	0.731	0.734	0.740	8	..	0.97	0.86	..
95	Tunisia	0.567	0.651	0.716	0.726	0.729	0.734	0.738	0.740	7	1.39	0.96	0.37	0.92
97	Saint Vincent and the Grenadines	..	0.681	0.718	0.733	0.733	0.734	0.736	0.738	-3	..	0.53	0.31	..
97	Suriname	..	..	0.710	0.735	0.740	0.732	0.734	0.738	-5	..	..	0.43	..
99	Mongolia	0.578	0.588	0.696	0.732	0.735	0.728	0.735	0.737	-3	0.17	1.70	0.64	0.84
100	Botswana	0.573	0.581	0.663	0.711	0.717	0.726	0.730	0.735	5	0.14	1.33	1.15	0.86
101	Jamaica	0.645	0.678	0.732	0.729	0.731	0.734	0.734	0.734	-2	0.50	0.77	0.03	0.45
102	Jordan	0.625	0.711	0.737	0.729	0.730	0.726	0.728	0.729	-3	1.30	0.36	-0.12	0.53
103	Paraguay	0.598	0.643	0.696	0.715	0.721	0.726	0.727	0.728	1	0.73	0.80	0.50	0.68
104	Tonga	0.654	0.675	0.699	0.707	0.720	0.723	0.723	0.725	2	0.32	0.35	0.41	0.36
105	Libya	0.724	0.780	0.798	0.728	0.697	0.714	0.721	0.724	-4	0.75	0.23	-1.08	0.00
106	Uzbekistan	..	0.599	0.669	0.696	0.701	0.713	0.717	0.720	4	..	1.11	0.82	..
107	Bolivia (Plurinational State of)	0.551	0.627	0.667	0.690	0.697	0.710	0.714	0.718	6	1.30	0.62	0.82	0.92
107	Indonesia	0.523	0.603	0.665	0.690	0.695	0.707	0.712	0.718	6	1.43	0.98	0.86	1.10
107	Philippines	0.593	0.632	0.671	0.696	0.701	0.708	0.711	0.718	3	0.64	0.60	0.76	0.66
110	Belize	0.610	0.640	0.695	0.705	0.710	0.714	0.714	0.716	-3	0.48	0.83	0.33	0.55
111	Samoa	0.633	0.651	0.698	0.703	0.707	0.710	0.709	0.715	-3	0.28	0.70	0.27	0.42
111	Turkmenistan	..	..	0.666	0.689	0.694	0.701	0.710	0.715	4	..	..	0.79	..
113	Venezuela (Bolivarian Republic of)	0.644	0.676	0.757	0.775	0.769	0.743	0.733	0.711	-44	0.49	1.14	-0.69	0.34
114	South Africa	0.627	0.631	0.664	0.693	0.701	0.705	0.707	0.709	-2	0.06	0.51	0.73	0.42
115	Palestine, State of	..	..	0.684	0.697	0.701	0.706	0.708	0.708	-6	..	..	0.38	..
116	Egypt	0.548	0.613	0.668	0.685	0.691	0.698	0.701	0.707	1	1.13	0.86	0.63	0.88
117	Marshall Islands	..	..	..	..	..	0.699	0.702	0.704	..	..	..	..	..
117	Viet Nam	0.483	0.586	0.661	0.683	0.688	0.696	0.700	0.704	1	1.95	1.21	0.70	1.31
119	Gabon	0.613	0.621	0.652	0.682	0.685	0.694	0.697	0.703	0	0.13	0.49	0.84	0.47
Medium human development														
120	Kyrgyzstan	0.640	0.620	0.662	0.686	0.690	0.694	0.696	0.697	-4	-0.32	0.66	0.57	0.29
121	Morocco	0.457	0.529	0.616	0.652	0.658	0.673	0.680	0.686	2	1.47	1.53	1.20	1.41
122	Guyana	0.548	0.616	0.649	0.671	0.674	0.677	0.680	0.682	-2	1.18	0.52	0.55	0.76
123	Iraq	0.560	0.595	0.636	0.645	0.649	0.667	0.671	0.674	4	0.61	0.67	0.65	0.64

Continued →

TABLE 2

HDI RANK	Human Development Index (HDI) Value								Change in HDI rank	Average annual HDI growth (%)			
	1990	2000	2010	2014	2015	2017	2018	2019	2014-2019[a]	1990-2000	2000-2010	2010-2019	1990-2019
124 El Salvador	0.536	0.615	0.668	0.668	0.668	0.671	0.670	0.673	-3	1.38	0.83	0.08	0.79
125 Tajikistan	0.617	0.555	0.638	0.652	0.652	0.657	0.661	0.668	-2	-1.05	1.40	0.51	0.27
126 Cabo Verde	..	0.569	0.632	0.654	0.656	0.660	0.663	0.665	-4	..	1.06	0.57	..
127 Guatemala	0.481	0.549	0.606	0.648	0.652	0.655	0.657	0.663	-1	1.33	0.99	1.00	1.11
128 Nicaragua	0.497	0.577	0.622	0.649	0.652	0.661	0.659	0.660	-3	1.50	0.75	0.66	0.98
129 Bhutan	..	..	0.574	0.618	0.628	0.646	0.649	0.654	1	..	..	1.46	..
130 Namibia	0.581	0.544	0.589	0.631	0.638	0.644	0.645	0.646	-2	-0.66	0.80	1.03	0.37
131 India	0.429	0.495	0.579	0.616	0.624	0.640	0.642	0.645	1	1.44	1.58	1.21	1.42
132 Honduras	0.519	0.566	0.610	0.616	0.618	0.630	0.633	0.634	0	0.87	0.75	0.43	0.69
133 Bangladesh	0.394	0.478	0.557	0.579	0.595	0.616	0.625	0.632	8	1.95	1.54	1.41	1.64
134 Kiribati	..	0.553	0.593	0.617	0.625	0.627	0.628	0.630	-3	..	0.70	0.67	..
135 Sao Tome and Principe	0.452	0.498	0.561	0.591	0.604	0.619	0.624	0.625	1	0.97	1.20	1.21	1.12
136 Micronesia (Federated States of)	..	0.546	0.601	0.604	0.612	0.616	0.618	0.620	-2	..	0.96	0.35	..
137 Lao People's Democratic Republic	0.405	0.471	0.552	0.589	0.598	0.608	0.609	0.613	1	1.52	1.60	1.17	1.44
138 Eswatini (Kingdom of)	0.541	0.465	0.510	0.568	0.581	0.597	0.605	0.611	5	-1.50	0.93	2.03	0.42
138 Ghana	0.465	0.494	0.565	0.590	0.590	0.602	0.606	0.611	-1	0.61	1.35	0.87	0.95
140 Vanuatu	..	..	0.590	0.594	0.598	0.601	0.603	0.609	-5	..	..	0.35	..
141 Timor-Leste	..	0.484	0.628	0.620	0.610	0.599	0.599	0.606	-12	..	2.64	-0.40	..
142 Nepal	0.387	0.453	0.537	0.576	0.583	0.588	0.596	0.602	0	1.59	1.72	1.28	1.54
143 Kenya	0.482	0.461	0.551	0.580	0.587	0.595	0.599	0.601	-3	-0.44	1.80	0.97	0.76
144 Cambodia	0.368	0.424	0.539	0.565	0.570	0.582	0.585	0.594	0	1.43	2.43	1.09	1.66
145 Equatorial Guinea	..	0.525	0.576	0.586	0.589	0.584	0.582	0.592	-6	..	0.93	0.30	..
146 Zambia	0.421	0.425	0.527	0.561	0.569	0.578	0.582	0.584	0	0.09	2.17	1.15	1.13
147 Myanmar	0.342	0.414	0.515	0.550	0.557	0.572	0.579	0.583	3	1.93	2.21	1.39	1.86
148 Angola	..	0.400	0.517	0.565	0.572	0.582	0.582	0.581	-4	..	2.60	1.31	..
149 Congo	0.500	0.461	0.520	0.560	0.580	0.574	0.573	0.574	-2	-0.81	1.21	1.10	0.48
150 Zimbabwe	0.478	0.430	0.482	0.547	0.553	0.563	0.569	0.571	1	-1.05	1.15	1.90	0.61
151 Solomon Islands	..	0.475	0.537	0.559	0.563	0.562	0.564	0.567	-3	..	1.23	0.61	..
151 Syrian Arab Republic	0.550	0.600	0.672	0.556	0.537	0.564	0.563	0.567	-2	0.87	1.14	-1.87	0.11
153 Cameroon	0.448	0.440	0.505	0.540	0.549	0.557	0.560	0.563	1	-0.18	1.39	1.22	0.79
154 Pakistan	0.402	0.447	0.512	0.530	0.536	0.550	0.552	0.557	2	1.07	1.37	0.94	1.13
155 Papua New Guinea	0.380	0.450	0.522	0.542	0.548	0.549	0.549	0.555	-2	1.71	1.50	0.68	1.31
156 Comoros	..	0.465	0.521	0.543	0.545	0.550	0.552	0.554	-4	..	1.14	0.68	..
Low human development													
157 Mauritania	0.397	0.464	0.505	0.531	0.536	0.540	0.542	0.546	-2	1.57	0.85	0.87	1.10
158 Benin	0.364	0.416	0.494	0.527	0.532	0.536	0.541	0.545	-1	1.34	1.73	1.10	1.40
159 Uganda	0.320	0.404	0.498	0.519	0.525	0.532	0.538	0.544	2	2.36	2.11	0.99	1.85
160 Rwanda	0.248	0.341	0.492	0.521	0.526	0.535	0.540	0.543	-1	3.24	3.73	1.10	2.74
161 Nigeria	..	..	0.482	0.523	0.526	0.531	0.534	0.539	-3	..	..	1.25	..
162 Côte d'Ivoire	0.404	0.421	0.468	0.492	0.503	0.525	0.534	0.538	7	0.41	1.06	1.56	0.99
163 Tanzania (United Republic of)	0.368	0.390	0.481	0.504	0.514	0.523	0.524	0.529	-1	0.58	2.12	1.06	1.26
164 Madagascar	..	0.462	0.511	0.520	0.522	0.526	0.527	0.528	-4	..	1.01	0.36	..
165 Lesotho	0.498	0.459	0.460	0.498	0.503	0.517	0.522	0.527	2	-0.81	0.02	1.52	0.20
166 Djibouti	..	0.360	0.454	0.492	0.499	0.510	0.518	0.524	3	..	2.35	1.61	..
167 Togo	0.406	0.427	0.466	0.493	0.499	0.506	0.510	0.515	1	0.51	0.88	1.12	0.82
168 Senegal	0.376	0.390	0.468	0.499	0.506	0.512	0.516	0.512	-3	0.37	1.84	1.00	1.07
169 Afghanistan	0.302	0.350	0.472	0.500	0.500	0.506	0.509	0.511	-5	1.49	3.04	0.89	1.83
170 Haiti	0.414	0.442	0.471	0.492	0.496	0.505	0.508	0.510	-1	0.66	0.64	0.89	0.72
170 Sudan	0.331	0.403	0.469	0.499	0.504	0.509	0.506	0.510	-5	1.99	1.53	0.94	1.50
172 Gambia	0.349	0.403	0.459	0.468	0.471	0.480	0.487	0.496	1	1.45	1.31	0.87	1.22
173 Ethiopia	..	0.292	0.421	0.455	0.462	0.474	0.478	0.485	5	..	3.73	1.58	..
174 Malawi	0.333	0.388	0.431	0.465	0.468	0.473	0.478	0.483	0	1.54	1.06	1.27	1.29
175 Congo (Democratic Republic of the)	0.369	0.349	0.435	0.460	0.464	0.475	0.478	0.480	0	-0.56	2.23	1.10	0.91
175 Guinea-Bissau	..	..	0.436	0.459	0.464	0.470	0.472	0.480	1	..	..	1.07	..
175 Liberia	..	0.435	0.455	0.478	0.477	0.481	0.480	0.480	-3	..	0.45	0.60	..
178 Guinea	0.282	0.340	0.416	0.452	0.457	0.471	0.473	0.477	1	1.89	2.04	1.53	1.83
179 Yemen	0.401	0.444	0.506	0.502	0.483	0.467	0.468	0.470	-16	1.02	1.32	-0.82	0.55
180 Eritrea	..	..	0.436	0.457	0.454	0.454	0.456	0.459	-3	..	..	0.57	..
181 Mozambique	0.227	0.307	0.401	0.425	0.433	0.446	0.452	0.456	2	3.07	2.71	1.44	2.43
182 Burkina Faso	..	0.293	0.384	0.413	0.422	0.439	0.443	0.452	3	..	2.74	1.83	..
182 Sierra Leone	0.287	0.295	0.399	0.438	0.431	0.443	0.447	0.452	-2	0.28	3.07	1.40	1.58
184 Mali	0.234	0.312	0.408	0.419	0.417	0.427	0.431	0.434	0	2.92	2.72	0.69	2.15
185 Burundi	0.299	0.300	0.411	0.438	0.437	0.434	0.431	0.433	-5	0.03	3.20	0.58	1.29

Continued →

TABLE 2 / HUMAN DEVELOPMENT INDEX TRENDS, 1990–2019   349

TABLE 2

HDI RANK	Human Development Index (HDI) Value								Change in HDI rank 2014–2019[a]	Average annual HDI growth (%)			
	1990	2000	2010	2014	2015	2017	2018	2019		1990–2000	2000–2010	2010–2019	1990–2019
185 South Sudan	..	..	0.410	0.428	0.425	0.426	0.429	0.433	−3	..	..	0.61	..
187 Chad	..	0.293	0.369	0.401	0.398	0.396	0.397	0.398	−1	..	2.33	0.84	..
188 Central African Republic	0.334	0.325	0.365	0.368	0.375	0.391	0.395	0.397	−1	−0.27	1.17	0.94	0.60
189 Niger	0.220	0.262	0.331	0.365	0.372	0.386	0.391	0.394	−1	1.76	2.37	1.95	2.03
Other countries or territories													
Korea (Democratic People's Rep. of)	..	..	..	..	..	..	..	..	..	..	..	..	..
Monaco	..	..	..	..	..	..	..	..	..	..	..	..	..
Nauru	..	..	..	..	..	..	..	..	..	..	..	..	..
San Marino	..	..	..	..	..	..	..	..	..	..	..	..	..
Somalia	..	..	..	..	..	..	..	..	..	..	..	..	..
Tuvalu	..	..	..	..	..	..	..	..	..	..	..	..	..
Human development groups													
Very high human development	0.782	0.826	0.870	0.885	0.889	0.894	0.896	0.898	–	0.55	0.52	0.35	0.48
High human development	0.567	0.629	0.705	0.730	0.735	0.744	0.748	0.753	–	1.04	1.15	0.73	0.98
Medium human development	0.433	0.492	0.571	0.601	0.609	0.624	0.627	0.631	–	1.29	1.50	1.12	1.31
Low human development	0.345	0.381	0.468	0.497	0.500	0.507	0.509	0.513	–	1.00	2.08	1.03	1.38
Developing countries	0.517	0.571	0.642	0.668	0.673	0.683	0.685	0.689	–	1.00	1.18	0.79	1.00
Regions													
Arab States	0.556	0.614	0.676	0.687	0.691	0.699	0.702	0.705	–	1.00	0.97	0.47	0.82
East Asia and the Pacific	0.517	0.595	0.688	0.718	0.724	0.735	0.740	0.747	–	1.42	1.46	0.92	1.28
Europe and Central Asia	0.662	0.675	0.739	0.772	0.775	0.785	0.787	0.791	–	0.19	0.91	0.76	0.62
Latin America and the Caribbean	0.632	0.690	0.736	0.756	0.759	0.762	0.764	0.766	–	0.88	0.65	0.44	0.67
South Asia	0.437	0.501	0.580	0.612	0.620	0.635	0.637	0.641	–	1.38	1.47	1.12	1.33
Sub-Saharan Africa	0.404	0.426	0.501	0.530	0.535	0.542	0.544	0.547	–	0.53	1.63	0.98	1.05
Least developed countries	0.353	0.403	0.489	0.513	0.520	0.531	0.534	0.538	–	1.33	1.95	1.07	1.46
Small island developing states	0.599	0.646	0.706	0.715	0.720	0.724	0.726	0.728	–	0.76	0.89	0.34	0.67
Organisation for Economic Co-operation and Development	0.786	0.835	0.874	0.888	0.891	0.896	0.898	0.900	–	0.61	0.46	0.33	0.47
World	**0.601**	**0.644**	**0.699**	**0.720**	**0.724**	**0.732**	**0.734**	**0.737**	**–**	**0.69**	**0.82**	**0.59**	**0.71**

Notes

For HDI values that are comparable across years and countries, use this table or the interpolated data at http://hdr.undp.org/en/data, which present trends using consistent data.

a   A positive value indicates an improvement in rank.

Definitions

Human Development Index (HDI): A composite index measuring average achievement in three basic dimensions of human development—a long and healthy life, knowledge and a decent standard of living. See *Technical note 1* at http://hdr.undp.org/sites/default/files/hdr2020_technical_notes.pdf for details on how the HDI is calculated.

Average annual HDI growth: A smoothed annualized growth of the HDI in a given period, calculated as the annual compound growth rate.

Main data sources

Columns 1–8: HDRO calculations based on data from UNDESA (2019a), UNESCO Institute for Statistics (2020), United Nations Statistics Division (2020b), World Bank (2020a), Barro and Lee (2018) and IMF (2020).

Column 9: Calculated based on data in columns 4 and 8.

Columns 10–13: Calculated based on data in columns 1, 2, 3 and 8.

TABLE 3

Inequality-adjusted Human Development Index

		Human Development Index (HDI)	Inequality-adjusted HDI (IHDI)			Coefficient of human inequality	Inequality in life expectancy	Inequality-adjusted life expectancy index	Inequality in education[a]	Inequality-adjusted education index	Inequality in income[a]	Inequality-adjusted income index	Income shares held by (%)			Gini coefficient
				Overall loss (%)	Difference from HDI rank[b]								Poorest 40 percent	Richest 10 percent	Richest 1 percent	
		Value	Value				(%)	Value	(%)	Value	(%)	Value				
HDI RANK		2019	2019	2019	2019	2019	2015-2020[c]	2019	2019[d]	2019	2019[d]	2019	2010-2018[e]	2010-2018[e]	2010-2017[e]	2010-2018[e]
Very high human development																
1	Norway	0.957	0.899	6.1	0	6.0	3.0	0.931	2.3	0.908	12.6	0.858	23.2	21.6	9.4	27.0
2	Ireland	0.955	0.885	7.3	-3	7.2	3.4	0.926	3.3	0.892	15.0	0.838	20.5	25.9	11.3	32.8
2	Switzerland	0.955	0.889	6.9	-1	6.8	3.5	0.947	1.8	0.883	14.9	0.841	20.2	25.5	10.6	32.7
4	Hong Kong, China (SAR)	0.949	0.824	13.2	-17	12.6	2.5	0.973	9.8	0.793	25.6	0.724	..	..	..	..
4	Iceland	0.949	0.894	5.8	2	5.6	2.4	0.946	2.8	0.900	11.7	0.841	23.7	22.5	7.6	26.8
6	Germany	0.947	0.869	8.2	-4	7.9	3.8	0.908	2.3	0.922	17.7	0.786	20.4	24.6	12.5	31.9
7	Sweden	0.945	0.882	6.7	0	6.5	2.9	0.938	3.7	0.884	13.0	0.828	22.2	22.3	9.0	28.8
8	Australia	0.944	0.867	8.2	-3	7.9	3.7	0.940	2.7	0.899	17.3	0.771	19.6	27.0	9.1	34.4
8	Netherlands	0.944	0.878	7.0	0	6.9	3.1	0.928	5.4	0.865	12.2	0.843	22.6	23.3	6.2	28.5
10	Denmark	0.940	0.883	6.1	4	6.0	3.6	0.903	2.9	0.894	11.4	0.853	22.8	24.0	10.7	28.7
11	Finland	0.938	0.888	5.3	7	5.3	3.0	0.924	2.2	0.907	10.6	0.835	23.4	22.6	10.1	27.4
11	Singapore	0.938	0.813	13.3	-15	12.8	2.5	0.954	11.0	0.751	25.0	0.750	..	..	14.0	..
13	United Kingdom	0.932	0.856	8.2	-3	7.9	4.1	0.905	2.7	0.902	17.0	0.769	19.0	26.8	12.6	34.8
14	Belgium	0.931	0.859	7.7	1	7.7	3.6	0.914	8.2	0.828	11.4	0.837	22.9	21.9	7.8	27.4
14	New Zealand	0.931	0.859	7.7	1	7.5	4.3	0.917	1.8	0.909	16.4	0.759	..	..	8.7	..
16	Canada	0.929	0.848	8.7	-1	8.4	4.6	0.916	2.7	0.870	18.1	0.766	19.1	25.1	13.6	33.8
17	United States	0.926	0.808	12.7	-11	12.1	6.3	0.848	2.8	0.875	27.1	0.711	15.4	30.5	20.5	41.4
18	Austria	0.922	0.857	7.0	3	6.9	3.7	0.912	2.9	0.840	14.1	0.821	21.3	23.0	9.3	29.7
19	Israel	0.919	0.814	11.4	-6	10.9	3.3	0.937	5.7	0.833	23.7	0.691	15.7	27.7	..	39.0
19	Japan	0.919	0.843	8.3	1	8.1	2.9	0.965	4.7	0.812	16.7	0.763	20.5	26.4	10.4	32.9
19	Liechtenstein	0.919	..	..	..	..	..	..	..	..	..	..	..	..	..	..
22	Slovenia	0.917	0.875	4.6	12	4.6	2.9	0.916	2.1	0.891	8.7	0.820	24.8	20.4	7.7	24.2
23	Korea (Republic of)	0.916	0.815	11.0	-2	10.7	3.0	0.941	8.8	0.789	20.2	0.731	20.3	23.8	12.2	31.6
23	Luxembourg	0.916	0.826	9.8	2	9.6	3.4	0.925	6.3	0.756	19.0	0.806	18.4	25.8	11.9	34.9
25	Spain	0.904	0.783	13.4	-10	13.1	3.0	0.949	16.9	0.691	19.5	0.732	18.4	25.4	11.9	34.7
26	France	0.901	0.820	9.0	2	8.9	3.8	0.927	9.5	0.740	13.5	0.804	21.1	25.8	11.2	31.6
27	Czechia	0.900	0.860	4.4	14	4.4	3.0	0.886	1.4	0.878	8.9	0.818	24.9	21.5	10.1	24.9
28	Malta	0.895	0.823	8.0	5	7.9	4.6	0.918	6.2	0.774	13.0	0.786	21.9	23.3	11.4	29.2
29	Estonia	0.892	0.829	7.1	9	6.9	3.6	0.871	2.3	0.862	14.8	0.758	20.9	22.5	11.1	30.4
29	Italy	0.892	0.783	12.2	-6	11.8	3.1	0.947	10.6	0.709	21.8	0.716	18.0	26.7	8.7	35.9
31	United Arab Emirates	0.890	..	..	..	..	5.2	0.845	18.2	0.656	..	..	18.2	21.4	22.8	32.5
32	Greece	0.888	0.791	10.9	-1	10.8	3.5	0.924	11.1	0.755	17.8	0.709	18.9	25.9	13.4	34.4
33	Cyprus	0.887	0.805	9.2	1	9.1	3.6	0.904	10.5	0.740	13.2	0.779	21.3	25.5	11.6	31.4
34	Lithuania	0.882	0.791	10.3	1	10.0	5.5	0.813	3.9	0.863	20.6	0.706	17.9	28.4	10.4	37.3
35	Poland	0.880	0.813	7.6	7	7.6	4.3	0.865	4.9	0.826	13.5	0.752	21.7	23.5	14.0	29.7
36	Andorra	0.868	..	..	..	..	..	..	10.0	0.648	..	..	..	..	..	..
37	Latvia	0.866	0.783	9.6	0	9.2	5.4	0.805	2.5	0.861	19.6	0.694	18.4	26.9	10.9	35.6
38	Portugal	0.864	0.761	11.9	-5	11.8	3.5	0.921	15.0	0.653	16.9	0.731	19.8	26.7	10.6	33.8
39	Slovakia	0.860	0.807	6.2	7	6.1	5.0	0.841	1.6	0.813	11.7	0.770	23.8	19.9	5.3	25.2
40	Hungary	0.854	0.791	7.4	6	7.3	4.2	0.838	3.1	0.796	14.5	0.743	21.1	23.9	12.1	30.6
40	Saudi Arabia	0.854	..	..	..	..	6.4	0.794	18.0	0.647	..	..	..	..	19.7	..
42	Bahrain	0.852	..	..	..	..	5.5	0.833	22.7	0.594	..	..	..	..	18.0	..
43	Chile	0.851	0.709	16.7	-11	15.9	6.3	0.868	10.4	0.726	31.1	0.567	15.5	36.3	23.7	44.4
43	Croatia	0.851	0.783	8.0	4	7.9	4.3	0.861	4.7	0.767	14.7	0.727	20.7	22.9	8.2	30.4
45	Qatar	0.848	..	..	..	..	5.7	0.874	11.8	0.581	..	..	..	..	29.0	..
46	Argentina	0.845	0.729	13.7	-4	13.2	8.6	0.797	6.0	0.804	25.2	0.606	14.9	29.9	..	41.4
47	Brunei Darussalam	0.838	..	..	..	..	7.6	0.794	..	..	..	..	..	..	..	..
48	Montenegro	0.829	0.749	9.7	0	9.4	3.6	0.844	7.8	0.740	16.9	0.673	15.9	27.7	8.5	39.0
49	Romania	0.828	0.730	11.8	-1	11.4	6.3	0.808	5.3	0.724	22.7	0.664	17.0	24.9	15.2	36.0
50	Palau	0.826	..	..	..	..	..	..	1.9	0.839	..	..	..	..	..	..
51	Kazakhstan	0.825	0.766	7.2	4	7.1	7.7	0.761	3.2	0.804	10.3	0.736	23.4	23.0	..	27.5
52	Russian Federation	0.824	0.740	10.2	2	10.0	7.1	0.751	4.2	0.789	18.8	0.683	18.3	29.9	20.2	37.5
53	Belarus	0.823	0.771	6.3	7	6.3	4.4	0.806	3.7	0.807	10.8	0.704	24.5	21.4	..	25.2
54	Turkey	0.820	0.683	16.7	-11	16.5	9.0	0.808	16.5	0.611	24.1	0.645	15.9	32.6	23.4	41.9
55	Uruguay	0.817	0.712	12.9	-1	12.6	7.9	0.821	6.5	0.715	23.4	0.614	16.3	29.7	14.0	39.7
56	Bulgaria	0.816	0.721	11.6	2	11.3	6.1	0.795	6.1	0.732	21.8	0.644	16.7	31.9	12.6	40.4
57	Panama	0.815	0.643	21.1	-17	20.1	12.0	0.792	11.4	0.620	36.9	0.542	11.9	37.1	..	49.2

Continued →

TABLE 3 / INEQUALITY-ADJUSTED HUMAN DEVELOPMENT INDEX 351

TABLE 3

SDG 10.1

HDI RANK		Human Development Index (HDI) Value 2019	Inequality-adjusted HDI (IHDI) Value 2019	Overall loss (%) 2019	Difference from HDI rank[b] 2019	Coefficient of human inequality 2019	Inequality in life expectancy (%) 2015-2020[c]	Inequality-adjusted life expectancy index Value 2019	Inequality in education[a] (%) 2019[d]	Inequality-adjusted education index Value 2019	Inequality in income[a] (%) 2019[d]	Inequality-adjusted income index Value 2019	Income shares held by (%) Poorest 40 percent 2010-2018[e]	Richest 10 percent 2010-2018[e]	Richest 1 percent 2010-2017[e]	Gini coefficient 2010-2018[e]
58	Bahamas	0.814	..	..	..	..	6.8	0.773	6.3	0.693	..	..	..	..	..	..
58	Barbados	0.814	0.676	17.0	-9	15.9	8.7	0.831	5.5	0.739	33.6	0.502	..	..	..	..
60	Oman	0.813	0.706	13.2	0	12.9	6.7	0.831	11.9	0.633	20.1	0.671	..	..	19.5	..
61	Georgia	0.812	0.716	11.8	5	11.5	7.9	0.762	4.1	0.826	22.5	0.582	18.0	27.5	..	36.4
62	Costa Rica	0.810	0.661	18.4	-11	17.5	7.1	0.862	11.6	0.642	33.9	0.521	12.8	36.3	..	48.0
62	Malaysia	0.810	..	..	..	..	6.1	0.811	12.1	0.638	..	..	15.9	31.3	14.6	41.0
64	Kuwait	0.806	..	..	..	..	5.9	0.803	22.1	0.497	..	..	..	..	19.9	..
64	Serbia	0.806	0.705	12.5	2	12.1	4.9	0.819	7.5	0.724	24.0	0.591	17.3	25.6	12.8	36.2
66	Mauritius	0.804	0.694	13.7	1	13.6	9.4	0.766	13.2	0.639	18.2	0.684	18.8	29.9	13.8	36.8
High human development																
67	Seychelles	0.796	0.670	15.8	-6	15.2	9.6	0.743	6.7	0.678	29.3	0.598	15.2	39.9	20.4	46.8
67	Trinidad and Tobago	0.796	..	..	..	..	14.9	0.701	..	..	..	..	..	..	..	..
69	Albania	0.795	0.708	10.9	7	10.9	7.2	0.836	12.3	0.655	13.2	0.648	19.5	24.8	8.2	33.2
70	Cuba	0.783	..	..	..	..	5.1	0.858	7.8	0.728	..	..	..	..	..	..
70	Iran (Islamic Republic of)	0.783	0.693	11.5	3	11.3	9.2	0.792	5.0	0.719	19.7	0.585	16.2	31.3	16.3	40.8
72	Sri Lanka	0.782	0.673	13.9	-1	13.8	7.0	0.815	12.0	0.657	22.4	0.568	17.7	32.9	..	39.8
73	Bosnia and Herzegovina	0.780	0.667	14.5	-3	14.2	5.4	0.835	17.0	0.590	20.2	0.603	19.8	25.1	9.0	33.0
74	Grenada	0.779	..	..	..	..	11.2	0.716	..	..	..	..	..	..	..	..
74	Mexico	0.779	0.613	21.3	-13	20.8	10.5	0.758	18.4	0.574	33.4	0.529	14.9	36.4	..	45.4
74	Saint Kitts and Nevis	0.779	..	..	..	..	..	..	..	..	..	..	..	..	..	..
74	Ukraine	0.779	0.728	6.5	16	6.5	7.4	0.742	3.6	0.770	8.5	0.675	24.0	22.0	..	26.1
78	Antigua and Barbuda	0.778	..	..	..	..	5.8	0.826	..	..	..	..	..	..	..	..
79	Peru	0.777	0.628	19.2	-8	18.8	10.8	0.779	17.0	0.614	28.6	0.519	14.8	32.1	..	42.8
79	Thailand	0.777	0.646	16.9	-2	16.7	7.9	0.810	18.3	0.557	23.8	0.596	18.3	28.1	20.2	36.4
81	Armenia	0.776	0.699	9.9	12	9.7	8.7	0.774	2.9	0.718	17.4	0.616	20.3	29.2	..	34.4
82	North Macedonia	0.774	0.681	12.0	8	11.8	7.9	0.791	8.4	0.646	19.2	0.619	17.9	23.8	7.7	34.2
83	Colombia	0.767	0.595	22.4	-12	21.6	10.7	0.787	18.6	0.555	35.5	0.483	12.1	39.7	20.5	50.4
84	Brazil	0.765	0.570	25.5	-20	24.4	10.9	0.766	21.2	0.547	41.0	0.442	10.4	42.5	28.3	53.9
85	China	0.761	0.639	16.0	2	15.7	7.9	0.806	11.7	0.580	27.4	0.557	17.2	29.3	13.9	38.5
86	Ecuador	0.759	0.616	18.8	-3	18.4	11.5	0.776	13.9	0.605	29.9	0.498	13.8	34.4	..	45.4
86	Saint Lucia	0.759	0.629	17.1	0	16.9	10.6	0.773	12.6	0.588	27.4	0.547	11.0	38.6	..	51.2
88	Azerbaijan	0.756	0.684	9.5	16	9.4	13.9	0.702	5.3	0.673	8.9	0.678	..	..	..	..
88	Dominican Republic	0.756	0.595	21.3	-7	21.1	17.0	0.691	15.8	0.560	30.4	0.544	15.6	35.2	..	43.7
90	Moldova (Republic of)	0.750	0.672	10.4	13	10.3	9.6	0.722	7.3	0.659	14.0	0.639	24.4	22.0	9.9	25.7
91	Algeria	0.748	0.596	20.3	-2	19.7	14.1	0.752	33.7	0.445	11.4	0.631	23.1	22.9	9.7	27.6
92	Lebanon	0.744	..	..	..	..	7.4	0.840	6.2	0.567	..	..	20.6	24.8	23.4	31.8
93	Fiji	0.743	..	..	..	..	14.9	0.621	..	..	..	..	18.8	29.7	..	36.7
94	Dominica	0.742	..	..	..	..	..	..	..	..	..	..	..	..	..	..
95	Maldives	0.740	0.584	21.1	-10	20.4	6.0	0.852	29.3	0.405	25.8	0.578	21.2	25.2	..	31.3
95	Tunisia	0.740	0.596	19.5	-1	18.9	9.0	0.794	30.7	0.458	16.9	0.583	20.1	25.6	10.7	32.8
97	Saint Vincent and the Grenadines	0.738	..	..	..	..	11.3	0.717	..	..	..	..	..	..	..	..
97	Suriname	0.738	0.535	27.5	-17	26.0	12.8	0.693	18.4	0.551	46.7	0.400	..	..	..	..
99	Mongolia	0.737	0.634	14.0	11	14.0	13.1	0.667	11.9	0.649	16.9	0.588	20.2	25.7	..	32.7
100	Botswana	0.735	..	..	..	..	19.4	0.615	23.3	0.518	..	..	10.9	41.5	22.6	53.3
101	Jamaica	0.734	0.612	16.6	4	15.9	10.0	0.754	5.6	0.651	32.0	0.466	..	..	..	..
102	Jordan	0.729	0.622	14.7	9	14.6	10.6	0.750	15.4	0.564	17.9	0.569	20.3	27.5	16.1	33.7
103	Paraguay	0.728	0.557	23.5	-7	22.8	13.8	0.719	16.7	0.531	37.8	0.452	13.9	35.9	..	46.2
104	Tonga	0.725	..	..	..	..	10.4	0.702	4.5	0.740	..	..	18.2	29.7	..	37.6
105	Libya	0.724	..	..	..	..	9.1	0.740	..	..	..	..	..	..	13.5	..
106	Uzbekistan	0.720	..	..	..	..	13.9	0.685	0.7	0.723	..	..	..	..	..	..
107	Bolivia (Plurinational State of)	0.718	0.546	24.0	-9	23.7	22.5	0.614	17.6	0.573	31.2	0.463	14.7	30.4	..	42.2
107	Indonesia	0.718	0.590	17.8	2	17.7	13.9	0.685	16.2	0.545	23.1	0.551	17.2	30.4	..	39.0
107	Philippines	0.718	0.587	18.2	-1	17.8	15.3	0.668	10.1	0.610	28.1	0.498	15.0	34.8	..	44.4
110	Belize	0.716	0.554	22.6	-5	21.6	11.1	0.747	15.9	0.584	37.9	0.390	..	..	..	..
111	Samoa	0.715	..	..	..	..	..	0.738	4.9	0.678	..	..	17.9	31.3	..	38.7
111	Turkmenistan	0.715	0.586	18.0	2	17.5	23.4	0.568	2.9	0.634	26.2	0.558	..	..	..	..
113	Venezuela (Bolivarian Republic of)	0.711	0.588	17.3	6	17.0	17.1	0.664	8.8	0.638	25.2	0.481	..	..	..	..
114	South Africa	0.709	0.468	34.0	-18	31.2	19.2	0.549	17.3	0.599	57.0	0.312	7.2	50.5	19.2	63.0

Continued →

TABLE 3

HDI RANK		Human Development Index (HDI) Value 2019	Inequality-adjusted HDI (IHDI) Value 2019	Overall loss (%) 2019	Difference from HDI rank[b] 2019	Coefficient of human inequality 2019	Inequality in life expectancy (%) 2015-2020[c]	Inequality-adjusted life expectancy index Value 2019	Inequality in education[a] (%) 2019[d]	Inequality-adjusted education index Value 2019	Inequality in income[a] (%) 2019[d]	Inequality-adjusted income index Value 2019	Income shares held by (%) Poorest 40 percent 2010-2018[e]	Income shares held by (%) Richest 10 percent 2010-2018[e]	Income shares held by (%) Richest 1 percent 2010-2017[e]	Gini coefficient 2010-2018[e]
115	Palestine, State of	0.708	0.613	13.4	16	13.4	12.0	0.732	11.6	0.599	16.6	0.524	19.2	25.2	15.8	33.7
116	Egypt	0.707	0.497	29.7	−9	28.7	11.6	0.707	38.1	0.383	36.5	0.455	21.8	26.9	15.8	31.5
117	Marshall Islands	0.704	..	..	..	..	..	..	4.3	0.677	..	..	..	..	..	..
117	Viet Nam	0.704	0.588	16.5	10	16.5	12.9	0.742	17.6	0.519	19.1	0.526	18.6	27.5	..	35.7
119	Gabon	0.703	0.544	22.6	0	22.5	22.8	0.552	23.5	0.498	21.2	0.588	16.8	27.7	10.9	38.0
Medium human development																
120	Kyrgyzstan	0.697	0.630	9.6	25	9.5	11.3	0.702	3.4	0.706	13.8	0.506	23.4	23.6	..	27.7
121	Morocco	0.686	..	..	..	..	13.0	0.759	..	..	..	..	17.4	31.9	15.0	39.5
122	Guyana	0.682	0.556	18.5	5	18.3	19.0	0.622	10.7	0.536	25.1	0.515	..	..	..	..
123	Iraq	0.674	0.541	19.7	2	19.4	15.9	0.655	29.7	0.392	12.7	0.618	21.9	23.7	22.0	29.5
124	El Salvador	0.673	0.529	21.4	1	21.1	12.5	0.718	29.1	0.393	21.8	0.523	17.1	29.4	..	38.6
125	Tajikistan	0.668	0.584	12.6	12	12.4	16.7	0.655	6.0	0.641	14.5	0.475	19.4	26.4	..	34.0
126	Cabo Verde	0.665	..	..	..	..	12.2	0.716	23.7	0.429	..	..	15.4	32.3	..	42.4
127	Guatemala	0.663	0.481	27.5	−2	26.9	14.6	0.713	30.8	0.359	35.4	0.433	13.1	38.1	..	48.3
128	Nicaragua	0.660	0.505	23.5	1	23.2	13.1	0.728	25.7	0.425	30.7	0.415	14.3	37.2	..	46.2
129	Bhutan	0.654	0.476	27.2	−2	26.3	17.1	0.660	41.7	0.289	20.0	0.565	17.5	27.9	..	37.4
130	Namibia	0.646	0.418	35.3	−14	33.6	22.1	0.524	25.0	0.438	53.6	0.318	8.6	47.3	21.5	59.1
131	India	0.645	0.475	26.4	−1	25.7	19.7	0.613	38.7	0.340	18.8	0.515	18.8	31.7	21.3	37.8
132	Honduras	0.634	0.472	25.6	−2	24.8	13.3	0.737	23.3	0.382	37.8	0.373	10.4	39.1	..	52.1
133	Bangladesh	0.632	0.478	24.4	3	23.7	17.3	0.669	37.3	0.332	16.6	0.492	21.0	26.8	..	32.4
134	Kiribati	0.630	0.516	18.1	8	17.9	24.7	0.560	9.6	0.537	19.4	0.457	..	..	..	..
135	Sao Tome and Principe	0.625	0.520	16.8	10	16.7	17.0	0.643	18.3	0.463	14.9	0.473	11.5	49.2	8.8	56.3
136	Micronesia (Federated States of)	0.620	..	..	..	..	16.1	0.618	..	..	26.4	0.410	16.2	29.7	..	40.1
137	Lao People's Democratic Republic	0.613	0.461	24.8	0	24.7	22.6	0.571	31.3	0.331	20.3	0.518	19.1	29.8	..	36.4
138	Eswatini (Kingdom of)	0.611	0.432	29.3	−5	29.0	25.1	0.463	24.1	0.423	37.9	0.410	10.5	42.7	18.2	54.6
138	Ghana	0.611	0.440	28.0	−3	27.8	24.2	0.514	35.1	0.365	24.1	0.454	14.3	32.2	15.1	43.5
140	Vanuatu	0.609	..	..	..	..	14.4	0.665	..	..	19.7	0.417	17.8	29.4	..	37.6
141	Timor-Leste	0.606	0.436	28.1	−2	26.7	21.7	0.596	44.9	0.281	13.6	0.495	22.8	24.0	..	28.7
142	Nepal	0.602	0.446	25.9	3	24.9	17.5	0.645	40.9	0.308	16.3	0.448	20.4	26.4	..	32.8
143	Kenya	0.601	0.443	26.3	3	26.2	22.5	0.557	22.9	0.412	33.1	0.379	16.5	31.6	15.0	40.8
144	Cambodia	0.594	0.475	20.0	10	19.9	18.1	0.628	27.3	0.352	14.3	0.485	..	..	..	..
145	Equatorial Guinea	0.592	..	..	..	..	34.6	0.390	..	..	..	..	..	..	17.3	..
146	Zambia	0.584	0.401	31.3	−2	30.6	26.5	0.496	20.4	0.443	44.8	0.292	8.9	44.4	23.1	57.1
147	Myanmar	0.583	..	..	..	..	22.8	0.560	26.9	0.339	..	..	21.9	25.5	..	30.7
148	Angola	0.581	0.397	31.7	−3	31.7	32.0	0.430	34.3	0.328	28.9	0.442	11.5	39.6	15.2	51.3
149	Congo	0.574	0.430	25.1	2	24.9	22.8	0.529	20.9	0.429	31.0	0.350	12.4	37.9	20.4	48.9
150	Zimbabwe	0.571	0.441	22.8	7	22.5	24.2	0.484	14.6	0.501	28.8	0.353	15.1	34.8	17.2	44.3
151	Solomon Islands	0.567	..	..	..	..	12.1	0.717	..	..	19.4	0.379	18.4	29.2	..	37.1
151	Syrian Arab Republic	0.567	..	..	..	..	13.0	0.705	..	..	..	..	..	..	14.7	..
153	Cameroon	0.563	0.375	33.4	−7	33.4	33.5	0.402	31.7	0.373	35.0	0.351	13.0	35.0	15.7	46.6
154	Pakistan	0.557	0.384	31.1	−4	30.2	29.9	0.510	43.5	0.227	17.2	0.489	21.1	28.9	..	33.5
155	Papua New Guinea	0.555	0.390	29.7	0	29.6	24.1	0.520	35.7	0.282	28.9	0.404	15.1[f]	31.0[f]	..	41.9[f]
156	Comoros	0.554	0.303	45.3	−21	44.2	28.9	0.485	47.6	0.252	56.0	0.228	13.6	33.7	14.1	45.3
Low human development																
157	Mauritania	0.546	0.371	32.1	−4	31.8	30.0	0.484	40.8	0.234	24.6	0.449	19.9	24.9	10.6	32.6
158	Benin	0.545	0.343	37.1	−10	36.9	34.9	0.418	43.7	0.269	32.0	0.358	12.8	37.6	17.5	47.8
159	Uganda	0.544	0.399	26.7	7	26.7	27.2	0.486	27.9	0.377	24.9	0.346	15.9	34.2	16.9	42.8
160	Rwanda	0.543	0.387	28.7	3	28.4	19.5	0.607	29.3	0.324	36.4	0.295	15.8	35.6	..	43.7
161	Nigeria	0.539	0.348	35.4	−2	35.2	37.1	0.336	40.4	0.297	28.1	0.423	15.1[f]	32.7	15.3	43.0[f]
162	Côte d'Ivoire	0.538	0.346	35.7	−4	35.3	33.3	0.388	45.6	0.246	27.0	0.433	15.9	31.9	17.1	41.5
163	Tanzania (United Republic of)	0.529	0.397	25.0	10	24.9	25.3	0.522	27.0	0.313	22.4	0.382	17.4	33.1	16.2	40.5
164	Madagascar	0.528	0.390	26.1	9	26.0	21.1	0.571	29.3	0.343	27.6	0.303	15.7	33.5	15.0	42.6
165	Lesotho	0.527	0.382	27.5	6	27.4	33.1	0.353	19.6	0.428	29.6	0.367	13.5	32.9	19.0	44.9
166	Djibouti	0.524	..	..	..	..	23.4	0.555	..	..	27.7	0.441	15.8	32.3	15.7	41.6
167	Togo	0.515	0.351	31.8	4	31.7	30.5	0.439	37.7	0.322	26.9	0.307	14.5	31.6	13.7	43.1
168	Senegal	0.512	0.348	32.0	4	31.2	21.2	0.581	46.4	0.185	25.9	0.392	16.4	31.0	13.0	40.3
169	Afghanistan	0.511	..	..	..	..	28.3	0.495	45.4	0.226	..	..	..	..	..	..
170	Haiti	0.510	0.303	40.6	−9	40.0	32.2	0.459	37.3	0.286	50.4	0.212	15.8	31.2	..	41.1

SDG 10.1

Continued →

TABLE 3 / INEQUALITY-ADJUSTED HUMAN DEVELOPMENT INDEX 353

TABLE 3

		Inequality-adjusted HDI (IHDI)			Coefficient of human inequality	Inequality in life expectancy	Inequality-adjusted life expectancy index	Inequality in education[a]	Inequality-adjusted education index	Inequality in income[a]	Inequality-adjusted income index	Income shares held by (%)			Gini coefficient
	Human Development Index (HDI)		Overall loss (%)	Difference from HDI rank[b]								Poorest 40 percent	Richest 10 percent	Richest 1 percent	
	Value	Value				(%)	Value	(%)	Value	(%)	Value				
HDI RANK	2019	2019	2019	2019	2019	2015–2020[c]	2019	2019[d]	2019	2019[d]	2019	2010–2018[e]	2010–2018[e]	2010–2017[e]	2010–2018[e]
170 Sudan	0.510	0.333	34.7	-3	34.3	27.4	0.506	42.5	0.198	33.0	0.369	19.9	27.8	11.2	34.2
172 Gambia	0.496	0.335	32.5	1	31.2	28.5	0.463	47.7	0.213	17.5	0.384	19.0	28.7	13.4	35.9
173 Ethiopia	0.485	0.348	28.2	8	27.3	24.9	0.538	43.5	0.193	13.4	0.405	19.4	28.5	14.3	35.0
174 Malawi	0.483	0.345	28.6	5	28.6	25.1	0.510	28.4	0.336	32.4	0.239	16.2	38.1	31.1	44.7
175 Congo (Democratic Republic of the)	0.480	0.335	30.2	4	30.2	36.1	0.400	26.8	0.363	27.6	0.258	15.5	32.0	18.1	42.1
175 Guinea-Bissau	0.480	0.300	37.5	-7	37.4	32.3	0.399	41.9	0.240	37.9	0.281	12.8	42.0	19.3	50.7
175 Liberia	0.480	0.325	32.3	1	31.8	29.8	0.476	42.9	0.243	22.7	0.296	18.8	27.1	12.0	35.3
178 Guinea	0.477	0.313	34.4	0	33.1	31.3	0.440	50.1	0.176	17.8	0.395	19.8	26.4	12.4	33.7
179 Yemen	0.470	0.321	31.7	4	30.9	24.7	0.534	46.1	0.189	21.8	0.327	18.8	29.4	15.7	36.7
180 Eritrea	0.459	..	..	..	..	21.4	0.560	..	..	..	..	..	..	14.3	..
181 Mozambique	0.456	0.316	30.7	4	30.7	29.8	0.441	33.8	0.262	28.4	0.273	11.8	45.5	30.9	54.0
182 Burkina Faso	0.452	0.316	30.1	5	29.5	32.0	0.435	39.2	0.190	17.3	0.382	20.0	29.6	14.3	35.3
182 Sierra Leone	0.452	0.291	35.6	-2	34.5	39.0	0.326	46.9	0.216	17.7	0.350	19.6	29.4	10.5	35.7
184 Mali	0.434	0.289	33.4	-1	32.4	36.7	0.383	43.9	0.160	16.6	0.393	20.1[f]	25.7[f]	9.5	33.0[f]
185 Burundi	0.433	0.303	30.0	5	29.6	28.5	0.457	39.5	0.252	20.9	0.241	17.9	31.0	14.6	38.6
185 South Sudan	0.433	0.276	36.3	-2	36.0	36.2	0.372	39.6	0.185	32.3	0.307	12.5[f]	33.2[f]	14.1	46.3[f]
187 Chad	0.398	0.248	37.7	-1	37.4	40.9	0.311	43.0	0.164	28.4	0.297	14.6	32.4	15.6	43.3
188 Central African Republic	0.397	0.232	41.6	-1	41.3	40.1	0.307	34.5	0.231	49.2	0.176	10.3[g]	46.2	30.9	56.2[g]
189 Niger	0.394	0.284	27.9	3	27.4	30.9	0.451	35.0	0.162	16.4	0.314	19.6	27.0	11.4	34.3
Other countries or territories															
Korea (Democratic People's Rep. of)	..	..	..	..	..	11.5	0.712	..	..	..	..	..	..	..	..
Monaco	..	..	..	..	..	..	..	..	..	..	..	..	..	..	..
Nauru	..	..	..	..	..	..	..	..	..	..	..	..	..	..	..
San Marino	..	..	..	..	..	..	..	..	..	..	..	..	..	..	..
Somalia	..	..	..	..	..	38.9	0.352	..	..	..	..	..	..	16.9	..
Tuvalu	..	..	..	..	..	..	..	10.5	..	..	..	17.4	30.7	..	39.1
Human development groups															
Very high human development	0.898	0.800	10.9	–	10.7	5.2	0.869	6.4	0.804	20.4	0.733	18.3	27.7	15.6	–
High human development	0.753	0.618	17.9	–	17.6	10.1	0.765	14.5	0.572	28.0	0.539	16.6	31.3	..	–
Medium human development	0.631	0.465	26.3	–	25.9	20.8	0.601	37.1	0.334	19.7	0.499	18.8	31.0	..	–
Low human development	0.513	0.352	31.4	–	31.3	30.8	0.441	37.9	0.263	25.1	0.375	16.7	31.9	16.0	–
Developing countries	0.689	0.535	22.4	–	22.3	16.7	0.657	25.5	0.439	24.6	0.531	17.4	31.3	17.7	–
Regions															
Arab States	0.705	0.531	24.7	–	24.3	15.0	0.681	32.5	0.391	25.4	0.563	20.7	26.6	15.8	–
East Asia and the Pacific	0.747	0.621	16.9	–	16.5	9.9	0.769	13.4	0.561	26.2	0.556	17.3	29.5	..	–
Europe and Central Asia	0.791	0.697	11.9	–	11.7	9.7	0.756	8.2	0.692	17.2	0.649	19.7	27.2	..	–
Latin America and the Caribbean	0.766	0.596	22.2	–	21.5	11.6	0.756	18.0	0.571	34.9	0.491	12.9	37.8	..	–
South Asia	0.641	0.475	25.9	–	25.4	20.2	0.613	37.5	0.339	18.5	0.515	19.2	30.9	..	–
Sub-Saharan Africa	0.547	0.380	30.5	–	30.5	29.7	0.449	34.1	0.310	27.6	0.394	15.4	33.9	16.4	–
Least developed countries	0.538	0.384	28.6	–	28.4	26.4	0.514	36.0	0.280	22.9	0.394	17.9	30.8	16.3	–
Small island developing states	0.728	0.549	24.6	–	24.2	16.7	0.667	22.0	0.493	34.0	0.504	..	..	..	–
Organisation for Economic Co-operation and Development	0.900	0.791	12.1	–	11.8	5.5	0.878	7.6	0.787	22.2	0.718	17.9	28.7	15.1	–
World	**0.737**	**0.587**	**20.4**	**–**	**20.2**	**14.7**	**0.692**	**22.1**	**0.497**	**23.8**	**0.589**	**17.6**	**30.6**	**17.1**	**–**

TABLE 3

Notes

a   See http://hdr.undp.org/en/composite/IHDI for the list of surveys used to estimate inequalities.

b   Based on countries for which an Inequality-adjusted Human Development Index value is calculated.

c   Calculated by HDRO from the 2015–2020 period life tables from UNDESA (2019a).

d   Data refer to 2019 or the most recent year available.

e   Data refer to the most recent year available during the period specified.

f   Refers to 2009.

g   Refers to 2008.

Definitions

Human Development Index (HDI): A composite index measuring average achievement in three basic dimensions of human development—a long and healthy life, knowledge and a decent standard of living. See *Technical note 1* at http://hdr.undp.org/sites/default/files/hdr2020_technical_notes.pdf for details on how the HDI is calculated.

Inequality-adjusted HDI (IHDI): HDI value adjusted for inequalities in the three basic dimensions of human development. See *Technical note 2* at http://hdr.undp.org/sites/default/files/hdr2020_technical_notes.pdf for details on how the IHDI is calculated.

Overall loss: Percentage difference between the IHDI value and the HDI value.

Difference from HDI rank: Difference in ranks on the IHDI and the HDI, calculated only for countries for which an IHDI value is calculated.

Coefficient of human inequality: Average inequality in the three basic dimensions of human development.

Inequality in life expectancy: Inequality in distribution of expected length of life based on data from life tables estimated using the Atkinson inequality index.

Inequality-adjusted life expectancy index: HDI life expectancy index value adjusted for inequality in distribution of expected length of life based on data from life tables listed in *Main data sources.*

Inequality in education: Inequality in distribution of years of schooling based on data from household surveys estimated using the Atkinson inequality index.

Inequality-adjusted education index: HDI education index value adjusted for inequality in distribution of years of schooling based on data from household surveys listed in *Main data sources.*

Inequality in income: Inequality in income distribution based on data from household surveys estimated using the Atkinson inequality index.

Inequality-adjusted income index: HDI income index value adjusted for inequality in income distribution based on data from household surveys listed in *Main data sources.*

Income shares: Percentage share of income (or consumption) that accrues to the indicated population subgroups.

Income share held by richest 1%: Share of pretax national income held by the richest 1 percent of the population. Pretax national income is the sum of all pretax personal income flows accruing to the owners of the production factors, labour and capital before the tax/transfer system is taken into account and after the pension system is taken into account.

Gini coefficient: Measure of the deviation of the distribution of income among individuals or households in a country from a perfectly equal distribution. A value of 0 represents absolute equality, a value of 100 absolute inequality.

Main data sources

Column 1: HDRO calculations based on data from UNDESA (2019a), UNESCO Institute for Statistics (2020), United Nations Statistics Division (2020b), World Bank (2020a), Barro and Lee (2018) and IMF (2020).

Column 2: Calculated as the geometric mean of the values in the inequality-adjusted life expectancy index, inequality-adjusted education index and inequality-adjusted income index using the methodology in *Technical note 2* (available at http://hdr.undp.org/sites/default/files/hdr2020_technical_notes.pdf).

Column 3: Calculated based on data in columns 1 and 2.

Column 4: Calculated based on IHDI values and recalculated HDI ranks for countries for which an IHDI value is calculated.

Column 5: Calculated as the arithmetic mean of the values in inequality in life expectancy, inequality in education and inequality in income index using the methodology in *Technical note 2* (available at http://hdr.undp.org/sites/default/files/hdr2020_technical_notes.pdf).

Column 6: Calculated based on abridged life tables from UNDESA (2019a).

Column 7: Calculated based on inequality in life expectancy and the HDI life expectancy index.

Columns 8 and 10: Calculated based on data from the Luxembourg Income Study database, Eurostat's European Union Statistics on Income and Living Conditions, the World Bank's International Income Distribution Database, the Center for Distributive, Labor and Social Studies and the World Bank's Socio-Economic Database for Latin America and the Caribbean, ICF Macro Demographic and Health Surveys and United Nations Children's Fund Multiple Indicator Cluster Surveys using the methodology *in Technical note 2.*

Column 9: Calculated based on inequality in education and the HDI education index.

Column 11: Calculated based on inequality in income and the HDI income index.

Columns 12, 13 and 15: World Bank (2020a).

Column 14: World Inequality Database (2020).

TABLE 3 / INEQUALITY-ADJUSTED HUMAN DEVELOPMENT INDEX   355

TABLE 4

Gender Development Index

		Gender Development Index		Human Development Index		SDG 3 Life expectancy at birth (years)		SDG 4.3 Expected years of schooling (years)		SDG 4.4 Mean years of schooling (years)		SDG 8.5 Estimated gross national income per capita[a] (2017 PPP $)	
				Value									
		Value	Group[b]	Female	Male	Female	Male	Female	Male	Female	Male	Female	Male
HDI RANK		2019	2019	2019	2019	2019	2019	2019[c]	2019[c]	2019[c]	2019[c]	2019	2019
Very high human development													
1	Norway	0.990	1	0.949	0.959	84.4	80.4	18.8[d]	17.4	13.0	12.8	58,548	74,280
2	Ireland	0.981	1	0.943	0.961	83.9	80.7	18.8[d]	18.6[d]	12.9	12.4	55,540	81,401[e]
2	Switzerland	0.968	2	0.934	0.965	85.6	81.9	16.2	16.4	12.7	13.6	57,840	81,137[e]
4	Hong Kong, China (SAR)	0.972	2	0.933	0.959	87.7	82.0	17.1	16.8	11.9	12.7	45,961	82,993[e]
4	Iceland	0.969	2	0.933	0.963	84.5	81.5	20.2[d]	18.0[d]	12.6[f]	13.0[f]	46,413	62,883
6	Germany	0.972	2	0.933	0.960	83.7	78.9	16.9	17.0	13.9	14.4	45,277	65,599
7	Sweden	0.983	1	0.936	0.953	84.6	81.0	20.4[d]	18.6[d]	12.7	12.4	47,709	61,287
8	Australia	0.976	1	0.932	0.955	85.4	81.5	22.4[d]	21.5[d]	12.8[f]	12.7[f]	39,287	56,954
8	Netherlands	0.966	2	0.926	0.960	84.0	80.6	18.8[d]	18.2[d]	12.2	12.7	46,815	68,685
10	Denmark	0.983	1	0.931	0.948	82.9	78.9	19.6[d]	18.3[d]	12.8[f]	12.4[f]	49,296	68,134
11	Finland	0.990	1	0.932	0.942	84.7	79.1	20.2[d]	18.6[d]	13.0	12.6	40,759	56,485
11	Singapore	0.985	1	0.931	0.945	85.7	81.5	16.7	16.3	11.2	12.1	71,387	103,421[e]
13	United Kingdom	0.970	2	0.916	0.944	83.0	79.6	18.0	17.0	13.2	13.2	33,323	59,135
14	Belgium	0.974	2	0.918	0.943	83.9	79.3	20.7[d]	18.8[d]	11.9[g]	12.2[g]	41,948	62,427
14	New Zealand	0.964	2	0.912	0.946	84.0	80.6	19.7[d]	17.9	12.7[f]	12.9[f]	31,233	50,693
16	Canada	0.986	1	0.922	0.935	84.4	80.4	16.7	15.7	13.4[f]	13.3[f]	39,459	57,734
17	United States	0.994	1	0.922	0.928	81.4	76.3	16.9	15.7	13.5	13.4	50,590	77,338[e]
18	Austria	0.964	2	0.903	0.937	83.9	79.2	16.4	15.8	12.2[f]	12.9[f]	39,386	73,528
19	Israel	0.973	2	0.904	0.929	84.5	81.3	16.8	15.6	13.1	13.0	29,665	50,819
19	Japan	0.978	1	0.906	0.927	87.7	81.5	15.2	15.3	13.1[h]	12.6[h]	30,584	55,869
19	Liechtenstein	..	..	..	..	..	..	13.8	16.0	..	..	..	..
22	Slovenia	1.001	1	0.916	0.914	84.0	78.6	18.3	16.8	12.6	12.7	33,885	42,312
23	Korea (Republic of)	0.936	3	0.881	0.941	86.0	79.9	15.9	17.0	11.4	12.9	27,734	58,309
23	Luxembourg	0.976	1	0.901	0.923	84.3	80.2	14.3	14.2	12.0[g]	12.6[g]	58,642	86,488[e]
25	Spain	0.986	1	0.896	0.909	86.2	80.8	18.0	17.2	10.2	10.3	32,881	49,356
26	France	0.987	1	0.895	0.907	85.5	79.7	16.0	15.3	11.3	11.7	39,478	55,375
27	Czechia	0.985	1	0.893	0.906	81.9	76.8	17.5	16.1	12.5[f]	12.9[f]	29,480	47,012
28	Malta	0.966	2	0.877	0.909	84.3	80.7	16.5	15.7	11.1	11.6	29,368	49,686
29	Estonia	1.017	1	0.896	0.882	82.7	74.4	16.8	15.2	13.6[f]	12.7[f]	27,086	45,984
29	Italy	0.968	2	0.875	0.905	85.5	81.3	16.4	15.8	10.2[i]	10.6[i]	31,639	54,529
31	United Arab Emirates	0.931	3	0.842	0.905	79.3	77.3	14.8	14.1	11.7[i]	12.4[i]	28,578	84,723[e]
32	Greece	0.963	2	0.869	0.902	84.7	79.8	17.5	18.1	10.3	10.8	24,062	36,476
33	Cyprus	0.979	1	0.876	0.895	83.0	78.9	15.4	14.9	12.1	12.3	31,881	44,533
34	Lithuania	1.030	2	0.894	0.868	81.4	70.3	17.1	16.2	13.1	13.0	30,987	41,389
35	Poland	1.007	1	0.880	0.874	82.6	74.8	16.9	15.3	12.5[g]	12.4[g]	24,827	38,850
36	Andorra	..	..	..	..	..	..	..	..	10.4	10.6	..	..
37	Latvia	1.036	2	0.879	0.849	80.0	70.2	16.8	15.5	13.4[f]	12.6[f]	25,758	35,584
38	Portugal	0.988	1	0.858	0.868	84.9	79.0	16.5	16.6	9.4	9.1	28,937	39,571
39	Slovakia	0.992	1	0.855	0.862	81.0	74.0	15.0	14.0	12.6[f]	12.8[f]	24,618	40,014
40	Hungary	0.981	1	0.844	0.861	80.3	73.2	15.5	14.9	11.7	12.2	23,170	40,316
40	Saudi Arabia	0.896	5	0.791	0.883	76.8	73.9	16.0	16.2	9.8	10.5	16,512	70,181
42	Bahrain	0.922	4	0.806	0.874	78.4	76.4	16.7	16.1	9.1	9.7	19,059	55,565
43	Chile	0.963	2	0.833	0.865	82.4	77.8	16.7	16.2	10.5	10.7	16,398	30,322
43	Croatia	0.990	1	0.848	0.857	81.6	75.3	16.0	14.5	11.1[g]	12.2[g]	23,775	32,689
45	Qatar	1.030	2	0.866	0.841	82.0	79.1	14.1	11.3	11.3	9.4	45,338	107,833[e]
46	Argentina	0.993	1	0.835	0.840	80.0	73.2	18.9	16.4	11.1[f]	10.7[f]	14,872	27,826
47	Brunei Darussalam	0.981	1	0.830	0.846	77.1	74.7	14.8	13.9	9.1[h]	9.2[h]	54,386	72,835
48	Montenegro	0.966	2	0.814	0.843	79.3	74.4	15.4	14.7	10.9[i]	12.3[i]	17,518	25,368
49	Romania	0.991	1	0.824	0.831	79.5	72.6	14.7	13.9	10.8	11.4	24,433	34,846
50	Palau	..	..	..	..	..	..	16.3[i]	15.3[i]	..	..	..	..
51	Kazakhstan	0.980	1	0.807	0.823	77.7	69.2	15.8	15.1	10.9[i]	11.9[i]	16,791	29,296
52	Russian Federation	1.007	1	0.823	0.817	77.8	67.1	15.3	14.8	11.9[i]	12.1[i]	19,694	33,640
53	Belarus	1.007	1	0.824	0.819	79.6	69.7	15.7	15.2	12.2[i]	12.4[i]	14,911	22,721
54	Turkey	0.924	4	0.784	0.848	80.6	74.7	16.0[f]	17.1[f]	7.3	9.0	17,854	37,807
55	Uruguay	1.016	1	0.814	0.801	81.5	74.1	17.1	15.1	9.2	8.6	15,445	25,008
56	Bulgaria	0.995	1	0.813	0.817	78.7	71.6	14.6	14.2	11.5	11.2	18,453	28,483
57	Panama	1.019	1	0.826	0.811	81.8	75.4	13.5	12.4	11.2[h]	10.0[h]	24,050	35,049
58	Bahamas	..	..	..	..	76.1	71.7	..	..	11.7	11.4	27,560	40,295
58	Barbados	1.008	1	0.816	0.809	80.5	77.8	16.8	14.0	11.0[k]	10.3[k]	12,656	17,370

Continued →

TABLE 4

		Gender Development Index		Human Development Index Value		SDG 3 Life expectancy at birth (years)		SDG 4.3 Expected years of schooling (years)		SDG 4.4 Mean years of schooling (years)		SDG 8.5 Estimated gross national income per capita[a] (2017 PPP $)	
		Value	Group[b]	Female	Male	Female	Male	Female	Male	Female	Male	Female	Male
HDI RANK		2019	2019	2019	2019	2019	2019	2019[c]	2019[c]	2019[c]	2019[c]	2019	2019
60	Oman	0.936	3	0.768	0.821	80.3	76.1	15.0	13.7	10.6[i]	9.4[i]	7,959	35,201
61	Georgia	0.980	1	0.800	0.817	78.1	69.3	15.5	15.0	13.2	13.1	9,475	19,864
62	Costa Rica	0.981	1	0.802	0.818	82.9	77.7	16.4	15.4	8.9	8.6	13,476	23,501
62	Malaysia	0.972	2	0.797	0.821	78.3	74.2	14.0	13.3	10.3	10.5	20,825	33,877
64	Kuwait	0.983	1	0.793	0.807	76.6	74.8	15.2	13.2	8.0	6.8	31,698	75,840[e]
64	Serbia	0.977	1	0.797	0.815	78.6	73.4	15.3	14.2	10.8	11.6	13,990	20,525
66	Mauritius	0.976	1	0.791	0.811	78.5	71.7	15.7	14.4	9.4[h]	9.7[h]	15,870	34,898
High human development													
67	Seychelles	..	..	..	..	77.4	69.9	15.3	13.1	9.9[i]	10.1[i]	..	..
67	Trinidad and Tobago	1.003	1	0.796	0.793	76.2	70.9	14.0[i]	12.0[i]	11.1[h]	10.9[h]	20,482	32,121
69	Albania	0.967	2	0.780	0.807	80.2	77.0	15.5	14.0	9.7[m]	10.6[m]	11,004	16,885
70	Cuba	0.944	3	0.754	0.799	80.8	76.8	14.7	13.9	11.2[i]	11.8[i]	5,714	11,567
70	Iran (Islamic Republic of)	0.866	5	0.709	0.819	77.9	75.6	14.6	15.0	10.3	10.4	4,084	20,637
72	Sri Lanka	0.955	2	0.759	0.794	80.3	73.6	14.5	13.8	10.6	10.6	7,433	18,423
73	Bosnia and Herzegovina	0.937	3	0.753	0.803	79.9	74.9	14.1[i]	13.5[i]	8.9	10.9	10,567	19,357
74	Grenada	..	..	..	..	75.0	70.1	17.0	16.2	..	..	..	..
74	Mexico	0.960	2	0.760	0.792	77.9	72.2	15.0	14.6	8.6	8.9	12,765	25,838
74	Saint Kitts and Nevis	..	..	..	..	..	..	14.0[i]	13.7[i]	..	..	..	..
74	Ukraine	1.000	1	0.776	0.776	76.8	67.1	15.3[i]	14.9[i]	11.3[k]	11.3[k]	10,088	16,840
78	Antigua and Barbuda	..	..	..	..	78.1	75.9	13.2[i]	12.1[i]	..	..	..	..
79	Peru	0.957	2	0.759	0.793	79.5	74.1	14.9	15.1	9.1	10.3	9,889	14,647
79	Thailand	1.008	1	0.782	0.776	80.9	73.5	15.8[i]	14.7[i]	7.7	8.2	15,924	19,737
81	Armenia	0.982	1	0.766	0.780	78.5	71.3	13.6	12.6	11.3	11.3	9,737	18,574
82	North Macedonia	0.952	2	0.753	0.791	77.8	73.8	13.8	13.4	9.4[i]	10.2[i]	11,698	20,027
83	Colombia	0.989	1	0.761	0.770	80.0	74.5	14.7	14.1	8.6	8.3	11,594	17,018
84	Brazil	0.993	1	0.760	0.765	79.6	72.2	15.8	15.1	8.2	7.7	10,535	18,120
85	China	0.957	2	0.744	0.777	79.2	74.8	14.0[i]	14.0[i]	7.7[h]	8.4[h]	12,633	19,308
86	Ecuador	0.967	2	0.743	0.768	79.8	74.3	14.9[i]	14.3[i]	8.7	8.9	7,874	14,211
86	Saint Lucia	0.985	1	0.752	0.763	77.6	74.9	14.7[i]	13.3[i]	8.8[i]	8.2[i]	11,476	17,851
88	Azerbaijan	0.943	3	0.730	0.774	75.5	70.5	13.0[i]	12.8[i]	10.2	10.9	8,919	18,664
88	Dominican Republic	0.999	1	0.759	0.760	77.4	71.0	15.0	13.5	8.8[i]	8.3[i]	12,449	22,740
90	Moldova (Republic of)	1.014	1	0.754	0.744	76.2	67.6	11.8	11.3	11.8	11.6	11,994	15,477
91	Algeria	0.858	5	0.671	0.782	78.1	75.7	14.8	14.4	7.7[i]	8.3[i]	3,296	18,891
92	Lebanon	0.892	5	0.691	0.774	80.9	77.1	11.1	11.5	8.5[n]	8.9[n]	6,078	23,124
93	Fiji	..	..	..	..	69.3	65.7	..	..	11.0	10.8	8,317	17,577
94	Dominica	..	..	..	..	..	..	12.3[m]	12.1[m]	7.0[m]	7.0[m]	7,908	22,931
95	Maldives	0.923	4	0.698	0.756	80.8	77.5	15.8	14.3	6.5	8.0	4,587	16,341
95	Tunisia	0.900	4	0.689	0.766	78.7	74.7	14.2[i]	14.0[i]	8.9[i]	8.7[i]	8,880	15,776
97	Saint Vincent and the Grenadines	0.965	2	0.724	0.750	75.1	70.3	13.8	12.5	9.4[i]	9.1[i]	9,504	19,093
97	Suriname	0.985	1	0.729	0.740	75.1	68.5	14.8[i]	13.7[i]	10.7[i]	9.7[i]	8,756	12,981
99	Mongolia	1.023	1	0.744	0.727	74.1	65.8	13.0	12.7[i]	9.5[k]	9.7[k]	15,276	17,677
100	Botswana	0.998	1	0.734	0.735	72.4	66.5	13.9[i]	12.4[i]	10.2[i]	9.3[i]	7,501	11,163
101	Jamaica	0.994	1	0.730	0.735	76.1	72.9	11.6[m]	11.1[m]	10.3[h]	10.7[h]	3,324	16,234
102	Jordan	0.875	5	0.664	0.758	76.3	72.8	13.0[i]	12.4[i]	8.5	8.5	8,855	15,483
103	Paraguay	0.966	2	0.714	0.739	76.4	72.3	14.6[i]	14.0[i]	11.3[h]	11.2[h]	4,311	8,416
104	Tonga	0.950	3	0.702	0.739	72.9	69.0	13.1[n]	12.6[n]	8.5[k]	7.2[k]	9,249	21,999
105	Libya	0.976	1	0.713	0.731	76.0	70.1	11.9	12.2	11.6	12.0	5,064	9,230
106	Uzbekistan	0.939	3	0.695	0.740	73.8	69.6	14.2[o]	14.2[o]	8.3	9.8	6,481	10,610
107	Bolivia (Plurinational State of)	0.945	3	0.696	0.737	74.5	68.7	13.7	13.5	7.8	8.6	7,902	14,966
107	Indonesia	0.940	3	0.694	0.738	74.0	69.6	13.5	12.8	9.6	9.2	7,843	11,694
107	Philippines	1.007	1	0.720	0.715	75.5	67.3	13.4	12.8	9.9[i]	9.9[i]	4,896	7,881
110	Belize	0.976	1	0.706	0.723	77.8	71.7	13.2[i]	12.3[i]	..	..	4,054	8,410
111	Samoa	..	..	..	..	75.5	71.3	13.2[i]	12.3[i]	..	..	4,054	8,410
111	Turkmenistan	..	..	..	..	71.7	64.7	10.9[i]	11.5[i]	..	..	10,493	19,461
113	Venezuela (Bolivarian Republic of)	1.009	1	0.712	0.706	76.0	68.3	13.8[i]	11.8[i]	10.6	10.0	5,173	8,973
114	South Africa	0.986	1	0.702	0.712	67.7	60.7	14.2	13.4	10.0	10.3	9,248	15,095
115	Palestine, State of	0.870	5	0.638	0.733	75.8	72.4	14.3	12.6	8.9	9.4	2,045	10,666
116	Egypt	0.882	5	0.652	0.739	74.4	69.7	13.3	13.3	6.8[i]	8.1[i]	4,753	18,039
117	Marshall Islands	..	..	..	..	..	..	..	..	10.7[i]	11.1[i]	..	..
117	Viet Nam	0.997	1	0.703	0.705	79.5	71.3	12.9[i]	12.5[i]	8.0[h]	8.6[h]	6,644	8,224

Continued →

TABLE 4 / GENDER DEVELOPMENT INDEX

357

TABLE 4

	Gender Development Index		Human Development Index		SDG 3 Life expectancy at birth (years)		SDG 4.3 Expected years of schooling (years)		SDG 4.4 Mean years of schooling (years)		SDG 8.5 Estimated gross national income per capita[a] (2017 PPP $)	
	Value	Group[b]	Value Female	Male	Female	Male	Female	Male	Female	Male	Female	Male
HDI RANK	2019	2019	2019	2019	2019	2019	2019[c]	2019[c]	2019[c]	2019[c]	2019	2019
119 Gabon	0.916	4	0.670	0.731	68.7	64.4	12.6[n]	13.4[n]	7.8[h]	9.6[h]	9,925	17,791
Medium human development												
120 Kyrgyzstan	0.957	2	0.677	0.707	75.6	67.4	13.2	12.7	11.2[i]	11.0[i]	2,971	6,798
121 Morocco	0.835	5	0.612	0.734	77.9	75.4	13.3	14.1	4.7[h]	6.6[h]	2,975	11,831
122 Guyana	0.961	2	0.662	0.688	73.1	66.9	11.6[i]	11.3[i]	8.9[i]	8.0[i]	5,359	13,512
123 Iraq	0.774	5	0.566	0.731	72.7	68.6	10.4[i]	12.2[i]	6.0[i]	8.6[i]	2,427	18,975
124 El Salvador	0.975	2	0.662	0.679	77.8	68.5	11.5	11.7	6.6	7.3	6,471	10,501
125 Tajikistan	0.823	5	0.586	0.712	73.4	68.9	10.7[i]	12.6[i]	10.2[m]	11.3[m]	1,440	6,427
126 Cabo Verde	0.974	2	0.655	0.672	76.2	69.5	13.0	12.4	6.0[i]	6.6[i]	5,453	8,573
127 Guatemala	0.941	3	0.639	0.679	77.2	71.4	10.6	10.9	6.6	6.7	5,451	11,629
128 Nicaragua	1.012	1	0.663	0.655	78.0	70.9	12.6[o]	12.1[o]	7.2[h]	6.6[h]	4,656	5,930
129 Bhutan	0.921	4	0.626	0.679	72.2	71.4	13.5	12.8	3.3	4.8	8,117	13,069
130 Namibia	1.007	1	0.648	0.643	66.5	60.7	12.7[i]	12.5[i]	7.3[h]	6.7[h]	8,482	10,287
131 India	0.820	5	0.573	0.699	71.0	68.5	12.6	11.7	5.4[i]	8.7[i]	2,331	10,702
132 Honduras	0.978	1	0.625	0.639	77.6	73.0	10.5	9.6	6.6	6.5	4,173	6,446
133 Bangladesh	0.904	4	0.596	0.660	74.6	70.9	12.0	11.2	5.7	6.9	2,873	7,031
134 Kiribati	..	..	..	..	72.3	64.2	12.2[i]	11.4[i]	..	..	..	..
135 Sao Tome and Principe	0.906	4	0.590	0.651	72.8	68.0	12.8[i]	12.6[i]	5.8[i]	7.1[i]	2,462	5,439
136 Micronesia (Federated States of)	..	..	..	..	69.6	66.2	..	..	..	..	..	..
137 Lao People's Democratic Republic	0.927	3	0.589	0.636	69.7	66.1	10.7	11.3	4.9[h]	5.7[h]	5,801	9,013
138 Eswatini (Kingdom of)	0.996	1	0.609	0.611	64.8	56.0	11.8[i]	11.9[i]	6.3[i]	7.2[i]	7,011	8,863
138 Ghana	0.911	4	0.582	0.639	65.2	63.0	11.4	11.6	6.6[h]	8.1[h]	4,073	6,432
140 Vanuatu	..	..	..	..	72.2	69.0	11.5[n]	12.0[n]	..	..	2,406	3,784
141 Timor-Leste	0.942	3	0.587	0.623	71.6	67.5	12.2[i]	13.0[i]	3.8[m]	5.6[m]	4,486	4,395
142 Nepal	0.933	3	0.581	0.623	72.2	69.3	13.0	12.6	4.3[h]	5.8[h]	2,910	4,108
143 Kenya	0.937	3	0.581	0.620	69.0	64.3	11.0	11.7	6.0[h]	7.2[h]	3,666	4,829
144 Cambodia	0.922	4	0.570	0.618	71.9	67.5	11.0[h]	11.9[h]	4.2[h]	5.8[h]	3,697	4,822
145 Equatorial Guinea	..	..	..	..	59.9	57.7	..	..	4.2[i]	7.6[i]	9,949	17,135
146 Zambia	0.958	2	0.569	0.593	66.9	60.8	10.7[m]	11.6[m]	6.3[m]	8.2[m]	3,380	3,270
147 Myanmar	0.954	2	0.564	0.592	70.1	64.0	10.9	10.5	5.0[m]	4.9[m]	3,174	6,881
148 Angola	0.903	4	0.552	0.611	64.0	58.4	11.0[m]	12.7[m]	4.0[m]	6.4[m]	5,205	7,022
149 Congo	0.929	3	0.555	0.598	66.0	63.1	11.6[n]	11.9[n]	6.1[k]	7.5[k]	2,500	3,259
150 Zimbabwe	0.931	3	0.550	0.590	62.9	59.8	10.5[i]	11.5[i]	8.1	8.9	2,375	2,985
151 Solomon Islands	..	..	..	..	74.9	71.3	9.7[i]	10.7[i]	..	..	1,974	2,523
151 Syrian Arab Republic	0.829	5	0.492	0.593	78.1	67.9	8.9[i]	8.8[i]	4.6[n]	5.6[n]	989	6,225
153 Cameroon	0.864	5	0.521	0.603	60.6	58.0	11.3	12.9	4.7[i]	8.0[i]	2,973	4,189
154 Pakistan	0.745	5	0.456	0.612	68.3	66.3	7.6	8.9	3.8	6.3	1,393	8,412
155 Papua New Guinea	..	..	..	..	65.8	63.3	..	..	4.0[h]	5.3[h]	3,767	4,814
156 Comoros	0.891	5	0.519	0.583	66.1	62.6	11.1	11.4	4.0[n]	6.0[n]	2,300	3,885
Low human development												
157 Mauritania	0.864	5	0.500	0.579	66.5	63.3	8.7	8.5	3.8[h]	5.6[h]	2,782	7,468
158 Benin	0.855	5	0.502	0.587	63.3	60.2	11.4	13.8	2.4[m]	5.5[m]	2,837	3,673
159 Uganda	0.863	5	0.503	0.582	65.6	61.0	10.6[m]	12.2[m]	4.9[m]	7.6[m]	1,591	2,671
160 Rwanda	0.945	3	0.528	0.558	71.1	66.8	11.2	11.2	4.0[i]	4.9[i]	1,876	2,444
161 Nigeria	0.881	5	0.504	0.572	55.6	53.8	9.4[m]	10.6[m]	5.7[m]	7.7[m]	4,107	5,692
162 Côte d'Ivoire	0.811	5	0.476	0.586	59.1	56.6	9.0	10.9	4.2[h]	6.4[h]	2,561	7,531
163 Tanzania (United Republic of)	0.948	3	0.514	0.542	67.2	63.6	8.2	8.0	5.8[h]	6.4[h]	2,222	2,978
164 Madagascar	0.952	2	0.513	0.539	68.7	65.4	10.2	10.2	6.4[n]	5.8[n]	1,273	1,921
165 Lesotho	1.014	1	0.529	0.522	57.6	51.2	11.7[i]	10.9[i]	7.2[i]	5.8[i]	2,471	3,849
166 Djibouti	..	..	..	..	69.4	65.1	6.7[i]	6.9[i]	..	..	4,151	7,077
167 Togo	0.822	5	0.464	0.565	61.9	60.2	11.5	13.8	3.5[i]	6.7[i]	1,220	1,989
168 Senegal	0.870	5	0.475	0.546	69.9	65.8	8.9	8.2	1.9[i]	4.6[i]	2,271	4,401
169 Afghanistan	0.659	5	0.391	0.593	66.4	63.4	7.7	12.5	1.9[h]	6.0[h]	819	3,566
170 Haiti	0.875	5	0.473	0.540	66.2	61.8	9.0[i]	10.4[i]	4.3[h]	5.2[h]	1,410	2,016
170 Sudan	0.860	5	0.466	0.542	67.2	63.5	7.7[i]	8.3[i]	3.3[h]	4.2[h]	1,981	5,679
172 Gambia	0.846	5	0.448	0.530	63.5	60.7	10.0[m]	9.8[m]	3.3[i]	4.6[i]	1,145	3,207
173 Ethiopia	0.837	5	0.442	0.527	68.5	64.7	8.3[i]	9.3[i]	1.7[m]	4.3[m]	1,642	2,771
174 Malawi	0.986	1	0.493	0.500	67.4	61.1	11.2[i]	11.3[i]	6.9[h]	5.2[h]	838	1,237
175 Congo (Democratic Republic of the)	0.845	5	0.439	0.520	62.2	59.1	8.6[i]	10.8[i]	5.3	8.4	907	1,218
175 Guinea-Bissau	..	..	..	..	60.2	56.3	..	..	..	..	1,647	2,361

Continued →

TABLE 4

		Gender Development Index		Human Development Index		SDG 3 Life expectancy at birth (years)		SDG 4.3 Expected years of schooling (years)		SDG 4.4 Mean years of schooling (years)		SDG 8.5 Estimated gross national income per capita[a] (2017 PPP $)	
				Value									
		Value	Group[b]	Female	Male	Female	Male	Female	Male	Female	Male	Female	Male
HDI RANK		2019	2019	2019	2019	2019	2019	2019[c]	2019[c]	2019[c]	2019[c]	2019	2019
175	Liberia	0.890	5	0.453	0.509	65.5	62.7	9.2[n]	10.4[n]	3.5[h]	6.2[h]	1,242	1,275
178	Guinea	0.817	5	0.428	0.524	62.1	60.9	8.0[j,m]	10.8[j,m]	1.5[m]	4.2[m]	2,266	2,554
179	Yemen	0.488	5	0.270	0.553	67.8	64.4	7.4[i]	10.2[i]	2.9[h]	5.1[h]	186	2,980
180	Eritrea	..	..	..	..	68.6	64.2	4.6[i]	5.4[i]	..	..	2,275	3,309
181	Mozambique	0.912	4	0.435	0.476	63.7	57.8	9.5	10.5	2.7[i]	4.5[i]	1,131	1,377
182	Burkina Faso	0.867	5	0.418	0.482	62.3	60.7	9.1	9.4	1.1[m]	2.3[m]	1,541	2,727
182	Sierra Leone	0.884	5	0.423	0.479	55.5	53.9	9.7[i]	10.6[i]	2.9[h]	4.5[h]	1,470	1,867
184	Mali	0.821	5	0.388	0.473	60.1	58.5	6.8	8.1	1.7[i]	3.0[i]	1,516	3,019
185	Burundi	0.999	1	0.432	0.432	63.4	59.8	11.0	11.1	2.6[m]	4.1[m]	866	640
185	South Sudan	0.842	5	0.384	0.456	59.4	56.4	3.5[n]	5.9[n]	3.9[i]	5.2[n]	1,759	2,247
187	Chad	0.764	5	0.342	0.448	55.7	52.8	5.9	8.8	1.3[m]	3.8[m]	1,244	1,868
188	Central African Republic	0.801	5	0.351	0.438	55.5	51.1	6.2[i]	8.9[i]	3.0[h]	5.6[h]	792	1,197
189	Niger	0.724	5	0.321	0.443	63.6	61.3	5.7	7.2	1.4[i]	2.8[i]	536	1,859
Other countries or territories													
	Korea (Democratic People's Rep. of)	..	..	..	..	75.7	68.6	10.4[i]	11.1[i]	..	..	..	..
	Monaco	..	..	..	..	..	..	..	..	..	..	..	..
	Nauru	..	..	..	..	..	..	11.8[i]	10.8[i]	..	..	..	..
	San Marino	..	..	..	..	..	..	12.8	13.3	..	..	..	..
	Somalia	..	..	..	..	59.1	55.7	..	..	..	..	..	..
	Tuvalu	..	..	..	..	..	..	..	..	..	..	..	..
Human development groups													
	Very high human development	0.981	–	0.886	0.903	82.4	76.8	16.6	16.0	12.0	12.2	33,668	55,720
	High human development	0.961	–	0.736	0.766	78.0	72.8	14.1	13.9	8.2	8.7	10,529	17,912
	Medium human development	0.835	–	0.567	0.679	70.8	67.9	11.7	11.4	5.3	8.1	2,530	9,598
	Low human development	0.861	–	0.474	0.551	63.0	59.9	8.7	10.1	3.9	6.0	2,043	3,446
	Developing countries	0.919	–	0.659	0.717	73.4	69.3	12.2	12.3	6.9	8.3	6,923	14,136
Regions													
	Arab States	0.856	–	0.636	0.743	73.9	70.4	11.9	12.4	6.5	8.1	5,092	23,923
	East Asia and the Pacific	0.961	–	0.731	0.760	78.0	73.1	13.7	13.6	7.7	8.4	11,485	17,827
	Europe and Central Asia	0.953	–	0.768	0.806	77.7	71.1	14.5	14.8	9.9	10.7	12,373	23,801
	Latin America and the Caribbean	0.978	–	0.755	0.772	78.7	72.4	15.0	14.3	8.7	8.4	10,708	19,046
	South Asia	0.824	–	0.570	0.692	71.3	68.7	11.9	11.5	5.5	8.4	2,393	10,416
	Sub-Saharan Africa	0.894	–	0.516	0.577	63.3	59.8	9.5	10.6	4.9	6.7	2,937	4,434
	Least developed countries	0.874	–	0.500	0.572	67.3	63.5	9.4	10.4	4.1	5.8	2,033	3,846
	Small island developing states	0.959	–	0.718	0.749	74.1	70.0	12.9	12.7	8.5	9.2	12,281	21,334
	Organisation for Economic Co-operation and Development	0.978	–	0.887	0.907	82.9	77.7	16.6	16.0	11.9	12.1	34,593	55,679
World		**0.943**	**–**	**0.714**	**0.757**	**75.0**	**70.6**	**12.7**	**12.7**	**8.1**	**9.2**	**12,063**	**21,323**

TABLE 4 / GENDER DEVELOPMENT INDEX 359

TABLE 4

Notes

a   Because disaggregated income data are not available, data are crudely estimated. See *Definitions* and *Technical note 3* at http://hdr.undp.org/sites/default/files/hdr2020_technical_notes.pdf for details on how the Gender Development Index is calculated.

b   Countries are divided into five groups by absolute deviation from gender parity in HDI values.

c   Data refer to 2019 or the most recent year available.

d   In calculating the HDI value, expected years of schooling is capped at 18 years.

e   In calculating the male HDI value, estimated gross national income per capita is capped at $75,000.

f   Based on data from OECD (2019b).

g   Updated by HDRO based on data from Eurostat (2019).

h   Based on projections from Barro and Lee (2018).

i   Updated by HDRO based on data from UNESCO Institute for Statistics (2020).

j   Updated by HDRO based on data from United Nations Children's Fund (UNICEF) Multiple Indicator Cluster Surveys for 2006–2019.

k   Updated by HDRO using projections from Barro and Lee (2018).

l   Based on data from the national statistical office.

m   Updated by HDRO based on data from ICF Macro Demographic and Health Surveys for 2006–2019.

n   Based on cross-country regression.

o   Updated by HDRO based on data from CEDLAS and World Bank (2020).

Definitions

Gender Development Index: Ratio of female to male HDI values. See *Technical note 3* at http://hdr.undp.org/sites/default/files/hdr2020_technical_notes.pdf for details on how the Gender Development Index is calculated.

Gender Development Index groups: Countries are divided into five groups by absolute deviation from gender parity in HDI values. Group 1 comprises countries with high equality in HDI achievements between women and men (absolute deviation of less than 2.5 percent), group 2 comprises countries with medium to high equality in HDI achievements between women and men (absolute deviation of 2.5–5 percent), group 3 comprises countries with medium equality in HDI achievements between women and men (absolute deviation of 5–7.5 percent), group 4 comprises countries with medium to low equality in HDI achievements between women and men (absolute deviation of 7.5–10 percent) and group 5 comprises countries with low equality in HDI achievements between women and men (absolute deviation from gender parity of more than 10 percent).

Human Development Index (HDI): A composite index measuring average achievement in three basic dimensions of human development—a long and healthy life, knowledge and a decent standard of living. See *Technical note 1* at http://hdr.undp.org/sites/default/files/hdr2020_technical_notes.pdf for details on how the HDI is calculated.

Life expectancy at birth: Number of years a newborn infant could expect to live if prevailing patterns of age-specific mortality rates at the time of birth stay the same throughout the infant's life.

Expected years of schooling: Number of years of schooling that a child of school entrance age can expect to receive if prevailing patterns of age-specific enrolment rates persist throughout the child's life.

Mean years of schooling: Average number of years of education received by people ages 25 and older, converted from educational attainment levels using official durations of each level.

Estimated gross national income per capita: Derived from the ratio of female to male wages, female and male shares of economically active population and gross national income (in 2017 purchasing power parity terms). See *Technical note 3* at http://hdr.undp.org/sites/default/files/hdr2020_technical _notes.pdf for details.

Main data sources

Column 1: Calculated based on data in columns 3 and 4.

Column 2: Calculated based on data in column 1.

Columns 3 and 4: HDRO calculations based on data from UNDESA (2019a), UNESCO Institute for Statistics (2020), Barro and Lee (2018), World Bank (2020a), ILO (2020) and IMF (2020).

Columns 5 and 6: UNDESA (2019a).

Columns 7 and 8: UNESCO Institute for Statistics (2020), ICF Macro Demographic and Health Surveys, UNICEF Multiple Indicator Cluster Surveys and OECD (2019b).

Columns 9 and 10: UNESCO Institute for Statistics (2020), Barro and Lee (2018), ICF Macro Demographic and Health Surveys, UNICEF Multiple Indicator Cluster Surveys and OECD (2019b).

Columns 11 and 12: HDRO calculations based on ILO (2020), UNDESA (2019a), World Bank (2020a), United Nations Statistics Division (2020b) and IMF (2020).

TABLE 5

Gender Inequality Index

	Gender Inequality Index		SDG 3.1 Maternal mortality ratio (deaths per 100,000 live births)	SDG 3.7 Adolescent birth rate (births per 1,000 women ages 15–19)	SDG 5.5 Share of seats in parliament (% held by women)	SDG 4.4 Population with at least some secondary education (% ages 25 and older)		Labour force participation rate[a] (% ages 15 and older)	
	Value	Rank				Female	Male	Female	Male
HDI RANK	2019	2019	2017	2015–2020[b]	2019	2015–2019[c]	2015–2019[c]	2019	2019
Very high human development									
1 Norway	0.045	6	2	5.1	40.8	95.4	94.9	60.4	67.2
2 Ireland	0.093	23	5	7.5	24.3	81.9[d]	79.9[d]	56.0	68.4
2 Switzerland	0.025	1	5	2.8	38.6	95.6	96.8	62.9	73.8
4 Hong Kong, China (SAR)	..	..	..	2.7	..	77.1	82.9	54.0	67.5
4 Iceland	0.058	9	4	6.3	38.1	100.0[d]	100.0[d]	70.8	79.2
6 Germany	0.084	20	7	8.1	31.6	95.9	96.3	55.3	66.6
7 Sweden	0.039	3	4	5.1	47.3	89.3	89.5	61.4	67.8
8 Australia	0.097	25	6	11.7	36.6	91.0	90.9	60.3	70.9
8 Netherlands	0.043	4	5	3.8	33.8	87.6	90.3	58.3	69.1
10 Denmark	0.038	2	4	4.1	39.1	91.2	90.9	58.2	66.3
11 Finland	0.047	7	3	5.8	47.0	100.0	100.0	55.5	62.8
11 Singapore	0.065	12	8	3.5	23.0	78.1	85.1	62.0	78.3
13 United Kingdom	0.118	31	7	13.4	28.9	78.0	79.3	57.6	68.1
14 Belgium	0.043	4	5	4.7	43.3	84.7	88.4	48.6	58.7
14 New Zealand	0.123	33	9	19.3	40.8	97.4[d]	96.9[d]	64.8	75.3
16 Canada	0.080	19	10	8.4	33.2	100.0	100.0	60.8	69.4
17 United States	0.204	46	19	19.9	23.7	96.1	96.0	56.1	68.2
18 Austria	0.069	14	5	7.3	38.5	100.0	99.8	55.1	66.6
19 Israel	0.109	26	3	9.6	23.3	87.9	90.7	59.7	68.5
19 Japan	0.094	24	5	3.8	14.5	95.3[e]	92.3[e]	52.7	71.3
19 Liechtenstein	..	..	..	..	12.0	..	..	..	..
22 Slovenia	0.063	10	7	3.8	22.3	97.2	98.3	53.4	63.4
23 Korea (Republic of)	0.064	11	11	1.4	16.7	80.4	95.5	52.9	73.1
23 Luxembourg	0.065	12	5	4.7	25.0	100.0	100.0	54.9	63.7
25 Spain	0.070	16	4	7.7	41.9	75.4	80.2	51.9	63.4
26 France	0.049	8	8	4.7	36.9	81.7	86.8	50.8	59.9
27 Czechia	0.136	36	3	12.0	20.6	100.0	99.9	52.9	68.5
28 Malta	0.175	40	6	12.9	14.9	78.7	85.6	46.0	67.1
29 Estonia	0.086	21	9	7.7	29.7	100.0	100.0	57.1	71.0
29 Italy	0.069	14	2	5.2	35.3	75.9	83.4	40.8	59.0
31 United Arab Emirates	0.079	18	3	6.5	50.0	76.0	81.0	52.4	93.4
32 Greece	0.116	29	3	7.2	20.7	62.0	73.2	44.2	59.8
33 Cyprus	0.086	21	6	4.6	17.9	79.9	83.8	57.8	68.3
34 Lithuania	0.124	34	8	10.9	21.3	94.3	97.4	56.5	67.7
35 Poland	0.115	28	2	10.5	27.9	83.1	88.5	48.6	65.5
36 Andorra	..	..	..	..	46.4	71.5	73.3	..	..
37 Latvia	0.176	41	19	16.2	30.0	100.0[d]	100.0[d]	55.7	68.4
38 Portugal	0.075	17	8	8.4	38.7	53.9	54.8	54.2	64.1
39 Slovakia	0.191	45	5	25.7	20.0	99.2	100.0	52.2	67.4
40 Hungary	0.233	51	12	24.0	12.6	96.4	98.4	48.5	65.5
40 Saudi Arabia	0.252	56	17	7.3	19.9	64.8	72.4	22.1	78.4
42 Bahrain	0.212	49	14	13.4	18.8	68.1	74.3	45.0	87.2
43 Chile	0.247	55	13	41.1	22.7	77.8	81.1	51.8	74.0
43 Croatia	0.116	29	8	8.7	20.5	94.6	97.4	45.4	57.5
45 Qatar	0.185	43	9	9.9	9.8	76.1	66.2	56.8	94.7
46 Argentina	0.328	75	39	62.8	39.9	59.2	54.8	50.7	72.7
47 Brunei Darussalam	0.255	60	31	10.3	9.1	69.5[e]	70.7[e]	57.8	71.0
48 Montenegro	0.109	26	6	9.3	28.4	88.0[f]	98.2[f]	46.5	62.8
49 Romania	0.276	61	19	36.2	19.6	88.2	93.6	45.3	64.7
50 Palau	..	..	..	..	13.8	96.9	97.3	..	..
51 Kazakhstan	0.190	44	10	29.8	22.1	99.3	99.6	62.7	75.5
52 Russian Federation	0.225	50	17	20.7	16.5	96.3	95.7	54.8	70.2
53 Belarus	0.118	31	2	14.5	34.9	87.2[f]	92.5[f]	57.7	71.8
54 Turkey	0.306	68	17	26.6	17.4	50.2	72.2	34.0	72.6
55 Uruguay	0.288	62	17	58.7	20.9	58.8	54.6	55.6	73.3
56 Bulgaria	0.206	48	10	39.9	25.8	94.4	96.4	49.2	62.0
57 Panama	0.407	94	52	81.8	21.1	74.8[g]	68.6[g]	53.4	79.9
58 Bahamas	0.341	77	70	30.0	21.8	88.0	91.0	68.1	81.6
58 Barbados	0.252	56	27	33.6	29.4	94.6[g]	92.2[g]	61.7	69.1
60 Oman	0.306	68	19	13.1	9.9	73.4	63.7	31.0	89.9

Continued →

TABLE 5 / GENDER INEQUALITY INDEX   361

TABLE 5

		Gender Inequality Index		Maternal mortality ratio	Adolescent birth rate	Share of seats in parliament	Population with at least some secondary education		Labour force participation rate[a]	
				SDG 3.1	SDG 3.7	SDG 5.5	SDG 4.4			
				(deaths per 100,000 live births)	(births per 1,000 women ages 15–19)	(% held by women)	(% ages 25 and older)		(% ages 15 and older)	
		Value	Rank				Female	Male	Female	Male
HDI RANK		2019	2019	2017	2015–2020[b]	2019	2015–2019[c]	2015–2019[c]	2019	2019
61	Georgia	0.331	76	25	46.4	14.8	97.2	98.6	57.4	80.8
62	Costa Rica	0.288	62	27	53.5	45.6	55.4	53.3	48.1	76.2
62	Malaysia	0.253	59	29	13.4	15.5	72.2	76.5	50.7	77.1
64	Kuwait	0.242	53	12	8.2	4.6	56.6	49.1	49.7	87.5
64	Serbia	0.132	35	12	14.7	37.7	86.3	93.6	47.4	62.8
66	Mauritius	0.347	78	61	25.7	20.0	65.8[e]	68.5[e]	45.2	72.0
High human development										
67	Seychelles	..	..	53	62.1	21.2	..	..	..	..
67	Trinidad and Tobago	0.323	73	67	30.1	32.9	74.5[e]	71.2[e]	50.1	70.2
69	Albania	0.181	42	15	19.6	29.5	93.7[h]	92.5[h]	46.7	64.6
70	Cuba	0.304	67	36	51.6	53.2	85.8[e]	89.1[e]	40.7	66.8
70	Iran (Islamic Republic of)	0.459	113	16	40.6	5.9	67.4	72.8	17.5	71.5
72	Sri Lanka	0.401	90	36	20.9	5.3	79.2	81.0	35.4	74.6
73	Bosnia and Herzegovina	0.149	38	10	9.6	21.1	74.0	89.3	35.4	58.1
74	Grenada	..	..	25	29.2	39.3	..	..	..	..
74	Mexico	0.322	71	33	60.4	48.4	62.2	64.2	44.2	78.5
74	Saint Kitts and Nevis	..	..	..	..	13.3	..	..	..	..
74	Ukraine	0.234	52	19	23.7	20.5	94.0[g]	95.2[g]	46.7	63.1
78	Antigua and Barbuda	..	..	42	42.8	31.4	..	..	..	..
79	Peru	0.395	87	88	56.9	30.0	58.9	69.4	70.3	85.1
79	Thailand	0.359	80	37	44.9	14.1	43.5	48.6	59.2	76.1
81	Armenia	0.245	54	26	21.5	23.5	97.3	97.2	47.1	65.9
82	North Macedonia	0.143	37	7	15.7	39.2	41.8[f]	57.7[f]	43.0	67.3
83	Colombia	0.428	101	83	66.7	19.6	55.7	53.0	57.3	80.9
84	Brazil	0.408	95	60	59.1	15.0	61.6	58.3	54.2	74.1
85	China	0.168	39	29	7.6	24.9	76.0[e]	83.3[e]	60.5	75.3
86	Ecuador	0.384	86	59	79.3	38.0	52.5	53.3	55.2	81.1
86	Saint Lucia	0.401	90	117	40.5	20.7	49.2	42.1	59.5	75.0
88	Azerbaijan	0.323	73	26	55.8	16.8	93.9	97.5	63.4	69.7
88	Dominican Republic	0.455	112	95	94.3	24.3	59.7	56.1	51.4	77.4
90	Moldova (Republic of)	0.204	46	19	22.4	25.7	96.6	98.1	40.5	46.0
91	Algeria	0.429	103	112	10.1	21.5	39.1[f]	38.9[f]	14.6	67.4
92	Lebanon	0.411	96	29	14.5	4.7	54.3[i]	55.6[i]	22.9	71.4
93	Fiji	0.370	84	34	49.4	19.6	79.4	78.2	38.5	76.5
94	Dominica	..	..	..	..	25.0	..	..	..	..
95	Maldives	0.369	82	53	7.8	4.6	45.4[h]	49.6[h]	41.6	84.2
95	Tunisia	0.296	65	43	7.8	22.6	42.4	54.6	23.8	69.4
97	Saint Vincent and the Grenadines	..	..	68	49.0	13.0	..	..	54.4	77.0
97	Suriname	0.436	105	120	61.7	31.4	61.5[f]	60.1[f]	38.8	63.7
99	Mongolia	0.322	71	45	31.0	17.3	91.5[f]	-86.1[f]	53.3	66.4
100	Botswana	0.465	116	144	46.1	10.8	89.6[g]	90.9[g]	65.4	76.9
101	Jamaica	0.396	88	80	52.8	19.0	70.0	62.4	59.8	72.5
102	Jordan	0.450	109	46	25.9	15.4	82.2[e]	86.1[e]	14.4	63.7
103	Paraguay	0.446	107	84	70.5	16.8	49.2	51.2	59.2	84.6
104	Tonga	0.354	79	52	14.7	7.4	94.0[g]	93.4[g]	45.7	74.3
105	Libya	0.252	56	72	5.8	16.0	70.5[g]	45.1[g]	33.9	65.3
106	Uzbekistan	0.288	62	29	23.8	16.4	99.9	100.0	52.4	78.1
107	Bolivia (Plurinational State of)	0.417	98	155	64.9	51.8	53.1	59.5	63.2	80.5
107	Indonesia	0.480	121	177	47.4	17.4	46.8	55.1	53.1	81.9
107	Philippines	0.430	104	121	54.2	28.0	75.6[e]	72.4[e]	46.1	73.3
110	Belize	0.415	97	36	68.5	11.1	79.0[f]	78.9[f]	49.9	80.6
111	Samoa	0.360	81	43	23.9	10.0	79.1[i]	71.6[i]	31.1	55.5
111	Turkmenistan	..	..	7	24.4	25.0	..	..	51.4	78.3
113	Venezuela (Bolivarian Republic of)	0.479	119	125	85.3	22.2	71.7	66.6	45.4	74.9
114	South Africa	0.406	93	119	67.9	45.3[j]	75.0	78.2	49.6	62.7
115	Palestine, State of	..	..	27	52.8	..	63.5	64.9	17.7	69.5
116	Egypt	0.449	108	37	53.8	14.9	73.5[e]	72.5[e]	21.9	70.9
117	Marshall Islands	..	..	..	..	6.1	91.6	92.5	..	..
117	Viet Nam	0.296	65	43	30.9	26.7	66.4[e]	78.2[e]	72.7	82.4
119	Gabon	0.525	128	252	96.2	17.9	66.2[e]	50.6[e]	43.5	61.8

Continued →

TABLE 5

	Gender Inequality Index		Maternal mortality ratio SDG 3.1 (deaths per 100,000 live births)	Adolescent birth rate SDG 3.7 (births per 1,000 women ages 15–19)	Share of seats in parliament SDG 5.5 (% held by women)	Population with at least some secondary education SDG 4.4 (% ages 25 and older)		Labour force participation rate[a] (% ages 15 and older)	
	Value	Rank				Female	Male	Female	Male
HDI RANK	2019	2019	2017	2015-2020[b]	2019	2015-2019[c]	2015-2019[c]	2019	2019
Medium human development									
120 Kyrgyzstan	0.369	82	60	32.8	19.2	99.1[e]	98.3[e]	44.8	75.7
121 Morocco	0.454	111	70	31.0	18.4	29.1[e]	36.0[e]	21.5	70.1
122 Guyana	0.462	115	169	74.4	31.9	70.9[e]	56.4[e]	43.9	68.5
123 Iraq	0.577	146	79	71.7	25.2	39.5	56.5	11.6	74.2
124 El Salvador	0.383	85	46	69.5	31.0	39.9	46.4	45.3	75.7
125 Tajikistan	0.314	70	17	57.1	20.0	93.3[h]	95.7[h]	31.3	52.8
126 Cabo Verde	0.397	89	58	73.8	23.6	28.8	31.2	53.3	67.6
127 Guatemala	0.479	119	95	70.9	19.4	38.6	37.5	39.9	86.3
128 Nicaragua	0.428	101	98	85.0	44.6	48.5[e]	46.8[e]	49.7	84.2
129 Bhutan	0.421	99	183	20.2	15.3	23.3	31.4	58.9	73.4
130 Namibia	0.440	106	195	63.6	37.0	40.6[e]	42.0[e]	56.1	63.3
131 India	0.488	123	133[k]	13.2	13.5	27.7[l]	47.0[l]	20.5	76.1
132 Honduras	0.423	100	65	72.9	21.1	32.2	29.6	52.0	85.9
133 Bangladesh	0.537	133	173	83.0	20.6	39.8	47.5	36.3	81.4
134 Kiribati	..	..	92	16.2	6.5	..	..	..	..
135 Sao Tome and Principe	0.537	133	130	94.6	14.5	31.5	45.8	41.4	74.4
136 Micronesia (Federated States of)	..	..	88	13.9	0.0[m]	..	..	..	..
137 Lao People's Democratic Republic	0.459	113	185	65.4	27.5	35.1[e]	46.2[e]	76.7	80.2
138 Eswatini (Kingdom of)	0.567	143	437	76.7	12.1	31.3[e]	33.9[e]	48.5	56.8
138 Ghana	0.538	135	308	66.6	13.1	55.7[e]	71.6[e]	63.6	71.9
140 Vanuatu	..	..	72	49.4	0.0[m]	..	..	61.0	78.8
141 Timor-Leste	..	..	142	33.8	38.5	..	..	61.9	72.7
142 Nepal	0.452	110	186	65.1	33.5	29.3[e]	44.2[e]	82.8	85.1
143 Kenya	0.518	126	342	75.1	23.3	29.8[e]	37.3[e]	72.1	77.3
144 Cambodia	0.474	117	160	50.2	19.3	15.1[e]	28.2[e]	76.3	88.9
145 Equatorial Guinea	..	..	301	155.6	19.2	..	..	54.8	67.1
146 Zambia	0.539	137	213	120.1	18.0	38.5[h]	54.1[h]	70.4	79.1
147 Myanmar	0.478	118	250	28.5	11.6	28.7[e]	23.5[e]	47.5	77.4
148 Angola	0.536	132	241	150.5	30.0	23.1[h]	38.1[h]	76.1	78.9
149 Congo	0.570	144	378	112.2	13.6	46.7[q]	51.3[q]	67.5	71.4
150 Zimbabwe	0.527	129	458	86.1	34.6	59.8	70.8	78.1	89.0
151 Solomon Islands	..	..	104	78.0	4.1	..	..	82.1	85.6
151 Syrian Arab Republic	0.482	122	31	38.6	13.2	37.1[e]	43.4[e]	14.4	74.1
153 Cameroon	0.560	141	529	105.8	29.3	32.7[f]	41.3[f]	71.1	81.1
154 Pakistan	0.538	135	140	38.8	20.0	27.6	45.7	21.9	81.7
155 Papua New Guinea	0.725	161	145	52.7	0.0[m]	10.0[e]	15.2[e]	46.3	48.0
156 Comoros	..	..	273	65.4	6.1	..	..	36.6	49.9
Low human development									
157 Mauritania	0.634	151	766	71.0	20.3	12.7[e]	25.0[e]	28.9	63.1
158 Benin	0.612	148	397	86.1	7.2	18.3[h]	33.9[h]	68.8	73.0
159 Uganda	0.535	131	375	118.8	34.9	27.5[h]	35.1[h]	67.0	73.9
160 Rwanda	0.402	92	248	39.1	55.7	10.9	15.8	83.9	83.4
161 Nigeria	..	..	917	107.3	4.1	..	..	47.9	57.9
162 Côte d'Ivoire	0.638	153	617	117.6	13.3	17.9[e]	34.4[e]	48.2	65.5
163 Tanzania (United Republic of)	0.556	140	524	118.4	36.9	12.0[e]	16.9[e]	79.6	87.3
164 Madagascar	..	..	335	109.6	16.9	..	..	83.4	88.9
165 Lesotho	0.553	139	544	92.7	23.0	33.0[q]	25.5[q]	60.2	75.9
166 Djibouti	..	..	248	18.8	26.2	..	..	50.7	68.8
167 Togo	0.573	145	396	89.1	16.5	27.6[f]	54.4[f]	76.3	78.9
168 Senegal	0.533	130	315	72.7	41.8	10.3	26.5	35.0	57.5
169 Afghanistan	0.655	157	638	69.0	27.2	13.2[e]	36.9[e]	21.6	74.7
170 Haiti	0.636	152	480	51.7	2.7	26.9[e]	40.0[e]	61.9	72.8
170 Sudan	0.545	138	295	64.0	27.5	15.4[e]	19.5[e]	29.1	68.2
172 Gambia	0.612	148	597	78.2	10.3	31.5[f]	44.4[f]	51.2	68.0
173 Ethiopia	0.517	125	401	66.7	37.3	11.5[h]	22.6[h]	73.4	85.8
174 Malawi	0.565	142	349	132.7	22.9	17.6[e]	26.1[e]	72.6	81.1
175 Congo (Democratic Republic of the)	0.617	150	473	124.2	12.0	36.7	65.8	60.7	66.3
175 Guinea-Bissau	..	..	667	104.8	13.7	..	..	65.8	78.7
175 Liberia	0.650	156	661	136.0	11.7	18.5[e]	40.1[e]	72.1	80.6
178 Guinea	..	..	576	135.3	22.8	..	..	62.7	60.2

Continued →

TABLE 5 / GENDER INEQUALITY INDEX 363

TABLE 5

HDI RANK	Gender Inequality Index Value 2019	Gender Inequality Index Rank 2019	SDG 3.1 Maternal mortality ratio (deaths per 100,000 live births) 2017	SDG 3.7 Adolescent birth rate (births per 1,000 women ages 15–19) 2015–2020[b]	SDG 5.5 Share of seats in parliament (% held by women) 2019	SDG 4.4 Population with at least some secondary education (% ages 25 and older) Female 2015–2019[c]	Population with at least some secondary education Male 2015–2019[c]	Labour force participation rate[a] (% ages 15 and older) Female 2019	Labour force participation rate Male 2019
179 Yemen	0.795	162	164	60.4	1.0	19.9[e]	36.9[e]	5.8	70.2
180 Eritrea	..	..	480	52.6	22.0	..	..	71.5	85.5
181 Mozambique	0.523	127	289	148.6	41.2	14.0	19.9	77.3	79.0
182 Burkina Faso	0.594	147	320	104.3	13.4	6.1[h]	12.3[h]	58.3	74.8
182 Sierra Leone	0.644	155	1,120	112.8	12.3	20.1[e]	33.0[e]	57.3	58.5
184 Mali	0.671	158	562	169.1	9.5	7.3[f]	16.4[f]	61.2	80.6
185 Burundi	0.504	124	548	55.6	38.8	7.5[h]	11.4[h]	80.4	77.8
185 South Sudan	..	..	1,150	62.0	26.6	..	..	71.0	73.8
187 Chad	0.710	160	1,140	161.1	14.9	1.7[h]	10.5[h]	63.9	77.5
188 Central African Republic	0.680	159	829	129.1	8.6	13.4[e]	31.3[e]	64.4	79.8
189 Niger	0.642	154	509	186.5	17.0	4.7	9.0	60.6	83.7
Other countries or territories									
Korea (Democratic People's Rep. of)	..	..	89	0.3	17.6	..	..	73.4	87.8
Monaco	..	..	..	..	33.3	..	..	..	..
Nauru	..	..	..	..	10.5	..	..	..	..
San Marino	..	..	..	..	25.0	..	..	..	..
Somalia	..	..	829	100.1	24.3	..	..	21.8	73.6
Tuvalu	..	..	..	..	6.3	..	..	..	..
Human development groups									
Very high human development	0.173	–	14	17.2	28.3	86.5	88.6	52.3	69.1
High human development	0.340	–	62	33.6	24.5	69.8	75.1	54.2	75.4
Medium human development	0.501	–	161	34.6	20.4	30.1	46.3	28.3	77.1
Low human development	0.592	–	572	102.8	22.2	17.2	30.1	57.7	72.3
Developing countries	0.463	–	224	47.2	22.7	53.0	62.3	45.6	75.7
Regions									
Arab States	0.518	–	135	46.8	18.0	49.3	55.8	20.7	73.0
East Asia and the Pacific	0.324	–	73	22.1	20.2	69.4	76.5	59.2	76.5
Europe and Central Asia	0.256	–	20	27.8	23.1	79.9	88.1	45.0	70.0
Latin America and the Caribbean	0.389	–	73	63.2	31.4	60.4	59.7	52.1	76.9
South Asia	0.505	–	149	26.0	17.5	31.3	48.4	23.2	77.0
Sub-Saharan Africa	0.570	–	535	104.9	24.0	28.8	39.8	63.3	72.7
Least developed countries	0.559	–	412	94.8	22.8	24.1	34.6	56.6	78.2
Small island developing states	0.458	–	207	57.7	25.1	59.1	62.8	51.9	70.6
Organisation for Economic Co-operation and Development	0.205	–	18	22.9	30.8	84.1	87.0	52.1	69.1
World	**0.436**	**–**	**204**	**43.3**	**24.6**	**61.0**	**68.3**	**47.2**	**74.2**

Notes

a Estimates modelled by the International Labour Organization.

b Data are average annual estimates for 2015–2020.

c Data refer to the most recent year available during the period specified.

d Based on data from OECD (2019b).

e Based on projections from Barro and Lee (2018).

f Updated by HDRO based on data from United Nations Children's Fund Multiple Indicator Cluster Surveys for 2006–2019.

g Updated by HDRO using projections from Barro and Lee (2018).

h Updated by HDRO based on data from ICF Macro Demographic and Health Surveys for 2006–2019.

i Based on cross-country regression.

j Excludes the 36 special rotating delegates appointed on an ad hoc basis.

k A special update by WHO, UNICEF, UNFPA, World Bank Group and United Nations Population Division (2019), communicated to HDRO on 7 September 2020.

l Refers to 2011.

m In calculating the Gender Inequality Index, a value of 0.1 percent was used.

Definitions

Gender Inequality Index: A composite measure reflecting inequality in achievement between women and men in three dimensions: reproductive health, empowerment and the labour market. See *Technical note* 4 at http://hdr.undp.org/sites/default/files/hdr2020_technical_notes.pdf for details on how the Gender Inequality Index is calculated.

Maternal mortality ratio: Number of deaths due to pregnancy-related causes per 100,000 live births.

Adolescent birth rate: Number of births to women ages 15–19 per 1,000 women ages 15–19.

Share of seats in parliament: Proportion of seats held by women in the national parliament expressed as a percentage of total seats. For countries with a bicameral legislative system, the share of seats is calculated based on both houses.

Population with at least some secondary education: Percentage of the population ages 25 and older that has reached (but not necessarily completed) a secondary level of education.

Labour force participation rate: Proportion of the working-age population (ages 15 and older) that engages in the labour market, either by working or actively looking for work, expressed as a percentage of the working-age population.

Main data sources

Column 1: HDRO calculations based on data in columns 3–9.

Column 2: Calculated based on data in column 1.

Column 3: WHO, UNICEF, UNFPA, World Bank Group and United Nations Population Division (2019).

Column 4: UNDESA (2019a).

Column 5: IPU (2020).

Columns 6 and 7: UNESCO Institute for Statistics (2020) and Barro and Lee (2018).

Columns 8 and 9: ILO (2020).

TABLE 6

Multidimensional Poverty Index: developing countries

	SDG 1.2 Multidimensional Poverty Index[a]		Population in multidimensional poverty[a]					Population in severe multidimensional poverty[a]	Population vulnerable to multidimensional poverty[a]	Contribution of deprivation in dimension to overall multidimensional poverty[a]			SDG 1.2 / SDG 1.1 Population living below income poverty line (%)	
	Year and survey[b]	Index	Headcount	(thousands)		Intensity of deprivation	Inequality among the poor			Health	Education	Standard of living	National poverty line	PPP $1.90 a day
Country	2008-2019	Value	(%)	In survey year	2018	(%)	Value	(%)	(%)	(%)			2008-2019[c]	2008-2018[c]
Estimates based on surveys for 2014–2019														
Afghanistan	2015/2016[D]	0.272[d]	55.9[d]	19,783[d]	20,783[d]	48.6[d]	0.020[d]	24.9[d]	18.1[d]	10.0[d]	45.0[d]	45.0[d]	54.5	..
Albania	2017/2018[D]	0.003	0.7	20	20	39.1	..[e]	0.1	5.0	28.3	55.1	16.7	14.3	1.7
Angola	2015/2016[D]	0.282	51.1	14,740	15,745	55.3	0.024	32.5	15.5	21.2	32.1	46.8	36.6	47.6
Armenia	2015/2016[D]	0.001	0.2	5	6	36.2	..[e]	0.0	2.7	33.1	36.8	30.1	23.5	2.1
Bangladesh	2019[M]	0.104	24.6	40,176	39,764	42.2	0.010	6.5	18.2	17.3	37.6	45.1	24.3	14.8
Belize	2015/2016[M]	0.017	4.3	16	16	39.8	0.007	0.6	8.4	39.5	20.9	39.6	..	..
Benin	2017/2018[D]	0.368	66.8	7,672	7,672	55.0	0.025	40.9	14.7	20.8	36.3	42.9	40.1	49.5
Botswana	2015/2016[N]	0.073[f]	17.2[f]	372[f]	388[f]	42.2[f]	0.008[f]	3.5[f]	19.7[f]	30.3[f]	16.5[f]	53.2[f]	19.3	16.1
Brazil	2015[N g]	0.016[d,g,h]	3.8[d,g,h]	7,856[d,g,h]	8,048[d,g,h]	42.5[d,g,h]	0.008[d,g,h]	0.9[d,g,h]	6.2[d,g,h]	49.8[d,g,h]	22.9[d,g,h]	27.3[d,g,h]	..	4.4
Burundi	2016/2017[D]	0.403	74.3	8,040	8,298	54.3	0.022	45.3	16.3	23.3	27.5	49.2	64.9	71.8
Cambodia	2014[D]	0.170	37.2	5,680	6,043	45.8	0.015	13.2	21.1	21.8	31.7	46.6	17.7	..
Cameroon	2014[M]	0.243	45.3	10,281	11,430	53.5	0.026	25.6	17.3	23.2	28.2	48.6	37.5	23.8
Chad	2014/2015[D]	0.533	85.7	12,089	13,260	62.3	0.026	66.1	9.9	20.1	34.4	45.5	46.7	38.4
China	2014[N i]	0.016[i,k]	3.9[i,k]	54,369[i,k]	55,464[i,k]	41.4[i,k]	0.005[i,k]	0.3[i,k]	17.4[i,k]	35.2[i,k]	39.2[i,k]	25.6[i,k]	1.7	0.5
Colombia	2015/2016[D]	0.020[d]	4.8[d]	2,335[d]	2,407[d]	40.6[d]	0.009[d]	0.8[d]	6.2[d]	12.0[d]	39.5[d]	48.5[d]	27	4.1
Congo	2014/2015[M]	0.112	24.3	1,178	1,273	46.0	0.013	9.4	21.3	23.4	20.2	56.4	40.9	37.0
Congo (Democratic Republic of the)	2017/2018[M]	0.331	64.5	54,239	54,239	51.3	0.020	36.8	17.4	23.1	19.9	57.0	63.9	76.6
Côte d'Ivoire	2016[M]	0.236	46.1	10,975	11,549	51.2	0.019	24.5	17.6	19.6	40.4	40.0	46.3	28.2
Cuba	2017[D]	0.002[d]	0.4[d]	50[d]	50[d]	36.8[d]	0.003[d]	0.0[d]	1.6[d]	25.8[d]	32.2[d]	42.0[d]	..	..
Dominican Republic	2014[M]	0.015[d]	3.9[d]	394[d]	412[d]	38.9[d]	0.006[d]	0.5[d]	5.2[d]	29.1[d]	35.8[d]	35.0[d]	22.8	0.4
Ecuador	2013/2014[N]	0.018[h]	4.6[h]	730[h]	782[h]	39.9[h]	0.007[h]	0.8[h]	7.6[h]	40.4[h]	23.6[h]	35.9[h]	25	3.3
Egypt	2014[D]	0.019[l]	5.2[l]	4,670[l]	5,083[l]	37.6[l]	0.004[l]	0.6[l]	6.1[l]	39.8[l]	53.2[l]	7.0[l]	32.5	3.2
El Salvador	2014[M]	0.032	7.9	495	505	41.3	0.009	1.7	9.9	15.5	43.4	41.1	29.2	1.5
Eswatini (Kingdom of)	2014[M]	0.081	19.2	210	218	42.3	0.009	4.4	20.9	29.3	17.9	52.8	58.9	28.4
Ethiopia	2016[D]	0.489	83.5	86,513	91,207	58.5	0.024	61.5	8.9	19.7	29.4	50.8	23.5	30.8
Gambia	2018[M]	0.204	41.6	948	948	49.0	0.018	18.8	22.9	29.5	34.6	35.9	48.6	10.1
Georgia	2018[M]	0.001[h]	0.3[h]	14[h]	14[h]	36.6[h]	..[e]	0.0[h]	2.1[h]	47.1[h]	23.8[h]	29.1[h]	20.1	4.5
Ghana	2014[D]	0.138	30.1	8,188	8,952	45.8	0.016	10.4	22.0	22.3	30.4	47.2	23.4	13.3
Guatemala	2014/2015[D]	0.134	28.9	4,694	4,981	46.2	0.013	11.2	21.1	26.3	35.0	38.7	59.3	8.7
Guinea	2018[D]	0.373	66.2	8,220	8,220	56.4	0.025	43.5	16.4	21.4	38.4	40.3	55.2	35.3
Guinea-Bissau	2014[M]	0.372	67.3	1,139	1,261	55.3	0.025	40.4	19.2	21.3	33.9	44.7	69.3	67.1
Guyana	2014[M]	0.014	3.4	26	26	41.8	0.008	0.7	5.8	31.5	18.7	49.8	..	..
Haiti	2016/2017[D]	0.200	41.3	4,532	4,590	48.4	0.019	18.5	21.8	18.5	24.6	57.0	58.5	24.2
India	2015/2016[D]	0.123	27.9	369,643	377,492	43.9	0.014	8.8	19.3	31.9	23.4	44.8	21.9	21.2
Indonesia	2017[D]	0.014[d]	3.6[d]	9,578[d]	9,687[d]	38.7[d]	0.006[d]	0.4[d]	4.7[d]	34.7[d]	26.8[d]	38.5[d]	9.8	4.6
Iraq	2018[M]	0.033	8.6	3,319	3,319	37.9	0.005	1.3	5.2	33.1	60.9	6.0	18.9	2.5
Jamaica	2014[N]	0.018[m]	4.7[m]	135[m]	138[m]	38.7[m]	..[e]	0.8[m]	6.4[m]	42.1[m]	17.5[m]	40.4[m]	19.9	..
Jordan	2017/2018[D]	0.002	0.4	43	43	35.4	..[e]	0.0	0.7	37.5	53.5	9.0	14.4	0.1
Kazakhstan	2015[M]	0.002[h]	0.5[h]	80[h]	83[h]	35.6[h]	..[e]	0.0[h]	1.8[h]	90.4[h]	3.1[h]	6.4[h]	2.5	0.0
Kenya	2014[D]	0.178	38.7	18,062	19,877	46.0	0.014	13.3	34.9	24.9	14.6	60.5	36.1	36.8
Kiribati	2018/2019[M]	0.080	19.8	23	23	40.5	0.006	3.5	30.2	30.3	12.1	57.6	..	..
Kyrgyzstan	2018[M]	0.001	0.4	25	25	36.3	..[e]	0.0	5.2	64.6	17.9	17.5	22.4	0.9
Lao People's Democratic Republic	2017[M]	0.108	23.1	1,604	1,629	47.0	0.016	9.6	21.2	21.5	39.7	38.8	23.4	22.7
Lesotho	2018[M]	0.084[l]	19.6[l]	413[l]	413[l]	43.0[l]	0.009[l]	5.0[l]	28.6[l]	21.9[l]	18.1[l]	60.0[l]	49.7	26.9
Libya	2014[P]	0.007	2.0	127	133	37.1	0.003	0.1	11.4	39.0	48.6	12.4	..	..
Madagascar	2018[D]	0.384	69.1	18,142	18,142	55.6	0.023	45.5	14.3	15.5	33.1	51.5	70.7	77.6
Malawi	2015/2016[D]	0.243	52.6	9,054	9,547	46.2	0.013	18.5	28.5	20.7	23.1	56.2	51.5	70.3
Maldives	2016/2017[D]	0.003	0.8	4	4	34.4	..[e]	0.0	4.8	80.7	15.1	4.2	8.2	0.0
Mali	2018[D]	0.376	68.3	13,036	13,036	55.0	0.022	44.7	15.3	19.6	41.2	39.3	41.1	49.7
Mauritania	2015[M]	0.261	50.6	2,046	2,227	51.5	0.019	26.3	18.6	20.2	33.1	46.6	31	6.0
Mexico	2016[N n]	0.026[m]	6.6[m]	8,097[m]	8,284[m]	39.0[m]	0.008[m]	1.0[m]	4.7[m]	68.1[m]	13.7[m]	18.2[m]	41.9	1.7
Mongolia	2018[M]	0.028[o]	7.3[o]	230[o]	230[o]	38.8[o]	0.004[o]	0.8[o]	15.5[o]	21.1[o]	26.8[o]	52.1[o]	28.4	0.5
Montenegro	2018[M]	0.005	1.2	8	8	39.6	..[e]	0.1	2.9	58.5	22.3	19.2	23.6	1.7
Myanmar	2015/2016[D]	0.176	38.3	20,325	20,579	45.9	0.015	13.8	21.9	18.5	32.3	49.2	24.8	2.0
Nepal	2016[D]	0.148	34.0	9,267	9,550	43.6	0.012	11.6	22.4	31.5	27.2	41.3	25.2	15.0
Nigeria	2018[D]	0.254	46.4	90,919	90,919	54.8	0.029	26.8	19.2	30.9	28.2	40.9	46	53.5
Pakistan	2017/2018[D]	0.198	38.3	81,352	81,352	51.7	0.023	21.5	12.9	27.6	41.3	31.1	24.3	3.9
Palestine, State of	2014[M]	0.004	1.0	42	46	37.5	0.003	0.1	5.4	53.3	32.8	13.9	29.2	1.0

Continued →

TABLE 6 / MULTIDIMENSIONAL POVERTY INDEX: DEVELOPING COUNTRIES　　365

TABLE 6

	Multidimensional Poverty Index[a]		Population in multidimensional poverty[a]						Population vulnerable to multidimensional poverty[a]	Contribution of deprivation in dimension to overall multidimensional poverty[a]			Population living below income poverty line (%)	
													SDG 1.2	SDG 1.1
			Headcount			Intensity of deprivation	Inequality among the poor	Population in severe multidimensional poverty		Health	Education	Standard of living	National poverty line	PPP $1.90 a day
	Year and survey[b]	Index	(%)	(thousands) In survey year	2018	(%)	Value	(%)	(%)		(%)			
Country	2008-2019	Value	(%)			(%)	Value	(%)	(%)		(%)		2008-2019[c]	2008-2018[c]
Papua New Guinea	2016/2018[D]	0.263[d]	56.6[d]	4,874[d]	4,874[d]	46.5[d]	0.016[d]	25.8[d]	25.3[d]	4.6[d]	30.1[d]	65.3[d]	39.9	38.0
Paraguay	2016[M]	0.019	4.5	305	313	41.9	0.013	1.0	7.2	14.3	38.9	46.8	24.2	1.6
Peru	2018[N]	0.029	7.4	2,358	2,358	39.6	0.007	1.1	9.6	15.7	31.1	53.2	20.5	2.6
Philippines	2017[D]	0.024[d]	5.8[d]	6,096[d]	6,181[d]	41.8[d]	0.010[d]	1.3[d]	7.3[d]	20.3[d]	31.0[d]	48.7[d]	21.6	6.1
Rwanda	2014/2015[D]	0.259	54.4	6,188	6,695	47.5	0.013	22.2	25.7	13.6	30.5	55.9	38.2	55.5
Sao Tome and Principe	2014[M]	0.092	22.1	43	47	41.7	0.008	4.4	19.4	18.6	37.4	44.0	66.2	34.5
Senegal	2017[D]	0.288	53.2	8,199	8,430	54.2	0.021	32.8	16.4	22.1	44.9	33.0	46.7	38.0
Serbia	2014[M]	0.001[h]	0.3[h]	30[h]	30[h]	42.5[h]	..[e]	0.1[h]	3.4[h]	20.6[h]	42.7[h]	36.8[h]	24.3	5.5
Seychelles	2019[N]	0.003[Lp]	0.9[Lp]	1[Lp]	1[Lp]	34.2[Lp]	..[e]	0.0[Lp]	0.4[Lp]	66.8[Lp]	32.1[Lp]	1.1[Lp]	39.3	1.1
Sierra Leone	2017[M]	0.297	57.9	4,338	4,432	51.2	0.020	30.4	19.6	18.6	28.9	52.4	52.9	40.1
South Africa	2016[D]	0.025	6.3	3,517	3,616	39.8	0.005	0.9	12.2	39.5	13.1	47.4	55.5	18.9
Sri Lanka	2016[N]	0.011	2.9	614	620	38.3	0.004	0.3	14.3	32.5	24.4	43.0	4.1	0.8
Sudan	2014[M]	0.279	52.3	19,873	21,874	53.4	0.023	30.9	17.7	21.1	29.2	49.8	46.5	12.7
Suriname	2018[M]	0.011	2.9	16	16	39.4	0.007	0.4	4.0	20.4	43.8	35.8	..	..
Tajikistan	2017[D]	0.029	7.4	661	678	39.0	0.004	0.7	20.1	47.8	26.5	25.8	27.4	4.8
Tanzania (United Republic of)	2015/2016[D]	0.273	55.4	29,415	31,225	49.3	0.016	25.9	24.2	21.1	22.9	56.0	26.4	49.1
Thailand	2015/2016[M]	0.003[h]	0.8[h]	542[h]	545[h]	39.1[h]	0.007[h]	0.1[h]	7.2[h]	35.0[h]	47.4[h]	17.6[h]	9.9	0.0
Timor-Leste	2016[D]	0.210	45.8	559	581	45.7	0.014	16.3	26.1	27.8	24.2	48.0	41.8	30.7
Togo	2017[M]	0.180	37.6	2,896	2,967	47.8	0.016	15.2	23.8	20.9	28.1	50.9	55.1	49.8
Tunisia	2018[M]	0.003	0.8	92	92	36.5	..[e]	0.1	2.4	24.4	61.6	14.0	15.2	0.2
Turkmenistan	2015/2016[M]	0.001	0.4	23	24	36.1	..[e]	0.0	2.4	88.0	4.4	7.6	..	..
Uganda	2016[D]	0.269	55.1	21,844	23,540	48.8	0.017	24.1	24.9	22.4	22.5	55.1	21.4	41.7
Viet Nam	2013/2014[D]	0.019[d]	4.9[d]	4,490[d]	4,677[d]	39.5[d]	0.010[d]	0.7[d]	5.6[d]	15.2[d]	42.6[d]	42.2[d]	6.7	1.9
Zambia	2018[D]	0.232	47.9	8,313	8,313	48.4	0.015	21.0	23.9	21.5	25.0	53.5	54.4	57.5
Zimbabwe	2019[N]	0.110	25.8	3,779	3,725	42.6	0.009	6.8	26.3	23.6	17.3	59.2	70	33.9
Estimates based on surveys for 2008–2013														
Algeria	2012/2013[M]	0.008	2.1	801	887	38.8	0.006	0.3	5.8	29.9	46.8	23.2	5.5	0.5
Barbados	2012[M]	0.009[m]	2.5[m]	7[m]	7[m]	34.2[m]	..[e]	0.0[m]	0.5[m]	96.0[m]	0.7[m]	3.3[m]	..	..
Bhutan	2010[M]	0.175[h]	37.3[h]	256[h]	282[h]	46.8[h]	0.016[h]	14.7[h]	17.7[h]	24.2[h]	36.6[h]	39.2[h]	8.2	1.5
Bolivia (Plurinational State of)	2008[D]	0.094	20.4	1,983	2,316	46.0	0.014	7.1	15.7	21.6	26.6	51.8	34.6	4.5
Bosnia and Herzegovina	2011/2012[M]	0.008[m]	2.2[m]	79[m]	73[m]	37.9[m]	0.002[m]	0.1[m]	4.1[m]	79.7[m]	7.2[m]	13.1[m]	16.9	0.1
Burkina Faso	2010[D]	0.519	83.8	13,083	16,559	61.9	0.027	64.8	7.4	20.0	40.6	39.4	40.1	43.7
Central African Republic	2010[M]	0.465[h]	79.4[h]	3,481[h]	3,703[h]	58.6[h]	0.028[h]	54.7[h]	13.1[h]	27.8[h]	25.7[h]	46.5[h]	62	66.3
Comoros	2012[D]	0.181	37.3	270	310	48.5	0.020	16.1	22.3	20.8	31.6	47.6	42.4	17.6
Gabon	2012[D]	0.066	14.8	260	315	44.3	0.013	4.7	17.5	31.0	22.2	46.8	33.4	3.4
Honduras	2011/2012[D]	0.090[q]	19.3[q]	1,668[q]	1,851[q]	46.4[q]	0.013[q]	6.5[q]	22.3[q]	18.5[q]	33.0[q]	48.5[q]	48.3	16.5
Liberia	2013[D]	0.320	62.9	2,674	3,033	50.8	0.019	32.1	21.4	19.7	28.2	52.1	50.9	40.9
Moldova (Republic of)	2012[M]	0.004	0.9	38	38	37.4	..[e]	0.1	3.7	9.2	42.4	48.4	9.6	0.0
Morocco	2011[P]	0.085[h]	18.6[h]	6,098[h]	6,702[h]	45.7[h]	0.017[h]	6.5[h]	13.1[h]	25.7[h]	42.0[h]	32.3[h]	4.8	1.0
Mozambique	2011[D]	0.411	72.5	17,524	21,371	56.7	0.023	49.1	13.6	17.2	32.5	50.3	46.1	62.9
Namibia	2013[D]	0.171	38.0	849	930	45.1	0.012	12.2	20.3	30.3	14.9	54.9	17.4	13.4
Nicaragua	2011/2012[D]	0.074	16.3	973	1,051	45.2	0.013	5.5	13.2	11.1	36.5	52.4	24.9	3.2
Niger	2012[D]	0.590	90.5	16,099	20,304	65.2	0.026	74.8	5.1	20.3	37.3	42.4	44.5	44.5
North Macedonia	2011[M]	0.010[m]	2.5[m]	52[m]	53[m]	37.7[m]	0.007[m]	0.2[m]	2.9[m]	62.5[m]	17.0[m]	20.5[m]	21.9	4.4
Saint Lucia	2012[M]	0.007[m]	1.9[m]	3[m]	3[m]	37.5[m]	..[e]	0.0[m]	1.6[m]	69.5[m]	7.5[m]	23.0[m]	25	4.7
South Sudan	2010[M]	0.580	91.9	8,735	10,083	63.2	0.023	74.3	6.3	14.0	39.6	46.5	82.3	42.7
Syrian Arab Republic	2009[P]	0.029[h]	7.4[h]	1,568[h]	1,253[h]	38.9[h]	0.006[h]	1.2[h]	7.8[h]	40.8[h]	49.0[h]	10.2[h]	..	..
Trinidad and Tobago	2011[M]	0.002[h]	0.6[h]	9[h]	9[h]	38.0[h]	..[e]	0.1[h]	3.7[h]	45.5[h]	34.0[h]	20.5[h]	..	..
Ukraine	2012[M]	0.001[d]	0.2[d]	109[d]	106[d]	34.5[d]	..[e]	0.0[d]	0.4[d]	59.7[d]	28.8[d]	11.5[d]	1.3	0.0
Yemen	2013[D]	0.241	47.7	11,995	13,593	50.5	0.021	23.9	22.1	28.3	30.7	41.0	48.6	18.8
Developing countries	–	0.108	22.0	1,243,895	1,291,125	49.0	0.018	9.8	15.2	25.8	29.6	44.5	20.7	14.7
Regions														
Arab States	–	0.077	15.8	48,627	53,025	48.5	0.018	7.0	9.4	26.1	35.2	38.8	26.0	4.9
East Asia and the Pacific	–	0.023	5.4	108,368	110,514	42.5	0.009	1.0	14.6	27.7	35.5	36.8	5.3	1.7
Europe and Central Asia	–	0.004	1.0	1,144	1,156	38.1	0.004	0.1	3.4	53.0	24.3	22.6	11.6	0.8
Latin America and the Caribbean	–	0.031	7.2	36,682	38,165	43.0	0.011	1.9	7.4	35.9	26.2	37.9	35.9	4.2
South Asia	–	0.132	29.2	521,093	529,846	45.2	0.015	10.3	18.4	29.2	28.5	42.3	22.9	18.2
Sub-Saharan Africa	–	0.299	55.0	527,980	558,420	54.3	0.022	32.9	17.9	22.4	29.3	48.4	43.4	45.7

TABLE 6

Notes

a   Not all indicators were available for all countries, so caution should be used in cross-country comparisons. When an indicator is missing, weights of available indicators are adjusted to total 100 percent. See *Technical note 5* at http://hdr.undp.org/sites/default/files/hdr2020_technical_notes.pdf for details.

b   *D* indicates data from Demographic and Health Surveys, *M* indicates data from Multiple Indicator Cluster Surveys, *N* indicates data from national surveys and *P* indicates data from Pan Arab Population and Family Health Surveys (see http://hdr.undp.org/en/mpi-2020-faq for the list of national surveys).

c   Data refer to the most recent year available during the period specified.

d   Missing indicator on nutrition.

e   Value is not reported because it is based on a small number of multidimensionally poor people.

f   Indicator on child mortality captures only deaths of children under age 5 who died in the last five years and deaths of children ages 12–18 who died in the last two years.

g   The methodology was adjusted to account for missing indicator on nutrition and incomplete indicator on child mortality (the survey did not collect the date of child deaths).

h   Considers child deaths that occurred at any time because the survey did not collect the date of child deaths.

i   Based on the version of data accessed on 7 June 2016.

j   Given the information available in the data, child mortality was constructed based on deaths that occurred between surveys—that is, between 2012 and 2014. Child deaths reported by an adult man in the household were taken into account because the date of death was reported.

k   Missing indicator on housing.

l   Missing indicator on cooking fuel.

m   Missing indicator on child mortality.

n   Multidimensional Poverty Index estimates are based on the 2016 National Health and Nutrition Survey. Estimates based on the 2015 Multiple Indicator Cluster Survey are 0.010 for Multidimensional Poverty Index value, 2.6 for multidimensional poverty headcount (%), 3,207,000 for multidimensional poverty headcount in year of survey, 3,281,000 for projected multidimensional poverty headcount in 2018, 40.2 for intensity of deprivation, 0.4 for population in severe multidimensional poverty, 6.1 for population vulnerable to multidimensional poverty, 39.9 for contribution of deprivation in health, 23.8 for contribution of deprivation in education and 36.3 for contribution of deprivation in standard of living.

o   Indicator on sanitation follows the national classification in which pit latrine with slab is considered unimproved.

p   Missing indicator on school attendance.

q   Missing indicator on electricity.

Definitions

Multidimensional Poverty Index: Percentage of the population that is multidimensionally poor adjusted by the intensity of the deprivations. See *Technical note 5* at http://hdr.undp.org/sites/default/files/hdr2020_technical_notes.pdf for details on how the Multidimensional Poverty Index is calculated.

Multidimensional poverty headcount: Population with a deprivation score of at least 33 percent. It is expressed as a share of the population in the survey year, the number of multidimensionally poor people in the survey year and the projected number of multidimensionally poor people in 2018.

Intensity of deprivation of multidimensional poverty: Average deprivation score experienced by people in multidimensional poverty.

Inequality among the poor: Variance of individual deprivation scores of poor people. It is calculated by subtracting the deprivation score of each multidimensionally poor person from the average intensity, squaring the differences and dividing the sum of the weighted squares by the number of multidimensionally poor people.

Population in severe multidimensional poverty: Percentage of the population in severe multidimensional poverty—that is, those with a deprivation score of 50 percent or more.

Population vulnerable to multidimensional poverty: Percentage of the population at risk of suffering multiple deprivations—that is, those with a deprivation score of 20–33 percent.

Contribution of deprivation in dimension to overall multidimensional poverty: Percentage of the Multidimensional Poverty Index attributed to deprivations in each dimension.

Population living below national poverty line: Percentage of the population living below the national poverty line, which is the poverty line deemed appropriate for a country by its authorities. National estimates are based on population-weighted subgroup estimates from household surveys.

Population living below PPP $1.90 a day: Percentage of the population living below the international poverty line of $1.90 (in purchasing power parity [PPP] terms) a day.

Main data sources

Column 1: Refers to the year and the survey whose data were used to calculate the country's Multidimensional Poverty Index value and its components.

Columns 2–12: HDRO and OPHI calculations based on data on household deprivations in health, education and standard of living from various household surveys listed in column 1 using the methodology described in *Technical note 5* (available at http://hdr.undp.org/sites/default/files/hdr2020_technical_notes.pdf). Columns 4 and 5 also use population data from UNDESA (2019a).

Columns 13 and 14: World Bank (2020a).

TABLE 6 / MULTIDIMENSIONAL POVERTY INDEX: DEVELOPING COUNTRIES   367

Human development dashboards

Quality of human development

Country groupings (terciles): Top third   Middle third   Bottom third

Three-colour coding is used to visualize partial grouping of countries by indicator. For each indicator countries are divided into three groups of approximately equal size (terciles): the top third, the middle third and the bottom third. Aggregates are colour coded using the same tercile cutoffs. See *Notes* after the table.

		Quality of health			SDG 4.c	SDG 4.a	Quality of education		SDG 4.1				SDG 7.1	SDG 6.1	SDG 6.2
					Pupil-teacher ratio, primary school	Primary school teachers trained to teach	Schools with access to the Internet		Programme for International Student Assessment (PISA) score			Vulnerable employment[a]	Rural population with access to electricity	Population using safely managed drinking-water services	Population using safely managed sanitation services
		Lost health expectancy	Physicians	Hospital beds			Primary schools	Secondary schools	Reading[b]	Mathematics[c]	Science[c]				
		(%)	(per 10,000 people)		(pupils per teacher)		(%)					(% of total employment)		(%)	
HDI RANK		2019	2010–2018[d]	2010–2019[d]	2010–2019[d]	2010–2019[d]	2010–2019[d]	2010–2019[d]	2018	2018	2018	2019	2018	2017	2017
Very high human development															
1	Norway	14.6	29.2	35	9	..	100	100	499	501	490	4.9	100.0	98	76
2	Ireland	14.2	33.1	30	16	..	..	..	518	500	496	10.6	100.0	97	82
2	Switzerland	14.2	43.0	46	10	..	100	100	484	515	495	8.9	100.0	95	100
4	Hong Kong, China (SAR)	..	..	..	13	97	99	95	524	551	517	5.7	100.0	..	..
4	Iceland	14.0	40.8	28	10	..	..	..	474	495	475	8.1	100.0	100	82
6	Germany	14.1	42.5	80	12	..	..	..	498	500	503	5.6	100.0	100	97
7	Sweden	13.8	39.8	21	12	..	..	..	506	502	499	6.1	100.0	100	93
8	Australia	15.2	36.8	38	..	..	100	100	503	491	503	10.6	100.0	..	76
8	Netherlands	13.6	36.1	32	12	..	100	100	485	519	503	12.7	100.0	100	97
10	Denmark	13.8	40.1	26	11	..	100	100	501	509	493	4.9	100.0	97	95
11	Finland	14.1	38.1	36	14	..	100	100	520	507	522	9.6	100.0	100	99
11	Singapore	12.2	22.9	25	15	99	..	..	549	569	551	9.7	100.0	100	100
13	United Kingdom	14.8	28.1	25	15	..	..	..	504	502	505	13.0	100.0	100	98
14	Belgium	14.4	30.7	56	11	..	100	100	493	508	499	10.2	100.0	100	97
14	New Zealand	14.9	35.9	26	15	..	..	..	506	494	508	12.1	100.0	100	89
16	Canada	14.3	26.1	25	..	..	..	..	520	512	518	10.7	100.0	99	82
17	United States	17.1	26.1	29	14	..	..	..	505	478	502	3.8	100.0	99	90
18	Austria	14.1	51.7	73	10	..	..	..	484	499	490	7.4	100.0	99	97
19	Israel	13.5	46.2	30	12	..	85	85	470	463	462	8.3	100.0	99	94
19	Japan	12.9	24.1	130	16	..	..	..	504	527	529	8.3	100.0	98	99
19	Liechtenstein	..	..	..	8	..	..	..	..	..	..	..	100.0	..	..
22	Slovenia	13.5	30.9	44	14	..	100	100	495	509	507	11.2	100.0	98	83
23	Korea (Republic of)	12.8	23.6	124	16	..	100	100	514	526	519	19.0	100.0	98	100
23	Luxembourg	14.4	30.1	43	8	..	..	..	470	483	477	5.6	100.0	100	97
25	Spain	13.8	38.7	30	13	..	100	100	..	481	483	11.0	100.0	98	97
26	France	13.7	32.7	59	18	..	98	99	493	495	493	7.4	100.0	98	88
27	Czechia	13.7	41.2	66	19	..	..	..	490	499	497	13.7	100.0	98	94
28	Malta	13.9	28.6	45	13	..	..	..	448	472	457	9.8	100.0	100	93
29	Estonia	12.7	44.8	46	11	..	100	100	523	523	530	6.1	100.0	93	97
29	Italy	14.3	39.8	31	11	..	70	88	476	487	468	16.9	100.0	95	96
31	United Arab Emirates	12.9	25.3	14	25	100	100	100	432	435	434	0.9	100.0	..	96
32	Greece	13.6	54.8	42	9	..	..	..	457	451	452	25.8	100.0	100	90
33	Cyprus	13.5	19.5	34	12	..	..	..	424	451	439	11.1	100.0	100	75
34	Lithuania	12.7	63.5	64	14	..	..	..	476	481	482	9.2	100.0	92	91
35	Poland	12.8	23.8	65	10	..	100	100	512	516	511	16.1	100.0	99	93
36	Andorra	13.8	33.3	..	10	100	100	100	..	..	..	..	100.0	91	100
37	Latvia	12.6	31.9	55	12	..	100	100	479	496	487	7.1	100.0	95	86
38	Portugal	14.1	51.2	35	12	..	100	100	492	492	492	11.8	100.0	95	85
39	Slovakia	12.8	34.2	57	16	..	100	100	458	486	464	11.8	100.0	100	83
40	Hungary	12.8	34.1	70	11	..	100	99	476	481	481	6.0	100.0	90	96
40	Saudi Arabia	13.5	26.1	22	14	100	100	100	399	373	386	3.0	100.0	..	78
42	Bahrain	13.6	9.3	17	12	100	100	100	..	..	..	1.1	100.0	99	96
43	Chile	13.6	25.9	21	18	..	..	..	452	417	444	22.7	100.0	99	77
43	Croatia	13.3	30.0	55	14	..	..	..	479	464	472	7.3	100.0	90	58
45	Qatar	13.1	24.9	13	12	49e	100	100	407	414	419	0.1	100.0	96	96
46	Argentina	12.8	39.9	50	17e	..	40	55	402	379	404	21.8	100.0	..	..
47	Brunei Darussalam	12.2	16.1	29	10	86	..	..	408	430	431	6.0	100.0	..	..
48	Montenegro	12.4	27.6	39	..	..	..	..	421	430	415	13.3	100.0	94	..
49	Romania	12.1	29.8	69	19	..	..	..	428	430	426	23.7	100.0	82	77
50	Palau	12.3	14.2	..	..	..	..	..	..	..	..	..	100.0	..	..
51	Kazakhstan	12.2	39.8	61	17	100	..	..	387	423	397	23.2	100.0	90	..

Continued →

		Quality of health			SDG 4.c	SDG 4.a Quality of education			SDG 4.1			SDG 7.1		SDG 7.1	SDG 6.1	SDG 6.2 Quality of standard of living
		Lost health expectancy	Physicians	Hospital beds	Pupil-teacher ratio, primary school	Primary school teachers trained to teach	Schools with access to the Internet Primary schools	Secondary schools	Programme for International Student Assessment (PISA) score Reading[b]	Mathematics[c]	Science[c]	Vulnerable employment[a]	Rural population with access to electricity	Population using safely managed drinking-water services	Population using safely managed sanitation services
		(%)	(per 10,000 people)		(pupils per teacher)		(%)					(% of total employment)		(%)	
HDI RANK		2019	2010-2018[d]	2010-2019[d]	2010-2019[d]	2010-2019[d]	2010-2019[d]	2010-2019[d]	2018	2018	2018	2019	2018	2017	2017
52	Russian Federation	12.6	40.1	71	21	..	..	..	479	488	478	5.4	100.0	76	61
53	Belarus	12.1	51.9	108	19	100	87	91	474	472	471	3.3	100.0	95	81
54	Turkey	13.5	18.5	29	17	..	..	..	466	454	468	27.0	100.0	..	65
55	Uruguay	13.0	50.8	24	11	100	100	100	427	418	426	24.3	100.0	..	..
56	Bulgaria	12.0	40.3	75	15	..	..	..	420	436	424	7.8	100.0	97	64
57	Panama	13.5	15.7	23	22	99	..	..	377	353	365	34.2	100.0	..	..
58	Bahamas	12.4	20.1	30	19	90	..	..	..	..	..	14.1	100.0	..	..
58	Barbados	12.5	24.8	60	14	76	..	..	..	..	..	15.8	100.0	..	..
60	Oman	12.4	20.0	15	10	100	100	100	..	..	..	2.6	100.0	90	..
61	Georgia	12.1	71.2	29	9	95 [e]	100	100	380	398	383	49.1	100.0	80	27
62	Costa Rica	13.4	28.9	11	12	94	59	61	426	402	416	21.1	100.0	94	..
62	Malaysia	12.5	15.4	19	12	97	97	96	415	440	438	21.8	100.0	93	89
64	Kuwait	13.8	26.5	20	9	79	..	..	..	..	..	1.1	100.0	100	100
64	Serbia	12.4	31.1	56	14	56	..	..	439	448	440	24.3	100.0	75	25
66	Mauritius	13.7	25.3	34	16	100	27	91	..	..	..	16.2	100.0	..	..
High human development															
67	Seychelles	12.5	21.2	36	14	85	100	100	..	..	..	..	100.0	..	..
67	Trinidad and Tobago	12.9	41.7	30	18 [e]	88 [e]	..	..	..	..	..	18.1	100.0	..	..
69	Albania	12.3	12.2	29	18	90	47	74	405	437	417	52.9	100.0	70	40
70	Cuba	13.0	84.2	53	9	100	13	49	..	..	..	23.1	100.0	..	44
70	Iran (Islamic Republic of)	14.1	15.8	16	29	100	11	36	..	..	..	41.4	100.0	92	..
72	Sri Lanka	13.4	10.0	42	22	83	12	23	..	..	..	39.0	99.5	..	..
73	Bosnia and Herzegovina	13.0	21.6	35	17	..	..	..	403	406	398	16.2	100.0	89	22
74	Grenada	12.7	14.1	36	16	63	72	100	..	..	..	..	100.0	87	..
74	Mexico	13.6	23.8	10	27	97	39	53	420	409	419	26.9	100.0	43	50
74	Saint Kitts and Nevis	12.5	26.8	..	14	72	100	100	..	..	..	..	100.0	..	..
74	Ukraine	12.5	29.9	75	13	87	58	95	466	453	469	14.9	100.0	92	68
78	Antigua and Barbuda	12.7	29.6	29	12	53	90	100	..	..	..	..	100.0	..	..
79	Peru	12.9	13.0	16	17	95	41	74	401	400	404	50.4	81.8	50	43
79	Thailand	12.8	8.1	..	17	100	99	97	393	419	426	48.5	100.0	..	..
81	Armenia	12.0	44.0	42	15	..	100	100	..	..	..	38.7	100.0	86	48
82	North Macedonia	12.1	28.7	43	15	..	..	..	393	394	413	19.0	100.0	81	17
83	Colombia	13.2	21.8	17	23	97	43	66	412	391	413	47.1	99.7	73	17
84	Brazil	14.0	21.6	21	20	..	62	83	413	384	404	27.9	100.0	..	49
85	China	11.7	19.8	43	16	..	96	98	555 [f]	591 [f]	590 [f]	45.4	100.0	..	72
86	Ecuador	12.6	20.4	14	24	72 [e]	39	71	..	..	..	46.7	100.0	75	42
86	Saint Lucia	13.3	6.4	13	15	89	100	100	..	..	..	29.6	100.0	..	..
88	Azerbaijan	11.3	34.5	48	15	100	54	62	389 [g]	420 [g]	398 [g]	55.2	100.0	74	..
88	Dominican Republic	12.3	15.6	16	19	95	23	..	342	325	336	40.4	100.0	..	..
90	Moldova (Republic of)	12.3	32.1	57	18	99	91	94	424	421	428	37.3	100.0	73	..
91	Algeria	13.0	17.2	19	24	100	..	..	..	..	..	27.0	100.0	..	18
92	Lebanon	13.8	21.0	27	12	..	90	94	353	393	384	26.9	100.0	48	22
93	Fiji	12.8	8.6	20	28	100	..	..	..	..	..	43.1	99.3	..	..
94	Dominica	12.7	11.2	..	13	66	100	93	..	..	..	..	100.0	..	..
95	Maldives	12.6	45.6	43 [e]	10	90	100	100	..	..	..	19.5	100.0	..	..
95	Tunisia	13.2	13.0	22	17	100	49	97	..	..	..	20.0	99.6	93	78
97	Saint Vincent and the Grenadines	12.8	6.6	43	14	61	100	96	..	..	..	19.9	100.0	..	..
97	Suriname	13.5	12.1	30	13	99	..	..	..	..	..	12.2	94.3	..	..
99	Mongolia	11.2	28.6	80	30	93	71	83	..	..	..	48.5	94.6	24	..
100	Botswana	13.1	5.3	18	24	99	..	86	..	..	..	25.9	27.9	..	..
101	Jamaica	12.8	13.1	17	25	100	84	73	..	..	..	35.8	97.6	..	..
102	Jordan	13.1	23.2	15	19	100	13	74	419	400	429	9.2	98.9	94	81
103	Paraguay	13.3	13.5	8	24	92	5	22	..	..	..	37.5	100.0	64	58
104	Tonga	12.4	5.4	..	22	92	..	..	..	..	..	52.2	98.9	..	..
105	Libya	14.0	20.9	32	..	..	..	..	..	..	..	5.7	6.6 [h]	..	26
106	Uzbekistan	11.0	23.7	40	22	99	89	89	..	..	..	42.0	100.0	59	..

Continued →

		Quality of health			Quality of education								Quality of standard of living			
						SDG 4.c	SDG 4.a		SDG 4.1				SDG 7.1	SDG 6.1	SDG 6.2	
					Pupil-teacher ratio, primary school	Primary school teachers trained to teach	Schools with access to the Internet		Programme for International Student Assessment (PISA) score			Vulnerable employment[a]	Rural population with access to electricity	Population using safely managed drinking-water services	Population using safely managed sanitation services	
		Lost health expectancy	Physicians	Hospital beds			Primary schools	Secondary schools	Reading[b]	Mathematics[c]	Science[c]					
		(%)	(per 10,000 people)		(pupils per teacher)		(%)					(% of total employment)		(%)		
HDI RANK		2019	2010-2018[d]	2010-2019[d]	2010-2019[d]	2010-2019[d]	2010-2019[d]	2010-2019[d]	2018	2018	2018	2019	2018	2017	2017
107	Bolivia (Plurinational State of)	12.4	15.9	13	18	90	8	19	..	..	..	63.2	86.0	..	23
107	Indonesia	12.4	4.3	10	17	..	..	61	371	379	396	47.9	96.8	..	..
107	Philippines	12.7	6.0	10	29	100	..	..	340	353	357	32.7	92.5	47	52
110	Belize	12.6	11.2	10	20	79	..	..	..	..	..	29.6	100.0	..	..
111	Samoa	12.3	3.4	10 e	30	..	14	23	..	..	..	30.0	100.0	59	48
111	Turkmenistan	11.2	22.2	40	..	..	..	..				25.2	100.0	94	
113	Venezuela (Bolivarian Republic of)	12.8	..	9	..	..	..	..				35.6	100.0	..	24
114	South Africa	13.8	9.1	23	30	..	..	..				10.3	89.6	..	..
115	Palestine, State of	13.9	..	..	24	100	85	95				23.1	100.0	..	..
116	Egypt	12.0	4.5	14	24	83	48	49				20.7	100.0	..	61
117	Marshall Islands	12.4	4.2	..	..	..	26					..	98.4	..	..
117	Viet Nam	11.7	8.3	32	20	100	..	..				54.1	100.0	..	..
119	Gabon	13.3	6.8	13 e	25	..	..	..				31.5	62.5	..	..
Medium human development																
120	Kyrgyzstan	11.6	22.1	44	25	95	41	44	..	..	..	33.8	100.0	68	..
121	Morocco	13.0	7.3	10	27	100	79	90	359	368	377	47.5	100.0	70	39
122	Guyana	13.3	8.0	17	23	70	..	..				25.5	90.0	..	..
123	Iraq	13.5	7.1	13	17 e	..	..	..				19.8	99.9	59	41
124	El Salvador	13.4	15.7	12	27	95	23	43				34.2	100.0	..	..
125	Tajikistan	11.1	21.0	47	22	100	..	..				41.8	99.3	48	..
126	Cabo Verde	12.4	7.8	21	21	99	16	100				35.2	96.9	56	..
127	Guatemala	13.3	3.5	4	20	..	9	44				37.5	93.6	56	..
128	Nicaragua	12.7	9.8	9	30	75	..	..				40.9	71.4	52	..
129	Bhutan	13.6	4.2	17	35	100	52	77				71.5	100.0	36	..
130	Namibia	13.0	4.2	27 e	25	96	..	..				31.0	35.5	..	..
131	India	14.5	8.6	5	33	70	..	..				74.3	92.9	..	..
132	Honduras	12.6	3.1	6	26	..	16	..				41.4	81.1	..	..
133	Bangladesh	13.4	5.8	8	30	50	4	35				55.3	78.3	55	..
134	Kiribati	11.9	2.0	19	25	73	..	..				..	100.0	..	..
135	Sao Tome and Principe	12.2	0.5	29	31	27	..	..				48.1	55.7	..	..
136	Micronesia (Federated States of)	11.6	1.8	..	20	..	..	..					78.7	..	..
137	Lao People's Democratic Republic	12.0	3.7	15	22	97	..	..				80.1	97.1	16	58
138	Eswatini (Kingdom of)	13.1	3.3	21	27	88	16	69				32.6	70.2	..	..
138	Ghana	12.2	1.4	9	27	62	8	20				68.7	67.3	36	..
140	Vanuatu	12.0	1.7	..	27	100 e	..	..				70.4	51.1	44	..
141	Timor-Leste	12.7	7.2	59 e	27	..	..	..				67.7	79.2	..	..
142	Nepal	13.5	7.5	3	20	97	..	..				78.4	93.5	27	..
143	Kenya	12.4	1.6	14	31	97 e	..	..				51.3	71.7	..	..
144	Cambodia	12.4	1.9	9	42	100	..	..				50.3	89.0	26	..
145	Equatorial Guinea	13.3	4.0	21	23	37	..	..				77.3	6.6	..	..
146	Zambia	12.8	11.9	20	42	99	6	..				78.1	11.0	..	..
147	Myanmar	12.4	6.8	10	24	95	0	6				59.1	54.8	..	..
148	Angola	12.8	2.1	..	50	47	3	17				66.0	3.8 i	..	..
149	Congo	12.9	1.6	..	44	80	..	..				76.0	20.2	45	..
150	Zimbabwe	12.3	2.1	17	36	86	..	..				64.7	20.0	..	..
151	Solomon Islands	10.9	1.9	14	25	76	..	12				65.7	63.5	..	..
151	Syrian Arab Republic	13.5	12.9	14	..	..	..	..				32.4	69.5	..	..
153	Cameroon	12.5	0.9	13	45	81	..	23				73.6	23.0	..	..
154	Pakistan	13.1	9.8	6	44	78	..	..				55.5	54.4	35	..
155	Papua New Guinea	12.8	0.7	..	36	..	..	..				77.9	55.5	..	..
156	Comoros	12.2	2.7	22	28	55	8	11				63.7	77.0	..	..
Low human development																
157	Mauritania	12.2	1.9	..	34	91	..	..				52.5	0.6	..	..
158	Benin	12.2	0.8	5	39	70	..	..				87.7	18.3	..	..
159	Uganda	12.8	1.7	5	43	80	..	..				75.2	38.0	7	..

Continued →

		Quality of health			SDG 4.c	SDG 4.a		SDG 4.1			SDG 7.1	SDG 6.1	SDG 6.2
							Quality of education					Quality of standard of living	
						Schools with access to the Internet						Population using safely managed drinking-water services	Population using safely managed sanitation services
				Pupil-teacher ratio, primary school	Primary school teachers trained to teach	Primary schools	Secondary schools	Programme for International Student Assessment (PISA) score			Rural population with access to electricity		
	Lost health expectancy	Physicians	Hospital beds								Vulnerable employment[a]			
	(%)	(per 10,000 people)		(pupils per teacher)		(%)		Reading[b]	Mathematics[c]	Science[c]	(% of total employment)	(%)		
HDI RANK	2019	2010–2018[d]	2010–2019[d]	2010–2019[d]	2010–2019[d]	2010–2019[d]	2010–2019[d]	2018	2018	2018	2019	2018	2017	2017
160 Rwanda	12.8	1.3	..	60	94	30	54	..	..	..	68.0	23.4	..	..
161 Nigeria	12.9	3.8	..	38	66	..	..	..	..	..	77.6	31.0	20	27
162 Côte d'Ivoire	12.5	2.3	..	42	100	..	..	..	..	..	71.2	32.9	37	..
163 Tanzania (United Republic of)	12.6	0.1	7	51	99	..	..	..	..	..	82.7	18.8	..	25
164 Madagascar	12.0	1.8	2	40	15	0	6	..	..	..	85.1	0.0	..	..
165 Lesotho	12.6	0.7	..	33	87	..	..	..	..	..	16.3	37.7	..	..
166 Djibouti	11.8	2.2	14	29	100	..	..	..	..	..	44.7	23.8	..	36
167 Togo	12.3	0.8	7	40	73	..	..	..	..	..	80.9	22.4	..	..
168 Senegal	12.6	0.7	3[e]	36	79	13	44	..	..	..	64.6	44.2	..	21
169 Afghanistan	14.6	2.8	4	49	..	..	..	..	..	..	79.7	98.3	..	..
170 Haiti	13.1	2.3	7	..	..	..	..	..	..	..	72.3	3.5	..	..
170 Sudan	12.9	2.6	7	38[e,j]	60[e]	..	..	..	..	..	50.4	47.1	..	..
172 Gambia	12.6	1.0	11	36	100	..	..	..	..	..	72.1	35.5	..	..
173 Ethiopia	12.5	0.8	3	55	85[e]	..	..	..	..	..	86.0	32.7	11	..
174 Malawi	12.6	0.4	13	59	91	..	..	..	..	..	59.2	10.4	..	..
175 Congo (Democratic Republic of the)	13.4	0.7	..	33	95	..	..	..	..	..	79.7	1.8	..	..
175 Guinea-Bissau	12.0	1.3	10[e]	52	39	..	..	..	..	..	75.7	10.0	..	..
175 Liberia	14.0	0.4	8	22	70	..	..	..	..	..	77.2	7.4	..	..
178 Guinea	12.0	0.8	3	47	75	..	..	..	..	..	89.4	19.7	..	..
179 Yemen	13.5	5.3	7	27	..	..	..	..	..	..	45.6	48.7	..	..
180 Eritrea	12.4	0.6	7	39	84	..	..	..	..	..	86.4	34.6	..	..
181 Mozambique	13.0	0.8	7	55	97	..	..	..	..	..	83.1	8.0	..	..
182 Burkina Faso	12.2	0.8	4	40	88	0	2	..	..	..	86.4	4.7[k]	..	..
182 Sierra Leone	12.5	0.3	..	28	61	1	4	..	..	..	86.1	6.4	10	13
184 Mali	12.2	1.3	1	38	52	..	..	..	..	..	81.0	25.4	..	19
185 Burundi	13.0	1.0	8	43	100	..	1	..	..	..	94.6	3.4	..	..
185 South Sudan	14.3	..	..	47	44	..	..	..	..	..	84.9	23.7	..	..
187 Chad	12.5	0.4	..	57	65	..	..	..	..	..	93.0	2.7	..	..
188 Central African Republic	12.7	0.7	10	83	..	..	..	..	..	..	91.4	16.3	..	..
189 Niger	11.9	0.4	4	36	62	..	..	..	..	..	93.7	11.7	..	10
Other countries or territories														
Korea (Democratic People's Rep. of)	11.2	36.8	143	20	..	..	..	..	..	..	87.8	55.0	67	..
Monaco	13.6	75.1	..	12	64	100	100	..	..	..	..	100.0	100	100
Nauru	11.6	13.5	..	40	100	..	..	..	..	..	..	100.0[i]	..	..
San Marino	13.7	61.1	..	7	90	100	100	..	..	..	..	100.0	100	77
Somalia	12.0	0.2	9	36[e]	..	..	..	..	..	..	87.2	14.6	..	..
Tuvalu	12.0	9.2	..	16	80	..	..	..	..	..	..	100.0	..	6
Human development groups														
Very high human development	14.2	31.2	52	14	..	–	–	–	–	–	10.2	100.0	95	87
High human development	12.3	17.0	31	19	..	–	–	–	–	–	41.9	98.8	..	..
Medium human development	13.9	7.9	7	32	73	–	–	–	–	–	67.0	83.5	..	..
Low human development	12.8	1.9	5	42	78	–	–	–	–	–	79.1	27.2	..	..
Developing countries	12.9	12.2	21	25	..	–	–	–	–	–	53.0	78.7	..	..
Regions														
Arab States	12.9	10.4	14	22	90	–	–	–	–	–	25.1	79.7	..	53
East Asia and the Pacific	11.9	15.8	36	18	..	–	–	–	–	–	46.4	96.3	..	..
Europe and Central Asia	12.5	26.9	48	17	..	–	–	–	–	–	28.0	100.0	79	..
Latin America and the Caribbean	13.4	22.7	18	21	..	–	–	–	–	–	33.2	93.0	..	..
South Asia	14.2	8.7	6	33	71	–	–	–	–	–	68.9	88.0	..	..
Sub-Saharan Africa	12.8	2.3	9	40	79	–	–	–	–	–	74.2	27.6	..	..
Least developed countries	12.9	2.7	7	38	77	–	–	–	–	–	73.2	39.3	..	..
Small island developing states	12.7	23.1	25	19	93	–	–	–	–	–	40.5	62.5	..	..
Organisation for Economic Co-operation and Development	14.5	29.2	47	15	..	–	–	–	–	–	12.8	100.0	92	84
World	**13.2**	**15.5**	**27**	**24**	..	–	–	–	–	–	**44.7**	**80.3**	..	..

Notes

Three-colour coding is used to visualize partial grouping of countries and aggregates by indicator. For each indicator countries are divided into three groups of approximately equal size (terciles): the top third, the middle third and the bottom third. Aggregates are colour coded using the same tercile cutoffs. See *Technical note 6* at http://hdr.undp.org/sites/default/files/hdr2020_technical_notes.pdf for details about partial grouping in this table.

a   Estimates modelled by the International Labour Organization.

b   Average score for Organisation for Economic Co-operation and Development (OECD) countries is 487.

c   Average score for OECD countries is 489.

d   Data refer to the most recent year available during the period specified.

e   Refers to a year from 2007 to 2009.

f   Refers to the cities of Beijing and Shanghai and the provinces of Jiangsu and Zhejiang.

g   Refers to Baku.

h   Refers to 2011.

i   Refers to 2015.

j   Refers to Sudan prior to South Sudan's secession.

k   Refers to 2014.

Definitions

Lost health expectancy: Relative difference between life expectancy and healthy life expectancy, expressed as a percentage of life expectancy at birth.

Physicians: Number of medical doctors (physicians), both generalists and specialists, expressed per 10,000 people.

Hospital beds: Number of hospital beds available, expressed per 10,000 people.

Pupil–teacher ratio, primary school: Average number of pupils per teacher in primary education.

Primary school teachers trained to teach: Percentage of primary school teachers who have received the minimum organized teacher training (preservice or in-service) required for teaching at the primary level.

Schools with access to the Internet: Percentage of schools at the indicated level with access to the Internet for educational purposes.

Programme for International Student Assessment (PISA) score: Score obtained in testing of skills and knowledge of 15-year-old students in reading, mathematics and science.

Vulnerable employment: Percentage of employed people engaged as contributing family workers and own-account workers.

Rural population with access to electricity: People living in rural areas with access to electricity, expressed as a percentage of the total rural population. It includes electricity sold commercially (both on grid and off grid) and self-generated electricity but excludes unauthorized connections.

Population using safely managed drinking-water services: Percentage of the population drinking water from an improved source that is accessible on premises, available when needed and free from faecal and priority chemical contamination. Improved water sources include piped water, boreholes or tubewells, protected dug wells, protected springs, and packaged or delivered water.

Population using safely managed sanitation services: Percentage of the population using an improved sanitation facility that is not shared with other households and where excreta are safely disposed of in situ or treated off site. Improved sanitation facilities include flush/pour flush toilets connected to piped sewer systems, septic tanks or pit latrines; pit latrines with slabs (including ventilated pit latrines); and composting toilets.

Main data sources

Column 1: HDRO calculations based on data on life expectancy at birth and healthy life expectancy at birth from IHME (2020).

Columns 2 and 12: World Bank (2020a).

Columns 3, 13 and 14: WHO (2020).

Columns 4–7: UNESCO Institute for Statistics (2020).

Columns 8–10: OECD (2019a).

Column 11: ILO (2020).

Life-course gender gap

Country groupings (terciles): Top third Middle third Bottom third

Three-colour coding is used to visualize partial grouping of countries by indicator. For each indicator countries are divided into three groups of approximately equal size (terciles): the top third, the middle third and the bottom third. Aggregates are colour coded using the same tercile cutoffs. See *Notes* after the table.

		SDG 4.2	SDG 4.1	SDG 4.1	SDG 4.1	SDG 8.5	SDG 4.4	SDG 8.5	SDG 8.3	SDG 5.5	SDG 5.5	SDG 5.4		SDG 1.3
		Childhood and youth					Adulthood							Older age
		Sex ratio at birth[a]	Pre-primary	Primary	Secondary	Youth unemployment rate	Population with at least some secondary education	Total unemployment rate	Share of employment in nonagriculture, female	Share of seats held by women — In parliament	In local government	Time spent on unpaid domestic chores and care work (% of 24-hour day)	(female to male ratio)	Old-age pension recipients
		(male to female births)	(female to male ratio)			(female to male ratio)	(female to male ratio)	(female to male ratio)	(% of total employment in nonagriculture)	(%)	(%)			(female to male ratio)
HDI RANK		2015-2020[b]	2014-2019[c]	2014-2019[c]	2014-2019[c]	2019	2015-2019[c]	2019	2019	2019	2017-2019[c]	2008-2018[c]	2008-2018[c]	2014-2019[c]
Very high human development														
1	Norway	1.06	1.00	1.00	0.96	0.98	1.01	0.94	47.5	40.8	40.8	15.3	1.2	0.87
2	Ireland	1.06	0.99	1.00	0.98	0.69	1.02	0.91	47.5	24.3	23.9	..	..	0.61
2	Switzerland	1.05	0.99	0.99	0.96	0.64	0.99	1.08	46.9	38.6	31.3	16.8	1.6	1.04
4	Hong Kong, China (SAR)	1.08	1.05	1.04	0.97	0.83	0.93	0.79	49.7	..	..	10.8	3.3	..
4	Iceland	1.05	1.03	1.00	0.99	0.80	1.00	1.00	48.5	38.1	47.0	..	..	1.12
6	Germany	1.05	0.99	1.00	0.94	0.80	1.00	0.81	46.7	31.6	27.5	15.9[d]	1.6[d]	1.00
7	Sweden	1.06	0.99	1.01	1.07	0.85	1.00	0.93	48.2	47.3	43.8	16.0	1.3	1.00
8	Australia	1.06	0.96	1.00	0.89	0.85	1.00	1.02	46.9	36.6	33.9	..	..	1.06
8	Netherlands	1.05	1.00	1.00	1.01	0.88	0.97	1.10	46.5	33.8	31.8	14.7[e]	1.6[e]	1.00
10	Denmark	1.06	0.99	0.99	1.01	0.89	1.00	1.11	47.8	39.1	33.3	15.6[e]	1.4[e]	1.02
11	Finland	1.05	1.00	0.99	1.10	0.77	1.00	0.92	49.0	47.0	39.1	14.5[d]	1.5[d]	1.00
11	Singapore	1.07	..	1.00	0.99	1.88	0.92	1.09	41.8	23.0	..	..	..	..
13	United Kingdom	1.05	1.00	1.00	1.03	0.66	0.98	0.87	47.2	28.9	34.3	12.7	1.8	1.00
14	Belgium	1.05	1.00	1.00	1.12	0.74	0.96	0.86	46.6	43.3	39.0	15.9[f]	1.6[f]	1.00
14	New Zealand	1.06	1.01	1.00	1.06	1.07	1.01	1.20	48.4	40.8	39.4	18.1[f]	1.7[f]	1.00
16	Canada	1.05	..	1.00	1.01	0.82	1.00	0.90	47.8	33.2	26.6	14.6	1.5	1.00
17	United States	1.05	1.01	0.99	0.99	0.76	1.00	0.97	46.3	23.7	..	15.4	1.6	0.87
18	Austria	1.06	0.99	1.00	0.96	0.89	1.00	0.95	46.7	38.5	23.1	18.3[d]	1.9[d]	0.99
19	Israel	1.05	1.00	1.01	1.02	1.16	0.97	1.02	47.6	23.3	17.1	..	..	..
19	Japan	1.06	..	..	..	0.73	1.03	0.89	44.3	14.5	12.9	14.4[d]	4.7[d]	..
19	Liechtenstein	..	1.04	0.97	0.81	..	..	..	..	12.0	39.1	..	..	..
22	Slovenia	1.06	0.98	1.00	1.02	1.46	0.99	1.23	46.3	22.3	33.7	..	..	..
23	Korea (Republic of)	1.06	1.00	1.00	0.99	0.82	0.84	0.90	42.3	16.7	18.6	14.0[d]	4.2[d]	0.96
23	Luxembourg	1.05	0.98	0.99	1.02	0.84	1.00	1.20	45.9	25.0	25.1	14.4[d]	2.0[d]	0.66
25	Spain	1.06	1.00	1.02	1.01	1.10	0.94	1.35	46.0	41.9	38.5	19.0[e]	2.2[e]	0.47
26	France	1.05	1.00	0.99	1.01	0.86	0.94	0.99	48.6	36.9	40.4	15.8	1.7	1.00
27	Czechia	1.06	0.97	1.01	1.01	1.10	1.00	1.52	45.0	20.6	27.1	..	..	1.00
28	Malta	1.06	0.99	1.00	1.00	0.58	0.92	1.16	41.0	14.9	26.3	..	..	0.43
29	Estonia	1.07	0.99	1.00	1.02	0.94	1.00	0.95	49.0	29.7	28.6	17.2[d]	1.6[d]	1.00
29	Italy	1.06	0.98	0.97	0.99	1.19	0.91	1.18	42.7	35.3	31.8	20.4	2.4	0.83
31	United Arab Emirates	1.05	0.95	0.98	0.92	2.26	0.94	3.88	17.2	50.0	..	..	..	..
32	Greece	1.07	1.01	1.00	0.94	1.05	0.85	1.63	41.6	20.7	..	17.5[d]	2.6[d]	..
33	Cyprus	1.07	0.99	1.00	0.98	0.84	0.95	1.24	46.2	17.9	..	..	..	0.77
34	Lithuania	1.06	0.99	1.00	0.96	0.86	0.97	0.99	51.5	21.3	29.4	..	..	1.00
35	Poland	1.06	0.99	1.00	0.97	1.02	0.94	1.02	45.2	27.9	26.9	17.6[d]	1.8[d]	1.00
36	Andorra	..	..	..	..	..	0.97	..	..	46.4	35.8	..	..	..
37	Latvia	1.07	0.99	1.00	0.99	0.75	1.00	0.76	52.0	30.0	34.0	..	..	1.00
38	Portugal	1.06	0.99	0.97	0.98	1.21	0.98	1.21	49.9	38.7	..	17.8	1.7	0.77
39	Slovakia	1.05	0.98	0.99	1.01	1.40	0.99	1.23	45.6	20.0	25.9	..	..	1.00
40	Hungary	1.06	0.96	0.99	1.00	0.84	0.98	1.04	46.5	12.6	30.5	16.6[d]	2.2[d]	1.00
40	Saudi Arabia	1.03	1.05	1.01	0.94	2.97	0.90	7.67	13.4	19.9	1.1	..	..	..
42	Bahrain	1.04	1.03	0.99	1.06	7.81	0.92	19.75	19.8	18.8	13.3	..	..	..
43	Chile	1.04	0.98	0.97	1.00	1.17	0.96	1.16	43.8	22.7	24.9	22.1[f]	2.2[f]	1.59
43	Croatia	1.06	0.98	1.00	1.05	1.54	0.97	1.59	46.3	20.5	26.4	..	..	..
45	Qatar	1.05	1.01	1.01	..	9.77	1.15	11.68	13.8	9.8	..	8.2	3.7	0.36
46	Argentina	1.04	1.01	1.00	1.04	1.29	1.08	1.22	42.4	39.9	..	23.4	2.5	..
47	Brunei Darussalam	1.06	1.01	1.01	1.02	1.03	0.98	1.16	42.8	9.1	..	..	..	..
48	Montenegro	1.07	0.90	0.95	1.01	0.81	0.90	1.11	43.6	28.4	27.8	..	..	..
49	Romania	1.06	1.00	0.99	1.00	0.96	0.94	0.78	43.3	19.6	12.5	19.0[d]	2.0[d]	1.00
50	Palau	..	1.17	0.88	1.11	..	1.00	..	..	13.8	..	..	..	..
51	Kazakhstan	1.07	1.02	1.02	1.01	1.09	1.00	1.30	48.6	22.1	22.2	17.9[d]	3.0[d]	1.00

Continued →

	SDG 4.2	SDG 4.1	SDG 4.1	SDG 4.1	SDG 8.5	SDG 4.4	SDG 8.5	SDG 8.3	SDG 5.5	SDG 5.5	SDG 5.4		SDG 1.3
		Childhood and youth						Adulthood					Older age
	Sex ratio at birth[a]		(female to male ratio)		Youth unemployment rate	Population with at least some secondary education	Total unemployment rate	Share of employment in nonagriculture, female	Share of seats held by women		Time spent on unpaid domestic chores and care work		Old-age pension recipients
									In parliament	In local government			
	(male to female births)	Pre-primary	Primary	Secondary	(female to male ratio)	(female to male ratio)	(female to male ratio)	(% of total employment in nonagriculture)	(%)		(% of 24-hour day)	(female to male ratio)	(female to male ratio)
HDI RANK	2015-2020[b]	2014-2019[c]	2014-2019[c]	2014-2019[c]	2019	2015-2019[c]	2019	2019	2019	2017-2019[c]	2008-2018[c]	2008-2018[c]	2014-2019[c]
52 Russian Federation	1.06	0.98	1.00	0.98	1.11	1.01	0.95	49.6	16.5	..	18.4	2.3	1.00
53 Belarus	1.06	0.96	1.00	0.99	0.67	0.94	0.58	51.6	34.9	48.2	19.2[d]	2.0[d]	..
54 Turkey	1.05	0.96	0.99	0.95	1.31	0.69	1.36	28.9	17.4	10.1	19.2	5.2	..
55 Uruguay	1.05	1.00	0.98	1.11	1.33	1.08	1.50	46.7	20.9	26.1	19.9	2.4	1.04
56 Bulgaria	1.06	0.98	0.99	0.97	0.88	0.98	0.85	47.5	25.8	27.2	18.5[e]	2.0[e]	1.00
57 Panama	1.05	1.02	0.98	1.06	1.89	1.09	1.62	42.7	21.1	9.0	18.0	2.4	..
58 Bahamas	1.06	1.08	1.00	1.06	1.36	0.97	1.08	48.2	21.8	..	..	..	..
58 Barbados	1.04	1.02	0.96	1.04	1.12	1.03	1.07	49.7	29.4	..	..	..	..
60 Oman	1.05	1.05	1.10	0.92	3.72	1.15	9.00	12.0	9.9	3.5	18.9	2.5	..
61 Georgia	1.07	..	1.01	1.01	1.21	0.99	0.82	43.9	14.8	13.5	..	..	0.92
62 Costa Rica	1.05	1.01	1.01	1.08	1.50	1.04	1.49	41.1	45.6	45.6	21.3[f]	2.6[f]	..
62 Malaysia	1.06	1.02	1.01	1.08	1.13	0.94	1.22	39.9	15.5	..	..	..	..
64 Kuwait	1.05	1.05	1.10	1.06	2.92	1.15	5.19	24.7	4.6	..	..	..	..
64 Serbia	1.07	0.99	1.00	1.01	1.11	0.92	1.17	45.2	37.7	31.2	19.2	2.2	..
66 Mauritius	1.04	1.01	1.03	1.06	1.70	0.96	2.22	38.5	20.0	26.2	..	..	..
High human development													
67 Seychelles	1.06	1.02	1.06	1.07	..	..	..	..	21.2	..	..	..	..
67 Trinidad and Tobago	1.04	..	..	..	1.04	1.05	1.09	43.2	32.9	..	..	..	..
69 Albania	1.09	1.01	1.04	1.01	0.80	1.01	0.90	39.2	29.5	43.6	21.7[d]	6.3[d]	..
70 Cuba	1.06	1.00	0.96	1.02	0.89	0.96	1.15	43.2	53.2	34.9	21.0	1.7	..
70 Iran (Islamic Republic of)	1.05	1.03	1.06	0.96	1.79	0.92	1.93	17.3	5.9	3.2	21.0	4.0	0.10
72 Sri Lanka	1.04	0.99	0.99	1.05	1.77	0.98	2.33	32.5	5.3	10.9	..	..	..
73 Bosnia and Herzegovina	1.07	..	..	..	1.26	0.83	1.25	37.9	21.1	18.6	..	..	..
74 Grenada	1.05	1.04	0.98	1.03	..	..	..	..	39.3	..	..	..	..
74 Mexico	1.05	1.03	1.00	1.08	1.35	0.97	1.14	41.6	48.4	45.0	28.1[f]	3.0[f]	0.84
74 Saint Kitts and Nevis	..	0.80	0.97	1.03	..	..	..	..	13.3	..	..	..	..
74 Ukraine	1.06	..	1.02	0.98	1.05	0.99	0.79	49.0	20.5	..	..	..	..
78 Antigua and Barbuda	1.03	1.11	0.99	0.96	..	..	..	..	31.4	66.7	..	..	0.95
79 Peru	1.05	1.00	0.97	0.95	1.31	0.85	1.06	46.7	30.0	26.2	22.7[f]	2.6[f]	..
79 Thailand	1.06	1.00	1.00	0.98	1.39	0.90	0.97	47.6	14.1	17.4	11.8[g]	3.2[g]	..
81 Armenia	1.11	1.08	1.00	1.04	1.38	1.00	1.03	43.9	23.5	9.0	21.7	5.0	1.17
82 North Macedonia	1.06	1.03	1.00	0.97	1.07	0.73	0.94	40.0	39.2	..	15.4[d]	2.8[d]	0.99
83 Colombia	1.05	..	0.97	1.05	1.75	1.05	1.71	45.9	19.6	17.9	18.2	3.4	..
84 Brazil	1.05	1.01	0.97	1.03	1.28	1.06	1.35	45.0	15.0	13.5	11.6	2.3	..
85 China	1.13	1.01	1.01	..	0.82	0.91	0.78	45.6	24.9	..	15.3	2.6	..
86 Ecuador	1.05	1.05	1.02	1.03	1.56	0.99	1.51	42.1	38.0	27.2	19.7	4.2	..
86 Saint Lucia	1.03	1.10	1.01	1.00	1.25	1.17	1.25	47.0	20.7	..	..	..	..
88 Azerbaijan	1.13	0.99	1.01	1.00	1.24	0.96	1.34	44.1	16.8	35.0	25.4	2.9	1.51
88 Dominican Republic	1.05	1.02	0.94	1.08	2.08	1.06	1.97	42.6	24.3	28.3	16.7	4.4	..
90 Moldova (Republic of)	1.06	1.00	1.00	0.99	0.85	0.98	0.61	52.8	25.7	35.6	19.5[d]	1.8[d]	..
91 Algeria	1.05	..	0.95	..	1.76	1.00	2.17	16.9	21.5	17.6	21.7[f]	5.8[f]	..
92 Lebanon	1.05	..	..	..	1.32	0.98	1.96	23.3	4.7	4.0	..	..	..
93 Fiji	1.06	..	0.98	..	1.94	1.02	1.52	33.5	19.6	..	15.2	2.9	..
94 Dominica	..	1.03	0.97	0.99	..	..	..	..	25.0	..	..	..	..
95 Maldives	1.07	1.03	1.02	..	0.71	0.92	0.95	21.7	4.6	6.1	..	..	..
95 Tunisia	1.06	1.02	0.99	1.14	1.12	0.78	1.75	25.0	22.6	48.5	..	..	..
97 Saint Vincent and the Grenadines	1.03	1.02	0.99	1.03	1.09	..	0.82	44.5	13.0	..	..	..	..
97 Suriname	1.08	1.00	1.00	1.32	2.42	1.02	2.65	37.6	31.4	35.6	..	..	..
99 Mongolia	1.03	1.00	0.98	..	1.50	1.06	0.89	47.7	17.3	26.7	17.6[f]	2.8[f]	..
100 Botswana	1.03	1.03	0.98	..	1.43	0.99	1.39	49.6	10.8	12.7	..	..	..
101 Jamaica	1.05	1.04	0.96	1.03	1.58	1.12	1.92	48.5	19.0	18.4	..	..	..
102 Jordan	1.05	0.99	0.98	1.03	1.85	0.95	1.82	16.6	15.4	31.9	..	..	0.20
103 Paraguay	1.05	1.01	..	..	1.40	0.96	1.40	42.9	16.8	20.8	14.5	3.4	0.80
104 Tonga	1.05	1.07	0.99	1.03	3.58	1.01	3.80	49.8	7.4	..	..	..	..
105 Libya	1.06	..	..	..	1.65	1.56	1.59	30.3	16.0	..	..	..	..

Continued →

		SDG 4.2	SDG 4.1	SDG 4.1	SDG 4.1	SDG 8.5	SDG 4.4	SDG 8.5	SDG 8.3	SDG 5.5	SDG 5.5	SDG 5.4	SDG 5.4	SDG 1.3
			Childhood and youth							Adulthood				Older age
		Sex ratio at birth^a		(female to male ratio)		Youth unemployment rate	Population with at least some secondary education	Total unemployment rate	Share of employment in nonagriculture, female	Share of seats held by women		Time spent on unpaid domestic chores and care work		Old-age pension recipients
		(male to female births)	Pre-primary	Primary	Secondary	(female to male ratio)	(female to male ratio)	(female to male ratio)	(% of total employment in nonagriculture)	In parliament	In local government (%)	(% of 24-hour day)	(female to male ratio)	(female to male ratio)
HDI RANK		2015–2020^b	2014–2019^c	2014–2019^c	2014–2019^c	2019	2015–2019^c	2019	2019	2019	2017–2019^c	2008–2018^c	2008–2018^c	2014–2019^c
106	Uzbekistan	1.06	0.96	0.99	0.99	1.08	1.00	0.94	40.6	16.4	..	..	..	..
107	Bolivia (Plurinational State of)	1.05	1.02	0.99	0.98	1.22	0.89	1.17	44.1	51.8	50.5	..	..	..
107	Indonesia	1.05	0.90	0.97	1.03	1.03	0.85	0.94	40.5	17.4	14.4	..	..	..
107	Philippines	1.06	0.96	0.96	1.11	1.44	1.04	1.24	43.6	28.0	29.1	..	..	..
110	Belize	1.03	1.05	0.95	1.04	2.63	1.00	2.22	43.0	11.1	31.0	..	..	..
111	Samoa	1.08	1.16	1.00	1.10	1.49	1.11	1.30	45.4	10.0	..	..	..	..
111	Turkmenistan	1.05	0.97	0.98	0.96	0.60	..	0.43	42.1	25.0	21.9	..	..	..
113	Venezuela (Bolivarian Republic of)	1.05	1.01	0.98	1.08	1.43	1.08	1.10	41.9	22.2	..	..	..	0.72
114	South Africa	1.03	1.00	0.97	1.09	1.16	0.96	1.15	44.6	45.3^h	40.7	15.6^d	2.4^d	..
115	Palestine, State of	1.05	1.00	1.00	1.10	1.84	0.98	1.82	15.9	..	21.2	17.8^d	6.0^d	..
116	Egypt	1.06	1.00	1.00	0.99	1.55	1.01	3.06	17.4	14.9	..	22.4^d	9.2^d	..
117	Marshall Islands	..	0.92	1.00	1.07	..	0.99	..	..	6.1	15.9	..	..	..
117	Viet Nam	1.12	0.99	1.02	..	1.07	0.85	0.90	46.9	26.7	26.8	..	..	..
119	Gabon	1.03	..	..	..	1.34	1.31	1.99	27.8	17.9	..	..	..	..
Medium human development														
120	Kyrgyzstan	1.06	1.00	0.99	1.00	2.00	1.01	1.33	38.4	19.2	..	16.8^f	1.8^f	..
121	Morocco	1.06	0.86	0.96	0.91	1.04	0.81	1.21	16.8	18.4	20.9	20.8	7.0	..
122	Guyana	1.05	..	..	..	1.64	1.26	1.57	41.4	31.9	..	..	..	..
123	Iraq	1.07	..	..	..	2.86	0.70	3.02	10.8	25.2	25.7	..	..	..
124	El Salvador	1.05	1.02	0.97	0.99	1.29	0.86	0.80	48.7	31.0	32.4	20.2	2.9	..
125	Tajikistan	1.07	0.87	0.99	..	0.95	0.97	0.85	27.3	20.0	..	..	..	..
126	Cabo Verde	1.03	1.01	0.93	1.10	1.28	0.92	0.89	47.1	23.6	28.4	..	..	0.71
127	Guatemala	1.05	1.02	0.97	0.95	2.03	1.03	1.72	43.1	19.4	10.6	19.5	7.5	0.50
128	Nicaragua	1.05	..	..	..	1.48	1.04	0.97	51.1	44.6	..	..	..	..
129	Bhutan	1.04	1.01	1.00	1.13	1.50	0.74	1.83	32.9	15.3	10.6	15.0	2.5	..
130	Namibia	1.01	1.04	0.97	..	1.07	0.97	0.94	50.9	37.0	45.1	..	..	..
131	India	1.10	0.92	1.15	1.04	1.07	0.59	0.97	15.9	13.5	44.4	..	..	..
132	Honduras	1.05	1.02	1.00	1.15	2.10	1.09	1.60	48.5	21.1	27.9	17.3	4.0	..
133	Bangladesh	1.05	1.04	1.07	1.16	1.50	0.84	1.88	20.7	20.6	25.2	..	..	..
134	Kiribati	1.06	..	1.07	..	..	..	..	..	6.5	..	..	..	..
135	Sao Tome and Principe	1.03	1.09	0.97	1.16	2.01	0.69	2.30	37.1	14.5	..	..	..	..
136	Micronesia (Federated States of)	1.06	0.89	0.98	..	..	..	..	..	0.0	1.5	..	..	..
137	Lao People's Democratic Republic	1.05	1.03	0.96	0.93	0.88	0.76	0.83	46.6	27.5	32.2	13.6	1.4	..
138	Eswatini (Kingdom of)	1.03	..	0.92	0.99	1.12	0.93	1.15	48.0	12.1	14.2	..	..	..
138	Ghana	1.05	1.02	1.01	1.00	0.97	0.78	1.06	51.2	13.1	3.8	14.4^d	4.1^d	..
140	Vanuatu	1.07	0.97	0.97	1.03	1.07	..	1.24	44.2	0.0	9.5	..	..	..
141	Timor-Leste	1.05	1.01	0.96	1.08	1.53	..	1.94	47.5	38.5	4.0	..	..	1.13
142	Nepal	1.07	0.91	1.02	1.07	0.60	0.66	0.73	40.3	33.5	41.0	..	..	..
143	Kenya	1.03	0.97	1.00	..	1.01	0.80	1.12	42.4	23.3	33.5	..	..	..
144	Cambodia	1.05	1.04	0.98	..	1.20	0.53	1.53	46.8	19.3	16.9	..	..	0.15
145	Equatorial Guinea	1.03	1.02	0.99	..	0.92	..	0.94	36.6	19.2	26.9	..	..	..
146	Zambia	1.03	1.08	1.02	..	1.08	0.71	1.15	42.8	18.0	7.1	..	..	0.22
147	Myanmar	1.03	1.02	0.96	1.09	1.49	1.22	1.67	44.4	11.6	..	..	..	..
148	Angola	1.03	0.89	0.87	0.64	0.91	0.61	1.02	44.2	30.0	..	..	..	..
149	Congo	1.03	..	..	..	0.93	0.91	1.14	49.1	13.6	..	..	..	..
150	Zimbabwe	1.02	..	..	..	1.27	0.84	1.23	45.5	34.6	12.0	..	..	..
151	Solomon Islands	1.07	1.02	1.00	..	1.54	..	1.06	48.7	4.1	..	..	..	..
151	Syrian Arab Republic	1.05	..	..	..	2.83	0.86	3.52	14.6	13.2	7.1	..	..	..
153	Cameroon	1.03	1.02	0.90	0.86	1.19	0.79	1.32	43.1	29.3	25.3	14.6^d	3.1^d	..
154	Pakistan	1.09	0.87	0.84	0.85	0.94	0.60	1.34	11.0	20.0	16.9	..	..	..
155	Papua New Guinea	1.08	0.99	0.91	0.73	0.61	0.66	0.40	46.3	0.0	..	..	..	..
156	Comoros	1.05	1.03	1.00	1.07	0.77	..	1.16	37.5	6.1	28.0	..	..	..
Low human development														
157	Mauritania	1.05	1.26	1.06	1.02	1.20	0.51	1.45	31.3	20.3	31.4	..	..	..
158	Benin	1.04	1.03	0.94	0.76	1.12	0.54	1.10	55.8	7.2	4.7	..	..	..

Continued →

				SDG 4.2	SDG 4.1	SDG 4.1	SDG 8.5	SDG 4.4	SDG 8.5	SDG 8.3	SDG 5.5	SDG 5.5	SDG 5.4		SDG 1.3
					Childhood and youth						Adulthood				Older age
				Sex ratio at birth[a]		(female to male ratio)		Youth unemployment rate	Population with at least some secondary education	Total unemployment rate	Share of employment in nonagriculture, female	Share of seats held by women		Time spent on unpaid domestic chores and care work		Old-age pension recipients
				(male to female births)	Pre-primary	Primary	Secondary	(female to male ratio)	(female to male ratio)	(female to male ratio)	(% of total employment in nonagriculture)	In parliament	In local government (%)	(% of 24-hour day)	(female to male ratio)	(female to male ratio)
HDI RANK				2015-2020[b]	2014-2019[c]	2014-2019[c]	2014-2019[c]	2019	2015-2019[c]	2019	2019	2019	2017-2019[c]	2008-2018[c]	2008-2018[c]	2014-2019[c]
159	Uganda			1.03	1.04	1.03	..	1.52	0.78	1.64	41.2	34.9	45.7	..	..	..
160	Rwanda			1.02	1.03	0.99	1.12	1.71	0.69	1.08	39.1	55.7	43.6	..	..	..
161	Nigeria			1.06	..	0.94	0.90	1.58	..	1.20	52.3	4.1	9.8	..	..	..
162	Côte d'Ivoire			1.03	1.02	0.93	0.77	1.26	0.52	1.26	47.8	13.3	15.0	..	..	..
163	Tanzania (United Republic of)			1.03	1.00	1.03	1.05	1.40	0.71	1.61	45.0	36.9	30.1	16.5[i]	3.9[i]	..
164	Madagascar			1.03	1.10	1.01	1.03	0.89	..	1.10	54.0	16.9		..	..	..
165	Lesotho			1.03	1.04	0.95	1.35	1.33	1.30	1.33	45.7	23.0	39.0	..	..	..
166	Djibouti			1.04	0.95	1.00	1.03	0.96	..	1.02	41.0	26.2	28.9	..	..	..
167	Togo			1.02	1.03	0.96	0.73	0.97	0.51	0.61	51.6	16.5	..	..	..	..
168	Senegal			1.04	1.13	1.13	1.10	1.38	0.39	1.23	43.0	41.8	47.6	..	..	..
169	Afghanistan			1.06	..	0.67	0.57	1.31	0.36	1.36	12.6	27.2	16.5	..	..	..
170	Haiti			1.05	..	..	..	1.57	0.67	1.50	55.8	2.7	..	..	..	..
170	Sudan			1.04	1.02	0.94	1.01	1.56	0.79	2.39	20.0	27.5		..	..	..
172	Gambia			1.03	1.06	1.09	..	1.89	0.71	1.87	39.1	10.3		..	..	..
173	Ethiopia			1.04	0.95	0.91	0.96	1.76	0.51	1.84	57.2	37.3	..	19.3[d]	2.9[d]	..
174	Malawi			1.03	1.01	1.01	0.98	1.16	0.67	1.40	48.5	22.9	14.6	..	..	..
175	Congo (Democratic Republic of the)			1.03	1.07	0.99	0.64	0.61	0.56	0.68	38.6	12.0		..	..	..
175	Guinea-Bissau			1.03				0.79	..	0.82	44.0	13.7		..	..	..
175	Liberia			1.05	1.01	0.99	0.77	0.96	0.46	0.66	49.2	11.7	..	6.3	2.4	..
178	Guinea			1.02	..	0.82	0.65	0.68	..	0.61	52.7	22.8	15.4	..	..	..
179	Yemen			1.05	0.90	0.87	0.73	1.47	0.54	2.09	5.0	1.0	0.5[j]	..	..	..
180	Eritrea			1.05	0.99	0.86	0.91	0.92	..	0.93	40.6	22.0		..	..	..
181	Mozambique			1.02	..	0.93	0.89	0.96	0.70	1.15	34.8	41.2		..	..	..
182	Burkina Faso			1.05	0.99	0.98	1.00	2.40	0.50	2.38	47.9	13.4	12.7	..	..	0.13
182	Sierra Leone			1.02	1.12	1.03	0.97	0.41	0.61	0.70	53.4	12.3	18.2	..	..	..
184	Mali			1.05	1.03	0.90	0.82	1.22	0.45	1.19	43.1	9.5	25.3	..	..	0.11
185	Burundi			1.03	1.04	1.01	1.11	0.44	0.66	0.54	26.2	38.8	19.1	..	..	..
185	South Sudan			1.04	0.95	0.71	0.54	0.86	..	1.21	30.2	26.6		..	..	..
187	Chad			1.03	0.92	0.77	0.46	0.75	0.17	0.83	48.9	14.9		..	..	..
188	Central African Republic			1.03	1.05	0.78	0.67	0.90	0.43	0.94	37.7	8.6		..	..	..
189	Niger			1.05	1.07	0.86	0.75	0.45	0.52	0.64	51.3	17.0	15.8[k]	..	..	..
Other countries or territories																
..	Korea (Democratic People's Rep. of)			1.05	..	1.00	1.01	0.78	..	0.75	39.1	17.6				
..	Monaco			..	..	..	..	..	..	..		33.3	..			
..	Nauru			..	0.94	0.95	1.02	..	..	..		10.5				
..	San Marino			..	1.04	1.16	0.89	..	..	..		25.0				
..	Somalia			1.03				0.98	..	0.97	18.0	24.3				
..	Tuvalu			..	0.94	0.92	1.14					6.3	10.4			
Human development groups																
	Very high human development			1.05	0.99	1.00	0.99	1.10	0.98	1.17	44.4	28.3	–	–	–	0.93
	High human development			1.08	0.99	1.00	..	1.19	0.93	1.16	43.2	24.5	–	–	–	..
	Medium human development			1.08	0.95	1.06	1.02	1.12	0.65	1.15	21.0	20.4	–	–	–	..
	Low human development			1.04	1.01	0.94	0.84	1.32	0.57	1.40	45.0	22.2	–	–	–	..
Developing countries				1.07	0.97	1.01	1.00	1.18	0.85	1.22	37.1	22.7	–	–	–	..
Regions																
	Arab States			1.05	0.98	0.97	0.96	1.79	0.88	2.63	16.3	18.0	–	–	–	..
	East Asia and the Pacific			1.10	0.99	1.00	..	0.92	0.91	0.82	44.9	20.2	–	–	–	..
	Europe and Central Asia			1.06	0.98	1.00	0.97	1.19	0.91	1.10	40.4	23.1	–	–	–	..
	Latin America and the Caribbean			1.05	1.02	0.98	1.04	1.37	1.01	1.34	44.1	31.4	–	–	–	..
	South Asia			1.09	0.93	1.07	1.02	1.11	0.65	1.15	16.5	17.5	–	–	–	..
	Sub-Saharan Africa			1.04	1.00	0.96	0.88	1.19	0.72	1.17	47.5	24.0	–	–	–	..
Least developed countries				1.04	1.00	0.95	0.92	1.25	0.70	1.48	37.7	22.8	–	–	–	..
Small island developing states				1.06	..	0.95	1.00	1.56	0.94	1.47	43.8	25.1	–	–	–	..
Organisation for Economic Co-operation and Development				1.05	1.00	1.00	1.00	1.03	0.97	1.12	45.0	30.8	–	–	–	0.91
World				**1.07**	**0.98**	**1.01**	**1.00**	**1.15**	**0.89**	**1.18**	**39.4**	**24.6**	**–**	**–**	**–**	**..**

Notes

Three-colour coding is used to visualize partial grouping of countries and aggregates by indicator. For each indicator countries are divided into three groups of approximately equal size (terciles): the top third, the middle third and the bottom third. Aggregates are colour coded using the same tercile cutoffs. Sex ratio at birth is an exception—countries are divided into two groups: the natural group (countries with a value of 1.04–1.07, inclusive), which uses darker shading, and the gender-biased group (all others), which uses lighter shading. See *Technical note* 6 at http://hdr.undp.org/sites/default/files/hdr2020_technical_notes.pdf for details about partial grouping in this table.

a	The natural sex ratio at birth is commonly assumed and empirically confirmed to be 1.05 male births to 1 female birth.
b	Data are average annual estimates for 2015–2020.
c	Data refer to the most recent year available during the period specified.
d	Refers to the population ages 10 and older.
e	Refers to the population ages 20–74.
f	Refers to the population ages 12 and older.
g	Refers to the population ages 6 and older.
h	Excludes the 36 special rotating delegates appointed on an ad hoc basis.
i	Refers to the population ages 5 and older.
j	Refers to 2006.
k	Refers to 2011.

Definitions

Sex ratio at birth: Number of male births per female birth.

Gross enrolment ratio, female to male ratio: For a given level of education (pre-primary, primary, secondary), the ratio of the female gross enrolment ratio to the male gross enrolment ratio. The gross enrolment ratio (female or male) is the total enrolment in a given level of education, regardless of age, expressed as a percentage of the official school-age population for the same level of education.

Youth unemployment rate, female to male ratio: Ratio of the percentage of the female labour force population ages 15–24 that is not in paid employment or self-employed but is available for work and is actively seeking paid employment or self-employment to the percentage of the male labour force population ages 15–24 that is not in paid employment or self-employed but is available for work and is actively seeking paid employment or self-employment.

Population with at least some secondary education, female to male ratio: Ratio of the percentage of the female population ages 25 and older that has reached (but not necessarily completed) a secondary level of education to the percentage of the male population ages 25 and older with the same level of education achievement.

Total unemployment rate, female to male ratio: Ratio of the percentage of the female labour force population ages 15 and older that is not in paid employment or self-employed but is available for work and is actively seeking paid employment or self-employment to the percentage of the male labour force population ages 15 and older that is not in paid employment or self-employed but is available for work and is actively seeking paid employment or self-employment.

Share of employment in nonagriculture, female: Share of women in employment in the nonagricultural sector, which comprises industry and services activities.

Share of seats held by women in parliament: Proportion of seats held by women in the national parliament, expressed as a percentage of total seats. For countries with a bicameral legislative system, the share of seats is calculated based on both houses.

Share of seats held by women in local government: Proportion of elected positions held by women in legislative/deliberative bodies of local government, expressed as a percentage of total elected positions in those bodies.

Time spent on unpaid domestic chores and care work: The average daily number of hours spent on unpaid domestic and care work, expressed as a percentage of a 24-hour day. Unpaid domestic chores and care work refer to activities related to the provision of services for own final use by household members or by family members living in other households.

Old-age pension recipients, female to male ratio: Ratio of the percentage of women above the statutory pensionable age receiving an old-age pension (contributory, noncontributory or both) to the percentage of men above the statutory pensionable age receiving an old-age pension (contributory, noncontributory or both).

Main data sources

Column 1: UNDESA (2019a).

Columns 2–4: UNESCO (2020).

Columns 5 and 7: HDRO calculations based on ILO (2020).

Column 6: HDRO calculations based on UNESCO Institute for Statistics (2020) and Barro and Lee (2018).

Column 8: ILO (2020).

Column 9: IPU (2020).

Columns 10 and 11: United Nations Statistics Division (2020a).

Columns 12 and 13: HDRO calculations based on United Nations Statistics Division (2020a).

Women's empowerment

Country groupings (terciles): `Top third` Middle third Bottom third

Three-colour coding is used to visualize partial grouping of countries by indicator. For each indicator countries are divided into three groups of approximately equal size (terciles): the top third, the middle third and the bottom third. Aggregates are colour coded using the same tercile cutoffs. See *Notes* after the table.

		SDG 3.1	SDG 3.7, 5.6	SDG 5.6	SDG 5.6	SDG 5.3	SDG 5.3	SDG 5.2	SDG 5.2			SDG 5.5		SDG 1.3
		Reproductive health and family planning				Violence against girls and women				Socioeconomic empowerment				
						Child marriage		Violence against women ever experienced[a]		Share of graduates in science, technology, engineering and mathematics programmes at tertiary level, female	Share of graduates from science, technology, engineering and mathematics programmes in tertiary education who are female	Female share of employment in senior and middle management	Women with account at financial institution or with mobile money-service provider	Mandatory paid maternity leave
		Antenatal care coverage, at least one visit	Proportion of births attended by skilled health personnel	Contraceptive prevalence, any method	Unmet need for family planning	Women married by age 18	Prevalence of female genital mutilation/cutting among girls and women	Intimate partner	Nonintimate partner					
		(%)	(%)	(% of married or in-union women of reproductive age, 15–49 years)	(%)	(% of women ages 20–24 who are married or in union)	(% of girls and women ages 15–49)	(% of female population ages 15 and older)		(%)	(%)	(%)	(% of female population ages 15 and older)	(days)
HDI RANK		2009–2019[b]	2014–2019[b]	2009–2019[b]	2009–2019[b]	2005–2019[b]	2004–2018[b]	2005–2019[b]	2005–2019[b]	2009–2019[b]	2009–2019[b]	2009–2019[b]	2017	2019
Very high human development														
1	Norway	..	99.2	..	..	..	..	27.0	..	10.9	28.5	32.8	100.0	..
2	Ireland	..	99.7	73.3	..	..	..	15.0	5.0	14.1	29.0	31.3	95.3	182
2	Switzerland	..	..	71.6	..	..	..	..	..	11.4	22.3	32.5	98.9	98
4	Hong Kong, China (SAR)	..	..	66.7	..	..	..	..	..	..	..	..	94.7	70
4	Iceland	..	98.2	..	..	..	..	22.4	..	10.3	35.2	44.0	..	90
6	Germany	..	98.8	80.3	..	..	..	22.0	7.0	19.2	27.6	28.6	99.2	98
7	Sweden	..	..	..	..	..	..	28.0	12.0	15.7	35.5	41.9	100.0	..
8	Australia	..	96.7	66.9	..	..	..	22.8	10.0	10.2	32.1	..	99.2	..
8	Netherlands	..	..	73.0	..	..	..	25.0	12.0	8.7	29.3	26.0	99.8	112
10	Denmark	..	95.3	..	..	..	..	32.0	11.0	12.7	34.2	26.6	100.0	126
11	Finland	..	100.0	85.5	..	..	..	30.0	11.0	12.4	27.4	36.8	99.6	147
11	Singapore	..	99.5	..	..	..	..	6.1	..	22.6	34.3	..	96.3	84
13	United Kingdom	..	..	..	..	..	..	29.0	7.0	17.5	38.1	34.9	96.1	42
14	Belgium	..	..	66.7	..	..	..	24.0	8.0	7.2	25.8	31.9	98.8	105
14	New Zealand	..	96.6	79.9	..	..	..	..	..	12.9	35.0	..	99.3	..
16	Canada	..	98.0	..	..	..	..	..	..	11.6	31.4	..	99.9	105
17	United States	..	99.1	75.9	9.0	..	..	..	..	10.4	34.0	40.9	92.7	..
18	Austria	..	98.4	79.0	..	..	..	13.0	4.0	14.3	25.9	32.0	98.4	112
19	Israel	..	..	..	..	..	..	..	..	..	..	34.8	93.7	105
19	Japan	..	99.9	39.8	..	..	..	..	..	..	..	..	98.1	98
19	Liechtenstein	..	..	..	..	..	..	..	..	33.8	40.7	..	..	..
22	Slovenia	..	..	..	..	..	..	13.0	4.0	14.5	33.3	40.5	96.9	105
23	Korea (Republic of)	..	100.0	82.3	..	..	..	..	..	14.4	25.2	..	94.7	90
23	Luxembourg	..	..	..	..	..	..	22.0	8.0	9.5	27.6	17.9	98.2	112
25	Spain	..	..	72.2	..	..	..	13.0	3.0	12.4	29.6	33.7	91.6	112
26	France	..	98.1	78.4	..	..	..	26.0	9.0	14.5	31.8	34.2	91.3	112
27	Czechia	..	99.8	..	..	..	..	21.0	4.0	13.9	35.6	26.6	78.6	196
28	Malta	..	99.7	..	..	..	..	15.0	5.0	10.3	27.8	30.0	97.0	126
29	Estonia	..	99.1	..	..	..	..	20.0	9.0	17.5	38.4	35.1	98.4	140
29	Italy	..	99.9	65.1	..	..	..	19.0	5.0	15.7	39.5	23.3	91.6	150
31	United Arab Emirates	..	99.9	..	..	..	..	..	..	22.2	41.5	15.8	76.4	45
32	Greece	..	99.9	..	..	..	..	19.0	1.0	20.2	40.1	29.8	84.5	119
33	Cyprus	..	98.3	..	..	..	..	15.0	2.0	8.9	38.3	27.0	90.0	126
34	Lithuania	..	100.0	..	..	..	..	24.0	5.0	12.3	29.6	38.6	81.0	126
35	Poland	..	99.8	62.3	..	..	..	13.0	2.0	15.3	43.4	41.2	88.0	140
36	Andorra	..	100.0	..	..	..	..	..	..	4.5	66.7	..	..	..
37	Latvia	..	99.9	..	..	..	..	32.0	7.0	10.2	31.1	43.5	92.5	112
38	Portugal	..	98.7	73.9	..	..	..	19.0	1.0	19.0	37.8	37.0	90.6	..
39	Slovakia	..	98.0	..	..	..	..	23.0	4.0	11.9	35.2	33.3	83.1	238
40	Hungary	..	99.7	61.6	..	..	..	21.0	3.0	12.2	31.7	35.9	72.2	168
40	Saudi Arabia	..	99.4	24.6	..	..	..	..	..	14.7	36.8	..	58.2	70
42	Bahrain	..	99.9	..	..	..	..	..	..	10.5	41.2	..	75.4	60
43	Chile	..	99.8	76.3	..	..	..	..	..	6.8	18.8	28.3	71.3	126
43	Croatia	..	99.9	..	..	..	..	13.0	3.0	17.6	38.9	24.3	82.7	208
45	Qatar	90.8	100.0	37.5	12.4	4	..	..	..	15.9	47.6	..	61.6 c	50
46	Argentina	98.1	93.9	81.3	..	..	..	26.9	12.1	9.1	43.5	33.1	50.8	90
47	Brunei Darussalam	99.0	99.8	..	..	..	..	..	..	33.7	54.3	32.3	..	91
48	Montenegro	97.2	98.8	20.7	21.0	6	..	17.0	1.0	..	..	28.2	67.6	126
49	Romania	76.3	97.1	..	..	..	..	24.0	2.0	20.3	41.2	34.2	53.6	126

Continued →

		SDG 3.1	SDG 3.7, 5.6	SDG 5.6		SDG 5.3	SDG 5.3	SDG 5.2	SDG 5.2			SDG 5.5		SDG 1.3
		Reproductive health and family planning				Violence against girls and women				Socioeconomic empowerment				
						Child marriage		Violence against women ever experienced[a]		Share of graduates in science, technology, engineering and mathematics programmes at tertiary level, female	Share of graduates from science, technology, engineering and mathematics programmes in tertiary education who are female	Female share of employment in senior and middle management	Women with account at financial institution or with mobile money-service provider	Mandatory paid maternity leave
		Antenatal care coverage, at least one visit	Proportion of births attended by skilled health personnel	Contraceptive prevalence, any method	Unmet need for family planning	Women married by age 18	Prevalence of female genital mutilation/cutting among girls and women	Intimate partner	Nonintimate partner					
				(% of married or in-union women of reproductive age, 15–49 years)		(% of women ages 20–24 who are married or in union)	(% of girls and women ages 15–49)	(% of female population ages 15 and older)					(% of female population ages 15 and older)	
		(%)	(%)							(%)	(%)	(%)		(days)
HDI RANK		2009–2019[b]	2014–2019[b]	2009–2019[b]	2009–2019[b]	2005–2019[b]	2004–2018[b]	2005–2019[b]	2005–2019[b]	2009–2019[b]	2009–2019[b]	2009–2019[b]	2017	2019
50	Palau	90.3	100.0	..	..			25.2	15.1	..	..	35.5	..	
51	Kazakhstan	99.3	99.9	53.0	15.5	7		16.5	1.5	14.1	31.6	..	60.3	126
52	Russian Federation	..	99.7	68.0	8.0	..		..	..	..	..	39.8	76.1	140
53	Belarus	99.7	99.8	71.2	7.0	5		..	..	15.4	27.4	..	81.3	126
54	Turkey	97.0	98.0	69.8	11.6	15		38.0	..	14.2	34.7	17.5	54.3	112
55	Uruguay	97.2	100.0	79.6	..	25		16.8	..	12.2	44.0	35.2	60.6	98
56	Bulgaria	..	99.8	..	..	..		23.0	6.0	12.5	36.9	39.3	73.6	410
57	Panama	99.1	92.9	50.8	24.2	26		14.4	..	10.3	43.2	43.5	42.3	98
58	Bahamas	..	99.0	..	..	..		..	..	..	..	..	..	91
58	Barbados	93.4	99.1	59.2	19.9	29		..	..	..	40.5	..	..	84
60	Oman	98.6	98.6	29.7	17.8	4		..	..	41.0	55.7	..	63.5[c]	50
61	Georgia	97.6	99.4	40.6	23.1	14		6.0	2.7	16.5	38.7	..	63.6	183
62	Costa Rica	97.6	99.0	70.9	13.7	21		35.9[d]	..	8.1	32.2	..	60.9	120
62	Malaysia	97.2	99.6	52.2	..	..		..	..	26.2	34.2	..	82.5	60
64	Kuwait	..	99.9	..	..	..		..	..	..	..	..	73.5	70
64	Serbia	98.3	98.4	58.4	14.9	3		17.0	2.0	20.3	42.6	33.6	70.1	135
66	Mauritius	..	99.8	63.8	12.5	..		..	..	14.8	36.0	31.0	87.1	98
High human development														
67	Seychelles	..	..	..	..	..		..	..	7.9	31.6	47.4	..	112
67	Trinidad and Tobago	95.1	100.0	40.3	24.3	11		30.2	19.0	..	..	..	73.6	98
69	Albania	88.4	99.8	46.0	15.1	12		21.0	1.3	15.2	46.7	41.3	38.1	365
70	Cuba	98.5	99.9	73.7	8.0	26		..	..	6.1	39.9	..	..	
70	Iran (Islamic Republic of)	96.9	99.0	77.4	5.7	17		..	..	31.5	31.2	..	91.6	270
72	Sri Lanka	98.8	99.5	61.7	7.5	10		..	..	..	40.6	22.5	73.4	118
73	Bosnia and Herzegovina	87.0	99.9	45.8	9.0	4		11.0	1.0	16.1	44.5	25.4	54.7	365
74	Grenada	..	100.0	..	..	..		..	..	11.6	40.9	..	..	90
74	Mexico	98.5	96.4	73.1	13.0	26		24.6	38.8	14.5	30.6	35.5	33.3	84
74	Saint Kitts and Nevis	..	100.0	..	..	..		..	..	..	..	..	..	91
74	Ukraine	98.6	99.9	65.4	4.9	9		26.0	5.0	13.7	28.8	..	61.3	126
78	Antigua and Barbuda	..	100.0	..	..	..		..	..	1.8	33.3	..	..	91
79	Peru	97.0	92.1	76.3	6.3	17		31.2	..	24.4	47.8	..	34.4	98
79	Thailand	98.1	99.1	78.4	6.2	23		..	..	15.0	30.1	31.0	79.8	90
81	Armenia	99.6	99.8	57.1	12.5	5		8.2	..	10.2	39.8	..	40.9	140
82	North Macedonia	98.6	99.9	40.2	17.2	7		10.0	2.0	18.0	47.4	28.2	72.9	270
83	Colombia	97.2	99.1	81.0	6.7	23		33.3	..	13.8	33.4	..	42.5	126
84	Brazil	97.2	99.1	80.2	..	26		16.7	..	10.7	36.6	38.6	67.5	120
85	China	99.6	99.9	84.5	..	..		..	..	..	..	..	76.4	128
86	Ecuador	..	96.0	80.1	8.8	20		40.4	..	8.0	29.2	37.1	42.6	84
86	Saint Lucia	96.9	100.0	55.5	17.0	24		..	..	..	..	..	..	91
88	Azerbaijan	91.7	99.4	54.9	..	11		13.5	..	14.6	35.1	..	27.7	126
88	Dominican Republic	98.0	99.8	69.5	11.4	36		28.5	..	7.0	40.0	50.2	54.1	98
90	Moldova (Republic of)	98.8	99.7	59.5	9.5	12		34.0	4.0	12.3	30.5	..	44.6	126
91	Algeria	92.7	..	57.1	7.0	3		..	..	30.9	58.2	..	29.3	98
92	Lebanon	..	..	54.5	..	6		..	..	18.0	43.3	..	32.9	70
93	Fiji	..	99.8	..	..	..		64.1	8.5	..	..	38.6	..	98
94	Dominica	..	100.0	..	..	..		..	..	..	..	..	..	84
95	Maldives	98.7	99.5	18.8	31.4	2	12.9	16.3	..	0.8	10.6	19.5	..	60
95	Tunisia	95.3	99.5	50.7	19.9	2		..	..	36.5	55.4	19.3	28.4	30
97	Saint Vincent and the Grenadines	..	98.6	..	..	..		..	..	..	..	..	..	91
97	Suriname	84.8	98.4	39.1	28.4	36		..	..	..	..	..	..	
99	Mongolia	98.7	99.3	48.1	22.8	12		31.2	14.0	14.4	34.1	43.0	95.0	120
100	Botswana	..	99.8	67.4	..	..		..	..	..	..	29.6	46.8	84
101	Jamaica	97.7	99.7	72.5	10.0	8		27.8	23.0	..	..	..	77.8[e]	56
102	Jordan	97.6	99.7	51.8	14.2	10		19.0	..	..	..	..	26.6	70
103	Paraguay	98.7	97.7	68.4	12.1	22		20.4	..	..	..	..	46.0	126
104	Tonga	99.0	..	34.1	25.2	6		39.6	6.3	..	..	40.3	..	..
105	Libya	..	..	27.7	40.2	..		..	..	..	..	..	59.6	98

Continued →

		SDG 3.1	SDG 3.7, 5.6	SDG 5.6	SDG 5.6	SDG 5.3	SDG 5.3	SDG 5.2	SDG 5.2			SDG 5.5		SDG 1.3
		Reproductive health and family planning				Violence against girls and women				Socioeconomic empowerment				
						Child marriage		Violence against women ever experienced[a]						
		Antenatal care coverage, at least one visit	Proportion of births attended by skilled health personnel	Contraceptive prevalence, any method	Unmet need for family planning	Women married by age 18	Prevalence of female genital mutilation/ cutting among girls and women	Intimate partner	Nonintimate partner	Share of graduates in science, technology, engineering and mathematics programmes at tertiary level, female	Share of graduates from science, technology, engineering and mathematics programmes in tertiary education who are female	Female share of employment in senior and middle management	Women with account at financial institution or with mobile money-service provider	Mandatory paid maternity leave
		(%)	(%)	(% of married or in-union women of reproductive age, 15–49 years)		(% of women ages 20–24 who are married or in union)	(% of girls and women ages 15–49)	(% of female population ages 15 and older)		(%)	(%)	(%)	(% of female population ages 15 and older)	(days)
HDI RANK		2009–2019[b]	2014–2019[b]	2009–2019[b]	2009–2019[b]	2005–2019[b]	2004–2018[b]	2005–2019[b]	2005–2019[b]	2009–2019[b]	2009–2019[b]	2009–2019[b]	2017	2019
106	Uzbekistan	99.4	100.0	..	..	7	..	..	..	21.4	24.6	..	36.0	126
107	Bolivia (Plurinational State of)	95.6	71.5	66.5	23.2	20	..	58.5	..	..	..	30.4	53.9	90
107	Indonesia	97.5	94.7	55.5	14.8	16	..	18.3	..	12.4	37.4	19.4	51.4	90
107	Philippines	93.8	84.4	54.1	16.7	17	..	14.8	..	17.8	36.3	29.3	38.9	105
110	Belize	97.2	94.0	51.4	22.2	34	..	22.2	..	11.7	41.8	41.7	52.3[e]	98
111	Samoa	93.3	82.5	26.9	34.8	11	..	46.1	10.6	..	..	41.6	..	28
111	Turkmenistan	99.6	100.0	50.2	12.1	6	..	..	..	..	..	..	35.5	..
113	Venezuela (Bolivarian Republic of)	97.5	99.1	75.0	..	..	..	..	..	..	..	..	70.0	182
114	South Africa	93.7	96.7	54.6	14.9	4	..	21.3	..	12.9	42.8	33.3	70.0	120
115	Palestine, State of	99.4	99.6	57.2	10.9	15	..	..	..	11.3	44.3	17.8	15.9	70
116	Egypt	90.3	91.5	58.5	12.6	17	87.2	25.6	..	7.7	36.9	..	27.0	90
117	Marshall Islands	..	92.4	..	..	26	..	50.9	13.0	..	..	..	..	..
117	Viet Nam	95.8	93.8	77.5	6.1	11	..	34.4	2.3	15.4	36.5	..	30.4	180
119	Gabon	94.7	..	31.1	26.5	22	..	48.6	5.0	..	..	..	53.7	98
Medium human development														
120	Kyrgyzstan	99.8	99.8	39.4	19.0	13	..	26.6	0.1	11.3	31.3	..	38.9	126
121	Morocco	88.5	86.6	70.8	11.3	14	..	..	..	17.8	45.3	..	16.8	98
122	Guyana	90.7	95.8	33.9	28.0	30	..	..	..	5.2	27.2	38.5	19.5	91
123	Iraq	87.6	95.6	52.8	14.3	28	7.4			..	..	..	19.5	98
124	El Salvador	96.0	99.9	71.9	11.1	26	..	14.3	..	8.9	23.1	43.1	24.4	112
125	Tajikistan	91.8	94.8	29.3	22.7	9	..	26.4	..	..	..	..	42.1	140
126	Cabo Verde	..	92.4	..	..	18	..	12.6	..	10.6	42.4	..	..	60
127	Guatemala	91.3	69.8	60.6	13.9	30	..	21.2	..	5.4	34.7	34.5	42.1	84
128	Nicaragua	94.7	96.0	80.4	5.8	35	..	22.5	..	..	..	53.7	24.8	84
129	Bhutan	97.9	96.2	65.6	11.7	26	..	15.1	5.8	..	..	..	27.7[e]	56
130	Namibia	96.6	..	56.1	17.5	7	..	26.7	..	7.7	42.5	48.2	80.7	84
131	India	79.3	81.4	53.5	12.9	27	..	28.8	..	26.9	42.7	13.7	76.6	182
132	Honduras	96.6	74.0	73.2	10.7	34	..	27.8	..	9.1	37.8	47.5	41.0	84
133	Bangladesh	75.2	52.7	62.3	12.0	59	..	54.2	3.0	8.2	20.6	11.5	35.8	112
134	Kiribati	88.4	..	22.3	28.0	20	..	67.6	9.8	..	..	..	..	84
135	Sao Tome and Principe	97.5	92.5	40.6	33.7	35	..	27.9	..	..	..	..	..	98
136	Micronesia (Federated States of)	..	..	..	..	..	..	32.8	8.0	..	..	18.2	..	..
137	Lao People's Democratic Republic	78.4	64.4	54.1	14.3	33	..	15.3	5.3	12.8	29.0	23.4	31.9	105
138	Eswatini (Kingdom of)	98.5	88.3	66.1	15.2	5	..	..	..	..	..	54.6	27.4[c]	14
138	Ghana	97.1	78.1	33.0	26.3	21	3.8	24.4	4.0	7.9	19.8	26.6	53.7	84
140	Vanuatu	75.6	..	49.0	24.2	21	..	60.0	33.0	..	..	28.5	..	84
141	Timor-Leste	84.4	56.7	26.1	25.3	15	..	58.8	13.9	..	..	..	..	84
142	Nepal	83.6	58.0	52.6	23.7	40	..	25.0	..	..	..	13.9	41.6	60
143	Kenya	93.7	61.8	60.5	14.9	23	21.0	40.7	..	11.2	30.7	..	77.7	90
144	Cambodia	95.3	89.0	56.3	12.5	19	..	20.9	3.8	6.0	16.7	20.2	21.5	90
145	Equatorial Guinea	91.3	..	12.6	33.8	30	..	56.9	..	..	..	..	..	84
146	Zambia	96.9	63.3	49.5	19.7	29	..	45.9	..	..	..	40.3	40.3	98
147	Myanmar	80.7	60.2	52.2	16.2	16	..	17.3	..	31.0	60.8	34.1	26.0	98
148	Angola	81.6	46.6	13.7	38.0	30	..	34.8	..	9.9	38.4	..	22.3[e]	90
149	Congo	93.5	91.2	30.1	17.9	27	..	..	..	7.5	20.8	..	21.0	105
150	Zimbabwe	93.3	86.0	66.8	10.4	34	..	37.6	..	20.9	28.8	..	51.7	98
151	Solomon Islands	88.5	86.2	29.3	34.7	21	..	63.5	18.0	..	..	25.1	..	84
151	Syrian Arab Republic	87.7	..	53.9	16.4	13	..	..	..	19.2	49.5	..	19.6[c]	120
153	Cameroon	87.0	69.0	19.3	23.0	31	1.4	51.1	5.0	16.1	32.3	..	30.0	98
154	Pakistan	86.2	69.3	34.2	17.3	18	..	24.5	..	..	..	4.2	7.0	112
155	Papua New Guinea	76.1	56.4	36.7	25.9	27	..	..	..	..	..	19.3	..	..
156	Comoros	92.1	..	19.4	31.6	32	..	6.4	1.5	..	..	..	17.9[c]	98
Low human development														
157	Mauritania	86.9	69.3	17.8	33.6	37	66.6	..	..	29.4	28.9	..	15.5	98
158	Benin	83.2	78.1	15.5	32.3	31	9.2	23.8	..	19.1	54.9	..	28.6	98

Continued →

		SDG 3.1	SDG 3.7, 5.6	SDG 5.6	SDG 5.3	SDG 5.3	SDG 5.2	SDG 5.2			SDG 5.5		SDG 1.3
		Reproductive health and family planning			Violence against girls and women				Socioeconomic empowerment				
					Child marriage		Violence against women ever experienced[a]		Share of graduates in science, technology, engineering and mathematics programmes at tertiary level, female	Share of graduates from science, technology, engineering and mathematics programmes in tertiary education who are female	Female share of employment in senior and middle management	Women with account at financial institution or with mobile money-service provider	Mandatory paid maternity leave
		Antenatal care coverage, at least one visit	Proportion of births attended by skilled health personnel	Contraceptive prevalence, any method	Unmet need for family planning	Women married by age 18	Prevalence of female genital mutilation/cutting among girls and women	Intimate partner	Nonintimate partner					
				(% of married or in-union women of reproductive age, 15–49 years)		(% of women ages 20–24 who are married or in union)	(% of girls and women ages 15–49)	(% of female population ages 15 and older)					(% of female population ages 15 and older)	
		(%)	(%)							(%)	(%)	(%)		(days)
	HDI RANK	2009–2019[b]	2014–2019[b]	2009–2019[b]	2009–2019[b]	2005–2019[b]	2004–2018[b]	2005–2019[b]	2005–2019[b]	2009–2019[b]	2009–2019[b]	2009–2019[b]	2017	2019
159	Uganda	97.3	74.2	41.8	26.0	34	0.3	49.9	..	..	..	25.5	52.7	84
160	Rwanda	97.6	90.7	53.2	18.9	7	..	37.1	..	12.1	35.4	33.2	45.0	84
161	Nigeria	67.0	43.3	27.6	23.1	43	19.5	17.4	1.5	..	..	28.9	27.3	84
162	Côte d'Ivoire	93.2	73.6	23.3	26.5	27	36.7	25.9	..	..	..	22.2	35.6	98
163	Tanzania (United Republic of)	98.0	63.5	38.4	22.1	31	10.0	46.2	..	..	..	17.3	42.2	84
164	Madagascar	85.1	46.0	44.3	16.4	40	..	..	..	14.9	31.0	24.5	16.3	98
165	Lesotho	91.3	86.6	64.9	16.0	16	..	..	..	6.4	24.8	..	46.5	84
166	Djibouti	87.7	..	19.0	..	5	94.4	..	..	..	..	..	8.8[c]	98
167	Togo	77.9	69.4	23.9	34.0	25	3.1	25.1	..	..	..	29.5	37.6	98
168	Senegal	97.1	74.2	27.8	21.9	29	24.0	21.5	..	..	..	..	38.4	98
169	Afghanistan	65.2	58.8	18.9	24.5	28	..	50.8	..	..	..	4.3	7.2	90
170	Haiti	91.0	41.6	34.3	38.0	15	..	26.0	..	..	..	..	30.0	42
170	Sudan	79.1	77.7	12.2	26.6	34	86.6	..	..	27.8	47.2	..	10.0[e]	56
172	Gambia	99.0	82.7	16.8	26.5	26	75.7	20.1	..	53.1	45.7	33.7	..	180
173	Ethiopia	73.6	27.7	40.1	20.6	40	65.2	28.0	..	..	17.3	21.1	29.1	90
174	Malawi	97.6	89.8	59.2	18.7	42	..	37.5	..	..	..	..	29.8	56
175	Congo (Democratic Republic of the)	88.4	80.1	20.4	27.7	37	..	50.7	..	11.0	25.1	..	24.2	98
175	Guinea-Bissau	92.4	45.0	16.0	22.3	24	44.9	..	..	..	..	..	..	60
175	Liberia	95.9	..	31.2	31.1	36	44.4	38.5	2.6	..	..	20.1	28.2	98
178	Guinea	80.9	55.3	10.9	17.7	47	94.5	..	..	..	..	..	19.7	98
179	Yemen	64.4	..	33.5	28.7	32	18.5	..	..	..	..	..	1.7[e]	70
180	Eritrea	88.5	..	8.4	27.4	41	83.0	..	..	21.8	27.8	..	..	60
181	Mozambique	87.2	73.0	27.1	23.1	53	..	21.7	..	5.6	29.3	22.2	32.9	60
182	Burkina Faso	92.8	79.8	32.5	23.3	52	75.8	11.5	..	10.1	20.6	24.0	34.5	98
182	Sierra Leone	97.9	86.9	21.2	24.8	30	86.1	48.8	..	..	..	..	15.4	84
184	Mali	79.5	67.3	17.2	23.9	54	88.6	35.5	..	..	..	..	25.7	98
185	Burundi	99.2	85.1	28.5	29.7	19	..	48.5	..	10.4	18.2	..	6.7[e]	84
185	South Sudan	61.9	..	4.0	26.3	52	..	..	..	..	..	..	4.7	90
187	Chad	54.7	24.3	5.7	22.9	67	38.4	28.6	..	..	..	..	14.9	98
188	Central African Republic	68.2	..	15.2	27.0	68	24.2	29.8	..	..	..	..	9.7	98
189	Niger	82.8	39.1	11.0	15.0	76	2.0	..	..	5.8	18.0	21.6	10.9	98
Other countries or territories														
..	Korea (Democratic People's Rep. of)	99.5	99.5	70.2	6.6	..	..	..	..	22.2	19.3	..	..	..
..	Monaco	..	..	..	..	..	..	..	..	..	..	..	..	..
..	Nauru	..	..	..	..	27	..	48.1	47.3	..	..	..	..	..
..	San Marino	..	..	..	..	..	..	..	..	9.7	36.0	..	..	630
..	Somalia	..	..	..	..	45	97.9	..	..	..	..	..	33.7[e]	98
..	Tuvalu	..	..	..	..	10	..	36.8	..	..	..	36.7	..	..
Human development groups														
	Very high human development	..	98.9	68.0	..	..	..	..	..	13.4	33.2	36.7	86.4	117
	High human development	97.9	97.7	75.2	..	..	..	..	..	..	..	..	64.2	118
	Medium human development	81.6	76.1	51.7	14.4	28	..	30.5	..	25.2	42.1	13.8	59.3	94
	Low human development	80.2	57.6	28.8	23.8	39	37.1	31.6	..	..	..	..	26.3	88
Developing countries		89.6	84.8	59.9	15.3	27	..	..	..	..	..	..	58.1	101
Regions														
	Arab States	87.0	91.7	47.5	16.1	20	..	..	..	19.6	48.1	..	26.9	75
	East Asia and the Pacific	98.0	96.5	76.2	..	..	..	..	..	..	..	..	..	95
	Europe and Central Asia	97.5	99.0	61.3	11.5	11	..	27.9	..	14.4	32.2	..	53.4	165
	Latin America and the Caribbean	97.2	95.1	75.7	..	25	..	23.8	..	12.0	34.5	..	52.0	97
	South Asia	80.5	77.7	52.8	13.3	29	..	31.0	..	..	41.1	13.4	64.9	118
	Sub-Saharan Africa	84.1	61.3	33.6	22.5	36	30.7	31.4	..	..	..	..	35.9	91
Least developed countries		82.1	59.7	38.0	21.4	40	..	38.3	..	..	..	..	28.3	88
Small island developing states		91.8	80.1	51.0	21.2	24	..	..	..	..	..	..	..	82
Organisation for Economic Co-operation and Development		..	98.7	71.2	..	..	..	..	..	12.9	32.6	36.7	84.6	122
World		89.6	86.7	61.2	..	..	..	..	..	..	..	..	64.5	110

Notes

Three-colour coding is used to visualize partial grouping of countries and aggregates by indicator. For each indicator countries are divided into three groups of approximately equal size (terciles): the top third, the middle third and the bottom third. Aggregates are colour coded using the same tercile cutoffs. See *Technical note 6* at http://hdr.undp.org/sites/default/files/hdr2020_technical_notes.pdf for details about partial grouping in this table.

a	Data collection methods, age ranges, sampled women (ever-partnered, ever-married or all women) and definitions of perpetrators and forms of violence vary by survey. Thus data are not necessarily comparable across countries.
b	Data refer to the most recent year available during the period specified.
c	Refers to 2011.
d	Refers to 2003.
e	Refers to 2014.

Definitions

Antenatal care coverage, at least one visit: Percentage of women ages 15–49 attended at least once during pregnancy by skilled health personnel (doctor, nurse or midwife).

Proportion of births attended by skilled health personnel: Percentage of childbirths attended by skilled health personnel (generally doctors, nurses or midwives) who are maternal and newborn health professionals educated, trained and regulated to national and international standards. They are competent to provide and promote evidence-based, human rights–based, quality, socioculturally sensitive and dignified care to women and newborns; facilitate physiological processes during labour and delivery to ensure a clean and positive childbirth experience; and identify and manage or refer women and/or newborns with complications. Traditional birth attendants, even if they receive a short training course, are not included.

Contraceptive prevalence, any method: Percentage of married or in-union women of reproductive age (15–49 years) currently using any contraceptive method.

Unmet need for family planning: Percentage of married or in-union women of reproductive age (15–49 years) who are fecund have an unmet need if they want to have no (more) births, or if they want to postpone or are undecided about the timing of their next birth, yet they are not using any method of contraception.

Child marriage, women married by age 18: Percentage of women ages 20–24 who were first married or in union before age 18.

Prevalence of female genital mutilation/cutting among girls and women: Percentage of girls and women ages 15–49 who have undergone female genital mutilation/cutting.

Violence against women ever experienced, intimate partner: Percentage of the female population ages 15 and older that has ever experienced physical and/or sexual violence from an intimate partner.

Violence against women ever experienced, nonintimate partner: Percentage of the female population ages 15 and older that has ever experienced sexual violence from a nonintimate partner.

Share of graduates in science, technology, engineering and mathematics programmes at tertiary level, female: Share of female tertiary graduates in science, technology, engineering and mathematics programmes among all female tertiary graduates.

Share of graduates from science, technology, engineering and mathematics programmes in tertiary education who are female: Share of female graduates among all graduates of tertiary programmes in science, technology, engineering and mathematics.

Female share of employment in senior and middle management: Proportion of women in total employment in senior and middle management.

Women with account at financial institution or with mobile money-service provider: Percentage of women ages 15 and older who report having an account alone or jointly with someone else at a bank or other type of financial institution or who report personally using a mobile money service in the past 12 months.

Mandatory paid maternity leave: The mandatory minimum number of calendar days that legally must be paid by the government, the employer or both. It refers to leave related to the birth of a child that is available only to the mother; it does not cover parental leave that is available to both parents.

Main data sources

Column 1: UNICEF (2020a).

Columns 2, 5 and 6: United Nations Statistics Division (2020a).

Columns 3 and 4: UNDESA (2020).

Columns 7 and 8: UN Women (2019).

Columns 9 and 10: UNESCO Institute for Statistics (2020).

Column 11: ILO (2020).

Columns 12 and 13: World Bank (2020b).

Environmental sustainability

Country groupings (terciles): Top third   Middle third   Bottom third

Three-colour coding is used to visualize partial grouping of countries by indicator. For each indicator countries are divided into three groups of approximately equal size (terciles): the top third, the middle third and the bottom third. Aggregates are colour coded using the same tercile cutoffs. See *Notes* after the table.

		SDG 12.c	SDG 9.4	SDG 9.4	SDG 15.1		SDG 6.4			SDG 8.4, 12.2	SDG 3.9	SDG 3.9	SDG 1.5, 11.5, 13.1	SDG 15.3	SDG 15.5
			Carbon dioxide emissions					Use of fertilizer nutrient per area of cropland				Environmental threats			
											Mortality rate attributed to		Number of deaths and missing persons attributed to disasters		
		Fossil fuel energy consumption	Production emissions per capita	Per unit of GDP	Forest area		Fresh water withdrawals	Nitrogen (N)	Phosphorus (expressed as P₂O₅)	Domestic material consumption per capita	Household and ambient air pollution	Unsafe water, sanitation and hygiene services		Degraded land	Red List Index
		(% of total energy consumption)	(tonnes)	(kg per 2010 US$ of GDP)	(% of total land area)	Change (%)	(% of total renewable water resources)	(kg per hectare)		(tonnes)	(per 100 000 population, age standardized)	(per 100,000 population)	(per 100,000 population)	(% of total land area)	(value)
	HDI RANK	2013-2015[b]	2018	2017	2016	1990/2016	2007-2017[b]	2018	2018	2017	2016	2016	2009-2019[b]	2015	2019
	Very high human development														
1	Norway	57.0	8.3	0.11	33.2	-0.1	0.8	127.0	25.3	21.8	9	0.2	4.4	..	0.939
2	Ireland	85.3	8.1	0.11	11.0	63.4	1.5			13.5	12	0.1	0.1	..	0.915
2	Switzerland	50.2	4.3	0.08	31.8	9.3	3.8	105.2	33.5	13.7	10	0.1	3.7	..	0.975
4	Hong Kong, China (SAR)	93.2	5.9	0.11	..	..	..	..	..	..	..	..	..	..	0.831
4	Iceland	11.3	10.8	0.13	0.5	213.7	0.2	97.1	16.9	14.9	9	0.1		..	0.863
6	Germany	78.9	9.1	0.20	32.7	1.0	15.9	112.5	16.9	14.7	16	0.6		..	0.984
7	Sweden	25.1	4.1	0.08	68.9	0.8	1.4	72.1	12.8	16.9	7	0.2	0.0	..	0.992
8	Australia	89.6	16.9	0.34	16.3	-2.8	3.2	45.1	30.5	37.9	8	0.1	0.0	..	0.821
8	Netherlands	93.5	9.5	0.19	11.2	9.4	8.8	..	..	13.7	14	0.2		..	0.940
10	Denmark	64.9	6.1	0.12	14.7	14.7	12.4	79.3	12.2	15.7	13	0.3		..	0.972
11	Finland	40.2	8.5	0.19	73.1	1.8	..	61.6	11.3	24.7	7	0.1[c]	0.1	1	0.990
11	Singapore	90.6	7.1	0.10	23.1	-5.5	83.2	..	..	32.6	26	0.1		..	0.853
13	United Kingdom	80.4	5.6	0.14	13.1	13.8	5.7	169.8	30.9	7.8	14	0.2	0.1	..	0.781
14	Belgium	75.9	8.7	0.19	22.6	..	21.8	195.0	21.3	16.1	16	0.3	..	11	0.986
14	New Zealand	59.7	7.3	0.19	38.6	5.1	3.0	..	..	24.2	7	0.1	0.0	..	0.623
16	Canada	74.1	15.3	0.35	38.2	-0.4	1.2	71.3	29.1	28.8	7	0.4	..	..	0.964
17	United States	82.4	16.6	0.27	33.9	2.7	14.5	72.6	25.4	20.3	13	0.2	1.2	..	0.833
18	Austria	65.7	7.7	0.17	46.9	2.6	4.5	82.0	22.4	15.8	15	0.1	0.0	..	0.894
19	Israel	97.4	7.7	0.23	7.7	26.7	67.3	103.9	12.6	13.0	15	0.2		..	0.723
19	Japan	93.0	9.1	0.23	68.5	0.0	18.9	88.0	80.3	9.0	12	0.2	0.4	..	0.776
19	Liechtenstein	..	4.0	..	43.1	6.2	..	..	..	..	..	..	..	..	0.993
22	Slovenia	61.1	6.9	0.21	62.0	5.1	2.9	115.8	38.7	13.4	23	0.1[c]	1.1	5	0.930
23	Korea (Republic of)	81.0	12.9	0.32	63.4	-4.1	..	135.4	90.0	15.9	20	1.8	0.3	..	0.702
23	Luxembourg	80.6	15.9	0.17	35.7	..	1.3	204.8	14.3	28.5	12	0.1[c]		4	0.987
25	Spain	73.0	5.7	0.16	36.9	33.6	28.0	61.6	25.4	11.9	10	0.2	0.1	18	0.854
26	France	46.5	5.2	0.12	31.2	18.5	12.5	117.5	22.5	11.9	10	0.3	2.4	12	0.872
27	Czechia	77.7	9.9	0.30	34.6	1.6	12.4	138.9	20.3	16.9	30	0.2	0.0	6	0.971
28	Malta	97.8	3.6	0.09	1.1	0.0	85.2	125.1	8.9	15.5	20	0.1[c]	..	..	0.884
29	Estonia	13.1	14.8	0.43	51.3	-1.4	13.9	56.2	13.4	35.0	25	0.1[c]	0.8	..	0.985
29	Italy	79.9	5.6	0.16	31.8	23.2	17.9	65.7	17.5	10.8	15	0.2	0.1	13	0.899
31	United Arab Emirates	86.1	21.3	0.32	4.6	32.1	1,708.0	185.3	50.8	22.5	55	0.1[c]	..	1	0.857
32	Greece	82.6	7.0	0.24	31.7	23.8	16.4	55.7	18.4	10.0	28	0.1[c]	..	16	0.845
33	Cyprus	92.9	6.3	0.23	18.7	7.2	27.7	60.1	40.1	19.5	20	0.3	1.4	19	0.982
34	Lithuania	68.0	4.8	0.14	34.8	12.3	1.1	74.1	23.9	15.3	34	0.1	..	3	0.989
35	Poland	90.3	9.1	0.30	30.9	6.5	16.7	96.0	29.4	18.5	38	0.1	..	5	0.972
36	Andorra	..	6.1	..	34.0	0.0	..	..	..	..	..	..	..	..	0.916
37	Latvia	56.7	3.7	0.14	54.0	5.8	0.5	57.2	20.2	17.0	41	0.1[c]	..	13	0.988
38	Portugal	77.0	5.0	0.18	34.6	-7.8	11.8	59.2	28.1	10.0	10	0.2	..	32	0.870
39	Slovakia	64.1	6.6	0.20	40.4	1.0	1.1	94.5	18.8	10.7	34	0.1[c]	..	4	0.961
40	Hungary	69.5	5.1	0.18	22.9	14.3	4.3	94.2	26.0	16.9	39	0.2	..	13	0.875
40	Saudi Arabia	99.9	18.4	0.34	0.5	0.0	883.3	47.8	26.3	25.0	84	0.1	..	4	0.907
42	Bahrain	99.4	19.8	0.47	0.8	145.9	132.2	..	..	28.6	40	0.1[c]	..	..	0.751
43	Chile	74.6	4.6	0.22	24.3	18.2	..	157.1	47.2	41.8	25	0.2	0.3	1	0.763
43	Croatia	70.7	4.5	0.18	34.4	3.8	0.6	113.5	40.7	10.1	35	0.1	0.6	..	0.897
45	Qatar	100.0	38.0	0.26	0.0	0.0	432.4	82.4	29.4	52.5	47	0.1[c]	..	6	0.821
46	Argentina	87.7	4.4	0.22	9.8	-22.9	4.3	28.8	17.1	16.1	27	0.4	0.0	39	0.849
47	Brunei Darussalam	100.0	18.5	0.22	72.1	-8.0	..	..	..	22.9	13	0.1[c]	..	..	0.861
48	Montenegro	64.7	3.2	0.22	61.5	32.1	..	..	..	13.4	79	0.1[c]	0.5	6	0.806
49	Romania	72.5	3.8	0.16	30.1	8.4	3.2	37.7	13.8	11.7	59	0.4	6.3	2	0.930

Continued →

	SDG 12.c	SDG 9.4	SDG 9.4	SDG 15.1		SDG 6.4	\multicolumn{2}{c	}{Use of fertilizer nutrient per area of cropland}	SDG 8.4, 12.2	SDG 3.9	SDG 3.9	SDG 1.5, 11.5, 13.1	SDG 15.3	SDG 15.5
		\multicolumn{2}{c	}{Carbon dioxide emissions}							\multicolumn{3}{c	}{Environmental threats}		
										\multicolumn{2}{c	}{Mortality rate attributed to}			
	Fossil fuel energy consumption	Production emissions per capita	Per unit of GDP	\multicolumn{2}{c	}{Forest area}	Fresh water withdrawals	Nitrogen (N)	Phosphorus (expressed as P_2O_5)	Domestic material consumption per capita	Household and ambient air pollution	Unsafe water, sanitation and hygiene services	Number of deaths and missing persons attributed to disasters	Degraded land	Red List Index
	(% of total energy consumption)	(tonnes)	(kg per 2010 US$ of GDP)	(% of total land area[a])	Change (%)	(% of total renewable water resources)	\multicolumn{2}{c	}{(kg per hectare)}	(tonnes)	(per 100 000 population, age standardized)	(per 100,000 population)	(per 100,000 population)	(% of total land area)	(value)
HDI RANK	2013-2015[b]	2018	2017	2016	1990/2016	2007-2017[b]	2018	2018	2017	2016	2016	2009-2019[b]	2015	2019
50 Palau	..	13.2	..	87.6	..	..	..	..	1.2	..	..	..	..	0.727
51 Kazakhstan	99.2	17.6	0.60	1.2	-3.3	20.7	3.5	4.1	29.1	63	0.4	0.0	36	0.867
52 Russian Federation	92.1	11.7	0.48	49.8	0.8	1.4	12.5	4.9	16.9	49	0.1	0.4	6	0.954
53 Belarus	92.4	6.9	0.34	42.6	11.1	2.4	69.5	18.0	17.5	61	0.1	..	1	0.970
54 Turkey	86.8	5.2	0.19	15.4	22.8	27.8	65.9	22.5	18.7	47	0.3	0.1	9	0.876
55 Uruguay	46.3	2.0	0.08	10.7	134.1	..	85.8	75.9	37.6	18	0.4	0.1	26	0.855
56 Bulgaria	71.0	6.3	0.33	35.4	17.6	26.6	92.1	19.2	7.6	26	0.1	0.0	14	0.941
57 Panama	80.7	2.6	0.11	61.9	-8.7	0.9	15.5	9.9	7.6	20	1.9	0.6	..	0.746
58 Bahamas	..	4.7	..	51.4	0.0	..	55.2	32.6	3.0	20	0.1	..	..	0.702
58 Barbados	..	4.5	..	14.7	0.0	..	28.8	20.9	2.3	31	0.2	1.4	..	0.898
60 Oman	100.0	13.9	0.38	0.0	0.0	116.7	93.9	28.3	31.7	54	0.1[c]	0.0	7	0.891
61 Georgia	72.2	2.6	0.25	40.6	2.6	2.9	95.9	8.4	6.8	102	0.2	0.2	6	0.871
62 Costa Rica	49.9	1.6	0.10	54.6	8.7	2.8	165.2	28.7	8.6	23	0.9	0.1	9	0.831
62 Malaysia	96.6	8.1	0.25	67.6	-0.7	1.2	46.2	36.8	19.3	47	0.4	0.0	16	0.769
64 Kuwait	93.7	23.7	0.34	0.4	81.2	..	..	..	29.6	104	0.1[c]	0.0	64	0.838
64 Serbia	83.9	5.2	0.49	31.1	9.9	3.3	41.7	7.9	11.8	62	0.7	0.0	6	0.957
66 Mauritius	84.5	3.8	0.17	19.0	-6.0	22.2	93.8	30.8	11.6	38	0.6	0.8	27	0.413
High human development														
67 Seychelles	..	6.7	..	88.4	0.0	..	30.2	7.6	2.3	49	0.2	1.0	12	0.686
67 Trinidad and Tobago	99.9	31.3	0.47	46.0	-1.9	8.8	138.3	10.6	19.9	39	0.1	0.1	..	0.806
69 Albania	61.4	1.6	0.13	28.1	-2.3	3.9	35.6	19.2	10.1	68	0.2	0.1	8	0.838
70 Cuba	85.6	2.5	0.11	31.3	63.2	18.3	15.0	6.6	7.7	50	1.0	..	..	0.663
70 Iran (Islamic Republic of)	99.0	8.8	0.38	6.6	17.8	..	34.3	6.0	14.8	51	1.0	0.0	23	0.842
72 Sri Lanka	50.5	1.1	0.09	32.9	-9.7	..	29.0	17.3	5.6	80	1.2	0.5	36	0.574
73 Bosnia and Herzegovina	77.5	6.5	0.57	42.7	-1.1	1.1	61.5	7.0	14.0	80	0.1	..	4	0.901
74 Grenada	..	2.4	..	50.0	0.0	7.1	..	..	1.0	45	0.3	..	..	0.675
74 Mexico	90.4	3.8	0.21	33.9	-5.5	19.0	50.1	31.1	10.0	37	1.1	0.5	47	0.677
74 Saint Kitts and Nevis	..	4.6	..	42.3	0.0	51.3	..	..	..	..	..	3.9	..	0.734
74 Ukraine	75.3	5.1	0.52	16.7	4.4	4.9	41.6	12.2	12.5	71	0.3	0.0	25	0.934
78 Antigua and Barbuda	..	5.9	..	22.3	-4.9	8.5	1.7	0.5	2.8	30	0.1	3.2	..	0.890
79 Peru	79.6	1.7	0.13	57.7	-5.3	0.9	51.2	15.6	15.4	64	1.3	0.5	..	0.729
79 Thailand	79.8	4.2	0.22	32.2	17.3	13.1	71.1	17.3	12.7	61	3.5	0.1	21	0.783
81 Armenia	74.6	1.9	0.20	11.7	-0.8	36.9	178.5	0.1	11.1	55	0.2	14.4	2	0.845
82 North Macedonia	79.4	3.5	0.27	39.6	10.3	8.2	39.0	9.0	14.5	82	0.1	..	..	0.970
83 Colombia	76.7	2.0	0.12	52.7	-9.2	0.5	57.1	19.9	6.8	37	0.8	0.8	7	0.749
84 Brazil	59.1	2.2	0.15	58.9	-9.9	0.8	80.6	80.3	17.4	30	1.0	0.1	27	0.900
85 China	87.7	7.0	0.45	22.4	33.6	20.9	208.5	58.0	25.0	113	0.6	0.0	27	0.743
86 Ecuador	86.9	2.5	0.20	50.2	-5.0	..	87.7	16.8	9.3	25	0.6	0.0	30	0.660
86 Saint Lucia	..	2.3	..	33.2	-7.2	14.3	13.2	13.6	..	30	0.6	2.8	..	0.838
88 Azerbaijan	98.4	3.7	0.20	14.1	37.7	36.9	50.6	0.0	9.2	64	1.1	..	..	0.910
88 Dominican Republic	86.6	2.3	0.14	41.7	82.5	30.4	72.8	24.3	5.8	43	2.2	..	..	0.733
90 Moldova (Republic of)	88.7	1.3	0.42	12.6	29.6	6.9	33.3	12.5	8.8	78	0.1	..	29	0.968
91 Algeria	100.0	3.7	0.23	0.8	17.8	84.0	8.2	6.9	9.0	50	1.9	0.0	1	0.908
92 Lebanon	97.6	3.5	0.34	13.4	4.9	40.2	65.6	47.3	10.0	51	0.8	0.2	..	0.919
93 Fiji	..	2.4	..	55.9	7.3	..	12.0	6.3	6.5	99	2.9	0.2	..	0.668
94 Dominica	..	2.5	..	57.4	-13.9	10.0	2.2	1.8	4.6	..	..	2.8	..	0.675
95 Maldives	..	3.0	..	3.3	0.0	15.7	58.9	3.2	6.8	26	0.3	0.2	..	0.850
95 Tunisia	88.9	2.7	0.21	6.8	63.5	103.3	14.4	7.5	9.3	56	1.0	0.2	13	0.974
97 Saint Vincent and the Grenadines	..	2.0	..	69.2	8.0	7.9	..	..	..	48	1.3	11.0	..	0.767
97 Suriname	76.3	3.1	0.25	98.3	-0.7	..	102.7	9.0	13.5	57	2.0	..	21	0.983
99 Mongolia	93.2	8.9	0.54	8.0	-0.6	1.3	30.4	0.6	34.5	156	1.3	6.3	13	0.950
100 Botswana	74.7	3.0	0.22	18.9	-21.7	1.6	80.9	4.3	29.5	101	11.8	0.0	51	0.974
101 Jamaica	81.0	2.8	0.30	30.9	-2.8	12.5	17.2	7.6	6.5	25	0.6	0.0	..	0.666
102 Jordan	97.6	2.4	0.32	1.1	-0.6	96.4	71.2	5.8	7.6	51	0.6	0.1	4	0.965
103 Paraguay	33.7	1.1	0.10	37.7	-29.1	0.6	27.6	46.0	12.5	57	1.5	0.1	52	0.950
104 Tonga	..	1.3	..	12.5	0.0	..	2.1	1.6	16.9	73	1.4	1.0	..	0.724

Continued →

	SDG 12.c	SDG 9.4	SDG 9.4	SDG 15.1		SDG 6.4	Use of fertilizer nutrient per area of cropland		SDG 8.4, 12.2	SDG 3.9	SDG 3.9	SDG 1.5, 11.5, 13.1	SDG 15.3	SDG 15.5
		Carbon dioxide emissions								Mortality rate attributed to		Environmental threats		
	Fossil fuel energy consumption	Production emissions per capita	Per unit of GDP	Forest area		Fresh water withdrawals	Nitrogen (N)	Phosphorus (expressed as P$_2$O$_5$)	Domestic material consumption per capita	Household and ambient air pollution	Unsafe water, sanitation and hygiene services	Number of deaths and missing persons attributed to disasters	Degraded land	Red List Index
	(% of total energy consumption)	(tonnes)	(kg per 2010 US$ of GDP)	(% of total land area[a])	Change (%)	(% of total renewable water resources)	(kg per hectare)		(tonnes)	(per 100 000 population, age standardized)	(per 100,000 population)	(per 100,000 population)	(% of total land area)	(value)
HDI RANK	2013-2015[b]	2018	2017	2016	1990/2016	2007-2017[b]	2018	2018	2017	2016	2016	2009-2019[b]	2015	2019
105 Libya	99.1	8.1	0.37	0.1	0.0	822.9	7.2	0.9	11.0	72	0.6	..		0.972
106 Uzbekistan	97.7	2.8	0.41	7.5	5.4	120.5	161.6	50.6	9.1	81	0.4		29	0.969
107 Bolivia (Plurinational State of)	84.2	2.0	0.29	50.3	-13.2	0.4	3.0	2.7	13.0	64	5.6	0.3	18	0.871
107 Indonesia	66.1	2.3	0.17	49.9	-23.8	11.0	63.1	15.9	7.5	112	7.1	0.2	21	0.751
107 Philippines	62.4	1.3	0.16	27.8	26.3	19.4	59.4	12.2	4.0	185	4.2	0.2	38	0.676
110 Belize	..	1.5	..	59.7	-15.8		87.7	55.4	11.5	69	1.0	0.3	81	0.845
111 Samoa	..	1.3	..	60.4	31.5		0.2	0.2	5.3	85	1.5	0.5	..	0.767
111 Turkmenistan	13.7	..	0.75	8.8	0.0		..	..	16.5	79	4.0		22	0.977
113 Venezuela (Bolivarian Republic of)	88.4	4.8	0.33	52.7	-10.6	1.7	79.0	27.9	6.7	35	1.4	0.1	15	0.828
114 South Africa	86.8	8.1	0.62	7.6	0.0	37.7	37.9	21.6	11.3	87	13.7	0.5	78	0.776
115 Palestine, State of	..	0.7	..	1.5	1.0	34.4	..	..				0.0	15	0.921
116 Egypt	97.9	2.4	0.21	0.1	67.3	112.0	342.3	68.9	7.9	109	2.0	3.2	1	0.914
117 Marshall Islands	..	2.6	..	70.2	..		..	..	2.0					0.838
117 Viet Nam	69.8	2.2	0.33	48.1	67.1		136.5	65.1	14.7	64	1.6	0.1	31	0.728
119 Gabon	22.8	2.5	0.10	90.0	5.5		12.6	7.4	6.0	76	20.6	..	16	0.956
Medium human development														
120 Kyrgyzstan	75.5	1.6	0.43	3.3	-24.8		18.3	1.6	8.4	111	0.8	0.3	24	0.985
121 Morocco	88.5	1.8	0.22	12.6	13.5	35.7	27.4	17.5	7.9	49	1.9	0.2	19	0.889
122 Guyana	..	3.1	..	83.9	-0.9	0.5	42.2	9.7	24.5	108	3.6	0.4	16	0.880
123 Iraq	96.0	5.3	0.24	1.9	3.4	42.9	34.5	12.5	6.3	75	3.0	20.9	26	0.793
124 El Salvador	48.4	1.1	0.13	12.6	-30.9		64.2	14.4	5.3	42	2.0	0.1	16	0.832
125 Tajikistan	46.0	0.6	0.23	3.0	1.9		9.3	3.9	3.5	129	2.7	0.1	97	0.990
126 Cabo Verde	..	1.2	..	22.5	57.3		..	..	6.9	99	4.1	0.2	17	0.904
127 Guatemala	37.4	1.1	0.13	32.7	-26.2		84.5	25.8	6.6	74	6.3	0.6	24	0.730
128 Nicaragua	40.7	0.9	0.16	25.9	-31.0	0.9	27.0	7.7	6.7	56	2.2	0.6	..	0.851
129 Bhutan	..	1.6	..	72.5	35.1	0.4	28.2	3.5	10.4	124	3.9	3.7	10	0.798
130 Namibia	66.7	1.7	0.17	8.3	-21.9		25.1	1.2	11.2	145	18.3	35.9	19	0.969
131 India	73.6	2.0	0.26	23.8	10.8	33.9	104.1	41.1	5.5	184	18.6	..	30	0.676
132 Honduras	52.5	1.0	0.23	40.0	-45.0		69.0	21.7	5.2	61	3.6	5.3	..	0.765
133 Bangladesh	73.8	0.5	0.14	11.0	-4.5	2.9	154.7	82.6	2.7	149	11.9	0.2	65	0.752
134 Kiribati	..	0.6	..	15.0	0.0		..	..	6.3	140	16.7			0.772
135 Sao Tome and Principe	..	0.6	..	55.8	-4.3	1.9	..	..	3.2	162	11.4	..		0.799
136 Micronesia (Federated States of)	..	1.3	..	91.9	..		..	..	2.3	152	3.6	9.2		0.697
137 Lao People's Democratic Republic	..	2.7	..	82.1	7.4		..	..	12.0	188	11.3	0.8		0.830
138 Eswatini (Kingdom of)	..	1.1	..	34.3	25.1		..	..	9.4	137	27.9	2.0	13	0.812
138 Ghana	52.5	0.6	0.12	41.2	8.6		7.5	5.5	7.0	204	18.8	0.5	14	0.847
140 Vanuatu	..	0.5	..	36.1	0.0		..	..	6.1	136	10.4	4.1		0.661
141 Timor-Leste	..	0.4	..	45.4	-30.1		..	..	7.7	140	9.9	0.2		0.854
142 Nepal	15.5	0.3	0.14	25.4	-24.7		54.7	20.9	3.9	194	19.8	1.9		0.831
143 Kenya	17.4	0.4	0.11	7.8	-5.8	13.1	9.5	2.3	3.2	78	51.2	1.8	40	0.798
144 Cambodia	30.6	0.6	0.19	52.9	-27.9		31.4	0.9	5.3	150	6.5	0.3	33	0.790
145 Equatorial Guinea	..	4.3	..	55.5	-16.3		..	..	19.2	178	22.3	1.3	19	0.822
146 Zambia	10.6	0.3	0.10	65.2	-8.2		38.6	9.6	8.4	127	34.9	0.1	7	0.875
147 Myanmar	44.3	0.6	0.10	43.6	-27.3		21.6	11.7	3.5	156	12.6	1.0	23	0.800
148 Angola	48.3	1.1	0.10	46.3	-5.3		4.2	1.2	4.9	119	48.8	0.9	20	0.932
149 Congo	40.5	0.6	0.11	65.4	-1.8		0.5	0.7	3.5	131	38.7	..	10	0.966
150 Zimbabwe	29.1	0.8	0.27	35.5	-38.0	16.7	15.9	11.8	3.4	133	24.6	2.3	36	0.792
151 Solomon Islands	..	0.3	..	77.9	-6.2		..	..	7.1	137	6.2	3.7		0.762
151 Syrian Arab Republic	97.8	1.7	0.79	2.7	32.1		0.9	0.6	10.6	75	3.7	0.2		0.940
153 Cameroon	38.3	0.3	0.08	39.3	-23.5		6.0	1.2	4.2	208	45.2	3.9	0	0.840
154 Pakistan	61.6	1.1	0.19	1.9	-43.5	81.0	110.1	40.2	4.4	174	19.6	0.1	5	0.859
155 Papua New Guinea	..	0.9	..	74.1	-0.2		31.7	2.9	10.2	152	16.3	0.4	21	0.836
156 Comoros	..	0.3	..	19.7	-25.3		..	..	3.5	172	50.7	0.7	22	0.745
Low human development														
157 Mauritania	..	0.6	..	0.2	-46.7		..	..	7.4	169	38.6	..	3	0.975
158 Benin	36.7	0.6	0.30	37.8	-26.0		14.1	8.1	5.2	205	59.7	..	53	0.910

Continued →

	SDG 12.c	SDG 9.4	SDG 9.4	SDG 15.1		SDG 6.4	SDG 8.4, 12.2			SDG 3.9	SDG 3.9	SDG 1.5, 11.5, 13.1	SDG 15.3	SDG 15.5
		Carbon dioxide emissions					Use of fertilizer nutrient per area of cropland			Environmental threats				
										Mortality rate attributed to		Number of deaths and missing persons attributed to disasters		
	Fossil fuel energy consumption	Production emissions per capita	Per unit of GDP	Forest area	Change	Fresh water withdrawals	Nitrogen (N)	Phosphorus (expressed as P_2O_5)	Domestic material consumption per capita	Household and ambient air pollution	Unsafe water, sanitation and hygiene services	Number of deaths and missing persons attributed to disasters	Degraded land	Red List Index
	(% of total energy consumption)	(tonnes)	(kg per 2010 US$ of GDP)	(% of total land area[a])	(%)	(% of total renewable water resources)	(kg per hectare)		(tonnes)	(per 100 000 population, age standardized)	(per 100,000 population)	(per 100,000 population)	(% of total land area)	(value)
HDI RANK	2013–2015[b]	2018	2017	2016	1990/2016	2007–2017[b]	2018	2018	2017	2016	2016	2009–2019[b]	2015	2019
159 Uganda	..	0.1	..	9.7	-59.3	1.1	1.2	0.7	2.9	156	31.6	0.3	22	0.755
160 Rwanda	..	0.1	..	19.7	53.1	..	3.1	4.9	2.9	121	19.3	0.3	12	0.884
161 Nigeria	18.9	0.6	0.09	7.2	-61.8	4.4	10.9	2.9	3.5	307	68.6	..	32	0.856
162 Côte d'Ivoire	26.5	0.3	0.12	32.7	1.7	1.4	4.6	3.3	3.0	269	47.2	0.2	14	0.905
163 Tanzania (United Republic of)	14.4	0.2	0.07	51.6	-18.3	..	9.1	3.7	3.2	139	38.4	0.1	..	0.701
164 Madagascar	..	0.2	..	21.4	-9.1	..	8.0	1.3	2.4	160	30.2	0.4	30	0.761
165 Lesotho	..	1.3	..	1.6	25.0	..	..	..	11.7	178	44.4	..	20	0.945
166 Djibouti	..	0.7	..	0.2	0.0	..	..	..	2.9	159	31.3	3.2	..	0.810
167 Togo	17.8	0.4	0.18	3.1	-75.4	..	1.5	0.7	4.2	250	41.6	0.1	12	0.862
168 Senegal	53.9	0.7	0.17	42.8	-11.9	..	11.3	6.1	3.2	161	23.9	0.0	6	0.941
169 Afghanistan	..	0.3	..	2.1	0.0	..	5.9	1.6	1.9	211	13.9	1.2	8	0.837
170 Haiti	22.0	0.3	0.19	3.5	-17.1	10.3	..	..	1.6	184	23.8	..	..	0.719
170 Sudan	31.7	0.5	0.11	..	..	71.2	8.2	0.2	5.4	185	17.3	0.9	12	0.928
172 Gambia	..	0.3	..	48.4	10.8	..	4.5	1.6	2.5	237	29.7	10.4	14	0.967
173 Ethiopia	6.6	0.1	0.07	12.5	..	8.7	23.5	9.2	3.2	144	43.7	0.0	29	0.847
174 Malawi	..	0.1	..	33.2	-19.7	..	23.2	6.2	3.3	115	28.3	7.1	17	0.808
175 Congo (Democratic Republic of the)	5.4	0.0	0.03	67.2	-5.0	..	0.7	0.1	2.3	164	59.8	..	6	0.891
175 Guinea-Bissau	..	0.2	..	69.8	-11.5	..	..	..	3.9	215	35.3	0.1	15	0.908
175 Liberia	..	0.3	..	43.1	-15.8	..	..	..	3.1	170	41.5	0.9	29	0.905
178 Guinea	..	0.3	..	25.8	-12.9	..	2.5	0.0	3.8	243	44.6	0.5	11	0.896
179 Yemen	98.5	0.4	0.14	1.0	0.0	..	2.6	0.3	2.3	194	10.2	0.7	..	0.859
180 Eritrea	23.1	0.1	0.08	14.9	-7.1	..	6.7	0.1	7.0	174	45.6	..	35	0.893
181 Mozambique	12.6	0.3	0.23	48.0	-13.0	0.7	4.5	0.7	2.4	110	27.6	0.1	..	0.817
182 Burkina Faso	..	0.2	..	19.3	-22.7	..	9.3	3.8	4.4	206	49.6	0.0	19	0.988
182 Sierra Leone	..	0.1	..	43.1	-0.3	..	..	..	7.0	324	81.3	12.7	18	0.931
184 Mali	..	0.2	..	3.8	-30.7	..	15.7	5.3	5.8	209	70.7	0.1	3	0.981
185 Burundi	..	0.0	..	10.9	-2.9	..	8.7	6.3	1.8	180	65.4	5.5	29	0.892
185 South Sudan	72.2	0.2	0.41	..	..	1.3	..	..	0.9	165	63.3	2.7	..	0.930
187 Chad	..	0.1	..	3.8	-29.2	..	..	..	2.5	280	101.0	..	34	0.916
188 Central African Republic	..	0.1	..	35.6	-1.8	..	0.1	0.0	3.4	212	82.1	0.0	13	0.937
189 Niger	24.1	0.1	0.11	0.9	-41.9	5.1	0.4	0.4	3.4	252	70.8	2.2	7	0.936
Other countries or territories														
.. Korea (Democratic People's Rep. of)	62.1	1.2	0.19	40.7	-40.2	..	..	..	3.6	207	1.4	..	..	0.918
.. Monaco	..	..	..	..	..	..	..	..	..	..	..	..	..	0.758
.. Nauru	..	4.7	..	0.0	0.0	..	0.0	0.0	..	..	..	..	..	0.769
.. San Marino	..	..	..	0.0	0.0	..	..	..	..	..	..	..	..	0.991
.. Somalia	..	0.0	..	10.0	-24.1	..	..	..	2.7	213	86.6	..	23	0.905
.. Tuvalu	..	1.0	..	33.3	0.0	..	..	..	1.1	..	..	..	..	0.833
Human development groups														
Very high human development	82.3	10.4	0.24	33.0	1.2	6.1	55.5	20.0	17.2	25	0.3	0.7	..	–
High human development	84.8	5.1	0.34	31.6	-3.8	6.1	106.6	39.7	17.7	94	1.9	0.3	26	–
Medium human development	68.9	1.6	0.23	31.6	-8.7	..	82.4	32.8	5.3	168	18.6	..	23	–
Low human development	..	0.3	..	23.7	-13.1	..	8.7	2.8	3.3	205	47.6	..	16	–
Developing countries	80.5	3.4	0.31	27.1	-6.4	8.5	74.1	28.5	11.5	133	14.0	0.6	23	–
Regions														
Arab States	95.5	4.8	0.29	1.8	-1.9	77.3	35.4	10.9	9.9	101	7.0	3.5	7	–
East Asia and the Pacific	..	5.5	..	29.8	3.9	..	139.8	40.3	19.7	114	2.2	0.1	..	–
Europe and Central Asia	87.0	5.5	0.30	9.2	8.6	20.4	43.2	13.4	14.9	67	0.5	0.3	28	–
Latin America and the Caribbean	74.5	2.8	0.18	46.2	-9.6	1.5	57.3	43.4	13.3	40	1.7	0.4	28	–
South Asia	76.9	2.0	0.26	14.7	7.8	25.4	97.3	38.3	5.5	174	17.1	..	23	–
Sub-Saharan Africa	39.2	0.8	0.25	28.1	-11.9	..	11.1	4.4	4.1	187	47.8	1.2	22	–
Least developed countries	..	0.3	..	29.1	-11.3	..	17.6	7.3	3.4	167	34.3	0.8	16	–
Small island developing states	..	3.2	..	69.4	1.3	..	..	..	9.6	92	8.9	..	..	–
Organisation for Economic Co-operation and Development	79.6	9.5	0.23	32.0	1.0	7.3	74.7	26.4	15.7	20	0.4	0.7	..	–
World	80.6	4.6	0.26	31.2	-3.0	7.7	69.7	26.0	12.3	114	11.7	0.7	20	–

Notes

Three-colour coding is used to visualize partial grouping of countries and aggregates by indicator. For each indicator countries are divided into three groups of approximately equal size (terciles): the top third, the middle third and the bottom third. Aggregates are colour coded using the same tercile cutoffs. See *Technical note 6* at http://hdr.undp.org/sites/default/files/hdr2020_technical_notes.pdf for details about partial grouping in this table.

a   This column is intentionally left without colour because it is meant to provide context for the indicator on change in forest area.

b   Data refer to the most recent year available during the period specified.

c   Less than 0.1.

Definitions

Fossil fuel energy consumption: Percentage of total energy consumption that comes from fossil fuels, which consist of coal, oil, petroleum and natural gas products.

Carbon dioxide emissions, production emissions: Total carbon dioxide emissions produced as a consequence of human activities (use of coal, oil and gas for combustion and industrial processes, gas flaring and cement manufacture), divided by midyear population. Values are territorial emissions, meaning that emissions are attributed to the country in which they physically occur.

Carbon dioxide emissions, per unit of GDP: Human-originated carbon dioxide emissions stemming from the burning of fossil fuels, gas flaring and cement manufacture, expressed in kilograms per unit of gross domestic product (GDP) in constant 2010 US dollars. Carbon dioxide emitted by forest biomass through depletion of forest areas is included.

Forest area: Land spanning more than 0.5 hectare with trees taller than 5 metres and a canopy cover of more than 10 percent or trees able to reach these thresholds in situ. It excludes land predominantly under agricultural or urban land use, tree stands in agricultural production systems (for example, in fruit plantations and agroforestry systems) and trees in urban parks and gardens. Areas under reforestation that have not yet reached but are expected to reach a canopy cover of 10 percent and a tree height of 5 metres are included, as are temporarily unstocked areas resulting from human intervention or natural causes that are expected to regenerate.

Fresh water withdrawals: Total fresh water withdrawn, expressed as a percentage of total renewable water resources.

Use of fertilizer nutrient: Total agricultural use of fertilizer nutrient—nitrogen (N) or phosphorus (expressed as P_2O_5), expressed per area of cropland. Cropland is the sum of arable land and land under permanent crops.

Domestic material consumption per capita: The sum of direct imports of materials and domestic extraction of materials minus direct exports of materials, measured in tonnes, divided by midyear population. A territorial (production-side) indicator, domestic material consumption measures the total amount of materials used in economic processes. It excludes materials that are mobilized during domestic extraction but do not enter the economic process. Domestic material consumption per capita, also referred to as metabolic profile, is an environmental pressure indicator that describes the average level of material use in an economy.

Mortality rate attributed to household and ambient air pollution: Number of deaths attributable to the joint effects of household and ambient air pollution, expressed per 100,000 population. The rates are age standardized. The diseases taken into account are acute respiratory infections (estimated for all ages), cerebrovascular diseases (estimated for adults older than age 25), ischaemic heart diseases (estimated for adults older than age 25), chronic obstructive pulmonary disease (estimated for adults older than age 25) and lung cancer (estimated for adults older than age 25).

Mortality rate attributed to unsafe water, sanitation and hygiene services: Number of deaths due to diarrhoea, intestinal nematode infections and protein-energy malnutrition that are attributable to inadequate water, sanitation and hygiene services, expressed per 100,000 population.

Number of deaths and missing persons attributed to disasters: Number of people who died during or directly after a disaster as a direct result of the event or whose whereabouts are unknown since the event, expressed per 100,000 population. It includes people who are presumed dead, for whom there is no physical evidence such as a body and for whom an official or legal report has been filed with competent authorities.

Degraded land: Rain-fed cropland, irrigated cropland, or range, pasture, forest and woodlands that have experienced the reduction or loss of biological or economic productivity and complexity resulting from a combination of pressures, including land use and management practices, expressed as a percentage of total land area.

Red List Index: Measure of the aggregate extinction risk across groups of species. It is based on genuine changes in the number of species in each category of extinction risk on the International Union for Conservation of Nature Red List of Threatened Species. It ranges from 0, all species categorized as extinct, to 1, all species categorized as least concern.

Main data sources

Columns 1 and 4: World Bank (2020a).

Column 2: Global Carbon Project (2020).

Columns 3, 9 and 12–14: United Nations Statistics Division (2020a).

Column 5: HDRO calculations based on data on forest area from World Bank (2020a).

Column 6: FAO (2020c).

Columns 7 and 8: FAO (2020b).

Columns 10 and 11: WHO (2020).

Socioeconomic sustainability

Country groupings (terciles): [Top third] [Middle third] [Bottom third]

Three-colour coding is used to visualize partial grouping of countries by indicator. For each indicator countries are divided into three groups of approximately equal size (terciles): the top third, the middle third and the bottom third. Aggregates are colour coded using the same tercile cutoffs. See *Notes* after the table.

		SDG 17.4					SDG 9.5			SDG 10.1		SDG 10.1	SDG 5	SDG 10.1
		Economic sustainability								Social sustainability				
		Adjusted net savings	Total debt service	Gross capital formation	Skilled labour force	Concentration index (exports)	Research and development expenditure	Dependency ratio Old age (65 and older)	Education and health expenditure versus military expenditure		Overall loss in HDI value due to inequality[c]	Gender Inequality Index[c]	Income share of the poorest 40%[d]		
			(% of exports of goods, services and primary income)		(% of labour force)			(per 100 people ages 15-64)	Military expenditure[a]	Ratio of education and health expenditure to military expenditure[b]					
HDI RANK		(% of GNI) 2015–2018e	2015–2018e	(% of GDP) 2015–2019e	2015–2019e	(value) 2018	(% of GDP) 2014–2018e	2030f	(% of GDP) 2015–2018e	2010–2017g	2010/2019h	2005/2019h	2005/2018
Very high human development														
1	Norway	18.2	..	29.0	84.3	0.357	2.1	31.9i	1.6	11.4	-0.9	-4.4	0.3
2	Ireland	16.1	..	43.8	85.0	0.269	1.1	27.8	0.3	33.5	-2.4	-5.0	0.2
2	Switzerland	16.9	..	22.3	87.3	0.246j	3.4	37.9	0.7	25.4	-0.3	-7.4	-0.1
4	Hong Kong, China (SAR)	..		18.9	77.0	0.286	0.9	43.2	..	..	..	..	..
4	Iceland	11.0	..	20.1	76.2	0.460	2.0	31.8	..	..	-1.4	-5.3	0.4
6	Germany	14.4	..	21.6	87.3	0.093	3.1	44.0	1.2	13.4	0.3	-2.3	-0.1
7	Sweden	17.8	..	25.2	87.1	0.097	3.3	36.4	1.0	17.6	-0.2	-2.0	-0.3
8	Australia	4.4	..	23.3	78.9	0.291	1.9	31.0k	1.9	6.9	0.3	-2.5	-0.2
8	Netherlands	19.2	..	21.2	78.6	0.083	2.2	40.8	1.2	13.6	-1.7	-4.6	0.1
10	Denmark	19.4	..	22.7	79.7	0.100	3.1	37.1	1.2	15.5	-0.7	-3.7	-0.6
11	Finland	10.8	..	24.0	90.5	0.143	2.8	43.1i	1.4	11.4	-3.6	-4.4	0.0
11	Singapore	34.7	..	24.9	84.0	0.239	1.9	34.5	3.1	2.1	..	-6.0	..
13	United Kingdom	3.0	..	17.4	84.4	0.111	1.7	34.8	1.8	8.4	-1.9	-3.7	0.0
14	Belgium	11.1	..	25.3	85.6	0.096	2.8	37.6	0.9	18.3	-1.0	-6.1	0.2
14	New Zealand	10.1	..	24.0	82.2	0.176	1.4	33.3	1.2	13.3	..	-2.3	..
16	Canada	6.0	..	22.7	92.0	0.147	1.6	36.7	1.3	13.1	0.1	-3.9	-0.2
17	United States	5.6	..	21.0	96.5	0.099	2.8	32.5	3.2	6.2	1.3	-1.8	-0.3
18	Austria	14.3	..	25.4	87.6	0.068	3.2•	38.5	0.7	21.7	-0.7	-3.8	-0.3
19	Israel	15.6	..	21.8	90.3	0.223	5.0	22.5	4.3	2.8	-1.0	-3.2	0.5
19	Japan	7.3	..	24.3	99.9	0.139	3.3	53.2	0.9	14.9	..	-3.1	2.1
19	Liechtenstein	..		..	..	..	..	..	..	..	..	..	..
22	Slovenia	11.8	..	20.7	92.1	0.177	1.9	41.8	1.0	13.2	-4.4	-5.2	0.1
23	Korea (Republic of)	19.2	..	31.2	86.0	0.198	4.8	38.2	2.6	4.6	-4.5	-3.8	0.1
23	Luxembourg	13.1	..	17.4	79.6	0.106	1.2	27.1	0.6	19.5	1.0	-5.2	-1.2
25	Spain	10.2	..	20.8	67.7	0.097	1.2	39.8m	1.3	11.6	3.6	-3.6	-0.6
26	France	8.9	..	24.2	85.7	0.089	2.2	40.4	2.3	..	-0.3	-7.1	-0.3
27	Czechia	10.2	..	26.3	95.4	0.127	1.9	35.3	1.1	12.7	-3.2	-0.8	0.4
28	Malta	..		20.0	63.5	0.308	0.6	41.9	0.5	29.5	..	-3.5	-0.2
29	Estonia	16.7	..	28.1	91.2	0.099	1.4	38.3	2.1	5.6	-3.6	-6.7	0.3
29	Italy	6.4	..	18.0	70.0	0.053	1.4	45.8	1.3	9.5	0.1	-6.5	-0.5
31	United Arab Emirates	..		23.8	52.4	0.231	1.3	6.4	5.6n	..	..	-13.4	..
32	Greece	-1.7	..	12.5	81.3	0.291	1.2	42.5	2.4	..	0.8	-3.1	0.0
33	Cyprus	8.1	..	19.1	85.0	0.374	0.6	27.0o	1.6	9.1	-2.5	-3.4	-0.2
34	Lithuania	11.2	..	16.7	96.4	0.115	0.9	45.2	2.0	7.2	-1.1	-3.2	-0.5
35	Poland	10.5	..	19.6	95.1	0.063	1.2	37.0	2.0	5.8	-3.7	-2.5	1.5
36	Andorra	..		..	..	0.189	..	..	..	..	..	..	..
37	Latvia	4.7	..	22.1	92.5	0.083	0.6	42.3	2.0	7.4	-1.6	-2.2	0.6
38	Portugal	4.6	..	18.9	56.6	0.080	1.4	44.3	1.8	7.7	0.0	-5.7	0.8
39	Slovakia	4.3	..	23.3	95.6	0.216	0.8	32.7	1.2	9.8	-1.0	0.1	0.5
40	Hungary	14.5	..	28.6	88.8	0.108	1.6	34.5	1.1	11.6	-1.8	-0.9	0.6
40	Saudi Arabia	17.2	..	27.3	58.7	0.557	0.8n	8.3	8.8	1.1n	..	-6.8	..
42	Bahrain	19.9	..	36.4	19.3	0.386	0.1	7.1	3.6	1.6	..	-2.9	..
43	Chile	0.5	..	22.8	71.3	0.324	0.4	26.0	1.9	7.4	-1.4	-3.0	1.9
43	Croatia	14.4	..	22.8	91.8	0.071	1.0	40.5	1.5	6.7	-6.9	-2.1	0.7
45	Qatar	29.3	..	44.4	43.9	0.463	0.5	5.7	1.5n	4.2	..	..	..
46	Argentina	5.0	45.0	18.2	66.9	0.227	0.5	19.7	0.9	17.0	-3.9	-0.9	1.7
47	Brunei Darussalam	30.4	..	38.7	78.8	0.624	0.3	14.4	2.4	2.0	..	..	..
48	Montenegro	..	63.7	31.1	92.0	0.218	0.4	30.1	1.5	..	-0.2	..	..
49	Romania	0.3	20.8	22.9	81.7	0.114	0.5	32.6	1.9	5.7	-0.2	-1.8	0.7
50	Palau	..		26.7	92.5	0.604	..	..	..	..	..	..	..

Continued →

	SDG 17.4					SDG 9.5					SDG 10.1	SDG 5	SDG 10.1
	Economic sustainability						Social sustainability						
	Adjusted net savings	Total debt service	Gross capital formation	Skilled labour force	Concentration index (exports)	Research and development expenditure	Dependency ratio Old age (65 and older)	Education and health expenditure versus military expenditure		Overall loss in HDI value due to inequality[c]	Gender Inequality Index[c]	Income share of the poorest 40%[d]
								Military expenditure[a]	Ratio of education and health expenditure to military expenditure[b]			
	(% of GNI)	(% of exports of goods, services and primary income)	(% of GDP)	(% of labour force)	(value)	(% of GDP)	(per 100 people ages 15-64)	(% of GDP)		Average annual change (%)		
HDI RANK	2015-2018e	2015-2018e	2015-2019e	2015-2019e	2018	2014-2018e	2030f	2015-2018e	2010-2017g	2010/2019h	2005/2019h	2005/2018
51 Kazakhstan	3.0	48.3	27.0	80.8	0.599	0.1	17.4	1.0	6.6	-6.8	-4.4	3.1
52 Russian Federation	8.2	19.6	23.1	96.1	0.327	1.0	31.1	3.9	1.7	-1.4	-3.3	1.1
53 Belarus	15.7	13.5	29.0	98.6	0.182	0.6	32.5	1.3	9.2	-4.2	..	0.6
54 Turkey	12.1	36.7	25.1	46.3	0.076	1.0	18.5	2.5	..	-3.8	-3.9	0.3
55 Uruguay	5.2	..	16.2	26.1	0.226	0.5	27.0	2.0	7.1	-2.4	-1.6	1.2
56 Bulgaria	15.1	15.3	19.5	87.9	0.092	0.8	37.2	1.7	7.4	0.3	-1.5	-0.8
57 Panama	25.8	..	41.3	54.2	0.144	0.1	17.4	0.0	..	-3.2	-1.1	1.7
58 Bahamas	-3.5	..	24.5	..	0.421	..	17.1	..	..	..	-0.4	..
58 Barbados	-0.6	..	15.7	..	0.158	..	35.4	..	..	..	-2.3	..
60 Oman	-17.5	..	23.2	..	0.447	0.2	6.0	8.2	0.7	..	-1.7	..
61 Georgia	9.6	23.7	26.8	93.4	0.210	0.3	29.5p	1.9	5.6	-4.0	-1.2	0.3
62 Costa Rica	16.9	18.3	17.9	44.0	0.262	0.4	22.6	0.0	..	-1.3	-1.4	-0.1
62 Malaysia	2.8	..	20.9	66.8	0.218	1.4	14.7q	1.0	7.7	..	-0.8	1.5
64 Kuwait	18.9	..	25.2	..	0.486	0.1	10.0	5.1	..	..	-3.2	..
64 Serbia	3.1	22.3	23.6	82.9	0.081	0.9	32.7r	1.9	6.2	1.8	..	..
66 Mauritius	3.0	23.3	20.0	61.7	0.219	0.3	26.7s	0.2	60.1	..	-0.9	-0.2
High human development												
67 Seychelles	..	..	31.6	95.2	0.424	0.2	19.2	1.4	5.1	..	..	..
67 Trinidad and Tobago	..	..	..	72.0	0.345	0.1	24.1	0.8	..	..	-0.9	..
69 Albania	-1.6	20.7	25.1	79.5	0.298	0.2n	32.7	1.2	..	-1.7	-3.7	-0.7
70 Cuba	..	..	12.0	69.4	0.236	0.4	33.8	2.9	7.1	..	-0.8	..
70 Iran (Islamic Republic of)	..	0.8	34.7	18.0t	0.525	0.8	14.1	2.7	4.0	..	-0.8	0.7
72 Sri Lanka	21.0	36.0	27.4	39.2	0.194	0.1	24.2	1.9	3.1	-2.3	-0.7	0.3
73 Bosnia and Herzegovina	..	10.8	21.3	83.6	0.100	0.2	37.5	1.1	..	-3.7	..	0.2
74 Grenada	..	8.4	..	..	0.208	..	18.8	..	..	..	..	..
74 Mexico	6.6	11.9	21.4	41.6	0.137	0.3	15.2	0.5	18.8	0.2	-2.0	1.5
74 Saint Kitts and Nevis	..	..	30.0	..	0.313	..	..	..	..	..	..	..
74 Ukraine	1.6	20.7	12.6	80.0	0.140	0.5	30.2u	3.8	3.8	-2.5	-3.4	0.6
78 Antigua and Barbuda	..	..	..	..	0.426	..	20.7	..	..	..	..	..
79 Peru	6.6	12.2	20.9	58.1	0.295	0.1	17.5	1.2	7.2	-5.1	-1.1	2.0
79 Thailand	15.0	5.4	23.9	38.8	0.079	1.0	29.6	1.3	5.4	-2.5	-0.5	1.1
81 Armenia	-4.2	29.9	17.4	79.9	0.265	0.2	26.1	4.8	3.4	-1.1	-3.3	0.2
82 North Macedonia	14.6	16.6	34.1	82.4	0.221	0.4	27.4	1.0	..	-3.6	..	2.9
83 Colombia	-2.0	40.8	22.3	59.9	0.341	0.2	19.3	3.2	3.7	-2.6	-1.0	0.7
84 Brazil	3.3	31.7	15.1	65.7	0.165	1.3	19.9	1.5	11.1	-0.7	-1.1	0.8
85 China	21.1	8.2	43.8	..	0.094	2.2	25.0	1.9	..	-3.9	-2.1	0.7
86 Ecuador	3.6	36.7	25.0	47.0	0.393	0.4	15.5	2.4	5.2	-0.8	-1.5	2.1
86 Saint Lucia	..	3.9	..	16.8	0.456	..	21.1	..	..	..	..	..
88 Azerbaijan	6.3	10.5	20.1	93.3	0.827	0.2	17.3v	3.8	2.4	-4.0	-0.4	..
88 Dominican Republic	19.3	15.1	27.3	48.0	0.189	..	15.7	0.7	10.0n	-1.7	-0.6	1.9
90 Moldova (Republic of)	4.6	12.9	26.3	65.2	0.188	0.3	24.6w	0.3	33.7	-2.8	-2.3	2.2
91 Algeria	21.2	0.5	44.3	40.3	0.486	0.5	14.0	5.3	2.8n	..	-1.8	..
92 Lebanon	-23.3	72.1	18.4	..	0.122	..	17.9	5.0	2.4	..	..	..
93 Fiji	..	2.0	..	62.5	0.221	..	12.5	0.9	5.3	..	-1.1	0.5
94 Dominica	..	16.5	..	..	0.409	..	..	..	..	..	..	..
95 Maldives	..	9.2	..	32.7	0.586	..	9.0	..	..	3.5	-0.7	1.4
95 Tunisia	-8.3	14.0	19.3	55.8	0.137	0.6	19.0	2.1	6.0	-2.9	-0.4	1.3
97 Saint Vincent and the Grenadines	..	12.3	..	..	0.307	..	20.0	..	..	..	..	..
97 Suriname	23.0n	..	36.2n	45.0	0.689	..	15.1	..	..	1.4	-0.9	..
99 Mongolia	-7.5	101.6	35.9	80.6	0.446	0.1	10.5	0.8	10.9	-1.0	-1.8	0.2
100 Botswana	20.5	2.4	33.2	34.0	0.888	0.5n	8.6	2.8	5.0n	..	-0.7	3.6
101 Jamaica	17.5	20.4	23.3	..	0.498	..	17.9	1.4	11.5	0.0	-1.0	..
102 Jordan	3.3	14.1	18.4	..	0.170	0.7	8.2	4.7	2.4	-3.0	-1.5	1.2
103 Paraguay	7.2	15.7	22.4	43.7	0.336	0.1	13.0	0.9	10.7	-0.6	-1.2	1.3

Continued →

Developing regions

Arab States (20 countries or territories)
Algeria, Bahrain, Djibouti, Egypt, Iraq, Jordan, Kuwait, Lebanon, Libya, Morocco, State of Palestine, Oman, Qatar, Saudi Arabia, Somalia, Sudan, Syrian Arab Republic, Tunisia, United Arab Emirates, Yemen

East Asia and the Pacific (26 countries)
Brunei Darussalam, Cambodia, China, Fiji, Indonesia, Kiribati, Democratic People's Republic of Korea, Lao People's Democratic Republic, Malaysia, Marshall Islands, Federated States of Micronesia, Mongolia, Myanmar, Nauru, Palau, Papua New Guinea, Philippines, Samoa, Singapore, Solomon Islands, Thailand, Timor-Leste, Tonga, Tuvalu, Vanuatu, Viet Nam

Europe and Central Asia (17 countries)
...baijan, Belarus, Bosnia and Herzegovina, Georgia, ...va, Montenegro, North... ...tan, Ukraine...

		Economic sustainability				SDG 9.5		Social sustainability			SDG 10.1	SDG 5	SDG 10.1
		Adjusted net savings	Total debt service	Gross capital formation	Skilled labour force	Concentration index (exports)	Research and development expenditure	Dependency ratio Old age (65 and older)	Military expenditure	Ratio of education and health expenditure to military expenditure	Overall loss in HDI value due to inequality	Gender Inequality Index	Income share of the poorest 40%
		(% of GNI)	(% of exports of goods, services and primary income)	(% of GDP)	(% of labour force)	(value)	(% of GDP)	(per 100 people ages 15-64)	(% of GDP)		Average annual change (%)		
HDI RANK		2015-2018	2015-2018	2015-2019	2015-2019	2018	2014-2018	2030	2015-2018	2010-2017	2010/2019	2005/2019	2005/2018
104	Tonga	9.3^a	7.2	33.4^a	72.3	0.300	..	10.8	..	..	..	-1.7	0.4
105	Libya	34.8^a	..	29.8^a	..	0.794	..	9.0	15.5^a	..	..	-2.1	..
106	Uzbekistan	26.7	5.8	39.8	..	0.342	0.1	11.3	3.6	..	..	..	..
107	Bolivia (Plurinational State of)	-0.8	9.6	19.9	47.6	0.380	0.2^a	13.7	1.5	..	-5.0	-2.0	4.7
107	Indonesia	12.9	26.0	33.8	42.0	0.134	0.2	13.5	0.7	7.4	0.1	-1.0	-1.1
107	Philippines	21.0	8.7	26.2	29.9	0.250	0.2	11.5	1.1	5.6^a	-0.4	-0.8	0.6
110	Belize	-3.9	10.1	19.0	43.5	0.267	..	10.5	1.3	9.8	-2.6	-1.1	..
111	Samoa	..	9.8	..	66.6	0.343	..	11.4	..	..	..	-1.7	0.5
111	Turkmenistan	..	..	47.2^a	..	0.643	..	10.8	..	..	-4.1	..	..
113	Venezuela (Bolivarian Republic of)	7.4^a	69.0	24.8^a	42.3	0.734	0.3	15.0	0.5	11.7^a	-2.2	-0.1	..
114	South Africa	-0.6	19.9	17.6	52.2	0.133	0.8	9.9	1.0	13.6	1.0	-0.9	-0.2
115	Palestine, State of	..	..	24.2	48.5	0.180	0.5^a	6.7^a	..	..	..	..	0.0
116	Egypt	3.6	15.0	16.7	57.2	0.152	0.7	10.2	1.2	3.8^a	0.8	-1.8	0.0
117	Marshall Islands	..	..	23.4	..	0.790	..	..	..	..	..	..	..
117	Viet Nam	13.5	7.1	26.8	39.4	0.188	0.5	17.9	2.3	4.1	0.1	-0.3	0.0
119	Gabon	20.4	7.7	22.4	35.5	0.546	0.6^a	6.4	1.5	4.5	0.7	-0.7	0.5
Medium human development													
120	Kyrgyzstan	7.1	31.3	32.9	92.7	0.364	0.1	11.3	1.6	7.3	-4.9	-4.2	0.9
121	Morocco	19.7	8.8	32.2	18.7^f	0.173	0.7^a	17.1	3.1	3.4^a	..	-1.5	0.3
122	Guyana	19.9	5.0	36.8	41.3	0.462	..	16.1	1.7	6.7	-0.1	-0.9	..
123	Iraq	-2.8	..	12.9	28.3	0.948	0.0	6.1	2.7	..	..	..	-0.6
124	El Salvador	5.1	45.8	19.1	41.1	0.213	0.0	16.3	1.0	10.4	-2.8	-1.6	2.5
125	Tajikistan	14.4	22.0	27.2	80.1^a	0.264	0.1	8.4	1.2	10.0	-4.6	-0.7	-0.2
126	Cabo Verde	19.2	5.6	35.3	59.8	0.332	0.1^a	10.4	0.6	19.2	..	..	1.9
127	Guatemala	1.8	26.7	14.5	18.2	0.136	0.0	9.5	0.4	23.7	-2.2	-1.4	1.3
128	Nicaragua	15.0	19.0	17.1	30.5	0.231	0.1	12.0	0.6	20.8	-0.5	-1.4	0.8
129	Bhutan	16.8	10.7	47.5	19.5	0.393	..	11.1	..	..	..	..	0.4
130	Namibia	0.0	..	12.7	66.7	0.267	0.3	6.6	3.3	2.7	-2.5	-1.2	0.3
131	India	17.7	11.4	30.2	21.2	0.139	0.6	12.5	2.4	3.1	-1.3	-1.7	-0.4
132	Honduras	19.4	28.1	22.3	28.2	0.222	0.0	10.0	1.7	8.4	-2.0	-0.7	2.5
133	Bangladesh	22.5	6.3	31.6	25.8	0.405	..	10.7	1.4	3.5	-2.1	-1.2	0.0
134	Kiribati	..	..	31.7	48.3	0.919	..	10.1	..	..	..	..	-3.3
135	Sao Tome and Principe	..	4.5	..	..	0.690	..	6.7	..	..	..	..	0.6
136	Micronesia (Federated States of)	..	..	..	65.0	0.829	..	9.7	..	..	..	..	..
137	Lao People's Democratic Republic	-6.0	14.6	29.0	34.2	0.244	0.3	8.5	0.2^a	29.7	0.0	-1.2	-0.9
138	Eswatini (Kingdom of)	5.0	..	13.1	17.9	0.340	0.3	6.0	1.5	8.0	-2.2	-0.3	-0.8
138	Ghana	-8.4	9.4	26.4	28.5	0.459	0.4^a	6.8	0.4	17.1	1.1	-0.5	-0.5
140	Vanuatu	25.3^a	2.1	26.4^a	10.1	0.243	..	7.0	..	..	..	..	..
141	Timor-Leste	-11.5	0.3	34.0	28.3	0.498	..	8.2	0.6	9.9	-1.9	..	1.5
142	Nepal	36.7	8.5	56.6	41.9	0.141	0.3^a	10.2	1.4	6.9	-2.3	-2.5	3.3
143	Kenya	-4.4	22.6	17.4	40.5	0.233	0.8^a	5.4	1.2	7.9	-2.1	-1.6	1.6
144	Cambodia	10.1	6.7	24.2	14.3	0.298	0.1	10.1	2.2	5.2	-3.9	-1.3	..
145	Equatorial Guinea	..	..	13.2	..	0.661	..	3.5	0.2	..	..	..	..
146	Zambia	20.3	14.6	39.2	39.1	0.680	0.3^a	4.3	1.4	6.3	-0.1	-1.1	-1.4
147	Myanmar	21.2	4.9	30.6	28.1	0.216	0.0	12.4	2.9	2.1	..	..	0.2
148	Angola	-37.1	21.9	17.9	10.3	0.934	0.0	4.6	1.8	1.5	-2.5	..	0.2
149	Congo	-39.9	3.2	18.8	..	0.624	..	5.4	2.5	2.0	-2.6	-0.7	-1.4
150	Zimbabwe	-15.8	11.7	9.3	63.5	0.394	..	5.4	2.2	6.4	-3.0	-0.8	..
151	Solomon Islands	..	5.6	..	18.7	0.711	..	7.6	..	..	..	..	3.4
151	Syrian Arab Republic	..	3.1^a	27.8^a	..	0.232	0.0	9.4	4.1^a	2.2^a	..	-0.1	..
153	Cameroon	-0.3	10.7	24.2	19.9	0.337	..	5.0	1.3	6.0	-0.2	-1.1	-1.7
154	Pakistan	4.0	19.9	15.6	27.8	0.204	0.2	8.3	4.0	1.5	-0.1	-0.8	-0.2
155	Papua New Guinea	..	26.1	..	26.7	0.294	0.0	6.9	0.3	13.3	..	0.6	..
156	Comoros	4.2	1.9	15.0	14.0	0.559	..	6.3	..	..	0.4	..	1.9
Low human development													
157	Mauritania	14.8	15.7	40.9	8.2	0.308	0.0	6.2	3.0	2.3	-1.1	..	1.5

Continued →

		SDG 17.4				SDG 9.5				SDG 10.1	SDG 5	SDG 10.1
		Economic sustainability							Social sustainability				
	Adjusted net savings	Total debt service	Gross capital formation	Skilled labour force	Concentration index (exports)	Research and development expenditure	Dependency ratio Old age (65 and older)	Education and health expenditure versus military expenditure		Overall loss in HDI value due to inequality	Gender Inequality Index	Income share of the poorest 40%
								Military expenditure	Ratio of education and health expenditure to military expenditure			
	(% of GNI)	(% of exports of goods, services and primary income)	(% of GDP)	(% of labour force)	(value)	(% of GDP)	(per 100 people ages 15-64)	(% of GDP)				Average annual change (%)		
HDI RANK	2015-2018	2015-2018	2015-2019	2015-2019	2018	2014-2018	2030	2015-2018	2010-2017	2010/2019	2005/2019	2005/2018
158 Benin	3.2	7.8	25.6	17.1	0.373	..	6.3	0.9	6.8	0.6	-0.5	-2.8
159 Uganda	-5.4	12.2	26.5	3.2	0.267	0.2	4.1	1.4	6.9	-2.1	-0.8	-0.1
160 Rwanda	-2.8	12.6	26.1	18.1	0.380	0.7	7.3	1.2	7.7	-2.8	-1.5	2.1
161 Nigeria	0.1	8.3	19.8	41.4	0.789	0.1ᵃ	5.2	0.5	..	-1.8	..	-1.1
162 Côte d'Ivoire	21.3	17.1	21.0	25.5	0.361	0.1	5.3	1.4	7.5	-0.1	-0.5	-0.4
163 Tanzania (United Republic of)	16.7	8.4	34.0	5.0	0.206	0.5ᵃ	5.3ᵃ	1.2	6.8	-1.5	-0.5	-0.2
164 Madagascar	4.9	2.7	21.9	18.5	0.213	0.0	6.4	0.6	15.7	-1.2	..	-1.5
165 Lesotho	6.8	3.6	32.1	..	0.288	0.0	8.7	1.8	8.0	-2.3	-0.3	1.7
166 Djibouti	40.8	57.8	25.0	..	0.185	..	9.4	3.7ᵃ	3.2ᵃ	..	..	-0.3
167 Togo	1.1	5.0	28.0	8.2	0.237	0.3	5.5	2.0	6.0	-0.4	-0.8	-0.9
168 Senegal	12.5	13.5	32.8	10.8	0.236	0.6	5.8	1.9	4.6	-1.3	-1.3	-0.5
169 Afghanistan	5.4	4.9	17.8	19.2	0.399	..	5.1	1.0	16.8	..	-0.9	..
170 Haiti	15.4	1.2	27.6	9.4	0.508	..	9.7	0.0	..	0.0	0.5	..
170 Sudan	-6.2	4.2	19.3	22.7	0.440	..	7.1	2.3	1.4ᵃ	..	-1.4	1.5
172 Gambia	-7.8	16.8	18.5	35.0	0.449	0.1	4.8	1.1	3.4	-2.0	-0.5	2.9
173 Ethiopia	8.4	20.8	35.2	6.9	0.287	0.3	6.4	0.6	12.3	-2.1	-1.3	-1.3
174 Malawi	-6.3	5.7	12.3	17.6	0.558	..	4.8	0.8	17.9	-1.3	-1.0	-0.7
175 Congo (Democratic Republic of the)	-7.9	2.4	25.3	43.0	0.545	0.4	5.9	0.7	7.4	-2.0	-0.4	-0.1
175 Guinea-Bissau	-2.2	1.9	11.3	..	0.875	..	5.1	1.6	4.3	-1.4	..	-4.8
175 Liberia	-99.4	2.8	22.8	21.1	0.395	..	6.4	0.8	15.0	-1.6	-0.2	0.3
178 Guinea	-10.2	2.2	30.6	..	0.502	..	5.4	2.5	2.4	-1.2	..	2.4
179 Yemen	..	14.6		29.7	0.378	..	5.4	4.0ᵃ	2.5ᵃ	-0.8	0.0	-0.6
180 Eritrea	..	..	12.6ᵃ	..	0.314	..	7.0	..	..	..	..	..
181 Mozambique	5.1	13.1	43.9	7.1	0.315	0.3	5.1	1.0	10.5	-4.3	-1.1	-1.8
182 Burkina Faso	0.6	3.5	26.0	5.0	0.658	0.7	4.8	2.1	9.3	-2.0	-0.5	2.3
182 Sierra Leone	-20.3	7.2	17.4	15.2	0.227	..	5.2	0.8	16.2	-1.1	-0.3	1.0
184 Mali	2.5	4.4	22.5	5.8	0.723	0.3	4.5	2.9	2.5	-1.5	-0.4	2.4
185 Burundi	-16.9	14.0	12.3	2.5	0.438	0.2	5.2	1.9	6.6	-2.3	-0.8	-2.1
185 South Sudan	-9.2	..	5.8	..		..	6.2	1.3	4.6	..	..	..
187 Chad	..	..	21.4	7.6	0.757	0.3	4.7	2.1	3.1	-0.5	..	-1.7
188 Central African Republic	..	..	23.2	..	0.336	..	5.0	1.4	2.2	-0.1	-0.1	-6.7
189 Niger	7.2	8.5	30.5	4.0	0.352	..	5.2	2.5	4.6	-2.1	-0.6	2.6
Other countries or territories												
Korea (Democratic People's Rep. of)	..	..	..	..	0.103	..	18.7	..	..	..	..	..
Monaco	..	..	..	..	..	..	..	..	..	..	..	..
Nauru	..	..	..	96.5	0.424	..	..	..	..	..	..	..
San Marino	..	..	19.1	51.9	..	..	..	..	..	..	..	..
Somalia	..	..	..	..	0.409	..	5.6	..	..	..	..	..
Tuvalu	..	..	..	50.1	0.578	..	..	..	..	..	..	..
Human development groups												
Very high human development	8.5	..	22.3	84.9	–	2.4	33.1	2.3	6.9	-0.9	-2.7	–
High human development	16.4	12.3	36.0	..	–	1.6	20.3	1.8	..	-2.4	-1.0	–
Medium human development	13.4	12.4	27.5	24.0	–	0.5	11.1	2.3	3.1	-1.4	-1.4	–
Low human development	2.9	10.0	24.0	21.5	–	0.2	5.6	1.0	4.2	-1.7	-0.6	–
Developing countries	15.2	14.0	33.1	33.9	–	1.3	14.7	2.1	4.5	-1.7	-0.9	–
Regions												
Arab States	12.4	16.3	26.2	41.7	–	0.7	9.7	5.5	1.6	-1.1	-1.2	–
East Asia and the Pacific	20.2	9.1	40.9	..	–	..	21.7	1.8	..	-2.8	-0.6	–
Europe and Central Asia	9.7	30.0	25.2	69.1	–	0.7	20.1	2.4	..	-3.3	-2.5	–
Latin America and the Caribbean	5.1	23.5	19.5	54.5	–	0.6	17.8	1.2	10.4	-1.4	-1.1	–
South Asia	17.1	12.1	29.9	22.6	–	0.6	11.9	2.5	3.1	-1.5	-1.3	–
Sub-Saharan Africa	-0.8	14.1	22.1	25.8	–	0.4	5.7	1.0	7.3	-1.5	-0.6	–
Least developed countries	8.4	11.1	29.4	19.6	–	..	7.0	1.5	3.5	-1.7	-0.8	–
Small island developing states	..	16.4	23.9	46.4	–	..	17.1	..	..	-1.8	..	–
Organisation for Economic Co-operation and Development	8.1	..	22.1	81.5	–	2.5	33.5	2.2	7.8	-0.7	-2.0	–
World	**10.8**	**14.5**	**26.3**	**47.3**	**–**	**2.1**	**18.0**	**2.2**	**6.7**	**-1.5**	**-0.9**	**–**

Notes

Three-colour coding is used to visualize partial grouping of countries and aggregates by indicator. For each indicator countries are divided into three groups of approximately equal size (terciles): the top third, the middle third and the bottom third. Aggregates are colour coded using the same tercile cutoffs. See *Technical note 6* at http://hdr.undp.org/sites/default/files/hdr2020_technical_notes.pdf for details about partial grouping in this table.

a This column is intentionally left without colour because it is meant to provide context for the indicator on education and health expenditure.

b Data on government expenditure on health and education are available in tables 8 and 9 and at http://hdr.undp.org/en/data.

c A negative value indicates that inequality declined over the period specified.

d A negative value indicates that inequality increased over the period specified.

e Data refer to the most recent year available during the period specified.

[...] bility variant.

Definitions

Adjusted net savings: Net national savings plus education expenditure and minus energy depletion, mineral depletion, net forest depletion, and carbon dioxide and particulate emissions damage. Net national savings are equal to gross national savings less the value of consumption of fixed capital.

Total debt service: Sum of principal repayments and interest actually paid in currency, goods or services on long-term debt; interest paid on short-term debt; and repayments (repurchases and charges) to the International Monetary Fund. It is expressed as a percentage of exports of goods, services and primary income.

Gross capital formation: Outlays on additions to the fixed assets of the economy plus net changes in inventories. Fixed assets include land improvements (such as fences, ditches and drains); plant, machinery and equipment purchases; and construction of roads, railways and the like, including schools, offices, hospitals, private residential dwellings and commercial and industrial buildings. Inventories are stocks of goods held by firms to meet temporary or unexpected fluctuations in production or sales as well as goods that are work in progress. Net acquisitions of valuables are also considered capital formation. Gross capital formation was form[...] known as gross domestic investment.

Skilled labour force: Percent[...]

Main data sources

Columns 1–3, 6 and 8: World Bank (2020a).

Column 4: ILO (2020).

Column 5: UNCTAD (2020).

Column 7: UNDESA (2019a).

Columns 9 and 12: HDRO calculations based on data from World Bank (2020a).

Column 10: HDRO calculations based on the Inequality-adjusted HDI time series.

Column 11: HDRO calculations based on the Gender Inequality Index time series.

Notes

Three-colour coding is used to visualize partial grouping of countries and aggregates by indicator. For each indicator countries are divided into three groups of approximately equal size (terciles): the top third, the middle third and the bottom third. Aggregates are colour coded using the same tercile cutoffs. See *Technical note 6* at http://hdr.undp.org/sites/default/files/hdr2020_technical_notes.pdf for details about partial grouping in this table.

a	This column is intentionally left without colour because it is meant to provide context for the indicator on education and health expenditure.
b	Data on government expenditure on health and education are available in tables 8 and 9 and at http://hdr.undp.org/en/data.
c	A negative value indicates that inequality declined over the period specified.
d	A negative value indicates that inequality increased over the period specified.
e	Data refer to the most recent year available during the period specified.
f	Projections based on medium-fertility variant.
g	Data refer to the most recent year for which all three types of expenditure (education, health and military) are available during the period specified.
h	The trend data used to calculate the change are available at http://hdr.undp.org/en/data.
i	Includes Svalbard and Jan Mayen Islands.
j	Includes Liechtenstein.
k	Includes Christmas Island, Cocos (Keeling) Islands and Norfolk Island.
l	Includes Åland Islands.
m	Includes Canary Islands, Ceuta and Melilla.
n	Refers to a year earlier than that specified.
o	Includes Northern Cyprus.
p	Includes Abkhazia and South Ossetia.
q	Includes Sabah and Sarawak.
r	Includes Kosovo.
s	Includes Agalega, Rodrigues and Saint Brandon.
t	Includes only intermediate education.
u	Includes Crimea.
v	Includes Nagorno-Karabakh.
w	Includes Transnistria.
x	Includes East Jerusalem.
y	Refers to 2009.
z	Includes Zanzibar.

Definitions

Adjusted net savings: Net national savings plus education expenditure and minus energy depletion, mineral depletion, net forest depletion, and carbon dioxide and particulate emissions damage. Net national savings are equal to gross national savings less the value of consumption of fixed capital.

Total debt service: Sum of principal repayments and interest actually paid in currency, goods or services on long-term debt; interest paid on short-term debt; and repayments (repurchases and charges) to the International Monetary Fund. It is expressed as a percentage of exports of goods, services and primary income.

Gross capital formation: Outlays on additions to the fixed assets of the economy plus net changes in inventories. Fixed assets include land improvements (such as fences, ditches and drains); plant, machinery and equipment purchases; and construction of roads, railways and the like, including schools, offices, hospitals, private residential dwellings and commercial and industrial buildings. Inventories are stocks of goods held by firms to meet temporary or unexpected fluctuations in production or sales as well as goods that are work in progress. Net acquisitions of valuables are also considered capital formation. Gross capital formation was formerly known as gross domestic investment.

Skilled labour force: Percentge of the labour force ages 15 and older with intermediate or advanced education, as classified by the International Standard Classification of Education.

Concentration index (exports): A measure of the degree of product concentration in exports from a country (also referred to as the Herfindahl-Hirschmann Index). A value closer to 0 indicates that a country's exports are more homogeneously distributed among a series of products (reflecting a well diversified economy); a value closer to 1 indicates that a country's exports are highly concentrated among a few products.

Research and development expenditure: Current and capital expenditures (both public and private) on creative work undertaken systematically to increase knowledge, including knowledge of humanity, culture and society, and the use of knowledge for new applications. Research and development covers basic research, applied research and experimental development.

Old-age dependency ratio: Ratio of the population ages 65 and older to the population ages 15–64, expressed as the number of dependants per 100 people of working age (ages 15–64).

Military expenditures: All current and capital expenditures on the armed forces, including peacekeeping forces; defence ministries and other government agencies engaged in defence projects; paramilitary forces, if these are judged to be trained and equipped for military operations; and military space activities.

Ratio of education and health expenditure to military expenditure: Sum of government expenditure on education and health divided by military expenditure.

Overall loss in HDI value due to inequality, average annual change: Annual compound change rate of the overall loss in Human Development Index (HDI) value due to inequality over 2010–2019.

Gender Inequality Index, average annual change: Annual compound change rate of the Gender Inequality Index value over 2005–2019, calculated as the annual compound change rate.

Income share of the poorest 40%, average annual change: Annual compound change rate of the income share of the poorest 40 percent of the population over 2005–2018, calculated as the annual compound change rate.

Main data sources

Columns 1–3, 6 and 8: World Bank (2020a).

Column 4: ILO (2020).

Column 5: UNCTAD (2020).

Column 7: UNDESA (2019a).

Columns 9 and 12: HDRO calculations based on data from World Bank (2020a).

Column 10: HDRO calculations based on the Inequality-adjusted HDI time series.

Column 11: HDRO calculations based on the Gender Inequality Index time series.

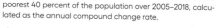

Developing regions

Arab States (20 countries or territories)
Algeria, Bahrain, Djibouti, Egypt, Iraq, Jordan, Kuwait, Lebanon, Libya, Morocco, State of Palestine, Oman, Qatar, Saudi Arabia, Somalia, Sudan, Syrian Arab Republic, Tunisia, United Arab Emirates, Yemen

East Asia and the Pacific (26 countries)
Brunei Darussalam, Cambodia, China, Fiji, Indonesia, Kiribati, Democratic People's Republic of Korea, Lao People's Democratic Republic, Malaysia, Marshall Islands, Federated States of Micronesia, Mongolia, Myanmar, Nauru, Palau, Papua New Guinea, Philippines, Samoa, Singapore, Solomon Islands, Thailand, Timor-Leste, Tonga, Tuvalu, Vanuatu, Viet Nam

Europe and Central Asia (17 countries)
Albania, Armenia, Azerbaijan, Belarus, Bosnia and Herzegovina, Georgia, Kazakhstan, Kyrgyzstan, Republic of Moldova, Montenegro, North Macedonia, Serbia, Tajikistan, Turkey, Turkmenistan, Ukraine, Uzbekistan

Latin America and the Caribbean (33 countries)
Antigua and Barbuda, Argentina, Bahamas, Barbados, Belize, Plurinational State of Bolivia, Brazil, Chile, Colombia, Costa Rica, Cuba, Dominica, Dominican Republic, Ecuador, El Salvador, Grenada, Guatemala, Guyana, Haiti, Honduras, Jamaica, Mexico, Nicaragua, Panama, Paraguay, Peru, Saint Kitts and Nevis, Saint Lucia, Saint Vincent and the Grenadines, Suriname, Trinidad and Tobago, Uruguay, Bolivarian Republic of Venezuela

South Asia (9 countries)
Afghanistan, Bangladesh, Bhutan, India, Islamic Republic of Iran, Maldives, Nepal, Pakistan, Sri Lanka

Sub-Saharan Africa (46 countries)
Angola, Benin, Botswana, Burkina Faso, Burundi, Cameroon, Cabo Verde, Central African Republic, Chad, Comoros, Congo, Democratic Republic of the Congo, Côte d'Ivoire, Equatorial Guinea, Eritrea, Kingdom of Eswatini, Ethiopia, Gabon, Gambia, Ghana, Guinea, Guinea-Bissau, Kenya, Lesotho, Liberia, Madagascar, Malawi, Mali, Mauritania, Mauritius, Mozambique, Namibia, Niger, Nigeria, Rwanda, Sao Tomé and Príncipe, Senegal, Seychelles, Sierra Leone, South Africa, South Sudan, United Republic of Tanzania, Togo, Uganda, Zambia, Zimbabwe

Note: All countries listed in developing regions are included in aggregates for developing countries. Countries included in aggregates for Least Developed Countries and Small Island Developing States follow UN classifications, which are available at www.unohrlls.org. Countries included in aggregates for Organisation for Economic Co-operation and Development are listed at www.oecd.org/about/membersandpartners/list-oecd-member-countries.htm.

Statistical references

Note: Statistical references relate to statistical material presented in this Statistical Annex and in the full set of statistical tables posted at http://hdr.undp.org/en/human-development-report-2020.

Alkire, S., U. Kanagaratnam and N. Suppa. 2020. "The Global Multidimensional Poverty Index (MPI) 2020." OPHI MPI Methodological Note 49. University of Oxford, Oxford Poverty and Human Development Initiative, Oxford, UK.

Barro, R. J., and J.-W. Lee. 2018. Dataset of Educational Attainment, June 2018 Revision. www.barrolee.com. Accessed 20 July 2020.

CEDLAS (Center for Distributive, Labor and Social Studies) and World Bank. 2020. Socio-Economic Database for Latin America and the Caribbean. www.cedlas.econo.unlp.edu.ar/wp/en/estadisticas/sedlac/estadisticas/. Accessed 15 July 2020.

CRED EM-DAT (Centre for Research on the Epidemiology of Disasters). 2020. The International Disaster Database. www.emdat.be. Accessed 22 July 2020.

Eurostat. 2019. European Union Statistics on Income and Living Conditions. EUSILC UDB 2018 – version of November 2019. Brussels. http://ec.europa.eu/eurostat/web/microdata/european-union-statistics-on-income-and-living-conditions. Accessed 10 January 2020.

FAO (Food and Agriculture Organization). 2020a. FAOSTAT database. www.fao.org/faostat/en. Accessed 21 July 2020.

———. **2020b.** FAOSTAT database. www.fao.org/faostat/en. Accessed 11 September 2020.

———. **2020c.** AQUASTAT database. www.fao.org/nr/water/aquastat/data/. Accessed 21 July 2020.

Gallup. 2020. Gallup World Poll Analytics database. https://ga.gallup.com. Accessed 30 March 2020.

Global Carbon Project. 2020. Global Carbon Atlas. www.globalcarbonatlas.org/en/CO2-emissions. Accessed 27 August 2020.

ICF Macro. Various years. Demographic and Health Surveys. www.measuredhs.com. Accessed 15 July 2020.

IDMC (Internal Displacement Monitoring Centre). 2020. Global Internal Displacement Database. www.internal-displacement.org/database. Accessed 22 July 2020.

IHME (Institute for Health Metrics and Evaluation). 2020. Global Burden of Disease Collaborative Network. Global Burden of Disease Study 2019 (GBD 2019) Disability-Adjusted Life Years and Healthy Life Expectancy 1990–2019. Seattle, WA. www.healthdata.org. Accessed 30 October 2020.

ILO (International Labour Organization). 2020. ILOSTAT database. https://ilostat.ilo.org/data/. Accessed 21 July 2020.

IMF (International Monetary Fund). 2020. World Economic Outlook database. Washington, DC. www.imf.org/external/pubs/ft/weo/2020/01/weodata/index.aspx. Accessed 15 July 2020.

IPU (Inter-Parliamentary Union). 2020. Parline database: Monthly ranking of women in national parliaments. https://data.ipu.org/women-ranking. Accessed 29 July 2020.

ITU (International Telecommunication Union). 2020. ICT Facts and Figures 2020. www.itu.int/en/ITU-D/Statistics/Pages/stat/. Accessed 2 September 2020.

LIS (Luxembourg Income Study). 2020. Luxembourg Income Study Project. www.lisdatacenter.org/data-access. Accessed 3 September 2020.

OECD (Organisation for Economic Co-operation and Development). 2019a. PISA 2018 Results in Focus. Paris. www.oecd.org/pisa/. Accessed 8 September 2020.

———. **2019b.** Education at a Glance 2019. Paris. www.oecd-ilibrary.org/education/education-at-a-glance-2019_f8d7880d-en. Accessed 15 July 2020.

UNCTAD (United Nations Conference on Trade and Development). 2020. Data Center. http://unctadstat.unctad.org. Accessed 11 September 2020.

UNDESA (United Nations Department of Economic and Social Affairs). 2011. World Population Prospects: The 2010 Revision. New York. www.un.org/en/development/desa/population/publications/trends/population-prospects_2010_revision.shtml. Accessed 15 October 2013.

———. **2018.** World Urbanization Prospects: The 2018 Revision. New York. https://esa.un.org/unpd/wup/. Accessed 25 August 2020.

———. **2019a.** World Population Prospects: The 2019 Revision. Rev 1. New York. https://population.un.org/wpp/. Accessed 30 April 2020.

———. **2019b.** International Migrant Stock: The 2019 Revision. New York. www.un.org/en/development/desa/population/migration/data/. Accessed 2 September 2020.

———. **2020.** World Contraceptive Use 2020. New York. www.un.org/en/development/desa/population/publications/dataset/contraception/wcu2020.asp. Accessed 21 July 2020.

UNECLAC (United Nations Economic Commission for Latin America and the Caribbean). 2020. Preliminary Overview of the Economies of Latin America and the Caribbean 2019. Santiago. www.cepal.org/en/publications/45001-preliminary-overview-economies-latin-america-and-caribbean-2019. Accessed 15 July 2020.

UNESCO (United Nations Educational, Scientific and Cultural Organization) Institute for Statistics. 2020. Data Centre. http://data.uis.unesco.org. Accessed 21 July 2020.

UNESCWA (United Nations Economic and Social Commission for Western Asia). 2020. Survey of Economic and Social Developments in the Arab Region 2018–2019. Beirut. www.unescwa.org/publications/survey-economic-social-development-arab-region-2018-2019. Accessed 15 July 2020.

UNHCR (Office of the United Nations High Commissioner for Refugees). 2020. UNHCR Global Trends 2019. Geneva. www.unhcr.org/globaltrends2019/. Accessed 4 August 2020.

UNICEF (United Nations Children's Fund). 2020a. UNICEF Data. https://data.unicef.org. Accessed 21 July 2020.

———. **2020b.** UNICEF Global Databases: Infant and Young Child Feeding: Exclusive Breastfeeding, Predominant Breastfeeding. July 2020. New York. https://data.unicef.org/resources/dataset/infant-young-child-feeding/. Accessed 25 August 2020.

———. **Various years.** Multiple Indicator Cluster Surveys. New York. http://mics.unicef.org. Accessed 15 July 2020.

UNICEF (United Nations Children's Fund), WHO (World Health Organization) and World Bank. 2020. Joint Child Malnutrition Estimates Expanded Database: Stunting. July 2020 Edition. New York. https://data.unicef.org/topic/nutrition/malnutrition/. Accessed 26 August 2020.

UN Inter-agency Group for Child Mortality Estimation. 2019. Child mortality estimates. www.childmortality.org. Accessed 26 August 2020.

United Nations Statistics Division. 2020a. Global SDG Indicators Database. https://unstats.un.org/sdgs/indicators/database/. Accessed 21 July 2020.

———. **2020b.** National Accounts Main Aggregates Database. http://unstats.un.org/unsd/snaama. Accessed 15 July 2020.

UNODC (United Nations Office on Drugs and Crime). 2020. dataUNODC database. https://dataunodc.un.org . Accessed 21 July 2020.

UNOHCHR (United Nations Office of the High Commissioner for Human Rights). 2020. Human rights treaties. http://tbinternet.ohchr.org/_layouts/Treaty BodyExternal/countries.aspx. Accessed 29 July 2020.

UNRWA (United Nations Relief and Works Agency for Palestine). 2020. "UNRWA in Figures 2019-2020." Amman. www.unrwa.org/resources/about-unrwa/unrwa-figures-2019-2020. Accessed 22 July 2020.

UN Women (United Nations Entity for Gender Equality and the Empowerment of Women). 2019. UN Women Global Database on Violence against Women. New York. http://evaw-global-database.unwomen.org. Accessed 10 June 2019.

WHO (World Health Organization). 2018. Global Health Observatory. www.who.int/gho/. Accessed 26 August 2020.

———. **2020.** Global Health Observatory. www.who.int/gho/. Accessed 21 July 2020.

WHO (World Health Organization) and UNICEF (United Nations Children's Fund). 2020. Estimates of national routine immunization coverage, 2019 revision (completed July 2020). https://data.unicef.org/topic/child-health/immunization/. Accessed 26 August 2020.

WHO (World Health Organization), UNICEF (United Nations Children's Fund), UNFPA (United Nations Population Fund), World Bank Group and United Nations Population Division. 2019. *Trends in Maternal Mortality: 2000 to 2017: Estimates by WHO, UNICEF, UNFPA, World Bank Group and the United Nations Population Division.* Geneva: World Health Organization. www.who.int/reproductivehealth/publications/maternal-mortality-2000-2017/. Accessed 4 August 2020.

World Bank. 2020a. World Development Indicators database. Washington, DC. http://data.worldbank.org. Accessed 22 July 2020.

———. **2020b.** Gender Statistics database. Washington, DC. http://data.worldbank.org. Accessed 21 July 2020.

World Inequality Database. 2020. World Inequality Database. http://wid.world. Accessed 20 August 2020.

		SDG 17.4				SDG 9.5			SDG 10.1	SDG 5	SDG 10.1
			Economic sustainability						Social sustainability			
							Dependency ratio	Education and health expenditure versus military expenditure		Overall loss in HDI value due to inequality[c]	Gender Inequality Index[c]	Income share of the poorest 40%[d]
	Adjusted net savings	Total debt service	Gross capital formation	Skilled labour force	Concentration index (exports)	Research and development expenditure	Old age (65 and older)	Military expenditure[a]	Ratio of education and health expenditure to military expenditure[b]			
	(% of GNI)	(% of exports of goods, services and primary income)	(% of GDP)	(% of labour force)	(value)	(% of GDP)	(per 100 people ages 15-64)	(% of GDP)		Average annual change (%)		
HDI RANK	2015-2018[e]	2015-2018[e]	2015-2019[e]	2015-2019[e]	2018	2014-2018[e]	2030[f]	2015-2018[e]	2010-2017[g]	2010/2019[h]	2005/2019[h]	2005/2018
104 Tonga	9.3[n]	7.2	33.4[n]	72.3	0.300	..	10.8	..	..	..	-1.7	0.4
105 Libya	34.8[n]	..	29.8[n]	..	0.794	..	9.0	15.5[n]	..	..	-2.1	..
106 Uzbekistan	26.7	5.8	39.8	..	0.342	0.1	11.3	3.6	..	..	..	..
107 Bolivia (Plurinational State of)	-0.8	9.6	19.9	47.6	0.380	0.2[n]	13.7	1.5	..	-5.0	-2.0	4.7
107 Indonesia	12.9	26.0	33.8	42.0	0.134	0.2	13.5	0.7	7.4	0.1	-1.0	-1.1
107 Philippines	21.0	8.7	26.2	29.9	0.250	0.2	11.5	1.1	5.6[n]	-0.4	-0.8	0.6
110 Belize	-3.9	10.1	19.0	43.5	0.267	..	10.5	1.3	9.8	-2.6	-1.1	..
111 Samoa	..	9.8	..	66.6	0.343	..	11.4	..	..	..	-1.7	0.5
111 Turkmenistan	..	..	47.2[n]	..	0.643	..	10.8	..	..	-4.1	..	..
113 Venezuela (Bolivarian Republic of)	7.4[n]	69.0	24.8[n]	42.3	0.734	0.3	15.0	0.5	11.7[n]	-2.2	-0.1	..
114 South Africa	-0.6	19.9	17.6	52.2	0.133	0.8	9.9	1.0	13.6	1.0	-0.9	-0.2
115 Palestine, State of	..	..	24.2	48.5	0.180	0.5[n]	6.7[x]	..	..	..	..	0.0
116 Egypt	3.6	15.0	16.7	57.2	0.152	0.7	10.2	1.2	3.8[n]	0.8	-1.8	0.0
117 Marshall Islands	..	..	23.4	..	0.790	..	..	..	..	..	..	..
117 Viet Nam	13.5	7.1	26.8	39.4	0.188	0.5	17.9	2.3	4.1	0.1	-0.3	0.0
119 Gabon	20.4	7.7	22.4	35.5	0.546	0.6[n]	6.4	1.5	4.5	0.7	-0.7	0.5
Medium human development												
120 Kyrgyzstan	7.1	31.3	32.9	92.7	0.364	0.1	11.3	1.6	7.3	-4.9	-4.2	0.9
121 Morocco	19.7	8.8	32.2	18.7[t]	0.173	0.7[n]	17.1	3.1	3.4[n]	..	-1.5	0.3
122 Guyana	19.9	5.0	36.8	41.3	0.462	..	16.1	1.7	6.7	-0.1	-0.9	..
123 Iraq	-2.8	..	12.9	28.3	0.948	0.0	6.1	2.7	..	..	..	-0.6
124 El Salvador	5.1	45.8	19.1	41.1	0.213	0.2	16.3	1.0	10.4	-2.8	-1.6	2.5
125 Tajikistan	14.4	22.0	27.2	80.1[v]	0.264	0.1	8.4	1.2	10.0	-4.6	-0.7	-0.2
126 Cabo Verde	19.2	5.6	35.3	59.8	0.332	0.1[n]	10.4	0.6	19.2	..	..	1.9
127 Guatemala	1.8	26.7	14.5	18.2	0.136	0.0	9.5	0.4	23.7	-2.2	-1.4	1.3
128 Nicaragua	15.0	19.0	17.1	30.5	0.231	0.1	12.0	0.6	20.8	-0.5	-1.4	0.8
129 Bhutan	16.8	10.7	47.5	19.5	0.393	..	11.1	..	..	..	..	0.4
130 Namibia	0.0	..	12.7	66.7	0.267	0.3	6.6	3.3	2.7	-2.5	-1.2	0.3
131 India	17.7	11.4	30.2	21.2	0.139	0.6	12.5	2.4	3.1	-1.3	-1.7	-0.4
132 Honduras	19.4	28.1	22.3	28.2	0.222	..	10.0	1.7	8.4	-2.0	-0.7	2.5
133 Bangladesh	22.5	6.3	31.6	25.8	0.405	..	10.7	1.4	3.5	-2.1	-1.2	0.0
134 Kiribati	..	..	31.7	48.3	0.919	..	10.1	..	..	..	..	..
135 Sao Tome and Principe	..	4.5	..	..	0.690	..	6.7	..	..	..	..	-3.3
136 Micronesia (Federated States of)	..	..	..	65.0	0.829	..	9.7	..	..	..	..	0.6
137 Lao People's Democratic Republic	-6.0	14.6	29.0	34.2	0.244	..	8.5	0.2[n]	29.7	0.0	-1.2	-0.9
138 Eswatini (Kingdom of)	5.0	2.3	13.1	17.9	0.340	0.3	6.0	1.5	8.0	-2.2	-0.3	-0.8
138 Ghana	-8.4	9.4	26.4	28.5	0.459	0.4[n]	6.8	0.4	17.1	1.1	-0.5	-0.5
140 Vanuatu	25.3[n]	2.1	26.4[n]	10.1	0.243	..	7.0	..	..	..	..	..
141 Timor-Leste	-11.5	0.3	34.0	28.3	0.498	..	8.2	0.6	9.9	-1.9	..	1.5
142 Nepal	36.7	8.5	56.6	41.9	0.141	0.3[n]	10.2	1.4	6.9	-2.3	-2.5	3.3
143 Kenya	-4.4	22.6	17.4	40.5	0.233	0.8[n]	5.4	1.2	7.9	-2.1	-1.6	1.6
144 Cambodia	10.1	6.7	24.2	14.3	0.298	0.1	10.1	2.2	5.2	-3.9	-1.3	..
145 Equatorial Guinea	..	..	13.2	..	0.661	..	3.5	0.2	..	..	..	..
146 Zambia	20.3	14.6	39.2	39.1	0.680	0.3[n]	4.3	1.4	6.3	-0.1	-1.1	-1.4
147 Myanmar	21.2	4.9	30.6	28.1	0.216	0.0	12.4	2.9	2.1	..	..	..
148 Angola	-37.1	21.9	17.9	10.3	0.934	0.0	4.6	1.8	1.5	-2.5	..	0.2
149 Congo	-39.9	3.2	18.8	..	0.624	..	5.9	2.5	2.0	-2.6	-0.7	-1.4
150 Zimbabwe	-15.8	11.7	9.3	63.5	0.394	..	5.4	2.2	6.4	-3.0	-0.8	..
151 Solomon Islands	..	5.6	..	18.7	0.711	..	7.6	..	..	..	..	3.4
151 Syrian Arab Republic	..	3.1[n]	27.8[n]	..	0.232	0.0	9.4	4.1[n]	2.2[n]	..	-0.1	..
153 Cameroon	-0.3	10.7	24.2	19.9	0.337	..	5.0	1.3	6.0	-0.2	-1.1	-1.7
154 Pakistan	4.0	19.9	15.6	27.8	0.204	..	8.3	4.0	1.5	-0.1	-0.8	-0.2
155 Papua New Guinea	..	26.1	..	26.7	0.294	0.0	6.9	0.3	13.3	..	0.6	..
156 Comoros	4.2	1.9	15.0	14.0	0.559	..	6.3	..	..	0.4	..	1.9
Low human development												
157 Mauritania	14.8	15.7	40.9	8.2	0.308	0.0	6.2	3.0	2.3	-1.1	..	1.5

Continued →

	Economic sustainability				SDG 9.5		Social sustainability			SDG 10.1	SDG 5	SDG 10.1
	SDG 17.4							Education and health expenditure versus military expenditure				
	Adjusted net savings	Total debt service	Gross capital formation	Skilled labour force	Concentration index (exports)	Research and development expenditure	Dependency ratio Old age (65 and older)	Military expenditure[a]	Ratio of education and health expenditure to military expenditure[b]	Overall loss in HDI value due to inequality[c]	Gender Inequality Index[c]	Income share of the poorest 40%[d]
	(% of GNI)	(% of exports of goods, services and primary income)	(% of GDP)	(% of labour force)	(value)	(% of GDP)	(per 100 people ages 15-64)	(% of GDP)		Average annual change (%)		
HDI RANK	2015-2018[e]	2015-2018[e]	2015-2019[e]	2015-2019[e]	2018	2014-2018[e]	2030[f]	2015-2018[e]	2010-2017[b]	2010/2019[h]	2005/2019[h]	2005/2018
158 Benin	3.2	7.8	25.6	17.1	0.373	..	6.3	0.9	6.8	0.6	-0.5	-2.8
159 Uganda	-5.4	12.2	26.5	3.2	0.267	0.2	4.1	1.4	6.9	-2.1	-0.8	-0.1
160 Rwanda	-2.8	12.6	26.1	18.1	0.380	0.7	7.3	1.2	7.7	-2.8	-1.5	2.1
161 Nigeria	0.1	8.3	19.8	41.4	0.789	0.1[n]	5.2	0.5	..	-1.8	..	-1.1
162 Côte d'Ivoire	21.3	17.1	21.0	25.5	0.361	0.1	5.3	1.4	7.5	-0.1	-0.5	-0.4
163 Tanzania (United Republic of)	16.7	8.4	34.0	5.0	0.206	0.5[n]	5.3[z]	1.2	6.8	-1.5	-0.5	-0.2
164 Madagascar	4.9	2.7	21.9	18.5	0.213	0.0	6.4	0.6	15.7	-1.2	..	-1.5
165 Lesotho	6.8	3.6	32.1	..	0.288	0.0	8.7	1.8	8.0	-2.3	-0.3	1.7
166 Djibouti	40.8	57.8	25.0	..	0.185	..	9.4	3.7[n]	3.2[n]	..	..	-0.3
167 Togo	1.1	5.0	28.0	8.2	0.237	0.3	5.5	2.0	6.0	-0.4	-0.8	-0.9
168 Senegal	12.5	13.5	32.8	10.8	0.236	0.6	5.8	1.9	4.6	-1.3	-1.3	-0.5
169 Afghanistan	5.4	4.9	17.8	19.2	0.399	..	5.1	1.0	16.8	..	-0.9	..
170 Haiti	15.4	1.2	27.6	9.4	0.508	..	9.7	0.0	..	0.0	0.5	..
170 Sudan	-6.2	4.2	19.3	22.7	0.440	..	7.1	2.3	1.4[n]	..	-1.4	1.5
172 Gambia	-7.8	16.8	18.5	35.0	0.449	0.1	4.8	1.1	3.4	-2.0	-0.5	2.9
173 Ethiopia	8.4	20.8	35.2	6.9	0.287	0.3	6.4	0.6	12.3	-2.1	-1.3	-1.3
174 Malawi	-6.3	5.7	12.3	17.6	0.558	..	4.8	0.8	17.9	-1.3	-1.0	-0.7
175 Congo (Democratic Republic of the)	-7.9	2.4	25.3	43.0	0.545	0.4	5.9	0.7	7.4	-2.0	-0.4	-0.1
175 Guinea-Bissau	-2.2	1.9	11.3	..	0.875	..	5.1	1.6	4.3	-1.4	..	-4.8
175 Liberia	-99.4	2.8	22.8	21.1	0.395	..	6.4	0.8	15.0	-1.6	-0.2	0.3
178 Guinea	-10.2	2.2	30.6	..	0.502	..	5.4	2.5	2.4	-1.2	..	2.4
179 Yemen	..	14.6	..	29.7	0.378	..	5.4	4.0[n]	2.5[n]	-0.8	0.0	-0.6
180 Eritrea	..	..	12.6[n]	..	0.314	..	7.0	..	..	..	..	..
181 Mozambique	5.1	13.1	43.9	7.1	0.315	0.3	5.1	1.0	10.5	-4.3	-1.1	-1.8
182 Burkina Faso	0.6	3.5	26.0	5.0	0.658	0.7	4.8	2.1	9.3	-2.0	-0.5	2.3
182 Sierra Leone	-20.3	7.2	17.4	15.2	0.227	..	5.2	0.8	16.2	-1.1	-0.3	1.0
184 Mali	2.5	4.4	22.5	5.8	0.723	0.3	4.5	2.9	2.5	-1.5	-0.4	2.4
185 Burundi	-16.9	14.0	12.3	2.5	0.438	0.2	5.2	1.9	6.6	-2.3	-0.8	-2.1
185 South Sudan	-9.2	..	5.8	..	..	..	6.2	1.3	4.6	..	..	..
187 Chad	..	..	21.4	7.6	0.757	0.3	4.7	2.1	3.1	-0.5	..	-1.7
188 Central African Republic	..	..	23.2	..	0.336	..	5.0	1.4	2.2	-0.1	-0.1	-6.7
189 Niger	7.2	8.5	30.5	4.0	0.352	..	5.2	2.5	4.6	-2.1	-0.6	2.6
Other countries or territories												
Korea (Democratic People's Rep. of)	..	..	..	..	0.103	..	18.7	..	..	..	..	..
Monaco	..	..	..	..	..	..	..	..	..	..	..	..
Nauru	..	..	..	96.5	0.424	..	..	..	..	..	..	..
San Marino	..	..	19.1	51.9	..	..	..	..	..	..	..	..
Somalia	..	..	..	..	0.409	..	5.6	..	..	..	..	..
Tuvalu	..	..	..	50.1	0.578	..	..	..	..	..	..	..
Human development groups												
Very high human development	8.5	..	22.3	84.9	—	2.4	33.1	2.3	6.9	-0.9	-2.7	—
High human development	16.4	12.3	36.0	..	—	1.6	20.3	1.8	..	-2.4	-1.0	—
Medium human development	13.4	12.4	27.5	24.0	—	0.5	11.1	2.3	3.1	-1.4	-1.4	—
Low human development	2.9	10.0	24.0	21.5	—	0.2	5.6	1.0	4.2	-1.7	-0.6	—
Developing countries	15.2	14.0	33.1	33.9	—	1.3	14.7	2.1	4.5	-1.7	-0.9	—
Regions												
Arab States	12.4	16.3	26.2	41.7	—	0.7	9.7	5.5	1.6	-1.1	-1.2	—
East Asia and the Pacific	20.2	9.1	40.9	..	—	..	21.7	1.8	..	-2.8	-0.6	—
Europe and Central Asia	9.7	30.0	25.2	69.1	—	0.7	20.1	2.4	..	-3.3	-2.5	—
Latin America and the Caribbean	5.1	23.5	19.5	54.5	—	0.6	17.8	1.2	10.4	-1.4	-1.1	—
South Asia	17.1	12.1	29.9	22.6	—	0.6	11.9	2.5	3.1	-1.5	-1.3	—
Sub-Saharan Africa	-0.8	14.1	22.1	25.8	—	0.4	5.7	1.0	7.3	-1.5	-0.6	—
Least developed countries	8.4	11.1	29.4	19.6	—	..	7.0	1.5	3.5	-1.7	-0.8	—
Small island developing states	..	16.4	23.9	46.4	—	..	17.1	..	..	-1.8	—	—
Organisation for Economic Co-operation and Development	8.1	..	22.1	81.5	—	2.5	33.5	2.2	7.8	-0.7	-2.0	—
World	**10.8**	**14.5**	**26.3**	**47.3**	**—**	**2.1**	**18.0**	**2.2**	**6.7**	**-1.5**	**-0.9**	**—**